ENCYCLOPEDIA OF THE RENAISSANCE   HC

ENCYCLOPAEDIA OF
THE RENAISSANCE

ENCYCLOPAEDIA OF
THE RENAISSANCE

Consulting Editor
Thomas G. Bergin, PhD, LHD, LittD, OBE
Sterling Professor Emeritus Romance Languages, Yale University

General Editor
Jennifer Speake, MA, BPhil

B.T. BATSFORD LTD, LONDON

Consulting Editor
Thomas G. Bergin, PhD, LHD, LittD, OBE

General Editor
Jennifer Speake, MA, BPhil

Contributors

D'Arcy Adrian-Vallance, BA
Evadne Adrian-Vallance, BA
Dr. Charles Avery, FSA
Virginia Bonito, PhD
Andrew Connor, BA
Graham Dixon, MA, BMus, PhD, FRCO
Mark L. Evans, BA, PhD
Rosalind Fergusson, BA
David Ferraro, BA, MA
Stephen Freer, MA
Derek Gjertsen, BA
Edward Gosselin, BA, MA, PhD
John Grace, MA, PhD
Dina Ickowicz, MA

T.H. Long, MA
Arthur MacGregor, MA, MPhil, FSA
Kate Murray, BA, MPhil
Andrew Pettegree, MA, DPhil
Andrew Pickering, BA, MA
David Pickering, MA
Sandra Raphael, BA, Dip Lib
Kenneth Scholes
J.B. Schultz, PhD
Mary Shields, PhD
Graham Speake, MA, DPhil
Jennifer Speake, MA, BPhil
David G. Wilkins, PhD
Edmund Wright, MA, DPhil

Picture Research
Juliet Brightmore

Cover Design
Robert Updegraff

CONTENTS

ACKNOWLEDGMENTS

Black and White Photographs
© 1987 Her Majesty The Queen: 212 (Windsor Castle, Royal Library), 420 (Windsor Castle, photo Courtauld Institute of Art). Alinari: 111, 182, 334, 373. Biblioteca Nazionale Centrale di Firenze: 160 (photo Guido Sansoni). British Library, London: 9, 125, 175, 288, 361. Reproduced by permission of the Chatsworth Settlement Trustees: 228 (photo Courtauld Institute of Art). Courtauld Institute of Art: 149. Fotomas Index, London: 65, 144, 425. Giraudon: 164, 168, 191. Arthaud-Giraudon: 258. Lauros-Giraudon: 358. Sonia Halliday Photographs: 298. Italian State Tourist Office: 15. A.F. Kersting: 357. Mansell Collection, London: 5, 24, 32 (above), 40, 47, 55, 68, 76, 101, 109, 146, 178, 185, 188, 193, 237, 242, 274, 321, 413. Phaidon Photo Archive: 117, 248, 313. Réunion des Musées Nationaux, Paris: 382. Graham Speake: 92. Staatliche Museen Preussischer Kulturbesitz (Gemäldegalerie), West Berlin: 319, 328 (photos Jörg P. Anders).

Color Plates
Plate XVI reproduced by Gracious Permission of Her Majesty Queen Elizabeth II. Plate XXI reproduced by kind permission of the Trustees of the Powis Castle Estate and the National Trust, photo Erik Pelham. Plate XVIII courtesy of Olivetti, photo Antonio Quattrone. Plates I, III, V, IX, X, XII, XIII, XVII, XIX, XXIII, XXIV, XXV, XXVI, XXVII, XXVIII, XXIX, photos SCALA.

Jacket
The Procession of the Magi, 1459. Fresco by Benozzo Gozzoli (1420-97), Palazzo Medici-Riccardi, Florence. Photo SCALA.

INTRODUCTION

The Renaissance, a vast cultural movement spanning some three centuries of European history, is so rich, so many-faceted, and so impressive in its achievements that it defies easy measurement or even accurate definition. An early aspect, and no doubt a determinant for the course of its development, was the rediscovery of the classics, studied without theological preconceptions for the first time since the dark ages. But, as Walter Pater (the nineteenth-century English critic) observed, the phenomenon of the Renaissance was of such complexity that humanism, as the cult of antiquity was styled, can be considered only one element or symptom. Indeed, even before the fourteenth century (the time of Petrarch, the pioneer of humanism) adumbrations of a new spirit were apparent in the culture of the Western world.

It is hard to imagine a figure more representative of what we have come to think of as "the Renaissance man" than the Emperor Frederick II—tolerant, inquisitive, and versatile—and born more than a century before Petrarch. The emergence of such a personality suggests that humanism was not spontaneously generated but had its roots in a combination of social, political and intellectual impulses that must have been at work in the collective subconsciousness of Europe, or at least of Italy, where the great movement had its beginnings.

Whatever may have been its genesis, the contributions of this dynamic age are manifold and spectacular. It was a period of exploration, inquiry, renovation, and renewal, characterized by a unique vitality. It is to the Renaissance that we owe the discovery of America and the Indies, the invention of printing, the Protestant Reformation, and in the field of arts and letters the unrivaled achievements of Michelangelo, Leonardo, Dante, Petrarch, and Boccaccio; overflowing the boundaries of its Italian birthplace, its genius later appeared in Montaigne, Shakespeare, and Cervantes, to invigorate the arts throughout Europe.

Perhaps more important than any individual inspiration, the Renaissance brought a new sense of freedom and a new appreciation of man and his potential: a legacy that has been the precious patrimony of all succeeding generations. For historians the age of the Renaissance had an ending, as all human things must, but in a deeper and truer sense the Renaissance is still alive. The creations of its great artists are still contemplated with awe, its paladins in letters are still read and indeed are still "best sellers"; with no less devotion if perhaps less rapture, the nature and significance of these unique centuries are still studied and analyzed by scholars.

It may not be inappropriate, as we grope for an understanding of the nature of the great era, to let two of its most memorable figures come to our assistance. In Canto XXI of the *Inferno* Dante puts into the mouth of the doomed Ulysses the following exhortation to his shipmates:

> To this, the last brief vigil of your senses
> That yet remains to you, do not deny
> Experience of that unpeopled world
> Which lies beyond the sun, unknown to all.
> Reflect upon the seed from which you spring.
> You were not made to live the lives of brutes,
> But rather to seek virtue and to learn.

And from Shakespeare we need only one brief but luminous phrase:

> Oh brave new world . . .

It is the enduring lesson of the Renaissance that the search for knowledge is for mankind not only a right but also a duty—and above all that the study of our world is joyous and exhilarating. In seeking the old world, the Renaissance—like Columbus, who was nourished in its climate—discovered the new and found the discovery both exciting and rewarding.

Thomas G. Bergin

Note: The text of this book is arranged alphabetically; this alphabetic arrangement is self-indexing. Asterisks before a word in the text denote a cross reference to a separate entry providing further information on the subject being looked up. References to plate numbers are given in certain of the articles (e.g.: See Plate I). These refer to the section of color plates included at the center of the book.

A

Aachen, Hans von (1552–1615) German painter. Despite his name, von Aachen was born at Cologne. Like Bartholomäus *Spranger, whom he later joined in Prague, and other northern artists of his time, von Aachen spent a long period as a young man in Italy, modifying his own German style with an Italian grace and roundedness of form, as well as warmer colours. He lived in Venice between 1574 and 1588, visiting Rome and Florence. On his return to southern Germany he painted portraits and historical and religious scenes, gaining a wide reputation (his patrons included the *Fugger family, who commissioned portraits). In 1592 Emperor Rudolf II appointed him court painter at Prague, although von Aachen did not move there until 1597. Here he was commissioned to paint mythological and allegorical subjects, such as his *Liberation of Hungary* (1598; Budapest). He also made many designs for sculptors and engravers, for example, for de *Vries's Hercules fountain in Augsburg.

abacus In early modern Europe, a system of parallel columns of lines representing successive powers of ten, on which the elementary operations of addition, subtraction, multiplication, and division, were performed with the aid of counters. The lines of this instrument, the line abacus or exchequer board, could be drawn in the dust, incised in wax, or carved on a board or table. In the absence of satisfactory algorithms for calculation such devices were used by officials, tradesmen, and schoolboys, but once satisfactory methods were developed, the abacus rapidly disappeared from general use. The system of pierced beads sliding along metal rods, though familiar today, originated in China and was little used in Renaissance Europe.

Abarbanel, Isaac (1437–1508) Jewish statesman, philosopher, and scholar. Born in Lisbon, he became a trusted state official under King Afonso V of Portugal, but on the king's death (1481) he was forced to seek refuge in Spain. Here he was minister of state under *Ferdinand and Isabella and was an early patron of *Columbus. He endeavoured to prevent the expulsion of the Jews from Spain (1492) by offering their Catholic Majesties a huge bribe, but was exiled with his co-religionists.

He went to Italy and then Corfu before ending his days as a servant of state in Venice. Abarbanel published several books of biblical exegesis, much used by Christian scholars; these commentaries were particularly noteworthy for their attention to social and political structures in biblical times.

Abarbanel, Judah *see* Leone Ebreo.

Abbate, Niccolò dell' (c. 1509–71) Italian painter. He first studied sculpture in his native Modena but it was his frescoes, particularly the *Martyrdom of St Peter and St Paul* (1547) in the church of S Pietro, for which he became known. The influence of his contemporaries *Mantegna, *Correggio, and *Parmigianino helped to form the mature style which followed his move to Bologna in 1548. The Palazzo dell'Università in Bologna contains some of his surviving mannerist landscapes. In 1552 Abbate was invited to the court of Henry II of France at Fontainebleau. Here, working with *Primaticcio, he introduced Mannerism to France and helped to create the Fontainebleau style, the first completely secular movement in French painting (*see* Fontainebleau). Few of his murals and easel paintings have escaped destruction; those that have are mainly graceful landscapes with pagan themes. See p. 2.

Abbot, George (1562–1633) English divine. Born at Guildford, the son of a clothworker, Abbot was educated at Guildford grammar school and Balliol College, Oxford. He helped prepare the Authorized Version of the Bible, first obtained a bishopric in 1609, and became archbishop of Canterbury in 1611. Abbot was a moderate Puritan, committed to Calvinistic principles and hostile to Rome and to the Arminians (*see* Arminianism) led by William Laud. In 1621 Laud availed himself of Abbot's accidental shooting of a gamekeeper to try to have him ejected from holy orders, but James I exercised his casting vote in Abbot's favour. A firm critic of Charles I's pro-Spanish and pro-Laudian policies, Abbot was suspended from his archiepiscopal functions for one year in 1627 after attacking a sermon defending Charles's arbitrary use of power. From then on Laud increasingly usurped Abbot's role as primate of England.

NICCOLÒ
DELL'ABBATE
Landscape with Eurydice. *The ancient myth of the death of Eurydice is re-enacted against a dream-like pastoral landscape. In the middle distance Orpheus charms the animals with his music.* (National Gallery, London)

Academia secretorum naturae (Accademia dei Segreti) The first scientific academy, founded at Naples by Giambattista *della Porta in 1560. Membership was open to those who had made some discovery in the natural sciences, which members presented at meetings held at della Porta's house. Its activities became the subject of ecclesiastical investigation (1580) and della Porta was ordered to close his academy.

academies In the Renaissance, associations of scholars, philosophers, writers, and (later) artists that more or less deliberately drew their inspiration from Plato's Academy in Athens in the fourth century BC. In the fifteenth century informal groups of scholars began to be referred to as "academies"; probably the earliest was the literary circle patronized by *Alfonso (I) the Magnanimous at Naples (*see* Neapolitan Academy), which later came to be known from its most eminent member as the Accademia Pontaniana. Study and appreciation of languages, literature, art, and thought of the classical world assumed different forms in different places. The intellectual world reflected in Plato's dialogues captured the imagination of Cosimo de' *Medici and Marsilio *Ficino, who founded the most famous of Renaissance academies, the Accademia Platonica (*see* Platonic Academy) at Florence in the early 1460s. In Venice the *Neakademia devoted itself to Greek studies, while the *Roman Academy concentrated on classical Rome. In the sixteenth and seventeenth centuries

nearly every Italian city had its academy, which often amounted to little more than a gentlemen's debating club, though some, like the *Accademia della Crusca, set themselves a more serious aim. Forerunner of later scientific academies was *della Porta's shortlived Accademia dei Segreti (*see* Academia secretorum naturae) at Naples in 1560. The *Accademia dei Lincei lasted rather longer. In the fine arts informal schools of teachers and pupils were often called "academies" from the fifteenth century onwards, but the first organized teaching academy was the *Accademia del Disegno founded in Florence in 1562, followed by the Roman Accademia di S Luca (1593).
Elsewhere humanist academies were slower to emerge. The French Académie des Jeux Floraux derived from a fourteenth-century troubadour festival at Toulouse, and in the Netherlands *chambers of rhetoric performed many of the functions of academies before the founding of the *Duytsche Academie in 1617. The Académie de la poésie et de la musique (1570–74) and the Académie du palais (1576–84) were less successful than the more haphazard grouping of the *Pléiade in introducing classical standards into French poetics. In England Spenser's *Areopagus may have had only a fictional existence.

Acarie, Barbe Jeanne (1566–1618) Founder in France of the Reformed (Discalced) Order of Carmelite nuns. Born in Paris, Mme Acarie was the daughter of a royal councillor, Nicolas Avrillot.

In 1582 she was married to Pierre Acarie by whom she had six children. A leading light in Parisian society, she became deeply involved in the Catholic reform movement and was a close friend of the *Bérulle family. In 1604 she introduced the Carmelite nuns into France and, after her husband's death (1613), entered their Amiens convent herself. On becoming a professed nun she adopted the name of Mary of the Incarnation (1615) and transferred to Pontoise (1616) where she remained until her death. She was beatified in 1791.

Accademia dei Lincei The scientific society founded in Rome in 1603 by Federico Cesi. Galileo and Giambattista della Porta were early members. It was revived in the 1870s to become the national academy of Italy, encompassing both literature and science among its concerns.

Accademia del Disegno The first true art academy, founded in Florence in 1562, mainly at the instigation of *Vasari. Its founder was Duke *Cosimo I de' Medici, who was joint head of the new institution with *Michelangelo. It had an elected membership of thirty-six artists; amateurs were also admitted. It gained enormous international prestige and enhanced the status of artists vis-à-vis the other Florentine guilds.

Accademia della Crusca The pre-eminent linguistic academy of Italy, founded in 1582 in Florence. Its object was the purification of the vernacular, symbolized in the academy's emblem of a sieve. It was the first academy to undertake the compilation of a standard dictionary; its *Vocabolario* (1612), which followed the linguistic principles advocated by *Bembo, exercised a powerful influence over the subsequent evolution of literary Italian. *See also questione della lingua*; Salviati, Leonardo.

Accademia Platonica *see* Platonic Academy.

Accademia Pontaniana *see* Neapolitan Academy; Pontano, Giovanni.

Acciaiuoli family Migrating from Bergamo in the twelfth century, the Acciaiuoli family became prominent Florentine businessmen and bankers and by the 1340s ran the third richest Italian bank. Niccolò Acciaiuoli (1310–65), who went to Naples (1331) to direct the family's interests there, became grand seneschal and virtual ruler of the kingdom under Queen Joanna I in 1348. He also founded (1342) the Certosa del Galluzzo near Florence. His nephew, Ranieri (died 1394), established himself in Greece, conquering Athens in 1388. Meanwhile, the family bank had been bankrupted (1345) by the combination of high Florentine taxation, loss of business in Rome due to strained relations between Florence and the papacy, and (from 1341) the default of Edward III of England on his loan repayments. The Acciaiuoli continued to play a major role in Florentine politics; in 1434 Agnolo Acciaiuoli helped the *Medici overcome the Albizzi, and the family's subsequent loyalty to the Medici brought them rewards in the form of important civil and ecclesiastical posts. Donato Acciaiuoli (1428–78), *gonfaloniere* of Florence in 1473, wrote commentaries on Aristotle and published a Latin translation of some of Plutarch's *Lives* (1478).

Accolti family A family from Arezzo that produced several distinguished churchmen, jurists, and authors in the fifteenth and sixteenth centuries. Benedetto Accolti (1415–64) taught jurisprudence at the university in Florence and in 1458 became chancellor of the Florentine republic, but he is chiefly remembered for his Latin history of the First Crusade, which was printed in 1532, translated into Italian in 1543, and furnished material for Tasso's *Gerusalemme liberata*. His brother Francesco (Francesco Aretino; 1416–c. 1484) was also a jurist and wrote a verse translation of Leonardo Bruni's *De bello italico adversus Gothos* (1528). Benedetto's son Bernardo (1465–1536), generally known to his contemporaries as Unico Aretino, was a poet who acquired considerable renown at several Italian courts as a reciter of impromptu verse. His comedy *Virginia*, based on a story in the *Decameron*, was first performed in 1493 and published in 1535, and a collected edition of his works, *Opera nova*, was first published in 1513. Another of Benedetto's sons, Pietro (1455–1532), was made a cardinal by Julius II and became archbishop of Ravenna in 1524. Pietro's nephew, another Benedetto (1497–1549), continued the family tradition of learned churchmen, becoming a cardinal under Clement VII.

Acosta, José de (1539–1600) Spanish naturalist and missionary. Born at Medina del Campo, Acosta joined the Jesuits in 1551 and accompanied them in 1571 to Peru where he remained until his return to Spain in 1587. In 1598 he became rector of the Jesuit college at Salamanca. While in South America he published (1583) a Quechua catechism, the first book to be printed in Peru. His *Historia natural y moral de las Indias* (1590), an influential and much translated work, introduced many to the distinctive flora and fauna of Latin America. They had originated, he argued, in the Old World and had spread to the New World via an undiscovered land bridge. He also pointed out Aristotle's error in claiming equatorial lands to be uninhabitable.

Adagia A collection of proverbs and allusions gathered from classical authors by *Erasmus. The first version, entitled *Collectanea adagiorum*, appeared in Paris in 1500 with a dedication to Lord Mountjoy. By the time of the second edition, *Chiliades adagiorum* (1508), published by the *Aldine press in Venice, Erasmus had expanded the collection from around 800 to over 3000, including a number of Greek sayings. The collection was accompanied by a commentary designed to inculcate an elegant Latin style, and the *Adagia* quickly became enormously successful, with numerous editions throughout the sixteenth century.

Adoration of the Lamb *see* Ghent altarpiece.

Adriano Fiorentino (Adriano di Giovanni de' Maestri; c. 1450/60–1499) Italian sculptor and medallist. Born in Florence, he was first recorded as a bronze founder in an inscription on the base of the *Bellerophon and Pegasus* (Vienna), a bronze statuette designed by *Bertoldo in Florence during the early 1480s. Adriano then moved to Naples, serving King Ferrante (Ferdinand I) and his commander-in-chief as military engineer and artillery founder, as well as producing medals of members of the house of Aragon and their court poet *Pontano. In 1495 Adriano was serving Elizabetta Gonzaga, Duchess of Urbino, and then her brother Gianfrancesco Gonzaga, Duke of Mantua. By 1498 he was in Germany, where he produced a bust in bell-metal of Elector *Frederick (III) the Wise in contemporary costume (Grünes Gewölbe, Dresden). A bronze statuette of *Venus* (Philadelphia) and one of a *Satyr* with pan-pipes (Vienna) are among Adriano's signed works on a small scale and herald the High Renaissance in sculpture.

Adrian VI (1459–1523), Pope (1522–23) Born Adrian Dedel in Utrecht, he served as boyhood tutor to *Charles V and subsequently (1516) became inquisitor-general of Aragon. On becoming pope he was immediately beset by the menace of the Turks in the east, the continued war between Charles V and *Francis I of France, and the revolt of *Luther in Germany. The significance of Adrian's pontificate lies in his aims rather than his achievements, notably his instruction (December 1522) to Father Chieregati, Rome's representative in Nuremberg, with its admission that reform in Christendom must be preceded by reform of the Curia itself. This broke the pattern established by the Renaissance popes and can be seen as the beginning of the *Counter-Reformation.

Aertsen, Pieter (1509–75) Netherlands painter. Aertsen was a student of Allaert Claesz. in Amster-dam, before moving to Antwerp about 1530, whence he returned to his native city in 1557. He painted a number of altarpieces, many of which were destroyed in the *iconoclasm that followed the arrival of Calvinism in the Netherlands. Aertsen was the creator of a new type of genre scene, featuring large figures of maids or cooks, surrounded by fruit, vegetables, and other provisions, in domestic interiors. Famous examples are the *Farmer's Wife* (1543; Lille) and *Market Woman at a Vegetable Stand* (1567; Berlin). The peasants, housewives, and domestic servants who populate these canvases have a grandeur and self-confidence prophetic of much later social realist works. Some of his paintings, such as the *Butcher's Shop with the Flight into Egypt* (1551; Uppsala) include well-known religious scenes in the background – a reversal of the customary order of priority. Aertsen's students included his sons Pieter ("Jonge Peer"; 1543–1603) and Aert 0081Pietersz. (1550–1612), as well as his nephew Joachim Beuckelaer (c. 1533–c. 1573). His style stimulated imitation as far afield as Italy, as is evident from certain canvases by Vincenzo Campi (1536–91), Bartolommeo *Passarotti, and Annibale *Carracci.

Agostino di Duccio (1418–81) Italian sculptor. Agostino was born in Florence, but his training is unknown, and his first dated work was in 1442 in Modena. In 1449 and 1454 Agostino appears in documents at Rimini, where he carved many marble panels in the interior of the *Tempio Malatestiano. Agostino's style is incisive and calligraphic; it was possibly inspired initially by Donatello's low reliefs, though not by their emotional content, of which the lesser sculptor was incapable. Between 1457 and 1462, Agostino was carving the façade of the oratory of S Bernardino in Perugia with reliefs of Christ in majesty, the Annunciation, and the saints in glory, surrounded by flying angels and statues in niches. After an unsuccessful year in Bologna, Agostino returned to Florence (1463), joined the guild of sculptors, and received (abortive) commissions for colossal statues on the cathedral (one of which eventually was carved by Michelangelo into his *David*). After carving several Madonna reliefs, one for the Medici (Louvre), he returned to Perugia, where he carved continuously until his death. His talents were better appreciated in this provincial city than in his native metropolis.

Agostino Veneziano (Agostino de' Musi; c. 1490–c. 1536) Italian engraver. Originally active in his native Venice, Agostino was influenced by Giulio *Campagnola and by Jacopo de' *Barbari. In 1516 he left Venice for Rome, where he became the foremost pupil of *Raimondi and, like Raimondi,

AGOSTINO DI DUC-
CIO *Swirling drapery ani-
mates this low-relief marble carving of an angel
drawing a curtain. (early
1450s; Tempio Malates-
tiano, Rimini)*

important in disseminating Italian Renaissance
themes and motifs through the medium of engraving. Raphael and Giulio Romano were among the
artists whose works were made more widely available through Agostino's prints.

Agricola, Georgius (Georg Bauer; 1494–1555)
German mineralogist and physician. Agricola
studied at Leipzig and several Italian universities
before graduating in medicine. He was physician
(1527–33) in the Bohemian mining town of Joach-
imsthal (now Jachymov in Czechoslovakia) before
returning to practise for the rest of his life at
Chemnitz in his native Saxony. His first scientific
publication was *Bermannus* (1530), a dialogue in
which the main speaker is a celebrated miner and

in which many minerals are first described under
their German names (e.g. bismuth). He published
numerous other geological and metallurgical
works, notably *De natura fossilium* (1530) (*see*
mineralogy). These culminated in *De re metallica*
(1556), the first systematic textbook of the subject,
issued, as all his scientific works had been, by the
publishing house of *Froben at Basle. Agricola
also wrote from practical experience on weights
and measures (*De mesuribus et ponderibus*, 1533),
on subterranean fauna (*De animantibus subterra-
neis*, 1549), and the plague (*De peste*, 1554).

Agricola, Johann (c. 1494–1566) German Protestant reformer. Agricola was born at Eisleben and
became a student of *Luther at Wittenberg. An

early venture was his collection of German proverbs (1528). Agricola found himself opposed by Luther for his denial of the necessity of the preaching of Mosaic and moral law as well as the Gospel (the antinominian heresy), and Luther's growing intolerance of dissent obliged Agricola to leave Wittenberg (1540) in order to avoid being put on trial. He became court preacher to Joachim II of Brandenburg and in 1548 helped prepare the Interim of *Augsburg. The resulting adiaphorist controversy, concerning whether or not certain actions or rites were matters of indifference to true Christian doctrine, became Agricola's main preoccupation as he unsuccessfully attempted to resolve it. He died during a plague epidemic.

Agricola, Rudolf (Roelof Huysman; 1442–95) Dutch humanist philosopher and scholar. Agricola was born near Groningen and became a pupil of Nicholas *Cusanus; he was, like him, one of the Brethren of the Common Life. From 1468 to 1479 he studied, though not continuously, at Padua and Ferrara and impressed Italian humanists with his fluency in Latin. He was also an accomplished Hebrew scholar who translated the Psalms into Latin. He had great enthusiasm for the works of Petrarch, whose biography he wrote. Unlike many Italian humanists Agricola remained a devout Christian, believing that though the study of the ancients was important it was not a substitute for the study of the scriptures. He used the phrase "Philosophia Christi" to describe his teaching, the object of which was to mediate between the wisdom of the ancients and Christian belief. These ideas exercised considerable influence over *Erasmus, his most distinguished pupil.

Agrippa von Nettesheim, (Henry) Cornelius (1486–1535) German lawyer, theologian, and student of the occult. Born near Cologne, of a family of minor nobility, he entered the service of the emperor and went to Paris (1506). There he studied the *Cabbala and around 1510 wrote *De occulta philosophia* (1531). In 1510 Agrippa was sent to London where he met *Colet. In 1515 he was teaching occult science at Pavia. He then moved to Metz but opposition forced him to leave and he settled in Geneva. He became a doctor in 1522 and was appointed physician to Louise of Savoy, queen mother of France, his duties consisting mainly of writing horoscopes. In 1530 Agrippa published his major work, *De vanitate et incertitudine scientiarum et artium*, a survey of the state of knowledge in which human learning is unfavourably compared with divine revelation. In 1528 he had been made historiographer to Charles V but hostility to his occult studies led to his disgrace. He was banished from Germany in 1535 and died

at Grenoble. His major contribution to the Renaissance was his scepticism.

Ailly, Pierre d' (1350–1420) French geographer and theologian. Born at Compiègne and educated at the university of Paris, d'Ailly pursued a clerical career, rising in 1411 to the rank of cardinal. Caught up in the *Great Schism, he broke with Pope Benedict XIII in 1408 and argued in his *Tractatus super reformatione ecclesiae* (1416) for the supremacy of Church councils over popes. He was also the author of *Imago mundi* (c. 1410), one of the foremost geographical texts of the period. The inspiration for the work remained predominantly classical; d'Ailly took little notice of the growing travel literature. A related work, *Compendium cosmographiae* (1413), did little more than repeat the geography of Ptolemy. Whereas, however, Ptolemy had assumed that both land and sea covered about 180° of longitude, d'Ailly extended the land mass to 225°. The implications of such a framework were not lost on Christopher *Columbus, a careful reader of d'Ailly.

Alamanni, Luigi (1495–1556) Italian poet and humanist. Alamanni was born in Florence and took part in the unsuccessful conspiracy of 1522 against Giulio de' Medici (later Pope *Clement VII) and was forced to flee to France. He returned and briefly served in the Florentine republican government of 1527–30, but thereafter lived in exile, enjoying the patronage of Francis I, Henry II, and Catherine de' Medici. As a protégé of the French court, he made many return journeys to Italy and maintained contacts with *Bembo, *Varchi, and other leading figures. In Florence he had been associated with the *Orti Oricellari, and from that time had been a close friend of *Machiavelli, who made Alamanni one of the speakers in *Arte della guerra*. Alamanni played an important role in the establishment of Italian cultural influence in sixteenth-century France. His works include *Flora* (1549), a comedy based on Roman models, *Antigone* (1556), a tragedy after Sophocles, *Avarchide* (1570), a minor epic imitative of the *Iliad*, and *Girone il cortese* (1548), which drew on medieval French material. Most influential, however, was *La coltivazione* (1546), a didactic blank-verse imitation of Virgil's *Georgics*.

Alarcón y Mendoza, Juan Ruiz de *see* Ruiz de Alarcón y Mendoza, Juan.

Alba, Fernando Alvarez de Toledo, 3rd Duke of (1507–82) Spanish nobleman. He served Charles I of Spain (who was also Emperor *Charles ·V) and *Philip II of Spain as military commander,

ALBA *A wooden statuette by an unknown sculptor shows Philip II's general slaying a monster with the three heads of Spain's arch-enemies: the pope, Queen Elizabeth of England, and the elector of Saxony, champion of Lutheranism. (Palacio de Liria, Madrid)*

political adviser, and administrator. In the service of Charles Alba fought the French (1524), attacked Tunis (1535), helped lead the imperial forces to their important victory over the German Protestant princes at *Mühlberg, and became commander-in-chief of the emperor's armies in Italy (1552). He was one of Philip II's leading ministers from 1559 until 1567, when he was ordered to the Netherlands to crush the Calvinist Dutch rebels and to reassert Spanish authority (*see*

also Netherlands, Revolt of the). His harsh rule as governor-general of the Netherlands fuelled Dutch hatred of Spain; worst hated was Alba's Council of Troubles (nicknamed *Tribunal of Blood by the Dutch) which set aside local laws, imposed heavy taxation, confiscated property, sent hundreds of Dutch to their deaths, and drove thousands more into exile. Lacking both money and sufficient naval resources, Alba lost control over parts of Holland. This failure, combined with the intrigues of his enemies at the Spanish court, led to his recall to Spain (1573) and house arrest (1579). Although Alba led the successful invasion of Portugal (1580), he never regained Philip II's favour.

Alberti, Leon Battista (1404–72) Italian architect and humanist. A member of a prominent merchant-banking family exiled by political opponents from its native Florence in 1402, Alberti, who was illegitimate, was born in Genoa and brought up by his father and stepmother in Venice. He attended Guarino's school in Padua and in the 1420s studied law at Bologna university. The Florentine ban against his family was lifted in 1428 and by 1432, when he was employed as a secretary in the papal chancery, Alberti had made his first visit to the city. There he became acquainted with such men as *Donatello, *Ghiberti, and *Masaccio, and with *Brunelleschi, to whom he dedicated the preface of his treatise *Della pittura* (On Painting; 1435), a work that contains the first description of *perspective construction.

Alberti's study of Vitruvius resulted in *De re aedificatoria*, a treatise on architecture, dedicated to Pope *Nicholas V in 1452 and published in 1485. This Latin edition was subsequently reprinted at Paris (1512) and Strasbourg (1541); the first Italian translation appeared in 1546, and French (1553) and Spanish (1582) versions were also printed during the sixteenth century. Alberti was employed by the pope on a number of architectural projects in Rome but his most famous buildings are in Florence, Rimini, and Mantua. In Florence he designed the Palazzo Rucellai (c. 1445–51), the classical forms of its façade being influenced by the Roman Colosseum, and the main façade of Sta Maria Novella (1456–70); in Rimini the famous *Tempio Malatestiano; and in Mantua the churches of S Sebastiano (1460–70) and S Andrea (c. 1470), in which the Tempio's triumphal-arch motif was again incorporated. Alberti's humanistic interests found expression in a number of prose works, notably *Della famiglia* (On the Family; 1435–41), *De iciarchia* (On the Ruler of his Family; 1470), and the first Italian grammar. Also a poet, mathematician, and engineer, Alberti exemplified his own belief that "men can do all things." He died in Rome.

Albertinelli, Mariotto (1474–1515) Italian painter. Albertinelli was born in Florence, where he trained under Cosimo *Rosselli. Through Rosselli he met Fra *Bartolommeo, with whom he collaborated for a number of years, for example on the altarpiece of Sta Maria della Quercia, near Viterbo. Albertinelli also painted an *Annunciation* for the Duomo in Volterra (1497), another now in the Accademia, Florence (1510), and a *Visitation* (1503; Uffizi). His works show the influence of Perugino and Leonardo da Vinci, as well as that of Fra Bartolommeo.

Albizzi, Rinaldo (degli) (1370–1442) A leading member of the Albizzi family which dominated the government of Florence between the revolt of the *ciompi (1378) and the *Medici seizure of power (1434). After his cousin Maso died (1417) Rinaldo took control of the oligarchic regime in Florence. He organized the unpopular and unsuccessful expedition against Lucca (1429–33), which was opposed by Cosimo de' *Medici. Rinaldo had him exiled (1433), but returning to Florence in 1434, Cosimo overthrew the Albizzi and sent Rinaldo into exile.

Albornoz, Egidio d' (Gil Alvarez Carrillo d'Albornoz; 1310–67) Spanish churchman. Albornoz was born at Cuenca, Castile. He fought bravely against the Moors, was a favourite of Alfonso XI, and became archbishop of Toledo (1338), but was exiled (1350) by Alfonso's son, Peter the Cruel. Albornoz was made a cardinal (1350) and appointed papal legate and vicar-general of Italy (1353–57, 1358–64) by Innocent VI to protect papal interests against Guelf Florence and to recover territory lost to the papacy (*see* Avignon, papacy at). His long series of wars made some gains and facilitated a papal return to Rome, briefly in 1367 and permanently in 1377. Often he merely legitimized existing local tyrants as papal vicars in return for a recognition of papal authority, without breaking their power. Of more lasting importance was his work in administration and education. His codification of the laws of the Papal State (*Constitutiones egidianae*, 1357) provided the model for papal government until 1816. In 1365 he founded the Spanish college at Bologna.

Albuquerque, Afonso (1453–1515) Portuguese admiral, second viceroy of Portuguese India. Born near Lisbon and educated at court, Albuquerque made his name during King Afonso V's invasion of Spain (1476). His first eastern expedition (1503) was to befriend the king of Cochin and build a fort there. He succeeded, and in 1506 he assisted Tristão da Cunha during his massive expedition to India. Over the next few years Albuquerque carried out a series of attacks on Arab cities, establishing Portuguese trading routes and rights. His outstanding success was his recapture of Goa in 1510, where he established a senate and appointed native administrators. Albuquerque's enlightened administration was extended to other territories he conquered, notably Malacca and the Spice Islands. His success aroused jealousies in the Portuguese court, and Lope Suàrez, a personal enemy, was appointed in his stead. Albuquerque died at sea and was buried at Goa, where his tomb became a shrine for Indians oppressed by his successors.

Alcalá (de Henares) A town in central Spain on the River Henares, east of Madrid. Identified with the Roman settlement of Complutum, it was refounded by the Moors in 1083; its present name derives from the Moorish word for "castle". During the Renaissance it became a centre of learning under the patronage of Cardinal *Ximénes, to whom a handsome marble monument remains in the church of the Colegiata. He founded the university there in 1500 (opened 1508); the chief university building, the college of S Ildefonso, dates from 1583. Many of the scholars whom Ximénes brought to Alcalá were engaged on the production of the great edition of the Bible known as the *Complutensian Polyglot.

alchemy The pseudoscience that in the Renaissance period was inextricably linked with the beginnings of chemistry. Renaissance alchemists inherited from their medieval forebears two main quests: for the process or substance (the philosopher's stone) that would transmute base metals to gold and for the universal medicine (panacea). The elixir of life, the principal goal of Chinese alchemy, was of minor importance as clearly contrary to Christian doctrine.

Alchemists in pursuit of the philosopher's stone, who beggared themselves buying materials for their experiments or poisoned themselves with their processes, were properly ridiculed. Nonetheless they frequently imposed upon the greedy and gullible; Ben Jonson's comedy *The Alchemist* (1610) is a comprehensive exposé of the tricks of this kind of alchemical trade. The Church regarded alchemy, along with other occult learning, with hostility, condemning alchemists with other "sorcerers" in its decrees. Gold-hungry Renaissance princes, with wars or other projects to finance, took a more pragmatic line. *Rudolf II attracted many occult practitioners from all over Europe to Prague, among them the alchemists *Dee, *Drebbel, and *Sendivogius.

ALCHEMY *In this illustration from the* Musaeum Hermeticum, *published at Frankfurt in 1625, the seven figures in the cave represent the seven terrestrial metals, while the figures above them hold the symbols for fire, water, and "fiery water", the last symbolizing the union of opposites in the philosopher's stone. The four elements of the Aristotelian world scheme appear in the corners of the design.*

Regarding the quest for the panacea, the theories of *Paracelsus greatly stimulated spagyrical medicine. (The Latin word *spagyricus* "alchemical" was apparently a Paracelsian coinage.) Some practitioners developed their researches in the direction of *iatrochemistry, but others, notably the Rosicrucians, interpreted the quest in spiritual as well as alchemical terms (*see* Rosicrucianism). The terminology of alchemy, conspiring with the pathological secretiveness of its practitioners, thwarted any incipient usefulness it might have had to the embryonic science of chemistry. Renaissance alchemists continued to rely on such texts as the thirteenth-century Latin versions of the Arab Geber, the writings of Arnold of Villanova and Albertus Magnus, and such venerable classics of obfuscation as the *Turba philosophorum* and pseudo-Aristotle, in which metals were called after their astrological equivalents – Sol (gold), Luna (silver), Saturn (lead), etc. – and other materials were identified in fanciful metaphors; a powerful acid, for example, would be called "the stomach

of the ostrich" in tribute to its digestive properties. To some, the whole alchemical enterprise itself became a metaphor for the purgation and salvation of the soul and the process became associated with the cosmic manipulations of the Renaissance *magus.

Alciati, Andrea (1492–1550) Italian lawyer and humanist. Alciati was a native of Milan and after legal studies at Pavia and Bologna he was professor of jurisprudence at Avignon (1518–22, 1527–29) and at Bourges. Alciati's main contribution was in the field of juristics; he published a number of treatises on the *Corpus Iuris Civilis*. However, his most famous book was *Emblemata* (1531), a repertory of allegorical images illustrated by woodcuts accompanied by Latin epigrams pointing up the interaction of the visual image and the ethical message (*see* emblems). This volume exercised a profound influence on the iconography of mannerist and baroque art. There were many later editions, each of which added further emblems.

Alciati also published a volume of notes on the historian Tacitus:

Aldegrever, Heinrich (1502–55/61) German print maker and painter. Aldegrever who was born at Paderborn, probably studied in *Dürer's workshop. About 1527 he settled at Soest, where he died. He executed relatively few paintings, mostly portraits, which are notable for their characterization. Aldegrever is best known for his numerous engravings of religious subjects, events from classical antiquity, genre scenes, portraits, and decorative motifs. These reveal the influence of Dürer, but also of Italian engravers including *Pollaiuolo and Robetta. His delicate, slender figures have a mannerist elegance, and his meticulous engraving technique, reminiscent of Dürer's own, allowed him to depict effects of light and texture with considerable fidelity. He also designed woodcuts, and may be characterized as the most significant north German print maker of the sixteenth century.

Aldine press The press set up in Venice by Aldus *Manutius in 1494/95, specializing in scholarly texts of Greek and Latin classics. Until 1515 many of them were edited by Marcus Musurus (1470–1517), one of the Venetian community of exiled Greeks. A folio Aristotle (1495–98) is an early example of the press's standards, though the *Hypnerotomachia Polifili (1499), a fine illustrated book, is probably more famous. Italian classics were also printed, among them Petrarch (1501) and Dante (1502), both edited by *Bembo.

Francesco Griffo, who cut the Aldine Greek type, modelled on Musurus's script, also made the first italic types, which appeared in a 1501 Virgil. A series of compact little books followed, the small format and italic type setting a fashion that was soon copied, especially in Lyons. Griffo's roman type, commissioned by Aldus in 1495, influenced *Garamond and other designers, though *Jenson's types and matrices had also been bought for the press. The Aldine device of a dolphin and anchor, found on coins of the Roman emperor Titus Vespasianus (39–81 AD), was used in a series of versions after 1502, as well as being copied by several French printers during the next century and many others thereafter.

From 1515 to 1533 the press was run by the founder's brothers-in-law, the Asolani, who failed to maintain its scholarly editing. Aldus's youngest son, Paulus (Paolo) Manutius (1512–74) took over in 1533 and concentrated on Latin classics, especially Cicero.

Aldrovandi, Ulisse (1522–1605) Italian natural historian. The son of a wealthy Bolognese notary, Aldrovandi was educated at the university of Bologna where he later became professor of natural history. Financially independent, he was free to pursue his interests through extensive European travel. In this manner he accumulated a good deal of information on European fauna, and preparation of this material for publication dominated the remainder of his life. By his death only the volumes on birds, *Ornithologiae* (1599–1634), and insects (1602) had begun to appear. Ten further volumes, dealing with almost every aspect of the animal kingdom, were edited by pupils and appeared before 1668. Despite his considerable first-hand experience, Aldrovandi continued to operate mainly in a literary tradition, according to tales from Strabo and Pliny the same authority as his own observations. Consequently while there was a place for the hydra and basilisk in Aldrovandi's bestiary, fossils were dismissed in his *Musaeum metallicum* (1648) as of little importance.

Aldus Manutius *see* Manutius, Aldus.

Aleandro, Girolamo (1480–1542) Italian humanist and diplomat. Born at Treviso, he studied at Padua and then Venice, where he met Aldus *Manutius. In 1508 he went to Paris on the advice of and with an introduction from Erasmus. *Budé was among his first private pupils. In 1509 he gave a course of lectures in Hebrew, Greek, and Latin at Paris and taught there intermittently until 1513. His *Lexicon Graeco-Latinum* appeared in 1512. After ill-health forced him to give up teaching he was employed as a papal envoy, having a notorious confrontation with *Luther in Germany in 1520–21. He became Vatican librarian (1519) under Leo X and later cardinal (1536). Aleandro was an influential teacher. Sometimes his classes numbered 1500 students and he was largely responsible for introducing *Greek studies to Paris.

Alemán, Mateo (1547–1615) Spanish novelist. Descended from Jews who had been forcibly converted to Catholicism, Alemán, who was born the son of a prison doctor in Seville, studied medicine in Salamanca and Alcalá but abandoned his studies before completion. His most important literary work, *Guzmán de Alfarache* (1599), is one of the earliest *picaresque novels. Such was its popularity throughout Europe that there were several pirated editions, as well as a spurious sequel, which appeared even before Alemán could complete the second part of his own work (1604). Success however did not alleviate his constant financial difficulties; he had supported himself in a series of insignificant administrative jobs, but in 1601 he was imprisoned for debt for the third time. Alemán's fortunes prospered only after he emigrated to Mexico (1608) with his patron Archbishop García Guerra, whose biography he published in 1613. His other minor works include a biography of St Anthony of Padua (1603) and *Ortografía Castellana* (1609), the latter containing some sensible proposals for the reform of Spanish spelling.

Alençon, Francis, Duke of *see* Francis, Duke of Alençon.

Alessi, Galeazzo (1512–72) Italian architect. Alessi was born in Perugia, for the cathedral of which he later designed the principal doorway (1568). He visited Rome in the late 1530s and his style was formed by his enthusiasm for classical architecture, especially as mediated by Michelangelo. His most distinguished work combines the dignity of the classical orders with sumptuous detail, as exemplified in the courtyard of the Palazzo Marino, Milan (1553–58). From 1549 onwards he designed a number of notable buildings in Genoa, among them the church of Sta Maria Assunta di Carignano (begun 1552) and some fine villas and palaces in the Strada Nuova (now the Via Garibaldi), which he himself may have laid out. Other examples of his work appear in the Certosa di Pavia (sarcophagus of Giangaleazzo Visconti), at Brescia (the upper part of the Loggia), and Bologna (gateway to the Palazzo Communale; c. 1555). His style was much admired and influenced buildings as far afield as Spain and Germany, especially after Rubens published *Palazzi di Genova* (1622), a study in which Alessi's Genoese work features prominently.

Alexander VI (Rodrigo Borgia; 1431–1503), Pope (1492–1503) He was born at Xativa, Spain, studied law at Bologna, and was first advanced in the papal service by his uncle Alfonso Borgia, Pope Calixtus III, under whom he became head of papal administration, a post which he held ably for thirty-five years (1457–92). Political corruption and immorality in the Vatican reached their height under Alexander, deeply involved as he was in the struggle between the leading Italian families for power and wealth (*see* Borgia family). His contribution to the secularization of the Curia probably enhanced the spreading popularity throughout Italy of preaching friars who condemned the papacy and called upon clergy and laity to repent. Alexander's pontificate was set against the background of the Wars of *Italy. When *Charles VIII of France invaded Italy (1494), seizing Rome and Naples, Alexander helped organize the League of Venice, an alliance between Milan, Venice, Spain, and the Holy Roman Empire, which was successful in forcing Charles to leave Italy.

However, in the interests of the Borgias, particularly of his son Cesare, he later adopted a pro-French policy and aided the French invasion that led to their occupation of Milan in 1499. Monies from the jubilee year, proclaimed by Alexander in 1500, were diverted to Cesare to help him finally crush the Orsini and Colonna families. The marriages of Alexander's daughter Lucrezia were also directed towards political ends.

During Alexander's pontificate Spain laid claim to the New World, following the discoveries of *Columbus, and it was Alexander who determined the Spanish and Portuguese spheres of influence there (*see* Tordesillas, Treaty of). He is also remembered as a patron of artists and architects, including *Bramante and *Pinturicchio.

Alfonsine Tables *see under* astronomy.

Alfonso I (1395–1458), King of Naples (1442–58; also as Alfonso V, King of Aragon (1416–58)) Known as Alfonso the Magnanimous, he was admired as a model prince and a devout Christian. The son of a Castilian prince, who became Ferdinand I of Aragon in 1412, and of Leonor of Albuquerque, he was brought up in Castile and moved to Aragon in 1412. In 1415 he married Maria of Castile; their marriage was unhappy and childless. After succeeding to Aragon in 1416 Alfonso angered his subjects by relying on Castilian advisers, but he did follow the Aragonese tradition of expansion in the Mediterranean. In 1420 he set out to pacify his Sicilian and Sardinian subjects and to attack the Genoese in Corsica. He arrived in Naples in 1421 and persuaded Queen Joanna II to adopt him as her son and heir in exchange for his help against the Angevin claimant to the throne of Naples. After quarrelling with Joanna in 1423 he returned to Spain and busied himself with Spanish problems until her death in 1435. Alfonso returned to Naples to claim his throne and succeeded in driving out his main rival, *René of Anjou, after seven years of struggle. He left the government of his other territories to viceroys and settled permanently in Naples from 1443. He reorganized its finances and administration and made his court at Naples a brilliant centre of learning and the arts. He died in battle against Genoa, leaving Naples to his illegitimate son, Ferrante (*Ferdinand I); his other domains passed to his brother John.

Alfonso II (1448–95), King of Naples (1494–95) The son of *Ferdinand I (Ferrante) and Isabella of Naples, Alfonso, who was cowardly and cruel, was very unpopular. Before succeeding his father, he was associated with and blamed for much of his father's misrule. Through his marriage to

Lodovico Sforza's sister, Ippolita, and through his sister's marriage to Ercole d'Este of Ferrara, Alfonso was involved in various Italian conflicts. He defeated Florence at Poggio (1479) and the Turks at Otranto (1481). When *Charles VIII of France was advancing on Naples early in 1495 Alfonso abdicated in favour of his son, Ferdinand II (Ferrantino), and died later the same year.

algebra While ancient mathematicians made enormous contributions to *geometry and *arithmetic, their achievements in algebra were less impressive. A tendency to solve problems geometrically, and the failure to develop a convenient symbolism, had led the Greeks in a different direction, but the subject was developed by Indian and Muslim mathematicians, who bequeathed to the Renaissance a number of simple rules for the solution of equations. While Renaissance mathematicians made significant advances in the theory of equations, they proved less successful in developing an adequate symbolism. There was little uniformity of symbolism, and notation was cumbersome and unhelpful. The simple equation

$$ax^2 + bx + c = 0$$

where x is the unknown, and a, b, c, stand for given numbers could not have been written before 1637. The equality sign ($=$) was introduced by Robert Recorde in 1537, and the custom of equating the function to zero was established by Descartes in 1637.

Exponents proved more troublesome. *Viète in 1591 had, following the Greek custom, written A^2, A^3, as AQ, and AC, where the Q and C stood for "quadratus" and "cubus" respectively. The modern convention of A^2 and A^3 dates, once more, from Descartes, as does the use of letters of the alphabet to stand systematically for the unknowns. Long before this *Tartaglia and *Cardano would have written the equation

$$x^3 + 6x = 12$$

as

cubus p: 6 rebus aequilis 12

which translates as

a cube plus 6 things equals 12.

Despite the opacity of their notation, Tartaglia and Cardano still managed to make the first major breakthrough in modern algebra. Neither Greek nor medieval mathematicians had worked out a suitable algorithm for the solution of cubic or higher equations. Algebra seemed stuck at the level of quadratics. In this latter field *Bombelli had shown how quadratics could be solved by completing the square, while solution by factorization was first worked out by *Harriot. Linear equations, by contrast, tended to be solved by a number of traditional rules. Known by such names as "the rule of false position" and "the method of scales", they could be applied quite mechanically.

There remained the cubic equation. In 1535 Tartaglia publicly solved thirty cubics in a competition with del Fiore. Four years later he revealed his algorithm to Cardano, who unhesitatingly published his own variant of the solution in *Ars magna* (1545). Cardano also reported on the solution of the biquadratic or quartic discovered by his pupil Ludovico Ferrari (1522–c. 1560). To advance further, however, required the possession of techniques unknown to Renaissance mathematicians.

Allori, Alessandro (?1535–1607) Italian painter. Allori was active in Florence, where he studied under his uncle *Bronzino, of whom he was a close follower. A visit to Rome (1554–56) also brought him under the influence of Michelangelo, which is visible in his frescoes from the early 1560s in SS Annunziata, Florence. He was patronized by Francesco I de' Medici and contributed paintings in the manner of Bronzino to the duke's Studiolo in the Palazzo Vecchio. Other work for the Medici includes decoration in the Salone of their villa at Poggio a Caiano. His later works, among them a *Birth of the Virgin* (1602; SS Annunziata, Florence) and an *Ascension* (1603; S Michele, Prato), are in a softer, more relaxed style. His son Cristofano (1577–1621) followed the emerging baroque tendency in Florentine art. Cristofano's best-known picture, *Judith* (Palazzo Pitti, Florence), incorporates portraits of the artist and his wife.

Altdorfer, Albrecht (c. 1480–1538) German painter, print maker, and architect. The son of an illuminator, Altdorfer became a citizen of his home town of Regensburg in 1505. A member of Regensburg city council since 1519, he was appointed surveyor of public buildings in 1526. In 1535 he was chosen as an ambassador to Vienna, possibly because of his knowledge of the region. By about 1503 he was probably at Mondsee near Salzburg; he returned to the Danube region in 1511. Together with Wolf *Huber and the young *Cranach, Altdorfer was a chief exponent of the so-called "Danube style". Possibly influenced by the pastoral poetry of Konrad *Celtis, these painters delighted in portraying the lush vegetation and dreamy enchantment of the German woods. This fascination with the luxuriance of nature is strongly apparent in Altdorfer's tiny Berlin *Satyr Family* (1507). Despite the emphatically Germanic location of this scene, the figures are Italian in derivation; the artist copied engravings after Mantegna from as early as 1506. In the Berlin *Nativity* (c. 1512) Altdorfer utilized dramatic lighting effects and one-point perspective with brilliant effect. This fundamental bent towards Mannerism developed still further in the eerie viewpoints and stunning colours of the now dismantled altarpiece (1517) for St Florian near Linz. The high point of Altdorfer's career is his Munich *Battle of the Issus* (1529), one of the great visionary paintings of all time. Depicted from an almost astral viewpoint, the forces of Alexander the Great pursue the hordes of Darius into Asia. The background landscape curves to reveal the rim of a spherical earth upon which Cyprus and the North African coast may be plainly seen, upside down, as though viewed from the north and an immense height. Altdorfer was also outstanding as a draughtsman of *chiaroscuro* drawings and a designer of woodcuts. He was arguably the most individual genius in German painting of the sixteenth century.

Altichiero (1320/30–1395) Italian painter. Altichiero was born at Zevio, near Verona, and was mainly active in Verona and Padua. His style was influenced by *Giotto and he himself had numerous followers. Frescoes by him can be seen in S Stefano and Sant' Anastasia in Verona and in the Santo and Oratorio di S Giorgio in Padua.

Alva, Duke of *see* Alba, Fernando Alvarez de Toledo, 3rd Duke of.

Amadeo, Giovanni Antonio (1447–1522) Italian marble sculptor. He was born in Pavia and is documented from 1466 working on sculpture for the magnificent new Certosa (Carthusian monastery) in his native town; in 1474 he was made jointly responsible with the brothers Mantegazza for its huge polychrome marble façade. Between 1470 and 1476 he carved the monuments and reliefs of the Colleoni chapel in Bergamo and in 1490 was employed on Milan cathedral. Apart from portraits, in which his work was influenced by classical prototypes, his sculpture was mostly carved in relief, with religious themes predominating.

Amberger, Christoph (c. 1500–61/62) German painter. Amberger was born at Augsburg and probably trained there under Hans *Burgkmair and Leonhard *Beck. In 1548 he met *Titian, then visiting Augsburg. Amberger's Berlin portrait of Charles V (c. 1532) was influenced by the Netherlandish court painter Jan *Vermeyen, who was at Augsburg in 1530. References to the Venetian painters *Palma Vecchio and Paris *Bordone appear in Amberger's Vienna portraits of a man and a woman (1539) and his Munich *Christoph Fugger* (1541). In the Berlin portrait of Sebastian Münster (c. 1552), Amberger eschewed this international mannerist style in favour of a more tradi-

tional German approach. His altar for Augsburg cathedral (1554) is similarly conservative, translating the late Gothic architectual motifs of *Holbein the Elder into a contemporary Italianate idiom.

Ambrose of Camaldoli *see* Traversari, Ambrogio.

Ambrosiana, Bibliotheca The chief library of *Milan, founded by the bishop of Milan, Cardinal Federico Borromeo (1564–1631), who named it after St Ambrose, patron saint of the city. It was the first public library in Italy and opened on 8 December 1609, with a collection of over 30 000 books and 12 000 manuscripts housed in the palace built by Borromeo between 1603 and 1609 on the site of the Scuole Taverna. The library was enriched by many private donations and bequests, as well as by the acquisitions of its agents travelling abroad.

Ambrosian Republic (1447–50) A Milanese regime established immediately after Duke Filippo Maria Visconti (*see* Visconti family) died without an heir. Twenty-four local notables – "captains and defenders of liberty" – named the republic in honour of St Ambrose, Milan's patron. Divisions within the ruling group, discontent from the lesser bourgeoisie, rebellion in subject cities, and the hostility of Venice brought the republic close to collapse. In autumn 1449 Francesco Sforza, a *condottiere* formerly in Duke Filippo Maria's employ and married to the duke's illegitimate daughter, besieged the city; in March 1450 the republic surrendered and Sforza was installed as duke of Milan.

Amerbach, Johannes (1443–1513) Swiss printer and publisher. He studied in Paris and then returned to Basle to set up a printing house (1475) with the principal aim of producing good texts of the works of the Church Fathers (*see also* patristic studies). He gathered round him a circle of scholars that included *Reuchlin, and in 1511 employed a Dominican, Johannes Cono of Nuremberg (1463–1513), to instruct his sons and any other interested parties in Greek and Hebrew in his own house, which became a virtual academy for northern European scholars. This intellectual tradition was continued by Amerbach's successor, *Froben.

Ames, William (Amesius; 1576–1633) English Puritan divine. Ames was born at Ipswich. Having gained a reputation as a controversialist while at Cambridge, he left England for the Netherlands after being forbidden to preach at Colchester by the bishop of London. Here he soon made a name for himself as the champion of Calvinism in his debate with the minister of the Arminians at Rotterdam in 1613. Between 1622 and 1633 he was professor of theology at Franeker university in Friesland where his reputation was such that he attracted students from all over Europe. Ill health led to his resignation and he died at Rotterdam a few months later.

Amman, Jobst (1539–91) Swiss-born print maker and designer of stained glass. The son of a choirmaster and teacher of rhetoric, Amman worked first as a stained-glass designer in his native Zürich before moving, successively, to Schaffhausen, Basle, and Nuremberg. Although he is not documented as an assistant of Virgil *Solis, he was effectively the latter's successor as the leading book illustrator in Nuremberg. His voluminous output included numerous ornamental and heraldic prints and title-pages, as well as narrative illustrations. He received numerous commissions from humanists and editors, such as Sigmund Feyerabend of Frankfurt. In 1574 he married the widow of a Nuremberg goldsmith and became a citizen of his adopted city. On account of his commissions he travelled widely: to Augsburg (1578), Frankfurt and Heidelberg (1583), Würzburg (1586–87), and Altdorf (1590). Amman's penetrating portraits, such as *Hans Sachs* and *Wenzel Jamnitzer*, and his genre works and studies, such as the *Series of Animals*, constitute his finest work.

Ammanati, Bartolommeo (1511–92) Italian sculptor. Born near Florence, Ammanati trained in the workshop of Pisa cathedral, where his first independent work is found (1536). In 1540 he tried to make his mark in Florence with a private commission for the tomb of Jacopo Nari, but it was sabotaged by the jealous *Bandinelli, leaving only the effigy and a good allegorical group of *Victory* (both Bargello, Florence). Ammanati left for Venice, where he was helped and influenced by his fellow-countryman Jacopo *Sansovino. His principal sculptures in north Italy were Michelangelesque allegories for the palace and the tomb of the humanist Marco Benavides (1489–1582) in the Eremitani church in Padua.

After Pope Julius III was elected (1550) Ammanati moved to Rome, where he executed all the sculpture on the monuments to members of the pope's family in S Pietro in Montorio. The portrait effigies and allegories are among Ammanati's masterpieces. Moving with Vasari to Florence, he entered the service of the Medici dukes. His spectacular fountain of Juno has six over-life-size marble figures mounted on a rainbow (components now in the Bargello). Ammanati's best-known sculpture is the fountain of Neptune in the Piazza della Signoria, Florence (c. 1560–75). The central figure

was carved out of a colossal block of marble already begun by Bandinelli before his death (1560); this inhibited Ammanati's treatment. More successful are the surrounding bronze figures of marine deities, fauns, and satyrs, modelled and cast under his supervision. These figures and his *Ops*, a female nude statuette, which Ammanati contributed (1572–73), to the Studiolo of Francesco de' Medici, epitomize his style, which concentrates on grace of form at the expense of emotion. Ammanati rivalled Vasari as a mannerist architect, with his amazingly bold but capricious rustication in the courtyard of the Palazzo Pitti (1558–70) and his graceful bridge of Sta Trinità (1567–70). By 1582 the Counter-Reformation so strongly influenced the sculptor that he denounced on moral grounds the public display of nude sculpture.

Amorbach, Johannes *see* Amerbach, Johannes.

Amsdorf, Nikolaus von (1483–1565) German Lutheran theologian. Probably born at Torgau on the Elbe, Amsdorf studied at Wittenberg, where he later met *Luther. He soon became a close friend and one of Luther's most determined supporters. Amsdorf assisted in the translation of the Bible and accompanied Luther to the Leipzig conference (1519) and the Diet of *Worms (1521). He became an evangelical preacher, spreading word of the Reformation at Magdeburg (1524), Goslar (1531), Einbeck (1534), and Schmalkald (1537). John Frederick, Elector of Saxony, appointed him bishop of Naumburg-Zeitz in 1542, a post he held until 1547. In 1548 he helped found the university of Jena, and, in the same year actively opposed the Interim of *Augsburg. From 1552 until his death he lived at Eisenach, remaining a conservative and influential Lutheran.

Amsterdam A Netherlands city and port on the Ijsselmeer, an inlet of the North Sea. As a small fishing village Amsterdam gained toll privileges from Count Floris V of Holland in 1275 and prospered during the Renaissance to become Holland's largest commercial centre by the late fifteenth century. Political developments, combined with the expansion of trade, fishing, and shipbuilding, made sixteenth-century Amsterdam one of the greatest financial and commercial centres. Its citizens rejected Spanish rule and adopted the Calvinist cause under the leadership of *William of Orange (1578); they profited from the Spanish recapture of Antwerp (1585) and the subsequent closure of the River Scheldt to trade. By the early seventeenth century Amsterdam had close to 100 000 inhabitants and could claim to be not only Europe's financial capital but also a centre of world trade, especially the tea and spice trades. Its insti-

AMMANATI Fountain of Neptune (*detail*). (*c. 1560–75; Piazza della Signoria, Florence*)

tutions included the Dutch East India Company (founded 1602), the Amsterdam exchange bank (founded 1609), and the Amsterdam stock exchange. The Nieuwe Kerk is the city's most notable surviving Renaissance building.

Amyot, Jacques (1513–93) French bishop and classical scholar. Born at Melun and educated at Paris university, he became professor of Latin and Greek at Bourges, where he began his work of translating classical authors: Heliodorus (*L'His-*

toire éthiopique, 1548), Longus (*Daphnis et Chloé*, 1559), and, above all, Plutarch. His translation of Plutarch's *Lives*, finally completed under the patronage of Francis I in 1559, supplied the writers and playwrights of several generations with characters and situations. Retranslated into English by Thomas *North (1579), this was Shakespeare's major source for his Roman plays. Amyot's version of Plutarch's *Moralia* appeared in 1572, completing a task that made him deservedly hailed by his contemporaries as "le prince des traducteurs".

Favoured by four successive French kings and tutor to two of them, Amyot was finally made bishop of Auxerre in 1570, where he spent the rest of his life.

Anabaptists A variety of separate religious movements on the radical wing of the *Reformation. The Anabaptists emerged from the underprivileged layers of society, often with exceptionally radical social, economic, and religious programmes. Features common to all included the practice of adult baptism (hence the term "Anabaptists", coined by their enemies), a belief in continual revelation, and a doctrine of separation from the unconverted. Consequently they gained a reputation as dangerous revolutionaries, intent on the destruction of the established social and religious order. Anabaptist activity in Münster (1532–35) marks the peak of their political influence. The existing order in Münster was overthrown by Dutch Anabaptists led by Jan Matthys, a baker of Haarlem, and Jan Leyden (John of Leyden) who hoped to turn the city into a New Jerusalem from which the spiritual conquest of the world could be directed. The chief centres of Anabaptist activity were Saxony, Zürich, Augsburg and the upper Danube, Austria, Moravia, the Tyrol, Poland, Lithuania, Italy, the lower Rhine, and the Netherlands.

anatomy Renaissance anatomists worked almost exclusively in the tradition established by Galen (*see* Galenism, Renaissance). The tradition is clearly seen in Mondino's *Anathomia* (1316), the leading textbook of the early Renaissance. It suffered from two basic weaknesses. In the first place, because of constraints on human *dissection, anatomists had often been forced to work with barbary apes and domestic animals. For this reason they readily followed Galen in describing the *rete mirabile*, a vascular structure they had all supposedly seen at the base of the human brain, despite the fact that it is found in the ox and the sheep but not in man. Once such fictions as the *rete mirabile* and the five-lobed liver entered the literature, they seemed impossible to eliminate. Secondly, anatomy was made to serve the misguided Galenic physiology. If Galen's system needed septal pores to allow blood to pass directly from the right to the left side of the heart, they were conveniently "seen" and reported. To overcome these difficulties it would be necessary to prefer the evidence of nature to the authority of an ancient textbook.

The first real signs of such a transfer of allegiance can be seen in the early sixteenth century. Monographs revealing this tendency were produced by *Leonardo da Vinci, Berengar of Carpi (d.1530), Charles Estienne (*see under* Estienne press) Gunther of Andernach (1487–1584), Sylvius (1478–1555), and, above all, *Vesalius. The new-style monograph used the full resources of Renaissance artists and printers to provide, for the first time, detailed realistic illustrations, whereas earlier works had provided no more than extremely crude stylized diagrams. Moreover, anatomy was becoming a subject of serious artistic study in its own right, with Leonardo and Antonio del *Pollaiuolo leading the way, followed closely by *Michelangelo. A detailed account of the fruits of anatomical studies for artists appears in *Lomazzo's *Trattato* (1584). The first printed anatomical figures appeared in the *Fasciculo de medicina* (1493); fifty years later the *De fabrica* of Vesalius contained some 250 detailed blocks by Jan Steven van *Calcar. At last anatomists had something objective against which to judge their own observations. They soon came to realize that items such as septal pores and five-lobed livers could not be found in the human body. Once having seen that the traditional account of human anatomy was questionable, anatomists could begin the serious task of restructuring their discipline. Part of this task involved the construction of a new vocabulary. Many terms such as "pancreas" and "thyroid" came from Galen himself; others came from Arabic and Hebrew sources; the bulk, however, came from Renaissance anatomists. The Renaissance also saw the emergence of the new discipline of comparative anatomy. *Belon in 1551 had written on the anatomy of marine animals, while Carlo Ruini in his *Anatomia del cavallo* (1599) tackled the anatomy of the horse. On the basis of such detailed monographs Giulio Casserio (1561–1616) could at last present genuinely comparative material in his *De vocis auditusque organis* (1601), a study of the vocal and auditory organs of man, cow, horse, dog, hare, cat, goose, mouse, and pig.

Andrea da Milano *see* Bregno, Andrea.

Andrea del Castagno (1417/19–1457) Italian painter. Castagno, so named after his birthplace, is an important innovator like *Masaccio before him; he introduced a rugged vitality into Florentine painting. Most of Castagno's few surviving paintings and documented lost works are frescoes, including his earliest known commission, the effigies of hanged criminals for the façade of the Bargello (then the communal prison) in Florence in 1440 (now lost). Castagno's serious and heroic figures and interest in movement are already apparent in his earliest frescoes at the chapel of S Tarasio at S Zaccaria, Venice (1442, in collaboration with the little-known Francesco da Faenza). His *Last*

Supper with Scenes of the Passion, which fills the end wall of the refectory at Sant'Apollonia, Florence (1440s), is painted in an unusually dark and rich palette and reveals his skill in difficult perspective effects (for which he was praised by Cristoforo *Landino in 1481), his taste for moments of intense drama, and his involvement in the antiquarianism of the early Renaissance in Florence. *The Trinity Adored by St Jerome and Two Female Saints* (c. 1454; SS Annunziata, Florence), a penitential subject, combines a mood of grave intensity with dramatic foreshortening, qualities also noted in Castagno's moving and tragic *Lamentation*, a design for a stained glass rondel in the drum of the dome of Florence cathedral (1440), in a programme that includes designs by Donatello, Ghiberti, and Uccello.

Castagno's work in Rome for Pope Nicholas V in 1454 has recently been identified as a much restored architectural decoration in the Biblioteca Graeca of the Vatican palace. Landino also praised Castagno for a technique full of spontaneity and liveliness and his ability to create figures which express movement; these traits are best expressed in the *Victorious David* (c. 1450; National Gallery, Washington), one of the few surviving Quattrocento parade shields, and the equestrian monument for Niccolò da Tolentino (fresco, 1455–56; Florence cathedral), which is a pendant and a foil for Uccello's *Hawkwood*. The *Famous Men and Women* frescoes from the Villa Carducci (c. 1450; now Uffizi, with fragments *in situ*) are among the most important surviving Quattrocento secular decorations; Castagno and his patron abandoned well-established iconographic prototypes to introduce Florentine literary figures (Dante, Petrarch, and Boccaccio) and Florentine military leaders (Niccola Acciaiuoli, Farinata degli Uberti, and Pippo Spano) into the company of heroic women from antiquity (Esther, the Cumaean Sybil, and Queen Tomryis). These impressive sculpturesque figures in illusionistic niches reveal Castagno's sources, for in monumentality and boldly massed drapery they recall Masaccio, while in the lucid, sharp outlines, vigorous drapery patterns, and even in pose they convey the impact of the sculpture of Donatello. They offer an appreciation of human dignity and accomplishment which is seminal to an understanding of Renaissance attitudes.

Andrea del Sarto (1486–1530) Italian painter. Andrea d'Agnolo di Francesco was born in Florence, the son of a tailor (hence "del Sarto"). At the age of seven he was apprenticed to a goldsmith, shortly thereafter to a Florentine painter Gian Barile (otherwise unknown), and finally to the eccentric but technically brilliant master *Piero di Cosimo. Internal stylistic evidence suggests that he may have spent time with Raffaellino del Garbo (c. 1466–c. 1524), a painter also known for technical proficiency, although not for innovation. Vasari reports that like many young artists Andrea drew from cartoons by Leonardo da Vinci and Michelangelo, thus absorbing the achievements of the leading artists of the High Renaissance. In style and temperament his leaning was to Leonardo. By about 1506 he had taken a studio near the Piazza del Grano with *Franciabigio, a pupil of *Albertinelli, the latter a partner of Fra Bartolommeo. The early interest in Leonardo and the connection to Fra Bartolommeo through Franciabigio reinforced Andrea's interest in classic compositional solutions, modulated tonal harmonies, and *sfumato*, as shown in *The Marriage of St Catherine* (1512–13; Dresden). He befriended the young sculptor Jacopo *Sansovino, pupil of Andrea Contucci (called Sansovino), and he and Franciabigio moved into a new studio near the SS Annunziata which they shared with Jacopo. The two painters soon received commissions for frescoes for the entrance courtyard of the Annunziata (1509–14; *Birth of the Virgin*, *Arrival of the Magi*, scenes from the life of St Filippo Benizzi) and for the little cloister of the Confraternity of the Scalzo (1511–26; scenes from the life of John the Baptist).

Andrea was influenced as much by the sculpture of the two Sansovinos as by the painters of his generation. The figures of Christ and John the Baptist and of Justice in the Scalzo grisaille murals are quoted directly from identical figures by Andrea Sansovino; Jacopo Sansovino made models for figures which appeared in Andrea del Sarto's paintings, for instance, the Madonna and the St John in the *Madonna of the Harpies* (1517; Uffizi). The painter collaborated with Jacopo on the design and decoration of the mock façade for the Florentine Duomo, one of the elaborate temporary ornaments commissioned for the state visit of Pope Leo X to Florence in 1515. He also worked on stage sets with one of his assistants, Bastiano (Aristotile) da *Sangallo, member of the prominent family of architects. These contacts with sculptors and architects help to explain Andrea's highly developed sense of volume and perspective in his figures and architecture. His figures display an earthbound naturalism in their breadth and volume, yet they exude grace and sensitivity. In 1516 he married the widow Lucrezia, whose features served as the model for his broad-faced Madonnas.

By 1509, with Leonardo in Milan, Michelangelo and Raphael in Rome, and Fra Bartolommeo visiting Venice, Andrea took his place as the premier painter in Florence. Gestures, poses, and compositional groupings in his paintings represent a continual dialogue with his distinguished contemporaries, translated into a pictorial language distinctly his own. Tender blues, delicate violets, and rose tints applied in soft brushwork but with a supreme understanding of form are the pictorial counterpart of the psychological balance between emotion and restraint in his figures.

Andrea worked almost his entire career in Florence. He travelled to France by invitation of Francis I in spring 1518, returning to Florence by summer the following year. His interest in Leonardo was renewed by the presence of that great master at the French court, while two new paintings that he saw there, the *St Michael* and the *Holy Family of Francis I* (both Louvre), presented a point of contact with Raphael's mature Roman style, as witness Andrea's *Caritas* (1518; Louvre) and *Pietà* (1524; Palazzo Pitti, Florence). Among Andrea's pupils and assistants are to be counted the leaders of the next generation of Florentine artists. His use of unconventional effects of colour and light were signals picked up by these young painters, particularly the great "mannerists" Pontormo and Rosso, as well as Vasari and Salviati. Andrea weathered the siege of Florence (1529–30) but died at the end of September 1530 in the plague that followed it.
See Plate I.

Andreoli, Giorgio (Maestro Giorgio; c. 1470–1553) Italian potter. He was born at Intra on Lake Maggiore into a family from Pavia, but is famous for his association with the *majolica works of Gubbio, where he was based from 1498. He held a monopoly in a distinctive ruby glaze, which is one of the most characteristic products of the Gubbio potteries.

Andrewes, Lancelot (1555–1626) English preacher and theologian. The son of a London merchant, Andrewes received an academic education. After taking holy orders (1580) he rose steadily in the Church through his learning (he is reported to have mastered fifteen languages) and his exceptional qualities as a preacher. Under James I, at whose court he regularly preached on Church feast days, he became successively bishop of Chichester (1605), of Ely (1609), and of Winchester (1619). He played a prominent role in the Hampton Court Conference (1604) at which it was decided to produce a new English version of the Bible; when the Authorized (King James) Version was published (1611), Andrewes's name headed the list of translators. Apart from a controversy with Cardinal *Robert Bellarmine concerning the oath of allegiance imposed after the Gunpowder Plot (1605), Andrewes published little in his lifetime, and his two most famous works,

Ninety-Six Sermons (1629) and *Preces Privatae* ("Private Prayers"; 1648), were collected posthumously. Nonetheless he had a formative influence upon Anglican theology and was renowned for his personal integrity as much as for his theological scholarship.

Anerio, Felice (c. 1560–1614) Italian composer. As a boy Anerio sang in the choirs of several major Roman institutions, and his first known composition is music for a Passion play (1582). He was *maestro di cappella* of the English College in Rome (1584–85) and *maestro* of the Vertuosa Compagnia dei Musici di Roma, a society founded (1584) by leading Roman musicians. In 1594 Anerio succeeded *Palestrina as composer to the papal choir. He was also appointed *maestro di cappella* to Duke Altaemps. Most of Anerio's earlier works are secular (madrigals and canzonettes); his sacred works were written largely during his period as papal composer. His Masses, psalms, responsories, and motets are strongly influenced by Palestrina's style, but use some more progressive devices such as frequent word repetitions to stress parts of the text. While Felice Anerio's roots lay firmly in the Palestrina tradition, his brother, Giovanni Francesco (1567–1630), wrote in a distinctly baroque style and concentrated on the small-scale motet with continuo.

Angela Merici, St (1474–1540) Italian religious, founder of the *Ursulines. She spent most of her life at Brescia, where she taught young girls and cared for ill and needy women. On a pilgrimage to the Holy Land (1524–25) she was smitten with temporary blindness. Urged by visions, she founded (1535) a religious community for women at Brescia which she called after St Ursula and of which she became superior in 1537. She was canonized in 1807.

Angeli, Pietro Angelo (Pier Angelo Bargeo; 1517–96) Italian humanist poet. His alternative name derives from his birthplace of Barga, near Lucca. *Siriade* (1591), a Latin epic on the crusader conquest of Jerusalem, was drawn upon by *Tasso for the *Gerusalemme conquistata* (see *Gerusalemme liberata*). Besides his Latin verse, Angeli also wrote pastoral poetry in Italian (*Poesie amorose*, 1589) and translated Sophocles' *Oedipus Rex* into the vernacular.

Angelico, Fra (c. 1395/1400–1455) Fra Angelico, who was born at Vicchio di Mugello, northeast of Florence, was known to his contemporaries by the secular name Guido di Piero and by the religious name Fra Giovanni da Fiesole. Vasari placed his birth about 1387, but reconsideration of documents points to a more likely date of about 1395/1400. The difference of a decade helps correct the older view of Fra Angelico as a painter in the Trecento tradition, and instead places him in the vanguard of artists working in the third and fourth decades of the Quattrocento.

He may have been trained by the miniaturist Battista di Biagio Sanguigni and by the painter Ambrogio di Baldese. A payment recorded to "Guido di Piero" in 1418 is evidence that the young artist was then still a layman; in 1423 his name appears as "Frate Giovanni di San Domenico di Fiesole". Thus he joined the Dominican Order at its house of S Domenico in Fiesole between 1418 and 1423, perhaps inspired by the preaching of the Dominican Fra Manfredi da Vercelli.

As a friar Angelico continued painting, operating a workshop at S Domenico until about 1440, then transferring it to S Marco in Florence, as fresco decoration of that convent was under way. Historical evidence indicates that Angelico was highly regarded in his lifetime both as an intellect and as a painter. Administrative capabilities led to his appointment as substitute *vicario* at S Domenico in 1435, and as *sindicho* at S Marco in 1443. Tradition has it that Pope Eugenius IV, rejecting a number of distinguished candidates for the vacant archbishopric of Florence, offered it to Angelico, but that the artist was instrumental in securing the appointment of Fra (later St) *Antonino to that position in 1446. In a lost epitaph for his tomb in Sta Maria sopra Minerva, Rome, Angelico was celebrated as "…consummate painter, who had no equal in his art"; in a poem by the sixteenth-century painter Giovanni Santi, the father of Raphael, he is mentioned alongside Fra Filippo Lippi and Domenico Veneziano as "Giovan da Fiesole frate al ben ardente."

Establishing a chronology for Angelico's œuvre poses problems of connoisseurship and dating, particularly for his earliest period. Notable among the early works are the *Annunciation* (1428–32; Museo Diocesano, Cortona) and the Linaiuoli tabernacle (1433–35; Museo di S Marco, Florence), in which Angelico demonstrated an interest in the new manner of Masaccio and Ghiberti. He employed skilful perspective and spatial continuity and contributed advances in the depiction of natural phenomena. The period 1438–45 is dominated by a commission from the church and convent of S Marco for the altarpiece of the *cappella maggiore* and for the fresco decoration of the public quarters and private cells of the convent. The design and concept, linking the entire group of fifty-four frescoes, are Angelico's, though the work is largely that of assistants. The meditative clarity, simplicity, and order reflect *Michelozzo's architectural schemes, emphasizing, through economy of detail, the didactic and doctrinal gestures of the saints and biblical figures represented. In contrast, the S Marco altarpiece is rich in sumptuous textiles and architectural devices used to project and delimit an original perspective scheme. In the *Deposition* (Museo di S Marco), a frieze of foreground figures gives way to a panoramic landscape, bathed in a light which renders spatial coherence to the composition.

Angelico was called to Rome in 1445. It was during this Roman sojourn that he probably frescoed the private chapel of Pope Nicholas V in the Vatican with scenes from the lives of St Stephen and St Lawrence; in these the figures and architecture take on a new volume and gravity. In 1449 he was elected prior of his convent.

Angelico's reputation and (certainly) his nickname depend on the appeal of precious images of the Madonna and Child framed in a glory of angels, delicately painted in enamel-like colours on a gold ground. But it is the power to translate the quality of the miniaturist's art into the scale and vocabulary of the modern mode which distinguishes him. The result is an edifying and pious pictorial language, brilliant in the balance struck between celestial vision and the laws of nature.

Anghiera, Pietro Martire d' *see* Peter Martyr (Pietro Martire d'Anghiera).

Anguisciola, Sophonisba (1527– c. 1623) Italian painter. A native of Cremona, Sophonisba was the daughter of a Piedmontese nobleman and one of the first Italian women to become an artist. She was a pupil of Bernardino Campi and became a noted portrait painter in the mannerist style, executing several self-portraits and depictions of prominent figures in society. Her best works include a family group portrait of her sisters playing chess (Museum Narodowe, Poznań, Poland). She moved to Madrid in 1559 and also worked in Sicily, only returning to Italy when an old woman.

Anjou, Francis, Duke of Alençon- *see* Francis, Duke of Alençon.

Anjou, houses of Three French dynasties whose power was initially based on the lower Loire region of France. The first house of Anjou lasted from the ninth century until it lost its territories to the French crown in the early thirteenth century; it also ruled England from 1154 to 1157. The second was founded in 1246 by Charles, brother of Louis IX of France and later king of Naples and Sicily. One line of his descendants ruled Naples, another Hungary. When Philip of Valois succeeded to the French throne in 1328, Anjou, which he had inher-

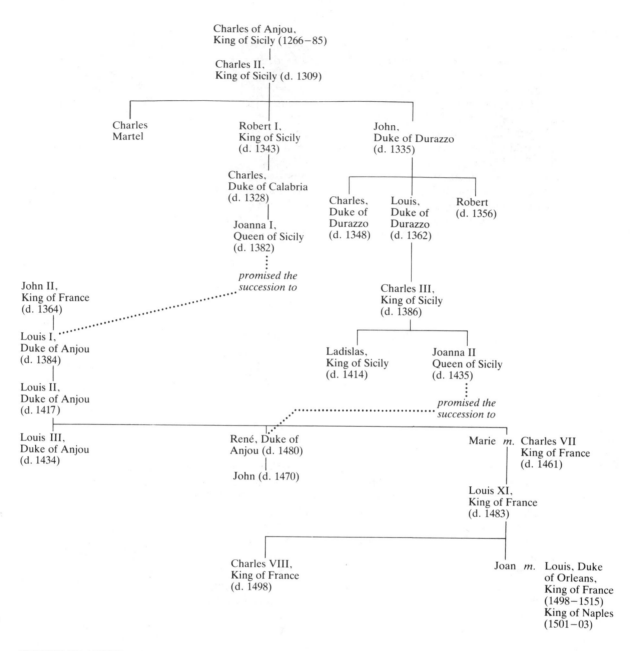

Charles of Anjou,
King of Sicily (1266–85)

Charles II,
King of Sicily (d. 1309)

Charles
Martel

Robert I,
King of Sicily
(d. 1343)

John,
Duke of Durazzo
(d. 1335)

Charles,
Duke of Calabria
(d. 1328)

Charles,
Duke of
Durazzo
(d. 1348)

Louis,
Duke of
Durazzo
(d. 1362)

Robert
(d. 1356)

Joanna I,
Queen of Sicily
(d. 1382)

*promised the
succession to*

John II,
King of France
(d. 1364)

Charles III,
King of Sicily
(d. 1386)

Louis I,
Duke of Anjou
(d. 1384)

Ladislas,
King of Sicily
(d. 1414)

Joanna II
Queen of Sicily
(d. 1435)

Louis II,
Duke of Anjou
(d. 1417)

*promised the
succession to*

Louis III,
Duke of Anjou
(d. 1434)

René, Duke of
Anjou (d. 1480)

Marie   *m.*   Charles VII
King of France
(d. 1461)

John (d. 1470)

Louis XI,
King of France
(d. 1483)

Charles VIII,
King of France
(d. 1498)

Joan   *m.*   Louis, Duke
of Orleans,
King of France
(1498–1515)
King of Naples
(1501–03)

HOUSES OF ANJOU   *The Angevin claim to Naples and Sicily*

ited from his mother, was reunited to the French crown. In 1351 the third house of Anjou was founded when John II of France invested his younger son Louis with Anjou. Joanna I of Naples promised Naples to Louis in 1379 and in the fifteenth century the later Angevins spent much of their time fruitlessly pursuing their claim to Naples. In 1480 *René I, the last male heir, died, and Angevin claims to Naples, Sicily, Hungary, and Jerusalem passed to the French crown.

Antico (Pier Jacopo di Antonio Alari Bonacolsi; c. 1460–1528) Italian sculptor, bronze-founder, and medallist. Born in Mantua and trained as a goldsmith, he had received his nickname by 1479 (when he used it to sign two medals) owing to his knowledge of antiquity, interest in archaeology, and brilliance at recreating in bronze statuettes some of the fragmentary masterpieces of Greco-Roman sculpture (e.g. the *Apollo Belvedere*, *Venus*, *Meleager*, and *Hercules and Antaeus*). He worked for various members of the *Gonzaga dynasty in and around Mantua, notably for Isabella d'Este, and visited Rome twice in the 1490s. His style is a sculptural counterpart to *Mantegna's in painting, emphasizing the smooth, rotund forms of the human body and contrasting their polished surfaces with intricately chiselled details in the hair, drapery, and accoutrements, which are often gilded, while the eyes are sometimes inlaid in silver.

Antiquaries, Society of A British society dedicated to the preservation of the national historic heritage. In its original form it was founded in 1572 by Archbishop Matthew *Parker with the collaboration of William *Camden and other scholars. Its early proceedings were preserved among Sir Robert *Cotton's papers and were published in 1720 as *A Collection of Curious Discourses*. James I suppressed the society in 1604, on suspicion of political intrigue, but it was formally revived in 1717.

Antonello da Messina (c. 1430–79) Sicilian-born Italian painter. Antonello probably trained initially with *Colantonio in Naples. His earliest surviving pictures, such as the London *Salting Madonna*, are however more profoundly conditioned by Netherlandish works than anything which Colantonio is known to have painted, so it seems likely that Antonello also received tuition from a Netherlandish painter, probably Petrus *Christus or a close follower. Antonello's Reggio *St Jerome in Penitence* and *Visit of the Three Angels to Abraham* and his London *Salvator Mundi* (1465) are distinctly Eyckian. His slightly later London *St Jerome in his Study* incorporates compositional motifs derived from Jan van *Eyck and Rogier van der *Weyden. It is plausible that this picture was executed during an undocumented visit to Venice (c. 1465–70), for Antonello's *St Gregory* polyptych (Messina; 1473) and *Fathers of the Church* altarpiece (Palermo) indicate a knowledge of both the figure style of *Piero della Francesca and the altarpieces of Giovanni *Bellini. His Syracuse *Annunciation* (1474) revolutionalizes a typical Netherlandish interior by the addition of a monumental figures and architectural motifs derived from Piero and the rigorous application of one-point perspective.

In 1475–76 Antonello was in Venice, where he painted the now fragmentary S Cassiano alterpiece (Vienna), partly modelled on Giovanni Bellini's lost altarpiece at the Venetian church of SS Giovanni e Paolo. In its turn, it was influential upon Venetian altarpieces to the end of the fifteenth century. Antonello's last major work, the Dresden *St Sebastian*, was also painted in Venice. In addition to religious works, Antonello painted a number of portraits which forcefully reinterpret a format initiated by Jan van *Eyck.

By far the most significant south Italian painter of the fifteenth century, Antonello's importance is far from merely local. He was the first Italian artist to be thoroughly conversant with the Netherlandish glazed oil technique and was a major influence upon the course of Venetian Renaissance painting.

Antoniazzo Romano (c. 1460–1508) Italian painter. Trained under the Umbrian followers of Fra *Angelico and Benozzo *Gozzoli, Antoniazzo was also influenced by *Melozzo da Forlì, *Perugino, *Botticelli, and *Ghirlandaio. He executed numerous frescoes in Rome and elsewhere and paintings by him of Madonnas and other religious subjects survive in several northern Italian galleries. During the second half of the fifteenth century he was the most significant painter working in Rome.

Antonino, St (Antonio Pierozzi; 1389–1459) Italian theologian, historian, and economist. Inspired by the preaching of John Dominici, Antonino joined the Dominican Order in 1405 at Cortona. From an early age he was greatly troubled by corruption in Church and society, and much of his life was spent in fighting this corruption. He became prior of the Dominican house in Fiesole in 1425. In 1436 or 1437, with the aid of Cosimo de' *Medici, he established the convent of S Marco in his native Florence. Between 1439 and 1445 he attended the Council of Florence (*see* Florence, Council of) and secured the lasting respect of the papacy. He received the archbishopric of Florence in 1446 but continued to live as a humble friar, spending what he could of the see's revenues on the poor. At the same time he appreciated the value of trade in relation to ecclesiastical wealth and was influential in lessening the Church's medieval distrust of commerce. Antonino was canonized in 1523, and his works continued to be widely published throughout the sixteenth century.

Antwerp A Netherlands (now Belgian) city and port on the River Scheldt, fifty-five miles from the North Sea. Antwerp was a Gallo-Roman foundation (about 200 AD), which was ruled by Franks or Frisians after the fall of Rome. By the early fourteenth century it was ruled by the dukes of Brabant and known for its flourishing trade with England, Venice, and Genoa and for its trade fairs. Antwerp's population grew rapidly from 20 000 in 1400 to 100 000 in 1550, overtaking Bruges as the leading mercantile centre in the Netherlands. In the first half of the sixteenth century Antwerp received its first cargo of pepper from Lisbon (1501) and became a centre for the spice trade; Antwerp at first prospered under *Habsburg rule (from 1477), pioneering the extension of credit and making the first public loan to the Netherlands government (1511). The Antwerp stock exchange is one of the oldest in Europe (established 1531). Later in the sixteenth century Antwerp's prosperity was destroyed by religious and political disputes. As an important Calvinist centre by 1560, Antwerp suffered severely during the revolt of the *Netherlands; a savage Spanish attack, the "Spanish fury" (1576), destroyed about a third of the town and killed about 7000 citizens. Later (1583), in the "French fury", the town was attacked by French troops under *Francis, Duke of (Alençon-)Anjou. After Spain recaptured Antwerp (1585) its power and wealth declined, crippled by the war and the closure of the River Scheldt to trade. During the Renaissance Antwerp was an important centre for arts and scholarship with its own school of painting in the late fifteenth century and numerous printing presses after the arrival of *Plantin (1548). It was also a centre for humanist scholarship. Antwerp's most notable building from the Renaissance period is the town hall (1561–66).

Antwerp Polyglot Bible see under Arias (y) Montano, Benito; Hebrew studies; Plantin press.

Aphrodite see under Venus.

Apian, Peter (Peter Bienewitz; 1495–1552) German astronomer, mathematician, and geographer. Educated at the universities of Leipzig and Vienna, Apian was later appointed to the chair of mathematics at Ingolstadt university. He established his reputation with the issue of a world map in 1520, and the subsequent publication of his *Cosmographia* (1524), a work of geography. He later published an arithmetical textbook, *Rechnung* (1527), which contained the first printed account of Pascal's triangle. In astronomy Apian's most important work was his *Astronomicum caesareum* (1540), containing a detailed description of five comets, one of which was the 1531 appearance of Halley's comet. Apian was also the first to note that the tails of comets invariably point away from the sun.

Apollo The classical sun-god, who was adopted into Renaissance iconography as the embodiment of reason and order, and thus particularly associated with philosophy. He was also closely associated with artistic creativity, and he appears as patron of the *Muses and *Graces in music, art, and literature. This concept is epitomized in the crude woodcut illustrating *Gaffurio's *Practica musice* (1496), showing a whole range of musical correspondences, with Apollo, crowned and holding a musical instrument, at the head of the picture, three dumpy Graces on his right, and below them medallions depicting the Muses.

Apollo's role as the creator of universal order through music is also celebrated in the myth of his victory in a musical contest with the satyr Marsyas (symbol of the irrational and uncontrollable), a subject treated by *Raphael in a fresco for the Stanza della Segnatura, as well as by Pietro *Perugino, *Giulio Romano, *Titian, and Guido *Reni. An allegory of the pursuit of artistic excellence was perceived in the story, taken from Ovid's *Metamorphoses*, of Apollo's pursuit of the nymph Daphne, who was transformed into a laurel tree at the instant that he caught her; the scene is depicted in a painting attributed to Antonio Pollaiuolo (National Gallery, London).

Aquaviva, Claudius (1543–1615) Italian theologian, fifth general of the Society of Jesus. Having joined the *Jesuits in 1567, Aquaviva was elected general in 1581, the youngest in the history of the society. He was faced with a variety of internal disputes, most importantly the claims of the Spanish Jesuits for special privileges; these he successfully opposed by defeating Spanish demands for an additional commissary-general for Spain. Aquaviva's writings include his *Directorium* (1591), a guide to *Ignatius Loyola's *Spiritual Exercises*, and his *Ratio Studiorum* (Method of Studies; 1586), a system of education for Jesuit schools, unchallenged until this century. His introduction of *Litterae Annuae* helped improve the society's efficiency, and during his time in office its membership increased from around 5000 to over 13 000. Aquaviva is honoured for his work in helping to preserve the society's Ignatian tradition during a time when Loyola's principles were seriously threatened.

Aragon, house of The royal family descended from Ramiro of Navarre who inherited the Pyrenean territory of Aragon in 1035. Succeeding generations enlarged the family's inheritance by judicious marriages and by conquest. By the end of the thirteenth century they had driven the Moors out of northern Spain and ruled Aragon, Catalonia, Valencia, and the Balearic Islands. Peter III's acquisition of Sicily after the ejection of the island's Angevin rulers following the Sicilian Vespers (1282) enabled the house of Aragon to become a major Mediterranean power, ruling over Sardinia, Naples, Sicily, and Athens, and enjoying the benefits of a flourishing maritime trade. Alfonso V, who had conquered Naples in 1442 (*see* Alfonso I), left Naples to his illegitimate son, Ferrante (*Ferdinand I), in 1458; his other domains passed to his brother. The last male heir, *Ferdinand II, whose marriage to Isabella of Castile prepared the way for the union of Spain, reunited Naples with the crown of Aragon in 1504.

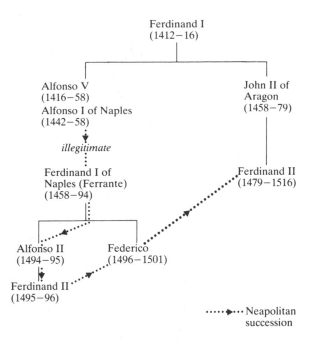

Ferdinand I
(1412–16)

Alfonso V
(1416–58)
Alfonso I of Naples
(1442–58)

John II of
Aragon
(1458–79)

illegitimate

Ferdinand I of
Naples (Ferrante)
(1458–94)

Ferdinand II
(1479–1516)

Alfonso II
(1494–95)

Federico
(1496–1501)

Ferdinand II
(1495–96)

·····▸··· Neapolitan
succession

HOUSE OF ARAGON *The simplified family tree (with regnal dates) shows the separation of the kingdom of Naples from that of Aragon in the mid-fifteenth century and the reunion of the two realms under Ferdinand II of Aragon.*

music, but his secular works are better known. There are extant 126 chansons and over 200 madrigals. The chansons were very popular, the earlier ones reflecting the influence of Josquin and the later ones written in Arcadelt's characteristic homophonic style, shifting between triple and duple time. All are of a sentimental nature and eschew licentious texts. In the madrigals, the text is of paramount importance, and musical effects are not permitted to interfere with its rhythmic requirements. One such madrigal, "Il bianco e dolce cigno" was consistently popular.

Arcadia The remote, mountainous area of southern Greece to which Virgil referred in his *Eclogues* and which thus passed into literary convention as the setting for the idealized world of the *pastoral. When writers revived the pastoral as a literary form in the Renaissance, it was the idealized landscape of Arcadia, not the reality, which dominated their works, and "Arcadia" became the title of more than one book. In 1504 a sequence of verse eclogues linked by prose narrative was published by the Neapolitan poet Jacopo *Sannazaro. The first pastoral romance, it concerns the unrequited love of the hero Sincero who retires into Arcadia to share the rustic life of the shepherds. Written in Italian, rather than Latin, it was a very popular and influential work. The *Arcadia* of Sir Philip *Sidney, a pastoral romance in prose, interspersed with lyrics, exists in two versions. The first was written between 1577 and 1580, but during the years 1580–84 Sidney undertook a radical revision of the work and added a third book. This version was published posthumously as *The Countesse of Pembroke's Arcadia* (1590). Common to both is the golden world of Arcadia itself and the trials and exploits of the two princes Musidorus and Pyrocles as they struggle to win their loves.

Aragona, Tullia d' (1508–56) Italian poet and courtesan. The daughter of a courtesan and possibly of Luigi, Cardinal of Aragon, Tullia attracted numerous aristocratic and scholarly admirers, including the Florentine historians Jacopo *Nardi and Benedetto *Varchi and the Paduan poet Girolamo *Muziano. She published poems, mainly imitating Petrarch, in *Rime* (1547), dedicated to Eleonora, wife of *Cosimo I de' Medici. Her *Dialogo dell'infinità d'amore* (1547) is a fashionable Neoplatonic essay on love.

Arca, Niccolò dell' (*or* Niccolò di Bari *or* Niccolò da Bologna) *see* Niccolò dell'Arca.

Arcadelt, Jacques (?1505–68) French or Flemish composer. Though little is known about his early life, there is evidence he may have spent time in Florence after 1532, when the Medici regained control there. On the assassination of Alessandro de' Medici (1537), Arcadelt probably moved to Venice and from 1540 he was in papal service in Rome. In 1544 he entered the employ of Charles of Lorraine, later archbishop of Reims, and settled in Reims until at least 1562. He may have belonged to the French court chapel and died in retirement in Paris.
Arcadelt almost certainly studied with Josquin *Des Prés; his Masses in particular show Josquin's influence. Arcadelt began by composing sacred

archeus A term introduced by *Paracelsus to denote the vital power of an organism to respond appropriately to various stimuli. Thus, the role of the archeus of the stomach was to extract the digestible parts of food and dispose of the remainder. A failure of the archeus would lead to poisoning and sickness. The notion persisted throughout the seventeenth century but finally disappeared before the growing acceptance of the mechanical philosophy.

architecture Humanist scholarship of the early fifteenth century, characterized by a nostalgic yearning for the bygone age of Roman splendour, had far-reaching repercussions within the visual arts. Classical literature, as well as antique monuments which survived throughout Italy, acted as testimonials to the glories of Rome before the

ARCHITECTURE *The masterpiece of Antonio I Sangallo, the pilgrimage church of the Madonna di S Biagio occupies a hill-top site at Montepulciano, near Cortona. Work was begun in 1518 on the church, which has a simple Greek cross plan. The dignified exterior exemplifies the poise of the most accomplished Renaissance architecture.*

influx of the barbarians and their foreign (Gothic) culture. Not surprisingly, architects were quick to translate the humanists' literary attempts to emulate antiquity into "the ancient manner of building". *Vitruvius, whose architectural treatise, *De architectura*, survived from antiquity, was known throughout the Middle Ages in Italy, but Poggio *Bracciolini's discovery (1414) of a superior manuscript of *De architectura* coincided with a surging interest in the principles of ancient building. The *editio princeps*, without illustrations, appeared at Rome (c. 1486); Fra *Giocondo published an illustrated edition at Venice in 1511; Cesariano's Italian translation followed in 1521, and Daniele *Barbaro's version came out in 1556, with illustrations by *Palladio.

Vitruvian theory centred upon three elements: utility, strength, and beauty. The concept of beauty was to preoccupy Renaissance architects from *Brunelleschi to Inigo *Jones. Vitruvius' notion of beauty derived from the modular interrelationship of every part of the whole, creating a harmonious and symmetrical unit. *Alberti, in his widely disseminated treatise *De re aedificatoria* (*editio princeps* 1485), defined beauty as "the harmony of all the parts ... fitted together with such proportion

and connection that nothing could be added, diminished, or altered but for the worse ...". This summarized the underlying principles of Renaissance architecture. Thus Alberti introduced large volutes on the upper storey of Sta Maria Novella (1456–70) in Florence in order to unify visually the nave and aisles, and Brunelleschi, in designing the Ospedale degli Innocenti (1421), also in Florence, laid out the plan on a grid system and ensured that the placement of the exterior doors mirrored the disposition of the interior spaces.

Vitruvius regarded architecture as an imitation of nature. For instance, he distinguished three column types, Doric, Ionic, and Corinthian, whose proportions and symbolism derived, respectively, from a man, matron, and young girl. This anthropomorphic view of architecture had a profound influence on Renaissance architects who were working in an age that celebrated man's individuality. However, the correct use of the vocabulary of orders was a High Renaissance phenomenon. *Bramante employed the Tuscan Doric order in the Tempietto in S Pietro in Montorio, Rome, as befitting a martyrium commemorating St Peter but *Francesco di Giorgio Martini, the early Renaissance theorist, took anthropomorphism to fanciful extremes in his sketches of young girls trapped within the confines of a column shaft.

Nineteenth-century art historians castigated the Renaissance masters for their imitation of pagan antiquity, but the Renaissance was not about imitation, rather the application of the antique to provide a new architectural vocabulary employed in a creative manner. Brunelleschi's Pazzi chapel in Florence, begun in 1429, has a portico carried on columns and pilasters on the interior walls which look as if they support an entablature, creating a visual harmony of forms and colours which derive from, but do not plagiarize, antique motifs. Alberti imposed a pedimented triumphal arch on the façade of the Mantuan church of S Andrea (c. 1470) and placed sarcophagi in arches along the side of the *Tempio Malatestiano in Rimini in emulation of the antique. Pagan temples, such as that of Minerva Medica in Rome, were to inspire a fascination in the circular form. Brunelleschi, Alberti, *Leonardo da Vinci, *Michelozzo and Bramante all experimented with circular forms in relation to church design. Its association with pagan worship lent the circular plan an air of controversy, although Alberti maintained that the circle, according to Neoplatonic theory, was appropriate to Christian piety, for it was the basis of divine harmony in nature. The problem remained, however, that a centrally planned church did not accommodate the need to separate clergy and laity according to Roman liturgy. Thus, although Bramante designed St Peter's, Rome, in the form of a Greek cross, it was built in the traditional basilica shape.

Secular architecture gave Renaissance architects far more scope in the use of antique vocabulary. Designs for *theatres show the gradual adaptation of classical plans to the different dramatic circumstances of the Renaissance. The urban *palazzo* emerged quite naturally from the classical *insula*, with its shops on the ground floor and living quarters on the *piano nobile*. Michelozzo's Palazzo Medici Riccardi (1444), with its rusticated basement and airy courtyard, has a massive classical cornice, and Alberti's Palazzo Rucellai (c. 1445–51) exhibits a network of superimposed pilasters on its façade. These examples of early Renaissance architecture are characterized by a superficial application of classical motifs. *Raphael's design for the Villa Madama (c. 1518) in Rome was a reinterpretation of an antique villa based upon the writings of Pliny the Younger.

Julius II's ambitious building programme, which included the reconstruction of St Peter's and the Vatican palace, as well as the development of new streets, moved the focus of Renaissance art from Florence to Rome. Working in the shadow of majestic classical monuments, architects were compelled towards a new and archaeologically pure interpretation of the antique. In 1515 Raphael was appointed superintendent of Roman antiquities, which prompted his scheme to measure and draw Roman remains. The newly uncovered Domus Aurea (Golden House) of Nero, with its rich *grotesque interior decoration, inspired the *all'antiqua* decoration of Raphael's Vatican Loggie (1518–19) and the façade of the Palazzo dell'Aquila (now destroyed). An increasing desire for a "Roman" quality in architecture, led to a greater monumentality in the handling of space and a greater plasticity in ornamentation. Bramante's design for the internal spaces of St Peter's shows apses and chapels scooped out of the heavy wall mass. The Roman Palazzo Vidoni Cafarelli, perhaps by Raphael (c. 1525), has a grandly sculpted façade with windows on the *piano nobile* set between paired columns. This rich and rhythmical façade contrasts with the flat surface of the Palazzo Rucellai, where the ornamentation is applied rather than organic. The Palazzo *Farnese, begun in 1517 to designs by Antonio da *Sangallo and modified by *Michelangelo, *Vignola, and Giacomo *della Porta, was the last great Roman monument of the High Renaissance. The huge wall expanse, enlivened by perfectly proportioned aedicules and bold quoins, and the imposing central doorway create a gravity and elegance that summarized the architectural aims of the period. Henceforth the High Renaissance buildings of Rome would combine with classical remains as a

source for architects such as Palladio, who would spread the new architectural vocabulary to northern Italy and beyond.

The Italian Renaissance was exported to the north in the wake of the French invasions of Italy, beginning in 1494 when the armies of Charles VIII marched into Lombardy. The spread of Renaissance values depended upon political and economic circumstances; after 1620, for instance, the Thirty Years' War precluded building on any scale in Germany and Austria during the first half of the seventeenth century, and abruptly curtailed the output of those architects, like Elias *Holl, who had transplanted the Italian ideals.

Without firsthand knowledge of remains of classical antiquity, the northern architects' response to Renaissance principles was fundamentally derivative. In France and England the Italian style of building was applied merely to surface decoration. The sixteenth-century French châteaux of *Chambord and *Chenonceau were sophisticated pastiches of Italian *palazzi*, with antique motifs superimposed upon the medieval French fortress plan. In England an extravagant expression of mainly medieval splendour emerged during the Elizabethan age (*see* Elizabethan style), 150 years after Brunelleschi initiated the Renaissance in Florence. The only country to employ a pure Italian style in the sixteenth century was Spain, although the exuberant *plateresque idiom was also in evidence at least until mid-century. The *Escorial, built for Philip II, displays an austere classicism, the centralized plan of its church recalling Bramante. However, by the seventeenth century this Italianate style was eclipsed by the excesses of the *Baroque. Elsewhere the deeply rooted Gothic traditions continued until the advent of Inigo Jones in England and Mansart and Le Vau in France in the seventeenth century.

Arcimboldo, Giuseppe (?1527–93) Italian painter. His early designs for stained-glass windows (1549–58) for the cathedral in his native Milan gave little hint of the bizarre later paintings for which he is best known. In 1562 he moved to the Habsburg court in Prague, where he designed court entertainments and ceremonies and painted settings for the imperial theatre. His grotesque oil paintings of symbolic figures composed of such objects as pieces of fruit, vegetables, and trees are said to have influenced twentieth-century surrealist painters (see Plate II); his depictions of *Summer* and *Winter* (Kunsthistorisches Museum, Vienna) are typical examples. He was made a count palatine by Emperor Rudolf II in 1592, a year before his death in Milan.

Arena Chapel (*or* Scrovegni Chapel) The chapel

built (1303–05) for Enrico Scrovegni on the site of a first-century Roman amphitheatre (arena) in Padua. The interior is decorated with frescoes by Giotto and his followers. The main decorative scheme, in three zones along the side walls, depicts the history of the Redemption in scenes from the lives of Mary and Jesus Christ. A fourth zone, below these, has allegorical figures of virtues and vices.

Areopagus The shadowy, perhaps fictitious, literary society of poets who aimed to reform English poetry along classical lines in the late 1570s. Chief among them were *Spenser, *Sidney, and Sir Edward Dyer (1543–1607), all protégés of the earl of Leicester, at whose house they could have met. The name derives from the hill northwest of the Athenian Acropolis, on which the tribunal of the ancient city used to meet.

Aretino, Francesco see under Accolti family.

Aretino, Leonardo see Bruni, Leonardo.

Aretino, Pietro (1492–1556) Italian poet, dramatist, and one of the most vigorous and inventive writers of the sixteenth century. The son of a shoemaker in Arezzo (the town from which he took his name), Aretino probably received little formal education. However, in 1510 he went to Perugia where he was soon welcomed into the company of cultivated men and was able to develop his interest in painting and poetry. In 1517 he moved to Rome, eventually joining the literary circle around Pope *Leo X. Here his lifelong love of political and ecclesiastical gossip surfaced in a series of vicious pasquinades that found favour with Cardinal Giulio de' Medici, whose rivals for the papacy Aretino lampooned (see Clement VII). Predictably, Aretino soon went too far with his pornographic illustrated collection of *Sonnetti lussuriosi* (Lewd Sonnets; 1524); he was eventually forced to retreat to Venice (1527) where he lived out his life in grand, if dissolute, style, surrounded by many of the great artists of the day.

Aretino continued his satirical campaigns, transforming Venice's somewhat unsophisticated broadsheets by his acute political comments. His six volumes of letters (1537–57) also demonstrate the great force and versatility of his writing. Known, in a phrase of *Ariosto's, as "il flagello dei principe" (the scourge of princes), Aretino never moderated his attacks on the powerful, many of whom placated him with gifts which became the chief source of his income. *Ragionamenti* (1534–36), in which Roman prostitutes discuss their eminent clients, shows him at his most venomous in his condemnation of moral and political corrup-

tion in Rome. His plays, on the other hand, lack the obsessively satirical intent of his prose works. The tragedy *Orazia* (1546) and his five comedies written between 1524 and 1544 are often considered to be some of the greatest works of the period. The comedies, which deal mainly with lower-middle-class life, are noticeably free from the conventions that dogged most other dramas of the time. Best known among them is *La cortigiana* (Life at Court), which was first performed in 1537. Aretino also tried his hand at the genres of poetry, devotional writing, and romantic epic.

Aretino, Unico (Bernardo Accolti) see under Accolti family.

Argyropoulos, John (c. 1415–87) Byzantine scholar. He was born into a noble family in Constantinople, where he became a priest. His first visit to Italy was before 1434; in that year he was lecturing at Padua on the works of Aristotle. In 1439 he attended Emperor John Palaeologus at the Council of *Florence. By 1441 he was back in Constantinople, but he returned to Italy in 1442, when he became rector of Padua university. Cosimo de' *Medici was one of his patrons and he was tutor to Piero, Cosimo's son, and to Lorenzo de' *Medici. When Lorenzo assumed power in Florence, Argyropoulos became a leading member of his *Platonic Academy, where he taught *Politian and other humanists. In 1456 he visited France, then returned to Florence, and eventually settled in Rome some time before 1471. He continued to expound the works of Aristotle and other Greek authors. The German scholar *Reuchlin was among his pupils. He wrote many original commentaries on Aristotle and translated a number of his works into Latin; much of Argyropoulos' original work remains unprinted. He was an important member of the first generation of Greek teachers in the West who helped to encourage the revival of classical learning.

Arias (y) Montano, Benito (1527–98) Spanish priest and writer. Arias Montano was born at Fregenal de la Sierra, near Badajoz, and studied oriental languages at Seville, Alcalá, and Leon. He accompanied the bishop of Segovia to the Council of *Trent, and was noted for his ability and erudition. He returned to a hermitage at Aracena, near Seville, and later was appointed professor of oriental languages and librarian at the Escorial. As editor of the Antwerp Polyglot Bible (1568–73) he was denounced to the Inquisition for attaching too much importance to the Hebrew and Aramaic texts; tried and acquitted, he afterwards retired to Seville. He was the author of theological and historical works, including one on Jewish antiquities (1593), and a poetic paraphrase of the Song of Solomon.

Ariosto, Ludovico (1474–1533) Italian poet. Ariosto was born at Reggio, in Emilia. He studied law by necessity and literature by inclination at Ferrara, then joined the household of Cardinal Ippolito d' Este, whom he served from 1503 to 1517. After this he entered the service of the cardinal's brother, Duke Alfonso I, who appointed him ducal commissioner at Garfagnana (1522). Ariosto spent three testing years there, after which he retired (1527) to Ferrara where he devoted his remaining days to meditation and the revising of his masterpiece *Orlando furioso*, which he had started in 1502 and completed only a few months before he died.

Ariosto's other major work belongs to the period 1517–25, a set of seven *Satires* or verse epistles in the Horatian manner, written in *terza rima* and depicting Ferrarese court life. Ariosto has also been seen as a pioneer dramatist, since his verse comedies, such as *I suppositi* (1509), though minor works in themselves, were the earliest vernacular plays based closely on Latin models which were to be a feature of European domestic comedy. He also supervised the building of a theatre at Ferrara in which his plays were performed. He died in Ferrara, having achieved recognition during his last years as Italy's greatest contemporary poet.

Aristotelianism, Renaissance The first printed edition of *Aristotle's Opera omnia* appeared in Padua in 1472–74; it was followed in the period 1495–98 by the publication of the Greek *princeps*. Thereafter the continuing importance of Aristotle to the Renaissance scholar is revealed by the publication of thirteen further editions of his collected works during the sixteenth century. For some, the Aristotelian canon was both comprehensive and authoritative. So much so, according to a well-publicized minority, that anything unrecorded by Aristotle was obviously fictitious. Such obtuseness was shown, for example, by the Paduan philosopher Cesare Cremonini in 1610 in response to Galileo's reported discovery of the moons of Jupiter. As they were unrecorded by Aristotle, Cremonini objected, they could not possibly exist. Equally dogmatic positions were adopted by *Ramus and *Bacon in opposition to Aristotle. Ramus had reportedly argued in Paris in 1536 that everything taught by Aristotle was false. More reasonably, Bacon had warned his contemporaries to apply themselves to "the study of things themselves. Be not for ever the property of one man."

The majority of scholars, however, adopted neither extreme position. For them Aristotle offered a comprehensive account of the universe, together with detailed textbooks on virtually all branches of knowledge. Consequently most scholars worked unthinkingly within the confines of Aristotelianism, and even those wishing to break free often found they could do no more than modify its basic structure. In many areas Aristotelian principles emerged from the Renaissance unscathed. When, for example, Newton entered Cambridge in 1661 he studied as an undergraduate Aristotelian physics, logic, rhetoric, ethics, and metaphysics. Missing from the list are astronomy and cosmology, the first disciplines, under the influence of *Copernicus, *Galileo, and *Kepler, to break away from their classical assumptions.

With regard to the more basic concepts of matter, motion, and change, less progress was apparent. Aristotle had rejected the atomism and the monism of his predecessors and argued that matter was formed from four basic elements: earth, air, fire, and water. While many Renaissance scientists quarrelled with details of this account, none could break away completely. The names of the elements might be changed and the numbers decreased to three, or increased to five or more, but the theory remained in essence Aristotelian. Equally, while all agreed that Aristotle's account of motion was inadequate, it was less easy to find an acceptable replacement. The problem lay with the motion of projectiles, falling bodies, and the planets. What kept them in motion? Aristotle's answer in terms of "natural" motion, or the action of the medium, had never proved popular, not even to otherwise committed Aristotelians. No significant advance could be made, however, until the concept of inertia was introduced into physics, and this was a post-Renaissance development. At a more fundamental level Aristotle had insisted that change of all kind must be explained in terms of his four causes: material, efficient, formal, and final. Thus, for Aristotle, a statue would have been caused by the material it was made from, the sculptor who made it (efficient cause), the object it represented (formal cause), and its final cause or purpose. While much of the Aristotelian vocabulary survived the Renaissance, some scholars began to question the value assigned to final causes. "Research into final causes", Bacon asserted, "like a virgin dedicated to God is barren and produces nothing."

Although Bacon's strictures found wide support among a later generation of physicists, Renaissance biologists remained uncompromisingly Aristotelian. Consequently, Aristotle's classification of animals on the basis of their modes of reproduction and development remained without serious challenge until the eighteenth century. In the field of generation, using concepts derived from his metaphysics, Aristotle argued that the female parent contributed the matter of the embryo and the male parent its form. It was precisely this view that William Harvey began to consider in the opening chapter of his *De generatione animalium* (1651).

As a final area of intellectual domination there remains Aristotelian logic. Despite the objections of Ramus and Bacon, the bulk of Renaissance logic textbooks worked exclusively within the parameters set out by Aristotle in the *Organon*, as indeed did the textbooks of the seventeenth and eighteenth centuries. It should, however, be remembered that traditions other than Aristotelianism were present during the Renaissance, and that, in their own way, *Neoplatonism, scepticism, and atomism exercised a comparable influence. *See also* criticism, literary.

Aristotle (384–322 BC) Greek philosopher. He was born at Stagira (hence allusions to him as "the Stagirite") and studied philosophy at Athens under *Plato for twenty years from 367. After short spells teaching at Assos in the Troad and Mytilene he became (342) tutor to Alexander the Great. In 335 he returned to Athens to found his own philosophical school, the disciples of which were known as Peripatetics on account of the master's habit of walking to and fro while teaching.

The huge quantity of Aristotle's surviving works cover a vast range of subjects: logic, physics, biology, psychology, metaphysics, politics, ethics, rhetoric, and poetry. Many of the treatises were known to medieval scholars in the West only through Latin translations of Arabic versions. Nonetheless his works were the basis of the predominant scholastic philosophy, and although there was some reaction against him in the Renaissance, especially in favour of *Plato, he continued to dominate philosophical and scientific discourse well into the seventeenth century (*see* Aristotelianism, Renaissance). In the sixteenth century his rediscovered *Poetics* became the basis of Renaissance literary theory (*see* criticism, literary), affecting the status and composition of both *epic and *tragedy.

arithmetic Both the Greeks and the Romans had represented numbers with letters of their alphabets, a custom that mattered little as long as problems were presented geometrically, and as long as calculations were performed on an *abacus. A more sophisticated arithmetic required a more lucid symbolism, which was first provided by the mathematicians of the Renaissance. Hindu numerals entered Europe through Islam. They were picked up by Gerbert in tenth-century Spain and later used by Leonardo of Pisa in his influential *Liber abaci* (1202). Consequently, by the time of the Renais-

sance, there was a growing need to develop appropriate algorithms in the new symbolism for the basic arithmetical operations of multiplication, division, subtraction, addition, exponentiation, and the extraction of roots. The result was a number of elementary textbooks appearing throughout Europe, all designed to convey the secrets of the new arithmetic to a public becoming increasingly concerned with numerical problems arising in commerce. Such works as Chuquet's *Le triparty* (1484), *Pacioli's *Somma* (1494), Recorde's *Grounde of Artes* (1540) and Stifel's *Arithmetica integra* (1544) performed this task in France, Italy, England, and Germany respectively. A bewildering variety of methods was presented, sufficiently complex to engender the belief that long division could be performed only by a professional mathematician.

The Renaissance also saw extensions to the concept of number. Cardano, for example, in his *Ars magna* (1545), accepted into mathematics the long-suspect negative and complex numbers. Later in the century decimals were introduced by *Stevin, and in 1614 John *Napier successfully introduced the notion of a logarithm. He had not, however, expressed his logarithms in terms of a decimal base. This latter innovation was carried through by Henry *Briggs who published in 1617 a table of logarithms to the base 10 of the numbers 1 to 1000.

Armada *see* Spanish Armada.

armillary spheres Astronomical instruments consisting of linked adjustable rings (the name derives from Latin *armilla*: bracelet) representing the circles of the celestial sphere such as the ecliptic and equator. A sphere in the centre represents the earth. Used by Hipparchus (second century BC) they were described by Ptolemy in his *Almagest* (*see* Ptolemaic system) and later became an indispensable tool of Renaissance astronomers. Fitted with sights (alidades), they could be used to make quite precise measurements. One of the most accurate of such instruments, with a diameter of nearly nine feet, was built by Tycho *Brahe at his Uraniborg observatory.

Arminianism A moderate reformed theology named after the Dutch theologian Jacob Arminius (1560–1609). With its insistence upon free will and the denial of the concepts of predestination and irresistible will, Arminianism was anti-Calvinistic and in Holland found expression in the sect of *Remonstrants, whose doctrines were set out in the Remonstrance of 1610. Suspected of pro-Spanish sympathies, the Dutch Arminians suffered bitter persecution after the Calvinists' triumph at the Synod of *Dort (1618–19).

"Arminianism" was the term adopted by English Puritans to describe the doctrines of William Laud who, like the Dutch Arminians, adopted a severely anti-Calvinistic policy and as bishop of London (1628–33) and, from 1633, archbishop of Canterbury, dominated religious affairs in England throughout Charles I's reign. "Laudianism", as it is more accurately described, emphasized the importance of vestments, ceremony, and decoration in church, ruled that the Communion table should be transferred to the east end of the church, and enhanced the authority of the clergy over the laity.

armour Body protection for soldiers in the fourteenth century saw a general trend away from the use of mail and towards the use of plate. In Scandinavia and eastern Europe lamellar armour composed of small plates laced or riveted together became widespread; it was worn under a leather jerkin. Elsewhere soldiers increasingly wore pieces of solid plate strapped onto their mail hauberks or attached to the inside of a leather jerkin to protect vulnerable joints and limbs. For mounted soldiers, whose legs were an easy target for foot soldiers, plate leg protection was evolved, comprising sabaton (foot), greave (shin), poleyn (knee), and cuisse (thigh) sections. By the end of the century armourers were attaching the pieces of limb protection to each other by metal strips known as lames, rather than to another garment. Leather straps and loose riveting provided the necessary flexibility. Armourers also began to demonstrate their skill in designing surfaces curved in such a way as to deflect an enemy's weapon point away from vulnerable body areas.

Two distinct styles in western European armour emerged during the fifteenth century – the Italian and the German. Italian armour is characterized by smoothness and roundness in the modelling of the individual pieces. Milan was an important centre of manufacture (*see* Missaglia family). The German style, more angular and spiky, is often referred to as "Gothic"; its main centres of manufacture were Innsbruck, Nuremberg, and Augsburg. These differences are exemplified in two common forms of head protection: the smooth cylindrical shape of the Italian barbut, based on ancient Greek helmet designs, and the prominent projections of the German sallet with its pointed neck guard. However, as both countries exported armour and armourers (Henry VIII employed first Italians and then, from 1515, Germans in his Greenwich workshops) elements from both soon blended in European armour.

In Germany in the early sixteenth century the armourers' craft received strong encouragement from the informed patronage of Emperor

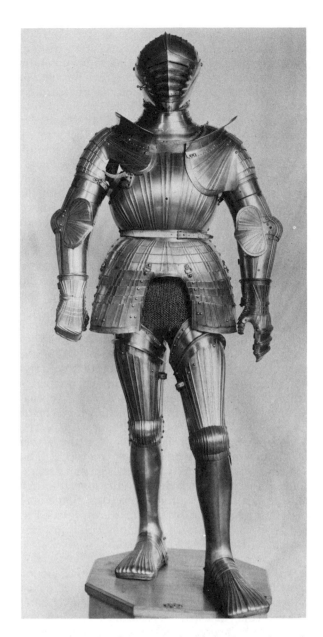

ARMOUR *A suit of armour in the Maximilian style, made around the beginning of the sixteenth century by Konrad Seusenhofer. (Kunsthistorisches Museum, Vienna)*

*Maximilian I. Among the famous makers who worked for Maximilian and his successors were the *Seusenhofers of Innsbruck and the *Helmschmieds of Augsburg. Maximilian's name is associated with the type of ridged plate that represented the most advanced scientific design attained in European armour, combining strength and flexibility to a marked extent. A curious vagary in this period was the attempt to reproduce in metal the puffed and slashed garments of contemporary civilian fashion, even down to simulation of the stitching. From the mid-sixteenth century changes in military strategy and increasing deployment of firearms made mobility more desirable than all-over body protection; plainer suits, often without the lower leg protection, became more common for practical purposes, while the parade or ceremonial armour of princes became increasingly ornate. The use of etching (in northern Europe) or embossing (predominantly an Italian fashion) for decoration naturally negated one of the primary functions of plate armour – to present a smooth surface off which a weapon point would glance.

Besides suits of armour for the battlefield, armourers also evolved specialist equipment to meet the rather different demands of the tournament. Heavily reinforced pieces protected the knight's left shoulder and arm, as the side that would take the brunt of his opponent's attack. A premium was placed on helmet design that protected the wearer against an opponent's lance; the English great helm and German frog-mouth helm are examples of this specialist type. For foot combat this kind of helmet restricted visibility to an impractical degree, so a helmet with a visor was used instead. The need to adapt armour for different purposes led to the evolution of the garniture, in which the basic suit of armour is provided with additional matching pieces for special applications, such as a tournament or a parade. Garnitures such as those made for Henry VIII of England and Emperor Charles V and preserved in such collections as the Tower of London or the Armería Real, Madrid, exhibit the armourers' ingenuity in the design and decoration of these sets, which of course only the rich and powerful could afford or needed. Sometimes matching sets of horse armour were provided as well; one such set was the ceremonial armour made for Eric XIV of Sweden in 1563.

Arrabbiati (the Enraged) The Florentine faction most hostile to *Savonarola. Its leaders were men of wealth, who, while they did not hanker after Medici rule, detested Savonarola's property tax and other measures against luxury and inequality.

ars nova (Latin: new art) A movement in French and Italian music named after *Ars nova musicae* (c. 1320), a treatise by Philippe de *Vitry. It marked a sharp break with the older music, the *ars antiqua*, which had practically ignored rhythm and from which the *ars nova* is distinguished by its rhythmical and contrapuntal innovations. Musical parts became more independent, and a greater use was made of instruments (the rebec, shawm, recorder, viol, lute, and portative organ). Originating in France, the *ars nova* was soon taken up in Florence, Bologna, Pisa, and elsewhere in northern Italy. Building upon the tradition of the troubadours and trouvères, the new art took a more casual approach to musical composition. More secular texts were set, and the Italian *madrigal was born, and the French *ballade* and *chace* – and the related Italian *ballata* and *caccia* – flourished. The Church was initially hostile to the *ars nova*; in 1324/25 Pope John XXII condemned the "lascivious wantonness" of de Vitry and others who practised the new art. Nevertheless, it entered the church in the form of the isorhythmic motet, in which the plainchant basis of liturgical compositions was broken into sections, each having the same set of internal time values. The leading exponents of the *ars nova*, besides de Vitry, were Guillaume de *Machaut and Francesco *Landini. In the later stages of the movement, the work of *Ciconia, a Walloon resident in Italy, is notable. His music foreshadows that of *Dufay and the Burgundian school of composers.

arte mayor In Iberian poetry, a verse line usually of eleven or twelve syllables with a strong caesura dividing the line into half-lines, each having two major stresses, giving an anapaestic rhythm. Towards the end of the fourteenth century, this metre gradually superseded the earlier *cuaderna vía* ("fourfold way"), a narrative stanza used by clerical poets (a fourteen-syllable line with strong caesura, arranged in four-line stanzas having a single rhyme, aaaa, bbbb, ...). Alfonso Álvarez de Villasandino (c. 1345–c. 1425) was especially influential in establishing *arte mayor* verse, and it was popularized by humanists like Juan de *Mena. The beginning of the *Siglo de Oro* is dated from a further metrical reform, inspired by Italian verse, introduced in the works (1543) of Juan *Boscán and *Garcilaso de la Vega. However, *arte mayor* continued to be used in some courtly verse until the eighteenth century.

Artemis see under Diana.

Arthur, legend of The cycle of stories, also known as "the matter of Britain", surrounding King Arthur and the Round Table. It grew from a tiny germ in medieval chronicles concerning a fifth- or sixth-century British general or chieftain who defied the Saxon invaders, was embroidered in the twelfth century, and then expanded into prose and verse romances by English, French, and German authors. Sir Thomas Malory stands at the intersection of medieval and Renaissance treatments of Arthurian legend with his prose *Morte Darthur*, written in the mid-fifteenth century, when the age of chivalry (if it had ever existed) was long past. It kept alive the ideals of love and war as the twin poles of a world populated almost exclusively by knights and ladies.

Perception of Arthur as a national hero was fuelled by the story that, like *Charlemagne, he would one day return and lead his people to great victories; twelfth-century writers had reported that on his tomb in Glastonbury were the words "Rex quondam et rexque futurus" (the once and future king). The quasi-historical aspect of Arthurian legend was first exploited by the Tudors. Hentry VII had his genealogy traced back to Arthur and christened his first-born son Arthur (1486–1502) in his honour. The Round Table in Winchester castle predates the Tudors but was repainted by Henry VIII with the Tudor rose for the visit of Emperor Charles V in 1522, and the names and motifs of Arthurian legend provided a framework for the neo-medieval tournaments laid on by Elizabeth I. As late as 1610 James I's eldest son Henry (1594–1612) was presented by "King Arthur" with a sword to restore chivalry in an entertainment scripted by Ben *Jonson.

Caxton, by enrolling Arthur as one of the Nine Worthies of the World (preface to *Morte Darthur*, 1485), guaranteed his place in innumerable pageants, but on a more serious literary level it was felt that Arthur ought to be the subject of a British national epic. Spenser's plan for The *Faerie Queene, set out in the letter to *Raleigh appended to the first edition (1590), seems to take this into account, but the completed part of the poem does not place Arthur in the centre of the action as might have been expected. Nonetheless, as the embodiment of the peculiarly Renaissance virtue of "Magnificence", he makes significant interventions in the affairs of the poem. As late as the 1640s Milton was still planning an Arthuriad, a national epic with Arthur as its hero.

artillery In the medieval period, any missile-throwing device, including the javelin-launching ballista and stone-hurling trebuchet. Introduced first by Greek and Roman engineers, their effectiveness against the increasingly massive castles of the late medieval period had become much reduced. Conditions changed in the fourteenth century with the introduction of the *cannon. Although the first certain reference to the cannon dates from 1326, it took time before the early primitive models could be adapted to the demands of field artillery officers. To begin with, *gunpowder needed to be improved. Made from saltpetre, sulphur, and charcoal, and ground into a fine powder known as serpentine, early samples tended to separate when transported over rough European roads, with unpredictable results. The solution came with the invention (c. 1425) of corned powder, in which the ingredients were first mixed into a wet paste before being allowed to dry.

Further problems arose over the question of mobility. Although never really solved, the introduction in the late 1300s of light two-wheeled carts known as ribauldequins gave artillery officers greater access to the battlefield. Such factors, together with improved cannon design, began to shift the balance of military power. Even the mighty fortress of Constantinople was unable to withstand such pressure and fell in 1453 to the artillery of Mehmet II (ironically, the technology was imported from the West). The power of artillery was again demonstrated when *Charles VIII of France invaded Italy in 1494 and managed without undue difficulty to destroy any town offering resistance.

It took longer, however, to adapt artillery to naval use. Although known to have been in use as early as 1338, guns were at first mounted only on the upper decks and it was not until the early sixteenth century that ports were cut in ships' hulls enabling cannon to be sited on the main deck. Thereafter the fire-power of ships continued to grow and, as at the battle of Lepanto in 1571, would henceforth be decisive in determining naval supremacy.

Ascensius, Jodocus Badius *see* Badius Ascensius, Jodocus.

Ascham, Roger (c. 1515–68) English humanist and writer. He was born near York and educated at Cambridge where he became a fellow of St John's (1534) and a reader in Greek. He attracted *Henry VIII's attention with his *Toxophilus* (1545), a treatise on archery, written (unusually for the time) in English. Between 1548 and 1550 he was tutor to the future *Elizabeth I, and then served Sir Richard Moryson, England's ambassador to *Charles V, for several years, during which he travelled widely on the Continent. A noted penman, he was appointed Latin secretary (1553) to *Mary I, which post he subsequently also held under Elizabeth. One of the leading English humanists of his day, Ascham strove to make the vernacular a vehicle of true eloquence; to facilitate this, he urged the adoption of Senecan and Ciceronian models, while abhorring excessive pedantry and affectation. He himself wrote simple, lively, lucid prose, often enhanced by vivid and humane observations. His best-known book, *The Scholemaster* (1570), was a landmark in educational theory, concerned not only with the teaching of Latin prose composition, but also with the nature and proper scope of education.

Aspertini, Amico (c. 1475–1552) Italian painter and sculptor. A native of Bologna, Aspertini was a pupil of *Ercole de' Roberti of Ferrara and assistant to both *Costa and *Francia, with whom he worked on the frescoes of the oratory of Sta Cecilia in S Giacomo Maggiore, Bologna (1506). Aspertini also visited Rome and Florence and absorbed features of the styles of such painters as *Signorelli,

*Pinturicchio, *Raphael, and Filippino *Lippi, whose works he studied in detail. Notable works include a series of reredoses and a cycle of frescoes (1508–09) in the church of S Frediano, Lucca. Other paintings are remarkable for their elements of fantasy. As a sculptor he collaborated on the portals of S Petronio, Bologna. His sketchbook in the British Museum shows his interest in antique models.

astrolabes Astronomical instruments formerly used to determine time, latitude, and the altitude of various celestial bodies above the horizon. The name means literally "a star-taking" (Greek *astrolabos*). An astrolabe consists of a flat circular plate (mater), usually made of brass, on which is engraved a stereographic projection of the heavens. Centred on one of the celestial poles, this normally shows the tropics, celestial equator, ecliptic, and the observer's zenith and horizon. Subsidiary plates which can be placed over the mater are often provided for use in different latitudes. Over the mater is fixed an adjustable rete, or fretted plate, showing the positions of the brightest stars. A sighting arm (alidade) is also attached. A simplified version of the instrument, known as the mariner's astrolabe, was available for use at sea. There was also a rare spherical form.

Although the planispheric astrolabe described above is not mentioned by Ptolemy (*see* Ptolemaic system), the principles behind its design were familiar to him, and through the influence of Islamic astronomers, particularly Masha'allah (eighth century AD), knowledge of the instrument passed to the West. Among early works on the subject to draw upon Masha'allah is Chaucer's *Treatise on the Astrolabe* (1391–92). Renaissance refinements of the astrolabe include two forms of the so-called "universal" astrolabe, suitable for use in any latitude: the *astrolabium catholicum* of *Gemma Frisius and the Rojas astrolabe, based on an orthographic projection first described by the Frisian Hugo Helt in Juan de Rojas's *Commentarii* (1550).

astrology The study of movements of stars and planets, traditionally divided into two distinct types: natural astrology, which simply predicted the motions of heavenly bodies and is now part of astronomy, and judicial astrology, which foretold future terrestrial events on the basis of celestial signs. The most significant branch of judicial astrology, genethliacal astrology, purported to throw light on human destiny by constructing natal horoscopes (i.e. horoscopes based on the aspect of the heavens at the exact time and place of the subject's birth).

Although the origins of astrology can be traced to Babylonian times, with the earliest known

ASTROLABES *The great Nuremberg astronomer Regiomontanus demonstrates how to use an astrolabe. The astrolabe shows the fine engraving characteristic of the best Nuremberg instruments of the period. (National Maritime Museum, London)*

horoscopes dating back to 409 BC, the fullest exposition of astrology in antiquity occurs in the *Tetrabiblos* of Ptolemy (fl. 127–48 AD), a work from which much of Renaissance, and indeed modern, astrology ultimately derives. This, in turn, was based largely on the prevailing assumptions of Hellenistic science. It was, at that time, reasonable to suppose that celestial events influenced human affairs; if ignorant sailors, Ptolemy argued, could predict the weather from the sky, how much more capable would learned scholars be to foresee its influence on man. The precise links between the heavens and earth were forged in terms of the traditional four elements. Planets were assigned properties on the basis of their supposed composition with, for example, the moon being classed as hot and moist, and *Saturn as cold and dry. As a moist heat was deemed beneficial, and a cold dryness damaging, it followed that the moon exercised a benign influence on man and Saturn a harmful one. Greater complexity was introduced by allowing celestial influences to be modified by a planet's position, both along the ecliptic (zodiac) and relative to other planets (aspects). The rules derived from these assumptions proved sufficiently comprehensive to allow astrologers to deal with almost any situation.

Opposition to astrology first arose within the Church; both Augustine and Aquinas set their great authority against it. Something of an astrological revival nonetheless occurred in the thirteenth century, through the writings of such figures as Arnold of Villanova, Pietro d'Abano, and, more significantly, Guido Bonatti whose *Liber astronomicus* served as the leading textbook of the early Renaissance. It was in fact Bonatti who was chosen by *Dante to represent astrology in the eighth circle of the Inferno, where he was depicted with his head on backwards and no ability to see ahead. Interest in astrology continued to grow and was well served by the newly developed printing press. Almanacs had appeared before Gutenberg but after he issued the first printed copy in 1448 they emerged with much greater frequency, variety, and number. However, they often provoked the hostility of an officialdom prone to suspect partisan motives behind political predictions. For this reason Pope Sixtus V issued a bull in 1586 condemning judicial astrology. In England the lucrative trade of almanac publishing was made the monopoly of the Stationers' Company, through which the state was able to exercise control over the content of the publications.

Scientific opinion appeared divided: such early Renaissance scholars as Nicholas *Cusanus and *Pico della Mirandola were critical, but astronomers of the standing of *Rheticus, *Kepler, and *Brahe openly practised as astrologers. It may have been, however, that in some cases their intellectual commitment was less urgent than their need to subsidize their astronomical researches. Astrology as a scientific discipline barely outlived the Renaissance. By the time of Newton, at the end of the seventeenth century, astronomers had begun already to rewrite their history and to dismiss much of their past, although Newton himself had an interest in the occult, including astrology.

astronomy The scientific study of celestial bodies (compare *astrology). At the beginning of the Renaissance, scholars accepted unquestioningly the *cosmology of Aristotle and the astronomy of Ptolemy (*see* Ptolemaic system). These views formed the background to *Dante's *Divine Comedy* and, more prosaically, were found expressed in the numerous editions of the popular thirteenth-century text, the *De sphaera* of Sacrobosco.

The first tasks facing the astronomers of the Renaissance were to acquaint themselves with the details of ancient astronomy and to develop new mathematical techniques to describe better the complexities of planetary motion. To this end such scholars as *Peuerbach, *Regiomontanus, and *Rheticus sought to establish accurate texts of Ptolemy's *Almagest* and related works, and to master and deploy the new language of *trigonometry, to astronomical observations. There followed developments which, by the time of the death of *Galileo (1642), had completely transformed man's view of the heavens. The traditional view that they were immutable and incorruptible was called into question by the discovery in 1572 by Tycho *Brahe of a *new star. Even more damaging were the observations in 1610 by *Galileo of the formerly unsuspected satellites of Jupiter, and the presence of mountains and craters on the moon. Further evidence of celestial corruptibility came in 1611 with Christoph *Scheiner's observations of sunspots. Additional difficulties were presented by the comet of 1577. Careful observation by Brahe revealed it to be a genuine feature of the heavens and not, as Aristotle had supposed, a transitory atmospheric phenomenon. Behind much of this success there lay an enormous improvement in the instruments available to astronomers. Brahe at his Uraniborg observatory developed such traditional instruments as *armillary spheres and *quadrants to the limits inherent in naked-eye observation. The greatest advance, however, came with the invention of the *telescope early in the seventeenth century. First applied to the heavens in 1610 by Galileo, it rapidly became the most fundamental tool of astronomy. Equally significant was the increasing accuracy of astronomical observations. Early Renaissance astronomers had relied upon the Alfonsine Tables (1252). When *Copernicus came to apply them in 1504 to an expected conjunction of Mars and Saturn he found the tables to be as much as ten days adrift. They continued in use, however, until 1551 when they were replaced by the Prutenic Tables compiled by Erasmus *Reinhold, the first tables to be based on the Copernican hypothesis. These, in turn, were superseded by the Rudolfine Tables (1627) which were prepared by Brahe and *Kepler and were to remain in use for the rest of the seventeenth century.

The period also saw an advance in the system of stellar nomenclature. Copernicus and his colleagues had, in the manner of Ptolemy, referred to stars as being located in the head, tail, or foot of a particular constellation. The modern system of identifying stars alphabetically by their brightness was introduced by Johann *Bayer in *Uranometria* (1603) and found quick support.

Equally significant were the more theoretical innovations associated with Copernicus and his successors. Since antiquity planetary orbits were taken as unquestionably circular, with the planets themselves, and all other heavenly bodies, moving with a pleasingly simple uniform motion around a central, stationary earth. In 1543 Copernicus initiated the first great astronomical revolution of modern science by replacing the central earth of antiquity with an equally stationary sun. The resulting heliocentric system remained dependent upon the traditional circular orbits of antiquity. Nor were they questioned by Brahe or Galileo. The break eventually came with Kepler. After spending several years trying to establish the orbit of Mars he finally saw that by assuming planets to move in elliptical orbits he would finally be able to make sense of the available data. He went on to propose in 1609 his first law: planets move in elliptical orbits, with the sun occupying one focus. Two other laws were formulated by Kepler. The second law tackled the problem of why planets move around the sun with varying speed by declaring that a radius vector joining the sun and planet would sweep out equal areas in equal times. In his third law Kepler noted the basic relationship between a planet's distance from the sun and its orbital period by noting that the square of the period varied as the cube of the distance. The harmonic law, as it became known, would later prove to be the key with which astronomers would work out the scale of the solar system. Kepler's laws also posed the problem of what held the system together, and why there seemed to be such a close relationship between the orbit and velocity of a planet and the sun. Kepler himself could do little more than talk unconvincingly of a magnetic attraction emanating from the sun. It remained for Newton, later in the century, to provide a firm dynamical basis for Kepler's laws with his introduction into astronomy of universal gravitation.

Athene (*or* Pallas Athene) *see* Minerva.

Aubigné, Theodore d'Agrippa d' (1551–1630) French poet, soldier, polemicist, and historian of his own times. After a studious youth at several European universities, Aubigné, an ardent Protestant, joined the Huguenot forces and served throughout the French religious wars, latterly as master of horse to Henry of Navarre. After Henry's accession (1589) as *Henry IV and conversion to Catholicism, Aubigné withdrew to his estates in Poitou, where he did much of his writing and became gradually estranged from his fellow Protestants. Haunted perhaps by his king's abjuration, he frequently depicts in his work the conflict between truth and outward show and celebrates the justice of an avenging deity, as in his epic poem, *Les Tragiques* (1616). His most interesting work is probably his *Histoire universelle* (1616–20), which deals with the years 1553–1602 and contains many lively eyewitness accounts of the events in which he played a part. Publication of the final volume of the history caused Aubigné to be proscribed, after which he lived in Geneva until his death.

Auerbach, Johannes *see* Amerbach, Johannes.

Augsburg A south German city on the junction of the Wertach and Lech rivers. Founded as a Roman colony (15 BC), Augsburg became the seat of a bishopric (759), an imperial free city (1276), and a member of the Swabian League (1331). Close to rich silver mines and situated on the principal trade route from the Mediterranean to northern and western Europe, Augsburg developed as a major banking and commercial centre in the fifteenth and sixteenth centuries. The *Fugger family, its leading merchants, became Europe's greatest bankers and lent large sums to the *Habsburgs and other princes. Augsburg was one of the first important centres of Renaissance arts and scholarship outside Italy. It was a centre for humanist scholars and the artists Hans *Holbein, Elder and Younger, were natives of the city. The oldest European settlement for the poor, the Fuggerei, was built in Augsburg in 1519. Notable buildings from the Renaissance period include the Gothic additions (1331–1432) to the eleventh-century cathedral, the church of SS Ulrich and Afra (1474–1604), and the town hall (1615–20).

Augsburg, Confession of The classic statement of Lutheran doctrine submitted to the Diet of Augsburg on 25 June 1530, and originally called the Articles of Schwabach. The diet had been called by *Charles V in his search for German unity at a time when the empire was threatened by Turkish invasion. The confession was compiled by *Melanchthon and approved by Luther prior to its presentation to the diet. It was divided into two parts, the first comprising twenty-one articles conciliatory and comparatively inoffensive to the Roman Church. The second part, however, consisted of seven articles attacking what the Lutherans considered its main abuses; these included aspects of Roman ceremony, certain clerical vows, and the secular authority exercised by its bishops. In response the Roman Catholics drew up the Confutatio presented in August 1530, rejecting any settlement based on the confession.

Augsburg, Interim of (1548) A peacetime agreement drawn up under the direction of Emperor *Charles V, designed to satisfy Lutherans without greatly offending Catholics. It admitted the universality and indivisibility of the Church, the seven sacraments, and the doctrine of transubstantiation, while allowing to the Protestant side the legality of clerical marriages and, to some extent, the doctrine of justification by faith. *See also* Leipzig, Interim of.

Augsburg, Peace of The treaty concluded on 25 September 1555 that ended the religious wars in Germany during the Reformation period. It was the product of the Diet of Augsburg, held between February and September that year. For the first time in the Christian West two confessions, Roman Catholicism and Lutheranism, were accorded equal legal recognition. This and the freedom it gave individual princes to choose their own and their subjects' religion marked the ultimate defeat of *Charles V's endeavours to create a unified Germany. In addition, Lutheran or Roman Catholic dissenters were to be allowed freedom to emigrate, Lutheran knights and towns within Roman Catholic states were to be allowed to maintain their form of worship, and all ecclesiastical lands secularized by the Lutherans before the treaty of Passau (1552) were to remain Lutheran. Although the exclusion of any concessions to other sects, most importantly the Calvinists, was to have serious repercussions, the Peace of Augsburg lasted for sixty-three years.

Aulic Council (*Reichshofrat*) The court council of the Holy Roman Empire from 1498 until the empire's dissolution in 1806. Attempting to make his government more effective, Emperor *Maximilian I established the council as his supreme executive and judicial body with responsibility for everything except finance and drafting documents. He appointed and paid the members who followed his court until settling permanently in Vienna. In 1559 Ferdinand I strengthened the council, especially in the exercise of the emperor's judicial powers. During the eighteenth century the Aulic Council grew stronger as its rival body, the *Reichskammergericht*, declined.

Aurispa, Giovanni (Giovanni Pichumerio; c. 1370–1459) Sicilian-born teacher of Greek and collector of manuscripts. He made two trips to the East (1405–13, 1421–23), principally to look for texts of Greek authors but also to take Greek lessons from Manuel *Chrysoloras. Aurispa recovered over 300 manuscripts, including the Venetian manuscript of the *Iliad* (MS. Venetus A), the Laurentian manuscript of Aeschylus, Sophocles, and Apollonius of Rhodes, and manuscripts of the Homeric Hymns and the Greek Anthology. In 1438 Aurispa was made a papal secretary by Eugenius IV. He died at Ferrara. Aurispa produced few works; he translated the commentary of Hierocles on the Golden Verses of Pythagoras (1474) and may have translated the works of Archimedes. His main importance lies in his efforts to copy and encourage the copying of Greek texts and to distribute them. He also drew attention in his teaching while professor of Greek at Florence to literary rather than philosophical values in Greek literature.

autobiography The narrative re-creation of the writer's own life, which only emerged as a distinct literary genre in the Renaissance. There are very occasional examples of autobiography in antiquity and in the Middle Ages; the *Confessions* (c. 400) of St Augustine of Hippo contains a celebrated account of his early life and spiritual quest, but no one else was to approach its degree of introspection for over a thousand years. *Dante's *Vita nuova* (c. 1292–1300) and *Petrarch's *Secretum* (1342–43) are autobiographical without being in the strict sense autobiographies. Rather, for the beginnings of secular autobiography, it is necessary to look to the personal records kept by Italian merchants from the late thirteenth century onwards. Some are merely accounts of business negotiations, but others, like the *Zibaldone quaresimale* (1457–85) of the Florentine Giovanni Rucellai, also contain passages of self-questioning. The first full-scale autobiography is arguably the *Commentarii* (1458–64) of Aenea Silvio Piccolomini, who became Pope *Pius II. While focusing on external events, and on the characters and politics of the period, it does contain an implicit portrait of the man himself. Perhaps the two most interesting and revealing Renaissance autobiographies, however, are the famous *Life* (or *Autobiography*) of Benvenuto *Cellini and *De vita propria liber* (*The Book of my Life*) of Girolamo *Cardano. Remarkable for its profound self-scrutiny, Cardano's document was written in his old age and not published until 1643. To find such an essay in the genre in England it is necessary to wait until the early seventeenth century and the *Life* of Edward, Lord Herbert of Cherbury (1582–1648), which traces his adventures from birth to 1624, and is a splendidly unabashed account of the author's own abundant virtues. *See also* biography.

auto sacramental (Spanish: sacramental act) A dramatic genre in Spain that reached its height in the seventeenth century with the *autos* of Pedro Caldéron de la Barca (1600–81). The *auto* was a one-act allegorical play in verse, originally dealing with an aspect of the Holy Eucharist; it derived from the tableaux which had traditionally been part of the procession accompanying the Eucharist as it was carried through the streets during the festival of Corpus Christi. These tableaux had developed into a dramatic form similar to that of the miracle and mystery plays in England and the Netherlands in the Middle Ages, and, like them, were mounted on carts and performed out-of-doors. The *autos* began to appear in Spain in the sixteenth century and were transformed by Caldéron from a simple form of pious entertainment into a significant new dramatic form. He exploited the allegorical elements of the *auto* and extended its range in the process, but after his death, it degenerated into farce until performances were finally prohibited by royal decree in 1765.

Averlino Antonio *see* Filarete.

Avignon, papacy at The period of papal exile from Rome when Avignon was the seat of seven popes (1309–78) and also of four who claimed the title during the Great Schism (1378–c. 1430). Following the bankruptcy of the papacy, the Frenchman Clement V (pope 1305–14), chose Avignon as his residence in 1309. During this so-called *Babylonian Captivity, all seven Avignon popes were French, as were most of the cardinals they appointed. All except Clement VI (pope 1342–52) were university trained and demonstrated considerable skill in handling papal business. The Avignon popes, particularly John XXII (pope 1316–34) were highly effective in reorganizing their finances, exploiting every possible means of extracting money from religious foundations and their subjects. These included the introduction of the annate (payment of a newly appointed bishop's first year's income) and the payment to the papacy of all incomes derived from vacant sees. Most importantly they helped prepare the way for Luther's conflict with Tetzel by their increased reliance on the sale of indulgences. Using such methods the Avignon popes eventually succeeded in collecting an income three times greater than that of the king of France.

In 1348 Clement VI bought the city of Avignon from Queen Joanna I of Naples. The papal palace (built 1316–70) and fortified walls remain there as witness to the popes' presence. Several Italian artists were attracted to Avignon to work on the papal palace; they include Simone *Martini and Matteo Giovanetti, who was responsible for the beautiful frescoes in the Chambre du Cerf and Grande Audience.

The new tradition of an Avignon-based papal seat was fundamental to the development of the Great Schism following the departure of Gregory XI (pope 1370–78) for Rome (1377) to restore order in the Italian Papal States. After the election of Urban VI (pope 1378–89) to the Roman seat in April 1378, the majority of Frenchmen among the cardinals (eleven out of sixteen), all chose to share in the election of the antipope, Clement VII, at Avignon in August of the same year. Although the schism was effectively ended by the abdication of the Avignon candidate, Benedict XIII, in 1417, Avignon continued to put up rival claimants until about 1430.

B

Babylonian Captivity The phrase adopted to describe the period 1305–78 when the papal seat was at Avignon instead of Rome. The allusion is to the biblical captivity of the Jews in Babylon that lasted for seventy years. The Babylonian Captivity followed the bankruptcy of the papacy and comprised seven pontificates before the return to Rome and the ensuing Great Schism. *See* Avignon, papacy at.

Bacchus The Roman god of wine, identified with the Greek god Dionysus, many of whose attributes he adopted. In classical mythology Dionysus was the son of Zeus (Roman Jupiter) and Semele, who was brought up by nymphs after his mother was destroyed by his father's thunderbolts. As the god associated with the intoxicating power of wine, he is accompanied by a train of creatures under its influence: the ecstatic women known as bacchantes or maenads, sileni, satyrs, and centaurs. The god himself often rides upon a panther or leopard. It is a train like this that comes upon Ariadne (whom, the legend says, Theseus abandoned on the island of Naxos) in the painting by *Titian (National Gallery, London), and other artists too were drawn to the pictorial qualities of the Bacchic entourage. The love of Bacchus and the mortal Ariadne, too, was susceptible to allegorical interpretation as the union of the soul with the divine being.
Michelangelo's statue of the drunken Bacchus with vine leaves in his hair and accompanied by a young satyr (Bargello, Florence) epitomizes the Renaissance impulse to imitate pagan antiquity – in this case so successfully that many contemporaries looked on it as a genuine classical piece, as Francisco da Hollanda records in his treatise on painting.

Bachelier, Nicolas (?1500–56) French architect. Bachelier was a native of Toulouse, the scene of his principal works. He was primarily influenced by *Serlio. Among the buildings definitely ascribed to Bachelier is the elegant Hôtel d'Assézat (1555) in Toulouse.

backstaffs Navigational instruments, also known as Davis's quadrants, for measuring the altitude of a celestial body. The ancestor of the backstaff, the cross-staff or Jacob's staff, was reputedly invented by a Jew from the Languedoc, Levi ben Gerson (1288–1324). It consisted of no more than a graduated staff and movable cross-piece(s) or transom(s). If the staff was pointed towards a celestial object and the transom suitably adjusted, the object's altitude above the horizon could be read off the staff. The instrument was used by surveyors and navigators, but it suffered from the disadvantage that the operator had to face the sun's glare whenever a measurement of solar altitude was required. The obvious solution was introduced by the English seaman John Davis (c. 1550–1605) in about 1594. His backstaff allowed the observer to stand with his back towards the sun and gain his reading by noting the position of the sun's shadow. The backstaff was the lineal ancestor of the sextant, which appeared in the late eighteenth century. It also proved to be yet one more discovery described in the unpublished manuscripts of Thomas *Harriot.

Bacon, Francis, 1st Baron Verulam, Viscount St Albans (1561–1626) English philosopher, lawyer, and politician. Bacon was born in London, the son of Sir Nicholas Bacon, and the nephew of Lord Burghley, both political advisers to Queen *Elizabeth. After studying law at Cambridge Bacon began his own political career by entering parliament in 1584. His career flourished under *James I, whom he served successively as solicitor-general, attorney-general, and, after 1618, lord chancellor. It ended abruptly in 1621 when, found guilty of corruption, he was fined £40,000 and imprisoned briefly in the Tower of London.
Bacon had earlier, in his *Advancement of Learning* (1605), begun the ambitious programme of working out the methodology of and laying the foundations for the newly emerging science of his day. Dismissive of traditional Aristotelian procedures (*see* Aristotelianism, Renaissance), he sought to develop new inductive methods, the exercise of which would lead more readily to scientific discovery. His *Instauratio magna* (The Great Renewal), an encyclopedic survey of all knowledge, was to have been his crowning achievement, but only a fragment, the *Novum organum* (1620), was completed before his death. Following his banish-

ment from court in 1621, Bacon did, however, manage to revise much of his earlier work in his *De augmentis scientiarum* (1623). In a further work, published posthumously as *The New Atlantis* (1626), Bacon described a utopian society which contained an institution called Solomon's House, charged with the organized study of nature. The suggestion was partially realized later in the century by the foundation of the Royal Society. Bacon is also known as a polished and epigrammatic essayist. Ten essays were published in 1597 while the third edition of the *Essays* (1625) contained an additional forty-eight pieces. He died from a chill contracted while attempting to see "why [chicken] flesh might not be preserved in snow, as in salt", leaving debts of £22,000.

Badius Ascensius, Jodocus (Josse Bade; 1462–1535) Flemish scholar and printer. He was born at Aasche, near Ghent, and after studying in Louvain and Bologna, he settled in Lyons (1492), teaching classics. There he married the daughter of the printer Jean (Johann) Trechsel (d. 1498) and became his editor, responsible for the first Lyons book printed in roman type ("Italian types"), a 1492 edition of the orations of Philippus Beroaldus. His illustrated Terence, first published in 1493, was reprinted over and over again. In 1499 he moved to Paris, working there in association with Jean Petit before starting on his own in 1503. In the next thirty years he produced about 800 books, among them Erasmus's early works. The designs of Badius's books sometimes used title-page borders modelled on manuscript ones; an example is his 1511 Cicero. His Thucydides translation of 1528 was printed in type bought from *Froben of Basle.

Badius was succeeded by his son-in-law, Robert *Estienne, and a subsequent dynasty of scholar-printers.

Baena, Juan Alfonso de (early fifteenth century) Spanish poet. A minor *converso* poet, Baena is remembered as the compiler of the *Cancionero de Baena*, a collection of 612 poems by fifty-four poets which was prepared for King John II of Castile in 1445. The anthology contains *canciones* (lyrics) and *decires* (narratives, satires, and panegyrics) dating from the reign of John I (1379–90) and extending into the fifteenth century. The lyrics are in octosyllabic lines, often varied with half-lines (*pie quebrado*); the narratives and satires are written either in octosyllabic lines or in twelve-syllable *arte mayor*. Linguistically, the anthology shows the change from the Gallego-Portuguese (or Galician-Portuguese) dialect used by Castilian poets in the thirteenth and fourteenth centuries to the Castilian Spanish adopted towards the end of

the fourteenth century. *López de Ayala is the earliest poet represented. Baena gives highest praise to the *trovador* Alfonso Álvarez de Villasandino (c. 1345–c. 1425). The collection as a whole reflects the Provençal and Galician troubadour tradition of courtly poetry. *See also cancionero.*

Baglioni family A powerful and wealthy Umbrian family, notorious in the Renaissance for its crimes. The Baglioni gained their wealth from employment as *condottieri in the thirteenth century and political power from Malatesta Baglioni (1389–1427), who was awarded territories by Pope Martin V and who virtually ruled Perugia. From 1488, after massacring or exiling their rivals, the Baglioni ruled Perugia through a council of ten family members. Giampaolo Baglioni (1470–1520) seized power after the murder of several leading Baglioni (1500) in family disputes. He tried to murder Pope *Julius II (1506) and was himself murdered on Pope *Leo X's orders. Ridolfo Baglioni was defeated and exiled by Pope *Paul III (*see* Salt War).

Baianism The doctrine of Michel de Bay (1514–89), a Louvain theologian more generally known as Baius. His writings on free will, righteousness, and justification (1563–64) were openly condemned by Pope Pius V in his bull *Ex omnibus afflictionibus* (1567) as false and heretical. Baianism, inspired by Augustinian doctrine, insisted upon man's total depravity and moral incapacity. In so doing it rejected the doctrine recognized at the Council of *Trent (1551) that rested upon the concept of man's preternatural innocence. Baius launched the first attack on man's freedom of will and denied the possibility of achieving spiritual and moral perfection in this life. His arguments were offensive to the Jesuits and were countered by their spokesman *Robert Bellarmine. The conflict between Baianism and the Jesuits during the sixteenth century anticipated that of the Jansenists and Jesuits during the seventeenth.

Baïf, Jean-Antoine de (1532–89) French poet and most learned member of the *Pléiade. Born in Venice, the natural son of the humanist Lazare de Baïf (c. 1496–1547), he received a classical education. He studied in Paris (1547) with *Ronsard under Jean Dorat, and together with Joachim *du Bellay, they formulated plans to transform French poetry by employing classical and neoclassical models. Baïf produced two collections of poetry, *Les Amours de Méline* (1552) and *L'Amour de Francine* (1555), in accordance with the principles they had laid down, followed by *Le Brave* in 1567, adapted from Plautus' *Miles gloriosus*. But his poetic gifts were inferior to his great learning, which is best displayed in his *Mimes* (1581) and in his many translations, including Terence's *Eunuchus* and Sophocles' *Antigone*. His interest in Platonic theories of the relation between music and poetry led him to set up (1567) a short-lived academy of the two arts with the musician Thibault de Courville.

Baïf is also remembered as an innovator in matters of language and versification, inventing a system of phonetic spelling and a new metrical form, the fifteen-syllable *vers baïfin*. His theories are expounded in *Etrènes de poesie francoêze en vers mezurés* (1574). Having received various marks of favour from Charles IX and Henry III during his last years, he died peacefully in Paris.

Balboa, Vasco Nuñes de (c. 1475–1517) Spanish explorer. Balboa was born into a good Estremaduran family and went to the West Indies in 1501. In 1510 he assumed command of an expedition to Darien, and, making friends with the native Indians, he heard rumours about the great ocean beyond the mountains west of the gulf of Darien. While at Darien Balboa heard that his enemies had complained of him to King Ferdinand, so, endeavouring to recover the king's favour, he set out on an expedition over the mountains, from which he caught his first sight of the Pacific Ocean (September 1513). A few days later he took possession of the new sea for the Spanish crown. He returned to Darien with considerable booty and when news of his exploits reached Spain the king rewarded him with the title of admiral. Nonetheless his enemies managed to frustrate his intended search for the gold of Peru and finally managed to have him executed for alleged treason at Acla, near Darien.

Baldovinetti, Alesso (c. 1426–99) Italian painter and mosaicist. His work, which was mainly in and around Florence, is documented by his diary recording his commissions. Some of his paintings, such as the *Madonna and Child* in the Louvre and the damaged *Nativity* fresco in SS Annunziata, Florence, have attractive, if unsophisticated, landscape views of the Val d'Arno in the background. Among his mosaics are decorations in the baptistery, Florence, and the tympanum over the south door of Pisa cathedral. The main influences visible upon his work are those of *Domenico Veneziano and *Andrea del Castagno.

Baldung Grien, Hans (Hans Baldung Grün; 1484/85–1545) German painter and print maker. While he was still a child, Baldung's family moved from his native Schwäbisch-Gmünd to Strasbourg, where he probably received his initial training. By about 1500 he was in Dürer's Nuremberg workshop, where he remained until 1508, when he returned to Strasbourg. There he remained for the rest of his career, save for the years 1512–17, when he was based at Fribourg. At Nuremberg Baldung contributed numerous woodcuts to the books *Beschlossen Gart* (1505) and *Speculum Passionis* (1507) by Ulrich Pinder and painted two altarpieces for Halle. The latter's remarkably lustrous colouristic effects imply knowledge of the early works of *Cranach. Baldung's key early work is the huge high altar of Fribourg minster. Although related to earlier compositions by Dürer, its central panel of the *Coronation of the Virgin* has a flamboyance of form and colour quite distinct from Dürer's disciplined style. Baldung's woodcuts of the same period, notably the famous *Witches* (1513), reveal a growing interest in the demonic. This tendency reached a high point of mingled horror and eroticism in the *Woman Embraced by Death* at Basle, painted in about 1517. With the coming of the Reformation to Strasbourg, Baldung's subject matter shifts away from religious themes, towards secular ones. These include portraits, such as the woodcut likeness of Luther (1521) and the oil painting of a young man in Nuremberg (1526). Baldung also painted genre scenes, such as the moralizing *Ill-Matched Couple* (1527) in Liverpool, and classical legends, such as *Pyramus and Thisbe* (1530) in Berlin. A highly intellectual artist, Baldung was far more than merely Dürer's greatest pupil. His style was always quite distinct from that of his master or any other painter, culminating in a highly personal contribution to European Mannerism.

Bale, John (1495–1563) English bishop, controversialist, and dramatist. He was born at Cove, Suffolk, and was a convert to Protestantism whose uncompromising views provoked great hostility (he was known as "Bilious Bale"). He was twice forced into exile – to Germany in 1540–47 and to Basle during Mary's reign (1553–58). However, Edward VI made him bishop of Ossory (1552) and under Elizabeth he ended his days in peace as a prebendary of Canterbury. He produced numerous polemical writings, a history of English literature, and several dramas, the most notable of which is *King John* (1548), often seen as the first English historical play.

balìa A committee with special powers, set up in an Italian city to handle particular constitutional situations. While overtly a republican institution, the Florentine *balìa* fell inexorably under the control of the *Medici during the fifteenth century.

ballade A French metrical form, not to be confused with the English "ballad". It consists of a poem of fixed form and strict rhyme scheme with three stanzas of either ten lines (*dizains*) or eight lines (*huitains*) each, the lines being most commonly of six or eight syllables; there is a concluding four-line *envoi*, in which the poet usually addresses his patron. All four parts end with the same line, constituting the refrain, though departures from the regular forms exist. The greatest exponent of the *ballade* was François Villon (1431–?).

ballet de cour A form of entertainment combining music, spectacle, dancing, song, and drama, evolved at the French court in the mid-sixteenth century. Catherine de' Medici, who would have encountered similar entertainments at the Florentine court in her youth, laid on the sumptuous *Balet comique de la royne* in 1581 to celebrate the marriage of her daughter, and the fashion for hugely expensive and spectacular shows of this nature continued in the reigns of Henry IV (1589–1610) and Louis XIII (1610–43). Costume designs surviving from the early seventeenth century, especially those by Daniel Rabel (1578–1637), indicate the grotesque and humorous, as well as the opulent, aspects of these *ballets. See also* masque.

Bandello, Matteo (1485–1561) Italian writer, cleric, diplomat, and soldier. Bandello was born at Castelnuovo Scrivia, near Tortona, and educated in Milan and at Pavia university. Among other appointments in Lombardy, he was tutor to Lucrezia Gonzaga. After the Spanish attack on Milan following the battle of *Pavia (1525), in which he lost his house and many documents, he fled to France. In 1550 he was made bishop of Agen, where he spent the rest of his life.

His works include a collection of Petrarchan verse (*Il Canzoniere*, 1544) and an Italian version of Euripides' *Hecuba*, but it was his prose *Novelle* (1554, 1573) containing 214 stories, which made him famous and initiated a new phase in narrative literature. Bandello did not aim at classical dignity in his writing, but he did help promote the vernacular as the literary language of Italy. Containing a extraordinary variety of tales, the collection was also an important source for later Renaissance playwrights who drew on it either directly or in translation (*Shakespeare, for instance, utilized Bandello's "Giulietta e Romeo").

Bandinelli, Baccio (1488–1560) Italian sculptor in marble and bronze. He was born in Florence and after training under his goldsmith father, worked with *Rustici, the sculptural associate of *Leonardo da Vinci. His career was dedicated to trying in vain to equal the sculpture of *Michelangelo, in a series of commissions from the *Medici

BANDINELLI Hercules and Cacus. *The sculpture records the exploit of Hercules in which he killed the giant Cacus, who had stolen some of the hero's cattle. (1534; Piazza della Signoria, Florence)*

dynasty, both in Florence and Rome. Much of his original monumental statuary can be criticized: for example, the *Hercules and Cacus* (1534; Piazza della Signoria, Florence), which he pretentiously carved as a pair of Michelangelo's *David*. His best work is either closely based on classical statuary, like the *Laocöon* in the Uffizi (1525), or is in low relief, like the *Prophets* in the choir of Florence cathedral (1555). As court sculptor to Duke Cosimo I, he was a rival of *Cellini. He also produced portraits, bronze statuettes, paintings, and drawings, most of which are still in Florence.

banking Renaissance banking was basically the same as medieval banking, with a few great houses offering merchant banking services (particularly long-distance money transfer and the provision of loans). The first such organization was that of the *Knights Templar, who by 1200 were in effect bankers to the kings of England and France. The thirteenth century saw the rise of the great Italian houses – the *Acciaiuoli, *Bardi, and Peruzzi of Florence, the Frescobaldi of Lucca, and others – who used the capital amassed in trade to move into banking. With kings always short of cash for major enterprises, especially wars, these bankers quickly became immensely wealthy and influential. However, this had its risks: the default of Edward III of England (1341) bankrupted the Peruzzi (1343), Acciaiuoli (1345), and Bardi (1346). Later banks, such as the *Medici, adopted a more decentralized organization, so the failure of one branch could not ruin the whole company, and in general took fewer risks.

Italian dominance continued until the end of the fifteenth century, when economic and political changes shifted the focus northwards. After 1494, when Charles VIII of France captured Florence, the Medici bank ceased to function. The great bankers of the sixteenth century were the *Fuggers of Augsburg, who had built their fortune in the silver and copper mines of Slovakia, the Welsers, also of Augsburg, and the Höchstetters. The commercial and financial capital of Europe was then Antwerp. However, the opening up of the world beyond Europe occasioned further changes; by the early seventeenth century the lead had passed to the Dutch, backed by the wealth from their East Indian empire.

What distinguished these firms were their international connections and the scale of their operations. Almost anybody with capital could, and did, lend money. For example, the English kings of the late fourteenth and early fifteenth centuries preferred to deal with syndicates of English merchants rather than the Italian houses. At a lower level, money-lenders and pawnbrokers abounded. The taking of interest – usury – was technically against canon law, but was generally practised, especially by the Jews upon whom, of course, canon law was not binding.

In the late sixteenth century there began to emerge a major change in banking: the provision of capital for loans by accepting deposits, on which interest was paid. This led to the establishment of firms that concentrated solely on banking, without a base in trade, commerce, or other industry. Such a "public bank", the Banco della Piazza di Rialto, was established in Venice in 1587, and in 1609 the Dutch launched the great Bank of Amsterdam.

Barbari, Jacopo de' (c. 1450–c. 1515) Italian painter and engraver. Barbari was a native of Venice and may have met *Dürer on the latter's visit to Italy in 1495, but little is known of his early career. He produced a grand woodcut panorama of Venice in twelve sheets, and the same year (1500) he moved to Nuremberg as painter to Emperor Maximilian I. During his peripatetic career in northern Europe he was immensely important in propagating Italian Renaissance motifs and style among northern artists. After a period (1503–05) serving Frederick (III) the Wise of Saxony, he moved to the Netherlands (c. 1508), working first for Philip of Burgundy and later for the Habsburg regent Margaret of Austria. His still life of a dead bird (1504; Munich) is a very early example of the genre. Among the artists who were deeply influenced by him were *Gossaert and van *Orley.

Barbaro, Daniele (1513–70) Italian nobleman and polymath. Barbaro belonged to a landed Venetian family and studied science, philosophy, mathematics, and literature in Padua. In 1545 he founded and became curator of the botanic garden there. In 1548 he was sent to England as ambassador and on his return (1550) was appointed patriarch of Aquileia, in which role he attended the Council of *Trent. He commissioned the Villa Barbaro (1560–68) at Maser from *Palladio, who had earlier provided the illustrations to Barbaro's edition of Vitruvius (1556), and engaged *Veronese to decorate the interior. Barbaro's *Pratica della perspettiva* (1568/69), giving an interesting account of the camera obscura, has some illustrative material borrowed from the 1566 edition of *Serlio's architectural treatise; the fact that this edition had been dedicated to Barbaro is still further evidence of his informed patronage.

Barbaro, Ermolao (Almoro di Zaccaria; 1453–c. 1493) Italian poet and scholar. He was born at Venice and studied at Rome under Pomponio *Leto, was crowned laureate at fourteen, and appointed professor of philosophy at Padua in 1477. There he corresponded with *Politian and *Pico della Mirandola and lectured on Aristotle. He went on a number of diplomatic missions for the city and was made patriarch of Aquileia by Pope Innocent VIII (1491). Unfortunately he failed to obtain the permission of the Venetian senate for this post and he was banished to Rome, where he died, probably of plague. His major scholarly activity was textual criticism (his *Castigationes Pliniae* (1492) emended over 5000 passages in Pliny's *Natural History*). He also edited Pomponius Mela (1493) and translated Themistius' Greek commentary on Aristotle (1480). His translation of Aristotle's *Rhetorica* into Latin was not printed until 1544.

Barbarossa ("Redbeard", Khair ed-Din; c. 1465–1546) Barbary pirate and admiral of the Ottoman fleet. Raised on Lesbos, he moved to Djerba with his three brothers when their father died. Scorning both the weakness of the Muslim rulers and the presence of Iberian invaders in North Africa, the brothers undertook a campaign of brutal piracy. They formed a principality on Djidjelli, but Spain captured their land in 1518. Barbarossa, now the head of the family, was saved from annihilation by the sultan of Turkey, and for the rest of his life he worked for the sultan. He conquered Tunis for the Ottomans (1534) and permanently loosened Spain's grip on North Africa.

Bardi family The Florentine family of Bardi won a large fortune and European influence through international banking. By 1310 they were the wealthiest family in Florence and used their position to secure political dominance. However, as part of Edward III of England's manoeuvres to finance the Hundred Years' War, they participated from 1338 in schemes to exploit the English wool trade though monopolistic syndicates, intended to repay the large loans they made to the king. These did not work, and Edward defaulted on his repayments (1341); by 1345 the Bardi were owed at least £103,000. This, combined with the burden of supporting Florence's war against Lucca, forced them into bankruptcy (1346), and they also lost their political power. The sole surviving evidence of the Bardi fortune can be seen in their gifts to the church of Sta Croce, Florence. Count Giovanni Bardi (1534–1612) was an intellectual leader in late sixteenth-century Florence, the patron of musicians, scholars, and poets, as well as being a composer himself.

Barends, Dirk (1534–92) Netherlands painter. He was born in Amsterdam and around 1555 travelled to Venice where he worked in the studio of Titian. Back in Amsterdam by 1562, he became known as a portrait painter and one of the earliest to produce a group portrait (*schuttersstuk*) of the kind made famous in the seventeenth century by such masterpieces as Rembrandt's *The Night Watch*. His style is characteristic of the Mannerism prevalent in the northern Netherlands during this period.

Barents, Willem (d. 1597) Dutch navigator, after whom the Barents Sea was named. Barents pioneered the *northeast passage to Asia. In 1594 his first attempt to find a route was defeated by the harsh climate of Novaya Zemlya, where he was following the western coastline. The following year a seven-ship convoy attempted to penetrate the strait between Vaigach Island and the continental coast. His third expedition, under Jakob van Heemskerck (died 1607), discovered Spitzbergen, but was aborted during the winter of 1596/97, when ice trapped their ship north of Novaya Zemlya, and the crew became the first Europeans to winter so far north. They only escaped in two home-built open boats in June 1597. Barents died later that month, en route for the Kola Peninsula where most of his shipmates eventually reached safety. *See also* Veer, Gerrit de.

Bargeo, Pier Angelo see Angeli, Pietro Angelo.

Bari, Niccolò di see Niccolò dell'Arca.

Baro, Peter (1534–99) French divine. Baro was born at Étampes and admitted to the ministry by Calvin himself at Geneva in 1560. He fled persecution in France a year later and settled in England. Here, under the patronage of Lord Burghley, he was appointed to a chair of divinity at Cambridge (1574). By 1581 his increasing toleration of the tenets of Rome was apparent and he aroused considerable hostility, including that of Queen *Elizabeth. He left Cambridge in 1596 and passed his remaining years in London. Baro was the first divine in England to interpret the creed of the Church of England upon definite ultra-Calvinistic principles and so anticipated the work of Bancroft and Laud.

Barocci, Federico (Il Baroccio; c. 1535–1612) Italian painter. Born and trained in Urbino, Barocci was also known as Fiori da Urbino and became celebrated for his innovative emotional style strongly influenced by the works of *Correggio. He visited Rome twice (1550, 1560) to study Raphael's works and was probably encouraged there by Michelangelo. On his second visit he worked with Federico *Zuccaro on the decoration of the ceiling of the Casino of Pius IV in the Vatican gardens (1561–63), which established his reputation as a leading Italian artist. Barocci spent the rest of his career in Urbino, where he enjoyed ducal patronage; he painted mainly religious subjects, aspects of which anticipated the Baroque. Later works included the *Madonna del Popolo* (1575–79; Uffizi), the *Vision of St Sebastian* (1595; Genoa cathedral), the *Nativity* (1597; Prado, Madrid), and a number of sensitive drawings. He was also a pioneer of the use of pastel chalks and often employed mannerist devices in his compositions.

Baronius, Cesare (Cesare Baronio; 1538–1607) Italian historian of the Roman Catholic Church. Baronius was born at Sora, educated at Naples, joined the Oratory in Rome in 1557, and eventually (1593) succeeded St *Philip Neri as its head. He became confessor to Pope *Clement VIII, who made him a cardinal and librarian of the Vatican.

He is best remembered for his twelve-volume *Annales ecclesiastici* (1588–1607), a justification of his faith by the history of the Church to 1199 AD, designed to counter the claims of the Lutheran *Centuriators of Magdeburg. Although poorly arranged, dull, and inaccurate, this work has long been praised as a pioneering accumulation of historical sources drawn from the Vatican and leading Italian libraries. Baronius's support, on the basis of his studies, for the papal claim to Sicily against that of Spain reputedly lost him the papacy, due to Spanish opposition. He also revised and corrected the Roman Martyrology (1586, 1589).

Baroque A movement in the arts that began in Rome at the end of the Renaissance and later spread throughout Europe and the colonies. Possibly deriving its name from the Spanish word *barrueco* (meaning an irregularly shaped pearl) and used at first as a term of abuse, the Baroque prospered chiefly in Roman Catholic countries, where it was employed as a medium for propaganda during the *Counter-Reformation and reached its climax in the mid-seventeenth century (the High Baroque). The Baroque saw a new emphasis upon naturalism and emotionalism and a new boldness in combining different art forms to achieve a complete balanced work of art. In architecture and sculpture, the principal exponent of the style was Giovanni Lorenzo Bernini (1598–1680), who invested his works with a sense of movement and emotional urgency, encouraging the spread of such ideas during his travels around Europe. Other notable architects active mainly in Rome included Francesco Castelli Borromini (1599–1667).

Pre-eminent artists in the Baroque inherited an interest in the classical tradition via *Mannerism and were deeply influenced by such masters as Michelangelo, Titian, and Raphael. Among the early exponents were *Caravaggio, whose command of such techniques as *chiaroscuro* contributed to the revolutionary atmosphere of realism and emotional seriousness; Annibale *Carracci, who broke new ground in rejecting some of the excesses of the mannerists; Pietro da Cortona (1596–1669), who specialized in overwhelming illusionistic ceilings (for example, those in the Palazzo Pitti, Florence); and later Rubens (1577–1640), who became acquainted with the Baroque in Rome between 1600 and 1608, before establishing himself as the greatest of the northern baroque artists.

The movement outside Italy subsequently produced a number of other important artists and architects, who combined Italian ideals with their own national characteristics, notably Vermeer and Rembrandt in the Netherlands, Velázquez in Spain, Balthasar Neumann in Germany, Poussin in France, and van Dyck, Inigo *Jones, Wren, and Vanbrugh in England. The baroque taste for ornate decoration ultimately achieved an extreme form in the highly decorated rococo style of the early eighteenth century.

Barros, João de (1496–1570) Portuguese historian and administrator. Barros was born at Vizeu and brought up at the court of King Emanuel I of Portugal, where he was a favourite of the king and also of Prince John, later King John III. In 1532 he was appointed head of the overseas administration, dealing with Portuguese trade with the East and colonial expansionism. Barros's own venture in colonialism, his 1539 expedition to Brazil, was a disaster and he suffered severe financial loss when his fleet was shipwrecked.

A chivalric romance, the *Crónica do Emperador Clarimundo* (1522), was his first published work. Later works include the humanist dialogue *Rópica pnefma* (1532) and one of the earliest Portuguese grammars (1539), but his crowning achievement is his history of Portuguese ventures in the East. This work, the *Asia*, appeared in four "Décadas" (1552, 1553, 1563, 1615); it was continued after his death by Diogo do *Couto. Barros, who modelled his style on that of Livy, celebrated his country's overseas discoveries and conquests from the vantage-point of his own position in the colonial administration, and the *Asia* is still a valuable record of the great years of Portuguese expansionism.

Barthélemy, Nicolas (1478–c. 1540) French Benedictine monk and writer. He was born at Loches, near Tours, and became prior of Fréteval, near Vendôme, and later of Notre-Dame-de-Bonne-Nouvelle, Orleans. He studied law at Orleans university and was a friend of *Budé. Among his poems in Latin were *Epigrammata et eydillia* (1532), and his drama *Christus Xylonicus* (1529) combined elements of the humanist approach to tragedy with aspects of the vernacular mystery plays. He is also known for having influenced Rabelais. His biographies of two dukes of Orleans, Charles the poet (1394–1465) and his son, later King *Louis XII, have survived in manuscript.

Bartholomew('s Day), Massacre of St *see* Massacre of St Bartholomew.

Bartolommeo, Fra (Baccio della Porta; 1472–1517) Italian painter and draughtsman. Born in Florence, Bartolommeo trained as an artist under Cosimo *Rosselli before joining the convent of S Marco and coming under the influence of its prior

*Savonarola. Early works from this period include the *Annunciation* (1497; Volterra cathedral) and the *Last Judgment* (1499; Museo di S Marco). After Savonarola's death Bartolommeo joined the Dominican Order (1500) and gave up painting until 1504, when he became head of the monastery workshop at S Marco. Works from this period, such as *Vision of St Bernard* (1507; Accademia, Florence) and *God the Father with SS Catherine of Siena and Mary Magdalene* (1509; Pinacoteca Civica, Lucca), show the influences of Bellini and Leonardo da Vinci and served to establish Bartolommeo as the foremost painter in Florence by 1510. His control of colour and composition is evident in many of his subsequent works, including *The Mystic Marriage of St Catherine* (1511; versions in Louvre and Uffizi) and his *Pietà* (1515; Palazzo Pitti, Florence). His later paintings were also influenced by the works of Raphael and Michelangelo. He also executed many notable drawings, for instance in his sketchbook, now in Rotterdam.

Basle A Swiss city on the Rhine, close to the French and German borders. First mentioned in 374, Basle became the seat of a bishopric in the fifth century and was the venue of the ecumenical council (1431–49) (*see* Basle, Council of). *Erasmus taught at Basle university (1521–29) and is buried in the city. During the first half of the sixteenth century Basle, which from at least as early as 1468 had boasted a printing press, became a focus for humanist learning and the Reformation. In 1522 *Oecolampadius persuaded the Basle magistrates that the Church should be reformed. After a popular rising, government of the city passed from the bishop to the magistrates and the Mass was abolished. Basle became an important centre of Protestantism, welcoming *Calvin in the 1530s. Notable buildings from the Renaissance period include the fifteenth-century St Paul's Gate, the Münster (1019–1528), the town hall (1504–21), and the church of St Martin.

Basle, Confessions of The earliest reformed confessions of faith, comprising the Basle Confession of 1534 (sometimes called the Confession of Mühlhausen) and the First Helvetic Confession of 1536 (sometimes called the Second Confession of *Basle). In 1529, under the guidance of the Zwinglian reformer, *Oecolampadius, Basle broke with Rome and joined *Zwingli's Christian Civic Alliance. The (first) Basle Confession was written by Oswald Myconius (1488–1552) but based on the work of Oecolampadius, and is a confession of moderate Zwinglianism, fully endorsing Zwingli's view of scripture. It held its place in the Church of Basle until 1872. The First Helvetic Confession

was compiled by Heinrich *Bullinger and, though also essentially Zwinglian, a Lutheran influence can be detected.

Basle, Council of A council of the Church that sat intermittently between 1431 and 1449. The calling of this council was urged upon Pope Martin V by Emperor Sigismund in the hope of making some kind of settlement with the Hussites (*see* Huss, Jan). This resulted in the drawing up in July 1436 of the Compacts of Prague, by the terms of which the Bohemians and Moravians were granted a considerable amount of ecclesiastical independence in return for oaths of fealty to Sigismund. With their legal recognition of divergent practices within Christendom, the Compacts marked a significant change in the Church's policy.

Even before the Compacts were drawn up, relations between the papacy and the council were not good. To thwart the council's attempts to restrict papal authority, Pope *Eugenius IV in 1437 announced the transfer of the council from Basle to Ferrara, later Florence, and, in 1443, Rome (*see* Florence, Council of). Only a small minority of those sitting on the council at Basle accepted this; the majority, declaring the Council's authority superior to that of the pope, remained at Basle and began the proceedings that led to Eugenius's so-called excommunication and deposition and the election of an antipope, Felix V, in 1439. These moves lost the council many supporters, and a lasting schism was avoided when the council submitted to Rome by securing the abdication of Felix, following the death of Eugenius (1447) and the election of *Nicholas V. The dissolution of the council in 1449 marked the end of the "conciliar period", which left a lasting papal suspicion of church councils.

Bassano, Jacopo da Ponte (1510/19–92) Italian painter. The son of Francesco da Ponte the Elder (c. 1475–1539), Bassano was born in Bassano and studied first under his father and then under Bonifacio Veneziano (de' Pitati) in nearby Venice. There contact with the paintings of *Titian stimulated in him the feeling for colour and light that is characteristic of much of his work. From the 1530s he worked mainly in Bassano. His style changed continually according to changing influences and around 1540 he adopted a mannerist style with graceful attenuation of figures, as in his *Adoration of the Magi* (Kunsthistorisches Museum, Vienna). This painting was one of a number which included peasants and animals; Bassano was one of the first painters of religious scenes to do this. The large rustic genre scenes that he produced after 1565 were also innovatory. Bassano's four sons included the painters Francesco the Younger (1549–92) and Leandro (1557–1622).

Baudart, Willem (1565–1640) Dutch scholar and reformed minister. Baudart was born at Deinze, near Ghent, but his parents fled from religious persecution to England, and he was educated at Sandwich and Canterbury. In 1577 the family returned to Flanders. Baudart studied at Leyden, Franeker in Friesland, Heidelberg, and Bremen, and became proficient in Hebrew and Greek. He returned to his native country in 1593 and filled posts at Kampen and Zutphen. In 1619 he was chosen as one of the translators of the Old Testament for the Dutch Bible commissioned by the Synod of *Dort. He retired to Leyden in 1626. Among his works were an index to the Hebrew, Greek, and Latin Bibles (1596) and a history of the Dutch war of liberation. His *Morgenwecker* (1610) was one of the most eloquent tracts written against the truce with Spain negotiated by *Oldenbarneveldt in 1609.

Bauhin, Gaspard (1560–1624) Swiss botanist and anatomist. His textbooks of anatomy (1588–1605) supplemented *Vesalius's illustrations, but in spite of his nomenclature of muscles, which is still used, his botanical books, *Phytopinax* (1596), *Prodromos theatri botanici* (1620), and *Pinax* (1623) are better known. The last, a concordance of the various names of about 6000 plants, remained an essential tool for at least 150 years. His descriptions classified related plants into genera and species, although his *Theatrum botanicum* remained unpublished, except for a first instalment edited by his son in 1658. His elder brother, Jean Bauhin (1541–1613), was also a physician and a botanist and one of the pupils of *Gesner. *Historia plantarum universalis*, posthumously published (1650–51) by his son-in-law, Jean-Henri Cherler, attempted to reconstruct Gesner's unfinished *Historia plantarum*. The book includes concise descriptions of over 5000 plants, mostly European, with a few from the Far East or America, and reflects Jean Bauhin's visits to *botanic gardens at Padua and Bologna, as well as his connection with a similar garden at Lyons.

Bayer, Johann (1572–1625) German astronomer. A Protestant lawyer from Augsburg, Bayer made a lasting contribution to *astronomy in his *Uranometria* (1603), in which he identified stars by assigning letters of the Greek alphabet to them, in order of brightness. Under this system Aldebaran, previously described as the star in the southern eye of Taurus, became α Tauri. He was, however, less successful with his attempts to reform the names of constellations. His posthumously published *Coelum stellatum christianum* (1627) proposed replacing their heathen names with biblical ones, but scholars continued to prefer such traditional names as Cassiopeia and Argo to his suggested Mary Magdalen and Noah's Ark.

Beaufort, Lady Margaret (c. 1441–1509), Countess of Richmond and Derby The daughter and heiress of John, Duke of Somerset, she was descended from Edward III through John of Gaunt, Duke of Lancaster. By her marriage to Edmund *Tudor, she was Henry VII's mother. A devout supporter of the new learning and encouraged by *John Fisher (later bishop of Rochester), Lady Margaret established chairs of divinity at Oxford and Cambridge (1502), founded Christ's College, Cambridge (1505), and bequeathed money for the foundation of St John's College, Cambridge. She was an early patron of *Caxton and Wynkyn de Worde.

Beaumont, Francis (?1584–1616) English dramatist. Born into an old established Leicestershire family, Francis was the younger brother of the poet Sir John Beaumont (1583–1627), who is remembered chiefly as an early exponent of the heroic couplet in English in such poems as the mock-heroic *Metamorphosis of Tobacco* (1602) and the narrative *Bosworth-Field* (1629). Francis followed John to Oxford (1597) and the Inner Temple (1600). In London he met and became the disciple of Ben *Jonson; it may have been through Jonson that Beaumont met John *Fletcher, who became his close friend and with whom he collaborated in the writing of plays from about 1606. Beaumont's best-known independent poem is the Ovidian *Salmacis and Hermaphroditus* (1602).

The first collected edition of the works of Beaumont and Fletcher appeared in 1647 and contained thirty-four plays and a masque; the 1679 edition raises the number to fifty-two plays and the masque. Scholars have disentangled the style of each dramatist so that it is possible to say with some confidence which works are truly collaborative efforts, which solely or mainly by Beaumont, and which by Fletcher alone or with a third party. Among the plays generally thought to be by Beaumont is *The Knight of the Burning Pestle*, a burlesque of knight-errantry written about 1609 and published in 1613; *The Maid's Tragedy*, written in 1611 and first printed in 1619, and *Philaster*, written in 1611 and printed in 1620, are two of the most successful products of the collaboration. Beaumont alone is thought to have written (1613) *The Masque of the Inner Temple*.

Beccadelli, Antonio (1394–1471) Italian poet. Born in Palermo (Latin: Panormus), the town from which he took his nom-de-plume, "Il Panormita", Beccadelli studied law and classical poetry in several northern Italian cities (1420–34). In 1425 he published a Latin poem that brought him immediate notoriety: *Hermaphroditus*, explicitly extolling homosexual love with a scandalous nonchalance. Copies of the poem, together with portraits of Beccadelli, were publicly burned. However, others hailed it as a masterpiece, Cosimo de' Medici accepted the dedication of the poem, and Beccadelli's undoubted scholarship and skill gained him the post of court poet at Pavia, which he held until he returned to Naples. There he founded (1442) the Academia Pontaniana (*see* Neapolitan Academy). He spent the rest of his life as a respected servant of *Alfonso (I) the Magnanimous, for whom he composed *De dictis et de factis Alphonsi regis* (1455), later to become the chief source of the legend of that monarch's magnanimity.

Beccafumi, Domenico (c. 1486–1551) Italian painter. Born near Siena, the son of a peasant named di Pace, Domenico took the name of his patron, Lorenzo Beccafumi. His studies took place in Siena and Rome. Returning to Siena in 1512, he worked on the decoration of the façade of the Palazzo Borghese and produced a mosaic for the church of S Bernardino (1517) and thirty-five biblical scenes for the marble pavement of the cathedral. In 1541 he went to Genoa where he painted a fresco, now lost, for Andrea *Doria, but he then spent the rest of his life in Siena, where he was the most important mannerist painter. His *Birth of Virgin* (1543; Pinacoteca, Siena) is a characteristic example of his mannerist style, with its elongated and foreshortened forms and its contrasts of light and dark. He also produced some sculpture, such as the bronze angels for the cathedral (c. 1548). His decoration of the ceiling of the Palazzo Bindi Sergardi anticipated the erotic tendencies of sixteenth-century Mannerism.

Beck, Leonhard (c. 1480–1542) German painter and woodcut designer. The son of an Augsburg manuscript illuminator, Beck was apprenticed to *Holbein the Elder in 1495, became his assistant, and was registered as an independent master in 1503. His early style was close to that of his master, although he was subsequently influenced by Hans *Burgkmair and Jörg Breu. Beck was involved with Hans Schäufelein, Breu, and Burgkmair on the large cycles of woodcuts known as the *Theuerdank* and *Weisskunig*, commissioned by Emperor Maximilian I. Unaided, he designed the 123 woodcuts of saints in another of Maximilian's commissions, the *Sipp-, Mag-, und Schwägerschaften*. A series of chalk drawings of considerable

force, portraying Augsburg artists and dated 1502–15, has also been attributed to Beck. His later portraits are often confused with those of his son-in-law and pupil, Christoph *Amberger.

Behmen, Jakob *see* Boehme, Jakob.

Belgic Confession (1561) Articles of faith drawn up in French by Guy de Brès, aided by Hadrian à *Saravia, for the Walloon and Flemish reformed churches. It was based on the *Gallican Confession of 1559. Dutch, German, and Latin translations were made; between 1566 and 1581 it was accepted by synods at Antwerp, Wesel, Emden, Dort, and Middelburg, and again by the major Synod of *Dort in 1619. Less polemical than its predecessor, it was the best statement of continental Calvinist doctrine; an English version was adopted by the reformed church of America.

Bellano, Bartolommeo (c. 1440–96/97) Italian sculptor. Born at Padua, the son of a goldsmith, Bellano is first documented in 1456 as an assistant to Donatello in Florence. By 1463 he was probably assisting Donatello with the bronze reliefs for the pulpits of S Lorenzo as his style is discernible in the angular chiselling of several panels. In 1467 he was in Perugia, making a statue of Pope Paul II, and Vasari claims that he served the pope in Rome too, but, by 1468 Bellano had settled again in Padua. He executed a marble revetment for the reliquary chest of St Anthony of Padua in the sacristy of the basilica (1469–72): the panel of the *Miracle of the Mule* is characteristic of his angular and linear style of marble carving. Between 1484 and 1488 he produced his masterpiece, a cycle of ten bronze reliefs of Old Testament stories for the interior of the basilica choir enclosure.

Bellarmine, St Robert *see* Robert Bellarmine, St.

Belleau, Rémy (1528–77) French scholar and poet. Belleau, who was born at Nogent-le-Rotrou, gained first the patronage of the Abbé de Choiseul and later that of Charles IX and Henry III. After taking part in the French campaign against Naples (1557), he settled at Joinville as tutor and counsellor to the Guise family. There he found inspiration for his popular pastoral in verse and prose, *La Bergerie* (1565–72). Described as a "painter of nature" by *Ronsard, his erstwhile associate at the Collège de Coqueret, Belleau was renowned for detailed descriptions that won him the reputation of a poetic miniaturist. He also wrote some didactic verse, a commentary on precious stones and their virtues, and *La Reconnue* (1557), an unfinished comedy in verse, but it was his translation of

BECCAFUMI Christ in Limbo. *(1530s; Pinacoteca, Siena)*

Anacreon's *Odes* (1556) that won him membership of the *Pléiade. He died in Paris.

Bellegambe, Jean (c. 1470–c. 1535) Flemish painter. Probably a native of Douai, then in the Spanish Netherlands, Bellegambe was a follower of Simon Marmion (active 1449–89) and became the foremost history painter in Flanders at that time, combining elements of Flemish and French art in his own work. He may also have been influenced by several other artists of northern Europe, notably Quentin *Metsys. Bellegambe's works include a polyptych (c. 1511; Notre Dame, Douai), two altar wings depicting the glorification of the Virgin (1526; Notre Dame, Douai), and an *Adoration of Infant Christ* (1528). Also the designer of buildings, furniture, frames, and embroidery, Bellegambe was idolized in Douai.

Bellini, Giovanni (c. 1430–1516) Italian painter. The son of the artist Jacopo *Bellini, Giovanni trained in his father's workshop alongside his brother Gentile (c. 1429–1507) and was the brother-in-law of *Mantegna, whose influence is clear on Giovanni's early works. He worked with Gentile on several large narrative cycles and at an early stage showed his skill as a draughtsman in a number of small devotional pieces, notably in his versions of the *Pietà*. Many of these early paintings, such as the *Agony in the Garden* (1465; National Gallery, London), use settings of natural landscapes and demonstrate Giovanni's masterly handling of light and colour. In 1483 he became state painter to the Venetian republic, a post he retained until his death. In this capacity he executed paintings in the doge's palace (destroyed by fire in 1577) and was commissioned for several major portraits, including the *Doge Leonardo Loredan* (1501; National Gallery, London).
Important altarpieces by Giovanni include that for the church of SS Giovanni e Paolo in Venice, influenced by Antonello da Messina, from which stemmed the *sacre conversazioni* for S Giobbe (c. 1483–85) and S Zaccaria (1505). His later works include the secular paintings the *Feast of the Gods* (c. 1514; National Gallery, Washington), painted for Alfonso d'Este, and his only known female nude, the *Toilet of Venus* (1515; Kunsthistorisches Museum, Vienna). Other works include many versions of the Virgin and Child, a *Transfiguration* (c. 1480; Frick College, New York), and *Sacred Allegory* (see Plate III).
Giovanni established Venice as an artistic centre on a level with Florence and Rome and was the teacher of such pupils as Giorgione, Titian, Palma Vecchio, and Sebastiano del Piombo. He also exerted considerable influence over succeeding artistic schools through his development of the use of pure oil colour as opposed to the use of tempera.

Bellini, Jacopo (c. 1400–c. 1471) Italian painter. The father of the artists Gentile (c. 1429–1507) and Giovanni *Bellini and the father-in-law of Andrea *Mantegna, Jacopo was born in Venice and was a pupil of Gentile da Fabriano. After visiting Florence and being exposed to the works of other leading Italian artists, Jacopo returned to Venice and by 1429 was established as the pre-eminent painter there. Very few paintings certainly by him survive and are all executed in a stiff Venetian Gothic style; those that are signed include *Virgin and Child* (Accademia, Venice), *Christ on the Cross* (Museo Civico, Verona), and two *Madonnas* (Lovere and Brera, Milan). Jacopo is best known, however, for his two surviving sketchbooks (Louvre and British Museum) containing many experimental drawings and designs that were later adapted by his sons in their own works. He received many commissions for religious works in Venice and Padua and in 1441 he triumphed over Pisanello in a competition to execute the portrait (now lost) of the ruler of Ferrara, Leonello d'Este. The master of a flourishing workshop, he died in Venice.

Belon, Pierre (1517–64) French zoologist. Although born into a poor family at Le Mans, Belon was allowed to pursue his education at the university of Paris through the support of his local bishop. He was further enabled to develop his interests in natural history by the patronage of the wealthy Cardinal Tournon and the later backing of *Francis I, with whose financial support he travelled through much of Europe and the Near East. He revealed the results of his researches in two works. In the first, *La nature et diversité des poissons* (1551), he described 110 species of marine animals. Like *Rondelet, Belon used the term fish to cover virtually all animals found in the sea; it was even allowed to include the hyena! Belon also published an early ornithological work, *L'Histoire de la nature des oyseaux* (1555). He died at the hands of a highwayman in the Bois de Boulogne. *See also* zoology.

Bembine Table An inscribed bronze table-top made in Rome in the first century AD and excavated in the 1520s from the ruins of the temple of Isis (hence its other name of "Isiac Table"). In 1527 it came into the possession of Cardinal *Bembo. Its hieroglyphs made it an intriguing object to Renaissance scholars (*see* Egyptian studies). An accurate engraving of it was made by Enea Vico (1559) and it was published in 1605 by Lorenzo Pignorio in his *Vetustissimae tabulae aenaea sacris Aegyptiorum simulachris coelatae accurata explicatio* (An accurate account of a most ancient bronze tablet engraved with sacred symbols of the Egyptians).

Bembo, Pietro (1470–1547) Italian scholar, poet, and humanist. Born at Venice, he was educated by Augurello, Barbaro, and Donato. He met Politian in 1491 and in the same year travelled to Messina to learn Greek from Constantine Lascaris. In 1493 he returned to Venice and edited Lascaris's Greek grammar for *Manutius, who also issued Bembo's editions of Petrarch (1501) and Dante (1502). *Gli Asolani* (1505), dialogues on love dedicated to Lucrezia *Borgia, brought Bembo to Urbino where he is depicted as the advocate of platonic love in Castiglione's *Courtier*. In 1513 in Rome Bembo published *De imitatione*, which championed Ciceronianism and led to his appointment as secretary (1513–21) to Pope Leo X, after which he went to Padua. In 1530 he published

Rime, a collection of his Italian poetry, and was nominated historian and librarian of the Venetian republic. In 1539 he became a cardinal and moved back to Rome, where he died.

Bembo was an important member of the sceptical group which flourished around Leo X, and was patron of the free-thinking *Pomponazzi. He was also an important figure in the revival of interest in vernacular poetry, starting a vogue for imitations of Petrarch. He showed a much greater sensitivity to form than did those humanists who concentrated on classical literature; his *Prose della volgar lingua* (1525), the first critical history of Italian literature since Dante, used Petrarch and Boccaccio as models for a vernacular which would be natural as well as artistic. *See also* Bembine Table.

Benedetto da Maiano (1442–97) Italian sculptor. A member of a notable artistic family of Florence, Benedetto trained as a stone carver and developed a style of decorative realism that reflected the influence of his master Antonio *Rossellino. His earliest surviving work was the shrine of S Savino (1472; Faenza cathedral), upon which he worked with his brother, the architect *Giuliano da Maiano. His best-known work, however, was his series of marble reliefs on the pulpit in Sta Croce, Florence (1472–75), sketches of which survive in the Victoria and Albert Museum in London; this shows the influence of *Desiderio da Settignano, *Donatello, Lorenzo *Ghiberti, and antique pieces. At about the same time he also worked on an altar for Sta Fina in the Collegiata at S Gimignano where he became familiar with the naturalistic style of Ghirlandaio. Benedetto's other works included a number of portrait busts, including one of Pietro Mellini (1474; Bargello, Florence), who commissioned the marble reliefs in Sta Croce, contributions to churches in Naples, the tomb of Mary of Aragon, a portrait bust of Filippo Strozzi (Louvre), and the altar of S Bartolo in S Agostino at S Gimignano (1494). His architectural pieces included the Palazzo Strozzi (begun c. 1490) in Florence.

Benivieni, Girolamo (1453–1542) Italian poet and humanist. A Florentine by birth, he joined the scholarly circle under the patronage of Lorenzo de' Medici. He is mainly remembered for his *Canzone d'amore* ("Ode to love"; c. 1487), a versification of *Ficino's translation of Plato's *Symposium*. When *Pico della Mirandola produced an extensive commentary on the poem, Benivieni's fame was assured. The poem greatly assisted the spread of *Neoplatonism and had an enormous influence on many other writers. After becoming a follower of *Savonarola, Benivieni wrote some religious poetry, undertook a study of Dante's *Inferno*, and translated one of Savonarola's treatises. He died in Florence and lies buried next to his friend Pico in the church of S Marco.

Bentivoglio family A powerful family in fifteenth-century Bologna. Giovanni I ruled for a short time (1401–02) before the *Visconti overthrew him. His son, Antongaleazzo held power briefly in 1420 before Pope Martin V expelled him. Annibale (d. 1445) successfully ejected the papal forces, and after his assassination his cousin, Sante, controlled Bologna (1445–63). Sante established a close relationship with the *Sforza and defined the extent of Bologna's independence from the papacy (1447). Giovanni II then governed Bologna, improving buildings and waterways, encouraging the arts and learning, and strengthening the army until he was forced into exile in Ferrara by Pope *Julius II (1506). Giovanni's son, Annibale II, was temporarily restored by the French (1511–12).

Bermejo, Bartolomé (died 1498) Spanish painter and designer of stained glass. He came from Cordova but is documented as being active in Barcelona from 1486. His *Pietà* (1490), commissioned for the cathedral there, is his masterpiece and shows both Flemish and Italian influence.

Bernardines *see under* Feuillants.

Bernardino of Siena, St (1380–1444) Italian Franciscan reformer. He was born at Massa di Carrara, between La Spezia and Pisa, and, during an epidemic, he took charge of a hospital at Siena. In 1402 he entered the Franciscan Order and became a popular preacher, exhorting his brethren to a stricter observance of their rule and condemning the evils of his time, especially usury and party strife. His devotion to the Holy Name of Jesus gave rise to the sobriquet "Apostle of the Holy Name". Suspected of heresy by the theologians of Bologna university, he was eventually exonerated. In 1439 he was present at the Council of *Florence, at which he played an active part. His simplicity led him to accept conventional notions about the guilt of the Jews and the power of witchcraft. He died at Aquila degli Abruzzi, on his way to preach at Naples.

bernesco A type of lyric burlesque named after the Florentine poet Francesco *Berni. It was anti-Petrarchan in spirit and consisted of a caricature of manners marked by grotesque details, outrageous comparisons, and bold paradox. Berni drew on a long tradition of humorous vernacular poetry and also on his immediate literary forebears Domenico di Giovanni (1404–49) and Luigi *Pulci.

No character, however exalted, was safe from his biting satire. His best-known successor in the mode was Charles de Sygognes (1560–1611).

Berni, Francesco (?1497–1535) Italian poet. Born at Lamporrechio, Berni became a canon in Florence (c. 1530). It is said that his death there was occasioned by his being poisoned by Duke Alessandro de' Medici when he refused that worthy's order to poison a cousin of the duke's. Berni's poems are mainly satirical and jocose, often on occasional topics (see bernesco). He was also famous for his *Rifacimento* (recasting) of *Boiardo's *Orlando innamorato* into his own Tuscan dialect. The *Rifacimento*, published posthumously in 1541, contains interpolated stanzas of Berni's own. Although much lauded by contemporaries, Berni's version is now rejected in favour of Boiardo's original.

Berruguete, Alonso Gonzales (c. 1488–1561) Spanish sculptor. Born at Paredes de Nava, the son of Pedro *Berruguete, Alonso followed his father's footsteps in visiting Italy (c. 1504–17). In Florence he was highly impressed by *Michelangelo's sculptural style, as is evident from his alabaster *Resurrection* in Valencia. Although Berruguete was appointed a court artist to *Charles V in 1518, he did not accompany the emperor when he moved to Germany in 1520, but remained in Valladolid where he enjoyed considerable patronage. His numerous large sculptured altarpieces, such as those for the monastery of La Mejorada (1526) and for S Benito at Valladolid (1527–32), reveal a debt to *Donatello. Although Berruguete's stylistic vocabulary was distinctly Italianate, the format of the large Spanish altarpiece with numerous subdivisions, bright colours, and ornate decoration was essentially late Gothic. The exaggerated, contorted style of his figures is decidedly anticlassical and reminiscent both of fifteenth-century wood carving and contemporary Italian Mannerism. Berruguete had numerous pupils but his style defied imitation.

Berruguete, Pedro (active 1483–1504) Spanish painter. Documents indicate that Berruguete, who was born at Paredes de Nava, was employed at the cathedrals of Toledo and Avila between 1483 and 1500 and that in 1502 he became a court painter to Philip the Handsome, later king of Spain. He specialized in large painted altarpieces of many panels, some of which were painted in collaboration with other artists. His attributed works indicate points of contact with the painted decorations of the studies of Federico da Montefeltro in Urbino and Gubbio in Italy (1473–80). However, Berruguete's Spanish œuvre is not of such high quality as these decorations, which

should more properly be ascribed to *Justus of Ghent as whose assistant Berruguete probably worked there. Berruguete's hybrid Italo-Flemish style is an important pointer to the early sixteenth-century reorientation of Spanish painting, away from Netherlandish and towards Italian models. His son, Alonso Gonzales *Berruguete, was an important sculptor.

Bersuire, Pierre (?1290–1362) French biblical scholar. He was born at St-Pierre-du-Chemin, but little else is known about his life. A friend of *Petrarch, whom he met at Avignon, Bersuire was probably a Franciscan monk and was apparently imprisoned for heresy at one time, before becoming prior of St-Éloi in Paris. He is remembered as the author of a widely influential translation of Livy, made in the 1350s, and also as one of the first scholars to use a classical model to dignify the vernacular. His biblical guide, the *Reductorium repertorium et dictionarium moral utriusque testament* (c. 1340) enjoyed considerable success, being issued twelve times by 1526.

Bertaut, Jean (1552–1611) French poet. He was born near Caen and, as tutor to the children of a noble family, was introduced to court life as a young man. Soon he was writing lyric and elegiac poetry strongly influenced by *Ronsard and *Desportes. He was appointed official court poet under Henry III, and again under Henry IV, and composed many occasional poems admired for their polished, graceful style. Later he turned to religious subjects and paraphrases of the psalms. Bertaut published two collections: *Recueil des œuvres poétiques* (1601) and *Recueil de quelques vers amoureux* (1602). He also held various positions at court and was eventually made bishop of Sées (1606) in Normandy, where he spent his last years.

Bertoldo di Giovanni (c. 1440–91) Italian maker of bronze statuettes and medals. Of obscure origin, perhaps born in Florence as an illegitimate son of Giovanni di Cosimo de' Medici, Bertoldo worked mainly in the circle of the Medici, especially of Lorenzo the Magnificent, and was influenced by the elderly Donatello. His earliest dated piece is a medal of 1469 showing Emperor Frederick III, while his most original one shows the scene in Florence cathedral of the *Pazzi conspiracy (1478) when Giuliano de' Medici was assassinated. His most famous work is a bronze panel showing a *Cavalry Battle* (Bargello), based on a fragmentary Roman sarcophagus in Pisa; it once decorated a mantelpiece in the Medici palace. His finest bronze group, cast by *Adriano Fiorentino, is *Bellerophon and Pegasus* (Vienna), which is indebted to the *Horse-tamers* of the Quirinal Hill, Rome. Bertoldo's several statuettes of Hercules show his firm grasp of the masculine anatomy in action. He was curator of the Medici sculpture collection.

Bérulle, Pierre de (1575–1629) French cardinal and statesman. He was born at Serilly, near Troyes, and educated by the Jesuits at the university of Paris. Bérulle later emerged as one of the leading lights of the *Counter-Reformation. In 1611 he established the Congregation of the French Oratory, an institution for the study of church history, Hebrew, and biblical criticism. As statesman he helped arrange Henrietta Maria's marriage (1625) to Charles I of England, concluded the treaty of Monzon (1626), and was instrumental in the reconciliation of Louis XIII with his mother Marie de' Medici. He was created cardinal in 1627 and a councillor of state; the latter post he soon relinquished as a result of Richelieu's opposition to his Austrian policy. His writings, including *Grandeurs de Jésus* (1623), were popular among the French Jansenists.

Bessarion, Cardinal John (c. 1395–1472) Greek-born humanist scholar, churchman, philosopher, and collector of manuscripts. Born at Trebizond, he was educated in Constantinople. In 1423 he heard Plethon lecture on Plato and was attracted to his ideas. Unlike Plethon however, he was a Platonist who could recognize the value in contemporary Aristotelianism and he endeavoured to reconcile the two systems. By substituting the original works of Greek genius for an outworn scholasticism, thus bringing men's minds back to the pristine sources of antiquity, Bessarion was the principal author of the philosophical Renaissance. Created archbishop of Nicaea (1437), he visited Italy with Emperor John VIII Palaeologus to join in discussions intended to bring about unity between the Eastern and Western Churches. His support for the Roman Church at the councils of Ferrara and *Florence recommended him to Pope Eugenius IV, who made him a cardinal (1439). From then on Bessarion lived in Italy, encouraging the spread of Greek studies. He received the archbishopric of Sipunto and the bishoprics of Sabina and Frascati, and his palace in Rome was a meeting-place for philosophers; refugee Greeks were especially welcome and he thus made a major contribution to the diffusion of Hellenism. He translated Aristotle's *Metaphysics* and also wrote Platonic treatises *De natura et arte* and *In calumniatorem Platonis*, the latter being an attack on *George of Trebizond. Despite this, he was not an uncompromising Platonist and his works made Platonism more hospitable to orthodox theology and encouraged theology to be more speculative. Bessarion's collection of 800 manuscripts, nearly

500 of them Greek, was presented (1468) to the Venetian senate and became the nucleus of the Bibliotheca *Marciana.

Beza (Théodore de Bèze; 1519–1605) French theologian and scholar. Born in Vézelay and educated at Orleans and Bourges as a Protestant, he practised law in Paris (1539), where his life was marked by worldliness and frivolity. In 1548 a serious illness effected a change in his outlook. He became a Calvinist and in November 1549 was appointed professor of Greek at Lausanne. There he helped *Calvin with a number of works, including the *De haereticis a civili magistratu puniendis* (1554), which justified the persecution of those who refused to accept Calvin's teaching. In 1558 he moved to Geneva. On Calvin's death (1564) Beza became his successor and wrote his biography. His main contribution to scholarship was his work on the New Testament; his editions influenced the Genevan English versions (1557, 1560) and the Authorized Version (1611). In 1581 he presented D (the Codex Bezae), one of the primary manuscripts for the text of the New Testament, to Cambridge university, but little attention was then paid to it. His play *Abraham sacrifiant* (1550) is claimed to be the first French tragedy; it was translated into English by Golding in 1575. Beza's inaccuracies as a historian originated many errors made by later writers. His lasting importance lies in modifications he made to the rigours of Calvin's rule. He broadened the appeal of Protestantism by adopting a more tolerant approach to the details of administration, though he remained firm on the central points of Calvin's doctrine.

Bibbiena, Bernardo Dovizi, Il (1470–1520) Italian churchman, diplomat, and author. Called after his birthplace of Bibbiena, near Florence, Bibbiena was a protégé of Cardinal Giovanni de' Medici, whom he followed into exile in 1494. Bibbiena worked assiduously on his patron's behalf and when Giovanni became Pope *Leo X (1513) he was rewarded by being made a cardinal and Leo's treasurer-general. He also undertook several important diplomatic missions. Bibbiena was a friend of Raphael, who painted his portrait, and his character is favourably depicted in Castiglione's *The Courtier*. Apart from his letters, Bibbiena is mainly remembered as the author of *La calandria*, a *commedia erudita* first performed at Urbino in 1513, which had many revivals and imitators during the Renaissance.

Bible, editions of Throughout the Middle Ages the Latin translation of the Bible made by Jerome in the fourth century AD (the Vulgate) remained the basis of Bible texts. It was some time before the new approaches to textual criticism made an impact on biblical scholarship. Conservative scholastic exegetes, exemplified by the theological faculty of the Sorbonne, branded as heresy the subjecting of scripture to the same kinds of critical test as secular literature. Moreover the Hebrew text of the Old Testament could not be studied without the help of Jewish scholars and this too aroused hostility (see Hebrew studies).

Hebrew printing began in Italy around 1475, and the first important editions of biblical texts were printed at Soncino, east of Milan (1485–86). The whole of the Hebrew Old Testament was printed in 1488. The next stage was the printing of the *Complutensian Polyglot at Alcalá (1514–17), though the edition was not published till 1522. In 1516 the first edition of the rabbinical Bible was published. The only other important edition of the Hebrew Bible in this period was the Antwerp Polyglot (1568–73) printed by *Plantin.

The edition of Erasmus (1516), with a parallel Latin translation by the editor, was the first published Greek text of the New Testament. Subsequent editions (1519, 1522) made considerable improvements and were used as the bases of Luther's and Tyndale's translations respectively. The first attempt at a really critical text of the New Testament appeared in 1534, but it was not until the Stephanus folio New Testament (1550) (see Estienne press) that a text appeared based on the collation of a large number of manuscripts.

Scholars also addressed the problem of a reliable text of the Vulgate. The Stephanus editions from 1528 onwards represented a major advance but were rejected by the Catholic authorities. The text finally accepted by the Church was the Sistine-Clementine version, first published (1590) under Pope *Sixtus V and reissued (1592) with extensive correction under *Clement VIII.

Bible, translations of Translations of the scriptures go back to the third century BC when the Septuagint was produced to satisfy the needs of Greek-speaking Jews in Alexandria. Jerome in the fourth century AD produced, in the Vulgate, a Latin translation which catered for the Western Church and became the Bible of the Middle Ages.

The impetus to translate the Bible into vernacular languages was part of the general reform movement which spread through northern Europe in the fifteenth and sixteenth centuries, and these translations were often made with a polemical purpose. For English students the first important name is that of John Wyclif whose translation, based on the Vulgate, appeared in 1382; the fact that nearly 200 manuscripts survive, containing all or a substantial part of the scriptures, shows the wide diffusion of this work. Wyclif's translation

was used to support a challenge to Church authority and Archbishop Arundel tried to suppress it. A similar series of events led *Luther to the production of his German Bible (New Testament 1522, Old Testament 1523–24), which had an immense impact not only upon the religious debate but also upon the *German language.

Wyclif's work circulated in England in manuscript; even so it reached a wide audience and travelled as far as Bohemia where it influenced the Hussite movement. The invention of printing had a profound impact on Bible translation, enabling new versions to gain currency with unprecedented speed. The study of Greek, encouraged by Florentine humanism, led to the study of the New Testament in the original language and eventually to translations from Greek rather than from Jerome's Latin version. William *Tyndale was the first to produce an English translation from Greek (1525). Religious pressures forced Tyndale out of England and the work was printed at Cologne. It received hostile treatment from the government, Sir Thomas *More being particularly opposed to it. Tyndale's work was the basis for Coverdale's Bible (1535), a translation which circulated in England with government approval as a consequence of the changed political climate. Matthew's Bible (1537) combines the work of Tyndale and Coverdale. Coverdale also edited the large format Great Bible (1539), designed to be read aloud from church lecterns. The Geneva Bible (1560) was the work of Protestant exiles on the Continent during Mary's reign, but its extreme Puritan marginalia made it unacceptable to the moderate Elizabethan Church, which countered with the Bishops' Bible (1568). English Protestant translations of the Bible in this period culminated in the Authorized Version of 1611 (also known as the King James Bible), which became the standard English Bible until the Revised Version of 1885.

The Reformation forced the Roman Church to produce its own vernacular translations of the scriptures. One of the earliest was the German version by Hieronymus *Emser (1527). An English Bible was published at Reims (New Testament 1582) and Douai (Old Testament 1609). The Douai-Reims text, with its strongly Latinate language, followed the Vulgate minutely, even to the point of reproducing nonsense, but nonetheless became the accepted version for the English Catholic community. The Polish Catholic Bible (1599) of the Jesuit scholar Bishop Jakub Wiyek (1541–97) has greatly influenced the Polish vernacular.

Following Luther's example, Protestant scholars all over Europe translated the scriptures into their native tongues. An early Lutheran New Testament was published in Sweden in 1526; it was associated with Olaus *Petri, who also worked on the complete Gustavus Vasa Bible of 1541. Another Lutheran New Testament was that published in 1529 by the Dane Christiern Pedersen (c. 1480–1554), who later collaborated on the so-called Christian III Bible (1550). In France *Lefèvre d'Étaples made a translation of the New Testament from the Vulgate (1523); his French Old Testament appeared five years later. *Olivetan, whose Bible was published in 1535, made the first French translation of the Old Testament direct from the Hebrew, but his New Testament is merely a revision of Lefèvre's. *Enzinas (Dryander) published *El Nuevo Testamento* in Antwerp in 1543, and a complete Spanish version by the friar turned Protestant, Casiodoro de Reina (died c. 1581), appeared at Basle in 1569. A Bible in Latin was produced by *Castellio in the late 1540s to save learned Protestants from the necessity of using the Vulgate.

Bicci, Neri di *see* Neri di Bicci.

Bidermann, Jakob (1578–1639) German Jesuit dramatist. Born at Ehingen, near Ulm, and educated at Augsburg, Bidermann entered the Society of Jesus in 1594. For eight years he was in charge of dramatic activities in the Jesuit school in Munich, before being sent to Dillingen university and finally to Rome, where he died. Bidermann was probably the greatest exponent of *Jesuitendrama*, plays written in Latin which were predominantly educational and propagandist in intent, but which nevertheless exerted a powerful influence not just in Germany, but throughout Europe. His most famous plays were *Cenodoxus* (1609) and *Belisarius* (1607). Most of his work draws on the Old Testament and legends of the saints.

Bigi (the Greys) The party that intrigued for the restoration of the *Medici during their period of exile from Florence (1494–1512) following the ousting of Lorenzo the Magnificent's son Piero. The Bigi triumphed in 1512 after the threat of invasion by Spanish troops had effectively wrecked the Florentine republic.

Binchois, Gilles de (c. 1400–60) Franco-Flemish composer. Binchois was probably born in Binche, near Mons, and from 1419 to 1423 was organist at the church of Ste Waldetrude, Mons. He was possibly in the service of the duke of Suffolk in the early 1420s but from at least 1431 served at the Burgundian court chapel, remaining there until 1453. On retirement he moved to Soignies, where he became provost at the church of St Vincent. Binchois is generally regarded as a major figure in fifteenth-century music along with *Dufay (whom he knew) and *Dunstable. Binchois's sacred music is simple in style; he wrote twenty-eight Mass sections, six Magnificats, and around thirty smaller works (motets and hymns). He is chiefly remembered for his secular compositions; he wrote around fifty-five chansons, mostly in the rondeau form, with texts dealing with courtly love. Nearly all are set for one voice and two instruments, with graceful melodies; they are symmetrical and pay great attention to the form of the poetic text.

biography The narrative re-creation of another person's life. Secular biography in the modern sense was very much a Renaissance invention. Saints' lives had been very popular reading in the Middle Ages, but non-devotional biography had tended to take the form of extended panegyrics of princely patrons; *Beccadelli's life of *Alfonso (I) the Magnanimous (1455) falls into this category. Another use to which biographical materials was often put was to demonstrate the futility of human affairs and in works of this kind the subject's motives and personality are strictly subordinated to the moral lesson; *Boccaccio's *De casibus virorum illustrium* was a leader in the genre, starting a tradition that survived well into the Renaissance with such works as the English verse biographies in the multi-author *Mirror for Magistrates* (1559). The prime classical inspiration for early biographers was Plutarch, whose *Parallel Lives* of Greek and Roman dignitaries was very widely read. In Italy in the fifteenth century Aenea Silvio Piccolomini (*see* Pius II) and Vespasiano da *Bisticci led the way in writing biographical accounts of their important contemporaries, often on the basis of personal knowledge. The culmination of the Italian biographical effort is reached in the following century with *Vasari's *Vite dei più eccellenti pittori, scultori, e architetti* (1550; revised and expanded edition 1568).

Before the seventeenth century, however, biography remained a comparatively under-exploited genre in most countries, although biographical material is of course embedded in letters and memoirs (as in the *Memoirs* of Pierre de *Brantôme). In England Sir Thomas *More's controversial *History of Richard III* (1543), written, though never finished, in both English and Latin around 1513, is a landmark in the evolution of biography, notable for the strikingly dramatic quality of the scenes and its insights into human motivation. The life of More himself was written (c. 1535) by his son-in-law William Roper (1496–1578) and between 1554 and 1557 George Cavendish (?1500–?1561) wrote his *Life and Death of Cardinal Wolsey*, both of them accounts of great and complex public figures by men who knew them intimately; neither biography was published until the following century. *See also* autobiography.

Biondo, Flavio (1392–1463) Italian historian and archaeologist. Born at Forlì and educated at Cremona, he was caught up in the politics of the time and lived in exile in Imola, Ferrara, and Venice until Eugenius IV employed him in the papal Curia in 1433. Though he had little interest in the speculative side of the Renaissance he was the first historian who showed awareness of the gap separating the classical from the medieval world. He published three volumes which collected the antiquities of Italy as far as they were then known: *Roma instaurata* (1440–63), *Roma triumphans* (1456–60), and *Italia instaurata* (1456–60). The effect of these books was to stimulate topographical research and encourage the development of chorography, the study of local history from surviving remains. They also influenced artists, particularly *Mantegna. Biondo's last work, left incomplete at his death, was his *Historiarum ab inclinatione Romane imperii decades* in forty-two books, dealing with the period 410–1441.

Biringuccio, Vannoccio (1480–c. 1539) Italian metallurgist. The son of a Sienese official, Biringuccio began his career in the arsenal of Pandolfo Petrucci, ruler of Siena. After a period of exile during which he worked in Parma, Ferrara, and Venice, he returned to Siena in 1530. In 1538, shortly before his death, he entered the service of Pope Paul III in Rome as superintendent of the papal arsenal. Biringuccio's observations on his lifetime's trade were published posthumously in his *Pirotechnia* (1540). Lavishly illustrated, it contained detailed accounts of the mining and extraction of ores, the blast furnace, the manufacture of cannon and gunpowder, and the production of glassware. There were ten editions of the work before 1678, including translations into English and French, keeping Biringuccio's work in wide use as a practical text well into the eighteenth century.

Bisticci, Vespasiano da (1421–98) Florentine bookseller, scholar, and biographer. He was agent for the three greatest collectors of manuscripts of the early Renaissance: Cosimo de' *Medici, Pope *Nicholas V, and Federico da *Montefeltro, Duke of Urbino. Manuscripts were exported from his factory all over Europe, even to England and Hungary. He was the largest employer of copyists in Europe and his reputation for craftsmanship maintained the market for manuscripts for some time after the invention of printing. On one occasion he and a team of forty-five copyists produced 200 volumes in twenty-two months for Cosimo's library in the Badia, Fiesole. He took a scholarly interest in the books his workmen produced and guaranteed the accuracy of the texts as well as the beauty of the execution. This interest helped him to make the contacts with scholars and humanists which he used in his *Vite d'uomini illustri del secolo XV* (written after 1480), which gives many biographical details not available elsewhere and is notable for its lack of malice.

Black Death *see under* plague.

Blaeu, Willem Jansz. (1571–1638) Dutch cartographer and astronomer. Born at Alkmaar, Blaeu served a two-year apprenticeship in Amsterdam, then developed his geographical and astronomical skills under the guidance of Tycho *Brahe. In 1596 he returned to Amsterdam, and established himself as a maker of both globes and scientific instruments. He also founded a publishing house (1599), specializing in cartography. Blaeu enjoyed universal acclaim for the quality of his work; his instruments and globes featured unprecedented precision, and he developed a new type of press for mapmaking. His most famous works are a world map issued in 1605, *Het Licht der Zeevaerdt* (*The Light of Navigation;* a three-volume sea atlas, 1608–21), and a magnificent series of atlases, beginning in 1638 and ongoing at the time of Blaeu's death. After Blaeu died, his son Jan (d. 1673) continued his work, the eleven-volume *Atlas Major* (1662) being the firm's greatest achievement.

Blahoslav, Jan (1523–71) Czech humanist scholar and theologian. Blahoslav was born in Přerov, northeast of Brno, and was a leading member of the *Czech Brethren, whose bishop he became in 1557. Under his leadership the brethren became a significant force on the Czech cultural scene. Blahoslav translated the New Testament into Czech (1564), and his version was incorporated virtually unaltered into the Kralice Bible (1588). His Czech grammar was influential in establishing Czech as a literary language, and he also contributed to musicology, producing the first theoretical treatise in the vernacular under the title *Musica* (1558) and a hymn book (1561) with well over 700 tunes.

block-books *see under* book illustration.

Bloemaert, Abraham (1564–1651) Dutch painter. Bloemaert was born in Gorinchem, the son of the architect Cornelis Bloemaert (c. 1540–95). Abraham trained in Utrecht, visited France (1580–83), and then settled in Utrecht, where he ran a school that attracted many pupils, including his own four sons. Apart from a brief sojourn in Amsterdam (1591–93), when his father was appointed city architect there, Abraham remained in Utrecht for the rest of his long life. A versatile artist, he painted biblical and mythological subjects in the mannerist mode made current in northern Europe by Frans *Floris and *Spranger. Bloemaert later came under the influence of *Caravaggio, as mediated by his pupil Gerard Honthorst (1590–1656) who studied in Italy between 1610 and 1620, and later still he adopted a more classical style. He was also a portraitist and a prolific and accomplished draughtsman, particularly notable for his landscape drawings.

Blois A French city on the River Loire. First mentioned in the sixth century, it was the seat of the powerful counts of Blois in the Middle Ages. The city was acquired by Louis of Orleans late in the fourteenth century and passed to the French crown when his grandson became *Louis XII of France (1498). In the sixteenth century Blois was an important administrative and royal centre. Its many Gothic and Renaissance buildings include the château with its famous *Francis I façade (1515–24). The château was the scene of the murder (1588) of the duke of *Guise by order of *Henry III.

BLOIS *The grand staircase on the courtyard façade of the Francis I wing of the château.*

Blondeel, Lancelot (1496–1561) Flemish painter, architect, designer, and engraver. He was born at Poperinghe, but became a master painter in the guild at Bruges in 1519. The chimneypiece (1530) for the Greffe du Franc, Bruges, is an example of his architectural work in the early Renaissance style, and Renaissance elements also appear in his triptych of *SS Cosmas and Damian* (1523; S Jacques, Bruges). In 1550 he and *Scorel were commissioned to restore the *Ghent altarpiece.

Blood, Tribunal (*or* **Council**) **of** *see* Tribunal of Blood.

Boccaccino, Boccaccio (c. 1466–1525) Italian painter. Boccaccino came from Ferrara and was influenced by the Ferrarese master *Ercole de' Roberti. He also adopted elements of the Venetian style. His best work was the frescoes he executed in the cathedral at Cremona between 1506 and 1519. Other works on religious subjects are preserved in the Accademia and Museo Correr, Venice. Galeazzo *Campi was among his Cremonese followers, and Boccaccino's son Camillo (1501–46) was among those who worked, like the Campi brothers, on the frescoes in S Sigismondo, Cremona.

Boccaccio, Giovanni (1313–75) Italian poet and scholar. He is one of the greatest figures in the history of European literature. The recovery and study of classical texts, which was the driving force behind Renaissance *humanism, can justly be claimed to have originated with Boccaccio and his older contemporary *Petrarch. Their determination that the classical ideal should permeate every aspect of life led to what has been called the "humanism of the vernacular": the ennobling not only of their native tongue, but also of everyday experience, under the influence of classical models. Boccaccio's birthplace is uncertain, but was probably either Certaldo or Florence. He spent his early years in Florence before being sent to Naples (c. 1328) to learn business in the service of the wealthy *Bardi family: his merchant father had apparently little sympathy with his son's literary aspirations. The dozen or so years Boccaccio spent in Naples were decisive for him, since it was there that he gained the support of King *Robert of Anjou, was introduced into the circle of humanists around the king, and began to write. It was also during this period that he fell in love with the mysterious "Fiammetta" (possibly Maria d'Aquino, the king's illegitimate daughter), who, like Dante's Beatrice or Petrarch's Laura, was to be the inspiration for his writing for many years. Among the works he produced at this time are the prose *Il filocolo* (c. 1336) and the verse *Il filostrato* (c. 1338); the latter was to be a major influence on Chaucer's *Troilus and Criseyde* (c. 1380–85). In 1341 he also finished *Teseida*, an epic in *ottava rima*, the verse metre which was to become the characteristic vehicle for Italian epic or narrative poetry. The following year he completed his *Ameto* (*see under* pastoral).

In all his early writings Boccaccio is an innovator, but it was the decade following his return to Florence (c. 1340) that saw him at the height of his powers, culminating in the composition of the *Decameron* (1348–53). During the period of the *Decameron's* composition Boccaccio received a series of appointments as ambassador, and in 1351 he was sent to recall the exiled Petrarch to Florence. His friendship with Petrarch was very significant; under his influence Boccaccio turned more and more towards scholarship, and together they traced the paths along which humanism was to develop. One result of these interests was that Boccaccio worked until the end of his life on a huge encyclopedia of ancient mythologies, the *De genealogiis deorum*. His biographical compilations, *De casibus virorum illustrium* ("On the fates of famous men") and *De claris mulieribus* ("On famous women") were mines of material for later writers. He wrote a biography of Dante (c. 1355) and in 1373 lectured in Florence on the *Divina commedia*. Later that year illness forced him to retire to Certaldo, where he died. When he died, within eighteen months of Petrarch, Franco *Sacchetti expressed the feelings of many when he said that all poetry was now extinct.

Boccador, Le *see* Domenico da Cortona.

Boccanegra, Simone (c. 1301–63) Doge of Genoa (1339–44, 1356–63) Born into a prominent Genoese family, Boccanegra was first appointed doge in the Guelf-Ghibelline crisis of 1339, the Genoese hoping that he would show leadership qualities similar to those of his great-uncle, Guglielmo (captain of the people, 1257–62). However, he failed to end the conflict, and his greed and heavy tax exactions led to his exile to Pisa (1344). He later participated in Genoa's revolt (1355) against the Visconti of Milan, who had taken control of the city in 1353, and was reappointed doge the next year. He remained in office until his sudden death, traditionally explained as the result of poisoning at a banquet. Verdi made him the hero of an idealized opera.

Bodin, Jean (1530–96) French lawyer and political philosopher. Born at Angers, he became professor of Roman law at Toulouse until he entered the service of the crown (1567). In 1581 he was involved in negotiations for the projected marriage of *Elizabeth I and Duke *Francis of Alençon. His reputation rests on his political writings, in particular, *Six livres de la république* (1576), which he himself translated into Latin (1586). The work expounds his theories of an ideal government based on a powerful hereditary monarchy kept in check by certain political institutions. It established Bodin as the founder of political science in France and was to exert a great influence on men like Montesquieu, Rousseau, and Hobbes. His wide-ranging works include *De la démonomanie* (1580), a denunciation of witchcraft, and a comparative study of religions, the *Colloquium Heptaplomeres*, written in 1588 but not published until the nineteenth century. He died in Laôn of the plague.

Bodleian Library The main library of Oxford university and one of the oldest and most important non-lending reference libraries in Great Britain. Founded originally in the fourteenth century, its first major benefactor was Humfrey, Duke of Gloucester (1391–1447), but by the mid-sixteenth century his collection of rare manuscripts had been dispersed. The library was refounded in 1598 by Thomas Bodley (1545–1613), diplomat and scholar. Originally designed as a fortress of Protestant learning, the library soon became a storehouse of valuable books and manuscripts, due partly to Bodley's arrangement whereby the Stationer's Company of London undertook in 1610 to give the library a copy of every book they printed, and also to a series of important acquisitions since Bodley's time, including John Selden's library in 1659, and the Tanner, Rawlinson, Malone, and Douce collections.

Boehme, Jakob (1575–1624) German mystic. The son of a farmer at Altseidenberg in Upper Lusatia, Boehme became a shoemaker in 1589. He moved to Görlitz in Silesia where he published his first work *Aurora, oder die Morgenröte im Aufgang* (1612). This mystical work aroused the wrath of the Lutheran pastor, Gregory Richter, who persuaded the municipal council to suppress Boehme's works. Boehme, however, continued writing; several more treatises, some of them published posthumously, were completed before his death at Görlitz. These include the devotional work *Der Weg zu Christo* (1623), *De signatura rerum* (1623) on cosmology (*see* signatures, theory of), and *Mysterium Magnum* (1623), a mystical interpretation of Genesis. Although obscure (especially in their use of Paracelsian terminology) and open to dualist and pantheistic interpretations, his works had a lasting influence on people as diverse as the Quaker George Fox, the Cambridge Platonists, and the great German Romantics.

Bohemian Brethren *see* Czech Brethren.

Boiardo, Matteo Maria (1441–94) Italian poet and courtier. Born at Scandiano, of which he became count, member of a prominent Ferrarese family, Boiardo received a classical education in Latin and Greek, law and philosophy. As a courtier he served the dukes of Ferrara – Borso, Ercole, and Sigismondo d'Este – and was appointed governor of Modena and later of Reggio.

Boiardo's works reflect the polished manners and the brilliant literary culture of the Este court. Among his earlier works are eclogues written in imitation of Virgil and translations of Herodotus and Apuleius. His reputation as one of the finest lyric poets of the fifteenth century rests on three *Amorum libri* (1499), comprising 180 poems, Petrarchan in style though not excessively so, which commemorate his love of Antonia Caprara. Boiardo's major work is the epic *Orlando innamorato*, of which he completed two books (1483) and left unfinished a third (1495). Drawing on French romances, which were in vogue at Ferrara, Boiardo combined heroic legends of *Charlemagne and his knights (as in the *Chanson de Roland*) with the romantic and fantastic matter of Britain (*see* Arthur, legend of); he also imposed courtly ideals of love and courtesy on cruder sources of popular origin. These innovations were carried further and refined by *Ariosto in *Orlando furioso*. Boiardo's text, which had regional features in its language, was Tuscanized by Francesco *Berni in 1541, and the original text was not recovered until the nineteenth century.

Bologna A north Italian city at the foot of the Apennines. Originally the Etruscan town of Felsina, Bologna prospered on account both of its position on an important trade route to Florence and of its textile industry, especially silk. Claimed by the papacy in 1278, the city suffered from the region's political turmoil and rivalries; it was dominated by a series of lords, notably the *Bentivoglio family during the fifteenth century. Pope *Julius II finally established papal authority over Bologna in 1506. The old and famous university of Bologna (founded in the eleventh century) attracted scholars from all over Europe during the period of the Renaissance; from the twelfth century its faculty of law led legal studies in Europe. The late sixteenth and early seventeenth century Bolognese school of artists included the *Carracci, Guido *Reni, Domenichino, and Francesco Albani. Notable palaces and churches from the Renaissance period include S Petronio and *Sanmicheli's Palazzo Bevilacqua (1477–82). The university was housed (1562–1800) in the Archiginnasio, remodelled for it by Antonio Morandi.

Bologna, Concord(at) of (1516) An agreement between Pope Leo X and Francis I of France, which revoked the Pragmatic Sanction of *Bourges and restored papal authority over the Gallican (French) Church. Nonetheless, Francis maintained a significant degree of control over ecclesiastical affairs in France under those clauses that stated that the king was to appoint archbishops, bishops, abbots, and conventual priors, and, subject to certain rules, the pope was to confirm the nominations. If two successive royal nominations were found to be invalid, the appointment lapsed to the pope.

Bologna, Giovanni (da) *see* Giambologna.

Bologna, Niccolò da *see* Niccolò dell'Arca.

Bombelli, Raffaele (c. 1526–73) Italian mathematician. Little is known of Bombelli's life other than that he was born at Bologna, became an engineer in the service of the bishop of Melfi, and was the author of *L'algebra* (1572). This was the first Italian text to be so called and contained notable advances in the history of equations, and in the development of an adequate algebraic symbolism. The analysis of the cubic equation proposed by *Tartaglia had led to a number of cases involving roots of negative numbers. Unsure of how to deal with such items, Renaissance mathematicians had classified them as irreducible cases and ignored them. Bombelli, however, made the first significant advance in the handling of such problems. In the field of symbolism he took the step of representing unknown quantities and exponents by special symbols. Though other systems came to be preferred, Bombelli had nonetheless shown the need for such expressions.

Bon, Bartolommeo *see* Buon, Bartolommeo.

Bontemps, Pierre (c. 1507–68) French sculptor. Assistant to *Primaticcio at *Fontainebleau, Bontemps is best known for his work on the tomb of Francis I and Claude de France and their children (1547–58) at the church of St Denis. The monument was designed by Philibert *Delorme; Bontemps worked on it alongside François Marchand. Bontemps also worked on a monument for the heart of Francis I in the same church, incorporating a number of features from the outdated Gothic tradition. After 1562 he became a religious fugitive.

book illustration The earliest illustrated books inevitably suffered by comparison with illuminated manuscripts. Some copies of early printed books have however been decorated as though they were manuscripts, for example, the Bodleian Library copy of Jenson's 1476 edition of Pliny's *Natural History*, enriched with splendid Florentine illumination. Printing was slow to kill the earlier craft in most of Europe, especially Italy (see Plate IV). Block-books, mostly German, with text and picture cut on the same block, began to be produced about 1430. The oldest surviving single woodcut is a St Christopher of 1423. Although *woodcuts and text were formed into books soon afterwards, no extant block-book bears a date before 1470, and by 1480 they were ousted by the spread of printing with movable type. Most block-books were intended for those who preferred stories in pictures, with as few words as possible, so the *Biblia pauperum* and other religious writings provided most of the material. Ornamental initials, sometimes printed in colour, and woodcuts soon appeared, to such an extent that about a third of all *incunabula are thus illustrated. Albrecht Pfister of Bamberg added woodcuts to his popular books in the 1460s, though the pictures were printed after the text. The quality of book illustration in Italy was soon the best in Europe, culminating in the *Hypnerotomachia Polifili* (1499). Engraving on metal was first used in Florence in 1477, though the process was not taken up until the middle of the next century. The use of roman or italic type in Italy led to smaller books with a lighter appearance than black-letter printing, an effect echoed in the illustrations (*see* typography).

In Germany the printers of Augsburg specialized in illustrated books, and Günther Zainer's *Golden Legend* (1471) has historiated initials echoing manuscript ones. A little later his brother Johann, working in Ulm, printed an edition of Aesop the illustrations of which were subsequently used in *Caxton's 1484 London edition, the first known example of a sort of borrowing that later became widespread. Schedel's *Liber chronicarum* (*Nuremberg Chronicle*), was printed in Nuremberg by Koberger in 1493, with nearly 2000 pictures from only 645 blocks, an economy allowed by using illustrations as decoration rather than an integrated complement to the text.

The first named illustrator was Erhard Reuwich, whose pictures for Breydenbach's *Peregrinationes in terram sanctam* (Mainz, 1486) are an essential part of the book. Later, professional illustrators like Hans (II) *Weiditz, who designed woodcuts for *Brunfels's herbal, were also given credit in print for their work.

In the 1530s and 1540s Basle became a famous centre for illustrated books. Dürer may have worked there in the 1490s, and his influence certainly refined the local style. The Holbein family lived there, though the books they illustrated were often printed in France, like the *Dance of Death* (Lyons, 1538). *Fuchs's herbal (1542) and *Vesalius's textbook of human anatomy (1548) were two famous Basle productions of this period.

*Emblem books were another development of the 1530s. Soon afterwards topographical books, illustrated by engravings, began to be published in Italy; the first, *Speculum Romanae magnificentiae* (Rome, 1548–68), has nearly 150 plates of monuments in the city. Some printers became specialists in engraving on metal, like the *de Bry family in Frankfurt and the Dutch printers of cartographic works like Ortelius's *Theatrum orbis terrarum* (1570) and Mercator's *Atlas* (1595).

*Plantin's Antwerp Polyglot Bible (1568–73) features both woodcuts and copper engravings. This printer, who encouraged the use of pictures, organized his illustrators on a grand scale, so that blocks from his store were often borrowed and used elsewhere. By the end of the sixteenth century, engravings, which allowed greater delicacy, were overtaking woodcuts for book illustration. The products of both methods were still coloured by hand, sometimes in the printers' own workshops, if coloured copies were required. The quality of the engraving, as in flower books like Crispin de Passe's *Hortus floridus* (Utrecht, 1614) is sometimes so fine that the addition of colour is the reverse of improvement.

Book of Concord *see* Concord, Book of.

book trade The distribution of printed books was able to follow patterns established by the commercial production and sale of multiple manuscript copies of texts in demand. Trade fairs, such as those of Frankfurt (originally two a year) and Lyons (four a year) existed before printing, but they were developed as useful centres for printers, publishers, and booksellers to meet. In 1498, for example, Koberger of Nuremberg was already ordering 100 copies of a book from Milan to be delivered to his representative at Frankfurt. For two centuries Frankfurt was the major marketplace for book dealers from Holland, Switzerland, France, and Italy, as well as Germany, though the censorship imposed there in 1576 sent Protestant publishers off to establish an alternative centre in Leipzig.

Printed catalogues helped to publicize books available at the fairs; individual publishers or printers issued them from the 1560s and joint ones were compiled by the fair organizers from 1590 in Frankfurt and 1594 in Leipzig. Hopeful predictions of publication dates were as common then as now, for in 1653 James Allestrye, an Englishman, complained that "it is a very usual thing for the booksellers of Germany to send the titles of their books to be put in the catalogue before they are printed, so that at present they are not to be had."

Even so, the choice was wide, for 22 000 books were listed between 1564 and 1600. The fairs were also appropriate places to buy and sell type or engage illustrators, translators, editors, or even authors.

Latin remained the predominant language of the printed book until at least 1500, so the market for books was effectively an international one from the start, and the size of editions printed in trading centres like Venice grew to reflect the demand for them. As German craftsmen became printers in other countries, they naturally turned to German merchants to sell their products elsewhere. Barrels of books packed in sheets followed trade routes all over Europe, with the reputations of the greatest printing houses, like those of *Estienne, *Froben, or *Plantin, being just as widespread. The growth of vernacular printing inevitably restricted the distribution of the books concerned, although, in the hands of publishers like the *Elzevir family, books in the main European languages were not necessarily printed in their native countries. Even *Caxton's first book in English was actually printed in Bruges. *See also* printing.

Bordone, Paris (1500–71) Italian painter. Bordone came from a noble family at Treviso and was probably a pupil of *Titian and of *Giorgione in Venice. Although there is very little originality in his pictures Bordone had a very successful career and was regarded as highly as Titian for the quality of his work and its rich colouring and chiaroscuro. An excellent portraitist, he received commissions from many parts of Europe, including the royal houses of Poland, Austria, and France, and he was knighted by King Francis II of France. He also painted mythological pictures such as his *Daphnis and Chloe* (National Gallery, London) and religious works, which included frescoes and numerous easel paintings, many still in Treviso. His *Fisherman presenting St Mark's Ring to the Doge* (Accademia, Venice) features a characteristically attractive architectural backdrop.

Borgia, Cesare (1475/76–1507) Italian soldier and nobleman. The second son of Rodrigo Borgia (Pope *Alexander VI) and Vanozza Catanei, Cesare was carefully educated and destined for the Church. His father made him archbishop of Valencia (1492) and cardinal (1493), but Cesare renounced holy orders after his brother's death. As part of a deal made between Alexander VI and *Louis XII of France, Cesare became duke of Valentinois and married (1499) Charlotte d'Albret, a sister of the king of Navarre. With his father's support Cesare began to conquer a state for himself in central Italy (1499–1503), making rapid advances in a successful military campaign and winning the title of duke of Romagna (1501). The model state he established was admired by many, and Cesare partly inspired *Machiavelli's concept of the prince. Alexander's death (1503) ruined Cesare. He was imprisoned by Pope *Julius II, released, and imprisoned again in Spain. In 1506 he escaped to Navarre and died at the siege of Viana, fighting for his brother-in-law.

Borgia, Lucrezia (1480–1519) Italian noblewoman. The daughter of Rodrigo Borgia (Pope *Alexander VI) and Vanozza Catanei, Lucrezia seems to have been a pawn in her family's intrigues, and accusations against her of poisoning and incest appear unfounded. Her marriage (1493) to Giovanni Sforza, lord of Pesaro, was annulled (1497) after her father quarrelled with the Sforza clan. Furthering his plan to strengthen the Neapolitan alliance, Alexander then married her to Alfonso of Aragon (1498), an illegitimate son of *Alfonso II of Naples. When this alliance collapsed Alfonso was murdered (1500), probably at Cesare's command. Lucrezia then married Alfonso d'Este, the duke of Ferrara's heir (1502). This apparently happy marriage produced seven children. Lucrezia devoted herself to charitable works and her children's education; after becoming duchess of Ferrara (1505) she made the court a centre for artists, poets, and scholars, among them *Titian and *Ariosto.

Borgia family A Spanish-Italian family of great power and influence during the late fifteenth and the sixteenth centuries, which has earned an unsavoury reputation for immorality, treachery, nepotism, and greed. Alfonso Borgia (1378–1458), the founder of the family fortunes, became Calixtus III (pope 1455–58). He was known not only for his enthusiasm for a crusade against the Turks but also for his nepotism, which led him to make his nephew, Rodrigo, a cardinal in his mid-twenties. As Pope *Alexander VI, Rodrigo schemed to advance the fortunes of his illegitimate children, Cesare and Lucrezia. The family also included a number of cardinals, a viceroy of Sardinia, a viceroy of Portugal, a general in Flanders, and a saint. St Francis Borgia (1510–72), great-grandson of Alexander VI, was third general of the Jesuits (1565–72) and did much to redeem his family's reputation: he founded the university of Gandia and his generosity led to the foundation of the *Gregoriana at Rome.

Borromeo, St Charles *see* Charles Borromeo, St.

Borromeo family An Italian family of Tuscan origin which from the twelfth century held land near Lake Maggiore. In the fifteenth century the family amassed great wealth from banking in Milan and acquired the title of counts of Arona. Notable members of the family include St *Charles Borromeo, a leading *Counter-Reformation figure, and Cardinal Federico Borromeo (1564–1631), archbishop of Milan from 1595 and founder of the Bibliotheca *Ambrosiana, for which he collected 9000 manuscripts. The family built beautiful gardens on the Borromean islands in Lake Maggiore.

Bos, Cornelis (c. 1506–56) Netherlands engraver. Bos was born at 's-Hertogenbosch, but many other details of his biography are uncertain. As a young man he seems to have studied in Rome under *Raimondi. By 1540 he was in Antwerp, but was forced to leave for religious reasons in 1544. He died in Groningen. Bos was particularly influential in his engravings after Italian or Flemish-influenced Italian paintings of his day, but he was also significant in his own original designs. His brother Balthasar (1518–80) was also a Raimondi-trained engraver.

Boscán de Almogáver, Juan (Juan Boscà Almugáver; c. 1492–1542) Spanish poet. Born at Barcelona into an aristocratic Catalan family, but brought up in Castile, Boscán was tutor to the future duke of *Alba and an attendant at the court of Charles V. There he met and became a friend of his younger fellow-poet, *Garcilaso de la Vega. In Granada in 1526 Boscán met the Venetian ambassador, Andrea *Navagiero, who suggested that Boscán try his hand at writing sonnets and other types of verse practised by Italian poets. Boscán, who was already acquainted with the hendecasyllabic line of Provençal and Catalan lyric poetry, rapidly mastered the Italian forms and introduced into Spanish the eleven-syllable metres that effected a transformation of Spanish poetry. He wrote *ottava rima in imitation of Ariosto, sonnets, tercets (*terza rima), and blank verse (verso suelto). Though the quality of his poetry cannot match that of Garcilaso, who also started to write in the Italian mode, the impact of his metrical innovations was enormous.

Published posthumously by Boscán's widow, Las obras de Boscán y algunas de Garcilaso de la Vega repartidas en quatro libros (The Works…in Four Books; Barcelona, 1543) is customarily taken as initiating the Golden Age (Siglo de Oro) of Spanish literature. At Garcilaso's urging, Boscán also translated Castiglione's The *Courtier (El Cortesano; 1534).

Bosch, Hieronymus (c. 1453–1516) Netherlands painter. Bosch's grandfather and father were both painters and he probably trained in the family workshop. In 1486/87 he joined the Brotherhood of Our Lady at the church of St Jan in his native town of 'sHertogenbosch; to this he apparently belonged for the remainder of his life. He executed works for Philip the Handsome and *Margaret of Austria, and after his death his paintings were avidly collected by *Philip II; thus, the better part of his œuvre is now in Spain. None of Bosch's paintings is precisely dated and, as his style changed relatively little, the course of his development remains elusive.

Bosch's pictures are primarily important for their subject matter. The Seven Deadly Sins (Madrid), originally a pair with a lost Seven Sacraments, depicts the Sins in a circular narrative strip with a circular painting of the Man of Sorrows in the centre and four roundels of the Four Last Things (Death, Judgment, Heaven, and Hell) around the main composition. The meaning of the picture is elucidated by a text scroll: "Beware, beware, God is watching." Other presumably early works include the Berlin St John on Patmos and the Washington Death of the Miser; both reveal a growing taste for the fantastic in the inclusion of tiny demonic figures. Demons appear in force in Bosch's extraordinary triptych The Haywain (Madrid). The shutters depict the fall of man, with the fall of Lucifer in the background, and, while in the centre panel men and women of every estate crowd around a haywain, drawn by devils towards hell, ignoring an apparition of Christ as the Man of Sorrows. Bosch's iconography probably relates to Isaiah's text, "All flesh is grass", and is evidently a denunciation of pride leading to materialism and sinfulness.

Temptation is the central theme of Bosch's Temptation of St Anthony triptych (Lisbon). In this painting the dilemma of the saint is almost lost in an extensive, stricken landscape, peopled by all manner of demons, some part animal or vegetable, of every conceivable shape and size. In Bosch's most famous work, The Garden of Earthly Delights (Madrid), three fantastic landscapes are presented. One shutter depicts the creation of man in a beautiful Eden filled with wonderful animals and flowers, and the other a black hell, lit by burning buildings, in which sinners are tormented by swarming devils, utilizing enormous musical instruments as instruments of torture. The central panel portrays an alien landscape filled to capacity with nude men and women, animals, and colossal fruits. While the subject matter is presumably a denunciation of hedonism, the painting is primarily memorable for its superb decorative patterns, glowing colours, and boundless wit.

Over the centuries innumerable theories, many of them as fantastic as the painter's imagery, have grown up around Bosch's work. His membership of a religious confraternity and his aristocratic patrons and collectors indicate that his own religious ideas and those embodied in his work were considered entirely respectable. The roots of his personal iconography lie so deep in popular belief that it is unlikely ever to be entirely understood. In a sense, his pictures are the ultimate exotic fruit of the taste for concealed religious symbolism that so proccupied fifteenth-century Netherlands artists.

Bosio, Antonio (c. 1576–1629) Maltese-born Italian archaeologist. The nephew of Giacomo Bosio, he succeeded his uncle as agent for the Knights of Malta in Rome. From 1593 he used his leisure time to explore the underground areas of ancient Rome, particularly the catacombs. These researches formed the basis for *Roma sotteranea*, which his executor published in 1634. The volume, often reprinted, was the first, and until the nineteenth century the fullest, work on the subject.

botanic (*or* physic) gardens Collections of growing plants designed originally to teach student physicians to recognize the sources of most of the medicines they used. The earliest were established in Italy in the sixteenth century, first at Pisa (1543) and Padua (1545) and soon in many other university towns, including Leipzig (1579), Leyden (1587), Montpellier (1592), Oxford (1621), and Paris (1635). From plants with known benefits, the scope of physic gardens grew to include newly introduced plants, whose possible virtues had still to be discovered; this innovation soon made the gardens attractive to visitors other than students. Herbaria (reference collections of dried plants) were added to the living ones, and *cabinets of natural history curiosities were often situated in botanic gardens too, as in Bologna, where *Aldrovandi was a professor and first director of the garden. A few private botanic gardens, like Cardinal Odoardo Farnese's in Rome and the short-lived one at Eichstätt, near Nuremberg, belonging to the Prince Bishop Johann Konrad von Gemmingen, had their contents described in print, as did many of the academic gardens.

botany Perhaps the most obvious feature of botany during the Renaissance is an increasing concern with the accurate identification of plants, including new ones brought to Europe by explorers of distant lands, and the emergence of schemes of classification to reduce the plant kingdom to an orderly pattern. Aristotelian botany, transmitted through the work of his pupil Theophrastus (first printed in 1483), divided plants into herbs, sub-shrubs, shrubs, and trees and gave some account of plant structure as well as descriptions of individual plants. *Herbals, practical handbooks of medical advice based on remedies from plants and other sources, which had a much wider audience, mainly relied on the work of Dioscorides. The famous Byzantine illustrated manuscript of the latter's *De materia medica*, made about 512, was rediscovered in Constantinople in the mid-sixteenth century and sold to the Holy Roman Emperor. This so-called Codex Vindobonensis is still safe in Vienna. Other manuscripts of Dioscorides had been copied and then printed, but this one remains a landmark for the quality of its illustrations, obviously made from live plants. Elsewhere naturalism was rarely seen in manuscript herbals until late in the fourteenth century, when, for example, the artist of the Carrara Herbal (British Library, MS. Egerton 2020) was certainly drawing from life rather than copying his illustrations from increasingly stylized ones in earlier manuscripts. Herbals spread some knowledge of plants among a wide public, for demand placed them among the earliest scientific books to be written and then printed in vernacular languages. Accurate illustrations were needed as one route to accurate identification, and the great herbals of the sixteenth century, foremost among them those of *Brunfels, *Fuchs, and *Mattioli, are distinguished by the quality of their pictures. The texts, in general, still dwell in the shadow of Dioscorides, though descriptions of local plants from northern Europe began to be added to those he had known. Mattioli's book, like some earlier herbals, included instructions on distillation in some editions, a skill considered necessary in the preparation of effective remedies. Even the sixteenth-century doctrine of *signatures, by which plants were said to help the parts of the body they resembled, necessitated reliable identification of the plants concerned.

Practical instruction in the study of plants was made easier by the establishment of *botanic gardens to teach medical students about the sources of their remedies. From the 1530s these gardens spread from Italy to most other parts of Europe, often in association with newly establishd professorships of botany (the first at Padua in 1533). Herbaria (reference collections of dried plants, both wild and cultivated) began to be made about the same time. The gardens soon became centres for the introduction of new plants as they were discovered, for it was assumed that anything new might have useful properties. Travellers imported new plants from the East and West Indies, Asia, and North and South America, among them cocoa, tobacco, and the potato. The Flemish botanist *Clusius helped to publicize these new introductions, ornamental as well as useful, by his descriptions and translations.

The greater the number of plants known, the

greater the need to classify them by a more sophisticated method than by grouping those with similar uses or effects. Bock's herbal (1539) echoed Theophrastus in its suggested divisions of the plant kingdom, adding observations of his own to support the arrangement. Other botanists proposed the form of leaves or other parts of plants as a basis for classification, but *Cesalpino's scheme, using the characters of seeds and fruit as criteria for subdividing the larger groups of trees, shrubs, and herbs, was the outstanding one of its period. Gaspard *Bauhin, in his *Pinax* (1623), grouped plants with common properties, and made divisions that roughly resemble genera and species, giving them distinctive names that foreshadow the standard binomial nomenclature developed in the eighteenth century by Linnaeus. Bauhin's system started with relatively simple plants like grasses and ended with more complex ones like trees, though he seems to have been puzzled by the question of an appropriate niche for the cryptogams. His classification seems a recognizable precursor of those of Ray and Tournefort later in the century, and even that of Linnaeus. The Swiss naturalist *Gesner also distinguished genera and species, but most of his botanical work remained unpublished until the eighteenth century.

As early as 1592, in his *Methodi herbariae*, Adam Zaluziansky von Zaluzian argued for the separation of botany from medicine, although this independence was not achieved until much later. Even so, the progression from early herbals, mixing plant descriptions with folklore and stylized illustrations, to more rigorous ones with accurate drawings from live specimens and accounts of new plants, shows the development of the science. The systematic recording and classification of all known plants established a base for the growth of botanical studies, as more material became available through exploration within Europe and elsewhere.

Botero, Giovanni (1544–1617) Italian political theorist. Botero was born in Cuneo, Piedmont, and was sent to a Jesuit seminary in Palermo, from which he joined the order. While a Jesuit he pursued his studies in a number of centres, including Paris, but in 1580 he left the order to take service with Cardinal (later St) *Charles Borromeo. After the latter's death (1584), Botero was secretary to Cardinal Federico Borromeo, but from 1599 he was tutor and adviser at the Turin court of Carlo Emanuele I, Duke of Savoy.

Botero's reputation as a political consultant was made by the publication of two works: *Cause della grandezza...delle città* (1588) and *Della ragion di stato* (1589). The former broke new ground with its analysis of factors determining the growth and prosperity of cities, and the latter argues, against

*Machiavelli, for Christian ethics as a viable component in political life. *Relazioni universali* (1596) expands his views on population studies, a field in which he often anticipates Malthus.

Botticelli, Alessandro di Mariano Filipepi (1444–1510) Italian painter. Botticelli was born into the family of a poor Florentine tanner and was apprenticed first to a goldsmith before becoming (1458/59) the pupil of Filippo *Lippi, whose assistant he seems to have remained until 1467. The influence of *Verrocchio, who also ran an important workshop in Florence at this time, is less definite but is perhaps visible in the earliest dated work by Botticelli, the figure of *Fortitude* from a series representing the Virtues (1470; Uffizi). The so-called *Madonna of the Rose-bush* (Uffizi) also dates from this early period.

In the 1470s Botticelli attracted the patronage of the Medici; portraits of family members and their adherents (with Botticelli himself on the extreme right) feature prominently in the Uffizi *Adoration of the Magi* (c. 1477). Moving in the circles surrounding Lorenzo de' *Medici (the Magnificent), Botticelli became imbued with their brand of *Platonism and created for the first time in Renaissance art a series of paintings in which pagan mythological subjects embody profound philosophical and even spiritual truths. There is doubt about the exact dates of these allegories, but at least two – La *Primavera and *The Birth of Venus* (both Uffizi; see Plate V) – were painted for the Villa di Castello on the outskirts of Florence, which was acquired by Lorenzo the Magnificent in 1477; the man who commissioned them was probably Lorenzo di Pierfrancesco de' Medici, a second cousin and ward of Lorenzo the Magnificent, for whom Botticelli certainly executed in the early 1490s a famous set of drawings illustrating Dante's *Divine Comedy*. *Minerva and the Centaur* (Uffizi) and *Mars and Venus* (National Gallery, London) are the other two mythological paintings in which decorative and allegorical elements perfectly combine to epitomize Platonic theory on the ideal relationship between beauty of form and truth.

Botticelli also continued a steady output of religious subjects, notable among which is the powerful fresco of St Augustine in his study (1480; Ognissanti, Florence). In 1481–82 he was in Rome, his only significant sojourn away from Florence; while there he was employed on the frescoes of the Sistine Chapel. Another venture at this time was the series of small illustrations to *Landino's edition of the *Divine Comedy* (1481). In the later 1480s he executed several altarpieces and the tondi known as the *Madonna of the Magnificat* and the *Madonna with a Pomegranate* (both Uffizi). The

Calumny of Apelles (Uffizi), which tells a story taken from Lucian, is a conscious exercise in the revival of the antique. He also painted frescoes in the Villa Lemmi (1486; Louvre) and a number of accomplished portraits.

According to *Vasari, Botticelli was profoundly influenced by *Savonarola; certainly Botticelli's brother Simone, who shared the artist's house from 1493, was one of the friar's most devout disciples. After 1498 there is no further record of any relationship between Botticelli and the Medici, and his latest works are all religious in character. Ecstatic religious feeling informs such works as the Munich *Pietà* and the London *Mystic Nativity* (1500). Later records show him on the committee of artists convened (1503–04) to decide the placing of Michelangelo's colossal *David* and finally note his burial in the garden of Ognissanti, Florence.

Bourgeois, Loys (c. 1510/15–c. 1560) French composer and theorist. Bourgeois, as a singer at the churches of St Pierre and St Gervais in Geneva, taught the choristers to lead congregational singing according to the monophonic Calvinistic Psalter. His book of psalm tunes (1551) proved highly unpopular with the Geneva council, who claimed that the new melodies confused congregations. Bourgeois was imprisoned, but was released the next day on the intercession of *Calvin. In August 1552 he took leave to visit Lyons and did not return. By 1560 he had moved to Paris. Bourgeois is chiefly known for his Calvinistic psalm settings, in which he adapted popular chansons and Latin hymns as well as composing new melodies for translations by *Marot and *Beza. He also wrote *Le droict chemin de musique* (1550), the first didactic manual in French dealing with singing and sight reading. In this he introduced the concept of solfège and advocated a simplified system of music theory and practice.

Bourges, Pragmatic Sanction of (1438) A decree of Charles VII, in response to a resolution of an assembly of prelates and delegates, named by the king, to regulate the affairs of the Church in France. It was designed to limit papal power in France, especially concerning nomination to bishoprics and other benefices, and to protect the liberties of the Gallican (French) Church. It was terminated by the Concord(at) of *Bologna (1516).

Bouts, Dirk (c. 1415–75) Netherlands painter. Bouts was born in Haarlem, but from 1445/48 until his death was based in Louvain. His key work is the *Last Supper* triptych (1464–67) for the Brotherhood of the Holy Sacrament at the church of St Peter's, Louvain. Its central panel reveals the early use of one-point perspective. For the municipal

authorities of his home town Bouts painted a *Last Judgment* triptych, of which the wings survive in Lille, and a diptych of *The Justice of the Emperor Otto*, now in Brussels, which was unfinished on his death. His London *Portrait of Man* (1462) may be a self-portrait. Bouts's angular and undemonstrative style is derived from Rogier van der *Weyden but has a peculiar intensity of its own. He had a number of followers, including his sons Dirk (died 1490/91) and Aelbrecht (died 1548).

Bracciolini, Poggio (1380–1459) Italian humanist scholar and collector of manuscripts. Born at Terra Nuova d'Arezzo and educated at Florence under John of Ravenna and Manuel *Chrysoloras, he attracted the attention of Coluccio *Salutati, who found work for him (1403) in the Curia, which he served for fifty years. In his capacity as secretary Poggio attended the Council of *Constance (1414–18); this gave him the opportunity to make four journeys to French and German monasteries in search of manuscripts. He discovered numerous manuscripts of classical authors, including hitherto unknown speeches of Cicero with the commentaries of the first century AD scholar Asconius, and important texts of works by *Quintilian, Valerius Flaccus, *Lucretius, Silius Italicus, *Vitruvius (*see also* architecture), and Statius. His Ciceronian discoveries in particular caused a sensation when they reached Italy. In 1418 Poggio accompanied Cardinal Henry Beaufort to England where he remained four years, occupying himself with *patristic studies and looking unsuccessfully for manuscripts. On his return to Rome he continued his textual studies and added archaeology to his interests. In 1453 he retired to Florence as chancellor and composed a history of the city covering the previous century.

Poggio was also famous as a story-teller and his *Liber facetiarum*, anecdotes often of a salacious and scandalous nature, became very popular (*see facetiae*). He was a great letter-writer, corresponding with most leading scholars of the day, and his letters are a valuable source of information; they include, for instance, an eyewitness account of the trial and execution of Jerome of Prague (1416). Poggio's last years were clouded by a furious quarrel with Lorenzo *Valla; he actually tried to have Valla murdered. The quarrel arose from Valla's insistence that Latin should be written according to classical models, while Poggio wrote Latin as if it were a living language. The feud marked a turning point in the resurrection of ancient literature: the stylistically naive approach of the first-generation humanists was replaced by a more self-consciously artistic observance of Ciceronian canons, which in turn led to the kind of extravagances later parodied by Erasmus.

Brahe, Tycho (1546–1601) Danish astronomer. The first important observational astronomer of modern times, Brahe was born at Knudstrup, the son of a nobleman, and educated at Leipzig university. After a tour of Europe, in the course of which he lost the tip of his nose in a duel, Brahe returned to Denmark and established his international reputation with his observation in 1572 of the first ever *new star to be recorded in the West. His report, *De nova...stella* (1573), was taken by many as proof of the inadequacy of the traditional Aristotelian *cosmology. With the financial support of the Danish king, Frederick II (1534–88), Brahe began to build at Uraniborg on the island of Hven the finest observatory of his day. With his nine-foot *armillary sphere and his fourteen-foot mural *quadrant, Brahe began to survey the heavens. Within a decade he had calculated the position of nearly eight hundred stars with an unparallelled accuracy. Whereas earlier astronomers had worked within a margin of error of 10′, Brahe reduced this to the 4′ recognized to be fairly close to the limits of naked-eye observation.

Although anxious to replace the unsatisfactory Prutenic Tables (*see* astronomy) with his own observations, Brahe proved to be the victim of his own imperious temperament. A quarrel with Frederick's successor, Christian IV (1577–1648), led to a withdrawal of patronage and forced Brahe to abandon Hven (1596). After several years' travel he settled finally in 1599 at the court of Emperor *Rudolf II in Prague. Appointed imperial mathematician, he set up his new observatory at Benatek outside Prague where, with the assistance of the young *Kepler, he began to prepare his observations for publication. Although Brahe died long before the work could be completed, it was finally published in 1627 by Kepler as the Rudolfine Tables.

At a more theoretical level Brahe was led, following his observation of the nova of 1572, and the comet of 1577, to reject the crystalline spheres of classical cosmology. He did not, however, as might have been expected, embrace the heliocentric system of *Copernicus, but instead proposed in his *De mundi aetherei recentioribus phaenominis* (On Recent Phenomena of the Aetherial World; 1588) his alternative *Tychonic system.

Bramante, Donato (c. 1444–1514) Italian architect. Born near Urbino, Bramante began his career as a painter, allegedly a pupil of *Piero della Francesca and *Mantegna who instilled in him an appreciation of classical antiquity as mirrored in the architecture of the Palazzo Ducale, Urbino. Little is known of him until 1497 when he entered the service of Duke Ludovico Sforza "il Moro" of Milan, who also patronized *Leonardo da Vinci. Leonardo's fascination with centrally planned forms and his understanding of *Brunelleschi's concept of perspective profoundly influenced Bramante, whose design for Sta Maria presso S Satiro, Milan (1482–86), displays an awareness of Brunelleschi's Pazzi chapel in Florence (1429–69) in its oblong plan with niches carved out of the wall mass; the coffered dome is evidence of an impressive implementation of antique style and techniques. Bramante's concern with harmonious spatial effects led him to create an illusionistic east end for this church – necessary because a street ran across the end of the building. His manipulation of real and illusionistic space also manifested itself in Sta Maria delle Grazie, Milan, begun in 1493; there the fictive roundels of the dome and fake pedimented windows in its base create an impression of clarity and light. The spatial solutions of the centrally planned east end reflect Leonardo's handling of volume in the *Last Supper* in the refectory of the same church. The cloisters of S Ambrogio (1497–98) demonstrate Bramante's increasing understanding of the classical language of orders. His use of basket capitals and tree-trunk columns in the Corinthian cloister shows a radical interpretation of Vitruvius.

In 1499 Bramante moved to Rome. Firsthand contact with Roman antique architecture introduced a new and weighty classicism to his designs. The cloister of Sta Maria della Pace, begun in 1500, has sturdy piers and attached Ionic columns on the ground floor, deriving from the Colosseum. This air of majestic gravity reached its apogee in the Tempietto (1502) at S Pietro in Montorio, Rome. The small circular structure, erected as a martyrium to St Peter, is reminiscent of the temple of Sibyl at Tivoli, with its classical entablature carried on a Tuscan Doric colonnade and rich frieze of metopes and triglyphs. It is the first monument of the High Renaissance and established a prototype for sixteenth-century church design. Bramante's Palazzo Caprini (1510, now destroyed) did the same for palace design in its symmetrical plan and repetitive use of simple but elegant elements.

Bramante's last years were spent in the service of Pope Julius II for whom he remodelled part of the Vatican palace. The Cortile di S Damaso was built as a series of open arcades and the Belvedere was linked to the palace by a classically inspired amphitheatre on three levels. His most important project was that of *St Peter's which, taking its cue from the Tempietto, was envisaged as a martyrium on a heroic scale. His plan – a Greek cross with four smaller Greek crosses in the angles – was to have been crowned by a huge cupola reminiscent of the Pantheon. Although only the central crossing was built according to his plan, Bramante's ideas were the starting point for all subsequent designs, and his work in Rome was the foundation of Roman High Renaissance architecture.

Brant, Sebastian (1457/8–1521) German humanist and poet. Famed in his time both as a poet and as a legal authority, Brant is remembered now as a major influence on German literature. Born at Strasbourg, he was introduced to humanism at Basle university, where from 1475 he studied law and then taught it. In Basle he also practised as a lawyer and selected and edited books for the city's printers. In 1501 he returned to Strasbourg, where he became municipal secretary and co-founded a literary society. Throughout his life he corresponded with other eminent humanists. His wide-ranging interests expressed themselves in poetry (composed initially in Latin but increasingly in German), translations from Latin and medieval German, legal and historical works, and secular pamphlets and broadsheets. It was, however, his

BRANT *Ships laden with fools, wearing jesters' caps and armed with the tools of their trades, adorn the opening page of the 1509 Latin translation of* Das Narrenschyff.

satirical poem *Das Narrenschyff* (1494; translated as *The Ship of Fools*) that proved most influential. It describes every imaginable type of fool, such as the complacent priest and deceitful cook, with the didactic aim of bringing the reader to recognize his own folly. An immediate popular success – not least because of its outstanding woodcuts – it went into numerous editions and was quickly translated into Latin, French, English, and Dutch.

Brantôme, Pierre de Bourdeille, Abbé et Seigneur de (c. 1540–1614) French chronicler, soldier, and courtier. Brantôme was born at Bourdeille (now Bourdeilles) and spent his early years at the court of *Marguerite de Navarre. He then studied in Paris and at the university of Poitiers before embarking on a military career. He fought in Italy, Spain, and Portugal, in Africa against the Turks, and supported the *Guise faction in the Wars of *Religion. Forced to retire through injury, after falling from his horse, he began to write his memoirs: these were published posthumously (1665–66) and include *Les Vies des hommes illustres et des grands capitaines*, an informative account of military life in the sixteenth century, *Les Vies des dames galantes*, an anecdotal exposé of the scandals of the French court, and *Discours sur les duels*.

Breda, Compromise of (1566) A petition by Dutch noblemen and burghers to the Habsburg regent, *Margaret of Parma, against the attempts of *Philip II of Spain to force Catholicism on the Netherlands. The scornful rejection of the petitioners as "beggars" and Philip's refusal to modify his religious policy were followed by an uprising (*see* Netherlands, Revolt of the).

Bregno, Andrea (Andrea da Milano; 1421–1506) Italian sculptor. He was born at Osteno, near Lugano, and was active in Rome from 1465, producing monumental decorative sculptures, tombs, and altars in marble. Gian Cristoforo *Romano was one of the pupils in this thriving workshop. In Rome he is principally noted for his work in Sta Maria del Popolo, while outside Rome he made the Piccolomini altar in Siena cathedral (1485), which has statues of saints by Michelangelo, and the tabernacle in Sta Maria della Quercia outside Viterbo (1490).

Briggs, Henry (1561–1631) English mathematician. Born at Warley Wood, near Halifax, and educated at Cambridge, Briggs served as professor of geometry at Gresham College, London (1596–1619), and as Savilian professor of geometry at Oxford from 1620 until his death. In 1615 he visited John *Napier, the inventor of logarithms, and they agreed to develop a system of decimal logarithms in which log. 1 = 0, and log. 10 = 1. Napier, however, was too old to undertake the prolonged labours involved in constructing the necessary tables, so the task fell to Briggs. In 1617 he published his *Logarithmorum chilias prima* in which the logarithms of the numbers 1 to 1000 were listed to fourteen decimal places. The tables were extended in his *Arithmetica logarithmica* (1624) to include the numbers up to 20 000 and from 90 000 to 100 000. The gap between 20 000 and 90 000 was filled by Adrien Vlacq (1600–66) in 1628. Briggs was also keen to see science applied in other areas. Consequently he worked with, among others, William *Gilbert on magnetism, merchants on the application of mathematics to navigation, and surveyors wishing to master the use of logarithms.

Briosco, Il *see* Riccio, Andrea di Ambrogio Briosco.

Briot, François (c. 1550–1616) French metal-worker. Briot was born in Damblain, but was active from 1579 in Montbeliard, in the county of Württemberg. He was celebrated as a master of pewter relief work, especially for his masterpiece, the Temperantia Dish (1585–90; Louvre), with its central allegorical figure of Temperance. Other works included the Mars Dish and, probably, the Suzannah Dish both of which were later imitated by Gaspar *Enderlein and other notable metal-workers at Nuremberg.

Broeck(e), Willem van den *see* Paludanus, Guilielmus.

Bronzino, Il (Agnolo Allori di Cosimo di Mariano; 1503–72), Italian painter. Born at Monticelli, near Florence, he was the pupil and adopted son of *Pontormo, whom he assisted in a number of works that included the decorations, now destroyed, in the chapel of S Lorenzo, Florence. Bronzino's first paintings are in the early mannerist style of Pontormo but they quickly developed away from the sensitivity of Pontormo towards the cold, courtly, artificial, and technically superb style of portraiture for which Bronzino is best known. As court painter to *Cosimo I de' Medici, he undertook portraits of the Medici and of eminent figures from the past like *Boccaccio, *Dante, and *Petrarch. The sitters appeared stiff, elegant, and reserved, set apart from the rest of humanity. Fine rich colours were used and, unlike most portraits of the day, dark forms were set against a light background. The development of European court portraiture was strongly influenced by these works. Bronzino also produced rather feelingless religious

paintings, whose grandness of design reflects his study of Michelangelo, and equally cold allegorical works such as *Venus, Cupid, Folly, and Time* (1546; National Gallery, London). Mannerist figure elongation is evident in both these categories. He also wrote poetry.

Brownism A separatist movement arising from the Church of England, out of which the Independent or Congregationalist churches developed. Robert Browne (c. 1550–1633) maintained that local gathered churches should reform their doctrines and practices without waiting for authority from the civil power. He established congregations at Norwich and elsewhere but on suffering harassment from the Church authorities, he and some of his disciples moved (1581) to Middelburg in the Netherlands. Browne soon returned and submitted to the Anglican authorities in the late 1580s; he was ordained in 1591 and from then until his death held the living of Achurch, Northamptonshire. In 1593 some of his principal followers were hanged. Later many emigrated to America; others became the predominant element in Cromwell's army

Brueghel, Jan ("Velvet" Brueghel; 1568–1625) Netherlands painter. Born in Brussels, Jan lost his famous father, Pieter, when he was only one year old. He received his initial training from his grandmother, Maria Bessemers, a miniaturist. Between 1590 and 1595 he was in Naples, Rome, and Milan under the patronage of Cardinal Federico Borromeo. In 1596 he returned to Antwerp where, a year later, he entered the artists' guild, of which he became dean (1602). In 1604 he visited Prague and in 1606 Nuremberg. Appointed court artist to Archduke Albert of Austria at Brussels in 1609, he also worked for Emperor *Rudolf II and King Sigismund of Poland. His collaborators included Rubens, Frans Francken II, Rottenhammer, and Joos de Momper; Daniel Seghers was his pupil. Breughel was famous for his brightly coloured historical subjects, filled with tiny figures, and for his landscapes and flower paintings. See Plate VI.

Brueghel, Pieter (c. 1525–69) Netherlands painter and print designer. Brueghel was possibly born near Breda and apparently trained in Brussels under Pieter *Coecke, whose daughter he married. He subsequently worked for Pieter Balten at Malines and for Hieronymus Cock in Antwerp. After Pieter Coecke's death, he visited Rome (1552–53), where he became acquainted with the miniaturist Giulio *Clovio. Thence, he returned to Antwerp, where he remained until 1563; he then moved to Brussels, where he subsequently died. As a young artist, Brueghel was principally a designer of prints for the publisher Hieronymus Cock. Such famous works as the *Big Fish Eat Little Fish*, published in 1557, and the cycles of the *Seven Deadly Sins* and the *Seven Virtues* reveal a perceptive study of the paintings of Hieronymus *Bosch, whose work remained internationally famous decades after his death. The moralizing subject matter of Brueghel's early designs for engravings conditioned the outlook of much of his subsequent painting. For example, the *Fall of Icarus* (c. 1555; Brussels) is essentially a condemnation of pride. In the Berlin *Netherlandish Proverbs* (1559), sometimes misunderstood as a compendium of folk customs, mankind's foolishness is expressed through illustrations of popular sayings. The *Combat Between Carnival and Lent* (also 1559; Vienna) is an ironic condemnation of the hypocrisy of both Protestants and Catholics, which inclines only slightly towards the latter, the artist's own co-religionists. An extremely important illustration of intellectual attitudes towards the religious strife in the Netherlands on the eve of the Dutch revolt, this painting reflects Brueghel's connections with the liberal humanistic circle of the geographer Abraham *Ortelius. References to the uneasy political situation in the Netherlands have also been divined in his *Road to Calvary* (1564; Vienna) and his *John the Baptist Preaching in the Wilderness* (1566; Budapest). There is a resurgence of Bosch's influence in Brueghel's paintings of 1562: the Brussels *Fall of the Rebel Angels*, the Antwerp *Dulle Griet*, and the Madrid *Triumph of Death*. However, naturalism reigns supreme in the five paintings of the *Months*, dated 1565 and currently divided between Vienna, Prague, and New York. Although the subject matter of these works derives from fifteenth-century manuscript illuminations, they are fundamentally innovatory as depictions not only of seasons but also of specific effects of weather.

For most of his career Brueghel was primarily concerned with the depiction of landscapes peopled with multitudes of tiny figures. Larger figures predominate in his *Peasant Dance* and *Peasant Wedding* (1566–67; Vienna). This development culminates in the Vienna *Parable of the Bird's Nest*, executed the year before his death. Brueghel was certainly the most accomplished landscape painter of the sixteenth century. On account of his penchant for peasant scenes, he is often considered as the originator of the genre scene popularized by seventeenth-century Dutch artists. However, the thrust of Brueghel's own peasant paintings was directed principally at questions of morality and the human condition. Historically, he may be considered as the artist who concluded the great chapter of northern painting initiated more than a century earlier by Jan van *Eyck.

Bruges A city in the province of West Flanders, Belgium, situated a few miles from the coast, to which it is now linked by canals. The Flemish name, Brugge (bridge), is of Norse origin. The town was a trading centre by 1000, the capital of Flanders, and chief residence of its counts. Although the capital moved to Ghent in the late twelfth century, Bruges continued as a major mercantile centre, especially for the wool trade with England, under the auspices of the *Hanseatic League; during the fourteenth century its bourse governed the rates of exchange in northern Europe. Like the burghers of the other rich Flemish cities, the merchants of Bruges stubbornly resisted any attempts by princes to encroach upon their privileges. In 1440 Bruges's defiance of its Burgundian overlord, *Philip the Good, brought upon it severe punishment, but generally it continued to thrive under Burgundian rule and under the early Habsburgs, and some fine buildings remain from this period. The silting up of the Zwyn, total by 1490, however, ended Bruges's position as a maritime trading centre and in the late sixteenth century it suffered depopulation and depression as a result of the revolt of the *Netherlands.

Bruges was a significant cultural centre during its fourteenth- and fifteenth-century heyday. Jan van *Eyck worked there, and later *Memling. The city's first printing press was set up in 1474/75 by *Caxton.

Brunelleschi, Filippo (1377–1446) Italian architect. He trained first as a goldsmith, but at some time (?1401) appears to have gone to Rome where his studies of antique monuments led him to formulate the law of perspective (developed by *Alberti in his treatise *Della pittura*) and provided him with structural solutions to technical building problems. His execution of the dome (1420) for the cathedral of his native Florence was an achievement of constructional engineering which looked to the Pantheon for inspiration and inaugurated the Renaissance in Italy. The lantern (1445–67) exemplifies Brunelleschi's experimental approach to the antique with the employment of inverted classical consoles, in place of flying buttresses.

The Ospedale degli Innocenti in Florence (1421–44) was hailed as the first Renaissance building, despite being influenced by Tuscan Romanesque form. The implementation of a strict modular system, based on the square and circle, to provide a regularized plan had a profound impact on town palace architecture. *All'antiqua* quotations are evident in the symmetrically aligned façade with arches carried on Corinthian columns, forming a loggia of pendentive vaults, which established a new canon of architectural beauty. Brunelleschi's preoccupation with the classically inspired values of harmony and geometric proportion is demonstrated in the basilica of S Lorenzo, begun in 1419. Using the square of the crossing as his module, Brunelleschi established a visual rapport between the semicircular arches of the nave arcade and the transverse arches of the side aisles. The combination of pietra serena and white plaster became Brunelleschi's decorative leitmotif, used to great effect in the old sacristy of the same church (1421–28). Once again, the design centred upon the interplay of a square, that of the main cella, and a circle, the umbrella dome. The transition of one shape into another was effected by the pendentives of the dome. A more sophisticated version of this design was realized in the Pazzi chapel (1429–69: Sta Croce, Florence), where a combination of grey Corinthian pilasters and arches incised onto the white plaster walls, with glazed terracotta reliefs in the spandrels, subtly emphasized the harmonious proportions of the interior. Although the Spanish chapel (Sta Maria Novella, Florence), a Tuscan Romanesque design, exerted a certain influence on the Pazzi chapel, Brunelleschi's stress on logical spatial organization is a typically Renaissance feature.

Brunelleschi's later designs are characterized by a more sculptural approach to the treatment of wall mass, suggesting a renewed study of antiquity. The incomplete Florentine church of Sta Maria degli Angeli (1434–37), with its alternating concave and convex niches scooped from the outer walls, is the first centrally planned church of the Renaissance, reflecting the temple of Minerva Medica, Rome. The radiating chapels of Sta Maria degli Angeli were adapted to the basilica of S Spirito (1434–82; Florence), the foundations of which were laid on a chequerboard grid. The flat pilasters of S Lorenzo were replaced by half-columns giving a richly plastic spatial rhythm. All of Brunelleschi's important works are in Florence, yet his fame spread to Milan and Urbino, influencing *Bramante and underlying the emergence of the High Renaissance in Rome. His claim to be considered the first Renaissance architect was acknowledged and established by his pupil and biographer, Antonio Manetti (1423–97).

Brunfels, Otto (1489–1534) German physician and botanist. His *Herbarum vivae eicones* (1530–36), the first of the great printed *herbals, was illustrated with plants drawn from nature by Hans (II) *Weiditz, using live models rather than earlier drawings. In spite of his artist's originality, Brunfels still concentrated on Dioscorides's plants instead of northern European ones.

Bruni, Leonardo (Leonardo Aretino; c. 1370–1444) Italian humanist scholar and translator. His

BRUNI *Bernardo Rossellino's effigy of the great humanist on his tomb in Sta Croce, Florence, shows Bruni apparently peacefully asleep, crowned with a laurel wreath and clasping a book – as in Vespasiano da Bisticci's account of his funeral.*

other name, "Aretino" derives from his native Arezzo. Bruni was a pupil of *Salutati and learned Greek from Manuel *Chrysoloras in Florence. His thorough knowledge of the language enabled him to make the first idiomatic translations of Greek literature. He spent most of his mature years as a papal secretary but in 1415 returned to Florence, where, like his master Salutati, he became secretary to the republic (1427–44).

Most of Bruni's translations were of prose works, although he also translated some passages of Homer and Aristophanes. In 1406 he produced a translation of Demosthenes' *De corona* and *De falsa legatione.* By 1414 he had begun to translate Aristotle's *Ethics.* Between 1414 and 1437 he translated six of Plato's dialogues, including the *Phaedo* and *Apology,* and he sought to reconcile Platonism with Christian doctrine. These translations were the means by which the political thought of Greece entered into the life of fifteenth-century Italy. Bruni also translated Plutarch's *Lives* – his Latin was the basis of all early vernacular translations – and works by Xenophon. In 1437, at the request of Humfrey, Duke of Gloucester, he translated Aristotle's *Politics*. He wrote *De interpretatione recta* to defend his theory of translation and also discoursed on Ciceronian prose rhythm.

As early as 1404 Bruni had begun work on his *Historiarum Florentini populi libri* in twelve books; this remained unfinished at his death. The work represented a new departure in *historiography, showing the influence of Petrarch and Salutati as well as classical models. It was translated into Tuscan and published by Acciaiuoli at Venice (1476). The estimate Bruni made of his own Latin scholarship can be gauged by the fact that he "restored" the lost second decade of Livy in his work *De bello punico primo*. Bruni was buried in Sta Croce, Florence, at public expense. With his friends Salutati and *Niccoli, he was one of the first to use "Humanitas" as a term for literary studies.

Bruno, Giordano (1548–1600) Italian philosopher. The son of a soldier, Bruno was born at Nola, near Naples, and joined the Dominican Order in 1563. For unknown reasons he was forced in 1576 to flee both Naples and his order. By this time he had already established his reputation as a teacher of the then fashionable discipline of mnemonics (*see* memory, art of) and was probably already committed to the hermetic neoplatonic views that he later expounded throughout his extensive European travels. After visiting Italy and Switzerland, he appeared at the court of *Henry III in Paris in 1581, and in 1585 he discussed his system with the scholars of Oxford. In 1591 he was arrested in Venice, extradited to Rome, and later tried and burnt at the stake as a heretic. Unfortunately, the precise nature of Bruno's offence remains a matter of speculation as the trial papers were not preserved. It is known, however, from his *Cena de le ceneri* (The Ash Wednesday Supper; 1584) that he supported the *Copernican system. More likely to have sent him to the stake were the claims, expressed in his *De l'infinito universo e mondi* (1584), that "there are innumerable suns, and an infinite number of earths revolve around these suns, just as the seven we can see revolve around the sun close to us."

Brussels A city in the Netherlands (now Belgium). By the late Middle Ages Brussels had developed from an island fort into a thriving market community at a road–river junction in the duchy of Brabant. Thousands of workers employed in the manufacture of luxury fabrics made a few merchant families very rich. These families abused their considerable political power and provoked a number of workers' revolts (1280, 1303, 1421); after the 1421 revolt the guilds of workers and craftsmen gained some political influence. The count of Flanders occupied Brussels briefly; his expulsion from the city (1357) was followed by the construction of strong city walls.

Under Burgundian rule Brussels prospered as a centre of art, learning, and administration. Its most distinguished artist at this time was Rogier van der *Weyden. Under Habsburg rule (from 1477) the guilds were excluded from the administration of the city by *Charles V (1528), but Brussels remained the administrative centre of the Netherlands. In 1577 radical supporters of the Calvinist cause seized power in Brussels, but the Spanish Habsburgs regained control in 1585. Notable buildings from the Renaissance period include the Coudenberg palace, the Hôtel de Ville (1402–54), and fine early seventeenth-century baroque buildings. Otto van *Veen and Rubens were attached to the court of the Habsburg archdukes in Brussels in the early seventeenth century.

Bucer, Martin (1491–1551) German reformer and theologian. Born at Schlettstadt, Bucer became a Dominican monk, but was won to the side of Reformation by Martin *Luther at the Heidelberg Disputation (1518), and embarked on a career as a Lutheran preacher. In 1523 he settled in Strasbourg where he remained for twenty-five years, emerging in this period as a leading figure among the reformers. He attempted to mediate in the eucharistic controversy between Luther and *Zwingli and later took a leading role in the conferences with leading Catholic theologians at Worms and Regensburg (1540–41) aimed at reuniting the Church. His organizational work at Strasbourg also had a profound influence, particularly on John *Calvin, who spent three formative years there.

Forced to leave Strasbourg in 1549 by the imposition of the *Augsburg Interim, Bucer settled in England, where *Cranmer secured for him the post of regius professor of divinity at Cambridge. Although he died less than two years later he exercised a major influence on the English Reformation, submitting at Cranmer's request detailed suggestions for the revision of 1549 Prayer Book (the *Censura*, 1550). His last work *De regno Christi*, a blueprint for a godly commonwealth, dedicated to King Edward VI, was published posthumously (?1557).

Buchanan, George (1506–82) Scottish humanist scholar. Buchanan was born at Killearn and attended St Andrews university (1524). In 1526 he moved to Paris, where he subsequently taught. Back in Scotland (1536) he became tutor to an illegitimate son of James V, but the furore caused by his verse satires against the friars forced him to flee back to France. There he established his reputation for scholarship and wrote some highly admired Latin poetry and four tragedies on classical models, including *Baptistes* (1554); *Montaigne was among his pupils who acted in these plays. Invited to Coimbra (1547), he fell foul of the Inquisition and was imprisoned (1549–51). He held several more teaching posts in Europe before returning to Scotland (c. 1560) where, although now openly a Protestant, he was tutor to Mary, Queen of Scots, and active in state affairs. After her downfall, in which Buchanan played a role by identifying her handwriting in the casket letters, incriminating her in Darnley's murder, he was tutor (1570–78) to young James VI, later *James I of England. Buchanan's major prose works were *De jure regni* (1579), which influenced seventeenth-century writers on the theory of kingship, and *Rerum Scoticarum historia* (1582).

bucintoro The state barge of the doge of Venice. The name derives from Italian *buzino d'oro* (golden barque). It headed the procession of boats in the Ascension Day ceremony of the *sposalizio del mar* (marriage of the sea), in which the doge sailed to the Porto del Lido and threw a consecrated ring into the Adriatic. The custom commemorated Venice's conquest of Dalmatia in 1000 AD. Remains of the last *bucintoro*, destroyed by the French in 1798 for the sake of its gold ornamentation, survive in the Museo Correr, Venice.

Budé, Guillaume (Budaeus; 1468–1540) French scholar and humanist. He was born in Paris and studied law at Orleans, before learning Greek with John Lascaris and Jerome of Sparta. He was employed as secretary and ambassador by Louis XII and as court librarian by Francis I, and helped the latter develop his idea of a university (the Collège Royal, later the Collège de France) to provide an alternative to the scholasticism of the Sorbonne. By his influence on Francis I he shaped the curriculum of the new institution to include the new learning that he had met on his diplomatic missions to Rome in 1503 and 1515, although he rejected the secular emphasis of the Italian scholars. Budé wrote on Roman law (*Annotationes ad Pandectas*, 1508), Roman coinage (*De asse eiusque partibus*, 1514), and the Greek language (*Commentarii linguae Graecae*, 1529). In 1532 he published *De philologia*, a general account of classical scholarship. J. C. Scaliger called him the greatest Grecian in Europe. Budé brought the critical

approach of humanism to the study of Christian texts and set an early example of that personal interpretation of the scriptures that led to the Reformation.

Bugenhagen, Johannes (1485–1558) German Lutheran theologian. After a career as a Premonstratensian canon at Treptow in his native Pomerania, Bugenhagen became, through a reading of *Luther's *De captivitate Babylonica ecclesiae*, an early convert to the Reformation. In 1521 he abandoned his post as rector of the city school in Treptow and enrolled as a theology student in Wittenberg, where he was appointed minister of the town church in 1523 and professor in 1535. He became one of Luther's closest friends and associates, serving as his confessor and assisting him in his New Testament translations. Although Bugenhagen remained in Wittenberg until his death, his most important work was undertaken in missions away from the city, particularly in northern Germany and Denmark. As the architect of numerous church orders (for Hamburg in 1529, Lübeck in 1531, and Denmark in 1537) Bugenhagen played an essential role in the establishment of the Reformation in these northern lands. His contribution to the Danish Reformation, during an extended stay of two years (1537–39), was particularly important. He translated several of Luther's works and was responsible for the production of a Lower German edition of Luther's Bible. He was one of the signatories of the *Saxon Confession.

Bull, John (?1562/63–1628) English composer, organist, and virginalist. As a boy chorister Bull sang at Hereford cathedral and the Chapel Royal. In 1583 he was appointed organist and master of the choristers at Hereford; on his dismissal from Hereford, he became a gentleman of the Chapel Royal (1586). Bull gained doctorates in music at both Oxford and Cambridge and in March 1597 was elected first public reader in music at Gresham College, London, on Elizabeth I's recommendation; this post he was obliged to resign in 1607 on account of his marriage. Throughout this period he continued his duties at the Chapel Royal. By 1610 he had probably entered the service of James I's heir, Prince Henry, to whose sister, Princess Elizabeth, he dedicated the first printed volume of virginal music: *Parthenia* (1613). In 1613 Bull was charged with adultery and fled to the Netherlands, never to return. Archduke Albert employed him at Brussels but he was dismissed the following year at the request of James I, displeased at the flight of his organist. In 1617 Bull was appointed cathedral organist at Antwerp, where he died.
Bull was a keyboard virtuoso and is chiefly remem-

bered for his keyboard music, which makes unprecedented technical demands on the player. Among his most astounding works are the hexachord fantasias, most suitable for organ. Bull's virginal music mainly comprises settings of pavans, galliards, and other dance tunes, employing brilliant technical and rhythmical devices. His canons, of which 200 survive, are extraordinary in their complexity and ingenuity.

Bullant, Jean (1520/25–1578) French architect. Born at Amiens, Bullant studied in Italy where he was influenced by the classical style. He returned to France in 1540 to enter the service of Constable Anne de *Montmorency, for whom he worked on the Château d'Écouen (c. 1555), and became the first French architect to make use of the colossal order by modelling his work on the Pantheon in Rome. Subsequent works included the Petit Château (Capitainerie) at Chantilly (c. 1561) and a bridge and gallery combining ancient Roman and mannerist ideals at Fére-en-Tardenois (1552–62). In 1570 Bullant succeeded *Delorme as architect to Catherine de' Medici, for whom he executed work at the Chapelle des Valois and the *Tuileries and drew up plans for the enlargement of the châteaux of St-Maur and *Chenonceau and for the Hôtel de Soissons. He was also the author of a treatise on architecture, *La Règle générale d'architecture, étude des cinq ordres de colonnes* (1564), which became a textbook for French architects.

Bullinger, Johann Heinrich (1504–75) Swiss reformer and theologian. The son of a parish priest, Bullinger studied in Germany before returning to take up his father's post in his native Bremgarten. In 1531 Bullinger was appointed minister in Zürich in succession to *Zwingli, where his resolute defence of the Zürich church preserved it through the many difficulties which followed Zwingli's death. In the eucharistic controversy Bullinger defended the Zwinglian position, but he also associated himself with *Bucer in attempts to reconcile the German and Swiss churches. In 1549 he and *Calvin made the important *Zürich Agreement (Consensus Tigurinus), which defined a common sacramental doctrine for the Zürich and Geneva churches. By this time Bullinger enjoyed a considerable international influence, largely through his enormous correspondence (12 000 surviving pieces). A prolific writer, he wrote sermons (published as the *Sermonorum decades quinque*) that had an enduring popularity, particularly in England where his reputation rivalled that of Calvin. Bullinger was also the architect of the Second *Helvetic Confession (1566) and the author of a history of the Reformation down to 1532.

Buon, Bartolommeo (Bartolommeo Bon; c. 1374–?1467) Italian architectural sculptor. Trained by his father Giovanni, Bartolommeo is first recorded collaborating with him on the façade of Sta Maria dell'Orto in his native Venice (1392). They next appear in 1422 working, with others, on the Ca d'Oro (until 1437); the large well-head in its courtyard, adorned with allegorical figures, is documented to Bartolommeo in 1427. From the late 1430s date a lunette over the entrance to the Scuola di S Marco and the Porta della Carta of the ducal palace, with its *Lion of St Mark*, statue of *Justice* and several *Virtues*, and many subsidiary ornaments. This is Buon's masterpiece. An important carving is the lunette of the *Madonna of Mercy* (now Victoria and Albert Museum, London) from the façade of the Misericordia, a charitable brotherhood. Buon's style, with its emphasis on luxuriant foliage and heraldry, is still basically Gothic and has an attractive boldness, owing to the relatively hard local stones he used, Verona red marble and Istrian limestone.

Buonarroti, Michelangelo *see* Michelangelo Buonarroti.

Buoninsegna, Duccio di *see* Duccio di Buoninsegna.

Buontalenti, Bernardo (c. 1536–1603) Italian architect, engineer, painter, and sculptor. Buontalenti was born in Florence and when he was eleven years old, his parents were ruined as a result of flooding and he was taken under the protection of *Cosimo I de' Medici. The duke had Buontalenti trained in architecture, painting, and sculpture and from 1567 employed him as a river engineer. Buontalenti built the Casino Mediceo in Rome in the early 1570s and the Casino di S Marco, now the Palazzo dei Tribunali, in Florence in 1574 in an exuberantly mannerist style. Parts of the Uffizi and Palazzo Vecchio are his, built in the 1580s. As a theatre architect and technician he was responsible for spectacular court productions and created special effects, costumes, and firework displays of a kind never seen before. He designed automata and waterworks for villa gardens and he even arranged a naval battle inside the Palazzo Pitti. He also worked on fortifications and wrote two books on military engineering. His best-known paintings are the miniatures he did for Francesco, son of Cosimo I, and his self-portrait in the Uffizi.

Bürgi, Jost (1552–1632) Swiss-born horologist and mathematician. After serving as court clockmaker to *William IV of Hesse-Kassel (from 1579), Bürgi moved in 1603 to a similar post at the Prague court of Emperor *Rudolf II. One of the first clockmakers to use second hands, Bürgi also introduced into his designs the cross-beat escapement and the remontoire, an ingenious device providing the escapement with a constant driving force. In mathematics Bürgi took the fundamental step in the 1580s of working out a comprehensive system of logarithms, a quarter century before *Napier published his own system. Bürgi's work remained unknown until 1620 when he published his *Arithmetische und Geometrische Progress-Tabulen*. By this time the glory had gone to Napier, and Bürgi's own role remained unrecognized until relatively recent times.

Burgkmair, Hans (1473–1531) German painter and print maker. Born at Augsburg, Burgkmair received his initial training from his father, and between 1488 and 1490 studied with Martin *Schongauer in Colmar. On his return to Augsburg (1490) he designed woodcuts for the printer *Ratdolt and assisted *Holbein the Elder with portraits and altarpieces. In 1498 he was admitted to the Augsburg guild. Burgkmair travelled to Cologne in 1503 and in about 1507 visited northern Italy, including Venice and Lucca. His portraits, such as the *Sebastian Brant* in Karlsruhe, are remarkable for their realism and psychological intensity. Classicizing architectural motifs of Italian derivation appear in his altarpieces, such as the Nuremberg *Virgin and Child* (1509). Burgkmair was a prolific designer of woodcuts, executing the largest part of the *Triumphal Procession of the Emperor Maximilian* and the *Weisskunig*. As a print maker he is important as a pioneer of the multicoloured *chiaroscuro* woodcut.

Butinone, Bernardino *see under* Zenale, Bernard(in)o.

Buxtorf, Johannes (I) (1564–1629) German Hebrew scholar. The son of a Protestant minister, Buxtorf was born at and studied at Marburg and later at Geneva and Basle under Beza. For thirty-eight years from 1591 he occupied the chair of Hebrew at Basle, rejecting attractive offers from Saumur and Leyden. To the study of Hebrew Buxtorf brought rabbinical learning acquired from the many scholarly Jews whom he befriended. His main works had an educational purpose: a number of elementary grammars and readers, a Hebrew-Chaldee *Lexicon* (1607), and a Hebrew reference grammar (1609). He also produced an edition of the Bible with rabbinic commentary and the Chaldean paraphrases (1618–19). His son Johannes II (1599–1664), followed him as professor of Hebrew at Basle and completed his father's *Lexicon Chaldaicum Talmudicum et Rabbinicum* (1639), which provided a scientific basis for the study of postbiblical Jewish writings.

Byrd, William (1543–1623) English composer. Although possibly born in Lincoln, Byrd at an early age became a pupil of *Tallis in London. He was organist and master of the choristers at Lincoln cathedral (1563–72) and became a gentleman of the Chapel Royal in 1570. In London Byrd's patrons included the earls of Worcester and Northumberland. With Tallis, Byrd was granted a crown patent for the printing and selling of part music and lined music paper; together they issued *Cantiones, quae ab argumento sacrae vocantur* (1575), which comprised Latin motets by both composers and was dedicated to the queen. In the 1580s, as a known recusant, Byrd suffered considerable yearly fines, though he was granted certain concessions, probably because the queen favoured his music. In 1587, after the death of Tallis, Byrd was left in sole possession of their patent, and with the printer Thomas East dominated English music printing until the expiration of the patent nine years later. Among Byrd's publications at this time were *Psalmes, Sonets and Songs* (1588), *Songs of Sundrie Natures* (1589), and *Cantiones sacrae* (1589). In the 1590s and 1600s Byrd wrote music for Catholic services; notable from this period are his three Mass settings and the two-volume *Gradualia* (1605, 1607). He died at Stondon Massey, Essex, where he spent the last thirty years of his life.

Byrd is chiefly remembered for his church music, notably his verse anthems (a form which he may have invented) and music for the Anglican service. Byrd's Latin motets, frequently with words lamenting a captive people, may have been composed as a solace to the persecuted Catholic community. The three-, four-, and five-part Masses are in a simple style with little word repetition and a restricted use of polyphony. Byrd was also well regarded for his keyboard music, including grounds, descriptive pieces, variations, pavans, and galliards. His best-known collection is the manuscript "My Ladye Nevells Booke" (1591).

Byzantium *see* Constantinople.

C

Cabbala A body of Jewish mystical literature, the name of which derives from the Hebrew *kabbalah*, with the literal meaning "that which is received by tradition". Originally an esoteric doctrine, it spread throughout Europe with the expulsion (1492) of the Jews from Spain. It is based on a number of texts of which the two most important are the *Sefer yetzirah* (Book of Creation; third–sixth centuries AD) and the *Zohar* (Splendour; c. 1300) of Moses de Leon of Granada. Though ignored by *Ficino, the Cabbala was introduced to Renaissance Italy by *Pico della Mirandola in his seventy-two *Conclusiones cabalisticae* (1486). Cabbalistic ideas were further expounded by *Reuchlin in his *De verbo mirifico* (1494) and the *De arte cabalistica* (1517), the first full-length work on the subject by a non-Jew. Thereafter the ideas became part of the general Neoplatonic intellectual background of the more scholarly Renaissance *magus.

At the heart of the system are the ten *sephiroth*, the divine attributes extending from *kether* to *malkuth* and relating God to the universe. Each of these is linked with one of the ten spheres of the heavens and, in an ever-widening system of correspondences, with all other aspects of nature. The divine names, suitably expressed in the twenty-two letters of the Hebrew alphabet, yielded power over their appropriate sphere of influence. At its crudest the Cabbala involved no more than the attempt to gain power over angels and demons through possession of their names, and was the camouflage adopted by the charlatan to impose on the gullible. To the Neoplatonist, however, it offered the means to apprehend a transcendent God and to understand the harmonies which so clearly existed in nature. As such, it ceased to exercise any serious influence in Western thought after the rise of the mechanistic philosophy in the seventeenth century. *See also* magic.

cabinets (*studioli, Wunderkammern, cabinets de curiosités*) Collections of rarities of art and nature through which the Renaissance originated the idea of the museum. The term "cabinets", it should be noted, refers to the collections themselves or to the rooms housing them, not to the cupboards in which they might be stored or displayed. Several present-day European museums can indeed trace their origins directly to such collections.

During the sixteenth and seventeenth centuries the European's conception of the world he lived in was constantly assailed. New territories populated by undreamt-of peoples, animals, and plants were discovered; scientific advances inconceivable in the medieval period were made at an ever-increasing rate. Cabinets encapsulated the products and apparatus of these discoveries, making them at once more tangible and more comprehensible. Within his cabinet the collector confronted the mysteries of the universe.

Universality was the theme common to almost all such collections: their ambitious aim was no less than the re-creation of the world in microcosm. Although this quest could result in an amazingly heterogeneous range of material, both natural and man made, most collectors were content to seek a purely symbolic completeness, in which certain items or categories of exhibit stood emblematically for each of the continents, for each of the elements, or for scientific, historical, mythological, or magical themes.

To the Renaissance prince a cabinet was as indispensable as a library: the two served complementary philosophical purposes and frequently occupied adjacent chambers. In Italy almost every princely household had its *studio*, that of Francesco I de' Medici (1541–87) being the most perfectly realized. Further north the Habsburgs and other noble dynasties populated Austria and Germany with numerous *Kunst- und Wunderkammern*: Archduke Ferdinand II's collection still exists at Schloss Ambras, near Innsbruck, and elements of other princely cabinets survive in Stuttgart, Munich, Berlin, Dresden, and elsewhere. Frederick III established one *Kunstkammer* in Denmark and Gustavus Adolphus another in Sweden. In France the ducal collections of Montmorency (1493–1567) and Orleans (1608–60) preceded the founding of the *cabinet du roi* in the seventeenth century. Their invariable purpose was for the personal recreation of their owners.

Cabinets were not solely the prerogative of noble households; many of the most influential were developed by scholars as resources for scientific study rather than for philosophical diversion. Such purposefulness can be detected in the cabinets of men like Ulisse *Aldrovandi and Ferrante Imperato (1550–1631) in Italy, of Konrad *Gesner (1516–65) in Zürich, of Bernard Paludanus (1550–1633) in the Netherlands, and Olaus Worm (1588–1654) in Denmark. Men like these systemized and classified the wonders of the world, while their publications described not only the contents of their cabinets but also the greater world which they represented.

From the early seventeenth century the numbers of private citizens of lesser means who founded collections began to increase. Some bourgeois collectors, like Pierre Borel (1620–71) of Castres, emulated their social superiors in forming cabinets as a basis for romantic contemplation. Others, such as Manfredo Settala (1600–80) of Milan, pursued more scientific goals. The John Tradescants at Lambeth (the elder died 1638; the younger 1608–62) were of a more practical bent, opening their collection to the public and deriving income from it. As the numbers of collectors increased, the universal nature of the prototype cabinets was abandoned in favour of collections specializing in specific aspects of natural history, art, or antiquity. Academic institutions also began to recognize the practical value of cabinets. That of the anatomy school at Leyden was perhaps the most famous, having opened its doors to the public from the early 1600s. At Oxford several smaller collections within the university were overshadowed by the founding (1683) of the Ashmolean Museum. Within the Royal Society in London, which received its charter in 1662, the aim of founding a museum with a precisely defined collecting programme, designed to produce comprehensive and systematic collections (particularly of natural history specimens), clearly demonstrates the extent to which the original concept of the cabinet of curiosities had become outmoded. *See also* botanic gardens; zoological collections.

Cabot, John (Giovanni Caboto; 1450–98) Italian navigator and explorer. Born in Genoa, Cabot moved to Venice in 1461. His trading voyages around the Mediterranean made him an expert navigator. In 1484 he moved to London, and then on to Bristol. The move was probably inspired by Britain's Atlantic position and status as a trading nation, encouraging Cabot's vision of a *northwest passage to Asia.

In 1496 Henry VII commissioned Cabot and his sons to colonize any territories they discovered for England; in return Cabot was to enjoy trading rights. On 2 May 1497 the *Matthew* sailed west for Asia with Cabot and eighteen sailors aboard. He landed on Cape Breton Island off the coast of Canada on 24 June and claimed it for England.

Convinced he had discovered Asia, Cabot returned to Bristol, where he easily found backing for a five-ship expedition. This sailed in May 1498. Cabot hugged the east coast of Greenland at first but later may have gone south along the east coast of America as far as Chesapeake Bay. Lack of supplies caused a mutiny, and Cabot was forced to return to England, where he died in obscure circumstances.

Cabot, Sebastian (1476–1557) Italian navigator. Probably born in Venice, then raised in England, Cabot was the son of John *Cabot, on whose northwestern voyages he began his career. In 1512 Henry VIII employed him as cartographer, an occupation he continued for King Ferdinand II of Aragon. Ferdinand's successor, Charles V, promoted Cabot to pilot major (1519). In 1525 he was sent to develop commercial relations with the Orient, but was distracted by fabulous tales of South America's wealth. For five years he explored the navigable rivers of the continent, before returning to a furious Charles V who banished him to Africa. In 1533 he was pardoned and reappointed pilot major. In 1548 Cabot returned to England where he ended his days as governor of the Merchant Adventurers. His 1544 world map shows details of his own and his father's American discoveries.

Cabral, Pedro Alvares (c. 1467–c. 1520) Portuguese explorer. Born in Belmonte of the lesser nobility, Cabral was appointed by King Emanuel I to command a fleet of thirteen ships and 1200 men bound for the East Indies. He set sail on 9 March 1500. He soon drifted westwards a long way off course, a mistake which some authorities suspect was premeditated. He became caught in the Atlantic's westerly currents, and made landfall in Brazil, which he claimed for Portugal. After ten days in Brazil, Cabral sent one ship home with news of his discovery, and sailed east for India with the rest. During the voyage seven vessels sank. Bartholomeu *Diaz was among the dead. After founding a factory at Calicut, Cabral returned to Portugal and retired.

Caccini, Giulio (c. 1545–1618) Italian composer and singer. Probably born in Tivoli or Rome, Caccini was taken to Florence by *Cosimo I de' Medici around 1565; his singing made a great impression there, and his fame spread throughout Italy. Caccini was among the musicians and intellectuals who frequented Count Giovanni Bardi's salon in Florence, and was acclaimed as the inventor of a new style of song, the *stile recitativo*, which was evolved there. Caccini's first mention as a composer was in 1589 when he contributed music for the marriage of Grand Duke Ferdinando I. In 1600 he was made musical director at the Medici court, remaining in their service until his death. His *Euridice* (1600) was the first published opera; it was written to rival Jacopo Peri's opera of the same name. His two songbooks, *Le nuove musiche* (1602, 1614), are collections for solo voice and figured bass. In the first there is a preface on the new style of singing and composition that Caccini had adopted; in the actual music, embellishments, which were normally improvised, are written out in full. Caccini's declamatory monody sought to capture the spirit of ancient Greek music, but is not noted for its lyricism.

Cádiz, Raid on (April 1587) The naval raid by Sir Francis *Drake on Cádiz, where *Philip II of Spain was gathering a fleet for the invasion of England. Taking advantage of ambiguous instructions from *Elizabeth I, Drake forced his way into the harbour, destroyed over thirty ships, and captured four vessels loaded with provisions. This raid cost Spain over 300 000 crowns and 13 000 tons of shipping, forcing Philip to delay the *Spanish Armada until 1588.

Cádiz, Sack of (June 1596) An attack on Cádiz led by Robert Devereux, Earl of *Essex, Lord Howard of Effingham, and Sir Walter *Raleigh. After defeating the Spanish fleet, Essex took 3000 men ashore and fought his way into the town, which surrendered. On his return to England with considerable booty he was greeted as a popular hero.

Caius, John (1510–73) English physician and humanist. He was born at Norwich and educated at Gonville Hall, Cambridge, and Padua university, where he studied under *Vesalius. Caius returned to Cambridge in the 1540s. In 1557 he received permission to renovate his old college; he became master in 1559, and ever since the college has been known as Gonville and Caius. Despite his munificence, his tenure was unhappy; suspected of wishing to introduce Catholicism into the college, Caius found himself involved in lawsuits, with dissension and expulsions being the order of the day. Much of his own time was spent editing a number of Hippocratic and Galenic texts. He also produced *A Boke or Counseill against...the Sweatyng Sicknesse* (1552), a prime account of the mysterious epidemic which swept through sixteenth-century Britain, and involved himself with controversies over the pronunciation of Greek and the relative antiquity of Oxford and Cambridge.

Cajetan, Thomas de Vio (Gaetano; 1469–1534) Italian theologian. His name derived from his birthplace of Gaeta. Cajetan entered the Dominican Order in 1484 and taught philosophy and theology at Padua, Paris, and Rome. He was general of the order (1508–18), and was appointed a cardinal in 1517 and bishop of Gaeta in 1518. He spoke for reform at the Lateran Council of 1512–17 and disputed with Luther in 1518. The elections of Charles V as king in Germany (1519) and of Pope Adrian VI (1522) were partly his doing. He opposed the divorce of Henry VIII from Catherine of Aragon. Cajetan was a prolific writer, and his commentary (1507–22) on the *Summa theologica* of St Thomas Aquinas remains an important contribution to Thomist philosophy. He was antagonistic towards Scotism, humanism, and Protestantism, but his approach to critical problems was remarkably modern.

Calcar, Jan Steven van (1499–1546/50) German painter and woodcut designer. Jan Steven was born at Kalkar and probably trained in the northern Netherlands. By 1536/37 he had moved to Venice, where he fell deeply under the influence of *Titian. In 1545 *Vasari met him in Naples, where he died. His œuvre is much confused with that of Titian and his workshop, but one of the best documented examples of his style is the portrait of Melchior von Brauweiler of Cologne, dated 1540, in the Louvre. Steven's chief claim to fame is his woodcut illustrations to Vesalius's *De humani corporis fabrica* (1543). This remarkable anatomical textbook, of considerable significance for the development of both medical science and figure painting, includes prints of dissected cadavers in dramatic action, reproducing the gestures and poses of living beings. See p. 76.

calendar A system for structuring years, determining their beginnings, and ordering their subdivisions. Julius Caesar, aided by Sosigenes, an Alexandrian astronomer, restructured the 355-day calendar of republican Rome. Ten days were added, together with, every fourth year, an extra day. The Julian year thus averaged 365.25 days, a close approximation to the 365.243 days of the tropical year. Though undetectable over short periods of time the discrepancy became evident with the passage of centuries. For example, by the sixteenth century, the vernal equinox, crucial to the calculation of Easter, had slipped from 21 March to 11 March. To tackle the problem Pope Gregory XIII in 1582 summoned to Rome astronomers, mathematicians, and theologians to advise him on calendrical reform. It was decided to cancel ten days: that 4 October 1582 would be followed by 15 October 1582. In addition, only centurial

years exactly divisible by 400 (1600 and 2000 for example) would be leap years. The effect would be to shorten the calendar year to 365.2425 days and so keep the vernal equinox tied much more closely to 21 March. The architect of the reform was Aloisio Lillo (1510–76), a physician at Perugia university. Though accepted immediately by Catholic states, the Gregorian calendar was ignored by most Protestant countries, and it was not until 1752 that Britain belatedly adopted the new system.

Caliari, Paolo *see* Veronese, Paolo.

Calixtus III, Pope *see under* Borgia family.

calligraphy The gothic, or black-letter, style of writing was used throughout western Europe in the later Middle Ages. There were local variations in the form of the letters, and Italian writing (*littera rotunda*) was less angular than that of northern Europe. In the fourteenth century, *Petrarch led the revival of interest in the classical Roman style.

He was the chief of a group of humanists at Florence, who studied manuscripts of ancient authors and inscriptions on coins and monuments. The early manuscripts available to them mostly dated from the tenth and eleventh centuries, with text in Carolingian minuscule script and display lines in monumental capitals. These became the basis of the Renaissance *littera antica*, which differs little from modern roman type.

Petrarch was followed by Coluccio *Salutati, chancellor of Florence, two of whose followers, Poggio *Bracciolini and Niccolò *Niccoli, developed their styles on divergent lines. Poggio continued the formal Roman tradition; in 1403 he went to Rome and became secretary to the pope, and his hand influenced a number of scholars and artists from Verona and Padua, including Andrea Mantegna. Niccoli produced a more cursive script, with taller and narrower letters, differing less from the current gothic. This was the origin of the italic hand, which was used for less formal writing and for the more popular, small-format books. One form of italic, the *cancellaresca*, was developed for more rapid writing in government offices and for commercial and private use.

From the mid-sixteenth century the italic style spread over the rest of western Europe, aided by popular copybooks, of which that by the papal scribe Arrighi was the first (1523). In Italy and Spain and to some extent in France and in England, italic was used for the vernacular languages as well as Latin. In Germany and Scandinavia its use was more or less confined to Latin. In England the bastard running secretary hand (a mixture of gothic and italic, with many variant forms of letters), was in common use till the early seventeenth century, but thereafter the italic prevailed and was the origin of the copperplate style from which modern handwriting is derived.

Greek texts began to be copied in Italy in about 1400. At first a clear simple style, introduced by Manuel *Chrysoloras, was used. Later, a formal script, favoured by Cretan scribes, was employed for liturgical texts, while a more mannered style, with extensive use of ligatures employed for the classics, influenced the printing of Aldus *Manutius. In the reign of Francis I, some Cretans at Fontainebleau cultivated a simpler style which is the basis of Greek type used today. *See also* typography.

Calvaert, Denys (Dionisio Fiammingo; 1540–1619) Flemish-born painter. Calvaert emigrated from his native Antwerp as a young man and around 1560 he was studying in Bologna under Prospero Fontana. After a short spell in Rome in the early 1570s, working on the Vatican, Calvaert returned to spend the rest of his life in Bologna, where he opened a very influential painting academy. Guido Reni was among his numerous pupils.

Calvin, John (1509–64) French reformer. Calvin was born at Noyon, Picardy, and was intended from an early age for a career in the Church. He spent six years studying in Paris (1523–28), mostly at the ultra-orthodox Collège de Montaigu, before moving to the more liberal atmosphere of the university of Orleans. In 1532 he published his first book, a commentary on Seneca's *De clementia*, a choice of subject which demonstrates the extent of his early interest in humanism and classical scholarship. His conversion to Protestantism occurred suddenly, probably in 1533; the following year he left France and settled in Basle in Switzerland. In 1536 he published *Christianae religionis institutio* (*The *Institutes of the Christian Religion*), a book which immediately established his own reputation among the reformers. A visit to Geneva this same year resulted in an invitation to remain and assist the local reformer, Guillaume *Farel, in his work; but Calvin and Farel soon alienated the local populace, and in 1538 they were expelled from the city. Calvin settled in Strasbourg, where he acted as minister to the small French church in exile and observed with approval Martin *Bucer's work in the city; he was able to put this experience to good use, when, in 1541, he was asked to return to Geneva.

Calvin acted quickly to assert his authority. His Ecclesiastical Ordinances (1541) defined the powers of the pastors and established the authority of the consistory, the assembly of pastors and laymen (elders) which exercised control over morals and doctrine within the city. Calvin's austere discipline inevitably aroused opposition, which reached its climax with the trial of Michael *Servetus (1553) and the exiling of the leading "Libertines" in 1555. Thereafter Calvin's authority in Geneva was unchallenged, and he enjoyed a steadily growing international influence. A tireless writer, Calvin published numerous biblical commentaries and smaller dogmatic works. He also re-edited the *Institutes*, which became by the time of the definitive 1559 edition a complete systematic theology of the Calvinist Reformation. His treatise on predestination, regarded as his characteristic doctrine, was published in 1552.

Calvinism The system of theology based on the teachings of John *Calvin, the reformer of Geneva. Calvin shared with *Luther a belief in the centrality of the Bible, the denial of human free will, and the doctrine of justification by faith alone. To these Calvin added predestination, the notion that God had predestined some to salvation and others to damnation. This doctrine, given greater emphasis still in the teaching of Calvin's successor *Beza, came in time to be the touchstone of Calvinist orthodoxy. On eucharistic doctrine Calvin took a middle position between Luther's beliefs and the symbolism of *Zwingli, gaining the support of the other leading Swiss churches in the important *Zürich Agreement (1549). Calvin favoured a strongly theocratic church polity, and his model of church government for Geneva (the Ecclesiastical Ordinances, 1541) proved extremely influential as Calvinism spread through Europe in the later part of the sixteenth century.

Important Calvinist churches were established in France (where the *Huguenots were of this persuasion), in the Netherlands (where Calvinism became the official state religion of the United Provinces in 1622), in Scotland, and in Eastern Europe. In England Calvinist theology exercised a significant influence on the doctrinal development of the Anglican Church (in the Thirty-nine Articles). It also took a firm hold among the early nonconformist groups, who carried it with them to North America.

Camaldolese Chart A world map commissioned in 1457 by King Afonso V of Portugal from the Italian cartographer Fra Mauro (d. 1460). It was produced in the Camaldolese monastery on the island of Murano, Venice, and incorporates information drawn from the voyages of Marco Polo and the exploration sponsored by *Henry the Navigator within the circular format of the ancient *mappa mundi*. Completed in 1459, it measures 6 feet 4 inches (190 cm) in diameter and is housed in the Marciana library, Venice.

Cambiaso, Luca (1527–85) Italian painter. The son of the painter Giovanni Cambiaso, Luca was born at Moneglia, near Genoa. He became the first, and most important, master of a native Genoese school of painters. The vivacity of his early pictures reflects the speed and impetuosity with which he is said to have worked, without the usual preparatory drawing and even painting large areas with both hands at once. The frescoes and oils painted in his maturity show greater moderation and are more graceful in style, but he continued to develop a simplification of form which in his drawings almost resembles cubism. Like Beccafumi, he often used light to dramatize his subjects, as in *The Virgin with a Candle* (c. 1570; Palazzo Bianco, Genoa). Cambiaso spent the last two years of his life decorating the Escorial with large frescoes at the invitation of Philip II of Spain, and died in Madrid.

Cambrai, League of (1508) An alliance formed at Cambrai in northeast France by Emperor Maximilian I, Louis XII of France, and Ferdinand II of Aragon, nominally against the Turks, but really in order to dismember the Venetian empire. It was joined by the pope and the dukes of Mantua and Ferrara, all of whom had territorial disputes with Venice. After some initial successes, beginning at Agnadello (1509), the league began to collapse in 1510, owing to the defection of the pope and Ferdinand, and by 1517 Venice had won back virtually all the territory it had lost.

Camden, William (1551–1623) English antiquarian and educationist. Born into a London painter's family, Camden attended St Paul's School before going to Oxford (1566–71). Patrons in London then supported his antiquarian researches until his appointment as second master at Westminster School (1575). This post, and his subsequent headmastership (1593–97) left him free time for extensive journeys researching his monumental topographical work *Britannia* (1586; 6th edition, much enlarged, 1607). This county-by-county survey was written in Latin and translated by Philemon Holland into English in 1610. In 1597 Camden was made Clarenceux King of Arms. He died at Chislehurst after a long illnes. Besides *Britannia*, his life's work, he also published *Annales* (1615).

Camerarius, Joachim (1500–74) German scholar. Camerarius, who was born in Bamberg, was a child prodigy. He studied Greek at Leipzig, then went to Wittenberg, attracted by the reputations of Luther and Melanchthon; he became the latter's close friend and biographer. In 1524 he published a Latin translation of Demosthenes' first *Olynthiac Oration*; the next year his commentary on Cicero's *Tusculan Disputations* brought him into contact with Erasmus. The wars of religion then forced him to leave Wittenberg and in 1526 Melanchthon made him professor of Greek and Latin at the new Protestant college in Nuremberg. In 1530 he attended the Diet of Augsburg and collaborated on the formulation of the Augsburg Confession. A moderate voice in Lutheranism, even as late as 1568 he was discussing with Emperor *Maximilian II the possibility of a Catholic–Protestant rapprochement. He moved subsequently to Tübingen (1535) and to Leipzig (1541), where he died. Camerarius was one of the leaders of the Renaissance in Germany, combining the roles of scholar, theologian, and diplomat. He made a significant contribution in many areas but his most lasting work was the many editions and translations of Greek and Latin authors he produced throughout a long working life; notable among these are his Greek editions of Ptolemy's *Tetrabiblos* (1535) and

Almagest (1538; with Simon Grynaeus) and the first complete modern edition of all Plautus' plays (1552).

Camillus of Lellis, St (1550–1614) Italian priest, founder of the Servants of the Sick (Camillians). Born in Abruzzi, he served in the Venetian army against the Turks, lost his fortune by gambling, and was employed (1574) as a labourer by the Capuchins. He tried to join their order and the Franciscan Recollects, but was rejected owing to ill health. He became bursar of a hospital in Rome, and, under the spiritual guidance of St *Philip Neri, became a priest in 1584 and established a congregation of priests and lay brothers, dedicated to nursing. As superior-general of this congregation until 1607, he did much to improve hospital methods and hygiene and to provide proper nursing and spiritual care for the dying. The Camillians won papal approval in 1586, and Camillus himself was canonized in 1746.

Camões, Luís Vaz de (1524–80) Portuguese poet. Many details of Camões's life are based on guesswork. Born in Lisbon, he appears to have been one of the old Galician aristocracy, impoverished but with prominent connections. He may have been educated at Coimbra: his work indicates a thorough classical education. He was at the court of John III in Lisbon in 1544. His love for a lady-in-waiting, Caterina de Ataide (called "Natercia" in his lyrics), was opposed by her family, who forced his withdrawal from the court. About this time he was writing lyrics and three plays, two in the native tradition of Gil *Vicente (*El Rei Seleuco, Filodemo*) and a comedy in the manner of Plautus (*Enfatriões*). After taking part in an expedition to Morocco, where he lost an eye in battle, he returned to Lisbon in an unsuccessful attempt to regain royal favour. In 1553 John III pardoned him for being involved in a street brawl in which a minor palace official died; the pardon contains hints that Camões was to go to India in the service of the crown. He was in the East until 1570, where he experienced shipwreck and the other common dangers faced by Portuguese adventurers of the time. He completed his masterpiece, *Os Lusíadas* (*The *Lusiads*; 1572), soon after returning to Lisbon and was granted a small pension by King Sebastian for his services in India. He died in poverty in an epidemic in Lisbon.
Although Camões was perhaps the greatest lyric poet of the Iberian peninsula and a master of the main Renaissance lyric forms (sonnets, odes, *canzone* [*canções*], eclogues, and elegies), virtually all of his non-epic poetry was published posthumously (1595; an expanded edition, *Rimas*, appeared in 1598). These early editions contained a number of unauthentic poems and only recently, since the 1930s, have there been attempts at critical editions of his complete works.

Campagnola, Giulio (c. 1482–c. 1518) Italian engraver. Born in Padua, Campagnola trained under Andrea Mantegna and by 1499 was executing work for the Ferrarese ducal court. His copies of works by Dürer popularized the latter throughout Italy, while his own technique anticipated later schools of engraving. He was also much influenced by Giorgione and engraved several prints after his paintings. By 1509 Campagnola was working in Venice; his pupils included his adopted son Domenico Campagnola (c. 1484–c. 1563).

Campana, Pedro de (Pieter de Kempeneer; 1503–80) Flemish artist. Although he was born in Brussels, Campana spent considerable time in Italy, where he worked at Bologna, Venice, and elsewhere. By 1537 he had moved to Seville. There he executed religious paintings for the cathedral, notably the *Descent from the Cross* (1547) and the *Group of Donors* (1555), which were typical of his many religious works in a broadly mannerist style. Having done much to popularize Italian ideals in Andalusia, Campana returned to Brussels where he ran a tapestry factory and was also active as a tapestry designer.

Campanella, Tommaso (1568–1639) Italian philosopher. Campanella was born at Silo, Calabria. Like *Bruno, he began his career by joining the Dominican Order (1582). After various quarrels with the authorities in Naples, Padua, and Rome, Campanella returned to his native Calabria to play a leading role in the revolt against Spanish rule. The revolt quickly collapsed and in 1599 Campanella found himself imprisoned in Naples. After undergoing repeated torture he was finally released in 1626 and spent the rest of his life based in Rome and, from 1634, Paris. During his prolonged imprisonment Campanella produced many books and poems. Best known is his utopian fantasy, *La città del sole*, written about 1602 but first published at Frankfurt in a Latin version, *Civitas solis*, in 1623. In the City of the Sun the "Solarians" regulate their lives by astrological principles; hermetic influences are also identifiable among them, and they admire Copernicus and consider Aristotle to be a pedant. Campanella also wrote an *Apologia pro Galileo* (1622) and *De sensu rerum et magia* (1620), both of which had also to be published by his disciple Tobias Adami at Frankfurt.

Campi family Italian painters from Cremona. Galeazzo (c. 1477–1536) was strongly influenced by *Boccaccino, and examples of his work survive in the Cremonese churches of S Sigismondo and Sant'Agostino. Galeazzo's son Giulio (c. 1500–72) was influenced by Giulio Romano and by Pordenone and worked with his brother Antonio (c. 1535–c. 1591) on the frescoes in S Sigismondo, in which is preserved the most important of his works, *The Madonna appearing to Francesco and Bianca Sforza* (1540); it was in honour of their marriage (1441) that the present church of S Sigismondo was begun in 1463. Giulio also painted frescoes of the life of St Agatha for the church of Sant'Agata, Cremona. A *Pietà with Saints* (1566) by Antonio is in the cathedral at Cremona and both Giulio and Antonio are represented by works in S Paolo Converso, Milan. Antonio also wrote a history of Cremona (1585), which he illustrated with his own engravings. The third of Galeazzo's sons, Vincenzo (1536–91), specialized in portraits with still lifes; typical of his output is the realistic *Woman with Fruit* (Brera, Milan). A cousin, Bernardino (c. 1522–c. 1592), also worked on S Sigismondo (1570); his works hint at the elegant manneristic style of *Correggio. A *Pietà* by Bernardino is in the Louvre.

Campin, Robert (1379–1444) Netherlands painter. He is now generally thought to be identical with the so-called Master of Flémalle, the painter of panels depicting St Veronica and the Virgin (1430–35; Städelesches Kunstinstitut, Frankfurt) that were thought to come from Flémalle, near Liège. Campin was born at Valenciennes and is recorded as a master at Tournai (now in Belgium) in 1406, becoming a citizen of the town in 1410. There his most famous pupil was Rogier van der *Weyden in the late 1420s.

Campin is considered one of the great innovators of the early Netherlandish school as he moved from the decorative but flat stylization of International Gothic to a mode in which realism and perspective played a more significant role. The triptych known as the Mérode altarpiece (c. 1428; Metropolitan Museum, New York) shows the Annunciation taking place in a pleasantly furnished bourgeois room; the townscape visible through the window behind St Joseph on the right wing has a faltering approach to perspective, which is more deftly handled in the *Nativity* (c. 1430; Dijon). A *Virgin in Glory with Saints* (1430–35; Musée Granet, Aix-en-Provence), the Werl altarpiece wings (1438; Prado, Madrid), and portraits of a man and a woman (1430–35; National Gallery, London) are among his later works. He is often compared with his greater contemporary, Jan van *Eyck.

cancionero (Portuguese: *cancioneiro*) In Iberian poetry, a verse anthology of songs and lyrics, usually of a particular era or school of poets, but also of individuals (those of Jorge *Manrique and Juan del *Encina, for example). The earliest anthologies are thirteenth century, the oldest being *El cancioneiro de Ajuda* of King Dinis of Portugal (1259–1325), a collection of Portuguese verse in the troubadour tradition of Provence. Other Gallego-Portuguese anthologies contain written versions of Galician folksongs. Major *cancioneros* are those of Juan Alfonso de *Baena (1445) and the *Cancionero de Stúñiga* (named after the first poet to appear in it, Lope de Stúñiga), which contains works chiefly from the court of Alfonso I of Naples (1443–58). The largest, the *Cancionero general* (1511), compiled by Hernando del Castillo, contains about 1000 poems by over 100 poets living from the reign of John II (1406–54) onwards. A similar Portuguese anthology is the *Cancionero geral de Resende* (1516), containing verses by 286 courtly poets of the late fifteenth and early sixteenth centuries writing in Spanish as well as Portuguese.

Candia The Venetian name for the largest city on the island of Crete, and, by extension, the name by which the whole island was commonly known in the Middle Ages. The word is a corruption of the Arabic name "Khandak", which refers to the great ditch that encompasses the ancient town. The Venetians took control of Crete in 1210 and subsequently made the town of Candia their capital and one of the major seaports in the eastern Mediterranean, fortifying it with walls, bastions, and gates. The military architect *Sanmicheli was put in charge of the work there in 1538. After a great siege (1648–69) the town fell to the Turks. It was renamed Herakleion in 1898.

Candida, Giovanni (active c. 1475–c. 1504) Italian medallist, diplomat, and author. Candida was possibly born at Naples, but by 1475 was a secretary at the Burgundian court. In 1477 he was resident at Bruges, and between 1482 and 1483 he entered the service of Louis XI of France. He wrote a short Latin history of France for Louis's successor, Charles VIII, and by 1491 was a royal counsellor on the first of several diplomatic missions to Italy. Candida's medallic style is Italianate and was probably learned in his youth from Mantuan and Florentine medallists. His portrait medals include likenesses of Maximilian of Austria and Mary of Burgundy, the young Francis I of France, and numerous French and Italian statesmen. A fine medallist, Candida had a delicate style and considerable powers of characterization, but his primary art-historical significance is as a forerunner of the Italian artists who worked in France during the early sixteenth century (*see* Fontainebleau).

Candido, Pietro see Witte, Pieter de.

Cane, Facino (c. 1350–1412) Italian mercenary soldier. A Piedmontese by birth, Cane led mercenary forces there and in Savoy from his youth up and established a reputation as a ruthless and efficient condottiere. The Genoese gave him a major command in 1394, and in 1397 he entered the employ of the *Visconti of Milan. By the death of Giangaleazzo (1402) he had become such a powerful figure in Milanese affairs that the new duke, the incompetent Giovanni Maria, relied for his position upon Cane's continuing support. Had it not been for his death, it is probable that Cane would have ousted the Visconti line from Milan. One of Duke Filippo Maria's first acts on succeeding his brother in 1412 was to establish his position by marrying Cane's widow, Beatrice, whom he later had put to death on a trumped-up charge of adultery (1418).

Cangrande see under Dante Alighieri; della Scala family.

cannon A large gun fired from a carriage or fixed platform. The first undisputed references to cannon date from the early fourteenth century. Using skills gained in the manufacture of bells, the earliest cannon were cast from bronze and muzzle-loaded. Such weapons, however, proved to be too expensive, too difficult to make, and too easily worn away, to be completely successful. Consequently, they were soon superseded by larger, more durable, wrought-iron models, forged from strips of iron and secured with hooped rings. These were replaced by cast-iron cannon which began to appear in the early sixteenth century. Although normally quite small, weighing no more than a few hundred pounds, giants like the fifteenth-century twelve-ton Mons Meg (Edinburgh Castle) were occasionally constructed.

Cano, Juan Sebastian del (died 1526) Spanish navigator. Born at Guetaria, on the Bay of Biscay, Cano commanded the *Vittoria*, one of the five ships that participated in *Magellan's celebrated voyage. The expedition set sail in 1519, and when Magellan was killed (1521), Cano became commander of the fleet. After visiting the Moluccas, Cano returned to Spain, landing at Seville on 8 September 1522. He was accordingly heralded as the first circumnavigator of the world, and was rewarded by the king with an engraved globe and a pension. In 1526 Cano left on another expedition to the Moluccas, but died at sea on 4 August.

Cano, Melchior (1509–60) Spanish theologian. In 1523 he became a Dominican friar at Salamanca.

He taught at Valladolid from 1533, and in 1543 became the first professor of theology at Alcalá. He defended Philip II in his political conflict with the papacy, and when in 1557 he was chosen as provincial of his order papal conformation of his appointment was long delayed. His doctrine of marriage, that the priestly blessing was the essential form of the sacrament, was controversial. His *De locis theologicis*, his principal work, was published in 1563.

Capnion see Reuchlin, Johann.

Capponi family A wealthy and influential Florentine family, established in the city from 1210. Although Gino (1350–1421) supported the *Albizzi, Neri (1388–1475) was a prominent supporter of the *Medici. Piero (1447–96) was employed as an ambassador by Lorenzo the Magnificent, but after the latter's death (1492) joined the anti-Medicean party, becoming head of the republic set up in Florence on the expulsion of Piero de' Medici in 1494. His defiance of *Charles VIII of France in 1494 is famous; the French king, backed by 12 000 troops, issued an ultimatum which Capponi tore up in his face, and when Charles said menacingly, "Then we shall sound our trumpets," Capponi retorted, "And we shall ring our bells" (i.e. summon the citizens to fight in the streets). The king backed off. Unluckily for the Florentine republic, Capponi was soon afterwards killed fighting in the ill-starred war against the Pisans.

During the second Medicean expulsion, Niccolò di Piero (died 1529) was twice elected *gonfaloniere* (1527, 1528) but he was forced to resign when his attempts to make peace with the Medicean pope Clement VII were construed as high treason. After the restoration of the Medici (1530) many of the family were forced into exile.

Capra, Villa see Rotonda, Villa.

Capuchins A branch of the Franciscans founded in the 1520s by Matteo di Bassi of Urbino, who wished to return to the original austerity of the Franciscan rule. The habit, based on St Francis's own garb, includes the pointed cowl (*capuche*) that gives the order its name. Despite initial disapproval from other Franciscans, the Capuchin rule was established in 1529 and their preaching and missionary zeal made them valued agents of the Counter-Reformation. In 1619 they were recognized as an independent order, by which time they had spread all over Europe.

Caravaggio, Michelangelo Merisi da (1573–1610) Italian painter. Born at Caravaggio, near

Bergamo, he was trained in Milan by an undistinguished mannerist and was influenced by contact with the works of Venetian painters. He was in Rome by 1592, where his tempestuous nature led to trouble with the police, and his refusal to adopt the method favoured in central Italy of careful preparation prior to painting caused controversy. Until his fortunes improved in 1597 he lived in poverty, painting still lifes and portraits and working for other painters; in that year the influence of Cardinal del Monte, who admired and bought his work, lead to a commission to decorate the chapel of S Luigi dei Francesi. Much of this work was subsequently rejected by the clergy on grounds of indecorum or theological error before it was finally finished in 1602. The same difficulties arose with his work in Sta Maria del Popolo (1600–01). In fact opinion about his work was sharply divided: paintings that were angrily rejected by some clergy were eagerly bought by cardinals and noblemen who admired them. The reason was Caravaggio's scorn for traditional idealized representations of religious subjects and his insistence on naturalism together with dramatic use of chiaroscuro (see Plate VII). Paintings such as the *Madonna di Loreto* (S Agostino, Rome) and the *Death of the Virgin* (Louvre) introduced sweat and dirt into religious art, and the bloated corpse of the dead Virgin is said to have been painted from a drowned prostitute.

Caravaggio's personal life also remained stormy: in 1603 he was involved in a libel action by Baglioni, who later became his biographer, and in 1606 he had to leave Rome after stabbing his opponent during a game of tennis. He fled to Naples and in 1607 to Malta where he was made a knight by the grand master of the *Knights Hospitaller, whose portrait he painted. However, after assaulting a judiciary he was imprisoned in 1608 but escaped to Sicily, pursued by agents of the knights. In 1609 he was wounded in a tavern brawl in Naples and he died of malaria the following year at the age of thirty-seven while on his way back to Rome where friends were attempting to arrange a pardon for him. The paintings produced in Naples, Malta, and Sicily showed an even greater economy of style than those of his Rome period. They were dark pictures with little colour and had an intense stillness new to his work. Caravaggio's work, produced in such a short time, inspired the Caravaggisti school in Spain and had a strong influence on the development of baroque painting.

Caravaggio, Polidoro Caldara da *see* Polidoro Caldara da Caravaggio.

Cardano, Girolamo (1501–76) Italian physician and mathematician. Born at Pavia, the illegitimate son of a Milanese lawyer, Cardano was educated at the universities of Pavia and Padua. After practising and teaching medicine in Milan and Pavia (1524–50), he spent some time travelling in France and Britain. While in London in 1552 he demonstrated his astrological skill by predicting that the dying *Edward VI would have a long life. On his return to Italy he held chairs of medicine in Milan, Pavia, Bologna, and Rome. Despite his conflict with *Tartaglia, Cardano was a mathematician of considerable originality. His *Ars magna* (1545) is recognized as the first modern algebra text, while he was also one of the earliest writers to tackle problems in probability theory. Among his many books, the best known are the encyclopedic *De subtilitate* (1550) on the natural sciences, augmented and supplemented by *De varietate rerum* (1557), and the dramatic and revealing account of his life, *De vita propria liber* (1643; translated as *The Book of My Life,* 1931).

Cariani, Giovanni Busi (1485/90–c. 1547) Italian painter. Cariani was born near Bergamo and became a pupil of Gentile *Bellini. He worked mainly in Venice, initially in the style of his teacher and those of the great Venetian masters *Giorgione, *Titian, and *Palma Vecchio, with the result that a number of pictures attributed to these masters are now thought by some to be his work. An example is the two heads in the Louvre, supposedly by Bellini. Cariani's first and last recorded paintings (1514 and 1541) are both lost, but some of his portraits and religious paintings have survived, as well as fragments of frescoes in Bergamo.

Carlo Emanuele I (1562–1630), Duke of Savoy (1580–1630) The son of Emanuel Philibert (*see* Savoy, house of), Carlo Emanuele pursued his father's ambitions to make Savoy a major Italian power and involved the duchy in frequent wars. He annexed some territory, but constant warfare strained the duchy's finances; among other enterprises, he took advantage of the conflict between France and Spain to make some gains for Savoy, but then failed in his attack on Geneva (1602). Carlo Emanuele promoted commercial development and made his court at Turin a centre of culture.

Carmelites, Reform of the The movement, originating in Spain, to restore the "primitive rule" in the houses of the Order of Our Lady of Mount Carmel. By the mid-sixteenth century, the Carmelite friars and sisters had largely departed from the original austerity prescribed for the order in 1209, some fifty years after its foundation. In 1562 St

*Teresa founded a small enclosed community of nuns at Ávila, dedicated to a stricter observance of the rule of the order. In 1568 St *John of the Cross founded the first community of reformed Carmelite friars at Duruelo, and the movement gradually spread. The Discalced Carmelites (as they were called because they wore sandals instead of shoes to symbolize the austerity of their regime) were poor, held no property as individuals, had no contact with the secular world, and led ascetic lives of prayer and contemplation. They encountered much opposition, particularly from those within the order who continued to follow the "mitigated rule", but in 1579 a separate province of the reformed Carmelites was constituted, and in 1593 they were confirmed as a distinct order by papal ordinance.

Caro, Annibale (1507–66) Italian scholar, poet, and translator. Caro was born at Civitanova Marche, near Ancona, and studied in Florence, where he was a friend of Benedetto *Varchi. After living for a time at the court of Naples, he became secretary to Cardinal Pierluigi Farnese and, after Pierluigi's murder (1547), to Cardinal Alessandro Farnese. A thoroughly professional man of letters, Caro wrote a comedy in prose, *Gli straccioni* ("The Ragamuffins"; 1554), which combined classical influence with characters based on real persons in the Rome of Caro's day, a collection of Petrarchan poems entitled *Rime* (1557), and satirical sonnets. His quarrel with Ludovico *Castelvetro, who had criticized one of his poems, resulted in Castelvetro's fleeing into exile after Caro had accused him of having Lutheran sympathies. Two works, published posthumously, firmly established Caro's reputation among future generations: *Lettere familiari* (1573, 1575), a collection of 1000 letters, rhetorical in style and modelled on Petrarch's; and the *Eneide* (1581), a blank-verse translation of the *Aeneid* which exercised an influence on Italian verse up to the nineteenth century.

Carpaccio, Vittore (c. 1457–c. 1526) Italian painter. A native of Venice, Carpaccio was probably taught by Lazzaro Bastiano (c. 1425–1512), by whom he was profoundly influenced, and also absorbed many features of the works of Gentile *Bellini and *Antonello da Messina. Although his career is poorly documented, Carpaccio was noted for his narrative skill and psychological insight and was commissioned by the Venetian confraternities (*scuole*) to execute several major cycles of large paintings, notably the nine pictures in *The Legend of St Ursula* (1490–95; Accademia, Venice), which was commissioned by the Scuola di Sant'Orsola. His cycle of nine *Scenes from the Lives of St George and Other Saints* (1502–07; also Accademia,

Venice), painted for the Scuola di S Giorgio degli Schiavone, represents his mature style and accurate observation of naturalistic detail. Subsequent cycles of scenes from the lives of the Virgin (c. 1504) and St Stephen (1511–20) are now scattered. Other works include an undated painting of *Courtesans* (Museo Correr, Venice), the altarpiece of the *Presentation of Christ in the Temple* (1510; Accademia, Venice), and his last dated works, the two organ shutters for the Duomo at Capodistria (1523). Much admired in the nineteenth century by John Ruskin and others, Carpaccio was also one of the first artists to execute notable townscapes, which have documentary value in depicting the life of contemporary Venice.

Carpi, Girolamo da (1501–56) Italian painter. A pupil of Benvenuto Garofolo in his native Ferrara, Carpi also visited Parma and Modena where he studied and made copies of the works of *Correggio and *Parmigianino. He undertook commissions for portraits and produced original compositions for churches in Bologna and Ferrara, including three pictures in the cathedral in Ferrara. He painted for a time in Rome and some of his work, for example the *Adoration of the Magi* for S Martino Maggiore in Bologna, shows the influence of the Roman style. His Roman sketchbook shows his interest in antique decorative motifs. He died in Ferrara.

Carracci, Annibale (1560–1609) Italian painter. The most gifted member of the Carracci family of Bologna, he trained as a fresco painter with his brother Agostino (1557–1602) and his cousin Lodovico in his native city. On study trips to Parma and Venice he admired the works of *Correggio and *Titian. His earliest surviving pictures are genre paintings, such as *The Butcher's Shop* (c. 1582; Christ Church, Oxford) and caricature drawings. Monumental compositions were what he came to excel at, and he painted a number of large altarpieces. In 1585 the Carracci founded an academy called the Incamminati in Bologna, the teaching at which aimed to revive the canons of classical art; it played an important part in the development of a classical baroque style.
In 1595 Carracci was invited to Rome by Cardinal Odoardo Farnese to decorate the ceiling of the Camerino in the Palazzo Farnese with frescoes on classical themes. Two years later he began a larger work which is considered to rank with *Michelangelo's Sistine ceiling and *Raphael's decorations in the Vatican and Farnesina, from both of which Carracci drew inspiration, namely the decoration of the ceiling of the Galleria Farnese in the Palazzo Farnese on the theme of *The Loves of the Gods*. This series of pictures within an illusionistic frame-

work of architecture and gilt frames required over 1000 preparatory drawings. It was completed in 1604. His easel paintings at this time consisted of landscapes and history paintings such as *Domine, Quo Vadis?* (c. 1602; National Gallery, London). This, like many of his pictures, in notable for its powerful use of gesture. The language of gesture in painting owes much to Carracci, as does the ideal classical landscape used by later artists such as Poussin. In 1605 Carracci became ill with what was described as *melancholia and he painted very little during the last five years of his life.

Carracci, Lodovico (1555–1619) Italian painter. Though less gifted than his younger cousin Annibale *Carracci, Lodovico was the dominant figure during their early partnership in their native Bologna. With the brothers Annibale and Agostino, Lodovico decorated the Fava, Magnani, and Sampieri palaces in Bologna in the 1580s and early 1590s, and with them founded a teaching academy there in 1585. This academy was run by him alone after his cousins left for Rome (1595) and was responsible for training most of the next generation of Bolognese painters including Domenichino, Guercino, and Reni. Lodovico's best paintings were produced during the ten years before he and his cousins parted company. They are remarkable for their forceful emotional expression.

Cartier, Jacques (1491–1557) French navigator, discoverer of the St Lawrence river. Born at St-Malo, Cartier was commissioned by King Francis I to find a *northwest passage to the Orient, and in 1534 he sailed with two ships and sixty-one men. He followed the coast of Newfoundland and established friendly relations with the Huron-Iroquois Indians, by whose word for village, "Canada", he named the territory. Cartier returned to France for the winter, but went back to Canada in 1535. He landed at the bay of St Lawrence on 9 August, then navigated the river as far as the site of Montreal. Inspired by tales of an enchanted land north of Mexico, Cartier then decided to explore the Ottawa river, but before doing this he returned to France with twelve Indian elders to convince a sceptical Francis I. In spring 1541 Cartier left St-Malo with five vessels, and from his camp at Cap Rouge, he navigated the Ottawa. He returned to France with many mineral samples but these were found to be worthless. Consequently, Cartier fell from royal favour, and the French lost interest in Canada. The true value of Cartier's work was not realized until the French opted to develop their Canadian territory.

cartography The science of maps, charts, and globes. As the golden age of discovery, the Renaissance is the period in which cartography became established and flourished. New discoveries led to maps becoming more detailed and accurate; consequently, cartography became of greater use to *exploration, and mutual development was promoted. Early Renaissance cartography was based on the work of the second-century Greek geographer Ptolemy, whose *Geographica* (first printed edition with maps, 1477) was the first ever atlas (although the term "atlas" was not widely used until *Mercator popularized it). The so-called T-O world maps of the medieval period persisted in early Renaissance publications. In 1492 the Nuremberg merchant Martin Behaim made a globe that still survives and so introduced a new dimension into cartography. Fra Mauro had portrayed the world in circular form as early as 1459 (*see* Camaldolese Chart).

In the late fifteenth and early sixteenth centuries, the Portuguese made best practical use of the development of cartography. Their Casa du India provided information for many explorers and merchants, and the maps (1520) of Garcia de Toreno were vital to *Magellan's circumnavigation of the world. The Portuguese had enough confidence in their cartographers deliberately to misplace certain territories within areas granted to them under the Treaty of *Tordesillas. The Italians and Germans continued to develop Ptolemy's ideas. In 1507 Martin Waldseemüller showed America as a separate continent for the first time (*see* Vespucci, Amerigo). Some years later Johann Schöner popularized globes.

From 1460 to 1540, German cartographers such as *Münster, Werner, and Philipp Apian revolutionized cartographers' instruments, and cartography developed as a science. *Gemma Frisius used a planimetrum, Waldseemüller developed the polymetrum (an early form of theodolite), and Apian's map of Bavaria (1579) introduced grid references. The most important individual was Gerardus *Mercator, inventor of the Mercator projection; this rectangular format for maps is still in common use. Using copperplate printing, which began to supersede the old woodcut technique around 1550, Mercator combined Ptolemy's data with technological developments to produce maps of unprecedented accuracy and proportion. Mercator's world map (1569) is the first example of his projection.

In 1579 *Saxton produced an atlas of England, the first ever national atlas. Bouguereau published the French counterpart, *Le Theatre Françoys*, in 1594. By 1620 most leading nations boasted comprehensive geographies and atlases.

Casaubon, Isaac (1559–1614) French classical

scholar. His Protestant family were refugees from the French religious wars, and Casaubon was born in Geneva. He was taught by his father until at the age of twenty he began intensive Greek studies in Geneva. His second wife was one of the printer Henry *Estienne's daughters. After lecturing in Geneva and Montpellier he was invited (1599) by *Henry IV to Paris, where his first official position was sub-librarian in the royal library. After Henry's murder (1610) Casaubon, declining to become a Catholic, came to England at the invitation of Richard Bancroft, Archbishop of Canterbury. He was enthusiastically received and at his death was buried in Westminster Abbey. Casaubon lacked extraordinary critical insight or linguistic knowledge but he had an enormous capacity for work and a desire to gain exhaustive understanding of the ancient world. The classical texts on which he wrote commentaries were well off the beaten track of scholarship, for example, Athenaeus (1600) and Strabo (1587). His massive commentary on Persius' *Satires* (1605) was prefaced by a study of Greek and Roman satirical poetry which was the first specialized work on a problem of ancient literary history.

Cassander, Georg (1513–66) Netherlands theologian and humanist. After early study in his native Bruges and at Ghent, Cassander went to Cologne with the intention of finding some means of reconciling the orthodox Catholic and reforming positions. In 1561 he published anonymously *De officio pii ac publicae tranquillitatis...in hoc religionis dissidio* (On the duty of pious and public peace...in the present dispute of religion). This volume involved him in fierce controversy; he found his moderate line attacked by the extremists on both sides, but he gained support from those who saw the importance of compromise as a means to unity. As well as his voluminous theological writings Cassander produced treatises on antiquarian subjects. His eagerness for unity sometimes led him to adopt views that were doctrinally suspect but he remained faithful to the authority of the Church. He died at Cologne.

cassoni Wooden chests used in Italy in the Renaissance period for domestic storage of garments, documents, and valuables. Pairs of *cassoni* were made for bridal trousseaux, with one bearing the husband's armorial and the other that of the bride. Early examples have painted panels depicting Roman triumphs and battles, and, in northern Italy, religious subjects. Others had gilded carving and intarsia decoration. Mannerist influences later introduced carved and polished wood versions of antique sarcophagi on lion-paw supports. A variant on the *cassone* was the *casapanca*, to which

a back and arms were added, enabling the piece to double as a storage chest and a seat. Being heirlooms, many *cassoni* survive. See p. 86.

Castagno, Andrea del *see* Andrea del Castagno.

Castellio, Sebastian (Sebastien Châteillon; 1515–63) Savoyard teacher and translator. Born at St-Martin de Fresne, near Nantua, Castellio was educated at Lyons and kept a school for young gentlemen there. After reading Calvin's *Institutio* he went to Strasbourg in 1540 and having met Calvin, he was converted to the reformed religion. He was appointed rector of the college at Geneva, but his humanism later brought him into conflict with Calvin. In 1552 he was appointed professor of Greek at Basle. He deplored the execution of *Servetus (1553) and broke entirely with Calvin and Beza after the publication of his tolerant tract concerning heretics in 1554. Castellio's Latin Bible, a version noted for its classical elegance, appeared between 1546 and 1551, and a French version came out in 1555. He was also a translator of Greek and Latin classics. His work on predestination was not published until 1578 and his answer to Calvin's criticisms only appeared in 1612.

Castelvetro, Lodovico (1505–71) Italian scholar and critic. Born in Modena, Castelvetro became one of the leading linguists of his day. His grasp of the historical evolution of Italian is demonstrated in his *Giunta fatta al Ragionamento di Messer Pietro Bembo* (1563) and in his commentaries on Petrarch's *Rime* and on the first part of Dante's *Inferno*. He also translated and wrote an influential commentary (1570) on Aristotle's *Poetics*. From 1560 he spent some years in exile after the Inquisition had condemned him for doctrinal irregularities, and he died at Chiavenna, north of Lake Como.

Castiglione, Baldassare (1478–1529) Italian writer and courtier. Born at Casatico, near Mantua, to minor landed gentry traditionally serving the dukes of Mantua, Castiglione was sent to Milan, where he acquired a fundamental education in the skills of a courtier under Duke Ludovico Sforza, "il Moro". After a brief stay at Mantua (1500–04), he entered the service of Guidobaldo da Montefeltro, Duke of Urbino, and his successor Francesco Maria della Rovere.
Guidobaldo, a distinguished soldier and statesman, scholar, patron of humanists and artists, collector and connoisseur, epitomized the ideal ruler, and Castiglione's years at Urbino, the setting of his major work The *Courtier*, were the happiest of his life. As Urbino's representative in Rome, Castiglione met leading humanists and formed a

CASSONI *An elaborate Florentine chest, one of a pair made for the marriage of a daughter of the Nerli family. (1472; Courtauld Collection, Courtauld Institute Galleries, London)*

friendship with Raphael. After the fall of Francesco della Rovere in 1515, Castiglione returned to Mantua. Following the death of his wife in 1520 he was ordained and in 1524 he was appointed papal nuncio to the court of Charles V in Spain. His final years were apparently lonely and especially troubled by the imperial sack of Rome (1527). He was made bishop of Ávila in 1528, the year *The Courtier* was published, and died in Toledo.

Catalan Atlas A set of manuscript charts created in 1375 in Majorca by Abraham Cresques for Charles V of France. The collection of beautifully decorated charts is in the *portolan style and contains the first major portolan of an area outside Europe. The Catalan Atlas is distinguished by the first fairly accurate maps of China, India, and Africa, and contains a large quantity of information about inland Europe and its navigable waterways.

Cateau-Cambrésis, Peace of (3 April 1559) A treaty principally between *Henry II of France and *Philip II of Spain, ending more than sixty years of conflict between France and Spain. France restored Savoy-Piedmont to Emanuel Philibert of Savoy and Corsica to Genoa. Henry II renounced his claim to Milan and accepted Spanish domination of Italy. France gained some fortresses and the bishoprics of Toul, Metz, and Verdun. England had to accept the French reconquest of Calais. The treaty marked the end of dynastic struggles and paved the way for religious wars.

Catena, Vincenzo di Biagio (c. 1470–1531) Italian painter. Catena was born into a patrician Venetian family and was influenced by fellow-members of the *Venetian school, at first *Cima da Conegliano and Giovanni *Bellini and later *Titian and *Giorgione. Many of Catena's paintings are *sacre conversazioni*. He was a friend of Giorgione, whose influence can particularly be seen in the delightful *Holy Family with a Kneeling Knight* (National

Gallery, London) and *The Vision of St Christina* (1520; Sta Maria Mater Domini, Venice). Among the eminent people who sat to him for a portrait was the poet Giangiorgio Trissino.

Catherine de' Medici (1519–89), Queen consort of France The daughter of Lorenzo de' Medici (d. 1519), Duke of Urbino, she married the future *Henry II in 1533. Artistic and energetic, Catherine designed the *Tuileries in Paris and the Château de *Chenonceau; she made a great impression on the French court, despite Henry's attachment to *Diane de Poitiers. After the death of her son Francis II (king 1559–60), she triumphed over the extremist *Guise faction, obtaining the regency of her next son, Charles IX (king 1560–74). The failure of initial attempts to reach a religious compromise increasingly involved Catherine in the Wars of *Religion. Alarmed at the Huguenot threat to Church and state, she approved the murder of leading Huguenots in the *Massacre of St Bartholomew (1572). The reign of her third son, *Henry III (1574–89), brought increasing disorder to France, but Catherine's efforts helped hold France together until the accession of *Henry IV (1589).

CATHERINE DE' MEDICI *Miniature by Clouet. (Victoria and Albert Museum, London)*

Catherine of Genoa, St (Caterina Fieschi; 1447–1510) Italian mystic. Born in Genoa, at sixteen she was married to Giuliano Adorno, who was rich, dissipated, and unfaithful. She found no consolation in a frivolous social life, and in 1473 experienced a religious conversion; some years later, she influenced her husband to change his way of life. They devoted themselves to nursing, and she became matron of a hospital in Genoa. Her prayer life was intense, she fasted rigorously, and received communion daily; the quality of her spiritual

experiences can be gauged from the compilation *Vita e dottrina* (1551).

Catherine of Siena, St (Caterina Benincasa; 1347–80) Italian mystic. The daughter of a prosperous Sienese dyer, Catherine rejected proposals of marriage to become a Dominican tertiary (1363). She travelled widely in Italy, accompanied by a band of disciples, including priests and nobles. Her spiritual experiences were remarkable, including receiving the stigmata (1375). Drawn into a public role by her fame, she attempted to mediate in an armed conflict between the papacy and some of the Italian cities led by Florence, and to unite the Christian powers in a crusade against the Turks. She also went to Avignon and helped to persuade Pope Gregory XI to return to Rome (1377). From 1378 she supported Urban VI against the antipope Clement (VII) and attempted to win Queen Joanna I of Naples over to Urban's side.

Catholic Majesties The title accorded to *Ferdinand (of Aragon) and Isabella (of Castile), and subsequently to other kings of Spain. It was said to have been bestowed upon Ferdinand by Pope Alexander VI in recognition of his having completed the reconquest of Spain from the Moors by the taking of Granada in 1492.

Cattamelata, Il *see* Gattamelata, Il.

Cavalcanti, Guido (c. 1250–1300) Italian poet. Born in Florence some time prior to 1257, Cavalcanti belonged to a prominent Guelph family. In 1267 he was betrothed to the daughter of a Ghibelline in one of several such engagements arranged to end the continual strife between the Guelph and Ghibelline parties. He represented the Guelphs in 1280 as a guarantor of peace and later served on the general council of the commune. Accused as a leader of the Guelph faction, on 24 June 1300 he was condemned to exile. Although the ban was soon lifted, Cavalcanti died in Sarzana on 29 August. Dante dedicated the *Vita nuova* to him and they exchanged sonnets, but the friendship may not have lasted; in the *Divine Comedy* Dante only refers briefly to his "disdain" (*Inferno* X 63). The principal Florentine contributor to the *dolce stil nuovo*, Cavalcanti wrote sonnets, ballads, and *canzoni*, fifty-two of which are extant.

Caxton, William (c. 1420–92) English merchant and printer. Caxton was born in Kent and after a career as a cloth merchant in Bruges, he learned to print in Cologne, probably with Johann Veldener. In partnership with Colard Mansion he then set up a printing press in Bruges, where the first book printed in English, his own translation of

Raoul le Fèvre's *Recuyell of the Historyes of Troye*, was finished in 1474 or early 1475. In 1476, leaving Mansion to go on printing in Bruges, he brought the first English press to a shop by the chapter-house of Westminster Abbey, where he printed about a hundred books, seventy-three in English. The first dated publication was Earl Rivers's translation of *Dictes or Sayengis of the Philosophres* (1477), the first illustrated one *Myrrour of the Worlde* (1481). About 1478 he printed Chaucer's *Canterbury Tales*, with an illustrated edition five years later, followed by Malory's *Le Morte Darthur* in 1485. As well as printing, Caxton imported and exported books and manuscripts. His successor, Wynkyn de Worde, had been his foreman from 1479.

Cecchino, Il *see* Salviati, Francesco.

celestial spheres (*or* globes) The representation of constellations and planets on the surface of a globe. The concept goes back at least to Eudoxus (fourth century BC), but the earliest surviving globe is the Farnese marble (c. 200 BC) in the Naples museum. The tradition persisted among Islamic astronomers and returned to the West in the thirteenth century through the Sicilian court of Frederick II. Islamic examples were generally made of engraved brass, but by the late fifteenth century printed paper gores were produced, which when cut out could be pasted onto a *papier mâché* or lath and plaster sphere. Elaborate and highly decorated globes were made during the Renaissance by such figures as *Apian, *Mercator, and *Blaeu. One with a diameter of five feet and on which a thousand stars were plotted was to be found at the Uraniborg observatory of *Brahe.

Celestina, La A novel in dramatic form by Fernando de *Rojas, first published anonymously in a sixteen-act version (1499) and later in a twenty-one act version. Originally entitled *La (tragi)comedia de Calisto y Melibea*, the story concerns a noble youth, Calisto, who falls in love with Melibea, the daughter of the Jew Pleberio. Calisto is persuaded to seek the help of the procuress or go-between Celestina, who succeeds in overcoming Melibea's resistance by appealing to her compassion. Celestina is killed in a quarrel over money with Calisto's corrupt servants. Calisto seduces Melibea but falls to his death when leaving her; Melibea commits suicide. The expanded version introduces Centurio, a braggart soldier, in the final acts, but the ending is the same. The book was enormously popular, with sixty reprints in the sixteenth century. Despite its sexual subject and outspoken language, the characters pay dearly for their sins and the novel never attracted the censure of the Inquisition.

Cellini, Benvenuto (1500–71) Italian goldsmith, die-engraver, sculptor, and writer. From two books written toward the end of Cellini's life, his *Autobiography* (1558–62) and *Treatises on Goldsmithing and Sculpture* (1565), we are better informed about his career and attitude to his patrons than about any other Renaissance artist. Born in Florence and originally trained as a goldsmith, Cellini moved from city to city to make his fortune and to escape punishment for his misdemeanours: from 1519 until 1540 he worked in and around the papal court and mint in Rome; from 1540 until 1545 he served Francis I of France at Paris and Fontainebleau, alongside *Rosso Fiorentino and *Primaticcio; back again in Florence, he turned his hand to major sculpture in bronze and marble for Duke *Cosimo I de' Medici. By 1560 his popularity as a court artist had declined and he resorted to writing.

The majority of Cellini's goldsmithwork and jewellery, described with loving detail in both *Autobiography* and *Treatises*, has been lost; his activities on a small scale may be judged only from seals, coins, and medals, of which several examples survive. Some drawings by him, or of lost works (e.g. the fabulous cope-clasp for Pope Clement VII), also exist, and he influenced most of the jewellery and precious metalwork of Italy, France, and Germany during the second half of the sixteenth century. Fortunately, Cellini's masterpiece of miniature sculpture does survive, in Vienna, the salt-cellar in gold and enamel which he had begun in Italy and finished for Francis I. It is a typically mannerist artefact – intellectual, ingenious, colourful, and a technical *tour de force*. Anatomical forms are distorted for grace of line, as in a modern fashion plate. Cellini's most ambitious project for the French king, a series of twelve over-life-size statues of classical deities in silver, was never completed, though his designs are probably reflected on a reduced scale in some of his later bronze statuettes. However, a great bronze lunette for a portal at Fontainebleau, showing the nymph of the fountain surrounded by the animals of the hunt, survives in the Louvre, and there is a drawing of one of the satyrs that flanked the portal as caryatids.

In 1545 Cellini, suspected of embezzling precious metal and gemstones, fled from France back to Florence. There he persuaded Cosimo I to commission a group of two over-life-size bronze figures – *Perseus and Medusa* (1545–54) – to match Donatello's *Judith and Holofernes* of a century earlier under the arches of the Loggia dei Lanzi. Cellini's original wax and bronze models are in the Bargello; they are much more elongated than the finished work.

A bronze study for the head of Medusa is in the Victoria and Albert Museum, London. The *Perseus and Medusa* is the most obviously mannerist sculpture in Florence. Its decorative marble pedestal comprises a repertory of mannerist motifs and contains four bronze statuettes of the ancestors of Perseus, as well as a narrative relief in bronze of Perseus rescuing Andromeda. Challenged by *Bandinelli to prove his worth as a sculptor by carving marble, Cellini produced several statues on classical themes, but his masterpiece in the medium is the *Crucifixion*, now in the Escorial.

Celtis, Konrad (1459–1508) German humanist and poet. Born a peasant near Würzburg, Celtis ran away at eighteen to study. He spent the next twenty years studying and teaching at a succession of universities – Cologne, Heidelberg, Erfurt, Rostock, Leipzig, Cracow, Nuremberg, Ingolstadt – before settling at Vienna university to teach poetry and rhetoric (1497). His travels included two years in Italy (1487–89), where he met many Italian humanists. Although generally disillusioned by Italy, he was inspired by *Leto's academy in Rome to start similar societies in Germany where humanists could meet and work together – most notably the "Sodalitas danubiana" in Vienna. *Peutinger and *Pirckheimer were among his friends and correspondents.

Celtis's own studies of Greek and Hebrew, his editions of Latin authors, and his Latin dramas were important in the humanist movement, as were his introduction of literary studies to various universities and his ideas on education. Resenting Italian cultural domination, he passionately wanted to revive German culture; significant here was his discovery (1492/93) at Regensburg of six Latin dramas by Hrosvitha von Gandersheim, a tenth-century nun, and his edition of Tacitus' *Germania* (1500). His great ambition was to write the first comprehensive geographical and historical survey of Germany, although only a few preparatory studies were completed. The first German to be crowned poet laureate by the emperor (1487), he was a gifted poet, as seen especially from his *Quattuor libri amorum* (1502). This is a semi-autobiographical verse narrative of four love affairs, highly entertaining, with an amoral sensuality. Celtis died in Vienna of syphilis.

Cenacolo *see Last Supper.*

Cenci, Beatrice (1577–99) Roman noblewoman. Her controversial execution under Pope *Clement VIII aroused great public interest and became the subject of numerous poems, dramas, and novels, notably Shelley's *The Cenci* (1819) and Moravia's *Beatrice Cenci* (1958). Treated with extraordinary cruelty by her father Francesco Cenci, Beatrice finally murdered him with the help of servants and other members of her family. They were all brought to trial, tortured, and sentenced to death, despite pleas for leniency on their behalf. The subsequent confiscation of the Cenci property was rumoured to have been the pope's real object in the prosecution.

Cenni di Peppi *see* Cimabue.

censorship The invention of *printing was quickly perceived by both secular and religious authorities in the Renaissance to be a massive threat to their ability to control the spread of subversive ideas. The idea of censorship was not new, but the laborious production of manuscripts by scribes could relatively easily be dealt with by seizure and destruction of the finished product, as authorized, for instance, in the case of Lollard texts in England by the Merciless Parliament of 1388. The rapid multiplication of copies by printing made it expedient to introduce mechanisms of control at an earlier stage of production. One widely employed method was to require printers to submit material they proposed to publish to be licensed by an official censor or other competent body before it could legally be printed.

The writings of the religious reformers were an obvious target for censorship (*see* Counter-Reformation). The Milanese senate issued an index of banned books in 1538 and other Italian cities soon followed suit. The Index Librorum Prohibitorum issued in 1557 and 1559 under Pope *Paul IV was the forerunner of all subsequent lists of publications forbidden to Roman Catholics by reason either of heterodoxy or immorality. It became usual for printers to cite on their title-pages their authority to print, a practice ridiculed by Milton in his great attack on licensing for the press, *Areopagitica* (1644): "Sometimes 5 *Imprimaturs* are seen together dialoguewise in the Piatza of one Title page, complementing and ducking each to other with their shav'n reverences..." Secular works also suffered the attentions of censor and expurgator; for instance, the writings of *Aretino and *Machiavelli were banned, Cinthio Fabrizi's obscene *Libro della origine delli volgari proverbi* (1526) provoked the initiation of censorship in Venice in 1527, and Boccaccio's *Decameron* suffered the indignity of expurgated editions in 1573 and 1582.

In England licensing for the press by the privy council was introduced in 1538. From 1557 the Stationers' Company was held responsible for the regulation of the book trade, and later decrees nominated various dignitaries as licensers. In 1586 the number of presses allowed per printer was strictly curtailed and their whereabouts limited to London, apart from one press each for the university cities of Oxford and Cambridge; unauthorized presses, such as those used to print the pamphlets in the *Marprelate controversy were rigorously pursued, and if found were destroyed. Furthermore, authors were liable to penalties of imprisonment, mutilation, or death for producing obnoxious material, and books themselves could be seized and burnt, as befell the satirical works of *Nashe and Gabriel *Harvey under an edict of 1599.

As the Counter-Reformation advanced in Europe, censorship of the visual arts was also attempted. The most notorious incidence of this is probably the employment of a number of artists, among them El Greco, to paint draperies over the naked figures in Michelangelo's *Last Judgment* in the Sistine Chapel. A similar trend was manifested in music when Philip II of Spain insisted that plainsong only was to be used for the religious services in the Escorial, as the polyphonic church music hitherto popular in Spain had secular tunes worked into it.

Centuriators of Magdeburg The collective name for the authors of *Historia ecclesiae Christi*, a history of the Church century by century until 1400, published at Basle from 1559 to 1574. Among the Centuriators were Matthias Flacius (Vlacic), Nicolaus von Amsdorf, Johann Wigand, Nicolaus Gallus (Hahn), and Matthäus Judex (Richter). The work was begun about 1550 at Magdeburg and continued from 1562 at Regensburg (Ratisbon). It is broad in conception, but often inaccurate in detail, and was cogently attacked by the Catholic historian *Baronius.

Cervantes Saavedra, Miguel de (1547–1616) Spanish novelist, poet, and dramatist. One of the large family of a poor and unsuccessful doctor at Alcalá de Henares, Cervantes had little formal education apart from a period at a Madrid school run by a follower of Erasmus. In 1569 he went to Italy, joined the Spanish army there, and was wounded in the naval battle of Lepanto (1571), losing the use of his left hand. After completing military service, he boarded a ship for Spain in 1575 with a written commendation by Don John of Austria, but was seized by Algerian pirates and held captive by the Turks in Algiers for five years while he vainly tried to raise the necessary ransom. When it was finally paid by the Trinitarian Friars in 1580 and he returned to Spain, he hoped for some reward for past services but was ignored. His marriage in 1584 was an unhappy one and his first attempt to earn a living by writing, the pastoral romance *La Galatea* (1585) was hardly successful.

He had a somewhat better return on his early plays for the Madrid theatre, but his circumstances did not improve. In 1587 he was forced to leave Madrid to work in Andalusia as a tax collector. He was imprisoned two or perhaps three times for debt or trouble with his bookkeeping and spent a number of years living in Seville. After Part I of *Don Quixote* appeared (1605), he spent the final and most productive years of his life in Madrid. Despite his fame and the immense success of *Don Quixote*, his grave in Madrid was unmarked.

Though Cervantes wrote verse and included many poetic passages in his prose works, he acknowledged that he had little talent for it. Early lack of success in the theatre did not discourage him from making a second attempt, and he collected his later plays in *Ocho comedias y ocho entremeses* (1615). The *entremeses*, one-act prose farces, proved especially congenial to his gift for comic dialogue and social satire. The twelve short stories collected in *Novelas ejemplares* (*Exemplary Novels*; 1613) contain his most interesting work after *Don Quixote*. A long romance, *Persiles y Sigismunda*, was published posthumously (1617) and translated into English two years later.

Cesalpino, Andrea (1519–1603) Italian physician and botanist. Cesalpino was born at Arezzo, studied at Pisa, and in 1555 succeeded Luca Ghini as director of the Pisan botanic garden. He moved to the Sapienza in Rome in 1592. *De plantis libri XVI* (1583) starts with botanical principles; following Aristotle's division of plants into trees, shrubs, shrubby herbs, and herbs, Cesalpino's pioneering classification concentrated on fruits and seeds, neglecting broader affinities. The greater part of his book contains descriptions of about 1500 plants, but with less advice on their uses than the herbalists provided.

Cesarini, Julian (1398–1444) Italian churchman. Cesarini was born in Rome and studied at Perugia and Padua, where he was a friend of *Nicholas of Cusa. He occupied several posts in the papal Curia, and in 1425 was sent on a diplomatic mission to John, Duke of Bedford, regent of France for Henry VI. In 1426 he was made a cardinal and transferred to England, where he met Cardinal Beaufort and the humanists patronized by the duke of Gloucester. In 1431 he was appointed papal legate in Bohemia, Germany, Hungary, and Poland, to direct a crusade against the Hussites. He presided at the Council of *Basle, which opposed the policy of Pope Eugenius IV and attempted to limit the papal power. Later, at the Council of Ferrara, which transferred to Florence, he negotiated a settlement with the Greek Church. In 1442 he went to Hungary to preach a crusade against the Turks, and was killed during the flight after the defeat of the Christian forces at Varna, Bulgaria.

chain of being The doctrine that all natural entities, whether mineral, vegetable, or animal, are linked in a single, continuous, unbroken sequence. It originated with Plato and began to lose its appeal only with the geological revolution of the late eighteenth century. The animal and vegetable kingdoms, it was claimed, are so connected that it was impossible to distinguish between the highest plant and the lowest animal – and so on throughout all parts of the natural world. Considered hierarchically the chain (or ladder) of being joined the lowest natural form in a continuous sequence ultimately to God himself. Further, according to the related principle of plenitude, the chain extended throughout the whole of nature. This latter view was apparently dramatically confirmed during the late Renaissance period by observations made through the newly invented *microscope. Every green leaf was shown to be swarming with animal life, while the animals themselves were also shown to be similarly inhabited.

chambers of rhetoric Amateur literary societies in France and, more significantly, the Netherlands, active from about 1400. The *rhétoriqueurs* (French) or *rederijkers* (Dutch) were mainly middle-class townspeople who formed associations similar to guilds in order to promote their love of poetry and drama. They were mostly encouraged by the civic authorities and they reciprocated by organizing public celebrations, but the religious upheavals of the sixteenth century caused many of the chambers to fall under suspicion of heresy, and by 1600 their heyday was generally over.
Like the *Meistergesang* guilds in Germany, the chambers of rhetoric were not usually innovative in their literary enterprises or particularly quick to respond to Renaissance ideas; they were however associated with the rise of secular drama in northern Europe, and the Dutch *Elckerlijk* (c. 1495) is probably the source for the English morality play *Everyman*. Significant Dutch writers associated with the *rederijker* tradition include: Cornelis Everaert (c. 1480–1556), playwright and member of De Drie Santinnen at Bruges; Matthijs de Castelein (1485–1550), author of the first Dutch treatise on poetry, *De Const van Rhetoriken* (1548); Colijn van Rijssele, the fifteenth-century author of the bourgeois drama cycle *De Spiegel der Minnen* (The Mirror of Love); Anna Bijns (1493–1575), a schoolmistress at Antwerp; Dirck *Coornheert; and Henrick *Spiegel. The fanciful names adopted by the chambers were expressed in mottoes and emblems: they included De Egelantier and 't Wit Lavendel at Amsterdam, Het Bloemken Jesse at Middelburg, Trou moet Blijcken at Haarlem, De Fonteine at Ghent, and De Violieren at Antwerp. *See also* Duytsche Academie.

Chambord, Château de A château in central France, on the left bank of the River Cosson, a tributary of the Loire, east of Blois. Erected on the site of a hunting lodge and surrounded by forest, the château was mainly built (1519–47) during the reigns of Francis I and Henry II and incorporated many Renaissance features. The design was by the Italian architect *Domenico da Cortona and was executed by Jacques Sourdeau, Pierre Neveu, and Denis Sourdeau. Although the château was laid out in a medieval Gothic style, its 440 rooms were decorated in a classical manner typical of the Renaissance; other details include a double spiral open staircase. See p. 92.

Champlain, Samuel de (1567–1635) French navigator, founder of Quebec, and governor of Canada. Hailed as the key figure in the establishment of French interests in America, Champlain was born at Brouage, his father a sea captain. Champlain fought for Henry IV in the religious wars as a youth and sailed to the West Indies for Spain in 1599, before his first visit to Canada in 1603. For the next five years he explored extensively, before founding Quebec in 1608. He then devoted himself to the welfare of this community, developing the fur trade and making frequent sorties into the hinterland. He became lieutenant of Canada in 1612, but was captured by an English expedition against Quebec in 1629 and taken to England. France regained Quebec in 1632, and Champlain returned the following year to end his days there.

chanson A French polyphonic song of the medieval and Renaissance periods. A generic term, "chanson" encompasses rondeaux, *ballades,* and virelais. *Machaut can be regarded as the first major chanson composer. In the second half of the fourteenth century composers regularly set poems polyphonically, usually in three parts, in a rhythmically complex manner. The chansons of *Dufay were refined, with a rich texture, inventive melodies, and rhythmic variety. Chanson style changed radically around 1500; Josquin *Des Prés and his contemporaries treated each voice independently, and the new technique of imitative counterpoint was used with repetition of phrases. In Paris in the 1530s and 1540s Attaignant published many chansons, notably those by *Sermisy and *Janequin; the Parisian chanson was much simpler in style and more chordal. In the 1550s and 1560s composers used more word-painting, with more variety of texture, though the genre

CHAMBORD *The fairyland roofscape hides over 360 chimneys among its turrets, gables, and pinnacles.*

never attained the scope of the *madrigal.

Chapman, George (?1559–1634) English poet, playwright, and translator. Little is known for certain about Chapman's life; he may have been born near Hitchin and have attended both Oxford and Cambridge universities without taking a degree. His earliest published poems, *The Shadow of Night* (1594) and *Ovid's Banquet of Sence* (1595), are remarkable mainly for their obscurity; Chapman was never one to wear his learning lightly, a failing also apparent in his continuation of *Marlowe's *Hero and Leander* (1598). He probably began writing for the stage in the mid-1590s, producing such comedies as *An Humorous Day's Mirth* (1599) and *All Fools* (1605). Satirical allusions to Scots in *Eastward Ho!* (1605) caused Chapman and his co-authors *Jonson and Marston to be briefly imprisoned. Chapman's best play is his tragedy *Bussy d'Ambois* (1607), the hero of which is his finest dramatic creation. Chapman's greatest achievement, however, was his translation of the whole Homeric corpus: the complete *Iliad* in rhymed fourteen-syllable lines appeared in 1611, followed by the *Odyssey* in rhymed decasyllables (1614–15) and the Homeric hymns (1616).

Charlemagne, legend of The cycle of narratives, also known as "the matter of France", that accumulated during the Middle Ages around the Frankish king Charlemagne (c. 742–814; emperor 800–814) and his knights (paladins). Much of the earliest material focuses on Charlemagne himself as the divinely appointed champion of Christianity against Islam, but the part of the Charlemagne cycle that really kindled the medieval imagination was the incident in 778 when the rearguard of the Frankish army was ambushed by Basques while returning from an abortive campaign in Spain and was annihilated at Roncesvaux in the Pyrenees. This historical kernel grew into the Old French *Chanson de Roland* (c. 1100), the epic tale of the rearguard's last stand under its commander Roland against overwhelming hordes of Saracens. The poem was translated into German as the *Rolandslied* (mid-twelfth century), and further material was added to the Roland theme in Spanish and Italian poems on the hero's exploits prior to Roncesvaux and in laments for the slaughtered knights. Grotesque, magic, and erotic elements were also attached to the Roland story, particularly in Italy, and *Pulci's *Morgante* attempts to blend these with the story of Roncesvaux. Roland, Italianized as Orlando, also appears as the hero of the two greatest Italian romantic epics, *Boiardo's *Orlando innamorato* and *Ariosto's *Orlando furioso*, in which the *materia cavalleresca* of Charlemagne's wars against the pagans provides the general narrative framework.

Charles V (1500–58), Holy Roman Emperor (1519–56) (also Charles I of Spain (1516–56), Archduke of Austria, Duke of Burgundy) A *Habsburg prince, the son of Philip (the Handsome) of Burgundy and Joanna (the Mad) of Castile, Charles inherited vast territories from each of his four grandparents. He succeeded *Maximilian I as Holy Roman Emperor, inheriting from him Austrian and other German territories. From Mary, heiress of Burgundy, Charles inherited the Netherlands, Franche-Comté, and other territories near the Rhine. From *Ferdinand of Aragon and Isabella of Castile came Spain, Spanish territory in North Africa and the New World, and

CHARLES V *Titian's full-length portrait captures the imposing presence of the emperor, whose favourite painter he became. (1532; Prado, Madrid)*

various Italian territories and claims. By his wife, Isabella of Portugal (1503–39), Charles had the future *Philip II of Spain; two of his illegitimate children – *Margaret of Parma and Don *John of Austria – also played prominent roles in the late sixteenth century.

Charles was an earnest, but not particularly intellectual, man. His favourite painter was *Titian. A devout, if rather unimaginative Catholic, he took his great responsibilities seriously and was determined to protect his faith both against the attacks of the *Ottoman Turks, who reached the gates of Vienna in 1529, and against the Protestants.

Charles was born in Ghent and educated in the Netherlands, where he succeeded his father in 1506 and assumed personal rule in 1515. He was later faced with serious revolts in some Netherlands cities, notably the revolt of Ghent which was ruthlessly suppressed in 1540. In Spain too there were rebellions early in his reign (*see* Comuneros, Revolt of the), but order was restored by 1522. Charles worked hard to reach an understanding with his Spanish subjects in the 1520s; during his reign Spanish power in the New World was developed and the monarchy in Spain became more unified and centralized.

In Germany, despite some attempts to reach a compromise, as for instance at the colloquy of *Regensburg, Charles had to confront the Protestant challenge and years of sectarian warfare until the Peace of *Augsburg (1555) suspended the religious struggle. In Italy, as Maximilian I had done, Charles continued to dispute French claims. The Wars of *Italy were the most obvious expression of Habsburg-Valois rivalry for mastery in Europe.

In 1556, exhausted by the burdens of his inheritance, Charles retired to the Spanish monastery of Yuste. His inheritance was divided; Spain, the Netherlands, and other Spanish territories went to his son, *Philip II of Spain. Austria, other German territories, and the Holy Roman Empire passed to his brother, *Ferdinand I.

Charles VIII (1470–98), King of France (1483–98) The only son of *Louis XI and Charlotte of Savoy, Charles was frail and not very intelligent. During his minority (1483–91), Anne de Beaujeu, his sister, and her husband were regents. They administered France soundly and by arranging Charles's marriage (1491) to Anne, heiress of Brittany, eventually secured Brittany for the French royal domain. This marriage infuriated Anne's erstwhile fiancé, *Maximilian I, and presaged the long Habsburg-Valois conflict. On attaining his majority Charles was able to pursue his dreams of conquest, chivalry, and a crusade against the Turks. His first step was to assert French claims in Italy. After making costly treaties to buy off possible enemies, Charles invaded Italy (1494). He met little opposition; *Savonarola welcomed him as a liberator to Florence, the pope opened the gates of Rome, and Naples surrendered without a fight. Charles was crowned king of Naples (May 1495), but France's enemies formed a league against her. Charles abandoned Naples to the Aragonese and fought his way back to France, where he died while preparing another Italian invasion.

Charles Borromeo, St (1538–84) Italian churchman, a leading *Counter-Reformation figure. Born at Arona, Borromeo was destined from childhood for the Church and in 1560 was appointed cardinal archbishop of Milan by his maternal uncle, Pope Pius IV. Until Pius IV died (1565) Cardinal Borromeo served in the Curia, playing an important part in the later sessions of the Council of *Trent and drafting the Roman catechism. After 1566 he devoted himself to the archdiocese of Milan. He reformed its administration, improved the morals of clergy and laity, supported the Jesuits, helped establish seminaries and religious schools, and aided the poor and sick. His heroic efforts during an outbreak of plague (1576–78) were much admired. He was canonized in 1610.

Charles the Bold (1433–77), Duke of Burgundy (1467–77) The son of *Philip the Good, Charles was a rash man, who inherited extensive territories. His great ambitions were to gain a royal title and to win Alsace and Lorraine, the lands dividing his domains in the Netherlands from those in the Franche-Comté. He came close to realizing his first ambition, when Emperor Frederick III was on the brink of making Burgundy a kingdom. In pursuit of his second ambition he acquired power in Alsace and attacked Lorraine (1475). Alarmed at the prospect of a Burgundian kingdom stretching from the North Sea to the Alps, his neighbours combined against him. He died fighting the Swiss at Nancy and left his daughter Mary as his heiress. Her marriage to *Maximilian I conveyed most of the Burgundian inheritance to the house of *Habsburg.

Charron, Pierre (1541–1603) French writer and moralist. Born in Paris, he was one of a family of twenty-five children. After studying law at Orleans and Bourges he practised as an advocate but became disenchanted with the profession. He turned to the Church and enjoyed a distinguished career as a preacher, becoming chaplain-in-ordinary to Margaret of Valois, first wife of Henry of Navarre. In 1588 he returned to Paris determined to join a religious order, but, when none would accept him because of his age, he retired to Bordeaux where he became close friends with Montaigne. Charron published anonymously a treatise on *Les Trois Vérités* (1593), which combined an apology for Catholicism with an attack on *du Plessis-Mornay. He died in Paris of a stroke.
Charron's most important work was *De la sagesse* (1601). The main thesis of this work was the incapacity of reason to discover truth and the need for tolerance on religious questions. The work was severely censured by the Sorbonne and was a forerunner of seventeenth-century deism.

Chaucer, Geoffrey (c. 1343–1400) English poet. Born the son of a rich London wine merchant, Chaucer was brought up in the household of the earl of Ulster. Captured by the French near Reims while serving with the English army, he was ransomed by Edward III (1360). He then visited Spain (1366) before joining the royal household in 1367. In 1369 or 1370 he produced his first important poem, *The Book of the Duchess*, commemorating the recently dead Blanche of Lancaster. He made two visits to Italy, the first on business with the Genoese (1372–73), the second (1378) negotiating with Bernabò Visconti of Milan. From 1374 to 1386 he was a customs controller in the port of London. Poems of the early 1380s include *The House of Fame, The Parliament of Fowls*, and *Troilus and Criseyde*. Around 1387 he began work on *The Canterbury Tales*. From 1385 he was associated with the county of Kent in some of his many official capacities and probably lived there until he moved to a house near Westminster Abbey in 1399. He was interred in the abbey the following year. Acknowledged by his Renaissance successors as the greatest of earlier English writers, Chaucer was an important figure to them on several counts, despite what seems to us the thoroughly medieval nature of his poetry. First, his learning was singled out for special admiration, for instance in the dedication to the first complete edition of his works, published in 1532. The moral lessons implicit in his poetry particularly appealed to an age which held that "wholesome counsel and sage advice" (William Webbe, *Discourse of English Poetry*, 1586) should be mingled with "delight".
However, it was in his role of "Dan Chaucer, well of English undefyled" (Spenser, *The *Faerie Queene* IV ii 32) that he most influenced the literature of the English Renaissance. Caxton's proem to his second edition of *The Canterbury Tales* (1484) praises Chaucer as "that noble and grete philosopher" who "enbelysshed, ornated, and made faire our Englisshe", and the theme was taken up by several subsequent writers on the development of the vernacular, although *Sidney in his *Defence of Poesie* was more guarded: "I knowe not whether to mervail more, either that hee [Chaucer] in that mistie time could see so clearly, or that wee in this cleare age, goe so stumblingly after him. Yet had hee great wants, fit to be forgiven in so reverent an Antiquitie." *See also* Deschamps, Eustache.

Cheke, Sir John (1514–57) English humanist. Cheke was born in Cambridge, where he became a fellow of St John's College (1529) and took his MA in 1533. He became first Regius Professor of Greek at Cambridge (1540), a canon of Christ Church, Oxford (1544), and tutor in Latin and Greek to King Edward VI. He was knighted in 1552, but, as a Protestant, upon Mary's accession he was imprisoned and then driven into exile (1554). English agents captured him near Brussels (1556), and he was brought back to England where he was forced to make a humiliating public abjuration of his faith. Consumed with remorse for his recantation, he died in London the following year. A renowned scholar, Cheke made a number of translations of Greek texts into Latin. He also took part in the controversy surrounding the pronunciation of Greek (*see* Greek studies), his letters opposing Stephen *Gardiner on the subject being published in Basle in 1555. This study of phonetics led him to evolve a reformed spelling for English which he used in gospel translations that he made around 1550 and in his letter to Sir Thomas *Hoby, published in the latter's translation of Castiglione (1561).

Chenonceau, Château de A château in central France, southwest of Paris, bridging the River Cher. Incorporating a single tower from an earlier building of the fifteenth century, the château was begun in 1513 by Thomas Bohier, the financial minister of Normandy, but was subsequently confiscated by Francis I and became a royal residence (1535). Noted for its combination of Gothic and Renaissance features, the château was inherited by Henry II who presented it to his mistress *Diane de Poitiers. She added an arched bridge spanning the Cher, designed by Philibert *Delorme. When the château passed to Catherine de' Medici this wing was enlarged (1570–78) by Jean *Bullant as the Grande Galerie.

chiaroscuro A term describing the handling of light and dark in the visual arts, particularly with regard to painting. Derived from the Italian words *chiaro* (lightness) and *oscuro* (darkness), chiaroscuro was first developed by artists during the fourteenth century as a means of heightening atmospheric qualities and achieving three-dimensional effects. The use of contrast of light and dark was also applied to manuscript illustration and, by *Ugo da Carpi and *Parmigianino, to woodcuts. Also referred to as *tenebrismo*, the effect was employed by numerous artists of the Renaissance, such as *Caravaggio (whose followers were sometimes called "tenebristi"), and reached its greatest heights in the works of Rembrandt.

Chigi, Agostino (1465–1520) Italian banker and patron of the arts. Also known as "Il Magnifico", Chigi was a member of a noted Sienese family and the founder of a major banking house in Rome (1485). As leasor (1500) of the papal alum mines and treasurer to the Church he exerted financial influence in several European countries and was in an ideal position to become acquainted with the foremost artists of his day. Peruzzi's masterpiece, the Villa *Farnesina, was built for Chigi near Rome and decorated by *Raphael, the most distin-

guished of the many artists who enjoyed his patronage. He was also a patron of scholarship and literature, under whose auspices the Cretan Zacharias Calliergis (c. 1473–c. 1524) set up the first Greek press in Rome and published an important edition of Pindar (1515).

Christian Majesty, His Most (*Rex Christianissimus*) A title accorded to the kings of France especially in papal correspondence of the fifteenth century onwards.

Christine de Pisan (c. 1364–c. 1430) Venetian-born French poet and prose writer. Christine de Pisan grew up at the court of Charles V of France, where her father was astrologer and physician to the king. Widowed with three children at the age of twenty-five, she began to write poetry to support her family: the success of her early love ballads encouraged her to embark on more serious works in defence of women, such as *Épître au dieu d'amour* (1399), *Cité des dames* (1405; translated as *The Book of the City of Ladies*, 1982), and *Livre des trois vertus* (1406). Her other writings include a biography of Charles V, *Livre des faits et bonnes moeurs du roi Charles V* (1404), and a number of patriotic stories, notably *Ditié de Jeanne d'Arc*. After the French defeat at Agincourt (1415) Christine took refuge in a convent, where she spent the latter years of her life.

Christus, Petrus (c. 1410–72/73) Netherlands painter. Born in Baerle, Christus became in 1444 a citizen of Bruges, which remained his base for the rest of his life. His style was directly conditioned by that of Jan van *Eyck, who was probably his master, and his early works such as the *Exeter Madonna* (Berlin) and a pair of triptych wings of 1452 (Berlin) are derived from Eyckian compositions. Christus's Frankfurt *Madonna and Child* (1457) reveals an early mastery of one-point perspective, which may have been learned in Italy. The latter hypothesis remains unproven, although Christus's work was appreciated in Italy shortly after his death and it seems likely that he influenced *Antonello da Messina. Christus's style was essentially a simplification and systemization of Jan van Eyck's, which nevertheless perpetuated his mentor's influence during a period when most Netherlands painters sought inspiration in the work of Rogier van der *Weyden.

chronicles *see under* historiography.

Chrysoloras, Manuel (1350–1415) Greek diplomat and teacher of Greek. Chrysoloras was born in Constantinople and was a pupil of Plethon. In 1393 he was sent by Emperor Manuel Palaeologus to seek aid from the Italian states against the Turks. He returned to Constantinople but was invited in 1395 to Florence, where he became professor of Greek; his pupils included Poggio *Bracciolini, Leonardo *Bruni, and Francesco Barbaro; he also translated Homer and Plato into Latin during his stay there. Chrysoloras then (1400) moved to Milan, Pavia, and Venice, remaining in the last for several years. He then went to Rome and in 1408 was sent to Paris as the Greek emperor's representative. In 1413 he served on the embassy that prepared the way for the Council of *Constance. He died en route for the council to represent the Greek Church. His *Erotemata* (printed 1484) was the first Greek grammar used in the West. His influence was important in introducing a more critical approach to literature based on a close study of language.

Cicero, Marcus Tullius (106–43 BC) Roman statesman and orator. Cicero was important to the Renaissance on two grounds: the morals that could be drawn from his writings and his private and public life and the example set by his prose style. The former first made him an object of interest to *Petrarch, who as a philosopher and moralist himself was struggling to reconcile the counter-claims of the active and the contemplative life. *Salutati was more swayed by admiration for Cicero's important career in public life, and his view of the Roman statesman generally prevailed among the Florentine humanists and was transmitted through them to later Renaissance moralists. It was Petrarch and a little later Poggio *Bracciolini who were responsible for discovering and preserving almost half the writings of Cicero that we still possess, including the letters of Atticus and a number of his most famous orations.

Cicero's status as a model for humanist prose writers struggling to free themselves from medieval Latin style likewise stemmed from Petrarch and grew virtually unchecked, with the backing of men like *Valla and the educationist *Guarino da Verona, for over a century. The powerful rhetoric of his orations, the easy familiarity of his letters, the lucid Latin of his philosophical treatises were all enthusiastically imitated. Inevitably there was a reaction; writers such as *Politian, rebuked for using un-Ciceronian vocabulary, defended their right to go beyond its limits in pursuit of self-expression, and *Erasmus wrote his *Ciceronianus* (1528) as a withering attack on the pedants who carried Ciceronianism to absurd extremes. Nevertheless, Cicero continued to be a major influence on Renaissance prose, not only in terms of style but also on account of his philosophy, since many writers found his Stoicism comparatively easy to reconcile with their Christianity. His dialogues on

friendship (*De Amicitia*) and old age (*De Senectute*) were often imitated, and the dialogue form was also carried over into philosophical or didactic works in the vernacular.

Ciconia, Johannes (c. 1373–1411) Franco-Flemish composer. He received his earliest musical education as a choirboy at St Jean l'Evangeliste, Liège, around 1385. Before 1400 he went to Padua where he became *magister* and a canon at the cathedral, posts which he retained until his death. Mass sections, motets, and secular works, including *ballate*, survive. An advanced approach to imitation is evident in his motets, some of which are ceremonial, occasional works. These date largely from his time in Padua, and include two isorhythmic pieces in honour of the city's bishop.

Cieco d'Adria, Il *see* Groto, Luigi.

Cigoli, Lodovico Cardi da (1559–1613) Italian painter. Born at Cigoli in Tuscany and brought up in the tradition of Florentine Mannerism, he was a pupil of Alessandro *Allori and *Santi di Tito but was more influenced by the works of *Michelangelo, *Pontormo, and *Andrea del Sarto. After travelling in Lombardy he returned to Florence, where he did paintings for the Palazzo Pitti at the request of the grand duke and frescoes in the church of Sta Maria Novella (1581–84) which mark the transition from Mannerism to the Baroque. His best-known work is the very fine painting for St Peter's in Rome, *St Peter Healing the Lame Man at the Beautiful Gate of the Temple*. His pictures all comprise fervent ascetic treatments of religious subjects, especially saints. Cigoli died in Rome.

Cimabue (Cenni di Peppi; c. 1240–c. 1302) Italian artist and mosaicist. Known by his nickname (meaning "bullheaded"), Cimabue was trained in the Byzantine style but was recognized by later scholars, including *Ghiberti and *Vasari – the latter began his *Lives* with an account of Cimabue's career – as marking the divide between the art of the Middle Ages and that of the Renaissance.

Although little is known of his life, Cimabue was in Rome in 1272, where he may have been influenced by the developing realism of sculptural art there, and in Pisa in 1302. The only surviving work certainly attributed to Cimabue is *Christ in Glory*, part of a large mosaic of St John in the apse of Pisa cathedral (c. 1302); other works probably by him include the badly deteriorated frescoes in the upper basilica at Assisi (c. 1290), the *Sta Trinità Madonna* (c. 1290; Uffizi), and the *Madonna with Angels* (c. 1290–95; Louvre). These pieces are notable for their combination of traditional Byzantine forms and a new naturalism, seen particularly in his handling of human figures. Another work, the *Crucifix* (c. 1290; Sta Croce, Florence), was badly damaged in the floods of 1966. Cimabue's approach was subsequently reflected in and indeed eclipsed by the revolutionary paintings of *Giotto, who may have been Cimabue's pupil, as evidenced by Dante in his *Divine Comedy*, in which the writer berates Cimabue for his pride and comments that "now Giotto hath the cry". Nonetheless, Cimabue is now generally recognized as the first herald of the ideals of the Renaissance and the most important artist in Italy before Giotto.

Cima da Conegliano, Giovanni Battista (c. 1460–1518) Italian painter. Born at Conegliano near Venice, Cima probably trained under Bartolommeo Montagna and later came under the influence of the style of Giovanni Bellini. His earliest authenticated picture, an altarpiece now in the museum at Vicenza (1489), demonstrates his control of colour and landscape; later works include paintings of the Madonna, the *Incredulity of St Thomas* (1504; National Gallery, London), and an altarpiece (1493) for the cathedral of Conegliano. Typical of his contemplative paintings is the *Madonna with Six Saints* (c. 1496–99; Accademia, Venice).

Cinquecento (Italian: five hundred) A term denoting artistic and cultural development in Italy during the sixteenth century. This period witnessed the culmination of the humanist movement in Renaissance Italy and the spread of mannerist ideals from such cultural centres as Venice, Ferrara, Mantua, and Rome under the patronage of the *Medici, *Este, *Gonzaga, and *Farnese families, and others. Leading Italian figures of the century included *Ariosto, *Machiavelli, and *Castiglione in literature, *Leonardo da Vinci, *Raphael, *Michelangelo, *Giorgione, *Titian, and *Correggio in painting, Michelangelo in sculpture, *Palestrina in music, and Michelangelo, Raphael, *Palladio, *Vasari, *Bramante, and *Peruzzi in architecture.

Cinthio (Giambattista Giraldi; 1504–73) Italian dramatist, critic, and writer. Cinthio (an epithet adopted in some of his verses) received a humanist education and taught rhetoric at the university of his native Ferrara (1541–62) until he fell from favour with Ferrara's Este rulers after a lengthy literary feud. He then taught in Pavia, returning to Ferrara shortly before his death. His *Orbecche* (1541), the first performance of tragedy in Italian, is important for introducing the Senecan model in the Renaissance: its main features are a five-act structure, emphasis on the horror of events, and a moralizing style. Three further tragedies, *Didone*,

Cleopatra, and *Altile* (c. 1543), were followed by the pastoral *Egle* (1545). Later plays look forward to the genre of tragicomedy. Cinthio's collection of *novelle*, *Hecatommithi* (*One Hundred Tales*; 1565) provided plots for his own plays and those of other dramatists, including Shakespeare (*Measure for Measure* and *Othello*). The theory of his dramatic practice was expounded in the discourse *Intorno al comporre delle commedie e delle tragedie* (1543) and a defence of the romance epic, such as *Ariosto's *Orlando furioso*, was argued in *Intorno al comporre dei romanzi* (1548).

ciompi The low-paid day-labourers in Florence's wool industry. In July 1378 the ciompi rebelled against their low wages and their subjection to their employers and the wool guild. They armed themselves and seized power with the help of artisans and shopkeepers. Having overthrown the oligarchy, they then forced through radical and democratic legislation. Their extremism and the worsening economic situation alarmed their allies, many of whom deserted them. The guilds were able to regain control late in August 1378 and to restore oligarchy to Florence.

Civitali, Matteo (1436–1501) Italian architect and sculptor in marble. Civitali was born and died in Lucca, and most of his work remains in the city or its environs. The cathedral at Lucca contains tombs by Civitali, a pulpit (1494–98), and the Tempietto del Volto Santo (1484), an octagonal marble shrine housing a wooden image of Christ believed to have been the work of Nicodemus. Civitali was the original architect of Lucca's Palazzo Pretorio (1492) and his statue stands in the portico there. Outside Lucca, Civitali has a lectern and candelabra in the cathedral at Pisa and statues of Old Testament figures in Genoa cathedral.

classics, study of *see* criticism, literary; criticism, textual; Greek studies; humanism; Latin studies.

Claudin *see* Sermisy, Claudin de.

Clavius, Christopher (Christoph Klau; 1537–1612) German mathematician and astronomer. Born at Bamberg, Clavius became a leading Jesuit and professor of mathematics at the Collegio Romano. His views were often sought by the Vatican on controversial scientific matters; thus, between 1588 and 1603, he wrote no fewer than five separate works defending the calendrical reforms of Pope Gregory XIII in 1582. Clavius was again called upon in 1611 to advise the Vatican authorities upon the reliability and seriousness of *Galileo's telescopic observations. While responding sympathetically to Galileo's work, he advised, nonetheless, that the observations did not constitute a convincing proof of the *Copernican system. The lunar mountains described by Galileo were covered, Clavius said, with a smooth but transparent crystalline surface. As a mathematician Clavius was known as the author of *Epitome arithmeticae* (1583) and *Algebra* (1608), widely used textbooks of arithmetic and algebra, and he also wrote a major treatise on gnomonics (1581).

Clemens (non Papa), Jacobus (c. 1510–55/56) Franco-Flemish composer. Clemens was succentor at Bruges cathedral (1544–45), and in late 1550 was at 's-Hertogenbosch. It is known that he spent some time in Ypres, but he also had links with Leyden and Dort. The reason for the "non Papa" (not the pope) in his name is uncertain, though it was probably coined as a joke, for Pope Clement VII died in 1534, and the name was not used in a publication until 1545. Clemens was a prolific composer known chiefly for his sacred works. He also wrote many chansons, and his Mass settings are, with one exception, parody settings on chansons and motets by contemporary composers. He is most remembered for his settings of *souterliedekens*, the Dutch psalms. These three-voice pieces were the first polyphonic settings of the psalms in Dutch, with the use of popular song melodies as *cantus firmi*.

Clement VII (1478–1534), Pope (1523–34) Clement was born Giulio de' Medici at Florence, a bastard nephew of Lorenzo the Magnificent. During the Medici exile from Florence (1494–1512) he travelled extensively in Europe, gaining valuable experience. He took an active part in the Lateran Council of 1512–17, being made archbishop of Florence and a cardinal in 1513, and he became political counsellor to his cousin Pope Leo X. He was a candidate for the papacy in 1521 and was elected pope in 1523. His policy was shifty and weak. He attempted to control Italy by supporting alternately Emperor Charles V and Francis I of France. After the sack of Rome in 1527 by imperial troops, he was imprisoned in the Castel S Angelo for several months. In 1530 he crowned Charles (already German king) as Holy Roman Emperor at Bologna. In 1533 he officiated at the wedding of his niece *Catherine de' Medici to the future Henry II of France. Clement's vacillations over Henry VIII's petition for a divorce from Catherine of Aragon were one of the causes of the king's repudiation of papal authority. His attempts to deal with Luther's revolt were also unsuccessful, and he failed to effect any reforms within the Roman Church. Clement VII was a wordly figure, concerned for the advancement of his family and

his own posthumous fame. He was a patron of such eminent artists as Raphael, Michelangelo, Benvenuto Cellini, and Sebastiano del Piombo (see Plate XXVII), and of Machiavelli and Copernicus.

Clement VIII (1536–1605), Pope (1592–1605) He was born Ippolito Aldobrandini at Fano, near Pesaro, and studied law at Padua, Perugia, and Bologna. He held numerous offices in the Roman Curia, became a cardinal in 1585, and was elected pope in 1592. Clement reduced Spanish influence in the college of cardinals, and recognized Henry IV as king of France in 1593. In 1598 he annexed Ferrara to the Papal States, after the death of the last duke without legitimate heirs. He arranged the Treaty of Vervins between France and Spain in 1598, and tried to resolve the controversy between the Jesuits and Dominicans concerning grace and free will. He was responsible for a new standard edition of the Vulgate (the Sistine-Clementine version) and for revisions of the missal, breviary, and pontifical.

clocks Though described by Lewis Mumford (*Technics and Civilization*) as "the key-machine of the modern industrial age", little of this significance can have been apparent in the turret clocks which first began to appear in the early fourteenth century. Driven by falling weights, located in towers, controlled by a verge and foliot escapement, and without hands, they served more as planetaria than clocks. In addition, however, to displaying such phenomena as the phases of the moon, and the motions of planets, they rang bells and, in this manner, marked out the liturgical day for monks and other clerics. Clocks soon, also, came to regulate the working day of many residents of the rapidly growing towns. Such early instruments were too massive and too expensive to make and maintain to be anything other than the property of princes or corporations.

After 1450 the turret clocks were joined by chamber clocks. A common early design was the drum clock, a squat cylinder with the dial on its uppermost surface. This advance was made possible by the invention of the spring drive. Springs, though portable, fail to deliver constant power as they unwind. The solution consisted of attaching the spring by a chain to a conically shaped fusee which acted as an equalizing force as the spring unwound. Improvements in this basic design, together with the use of more accurately produced parts, allowed clockmakers to introduce the minute hand sometime in the 1470s. The second hand followed almost a century later in the decade 1560–70. A more fundamental advance came with the pendulum clock; conceived by *Galileo in 1637, the first such clock actually constructed was the

CLOCKS *This drum clock by Jacob Zech is the earliest surviving spring-driven clock with a fusee. (1525; Society of Antiquaries, London)*

work of Christian Huygens in 1653. The improvement in time-keeping was astonishing: the best clocks had previously varied by about fifteen minutes a day, but early pendulum clocks reduced this to no more than fifteen seconds.

Clouet, François (c. 1510–72) French artist. Born at Tours, the son of the Flemish-born painter Jean (*or* Janet) Clouet (c. 1485–1541), François Clouet inherited his father's position as official painter to Francis I. Subsequently painter to Henry II and Charles IX, Clouet continued in the tradition established by his father, executing notable portraits of the Valois court and a number of genre paintings. His portraits include those of Diane de Poitiers (National Gallery, Washington), Pierre Quthe (1562; Louvre), Charles IX (1570; Kunsthistorisches Museum, Vienna), and *Lady in her Bath* (c. 1570; National Gallery, Washington), which was probably modelled on Marie Touchet, mistress of Charles IX. Although his formal portraits were influenced by the works of his father, his more informal works bore the mark of Italian artists, while his genre paintings followed the style of the Netherlandish school. Clouet was also noted as a brilliant draughtsman and many of his drawings survive in the Musée Condé in Chantilly.

Clovio, Giulio (Jure Clović; 1498–1578) Croatian-born painter. Clovio was born in Grizane, but lived in Italy after 1516 and probably studied under *Giulio Romano in Rome. After the sack of Rome (1527), in which he was captured, Clovio escaped and took holy orders. He was renowned as a miniaturist, demonstrating his pre-eminence in this field

in such sequences as his illustrations of the victories of Emperor Charles V (British Library) and those in the manuscript life of Federico, Duke of Urbino (Vatican Library). Other commissions included decorations in the Palazzo *Farnese and a *Pietà* (1553; Uffizi). Clovio also helped and encouraged the young El *Greco on his arrival in Rome.

Clusius, Carolus (Charles de l'Ecluse; 1526–1609) Franco-Flemish physician and botanist. Clusius was born in Arras. From his travels in Spain, Portugal, France, Hungary, and Austria he introduced many new garden plants, especially bulbs, to western Europe. The imperial garden in Vienna, which he controlled from 1573 to 1587, was a source of plants from the East, including tulips from Turkey. Among his books are botanical translations from Spanish and his *Rariorum plantarum historia* (1601), prepared during his years as professor at Leyden, where he replanned the university's botanic garden in 1594.

Cochanovius, Joannes *see* Kochanowski, Jan.

Cochlaeus, Johannes (Johann Dobneck; 1479–1552) German humanist and Roman Catholic controversialist. He was born at Wendelstein, near Schwabach, and studied philosophy at Nuremberg (where he was a protégé of *Pirckheimer) and Cologne. He was a Platonist and critical of the scholastics. About 1518 he was ordained priest in Rome, and from 1521 he was a bitter opponent of Luther. In 1525 he strenuously opposed the printing of *Tyndale's New Testament at Cologne. From 1526 he was a canon of Mainz, transferring to Meissen around 1535 and thence to Breslau (Wroclaw, now in Poland) in 1539. His history of the Hussites in twelve books and his commentary on the words and deeds of Luther in the period 1517–46, both appeared in 1549.

Codussi (or Coducci), Mauro (c. 1440–1504) Italian architect. Although he was born near Bergamo, Codussi was active from 1469 in Venice, where he developed a distinctive style based upon the classical architecture of Florence and central Italy. Early buildings included the church of S Michele in Isola (1469–79), which was the first Renaissance church in Venice. S Zaccaria (1483) and the Scuola Grande di S Marco (1485–95) are notable for their façades. The influence of Alberti's principles of architecture is evident in many of Codussi's buildings, including his best-known edifices, the Torre dell' Orologio (1496–99) and the Procurazie Vecchie (begun 1496) on the Piazza S Marco. Other major projects undertaken by Codussi were the churches of Sta Maria Formosa (rebuilt 1492–1502) and S Giovanni Crisostomo (c. 1500), the latter being the first centrally planned Venetian church, the Scuola Grande di S Giovanni Evangelista (1498), with its famous double staircase, and the Palazzo Corner-Spinelli (c. 1490) and Palazzo Vendramin-Calerghi (1501–09), both Lombardesque in style, but incorporating innovatory features, such as the free-standing classical orders on the façade of the latter palace.

Coecke van Aelst, Pieter (1502–50) Netherlands painter, print maker, and author. Coecke, who was born in Aelst, is believed to have studied under Bernard van *Orley and is recorded as a master at Antwerp in 1527. He visited Italy (c. 1530) and Constantinople (1533) and in 1535 may have accompanied Emperor Charles V on his Tunis campaign. He was still at Antwerp in 1544, but 'subsequently moved to Brussels, where he died. He had a large workshop with many pupils, including the young Pieter Bruegel. His wife, Meyken Verhulst, was also an artist. No surviving paintings of Coecke's can be identified with absolute certainty. His most famous composition, the *Last Supper* (c. 1527), is loosely based upon *Leonardo da Vinci's famous fresco; it exists in several versions, all possibly replicas of a lost original. Coecke's numerous prints were highly influential and he also designed tapestries and stained glass. His most important work, however, was his summary of Vitruvius's book on architecture and his translation of *Serlio (1539).

Coelho, Alonso Sánchez (Alonso Sánchez Coello; c. 1531–88) Spanish painter of Portuguese extraction. Born at Benifayó near Valencia, Sánchez

Coelho was educated in Flanders and Portugal and later studied in Brussels, where he became a pupil of Antonio *Moro (Anthonis Mor van Dashorst). In 1571 he succeeded his master as court painter to Philip II of Spain and established himself as a leading portraitist and royal favourite. Also influenced by Titian, he portrayed members of the Spanish court with great dignity and formality, as in his portraits of Elizabeth of Valois (c. 1560; Kunsthistorisches Museum, Vienna), Philip II (c. 1575; Prado, Madrid), and their daughter Infanta Isabella Clara Eugenia (1579; Prado, Madrid), later ruler of the Netherlands. Besides these portraits, which laid the foundation of the Spanish tradition of portraiture, Sánchez Coelho also produced a number of religious paintings for the Escorial, most of which were conventional and unremarkable. A portrait of St Ignatius Loyola (1585) is now lost.

Cognac, League of see under Italy, Wars of.

coins see under numismatics.

Colantonio (mid-fifteenth century) Italian painter. Active in Naples from about 1440 to 1470, Colantonio was notable chiefly for his fusion of Flemish and Italian artistic styles. Colantonio was apparently familiar with the works of van *Eyck, among others, and employed many features of Flemish style in the extant paintings *St Vincent* (c. 1456), painted for S Pietro Martire, and *St Jerome* (Museo Nazionale, Naples), painted as part of an altarpiece for the church of S Lorenzo. A notable polyptych for S Severino is now lost. Colantonio's successful blend of Flemish and Italian was subsequently imitated by his own pupil *Antonello de Messina.

Colet, John (?1467–1519) English humanist and educator. Born in London and educated at Oxford (1483–90), he went in 1493 to France and Italy to complete his studies; in Paris he met *Budé and in Florence he studied Plato and Plotinus. He also applied the newly discovered principles of textual criticism to the Church Fathers. In 1496 he returned to Magdalen College, Oxford, where he introduced the study of Greek. In 1499 he met Erasmus at Oxford, subsequently exercising considerable influence on the latter's approach to the study of the Bible. In 1505 Henry VII made him dean of St Paul's cathedral. In 1509 he founded St Paul's School, the statutes of which formed a model for other schools. Colet's approach to the scriptures was to interpret them as living literature, going directly to the text rather than engaging in the mystical allegorization characteristic of Florentine Platonism.

Coligny, Admiral Gaspard de Châtillon (1519–72) French *Huguenot leader in the Wars of *Religion. He served in Italy and was colonel-general of the infantry before his appointment as admiral of France (1552). While a prisoner of war of Spain (1557–59), after the French defeat at *St-Quentin, Coligny converted to Calvinism. He wished to reach a compromise with the French monarchy, but after 1569 became the most important Huguenot military leader. The *Guise family, who blamed Coligny for the assassination of Francis, Duke of Guise (1563), ensured that Coligny was one of the first Huguenots to die in the *Massacre of St Bartholomew (1572), even though he enjoyed the personal regard of the king.

Colleoni, Bartolommeo (1400–75) Italian condottiere. Born near Bergamo, Colleoni first fought (1419) as a condottiere in southern Italy under the leadership of Braccio da Montone and then Muzio Attendolo (*see* Sforza family). Colleoni served Venice on several occasions after 1431 and was highly esteemed for his skilful use of light field artillery. Anxious to retain the loyalty of such an able soldier, Venice made Colleoni its commander-in-chief (1454) and paid him lavishly. Colleoni lived luxuriously in his castle of Malpaga near Bergamo,

COLLEONI *The great condottiere left money to the Venetian signoria on the understanding that he should be commemorated by an equestrian statue like those of the ancient Roman emperors. Commissioned from Verrocchio but completed after the latter's death by the Venetian bronze-founder Alessandro Leopardi, it was not set up, as Colleoni had intended, in the Piazza S Marco, but in its present less conspicuous position outside the church of SS Giovanni e Paolo. (c. 1479–88)*

where he received condottieri and also extended to artists and men of letters a cordial welcome that earned him a reputation as a patron of the arts. *Verrocchio created the famous bronze equestrian statue of Colleoni (Venice) after Colleoni's death.

Colman family *see* Helmschmied family.

Colocci, Angelo (1474–1547) Italian humanist. Colocci was born at Iesi and from 1497 was a papal secretary, first to Leo X and then to Clement VII. According to Pomponius Leto, Colocci was the true inspiration of Roman humanism. In 1537 he was made bishop of Nocera Umbra. He combined an interest in classical literature with a lively involvement in vernacular poetry, particularly the study of the origins of Italian poetry in Provence. He was himself a poet in both Latin and Italian and his house in Rome was a centre for the discussion of literary theory and scholarship. He collected manuscripts and inscriptions but his collections suffered in the sack of Rome (1527). The surviving manuscripts are now in the Vatican library but the collection of inscriptions was dispersed. Colocci is a good example of the humanists' ability to reconcile the demands of religious orthodoxy with allegiance to the values of the classical world.

Colombe, Michel (1430/35–c. 1515) French sculptor. Born in Brittany, Colombe was a member of a family of artists and brother of the miniaturist Jean Colombe (d. 1529), who is associated with the Apocalypse manuscript in the Escorial (1482) and the completion of *Les Très Riches Heures du duc de Berry* (1485; Chantilly). Little is known of his early years, from which no works survive, and he is celebrated chiefly for just two sculptures. His masterpiece is the tomb (1502–07) of Francis II of Brittany and Marguerite de Foix in Nantes, with allegorical figures; his other work is the marble relief of St George and the dragon (1508–09; Louvre) for the altarpiece of the château de Gaillon. The former of these works was designed by the sculptor Jean Perréal and also worked on by Girolamo da Fiesole; both works demonstrate Colombe's successful combination of the French Gothic style with the artistic ideals of the Italians.

Colonia, Simón de (died c. 1511) Spanish architect of German extraction. His father Juan (died 1481) came to Burgos in the 1440s and built the spires at the western end of the cathedral, and Simón succeeded his father in the post of master of the works there. His two chief monuments are the octagonal Capilla del Condestable (1482–94) at Burgos and the façade of the church of S Pablo, Valladolid (1490–1504), both in the early *plateresque style. Simón's son Francisco (died c. 1542) collaborated with him at Valladolid and succeeded him as master of works at Burgos (1511).

Colonna, Francesco see under Hypnerotomachia Polifili.

Colonna, Vittoria (1492–1547) Italian poet. A member of an illustrious Roman Ghibelline family, she was betrothed at the age of four and at nineteen married to Ferdinando d'Avalos, Marquis of Pescara, to whom she was devoted. After his untimely death (1525) she lived mainly in convents, eventually settling in Rome; she became associated with religious reformers, though she remained within the Church through the influence of her adviser, Cardinal Reginald *Pole. Her many literary friendships and correspondents included Aretino, Bembo, Castiglione, Sannazaro, and particularly Michelangelo, who addressed a number of poems and letters to her. Her own poems, *Rime* (published several times between 1538 and 1544), are mainly Petrarchan sonnets influenced by Bembo and are concerned with the memory of her husband and with Neoplatonic and religious subjects.

Colonna family A noble Roman family, whose members were senators and cardinals from the thirteenth century. During the fourteenth century the Colonna's bitterest rivals for power were the Caetani and Orsini families. As Pope Martin V (1417–31), Oddone Colonna increased his family's wealth and power with generous grants of land in the Papal States. The next pope, *Eugenius IV (1431–47), tried unsuccessfully to force the family to return its estates, and over a century of bitter conflict with the papacy followed, especially when the *Borgia family was in the ascendancy. The power of the Colonna was eventually brought under control and the family was reconciled with the papacy in the later sixteenth century.

colossal (or giant) order An architectural device in which columns or pilasters rise for more than one storey in a façade. Originally devised by the Romans and used on such edifices as triumphal arches, the style was revived during the Renaissance, being reintroduced by Michelangelo who first incorporated it into the Capitol at Rome. After the Renaissance the colossal order was taken up by the baroque movement and, later, by such eighteenth-century architects as Sir John Vanbrugh and Nicholas Hawksmoor.

Columbus, Christopher (Cristoforo Colombo; 1451–1506) Italian explorer, credited with the discovery of the Americas. Columbus was born Genoa and initially joined the family wool-weaving business, having received little education. At fourteen he went to sea, and by 1477 had been to the Levant, Iceland, Ireland, Portugal, and England. After settling in Lisbon, he married in 1479 and solicited patronage for an Atlantic expedition in search of a route to Asia. The king of Portugal refused, and Columbus left for Spain (1484). Through the aid of influential churchmen, Columbus eventually convinced Queen Isabella of the validity of his ideas; in turn, she persuaded King Ferdinand. On 3 August 1492 Columbus sailed from Saltes, an island near Palos, with 120 men and three small ships, led by the *Santa Maria*. He went first to the Canary Islands, then sailed westwards. In October he reached the Bahamas, much to the relief of his terrified crew. He proceeded to Cuba and Haiti (Hispaniola), where he founded the first Spanish settlement in the New World. On his return to Spain with gold, plants, birds, and six Indians, he was immediately made a grandee.

On 24 September 1493 Columbus set sail again. During the next three years he refounded the Hispaniola colony at Isabella and thoroughly explored and attempted to chart the West Indies. His third voyage in 1498 achieved the discovery of the South American mainland, but mischief-makers persuaded Ferdinand to supplant Columbus as governor of Hispaniola, and Bobadilla, the new governor, sent Columbus back to Spain in chains (1500). On his arrival, however, he was triumphantly vindicated, and in 1502 he set off to search for a route to Asia between Cuba and South America. This failed for obvious reasons, and Columbus returned (1504) to Spain much weakened in health. He died at Valladolid, but in 1542 his remains were transferred to Hispaniola.

comedy There is little evidence of any significant staged comedy between the death of Terence (159 BC) and the late Middle Ages, when comic elements re-emerge in liturgical offshoots: in the buffoonery and clowning that formed part of the mystery play and in the comic Vice of the later morality play and *interlude. In these, comic passages ridiculed everyday foibles, favourite subjects being love and money – that is, infidelity and financial chicanery. In France, the Feast of Fools was introduced in cathedral liturgies between Christmas and the Octave of the Epiphany (13 January) and gave an opportunity to the lower clergy to poke fun at their superiors with a parody sermon (*sermon joyeux*), an ass led into the church to add its bray to the responses, and other farcical proceedings. Secular farces, of which some 150 examples (each about 500 lines of octosyllabic verse) survive, evolved from these origins in France. Although there were doubtless many comic performances of some kind in the fourteenth and fifteenth centuries, they were apparently not considered worth preserving and documentation is therefore scarce. Under the auspices of the *chambers of rhetoric medieval farce persisted well into the sixteenth century in the Netherlands; several such farces, known as *esbattements*, in a collection from this period made in Haarlem are representative of the genre. Furthermore, as with *tragedy, comedy was not in the medieval view conceived of as a dramatic production. The statement by Vincent of Beauvais (c. 1190–c. 1264) in the *Speculum maius*, that a comedy is a poem which begins in misfortune and concludes happily, is the same general conception echoed by Dante in explaining the purpose of the *Divine Comedy* (Epistle to Cangrande). Chaucer's one use of the word, at the end of *Troilus and Criseyde* (V 1788), reflects a similar understanding. The revival of theatrical comedy in the Renaissance can be traced to the production in Ferrara in 1486 by Duke Ercole d'Este of Plautus' *Menaechmi*. *Ariosto, who was taken to this performance by his father, subsequently supervised theatricals at the Este court and took Roman comedy as his model, first in *La cassaria* (1508). The *commedia erudita* was soon well established in Italy and with the rise of the *commedia dell'arte* a rich and varied theatrical tradition emerged, with fruitful interaction between the two types of comedy. Productions in Latin or translations or adaptations of Plautus and Terence were common elsewhere as well in the early sixteenth century. In England Henry VIII ordered two performances of Plautus in 1526 as part of an entertainment for the French ambassador, and the boys of St Paul's School acted Terence's *Phormio* before Cardinal Wolsey. In France *Ronsard translated Aristophanes' *Plutus* and Étienne *Jodelle is credited with the first French comedy, *Eugène* (1552). Jacques *Grévin, Jean de *La Taille, Rémy *Belleau, and Jean-Antoine de *Baïf also adapted Plautus and Terence directly or were influenced by them via Italian works. Other early translators or adapters include Jean Meschinot (c. 1420–91), Octavien Saint-Gelais (1468–1502), and Charles Estienne (1504–64). Most French comedy before Molière was written in octosyllabic verse, but the prose comedies of La Taille, *Larivey, and *Tournèbe are notable exceptions.

In Spain, Bartolomé de *Torres Naharro distinguished (in *Propalladia*, 1517) two types of play: the *comedia a noticia* (comedy of wit, emphasizing plot and intrigue) and the *comedia de apariencia* (or *de tramoya* or *de ruido*), the comedy of spectacle depending on stage machinery, scene changes, etc. The former type flourished in the voluminous work of Lope de *Vega, whose thoroughly anti-classical

recommendations in *Arte nuevo de hacer comedias* (c. 1607) include mixing comic and tragic elements and ignoring the unities.

In England the earliest important works are Nicholas *Udall's classical academic comedy *Ralph Roister Doister* (written c. 1553), *Gammer Gurton's Needle* (performed 1566), and George Gascoigne's *Supposes* (performed 1566), the first surviving prose comedy, which Gascoigne adapted from Ariosto's *I suppositi*. All three were first produced in an academic setting: in a London school, at Christ's College, Cambridge, and at Gray's Inn, respectively. Otherwise the works of *Shakespeare and Ben *Jonson, written for the public theatre or court performance, overshadow other English comedies. It has been noted that Shakespeare wrote every type of comedy – Plautine, romantic, pastoral, farce and the "dark" comedies – except satirical. This gap was filled by Jonson, whose plays are perhaps the best illustrations of the most common Renaissance view of comedy: a strong emphasis on its reformatory function in mercilessly exposing and ridiculing the vices and follies of man. Not only did Jonson observe the rules of classical construction, but he also developed a theoretical framework for his satire in the early comedies of humours and went on to write two of the comic masterpieces of the English theatre, *Volpone* and *The Alchemist*.

Commandino, Federico (1509–75) Italian humanist and mathematician. Born into a noble family at Urbino, Commandino, after studying philosophy and medicine at Padua university, returned to his native land as tutor and physician at the court of the duke of Urbino. More importantly, Commandino began to collect and to translate into Latin the major surviving texts of Greek *mathematics. Beginning in 1558 with an edition of Archimedes, Commandino went on to issue Latin translations of the *Conics* of Apollonius (1566), the *Elements* of Euclid (1572), and the *Pneumatics* of Hero (1575). He also wrote an original treatise on the centre of gravity of solid bodies (1565). At his death Commandino was working on an Italian translation of Euclid's *Elements*.

***Commedia, Divina** see Divine Comedy.*

commedia dell'arte (comedy of the craft) The improvisational comedy that takes its name from the actor's craft, in the sense of both his technique and the guild of actors. Created by Italian theatrical troups, it flourished from the mid-sixteenth to the end of the eighteenth centuries. A number of stereotyped characters were played by actors who specialized in particular roles and performed extempore from a three-act scenario that provided a mere outline of the proceedings. The emphasis was on broad comic action with all manner of theatrical business, including acrobatics, and a traditional stock of verbal and visual jests (*lazzi*). The characters were readily identifiable: Pantalone, the grasping Venetian merchant; Graziano, the pedantic Bolognese lawyer; the *miles gloriosus*, or braggart soldier, often a Spaniard (Captain Matamoros); lovers whose language was Petrarchan and Tuscan; comically coarse female servants (Franceschina); and a number of *zanni* (zanies, buffoons). The Bergamask Arlecchino and Neapolitan Pulcinella survive as Harlequin and Punch. The masked actors drew on a variety of sources and traditions and developed an enormous repertoire of dialogue and gesture. Since actors also performed in the *commedia erudita*, literary theatre was both enriched by and was a source for the *commedia dell'arte*. Guilds – for example, the Gelosi, Desiosi, Confidenti, Uniti, Accesi – were formed in the mid-sixteenth century (the first recorded in 1545) and they spread the influence of the *commedia dell'arte* throughout Europe. Distinguished, highly respected, and academically honoured actors and families of actors – for example, Francesco and Isabella Andreini and the nobleman Flaminio Scala – directed some of the *commedia dell'arte* companies.

commedia erudita (erudite comedy) Italian vernacular comedy of the sixteenth century that imitated the Latin comedies of Plautus and Terence. While the action, construction, and certain stock characters were derived from the Roman models, and the unities of time (a single day) and place were observed, the settings were contemporary Italian urban ones; the actions involved more than one plot and these drew on a wealth of postclassical stories and novellas as well as on the Latin sources. Typically the problems faced by lovers are finally resolved in marriage after much intrigue and trickery involving mistaken identities and disguises, conniving servants and other clever, shady, or gullible comic types. Major examples of the *commedia erudita* are *La cassaria* (*The Coffer*; 1508) by *Ariosto, *La calandria* (*The Follies of Calandro*; 1513) by *Bibbiena, and *La mandragola* (*The Mandrake Root*; 1518) by *Machiavelli. *La calandria* and Plautus' *Menaechmi* respectively provided inspiration for *Firenzuola's *La triunizia* and *I lucidi* (both 1549). Later examples tend to have more intricate plots, to develop moral and romantic elements, and to show the increasing influence of the *commedia dell'arte*. Among the many writers of the type are Francesco d'Ambra (1499–1558), who wrote the prose play *Il Furto* (acted 1544) and *I Bernardi* and *La cofanaria* (acted 1547/65) in verse, Anton

Francesco *Grazzini, Giovanni Maria Cecchi (1518–87), Pietro *Aretino, Annibale *Caro, and Giambattista *della Porta.

Common Life, Brothers and Sisters of the The name adopted by the followers of Gerard Groote (1340–84), a widely travelled Carthusian monk and mystic based in Holland. Groote's aim was to keep religion simple, devout, and charitable. The Brethren of the Common Life were a semimonastic order of laymen and clergy dedicated to the cultivation of inner spirituality and good works. Their classic statement of belief is encapsulated in the *Imitatio Christi (Imitation of Christ)*, attributed to Thomas à Kempis (c. 1380–1471), the most celebrated mystical work ever written and widely read during his lifetime. Although essentially medieval and conservative, the book was to have lasting significance in its tendency to personalize religion and minimize the importance of formal Christianity. The brethren's emphasis on inner spirituality greatly influenced Christian humanists and some of the reformers. Both *Erasmus and *Luther were educated by members of the movement, which was at its peak during the second half of the fifteenth century.

communications The improvement in trade and transport during the Renaissance was modest compared to that of later centuries. Travel by land and sea was still slow and dangerous. At sea most ships hugged the Mediterranean or northern coasts, but improved *navigation and ship design in the fifteenth century made sailors bolder. The development of the sea-going caravel by Portugal (c. 1430) opened the way for the conquest of the world's oceans. By the late sixteenth century Europe was part of a global network of maritime communications.

Major rivers like the Po, Adige, Ebro, and Rhine were still prime routes for travel and trade, but were becoming unpopular because of frequent tolls, marked by chains stretched across the river. Waterways were further improved by canal locks in the fourteenth century.

Travel by land was slow; at best a traveller covered sixty miles in twenty-four hours. Most travellers were pedestrians, sometimes with pack animals. Some roads were improved by paving, especially near big cities, and with adequate hostelries and policing roads could be tolerably pleasant, but most were muddy tracks, full of potholes and vulnerable to brigands. Vehicles were improved by movable front axles in the late fifteenth century and the first coaches appeared in the late sixteenth century.

Complutensian Polyglot (1522) A six-volume

Spanish edition of the Bible that made the text available for the first time in parallel columns of Greek, Latin, and Hebrew. Begun in 1502, it was edited and financed by Cardinal Francisco *Ximénes de Cisneros, who was Queen Isabella's confessor and the founder of the university of Alcalá (Latin name: Complutum), the town after which this Bible is known. The Complutensian Polyglot is an outstanding early example of humanist scholarship employed in the service of religious reform within the orthodox Church.

Compromise of Breda see Breda, Compromise of.

Comuneros, Revolt of the (1520–21) The rebellion of the Spanish nobility and commoners against their Flemish-born king, Charles I (Emperor *Charles V). On his first visit to Spain (1517), the new king enraged the nobles by his partiality for his Flemish advisers, upset the commoners by making heavy financial demands, and united the two parties against him by his manifest intention of ruling Spain as an absentee while pursuing his European ambitions. Open disaffection broke out in 1520, and for a time Charles's position seemed seriously threatened. The king however managed to win round part of the malcontent aristocracy, certain towns, notably Seville, remained loyal, and after a defeat was inflicted on the rebels at Villalar in April 1521, the revolt collapsed, leaving Charles with enhanced power and prestige.

conceptismo see under Góngora y Argote, Luis de; Quevedo y Villegas, Francisco Gómez de.

concetto (literally, concept or idea) From the seventeenth century a term also having the specialized meaning "literary conceit", essentially an elaborate and striking metaphor drawing a parallel between two very unlike objects, qualities, or experiences. Two types are usually distinguished: the Petrarchan conceit, as employed by *Petrarch in his love poems, by his imitators, (for example, the French and Elizabethan sonneteers) and by *Tasso; and the metaphysical conceit, especially associated with the verse of John Donne and the English Metaphysical poets. The Petrarchan figure typically compares the beloved's beauty (or the lover's emotions) to very dissimilar concrete objects, often with hyperbolic exaggeration. In many of Petrarch's imitators, this amounts to nothing more than the trite and conventional love imagery which Shakespeare deflates in his sonnet beginning "My mistress' eyes are nothing like the sun."

Concord, Book of (1580) The publication comprising the Lutheran statement of doctrine known as the Formula of *Concord, the three ecumenical creeds, Luther's two catechisms, the Confession of *Augsburg, the Apology for the Confession of Augsburg, and the *Schmalkaldic Articles. The book was accepted by eighty-six rulers, princes, and imperial cities, but rejected by many others, including the king of Denmark who threw his copy into the fire. It was first published in German at Dresden, and a Latin edition appeared in 1584.

Concord, Formula of (March 1577) A formulation of Lutheran faith. Its original inspiration lay in a series of articles by Jakob Andreae (1528–90) that had resulted in the Swabian-Saxon Formula of Concord (1575) and the Torgau Book (1576). The Formula of Concord clarified the Lutheran position concerning doctrines associated with *Melanchthon and *Calvin by rejecting the former's doctrine of the Eucharist and the Calvinist doctrine of predestination. It proved to be only a partial settlement of Lutheran debates since many Lutherans, especially those outside Germany, rejected its conclusions, including the king of Denmark and several important cities. For this reason the Formula never possessed the authority of the Confession of *Augsburg.

condottieri Mercenaries employed by Italian states under the system of condotte ("contracts"). Initially they were mainly foreigners, but condottieri of Italian origin grew in number as men like Niccolò *Piccinino, Francesco Sforza (see under Sforza family), and Bartolommeo *Colleoni realized the financial and social opportunities afforded by mercenary activity. Facino *Cane in Milan during the rule (1402–12) of the weak Giovanni Maria Visconti is a prime example of the over-powerful condottiere. Condottieri came from all classes. They were regarded, in Machiavelli's venomous criticism of the system, as treacherous and dedicated to the perpetuation of strife. They studied war as an art, relying mainly on cavalry armed with lances, and their heyday passed with the development of infantry and artillery in warfare.

Consensus Tigurinus see Zürich Agreement.

Constance, Council of (1414–17) The Church council convoked at Constance in southern Germany by Pope John XXIII, at the insistence of Emperor Sigismund. It is an important landmark in the history of the movement for conciliar government of the Church, and in 1415 it declared itself a "general council", that is the supreme authority within Christendom, over and above that of popes. When the council convened in 1414 there were three cardinally elected popes, one in Rome, one at Avignon, and one at Pisa. The council was successful in ending this state of affairs, the *Great Schism (*see* Avignon, papacy at), by deposing two of the contending popes and ensuring the abdication of the third. In their place the council promoted Oddone Colonna as Martin V (pope 1417–31).

In accordance with the wishes of Sigismund, the council took action against the potentially heretical and revolutionary Bohemian Hussites. Employing its new-found authority the council condemned and executed the movement's leaders, Jan *Huss and Jerome of Prague. When the council dissolved itself (1417) it left as its legacy legislation that made possible the claims of supremacy made by Church councils during the next fifty years. Although power was restored in full to the papacy by the end of the century, the Council of Constance had demonstrated papal fallibility, and support for representative conciliar government remained.

Constantinople (formerly Byzantium; now Istanbul) The city on the European shores of the Bosphorus straits, now in Turkey. Its commanding position at the entrance to the Black Sea ensured its commercial and strategic significance ever since its foundation as the Greek colony of Byzantium in 667 BC. It was refounded by Constantine the Great in 330 AD as Constantinopolis, the New Rome in the East. When the Roman empire split in 395 AD, Constantinople became the capital of the eastern part. Theological differences and rivalry between the patriarchate in Constantinople and the papacy in Rome led to schism in 1054. In 1204 forces of the Fourth Crusade, under Venetian leadership, sacked Constantinople. Attempts were made to heal the breach at the councils of Lyons (1276) and Florence (1439), but Western Christendom lacked the will to come to the aid of the Byzantine emperor in the face of the growing threat from the *Ottoman Turks. In 1453 Constantinople fell to the forces of Sultan Mehmet II.

Diplomatic contacts between Constantinople and the West in the fourteenth and early fifteenth centuries first alerted western scholars to the treasures of classical Greek literature that had been preserved by Byzantine copyists; envoys from the East tarried in Italy to teach Greek to local scholars and these scholars sometimes visited Constantinople and returned home laden with Greek manuscripts (*see* Aurispa, Giovanni; Filelfo, Francesco). As the Turks advanced, learned refugees from former Byzantine lands fled

CONSTANTINOPLE *The panorama by Pieter Coecke van Aelst, made on his visit in 1533, shows the western European's interest in the antiquities and buildings of the great city and the exotic appearance of its inhabitants.*

westwards, bringing with them their knowledge of Greek.

Once Constantinople was under Turkish rule few westerners were enthusiastic about attempting to regain it for Christendom, despite some papal efforts to muster a crusade in the 1450s and 1460s; most people were much more concerned about the threat nearer home, as the Ottomans menaced the heartland of Europe. Nonetheless there was some limited contact between Constantinople and the West during the sixteenth century. The mercantile nations such as England saw it as a promising destination for trading missions, while other visitors, like Pieter *Coecke van Aelst, who went there in 1533, were primarily interested in observing what they saw as the exotic ways of the Muslim infidels.

contado The territory adjoining an Italian city that was subject to the laws and taxes of that city.

Contarini, Cardinal Gasparo (1483–1542) Italian Catholic reformer. Born into a leading Venetian family, Contarini studied philosophy and natural science at Padua before turning to theology. He experienced spiritual conversion in 1511 and remained throughout his life sympathetic to Erasmian doctrine and humanist principles. In 1518 he became an ambassador abroad and developed a profound knowledge of Rome and the imperial court. Having been made a cardinal (1535) by *Paul III, in 1536 he was appointed head of a commission designed to initiate reform of the Church. In his work as commissioner and as papal legate at *Regensburg (1541) it is evident that Contarini failed fully to appreciate the fundamental spiritual conflict between Protestant and Catholic in his assumption that formal reorganization of the Church, coupled with certain concessions to the Lutheran doctrine of justification by faith, would achieve reconciliation. Criticized on account of his *Epistola de justificatione* (1541) as a "crypto-Lutheran" and embittered by his failure at Regensburg, Contarini died the following year. Although he never shared in the true spirit of the coming *Counter-Reformation, Contarini played a part through his keen support of *Ignatius Loyola during the early 1540s. Besides works on theological topics and ecclesiastical reform, Contarini wrote (1523/24) a renowned book on Venetian statecraft, *De magistratibus et republica Venetorum* (1543).

contrapposto A pose used especially in sculpture in the round whereby the torso of the sculpted figure is twisted and its weight thrown into one leg. This device was developed originally by the ancient Greeks in the fifth century BC and later revived in Renaissance Italy by *Leonardo da Vinci and others, being employed to great effect in Michelangelo's *David* (Accademia, Florence). The pose was equally adapted to both draped and nude figures and introduced both tension and realism, with an aesthetically interesting play of light on the different angles and masses of the sculpture. It was also used at an early date by Donatello and Verrochio, and exaggerated *contrapposto* (*figura serpentinata*) became a favourite device of the mannerist sculptors like Cellini and Giambológna.

Contucci, Andrea *see* Sansovino, Andrea.

converso In Spain, a Jew who had been converted to Christianity. Although *conversos* and descendants of *conversos*, such as Álvaro de *Luna, rose to high office in fourteenth- and fifteenth-century Spain, antisemitism was a constant factor and was institutionalized in the persecutions conducted by the *Spanish Inquisition. Curiously, some of the most zealous persecutors of the Jews were themselves of *converso* stock – the antipope Benedict XIII (Pedro de Luna; died 1423) and *Torquemada, to name but two. Particularly at risk were the *marranos*, professed converts, either Jews or Moors, who continued to practise their ancestral religion in secret.

Coornheert, Dirck Volckertsz. (1522–90) Dutch humanist and scholar. As a young man Coornheert, who was born in Amsterdam, read widely on religious matters, eventually adopting a brand of evangelical humanism which brought him into conflict with both Catholics and reformers. From 1566 he was also associated with William of Orange in the political struggle against Spain, an involvement which forced him to withdraw into exile in 1568, where he acted as the prince's political agent in Cleves. Returning to Holland in 1572, Coornheert became embroiled in a serious theological controversy with orthodox Calvinists, defending his views on free will. His writings influenced the young Arminius (appointed to refute Coornheert but in large measure persuaded by him), and he is consequently seen as one of the forebears of *Arminianism.

A truly versatile figure, Coornheert was also an engraver and book illustrator, illustrating *Noot's *Das Buch Extasis* (1576). From 1577 he was a notary at Haarlem, but moved to Delft and finally Gouda in 1588. He translated works by Cicero, Boethius, and Seneca, the *Odyssey*, and various tales from Boccaccio's *Decameron*. He also wrote poetry and plays and in his prose works, many of them polemics against the Calvinists, he strove to improve the quality of his native language. *Zedekunst* (1586) is modelled on the ethical treatises of the ancient stoics. He also began, but left incomplete, a Dutch version of the New Testament.

Copernican system The cosmological scheme advanced in *Copernicus's *De revolutionibus* (1543), contrary to the traditional geocentric astronomy of Ptolemy (*see* Ptolemaic system). In the Copernican system the universe is centred upon the sun, around which the earth and all other celestial bodies revolve with uniform motion in perfectly circular orbits; in addition the earth rotates daily around its own axis (*see* cosmology, Fig. 2). In this simple manner Copernicus accounted for the observed rotation of the heavens by the daily movement of just one body. Many, however, considered it most implausible to suppose that the earth could move in such a manner. Buildings would collapse, it was objected, and stones dropped from a hand would not fall directly to the ground. Cavils of this kind continued to be raised for some time; until, in fact, they were only dispelled by the better analysis of the nature of motion offered by *Galileo and his successors.

On the matter of planetary orbits, however, Copernicus appears less innovatory. Like Ptolemy, he assumed without question that planets moved in circular orbits with a uniform velocity. Such a theory is far too simple to describe the planets' paths as they move in their elliptical orbits with their varying velocities. Thus, to account, for example, for their variable velocities and their constantly changing distances from the sun, Copernicus found it necessary to locate each of the planets on its own epicycle. In this way he found himself as dependent upon eccentrics and epicycles as any Ptolemaic astronomer. It has been calculated that he actually increased the number of such constructions from the forty of the *Almagest* to the forty-eight found in *De revolutionibus*. Complications of this kind persisted in *astronomy until the time of *Kepler and his realization that planets moved in elliptical orbits. Damaging theological objections remained. In the Bible Joshua, for instance, had commanded the sun, not the earth, to stand still (Joshua 10:12–13). Consequently, in 1616 the Holy Office placed *De revolutionibus* on the *Index Librorum Prohibitorum where it remained until 1822.

Copernicus, Nicolaus (1473–1543) Polish astronomer. The son of a merchant, Copernicus was born at Torun and educated at Cracow university and at various Italian universities where he studied medicine and law. On his return to Poland in 1506 he served as physician and secretary to his uncle Lucas, Bishop of Ermland. On his uncle's death (1512), Copernicus took up the post of canon of Frauenburg cathedral to which he had been appointed in 1499. By this time he had already abandoned the traditional astronomy of antiquity (*see* Ptolemaic system) and had begun to formulate the revolutionary system with which his name has been associated (*see* Copernican system). The new system was first described in his *Commentariolus*, a brief tract completed sometime before 1514 and circulated in manuscript to interested scholars. Thereafter he worked out the details of the new system in an exact and comprehensive manner in his *De revolutionibus orbium coelestium* (1543; translated as *Concerning the Revolutions of the Heavenly Spheres*, 1952). Although it was complete in manuscript by 1530 Copernicus seemed, for no very clear reason, reluctant to publish his work. It was not, in fact, until *Rheticus arrived in Frauenburg in 1539 and intervened that Copernicus reluctantly allowed its publication. The work finally appeared just in time, according to popular legend, for it to be shown to Copernicus on his deathbed. There were other dimensions to the career of Copernicus. For much of his life Poland was under threat from the *Teutonic Knights and Copernicus found himself on more than one occasion besieged by them and called upon to negotiate with them. He also, in his *De monete* (1522), wrote on the topic of Poland's debased currency, and, according to some scholars, is to be credited with the first formulation of the principle, later known as Gresham's law, that "bad money drives out good" (*see* Gresham, Sir Thomas).

Cornaro, Caterina (1454–1510), Queen of Cyprus (1472–89) A Venetian noblewoman, she married James II of Cyprus (1472) in order to ally Cyprus with Venice. James died (1473), leaving Cyprus to Caterina and her unborn child (James III). After the infant James III died (1474) Caterina needed Venetian support to suppress numerous conspiracies, but Venice gradually usurped her power and forced her abdication (1489). Retiring to Asolo, near Treviso, she entertained literary figures, including Pietro *Bembo who entitled his dialogue on love *Gli Asolani* (1505).

Cornaro, Luigi (1467–1566) Italian dietician. A member of the powerful Cornaro family of Venice, he spent the first forty years of his life indulging his passion for food and drink. Threatened by his physician with death if he continued to indulge himself, Cornaro resolved to restrict his diet drastically. Initially it was reduced to a daily intake of twelve ounces of food and fourteen ounces of wine. Eventually, however, it was reduced to a single egg a day. Details of Cornaro's austere regime were revealed in his *Discorsi della vita sobria* (1558). Assuming the accuracy of his birth date, Cornaro lived to be ninety-eight.

Cornelisz., Cornelis (Cornelisz. van Haarlem; 1562–1638) Dutch painter. Cornelisz. studied under Pieter Pietersz. (Jonge Peer) in his native Haarlem before visiting Rouen and Antwerp. Back in Haarlem (1583) he collaborated with *Goltzius and Carel van *Mander in their academy. Cornelisz., who specialized in history and portrait painting, retained a strong mannerist influence throughout his working life. His bravura approach to figure drawing and foreshortening is exemplified in *The Massacre of the Innocents* (1591; Haarlem).

Corpus Hermeticum *see under* hermeticism.

Correggio, Antonio Allegri (c. 1489–1534) Italian painter. He took his name from his birthplace, Correggio, east of Parma, but otherwise little is known of Correggio's life. The obvious influence of *Mantegna on his work suggests that he may have studied in Mantua. Another influence was that of *Leonardo da Vinci, seen in the softness that is characteristic of all but his earliest work; Correggio's figures are however more sensual and

CORREGGIO Madonna and Child with SS Jerome and Mary Magdalene. *The face and gesture of St Mary Magdalene have an erotic tenderness familiar from some of Correggio's secular mythologies. (1520s; Pinacoteca, Parma)*

fleshy than Leonardo's. In about 1518 he went to Parma, where the following year he decorated a ceiling in the convent of S Paolo, before working on the dome of the church of S Giovanni Evangelista (1520–23). The resulting fresco depicted the twelve apostles on clouds around the figure of Christ ascending into heaven, sharply foreshortened as if seen from below. The same technique (known as *sotto in su*) was used with more daring foreshortening in his *Assumption of the Virgin* in the dome of Parma cathedral (1526–30), which again presents to the spectator standing beneath it a visually convincing ascent into heaven. Although the work was described by one contemporary as "a hash of frogs' legs", this masterly illusionism of Correggio's, a development of that first used by Mantegna, set the style for almost all future ceiling decorations.

Correggio's oil paintings were equally bold in their composition, particularly his altar paintings, in which he also experimented with artificial effects of light. As well as religious paintings he painted a number of voluptuous mythologies, such as *The Loves of Jupiter* for Federico Gonzaga (1530 onwards; various locations). He died in Correggio, having produced work that was to influence both baroque and rococo artists.

Corteccia, Francesco (1502–71) Italian composer and organist. From 1515 he served the church of S Giovanni Battista, Florence, in various capacities and was organist there from 1535 to 1539. In 1540 Corteccia was appointed *maestro di cappella* at S Giovanni Battista, at the cathedral, and at the Medici court. Corteccia made a substantial contribution to the early madrigal; he wrote many for particular occasions, the most famous being those composed for the wedding of Duke *Cosimo I to Eleonora of Toledo (1539). Corteccia also wrote a prologue, five *intermedii*, and an epilogue for the comedy, *Il comodo*, by Antonio Landi, which was performed at the wedding banquet. The *intermedii* were written for solo singers, ensemble, and varying combinations of instruments to depict different times of the day; these were published in Corteccia's madrigal collection of 1547. His considerable output of liturgical music is less progressive than his secular compositions.

Cortegiano, Il *see Courtier, The.*

Cortes, Hernando (1485–1547) Spanish soldier, conqueror of Mexico. Born at Medellin, Estremadura, Cortes studied law at Salamanca before emigrating to Hispaniola (1504). He married and farmed there until 1511, when he sailed with Diego Velázquez to Cuba, where he became chief magistrate of Santiago.

His eleven-ship expedition to Yucatan made landfall early in 1519. He founded a settlement at Vera Cruz and made contact with the native Indians, who were awestruck by the white men with their guns, ships, and horses. After burning his ships to discourage desertion, Cortes marched to Tenochtitlan, the Aztec capital (now Mexico City). Montezuma, the Aztec emperor, greeted Cortes as a representative of the gods, but an Aztec attack on the Spaniards at Vera Cruz soon shattered the myth of the Spaniards' divine invulnerability. Cortes went on the offensive, threw Montezuma into chains, and forced him to acknowledge Spanish sovereignty, Having drawn off some of his troops to defeat an expedition sent by Velázquez to supplant him, Cortes returned to Tenochtitlan to find fighting between the Spanish garrison in the city and the Aztecs. Montezuma was killed by his subjects while appealing for peace. The Spaniards fought their way out with heavy losses, but in July 1520 decisively defeated the Aztecs in the plain of Otumba. In August 1521 Cortes recaptured and destroyed Tenochtitlan.

Cortes's account of the conquest, in five letters to *Charles V, was published, together with the first map of Mexico, in 1524. The fall of the Aztec empire allowed Cortes to develop Mexico as a Spanish colony. He also made expeditions into Honduras (1524–26) and lower California (1536). However, Charles never entirely trusted Cortes and, despite receiving the title of marquis of Oaxaca (1529), Cortes found his authority was curtailed and he was passed over for viceroy (1535). Disillusioned, he returned to Spain around 1540 but still failed to win Charles's confidence. He eventually retired to die on his estate near Seville.

Coryate, Thomas (?1577–1617) English traveller and writer. Born at Odcombe, Somerset, Coryate studied at Winchester and Oxford, but failed to graduate. As a young man he lived in the court of James I, earning his keep as an unofficial court jester, and by exploiting his opportunistic talents to the full. In 1608 he walked through France, Switzerland, and Italy, covering 2000 miles in five months. His anecdotal account of the journey was published as *Coryate's Crudities* (1611). The following year he set out for the East, sending home reports of his experiences. Still travelling, he died in Surat, India.

Cosimo I de' Medici (1519–74), Duke of Florence (1537–74), first Grand Duke of Tuscany (1569–74) Cosimo assumed power as a youth of eighteen after his distant cousin Alessandro's assassination. Initially supported by *Charles V, Cosimo extended the Medici domains throughout Tuscany and in 1557 acquired Siena from the Spaniards, despite the efforts of *Francis I's soldiers.

Cosimo and his officials established an efficient modern despotism. Tuscan government was integrated and public services were centred on the *Uffizi, designed by Cosimo's superintendent of buildings, Giorgio *Vasari. Other public works included road building, the completion of the Palazzo Pitti for Cosimo by Bartolommeo *Ammanati, the refurbishing of the Palazzo Vecchio, and the Boboli Gardens. Cosimo supported the *Accademia della Crusca, Etruscan archaeology, and artists, such as *Michelangelo, *Pontormo, and *Bronzino. In 1564 he resigned active government to his son Francesco.

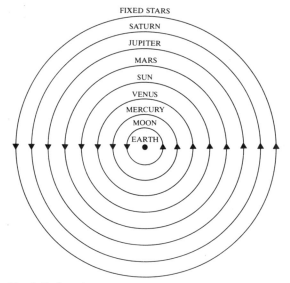

Fig. 1. Ptolomaic system
COSMOLOGY

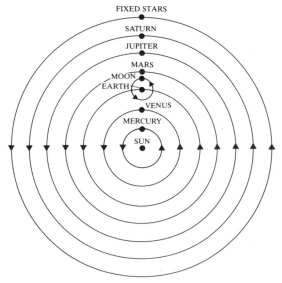

Fig. 2. Copernican system

cosmology The study of the nature of the universe. Traditional Renaissance cosmology derived ultimately from the metaphysics of Aristotle and the astronomy of Ptolemy (*see* Ptolemaic system). The universe was divided into two fundamentally distinct parts. In the heavens celestial objects, composed from an incorruptible, quintessential matter, were carried around the earth by solid crystalline spheres. All such bodies moved in circular orbits with a perfectly uniform motion (Fig. 1). In contrast, below the sphere of the moon a more degenerate matter, subject to change and composed from the four elements (earth, air, fire, and water), moved in more complex and varied ways. Superimposed upon this basically rational scheme there emerged a number of less realistic correspondences of which *astrology is the best known. By the sixteenth century traditional cosmology was under threat. *Copernicus had shown that alternatives to Ptolemy could be plausibly developed (Fig. 2), while observations by *Brahe of comets revealed the nonexistence of crystalline spheres. Work by *Galileo demonstrated that the heavens were no less corruptible than the earth. The final rejection of the traditional cosmology came with Descartes and his presentation of a more viable mechanical system.

Cossa, Francesco del (1436–c. 1478) Italian painter. Born in Ferrara, Cossa was possibly a pupil, and later a rival, of Cosimo *Tura in that city. He also absorbed the influence of Mantegna and the Florentine painters, while his best-known work, the fresco series the *Months* (completed 1470) in the Palazzo di Schifanoia in Ferrara, clearly draws on parallel works by Piero della Francesca. Painted for the Este family, the series combines astrological themes with scenes of the daily life of the court and includes contributions by several of Cossa's pupils. Cossa then spent seven years in Bologna, where he executed a notable polyptych for the altar of S Petronio (c. 1474), which included the *Crucifixion* (National Gallery, Washington) painted in the style of *Andrea del Castagno.

Costa, Lorenzo di Ottavio (c. 1460–1535) Italian painter. Born in Ferrara, Costa probably trained under *Tura and was also influenced at an early stage by the works of Ercole de' Roberti and Francesco del Cossa. Paintings from this period include *The Concert* (National Gallery, London). In 1483 he went to Bologna where he executed work for the Bentivoglio court, decorating the Bentivoglio palace and going into partnership with the Bolognese artist Francesco *Francia. After succeeding Mantegna as court painter at Mantua (1506) his style became softer and more atmos-

pheric in quality. Later works, which had a profound influence upon Giorgione, include two *Allegories* (Louvre) painted for Isabella d'Este. In his last years his reputation in Mantua was somewhat eclipsed by that of *Giulio Romano.

COSSA *A detail from* Mars and Venus. *The god of war kneels as a captive before Venus, who rides in triumph on a swan-drawn barge. This allegory of the power of love is part of Cossa's decorations for the Palazzo di Schifanoia in Ferrara.*

Coster, Samuel (1579–1665) Dutch dramatist and surgeon. Coster is important as the founder of the *Duytsche Academie in his native Amsterdam and for his Senecan-type tragedies. His *Iphigenia* (1617) was one of the anti-Calvinist satires that brought the academy into disfavour with the authorities; in other respects the tragedies, which also include *Ithys* (1615) and *Polyxena* (1619), exhibit the usual Senecan bias towards bloodcurdling horrors. Coster's farces, including *Teeuwis de Boer* (performed 1612), are written in the old *rederijker* mode (*see* chambers of rhetoric) and show little awareness of Renaissance trends.

Coster's Academie *see* Duytsche Academie.

costume With the disappearance of ancient Roman dress, even in Italy, the standard differentiation between male and female clothing was established in the early Middle Ages throughout

Europe: men in trousers (or hose) and women in skirts. In the later Middle Ages clothing became one of the principal indicators of social class, and sumptuary laws were in force in most countries to ensure that the distinctions were observed. These laws also operated to protect home-produced textiles against encroachments by foreign goods. Another area with which sumptuary laws were often concerned was the banning of fashions that might encourage sexual licence: low-cut dresses for women, exaggerated codpieces for men.

Sheep for wool and flax for linen had been familiar in Europe since prehistoric times. Silk came from the East as a luxury import until silkworm eggs were brought to Constantinople around 550 AD, and from there spread around the Mediterranean shores. Genoa, Venice, Florence, Lucca, and Milan were famous silk manufacturing centres in the Middle Ages, and in 1480 Louis XI of France set up silk weaving at Tours, an initiative followed in 1520 by Francis I, who started the Rhone valley silk industry, based on Lyons and staffed by Genoese and Florentine weavers. Furs, mainly from central and northern Europe, were worn both as necessities and luxuries; as an item of male attire the wearing of certain prestigious furs was restricted to those of royal blood, and sumptuary laws often regulated very minutely the type and quantity of fur allowable to any particular social class.

By the late fourteenth century international vagaries of fashion can be discerned. Peasant dress varied according to locality and was more dependent upon local products, but the clothes of the prosperous merchant classes and of the aristocracy show pronounced and well-documented trends. Ostentatious impracticality in dress displayed the leisured status of well-born ladies, who wore trailing skirts, long sleeves, and elaborately horned or pinnacled headdresses, which reached the peak of extravagance in fifteenth-century France and Burgundy. At the same time courtiers affected the poulaine, an extremely long and tapering toe to the shoe; such shoes were known as "crakows", a word which, like "poulaine", indicates the Polish origin of the fashion. An English statute of 1464 banned any cobbler or leatherworker from making poulaines more than two inches long. By the end of the century abruptly squared-off toes became the rage.

In the sixteenth century men's outer clothes were frequently "slashed", that is decorated with numerous parallel cuts to show off the garment underneath; this fashion was even imitated in *armour. Later they also practised "bombasting" or stuffing their garments with cottonwool or similar padding. A corresponding move away from the natural line of the body is seen in women's use of the farthin-

gale or hooped petticoat in the same period. Costume became a major form of display in Renaissance courts, particularly on such state occasions as the *Field of the Cloth of Gold. *Jewellery was attached to it in profusion, modest lace collars or frills swelled to huge ruffs, and the art of the embroiderer in gold and silken threads was lavishly employed. At a slightly lower social level the law of the land still tried to tie the wearing of certain garments to social or military obligations; thus a Tudor gentleman whose wife wore silk petticoats and velvet kirtles, the cloth for which was an imported luxury, would be expected to provide one light cavalry horse with its accoutrements in time of war.

Cotton, Sir Robert Bruce (1571–1631) English politician and bibliophile. Born in Denton, Huntingdonshire, the son of a wealthy landowner, Cotton was educated at Cambridge university, and then moved to London where he began his political career in 1601 as member of parliament for Newtown. By this time he had begun to assemble one of the finest collections of books and manuscripts ever seen in private hands. Used by many contemporary scholars, such as *Bacon, *Camden, and *Speed, it contained such items as the Lindisfarne Gospels and the manuscript of *Beowulf*. Although initially on good terms with *James I, Cotton was arrested in 1615 for involvement in the poisoning of Sir Thomas *Overbury (1613). Released soon afterwards, he was later suspected by *Charles I of sedition and arrested once more in 1629. Although released in the general amnesty of 1630 he was denied access to his own library. The collection itself was placed in the British Museum in 1753 where it remains today.

Council of Ten The Venetian body mainly responsible for state security. Its establishment dates from the investigation into Baiamonte Tiepolo's conspiracy (1310). Members were chosen for one year and could not serve consecutive terms of office. The numbers on the council varied and included the *doge and his six councillors. The council employed spies, received reports, conducted secret diplomacy, and sometimes ordered assassinations. It supervised the manufacture and distribution of artillery and munitions until 1582. After the appointment of three inquisitors of state (1539) for the secret investigation and punishment of crimes, the council was widely perceived as a sinister organization.

Counter-Reformation The reform of ecclesiastical abuses and the vitalization of spirituality were lively concerns in the decades before Brother Martin Luther's posting of the Ninety-five Theses and the beginning of the Protestant *Reformation. The early sixteenth-century Catholic Reformation continued after 1517 until, by the 1530s, it had become a vast movement of spiritual and moral renewal. The Catholic Reformation (meaning originally the reformist movement within the unitary pre-1517 Church) was therefore independent of the Protestant Reformation (meaning the reformation led by those who either removed themselves from the Roman communion or were excommunicated from that communion) and was not necessarily directed against it. Intellectuals such as Jacques *Lefèvre d'Étaples, Desiderius *Erasmus, Francisco de *Quiñones, and Juan de *Valdés (to name but a few) were all representatives of this movement. To the degree that the Council of *Trent disciplined and revitalized the ecclesiastical offices of the Church, it too was part of the Catholic Reformation. However, after 1540 there was also a desire to combat Protestantism, to counterattack, and to regain lost ground. This movement is called the Counter-Reformation. It was destructive of some of the most liberal trends of the earlier sixteenth-century Church, and it created the psychology and worship of Roman Catholicism until Vatican II in the 1960s.

The Counter-Reformation can best be discussed under the headings of theology, psychology, triumphalism, and mysticism. First, theology. Since Protestant ideas and Catholic spiritualist notions (understood to their disadvantage in the context of the Counter-Reformation) had been spread largely by preachers and the new printing press (for example, between 1517 and 1526 there were over 2000 editions of works by Luther), ecclesiastical and temporal authorities deemed it necessary to "protect" their flocks against dangerous proselytizing. Kings, princes, and civic authorities strengthened *censorship. In 1520 the first index of prohibited books was issued by Henry VIII who sought to protect England from Lutheran ideas. To guide civil authorities, the papacy finally (1559) issued its more famous *Index librorum prohibitorum. Local inquisitions and courts also took action against heretical theology. The Roman Inquisition was re-established in 1542 to rid Italy of heresy. French provincial *parlements* actively tried heretics. Temporal lords began requiring printers to acquire royal "licences" before allowing them to publish books. Should unwelcome books be published, the press could then be shut down by revoking its licence. The Roman Catholic Church organized an elaborate censorship system by which texts had to obtain a *nihil obstat* ("there is nothing objectionable") and an *imprimatur* ("it may be printed") before the press could run. It is paradoxical that the same invention, the printing press, could lead to the expansion of scholarship and the dissemination of ideas as well as to modern censorship.

The Counter-Reformation period also saw the foundation of new religious orders such as the Society of Jesus (*Jesuits). Founded by *Ignatius Loyola and a handful of companions in 1534, the order quickly grew in numbers and spread throughout western Europe. Ignatius was a soldier-mystic and, at one point, a near heretic. His *Constitutions* (first drawn up between 1547 and 1550) laid down a strict organization for the Jesuits. His *Spiritual Exercises*, the method of prayer and meditation followed by the first generation of Jesuits, exemplify the commitment, ardour, and discipline of the Counter-Reformation "Christian soldier", very different from the early sixteenth-century Catholic-Reformation model offered in Erasmus's *Enchiridion militis christiani* (1504; *Handbook of the Christian Soldier*). The single-minded passion of the Counter-Reformation is reflected in Ignatius's words: "To arrive at complete certainty, this is the mental attitude we should maintain: I will believe that the white object I see is black if that should be the decision of the hierarchical church."

The Council of Trent (1542–65) solidified the theological armamentum of the Counter-Reformation Church. Taken as a whole, the council was as dogmatic and militant as Ignatius Loyola for the Catholic camp and John *Calvin for the Protestant side. The council, a long time in coming into being and sometimes precarious in its existence, managed to define Roman Catholic doctrine for the next 400 years. It countered Protestant doctrines, issue by issue, and in this way it set forth a basically systematic ordering of Roman Catholic doctrine, thus making crystal clear who was a Catholic and who a Protestant. As one historian has noted, the medieval Church was generally more ecumenical and permissive theologically than was the post-Tridentine religious world. Peaceful coexistence of competing theological ideas was no longer possible during the Counter-Reformation era.

While there was a clear doctrinal gap between the Counter-Reformation Church and the various Protestant churches after 1560, there was also a growing psychological gap in terms of devotional practice and style of piety between the two sides. Counter-Reformation piety was characterized by a heated emotionalism, especially for the laity. The religious paintings of the late sixteenth and seventeenth centuries aimed at suggesting ideal worship practices: weeping, distorted figures, exaggerated gestures, and eyes turned piously toward heaven. Artistic examples of tearful repentance and contrition abounded: St Peter shedding tears after having denied Jesus; St Mary Magdalene's remorse for her earlier life. To encourage the Catholic viewer to share the tears and agonies of Christ on the cross as well as the martyrdoms of the saints, these scenes were pictured in gruesome detail: St Agatha having her breasts torn away; St Edward with his throat cut. Death became as much a preoccupation as it had been in the fourteenth-century plague years and quite unlike the halcyon days of the Renaissance when the epitaph on a cardinal's tomb (1541) read, "Why fear death, which brings us rest?" Now, the typical Counter-Reformation tombstone might read, "Ashes, ashes, nothing but ashes".

Triumphalism was an aspect, one could argue, of the psychology of the Counter-Reformation. However, it is distinct enough to be discussed separately. The Counter-Reformation Church was on the march in several regards. First, every attempt was made to enrich the ceremonial and feasts of the Catholic Church. The consecrated Host was displayed on feasts, proclaiming the Catholic doctrine of the Real Presence of Christ in the Eucharist, as opposed to the Protestant denials of this doctrine by *Zwingli and others. The feast of Corpus Christi was also a child of the Counter-Reformation and served triumphantly to underline the eucharistic doctrine of the Roman Catholic Church. Frescoes in St Peter's, Rome, showed Peter walking on water and healing the sick, asserting artistically the primacy of Peter and his successors against the Protestant denials of the authority of the pope. Even in New Spain the Church adopted an assertive posture, trying to make up for the falling away of Protestants from the Catholic fold in Europe by bringing new, Amerindian members into the Roman communion. And the churches of the New World were decorated just as lavishly as in Europe. In sum, the Counter-Reformation had succeeded in halting the victories of Protestantism and had begun to turn them back. The observer in 1540 might well have thought all of Europe would soon become Protestant. However, a few decades later, the same observer attending the triumphant polyphonies of *Palestrina in the Jesuit church of Gesù in Rome would see the Church once more sure of itself doctrinally and psychologically.

Mysticism was at the heart of Counter-Reformation religious emotion. In few other periods have there been such attractive mystics as at this time. Of these the two most prominent were St *Teresa of Ávila and St *John of the Cross. As individual as these two visionaries and reformers were, they are completely in harmony with the general qualities of Counter-Reform and the Council of Trent. One reason for their appeal is the harmony between the Tridentine doctrinal decrees and the assumptions of mysticism. Mystics such as Teresa and John believed that man, with the help of God's grace, could gradually perfect himself and briefly unite with God. Mysticism is totally unlike the assumptions of classical Protestantism (as exemplified by Luther and Calvin), for it is optimistic about man and God. In the mystics' planned and ordered meditations, spiritual exercises, and rigorous training of the will, sixteenth-century Roman Catholic mysticism complemented a theology which affirmed the freedom of the will, man's ability to cooperate in his own salvation, and the efficacy of good works and charity.

Courtier, The (*Il cortegiano*; 1528) The book by Baldassare *Castiglione, describing the accomplishments of the ideal courtier and portraying the court of Urbino shortly before the death of Duke Guidobaldo da Montefeltro in 1508. Written and gradually expanded between 1508 and 1524, the work, following Plato and Cicero's *De oratore*, is cast in dialogue form as the lively informal conversations of a group of courtiers and ladies. Popularizing humanist (Aristotelian and Ciceronian) ideals of the model citizen, Castiglione depicts the courtier, though necessarily of noble birth and trained in arms, as a gentleman, learned, a connoisseur, of cultivated tastes and sensibility, excelling at a variety of civilized pursuits but always with effortless grace (*sprezzatura*). The book was soon widely translated (into English by Sir Thomas *Hoby, 1561) and left a deep and lasting impact on European manners.

Couto, Diogo do (1542–1616) Portuguese historian. Born in Lisbon and educated at the Jesuit college there, do Couto sailed to India (1559), where he spent virtually all of his adult life. Philip II appointed him as royal historiographer, a position he used to expose the decadence of Portuguese affairs in the subcontinent, most notably in *Dialogo do soldado prático*. From 1602 do Couto also continued *Barros's *Décadas da Asia* on the Portuguese imperial adventure in the East. He died in Goa.

Covarrubias, Alonso de (c. 1488–1564) Spanish architect and sculptor. Covarrubias was evidently trained in the Gothic tradition and, as one of the nine consultants on Salamanca cathedral, had an opportunity at an early age to practise in an essentially Gothic style. However, his subsequent works were executed in a manner influenced by contemporary Italian trends and became good examples of the *plateresque style in Spain. Many of his most important works were executed in Toledo, where from 1504 he worked on the hospital of Sta Cruz with the late Gothic architect Enrique *Egas; on Egas's death (1534) Covarrubias succeeded him as master mason at Toledo cathedral. Of his work there, the chapel of the New Kings (1531–34) survives as a testament to his skill. Other works included the church of the Piedad at Guadalajara (1526), a fine staircase at the archbishop's palace at Alcalá (c. 1530), and the rebuilding of the Bisagra Neuva gate at Toledo (1559). As architect to the royal castles he also oversaw the rebuilding of the Alcázar at Toledo (1537–53) for Charles V.

Covilhã, Pero da (died 1525) Portuguese explorer. Covilhã, who was called after his birthplace in Beira, served at both the Castilian and Portuguese courts before being dispatched (1487) to explore the overland trade routes to the East and to discover the country of Prester John (i.e. Ethiopia). At the same time Bartholomeu *Diaz was sent to look for the southern sea route round Africa. From Barcelona Covilhã went via Naples to Rhodes and Egypt, and then to the Arabian peninsula and India. On his way back to Cairo he made a detour down the East African coast. From Cairo he sent back to Portugal a report on the feasibility of his route for the spice trade and then set out via Arabia for Ethiopia. There he was detained as an honoured prisoner of state for the remainder of his life.

Cracow A city in Poland on a strategic site on the left bank of the Vistula. Traditionally said to have been founded about 700 AD by a mythical Prince Krak, Cracow was nearly destroyed by the Tatars in 1241, but the rebuilt town prospered and in 1305 became the capital of the Polish kings, who continued to be crowned and buried in Cracow's cathedral of St Stanislas until 1764. Cracow university was founded in 1364 and played a leading role in strengthening the ties of the Polish Church with the West; the university library is housed in the fine fifteenth-century university buildings. Besides being famous as an intellectual centre in the fifteenth and sixteenth centuries, Cracow is famous for the number and beauty of its churches; the cathedral, which was substantially rebuilt in the fourteenth century, houses masterpieces by Veit *Stoss, Pieter *Vischer, Guido *Reni, and others, and the Marienkirche contains Stoss's great altarpiece of the Virgin. The former royal castle on the rocky outcrop known as the Wawel was rebuilt in the Italian Renaissance style under King Sigismund I (reigned 1506–48), who married (1518) Bona Sforza of Milan, under whose influence the court at Cracow became a major northern centre of Renaissance culture. The Sigismund chapel in the cathedral (1519–30) is an outstanding example of pure Italian Renaissance style.

Cranach, Lucas (1472–1553) German painter and print maker. Born at Kronach and initially trained by his painter father Hans, Cranach had become established at Coburg by 1501. Subsequently he travelled through the Danube area to Vienna, where he stayed until 1504 and established contact with humanists at the university. His Winterthur portraits of Dr Johannes Cuspinian and his wife, his Berlin/Nuremberg portraits of Stephan Reuss and his wife, and his Berlin *Rest on the Flight into Egypt* all date from this period. Distinguished by vibrant warm colours and lush landscape backgrounds, these are key early works of the so-called *Danube school.

In 1505 Cranach was appointed court painter to Elector Frederick the Wise at Wittenberg, succeeding the itinerant Venetian Jacopo de' *Barbari. Shortly after this, Cranach's style began to change. His *Martyrdom of St Catherine* (1506; Dresden) has a strongly decorative surface design and a light, transparent colouring reminiscent of *Dürer. Around 1506 Cranach began to produce woodcuts. Like *Burgkmair, he pioneered the two-tone *chiaroscuro* print, of which his 1507 *St George* is an early example. In 1509 Cranach visited the Netherlands. His Frankfurt *Holy Kinship* triptych (1509) revels the influence of *Metsys in its subject matter and perspectively deep architectural setting, but the shallow surface linearity of its figure grouping indicates Cranach's own future development. These decorative qualities are manifest in the full-size, full-length portraits of Duke Henry the Pious and Duchess Catherine (1514; Dresden). Both figures are portrayed in brightly coloured court dress against a flat black background, the effect emphasizing both silhouette and detail in a "heraldic" manner, reminiscent of a playing card. At Wittenberg Cranach became closely associated with Martin *Luther, who became godfather to one of the painter's children. Cranach's woodcut *Luther as Junker Jörg* (1521–22) is the first of a long series of portraits of the reformer. After the coming of Lutheranism to Saxony, Cranach concentrated increasingly upon portraits, secular themes from classical antiquity, and small religious pictures. With his Frankfurt *Venus* (1532) he perfected a particular type of slender, palid female nude which he and his workshop repeated in numerous variants until the mid-century, usually in pictures of *Venus and Cupid*, *Lucretia*, *The Nymph of the Fountain*, *Adam and Eve*, and *The Judgment of Paris*. Iconographically, an interesting departure in his later career is a series of religious pictures on novel themes acceptable to Protestant theology, such as *Christ and the Children* and *Allegory of the Old and New Testaments*. He also painted a small number of large, multi-figure compositions set against landscape backgrounds, such as the Madrid *Stag Hunt* (1545) and the Berlin *Fountain of Youth* (1546). In 1550 Cranach followed his master, Elector John Frederick, to Augsburg and in 1552 to Weimar. He died there the following year while engaged upon a large triptych, the *Allegory of Redemption*, subsequently completed by his son, Lucas Cranach the Younger (1515–86). By then Cranach was the most influential and sought-after painter in northern Germany. The author of an unique and particularly successful form of German *Mannerism, he was also the principal visual apologist of the Reformation.

Cranmer, Thomas (1489–1556) Archbishop of Canterbury (1533–56). A learned theologian and an early admirer of *Luther, in 1532 he visited leading Lutherans in Germany, where he married the niece of *Osiander. He already enjoyed royal favour for supporting *Henry VIII's first divorce, and despite his marriage, which was in contravention of his clerical vows, he became the first Protestant archbishop of Canterbury in 1533; subsequently he aided the king in his three later divorces. During *Edward VI's reign (1547–53) Cranmer worked to make the Church of England a truly Protestant Church. He encouraged publication of a new Bible in English and wrote much of the 1549 and 1552 Books of Common Prayer. *Mary I stripped him of his office. Sentenced as a heretic, Cranmer died bravely at the stake.

Credi, Lorenzo di (Lorenzo d'Andrea d'Oerigo; 1459–1537) Italian painter, sculptor, and goldsmith. Credi was born in Florence and became a pupil with Perugino and Leonardo da Vinci in the workshop of Andrea del Verrocchio. He exhibited considerable skill as a draughtsman and after Verrocchio's death he became the head of the most flourishing artistic workshop in Florence. He himself produced numerous pictures of seated Madonnas, including the *Madonna and Saints* altarpiece in Pistoia (1510). Other works were highly imitative of Leonardo's early paintings. Among his best drawings is his *Self-Portrait* (c. 1490; National Gallery, Washington).

Crete *see under* Candia.

criticism, literary Theoretical discussion of the nature, kinds, and purpose of literature (as opposed to "practical" or applied criticism or guides to technique) originated and attained most sophistication in Italy. The common assumption in Renaissance criticism, as in the neoclassicism which succeeded it, was that literature imparted knowledge or truths. This view was usually stated in the Horatian formulation, that poetry combined delight and instruction, *dulce et utile*, these functions being taken rather simply and distinctly,

with scant attention to their possible interactions. In the first part of the fifteenth century in Italy, the recovery of classical authors, the cultivation of Latin style, and the role of classical rhetoric in the humanist conception of the active, public life produced the ideal of a poet-orator, emulating the ancients and bringing honour to his city and himself. By the end of the century, vernacular literature was thriving and soon reached full maturity. Systematic criticism developed in the course of the sixteenth century, stimulated by the publication of Aristotle's *Poetics* (the Aldine edition of the Greek text appeared in 1508). The commentaries and poetic treatises that followed were mainly concerned with the theory of imitation, with the genres, and with related matters arising from the interpretation of Aristotelian ideas. The *Poetics*, transmitted in the Middle Ages through Averroes's commentary, was freshly translated into Latin (by Giorgio Valla, 1498, and Alessandro Pazzi, 1536) and Italian (Bernardo Segni, 1549). Commentaries on it were written by Francesco Robortello (1548), Vincenzo Maggi (1550), and Lodovico *Castelvetro (1570). While admitting imitation (of anything, not merely human actions and emotions) as an object of the literary work, Robortello is concerned with rhetorical persuasion rather than Aristotelian description and maintains the emphasis on the Horatian goals of moral instruction and aesthetic pleasure (one source of which is the marvellous). Castelvetro strays further from Aristotle's descriptive intention by reducing formal analysis, stressing rhetorical effect, and admitting only pleasure as the purpose of the literary work. The imitation of models – specifically of Virgil and Cicero for Latin verse and prose, with Petrarch and Boccaccio as the vernacular equivalents – was central in Pietro *Bembo's arguments (*De imitatione*, 1512; *Prose della volgar lingua*, 1525) and decisive in resolving the *questione della lingua*. *Vida's *De arte poetica* (1527), a verse treatise in the Horatian style which continued to influence eighteenth-century neoclassicism, accepted imitation as the goal of poetry, Virgil as the ideal model, and epic as the supreme genre. *Trissino's *Poetica* (parts 1–4, 1529; 5–6, essentially a translation of the *Poetics*, 1563) is perhaps the most important early vernacular treatise, with extensive treatment of prosody and rhyme and examples drawn from Italian poetry to illustrate points. *La poetica* (1536) by Bernardino Daniello of Lucca (c. 1500–65), a disciple of Bembo, is the earliest work to take up the question of verisimilitude. *Cinthio's two theoretical discourses on drama and romance comment on many critical issues and are notable for a certain originality. Though influenced by Aristotle, he prefers the Roman and Senecan to the Greek model in tragedy and defends Ariosto

LORENZO DI CREDI
Madonna and Child with
Saints.

and the romance (as a legitimate and distinct type of narrative). The dialogue *Naugerius* (1555) by Girolamo Fracastoro (1498–1553) takes into account the theories of Plato, Aristotle, and Horace. Julius Caesar *Scaliger (*Poetices libri septem*, 1561) emphasizes the didactic and moral purpose of art, which is held to be superior to nature, ranks Virgil above Homer, and gives clear definition to the genres. Minturno's work (*De poeta*, 1559; *Arte poetica*, 1563) is the most comprehensive of Renaissance poetics in its coverage of the mimetic theory, the rules of decorum and definition of genres (adding lyric to the traditional ones of drama and narrative), and influenced *Tasso, *Ronsard, *Sidney, and later neoclassicism. The *Della rhetorica* (1562) of Francesco *Patrizi presents a Platonic view opposed to the dominant Aristotelianism.

In France critical theorizing began with the poets of the *Pléiade, whose ideals were definitively stated in *du Bellay's *Défense et illustration de la langue française* (1549). It was much indebted to *Speroni's *Delle lingue* (1542), which followed Bembo in arguing for the imitation of classical models as a means of improving the vernacular.

De Bellay's manifesto greatly enhanced the prestige of French – a suitable vehicle, he argued, for the most exalted subjects – and promoted the influence of Greek, Latin, and Italian forms of French verse. The excesses (especially in diction) and artificiality that eventually resulted were successfully countered by *Malherbe, who laid the foundations for French neoclassicism.

Although *Bacon and *Ascham in England expressed misgivings about the use of the vernacular in preference to Latin, the *English language was both unified and solidly established in literary use in the sixteenth century and consequently one dimension of critical debate, so important in Italy and France, was minimized. More common than critical treatises in Elizabethan England were practical guides to writing or versifying, such as, for example, Gascoigne's *Certayne Notes of Instruction Concerning the Making of Verse or Rhyme in English* (1575) and Puttenham's *Arte of English Poesie* (1589). The outstanding work of apologetics, reflecting a number of the principal themes of Renaissance criticism, was Sir Philip *Sidney's *Defence of Poesie* (1595). Probably written in the early 1580s, this treatise contains a list, significant in its brevity, of English literary works considered by Sidney as worthy of critical attention in that they possessed "poeticall sinnewes": Chaucer's *Troilus and Criseyde*, *The Mirror for Magistrates*, Surrey's lyrics, and *Spenser's *Shepheardes Calender*.

criticism, textual As defined by the scholar poet A. E. Housman, "the science of discovering error in texts and the art of removing it". In as much as it is a matter of the application of common sense to emend slips of the the pen or keyboard, we practise it every day when we try to read a newspaper. In as much as it is a matter of the application of a set of rules (all of which are firmly based on common sense) to facilitate the restoration of a classical or biblical text, it is the product of a gradual but erratic development at the hands of scholars from the time of the Alexandrians (third century BC) to the present.

The Alexandrians, notably Callimachus, Aristophanes of Byzantium, and Aristarchus, were concerned to ensure the survival of all extant Greek literature in its purest (i.e. most accurate) form. This involved the acquisition and collation of the oldest and best manuscripts by means of which a "critical" edition approximating as closely as possible to the author's own words could be produced for the benefit of future readers. Their prime legacy to subsequent generations of textual critics was fidelity to tradition, and this remained the aim of the best scriptoria (centres of copying) throughout antiquity and for most of the Middle Ages.

During the fourteenth century scribal practices began to change. Less attention was given to the tradition, far more to the exercise of subjective "correction" of texts to make them conform with arbitrary notions of authenticity or readability. Motives varied from bowdlerization to meddling for its own sake, but most alterations that were deliberately introduced were the result of downright stupidity.

Happily there were exceptions. Demetrius Triclinius, for example, a schoolmaster in Thessalonica in the first quarter of the fourteenth century, made a notable contribution to the transmission of Greek tragedy and was personally responsible for the survival of about half of the plays of Euripides that we know today. In the West the Italian scholar and poet *Petrarch made similar contributions to the transmissions of Livy and Propertius.

In the fifteenth century, as the humanist tradition grew, and with it the fashion for collecting books and in particular the literature of the ancients, the pressure mounted on scribes to make more and more copies. The sudden proliferation of poor-quality texts was inevitable, but scholarly standards continued to be upheld in some quarters.

Lorenzo *Valla, who went so far as to emend the Vulgate itself, exposed the so-called Donation of Constantine, purportedly a fourth-century document, as a later medieval forgery on historical and linguistic grounds. Angelo *Politian, probably the first Italian to be equally at home in Latin and Greek, saw his way through the welter of humanist copies to establish principles about the earliest recoverable stage of a textual tradition that were not to be superseded for three centuries.

Coincident with the proliferation of ancient texts was the invention of *printing. Most of the principal classical Latin authors had found their way into print by the end of the fifteenth century. Typographical difficulties held up the printing of Greek texts, but by the time of his death in 1515 Aldus *Manutius had overseen the first printing of most of the major authors. The survival of ancient literature was finally ensured, but the price was the quality of the text. In their haste to publish printed versions the early printers had often seized the first manuscript that came to hand, giving it at best a veneer of critical attention. For the next 300 years the activity of textual critics was to be dominated by the need to unpick the tangled web created by these first editions.

Crivelli, Carlo (c. 1435–c. 1495) Italian painter. Born in Venice, Crivelli probably trained in the *Vivarini family workshop and was later influenced by the painters of Padua, including Schiavone and Mantegna. After being imprisoned for adultery Crivelli left Venice and settled in Ascoli Piceno in the Marches (1468), developing a contemplative and highly ornamental style and concentrating upon executing religious scenes. Major paintings include the *Madonna della Passione* (c. 1457; Museo di Castelvecchio, Verona), a *Pietà* (1485; Museum of Fine Arts, Boston), and the *Madonna della Candellata* (c. 1490; Brera, Milan), but he is best known for the *Annunciation* (1486; National Gallery, London), an exotic and eccentric masterpiece.

Croce, Giovanni (c. 1557–1609) Italian composer. A native of Chioggia, near Venice, and pupil of Gioseffo *Zarlino, Croce sang in the choir of St Mark's as a boy. He took holy orders before 1585 and was employed for much of his life at the church of Sta Maria Formosa. In 1603 he became *maestro di cappella* at St Mark's. Croce wrote in an essentially conservative style; his madrigals and canzonettes are lightly textured with attractive melodies, and his sacred compositions are generally small-scale, with simple melodies and straightforward harmonies. The posthumously published *Sacre cantilene concertate* (1610) shows the adoption of the more modern *concertato* style. Croce's main influence outside Italy was as a madrigalist, and his contribution to *Il trionfo di Dori* (1592) probably inspired *Morley to compile *The Triumphs of Oriana*.

Crocus, Cornelius (c. 1500–50) Dutch educationist and playwright. Crocus was born in Amsterdam and after studying at Louvain was ordained a priest. He then became (1528) headmaster in Amsterdam, a post which he held until the year before his death, when he resigned it in order to travel on foot to Rome, where he was received by Ignatius Loyola into the Jesuit Order. He engaged in religious controversy against *Luther and the *Anabaptists, wrote a popular textbook to assist children to form a correct Latin style (1536), and composed several Latin dramas for performance in schools. Of these the *Coemedia sacra Joseph* (1535) was the most successful, achieving over twenty editions and being imitated as far afield as Poland (*see* Rej, Mikołaj).

Croll, Oswald (c. 1560–1609) German chemist and physician. The son of the mayor of Wetter, near Marburg, Croll studied at a number of German universities, then spent several years travelling throughout Europe. Thereafter he practised medicine and in about 1602 entered the service of Prince Christian of Anhalt-Bernberg. He is also reported to have served subsequently as a councillor to Emperor *Rudolf II. As a scientist Croll is best known for his *Basilica chymica* (Royal Chemistry; 1609), a highly influential text which did much to spread the ideas of *Paracelsus throughout Europe. The work also contained his *De signaturis*, an account of the widely held doctrine of *signatures.

Cromwell, Thomas (c. 1485–1540) English statesman. The son of a blacksmith at Putney, Cromwell fought for the French in Italy before qualifying as a lawyer. In 1514 *Wolsey appointed him collector of the see of York's revenues. Cromwell entered parliament in 1523 and was made a privy councillor in 1531. As *Henry VIII's most trusted servant in the 1530s, Cromwell became chancellor of the exchequer (1533), lord privy seal (1536), lord high chamberlain (1539), and earl of Essex (1540). From 1535, as Henry's vicar-general, Cromwell carried out the English Reformation, dissolving the monasteries and confiscating their property (1536–39). He arranged the king's fourth marriage to Anne of Cleves, but when the marriage failed Cromwell fell from favour and was executed.

Cronaca, Simone, Il (Simone del Pollaiuolo; 1457–1508) Italian architect. Cronaca was born in Florence and mainly worked there, apart from a period in Rome (1475–85), where he gained an understanding of classical architecture. In 1495 he built the Sala del Consiglio (now Sala dei Cinquecento) of the Palazzo Vecchio to accommodate the council instituted by *Savonarola on the lines of the Venetian *Maggior Consiglio. He carried on *Benedetto da Maiano's work on the Palazzo Strozzi, probably designed the Palazzo Guadagni, and also executed Giuliano da *Sangallo's design for the vestibule and sacristy of S Spirito. The church of S Salvatore al Monte, near Florence, which Cronaca built at the end of his life, is a model of classical simplicity and restraint, and was praised by Michelangelo.

cross-staff *see under* backstaffs.

cryptography The science of devising and deciphering codes and ciphers. Simple ciphers were well known in antiquity. Like the basic Caesar alphabet, in which plaintext letters were replaced by letters three places further along the alphabet, they were invariably simple substitution ciphers. Such methods were readily employed in the Renaissance, for example, in the correspondence of the Avignon popes during the *Great Schism. Before long, however, skilled cryptographers such as François *Viète could be found attached to most courts, happily reading the encoded correspondence of their enemies.

The obvious step of complicating the cipher by using different alphabets to encode different parts of the plaintext was first proposed by *Alberti. Later generations of Renaissance cryptographers were left to work out precisely how polyalphabetic substitution could be deployed in practice. Alberti himself attempted to introduce polyalphabeticity by the use of two cipher discs, the setting of which could be changed for the encoding of each letter. A further step was taken by *Trithemius in his *Polygraphia* (1518) in which he replaced the cipher discs of Alberti with the more familiar and useful rectangular tableau of alphabets. Precisely how such complicated ciphers could be made to operate with easily remembered and easily changed keys was shown by Giovanni Belaso in *La cifra* (1553). The various innovations of Alberti, Trithemius, and Belaso were assembled and presented in a more convenient form by Blaise de *Vigenère in his *Traicté des chiffres* (1586). To their work he added the important notion of an autokey which, by using the plaintext as the key, endowed such ciphers with considerable security. So successful did Vigenère ciphers prove to be that they remained, when carefully constructed, indecipherable until the work of Friedrich Kasiski in the mid-nineteenth century.

Cueva, Juan de la (1543–1610) Spanish dramatist. On returning from Mexico (1577), where he had gone with his brother in 1574, Cueva wrote plays for the public theatre in his native Seville. These were produced between 1579 and 1581, after which he devoted himself to verse and other writing, none of which is significant. *Exemplar poético*, a verse treatise on poetics, appeared in 1609. *La Conquista de Bética* (1603), his attempt at epic on a patriotic subject, has more historical than literary interest. His fourteen surviving verse plays, ten comedies and four tragedies, were published as *Comedias y tragedias* (1584). Three are based on classical subjects (for example, a tragedy on the death of Virginia, taken from Livy) and three on fictional sources. His important contribution, however, was introducing material drawn from Spanish historical chronicles and ballads. Examples of these are *La muerte del rey Don Sancho (The Death of King Sancho)* and *Los siete infantes de Lara (The Seven Infantes of Lara)*. His allegorical play, *El infamador*, has similarities to the Don Juan legend and influenced *Tirso de Molina's *Burlador de Sevilla* (1630). Cueva's mediocre work is rhetorical, Senecan, and scarcely dramatic at all, but in adapting national themes for the stage he anticipated the truly Spanish drama of great playwrights of the Golden Age like Lope de *Vega.

culteranismo *see under* Góngora y Argote, Luis.

Cupid (*or* Amor) The god of love, usually depicted as a young winged boy with bow and arrows and flaming torches. He is the Roman equivalent of the Greek Eros, and is generally shown in the company of his mother *Venus (Greek Aphrodite). Another characteristic feature is that Cupid is often depicted as blind, or at least blindfolded, as in Botticelli's *Primavera* and *Titian's *The Blindfolding of Amor* (Galleria Borghese, Rome); the Renaissance Neoplatonic interpretation of the blindness of love rejected the original notion that it symbolized uncomprehending animal passion and exalted it into a symbol of love's superiority to both body and intellect. Cupid also features in two other scenes that were vehicles of Neoplatonic allegories: Mercury teaching Cupid to read (an allegory of intellectual love), exemplified by Correggio's picture of the subject in the National Gallery, London, and the love of Cupid and *Psyche (the desire of the soul for divine love and their eventual union).

Following the Hellenistic tradition that there was not just one Eros, but a number of Erotes, Renaissance painters often depict several Cupids attending on Venus. These have a decorative function indistinguishable from that of the *putti* (Italian: young boys) found in both sacred and profane art.

Cusanus, Nicholas (Nicholas of Kues *or* Cusa; 1401–64) German philosopher and theologian. Born at Kues on the Moselle, the son of a poor family, he entered the service of Ulrich, Count of Manderscheid, who supported him first while he studied at Deventer with the Brethren of the Common Life, then at Padua where he became a doctor of law (1423). He entered the Church and was entrusted with several important diplomatic missions, eventually becoming papal legate in Germany (1440–47). Nicholas V made him a cardinal (1448) and bishop of Brixen (1450). In 1451 he was sent to Germany to reform the monasteries but came into conflict with his secular lord, Archduke Sigismund, and was for a time imprisoned. He retired to Umbria where he died. His valuable library was left to the hospital he founded in Kues.

Cusanus was important both as a philosopher and as a Church reformer. He rejected scholasticism and in *De docta ignorantia* (1440) he maintained that humans could gain no certain knowledge and that God can only be apprehended by intuition. This idea was basic to the mysticism of Giordano *Bruno. Cusanus was also a scientist and mathematician. He proposed reforms of the *calendar similar to those later undertaken by Pope Gregory XIII, anticipated part of the Copernican theory by claiming that the earth rotated and was not the centre of the universe, and professed in *De quadratura circuli* to have squared the circle.

Cyriac of Ancona (Ciriaco de' Pizzicolli; 1391–1452) Italian merchant and antiquarian with a particular interest in classical Greece. He travelled in Italy, Egypt, Greece, and the Near East, drawing monuments, copying inscriptions, and collecting manuscripts, statuettes, and medallions. His notebooks (Commentaries) and collection, although not published until the mid-eighteenth century, proved valuable to archaeologists and classical scholars.

Czech Brethren (*or* Bohemian Brethren) A group representing a radical but peaceful side of the Hussite church of Bohemia. After the suppression of the militant Taborites in 1434, the Czech Brethren became the group most closely associated with the evangelical and social views of the early Hussites. Although possessing a sectarian tendency in their discipline and organization, they did demonstrate a desire for Protestant unity. Connections were established between Wittenberg and the brethren and it was for them that Luther wrote his *Adoration of the Sacrament* (1523). Under the leadership of Jan Augusta in 1532, they endeavoured to create greater unity through negotiation with Luther, Calvin, and Bucer, but this bore little fruit. The brethren suffered persecution between 1548 and 1552 and many fled to Poland and Prussia. *Maximilian II granted the Czech Brethren freedom to practise their religion (1575), and under *Rudolf II they played a leading role in education, but after the battle of the *White Mountain (1620) they were dispersed and eventually merged with other groups. *See also* Blahoslav, Jan.

D

Daddi, Bernardo (active 1290–c. 1349) Italian painter. A gifted pupil of *Giotto, Daddi absorbed the seriousness of his master and combined it with the lyrical grace of the painters of Siena, becoming the leading artist in Florence during the 1340s. His earliest dated work was the *Madonna* triptych (1328; Uffizi), which was based upon Giotto's *Madonna Enthroned*, originally in the same church. The influence of the Sienese school is evident in Daddi's *Enthroned Madonna* (c. 1340; Uffizi), which reflects the style of the Lorenzetti brothers and Simone Martini in particular. Daddi also painted a number of notable smaller panels, such as *The Story of St Cecilia* (Museo Civico, Pisa), which demonstrate his skill in the handling of colour. Other works still in Florence include a *Madonna* (1347; Orsanmichele) and two frescoes showing the martyrdoms of SS Lawrence and Stephen (Sta Croce). Daddi's influence remained profound throughout the fourteenth century.

Dalmau, Luis (fifteenth century) Spanish artist. A native of Valencia, Dalmau visited Bruges (1431) and Flanders before returning to Spain by 1437. There he worked as court painter to Alfonso V of Aragon (*Alfonso I of Naples). An admirer of van Eyck, he imitated the approach of the Flemish school in his own *Virgin of the Councillors* (1445; Barcelona museum), which was painted in the already outdated International Gothic style and is his only surviving documented work.

dance of Death (*danse macabre, Totentanz*) A pictorial and literary theme originating in the late Middle Ages, in which Death, usually in the form of a skeletal musician, leads away representatives of every class of society, from pope to beggar, from emperor to peasant. The dance of Death appeared first in the form of murals in churches, the earliest being recorded in Paris, dating from the mid-1420s (now destroyed). Other early examples of dance of Death murals were to be found elsewhere in France, in England, Switzerland, Germany, and Italy. It was also treated in other media – stained glass, tapestry, embroidery, and sculpture.
The first printed edition of a dance of Death cycle combining verses and woodcuts issued from the Parisian press of Guyot Marchant in 1485. Prior to that, manuscript versions of the dance of Death texts had appeared in both Spain (*Dança general de la muerte*, c. 1400) and Germany (the Lübeck *Totentanz*, 1463). The most famous treatment of the theme was by Hans *Holbein the Younger in a series of fifty woodcuts designed about 1523/24 and printed at Lyons in 1538.

Daniel, Samuel (1562–1619) English poet. Daniel was probably born near Taunton, went to Oxford in 1579, and then may have visited Italy. In the 1590s he was tutor to William Herbert, and from this congenial literary milieu he published his first poems, the sonnet sequence *Delia* and the *Complaynt of Rosamond* (both 1592). His Senecan tragedy *Cleopatra* was published in 1594. The first edition of his major work, a long poem in eight-line stanzas on the *Civil Wars* (i.e. the Wars of the Roses), appeared in 1595; a considerably revised and enlarged version came out in 1609, showing Daniel's subtle and thoughtful approach to political philosophy. His *Defence of Rhyme* (1602) is a refutation of Campion's tract on the unsuitability of rhyme in English verse. He wrote a number of court masques and was eventually put in charge of a troupe of boy actors, the Children of the Queen's Revels (1615–18). He was a friend and brother-in-law of John *Florio.

Daniele (Ricciarelli) da Volterra (1509–66) Italian painter and sculptor. Trained under Sodoma, Daniele is best known as a close associate of Michelangelo. After moving to Rome in about 1541, he executed several notable frescoes, the most celebrated being the *Deposition* (1541) in the Orsini chapel in Sta Trinita dei Monti, in which his skill as a draughtsman is evident. Daniele is, however, usually remembered as the artist who was commissioned to paint loincloths on the nude figures in Michelangelo's *Last Judgment* in the Sistine Chapel – for which he acquired the nickname "Il Braghettone" (the breeches maker). He also produced a bronze portrait bust (c. 1564; Bargello, Florence, and Louvre) of Michelangelo and was present at the latter's deathbed.

danse macabre *see* dance of Death.

Dante Alighieri (1265–1321) Italian poet. Alighiero d'Alighiero, Dante's father, was a Florentine Guelph typically belonging to the lower nobility. His mother died while he was a child; his father remarried and had nine children by his second wife. Dante received a sound education though little is known of it in detail; he studied rhetoric under Brunetto Latini and in his youthful verse came under the influence of *Cavalcanti. His marriage, to Gemma di Manetto Donati, was arranged, taking place soon after his father's death in 1283; there were two sons (Pietro and Jacopo) and perhaps daughters by the marriage.

Dante fought in the battle of Campaldino (1289) and for several years took part in public life. He was one of the six priors (chief officials of the council) of Florence in 1300 when strife between the Black and White factions of the Guelph party led to the exile of Cavalcanti, among others. The following year Dante, who opposed papal policies, was taking part in a delegation to Boniface VIII when the Blacks seized control of Florence and condemned him to exile. The possibility of returning only arose when Emperor Henry VII, whom Dante supported, entered Italy in 1310, but the failure of the emperor's cause and his unexpected death (1313) put an end to Dante's hopes. The long period of exile was spent in apparently extensive wanderings, during which Dante found refuge with Cangrande della Scala in Verona and finally with Guido da Polenta in Ravenna, where he died. The *Vita Nuova* (*New Life*; 1292–1300), lyrics joined by prose commentaries, concerns Dante's love for Beatrice, a figure who later plays a major role in the *Divine Comedy*. The historical existence of Beatrice is doubtful; she was perhaps the daughter of Folco Portinari, later the wife of Simone de' Bardi, and died in 1290. Dante says that he met her when she was nine and again when she was eighteen years old. He finds solace for his grief at her death in the consolation of philosophy (as conceived by Cicero and Boethius). The *Convivio* (*Feast*; 1304–08) and the Latin treatise *De vulgari eloquentia* (*On Eloquence in the Vernacular Tongue*; after 1304) are unfinished. The former alternates poems with prose explanations but only four of the proposed fourteen sections are complete. The latter discusses the origin and growth of languages and the use of the vernacular in poetry; it looks forward to issues raised in the *questione della lingua*. Among other works are *De monarchia* (*On World Government*), a treatise of doubtful date presenting Dante's argument for a temporal power centred in Rome, and *Canzoniere*, poems inspired by Beatrice but excluded from *Vita Nuova*. Dante also wrote a number of other miscellaneous poems and several Latin epistles.

Dante chair *see under* furniture.

Danti, Vincenzo (1530–76) Italian goldsmith and sculptor. His earliest sculpture is a monumental bronze figure, *Pope Julius III Enthroned*, outside the cathedral (1553–56) of his native Perugia. From 1557 until 1573 Danti worked as a court sculptor to Duke Cosimo I in Florence. His masterpiece there was a bronze group on the baptistery, the *Beheading of St John the Baptist* (1571): these and all his other figures are gracefully elongated and set in balletic poses characteristic of mannerist sculpture. For the Medici he cast in bronze a large narrative relief of *Moses and the Brazen Serpent* for the altar frontal of a chapel and a cupboard door (1561), both now in the Bargello, as well as a statuette of *Venus Anadyomene* for the Studiolo of Francesco I in the Palazzo Vecchio (c. 1573). Danti also carved marble statuary during the 1560s (e.g. *Honour triumphant over Falsehood* and *Duke Cosimo I*, both in the Bargello). He published in 1567 a treatise on proportion and retired after 1573 to Perugia, where he was appointed public architect and was a founder member of the Accademia del Disegno. Danti's sculpture has a delicacy of detail and an elegance of line reminiscent of other goldsmiths-turned-sculptor, such as *Ghiberti and *Cellini.

Danube School The collective name given various sixteenth-century artists working in the region of the River Danube in southern Germany and Austria. Although links can be established between particular individuals, the artists never functioned as a group, and opinions differ widely on exactly which artists should be accounted members. The unifying theme of their work, however, is love of landscape for its own sake; the Danube artists can be seen to have introduced landscape painting into German art. The painters usually seen as having developed the Danube style are Lucas *Cranach in his early years, Jörg Breu (c. 1475–1537), and Rueland Frueauf the Younger, all of whom probably visited Vienna during the first five years of the sixteenth century. The workshop of Jörg Kölderer, court painter to Emperor Maximilian I, may have provided a focus here. Albrecht *Altdorfer is generally considered the outstanding representative of the Danube style, which was continued by Wolfgang *Huber and many other minor figures. It is usually taken to apply to painters, but sculptors, architects, and other artists were also influenced by it.

Danzig (Polish: Gdansk) A city and port at the mouth of the River Vistula on the Baltic Sea, now in north Poland. First mentioned as a Polish city in the late tenth century, Danzig gained municipal self-government (1260) and became an important Hanse town (*see* Hanseatic League) and trading centre by the end of the Middle Ages. After its long occupation by the *Teutonic Knights (1308–1466), Danzig was regained by King Casimir IV of Poland. Under Polish rule in the fifteenth and sixteenth centuries Danzig became the most prosperous Baltic port, exporting grain and timber and developing a successful shipbuilding industry; its first warship was launched in 1572. In 1520 Danzig was involved in the Polish Teutonic war. In 1525 King Sigismund I of Poland intervened to crush the artisans who had seized church property and proclaimed the city's adherence to *Luther.

Datini, Francesco di Marco ("the Merchant of Prato"; c. 1335–1410) Italian merchant. From his home town of Prato, near Florence, he built up a trading empire in northern Italy, Avignon, Aragon, and Majorca. After 1378 he settled in Florence, joined the silk guild there, and used his surplus wealth to embark on banking. His letters and account books have survived, affording an unparalleled insight into the life and values of a wealthy bourgeois in fourteenth-century Italy.

Daucher, Hans (c. 1485–1538) German sculptor. Active in Augsburg, Hans was the son of the sculptor Adolf Daucher (c. 1460/65–1523/24) and executed a number of works for Emperor Charles V and the dukes of Württemberg. Noted for his small decorative bronze figures, he also produced the influential group of *Christ with the Virgin and St John* for the altar of the Fugger Chapel in Augsburg.

Daurat, Jean (Jean Dorat *or* Dinemand; 1508–88) French humanist scholar and poet. Daurat was born at Limoges. As principal of the Collège de Coqueret from 1547, he numbered among his pupils *Baïf, *Ronsard, *Belleau, and other members of the group that became known as the *Pléiade, to whom he communicated his love of classical literature. His work on the texts of the Greek dramatists, whom he also translated, his lectures on Homer, and his study of Pindar and later Greek poets ensured his place in the history of scholarship. In 1555 Daurat became tutor to the children of Henry II; from 1556 until his retirement in 1567 he held the chair of Greek at the Collège de France. Daurat wrote prolifically in Greek and Latin throughout his academic career, publishing (under his Latin sobriquet "Auratus") a collection of his poetry, *Poemata*, in 1586. He did not, however, excel as a writer of French verse.

David, Gerard (active 1484–1523) Netherlands painter. He was born at Oudewater, near Gouda, and in 1484 entered the Bruges painters' guild, of which he became dean in 1501. He was admitted to the Antwerp guild in 1515, but had returned to Bruges by 1519. Few of David's works are documented, but a large group of paintings is attributed to him. His early work, such as the London *Christ Nailed to the Cross*, has a brutal realism related to Hugo van der *Goes's work and the Dutch tradition. In the Bruges *Justice of Cambyses* diptych (1498) the flaying alive of the unjust judge is depicted with an excruciating objectivity. The slightly later altar shutter of *Canon Bernardinus de Salviatis and Three Saints* (London) reveals a perceptive study of the work of Jan van *Eyck. A high point in David's art is reached with the strikingly monumental Bruges triptych of *The Baptism of Christ* (c. 1509). Later artists, including *Metsys and *Gossaert, began by following David's precepts before discovering a new formal vocabulary in Italian art.

Davis's quadrant *see* backstaffs.

de Bry family A family of engravers including Theodor (1528–98), a refugee from Liège, and his sons Johann Theodor (1561–1623) and Johann Israel (fl. 1570–1611). Frankfurt, a centre for the production and sale of illustrated books, was their home from 1590, though Theodor worked in England in the late 1580s. All three worked on the *Collectiones peregrinationum...* (*Grands et petits voyages*), which was begun in 1590. After the death of Johann Theodor his son-in-law Matthäus Merian (1593–1650) of Basle, a member of another family of engravers, took over and finished the book in 1634. The 1590 part includes a section on America, with several pictures based on drawings by John White, an official artist with Raleigh's expedition to Virginia in 1585. Johann Theodor de Bry also produced a *Florilegium novum* in 1611, one of the most famous flower-books of the period.

Decameron, the The collection of stories written by *Boccaccio between about 1348 and 1353 and related in the fictional framework of a court set up for ten days (hence the title) in the Tuscan countryside by ten young people fleeing from the plague in Florence. The hundred stories (one per day from each of the seven ladies and three youths) range in tone from the most exalted and refined to the pornographic and comprise the first great masterpiece of Italian prose. *Bembo later proposed it as the ultimate model for prose writing in the vernacular. The *Decameron* also contains some of Boccaccio's greatest lyric poetry in the *canzone* with which each day ends. The work's influence throughout Europe is incalculable, with stories like that of patient Griselda, the archetypal submissive wife, being retold in many different forms in several languages.

DE BRY *The titlepage of the 1612 edition of Johann Theodor de Bry's* Florilegium novum *advertises the book's outstanding copperplate engravings.*

Dedekind, Friedrich (c. 1525–98) German satirist. Born in Hannover, Dedekind became a Protestant pastor. While a student at Wittenberg he wrote *Grobianus sive de morum simplicitate libri duo* (1549), one of the famous satires of the age. A book of anecdotes in Latin verse, which owes much to *Brant's *Narrenschyff*, it lampoons boorish, selfish behaviour (particularly table manners) by ironically praising it. The book went into twenty editions in the sixteenth century, with others in the seventeenth. Freely translated into German in 1551, it was even more popular in this form. Dedekind's later works are less noteworthy.

de Dominis, Marc Antonio (1566–1624) Dalmatian churchman. A brilliant student and teacher and member of the Jesuits, de Dominis left the order in 1596 and six years later became archbishop of Spalato. Siding with the Venetians in their protests against papal claims and eventually

repudiating the pope's authority, he was obliged to relinquish his archbishopric (1616) and flee to England. He was warmly received by James I and made dean of Windsor and master of Savoy (1617) and the same year began publication of his classic indictment of Rome, *De republica ecclesiastica*. Personal conflicts and political considerations led to his departure from England and attempted reconciliation with Rome in 1622 by means of a vehement attack on the Anglican Church (1623). He died in Rome, a captive of the Inquisition.

Dee, John (1527–1608) English mathematician, antiquary, and magus. The son of a London gentleman, Dee was educated at Cambridge and Louvain. He led an extremely varied life, travelling widely throughout Europe, and moving easily from mathematics to antiquarianism, and from commercial activity to occultism. In this last field Dee was to be found in 1586 in Prague with the medium Edward Kelley conjuring up spirits and supposedly conversing with them. More practically, Dee advised the Muscovy Company on the possibility of a *northeast passage to China and on the development of improved navigational instruments. As well as being the author of such hermetic texts as his *Monas hieroglyphica* (1564), he also contributed a famous *Preface* (1570) to the first English translation of Euclid, in which he argued eloquently for the need for technically trained workers to develop England's trade and industry. At his Mortlake home Dee had assembled one of the finest libraries in England. It was sufficiently impressive to attract visits from Queen *Elizabeth in 1575 and 1580, but in 1583 it was partially destroyed by a mob on account of Dee's reputation as a wizard.

Defenestration of Prague (1419) The incident marking the beginning of the Hussite revolution in Bohemia. Popular support for Jan *Huss expressed after his execution (1415) prompted King Wenceslas to impose upon Prague a town council of reactionary German merchants. Their persecution of leading Bohemian reformers led to a rising by the Prague mob which resulted in the magistrates' being hurled out of the windows of the town hall and impaled on pikes held by the mob below. Less than three weeks later (16 August 1419) Wenceslas died of a stroke, and the Hussite wars began in earnest.

Defenestration of Prague (1618) The incident that sparked off the Thirty Years' War. When Ferdinand (1578–1637), Archduke of Styria, was elected king of Bohemia (1617) and chosen to succeed Matthias as emperor, the Bohemian Protestants feared for their religious and civil freedom. In May 1618, invading the Hradschin

Palace, Prague, they broke up a meeting of the imperial commissioners by throwing two Catholic councillors and their secretary out of the window.

della Casa, Giovanni (1503–56) Italian churchman, diplomat, and writer. Belonging to a prominent Florentine family, Della Casa was probably born at Mugello and he studied literature and law at Bologna and Greek at Padua before going to Rome in 1532. He followed an administrative and diplomatic career in the Church, becoming archbishop of Benevento and papal nuncio to Venice in 1544. During the pontificate of Julius III he withdrew to Venice and devoted himself to writing (1551–55). He was recalled by Pope Paul IV and made Vatican secretary of state a year before his death. The Petrarchan poems collected in *Rime* (1558) were much admired by contemporaries, but he is chiefly remembered for the influential and widely translated prose work *Il Galateo* (1558), in which an older gentleman advises a younger on manners and conduct and tells stories to make moral points. It is indebted both to Boccaccio's *Decameron* for an informal un-Ciceronian style and to Castiglione's *Courtier* for its ideals of behaviour.

della Porta, Giacomo (c. 1537–1602) Italian architect. Born in Rome, della Porta trained under Michelangelo and was later influenced by *Vignola, developing a style based upon academic Mannerism. He is best known for completing works by Michelangelo, including the Palazzo dei Conservatori on the Capitol and, most notably, the dome of St Peter's basilica (1586–90), to the designs for which he and Domenico *Fontana made a number of alterations. Sometime after 1572 della Porta completed the façade for Vignola's Gesù, the mother church of the Jesuit order, and then incorporated features of Vignola's design into several of his own churches in Rome, including Sta Maria dei Monti (1580–81), S Atanasio (1580–83), and S Andrea della Valle (1591).

della Porta, Giambattista (c. 1535–1615) Italian natural philosopher, crytographer, and dramatist. After a period of study and travel throughout Europe, Porta returned to his native Naples where he published his *Magia naturalis* (1558; translated as *Natural Magick*, 1658). An immensely successful work (some twenty-seven editions are known), it distinguished between the magic of sorcery, which della Porta rejected, and natural magic. Under this latter term he included familiar yet mysterious phenomena taken from such fields as magnetism, hydraulics, optics, and chemistry, and sought to explain them in terms of attractions, sympathies, fascinations, and antipathies. The book also contains one of the earliest descriptions of the camera obscura. More original, although less well known, is his *De furtivis literarum* (On Secret Writing; 1563), a work of *cryptography in which he provided solutions to a number of simple polyalphabetic ciphers. His *Phytognomonica* (1589) expounds the doctrine of *signatures. Della Porta was also a leading figure in two early scientific societies. He helped to establish in Naples in 1560 the *Academia secretorum naturae, the first such modern society, and in 1610 he became a member of Cesi's *Accademia dei Lincei in Rome. In addition, from 1589 onwards, della Porta also published some twenty plays in prose and verse, some of which were translated in England and France.

della Porta, Guglielmo (c. 1500–77) Italian sculptor. Born in Milan, Guglielmo is first recorded working with other, older members of his sculptor family at Genoa in 1534. In 1537 he went to Rome, where he became the principal sculptor to Pope *Paul III. He was appointed to the office of the papal seal (*piombatore*) upon the death of its holder, the painter *Sebastiano del Piombo (1547), and executed busts of the pope in bronze and marble. He was an admirer of Michelangelo, until their dispute over the nature and location of a monument to Paul III in St Peter's, of which Michelangelo was architect: this was Guglielmo's major work and now stands to the left of the high altar, though he had initially hoped that it would stand free under the dome. The bronze seated portrait statue of the deceased pope was a major contribution to a series in St Peter's ranging from St Peter himself, through Pollaiuolo's Pope Innocent VIII, to the baroque figures by Bernini and Algardi. The reclining *Virtues* below recall Michelangelo's *Times of Day* in the Medici chapel. Della Porta was a prolific draughtsman and also produced many smaller statuettes and reliefs of religious subjects in gold, silver, or bronze.

della Robbia, Luca (1399/1400–1482) Italian sculptor. Luca della Robbia's significance as a sculptor in marble and bronze has been overshadowed by the popularity of his and his family's works in terracotta. The complex steps and secret formulas which Luca invented employed the lead-based glazes already in use by ceramicists to create enamelled terracotta sculpture; they became the basis for a family industry in his native Florence, which was continued by his nephew Andrea (1434–1525) and other relatives into the sixteenth century. Luca was trained as a marble carver, however, and his first important commission was for ten marble reliefs for an organ loft (known as the Cantoria) for the cathedral of Florence (1431–38; Museo dell'

Opera del Duomo), the classical design of which was probably suggested by Brunelleschi. Luca's figures of singing, dancing, and music-making angels combine naturalism, as seen in the ease of movement and well-observed detail, with idealism, evident in the beauty of the figures and the classically balanced compositions. Luca's reliefs offer a refined degree of surface finish which is impressive but not, as Vasari was the first to point out, completely appropriate for works to be seen from a distance in the relatively dark interior of the cathedral.

More satisfying are Luca's first large coloured terracotta reliefs, the *Resurrection* and the *Assumption of Christ* (1442–45, 1446–51), in lunettes above the sacristy doors and near the location of Luca's and Donatello's pendant *Cantorie*: the luminous colours and lucid, Renaissance compositions of Luca's terracottas enhance their readability in the dark interior. Enamelled terracotta proved an ideal and relatively economical medium for both interior and exterior architectural decoration, and Luca contributed to a number of important Florentine monuments, including Michelozzo's tabernacle at S Miniato (1448), Brunelleschi's Capella dei Pazzi (c. 1442–52; *Twelve Apostles, St Andrew*, cupola), the Medici palace (c. 1460; *Labours of the Months*, for the *studietto* of Piero de' Medici, now Victoria and Albert Museum, London), and a ceiling with *Virtues* for the chapel of the cardinal prince of Portugal at S Miniato (1461–66). Luca also combined marble reliefs with enamelled terracotta, as in the tabernacle (1441–42) now at Peretola and the monument of Bishop Benozzo Federighi (1454–57; now Sta Trinita). Luca's blue and white Madonna and Child compositions are among the sweetest and most serene of Quattrocento relief Madonnas; they offer a convincing sense of physical presence in concert with a gentle humanity. He also used enamelled terracotta for such free-standing sculptures as *Two Kneeling Angels Carrying Candlesticks* (1448–51; cathedral, Florence) and a *Visitation* (before 1445; S Giovanni Fuorcivitas, Pistoia).

Between 1464 and 1469 Luca collaborated with Michelozzo and Maso di Bartolommeo in the design and execution of a set of bronze doors with saints for the cathedral sacristy. The Florentine biographer Antonio Manetti (1423–97) included Luca in his *Uomini singolari in Firenze* (Illustrious Men of Florence), crediting him with the innovation of enamelled terracotta and praising him as a moral and intellectual individual.

della Rovere family A Ligurian family of obscure origins which acquired wealth, power, and status during the papacy of Francesco della Rovere (Pope *Sixtus IV; 1471–84). An enthusiastic nepotist, Sixtus generously bestowed cardinal's hats and lordships on his nephews. Giovanni della Rovere (1457–1501), whom Sixtus made lord of Senigallia, married the daughter of the last Montefeltro duke of Urbino; their son succeeded to the duchy in 1508 and the della Rovere family ruled Urbino until the extinction of the line in 1631. Sixtus made his nephew Giuliano a cardinal (1471); as *Julius II (pope 1503–13), Giuliano proved to be one of the ablest and most efficient Renaissance popes and further enhanced his family's prestige. He was known for his opposition to simony and nepotism.

della Scala family The rulers of Verona from 1259 to 1387. Mastino I (d. 1277) was the first to control Verona. Della Scala power in northeast Italy reached its highest point under Cangrande I (1311–29), who conquered Vicenza (1312–14), Padua (1317–18), Bellino, and Feltre and was imperial vicar of Mantua (1327). The family's fortunes declined when Mastino II (died 1351) provoked a hostile Florentine-Venetian coalition and lost all his territories except Verona and Vicenza. The *Visconti defeated the della Scala and annexed their territories in 1387. The della Scala were admired for their public works and patronage of scholarship and letters; *Dante was sheltered by them in Verona in the early fourteenth century.

Delorme, Philibert (Philibert de l'Orme; c. 1510–70) French architect. The son of a master stonemason in Lyons, Delorme became acquainted with contemporary Italian works, as well as with the antiquities, while living in Rome (c. 1533–36), where he executed work for Pope Paul III. Delorme returned to Lyons in 1536 and the same year designed the Hôtel Bullioud there for the finance minister of Brittany. In 1540 he was appointed controller of fortifications at Lyons and subsequently embarked (1541–47) upon his first major building, the château of St-Maur-des-Fosses near Paris for Cardinal Jean du Bellay, whom Delorme had met in Rome. Appointed superintendent of buildings under Henry II in 1548, Delorme built for him the Château-Neuf at St Germain-en-Laye (1557), and for Henry's mistress *Diane de Poitiers, the Château d'Anet (1547–52) and the bridge at *Chenonceau (1556–59). Although Delorme fell from favour after Henry's death in 1559, he was later commissioned by Catherine de' Medici to build the palace of the *Tuileries in Paris (1564), his last major work.

Noted for his success in combining Italian humanist ideas with traditional French achitecture, Delorme also wrote two books on architectural theory, *Nouvelles Inventions pour bien bastir* (1561) and *L'Architecture* (1567); of the latter only the first part of a projected nine appeared. He designed the tomb of Francis I at St-Denis (1547), and also undertook additions to the palace of Fontainebleau (1548–58) and work on Notre Dame. Most of his buildings are now destroyed.

Deschamps, Eustache (c. 1346–c. 1406) French poet. Born at Vertus and educated by Guillaume de *Machaut, Deschamps went on to study law at Orleans and served Charles V and Charles VI in a variety of diplomatic and administrative offices, including that of *maître des eaux et forêts* in Champagne and Brie. He wrote poetry in his spare time and after his retirement, producing over a thousand ballades and nearly two hundred rondeaux on patriotic and moral as well as traditional themes; one of his ballades is addressed to the English poet Geoffrey Chaucer, "grant translateur" (great translator). Deschamps's other writings include an important treatise on versification, *Art de ditier* (1392); a satire on women, *Miroir de mariage*; and a number of dramatic works, notably the *Farce de Maître Trubert et d'Antroignart*.

Desiderio da Settignano (c. 1430–64) Italian sculptor. Few facts are known about this precocious and brilliant, but short-lived sculptor. Born in the stone-quarrying village of Settignano, near Florence, he probably learned to carve from his family and later collaborated closely with Antonio *Rossellino. He was influenced by Donatello, but cannot have been trained by him, for the master was in Padua during the relevant decade. Desiderio was a successful imitator of Donatello's shallow-relief carvings (*rilievo *schiacciato*), which he used specially for Madonna reliefs. He was not interested in the darker, dramatic side of Donatello, but excelled in sweeter subjects, such as portraits of women and children. His two main commissions, both in Florence, were: the Marsuppini monument in Sta Croce (c. 1453), which was an elaboration on the theme of Bernardo Rossellino's Bruni monument, and the altar of the sacrament in S Lorenzo (finished 1461).

Des Périers, Bonaventure (c. 1510–c. 1544) French writer and humanist. He was born at Arnay-le-Duc and after collaborating with *Olivetan on his translation of the Bible and with *Dolet on the *Commentarii linguae latinae*, Des Périers became *valet de chambre* and secretary to *Marguerite de Navarre, whom he assisted with the transcription of her *Heptaméron*. In 1537 he produced the controversial *Cymbalum mundi*, a satirical attack on Christianity in the form of four allegorical dialogues, which was banned soon after publication. Des Périers is believed to have committed suicide in 1544. His *Nouvelles Récréa-*

tions et joyeux devis, a collection of short stories providing a lively and realistic picture of sixteenth-century society, was published posthumously in 1558.

Desportes, Philippe (1546–1606) French poet. Born at Chartres, Desportes entered the French court during the reign of Charles IX and enjoyed the patronage of the duke of Anjou, with whom he travelled to Poland. After the latter's accession to the French throne as Henry III Desportes superseded *Ronsard as court poet and received a number of lucrative benefices, including the abbacy of Tiron. Desportes's love poetry, stylistically influenced by *Petrarch, *Ariosto, and other Italian poets, consists largely of sonnets and elegies commissioned by his patrons for their mistresses: his *Premières Oeuvres* appeared in 1573 and his *Dernières Amours* in 1583. In the latter part of his life Desportes produced a series of translations of the Psalms, which brought adverse and perhaps unmerited criticism from his enemy *Malherbe.

Des Prés, Josquin (c. 1440–1521) French composer. First mentioned as a singer at Milan cathedral in 1459, he was in the employ of Duke Galeazzo Maria Sforza by 1474. After the duke's assassination (1476) Josquin joined the service of his brother, Cardinal Ascanio Sforza, with whom he travelled to Rome in 1484. From 1486 Josquin sang in the papal choir. Around 1501 he appears to have been in France, possibly as unofficial court composer to King Louis XII. His five-part *De profundis clamavi* may have been written for Louis's funeral in 1515. From 1503 to 1504 he was *maestro* to Duke Ercole d'Este. In 1505 Josquin was back in France, at Condé-sur-l'Escaut, where he was provost at the cathedral, and where he died. Josquin is generally regarded as the greatest composer of the High Renaissance. In the last two decades of his life his music was disseminated through printing, and his fame is partly due to the work of the Venetian printer *Petrucci. Josquin was a prolific composer; about twenty Masses, a hundred motets, and seventy-five secular works survive. He developed the techniques of Mass composition, notably the canon, paraphrase, and parody styles. In the late *Missa Pange lingua* the hymn melody underlies all the movements of the work, but it is subtly paraphrased rather than being employed as a *cantus firmus*. Josquin's motets are less conservative in style. For his many chansons he elaborated on melodies from popular music of the time. The compositional techniques he employed are similar to those found in his sacred works; through abandoning the *formes fixes* in his secular music he opened the way for greater stylistic variety.

Deutsch, Niklaus Manuel (c. 1484–1530) Swiss artist, poet, soldier, and statesman. Born in Berne, Deutsch popularized many of the concepts of the Italian Renaissance in northern Europe and adopted them himself in portraits, drawings, and paintings, mostly executed between 1515 and 1520. Many of his works dwell on the morbid subjects of ghosts and death, as in the case of his best work *The Dance of Death*, painted for the Dominican monastery at Berne and, having been destroyed in 1660, now only known by copies. Other works include a *Judgment of Paris*, a *Pyramus and Thisbe*, and a *Beheading of John the Baptist*. Deutsch was also an active member of the Berne city councils, a proponent of the Reformation, and author of such satires on ecclesiastical affairs as *Der Ablasskrämer* (1525) and *Testament der Messe* (1528).

Devereux, Robert, Earl of Essex *see* Essex, Robert Devereux, Earl of.

Devotio Moderna (Modern Devotion) A lay religious movement that emerged in the late fourteenth century. It was founded by Gerard Groote (1340–84), whose followers were known as the Brothers and Sisters of the *Common Life. Their aim was to keep religion simple, devout, and charitable, and they played an important part in restoring monastic virtues among the laity and in the monasteries themselves. Devotio Moderna has been criticized as anti-intellectual and anti-theological, but has also been praised as the source of all religious reforms during the sixteenth century.

Diana In Roman antiquity, the virgin goddess of the hunt, frequently identified with the Greek goddess Artemis, sister of Apollo. Diana was endowed by medieval and Renaissance iconographers with many of the attributes of Artemis, in particular the latter's association with the moon. As patroness of chastity, Diana was often evoked by artists and writers who wished to compliment a lady, and in the case of Elizabeth I of England the eulogizing of the queen as Diana, under a variety of names, became a cult, strongly promoted by the cult object herself. She appears for instance as Cynthia (one of Artemis' names) in Raleigh's poem "The Ocean to Cynthia" and as Belphoebe in Spenser's *Faerie Queene* (Phoebe was another of Artemis' names).

The myth of Actaeon, who surprised Artemis/Diana bathing with her nymphs and was turned into a stag and torn to pieces by his own hounds, is the subject of a fine painting by Titian (c. 1560; Harewood House). A marble statue of Diana in the character of a huntress, with stag and bow (c. 1549), which formerly stood in the grounds of *Diane de Poitiers's Château d'Anet, is attributed

to *Goujon, the subject a compliment to his patroness.

Diana, La (1559) A Spanish pastoral romance by Jorge de *Montemayor. It was an immense success, especially among the courtly audiences previously devoted to the romances of chivalry. The prose narrative, in seven chapters with interspersed lyrics, essentially concerns the love of Sereno for Diana, who is married to Delio. The meandering story, with passages of rich descriptive detail, involves an enchantress and magicians, a magic potion, nymphs, and a number of other complications, marvels, and relationships. Love is portrayed as irrational and painful but ennobling. Though a lesser work than Sannazaro's *Arcadia*, which it imitates, it was frequently reprinted and widely translated; it influenced a number of later pastoralists, in Spain notably Gaspar Gil Polo (*Diana enamorada*, 1564) and Cervantes (*La Galatea*, 1585). In England it influenced Sidney's *Arcadia*.

Diane de Poitiers (1499–1566) French noblewoman. Beautiful and talented, Diane married Louis de Brézé, Grand Seneschal of Normandy, in 1515. As mistress of *Henry II from the mid-1530s, she exerted considerable influence at the French court, forcing Queen *Catherine de' Medici to accept second place. Taking advantage of court rivalries between *Montmorency and the *Guise she played a decisive role in the allocation of positions of power and profit. She also patronized the architect *Delorme, who built her Château d'Anet (1547–52), and the sculptor *Goujon. After Henry II's death (1559) the widowed queen took her revenge and drove Diane from court.

Díaz del Castillo, Bernal (c. 1492–c. 1581) Spanish historian and soldier. Born at Medina del Campo, he sailed to Central America with de Avila in 1514. Subsequently he joined several expeditions, serving Cortes during the invasion of Mexico (1519) and the expedition to Honduras (1524–26). In 1568 he wrote *Historia verdadera de la conquista de la Nueva Espana* (The True History of the Conquest of New Spain; 1632) which contains vivid eyewitness accounts of personalities, events, and places involved in the conquest of Mexico.

Diaz de Novaes, Bartholomeu (died 1500) Portuguese navigator, discoverer of the Cape of Good Hope (1488). Diaz was of noble parentage, although the date and place of his birth are unknown. His first major voyage was to the Gold Coast as navigator in 1481. King John II was impressed by Diaz and in 1487 sent him with three ships to chart the African coast and explore possible routes to India. A prolonged storm forced him southwards and by the time he sailed north again, he had unknowingly rounded the Cape of Good Hope. He followed the coast eastwards as far as the Great Fish River before discontent among his crew forced him to turn back, but he did not return before ascertaining the north-eastwards trend of the coast. This confirmed the feasibility of a route round Africa to India. Diaz was received enthusiastically when he arrived back in Lisbon, but with Vasco da *Gama established as court favourite he was never given independent command again. He was lost at sea off the Cape of Good Hope on *Cabral's expedition.

Digges, Leonard (c. 1520–71) English mathematician. Little is known of Digges's early life other than that he was born in Kent, trained as a lawyer, and was caught up in the rebellion of Sir Thomas Wyatt. Sentenced to death in 1554, he was later reprieved. Digges belonged to the first generation of English mathematicians who sought to apply their newly acquired skills to the practical arts. To this end he produced some of the earliest surviving English texts on surveying (*Tectonicon*, 1556), geometry (*Pantometria*, 1571), and, as augmented by his son Thomas Digges (died 1595), the application of the "Science of Numbers" to military matters (*Stratioticos*, 1579).

Discalced Carmelites *see under* Carmelites, Reform of the.

dissection Little dissection of human cadavers took place before the Renaissance. Consequently, much of the anatomical knowledge of antiquity was derived misleadingly from the study of barbary apes, domestic animals, and the occasional human corpse. The main source of bodies for Renaissance students were those presented for autopsy. Outside this, anatomists were forced back on their own resources. As a result medical students, as in Bologna in 1319, found themselves prosecuted for grave robbing. Although arrangements were made in 1442 to allow the medical school to receive two executed corpses annually, the supply remained quite inadequate. Consequently, *Vesalius could still be found a century later haunting cemeteries and competing with marauding dogs for skeletal remains. In his entire career he seems to have seen no more than six female corpses.

Even when corpses were available, the anatomical custom of the day did little to advance knowledge. The actual dissection itself was often conducted by an illiterate demonstrator while the anatomist himself merely read from a supposedly authoritative text. Given the conditions under which they had to work, it is hardly surprising that few Renaissance anatomists could feel sufficiently confident in their work to challenge the authority of their dissecting manuals. *See also* anatomy; Galenism, Renaissance.

Divine Comedy The poem by *Dante, begun in exile in 1306 and allegorically describing the poet's (by implication mankind's) journey through life to salvation. The *Commedia* (as originally entitled, "divine" being a later addition) is the central and culminating literary work of medieval Europe. It is systematically structured in *terza rima*, with three *cantiche* (*Inferno*, *Purgatorio*, *Paradiso*), each having thirty-three *canti* (plus an introductory canto to the *Inferno*), and with each of the realms having nine subdivisions.

The action takes place in the year 1300. The poet is lost in a wood and unable to escape. Virgil, representing Reason, is sent by Beatrice, representing divine Revelation, to guide the poet's descent into Hell so that through a knowledge of sin he may acquire humility and finally ascend to Paradise. Dante's judgments on a number of people and issues are reflected in the historical persons who populate Hell and in the imaginative punishments meted out to them. The penitential mood continues, but with renewed hope, in *Purgatorio*, at the end of which Virgil vanishes and Dante is reunited with Beatrice. *Paradiso* is devoted to an exposition of religious life and the poetry is gradually simplified to an imagery of light as the work ends with a vision of divine love.

Manuscripts extant from the period up to Dante's death (1321) number 600, and the first printed edition (1472) was followed by many others. *Boccaccio instituted the first public lectures on Dante in Florence (1373), and a vast amount of critical commentary has accumulated since.

Divino, El *see* Morales, Luis de.

Dodoens, Rembert (1517–85) Flemish physician and botanist. His *Crüydeboeck* (1554) owes much to *Fuchs's herbal, including its illustrations. *Clusius translated it into French (1557), a version used by Henry Lyte for his *Niewe Herball* (1578). Lyte's translation and Dodoens's last book, *Stirpium historiae pemptades sex* (1583), were among *Gerard's sources for his *Herball*.

doge The head of state or chief magistrate in the republic of Genoa (1339–1797) and Venice (697–1805). Influential in medieval times, the Venetian office of doge became increasingly ceremonial with real power residing in the *Maggior Consiglio. While the dogate in Venice played an important role in the city's admired constitutional stability, the Genoese doges tended to have short and tumultuous terms of office until the sixteenth century when Andrea *Doria reformed the system with biennial elections to the position. The dogate in both cities was abolished by Napoleon.

dolce stil nuovo The "sweet new style" of lyric verse between about 1250 and 1300. The term was coined by *Dante (*Purgatorio* XXIV 57), who lists Guido Guinizelli (c. 1240–76), *Cavalcanti, and himself among the practitioners (*De vulgari eloquentia*). Later critics have added other names. It greatly influenced *Petrarch and through him many later poets. Characterized by musicality, the spiritualization of courtly love conventions, and a mystical and philosophical strain in the close analysis of love, the style was adopted in sonnets, *canzoni*, and ballads, the culminating examples being the poems inspired by Beatrice and gathered by Dante in his *Vita nuova*.

Dolet, Étienne (1509–46) French humanist and printer. Born at Orleans, Dolet was forced to abandon his law studies at Toulouse on account of his outspoken involvement in several controversial issues. He moved to Lyons, where he produced his two major works: *Dialogus de imitatione ciceroniana* (1535), in which he defended his fellow-Ciceronians against the attacks of *Erasmus, and *Commentarii linguae latinae* (1536–38), a significant contribution to Latin scholarship. In 1538 he set up as a printer, publishing the works of his friends *Marot and *Rabelais and his own translations of classical literature and the scriptures. He was the first to translate Platonic dialogues into French. Dolet was imprisoned at least four times: on the first occasion he had been accused of killing a painter, apparently in self-defence, for which he received a royal pardon; he subsequently faced three charges of atheism, based on his publication of allegedly heretical writings, notably a dialogue (attributed to Plato) denying the immortality of the soul. He was burned at the stake in the Place Maubert, Paris.

Domenico da Cortona (Le Boccador; 1470–1549) Italian architect and woodcarver. Domenico executed most of his best-known works in France, where he arrived in 1495 at the summons of Charles VIII. Responsible for the furthering of many Italian ideas in France, Domenico probably designed the wooden model for the Château de *Chambord, which was begun in 1519. A development of the designs of Giuliano da Sangallo, the model included such novel features as a double central staircase and had a profound influence upon subsequent architects in France. Other works included the design of the Hôtel de Ville in Paris (1532).

Domenico Veneziano (died 1461) Italian painter. Probably a native of Venice, Domenico was first recorded in Perugia in 1438, when he wrote to the Medici family asking for commissions; he settled in Florence in 1439. Noted for his interest in the effects of light upon colour, Domenico was employed upon a fresco cycle in S Egidio in Florence (1439–45), now lost, upon which he was assisted by *Piero della Francesca. Only two signed works by Domenico survive, the earlier being the Carnesecchi tabernacle (c. 1440; National Gallery, London), which reveals the influence of Masaccio. His greatest work was the altarpiece (c. 1445; Uffizi and elsewhere) painted for the church of Sta Lucia de' Magnoli in Florence, an early example of the *sacra conversazione*, showing the Madonna and Child with four saints. One of the predellas from this altarpiece, an exceptionally beautiful and hieratic *Annunciation*, is in the Fitzwilliam Museum, Cambridge. Other works sometimes attributed to Domenico include several profile portraits, an *Adoration of the Magi* (date unknown; Staatliche Museen Preussischer Kulturbesitz, Berlin), and *SS John and Francis* (Sta Croce, Florence), which echoes the style of *Andrea del Castagno.

Donatello (Donato di Betto Bardi; 1386–1466) Italian sculptor. A Florentine by birth, Donatello was the greatest sculptor of the early Renaissance and one of its key figures, alongside *Ghiberti, *Masaccio, *Brunelleschi, and *Alberti. He was one of the pioneers of linear perspective. Deeply concerned with the revival of Greco-Roman culture and realism in art, he nonetheless remained sincerely Christian.

First documented as an assistant to Ghiberti on the models for the reliefs on the north doors of the baptistery (1404–07), Donatello became a rival, allying himself with Brunelleschi. For public corporations such as the board of works of the cathedral and the guilds of Florence, he carved a succession of over-life-size statues in marble that indicate his rapid progress away from his Gothic beginnings (e.g. the marble *David*; now Bargello, Florence), via a transitional statue, *St John the Evangelist*, for the cathedral façade (1408; now Museo dell'Opera del Duomo, Florence), to full-blown Renaissance figures like *St Mark* (1411–13; Orsanmichele) and *St George* (1415; Bargello). These were followed by a series of increasingly expressive statues of Old Testament prophets for the campanile (1415–36; now Museo dell'Opera del Duomo). By imaginatively combining his study of Roman portrait statuary with his observation of contemporary Florentines, Donatello single-handedly created a new sculptural style with a maximum dramatic effect. He later pursued this vein in woodcarvings of *St John the Baptist* (1438; Frari

Dondi, Giovanni de

church, Venice) and *St Mary Magdalene* (c. 1455–60; Museo dell'Opera del Duomo).

Donatello also invented *rilievo *schiacciato,* a technique of very shallow carving for narrative reliefs which approximated the effect of drawing and shading on paper; this allowed the sculptor much greater freedom to suggest depths, movement, and emotion. The progressive milestones in this mode are *St George and the Dragon* (c. 1415; Bargello); the *Ascension of Christ* (Victoria and Albert Museum, London); the *Assumption of the Virgin* (S Angelo a Nido, Naples); the *Feast of Herod* (c. 1435; Musées des Beaux-Arts, Lille). These reliefs are quite unparalleled and were imitated only by *Desiderio da Settignano and by *Michelangelo in his youth. His friezes of *putti* on the Cantoria of the Duomo in Florence and on the external pulpit of Prato cathedral, both carved in the 1430s, show his highly individual interpretation of antique motifs.

Donatello's favourite patron was Cosimo de' *Medici, for whom he created many and various sculptures, including the reliefs in Brunelleschi's old sacristy and, later, the bronze pulpit in S Lorenzo, and for the newly built Medici palace the bronze statues of *David* (Bargello) and *Judith and Holofernes* (Palazzo Vecchio). Outside Florence, his greatest sculpture is in Padua, where he spent a whole decade (1443–53): this comprises the first surviving equestrian monument since ancient times, the statue to *Gattamelata, and statues and panels for the high altar of the basilica (il Santo). Donatello also worked in Rome and Siena. In each of these artistic centres, his fully developed Renaissance style made a great impact on the local schools, which were fundamentally still late Gothic in character and mood. In Padua and Siena, where he worked exclusively in bronze, he founded a strong tradition – *Bellano, Severo, and *Riccio in Padua, *Vecchietta and *Francesco di Giorgio in Siena. In his native Florence his principal followers were, in marble carving, Desiderio da Settignano and *Michelozzo, and, in bronze casting, *Verrocchio, *Pollaiuolo, and *Bertoldo. The latter formed a living link between the elderly Donatello and Michelangelo.

Dondi, Giovanni de (1318–89) Italian astronomer and horologist. Born at Chioggia, near Venice, the son of a physician and clock maker, Dondi followed his father Jacopo (1293–1359) and taught medicine and astronomy at the universities of Padua and Pavia. Jacopo was reported to have built an astronomical clock in 1344 in Padua. Shortly afterwards, probably with his father's help, Giovanni began work on his own clock. Completed in 1364, it was sited in the Visconti castle in Pavia. Though long since destroyed, details of the clock

GIOVANNI DE DONDI *A reconstruction of Dondi's famous astronomical clock, made with the aid of Dondi's manuscript account of his invention. (Smithsonian Institute, Washington)*

are preserved in Giovanni's lavishly illustrated 130 000-word manuscript. More concerned with celestial movements than the hourly recording of time, the brass weight-driven clock had seven sides, displaying much astronomical and calendrical information. It contained the most advanced gearing then constructed and remained unsurpassed in design until the mid-sixteenth century.

Doni, Anton Francesco (1513–74) Italian writer. The son of a Florentine tradesman, Doni joined the Servite order at an early age but left it in 1540, thereafter supporting himself by his writings. After Pietro *Aretino, he was the most distinguished of the authors known as the *poligrafi,* whose lively vernacular works were aimed at a popular audience and printed mainly in Venice. Often critical of or disillusioned with many humanist ideals, Doni's works include *La zucca* (1551; *The Gourd*), a collection of stories and proverbs; *I marmi* (1553; *The Marble Steps*), imaginary conversation overheard on the steps of Florence's Duomo; and *I mondi* and *Gl' inferni* (1553), dialogues on seven imaginary worlds and hells.

Don Quixote (*El ingenioso hidalgo Don Quixote de la Mancha*) The comic prose masterpiece by Miguel de *Cervantes Saavedra, published in two parts (1605, 1615). In the prologue to Part I (fifty-two chapters), Cervantes declares his intention of ridiculing the romances of chivalry. The elderly *hidalgo* Don Quixote has gone mad from reading too many of them and so, emulating Amadís de Gaula and other knights errant, he set out from his village on his nag Rocinante in search of adventure. Sancho Panza, whose peasant realism and unheroic character contrast with Quixote's idealistic credulity, becomes his "squire". The episodes, in which Quixote's delusion transforms windmills into giants, peasant girls into princesses, range from farce to social satire and high comedy. A vast number of brilliantly sketched characters are introduced, but the action is interrupted by digressions and long interpolated tales. Part II (seventy-four chapters), which Cervantes hastily completed because an unknown author ("Alonso Fernández de Avellaneda") had published a spurious sequel in 1614, continues the adventures but with fewer digressions and a much greater unity of action. In the course of events, the characters of Quixote and Sancho acquire a new depth until finally Quixote returns home, recovers his sanity, and dies. The book's success was immediate and its influence enduring. It was translated into English (by Thomas Shelton, 1612–20) and French (1614–18) in Cervantes's lifetime, and into Italian shortly afterwards (1622–25).

Dorat, Jean *see* Daurat, Jean.

Dordrecht, Synod of *see* Dort, Synod of.

Doria, Andrea (1466–1560) Genoese statesman, admiral, and patron of the arts. After fighting for the papacy and Naples he fitted out eight galleys to defeat the Barbary pirates and the Turks in the Mediterranean and won great acclaim by defeating the Turkish fleet at Pianosa (1519). He helped *Francis I take Genoa (1527), but changed sides (1528), obtained *Charles V's protection, and drove the French out. He then established his authority over Genoa, suppressing conspiracies and developing oligarchic rule. As grand admiral of the imperial fleet he helped Charles V take Tunis (1535). He came out of retirement to lead the Genoese reconquest of Corsica (1559).

Doria, Gian Andrea (1539–1606) Genoese nobleman, grand-nephew and heir of Andrea *Doria. When Andrea retired (1555) he handed over the command of his squadron to Gian Andrea, whose record as a naval commander is disappointing; he failed to take Djerba (1560) and his squadron performed poorly for the imperial fleet at *Lepanto (1571). After his grand-uncle's death Gian Andrea joined the older Genoese nobility in their struggle for power against the newer nobility.

Dort, Synod of (1618–19) An assembly of the Dutch Reformed Church at Dordrecht (Dort), to settle disputes arising from the Arminian Remonstrance to the states general of the United Provinces. The official delegates were all Gomarists, that is, strict Calvinists. Representatives of the *Remonstrants were heard, but took no part in the procedure, and were eventually expelled. Emissaries from German, Swiss, and British churches were present, the English delegation including three future bishops and John Hales, chaplain to the ambassador. A new Dutch version of the Bible was commissioned, and arrangements were made for a new catechism and for the censorship of books. Five sets of articles were approved, asserting the doctrines of election not dependent on belief, limited atonement (for the elect only), the total depravity of man, irresistible grace, and the impossibility of the elect's falling into sin. The authority of the *Belgic Confession and the *Heidelberg Catechism was also endorsed. As a result of this sweeping victory for Calvinism, many Arminian ministers were deprived, *Grotius was imprisoned, and *Oldenbarneveldt beheaded.

Dossi, Dosso (Giovanni di Luteri; c. 1480–1542) Italian painter. He was born in Mantua or Ferrara but little is known about his early life. The romantic approach to landscape which is apparent particularly in his early work indicates the influence of *Giorgione. He may also have had contact with *Titian. By 1512 he had left Venice for Mantua, where with his elder brother Battista (died 1548) he carried out for the duke of Mantua decorations which revealed the possible influence of *Correggio. In 1517 the brothers were working for Alfonso I, Duke of Ferrara, producing tapestries and entertainments, the latter with the poet *Ariosto. Although Dosso Dossi has been accused of poor draughtsmanship he was the leading figure in the school of Ferrara in the sixteenth century. One of his most famous paintings, *Circe* (1530; Galleria Borghese, Rome) is an example of the mysterious atmosphere he was able to create with effects of light. The equally well-known *Circe and her Lovers in a Landscape* (National Gallery, Washington; see Plate VIII), the second version of an earlier painting, is an example of his later work with rich exotic landscapes. Dossi died in Ferrara.

Douglas, Gavin (?1474–1522) Scottish churchman and poet. The son of the fifth earl of Angus, Douglas studied at St Andrews (1489–94), received his first ecclesiastical appointment in 1496, and became provost of St Giles, Edinburgh, about five years later. His allegorical poems *The Palace of Honour* and *King Hart*, not published until long after his death, were probably written between this time and 1513. His translation of Virgil's *Aeneid* into Scots, the first in Britain, was completed in July 1513, but not published until 1553. Douglas's prologues to each book of the *Aeneid* are some of his finest original verse, and the translation itself, in vigorous heroic couplets, makes up in energy what it lacks in accuracy. After James IV's death at Flodden (1513), Douglas's career was embroiled in politics, and he was only installed as bishop of Dunkeld (1516) with much help from the widowed queen. Further upheavals sent him into exile in London (1521), where he died.

Dovizi, Bernardo see Bibbiena, Bernardo Dovizi, Il.

Dowland, John (1563–1626) English composer and lutenist. Dowland is first mentioned as being in the service of Sir Henry Cobham, ambassador (1579–83) to France. While there he converted to Catholicism. After his return to England, probably in 1584, Dowland's music was performed at court, but on the rejection of his application for the post of queen's lutenist (1594) he went abroad again, travelling through Germany and Italy. In 1596 or 1597 he was back in England and published his *First Booke of Songes or Ayres of Foure Partes with Tableture for the Lute* (1597), an anthology of songs for solo voice and lute or four-part ayres; it was very popular and reprinted at least four times. By 18 November 1598 Dowland was lutenist at the court of Christian IV of Denmark, where he remained until his dismissal in 1606.
After his return to England, Dowland entered the service of Lord Walden. Though at this time he complained of neglect and criticism from younger lutenists, Dowland was enjoying considerable respect and popularity both in England and on the Continent. His famous *Lachrymae* (1605) was widely used in arrangements by other composers, and references to it in contemporary theatrical and literary works reflect its enormous popularity. He was finally appointed one of the king's lutes in 1612. Dowland wrote many attractive dance tunes and fantasias, but is chiefly remembered for his melancholy songs, in which chromaticism and discord are used to great effect.

Drake, Sir Francis (c. 1540–96) English sea captain and popular hero of the Elizabethan age. Drake first became rich and famous through his exploits against Spain in the Caribbean (1567–68) and in 1572 he received a royal commission as a privateer. With *Elizabeth I's support he led the first English expedition to circumnavigate the world (1577–80), bringing back with him on the *Golden Hind* a rich cargo of treasure and spices seized from the Spaniards. The queen recognized the feat by coming on board his ship to knight him. In 1585 Drake led another successful expedition against Spain in the New World, and in 1587 his raid on *Cádiz ("singeing the king of Spain's beard") cost the Spaniards thousands of tons of shipping and supplies. Drake played a prominent part in the defeat of the *Spanish Armada (1588). He died of fever off Panama, while leading yet another attack on Spain's overseas empire.

drama see comedy; *commedia dell'arte*; *commedia erudita*; interlude; masque; pastoral; *sacra rappresentazione*; theatres; tragedy.

Drayton, Michael (1563–1631) English poet. Born at Hartshill, Warwickshire, Drayton spent his youth in the household of the local Goodere family, before moving to London in about 1591. There he published the pastoral poems *Idea* (1593) and the fine sonnet sequence *Ideas Mirrour* (1594). The lady celebrated in these poems, Anne Goodere, remained the object of his poetic devotion for many years, though Drayton apparently died a bachelor. Drayton was both prolific and versatile as a poet. In 1596 he published the historical poem *Mortimeriados*, which he later recast in *ottava rima* as *The Barrons Warres* (1603). *England's Heroical Epistles* (1597), letters in rhyming couplets between famous English lovers such as King Henry II and Rosamond, were modelled on Ovid's *Heroides*; they were very popular and are among Drayton's best work. Around this time he was also writing for the theatre, and in 1607 was associated with the Children of the King's Revels at the Whitefriars Theatre. Drayton's patriotism is stirringly expressed in his fine "Ballad of Agincourt" (c. 1605) and he devoted many years to his principal work, the topographical epic *Poly-Olbion* (1622), written in hexameter couplets and divided into thirty "Songs" celebrating British landscape and history. Numerous editions of his poems appeared throughout the early 1600s and the *Muses Elizium* (1630) is the latest expression of the Elizabethan pastoral tradition.

Drebbel, Cornelis (1572–1633) Dutch inventor and alchemist. A native of Alkmaar, Drebbel trained as an engraver under his brother-in-law

DREBBEL *A detail from Hendrik Staben's picture of the visit of the Archdukes Albert and Isabella to the studio of Rubens shows a Drebbel* perpetuum mobile *(which apparently functioned by barometric pressure) on the table by the window. (Musées Royaux des Beaux-Arts de Belgique, Brussels)*

Hendrick *Goltzius, but subsequently turned his hand to hydraulic engineering. In the early 1600s he migrated to England, where he tried to attract James I's patronage by presenting him with a supposed *perpetuum mobile*. Drebbel was later involved in plans to drain fenland in East Anglia and was famous as the inventor of a scarlet dye which he and his sons-in-law exploited at their dyeworks in Bow, London. Among his many inventions was a submarine, which he demonstrated in the River Thames, apparently having found means of supplying himself with oxygen under water.

dress *see* costume.

Dryander, Francis *see* Enzinas, Francisco de.

du Bartas, Guillaume de Salluste, Seigneur (1544–90) French poet. A Huguenot gentleman born at Montfort, near Auch, du Bartas entered the service of Henry of Navarre, for whom he accomplished a number of diplomatic missions, including a visit to the court of King James VI of Scotland. His poetry was influenced in style by the techniques developed by the *Pléiade and in content by his Protestant faith; early works include the epics *Judith* and *Le Triomphe de la foi* (1574). Du Bartas's most significant achievement was *La Semaine ou la Création du monde* (1578), a didactic account of the creation of the world in seven cantos, which was highly acclaimed in France on publication but was subsequently criticized on stylistic grounds; it was well received in England, however, in translation (*see* Sylvester, Joshua). The *Seconde Semaine*, a continuation of the Old Testament story leading to a complete history of mankind, remained unfinished at du Bartas's death.

du Bellay, Joachim (1522–60) French poet. Born at Liré of noble parentage, du Bellay was the cousin of the cardinal and diplomat Jean du Bellay (c. 1493–1560) and the general and writer Guillaume du Bellay (1491–1543). After studying law at Poitiers he went to Paris, where he made the acquaintance of *Ronsard and joined him at the Collège de Coqueret. He became a member of the *Pléiade, and his early sonnets, notably *L'Olive* (1549), the first French sonnet sequence, were heavily influenced by *Petrarch; the Pléiade's manifesto, *La Défense et illustration de la langue française* (1549; translated as *Defence and Illustration of the French Language*, 1939), was his other major work of this period. In 1553 du Bellay accompanied his cousin Jean on a mission to Rome, a four-year exile that was to inspire some of his finest poetry: *Les Antiquités de Rome* (1558) is a melancholy contemplation of the grandeur and decadence of the ancient city; *Les Regrets* (1558) reflects his disillusionment with life at the Vatican and his homesickness for France. Du Bellay's other works include a collection of Latin poems and *Divers jeux rustiques*, both also published in 1558, after the poet's return to his native country.

Dubroeucq, Jacques (1500/10–1584) Flemish sculptor and architect. Dubroeucq, who was born near Mons, became acquainted with the ideals of the Italian Renaissance while travelling in Italy sometime before 1535; there he studied the works of Ghiberti, Michelangelo, Sansovino, and others. He executed his best works, a series of carvings for the cathedral of Ste Waldetrude at Mons (1535–48), after his return to the Netherlands – although much of this decoration was destroyed during the French Revolution. In 1545 he was honoured by the appellation of "master artist of the emperor"

(Charles V) and for Charles's sister *Mary of Hungary, regent of the Netherlands, he built and decorated the castles of Binche and Mariemont. Dubroeucq was also notable as the teacher of the sculptor *Giambologna.

Dubrovnik *see* Ragusa.

Duccio di Buoninsegna (c. 1260–c. 1318) Italian painter. As the first great Sienese artist Duccio's influence in Siena is comparable with *Giotto's in Florence. Whereas Giotto's art was revolutionary in its pursuit of naturalism, Duccio kept his ritualistic art within the Byzantine framework, yet brought to it a new narrative power in his use of facial expression, his rich and subtle colours, and dramatic arrangement of scenery. Little is known of his life except that despite several probably political clashes with the Sienese government, Duccio achieved a position of wealth and influence. His first known commission (1285) was a *Madonna* for the Florentine church of Sta Maria Novella. It is generally agreed that this is the imposing Rucellai *Madonna* (Uffizi).

The only work which can certainly be attributed to Duccio however is the double-sided *Maestà*, which he was commissioned to paint in 1308 for the high altar of Siena cathedral. It was completed and carried there in procession in 1311, but was dismembered in 1771 and while much remains in the Museo dell'Opera in Siena, other panels are scattered abroad or lost. The Madonna and Child are noted for their depth of character and solidity of form, while sixty other panels depicting the life of Christ and the saints illustrate Duccio's narrative power and the new infusion of emotion into old Byzantine models. Like the small *Madonna of the Franciscans* (1290; Pinacoteca, Siena), usually ascribed to him, the *Maestà* was remarkable also for its exquisite use of colour and of gold as both decoration and an essential feature of the composition. Duccio stood for the transition from Byzantine to Gothic, influencing Sienese painters including Simone *Martini and the *Lorenzetti brothers well into the fifteenth century, and his sense of composition and drama heralds even later Renaissance developments.

Ducerceau family (*or* Du Cerceau family) A French family of architects and designers, who were active from the mid-sixteenth century to the mid-seventeenth century. Jacques Androuet (c. 1520–c. 1585) established the family's reputation with his collections of architectural and decorative engravings, including *Les plus excellents bastiments de France* (1576, 1579), which bear witness to the influence of Italian works, with which he became acquainted during visits to that country early in his career. His patrons included the French royal family and he worked on several châteaux, although nothing now remains of these buildings. His engravings are valuable evidence for works now lost or severely damaged, such as *Rosso Fiorentino's, *Primaticcio's, and Thiry's at *Fontainebleau. His son Baptiste Androuet (1545–90) succeeded him as a leading architect; his only surviving work is the Pont-Neuf in Paris, begun in 1578. In 1584 Henry III made him supervisor of the royal office of works and he may have been employed on the Hôtel d'Angoulême and the Hôtel de Lamoignon (1584) in Paris. Two other sons, Jacques (c. 1550–1614) and Charles (died 1606), were also active as architects. Baptiste's son Jean (1585–1649) was a notable designer of private houses under Louis XIII, producing the Hôtel de Sully (1624–29) and the Hôtel de Bretonvillieurs (1637–43) as well as the horseshoe stairs at Fontainebleau (c. 1630).

Dudley, Robert, Earl of Leicester *see* Leicester, Robert Dudley, Earl of.

Dufay, Guillaume (c. 1400–74) French composer. Dufay was probably born in Cambrai, where he sang in the cathedral choir as a boy. Some of his compositions from the early 1420s were written for the Malatesta family in Pesaro. By 1426 he seems to have been back in France and by 1430 he held benefices at Laôn cathedral, Nouvion-les-Vineux, and St Géry in Cambrai. In 1428 Dufay joined the papal choir. By the time he left the choir in 1433 he was one of the most famous musicians in Europe. Dufay had close associations with two famous families, the *Este and the house of *Savoy. A notable occasion to which he contributed music was the marriage in 1434 of Louis, son of Duke Amadeus VIII of Savoy. In 1436, back in the papal choir, Dufay wrote one of his most famous works, *Nuper rosarum flores*, for the dedication of *Brunelleschi's dome of Florence cathedral. From 1440 Dufay was again in Cambrai as a canon at the cathedral, and apart from seven years in Savoy from around 1451, he spent the rest of his life there.

Dufay was no great innovator, but a master of the established techniques of composition. His secular works consist mainly of rondeaux; he also composed in the standard *ballade* and *virelai* form of his day. His sacred works show more development of style; the early Masses are in single and paired movements, where the later ones, such as the *Missa sine nomine*, are in cyclical, musically unified forms, as found in English Masses of the period. The motets were written for special occasions and are extraordinary in their complexity. The leading composer of his day, he greatly influenced his contemporaries, and his works were copied and performed throughout Europe.

Dunstable, John (c. 1390–1453) English composer. There are no certain details of Dunstable's career, but it is probable that he served John, Duke of Bedford, and the church where he is buried, St Stephen's, Walbrook, in London, belonged to the duke until 1432. Dunstable's importance as a composer was recognized by contemporaries both in England and on the Continent. Much of his work survives in Italian and German manuscripts. The overwhelming majority of Dunstable's surviving works are sacred and for three voices. Many use plainsong as a basis, and complex isorhythmic techniques are frequent. Some pieces are more declamatory, and here the clear presentation of the text becomes paramount. Dunstable's style was dubbed the *contenance angloise* (English sweetness) among continental musicians, but he cannot be regarded as an innovator. He wrote two complete Mass settings, often regarded as the earliest musically unified approaches to the genre. Though the song "O rosa bella" is well known, secular music hardly figures in his output, in which votive antiphons and motets predominate.

Duperron, Jacques Davy (1556–1618) Swiss-born churchman and statesman. Duperron was born at Berne, the son of French Huguenot refugees. In 1573 he went to Paris, and studied the Fathers of the Church, the schoolmen, and Roman Catholic theologians. He was received into the Roman Church by the Jesuits (c. 1578). He became a friend of King Henry III and after the king's death (1589), he supported first Cardinal de Bourbon, then the Protestant Henry IV, whose conversion he effected in 1593. In 1595 he obtained papal absolution for the king. Duperron took part in the conference at Nantes, and in 1600 he had the advantage in a theological disputation with the Protestant *du Plessis-Mornay. Since 1591 he had been bishop of Evreux, and he was made cardinal in 1604 (when he went to Rome as the king's *chargé d'affaires*) and archbishop of Sens in 1606. In 1607 he reconciled Pope Paul V and the Venetians, whom the pope had placed under an interdict on account of their defiant assertion of secular control in matters affecting the property and buildings of the Church. Duperron was a defender of ultramontanism, and corresponded with James I on the question of the true church.

du Plessis-Mornay, Philippe (1549–1623) French politician and religious leader. Born at Buhi in the Vexin into one of France's most distinguished families, he was converted by his mother to Calvin-ism and after study in Germany he became attached to *Coligny. The *Massacre of St Bartholomew forced him to take refuge in England. Returning to France, he became an adviser to Henry of Navarre and wrote extensively in favour of the Huguenots and religious toleration; these works included his *Traité de la vérité de la religion chretienne* (1581). He was employed in many official roles – ambassador to Spain and Flanders, governor of Saumur – and after Henry's coronation as Henry IV he acted as mediator between the Huguenots and the king, being instrumental in the promulgation of the Edict of *Nantes. He lost favour after the publication of *De l'institution, usage, et doctrine du saint sacrement de l'eucharistie en l'Eglise ancienne* (1598). In 1611 he published an overt attack on the Catholic church. Marie de' Medici restored him to favour because of his efforts to avert religious war after Henry IV's death but following the Huguenot uprising of 1620 he fell once more from grace. His standing can be gauged from his nickname, "the Pope of the Huguenots".

Dürer, Albrecht (1471–1528) German painter, draughtsman, print maker, and art theorist. Dürer was born at Nuremberg and initially trained as a goldsmith under his father. However, he probably never executed metalwork independently, and he began (1486) a second apprenticeship with the Nuremberg painter and woodcut designer Michael *Wolgemut. Dürer had early experience of printing through his godfather, Anton Koberger, who printed illustrated books in collaboration with Wolgemut. In 1490 Dürer travelled on the Upper Rhine, becoming familiar with the work of the Housebook Master, and in subsequent years worked, primarily as a woodcut designer, in Strasbourg and Basle. In 1494 he returned home, married, and set up on his own account. Copying engravings by Mantegna seems to have motivated him to visit Venice, via the Tyrol, before the year's end.

In Italy Dürer strengthened his acquaintance with Mantegna's work, studied the paintings of *Bellini, and encountered works by artists from other regions of Italy, including *Pollaiuolo. His alpine views, executed in 1494–95, are the earliest topographical watercolours in existence. Other early drawings, such as the Berlin *Lobster* (1495), reveal his interest in natural history. After his return to Nuremberg he executed the remarkable and expressive *Apocalypse* woodcuts (1498), the first book to be conceived, executed, printed, and published by an artist. This and later series of woodcuts, such as the *Large Passion* (1510), the *Small Passion* (1511), and *The Life of the Virgin* (1511), abandoned the primitive formality of

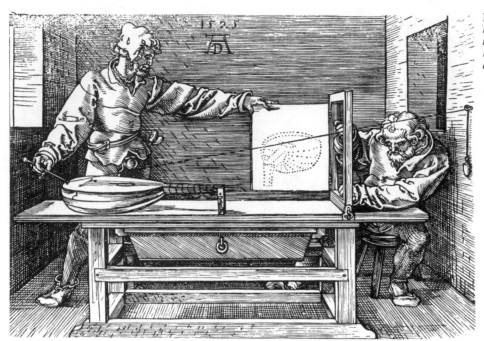

earlier northern prints for new realms of naturalism. Between 1498 and about 1520, their example transformed the woodcut as an illustrative medium.

From the beginning of his career, Dürer painted portraits. His most famous self-portraits are those of 1498 (Madrid) and 1500 (Munich). After his return from Venice, Dürer refined his Italian experiences in numerous drawings, prints, and paintings, but a work such as the Paumgärtner altarpiece (c. 1500; Munich) remains essentially a northern triptych, despite incorporating deep perspective and Italianate figure types. In 1500 Dürer became acquainted with the itinerant Venetian painter and print maker Jacopo de' Barbari, then based in Nuremberg, and his researches took a major step forward. He devoted a series of studies to the nude, which culminated in the engraved *Fall of Man* (1504), the first northern work to embody the proportional theories of Vitruvius. Between 1503 and 1505 Dürer also became increasingly familiar with the work of *Leonardo da Vinci, presumably via drawings made available to him through his friend Willibald *Pirckheimer. Dürer's engraved *Small Horse* (1505) utilizes Leonardo's canon of equine proportions.

Between 1505 and 1507 Dürer was based in Venice where he worked upon the altarpiece of *The Madonna of the Rosegarlands* (Budapest) for German merchants resident in the city. He wrote an account of his stay in the form of letters to Pirckheimer. Dürer was on good terms with the ageing Bellini, although he was ostracized by other

Venetian artists, who presumably feared him as a competitor. Although painted after his return to Germany, his lost Heller altarpiece (1509) indicated that Dürer encountered the works of *Raphael and Filippino *Lippi during this visit to Italy. Magnificent preparatory drawings for the Heller altarpiece survive, one of which, *Praying Hands* (Vienna), has become a popular symbol of faith throughout Christendom. Dürer's last major altarpiece was the Vienna *Adoration of the Trinity* (1511), the Italianate frame of which survives in Nuremberg. Thereafter, both artist and city turned increasingly towards Lutheranism and the market for large-scale religious works was considerably reduced.

Although Dürer had practised the engraver's art with consummate skill since his youth, his finest engravings are the "Three Master Prints" of 1513–14: *The Knight, Death, and the Devil, St Jerome in his Study*, and *Melancholia I* (*see* melancholia). Each displays Dürer's remarkable ability to render light and texture, which caused Erasmus to dub him "the Apelles of the Black Lines". From 1512 onwards Dürer became increasingly involved with the decorative printing projects of Emperor Maximilian I, such as the *Triumphal Arch* and *Triumphal Procession* woodcut series. His 1520–21 visit to the Netherlands was ostensibly to ensure renewal of his imperial pension by the newly crowned *Charles V. Dürer's diary of the visit and numerous drawings which he made in the Netherlands provide a detailed account of the trip. While there he made the acquaintance of several important painters, was enthralled by Aztec treasures recently brought from Mexico, and acquired a set of prints after Raphael, with whom he had previously exchanged drawings.

During his last years Dürer painted some of his finest small portraits, including those of Jacob Muffel and Hieronymus Holzschuher (both 1526; Berlin). From the same year dates his last large painting, the Munich *Four Apostles* diptych, which has a distinctly Lutheran iconography. Since 1512 he had been increasingly drawn towards theoretical studies, which culminated in the publication of his three illustrated books on geometry (1525), fortification (1527), and human proportions (1528). Dürer's publications, prints, and students, the last including *Aldegrever, *Baldung, and *Kulmbach, broadcast his influence throughout Europe. The most significant northern artist of the Renaissance, he was also probably the greatest print maker and the most important German artist of all time.

Dutch East India Company An amalgamation of over sixty rival companies which was granted a charter by the Netherlands states general in 1602. Formed to regulate and protect Dutch trade in the Far East, the company enjoyed considerable privileges, which included the power to make treaties and establish colonies, the right to maintain armed forces, a trade monopoly, and tax exemptions. From its Jakarta base the company expelled its Portuguese rivals from Ceylon (1638–58) and Malacca (1641); in 1652 it established the Cape of Good Hope colony. The company had 150 trading vessels, forty warships, and 10 000 soldiers by 1669, but soon declined due to English competition, waning Dutch power, and rising debts. It was disbanded in 1798.

Dutch language The language spoken in the modern kingdom of the Netherlands (where it is called Nederlands) and in northern Belgium, or Flanders (where it varies slightly from Nederlands and is called Vlaams). There are also small pockets of Dutch speakers in the French *département* of Nord, in former Dutch dependencies overseas, and in North America. The High Dutch spoken by seventeenth-century settlers in South Africa evolved and was simplified over 250 years until it was recognized as a distinct language, Afrikaans. Dutch is based mainly on Old Franconian, the Germanic dialect of the northern Franks, who, with the Saxons and the Frisians, settled the area in the Dark Ages. In the early Middle Ages the dialect of Bruges, by reason of the town's dominance as a trading counter of the *Hanseatic League, came to the fore, but in the fourteenth century the duchy of Brabant began to gain the ascendancy. Flanders passed to *Philip the Bold,

Duke of Burgundy, in 1384, and in the fifteenth century the Burgundians were the dominant power in the Low Countries. Throughout the Middle Ages the literary influence of France was strong in the area.

Resistance to Habsburg rule in the sixteenth century eventually centred on the northern province of Holland, and the form of the language there became the language of nascent nationalism. After the Spanish recapture of Antwerp in 1585, the dialects of refugees from the south affected northern Dutch in several ways; the southerners' diphthongal pronunciation of words such as *huis* (house) and *vijf* (five), formerly pronounced in the north as monothongs, became a permanent feature of the language. The concepts of purity and correctness in language were promoted in prose by Renaissance writers like *Coornheert. The *Statenbijbel*, the Dutch translation of the Bible authorized by the Synod of *Dort, contains many instances of the more formal usages of the south dignifying the colloquial language of the north.

du Vair, Guillaume (1556–1621) French statesman and philosopher. A Parisian by birth, du Vair became a supporter of Henry of Navarre and made his name as an orator with such speeches as *Exhortation à la paix* (1592). After Henry's accession to the French throne he served in a number of important offices, culminating in his appointment as lord chancellor (1615) and bishop of Lisieux (1616). His writings include the treatises *De la sainte philosophie* and *De la philosophie morale des Stoïques*, translations of Epictetus and Demosthenes, and the *Traité de la constance et consolation ès calamités publiques* (1593; translated as *A Buckler against Adversitie*, 1622), which applies the philosophy of Stoicism to the Christian faith. Du Vair's influence can be traced in the poems of his contemporary *Malherbe and in the works of the French philosophers of the seventeenth century.

Duytsche Academie (*or* Coster's Academie) A learned society founded in Amsterdam in 1617 by Samuel *Coster. Coster had been a member of De Egelantier (*see under* chambers of rhetoric), but he considered its activities were too frivolous and therefore launched his own academy along the lines of the Italian Renaissance *academies, with an ambitious programme of mathematical, philosophical, and linguistic instruction to be given in Dutch. The academy was also to produce plays; this was the only part of the programme carried through, but the virulently anti-Calvinist stance of its dramas brought it into collision with the authorities. In 1635 it merged with De Egelantier.

E

East India Company An English trading company granted a charter by Elizabeth I in 1600. Launched with £30,000 capital and a monopoly of trade to the Far East, the company established factories in Java and the Spice Islands. After conflict with the Dutch (*see* Dutch East India Company) in the 1620s the company concentrated its trading activities on India. The decline of the Mughal empire and wars with France in the seventeenth and eighteenth centuries enabled it to accumulate extensive and wealthy territories in India, where it survived until 1873.

Ebreo, Leone *see* Leone Ebreo.

Eccard, Johannes (1553–1611) German composer. Eccard received his earliest musical training in his native Mühlhausen. From being a chorister at the Weimar court, he moved in 1571 to the Hofkapelle in Munich, where he was a pupil of *Lassus. In the late 1570s he was in the household of the Augsburg *Fugger family, before joining (1579) the chapel of the margrave of Brandenburg-Ansbach in Königsberg. He was assistant *Kapellmeister* until 1604 when he succeeded to the senior post. In 1608 the new elector gave Eccard responsibility for music at his Berlin court. A Lutheran composer, Eccard made much use of the chorale melodies in his works; his 1597 publication of sacred music contains simple harmonizations, but other volumes of his work develop the complex genre of the chorale motet, of which he was one of the major exponents.

Eck, Johann (Johann Maier of Eck; 1486–1543) German theologian and polemicist. Professor of theology (1510–43) and chancellor at the university of Ingolstadt in Bavaria, Eck was the first and most persistent of Luther's adversaries. His attack was initially launched against Luther's supporter, Andreas Carlstadt (c. 1480–1541), which led to a formal disputation at Leipzig in June and July 1519. Eck's various assaults on Luther were published and widely circulated, and his accusations, including an association of Luther with Jan *Huss, forced Luther to define his position concerning the authority of the Bible, the character of Christ's Church, and the papacy and Church hierarchy. Eck helped draw up the *Confutatio* declaring Charles V's total rejection of Protestant principles that was read at the Diet of Augsburg (1530). He was one of the three Catholic spokesmen in the debates at the Colloquy of *Regensburg in 1541.

eclogue *see under* pastoral.

education In the Middle Ages education had been mainly under ecclesiastical control and was designed for those who were intended for a clerical career. This was true of the schools maintained by trade guilds no less than of the (Latin) grammar schools and choir schools supported by cathedral and collegiate churches.

From the fourteenth century onwards secular influences began to gain ground, and more importance was attached to training in the *liberal arts, especially *rhetoric. The Latin literature of pagan antiquity was studied for its own sake, and the revival of Greek learning in the West was begun by Manuel *Chrysoloras, who was invited to Florence from Constantinople in 1395. The *De ingenuis moribus et liberalibus studiis* (On Gentle Manners and Liberal Studies), written about 1402 by Pietro Paolo Vergerio (1370–1444) of Padua, argued in favour of a system of education that maintained a harmony of body and spirit. A number of boarding schools were founded in northern Italy in the early fifteenth century; *Vittorino da Feltre founded schools at Padua, Venice, and Mantua. This last, which enjoyed the patronage of the duke of Mantua, aimed at making learning pleasant and was known as *La Giocosa*. The instruction was entirely in Latin, and the subjects were mainly those of medieval schools, but the methods were revolutionary, including the teaching of mathematics by means of arithmetical and geometrical games. Leon Battista *Alberti's treatise *Della famiglia* (1435–41) emphasized the importance of the home background in education. He wrote in Italian, rather than Latin, as he wished to influence a wide public. The classical source for much of the educational theory behind these Italian projects was *Quintilian, whose first two books were known at the beginning of the fifteenth century.

In France, Spain, and England the new learning was first promoted in circles connected with the royal court. Literacy and even scholarship began to be perceived by the upper classes as fitting attainments for gentlemen, rather than as the prerogative of despised "clerks". In England the first of the public schools (schools maintained by a corporation or body of trustees), had been founded at Winchester in 1382 by Bishop William of Wykeham, sometime lord chancellor. Many more such schools were established in the fifteenth and sixteenth centuries; in the latter part of the period some of the founders were merchants. Numerous grammar schools also originated at this time. The most important English treatises on education were *The Boke named the Governour* (1531) by Sir Thomas *Elyot and *The Scholemaster* (1570) by Roger *Ascham, tutor to Princess (later Queen) Elizabeth. Both emphasized the importance of teaching English as well as Latin and included physical exercise as a curriculum subject. Furthermore, Ascham deplored the harsh methods used by many of his contemporaries. The elementary education of the poorer classes mostly depended on small endowments given or left by the pious to parish churches. At this level provision was made for the education of girls as well as boys. The higher education of girls was practically confined to the home. An outstanding example was the education which Sir Anthony Cooke (1504–76), sometime tutor to King Edward VI, provided for his daughters. They were instructed in Latin and Greek, as well as the more traditional feminine accomplishments, such as music and embroidery. In the Netherlands princely and aristocratic patronage was less important, but the increasing wealth and power of the burghers produced a demand for a broader system of education. The ground had been prepared in the fourteenth century by the Brothers and Sisters of the *Common Life (a mixed lay and religious association), who founded hostels for students and later, schools. *Erasmus, who was educated at their school at Deventer, became the author of several treatises embodying liberal educational ideals. He emphasized the importance of Greek and Latin and neglected the vernacular, but nonetheless related education to experience of life both before and after the years of formal schooling and regarded it as a continuous process.

In France the most influential writers were *Ramus and *Montaigne, and in Germany Johannes *Sturm, head of the academy of Strasbourg. The Spaniard Juan Luis *Vivès, who worked in France, the Netherlands, and England in the early sixteenth century, wrote treatises on education, including the education of women and the poorer classes. In Germany the Reformation led to the foundation of many new primary and secondary schools. *Melanchthon and *Bugenhagen were responsible for a complete reorganization of the system. Religious instruction and the teaching of reading and writing were done for the first time in the German language. The work was divided into stages, and the pupils had to master the work of each before passing to the next.

The Counter-Reformation movement in the Roman Church also produced many new schools and teaching orders such as the *Piarists. The *Jesuits, following the pedagogic precepts of their founder, Ignatius Loyola, maintained a very rigid educational system, primarily intended for the training of the clergy, but very influential too in the education of laymen. Whatever utilitarian purposes may have been served incidentally by their systems of education, the preceptors of the Renaissance period never lost sight of their highest ideals, the pursuit of knowledge and the attainment of virtue. *See also* universities.

Edward VI (1537–53), King of England and Ireland (1547–53) The son of *Henry VIII and his third wife, Jane Seymour, Edward was intelligent and well educated. He succeeded to the throne under the regency of his uncle, Edward Seymour, Duke of Somerset, but by the end of 1549 John Dudley, Duke of Northumberland, had supplanted Somerset. Edward was brought up to support the Protestant cause, and during his reign Cranmer's Book of Common Prayer (1549) and the Forty-Two Articles of Religion (1553) were published. Shortly before his death Edward excluded his half-sisters Mary and Elizabeth from the succession in favour of his cousin, Lady Jane Grey, Northumberland's daughter-in-law.

Egas, Enrique de (c. 1445–c. 1534) Spanish architect. He was probably born at Toledo, where his father Egas (died 1495) and uncle Hanequin (died c. 1475) were associated with work on the cathedral. Although Enrique and his brother Anton adopted the name of their father as their family name, it seems likely that the family was an offshoot of a well-known Brussels family of masons called Coeman. Enrique became cathedral architect at Toledo (c. 1498) before moving to Granada, where he designed the chapel royal (1506) and the cathedral (1521), although the latter was remodelled and completed by Diego de *Siloe. Although he worked mainly in the *plateresque style, Enrique was not unaware of Italian Renaissance developments. He also designed buildings in Valladolid and Santiago de Compostela, his cruciform hospital plan for the latter town (1501) being subsequently copied for the Sta Cruz hospital in Toledo (1504) and at Granada (1511).

Egmont, Lamoraal (1522–68) Dutch nobleman. Born in Hainaut (now in Belgium), Egmont served *Charles V in Algiers, Germany, and France. He led the Spanish cavalry to victory against France at St-Quentin (1557) and Gravelines (1558), and served Philip II of Spain as councillor and governor of Flanders and Artois, where he was idolized by his countrymen. Although a loyal subject, a Catholic, and a courtier, Egmont courageously opposed Philip's harsh policies in the Netherlands. He was treacherously seized by the duke of *Alba and executed with the count of Horn after a summary trial. His execution marked the start of the revolt of the *Netherlands.

Egyptian studies The Renaissance made contact with ancient Egypt almost exclusively through the medium of classical Greek and Latin literature. The second book of Herodotus' *Histories* and references scattered through Pliny's *Natural History* provided the basis for Renaissance ideas about the material life of ancient Egypt. Plutarch's *On Isis and Osiris* provided information about the mystical aspects of Egyptian religion. The major interest of Renaissance students was in the contribution of Egypt to hermetic, gnostic, and other pagan systems which were supposed to have affected Christianity in various ways (*see* hermeticism). Hieroglyphs, the ancient Egyptian system of writing, were the main focus for this interest. Early Christian writers, such as Cassiodorus and Rufinus, had taught that hieroglyphs were purely ideographic writing used by Egyptian priests to foreshadow divine ideas. Renaissance interest was stimulated by Cristoforo de' Buondelmonti's purchase, on the island of Andros in 1419, of a manuscript of the *Hieroglyphica*, attributed to Horapollo. Another early traveller to take notice of hieroglyphs was *Cyriac of Ancona, who visited Egypt in 1435 and copied a hieroglyphic inscription for Niccolò *Niccoli. *Ficino hailed Horapollo as a major source of information about Egyptian mysticism and its relation to Neoplatonism, and his work was mined as a source of esoteric wisdom and *imprese*. It also influenced the *Hypnerotomachia Polifili* (1499). The *editio princeps* of Horapollo was printed by Aldus (1505) and a Latin translation was published in 1517. Other early writers whose works on the ancient Egyptian mysteries were known to the Renaissance included Plotinus and Iamblichus, of whom Latin translations by Ficino appeared in 1492 and 1497 respectively.
Valeriano Bolzanio (c. 1443–1524) and his nephew Piero (*see* Valerianus, Pierius) summed up in their researches the state of Renaissance Egyptology in the mid-sixteenth century. Piero's *Hieroglyphica* (Basle, 1556) is an exhaustive account of contemporary speculation which established connections between hieroglyphs and the symbolism of medieval lapidaries and bestiaries. Increased contact with Egypt in the later sixteenth century extended the range of primary sources available and the re-erection in Rome of the many obelisks brought to the city in the time of the empire – the obelisk of Caligula in St Peter's Square (1586) and of Augustus in front of the Lateran Palace (1588) are examples – provided a further stimulus to the study of hieroglyphs (*see also* Bembine Table). Pietro della Valle (1586–1652) travelled extensively in the Levant (1614–26), bringing back with him to Italy Egyptian mummies and Coptic manuscripts. The learning of the whole period is summed up in the three massive volumes of Athanasius Kircher's *Oedipus Aegyptiacus...* (Rome, 1652–54).

Eight of War *see under* Eight Saints, War of the.

Eight Saints, War of the (1375–78) A conflict between Florence and its supporters and the papacy over the secular power of the papacy in central Italy. The war was ended by the compromise Peace of Tivoli (1378). The threat the war posed to the security of Rome prompted Gregory XI to end the papacy's seventy-year exile in Avignon. The "saints" referred to were the eight officials who exacted war taxes from the clergy, here confused with the Eight of War (*otto della guerra*), who conducted Florence's military operations.

Eldorado (Spanish: the gilded one) The name given in the early sixteenth century to a South American Indian ruler near Bogota. According to legend, he covered his body with gold dust for religious ceremonies, then plunged into a sacred lake to wash while his subjects threw gold and jewels into the water. From 1538 Spanish adventurers searched for him; they failed to find his great treasure but the area they explored came under Spanish rule. Later the quest shifted to the Orinoco and Amazon valleys, and Eldorado came to mean a fabulously rich country. Among the many who sought its gold were Gonzalo Pizarro (in 1539), Francisco de Orellana (in 1541–42), and Sir Walter *Raleigh (in 1595 and 1617–18). The legendary gold encouraged rapid exploration and conquest of much of America by Spain and other European powers.

Elizabeth I (1533–1603), Queen of England and Ireland (1558–1603) The daughter of *Henry VIII by his second wife, Anne Boleyn, Elizabeth led an insecure life until her accession to the throne. Her father had her mother beheaded, Elizabeth was declared illegitimate (1536), and her sister, *Mary

ELIZABETH I *Federico Zuccaro's chalk drawing was made from life in London in May 1575. (British Museum, London)*

I, imprisoned her in the Tower of London (1554) on suspicion of treason. Yet, Elizabeth's reign was one of the most successful in English history. It saw the defeat of Catholic Spain, a generally acceptable religious settlement, rising prosperity, expansion overseas, a great literary age, and the emergence of England as a world power.

Elizabeth soon ended years of religious turmoil with the establishment of a moderately Protestant Anglican Church. Attempts to restore Roman Catholicism continued, but Elizabeth had little difficulty in thwarting various plots to place her Catholic cousin, *Mary, Queen of Scots, on the throne of England. The pope had excommunicated Elizabeth in 1570, but it was not until after the execution of Mary on Elizabeth's orders (1587) that the *Spanish Armada was sent to invade England (1588). The defeat of the Armada was a great triumph for Elizabeth and her navy, confirming England's status as a great power.

Elizabeth never married, but used her eligibility as a powerful weapon in diplomatic negotiations until she was well into her fifties (*see* Francis, Duke of Alençon). She seems to have loved Robert Dudley, Earl of *Leicester. Elizabeth always retained the affection of her subjects, she managed the House of Commons shrewdly, and she had the ability to choose her ministers wisely; two of them in particular, William Cecil (1520–98) and Francis Walsingham (1532–90), were responsible for sound economic and administrative reforms. Elizabeth was succeeded by her Stuart cousin, *James I of England and VI of Scotland.

Elizabethan style The English architectural and decorative style associated with the reign (1558–1603) of Elizabeth I. During this period the assimilation of Renaissance models, begun in the preceding *Tudor period, gathered momentum, although much Elizabethan work was still medieval in character with an often idiosyncratic application of half-understood Renaissance motifs. One characteristic form of decoration was the low-relief carving in intricate geometrical patterns known as strapwork, which entered England from the Low Countries and was much used on *furniture and on plaster ceilings. The predominantly oak furniture was usually heavily carved, with bulbous pillar supports that reached massive proportions in the 1580s and 1590s; an assortment of classical motifs (lion masks, acanthus scrolls, caryatids, Ionic columns, etc.) would also appear on the same pieces.

Architectural innovations were predominantly secular and domestic. The houses of Elizabethan magnates, influenced by the increasing circulation of illustrated books on architecture, began to show a bias towards symmetry; this was exemplified in the E-shaped ground plan of country houses, with a formal entrance porch in the centre forming the short stroke of the E and two long wings protruding at right angles from the main block. A grand staircase and a long gallery were fashionable interior features. Fireplaces became elaborate stone edifices, often inlaid with coloured marbles. *See also* Jacobean style.

Elsheimer, Adam (1578–1610) German painter. Elsheimer studied painting in his native Frankfurt, where he came under the influence of exiled Dutch landscape painters living in the area. In Italy from 1598, he visited Venice and lived in Rome, absorbing the influence of Italians such as *Caravaggio, *Veronese, and the Bassano family. He met Rubens and other Dutch painters there, through whom he influenced the development of northern European art. Elsheimer's usually small, very delicate paintings, often executed in oil on copper, were widely popular. His subject matter is usually biblical or mythological, with figures and an idyllic landscape setting assuming equal importance, as in *Tobias and the Angel* (National Gallery, London). He is noted especially for his rich colours and effects of light, frequently achieved in night scenes. Elsheimer died in Rome, following his release from imprisonment for debt.

Elyot, Sir Thomas (c. 1490–1546) English writer and diplomat. His place of birth and education are uncertain, but in 1511 he became clerk of assize on the western circuit, on which his father was a judge. He attracted the patronage of *Wolsey and then of *Cromwell, becoming a close friend of the latter by 1528. After having been knighted in 1530, Elyot led embassies to Charles V in 1531 and 1535. In 1531 his first and most famous publication appeared, *The Boke named the Governour*; dedicated to Henry VIII, it was an appeal for humanistic values in the education of the aristocracy. *Pasquil the Plain* (1532) extols the virtues of free speech against flattery. The medical treatise *The Castel of Health* (1534) was novel in that it was written in the vernacular and by a layman. Among Elyot's other works, the most significant is his Latin-English *Dictionary* (1538).

Elzevir press The press founded by the Elzevirs, a Dutch family of printers, publishers, and booksellers, who spread from a base in Leyden to The Hague, Amsterdam, and Utrecht, and were active from about 1580 to 1712. The founder of the dynasty, Louis (1546–1617) left Louvain to work for *Plantin in Antwerp, before settling in Leyden in 1580 as a binder and bookseller, eventually associated with the local university. His publishing started in 1593 with an edition of Eutropius, and classical authors continued to be the main stock of the firm. Louis's son Bonaventura (1583–1652) and grandsons Abraham (1592–1652) and Izaak (1596–1651) – the offspring of Louis's oldest son, Matthias – began the series of pocket classics in 1629, providing accurate texts for a large market. These little thirty-twomos, with their narrow margins and solid slabs of type, often with engraved title-pages, became the family's most famous product. Izaak, who had established a press of his own in 1616, became printer to the university of Leyden in 1620, and his successors retained the office. Grotius was the first contemporary published by the Elzevirs, starting in 1609, and the Amsterdam branch, established by Louis III (1604–70) in 1639, concentrated on modern books in Dutch, German, English, and French until the death of Daniel Elzevir (1626–80), Bonaventura's son, when it was wound up. The Leyden branch lasted a little longer, under the control of Abraham's grandson, Abraham II (1653–1712). The Elzevirs, from Louis I on, sold new or second-hand books throughout Europe, an activity just as important as their printing and publishing.

emblems Symbolic pictures to which were added a few words, a motto or a short verse, to explain extra layers of meaning attached to the objects in the illustration, that is, a graphic expression of a thought. Emblematic devices are probably most familiar now as printers' marks, like the *Aldine press dolphin and anchor, glossed as "Hasten slowly". Francis Quarles, author of the best-known English emblem book, which appeared in 1635, said "An Emblem is a silent parable."

The Renaissance taste for emblems may have grown from study of Roman medals and Egyptian hieroglyphs. It was reinforced by the publication of collections of them in books; the first, Andrea *Alciati's *Emblemata*, printed in Augsburg in 1531, with woodcuts by Jörg Breu, initiated a fashion that lasted over a century. A Paris edition with better illustrations by Mercure Jollot followed in 1534, with a first French translation two years later and a German one in 1542, all issued by *Wechel. In 1546 the *Aldine press printed more of Alciati's emblems, followed by Lyons printers who put them

EMBLEMS *A variation on the theme of beating swords into ploughshares, Alciati's emblem on the motto* Ex bello pax *(from war, peace) has a helmet functioning as a beehive.*

into French, Spanish, and finally Italian, in 1549. The first English emblem book, Geoffrey Whitney's *A Choice of Emblemes* (Leyden, 1586) was overshadowed by Quarles's later collection. Dutch printers produced most emblem books, and the *Plantin press kept the fashion alive by diverting them to educational or spiritual themes expressed in allegories. A book of this kind marking the Jesuits' centenary, *Imago primi saeculi Societatis Jesu*, was issued by Moretus in 1640.

Emser, Hieronymus (1478–1527) German humanist and Roman Catholic controversialist. Emser was born at Ulm and studied at Tübingen, where he learnt Greek from Dionysius (the brother of Johann) *Reuchlin, and at Basle. In 1501 he became chaplain to Cardinal Raimund von Gurk, and in 1504 secretary to Duke George of Saxony. Initially he was in sympathy with *Luther and the reformers, but he wished rather to see the Church reformed from within, without making any doctrinal break. From 1519 he was engaged in violent controversy with Luther and in 1527 he produced a German Bible, with introduction and notes, to counteract the effect of Luther's.

Encina, Juan del (1469–c. 1529) Spanish poet, dramatist, and musician. Known as the father of the Spanish theatre, he was born near Salamanca and studied there under *Nebrija. He took minor orders and from 1492 to 1495 was in the service of the duke of Alba, at whose palace he produced his first pastoral entertainments which included his own music. These were dialogues of shepherds and rustics which combined classical material – Encina had translated Virgil's *Eclogues* at the age of twenty-one – with verse forms and songs of popular origin. About 1500 Encina went to Rome, serving as choirmaster under Alexander VI and Leo X. He was ordained in 1519 and went on a pilgrimage to Jerusalem where he said his first Mass. He spent his final years as prior of León cathedral.

The first edition of his *Cancionero* (1496) contained eight plays, his lyric poetry, and an introduction on Spanish poetry. Subsequent editions (1507, 1509) printed two other plays each, and sixty-eight of his musical compositions have survived as well. Three of his early dramatic pieces are religious *representaciones* (compare the *sacra rappresentazione* in Italy), written for particular days (Christmas, Good Friday, and Easter); the rest are dramatic secular pastoral plays, carefully plotted and frequently comic. They are written in octosyllabic verse in various stanzaic forms and are accompanied by music and dancing, with which almost all of them end. The best show the influence of Italian pastoral drama, for example, *Egloga de Plácida y Vitoriano*, first produced in Rome in 1512

and containing a character, the hag Eritea, based on Celestina (*see Celestina, La*). Encina popularized a type of peasant speech for his comic characters that was often imitated by his successors; called *sayagués* and supposedly originating in the village of Sayago, near Salamanca, it was in fact an artificial comic invention employed by Encina simply to characterize his comic shepherds and give the impresssion of local colour.

Encomium Moriae *see Praise of Folly, The*.

Enderlein, Gaspar (1560–1633) German metalworker. Enderlein was born in Basle but became a master in Nuremberg in 1586. He was profoundly influenced by the work of François *Briot, whose Temperantia Dish provided the model for Enderlein's own Temperantia Dish. An accompanying ewer was modelled upon the Mars Dish by Briot and the Suzannah Dish, also probably by Briot.

English language The Renaissance period saw English evolve from the stage known as Middle English to that known as Early Modern English. Middle English was characterized by a number of dialects; the language of Chaucer, a late fourteenth-century Londoner, was very different from that of his anonymous northwestern contemporary who wrote *Sir Gawain and the Green Knight*. In the fifteenth century pressure towards a standard form of English began to emerge. This pressure was partly administrative, as English supplanted French and Latin in official records, and partly social or educational. As an instance of the latter, members of the Norfolk Paston family who had spent time in London or at the universities began to use word forms characteristic of London dialect rather than of their native county.

Printing was a major factor in the standardization of the language. *Caxton complained of the troublesome variety of English dialects and told the story of a northcountryman who ordered "eggys" in a Kentish hostelry, only to be chided by the hostess for speaking French; another customer intervened to explain that he wanted "eyren", then still the usual word for "eggs" in the southeast. A century later Puttenham in his *Arte of English poesie* (1589) stipulated a famous model for correct English: "the usuall speach of the Court, and that of London and the shires lying about London within lx. myles, and not much above". It was this standard that generally prevailed among educated persons.

The superior status of Latin as an ancient, learned, and international language meant that English was at first discounted as a medium of educated discourse. Sixteenth-century writers, while acknowledging Chaucer's greatness, saw that his language had become obsolete within 150 years and feared to entrust their profoundest thoughts to such an impermanent and insular vehicle. Even in the early seventeenth century Sir Francis Kynaston tried to guarantee Chaucer's standing by publishing a Latin version of the latter's *Troilus and Criseyde* (1635). Among the first educationists to defend the vernacular was Richard Mulcaster, whose *Elementarie* (1582) contains a spirited defence of English as "a tung of it self both depe in conceit, and frank in deliverie"; in his opinion, no language "is better able to utter all arguments, either with more pith, or greater planesse than our English tung is." The latter point was amply proved by the many translations made in the period, in particular those of the Bible, which invested the vernacular with both dignity and authority.

To establish a standard English, attention needed to be paid to three main areas: *orthography, syntax, and vocabulary. Spelling reformers considered that the system should be overhauled to enable the written language to reflect more accurately the sounds of contemporary speech; to this end John Hart even suggested in his *Orthographie* (1569) that new symbols should be introduced into the alphabet. In the field of syntax several innovations that had arisen in the Middle English period generally supplanted older usages. One important one was the use of the auxiliary verb "do" to form negative or interrogative sentences; Shakespeare exhibits both kinds of question within a few lines: "Do you busy yourself with that?" (new) and "Spake you with him?" (obsolescent) (*King Lear* I ii). Another change, which manifested itself around 1600, was the use of "its" insteads of "his" for the neuter form of the genitive or possessive pronoun.

Vocabulary reflected the new linguistic consciousness and the new demands made upon the vernacular. An estimated 10 000 new words were adopted from Latin, Greek (often via Latin), Italian, French, and other languages during the Renaissance period. Linguistic critics fell into two camps: those who held that English could provide from its own native resources all the words necessary and those who believed that foreign importations were the best route to an enriched vocabulary. Spenser was praised for having taken the former option in *The Shepheardes Calender*; "he hath laboured to restore, as to their rightfull heritage such good and naturall English words, as have ben long time out of use and almost cleane disinherited" wrote E.K. in his commendatory letter, contrasting Spenser with those who "have made our English tongue, a gallimaufray or hodgepodge of al other speches." The contemporary term for those who imported and coined words to an excessive degree was "inkhornist". Most of their bizarre

affectations quickly died, but other words that had a genuine role to play in English took root and flourished.

engraving Engraving is an intaglio printing process, whereby a metal plate, usually of copper, is incised with an image. The plate is then inked and the residue of ink is wiped off so that the ink remains only in the engraved furrows of the plate. A piece of damp paper is then laid against the plate and both are rolled through a heavy press, somewhat like a clothes mangle. Under this intense pressure, the damp paper is forced into the ink-filled furrows so that an impression of the image is embossed upon the paper. The final image is a reverse impression of that incised upon the plate. The earliest form of engraving, and that most used during the Renaissance, is line (or copper) engraving, in which a sharp metal tool with a V-shaped section is pushed by hand pressure across the plate, rather like a plough. The tool, known as a burin, throws up metal shavings and leaves a V-shaped groove, which constitutes the line subsequently inked. This technique derived from that used by sculptors to chase the surface of bronze statues. The earliest dated print executed in this technique is of 1446.

Dry-point engraving is a simpler, but less commercially viable, technique, in which the image is trans-

ENGRAVING *The inscription under Lucas van Leyden's 1525 self-portrait proclaims that he himself made the engraving, rather than merely producing a design to be engraved by another hand.*

ferred to a metal plate by a sharp stylus of hard steel. The stylus throws up a raised metal edge to the furrow, known as "burr". The latter is retained when the plate is inked, so that it adds a rich, broken edge to the printed image. However, the pressure of printing rapidly crushes the burr, so that no more than a few dozen impressions may be made with this technique. The most outstanding early master of dry-point engraving was the Dutch Master of the Housebook, active about 1480, who was influential upon Albrecht *Dürer.

Etching is a further method of engraving, in which the plate is covered with a ground impervious to acid, upon which the engraver draws with a needle, exposing the copper where he wishes to print. The plate is then immersed in acid, which eats a line in the plate where the needle has exposed the copper, while leaving the covered area unaffected. The line produced by this technique has an irregular, broken form of greater variety than that produced by line engraving. Although Dürer experimented with etching as early as 1515, the technique was little used until the seventeenth century, since when it has become increasingly popular.

The earliest known engraver, the German Master of 1446, was followed by a number of outstanding northern masters, including the Master of the Banderoles, the Master of the Playing Cards, the *Master E.S., and Martin *Schongauer, who refined the technique of line engraving to a high level. In Italy a number of anonymous masters started producing engravings almost contemporaneously with their northern counterparts. The earliest major Italian engravers whose names are known were Antonio *Pollaiuolo and Andrea *Mantegna. However, both were primarily active in other fields and they produced relatively small editions of prints, which were nevertheless extremely influential. Albrecht Dürer was the greatest print maker of the Renaissance. He made numerous technical refinements, which permitted engraving to reproduce effects of light and texture with a much higher fidelity than had previously been possible. Dürer's example stimulated a remarkably accomplished series of followers, including the Germans Albrecht *Altdorfer, Urs *Graf, Hans *Baldung, Lucas *Cranach, and Hans Sebald Beham (see under Little Masters (of Nuremberg)), as well as the Netherlander *Lucas van Leyden. In Italy the most outstanding school of engraving of the early sixteenth century was that of Venice, the leading masters of which were Jacopo de' *Barbari, Giulio *Campagnola, and Marcantonio *Raimondi. Raimondi, who was profoundly influenced by Dürer, moved to Rome about 1510, where he specialized in prints after the paintings of Raphael. Subsequently, a decline in original engraving set in, which lasted until well into the following century. The growing market for prints, which expanded throughout the Renaissance, was satisfied by a highly organized print trade, in which painters prepared design drawings which were subsequently engraved by specialist engravers.

Enzinas, Francisco de (Francis Dryander; ?1520–70) Spanish scholar, translator, and reformer. Enzinas was born at Burgos and studied at Wittenberg, where he was influenced by Luther's teaching. He produced the first translation of the New Testament into Spanish, which was published at Antwerp in 1543. This translation incurred the displeasure of Charles V because it was based on the Greek text of Erasmus and because of Enzinas's marginalia, which expressed unorthodox opinions. He also printed in capitals the verses of Romans iii which provided one of the main supports for those who endorsed justification by faith. Enzinas was therefore imprisoned (1543) at Brussels but he managed to escape to Antwerp two years later. He journeyed widely and in 1546 came to England, where he was professor of Greek at Cambridge until the accession of Mary forced him to leave. He even travelled as far as Constantinople, founding a Protestant colony there. His works included a history of religion in Spain and Spanish translations of Lucian (1550) and Plutarch (1551). He also wrote memoirs in Latin which remained in manuscript until the nineteenth century.

epic A long narrative poem written in a heightened style concerning a heroic character whose legendary or historical actions are central to his culture, race, or nation. "Primary" or traditional epics, like the Homeric poems, derive from an heroic age and celebrate a war or similar event and the hero's role in it. "Secondary" or literary epics are by known individual poets writing in deliberate imitation of "primary" models. Virgil's *Aeneid* is both the outstanding example of the literary epic and the model, in turn, for most succeeding European epic poets.

In addition to the great national or cultural significance embodied by the epic hero and his actions, there are a number of other conventional features of both types of epic. The setting is suitably extensive, often representing the whole of the known world (as in the *Odyssey*) and more, for example, the underworld in classical epics and the entire Christian cosmos in Milton's *Paradise Lost* (1667). Divine beings or other supernatural agents take part, often actively, in the events. The exalted and ceremonial language appropriate to the action is also characterized by a number of conventions, for example, detailed catalogues of people, things, and places; set speeches reflecting the character of the speaker, who may also bear a stock epithet (*pius Aeneas, fidus Achates*); and epic similes involving elaborate comparisons. The poem usually starts *in medias res* after an invocation of the Muse and a question put to her, the answer to which is the narrative itself. The most important early theoretical comments on the epic are contained in Aristotle's *Poetics*, though they have survived only in mutilated form.

In the Renaissance, the nature of the epic was the subject of intense discussion in sixteenth-century Italy following the recovery of the *Poetics* and the dissemination of classical literary theory. Previously known mainly through a commentary by Averroes, the *Poetics* became available in much improved translations: into Latin by Giorgio Valla (1498) and Alessandro Pazzi (1536), and into Italian by Bernardo Segni (1549). Although Aristotle had ranked epic second to tragedy in the hierarchy of genres, this judgment was ignored by Renaissance critics, and epic was promoted to top place – "the best and most accomplished" as Sidney called it (*Defence of Poesie*, 1595). The Homeric epics with which Aristotle was concerned were eventually given serious consideration, but Virgil remained the most significant epic model for Renaissance poets and critics. Thus *Vida in *De arte poetica* (1527) proclaims the epic as the noblest of all genres and Virgil as the best model. Many other critics and poets reflect or adapt Aristotelian principles in commenting on the epic. *Trissino in *La poetica* (1529) cites Aristotelian criteria; he modelled his own blank-verse epic, *La Italia liberata da' Gotthi* (1547–48), on Homer. *Cinthio in *Discorsi intorno al comporre dei romanzi* (1548) attempted to defend Ariosto and the romance by categorizing them in a separate slot from the epic as classically conceived. Minturno (Antonio Sebastiani) argued for an epic having classical unity of action while taking Christian and romance material as proper subject matter (*L'arte poetica*, 1564). *Castelvetro (*Poetica d'Aristotele vulgarizatta et sposta*, 1570) opposed a rigid application of Aristotelian criteria to later works.

Among Renaissance poems of epic scope, the *Divine Comedy* occupies a special place at the very beginning of the period, but it lacks an epic hero in any traditional sense. *Petrarch's *Africa*, *Sannazaro's *De partu virginis*, *Vida's *Christus*, and *Trissino's epic are the best representatives of humanist classicism. Owing more to the medieval romance and the poetry of chivalry, which included such "primary" material as the legends of *Arthur and of *Charlemagne and the Twelve Peers – though the *Chanson de Roland* itself was not known in the Renaissance – are *Boccaccio's *Teseida*, with its erotic interest, *Pulci's *Il morgante*, *Boiardo's *Orlando innamorato*, *Ariosto's *Orlando furioso*,

and *Tasso's *Rinaldo*. Tasso's *Gerusalemme liberata* and, for theory, his *Discorsi del poema eroico* (1594) form a final, if inconclusive, attempt in Italy to reconcile neoclassical ideals of unity and moral purpose with the marvels, love interest, and multiplicity of event of the romance tradition.

The divergence between the "unified" classical epic and the "diversified" romantic epic manifested itself in the literatures of other European countries. In France *Ronsard attempted a national epic on the theme of the French monarchy; its feeble plan, ill-advised choice of metre (decasyllables, as opposed to the more eloquent alexandrine) and wooden diction condemned *La Franciade* (1572) to abandonment after only four of the projected twenty-four books had been completed. In England Spenser's *Faerie Queene*, also unfinished, combined grandeur of conception with poetic power in the execution, but its allegorical character and multiplicity of action disqualified it as an epic contender in the classical style. The most successful Renaissance epic under the classical rules is Camões' *Lusiad*, in which the excitement of Portugal's imperial adventure in the East breathes new spirit into the ancient conventions.

Growing unease with national or family pride as warranting the high seriousness of epic treatment led some poets to turn to religious themes for their subject matter. *La Semaine* (1578) of *du Bartas achieves epic dignity in its theme (the creation of the world) and occasionally in its treatment. The Christian theme was also exploited in seventeenth-century England, by Abraham Cowley in his unfinished *Davideis* (1656) and of course by Milton in *Paradise Lost* and *Paradise Regained* (1671).

Epicurus (341–270 BC) Greek philosopher. He was better known in the Middle Ages by repute than by any surviving writings, but he was generally mentioned with disapproval by Christian authors, who travestied his philosophy as teaching that the highest good is pleasure, while omitting to note that Epicurus defined pleasure as the practice of virtue. His atomism also was objectionable in that it suggested a random material origin for the world, as opposed to a divine plan. Finally, his doctrine that the gods did not involve themselves with human affairs contradicted Christian belief in divine intervention through the incarnation. Epicureanism and atheism were therefore frequently bracketed. Debate about his philosophy was fuelled in the Renaissance after the discovery of the work of his major Roman follower, *Lucretius.

Epistolae obscurorum virorum (*Letters of Obscure Men*) A brilliant satire originating in the controversy between the humanist Johann *Reuchlin and the converted Jew Johann Pfefferkorn.

Pfefferkorn, supported by theologians, wanted Hebrew literature confiscated and destroyed, while Reuchlin, who had initiated *Hebrew studies in Germany, pleaded for toleration; a bitter feud developed. In 1514, in self-defence, Reuchlin published some letters from eminent European scholars to him, the *Clarorum virorum epistolae* (Letters of Famous Men). The *Epistolae obscurorum virorum* appeared anonymously the following year, written mainly by the humanist Crotus Rubeanus; ostensibly they were letters from sycophantic academic theologians to one of Pfefferkorn's supporters, Ortivin Gratius, but they were soon recognized as a humanist joke. In them the fictitious theologians reveal themselves as petty and complacent, occupied with the most trivial scholastic problems, food, drink, and sex. Their absurd names and appalling Latin intensify the humour. In 1517 another book of letters appeared, more directly concerned with the Reuchlin affair (mainly by Ulrich von *Hutten). The *Epistolae* resulted in much advantageous publicity for Reuchlin's stance and for the humanist cause.

Equicola, Mario (c. 1470–1525) Italian humanist courtier and diplomat. Born at Alvito, Calabria, Equicola was mainly associated with the house of Este. As early as 1505 he composed a treatise on the phrase "Nec spe nec metu" (neither in hope nor in fear), which was Isabella d'Este's favourite motto, and in 1519 she appointed him her secretary. In this capacity he travelled with her on a pilgrimage to St Mary Magdalene at Ste-Beaune; his account of the trip still survives. His letters give valuable insights into the private lives of Isabella and her extensive family connections. He became involved in the quarrel between Isabella and her son Federico d'Este, and died in Mantua. His *De natura de amore* (1525) shows the influence of Ficino's theories of Platonic love.

Erasmus, Desiderius (?1469–1536) Dutch humanist scholar. Erasmus, who was illegitimate, was probably born in Rotterdam. He entered *Hegius's school at Deventer (1478), where, although the curriculum was still largely medieval, he made some contact with the new learning from Italy. In 1487 he joined the monastery of Steyn, near Gouda, but the monastic life was uncongenial and in 1495, as secretary to the bishop of Cambrai, he went to Paris to study theology. He found the course uninspiring and extended his reading in classical literature. In 1499 one of his private pupils, Lord Mountjoy, brought him to England where he met *Colet at Oxford. Colet's historical approach to the Bible so stimulated Erasmus that when he returned to Paris (1500) he was determined to equip himself fully as a scholar. He learnt Greek

ERASMUS *Despite the formality of the pose, this portrait, one of several by Hans Holbein the Younger, hints at the sitter's wry humour. (1523; private collection)*

and read widely. In 1504 he published *Enchiridion militis christiani* (Handbook of the Christian Soldier), a plea to return to the simplicity of the early Church and the pristine doctrine of the Fathers. This he followed with an edition of *Valla's annotations on the New Testament (1505), thereby indicating his chosen path in scriptural criticism.

In 1506 Erasmus visited Italy as director of studies to the sons of Henry VII's physician. In 1508 he published at the *Aldine press an expanded edition of his *Adagia*; the work made his European reputation. From Venice he went to Rome, where he was invited to stay, but Lord Mountjoy recalled him to England. He used his experiences to produce the satirical *Encomium Moriae* (1511; The *Praise of Folly*) with a dedication to Sir Thomas More. Between 1509 and 1514 Erasmus was at work in London and Cambridge on his Greek New Testament and an edition of the letters of St Jerome. He found a publisher in Johann *Froben of Basle; both works appeared in 1516. Erasmus used only a few manuscripts of the New Testament and his edition lacked serious critical scholarship but, the *Complutensian Polyglot apart, his text was the first Greek New Testament printed.

Erasmus had reached the peak of his fame. But the spread of the Reformation in northern Europe involved him in bitter controversy which clouded his later years. *Luther felt that he detected seeds of radical criticism of the Catholic Church in Erasmus's writings, and he failed to understand how Erasmus could refuse to follow these lines of reasoning to their logical conclusion. The temperaments of the two men were fundamentally different; Erasmus was appalled at the vitriolic emotional tone of the reformers which seemed to him a negation of of the reason that was God's special gift to man.

In 1517 Erasmus settled at Louvain where he worked on a second edition of his New Testament (1519). In 1521 religious persecution forced him to move to Basle where he helped Froben by editing an extensive series of patristic writers and produced the final version of his *Colloquia* (1526), a set of dialogues, started around 1500, in which he exemplified his ideal of civilized humane discussion of topical matters. He also wrote (1528) against *Reuchlin on the pronunciation of ancient Greek (*see* Greek studies). In 1529 he was forced to leave Basle for Fribourg, but he returned in 1535 to die there.

Erasmus exercised a profound influence over the northern Renaissance, despite the apparent failure of his ideals. He exploited the printing press to the full and his published work runs into dozens of volumes, including editions of classical authors and the Church Fathers, manuals of prose style which show his characteristic common sense, works of moral instruction such as the *Institutio principis Christiani* (1516), and satirical squibs like the *Encomium Moriae*. The fundamental principle of Erasmian humanism is awareness and recognition of free will, from which follows the individual's responsibility for his own actions. Erasmus remained concerned to the last to spread true religion and unity in the fellowship of Christ through humane learning.

Erastianism Secular control of the Church, even in ecclesiastical affairs. Erastianism is named after a Swiss theologian, Thomas Lüber (c. 1524–83), better known by his humanist pseudonym of Erastus. Erastus's *Explicatio gravissimae quaestionis* was published in London in 1589. This was a collection of theses circulated by Erastus after coming to Heidelberg in 1558 to serve as physician to the elector palatine. Initially written in defiance of attempts to impose Calvinist consistories and discipline upon the Palatinate, the *Explicatio* was employed to justify demands for greater state control of the Church during the late sixteenth and seventeenth centuries. The term is frequently erroneously used to describe the Tudor view of ecclesiastical government, particularly that of the Henricians.

Ercilla y Zúñiga, Alonso de (1533–94) Spanish poet. Belonging to a noble family, Ercilla was born in Madrid and served Philip II as a page. He later spent seven years (1556–63) in America, serving as a captain with forces in Chile. On his return to Spain he married well and lived at court as a favourite of Philip II. His poem, *La Araucana* (Part I, 1569; Part II, 1578; complete edition, 1589), is the first important literary work to emerge from America and the greatest Spanish epic of the Golden Age. Its thirty-seven cantos, written in *octava real* (hendecasyllabic eight-line stanzas, rhyming abababcc, a form introduced by *Boscán in imitation of Ariosto's *ottava rima*), are concerned with the Spanish capture of the Arauco valley in Chile. In itself a minor battle, in which Ercilla himself took part, the conflict is raised to epic grandeur, however, by striking descriptive passages. The Araucanian Indians and their leaders are sympathetically portrayed, courageous even in defeat. A section of the poem contains a "prophetic" passage on the battle of Lepanto.

Ercole de' Roberti (Ercole de Ferrara; c. 1450–96) Italian painter. A native of Ferrara often confused with the Bolognese painter Ercole di Giulio Cesare de' Grandi, Ercole de' Roberti was influenced by Giovanni *Bellini and was probably a pupil of *Cossa. After assisting Cossa on the frescoes of the Palazzo Schifanoia and on the altarpiece of S Lazzaro (now destroyed) in Ferrara and the Griffoni altarpiece at Bologna (c. 1476), Ercole de' Roberti established his reputation with a large altarpiece, *Madonna Enthroned with Saints* (1480/81; Brera, Milan), painted for Sta Maria in Porto at Ravenna. He then became court painter to the *Bentivoglio rulers of Bologna, in which post he executed portraits of Giovanni II and his wife Ginevra (National Gallery, Washington) before returning to Ferrara in 1486, where he succeeded *Tura as court painter to the Este family. Paintings from this last period included the *Harvest of the Manna* (National Gallery, London), a *Pietà* (Liverpool), and *The Way of the Cross* (Dresden).

Eros *see under* Cupid.

Escorial A royal palace, mausoleum, and Jeronymite monastery in central Spain. Sited northwest of Madrid, in the Guadarrama mountains, this massive complex, which constitutes the most important work of architecture of the Spanish Renaissance, was commissioned as a mausoleum for Emperor Charles V by Charles's son *Philip II. Built between 1562 and 1584, the Escorial was originally designed by Juan Bautista de Toledo (died 1567) and completed by Juan de *Herrera. Philip himself, according to Fray José de

*Sigüenza, took a close interest in his "royal foundation of S Lorenzo del Escorial" and was responsible for many details. Juan de Herrera revised the plan under the influence of the works by Serlio, Vignola, and Michelangelo – notably St Peter's in Rome – and also redesigned the great church (1572) that stands at the centre of the grid pattern of buildings. A library was added in 1592 and contains nearly 5000 manuscripts and 40 000 printed books. Paintings for the interior of the Escorial were commissioned from many notable artists, including *Titian, *Tibaldi, Federico *Zuccaro, *Fernández de Navarrete, and El *Greco. The principal sculptors employed were Leone and Pompeo *Leoni. All Spanish monarchs since Charles V have been buried in the mausoleum here, with the exception of Alfonso XII.

essay The name adopted by *Montaigne for a short prose composition dealing with a single topic in a fairly subjective manner and relaxed style. Montaigne saw his own *Essais* as "attempts" to express in writing his personal reflections and experiences; they provided for their author a means of self-discovery and have preserved for posterity an intimate and comprehensive picture of the man himself – his physical appearance, moral attitudes, erudition, and philosophy. In Britain the essay form was adopted by Montaigne's contemporary Francis *Bacon. Bacon's pithy and compelling expositions on such universal topics as "Riches", "Deformity", "Gardens", "Friendship", and "Revenge" were immediately popular, though less intimately self-revelatory than Montaigne's essays.

Essex, Robert Devereux, Earl of (1567–1601) English nobleman, courtier, and soldier. He was the elder son of Walter Devereux, 1st Earl of Esssex, and achieved distinction at an early age as a soldier in the Netherlands on the expedition (1585) led by his stepfather, Robert Dudley, Earl of *Leicester. After Leicester's death (1588), Essex became one of Queen Elizabeth's favourites, despite the fact that in 1590 he married Frances, the widow of Sir Philip *Sidney. Essex's sack of *Cádiz (1596) marked the zenith of his career. The following year his expedition to the Azores was a failure, enabling his numerous enemies at court to seize the initiative. He was sent to crush a revolt in Ireland (1599) but disobeyed instructions, causing Elizabeth to imprison him briefly in the Tower of London. He then attempted to raise London against the aged queen, but the revolt failed; he was tried and executed for high treason. Essex was a considerable patron of writers, and his own poems were highly valued by his contemporaries.

Est, Willem Hessels van *see* Estius.

Este, Isabella d' (1474–1539) Italian noblewoman. She was the daughter of Ercole I d'Este (1431–1505), Duke of Ferrara, who ensured that she received a thorough humanistic education. Battista *Guarino was among her tutors. In 1490 she married Gianfrancesco II Gonzaga, Marquess of Mantua, whose military prowess she complemented with her own skill in diplomacy. During her husband's frequent prolonged absences she ably protected the interests of Mantua and Ferrara aginst papal encroachments and after his death (1519) continued as a trusted counsellor to her eldest son, Federico II (1500–40).
Isabella is however chiefly remembered for the extraordinary cultural flowering she brought about in Mantua. Both she and her husband were keenly interested in choral and organ music, and Isabella's music room survives in the Reggia de' Gonzaga, Mantua, decorated with wooden inlays of musical motifs by Tullio *Lombardo. *Leonardo da Vinci, *Titian, *Mantegna, *Raphael, *Giulio Romano, *Francia, and *Perugino were among the artists she patronized. *Castiglione, *Ariosto, *Trissino, Mantovano (Battista *Spagnoli), and *Bandello were beneficiaries of her literary patronage.

Este family A dynasty powerful in northern Italy from the thirteenth century, when Obizzo II became perpetual lord of Ferrara (1264), despite papal claims to the title. Este power was considerably extended by Niccolò III (lord 1393–1441), by Borso (lord 1450–71), who became duke of Modena and Reggio (1452) and duke of Ferrara (1471), and by Ercole I (duke 1471–1505), who allied his family by marriage with the royal line of Naples and with the *Bentivoglio, *Gonzaga, and *Sforza families. Ercole I encouraged the arts; he beautified Ferrara and patronized *Ariosto. His daughters by Eleonora of Aragon, Isabella (1474–1539) (*see* Este, Isabella d') and Beatrice (1475–97), carried the Ferrarese enthusiasm for music, art, and literature to their husbands' courts, Isabella to Mantua and Beatrice to Milan. Other Este patrons of the arts included Niccolò II (lord 1361–88), who built the Castello Estense, Alberto V (lord 1388–93), who founded the university of Ferrara, and Leonello (lord 1441–50) who was educated by *Guarino da Verona and encouraged scholars and artists, among them *Alberti, *Veronese, *Pisanello, Jacopo *Bellini, van der *Weyden, and *Mantegna. In 1502 Alfonso I (duke 1503–34) married as his second wife Lucrezia *Borgia; in their time the Ferrarese court was renowned for its brilliance. When Alfonso II (duke 1559–97) died without an heir the papacy recovered

Ferrara, but a junior Este branch continued to rule Modena and Reggio.

Estienne press (Latin: Stephanus) The press established by a dynasty of scholar-printers who worked in Paris and Geneva from 1502 to 1674. The first was Henry I Estienne (died 1520), whose widow married his partner, Simon de Colines. He in turn trained his stepson Robert (1503–59) who took over the press in 1526, later receiving the royal appointment to Francis I of France. Robert's Latin thesaurus (1531; enlarged edition 1543) was followed by several bilingual dictionaries, while his editions of the Bible, including a Greek/Latin New Testament (1551), the first to divide the chapters into numbered verses, combined his scholarship and his Christianity. In the 1540s five priced catalogues of his books were issued.
Robert's Calvinist sympathies took him to Geneva in 1550, while his brother Charles (1504–64) continued printing in Paris. Charles was a man of extensive learning, compiler of the popular *Praedium rusticum* (1554) collection of agricultural tracts and author of the first French encyclopedia (1553) and of the anatomical textbook *De dissectione* (1548). There he was followed by his nephew Robert II (1530–71), who also became a royal printer in 1564. In Geneva Robert I was succeeded by his sons Henry II (1528–98), who brought out a Greek thesaurus (1572) to match his father's Latin one, and Francis (1537–82). His grandson Paul (1567–1627), son of Henry II, eventually returned to Paris, where his son Antoine (d. 1674) was the last of the dynasty and another royal printer.
The Estienne books combined scholarship and good design in a long series of sixteenth-century classical editions, from the Paris complete Cicero to the Geneva first editions of Anacreon and Plutarch.

Estius (Willem Hessels van Est; 1542–1613) Dutch Roman Catholic martyrologist and commentator. He was born at Gorinchem (Gorcum), educated at Utrecht, and from 1561 studied at Louvain under Michel Baius (*see* Baianism). From 1582 he was professor of theology at Douai, becoming chancellor of the university in 1595. His history of the martyrs of Gorcum (killed by the Protestants) appeared in 1603. He was the author of commentaries on the works of Peter Lombard, the epistles of St Paul, and the catholic epistles and also made notes for an edition of St Augustine. His zeal against the Protestants was such that it led him to defend the murder of *William the Silent, Prince of Orange (1584).

etching *see under* engraving.

Eugenius IV (1383–1447), Pope (1431–47) Born in Venice as Gabriele Condulmaro, Eugenius followed Pope Martin V's example in battling for restoration of papal supremacy over the Church. In December 1431 he attempted to exert this authority by adjourning the Council of *Basle and ordering its members to reassemble at some later date in Bologna. The council refused to adjourn and reasserted the counter-claim of conciliar supremacy. Eugenius gave way and in 1433 withdrew the decree of dissolution. In 1434 riots in Rome compelled him to flee to Florence, which remained his headquarters for nine years; in this time he met many leading writers and artists. Eugenius decreed the dissolution of the council again in September 1437 and ordered its removal to Ferrara to discuss the possibility of reconciliation with the Greek Church. In consequence, those who remained in council at Basle deposed Eugenius (1439) and elected in his place Duke Amadeus VIII of Savoy as Pope Felix V (1439–49). In the same year Eugenius succeeded in passing a short-lived act of union between Greek and Roman churches, thus increasing his prestige and undermining that of the council. This proved to be a lasting victory. He then returned to Rome (1443) where he died.

Euphuism The English prose style that took its name from the romance *Euphues* (1578, 1580) by John *Lyly. Its principal characteristic is the elaborate patterning of sentences by means of antithesis, alliteration, and similar rhetorical devices. It also makes heavy use of mythological and other allusions. A typical example is the metaphor used by Philautus: "as the fish Scolopidus in the flood Araris at the waxing of the Moon is as white as the driven snow, and at the waning as black as the burnt coal, so Euphues, which at the first increasing of our familiarity was very zealous, is now at the last cast become most faithless." This highly artificial shaping of prose was a radical departure from the rambling constructions of Lyly's contemporaries and set a considerable fashion.

Eustachio, Bartolommeo (1520–74) Italian anatomist. Born the son of a physician at San Severino, Eustachio followed his father in his choice of career. He was initially physician to the duke of Urbino and to his brother Cardinal Giulio della Rovere, and then (1549) moved to Rome where he taught at the papal college, being appointed professor of anatomy in 1562. In his best-known work, *Opuscula anatomica* (1564), Eustachio described the anatomy of the ear, identifying the eponymous Eustachian tube which joins the middle ear to the nasopharynx. The work also contained a description of the kidney in which Eustachio provided the first published account of the adrenal glands. Much of the impact of Eustachio's work, however, was lost by the absence of the illustrative plates. Discovered many years after his death, they were finally published in 1714.

Eworth, Hans (Hans Ewoutsz.; c. 1515–c. 1574) Flemish portrait painter. Eworth was born in Antwerp and may possibly be identified with the "Jan Euworts" mentioned as a freeman of the St Luke guild in that city in 1540, but his fame dates from his arrival in the late 1540s in England, where he spent the rest of his life. The earliest of his dated paintings, signed with his monogram HE, is from the year 1549. Thirty-five portraits can either definitely or probably be attributed to him, many of them of Roman Catholic notables in the circle of Mary I. He was also a painter and designer for court fêtes. His early allegorical picture of Sir John Luttrell (1550; Courtauld Institute, London) shows the influence of the Fontainebleau painters; later paintings are more reminiscent of Holbein and Clouet. His masterpiece is the double portrait traditionally identified as Frances Brandon, Duchess of Suffolk, and her second husband and erstwhile secretary, Adrian Stokes (1559; private collection); a more plausible theory is that they are Mary, Baroness Dacre, and her son Gregory, 10th Baron Dacre.

exploration The Renaissance era was the heyday of exploration by European adventurers. During the fifteenth and sixteenth centuries, explorers from the leading European merchant nations traversed all the major seas and plotted their coastlines. Much of early Renaissance exploration was inspired by medieval tales of Prester John, the legendary African Christian king with hoards of treasure, and by the travels (1271–92) of Marco Polo, who reported on the riches of the Orient.
Although individuals like Fernão *Pinto and Matteo *Ricci made epic journeys by land, Renaissance explorers were predominantly mariners, sponsored by monarchs and merchants to establish trading links with Asia. The Portuguese were the first great nation of explorers. Using developments in navigational instruments and *cartography, they drew inspiration from the enthusiasm of Prince *Henry the Navigator. Although serious exploration down the West African coast began in the early fifteenth century, it was not until 1488 that *Diaz rounded the Cape of Good Hope and turned northeast along the African coastline. In the same year *Covilhã reached India via the "overland" route, although Vasco da *Gama did not open up the southern sea route to India until 1498.
By the mid-fifteenth century the Spaniards had developed an interest in exploration. In 1474 an Italian named Paolo del Pozzo Toscanelli advocated sailing west to Asia – a theory based on Ptolemy's notions about the extent of the Asian land mass. The Spaniards adopted this theory and sponsored Christopher *Columbus, who made landfall on the Caribbean islands in 1492, believing them to be outposts of Asia. It was twenty years before the existence of America as a separate continent was established, and consequently, the intervening years saw an extensive search for a strait through America to the Orient. This meant that the east coast of America was extensively mapped within ten years, as various explorers searched for the supposed passage north or south from the Caribbean. The first atlas of the Americas was produced by Cornelis Wytfliet in 1597.
Although the treaty of *Tordesillas (1494) gave both Spain and Portugal spheres of influence in the Caribbean, the Spanish made best use of their opportunities, while the Portuguese continued to favour eastern routes to Asia. By 1519 Spain had established Panama as a base for incursions into the South American mainland. Rapid colonization followed, and with it came riches beyond the wildest dreams of the explorers (see Pizarro, Francisco). Based on Hispaniola in the Caribbean, the Spaniards were well placed to explore the new continent. De Solis discovered the Rio de la Plata in 1516, and *Cabral discovered the delta of the Amazon, which was navigated by Orellana in 1542. By 1600 coastal mapping of South America was complete.
In 1521 Magellan's lieutenant del *Cano achieved the first circumnavigation of the globe after Magellan had persisted with a southerly course down the coast of South America until he pased through the strait that bears his name. As exploration became global, England, Holland, and France slowly adopted increasingly active exploration policies. Although Sebastian *Cabot and *Cartier made pioneering attempts to find a direct route to the Orient by searching for a *northwest passage, it was not until the late sixteenth century that men such as *Linschoten and *Hakluyt inspired widespread northern European interest in exploration. France and Holland undertook trading ventures in the Far East, while Hakluyt's *Principall Navigations* ignited exploration fever in England. The 1550s had seen England's initial search for a *northeast passage and the establishment of valuable trade links with Russia (see Muscovy Company). Between 1576 and 1578 Francis Drake retraced Magellan's famous voyage. He confirmed that the Atlantic and Pacific oceans met and explored the southern Pacific and the west coast of America. By the end of the Renaissance period, the explorers of the age had sailed and charted the whole world except for its farthest extremities.

explosives *see* gunpowder.

Eyck, Hubert van (died 1426) *and* **Jan van** (active c. 1422–41) Dutch painters. Almost nothing is known of Hubert van Eyck, except that he was apparently Jan's elder brother and that both artists were born at Maaseyck and contributed to the *Ghent altarpiece. Jan is first documented at the court of the count of Holland at the Hague in 1422. In 1425 he was appointed court painter to *Philip the Good, Duke of Burgundy, at Bruges. He was highly esteemed by his master, who sent him on secret missions and embassies to Spain and Portugal, intervened when the ducal exchequer sought to reduce his salary, presented his children with baptismal gifts, and, finally, assisted his widow. Within a few years of his death, Jan's fame had reached almost legendary proportions as far afield as Italy; in the following century Vasari praised him as the "inventor" of oil painting. While this is not strictly true, Jan certainly grasped the new medium's potential for rendering effects of light and texture with a fidelity previously unimaginable.

The remarkable verisimilitude of Jan's technique was partially anticipated by earlier Franco-Flemish manuscript illuminators, but it is unlikely that he began his career as a miniaturist. The famous miniatures from the Turin-Milan Hours, which are sometimes believed to be his earliest works, are, more probably, late productions from his workshop. Jan's stunning technical virtuosity appears, already fully developed, in his earliest surviving panel paintings, such as the Berlin *Madonna in a Church* and the Washington *Annunciation*, both of which probably date from the 1420s. The latter includes numerous sculptural and architectural details which portray religious scenes related to the Annunciation. This "disguised symbolism" became a recurrent device in early Netherlandish painting, but Jan was its greatest and most sensitive exponent. The accurate forms of Romanesque and Gothic architecture with which Jan evoked the contrast between the Old and New Testaments imply a level of antiquarian research in advance even of contemporary Florentine artists.

Although the two brothers' respective contributions to the Ghent altarpiece (1432) have yet to be disentangled, the great polyptych has certain stylistic anomalies suggestive of two different hands. It seems probable that Hubert established the ambitious iconographic programme of the altarpiece and painted much of its interior before his death. Between 1426 and 1432 Jan probably reworked some of his brother's panels and painted most, if not all, of the exterior. The seeds of much of Jan's subsequent artistic development are to be found in this compendium, which is the most significant northern altarpiece of the fifteenth century. Jan's slightly later *Madonna of Chancellor Rolin* (Paris) includes a breathtaking panorama of a city. His *Arnolfini Wedding* (1434; London) records the making of a marriage vow and may have a quasi-legal significance as a form of pictorial "wedding certificate". The tiniest details are painted with an almost microscopic accuracy both in this painting and the 1436 *Madonna of Canon van der Paerle* (Bruges), although the latter also reveals a new monumentality and simplification of form. Jan also painted a series of independent portraits, such as that of his wife (1439; Bruges), which are remarkable for their dispassionate naturalism. The monumentality of his conceptions belies the fact that most of his pictures are quite small; for example, the Antwerp *Virgin by the Fountain* (1439) measures less than eight by five inches. Jan's closest follower was Petrus *Christus, who may have completed some pictures apparently unfinished at his master's death. Generally, however, the style of Rogier van der *Weyden was more easily assimilated and was consequently more influential upon subsequent Netherlands painters. Although too demanding to be readily emulated, Jan's method established a permanent standard of excellence. His paintings, more than those of any other artist, defined the outlook and priorities of northern painters before *Dürer.

F

Faber, Johann (1478–1541) German theologian. He was born at Leutkirch near Memmingen and studied at Tübingen and Fribourg. In 1518 he joined the diocesan bureaucracy of the bishop of Constance. At first he sympathized with the reformers, especially with his friend *Erasmus, but later he became a strong supporter of the old order; his knowledge of philosophy and science was valuable to his side in the debate. His treatise *Malleus in haeresim Lutheranam* (1524) earned him the nickname of "hammer of the heretics". Among his diplomatic missions was the occasion when the future Emperor Ferdinand I sent him to England to enlist the support of Henry VIII against the Turks. From 1530 Faber was bishop of Vienna.

Faber Stapulensis *see* Lefèvre d'Étaples, Jacques.

Fabricius, Girolamo (Fabricius ab Aquapendente; 1537–1619) Italian anatomist. A student of *Falloppio at Padua, Fabricius followed him as professor of anatomy in 1565. He is best known for his *De venarum ostiolis* (On the Valves of Veins; 1603) in which he published the first description of these valves. The work had a profound influence on his most famous pupil, William Harvey (1578–1657), the discoverer of the circulation of the blood. Fabricius also worked extensively in the field of embryology, paying particular attention in his *De formato foetu* (1600) to evidence derived from a wide variety of species. He remained nonetheless an Aristotelian, concerned predominantly with the analysis of embryological development in terms of material, efficient, formal, and final causes. It was consequently within this framework that Fabricius, in his *De formatione ovi et pulli* (On the Formation of the Egg and Chick; 1612), sought to understand the embryology of the chick.

facetiae (Latin: jests) Humorous, often indecent, anecdotes and stories, akin to the medieval *fabliaux*, which circulated in Latin among the humanist scholars of the Renaissance. Poggio *Bracciolini's *Facetiae* or *Liber facetiarum*, the chief butts of which were the monastic orders and the secular clergy, was the first and one of the most popular books in the genre.

faenza (French: faience) The type of *majolica that takes its name from the Italian town of Faenza, midway between Bologna and Rimini, which between 1450 and 1520 had about forty active potteries. The most famous of these was the Ca' Pirota. Faenza products were reputed for excellent painting and the use of a fine red colour. Arabesques, grotesques, and trophies *en camaieu* on blue or yellow grounds are usual. Plate backs carry concentric circles or spirals in lapis blue on pale blue.

Faerie Queene, The An epic poem by Edmund *Spenser. Probably begun shortly before 1580, it was left incomplete at the poet's death, with only six books and a fragment of a seventh, out of a projected twelve, having been written. The first three books appeared in 1590, the second three in 1596. The poem is composed in a nine-line stanza with a demanding rhyme scheme, the so-called Spenserian stanza. Spenser's language is notable for its archaisms. The poem is dedicated to Queen Elizabeth and in one sense is an elaborate tribute to her; it is also a complicated allegory, functioning on both moral and political levels, with each book narrating the adventures of a particular knight, representing one of the twelve moral virtues. Thus the first book concerns the Red Cross Knight, or holiness, who has to liberate himself from the wiles of Duessa (Mary Queen of Scots as champion of the Roman Catholic Church) in order to win Una, or truth.

Falconetto, Giovanni Maria (1468–1535) Italian architect. Working chiefly around Padua, Falconetto designed a number of edifices based on classical forms, notably the loggia and odeon in Padua (1524), which later became part of the Palazzo Giustiniani. He was also responsible for the much admired town gates in Padua, the Porta S Giovanni (1528) and the Porta Savonarola (1530). Falconetto was also a painter; a fresco of the *Annunciation* (1514; S Pietro Martire) and architectural frescoes (1503; Duomo) survive in his native Verona.

Falier, Marino (1274–1355) Venetian nobleman. He was elected doge (1354) after many years as ambassador and naval commander. Turning against his fellow patricians, he plotted with commoners to overthrow the oligarchy, but the plot was discovered and Falier was executed. His story inspired Byron's *Marino Faliero (1821)*.

Falloppio, Gabriele (1523–62) Italian anatomist. A pupil of *Vesalius at Padua, Falloppio first served as professor of anatomy at Pisa before returning in 1551 to Padua to occupy the chair once held by his teacher. In his only published work *Observationes anatomicae* (1561), he threw considerable light on the female reproductive organs. The terms "vagina" and "clitoris" were coined and the eponymous Fallopian tubes were fully described. Despite this, he failed to identify the role of the ovaries in reproduction. Falloppio also worked on the anatomy of the head and succeeded in revealing several new structures in the ear. Before he could pursue his investigations further he died of pleurisy at the age of forty.

Family of Love (Familia Caritatis) An obscure branch of *Anabaptists founded (c. 1540) by Hendrick Niclaes (c. 1502–c. 1580) in the Netherlands. It became best established in England during the second half of the sixteenth century through to the end of the seventeenth. A pantheistic and antinomian sect, the Familists were persecuted by Elizabeth I during the 1580s but survived and spread, enjoying a revival of popularity during the 1650s before being amalgamated into other dissenting bodies toward the end of the century.

Fancelli, Domenico di Alessandro (1469–1519) Italian sculptor. A native of Settignano, near Florence, Fancelli was one of the first sculptors to introduce the ideals of the Italian Renaissance into Spain. He executed most of his work at Carrara but frequently visited Ávila and Granada to install his pieces. His major works include the tombs of Cardinal Hurtado de Mendoza (1509; Seville cathedral), of Prince John (1511; S Tomás, Ávila), and of Ferdinand and Isabella (1517; Chapel Royal, Granada). He died at Zaragoza.

Farel, Guillaume (1489–1565) French Swiss reformer. Born at Gap, he studied in Paris and taught Greek and philosophy there. In 1521 he was converted to the reformed faith and soon fled to Basle (1524). He preached in several towns in and near Switzerland, attended a synod of the Waldensians (Vaudois), and settled in Geneva, where he invited Calvin to join him in 1536. Both were expelled (1538) for refusing to impose the usages of Berne on the Genevan church; Farel spent the rest of his life at Metz and Neuchâtel (where he died), with occasional visits to Geneva, to which

Calvin had returned in 1541. His writings were extensive, but marred by hasty composition. His *Maniere et fasson* (1533) was the first reformed liturgy in French.

Farnese, Alessandro (1545–92), Duke of Parma (1586–92) He was the son of Duke Ottavio Farnese of Parma and Margaret, the illegitimate daughter of Emperor Charles V (*see* Margaret of Parma). Brought up in Spain, Farnese accompanied his uncle, Don *John of Austria, to *Lepanto and then (1577) was sent to reinforce him in the Netherlands. On Don John's death (1578) Farnese succeeded him as governor-general and proved to be an astute diplomat, winning the discontented Catholic nobles of the southern provinces over to the Spanish cause under the treaty of Arras (1579). Combining diplomacy with military skill, Farnese won back the lost Habsburg territories, with the exception of Holland and Zeeland. He captured Antwerp in 1585 after a famous siege, but Spanish energies were then dissipated in preparations for the attack on England (*see* Spanish Armada) and the Dutch, under *Maurice of Nassau, regained confidence. A sortie into France (1590) to assist Paris against the forces of Henry of Navarre (*Henry IV) further weakened Farnese's position and he was now fighting the Dutch in the north and the French Protestants in the south. Worn out, he died near Arras.

Farnese, Palazzo A Roman palace commissioned by Cardinal Alessandro Farnese (later Pope *Paul III) and designed in the Florentine style by Antonio da *Sangallo the Younger. Building began in 1517; after Sangallo died (1546) Michelangelo became the chief architect, introducing a number of alterations in the mannerist style. In the 1560s *Vignola took charge of the works until his death in 1573, when Giacomo *della Porta took over, completing the building in 1589. The interior of the palace was decorated with frescoes by Annibale *Carracci, notably the Galleria, which was decorated with mythological scenes. The palace is now occupied by the French embassy.

Farnese family A family from central Italy who ruled Parma and Piacenza from 1545 to 1731. From the twelfth century the family had served the papacy in war and they owed their political power to Alessandro Farnese who became *Paul III (pope 1534–49) and made his son, Pierluigi (1503–47), duke of Parma and Piacenza. Pierluigi's eldest son, Cardinal Alessandro Farnese (1520–89), supported the arts and scholarship and completed the Palazzo *Farnese. Pierluigi's second son, Ottavio (1521–86), married *Charles V's illegitimate daughter, Margaret (*see* Margaret of Parma);

their son, Alessandro *Farnese, was an outstanding general. When the last Farnese duke died without an heir (1731) the duchy passed to Don Carlos of Spain.

Farnesina, Villa A villa outside Rome, built for the Sienese banker Agostino *Chigi. A fine example of Renaissance architecture, the villa was constructed between 1509 and 1521 by Baldassare *Peruzzi, decorated by *Raphael and *Sodoma, and set in gardens that reached to the bank of the Tiber. The building's two storeys were divided into equal bays by Tuscan pilasters, while the exterior walls were also covered with fresco decorations. The villa acquired its modern name after its purchase (1580) by the great patron of the arts Cardinal Alessandro Farnese.

Farrant, Richard (c. 1528–80) English composer. He appears to have joined the Chapel Royal under Edward VI and retained his post under Mary, but resigned in 1564 to direct the music at St George's Chapel, Windsor. He was appointed master of the Chapel Royal choristers in 1569, and kept his position as well as that in Windsor until his death. A service and three anthems are all that remain of his church music. Although not numerous, his works were popular and survive in a large number of sources. Farrant formed a dramatic company from the Windsor choristers; he wrote several plays, none of which survives.

Fauchet, Claude (?1530–?1602) French magistrate and historian. After studying law in his native Paris and in Orleans, Fauchet embarked on a successful legal career, rising to the office of president of the *cour des monnaies* (1581). He also made his name as a historian with such works as *Antiquités gauloises et françaises* (1579–1602) and *Recueil de l'origine de la langue et poésie française* (1581), a major contribution to French literary history. Forced to leave Paris after the *Journée des Barricades (1588), Fauchet returned in 1594 to find his library pillaged and his fortune ruined. He died in poverty.

Faust, legend of The story of a theologian whose thirst for knowledge leads him to sorcery and a pact with the Devil. In 1587 the Frankfurt printer Johann Spies published the anonymous and immediately popular *Historia von D. Johann Fausten*. Little is known about the historical George Faust (*or* Sabellicus; c. 1480–1540), a scholar and quack whose presence is recorded at various German universities in the early sixteenth century. Tales of his exploits combined with material from elsewhere (such as the motif of the pact with the Devil and the contemporary interest

in witchcraft) to produce a legend that has resounded in literature ever since. Faust's demonic companion, Mephistopheles, for twenty-four years shows him the world and its pleasures, helps him with magic pranks (an important element in comic treatments of the theme), brings him Helen of Troy as his mistress – and ultimately claims his soul. The power of the legend lay in its combination of Renaissance and Reformation ideas. It is the ungodly arrogance of Faust's intellectual curiosity (and especially his interest in the pagan classical world) which in the eyes of the moralizing Lutheran author merits his damnation. The *Historia* was translated into English before 1592 and inspired *Marlowe's tragedy *Dr Faustus*.

Feliciano, Felice (1433–c. 1479) Italian epigraphist, antiquary, and calligrapher. Feliciano was born in Verona. At some time in the 1460s he devised a way to form monumental Roman capitals on mathematical rules derived from the study of ancient inscriptions at Rome, Ravenna, and elsewhere; a collection of these, dedicated to Mantegna, has survived in manuscript. The effect of these studies can be seen in inscriptions on many Renaissance commemorative statues. He also wrote a number of calligraphic manuscripts in a hand which exercised a considerable influence over later manuals of penmanship. His interest in antiquities earned him the name "L'Antiquario". He also wrote poetry in the vernacular, and his interests included printing and alchemy, the latter causing him to spend much time and money on the search for the philosopher's stone.

Feltre, Vittorino da *see* Vittorino da Feltre.

Ferdinand I (1503–64), Holy Roman Emperor (1558–64) Ferdinand was born at Alcalá de Henares, the younger brother of Emperor *Charles V, whose career and personality overshadowed his own. In 1521 Ferdinand married Anna of Hungary, and Charles granted him extensive territories in central Europe, in which Ferdinand acted as his brother's representative. At Vienna, which he made his capital from 1530, he gathered around him a circle of scholars and artists and founded a notable collection of books and coins. In 1531 Charles rewarded Ferdinand for his loyalty with the title of king of the Romans, thus designating him heir to the empire.

After the death of Ferdinand's childless brother-in-law, Louis II of Hungary and Bohemia, at *Mohács, Ferdinand was elected king of both realms (1526), but a strong Hungarian nationalist party under John Zapolya resisted. War dragged on until Hungary was split between the claimants (1538), and even after Zapolya's death (1540)

Ferdinand's claim was contested by Zapolya's son, supported by the Turks and other enemies of the Habsburgs. The rise of Protestantism in the Habsburg lands was the second main issue of Ferdinand's reign, which he attempted to handle by negotiation and compromise.

Charles's attempts to secure the imperial succession for his son (later *Philip II of Spain) occasioned a temporary rift between the brothers around 1550, but thereafter Ferdinand increasingly took charge of imperial business. In 1555 he achieved the important religious settlement of the peace of *Augsburg. His own short reign as emperor, following Charles's abdication (1556) was taken up with the perennial problems of the Turks and religious strife. He was succeeded by his son *Maximilian (II).

Ferdinand I (Ferrante; 1423–94), King of Naples (1458–94). He was the illegitimate son of *Alfonso I of Naples (Alfonso V of Aragon), who on his death left his Aragonese possessions to his brother John and Sicily and Naples to Ferdinand. Educated by *Valla, Ferdinand inherited his father's enlightened attitude to patronage of the arts and scholarship, but his reign was much troubled by papal opposition (on account of Ferdinand's illegitimacy Calixtus III refused to recognize him on his accession), wars with the Turks and with the Angevin claimant to the Neapolitan throne, and baronial insurrections. He is notorious for his massacre of his nobles in 1485 after they had surrendered on Ferdinand's unequivocal promise of an amnesty. He was succeeded by *Alfonso II, his son by Isabella of Clermont.

Ferdinand II (1452–1516), King of Aragon (1479–1516), and **Isabella I** (1451–1504), Queen of Castile (1474–1504). In 1469 the marriage of these two heirs to Spain's principal kingdoms prepared the way for a united Spain. While respecting the different laws and customs of their domains Ferdinand and Isabella diminished feudal and local rights and extended the authority of the crown. They quelled overmighty lords and retrieved lands lost by earlier rulers. Relying on officials personally loyal to them, they strengthened their authority through *hermandades*, viceroys, and a reformed conciliar system. They also gained great prestige as patrons of learning and the arts. By the time Ferdinand died their territories had been extended to cover the whole Iberian peninsula except Portugal. In 1492 they completed the Christian Reconquest (Riconquista) with the capture of Granada, the last Moorish stronghold in Spain, and went on to take Algiers in 1510. Cerdagne and Roussillon were acquired by treaty in 1493 and Navarre was conquered by Ferdinand in 1512. He had further increased his Mediterranean empire by conquering Naples in 1504, and his and Isabella's support for Christopher *Columbus brought Spain great wealth and vast territories in the New World.

In 1494 Pope *Alexander VI recognized their loyalty to the Church by proclaiming them "the Catholic Kings"; this loyalty was principally shown by their support for the *Spanish Inquisition which was established in 1478 under *Torquemada. The Inquisition was concerned with the conversion of Jews and Moors, and was ultimately responsible for the expulsion from Spain of the Jews (1492) and the Muslim Moors (1500). The Catholic Kings presided over reforms which strengthened and purified the Church in Spain.

When Isabella died without a son, Castile passed to her mad daughter, Joanna, who had been married (1496) to the Habsburg heir, Philip the Handsome of Burgundy. As Ferdinand's second marriage proved childless, at his death all the domains of Ferdinand and Isabella passed to their Habsburg grandson, Charles I of Spain (also Emperor *Charles V).

Fernández, Gregório (Gregório Hernández; c. 1576–1636) Spanish sculptor. Active chiefly in Valladolid, Fernández produced numerous painted sculptures with a religious theme, many of which were intended for use in religious processions. His best pieces included dramatic figures of the dead Christ, such as that in the S Cristo monastery at El Pardo near Madrid (1605), which bore the influence of classical works as well as the Gothic tradition. Other works, which marked Fernández out as a master of baroque naturalism, include *St Veronica* (1614), a *Pietà* (1617; Valladolid museum), and the high altar for Plasencia cathedral (1624–34).

Fernández de Navarrete, Juan (El Mudo; c. 1526–79) Spanish painter. His nickname, "El Mudo", arose from the fact that he was a deaf-mute. Fernández was born in Logroño, studied in Italy under Titian, and became painter to King Philip II in 1568. From 1576 he also helped in the decoration of the Escorial near Madrid, producing a series of altarpieces for the church there, among them a striking *Burial of St Lawrence* (1579). He died in Toledo.

Fernel, Jean François (1497–1558) French physician. An innkeeper's son, Fernel studied medicine at the university of Paris where, in 1534, he was appointed professor of medicine. Soon afterwards he became physician to *Henry II after successfully treating his mistress, *Diane de Poitiers. He was also responsible with his *Medicina* (1554), a work known in some thirty editions, for one of the leading medical textbooks of his day. In a more controversial work, *De abditis rerum causis* (On the hidden causes of things; 1548), he sought to develop a more rational system of medicine by denying the relevance of astrology and other occult sciences to his profession. Much earlier Fernel had published a work of geodesy, *Cosmotheoria* (1528), in which he measured the length of a degree of meridian with notable accuracy.

Ferrabosco, Alfonso (1543–88) Italian composer. Born at Bologna into a family of musicians (his father, Domenico Ferrabosco (1513–74), was a well-known composer in Italy), Ferrabosco was first active as a musician in Rome, but by 1562 was in England in the employ of Queen Elizabeth. He travelled abroad many times, and by 1582 had entered the service of the duke of Savoy in Turin, thus breaking his promise of lifelong service to Elizabeth. Ferrabosco did much to interest English composers in Italian music; his madrigals were particularly influential, sixteen of them being included in the anthology *Musica transalpina* (1588). His son, Alfonso II (c. 1575–1628), was born in Greenwich and became a violinist, teacher, and composer at the courts of James I and Charles I. He collaborated with Inigo Jones and Ben Jonson in the production of court masques and composed fantasias for viol consort.

Ferrante *see* Ferdinand I, King of Naples.

Ferrara A northern Italian city state on a branch of the River Po. A Lombard town in the eighth century, Ferrara became an independent commune under the papacy in the tenth century. Ferrara, with its population of about 30 000 in 1500, was too small to compete politically with the larger Italian city states, but it was an important regional power and a prosperous focus of agriculture and trade.
Under *Este rule (1264–1597), Ferrara was an important centre of letters and the arts. Its university was founded in 1391. In the fifteenth and sixteenth centuries it was the home of distinguished literary figures (*Boiardo, *Ariosto, *Tasso) and artists (*Tura, the *Dossi, *Cossa). The sixteenth-century Este court was also renowned for its music, particularly its women singers, and attracted composers, such as *Luzzaschi and *Gesualdo. Notable Renaissance buildings include the Castello Estense, the Palazzo di Schifanoia, and the Palazzo dei Diamanti, which takes its name from the diamond emblem of the Este on the façade. Ferrara went into decline when the papacy regained control in 1598 after the death of Alfonso II d'Este without an heir.

Ferrara, Council of *see under* Florence, Council of.

Ferrari, Gaudenzio (c. 1475–1546) Italian artist. Born at Valduggia in Piedmont, Gaudenzio worked in Lombardy, Piedmont, and Milan. Early influences upon his style included those of Leonardo da Vinci and Perugino, although he also borrowed from the works of notable German artists, Pordenone, and Lotto in developing his own highly emotional approach. His earliest works were chapel decorations executed at Varallo in northern Italy, where he also painted a major fresco cycle on the life of Christ at the Sacro Monte (begun in 1517). This cycle was unusual in that it incorporated a number of terracotta figures, also by Gaudenzio, to enhance the three-dimensional effect. Other frescoes painted in Lombardy included series in S Cristoforo in Vercelli (1529–32) and for the dome of Sta Maria dei Miracoli in Saronno (1534), which indicates the influence of Correggio.

Ferreira, António (1528–69) Portuguese poet and dramatist. He was born in Lisbon and studied at Coimbra, where he came under the influence of the humanist Diogo de Teive. His life was spent as a judge in Lisbon, where he died a victim of the plague. His poems, *Poemas lusitanos* (1598), were published by his son. A friend and the outstanding disciple of Sá de *Miranda, Ferreira was an admirer of Virgil and Horace and wrote epigrams, epistles, eclogues, and odes as well as Petrarchan sonnets. He strongly defended the use of Portuguese (as opposed to Latin or Spanish), urged the reform of literature through the new metres (as introduced by *Boscán, *Garcilaso de la Vega, and Miranda) and the revival of classical models. He wrote two mediocre prose comedies, *Bristo* and *O Cioso* (published with Miranda's comedies, 1622). His *Tragedia de Dona Inês de Castro* (written after 1553; published 1586), a five-act blank-verse play based on classical Greek models and concerned with a famous historical incident, is the most important and successful tragedy of Renaissance Portugal.

Festa, Costanzo (c. 1490–1545) Italian composer. Festa's works mark the emergence of native Italian composers from the lengthy period of dominance by Flemish musicians. Festa probably came from Tuscany, and his earliest works are found in the Medici Codex of 1518, which was compiled on the marriage of Lorenzo II de' Medici, nephew of Pope Leo X. In the early 1510s Festa seems to have been employed at the French court. In 1517 he joined the papal choir in Rome, remaining a member until his death. Despite his ecclesiastical duties, Festa's historical importance is as one of the earliest madrigalists; the first publication to use the word "madrigal", the anthology *Madrigali de diversi musici libro primo* (1530), contains compositions by him. His madrigals are less substantial than his motets, though they show a good deal of textural variety. Some are complex in their use of counterpoint while others are consistently homophonic.

Feuillants Reformed Cistercians named after Les-Feuillans, near Toulouse, where their order was founded in 1577 by Abbot Jean de la Barrière (1544–1600). Encouraged by Henry III, the Feuillants were established in Paris and played a major part in the reform of the capital. By the time they were given status as an independent order (1589), the Feuillants had spread to Italy, where they were known as Bernardines. The order became less austere during the seventeenth century but remained influential until its demise at the end of the Napoleonic wars.

Fiammingo, Dionisio *see* Calvaert, Denys.

Ficino, Marsilio (1433–99) Italian humanist scholar and philosopher. He was born at Figline, near Florence, and taken at an early age into the household of Cosimo de' *Medici. In stressing the divine origins of both Christian and pagan revelations, he played a seminal role in the Renaissance process by which the inspiration of Greek and Roman antiquity, as preserved in the Platonic and Neoplatonic traditions, was absorbed and revived in the Christian world of fifteenth-century Europe. In 1462 he became head of the *Platonic Academy, which was based at Cosimo de' Medici's villa at Careggi and from where Ficino corresponded with admirers all over Europe, including John *Colet and Johann *Reuchlin. A proficient Greek scholar, Ficino undertook a new translation of Plato's works into Latin. This translation, completed in 1477, aroused interest in Platonism throughout Europe and remained the standard Latin text of Plato's work for over a century. Ordained priest in 1472 and appointed a canon of Florence cathedral in 1484, Ficino made explicit his defence of Platonic philosophy in a Christian context with his influential *De Christiana religione* (1476) and *Theologia Platonica* (1482), arguing in the latter his belief in the immortality of the soul. He wrote a number of biblical commentaries, but his interest in mysticism, first manifested in his work on the Hermetic *Pimander* (1471), continued to play a major role in his thought; in his later years he translated Plotinus (1492), (pseudo-) Dionysius the Areopagite (1496/97), and Iamblichus (1497). The mystical strain in his philosophy led in 1489 to his being accused of the practice of magic, but his

influential friends saved him from the usual consequences of such a charge. The bulk of his *Epistolae*, published in 1495 and covering the period 1473–94, formulate his official pronouncements on Platonic questions. *See also* Neoplatonism, Renaissance.

Field of the Cloth of Gold The field near Calais where *Francis I of France met *Henry VIII of England in June 1520. Public and private negotiations were accompanied by a lavish court spectacle and show of friendship between the two monarchs. Henry VIII was able to display himself as a great and powerful European monarch, but the meeting had little real significance. *Wolsey was already negotiating with *Charles V and England joined the emperor's anti-French alliance in 1521.

Filarete (Antonio Averlino; c. 1400–69) Italian sculptor and architect. Filarete was born in Florence. His nickname is derived from the Greek, meaning "lover of virtue", and is typical of his rather clumsy and pedantic attempts to emulate the sculpture and architecture of antiquity. His masterpiece is the huge west door of St Peter's, Rome, cast in bronze, with enamelled and gilded decoration, about 1445. A reduced version of the Roman statue of Marcus Aurelius is the earliest datable bronze statuette of the Renaissance and was presented in 1465 to Piero de' Medici, to whom in the same year Filarete dedicated one copy of his imaginative *Treatise on Architecture*. This was devoted to an ideal city named Sforzinda, after a prominent Milanese patron. His principal surviving building is the hospital in Milan (1456–65), where Lombard ornamented brickwork is combined with Brunelleschian Renaissance forms.

FILARETE *An imaginary building from Sforzinda.* (*Biblioteca Nazionale, Florence*)

Filelfo, Francesco (1398–1481) Italian scholar, teacher, and rhetorician. Born at Tolentino, he studied at Padua, where he was appointed professor at eighteen. In 1419 he travelled to Constantinople to learn the language and acquire Greek manuscripts. There he married Theodora, daughter of his teacher John Chrysoloras. He returned to Venice (1427) with over forty manuscripts, but was dissatisfied with his reception and moved on, first to Bologna, then to Florence. He quarrelled with the Florentine humanists and Cosimo de' Medici and had to leave the city (1434) for Siena; eventually he reached Milan (1440) where he remained, apart from a visit to Rome (1475). In 1481 he was invited back to Florence, but died there soon afterwards. Filelfo's quarrelsome temperament made him highly unpopular. Nevertheless, at the time of his death his reputation as a scholar was deservedly known throughout Italy.

Finiguerra, Maso (1426–64) Italian goldsmith, designer, and engraver. Born in Florence, Maso was praised by Vasari and Benvenuto Cellini as a print maker and a master of niello, a type of decorative silverwork in which silver is incised with a black metallic compound. As a young man he may have assisted *Ghiberti on the east door of the baptistery in Florence and he was later associated with Antonio *Pollaiuolo, several of whose paintings Maso may have reproduced in a series of copperplate engravings (1459–64). Although Maso did not actually invent the process of copper engraving as Vasari claimed, he was instrumental in developing its use as an extension of niello work. Few works by Maso survive; among those that are often attributed to him are the Thewalt cross (c. 1464; Metropolitan Museum of Art, New York) and a series of engravings, the *Seven Planets*.

Fioravanti, Aristotele (c. 1415–c. 1485) Italian architect and engineer. Born in Bologna into a family of architects, Fioravanti is remembered chiefly for his spreading of Renaissance ideas throughout Europe in the course of his many travels. After work in Rome, Bologna, and Milan, and other major Italian artistic centres, Fioravanti was invited to Hungary in 1467 where he worked for a short time for King *Matthias Corvinus. In 1475 he was summoned to Russia to build the cathedral of the Assumption (*Uspenskii Sobor*) on the Kremlin, combining elements of conventional Russian church architecture with features of Renaissance design. He died in Moscow.

Fiori da Urbino *see* Barocci, Federico.

fire For Aristotle fire itself was one of the four elements. Combined from the hot and the dry, it was as much a substantial part of the universe as the other elements; earth, water, and air. The assumption, however, began to be questioned by the chemists and alchemists of the Renaissance. *Paracelsus, for example, held that matter was composed of the three elements, salt, sulphur, and mercury, with sulphur serving as the element of combustibility in matter. While man cannot live, he argued, without earth, water, or air, "it is well possible for a man to be bred, and to live without fire." *Cardano was equally dismissive of Aristotelian theory. He accepted the elemental nature of earth, air, and water but insisted, perceptively, that fire was simply a mode of motion, a view repeated later by *Bacon in his *Novum organum* (1620). It did not, however, persist; Robert Boyle (1627–91) and later generations of chemists rejected Bacon's view and argued instead for the separate existence of particles of fire.

firearms Portable weapons from which projectiles are fired by an explosion (*compare* cannon). The earliest firearms, the arquebuses, emerged in the late fourteenth century. They were merely long, smooth-bored barrels, with a touch-hole through which a hot iron ignited the priming powder. So cumbersome were they, and so prolonged was the loading process, that they initially required the protection of an equal number of pikemen. These weapons were soon replaced by matchlocks operating on the more convenient principle of firing the gun with the aid of specially prepared, smouldering rope. The matchlock, despite such disadvantages as being difficult to fire in the rain, was unchallenged throughout the fifteenth century. Shortly after 1500, however, there arose competition from the wheel-lock, designed, according to one tradition, by *Leonardo da Vinci. In this case a piece of iron was held against a spring-loaded wheel; when the trigger was pulled the wheel revolved and the resulting sparks from the iron were directed into the priming pan. The principle was simplified in the flintlock, which began to appear from about 1620 and, in one form or another, survived until the development of the percussion cap in 1807. One further improvement was the introduction of rifling in about 1500. Although used initially in hunting weapons, rifling was put to military use by Christian IV of Denmark early in the seventeenth century. See Plate XXIX.

Firenzuola, Agnolo (Michelangelo Girolamo; 1493–1543) Italian writer. Firenzuola was born in Florence and after studying law, he became a monk in 1517. He was released from vows in 1526 after visiting the papal court in Rome, where his literary friends included *Aretino, *Bembo, *della Casa, and others. He returned to Florence in 1534 and spent the rest of his life as abbot of a church near Prato. His posthumously published works were widely known in manuscript during his life. He wrote two comedies, translated Apuleius (*Asino d'oro*, 1550), and wrote treatises on feminine beauty and orthography. His major works are *Ragionamenti d'amore* (1548; *Discourses on Love*), comprising an uncompleted group of *novelle* imitating the *Decameron*, and *Prima veste dei discorsi degli animali* (1548; *First Version of the Animals' Discourses*), a faithful rendering of the Spanish version of tales from India, the *Panchatantra*.

Fischart, Johann ("Der Mentzer"; 1546–90) German writer. His nickname might indicate that he was born in Mainz. Following several years travelling and studying in France, Holland, England, and Italy, Fischart gained his doctorate in law at Basle in 1574. For a time he worked as a proofreader for his brother-in-law, a Strasbourg printer, before taking a post as magistrate near Saarbrücken in 1580. Fischart's writings include translations and paraphrases of Greek, Latin, French, Dutch, and earlier German works, and also many didactic satires, such as *Till Eulenspiegel* (1572), a verse account of the folk hero's adventures. As a Protestant, he frequently used satire to attack the Roman Catholic Church. In the tradition of *Brant and *Murner, his satirical style also owes much to Rabelais, the first book of whose *Gargantua et Pantagruel* he paraphrased in German. His most acclaimed original work is the poem *Das glückhafft Schiff von Zürich* (1576), describing a day's boat journey; it is modelled on the classical epic.

Fisher, St John *see* John Fisher, St.

Flémalle, Master of *see* Campin, Robert.

Fletcher, Giles, the Elder (1546–1611) English lawyer, diplomat, and writer. Born in Watford and educated at Eton and Cambridge, Fletcher gained his doctorate in law in 1581. From 1587 to 1605 he was remembrancer of the City of London. A diplomatic mission to Scotland (1586) was followed by one to Germany and then to Russia (1588), where he secured important concessions for English merchants, despite a hostile reception from the tsar. His frank account of *The Russe Commonwealth* (1591) was suppressed on publication on account of the English traders' fears that it would antagonize the Russians. He also wrote a cycle of sonnets entitled *Licia* (1593) and a quantity of Latin verse. His sons Giles the Younger and Phineas were also poets.

Fletcher, Giles the Younger (c. 1585–1623) English poet. The younger son of Giles *Fletcher the Elder, he was born in London, went to Cambridge in 1603, and became reader in Greek grammar there in 1615. About 1618 he left Cambridge and in 1619 became rector of Alderton, Suffolk, where he spent the rest of his life. His chief work, the long devotional poem *Christ's Victorie and Triumph* (1610), acknowledges a debt to both *du Bartas and *Spenser.

Fletcher, John (1579–1625) English dramatist. Born at Rye, the son of a clergyman, Fletcher is chiefly remembered for his collaboration with Francis *Beaumont. His earliest known independent play is the pastoral *The Faithful Shepherdess* (1608/09); before then little is known of his life. Fletcher also probably collaborated with *Shakespeare on *The Two Noble Kinsmen* and with Massinger, Rowley, and Middleton. He is reported to have died of the plague.

Fletcher, Phineas (1582–1650) English clergyman and poet. He was born at Cranbrook, Kent, the elder son of Giles *Fletcher the Elder, and was educated at Eton and Cambridge. While a fellow at King's College, Cambridge (1611–16), he wrote (1614) the pastoral play *Sicelides* (1631). He became chaplain to Sir Henry Willoughby, who in 1621 presented him to the living of Hilgay in Norfolk, where he remained for the rest of his life. The contents of his volume of verse *The Purple Island…with Piscatorie Eclogs* (1633) were written in his youth. The title poem, an allegory of the human body, is strongly influenced by Spenser, and the "Piscatorie Eclogs" trace their origin to *Sannazaro (*see also* pastoral).

Florence A city state situated on the River Arno in Tuscany, central Italy. Florence was founded as the Roman military colony of Florentia. During the late Middle Ages it developed from a small city of moneylenders and cloth manufacturers to become a major Italian power and a dominating European influence during the period of the Renaissance. Its vernacular was the basis of the modern Italian language; in political and social development it gave Europe the model of an ideal prince and the first example of a genuine bourgeoisie. The *Bardi, *Medici, and other banking and commercial houses extended their power and influence throughout Europe. In learning and the arts Florence led the Renaissance.

During the earlier years of the Renaissance Florence's achievements were made in the face of political turmoil. Throughout the fourteenth century it was a battleground for the conflict of *Guelfs and Ghibellines, and it was constantly threatened by Milanese expansionism. Its merchant oligarchy was riven by feuds and threatened by the poorer citizens, notably in the revolt of the *ciompi (1378). By 1434 the Medici family had established their power in the city; the rich merchant families were generally prepared to accept Medici rule, which preserved the republican forms of government, gave them stability, and extended Florence's power over Tuscany, but the city did free itself briefly from the Medici for two periods during the Wars of *Italy (1494–1512; 1527–30).

Renaissance Florence was the centre for such architects, painters, and sculptors as *Alberti, *Brunelleschi (who designed the cathedral dome), *Cellini, *Donatello, *Ghiberti, *Leonardo da Vinci, *Masaccio, *Michelangelo, *Uccello, and *Vasari. In letters and scholarship Florence was the centre of Platonic studies under *Ficino, and the home of *Boccaccio, *Dante, *Galileo, *Machiavelli, and *Petrarch. It was also the birthplace of the navigator Amerigo *Vespucci.

A large and a prosperous city with close on 100 000 inhabitants in the late fifteenth century, Florence is famous for the magnificent Renaissance buildings which have survived there. These include several fine churches (Sta Croce, the Duomo), palaces (della Signoria, Pitti, Rucellai, Strozzi, *Uffizi), and other public works (Boboli gardens, Ponte Vecchio).

Florence, Council of The Church council that secured a short-lived reconciliation between the Western (Roman Catholic) and Eastern (Greek Orthodox) Churches and reasserted papal supremacy over the councils. It was in fact held in three cities – Ferrara (1438–39), Florence (1439–43), and Rome (1443–45). In 1437 Pope *Eugenius IV dissolved the Council of *Basle and ordered the next assembly to meet at Ferrara. The new council was to seek a religious reconciliation with the Greeks who were soliciting support against the *Ottoman Turks; Ferrara was considered to be a mutually convenient location for talks. The Council of Basle, offended by the pope's command to dissolve, continued to sit, refused to recognize the Ferrara Council when it met in 1439, deposed Eugenius, and elected in his place Felix V (antipope 1439–49).

Despite this, negotiations began with the Greek emperor, John VIII Palaeologus, and Joseph, Patriarch of Constantinople, resulting in the Decree of Union, promulgated on 6 July 1439 at Florence. By this decree the Greeks accepted the Latin statement of doctrine, including the contentious *Filioque* (and from the Son) clause in the Creed. Although some points, including the concept of papal primacy, caused much difficulty, eventually all the Greek bishops, except Mark of

Ephesus, accepted its dictates, though many were to recant shortly after. Hugely advantageous to papal prestige, the decree assured popular recognition of Eugenius's primacy in the West as well as the legality of his council at Florence. The members of the schismatic Basle assembly were excommunicated for heresy, and in 1441 the Bull *Etsi non dubitemus* declared the subservience of councils to popes. The remaining work of the council was directed at attaining further unions with other Eastern Churches before its dissolution in 1445.

The Council of Florence was also significant in the incidental role it played in bringing from the East scholars of the calibre of *Bessarion and *Plethon, who inaugurated *Greek studies in Italy.

Florentine Academy *see* Orti Oricellari; Platonic Academy.

Florio, John (?1553–1625) English courtier and translator of Italian descent. His father was an Italian Protestant refugee and Florio may have spent part of his youth abroad during Mary I's reign. He obtained the patronage of the earl of *Leicester in the 1570s and in 1603 became reader in Italian to Queen Anne. His *Worlde of Wordes*, an Italian-English dictionary which appeared first in 1598, was brought out in an enlarged edition in 1611 with a dedication to the queen. He also published a well-received translation of Montaigne's *Essays* (1603). In 1620 he retired to Fulham, where he died of the plague.

Floris, Cornelis (Cornelis de Vriendt; c. 1514–75) Netherlands sculptor and architect. A native of Antwerp and brother of Frans *Floris, Cornelis seems to have received his initial training from one of the early Netherlands Italianist artists, possibly Pieter *Coecke. In 1538 he was in Rome, whence he had returned to Antwerp by the following year. Floris published two volumes of engravings: one, with various adaptions of grotesque ornament, was published in 1556 and the other, with numerous designs for funeral monuments, in 1557. He executed numerous tombs, church screens, and other ecclesiastical furnishings in the Netherlands, and as far afield as north Germany and Scandinavia. However, his most famous work was the new town hall at Antwerp (1561–66), one of the key monuments of Flemish mannerist architecture. Floris's principal student was Hans *Vredeman de Vries.

Floris, Frans (Frans de Vriendt; 1516–70) Netherlands painter. The brother of Cornelis *Floris and the most famous pupil of Lambert *Lombard, Floris was registered as a member of the guild in his native Antwerp in 1540. Shortly afterwards he visited Rome, where he was deeply impressed by the Italian mannerists such as *Vasari, *Salviati, *Bronzino, and *Zuccaro. By 1547 he had returned home, where he worked for William of Orange and other illustrious patrons as a painter and designer of festival decorations and the like. His most famous painting, the *Fall of the Rebel Angels* (1554; Antwerp), includes numerous direct quotations from Michelangelo's *Last Judgment*. His own later *Last Judgment* (1565; Vienna) utilizes an expressively dynamic asymmetrical composition which suggests the influence of Tintoretto. Floris's style represents an extremely Italianate formulation of northern Mannerism, although his drawing has a linearity and his subject matter a sense of fantasy, both of which recall the northern late Gothic tradition. He was also capable of remarkably naturalistic portraits, of which a fine example is the *Falconer's Wife* (1558; Caen). From the mid-sixteenth century Floris's workshop was probably the most dynamic art centre in the Netherlands with, reputedly, more than a hundred pupils.

Flötner, Peter (active 1522–46) Swiss sculptor and engraver. Born in Thurgau, Flötner moved to Nuremberg in 1522, shortly after his first journey to Italy, which he revisited soon after 1530. His Stuttgart bronze horse (c. 1520–30) seems to reflect the naturalistic trend in late Gothic, but his masterpiece, the Nuremberg Apollo fountain (1532), is an entirely classical conception. Ultimately based upon the composition of an engraving by Jacopo de' Barbari, its formal clarity is remarkable. "Local colour" is confined to its base, which incorporates an agitated crowd of *putti* and sea creatures. This contrast corresponds to certain developments in contemporary Italian Mannerism. Flötner was deeply conscious of the distinction between the German and Italian traditions: a caption on a print which he executed during the 1530s actually describes the sculptor's ability to work in "Italian" and "German" manners. His influence was broadcast by small sculptures and engravings.

Fludd, Robert (1574–1637) English physician and Rosicrucian. Fludd was born at Bearsted, Kent, attended Oxford university (1591–97), and then travelled abroad, studying chemistry and medicine and becoming acquainted with the tenets of the shadowy Rosicrucians. After several false attempts, he became a fellow of the College of Physicians (1608) and practised successfully in London. He published an *Apologia* (1616) for the Rosicrucians, and their programme underlay most of his medical and philosophical writings, all of them in Latin, and unkindly characterized by an early biographer as "great, many, and mystical".

He was however shrewd enough to be one of the first of his profession to accept, in *Medicina Catholica* (1631), Harvey's account of the circulation of the blood.

Fontainebleau A town and former royal château south of Paris. Set in parkland and forest, the medieval palace was used as a hunting residence but it was pulled down by *Francis I, who wanted to enhance his prestige by building a magnificent palace in the new Renaissance style. Two schools of painting and architectural decoration were associated with Fontainebleau during the sixteenth century. The first was the more important and was based on the court of Francis I, who brought a number of leading artists from Italy and other countries to work on the interior of the newly rebuilt château. Chief of these artists were *Rosso Fiorentino, who arrived in 1530 and was responsible for the Galerie François I (c. 1533–44). *Primaticcio, who joined Rosso in 1532, is best remembered for the decoration of the Galerie d'Ulysse. Other visiting artists were Benvenuto *Cellini and Niccolò dell' *Abbate as well as French and Flemish artists, such as Leonard Thiry (died c. 1550), who was strongly influenced by Rosso and Primaticcio. Although many of their decorations were later lost or damaged, they introduced numerous ideas of the Italian Renaissance and provided the basis of the international mannerist style.

The second school of Fontainebleau was established under *Henry IV, but never equalled the

FONTAINEBLEAU *A detail from Primaticcio's painted and stucco decoration in the Chambre de la Duchesse d'Étampes.*

impact of its predecessor. Henry greatly enlarged the château, adding the Cours des Offices and the Cours des Princes and landscaping the grounds. Artists of the second Fontainebleau school included the Flemish painter Ambroise Dubois (1543–1614), Toussaint Dubreuil (1561–1602), and Martin Fréminet (1567–1602).

Fontana, Annibale (c. 1540–87) Italian sculptor and medallist. He was active in and around Milan, making two statues for the dome piers of Sta Maria presso S Celso and some very fine candelabra for the Certosa di Pavia (1580). Among his portrait medals is one of *Lomazzo.

Fontana, Domenico (1543–1607) Italian architect and engineer. Born at Melide, near Lugano, he was probably in Rome by 1563 and by 1574 he was working for Cardinal Montalto (Felice Peretti), who in 1585 was elected Pope Sixtus V. Fontana thus became architect to the papacy and the following year he achieved fame by transporting the Egyptian obelisk formerly in the Circus Nero to its present site outside St Peter's. This feat of engineering, which he described in an illustrated folio volume entitled *Della trasportatione dell'obelisco Vaticano...* (1590), marked the start of the extensive replanning, demolition, and building that he carried out in Rome. One major work was the completion, with Giacomo *della Porta, of the dome of St Peter's from Michelangelo's model (1586–90). Fontana is not considered to have been a great architect and he has been accused of destroying or spoiling a number of buildings better than his own; his Sistine library (1587–90) in the Vatican, for example, mars *Bramante's Belvedere court. Fontana even considered converting the Colosseum into a wool factory. Pope Clement VIII dismissed him from his post for misappropriating public money (1592), after which Fontana worked in Naples, mainly on the Palazzo Reale, remaining there until his death.

Fontana, Prospero (1512–97) Italian painter. A native of Bologna, Fontana travelled widely and assisted a number of notable artists on decorative projects, including Pierino del Vaga, Vasari, and Zuccaro. Painting in a strongly mannerist style, he worked in such artistic centres as Genoa, Rome, Florence, and Fontainebleau, where he assisted *Primaticcio (c. 1560), but he is chiefly associated with the Bolognese school. Fontana was the earliest teacher of Lodovico *Carracci, while his other pupils included his own daughter Lavinia (1552–1614), whose fame as a portraitist ultimately eclipsed that of her father. She painted many eminent people, both in Bologna and in Rome,

and a self-portrait is to be found in the Palazzo Pitti, Florence.

Foppa, Vincenzo (c. 1427–1515) Italian painter. Born near Brescia, Foppa probably trained in Padua, possibly as a pupil of Squarcione. He subsequently became the foremost painter in Lombardy and Milan until the advent of Leonardo da Vinci. His earliest dated work is a *Crucifixion* (1456; Bergamo), strongly influenced by Jacopo Bellini, from whom Foppa derived his interest in colour and light. Later works also bear the influence of Provençal and Flemish art, as well as the paintings of Bramante, as seen in Foppa's frescoes in Milan of the life of St Peter Martyr (1466–68) and the martyrdom of St Sebastian (1485). Other works include *Boy reading Cicero* (Wallace Collection, London) and *Epiphany* (National Gallery, London).

Forment, Damián (c. 1480–1540) Spanish sculptor. Born in Valencia, Forment was probably trained in Florence, returning to Valencia in 1500 for nine years before establishing a studio in Zaragoza, where he remained until his death. In 1509 he began work on an altar for the cathedral of El Pilar in Zaragoza, in which he combined Gothic elements with Renaissance figures and demonstrated his artistic debt to Donatello. The author of numerous notable altarpieces in alabaster, Forment executed further works for Huesca cathedral (1520–24), the monastery church at Poblet (1527), and S Domingo de la Calzada (1537–40), the last of which also betrayed the influence of Alonso *Berruguete. During the course of these works, Forment gradually exchanged features of Gothic style for those of the Italian Renaissance, and his later pieces were some of the first mannerist works undertaken in Spain.

Formula of Concord *see* Concord, Formula of.

Forster, Georg (c. 1510–68) German doctor and musician. Born in Amberg, Forster received his earliest musical training at the court in Heidelberg. A friend of *Luther and *Melanchthon, he devoted most of his life to the study and practice of medicine. His greatest contribution to music was the compilation of the *Frische teutsche Liedlein* (1539–40). In this sizeable publication he collected *Tenorlieder* by about fifty composers active during the previous half-century to form a representative and useful anthology. His achievement as a musical compiler outweighs his importance as a composer. He died in Nuremberg, where all his publications had been issued.

Foscari, Francesco (1373–1457), Doge of Venice

165

(1423–57) He was born into a noble Venetian family and held several of the highest offices in the republic before being elected doge at the early age of forty-nine. His expansionist policies resulted in Venice's obtaining Bergamo and Brescia (1428), but war with the *Visconti of Milan in the 1430s weakened the republic and checked its further territorial advance. Of all Foscari's children by his two wives, only Jacopo survived into adulthood, and the doge's life after 1444, when the first accusations of corruption were brought against his son, was darkened by Jacopo's crimes and exile. Jacopo died in Candia in January 1457, and the elderly doge was so shattered by grief that he was unable to carry on the business of government and was forced to resign. He died two days later. This tragedy was the basis of Byron's play *The Two Foscari* (written 1821) and Verdi's opera *I due Foscari* (1844).

Fouquet, Jean (active c. 1443/47–81) French manuscript illuminator and painter. The earliest fixed point in Fouquet's career is his visit to Italy (1443/47). Previous to this, it seems likely that he studied under the Bedford Master in Paris and, possibly, in the Netherlands. After his return home (?1449) he was based in his native Tours, working primarily for members of the French court. In 1475 he was appointed painter to Louis XI.

Fouquet's key work of manuscript illumination is the dismembered Book of Hours of Étienne Chevalier, which probably dates from between 1452 and 1461, and of which the largest surviving part is preserved in Chantilly. The Munich Boccaccio, illuminated by Fouquet and his *atelier*, was begun about 1459; at about the same time he began decorating the Paris *Grandes Chroniques de France* for King Charles VII. In 1465 he executed a single miniature for the Book of Hours of Charles de France, brother of Louis XI. This and other undated illuminations, probably of the same decade, indicate how the Hours of Étienne Chevalier remained the model for his devotional miniatures. His frontispiece to the *Statutes of the Order of St Michel* in Paris dates from about 1470 and his illuminations in the duke of Nemours's copy of the *Antiquités Judaïques* were completed by 1476. His latest manuscript illuminations are a series of detached pages in Paris and Amsterdam from a manuscript of the *Histoire ancienne*. Fouquet's few surviving panel paintings comprise the portraits of Gonella (Vienna), Charles VII (Paris), Guillaume Jouvénal des Ursins (Paris), the divided diptych of Étienne Chevalier and the Virgin (Berlin and Antwerp), and the large *Deposition* altarpiece (Nouans).

Fouquet's style, originally of Franco-Flemish derivation, was transformed by his experiences in Italy and his work reveals ideas appropriated from Fra *Angelico, *Andrea del Castagno, *Donatello, and even *Giotto and *Duccio. A highly intellectual artist, he employed classical architectural details to "label" specific non-French locations, including Italy, the classical world, and even paradise. He understood Alberti's system of one-point *perspective, but did not adopt it wholeheartedly as its use threatened to disrupt the unity of text and pictures in his manuscripts. The most significant French artist of the fifteenth century, he profoundly influenced later illuminators such as Jean Bourdichon (died 1521) and Jean Perréal (died 1530).

Fracastoro, Girolamo (c. 1478–1553) Italian physician, poet, and astronomer. Coming from a wealthy Veronese family, Fracastoro was educated at the university of Padua, where he also taught briefly. In 1508 he returned to Verona to run the family estates. He managed nonetheless to produce two important medical works. The first, a poem in Latin hexameters called *Syphilis sive morbus gallicus* ("Syphilis or the French disease"; 1530), not only introduced the term "syphilis" to medical parlance but also contained a detailed description of the disease. In the second work, *De contagione* (1546), Fracastoro argued that some diseases spread by *seminaria contagium* (contagious seeds). No attention was paid to his suggestive ideas. He was also ahead of his time in postulating that fossil mussels discovered (1517) in rocks at Verona were remains of creatures that had once lived in the vicinity. In astronomy Fracastoro proved less innovative. His *Homocentrica* (1538) insisted against Ptolemy (*see* Ptolemaic system) that all heavenly bodies move, without epicycle or eccentric, around the sun in circular orbit. His dialogue *Naugerius, sive de poetica* appeared in a collected edition of his works in 1555; it emphasizes the universality of poetry.

Francavilla, Pietro (Pierre Francheville *or* Francqueville; 1548–1615) Belgian-born French sculptor. Francavilla was born at Cambrai. Initially discouraged from his vocation, he went to Paris as a teenager to learn drawing, before going (1566) to Innsbruck to work with a compatriot, Alexander Colyn, on the tomb of Emperor Maximilian. He was patronized by Archduke Ferdinand of Tyrol and in 1571/72 he went to Rome and Florence with a letter of introduction from Ferdinand to *Giambologna, then established as court sculptor to the Medici. Francavilla went into partnership with Giambologna, taking on (1574) a big commission from Abbot Bracci for garden statuary (now distributed between the Victoria and Albert Museum, the Orangery,

Kensington Palace, in London, and the Wadsworth Atheneum, Hartford, Conn.). Soon afterwards Francavilla assisted Giambologna on the Grimaldi chapel in Genoa and then carved two colossal statues, *Janus* and *Jupiter* (signed and dated 1585), for the Grimaldi palace there; he also carved six statues for the Senarega chapel in Genoa cathedral. Back in Florence, Francavilla helped execute Giambologna's two great marble groups of the *Rape of the Sabines* and *Hercules slaying a Centaur* for the Loggia dei Lanzi. He helped Giambologna with the marble statuary in the Salviati chapel (S Marco) and carved five statues of his own for the Niccolini chapel (Sta Croce). His collaboration with Giambologna is specified in inscriptions on portrait statues of Ferdinando I de' Medici in Arezzo and Pisa.

Francavilla left Florence for France (1604) at the behest of Queen Marie de' Medici, to erect on the Pont-Neuf a bronze equestrian statue of her husband King Henry IV, which was being produced in Giambologna's Florence workshop. In his studio in the Louvre Francavilla modelled four slaves to adorn the corners of its pedestal, and after his death they were cast in bronze by a pupil; these survive (Louvre), but the statue was destroyed in the French Revolution.

Francavilla's style closely echoes Giambologna's and he frequently used his models. In his major works it is hard to determine whether he contributed anything more than competent carving in marble on a grand scale of a design by the greater sculptor. In his defence it should be noted that virtually all Giambologna's sculpture in marble or bronze was produced by close collaboration with just such skilled assistants.

Francesco di Giorgio Martini (1439–1502) Italian architect and architectural theorist. Trained as a painter and sculptor in *Vecchietta's workshop in his native Siena, Francesco subsequently turned to architecture. He wrote his influential *Trattato dell'architettura civile e militare* about 1482. Using *Vitruvius and *Alberti as springboards, Francesco attempted to rationalize and codify architectural practice, using illustrations to clarify his theories. His drawings display eccentric adaptations of Vitruvius' anthropomorphism and an idiosyncratic approach to classical design.

In his capacity as military engineer, Francesco travelled to Milan, Naples, and Urbino, pioneering a design for the angled bastion, and in 1477 he succeeded Luciano *Laurana as architect to Federico da Montefeltro. Moving to Urbino, he probably continued construction of the Palazzo Ducale there and provided plans for the ducal palace in Gubbio, as well as building many fortresses in the Marches. His architectural work is poorly

documented, but his singular style makes attribution fairly secure. His hallmarks include the use of arches supported on piers and capitals with flat fluting, evidenced in the Palazzo Ducale, Urbino, and the Palazzo Communale, Iesi (1486–98); superimposed pilasters whose capitals are formed by the stringcourse, executed in S Bernadino, Urbino (1482–90) and Sta Maria del Calcinaio, just outside Cortona (completed 1516); and the deployment of classical lettering in the courtyards of the ducal palaces of Urbino and Gubbio. Having maintained professional links with Siena throughout his career, Francesco returned there in 1497 after a six-year stay in Naples to advise on military fortifications. A *Nativity* in the Pinacoteca, Siena, is a good example of his work as a painter, among several paintings in the same gallery.

Francheville, Pierre *see* Francavilla, Pietro.

Francia, Francesco Raibolini (1450–1517/18) Italian painter and goldsmith. A native of Bologna, Francia began practising as a goldsmith before turning to painting in 1486. Influenced initially by the Ferrarese artists, Francia entered into partnership with Lorenzo *Costa, with whom he worked until 1506 when Costa left for Mantua. Early works, such as his *Madonna enthroned with Saints* (Pinacoteca, Bologna), exemplify the austerity of the Ferrarese school but later works, under the influence of the paintings of Raphael and Perugino, are executed in an increasingly soft style. Other works include several pictures of the Madonna and the more personal portrait *Federico Gonzaga as a Boy* (1510; Metropolitan Museum of Art, New York).

Franciabigio, Francesco di Cristofano (1482–1525) Italian painter. A notable member of the Florentine school, Franciabigio was a pupil of Albertinelli and Piero di Cosimo and was also influenced by Raphael and Andrea del Sarto. He collaborated with Andrea del Sarto on a series of paintings in SS Annunziata in Florence (1513) and in the Chiostro dello Scalzo in Florence, where Franciabigio painted a *Last Supper*. The two artists established a workshop together and Franciabigio went on to decorate the Medici villa at Poggio a Caiano with del Sarto's pupil Pontormo, executing the celebrated *Triumph of Cicero* there. Franciabigio was also noted for his introspective portraits of young men. Other works which bear the stamp of Raphael include the *Madonna del Pozzo* (c. 1508; Accademia, Florence).

Francis I (1494–1547), King of France (1515–47) Francis was born at Cognac, the son of Charles of Valois and Louise of Savoy, and was brought

FRANCIS I *The king's salamander emblem adorns a wall at the royal château at Blois.*

up as heir-presumptive to *Louis XII, whose daughter Claude (died 1524) he married in 1514. He and his sister Marguerite (*see* Marguerite de Navarre) both received a sound education, and Francis early manifested his lifelong love of hunting, chivalric tournaments, and other vigorous sports.

Inheriting Louis's policy of intervention in Italy, Francis soon after his accession led a campaign that resulted in his victory (1515) at Marignano, southeast of Milan; this left him in possession of Milan and Genoa and he also acquired Parma and Piacenza. By 1523, however, these gains had been negated by the intervention of the newly elected emperor, Charles V, and Francis's efforts to recover the territories ended in his defeat and capture at the battle of *Pavia (1525). Taken to Madrid as a prisoner, he signed a treaty renouncing his Italian ambitions (1526). After this his only territorial advance in the area was the conquest of Savoy and part of Piedmont in 1536. Although he married the emperor's sister as his second wife (1530), Francis wavered for the rest of his reign between allying himself with the Habsburg interests and conspiring against them.

At home Francis's reign was marked by a considerable increase in the monarch's power. Initially sympathetic towards the Protestants, he became from the mid-1530s increasingly repressive in his attitude to religious dissent, culminating in a shameful massacre of the Waldenses (1545). Dominated by his mistresses and favourites, Francis was vain and extravagant, but it was through his patronage that the Italian Renaissance

first made an impact upon French art and architecture (*see* Fontainebleau). He invited *Leonardo da Vinci to France in 1515, and *Cellini, *Primaticcio, *Rosso Fiorentino, and *Serlio were later and more influential Italian visitors. Prompted by *Budé, Francis founded (1530) the lectureships that were the basis for the Collège de France. Among the humanist scholars and writers whom he encouraged was Clément *Marot.

Francis, Duke of Alençon (1554–84), Duke of Anjou (1576–84) The youngest son of *Henry II of France and *Catherine de' Medici, Francis received the duchy of Alençon in 1566. After his elder brother Henry had succeeded to the throne (1574) as *Henry III, Francis succeeded him as duke of Anjou. Although stunted in stature and scarred by smallpox, from 1572 he was the apparently favoured suitor of *Elizabeth I, who nicknamed him her "petite grenouille" (little frog). He visited her in England three times and in 1581 she even announced her firm intention of marrying him. In 1580 the duke was offered limited sovereignty over part of the Netherlands in return for aid against Spain, but impatience at these limitations and military setbacks induced him to turn his troops against Antwerp (1583), the so-called "French fury". He was repulsed and withdrew to France, where he died.

Francis de Sales, St (1567–1622) French churchman and leader of the French Counter-Reformation. Born at Sales in Savoy, he was educated in Annecy, Paris, and Padua. On being ordained (1593) he embarked on the reconversion of much of the Calvinist population of Chablais. In 1602 he was made titular bishop of Geneva, making his headquarters at Annecy. An exceptionally active preacher and prolific writer of letters, he inspired many other French Catholic reformers, including St Jeanne de Chantal (1572–1641), who founded the Congregation of the Visitation in 1610. He wrote two classic books of devotion, *Introduction to a Devout Life* (1608) and *Treatise on the Love of God* (1616), in which he drew up a scheme of devout life attainable by all, laity as well as clergy. He was canonized in 1665.

Francis Xavier, St (1506–52) Jesuit missionary. A Basque of noble extraction, Xavier was born in Navarre. He was one of the small group of original followers that *Ignatius Loyola gathered together in Paris, and with him he took a vow of poverty and chastity in 1534. With Simon Rodríguez, Xavier succeeded in turning Portugal into a Jesuit stronghold by gaining both popular and royal support. In accordance with the wishes of Pope Paul III he set out for the Indies in 1541 with the intention of reasserting Christianity and making new conversions in the Portuguese colonies. Travelling via Mozambique he arrived at Goa in 1542 where he remained for five months. Having had some success among the colonists he travelled to Cochin, Ceylon, Malacca, the Moluccas, and Japan (1549), before returning to Goa in 1551. He then set right certain abuses that had developed in his absence and set sail again, this time with a view to realizing the conversion of the Chinese empire to Christianity. He is reputed to have converted many thousands on the way but never actually reached China for he died of fever in December 1552 on the island of Sancian, just thirty miles short of his destination. Although Xavier is popularly considered to have been the greatest missionary since St Paul, his critics believe that his work would have been of more lasting effect had he concentrated his mission on a single colony or country. Together with Ignatius Loyola, he was canonized in 1622.

Francisco da Hollanda (c. 1517–84) Portuguese artist and art theorist. He was born in Lisbon, where his father, a Netherlands miniaturist, had settled. King John III sent him to Rome in 1537 to study architecture; while there he met many major artists, including Michelangelo, and made an interesting album of archeological drawings, including some of frescoes in the Domus Aurea of Nero that are now destroyed. Francisco's famous *Quatro dialogos da pintura antiga*, recording conversations in Rome in 1538, appeared in his *Tractato de pintura antiga* (1548).

Franck, Sebastian (1499–1542) German theologian and humanist. Franck was born at Donauwörth and after studying at Ingolstadt and Heidelberg he was ordained priest. In about 1525 he became a Lutheran, but later developed an undogmatic form of religion and argued in favour of freedom of thought. This antagonized both reformers and traditionalists in Germany, and he retired to Basle. His major historical work, *Chronica*, appeared in 1531 and an index to the Bible in 1539. He also produced German versions of an anti-Anabaptist tract by Althamer (1528) and of Erasmus's *Praise of Folly* (1534). *Die deutschen Sprichwörter* (1541) was a major compendium of German proverbs.

François I style A trend in the visual arts in France initiated during the reign (1515–47) of Francis I. An enthusiastic patron of the arts, Francis modelled himself upon the Italian princes and actively encouraged the adoption of the ideals of the Italian Renaissance, chiefly through the building and decoration of a number of major French châteaux. Italian artists such as *Rosso Fiorentino, *Leonardo da Vinci, and *Primaticcio were brought to France to work at *Blois, *Chambord, *Fontainebleau, and elsewhere, providing the impetus for a national style incorporating both Gothic and humanist elements. As well as the châteaux, other works from this period in which this fusion of styles can be detected include tapestries, paintings, and furniture.

Frankfurt (Frankfurt-am-Main) A city in western Germany on the River Main. Celtic in origin, the site became a Roman settlement; its name, which dates from the early sixth century, means "crossing of the Franks". From the late Middle Ages Frankfurt prospered on account of its trade fairs (from 1240) and it became an international commercial centre during the Renaissance. Its stock exchange was founded in 1585. Despite its prosperity the city retained its rural character until the sixteenth century. Frankfurt became an imperial free city in 1372 and was an imporant base of Habsburg power by the late fifteenth century. In 1485 the imperial Diet met there. In 1519 it was the scene of the election of Emperor *Charles V. Later the city joined the Lutheran cause until it was forced into submission by Charles (1546).

Franqueville, Pierre *see* Francavilla, Pietro.

Frederick III (1415–93), Holy Roman Emperor (1452–93) The son of Duke Ernest of Styria and Carinthia, Frederick was born in Innsbruck; on his father's death (1424) he was brought up by his uncle, Count Frederick of Tyrol. From 1435 he was co-ruler with his brother Albert (died 1463) of Styria and Carinthia. In 1440 he was chosen German king but his alliance with the papacy through the Concordat of Vienna (1448), which was engineered by the future Pope *Pius II, occasioned great discontent among his subjects, who resented his pledge of their obedience to Rome. Nonetheless Frederick was crowned emperor in Rome by Pope Nicholas V in 1452. Friction with his brother Albert and incursions by his neighbours, the most dangerous of them *Matthias Corvinus of Hungary, caused Frederick to seek to establish his position by an alliance with Duke *Charles the Bold of Burgundy. Negotiations broke down in 1473, when Charles demanded the title of king, but after Charles's death (1477), Frederick was able to bring about the marriage of the duke's heir, *Mary of Burgundy, with his son, the future Emperor *Maximilian I, and thus secured the great Burgundian inheritance for the house of Habsburg. Frederick spent his last years in retirement at Linz where he indulged his passion for alchemy, astronomy, and botany.

Frederick (III) the Wise (1463–1525), Elector of Saxony (1486–1525) An efficient ruler who urged constitutional reform in the empire, Frederick welcomed to his court at Wittenberg scholars and such great artists as *Dürer, *Meit, and *Cranach. He befriended the humanist scholar George *Spalatin and established the university of Wittenberg (1502), where he chose Martin *Luther as professor of philosophy (1508). Frederick protected Luther, refusing to implement the papal bull against him (1520) and sheltering him at Wartburg castle after the imperial ban on him (1521). In 1524 Frederick accepted Luther's reformed doctrines.

French language The romance language of France, also spoken in parts of Belgium, Switzerland, eastern Canada, and in other areas of the former French colonial empire, for example in Africa and the Caribbean.

French developed from Vulgar Latin as spoken by Roman settlers in Gaul (conquered by Julius Caesar, 58–51 BC). Pre-Roman Gaul was inhabited mainly by Celtic tribes, though there were Basques in Gascony and Marseilles had been settled by Greek and Phoenician merchants since about 600 BC. (Provence had become a Roman colony in the second century BC.) Vulgar Latin replaced Gaulish (Celtic) after Caesar's conquest; a few hundred French words – *chemin*, for example – are of Gaulish origin, but in vocabulary and structure the language is primarily derived from Latin. Christianity, introduced in the first century AD, spread rapidly, and a distinctive Gallo-Roman society gradually emerged with its capital at Lugdunum (Lyons). There were incursions by Germanic tribes from the third century AD. One of these, the Franks, was led by Clovis (from 481), who defeated both the other barbarian tribes and the Roman governor and established the Merovingian dynasty at Paris, where it ruled until the last Merovingian was overthrown in 751 by Pepin the Short, father of Charlemagne. A few hundred words of Frankish origin – *guerre*, *honte* ("shame"), *riche*, *danser*, for example – survive in modern French; Old French contained many more that are now no longer in use. By the ninth century French (of which there were a number of dialects) was significantly different from Latin. The earliest extant document in French, the *Serments de Strasbourg* (842), transcribed by the chronicler Nithard (a grandson of Charlemagne), contains the oaths sworn in French and German by the sons of Louis I (Louis the German and Charles the Bald) against their brother Lothaire. The earliest literary text, the *Séquence de Ste Eulalie* (c. 880), was written down soon afterwards.

French evolved in quite different northern and southern forms during the Middle Ages, the line of division extending roughly from the mouth of the Gironde to the Alps. South of this divide, the language came to be known as the *langue d'oc* (*oc*, "yes", from Latin *hoc*); north of it, a number of related dialects were called the *langue d'oïl* (*oïl*, "yes", from Latin *hoc ille*). From the twelfth century the dialect of the Île-de-France – and of Paris, the ancient Frankish capital – gradually came to be preferred over the numerous other dialects (of Normandy, Anjou, Picardy, Champagne, etc.) of the *langue d'oïl*. And in the thirteenth century, the Albigensian crusade helped establish the *langue d'oïl* in the south as well. Literature in the *langue d'oc*, such as that of the Provençal troubadours, which was of major importance in the Middle Ages, began to decline after this time, though Provençal continued as a spoken language, and a number of words borrowed from it persist in modern French vocabulary (*asperge*, *bastide*, *béret*, *cadeau*).

Old French (ninth to thirteenth centuries) and Provençal retained two (nominative and oblique) of the six cases of the Latin noun, but otherwise changes, typical of most other romance languages, gradually occurred: indefinite and definite articles developed from *unus* and *ille*; new analytic constructions (as in the perfect tense of verbs and the comparison of adjectives) replaced Latin synthetic constructions; and complex changes took place in pronunciation and semantics. In the Middle French period (fourteenth and fifteenth centuries), inflections were reduced to their modern minimal levels, resulting in a more settled word order, and the dialect of the Île-de-France became dominant. In the early sixteenth century French, by royal decrees (1520, 1539), supplanted Latin as the dominant language in the legal and official spheres. The authority of Calvin's theological writings in French and translations of the Bible made French acceptable as a medium of religious discourse, while humanists and members of the *Pléiade explored its possibilities as a literary medium on a par with the classical languages. These developments resulted in a great expansion of the vocabulary, with learned borrowings especially from Latin.

The following century was characterized by attempts to control and refine the language, mainly promoted by the Académie Française, which was founded by Richelieu in 1635. The task of compiling an authoritative dictionary was undertaken by Claude Favre de Vaugelas (1585–1650), as editor, and the poet Jean Chapelain (1595–1674). Progress was slow, however, and the *Dictionnaire universel des arts et sciences* (1690) by the Académicien Antoine Furetière (1619–88) appeared first, the first modern encyclopedic dictionary. The Académie's

Dictionnaire (1694) in four volumes originally arranged words by families (roots) rather than alphabetically and was (and remains) concerned with establishing acceptable literary and polite usage rather than describing the language in detail. Subsequent editions, of which there have been eight, have been arranged alphabetically. Other noteworthy early lexicographical works are Robert Estienne's *Dictionnaire françois-latin* (1539), Jean Nicot's *Trésor de la langue françoise* (1606), Gilles Ménage's *Dictionnaire étymologique* (1650), and César-Pierre Richelet's *Dictionnaire françois* (1680).

frescoes Wall paintings executed upon plaster, most notably by Italian artists during the sixteenth century. The medium of fresco (Italian "fresh") was originally developed in the ancient world before being adopted by artists of the Renaissance in the decoration of public buildings, churches, and private houses. In the most permanent form, *buon fresco*, the wall is first plastered and then the basic cartoon is transferred to this surface. Next, an area sufficient for one day's work is coated with plaster in a stage known as the *intonaco*. Dry powder pigment is mixed with water or lime-water and then painted onto the still damp plaster with which it reacts so that the paint becomes part of the actual wall as opposed to a superficial layer. In a more primitive form of fresco, *fresco secco*, the pigment is applied to dry plaster and is consequently more likely to flake off, as happened notoriously in the case of Leonardo da Vinci's *Last Supper* in Milan. Exponents of fresco painting in the early Renaissance included *Giotto in Padua and Florence, *Masaccio in Florence, and *Piero della Francesca in Arezzo and Rimini. It reached its height, however, in the sixteenth century under the direction of *Raphael, best known for his decorations in the Stanze of the Vatican, and *Michelangelo, whose ceiling and *Last Judgment* for the *Sistine Chapel in Rome provided an inspiration for many subsequent fresco artists. Other leading Renaissance artists in this medium, all of whom worked with numerous assistants and combined with other painters on certain cycles, included *Rosso Fiorentino, *Andrea del Sarto, *Pontormo, *Vasari, *Bronzino, *Beccafumi, *Giulio Romano, *Correggio, and Paolo *Veronese.

Frisius, Gemma *see* Gemma Frisius.

Froben, Johann (1460–1527) Swiss scholar and printer. Froben was born at Hammelburg, Bavaria, and after studying in Basle started printing there in 1491, in partnership with *Amerbach and Petri and mostly in Greek, Latin, or Hebrew. The scholars he employed as editors included his friend

*Erasmus, whose Greek New Testament (1516) he printed, as well as many of his other works. Among Froben's authors was Martin *Luther, at least until his disagreement with Erasmus. Well-printed scholarly texts from Froben, among them St Jerome in nine volumes (1516) were distributed all over Europe. He sold type as well as books, once he had adopted roman faces, and introduced the use of italics for quotations. His situation in Basle allowed him to employ the Holbeins, who contributed initials, borders, and other decorations to his books after 1516. His son Hieronymus (1501–65) and grandson Ambrosius (1537–95) continued his work.

Froment, Nicolas (c. 1430–c. 1484) French artist. Originally from Uzès in Languedoc, Froment was active chiefly in Avignon where he established an important school with Enguerrand Quarton in about 1450. Two documented works by Froment survive, both altarpieces: *The Resurrection of Lazarus* (1461; Uffizi) and *Mary in the Burning Bush* (1475–76; cathedral of St-Sauveur, Aix-en-Provence). The former work was painted for *René of Anjou and includes portraits of the king and his wife, while the latter painting demonstrates the artist's control of sculptural form. Despite the lack of polish in these works, they contributed greatly to the introduction of both the ideals of the Italian Renaissance and the realism of Flemish art in subsequent French painting.

frottola A form of secular Italian song which flourished at the end of the fifteenth century and the beginning of the sixteenth. Although the frottola was a specific poetic form, alternatively known as the barzelletta, it was also used as a generic term for Italian secular songs of other poetic forms, such as the strambotto, oda, or canzona. The main centre for the frottola was Mantua, where Isabella d'Este, daughter of Duke Ercole I, encouraged the form. The major collection of frottolas is in eleven books published by *Petrucci in Venice (1504–14). Frottolas are simple in style and were written for varying numbers of performers. They were given in the theatre, sometimes as part of *intermedii. The frottola has been viewed as a precursor of the *madrigal, but some would argue that it represents a distinct strand in musical history.

Frueauf, Rueland, the Elder (c. 1445–1507) Austrian painter. Active in his native Salzburg from about 1478, Frueauf worked at first largely for the Benedictine monks there. His style was influenced by the work of Konrad *Laib, who had painted in Salzburg a few decades earlier; like Laib, Frueauf paid much attention to the expressive power of his figures (as in the Munich *Man of*

Fuchs, Leonhart

Sorrows), which he set in carefully observed landscapes. He died in Passau, to which he had moved in 1497. His son, Rueland Frueauf the Younger (died after 1534), worked in Passau, following his father's style.

Fuchs, Leonhart (1501–66) German physician and botanist. His *De historia stirpium* (1542), followed by a German edition (1543) and many later ones, described about 400 native plants and a hundred foreigners (including North American maize) with illustrations that were copied in many other herbals. The descriptions are arranged alphabetically, with no attempt at classification.

Fugger family The foremost of the trading and banking dynasties that arose in southern Germany, and most notably in Augsburg, during the fourteenth and fifteenth centuries. The pre-eminent position of the Fuggers was largely the result of their acquisition of mining concessions in copper, gold, silver, and quicksilver from the Habsburg

FUGGER FAMILY *Jakob Fugger dictates to a clerk in his accounting house. Behind them, named files indicate the extent of the Fugger financial empire – from Cracow to Lisbon, from Antwerp to Venice. (Herzog Anton Ulrich-Museum, Braunschweig)*

emperors, at a time when European demand for precious metals was rising rapidly. Under the direction of Jakob Fugger ("the Rich"; 1459–1525) between 1478 and 1525, the family fortunes reached their peak, with trading interests extending from the Far East to the New World, and the family acting as bankers to the Habsburgs and the Roman Curia. During this period and throughout the sixteenth century the Fuggers were great patrons of art, commissioning artists and sculptors for portraits and buildings, including a family chapel in Augsburg. Decline set in during the later sixteenth century, however, when the Habsburgs demanded increasingly large and risky loans to finance their wars. Ruined by the Spanish bankruptcies of 1557, 1575, and 1607, the family retired to its country estates.

furniture The Gothic tradition in domestic furnishings, extant throughout Europe before the Renaissance, was less firmly entrenched in Italy than elsewhere, so that the changes consequent on the Renaissance were more of a return to the ancient familiar classicism than the embracing of a new style.

Increasing sophistication in the style of life in Italy from the mid-fifteenth century demanded more and better furniture. Italian Renaissance furniture, principally of walnut, is strongly influenced by classical architecture, and the function is often subordinated to the form. Much is of elegant simplicity ornamented with uncomplicated carving, but other display furniture is more elaborately shaped, covered in gesso, painted, and gilded. Several new forms appear, notably *cassoni replacing Gothic coffers and chests. A characteristic chair, with an X shape and folding construction, derives from the Roman curule chair and is known as a Dante chair. The fashion for tables with tops of marble inlaid with coloured marble or semi-precious stones probably originated in Milan in the mid-sixteenth century and was reinforced by the foundation of the *opificio delle petre dure* in Florence in 1599. Monumental sideboards of classical architectural inspiration also appeared. Beds became increasingly luxurious, with covers of rich velvets and gold embroidery, while throughout the interior fabrics and Turkey carpets were used for sumptuous effect.

In France Italian styles were first adopted after Charles VIII's capture of Naples (1495). Subsequently Italian craftsmen were employed at Amboise and Fontainebleau; other furniture-making centres were in the Île de France and Burgundy. Walnut displaced oak and the refined and delicately carved furniture was often inlaid with ivory, marble, and marquetry. New forms were a light and elegant "caquetoire" (gossip)

172

lady's chair, fixed-top (as opposed to trestle) tables, and armoires in two stages, the upper one with several small enclosed drawers. The exuberance of early Renaissance carving with its medallions and grotesques was gradually mellowed by more restrained classical features, except in the Dijon area, where a school of rich regional carving, inspired by Hughues Sambin, flourished.

In England the Italian Renaissance style was less readily absorbed and developed into an idiosyncratic formula in which basically Gothic forms were merely decorated with Renaissance motifs (*see* Elizabethan style). Gradually new construction techniques introduced by continental craftsmen were adopted and new ideas emerged, such as the draw-leaf tables (mid-sixteenth century) and farthingale chairs (c. 1600). Typical Elizabethan features were heavy bulbous carved sections on legs and bed pillars, with carved strapwork often incorporating cabochons. Romayne work (a carved roundel featuring a head in profile) was especially popular in the first half of the sixteenth century, and is found in Italy, France, Portugal, and Spain, as well as England. In the Iberian peninsula classical motifs were often incongruously combined with the Moorish (mudéjar) style of intricate, abstract, curvilinear decoration. In Germany some cities like Augsburg and Nuremberg developed a specialist decorative line in perspective intarsia work.

G

Gabrieli, Andrea (c. 1510–85) Italian composer. He was a singer at St Mark's, Venice, in 1536 and organist at S Geremia there in 1557. In 1562 he was in the service of Duke Albrecht V of Bavaria; accompanying him on a state visit to Frankfurt, he met *Lassus in Munich. From 1566 until his death Gabrieli was organist at St Mark's. Gabrieli was a prolific composer; his works include keyboard music, notably canzonas and ricercars, which forms he developed, madrigals, and sacred music. He also wrote music for ceremonial occasions, such as the celebrations following the victory against the Turks at *Lepanto (1571). Gabrieli's compositions show the influence of Lassus and *Willaert, and he is acknowledged as one of the foremost native Venetian composers who emerged after a long period of Flemish dominance. He was the uncle and teacher of Giovanni *Gabrieli.

Gabrieli, Giovanni (c. 1555–1612) Italian composer. The nephew of Andrea *Gabrieli, he almost certainly studied with his uncle and like him worked for Duke Albrecht V in Munich; in 1575 he collaborated in a madrigal collection by composers who served the duke. Around 1579 he left Munich and in 1584 was back in Venice as temporary organist at St Mark's. He obtained the permanent post, and that of organist at the Scuola Grande di S Rocco, in 1585 and kept both until his death. For both institutions Gabrieli wrote ceremonial music, much of which he published in his *Sacrae symphoniae* (1597). This contains music for two or more choirs, some with instruments, and shows a development from his earlier works which were influenced by his uncle. Around 1605 his style became more progressive; solo voices, obbligato parts for specific instruments, and basso continuo are used in varied combinations. Gabrieli also composed instrumental music; his *Canzoni e sonate* (1615) contains elaborate music for large ensembles.

Gaddi, Agnolo (c. 1350–96) Italian painter. The son of Taddeo *Gaddi, Agnolo Gaddi worked in the Vatican as assistant to his brother Giovanni before embarking upon his own prosperous career. He was the last Florentine painter stylistically descended from *Giotto and, like both Giotto and his own father, painted a series of frescoes in Sta Croce, Florence (sometime after 1374). His most important work there was in the choir, illustrating the *Legend of the True Cross* (1388–93), in which his sacrifice of expression to design and highly decorated style anticipate the more refined paintings of his pupil Lorenzo Monaco and subsequent artists. He also designed a number of medallions, worked on statues, and painted other notable frescoes in Prato cathedral (1392–95) and S Minato al Monte, Florence (1393–96).

Gaddi, Taddeo (c. 1300–c. 1366) Italian painter. Son of the artist Gaddo Gaddi (c. 1250–1330) and godson of *Giotto, Gaddi was a prominent member of the Florentine school of painters and worked directly under Giotto, as his chief assistant, for twenty-four years. His best-known fresco cycle, the *Life of the Virgin* in the Baroncelli chapel in Sta Croce, Florence, was undertaken as an independent commission in 1332 and completed in 1338. The cycle demonstrates Gaddi's devotion to the manner of Giotto, which he later passed on to his son Agnolo *Gaddi, as well as his excellence as a narrative painter in a style parallel to that of such contemporaries as Bernardo *Daddi. By 1347 he was sufficiently admired to head a list of candidates to paint the altarpiece for S Giovanni Fuorcivitas in Pistoia (completed 1353). He also painted a series of scenes from the lives of Christ and St Francis on the panels of a sacristy cupboard door, based on similar works by Giotto.

Gaffurio, Franchino (1451–1522) Italian composer and theorist. A native of Lodi, he became a priest and singer at the cathedral there in the eacly 1470s. From 1474 he lived in various Italian cities, and in Naples he met the theorist *Tinctoris, who apparently became his closest friend. It was in Naples that he wrote his *Theoricum opus* (1479–80), his first original theoretical writing. After short periods in Lodi and Bergamo he became *maestro* at Milan cathedral in 1484, remaining there until his death. Though he left a large number of Masses and motets, Gaffurio is best known for his theoretical writings, which mainly date from his time in Milan. The *Practica*

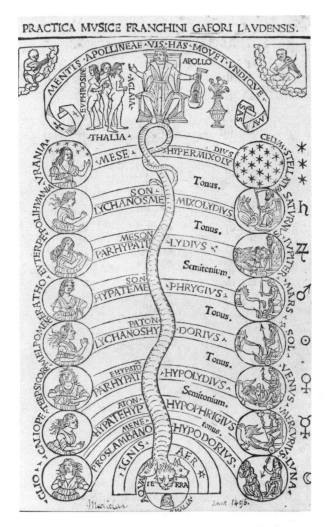

GAFFURIO *The titlepage of Gaffurio's* Practica musice *(1496) encapsulates a whole range of correspondences and connections believed by Renaissance theorists to underpin the musical universe.*

musice (1496) is of major importance; it deals with the interpretation of chant, poetic metres and mensuration, counterpoint, and musical proportions. Most of Gaffurio's music was composed for the Ambrosian liturgy celebrated in Milan cathedral. Like *Weerbeke, he composed for the Mass Ordinary.

Galateo, Il *see under* della Casa, Giovanni.

Galenism, Renaissance Galen's works became widely available in print during the early sixteenth century. A Latin *Opera* was published in 1490, while the Greek *editio princeps* appeared in 1525. In addition, such important works as *On the Use of Parts*, *On Natural Faculties*, and *On Anatomical Procedures* were all available in separate Latin editions. Their main appeal to Renaissance schol-

ars lay in the comprehensive systems of anatomy, physiology, and medicine developed in Galen's numerous works. By the mid-sixteenth century, however, *Vesalius and *Falloppio began to challenge details of his anatomy, arguing there were aspects of human anatomy ignored by Galen and other features misdescribed. They therefore sought to create a more accurate and detailed system of human anatomy.

Galenic physiology, however, proved to be more durable. The body operated, Galen argued, through three interacting systems. Natural spirits were transmitted through the venous system; vital spirits through the arterial system; and animal spirits through the nervous system, with areas of interaction in the liver, heart, and brain. Galen rejected the idea of the circulation of the blood and proposed instead that it ebbed and flowed, somewhat like the tides. Carried with it were the vital and natural spirits which, together with the animal spirits, were responsible for such distinctive vital phenomena as growth, motion, heat, and sensation. The system remained unchallenged during the Renaissance and only gradually collapsed after the publication in 1628 of Harvey's *De motu cordis*.

Even more successful was the system of medicine constructed by Galen. Derived from Hippocratic principles, it saw man as ultimately composed of the four elements: earth, air, fire, and water. These in turn, depending on how they combined, produced the four humours: blood, phlegm, yellow bile (choler), and black bile (melancholy). If the humours were mixed harmoniously, health followed; any imbalance produced disease. The most obvious causes of such an imbalance were diet and climate. Consequently, treatment consisted largely of redressing the defects; for example, the effects of an excessively "hot and dry" diet were neutralized by switching to "wet and cold" foods and herbs. Though, in essence, the system long outlasted the Renaissance, it nevertheless faced sustained opposition from *Paracelsus and the proponents of *iatrochemistry.

Galilei, Vincenzo (c. 1525–91) Italian music theorist and composer. He studied the lute in his youth, and later musical theory with *Zarlino in Venice. He had settled in Pisa by the early 1560s and married (1562) a member of the local nobility by whom he became the father of *Galileo Galilei. In 1572 he returned to Florence where his principal patron was the Florentine noble Giovanni Bardi. Galilei was at the forefront of attempts to revive the ancient Greek notion of the union of music and poetry through monody. His surviving compositions include madrigals, songs, and lute music, but he is best known for his theoretical writings.

175

Galileo Galilei

His *Dialogo della musica antica e della moderna* (1581) attacked Zarlino's theories, declaring that the Greek "modes" were quite different from the church modes, and that Greek tuning was not as Zarlino claimed. He condemned counterpoint and maintained that vocal writing should follow the form of ancient Greek music which always had a single melodic line.

Galileo Galilei (1564–1642) Italian physicist and astronomer. The son of Vincenzo *Galilei, Galileo studied at the university of his native Pisa, where in 1589 he began his academic career as a mathematics lecturer. Quarrels with colleagues forced him in 1592 to seek a comparable post in Padua. While in Padua he made one of the most dramatic scientific discoveries of all times. Early in 1610 he turned the newly invented telescope to the heavens and, observing such totally unexpected phenomena as the satellites of Jupiter and the mountains of the moon, he realized immediately that he had thereby destroyed the plausibility of the still widely accepted Aristotelian *cosmology. Galileo quickly published his observations in his *Sidereus nuncius* (1610; translated as *The Starry Messenger*, 1880), a work which, though it led him into controversy, won him an international reputation.

Sidereus nuncius also won him the patronage of Grand Duke Cosimo II (1590–1620), who persuaded him to return to Florence. Further controversies followed. In 1613 he clashed with Christoph *Scheiner on the nature of sunspots; during the same period he disputed with Ludovico Colombe on the issue of why thin bodies float on water. A further controversy, on the nature of comets, began in 1618 and continued for several years.

Galileo's debating skills and savage wit may well have gained him the upper hand in various disputes, but only at the expense of creating a number of powerful enemies. Consequently when they heard that Galileo was openly defending the *Copernican system they began to protest against this expression of beliefs contrary to scripture. Though warned by Cardinal *Robert Bellarmine in 1616 to be less forthright, Galileo chose to publish his thinly camouflaged views in dialogue form. When it appeared as *Dialogo dei due massimi sistemi del mondo* (1632; translated as *Dialogue on the Great World Systems*, 1953), Galileo found himself summoned to Rome. Abandoned by his patrons and friendless in Rome, Galileo had little choice, under threat of torture, other than to declare as erroneous the Copernican claim that the earth moved around the sun. Placed under house arrest in his villa at Arcetri, and with the *Dialogo* banned, Galileo spent the last years of his life tended by his daughter and his students. The exile did, however, allow him to complete a long contemplated treatise on the nature of motion, *Due nuove scienze* (1638; translated as *Two New Sciences*, 1914). The work shows Galileo struggling to develop a new science of motion and formulating in the process an early version of the law of inertia.

One further feature of Galileo's work lies in the fact that he was one of the first to appreciate the true nature of the newly emerging science. The book of nature, he declared, is written in the language of mathematics. Further, he went on, physics must concern itself with such "primary qualities" of matter as shape, size, weight, and position, which can be treated quantitatively. In this matter, while his account of motion and other such topics may long have been superseded, his vision of science and its method has been preserved largely intact.

Gallego, Fernando (c. 1440–c. 1509) Spanish painter. Mainly active in Salamanca, Gallego is noteworthy for his introduction of Flemish characteristics into Castilian painting. Dirk *Bouts is an obvious influence in Gallego's work. He painted an altarpiece of *S Idelfonso* (c. 1467) for Zamora cathedral, a triptych of the *Virgin and Saints* for Salamanca cathedral, the now almost destroyed ceiling of the old library of Salamanca university (before 1493), and paintings of scenes from the Passion and a *Christ in Majesty* in the Prado.

Gallican Confession (Confessio Gallicana) The Calvinist confession of faith drawn up at the first national synod of Protestants in Paris in 1559. The synod, called out of fear of persecution by Henry II, lasted four days and confessed adherence to Calvin's doctrines as revised by Antoine de la Roche Chandieu (1534–91). This confession written in French and comprising thirty-five articles was confirmed, in modified form, by the synod of La Rochelle (1571).

Galvão, Antonio (?1490–1557) Portuguese historian. Galvão was the first major historian to marshal a comprehensive knowledge of the voyages of all the leading Renaissance explorers, regardless of nationality. Galvão went to India in 1527 and rose to become governor of the Moluccas (1536–40), before his abilities led him to be offered the throne of Ternate. He declined, but on his return to Portugal (1540) he found he was out of favour and lived the rest of his life in anonymity and poverty, dying in Lisbon. His works remain among the most accurate and thorough of the period, especially *Livro dos descobrimentos das Antilhase India*, which was published in Lisbon in

1563 and translated into English by Hakluyt in 1601.

Gama, Vasco da (c. 1460–1524) Portuguese navigator. Emanuel I of Portugal employed da Gama to continue the search for the sea route to India. Sailing from Lisbon with four ships in July 1497, he successfully rounded the Cape of Good Hope in November that year. On Christmas Day 1497 he landed in Natal, naming it in honour of Christ's birthday. The expedition visited Mozambique, Mombasa, and Malindi before crossing the Indian Ocean, with the help of a local pilot, to Calicut in May 1498. Warmly received by Calicut's Hindu ruler, da Gama left some Portuguese behind and took some Hindus with him. Despite unfavourable winds and many deaths from scurvy, da Gama returned triumphantly to Lisbon in September 1499 with two ships heavily laden with spices. Rewarded with honours and a pension, da Gama returned to Calicut (1502–03) to avenge the murder of the men he had left there in 1498. Shortly before his death in Cochin he was appointed viceroy of India.

Garamond, Claude (c. 1500–61) French type designer, cutter, and founder. The design and manufacture of type formed a part of printers' work until Garamond concentrated on these processes alone. He worked in Paris, where he may have been influenced by the work of the printer Geoffrey Tory, who wrote the first treatise on type design, *Champfleury*, in 1529. Garamond's family of roman types, first used by Robert *Estienne in 1531 in a book by Jacques Dubois (Sylvius), *In linguam Gallicam isagoge*, included capitals, small capitals, and lower-case letters. They became European leaders for about 200 years, with many later versions too. Garamond designed roman and italic types to complement each other, as part of the same series. His customers for type included *Plantin, so that the best surviving collection of his punches and matrices is now in the Plantin-Moretus Museum in Antwerp.

Garcilaso de la Vega ("El Inca"; c. 1540–1616) Spanish writer on Inca history, rituals, and mythology. Garcilaso was born at Cuzco, the son of a Spanish sea captain and an Inca noble. He went to Spain in 1560. In 1590 his Spanish translation of the *Dialoghi di amore* by *Leone Ebreo was published. His own writing displays great affection for his theme and he contradicts many Spanish chroniclers by siding with the Incas over many key issues. His most famous works are *Comentarios reales* (1609) and *Historia general del Peru* (1617).

Garcilaso de la Vega (1501–36) Spanish poet.

Born in Toledo into one of the most distinguished aristocratic families of Castile, as a youth Garcilaso served Charles V in the imperial bodyguard and, apart from a brief period of disfavour (1532), remained a member of the highest court circle. A model courtier, he successfully combined the aristocrat's profession of arms and his literary vocation. In 1525 he married the noblewoman Elena de Zúñiga, but the following year fell in love with Isabel Freire, a lady-in-waiting at the court, the "Elisa" of his poems. The unhappiness of this affair was increased by Isabel's own marriage in 1529 and by her early death in childbirth a few years later. In 1532 Garcilaso left Spain, exiled briefly to the Danube for a minor offence that displeased the emperor. He then went to Naples where he met *Tasso, Juan de *Valdés, and others. He took part in the Tunis campaign in 1535 and the following year was fatally wounded in an unimportant skirmish near Fréjus during Charles V's invasion of France.

The greatest Spanish poet of his age, Garcilaso established Petrarchan hendecasyllabic metre and the sonnet and *canzone* in Spanish poetry. He also introduced the *lira*, a five-line stanza of eleven- and seven-syllable lines rhyming ababb. His works, with those of his friend *Boscán, were published by Boscán's widow in 1543, the year which marks the beginning of Spain's *Siglo de Oro*. The poems include about forty sonnets, five *canciones*, three eclogues, two elegies, a verse epistle to Boscán, and eight *coplas* in traditional Spanish metre. *Églogas* I and III are concerned with "Elisa"; I shows the influence of Petrarch and Sannazaro's *Arcadia* and III the purely classical inspiration of Virgil and Ovid. Garcilaso also wrote the prologue to Boscán's translation of The *Courtier* (done at Garcilaso's suggestion). His œuvre rapidly assumed the status of a classic, with editions in 1574 and in 1580, the latter by Fernando de *Herrera.

gardens The designers of Italian gardens of the Renaissance revived and developed the plans of the ideal villa gardens described by Pliny. *Alberti directed the choice of sloping sites, with terraces giving views of the scenery beyond the garden, while within its boundaries avenues, loggias, or pergolas covered with vines provided shade, and fountains, pools, and statues added symbolic decoration to regular patterns of clipped evergreens or groves of trees. Cypress, juniper, bay, and ilex were among the plants used, with flowers or fragrant herbs often confined to a small, private, walled *giardino segreto* near the house, as the designs made plants subservient to symmetry. Many of these features may be seen in the illustrations to Colonna's *Hypnerotomachia Polifili* (1499). Grottoes were favourite embellishments,

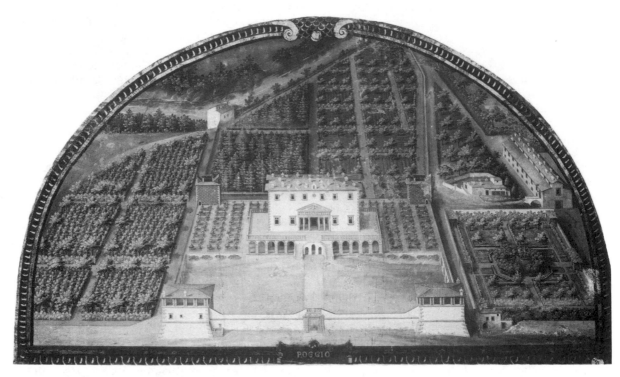

GARDENS *Justus Utens's view of the Medici villa at Poggio a Caiano shows the formal layout of the grounds. By such layouts Renaissance garden designers expressed man's mastery over nature and their delight in ordering it into harmonious patterns. (1599; Museo Topographico, Florence)*

and hydraulic automata were almost invariably added to fountains in the most fashionable gardens, first in Italy, as at the Villa d'Este (admired by Montaigne in the 1580s), and later in France, Germany, and England. Hero of Alexandria's *Pneumatica* (first printed in Latin in 1575 and in Italian in 1589) was a source book for these toys.

Gardens of this kind may be said to demonstrate man's control of nature rather than the luxuriance of the plant world. In France Charles Estienne's *Praedium rusticum* (1554) and its French version, *La Maison rustique* (1564), gave more encouragement to the enjoyment of plants arranged in parterres. However, Italian influence, filtered through the work of architects like Philibert *Delorme and Jacques Androuet *Ducerceau, persisted in the grandest gardens, like those of the Château d'Anet.

Around 1600 florilegia or flower books, often records of the contents of particular gardens, show greater interest in the cultivation of an increasing variety of plants. Some were new introductions, like the tulips brought from Turkey to western Europe in the mid-sixteenth century. Pierre Vallet's *Le Jardin du Roy très Chrestien Henry IV* (1608) illustrates fritillaries, tulips, hyacinths, crocuses, narcissi, and lilies, among many other plants,

including a selection of roses, and Basil Besler's *Hortus Eystettensis* (1613) presents a catalogue of a princely German garden in an appropriately lavish format, for systematic collections of plants were not confined to academic *botanic gardens.

Gardiner, Stephen (c. 1490–1555) English churchman. Through his mother Gardiner was a second cousin of Henry VIII. At Cambridge he was made doctor of both canon and civil law and master of Trinity Hall from 1525. He was tutor to a son of the duke of Norfolk, and in 1526 became secretary to Cardinal Wolsey, whom he accompanied to France. In 1528 he went as ambassador to the pope and was active in the attempt to obtain from the universities of Europe opinions favourable to the king's divorce from Catherine of Aragon. In 1531 he was appointed bishop of Winchester. Gardiner supported the breach with Rome, but opposed the further reforms planned by Cromwell and Cranmer. After the accession of Edward VI, he was imprisoned (1548) and deprived (1551). He was restored to his bishopric by Mary and was also created lord chancellor, in which roles he played an important part in the Catholic reaction.

Gargantua* and *Pantagruel A cycle of four (or five) satirical novels by François *Rabelais, inspired by the successful chapbook *Les Grandes et Inestimables Chroniques du grand et énorme géant Gargantua* (1532). *La Vie estimable du grand Gargantua, père de Pantagruel*, chronologically the first novel of the series, was published in 1534, two years after *Les Horribles et Épouvantables Faits et prouesses du très renommé Pantagruel* (1532); *Le Tiers Livre des faits et dits héroïques du noble Pantagruel* and *Le Quart Livre de Pantagruel* appeared in 1546 and 1552. (The *Cinquième Livre* (1564), which continues the story of Pantagruel in the style of Rabelais, is of doubtful authenticity.) *Gargantua* deals with the birth and childhood of the giant Gargantua, son of Grandgousier; his education in Paris (an opportunity for a satirical attack on the Sorbonne); the war between Gargantua and King Picrochole; and the foundation of the abbey of Thélème, the motto of which is "Fay ce que vouldras" ("Do what you will"). *Pantagruel* tells the story of Gargantua's son, a giant of enormous strength and appetite, his friendship with the cunning rogue Panurge, and his conquest of the kingdom of the Dipsodes. Both novels are written in mock-heroic style and reveal the extent of Rabelais's learning in the fields of medicine, theology, and law. They satirize a variety of institutions, notably the Church: the intensification of these attacks in the *Tiers Livre* and *Quart Livre* led to their condemnation by the Sorbonne.

Garnier, Robert (c. 1544–90) French tragic dramatist. Garnier was born at La Ferté-Bernard and studied law at Toulouse, where he won prizes for his poetry at the annual competition of the Jeux Floraux. After a period of service at the bar in Paris he was appointed to a number of important legal posts in the provinces. As a member of Henry II's Grand Conseil, he expressed his patriotism in the *Hymne de la monarchie* (1567). Garnier's dramatic works reveal his preoccupation with moral and religious issues; his early plays, which were heavily influenced by Seneca, include *Porcie* (1568), *Hippolyte* (1573), *Marc-Antoine* (1578), and *Antigone* (1580). With *Bradamante* (1582), inspired by Ariosto's *Orlando Furioso*, Garnier pioneered the genre of tragicomedy in French literature. The tragedy *Les Juives* (1583), generally considered to be his finest work, deals with the Old Testament story of the sufferings of Zedekiah and his family at the hands of Nebuchadnezzar.

Garofalo, Il (Benvenuto Tisi; 1481–1559) Italian painter. The most prolific of the sixteenth-century Ferrarese school, Garofalo studied in Cremona and visited Venice and Rome, where he came under the influence of *Raphael. He served his first apprenticeship with Domenico Panetti and, after settling in Ferrara, associated with Dosso *Dossi, whose influence is evident in the treatment of landscape backgrounds in several of Garofalo's works, including his pictures of the Nativity (pre-1520) and his fine *Sacrifice to Ceres* (1526). Others of his works, the majority of which are competent but unoriginal, can be seen in certain Ferrarese churches, most notably the *Madonna del Pilastro* in S Francesco. He went blind in 1550.

Gattamelata, Il (Erasmo da Narni; 1370–1443) Born in Padua the son of a baker, Gattamelata served his military apprenticeship under Braccio da Montone and Niccolò *Piccinino before serving in the Florentine and papal armies. It is unclear how he acquired his nickname, which means "honeyed cat". In 1434 he entered the service of Venice. During the republic's wars with the *Visconti of Milan, he developed a reputation for resourcefulness, determination, and leadership. His most famous exploit was to have his army drag five galleys and twenty-five other vessels overland from Mori on the Adige to Lake Garda to launch a surprise attack on a Milanese transport station. The tale is marred only by the failure of the raid. By the time he died, Gattamelata was captain-general of Venice, a position that earned him a state funeral and an equestrian statue by *Donatello, which stands outside the church of the Santo in Padua.

Gazes, Theodore (Theodore Gaza; c. 1400–75) Greek scholar and teacher of Greek. Born at Thessalonica, he came to Italy in 1430 and lived at Mantua, supporting himself by giving Greek lessons and copying manuscripts while learning Latin from *Vittorino da Feltre. He was made professor of Greek at Ferrara (1447) but in 1450 went to Rome at the invitation of Pope Nicholas V. In 1456 he moved to Naples and in 1459 to Calabria, where he died. He wrote a Greek grammar in Greek, which was printed in Venice (1495) and long remained a standard textbook, and he translated many Greek authors into Latin, including Aristotle, Theophrastus, and John Chrysostom.

Gemistus Plethon *see* Plethon, George Gemistus.

Gemma Frisius (Gemma Regnier; 1508–55) Dutch mathematician, astronomer, and geographer. Born at Dockum, East Friesland, he became a pupil of Peter *Apian and was educated at the university of Louvain, where he was appointed professor of medicine (1541). In his *Libellus de locorum describendorum ratione* (Little book on a method for delineating places), incorporated in his 1533 edition of Apian's *Cosmographia*, Frisius published the first clear description of how maps could be constructed more accurately using triangulation. Less immediate in its application (on account of the lack of sufficiently reliable timepieces) was Frisius's proposal in *De principiis astronomiae et cosmographiae* (1530) that longitude at sea and elsewhere could be determined with the aid of portable clocks. His *Arithmeticae practicae methodus facilis* (1540), judging by the fifty-nine editions known from the sixteenth century, proved to be one of the most successful mathematical textbooks of the period. Frisius was also known as a maker of globes, *astrolabes, and other mathematical and astronomical instruments.

Geneva (French: Genève; German: Genf; Italian: Ginevra) A Swiss city in the Rhone valley on the southwest corner of Lake Geneva. Occupied from the Stone Age, the site was first a Celtic city, then Roman, becoming the seat of a bishopric (379) and the domain of the hereditary counts of Geneva (1034–1401). After the family of the counts died out, Geneva owed a triple allegiance to its bishop-prince, its municipal government, and Savoy. During the fifteenth century the great trade fairs brought expansion and prosperity to the city, while its citizens resisted not only the increasing power of the bishop but also the claims of the dukes of Savoy to control its destiny.

In 1535 Guillaume *Farel persuaded the city to expel the bishop and his clergy and to adopt the reformed faith. It was Farel who invited *Calvin to settle in Geneva, and except for a brief period when the opposition regained power Calvin spent the rest of his life in the city (1536–38; 1541–64). Under Calvin's guidance Geneva became a virtual theocracy – the "Protestant Rome"; it welcomed Protestant refugees from all over Europe, it published Calvinist tracts, and it trained theologians at its academy (*see* Genevan Academy) and university to carry the Calvinist faith from Geneva to England, Germany, the Netherlands, Scandinavia, Scotland, and eventually to America. The refugees also played an important part in the development of Geneva's prosperous banking and watchmaking activities in the sixteenth century.

Late in the sixteenth century Geneva had to fend off aggression from Savoy; after the failure of the duke of Savoy's surprise attack (1602) Geneva's independence was guaranteed by the treaty of St-Julien (1603). Notable buildings that have survived from the Renaissance period include St Peter's cathedral and the town hall.

Genevan Academy The famous school in Geneva founded by Calvin in June 1559 and completed in 1564, of considerable importance to the spread of Calvinism. Calvin's main intention was that his academy would prepare ministers to preach the gospel. Its outstanding academic reputation and brilliant teachers, including *Beza, the first rector, and Jacob Arminius (1560–1609) (*see* Arminianism) attracted students from all over Europe. Divided into two parts, primary and secondary, the academy awarded no degrees, merely certificates of attendance. At Calvin's death it numbered 1500 students.

Genga, Girolamo (1472–1551) Italian painter. Genga was born and worked for much of his life in Urbino. He collaborated with his master *Signorelli before going with *Perugino to Florence (1502), where he studied perspective. Back in Urbino he was both painter and architect, completing the top storey of the ducal palace there in about 1536. He also restored and decorated the Villa Imperiale near Pesaro for the duke of Urbino, endowing it with handsome wall-paintings, fine stuccoed ceilings, and majolica tiled floors.

Gennadius (George Scholarius; c. 1400–c. 1468) Greek scholar and theologian. Perhaps born in Constantinople (the details of his early life are obscure), he came to Italy in 1438 as counsellor to Emperor John Palaeologus at the Council of *Florence. Here he wrote works attacking *Plethon on both theological and philosophical grounds. On the schism between Eastern and Western Churches, Scholarius advocated compromise and drew up a form of agreement ambiguous enough to be accepted by both, but on his return to Greece, he completely changed his position and opposed the union. In 1448 he became a monk and took the name Gennadius. Mehmet II made him patriarch of Constantinople (1453) and he composed an exposition of Christian belief for the sultan's use, but he found the strain of being patriarch of a Muslim city too much and retired to Serrae in Macedonia where he died. Very few of Gennadius's works have been printed.

Genoa A northwest Italian city state and port on the Ligurian Sea. A Roman settlement (third century BC), Genoa was frequently invaded by Arabs and Germans after the fall of Rome. By the twelfth century the city had established a republic that reached the peak of its power under the Doria and Spinola families late in the thirteenth century. Political rivalries and foreign intervention brought years of turmoil to Genoa. The Doria and other leading noble families were expelled by Simone *Boccanegra (1339), but he and his successors were unable to consolidate their authority. At various times Genoa was ruled by Savoy, France, and Milan. It was conquered by France (1499) and sacked by Spain (1522) during the Wars of *Italy. In 1528 Andrea *Doria achieved a measure of political stability by expelling the French and setting up an oligarchic republic with the support of Emperor *Charles V. The civil war (1573–76) between the old and the new aristocracy was ended by the intervention of Spain and the papacy and by the new constitutional settlement which abolished the distinctions between the old and the new nobility.

At the beginning of the Renaissance period Genoa was a major Mediterranean trading power with outposts in the Near East: during the fourteenth and fifteenth centuries its power and its trade were checked by the advances of Aragon, the loss of trading stations to the Ottoman Turks, the rivalry of Venice, and the discovery of the sea route to India. Despite these setbacks Genoa was still an important commercial power in the sixteenth century. Its bankers pioneered the use of credit and lent money throughout Europe.

Christopher *Columbus was one of its most notable citizens. Its outstanding buildings from the Renaissance period include the palaces of the Strada Nova (now the Via Garibaldi) from the second half of the sixteenth century and parts of the Palazzo di San Giorgio.

Gentile de Fabriano (Niccolò di Giovanni di Massio; c. 1370–1427) Italian painter. The most accomplished exponent of the international Gothic style, Gentile first became famous for his work in northern Italy. His productions are stylistically linked with paintings of the Lombard school, in which he may have trained. In 1409 he was commissioned to execute frescoes (now destroyed) in the doge's palace in Venice, later completed by his artistic heir *Pisanello. Further commissions followed in Brescia, Siena, Florence, Orvieto, and Rome, where he painted frescoes in the basilica of S John Lateran, which – like the greater part of Gentile's work – are now lost. The *Adoration of the Magi* (see p. 182), considered to be his surviving masterpiece, is the quintessential international Gothic painting. Commissioned for a family chapel in the sacristy of Sta Trinità, Florence, it depicts an exotic procession approaching the Virgin and Child through a fantastic landscape and is crammed with richly decorative natural detail. Among Gentile's other major extant works is the altarpiece known as the Quaratesi polyptych (1425), made for the Quaratesi family of Florence, which features a notable painting of the Madonna (London; other panels elsewhere). Such works greatly influenced the course of Florentine art.

geometry After the great triumphs of antiquity in the *Elements* of Euclid and the *Conics* of Apollonius, advances in geometry were sparse during the medieval period. The first task facing the Renais-

sance scholars was to recover the texts of the ancient geometers. *Ratdolt first issued the *Elements* in a Latin translation in 1482; the Greek *princeps*, edited by Simon Grynaeus, appeared in 1533. Numerous other editions, including translations, introductions, summaries, and commentaries appeared throughout the sixteenth century. Apollonius' *Conics* was first printed in Memo's 1537 Latin edition, while much of Archimedes was made available in Tartaglia's edition of 1543.

Given the completeness of Euclid, there was in fact little for the Renaissance mathematician to add, and, when a major advance in geometry did come, it took place in analytical and not classical geometry. The roots of this discipline lay more in the works of Archimedes and Apollonius than in those of Euclid. Archimedes had worked out a number of techniques for determining the areas of curved figures. The area of a parabolic segment, for example, was shown by him to be 4/3 the area of a triangle inscribed in it. Such problems, however, only began to appeal to modern mathematicians towards the end of the Renaissance. Luca Valerio, in his *De quadratura parabolae* (1606) did little more than survey the earlier work of Archimedes. Other early attempts to develop analytical geometry were made by *Stevin in his *Statics* (1586) and by *Kepler in his *Nova stereometria* (1615); it remained, however, for such later scholars as Descartes and Newton to develop the subject.

While not, therefore, in the centre of Renaissance mathematics, classical geometry could still excite and benefit scholars in other fields. Such artists as *Dürer, for example, made a serious study of Euclid to gain a better understanding of the principles of perspective and proportion. Dürer, in fact, wrote two geometrical works: *Underweysung der Messung* (1525), on constructions with compass and ruler, and *Vier Bücher von menschlicher Proportion* (1528), on human proportion. Similar interest was shown in the subject by surveyors, astronomers, physicists, and architects. Much of the astronomy of the heavens and of the physics of motion was worked out by Renaissance savants not in the observatory or laboratory but at the drawing board, using purely geometrical techniques. Thus, *Copernicus in his *De revolutionibus* (1545) could offer his work to the judgment of "learned mathematicians", a view echoed by *Leonardo da Vinci who opened his lost *Trattato della pittura* with the warning: "Let no one who is not a mathematician read my works."

George of Trebizond (?1395–1484) Cretan-born teacher of Greek. His family came from Trebizond on the Black Sea. Brought to Venice (1417) by the elder Ermolao Barbaro, who employed him as a copyist and had him taught Latin, he mastered the

GENTILE DE FABRIANO Adoration of the Magi *(detail). The central lunette of this large panel shows the Magi with their entourage winding their way through hilly countryside to Bethlehem, here depicted as an Italian hill-top castle. They clearly enjoyed some sporting diversions along the route; besides the more usual hounds and falcons, hunting leopards are perched on the backs of the horses immediately in front of the three kings. (1423; Uffizi, Florence)*

language so well that he became a public teacher of Latin literature at Venice, Padua, and Vicenza. Pope Eugenius IV used George's knowledge of Greek at the Council of Florence (1438) and subsequently appointed him apostolic secretary and professor at Rome, which aroused the jealousy of Italian humanists. George was a pioneer of Greek studies in Italy but his own bad temper, expressed in his feud with *Bessarion, who accused him of faulty translations of Aristotle (1464), and the greater abilities of the scholars who came to Rome in the papacy of Nicholas V eclipsed his fame and he died senile and impoverished.

Gerard, John (1545–1612) English barber-surgeon and gardener. Born in Nantwich, Gerard travelled abroad before settling in London to pursue his medical career. In 1596 he published a catalogue of plants in his Holborn garden. His *Herball* (1597; with woodcuts borrowed from Frankfurt) and its revised version by Thomas Johnson (1633; with new blocks taken from *Plantin's stock) had great influence during the next 150 years. It contains new observations on both wild and cultivated plants, combined with descriptions drawing on the work

of *Turner, *Dodoens, and Matthias l'Obel.

Gerhaert van Leyden, Nicolaus (c. 1430–73) Netherlands sculptor. Born at Leyden, Gerhaert is first documented in 1462 as executing the vigorously carved tomb of Archbishop von Sierck in Trier. Between 1463 and 1467 he was in Strasbourg, after which he moved to Wiener Neustadt, where he died. Assessment of Gerhaert's development is rendered difficult by the destruction of his early sculptures in Holland and of his chief work, the high altarpiece of Constance cathedral (1465–67). The latter, in particular, was deeply influential upon south German sculptors. Only three fragments survive from his sandstone portal (c. 1464) for the new chancellery in Strasbourg. One of these astonishingly realistic heads is probably a self-portrait. Gerhaert's best-known work is the sandstone crucifix (1467) in Baden-Baden parish church. His last years were spent working on the flamboyant and expressive red marble tomb effigy of Frederick III in Vienna cathedral. Gerhaert's productions possess an entirely novel dynamism and expansiveness combined with profound characterization. The widespread diffusion of his style was stimulated both by his extensive travels, from Holland to Austria, and by numerous prints influenced by his work.

Gerhard, Hubert (c. 1545–1620) Netherlands sculptor. One of the leading mannerist sculptors in Northern Europe, Gerhard was clearly influenced by his training in Italy. For the earlier part of his career he worked mainly for the *Fugger family in Augsburg (from 1581) and Duke Wilhelm V of Bavaria in Munich (from 1584). His Augsburg commissions included the Augustus fountain (erected in 1594 to celebrate the city's centenary), which first incorporated the newest Italian ideas into monumental German sculpture, and many figures and fittings for Hans Fugger's new castle at Kirchheim (1583–95), including the courtyard fountain showing Mars and Venus embracing. The first sculptor of note to work in Munich for many years, he made sculptures for Wilhelm's palace there (the Residenz) and for the church of St Michael which Wilhelm was building for the Jesuits. After Wilhelm abdicated (1597), Gerhard moved to the court of his successor, Archduke Maximilian I, at Innsbruck.

German language During the period 1350–1650 (the Early New High German period) the foundations of modern German were laid. The language previously consisted of regional spoken dialects with a standardized literary language used for courtly poetry. Otherwise Latin was the usual written language. The Early New High German period saw the simplification of case endings and changes in certain vowel sounds; but the most significant development was the emergence of a standardized written language, as writing became more widespread, encompassing new spheres, from trade to expression of the emotions. The chief promoting factors were the increase in trade and business, the advent of *printing, and the Reformation; the impact of *humanism was more complex.

Humanism in Germany did not give rise directly to a vernacular literary florescence, as in Italy, France, and England. By their use of Latin for education and poetry as well as for communication, the humanists even retarded German linguistic growth. Also, the Reformation channelled the energies of many scholars away from the refinement of literary skills and into religious disputes. The humanists mainly exerted a literary influence through their translations of works in Latin and romance languages (one by-product of this was an influx of new vocabulary into German in the form of loan words from these languages). Humanist literature, however, on the whole remained separate from the popular vernacular literature

(such as the *Schwänke), which was flourishing by the sixteenth century as the new middle classes began to provide their own literary entertainment. The nationalistic concern of some humanist scholars was also significant, as they directed their attention to German literary achievements. This motivated the rediscovery of forgotten manuscripts in the vernacular, the publication of the first German dictionaries in the late fifteenth century, and the production of German grammars in the sixteenth. Scholarly interest in the German language flourished in the seventeenth century with the formation of societies to unify and purify the language, such as Die Fruchtbringende Gessellschaft ("the fruitful society") founded in Weimar in 1617, and with Martin Opitz's championship of German as a language fit for poetry in his *Buch von der Deutschen Poetery* (1624). Latin remained the language of scholarship until very late, however; only in 1681 did the number of German-language books printed in Germany exceed those in Latin, and German only began to be used for university lectures in 1687.

The increasing standardization of German during the period is attributable largely to the growth of trade and business. Merchants generally did not know Latin, and the prosperous activities of the *Hanseatic League in the fourteenth and fifteenth centuries resulted in the incipient development of a standardized written language based on Low German (i.e. North German) dialects. German also came to be used as the language of documentation in the chancelleries of local princes; this was instrumental in introducing standardization in other regions in the fifteenth century. Most notable were a southern standard based on the *Kanzleisprache* (chancellery language) of the imperial court, and an east central standard (in, for example, Saxony). As the economic power of the north declined, the southern and central forms gained in importance. The process of regional standardization was furthered by printing, as it both satisfied and stimulated the growing demand for the new scholarship and literature. As printers strove to achieve the widest possible sales, they reduced regional variation in their texts and took care over orthographic consistency. The sixteenth century saw five regional standards of German in use among printers. Again, as the major centres of printing were in central and southern Germany, this strengthened the linguistic importance of these areas over the north.

The final step in the evolution of a written standard was *Luther's translation of the Bible, published between 1522 and 1534. His was not the first, but it was outstanding in its scholarship and in the power of its appeal. In order to spread his message as widely and clearly as possible, Luther deliberately used everyday (even vulgar) language, introducing a new vitality and vividness to the stilted written forms then in use. A measure of his success were the 100 000 copies printed by Lufft's press in Wittenberg alone between 1534 and 1584. As well as achieving a literary masterpiece, Luther exerted a decisive linguistic influence throughout Germany; even subsequent Catholic translations drew on his usage. The form of German that Luther used was east central German, modified with usages from other areas and extended by his own innovations to cover a variety of registers. This form became the basis of modern standard German.

Gerusalemme liberata (1581) An epic poem in twenty cantos by Torquato *Tasso. Although he had completed his masterpiece by 1575, Tasso remained dissatisfied, troubled by both aesthetic and religious qualms, and the poem underwent several revisions after its first publication. Retitled *Gerusalemme conquistata*, the latest of these appeared in 1593, a sorry testimony to Tasso's urge to appease Counter-Reformation morality and academic rules. Like *Boiardo and *Ariosto, his predecessors at the Este court in Ferrara, Tasso wrote in **ottava rima*, aiming to produce a Christian epic founded on historical truth without, however, foregoing the appeal of the chivalric and marvellous elements (*materia cavalleresca*) of earlier romances based on the legends of *Arthur and *Charlemagne and Roland. His subject was the climax of the First Crusade, the siege and conquest of Jerusalem in 1099 by the army of Godfrey of Boulogne. To the historical participants – Godfrey, Baldwin, Tancred, Raymond of Toùlouse, Bohemond, Peter the Hermit, and Solyman, Sultan of Nicaea – Tasso added essential fictional characters: Rinaldo (introduced as the ancestor of the Este), the enchantress Armida, Argante, and Clorinda and Erminia, who are romantically involved with Tancredi. The Christians defeat the many stratagems of the forces of evil and the poem concludes as Godfrey leads the triumphant crusaders to the Holy Sepulchre. It was translated into English in 1594 and 1600 and influenced parts of Spenser's *Faerie Queene*.

Gesner, Konrad (1516–65) Swiss naturalist and bibliographer. The son of a Zürich artisan, Gesner was educated at the university of Basle. After continuing his education in Paris and Montpellier, he returned to Switzerland in 1641 to become professor of Greek at Lausanne university. He later turned to medicine, becoming in 1541 chief physician of Zürich. A prolific author, Gesner wrote more than eighty works, the best known of which is his comprehensive five-volume *Historiae animalium* (1551–87). A related *Historiae plantarum*, with 1500 illustrations, appeared posthumously (1751–

59). Much shorter, but more perceptive, is Gesner's *De omni rerum fossilium genere* (1565), in which he proposes a possible organic origin for fossils (*see* mineralogy). In the field of bibliography Gesner's major work is *Bibliotheca universalis* (1545–49) in which he listed and summarized all known Greek, Latin, and Hebrew works. He died in Zürich of the plague.

Gesualdo, Carlo (c. 1561–1613) Italian nobleman and composer. Born in Naples, Gesualdo held the title of prince of Venosa. Following the widely publicized murder of his wife and her lover (1590), Gesualdo retired to his estate at Gesualdo near Avellino. In 1594 he went to Ferrara to marry Leonora d'Este, niece to the reigning duke. In the same year his first two books of madrigals were published in Ferrara. Gesualdo suffered from melancholy, and spent most of the rest of his life on his estate at Gesualdo; his letters from this period reveal an extraordinary sensitivity. He published in all six books of madrigals, two of motets, one of responsories, and some keyboard works. It is for his madrigals that he is chiefly remembered; chromatic harmonies and the juxtaposition of fast and slow movements result in a mannered, idiosyncratic style which was much admired, though little imitated.

Ghent The capital of the modern province of East Flanders, Belgium, situated at the junction of the Scheldt and Lys rivers. Ghent supplanted neighbouring Bruges as seat of the counts of Flanders in the late twelfth century but its wealthy merchant class soon gained a measure of independence from its feudal overlord and a degree of democratic self-government which was mainly in the hands of those connected with the cloth industry. Ghent passed with the rest of Flanders to Burgundian and then Habsburg rule, and in the sixteenth century played a prominent role in the attempt to throw off the Spanish yoke. It rebelled and was severely crushed by Charles V in 1540, and in 1576 the leaders of the Netherlands patriots met there to sign the Pacification of Ghent as a compact for preserving their lands from Habsburg despotism. It was regained for Spain by Alessandro *Farnese, Duke of Parma, but depopulation and religious persecution had wrecked its prosperity, and the closing of the Scheldt to trade (1648) ended its chances of recovery.
The cathedral of St Bavon contains the van *Eyck brothers' great masterpiece, *The Adoration of the Lamb* (*see* Ghent altarpiece). The town hall has one Flamboyant Gothic façade (1518–33) and one in the Renaissance style (1595–1628).

Ghent altarpiece (*Adoration of the Lamb*) (1432)

A polyptych painted for the cathedral of St Bavon, Ghent, by Hubert and Jan van *Eyck. The subject matter of the two-tier, shuttered altarpiece is complex. The lower register of the interior features *The Adoration of the Lamb of God by the Elect* (hence the altarpiece's alternative name), and the upper shows God the Father enthroned between the Virgin and St John the Baptist, musical angels, and Adam and Eve. On the lowest level of the exterior, Jodocus Vyd and his wife, patrons of the altarpiece, kneel in prayer before two simulated statues of St John the Baptist and St John the Evangelist. These figures are surmounted by an Annunciation, and, at the top, pictures of the prophets and sibyls who foresaw the Virgin Birth. Each of the polyptych's twenty separate panels has the same high finish and extraordinary attention to detail, and the relative contributions of the two brothers van Eyck remain controversial among art historians.

Ghibellines *see* Guelfs and Ghibellines.

Ghiberti, Lorenzo (1378–1455) Italian sculptor. Unlike many other Florentine sculptors, Ghiberti, who trained as a goldsmith, specialized exclusively in bronze casting. The Renaissance is often taken as beginning with the competition (1401) to find the executant of the doors for the baptistery, which Ghiberti won – narrowly – from *Brunelleschi, both submitting specimen panels in relief of the *Sacrifice of Isaac* (Bargello, Florence). Ghiberti is famed for the two sets of great bronze doors he

GHIBERTI Jacob and Esau. *A panel from the "Gates of Paradise" narrates the story of Jacob, who, aided by his mother Rebecca, tricked his aged father Isaac into giving him the blessing that by rights should have been bestowed upon Jacob's elder brother Esau. (c. 1435; Baptistery, Florence)*

produced: those now on the north of the baptistery took him the first half of his career (1403–24); those on the east, facing the façade of the cathedral (called by Michelangelo the *Gates of Paradise*), preoccupied him from 1425 until 1452. His style developed considerably from the twenty-eight small decorative panels of the earlier doors to the ten great panoramic narrative scenes of the later ones.

It is an oversimplification to regard Ghiberti as a Gothic artist, in diametric contrast with Brunelleschi and *Donatello as representatives of the Renaissance, for there are many debts in his work to Greco-Roman sculpture, which he personally collected and on which he advised others. Ghiberti's genuinely transitional style was greatly appreciated in his day and was probably more popular than Donatello's demanding and dramatic mode. Ghiberti's three bronze statues for the guildhall, Orsanmichele, are also far less intensely characterized than Donatello's: *St John the Baptist* (1412), still very Gothic in treatment; *St Matthew* (1419), a truly Renaissance statue, derived from those of ancient Roman senators; and *St Stephen* (1426–28), a rather bland young prelate.

Ghirlandaio, Domenico (Domenico di Tommaso Bigordi; 1449–94) Italian painter. The best fresco painter of his generation and extremely prolific, Ghirlandaio was the son of a Florentine goldsmith and established a flourishing workshop there with the assistance of his relatives. Later, *Michelangelo served him as an apprentice. One reason for Ghirlandaio's popularity was his inclusion in his paintings of portraits of his friends and contemporary Florentine dignitaries, as seen in the fresco cycle *Christ Calling the First Apostles* in the Sistine Chapel in Rome (1481–82), painted in the already old-fashioned style of *Masaccio. Most of Ghirlandaio's frescoes were painted in Florence and are notable for their complex composition and technical excellence; chief among them are those in the Sassetti chapel, Sta Trinità (scenes from the life of St Francis; c. 1485) and in the choir of Sta Maria Novella (scenes from the lives of the Virgin and St John the Baptist; c. 1490), which were again remarkable for their control of prosaic naturalism. Best known of his other paintings is *Old Man and his Grandson* (1480), which combines genuine tenderness with uncompromising reality. Ghirlandaio's son, Ridolfo (1483–1561), also distinguished himself as a portrait painter.

Giambologna (Jean Boulogne, *alias* Giovanni (da) Bologna; 1529–1608) Flemish-born sculptor. Giambologna was born at Douai and trained under the Flemish sculptor *Dubroeucq on the roodloft for Ste Waldetrude, Mons (now Belgium). In about 1550 he travelled to Rome to study classical and Renaissance sculpture and met Michelangelo. He was encouraged to settle in Florence and by 1558 was in the pay of the Medici. He grafted an understanding of Michelangelo's style onto his fresh knowledge of classical Hellenistic sculpture which had recently been excavated in Rome.

Giambologna developed Michelangelo's earlier ideas for sculptures with two or three figures in a series of marble masterpieces that span his career: *Samson slaying a Philistine* (1560–62; Victoria and Albert Museum, London); *Florence triumphant over Pisa* (1565–80; Bargello, Florence); *The Rape of a Sabine* (1579–83; Loggia dei Lanzi, Florence); *Hercules slaying a Centaur* (1594–99; also Loggia dei Lanzi). These made him the most influential and sought-after sculptor in the whole of Europe for half a century (1560–1610). Giambologna also excelled in modelling sculpture to be cast in bronze, a medium Michelangelo had abhorred; he must have been encouraged by the success of Cellini's *Perseus*, unveiled just as he arrived in Florence (1554). His own first success was a fountain of Neptune in Bologna (1563–67), where he also invented his most enduringly successful, and widely reproduced, composition in bronze, a flying Mercury (examples at different scales in Bologna, Florence, Naples, Paris, and Vienna). Exploiting the potential of metal for statues with widely flung limbs and accessories, he produced a series of *Labours of Hercules* and other aggressively masculine subjects; his statuettes of females are composed differently, with their bent limbs wound round their bodies in a fascinating sequence of angles and sensuous curves.

Giambologna revitalized, mainly for religious themes, the Florentine tradition of narrative reliefs in bronze. But his greatest contribution to the development of sculpture was the equestrian monument of Duke Cosimo I (1587–93; Piazza della Signoria, Florence); this gave a fresh impetus to a tradition which was then followed throughout the capitals of Europe. His own studio produced other similar equestrian portraits of the reigning Duke Ferdinando I de' Medici (Piazza SS Annunziata, Florence), of King Henry IV of France (Paris, destroyed in the French Revolution), and of King Philip III of Spain. These were imitated in London by Le Sueur's statue of King Charles I (1630; Trafalgar Square).

The spread of Giambologna's elegant, courtly style was ensured by the wide distribution of his bronze statuettes and the number of his pupils who went to work all over Europe. Giambologna's career links that of Michelangelo, whom he imitated, to that of Bernini, founder of the Baroque in Rome. See Plate IX.

186

giant order *see* colossal order.

Gibbons, Orlando (1583–1625) English composer. He sang in the choir of King's College, Cambridge, from 1596/98 before becoming a student at the university. In about 1603 he became a member and probably organist of the Chapel Royal. In 1623 he was appointed organist of Westminster Abbey, and in 1625 is recorded as also being senior organist at the Chapel Royal and a musician in the king's private music. He died in Canterbury, awaiting with Charles I's retinue the arrival of Charles's bride, Henrietta Maria. Gibbons wrote many keyboard pieces and a number of consort works, but is most famous for his church music, all for the Anglican rite. In his verse anthems soloists and chorus alternate in an expressive treatment of the text; many of these works may be accompanied by either viols or organ.

Giberti, Gian Matteo (1495–1543) Italian churchman. Giberti, who was illegitimate, was born in Genoa and as a young man he attracted the patronage of Cardinal Giulio de' Medici. When his patron became Pope Clement VII (1523) Giberti virtually ran the papal Curia and strongly encouraged the pope in his anti-imperial diplomacy. In 1524 he was appointed bishop of Verona, and after the sack of Rome (1527) he settled in his diocese and undertook far-reaching reforms, aimed at raising the quality of the Church's pastoral life and the efficacy of its ministry. His methods were studied with attention by Cardinal (later St) *Charles Borromeo. Under Pope Paul III Giberti continued to be a trusted papal adviser, and his work is seen as preparing the way for the Council of *Trent. He was also an able patristics scholar, publishing several editions of the Church Fathers.

Gilbert, Sir Humfrey (c. 1539–83) English explorer and soldier. He served in Le Havre (1563) and Ireland (1567–70 and 1579) and in 1572 commanded 1500 English volunteers assisting the Dutch struggle against Spanish rule. In 1566 he failed to persuade Queen Elizabeth to support his proposed search for a *northwest passage from England to the East; later she rejected his plans to prey on Spanish treasure ships. Armed with a royal charter to settle heathen land, he embarked on his first and unsuccessful expedition (1578–79) to North America. On his second expedition (1583) he annexed Newfoundland for England, but went down with his ship on the homeward voyage.

Gilbert, William (1544–1603) English physician and physicist. After reading medicine at Cambridge, and a period of European travel, Gilbert moved to London in 1573. His practice flourished, culminating in his becoming physician to Elizabeth I and, in 1600, president of the College of Physicians. It is, however, on *De magnete* (1600), long recognized as the first major work of British science, that Gilbert's reputation rests. Dedicated to those who seek knowledge from things, not books, the work made one of the first serious attempts to show the value of the newly established experimental method. In his most unexpected conclusion he demonstrated that the earth itself was a magnet, with lines of force running between the poles. No traditionalist, Gilbert was intensely critical of Aristotle, while at the same time supporting the claim of Copernicus that the earth rotates.

Gioconda, La see *Mona Lisa*.

Giocondo, Fra (Giovanni da Verona; 1433–1515) Italian architect. Best known for his edition of Vitruvius (1511), Giocondo was frequently consulted by other leading architects, and his collection of drawings of details of classical ruins in Rome was a valuable resource both to them and to his patrons. He worked in both Italy and France, often as architectural adviser, but also responsible for garden design (at Naples and Blois). In his native Verona he worked on the Palazzo del Consiglio (1476–88), in Naples (1489–93) he was responsible for fortifications, and in Paris he built the Pont-de-Notre-Dame (1500–08). He also designed the defences of Venice (c. 1506), built city walls at Treviso (1509), and, following Bramante's death in 1514, became supervisor at St Peter's in Rome, sharing the post with Raphael and Giuliano da Sangallo.

Giolito, Gabriele (fl. 1538–78) Italian printer. The most important member of a Piedmontese family of printers and publishers, Giolito settled in Venice in 1538. In the next forty years he published about 850 books, including many editions of Ariosto and reprints of Petrarch, Boccaccio, and Dante, as well as translations. As the intellectual climate changed and the power of the Inquisition grew, Giolito concentrated on books of spiritual advice. The decorated initials and title-pages of his books, with borders and panels of printers' flowers and fine woodcut illustrations, set new fashions, like those for enclosing whole scenes in initials (an echo of manuscript illumination) or packing a series of small illustrations into one picture. His sons took over his firm, but they were less successful and it did not survive beyond 1606.

Giorgio, Maestro see Andreoli, Giorgio.

Giorgione (Giorgio Barbarelli *or* Giorgio del Castelfranco; c. 1476–1510) Italian painter. Born at Castelfranco in the Veneto, Giorgione was a pupil of Giovanni *Bellini at Venice during the 1490s and probably met *Titian there. Little is known of his life, and only a few paintings are firmly attributed to him; however, there is general agreement that he initiated the High Renaissance style in Venetian art. His early works, such as the Castelfranco *Madonna Enthroned* (c. 1500) with its dreamy figures and passive mood, and *Judith* (c. 1504; Leningrad), were profoundly influenced by the styles of Bellini, *Gentile, and (increasingly) *Leonardo da Vinci. *The Tempest* (c. 1503; Venice) is an evocative pastoral scene in which landscape for the first time is treated for its own sake, rather than as a background, and established a genre in Venetian art. In this and other works, such as *Sleeping Venus* (Dresden), finished by Titian, *The Three Philosophers* (Vienna) finished by *Sebastiano del Piombo, and *Laura* (1506; Vienna), a portrait of a young woman, Giorgione experimented with qualities of mood and mystery, experiments that Titian went on to develop after Giorgione's death of the plague. Among his mature portraits is a fine one of a Knight of Malta (Uffizi), with an intense, brooding gaze. Other works probably by Giorgione include *The Pastoral Concert* (Louvre), *Christ Carrying the Cross* (Boston), and *Adoration of the Shepherds* (Washington), although several works are lost. Also active as a musician and poet, Giorgione, although controversial in his time, played a crucial role in the development of High Renaissance art, as expanded in the works of Titian.

Giotto (di Bondone) (c. 1267–1337) Italian painter. Born near Florence, Giotto, above all his contemporaries, is credited with effecting the transformation of European art from the earlier flat Byzantine model to the humanistic naturalism of the Italian Renaissance. Tradition has it that he was a pupil of the Florentine artist *Cimabue, who was lauded with Giotto in Dante's *Purgatorio* as the greatest of all artists. Giotto's early works also show the influence of Pisano and other contemporary sculptors in his adoption of a new three-dimensional realism. Giotto's work most celebrated among his contemporaries was the mosaic *Navicella* (c. 1300) for St Peter's, now largely destroyed.

More influential in the long term were his frescoes for the *Arena Chapel, Padua (begun c. 1305). This cycle, the *Lives of the Virgin and Christ*, covers most of the interior of the chapel and epitomizes Giotto's achievement as the first great creative personality of European painting. The three tiers of scenes are remarkable for their rejection of colour and conventional elegance and for their

GIOTTO The Meeting of Joachim and Anna at the Golden Gate. *(c. 1305: Arena Chapel, Padua)*

concentration upon moral content, expressed with a simplicity and dignity hitherto unknown. Giotto's altarpiece of the *Madonna Enthroned* for Ognissanti, Florence (c. 1310; Uffizi) and his frescoes for the chapels of the Bardi and Peruzzi families in the church of Sta Croce, Florence, painted during the 1320s, consolidated his reputation as the most important painter of the Trecento. Also often attributed to him is the fresco cycle in the upper church of S Francesco at Assisi (c. 1297– c. 1305). In Florence, where he was director of public works, he was entrusted with the major architectural commission for the building of the campanile of the cathedral (1334). An ugly but witty man, Giotto exercised enormous influence upon almost all the Florentine painters that succeeded him, including *Masaccio and *Michelangelo.

Giovanni (da) Bologna *see* Giambologna.

Giovanni da Udine (Giovanni Recamador; 1487– 1561/4) Italian painter and architect. Born at Udine, he was a pupil of *Raphael in Rome and played a leading part in the decoration of the Vatican Loggie (1517–19) and the Villa Madama (1520), together with such colleagues as *Giulio Romano. He made extensive use of *grotesques in his decorative style, which lent itself particularly well to stucco and fresco, and after his return to Udine he was made responsible for all public architectural projects there (1552), as well as continuing his decorative work. His graceful style was imitated throughout Europe during the eighteenth century by neoclassical designers. His other works include stained-glass windows, incorporating arabesque features, in Florence.

Giovanni da Verona *see* Giocondo, Fra.

Giovanni di Paolo (c. 1403–82) Italian painter. A native of Siena, Giovanni may have been a pupil of Taddeo di Bartolo and probably never visited the other artistic centres in Italy, thus remaining virtually unaffected by the growing trend towards naturalism and classical humanism in such cities as Florence. Instead Giovanni was, with *Sassetta, the leading exponent of the mystical and conservative style of the fifteenth-century Sienese school and was dubbed the "El Greco of the Quattrocento" by Berenson. Although archaic in form, works such as *St John in the Wilderness* (date unknown), *Purification of the Virgin* (1447–49), and the *Madonna* altarpiece in Pienza cathedral (1463) illustrate Giovanni's ability as a narrative painter. At his best Giovanni expresses a dramatic and tormented intensity, which has been seen by some to anticipate mannerist and expressionist art; at his worst he repeats the conventional formulae of medieval decoration. For many years his work was neglected but the twentieth century has seen a revival in critical interest, despite the fact that he was already outmoded in his own time and had no very profound influence upon his immediate successors.

Giovio, Paolo (1483–1552) Italian historian and biographer. Educated as a doctor, Giovio left his native Como to become a servant of the papacy under Leo X (1513) and spent most of his life at the papal court, where he acquired an intimate knowledge of its affairs. Clement VII made him bishop of Nocera (1528); he withdrew from Rome in 1549, having failed to become a cardinal under Paul III, and ended his life in Florence. His major work, *Historiae sui temporis* (1550–52), covers the years 1494–1547. He also wrote a commentary on Turkish affairs (1531), a work on heraldry, and biographies (of Leo X, Ferdinando d'Avalos, and others), and encouraged *Vasari to write his lives of artists.

Giraldi Cinthio, Giambattista *see* Cinthio.

Giuliano da Maiano (1432–90) Italian architect. A member of a leading artistic family of Florence in the fifteenth century, Giuliano trained with his brother, the sculptor *Benedetto da Maiano, as a stone-carver and later collaborated with him on a number of projects, including the shrine of S

Savino (1472; Faenza cathedral) and a chapel for Sta Fina in the Collegiata at S Gimignano (1468). Following in the artistic footsteps of *Brunelleschi and *Michelozzo, Giuliano worked on the Palazzo Pazzi in Florence (c. 1460–72) and designed Faenza cathedral (1474–86), the vaulting of the nave in the cathedral of Loreto (post-1481), and a royal villa in Naples, the Poggio Reale (1484–90), now destroyed. He also executed several notable carvings in wood.

Giulio Romano (Giulio Pippi; c. 1492–1546) Italian painter and architect. Born in Rome, Giulio worked in Raphael's workshop as a child and by the time of Raphael's death (1520) had become the chief assistant there, engaged on Raphael's frescoes in the Stanza dell'Incendio in the Vatican (completed in 1517) and in the Loggie (completed in 1519). After Raphael's death, Giulio completed several other works, including the Sala di Constantino frescoes at the Vatican (1524) and the *Transfiguration* (1517–22), as well as original paintings of his own, such as the altarpiece for Sta Maria dell'Anima in Rome (c. 1523) and the *Stoning of St Stephen* (1523) for S Stefano in Genoa.

After further work at the Villa Madama and the Villa *Farnesina with *Giovanni da Udine, he moved to Mantua, where he was obliged to remain after a scandal erupted over his implication in some obscene engravings. There he dominated artistic affairs and, at the invitation of Federico II Gonzaga, embarked upon his masterpiece, the Palazzo del *Tè (c. 1525). Constructed and decorated under Giulio's direction, the palace is a monument to the mannerist style that he helped to create (see Plate X). He also worked in the Reggia dei Gonzaga in Mantua, in a style anticipating the Baroque, built a mannerist-style house for himself and his family (1544–46), and in 1545 began the rebuilding of Mantua cathedral after his own plans. He enjoyed considerable fame even beyond the borders of Italy; Shakespeare, for instance, refers to him as "that rare Italian master" (*Winter's Tale* V ii).

Giunti (*or* **Junta**) **press** A printing house first established by Luca-Antonio Giunti (1457–1538) in Venice in the 1480s, specializing in liturgical works. The more important branch of the firm was at Florence, where Filippo Giunti (1450–1517) printed from 1497 until his death. The business was carried on by his descendants until the early seventeenth century. The Venetian branch of the family lasted until 1642, and there was a third branch printing at Lyons from 1520 to 1592. Filippo Giunti printed the first Greek edition of Plutarch's *Lives* (1517) but the quality of scholarship in Giunti editions was generally well below that of works from the *Aldine press.

Glareanus, Henricus (Henry of Glarus *or* Heinrich Loris; 1488–1563) Swiss musical theorist and humanist. As a child and young man Glareanus studied in Berne and Rottweil with Michael Rubellus, and in 1506 he began his studies of philosophy, theology, mathematics, and music at Cologne university. He made a reputation for himself by writing Latin poems and was awarded the poet's laurel by Emperor Maximilian in 1512. In 1514 he returned to Basle, where he met *Erasmus, who became a great influence on his thinking. In 1529 Glareanus became professor of poetry at the university of Fribourg, and later professor of theology. He wrote a treatise on geography (1527) and several musical treatises, the most important being his *Dodecachordon* (1547), in which he propounds his theory of twelve church modes. This had considerable influence on late Renaissance composers.

glass During the Renaissance the fine glass of Venice was pre-eminent, widely exported into northern Europe and coveted by the nobility. In the mid-fifteenth century an influx of expert Islamic glass-workers into Murano (the centre of Venetian glass manufacture) stimulated an already established glass industry. Strictly enforced guild rules of secrecy protected the Venetian product from effective competition.

From about 1450 output included goblets, cups, and bowls of dark red, green, and blue glass, modelled on shapes used by contemporary metal workers. These were painted in enamels in contrasting colours with historical and mythological scenes and on betrothal goblets medallion portraits of bride and groom (see Plate XI). This style was later superseded by painted geometric and fish-scale decoration, with imitations of inset jewels.

Towards the end of the fifteenth century a clear colourless glass called *cristallo* was developed. Its great ductility and rapid cooling allowed glass blowers to make thin-walled vessels, tazzas, and other items of austere, unadorned beauty. Gradually this *cristallo* ware became more ornamented, with fantastic applied winged shapes and handles. Admiration for antique Roman glass led to the revival of millefiori and mosaic glass, and to the imitation of natural stones like aventurine and chalcedony. Similarly the Roman use of rope-like decoration inspired the well-known *latticino* ware with interlaced white threads in the glass. Another widely practised technique produced cracked-ice glass, particularly effective when used for water jugs and bowls.

Eventually migrant workers from Genoa, not bound to secrecy, enabled many northern European centres to produce imitative glassware in what was called "façon de Venise". In Germany there was a different indigenous glass-making tradition, with beakers and stemmed glasses, almost always in green glass, often with prunt decoration. The classic German wine glass, the *roemer*, was an early sixteenth-century development. Around 1600 Kaspar Lehmann (1563–1622), jewel-cutter to Emperor Rudolf II, pioneered the technique of decorative glass cutting, a move that heralded the predominance of Bohemian glass in the post-Renaissance period.

Goes, Hugo van der (c. 1440–82) Flemish artist. Probably born at Ghent, Hugo van der Goes was accepted as a master in the painters' guild there in 1467, although few other details of his early life are known. He executed decorations for such public events as the marriage of *Charles the Bold and Margaret of York (1468) and a number of paintings reflecting the influence of Jan van *Eyck and Rogier van der *Weyden, notably a diptych begun in 1467. Having been made a dean of the painters' guild in 1474, Hugo entered the Augustinian monastery of the Red Cloister, near Brussels, as a lay brother in 1475 and, in the same year, produced his master work, the *Portinari altarpiece (see Plate XII). Subsequent works from this period, such as two panels probably designed as organ shutters (1478–79; National Gallery of Scotland, Edinburgh) and the *Death of the Virgin* (c. 1480; Musée Communal, Bruges) demonstrate Hugo's skill as a draughtsman and are characterized by a sense of religious intensity. In his last years Hugo became increasingly depressive, attempting suicide in 1481 and dying insane the following year.

Góis, Damião de (1502–74) Portuguese humanist and chronicler. A member of a noble family, Góis was born at Alenquer and grew up at the court of King Emanuel (I) the Fortunate. Emanuel's son and successor, John III, appointed him secretary to a Portuguese factory in Antwerp (1523), and he later travelled widely on a number of missions as a government servant. In 1533 he resigned his post to devote his time to study, in which he was advised by his friend Erasmus. In Padua (1534–38) he met Pietro Bembo. After marrying Johanna van Hargen, a Dutch noblewoman, he lived for six years in Louvain. He became keeper of the Portuguese national archive in Lisbon in 1548 and in 1558 was appointed official court chronicler. Towards the end of his life, Góis was imprisoned by the Inquisition and deserted by his family. He probably died at his family estate at Alenquer, a few miles north of Lisbon. His most important works, written in both Portuguese and Latin, are the chronicles of Emanuel I and John III: *Crónica do felicíssimo rei Dom Emanuel* (four parts; 1566–67) and *Crónica do príncipe Dom João* (1567). He also wrote a Latin treatise on the religion and customs of Ethiopia (1540).

Golden Fleece, Order of the (French: La Toison d'Or) The chivalric order founded at Bruges (1430) by *Philip the Good of Burgundy and pledged to uphold chivalry and the Catholic religion. The dukes of Burgundy served as grand masters and presided over the chapters, settling disputes between member knights, who had the right to trial by their peers on charges of heresy, treason, and rebellion. By the marriage (1477) of Mary of Burgundy, daughter of Duke *Charles the Bold, to Maximilian (later Emperor *Maximilian I) the grand mastership passed to the house of *Habsburg.

GOLDEN FLEECE *Antony of Burgundy wears the insignia of the order in Rogier van der Weyden's portrait. (Musée Condé, Chantilly)*

Goltzius, Hendrick (1558–1618) Dutch print maker and painter. Goltzius was born at Mulbrecht and studied under his father, Jan Goltz II, and with Dirck Volckertsz. *Coornheert. At Haarlem he was influenced by Bartholomäus *Spranger. His *chiaroscuro* woodcut of *Proserpine*,

an agitated mannerist conception, is typical of his early style. He was a virtuoso engraver, and his skill with the burin is exemplified by his famous print of the *Standard Bearer*. After a visit to Rome (1590) Goltzius adopted a more classical style. It was Goltzius's technical skill that most impressed his contemporaries. Van *Mander praised his ability to reproduce the styles of other artists, including Dürer, Lucas van Leyden, Raphael, and Parmigianino. Each of his six engravings of the *Life of the Virgin* is an expert imitation of a different artist's style. Goltzius also produced numerous drawings, including life-size works such as the *Venus, Ceres, and Bacchus with a Self-Portrait* (Leningrad). His paintings, however, lack the immediacy of his graphic work. Goltzius's wit and audacity reflects contemporary Mannerism and his technical mastery the northern tradition. His naturalistic studies hint at the future of seventeenth-century Dutch art.

Gomarists The extreme Calvinists in early seventeenth-century Holland, who took their name from their leader Francis Gomar (1563–1641), the principal opponent of *Arminianism. *See also* Dort, Synod of.

gonfaloniere The official responsible for a district of an Italian city. In Florence the title was attached to the chief member of the council of magistrates. The word derives from *gonfalone* (military banner), which, by extension, also came to mean a subdivision of a city with its own section of militia.

Góngora y Argote, Luis de (1561–1627) Spanish poet. Born into a prominent and cultured family at Cordova, Góngora appears to have been a precocious child. He attended Salamanca university but took no degree. As a young man, he was given to gambling, love affairs and, from about the age of twenty, verse writing. In 1585 he became a deacon and prebendary at the cathedral of Cordova, a post that he held until 1611, travelling widely on missions for the chapter. In 1589 twelve of his *romances* (ballads) appeared anonymously in an anthology; a number of shorter poems were also anthologized later in Pedro Espinosa's *Flores de poetas ilustres* (1605). In the meantime he had met his contemporary Lope de *Vega Carpio, whom he disliked, and while staying at the court in Valladolid had been lampooned by *Quevedo, the first of many attacks. In 1613 two works, which had earlier circulated in manuscript, set off the great controversy over *culterano* style: *Fábula de Polifemo y Galatea*, based on Ovid (*Metamorphoses* XIII), in 504 *octavas reales* (*ottava rima*), and *Soledad primera* (1091 verses), the first of an uncompleted four-part work, *Soledades*, of which only 979 further lines of *Soledad segunda* were finished. Góngora insisted on an allegorical reading of this poem, which deals with the journey and experiences of a youth shipwrecked on a strange shore, all rendered in a style of the utmost artificiality.

In 1617 Góngora, hoping to make his way at court, moved to Madrid, was ordained, and became a chaplain to King Philip III. The decision was unfortunate; he failed to advance as expected, his debts increased, and his health worsened. While collecting his works for publication, he suffered a stroke and lost his memory, dying a few months after returning to Cordova. His works, however, were published later the same year. *Culteranismo* (*culto*: polished, learned, "witty"), which Góngora's style exemplifies – but which he himself was quite capable of parodying, as in *Fábula de Piramo y Tisbe* (1618) – is conventionally said to involve surface elaborations, excessive metaphor, Latinate word order, inversions, and other devices, and is contrasted to *conceptismo*, in which the "wit" (*agudeza*) derives from meaning catachresis, ambiguity, etc. But a simplified opposition between the two is misleading, and the *culterano* style was not a novelty, as Lope de Vega claimed. The quarrel ignited by Góngora's verse reflects older stylistic arguments over Ciceronian elegance versus Senecan brevity, and distinctions such as those made by Quintilian between figures of speech and figures of thought. Of Góngora's shorter poems, his ninety-four ballads (*romances*) excel the rest. He also wrote 166 sonnets, 121 *letrillas*, and a number of other lyrics; many more are doubtfully ascribed to him.

Gonzaga family The dynasty that ruled Mantua (1328–1707) as marquesses (1433–1530) and dukes (1530–1707) and Montferrat as marquesses (1536–74) and dukes (1575–1707). The Gonzaga were feudal nobility near Mantua in the twelfth century. During the Renaissance the family included cardinals, a saint, *condottieri, and many patrons of the arts and scholarship. Luigi was the first Gonzaga to become captain-general of Mantua (1328). Gianfrancesco, a brave soldier and a patron of the arts and humanist scholarship, was made marquess by the emperor (1433). The first Gonzaga duke of Mantua was Federico II (1500–40), who also acquired Montferrat by his marriage (1531) to Montferrat's heiress, Maria Palaeologo. Gianfrancesco II (1466–1519) and his wife, Isabella d'Este, made the Mantuan court a glittering centre for the arts and scholarship. St Aloysius Gonzaga (1568–91), who died shortly before his ordination, is the patron of Catholic youth. The direct male line ended in 1627; after a war of succession

Mantua passed to a French branch, the Gonzaga-Nevers.

Gossaert, Jan (Mabuse; c. 1478–1533/36) Flemish painter. Gossaert derived his assumed name of Mabuse from his family home in Maubeuge in Hainaut (now in Belgium). He was the first artist to introduce the style of the Italian Renaissance into the Low Countries. First documented as belonging to the Antwerp painters' guild in 1503, Gossaert began by producing works full of richly ornate detail and flamboyance. The influence of Hugo van der *Goes, Gerard *David, Albrecht *Dürer, and Jan van *Eyck is also evident in such early paintings as the *Adoration of the Magi* (c. 1512; London), the Malvagna triptych (c. 1511; Palermo), and the *Agony in the Garden* (Berlin).

In 1508 Gossaert visited Italy in the service of Philip of Burgundy, bastard son of *Philip the Good, and was exposed for the first time to the art of the Italian Renaissance. Although he failed to understand the essence of the movement, he employed many features of the Italian style in his work on his return and continued to study it through the engravings of Marcantonio *Raimondi and Jacopo de' *Barbari. *Neptune and Amphitrite* (1516; Berlin), his first dated work, differs greatly from earlier efforts, with its Dürer-type figures placed incongruously in a Doric temple and its much more simple and direct execution. Later paintings, such as *Venus and Cupid*, *Danäe* (Munich), and *Hercules and Deianira* (1517; Birmingham) often present nude figures in elaborate architectural settings, painted with the acuteness of observation characteristic of Flemish art. Gossaert also excelled as a portrait painter and his patrons included the Danish royal family and Cardinal Carondelet. After Philip of Burgundy's death (1524) Gossaert retired to Middelburg, where he died.

Goudimel, Claude (c. 1516–72) French composer. Goudimel studied at Paris university and then worked with the publisher Nicolas du Chemin as proofreader and later partner. From 1557 he lived at Metz, where he composed his first complete Psalter (1564). He was killed in Lyons in the *Massacre of St Bartholomew. Although Goudimel wrote Masses, motets, and chansons, it is for his psalm settings that he is noted. These all treat French translations of the texts and range in style from motet-like works to simple harmonizations.

Goujon, Jean (c. 1510–c. 1568) French sculptor. The early years of Goujon's life are obscure but he was probably born near Rouen, where he executed his first documented work, the fine Corinthian columns supporting the organ loft in the church of St Maclou (1540). The tomb of Louis de Brézé (husband of *Diane de Poitiers) in Rouen has also been ascribed to him and shares the same classical influence evident in subsequent works. His mature style first showed itself in a notable rood screen for St Germain-l'Auxerrois in Paris (c. 1544; Louvre), upon which he collaborated with the architect Pierre *Lescot. Goujon also collaborated with Lescot upon his finest work, the Fontaine des Innocents (1547–49; Louvre), which is clearly influenced by the style of Benvenuto *Cellini.

Later works, similarly distinguished by strong classical elements, include decorations for the interior and exterior of the *Louvre, notably the caryatids of the Salle des Caryatides (extensively restored in the nineteenth century), and – again with Lescot – work at the Hôtel Carnavalet. No works after 1562 are known and Goujon eventually died in Bologna, an exile from religious persecution. He also contributed comments on sculptural ornamentation in an appendix to the first French edition (1547) of the *De architectura* of Vitruvius, as well as a number of woodcut illustrations for the book.

Gozzoli, Benozzo di Lese (1420–97) Italian painter. Celebrated as a painter of frescoes in the early Renaissance, Gozzoli was apprenticed as a goldsmith and worked (1444–47) with *Ghiberti on the baptistery doors in his native Florence. He also assisted Fra *Angelico, working with him at the Vatican and in the cathedral at Orvieto (1447), but maintained a more secular approach in his own frescoes at Viterbo and Perugia (1453–56). In 1459 Piero de' Medici, who shared Gozzoli's taste for pageantry, chose him to decorate the chapel in the Palazzo Medici-Riccardi, Florence. The *Procession of the Magi* is Gozzoli's masterpiece, covering three of the chapel's walls and revealing him as an artist of considerable decorative talent and ability as a portraitist. A number of his contemporaries, including Lorenzo and Cosimo de' Medici, are depicted among the figures. A major fresco cycle of Old Testament scenes (1468–84) in the Campo Santo at Pisa, where he died, is much damaged.

Graces In classical mythology, the three daughters of Zeus, the personifications of grace and beauty, known to the Greeks as Charites and to the Romans as Gratiae. Their names were Aglaia, Euphrosyne, and Thalia. They were often depicted or described in the company of the *Muses or *Apollo or as attendants on *Venus, and the Renaissance artists and poets accepted these associations as part of the iconography. Annibale Carracci, for instance, in a picture in the Kress Collection, National Gallery, Washington, shows

GOZZOLI The Journey of the Magi *(detail). Among the followers of the Magi, many of them portraits of his Florentine contemporaries, the artist has included himself and signed his work by means of the inscription on his cap. (1459; Palazzo Medici-Riccardi, Florence)*

the Graces adorning the goddess of love at her toilette.

Characteristically the Graces are shown linked together in a dancing group in such a way that two face the viewer and the third has her back turned, as in Raphael's stucco roundel in the Loggie of the Vatican. This image was interpreted by the Stoic writers of antiquity as an allegory of liberality – giving, receiving, and returning benefits – and the interpretation was inherited by the Renaissance along with the icon. To the Neoplatonists, the dancing Graces, being closely associated with Venus, were emblematic of the operations of love in the universe, moving in a ceascless circle (*see also* Primavera, La).

Graf, Urs (c. 1485–c. 1528) Swiss artist, goldsmith, and designer. Graf was born in Solothurn and was probably taught by his goldsmith father before being apprenticed at Strasbourg. He led a somewhat irregular life, but in 1509 he settled at Basle, where he executed his chief work as a goldsmith: a reliquary for the monastery of St Urban (1514; now lost). He was exceptionally talented as a draughtsman; over 200 drawings by him survive, many depicting mercenaries and courtesans and others with evocatively drawn mountain landscapes. Graf also made engravings and designs for woodcuts, stained glass, and goldsmith's work, and the Basle publisher *Froben employed him to ornament his books.

Granada A city in southern Spain on the slopes of the Sierra Nevada. A fifth-century BC Iberian settlement, Granada was refounded in the seventh century AD and taken by the Moors in the eighth century. It became the capital of the Moorish state of Granada and an important centre of Islamic learning and culture. The Alhambra (completed in the fourteenth century) is a supreme example of Moorish architecture. In 1492 the Catholic monarchs, *Ferdinand and Isabella, completed the Reconquista by driving the Moors out of Granada. Under Castilian and Spanish rule Granada's importance declined, and the expulsion of the Jews (1492) and the unconverted Moors (1502) deprived Granada of many enterprising citizens. The Moriscos (Moors who had converted to Christianity) were harried by the *Spanish Inquisition until their final expulsion (1610).
In addition to the Alhambra the monastery of S Jerònimo (1492), the Carthusian monastery (1516), and the cathedral (1523–1703) have survived from the Renaissance period. The Catholic university of Granada was founded in 1531.

Granjon, Robert (fl. 1545–89) French type designer, type cutter, and printer. The son of a printer, Granjon worked in his native Paris, Lyons (1556–62), and Rome (c. 1578–89), where he cut types for the Typographia Vaticana and oriental founts, including Arabic, for the religious propaganda of the Stamperia Orientale Medicea. His cursive *civilité* type was designed in 1557, but never achieved the widespread popularity of italics, though Granjon's roman and italic faces were spread across Europe by Dutch founders. His Greek, Syriac, and *civilité* founts were used in *Plantin's polyglot Bible (1568–73) and he worked for the Plantin press for many years. He is credited with being the first to make printers' flowers as units of decoration to be used in borders or headpieces.

Granvelle, Cardinal Antoine Perrenot de (1517–86) Burgundian aristocrat and churchman. He became bishop of Arras (1540), archbishop of Malines (1560), and cardinal (1561). *Philip II appointed this loyal servant of the Spanish Habsburg monarchy president of the council of state of the Netherlands, where he advised the regent, *Margaret of Parma, and was known for his religious orthodoxy and defence of political absolutism. His opposition to Dutch pleas for political reforms and religious toleration made him so unpopular that he was removed from the Netherlands (1564) and sent to serve Philip in various capacities in Italy (1565–79). Finally, as secretary of state in Spain (1579–86) he directed the campaign against the Dutch and negotiated the union of the Portuguese and Spanish crowns (1580). Granvelle was also a great patron of artists, both on his own behalf and for Charles V and Philip II. He was a personal friend of the sculptor Leone *Leoni and of *Titian, and was a noted collector, many of whose treasures passed (1597) after his death into the collection of *Rudolf II.

Grazzini, Anton Francesco (1503–84) Italian writer, poet, and dramatist. Grazzini was born in Florence; otherwise little is known of his early life and education. One of the founders of the Accademia degli Umidi (1540), which worked to promote the vernacular in literature, he adopted the name "Il Lasca" (Roach). In 1582 he helped found the *Accademia della Crusca. He is remembered for the realistic *novelle* about Florence collected in *Le cene* (*The Suppers*), which was not published until 1756. To contemporaries he was best known as a poet of burlesque verses and Petrarchan lyrics. He also wrote seven comedies and edited the poetry of Francesco *Berni (1548) and others.

Great Schism The division in Western Christendom in the period 1378–c. 1430 when rival popes existed at Rome and at Avignon. *See under* Avignon, papacy at.

Greco, El (Domenikos Theotokopoulos; 1541–1614) Spanish painter. Born in Crete, El Greco (the Greek) was the most outstanding Spanish artist of the sixteenth century and the last great painter of the Renaissance. Probably first apprenticed as a painter of religious works in the Greco-Byzantine tradition, El Greco studied under Titian in Venice during the 1560s, inheriting from him his taste for sensuous colour and also absorbing the influences of Bassano, Michelangelo, and, above all, Tintoretto. It is said that he had to leave Italy after offending the Roman art establishment by offering to repaint Michelangelo's *Last Judgment*.
By the time he moved (1577) to Toledo in Spain El Greco had rejected the three-dimensional space and solidly depicted figures of the High Renaissance and was building his own very individual

style from a fusion of Venetian Renaissance and Florentine-Roman mannerist styles. At Toledo he embarked upon an important series of religious paintings, beginning with two altarpieces, a *Trinity* and an *Assumption*, and the painting *The Disrobing of Christ* (1579). *The Adoration of the Name of Jesus*, also known as *The Dream of Philip* (c. 1580; see Plate XIII), and *St Maurice* (1582) represented attempts to attract Philip II's patronage but they were rejected, as their stormy harsh colours and emotional intensity were regarded as eccentric and not conducive to devotion. Relying on commissions in Toledo, where he spent the rest of his life, El Greco continued to move away from naturalism in order to express the hallucinatory quality of his supernatural vision as an artist. This is seen most clearly in such mature works as *The Burial of Count Orgaz* (1586), *The Agony in the Garden* (c. 1597–1603), and *The Assumption* (1613). He also demonstrated his penetrating psychological insight in several portraits, including those of Cardinal Guevara (c. 1600) and Félix Paravicino (1609), visionary landscapes such as *Toledo* (c. 1595–1614), and one mythological subject, *Laocoön* (c. 1610). Although he was too individual an artist to have many direct artistic heirs, apart from his own son Jorge Manuel Theotokopouli (1578–1631), El Greco has nonetheless had an impact upon twentieth-century art, with modern artists finding an affinity with his figural distortion and concentration upon the imaginary and spiritual aspects of art.

Greek studies Knowledge of Greek had practically disappeared in western Europe by the eighth century AD. For the next 500 years Europe depended on translations of Greek works into Latin, either made directly by late antique writers like Boethius or from Arabic versions of the originals. It was not until Petrarch's time that Greek began to be taught extensively in the West, though some twelfth-century scholars had a knowledge of the language. The first teachers in fifteenth-century Italy were either Sicilians or southern Italians who lacked idiomatic knowledge or envoys from Constantinople whose main preoccupation was with the threat from the Turks; the teaching was inevitably haphazard. It became more systematic with the appointment, at the instigation of Coluccio *Salutati and others, of Manuel *Chrysoloras as professor of Greek at Florence, where he taught from 1396 to 1400. From this time Greek studies evolved steadily in Italy using the talents not only of other Greek immigrants such as *George of Trebizond and Gemistus *Plethon but eventually native Italians such as *Politian. The first Greek book to be printed in the West was Constantine Lascaris's grammar, *Erotemata* (Milan, 1476).

France was the first country outside Italy in which Greek studies developed, though teaching was at first largely in the hands of Greeks such as Janus Lascaris, who visited France three times between 1495 and 1534, or Italian scholars such as *Aleandro; their main emphasis was on the acquisition of the language. Second-generation French Hellenists included *Budé, *Rabelais, Robert Estienne, and Étienne *Dolet. The emphasis of this second generation was on literature, but increasingly Greek scholars in France were forced to adopt one side or the other in the Reformation struggle. *Erasmus played a key role in this controversy with his edition of the Greek New Testament (1516). Religious controversy also accompanied the gradual extension of Greek studies into northern Europe. The activities of *Reuchlin in Germany (*see also* Hebrew studies) provoked a reaction by traditionalists, which led to the satirical scholarly feud of the *Epistolae obscurorum virorum*. *Luther was led to formulate some of his central doctrines as a result of his contact with the original New Testament text, though Erasmus deplored the conclusions he drew, and thereafter it was impossible to free the study of Greek in Germany from theological implications.

The study of Greek in England began at Oxford and Canterbury in the 1460s. George Neville, a younger brother of Warwick the Kingmaker, had Greek scholars attached to his household during his time as chancellor of Oxford (1453–56, 1461–72). A number of extant manuscripts were written by the scribe George Serbopoulos between 1489 and 1500 at Reading Abbey. Greek was first formally taught at Oxford (1491) by William *Grocyn whose fellow-pupil in Italy was *Linacre. A chair of Greek was established at Oxford in 1516 and some years later at Cambridge where Erasmus had lectured in 1511 at Bishop (later St) *John Fisher's request. As in the rest of northern Europe, the study of Greek was associated in England with developments in theology and there was a strong reaction against Greek, particularly at Oxford.

One topic that occasioned much controversy was the correct pronunciation of Greek. The fifteenth-century Greek immigrants recognized that their pronunciation differed from that of the ancient Greeks. Reuchlin derived his pronunciation from his Greek contemporaries, rendering the vowels η ι υ and diphthongs ει οι and υι like the Italian i. His so-called itacistic pronunciation was propounded in *Melanchthon's *Institutiones linguae Graecae* (1518) and Erasmus published his counter-proposals in *De recta Latini Graecique sermonis pronuntiatione* (1528). German and Italian scholars generally retained the Reuchlinian pronunciation while the Erasmian standard prevailed elsewhere.

The importance attached to the study of Greek by the early humanists had far-reaching implications. Greek philosophy encouraged the more radical aspects of humanism and the study of the language inculcated a critical approach that insisted on close attention to the actual words of the text rather than the revamping of scholastic commentaries and interpretations. The study of Greek carried with it the seeds of many preoccupations of the sixteenth-century reformers.

Greene, Robert (1558–92) English writer. Greene, who was probably born at Norwich, went up to Cambridge in 1575. There he made friends with *Nashe, who later supported him against the attacks of Gabriel Harvey. Greene then travelled abroad before settling to a life of dissipation, supported by writing, in London. He perhaps contributed to the *Henry VI* plays that were later recast by Shakespeare (whom Greene attacked in his autobiographical *Groatsworth of Wit* (1592)). Of his five independent plays, the lighthearted *Friar Bacon and Friar Bungay*, acted in 1594, is the best. His prose works include the romances *Pandosto* (1588) and *Menaphon* (1589; republished as *Greene's Arcadia*, 1599). His numerous pamphlets embrace a variety of topics and moods: for example, *Euphues, his Censure of Philautus* (1587) takes up *Lyly's theme and style (*see* Euphuism), but his most popular works were the so-called "conny-catching" pamphlets, describing in racy prose the lives and trickery of London's rogues.

Gregoriana The Jesuit college founded in Rome as the Collegium Romanum by St *Ignatius Loyola in 1551. Between 1582 and 1584 it was endowed and made into a university by Pope Gregory XIII. It was the earliest modern seminary and the model for later foundations. The college's influence on the course of the Counter-Reformation was very great, many of its pupils becoming missionaries and teachers in northern Europe and the Far East.

Gresham, Sir Thomas (1519–79) English merchant and financier. Gresham was born in London, of which his father, Sir Richard Gresham (?1485–1549), was lord mayor in 1537. After attending Caius College, Cambridge, Gresham was apprenticed to his uncle and in 1543 became a member of the Mercers' Company. He then became the Antwerp agent for Henry VIII, Edward VI, Mary, and Elizabeth until war compelled his return to England (1567). He was an acute financier and his name is (wrongly) associated with the formulation of the economic law that "bad money drives out good." In 1565 he proposed the building of the Royal Exchange and under his will he made provision for the rents from the exchange to be used to found a college in London at which seven chairs were to be endowed (in astronomy, divinity, geometry, law, music, physic, and rhetoric). The early Gresham professors of astronomy and geometry were particularly significant in establishing a practical scientific tradition in London.

Greville, Fulke (1554–1628) English statesman, courtier, and writer. The son of a Warwickshire landowner, Greville entered Shrewsbury school (1564) where he became friends with Philip *Sidney, whose biography he later wrote. Greville went on to Cambridge (1568) and then accompanied Sidney to court (1577) and on journeys abroad, although the queen, with whom Greville was a great favourite, thwarted his more ambitious travel plans. In 1583 Greville entertained Giordano *Bruno at his London home; among his friends and protégés were *Spenser, Francis *Bacon, *Camden, and *Daniel. He first became MP for Warwickshire in the 1590s and was granted several official posts such as secretary for Wales (1583) and treasurer of the navy (1598). James I continued Elizabeth's generous patronage of Greville, creating him Baron Brooke in 1621. Greville was stabbed to death by a disgruntled servant.
Most of Greville's literary works appeared posthumously (1633) in a volume that included his long verse tracts on humane learning, fame and honour, and war, his Senecan tragedy *Mustapha* (unauthorized first edition, 1609), and his collection of songs and sonnets entitled *Caelica*. His biography of Sidney appeared in 1652.

Grévin, Jacques (1538–70) French playwright, poet, and physician. Grévin was born at Clermont-en-Beauvaisis and studied medicine at the university of Paris. He was a friend of *Ronsard and sympathetic to the latter's promotion of classical standards in French literature. *La Trésorière*, based on an earlier lost comedy called *La Maubertine*, was first performed at the college of Beauvais in 1558. His tragedy *Jules César* (1560) was based on a Latin play by *Muret. Grévin's poetry, published in *Olimpe* (1560), is reminiscent of Ronsard, but about this time Grévin was converted to Protestantism and their friendship was broken off. Grévin became physician to Margaret of Savoy in 1561 and moved to her court at Turin, where he died. His *Théâtre* (1562) contains *Les Ébahis*, his most important, but also his most indecent, play.

Grien, Hans Baldung *see* Baldung Grien, Hans.

Grimani, Cardinal Domenico (1461–1523) Italian humanist and patron of the arts. He was the son of Doge Antonio Grimani of Venice and served the papal Curia, becoming apostolic secretary and protonotary in 1491. From 1497 to 1517 he was patriarch of Aquileia (and was succeeded by three of his nephews). He was employed by Venice as envoy to the pope. He was a collector of coins, cameos, paintings, and antique sculptures, many of which passed to the Venetian state at his death. In 1489 he obtained the Grimani Breviary, now in the *Marciana library.

Grocyn, William (c. 1446–1519) English humanist and scholar. Very little is known about his life before his matriculation at New College, Oxford (1465). In 1481 he was appointed reader in divinity at Magdalen College. In 1488 he went to Italy to study Greek at Florence and Rome with Chalcondyles and Politian. He returned in 1491, was ordained priest, and began to teach Greek at Exeter College, Oxford, the first time in England the subject had been taught publicly; *Erasmus and *More were among his pupils. Some impression of Grocyn's character can be gained from Erasmus's letters; he comes across as a man who combined traditional scholastic theology with a respect for the new learning. Grocyn died at Maidstone, leaving a library of 105 printed books and seventeen manuscripts. None of Grocyn's own writings survives; his importance today rests on his consistent encouragement of humanism in England and his embodiment of the highest standards of scholarship.

Grolier, Jean, Viscount d'Aguisy (1479–1565) French nobleman and humanist bibliophile. Grolier was born in Lyons (hence his *ex libris* "Grolerii Lugdunensis et Amicorum" – "of Grolier of Lyons and Friends") and was the friend of many distinguished humanists, including Aldus *Manutius, whom he met while ambassador in Italy (1510–35), and *Budé. Many books in Grolier's extensive library were handsomely bound with stamped patterns of interlaced geometrical designs and gold tooling; these bindings in the Grolier style are much sought after by collectors. Among the craftsmen who worked for him were Étienne Roffet (d. 1548) and Geoffrey Tory (c. 1480–1533), both bookbinders to the French kings. In 1545 Grolier became treasurer of France.

Groot, Hugo de *see* Grotius.

Groote, Gerard *see under* Common Life, Brothers and Sisters of the; Devotio Moderna.

grotesques Fanciful mural or sculptural decorations incorporating human, animal, and plant forms, originally used in ancient Roman buildings and revived by Renaissance artists in various media. Such decorations were found during

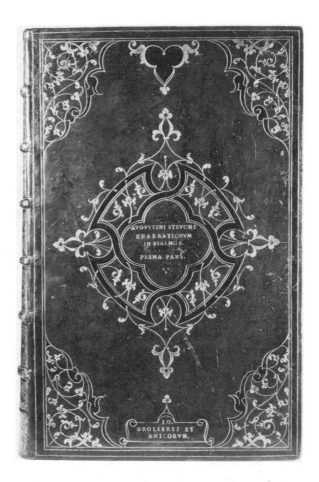

GROLIER *The cover shows Grolier's characteristic inscription and graceful interlacing. (Victoria and Albert Museum, London)*

excavations of Roman houses at the beginning of the sixteenth century, notably at the Golden House (Domus Aurea) of Nero: the term "grotesque" is derived from the Italian *grotteschi* (paintings found in grottoes, i.e. excavated chambers). Raphael and his followers quickly established grotesque motifs as a facet of their style, particularly in their frescoes. Early examples of grotesque ornament in architecture occur in Pinturicchio's cathedral library ceilings at Siena (1502), Perugino's ceiling of the Cambio in Perugia (c. 1500), and Signorelli's embellishments in Orvieto cathedral (1499–1504).

Grotius (Hugo de Groot; 1583–1645) Dutch jurist, statesman, theologian, playwright, and poet. Grotius was born at Delft and went in 1594 to study law at Leyden before visiting Orleans (1598) where he took a doctorate. He settled at The Hague (1599) to practise law. Grotius had been an accomplished Latinist at an early age, editing Martianus Capella when he was just fifteen years old; he wrote some fine Latin verse and of his three Latin dramas on biblical subjects – *Christus patiens*, *Sophomphaneas*, and *Adamus exul* – the last is best remembered as having suggested to Milton the subject of *Paradise Lost*. In 1603 the states general appointed Grotius official historiographer. For the Dutch East India Company, by whom he was employed as an advocate, he wrote (1604) *De jure praedae*, arising out of the company's claim to the prize of a Portuguese galleon captured in the East. This case led him to formulate his theory of the ocean's being free to all nations (*mare liberum*), a concept rejected by the English lawyer John Selden in *Mare clausum* (1635). His commission from the states general resulted in *De antiquitate reipublicae Bataviae* (1610), justifying the revolt of the United Provinces from Spain.

Grotius was made advocate-fiscal of Holland, Zeeland, and West Friesland (1607) and then in 1613 pensionary of Rotterdam, which gave him a seat in the states general. The same year he visited England and this may have encouraged him in his *Arminianism. The conflict between the *Remonstrants, under *Oldenbarneveldt, and the *Gomarists, who had the support of *Maurice of Nassau, came to a head in 1618; as a leader on the Remonstrant side, Grotius was sentenced in 1619 to life imprisonment. In the castle of Loevestein he continued his scholarly activities, and in 1621 his wife contrived his escape, concealed in a chest that his warders thought contained books. He went via Antwerp to Paris, where Louis XIII gave him a pension, and thence to a château lent to him near Senlis. There he completed *De jure belli et pacis* (1625), which he had first drafted in 1604. This book, now recognized as a cornerstone of international law, quickly became immensely famous, but Grotius' enemies in Holland remained implacable; apart from a six-month period in 1631–32 he spent the rest of his life in exile in France or Germany and finally as France's ambassador in Stockholm. Unhappy in this post, he obtained his recall, but died at Rostock on the way south after a stormy journey. In addition to his legal and historical writings, Grotius wrote on theological matters; his *De veritate religionis Christianae* (1627) and *Via et votum ad pacem ecclesiasticam* (1642) both suggest means of reconciliation between opposing Christian sects by playing down doctrinal differences and playing up grounds for accommodation.

Groto, Luigi (1541–85) Italian poet and playwright. Known from his birthplace and disability as Il Cieco d'Adria (the Blind Man of Adria), Groto wrote mainly in Italian but also in Latin, Spanish, and Venetian dialect. His works, both the extravagant and metrically complex verses of *Rime* (1577) as well as the plays, show mannerist tendencies. The plays include the tragedies *Dalida* (1572), a Senecan horror drama, and *Hadriana* (1578), a dramatization of the Romeo and Juliet story. His comedies are *Emilia* (1579), *Tesoro* (1580), and *Alteria* (1584).

Grün, Hans Baldung *see* Baldung Grien, Hans.

Guarini, Battista (1538–1612) Italian poet. Belonging to the Ferrarese family of the distinguished humanist *Guarino da Verona, he probably studied at Padua. He was appointed professor of rhetoric in Ferrara (1557–67), subsequently serving the Este court in secretarial and diplomatic roles. Guarini also succeeded *Tasso as court poet after the latter's disgrace in 1577. His final years were marred by quarrels with patrons and his children. He wrote lyrical verse and madrigals, a comedy called *La idropsica* (1583; *The Dropsical Woman*), a treatise on government, and a dialogue on letter-writing. He is remembered for the immensely popular and influential pastoral play, *Il pastor fido* (1589; *The Faithful Shepherd*), which stirred up a far-reaching critical debate. Guarini's controversial innovation was in mixing the noble and sentimental styles to create a new genre, his "pastoral tragicomedy", which went far beyond its model, Tasso's *Aminta*, in combining heroic and pastoral elements.

Guarino, Battista (1434–1503) Italian humanist scholar and educator. He was the son of *Guarino da Verona and he followed his father's footsteps in his native Ferrara, teaching Greek to scholars who came to him from as far afield as Germany and England. Of his pupils, the one who probably had the greatest impact on Greek studies was Aldus *Manutius. In 1459 he composed the treatise *De ordine docendi et studendi* which embodies his father's ideas on the teaching and studying of classical languages. His *Poemata* appeared in 1496, and he was also responsible for several editions and translations.

Guarino da Verona (Guarino Guarini; 1374–1460) Italian humanist scholar and educator. Guarino left his native Verona to study Greek with *Chrysoloras in Constantinople (1403–08), bringing back with him over fifty Greek manuscripts. Guarino taught Greek in several Italian centres – Florence (1410–14), Venice (1414–18), and Verona – before settling finally in Ferrara (1429), which he made into a showplace of humanism. As tutor to the young Leonello d'Este, Guarino was able to put into practice his theories about the education of the model prince, but he is best remembered for his services to the study of Greek, which he insisted was of equal importance with Latin. Many fifteenth-century scholars learnt their Greek from Guarino, including *Vittorino da Feltre. He used his classical studies as the basis for his influential book on the rules of grammar, *Regulae grammaticae* (1418), and translated into Latin Plutarch's treatise on education.

Guas, Juan (died 1496) Spanish architect and sculptor. A Frenchman in origin, Guas may have trained in Brussels before emigrating to Spain in the 1450s. He was master of works at the cathedrals of Segovia (1473–91) and Toledo (1483–95) and in his capacity as architect to Queen Isabella designed one of the foremost monuments in the Gothic-plateresque idiom, the monastery of S Juan de los Reyes (1479) at Toledo.

Ghibellines Labels attached to Italian political factions in the thirteenth and fourteenth centuries. They derived respectively from the German *Welf* (a Bavarian family that competed for the German throne against the Hohenstaufen in the twelfth and early thirteenth centuries) and *Waiblingen* (a Hohenstaufen castle). Originating as factional names in Florence, the terms were first widely used during Emperor Frederick II's conflict with the papacy (1227–50), when a Guelf opposed the claims of the Hohenstaufen emperor to authority in Italy and was sympathetic to the pope, while a Ghibelline supported Frederick. Already, however, they were also convenient tags for inter- or intra-city political rivalries, and their original function was lost with the extinction of the direct Hohenstaufen line in 1268. The Guelf label then became associated with French ambitions and with political conservatism, while, in the early fourteenth century, the *Visconti of Milan and *della Scala of Verona emerged as the leading Ghibellines. The last conflict in Italy between the empire and papacy, in the reign of Louis of Bavaria (1324–47), temporarily revived the original significance of the terms. Thereafter their importance rapidly declined.

Guerrero, Francisco (1528–99) Spanish composer. Born in Seville, Guerrero studied music with *Morales. He sang at Seville cathedral (1542–46) until his appointment as *maestro de capilla* at Jaén cathedral. In 1549 he returned to Seville as singer, then assistant *maestro*, at the cathedral, becoming *maestro de capilla* there in 1574. In 1581 he was granted leave of absence to visit Rome, and in 1588 went to the Holy Land. Many of his works were published in France and Italy, and were performed long after his death, especially in Latin America. He wrote many secular songs with alternative sacred texts, but is chiefly remembered for his sacred compositions. He published Masses, requiems, motets, psalms, and Passions in a flowing polyphonic style; they were much admired on account of their complex canonic devices.

Guevara, Fray Antonio de (1480–1545) Spanish bishop, courtier, and writer. From a prominent family, Guevara, who was born at Treceño, grew up at the court of Ferdinand and Isabella and for a time was page to their son Don Juan (died 1497). He became a Franciscan friar and left the court when Queen Isabella died (1504), returning to serve as preacher and chronicler under Charles V. He became bishop of Guadix and finally of Mondoñedo in 1537.

Guevara was steeped in classical learning and particularly influenced by Cicero; his own style, however, was extravagantly ornate, and his view of his material was medieval: he missed no opportunity to include anecdotes, digressions, and curious lore, often passing off fanciful lies as truths. The *Libro áureo de Marco Aurelio (Golden Book of Marcus Aurelius*; 1528) first published anonymously and extremely popular in Spain and elsewhere (it was translated into English in 1532 by Lord Berners), is presented as a series of letters addressed to the Roman emperor Marcus Aurelius on the virtues of an ideal ruler. It was later included in an enlarged, moralizing "mirror for princes" work entitled *Reloj de príncipes* 1539; translated as *The Diall of Princes* by Thomas *North, 1557). His *Epistolas familiares* (I, 1539; II, 1541) are 112 highly rhetorical essays, mainly cast as letters to various eminent people. Guevara's rhetorical excesses and ability to invent when it suited him were criticized even in his own day. His other works include lives of some of the Roman emperors, a handbook for courtiers, and a panegyric on rural life.

Guicciardini, Francesco (1483–1540) Italian historian and statesman. A member of one of the most distinguished Florentine families, Guicciardini became related to another (the Salviati) by his marriage in 1508. He received a classical education, studied law, and as ambassador to Spain (1511) embarked on a long and active career that gave him an intimate knowledge of the political affairs of the period. After the return of the Medici to power in Florence in 1512, Guicciardini was made a member of the *signoria* (1515) and under Leo X was successively governor of Modena, Reggio, and Parma (1516–19), during which time he met and became a friend of *Machiavelli. Under Clement VII, he served as president of Romagna (1524), represented the pope in Florence (1530), and was governor of Bologna. After Clement's death (1534), he acted as adviser to Alessandro de'

Medici until his assassination (1537), and then helped to secure the succession of Cosimo de' Medici, who subsequently forced his retirement from politics.

None of Guicciardini's works was published in his lifetime, a number were left unfinished, and only his major *Storia d'Italia* (1561) – covering events from the first French invasion to the death of Clement VII (i.e. 1494–1534) – appeared during the sixteenth century. It was translated into English in 1579. His work represents an important advance in historical scholarship, especially in the scrupulously critical use of sources and in its psychological emphasis. Guicciardini's other works include *Storie fiorentine* (written 1508–09; published 1859), a history of Florence 1378–1509, *Ricordi* (*Maxims and Reflections*), and *Considerazioni sui discorsi del Machiavelli*.

Guise family A prominent Roman Catholic family in sixteenth-century France. Claude de Lorraine was awarded the duchy of Guise (1527) for military service to *Francis I. His daughter, Mary of Guise, married James V of Scotland and was mother of *Mary, Queen of Scots. The attack by the second duke, Francis, on Huguenots at Vassy (1562) precipitated the (French) Wars of *Religion; Francis himself was assassinated by Huguenots in 1563. In order to avenge his father's murder, Henry, the third duke, fought bravely for the Catholics and also directed the murder of *Coligny (1572). Determined to resist the accession of the Huguenot prince Henry of Navarre (later *Henry IV), Guise forced *Henry III to make him lieutenant-general of the kingdom with wide powers in 1588. In December that year Henry III had Guise assassinated.

gunpowder An inflammable mixture of charcoal, sulphur, and saltpetre (potassium nitrate), used in warfare. Greek fire, deployed in the defence of Constantinople from the seventh century, seems to have been made from naphtha, and there were other similar substances known from very early times, but all required an external power to launch them. The first reference to a different kind of weapon comes from ninth-century China with a description of a mixture of gunpowder's ingredients. By 1240 the secret had reached Islam, where it was referred to as *thalj al-Sin* or Chinese snow. The same ingredients were noted anagrammatically in the West by Roger Bacon a few years later, and by the early fourteenth century the formula had become widely known. The *cannon followed soon after.

There remained two further questions to worry the Renaissance chemist. Until the present century only natural supplies of saltpetre, derived from manure collected in stables, were available. Supply was therefore limited and expensive. Further, the original fine powder tended to be unpredictable and to separate under field conditions. *See also* artillery; firearms.

Gunter's quadrants *see under* quadrants.

Gustavus I Vasa (1496–1560), King of Sweden (1523–60) After Christian II of Denmark murdered his father and uncles (1520) Gustav Eriksson led the struggle for independence from Denmark, drove the Danes out of Sweden, and was elected king. Despite the continuing Danish threat and the resentment of the great nobles whose power he systematically reduced, Gustavus Vasa created a strong monarchy and gave Sweden years of stable government. His need for money prompted him to take control of the Catholic Church's property (1527); eventually he made Sweden Lutheran (1544). He persuaded the diet to pronounce the monarchy hereditary (1544), created a strong standing national army, and founded the Swedish navy. Although he cared little for learning and the arts, he was an expert orator and a lover of music.

Gutenberg, Johann (c. 1399–1468) German printer. Although no surviving printed work bears his name, Gutenberg is usually considered the inventor of printing from movable type. His training as a goldsmith may well have helped him to solve the problems of casting the individual letters. In the 1430s he seems to have been experimenting with printing presses in Strasbourg, but by 1448 he was back in his native Mainz, where he borrowed money from a lawyer, Johann Fust, to continue his work. Another loan helped to pay for the six presses and assistants used in the production of the 42-line (or Mazarine) Bible between about 1450 and 1456. Part of the Mainz Psalter, dated 1457, may also have been Gutenberg's work, though it was published by Fust and Peter Schöffer, Gutenberg's foreman and successor, after Fust called in his loan in 1455 and took over books, presses, and type when his debtor was unable to repay what he had borrowed. Only forty-eight copies of the 42-line Bible, most of them imperfect, have survived from the 200 printed, but several smaller fragments printed before 1456, including calendars, indulgences, and copies of Donatus' grammar, are also attributed to Gutenberg.

After his break with Fust, Gutenberg's life is less well documented, though he was given an appointment by the archbishop of Mainz in 1465. He still owned some printing equipment when he died, but no more books were produced during the last decade of his life.

Guzmán de Alfarache (Part I, 1599; Part II, 1604) A novel by Mateo *Alemán. One of the first *picaresque novels, it became extremely popular, was widely translated, and established the fashion for the genre for the next fifty years. The hero recounts his life of crime, his thefts, deceits, the desertion of his rich wife (Alemán's own marriage was unhappy), and other escapades, until he is finally apprehended, condemned to the galleys, and repents. The novel is much longer than its predecessor, *Lazarillo de Tormes*, and has none of its mirth and satirical quality. Moral commentaries on each episode outweigh the narrative element and reflect a pessimistic loathing of the nastiness of life and of man's evil nature when unredeemed by grace. It was translated into English by James Mabbe under the title of *The Rogue* (1622).

H

Habsburg, house of The German princely family that took its name from Habsburg Castle in Switzerland and supplied sovereigns of the Holy Roman Empire, Austria, Spain, Hungary, and Bohemia. Werner I, the first Count Habsburg, died in 1096. The first Habsburg to be elected Holy Roman Emperor (1273) was Rudolf I (1218–91); subsequent Habsburgs ruled the empire from 1298 to 1308 and from 1438 to 1740, with successive generations enlarging their domains by diplomacy, conquest, and marriage. In 1477 the marriage of *Frederick III's heir, Maximilian (I) to Mary, heiress of *Charles the Bold of Burgundy, added the Netherlands to the Habsburg territories. Maximilian's grandson, *Charles V, also inherited Spain from his mother Joanna, daughter of *Ferdinand and Isabella. After Charles V's reign one branch of the family ruled Spain, the Netherlands, and the New World territories; the other branch held the imperial title and ruled the family's German lands. The death of Charles II of Spain in 1700 ended the Spanish Habsburg line. The direct male line in Germany ended with the death of Emperor Charles VI in 1740. His daughter, Maria Theresa, married Francis of Lorraine and the Habsburg-Lorraine family continued as emperors until the Holy Roman Empire was abolished in 1806; subsequently they ruled as emperors of Austria until 1918.

Hadrian VI *see* Adrian VI.

Hakluyt, Richard (c. 1552–1616) English geographer. Born near London of a wealthy family, Hakluyt excelled as a scholar and was educated at Westminster and Oxford. After ordination (1578) he remained at Oxford, lecturing on both geography and navigational technology. He also took pains to befriend the great merchants and navigators of the day. In 1583 he went to Paris, where for five years he was chaplain to the English embassy and simultaneously accumulated a mass of information about foreign settlements and trade. He returned to devote his life to promoting colonial expansion through his publications, putting much emphasis on the value of America. Hakluyt's *Principall Navigations, Voyages, and Discoveries of the English Nation* first appeared in 1589, and the three-volume second edition (1598–1600) is indispensable to any study of the theme in this period.

Hamlet The tragedy by *Shakespeare written about 1600 and first published in a corrupt form (Bad Quarto) in 1603 and a better version (Good Quarto) in 1604/05. The plot is based on an episode in the twelfth-century Danish history of Saxo Grammaticus, which was amplified by Belleforest in *Histoires tragiques* (1576) and was the subject of an earlier tragedy (the so-called Ur-Hamlet), now lost, possibly by Thomas *Kyd. The play contains melodramatic elements common to other Elizabethan and Jacobean revenge tragedies, such as the ghost of the murder victim and the real or feigned madness of the hero, but the complexity of the character of Hamlet himself sets it apart from its fellows; the play has evoked generations of critical speculation and the title role remains the supreme challenge for an English tragic actor.

Hampton Court Conference (1604) A Church conference convened at Hampton Court Palace under the presidency of James I for the purpose of considering the demands of the Puritans embodied in the Millenary Petition of 1603. This petition, so called on account of its purportedly having a thousand supporters in the ministry, objected to a number of rites and ceremonies practised by the Church of England. John *Rainolds was the leading spokesman for the Puritans, and the archbishop of Canterbury, Richard Bancroft (1544–1610), led the bishops' side. Few concessions were made to the Puritans, and James, who maintained that the logic of their position meant "no bishop, no king", lent his support to the bishops. He did however back Rainolds's suggestion that a new English translation of the Bible should be made; a strong panel of theologians and scholars was set up to undertake the work, which was published in 1611 as the Authorized Version or King James Bible (*see also* Bible, translations of).

Hampton Court Palace A palace built on the north bank of the River Thames, 14 miles (23 km) upstream from central London. Construction began at the behest of Cardinal *Wolsey in 1515.

The palace later passed into the hands of *Henry VIII, who made numerous alterations to it and adopted it as his favourite residence. Although the palace was built very much in the English *Tudor style, with red-brick turreted battlements and Gothic motifs, it also includes many features reminiscent of the Italian Renaissance, with terracotta medallions (c. 1521) by the Tuscan sculptor Giovanni da Maiano adorning the gateways and much classically derived decoration. The Great Hall, for instance, combines Renaissance-style carvings and gilding with a traditional open timber roof, while the rest of the palace is laid out in the symmetrical fashion favoured by the Italians.

Handl, Jacob (1550–91) Slovenian composer. Born in Ribnica near Ljubljana, Handl went to Austria in the mid-1560s. In 1574 he was a singer in the chapel of Emperor Maximilian II in Vienna. After leaving there (1575) he travelled through Austria, Bohemia, Silesia, and Moravia, becoming choirmaster to the bishop of Olomouc (c. 1579). By mid-1586 he was cantor at the church of St Jan na Brzehu in Prague, where he remained until his death. Handl was prolific in his composition of Masses, motets, German songs, and secular works, many of which show the influence of Franco-Flemish composers. Criticized during his lifetime for the complexity of his music, he included in his four-volume *Opus musicum* (1586–91) two pieces scored for twenty-four voices.

Hanseatic League A league of northern European and Baltic trading towns formed in the thirteenth century under the leadership of Lübeck. The word *Hanse* is Middle High German for "fellowship", and the league was an association to enforce a common commercial code in an area over which no single prince could impose an effective set of laws to govern trade. Despite the opposition of the Danish kings in the fourteenth century, the merchants of the Hanse combined successfully in political and commercial initiatives until the rise of Dutch maritime power, which, with Burgundian encouragement, broke their monopoly of the Baltic trade. Their trading counters extended across Europe from London to Novgorod, and their wealth, privileges, and prestige, if not their political power, survived in a number of places well into the sixteenth century.

Harington, John (1561–1612) English courtier and writer. Born to parents who had loyally served *Elizabeth I during her perilous youth, Harington became the queen's godson. From 1582, after an education at Eton, Cambridge, and the Inns of Court, he divided his energy between place-seeking in London and beautifying his country estate of

HARINGTON *The translator's portrait appears on the title-page of Harington's 1591 English version of* Orlando furioso.

Kelston, near Bath. His wit attacted attention, but also landed him in trouble. After he had circulated around the court his translation of an indecent episode from Ariosto's *Orlando furioso*, the queen banished him from her presence until he had translated the whole poem. One of the greatest Elizebethan translations, this was published in 1591.

In 1596 Harington was again in disgrace, this time with his *Metamorphosis of Ajax*, an indelicate discourse on water closets. More dangerous was his association with the earl of Essex, who knighted him (1599) in the course of his Irish expedition; on the failure of Essex's rebellion Harington managed to exonerate himself, but was unable to win Elizabeth's pardon for the earl. After James I's accession, Harington obtained little further royal patronage. His letters and other writings, giving an interesting insight into Harington's character and that of the late Elizabethan court, were published as *Nugae Antiquae* (1769).

Harriot, Thomas (1560–1621) English mathematician, astronomer, and physicist. Born and educated at Oxford, Harriot accompanied Sir Richard Grenville as a surveyor on his 1585 trip to Virginia and published his account of the expedition in *A Briefe and True Report of the New-Found Land of Virginia* (1588). Shortly afterwards he entered the service of the remarkable ninth Earl of Northumberland, the so-called "wizard Earl", Henry Percy. From 1590 until his health broke down in 1615, Harriot produced a number of important works, none of which was published until long after his death. The first to appear, *Artis analyticae praxis ad æquationes algebraicas resolvendas* (1631), revealed his power as a mathematician. He also appears to have worked out, at about the same time as *Kepler, that planets move in elliptical orbits and to have anticipated *Galileo's telescopic observations of the heavens and *Snell's derivation of the law of refraction.

Harvey, Gabriel (?1545–1630) English scholar and literary critic. Harvey's father was a prosperous ropemaker of Saffron Walden, Essex, who sent his son to Cambridge, where he became a fellow of Pembroke Hall (1570). There he became friendly with *Spenser, who celebrated him as "Hobbinol" in *The Shepheardes Calender* (1579) and corresponded with him on poetic topics. Part of their correspondence was published in 1580 as *Three proper and wittie, familiar Letters*, with a two-letter sequel; in one of the former Harvey writes scathingly of The *Faerie Queene, a judgment for which posterity has mercilessly ridiculed him. Harvey claimed for himself the title "father of the English hexameter" and tried to introduce classical metres into English verse. His vanity, pedantry, and quick temper won him many enemies both inside the university and beyond, although his outstanding abilities were also widely recognized. In the early 1590s he was drawn into a vituperative pamphlet controversy with Robert *Greene and Thomas *Nashe, which was eventually (1599) stopped by official decree and confiscation of Nashe's and Harvey's offending works. Thwarted in his attempts (1585, 1598) to become master of Trinity Hall, Cambridge, Harvey retired to his home town, where he died.

Hassler, Hans Leo (1564–1612) German composer. Born in Nuremberg, he received his earliest musical training from his father. In 1584 he became one of the first German musicians to study in Venice, as a pupil of Andrea *Gabrieli. In 1586 he was appointed chamber organist to Octavian II Fugger in Augsburg, where he published many works and established a wide reputation. In 1600 he returned to Nuremberg as director of the town's music. In 1604 he moved to Ulm, and in 1608 was appointed chamber organist to Christian II, Elector of Saxony, in Dresden. He died in Frankfurt as court *Kapellmeister*.
Though a Protestant, Hassler's early works are all for the Roman rite. His Masses and motets show the influence of the Venetians in their polychoral techniques and rich sonorities. He was also famous for his Italian madrigals and canzonettes. His rather conservative German church music, though often using Lutheran melodies, shows the influence of *Lassus. His lieder were widely known; the tune of his love-song, "Mein G'müt ist mir verwirret" (1601), was used for the Lutheran hymn, "O Haupt voll Blut und Wunden" which features in Bach's St Matthew Passion.

Hebrew studies Curiosity about the Hebrew language dates in Western Christendom from the time of the Church Fathers, notably St Jerome (337–420). During the Middle Ages, Hebrew's unfamiliar alphabet was thought by many Christians to possess talismanic powers, but isolated scholars, with the aid of learned Jews, did pursue the subject more seriously. In thirteenth-century France and Spain public disputations between Jews and Christians on matters of faith disseminated some knowledge of Jewish thought, but too often resulted in increased antisemitism and the burning of Hebrew books. The object of the Hebrew studies of such men as Robert Grosseteste (1175–1253) and Roger Bacon (?1213–?1294) was primarily the conversion of the Jews.
In the Renaissance the principal spur to Hebrew studies was the desire for better understanding of the Bible. John *Colet in 1497 stressed the importance of access to the original Hebrew version of the Old Testament and to Jewish commentaries on it. The idea was given wider currency by *Erasmus in his introduction to his 1516 New Testament. The Reformation, with its emphasis on the Word of God, stimulated all aspects of biblical scholarship. *Luther and *Tyndale, as Bible translators, were both competent Hebraists, as were *Zwingli, *Melanchthon, *Bullinger, and *Calvin.
In the pre-printing era access to Hebrew texts had been a problem. Gianozzo Manetti (1396–1459), secretary to Pope *Nicholas V, was instrumental in starting the collection of Hebrew manuscripts at the Vatican, where Pope *Sixtus IV later endowed Hebrew *scriptores*. The first printed Hebrew book appeared in 1475, with the first complete Hebrew Bible following in 1488, although before 1500 printing in Hebrew was confined to Italy, Spain, and Portugal. Two outstanding sixteenth-century printers of Hebrew were Daniel Bomberg (died 1549) at Venice and the Basle printer *Froben. Both were assisted by the best Jewish and Christian Hebraists of their day. The renowned Hebrew teacher Elias Levita (1468–1549) published his famous treatise on the Masoretic text of the Bible (1538) while working for Bomberg, and the following year Sebastian *Münster published the second edition of Levita's work in Basle. Later *Arias Montano was a regular reader for the Antwerp house of *Plantin, which issued his Polyglot Bible (1568–73), in which the

Hebrew text was printed with type obtained from Bomberg's descendants.

At first Hebrew studies spread mainly through personal contacts between individual scholars. Notable teachers were Levita and Obediah Sforno (1475–1550); the latter succeeded Jacob Loans (died 1506) as Reuchlin's tutor. *Reuchlin in Germany and *Pico della Mirandola in Italy were eminent early advocates of Hebrew studies, and through them the *Cabbala became known to Renaissance scholars. Despite antisemitic prejudice, which hardened in Catholic countries during the Counter-Reformation, Hebrew teaching gradually became institutionalized as part of the enthusiasm for the new learning. Chairs of Hebrew were established at Bologna (1488) and Rome (1514) universities. In England Henry VIII founded a Hebrew professorship at Cambridge in 1540 and Hebrew was taught at the London Merchant Taylors' School from its foundation (1561).

Heemskerck, Jakob van see under Barents, Willem.

Heemskerck, Maarten van (1498–1574) Netherlands painter. He was born at Heemskerck, near Alkmaar, and after working under the obscure artists Cornelis Willemsz., in Haarlem and Jan Lucasz. in Delft, Heemskerck entered the studio of Jan van *Scorel at Haarlem (1527). Initially Scorel's student, he seems subsequently to have become his collaborator, and their works are sometimes confused. Between 1532 and 1536 Heemskerck was living in Italy, principally at Rome, where he recorded his impressions of classical architecture and sculpture in two sketchbooks (West Berlin). After his return from Italy he specialized in religious paintings and classical allegories, redolent with architectural and decorative motifs copied from ancient monuments and the works of contemporary Italian mannerist painters. The flamboyancy of these narrative paintings contrasts markedly with the sober naturalism of his portraits. Both these aspects of his style find expression in the *Self-Portrait* (1553; Fitzwilliam Museum, Cambridge) in which his massive bearded head is set against the backdrop of a view of the Colosseum, like an allegory of the aspirations of northern visitors to Rome.

Heere, Lucas de (1534–84) Flemish painter. Born in Ghent, de Heere was taught by Frans *Floris and himself taught Carel van *Mander in the late 1560s. He worked in France and England as well as Ghent, where his *Solomon and the Queen of Sheba* (1559) is in St Bavon's cathedral. Also attributed to him is the design of the famous Valois tapestries (1582; Uffizi), woven in Flanders to celebrate the arrival there of the soon-to-be-discredited *Francis, Duke of (Alençon-)Anjou, in his role of "defender of the liberties of the Netherlands".

MAARTEN VAN HEEMSKERCK Self-Portrait. *The formula by which a visitor is depicted against a backdrop of antiquities was enthusiastically taken up by eighteenth-century portraitists like Pompeo Batoni, who painted the Grand Tourists in Italy. (1553; Fitzwilliam Museum, Cambridge, England)*

Hegius, Alexander (Alexander von Heek; c. 1433–98) German humanist and educator. He was born at Heek, Westphalia, and was at one time a pupil of Thomas à Kempis. He opened a school at Deventer, Holland, in 1474. Through this school passed many of the leading figures of the northern Renaissance, including *Erasmus and *Adrian VI. Hegius produced a number of works which were published posthumously but his importance rests more on his teaching methods. He rejected the formalism of medieval scholastic education and insisted on the need to go directly to the classical texts. Although Hegius stressed the importance of Greek, his knowledge of the language was considerably inferior to his grasp of Latin.

Heidelberg A city in southwest Germany on the River Neckar. Probably of twelfth-century origins, the city was the capital of the Rhenish Palatinate until 1720. Heidelberg has the oldest university in Germany, founded by Elector Palatine Rupert I and chartered by Pope Urban VI in 1386. In the second half of the fifteenth century the university was a centre of humanist studies, where Rudolf *Agricola ("the father of German humanism") taught Greek. By 1540 Heidelberg was described as the most Lutheran city in Germany. The Elector Palatine Frederick III the Pious made the Palatinate a haven for persecuted Calvinists and the university taught Calvinist youth from all over Europe. In 1562 Frederick III supported the promulgation of the *Heidelberg Catechism, hoping it would provide the basis for a reconciliation between the different Protestant groups. Although no reconciliation was achieved the catechism is still widely used. Notable buildings from the Renaissance period that have survived the Thirty Years' War and the French sack (1693) include sixteenth-century additions to the medieval castle, the church of the Holy Ghost (1400–36), the Marstall (1590), and the Haus zum Ritter (1592). *See also* Palatina, Bibliotheca.

Heidelberg Catchism (1562) A reformed confession of faith, written by Kaspar Olevianus and Zacharias Ursinus, both of Heidelberg. It maintained the doctrines of *Calvin and *Bullinger, but moderately expressed to conciliate the Lutherans. It was accepted by the annual synod of the Palatinate in 1563 and at *Dort in 1619, and was translated into English in 1572.

Helmschmied family (*or* Kolman family) A family of Augsburg armourers, successive generations of which worked for emperors and princes from the last quarter of the fifteenth century. Their work is signed with the mark of a helmet. Lorenz Helmschmied (1445–1516) made a complete set of armour for horse and rider for Emperor Frederick III (1477; Vienna) and in 1491 was appointed chief armourer to Frederick's son Maximilian (I), for whom he made many fine pieces. Lorenz's son Kolman (1471–1532), who worked independently from 1500, produced complete garnitures for Charles V, such as the "K.D." garniture (c. 1526), parts of which survive in the Armería Real, Madrid. The family workshop's tradition of creating richly decorated parade armour was further developed by Kolman's son Desiderius (1513–c. 1578) under the patronage of Philip0 I.

Helvetic Confessions (1536, 1562) Two confessions of faith of the reformed church in Switzerland. The earlier was compiled by *Bullinger, Myconius, and others. It is sometimes referred to as the second Confession of *Basle. The second was written by Bullinger, and a revised version was published in 1566 as the official creed of the Swiss cantons. By 1578 it had been adopted by several reformed churches.

Henri II style A movement in the visual arts in France during the reign (1547–59) of *Henry II. Succeeding *Francis I as patron at *Fontainebleau, Henry II continued to foster the ideals of the Italian Renaissance by favouring French artists who had assimilated Italian concepts and adapted them to traditional French modes. Talented French architects such as Pierre *Lescot and Philibert *Delorme were employed upon the building of major châteaux, such as those at St-Maur (1541) and Anet (1547–52), while the beginning of the construction of the *Tuileries was instrumental in the creation of an entirely new school of French decoration. As well as architecture, other fields in which French artists developed a national style based upon Italian ideals included tapestries and medals.

Henri IV style A movement in French architecture associated with the reign (1589–1610) of *Henry IV. A noted patron of the arts, Henry revolutionized contemporary attitudes towards town planning through his pragmatic redevelopment of Paris, overseeing such projects as the building of the Pont-Neuf (begun 1599), and the laying out of extensive public squares, notably the Place Dauphine (begun 1607). Henry also developed his ideas about architecture through a number of major building projects, such as the Cours des Offices at *Fontainebleau (1606–09) and the Place Royale (planned in 1603).

Henry II (1519–59), King of France (1547–59) Henry was the second son of *Francis I, and he became dauphin on the death of his elder brother in 1536. His marriage (1533) to *Catherine de' Medici gave him four sons (Francis II, Charles IX, *Henry III, *Francis of Alençon), but he neglected Catherine in favour of his mistress, *Diane de Poitiers. Henry reformed his administration and established the *chambre ardente* to stamp out heresy. His Edict of Écouen (1559) paved the way for harsh measures against *Huguenots. Henry's foreign policy was dominated by the continuing war against the *Habsburgs, mainly in Spain and northeast France. By the Treaty of Chambord (1552) he helped German Protestant princes against *Charles V in exchange for the freedom to take Verdun, Metz, and Toul. Despite successes by Francis of Guise, including the capture of Calais (1558), Henry decided on peace. Financial difficulties, some setbacks in battle, and his eagerness to concentrate his efforts on the elimination of heresy lead to the Peace of *Cateau-Cambrésis (1559). Henry was mortally injured while jousting in a tournament.

Henry III (1551–89), King of France (1574–89) The third son of *Henry II and *Catherine de' Medici, Henry abandoned the Polish throne, to which his mother had arranged his election (1573), to succeed his brother Charles IX as the last *Valois king of France. His reign was overshadowed by religious conflict. When the Protestant Henry of Navarre (later *Henry IV) became heir to France (1584), Henry was faced with the wrath of the diehard Catholics led by the *Guise family. Losing control of Paris, Henry had to grant wide powers to the duke of Guise (1588), but then arranged Guise's assassination (December 1588) at Blois. Henry III was in turn assassinated by a fanatical friar. Henry had cultivated tastes, but his attachment to his *mignons* (effeminate young men) discredited the French court.

Henry IV (1553–1610), King of France (1589–1610), King of Navarre (1572–1610) Born at Pau, the son of Antoine de Bourbon and Jeanne d'Albret, Queen of Navarre, Henry was brought up a Protestant, but forced to renounce his faith following the *Massacre of St Bartholomew (1572), which was shortly after his marriage to the king's sister, Margaret of Valois. He escaped from the French court in 1576 and rejoined the *Huguenot forces. The political and religious conflicts intensified after Henry was designated heir to the throne (1584), but he was reconciled to *Henry III shortly before the king's assassination (1588). The dying king acknowledged Henry of Navarre as his heir. On his accession as the first Bourbon king of France, Henry IV had first to establish his power; his conversion to Catholicism helped persuade Paris to accept him (hence his reputed comment,

"Paris is well worth a Mass"), but he was still opposed by the hardline Catholics. Gradually he gained control of all France and in 1598 granted the Huguenots religious toleration by the Edict of *Nantes.

Relying on trusted advisers like *Sully, the king started restoring order and prosperity. It was his declared aim that even the poorest peasant should be able to afford a chicken in his pot on Sundays. He reformed the administration and put the royal finances to rights. He encouraged the economy, especially agriculture and the cloth industry: the improvements in communications included an impressive network of canals. A programme of public works beautified Paris. In foreign affairs Henry IV opposed Spanish power, but he helped negotiate the 1609 truce between the Netherlands and Spain. Henry IV had no children by Margaret, whom he divorced in 1599; by his second wife, Marie de' Medici, niece of the grand duke of Tuscany, he had six. He also had numerous love affairs. Despite his general popularity, he was assassinated by a Roman Catholic fanatic, François Ravaillac, leaving his kingdom to his young son Louis XIII, under the regency of Marie de' Medici.

Henry VIII (1491–1547), King of England (1509–47), and Ireland (1540–47) The second son of *Henry VII and Elizabeth of York, he was descended from the houses of both Lancaster and York. Henry was a popular and accomplished young king, with an interest in *humanism. Later in his reign many regarded him as a ruthless tyrant whose hands were stained with much innocent blood.

Henry first married (1509) Catherine of Aragon, widow of his elder brother Arthur. He soon embarked on an ambitious foreign policy, which proved expensive and fruitless. He defeated France at the battle of the Spurs (1513), then confirmed an alliance with *Francis I at the *Field of the Cloth of Gold (1520), but soon afterwards was again at war with France.

Henry was well served by his chief minister, *Wolsey, until slow progress in the king's divorce from Catherine caused Wolsey's disgrace. Catherine had borne one healthy daughter, later *Mary I, but Henry wanted a son to secure the succession. With the support of Thomas *Cromwell and Archbishop *Cranmer Henry divorced Catherine in defiance of the pope and married Anne Boleyn (1533). This precipitated the English Reformation which made Henry the supreme head of the Church of England and the master of its wealth – a strange irony in that he had earlier been honoured by Pope *Leo X for his opposition to Luther. Anne Boleyn had a daughter, later *Elizabeth I, but was beheaded to make way for Henry's third wife, Jane Seymour, who died (1537) shortly after giving birth to a son, later *Edward VI. Cromwell then persuaded the king to marry the Lutheran princess, Anne of Cleves. A speedy divorce and Cromwell's execution followed. A fifth marriage to Catherine Howard ended in her execution (1542). Finally he married Catherine Parr, who survived him.

Henry, particularly in his early days, enjoyed a reputation as a patron of learning and the visual arts. He personally engaged in the religious controversies of the day with his *Assertio septem sacramentorum contra M. Luther* (1521) and is credited with writing a number of songs and ballads. *Holbein the Younger worked for him in the 1530s. Using assets acquired by the seizure of Church property, particularly after Wolsey's fall, Henry also embarked on major building projects, most notably at *Hampton Court Palace and Nonsuch.

Henry of Glarus *see* Glareanus, Henricus.

Henry the Navigator (1394–1460) Prince of Portugal. The younger son of John I of Portugal, he was renowned for fostering science and exploration. His home at Sagres was a centre of information about navigation, maps, new lands, and improved shipbuilding techniques. Henry himself did not travel, but he masterminded the exploration of the Atlantic coast of Africa, and his expeditions reached the Senegal coast, Madeira, and the Azores. He alerted Portugal to the opportunities to be won by exploration and after his death the Portuguese continued his work by opening the route to India via the Cape of Good Hope and by discoveries in the Americas.

herbals Collections of descriptions of plants and their medicinal uses. Many derive from Dioscorides' guide, compiled in the first century AD, of which the oldest surviving manuscript, the Codex Vindobonensis, was made in 512 in Byzantium; the family of herbals based on it, comprising manuscript or printed translations and adaptations, flourished until the seventeenth century. Latin versions often combine Dioscorides' text with another by pseudo-Apuleius (Apuleius Platonicus), collected from Greek sources about 400 AD and among the first to be printed, in Rome in the 1480s. The Mainz printer, Peter Schöffer, produced the Latin *Herbarius* (1484) and its larger German companion (1485), one of the first scientific books in the vernacular. The Latin one described about 150 plants, the German nearly 400. Both were illustrated, the German pictures drawn in part from nature, though the third Mainz herbal, *Hortus sanitatis* (1491) reverted to more primitive illustrations. The great herbals of *Brunfels,

*Fuchs, and *Mattioli, in Latin and the vernacular, first appeared from 1530 to 1544, still leaning on Dioscorides but also describing and illustrating new plants without medicinal uses. *Turner, *Dodoens, and *Clusius continued to enlarge botanical knowledge, though the influence of *Gerard's *Herball* probably lasted longer than most. The doctrine of *signatures, based on the supposed resemblance of particular plants to the parts of the body they affected, was explained most fully in Giambattista *della Porta's *Phytognomonica* (1588). As *botany became an independent study, herbals were once more restricted to medicinal plants.

Hercules (Greek: Heracles) The greatest of the heroes of ancient mythology, who played a leading role in a number of myths. He was the son of Zeus (Jupiter) by the mortal Alcmene and gave early promise of his great strength when he strangled two deadly serpents sent to kill him in his cradle by Zeus' jealous wife Hera (Juno). An episode from his youth became a moral fable generally referred to as the Choice of Hercules: Virtue and Pleasure appear to the hero in a dream, acquaint him with what each has to offer, and ask him to choose between them, which he does in favour of the former. This choice underlies the action of Ben Jonson's masque *Pleasure Reconciled to Virtue*. A similar decision confronts the young Scipio in the painting by Raphael entitled *The Dream of Scipio* (National Gallery, London). The Florentine humanist Cristoforo *Landino examined the moral interpretation of the Hercules myths in his *De vera nobilitate* (On true nobility), and *Salutati too subjected them to extended allegorical scrutiny.

The most famous of Hercules' exploits are those grouped under the title of the Twelve Labours of Hercules. The first of these was the slaying of the Nemean lion; thus he is often depicted as wearing a lionskin. Another of his labours was to fetch the apples of the Hesperides, and he is also sometimes shown holding these fruits, as in the colossal Farnese Hercules, a Roman copy of a Greek original, excavated from the baths of Caracalla in Rome and known and admired in the Renaissance. The Twelve Labours and Hercules' other adventures afforded material for studies of the mature male nude in vigorous action; *Pollaiuolo, for instance, treated the subject of Hercules' wrestling with Antaeus both in a bronze statuette (Bargello, Florence) and in a painting (Uffizi), and the contest is also the subject of a painting by *Baldung (1530; Breslau).

hermandad (brotherhood) A form of organization originally established by medieval Castilian towns to protect their interests and maintain law and order. *Ferdinand and Isabella reorganized the *hermandades* and combined them with a central council (1476). *Hermandad* tribunals of unpaid local officials (*alcaldes*) reduced crime by their savage punishment of criminals. Their police, who could call on the central council's soldiers for help, had many successes in suppressing brigandage and maintaining law and order. Partly because the system was expensive and partly because its success made it seem less necessary, Ferdinand and Isabella agreed to the abolition of the central council in 1498. After this, local *hermandades* tended to deteriorate into inefficient rural police forces.

Hermes In classical Greek mythology, the messenger of the gods. The Romans identified him with their indigenous god Mercurius (Mercury), patron of trade and traders, and, by a logical extension, of travellers. One of Hermes' roles was to lead the souls of the dead to Hades; ancient Greek funerary vases often depict him in this capacity of conductor of souls (*Psychopompos*). In art he is generally shown as a youth wearing a broad-brimmed, often winged hat (*petasos*) and winged sandals and carrying a serpent-entwined staff (*caduceus*). One myth tells how he invented the lyre and gave it to *Apollo to appease the senior god for the theft of some cattle; he is therefore sometimes associated in art and literature with Apollo and the *Muses and *Graces. He was also the god of eloquence and a bringer of dreams.

In the esoteric philosophy of the late antique world, Hermes was conflated with the Egyptian god Thoth, and a whole body of mystical writings was attached to his name (*see* hermeticism). This made him an object of special interest to the esoteric philosophers of the Renaissance, the Florentine Neoplatonists who rediscovered the ancient texts and believed that they contained profound truths that would only be revealed to the initiated. As the go-between between natural and supernatural worlds, Hermes was invested with the symbolic role of mystagogue, instructing the candidates for initiation in the divine wisdom. Boccaccio calls him an "*interpres secretorum*" (interpreter of secrets) in *De genealogiis deorum*.

hermeticism A body of esoteric doctrine deriving its name from its supposed author, Hermes Trismegistus (Hermes Thrice Greatest), the Greek equivalent of Thoth, Egyptian god of wisdom. From the second century AD onwards a collection of treatises was formed which became known as the Corpus Hermeticum and came to include gnostic and cabbalistic material as well as more conventionally Neoplatonic works. Some of this was known to medieval thinkers, but the main body of hermetic writings was not available until 1460 when a Greek manuscript of the Corpus Hermeticum was brought to Florence. Lorenzo de' Medici commissioned a Latin translation of it from Ficino as a preliminary to his translation of Plato. This was published in 1471 and made available to scholars such mystical texts as the *Poimandres*, *Asclepios*, and the *Emerald Table*, which the Renaissance saw as the source of Plato's doctrines, believing that the Corpus was an authentic record of Egyptian wisdom. Hermetic doctrines formed part of the philosophical basis of *Pico della Mirandola's 900 theses and he began his *Oratio de dignitate hominis* (1486) with a quotation from the *Asclepios*.

The association of Platonism with hermetic ideas fundamentally coloured Renaissance concepts of Plato. Christian theologians selected the less magical passages of the Corpus to provide support for Christian philosophy, some enthusiasts claiming that this was the fount of the wisdom of Moses who, the Bible says, was "learned in all the wisdom of the Egyptians" (Acts 7:22). Magicians and astrologers, such as John *Dee, saw in the Corpus a systematic body of ancient wisdom that supported their animism. Giordano *Bruno is a striking example of the influence of hermeticism on a Renaissance thinker; he rejected the Christian interpretation of the Corpus and saw it as a body of pure Egyptian doctrine from which he derived a complex structure of natural philosophy. The progress of a more scientific approach to ancient texts led to the discounting of an ancient Egyptian origin for the Corpus Hermeticum. *Casaubon demonstrated its post-Christian date and the doctrines gradually declined in importance, though they exercised an influence on later Rosicrucians.

Hernández, Gregório *see* Fernández, Gregório.

Héroet, Antoine (died 1568) French poet and churchman. Born in Paris, Héroet published his major work *La Parfaicte Amye* (1542) at Lyons; its idealized portrait of the beloved was heavily influenced by the Italian Neoplatonism characteristic of the writings of Maurice *Scève and his Lyonnaise disciples. Héroet also made some translations from the classics, but after he was ordained he gave up writing secular verse. He rose to become bishop of Digne. *Marot and *Ronsard were among his contemporary admirers.

Herrera, Fernando de (1534–97) Spanish poet. Coming from a poor family of Seville, Herrera took minor orders and obtained a small benefice which allowed him to pursue his literary interests. He was a prominent member of a *Tertulia* (literary circle) associated with the Conde de Gelves, which included Juan de la *Cueva and other poets, clergymen, and scholars. Most of Herrera's Petrarchan love poetry – more elaborate but less delicate and subtle than *Garcilaso's, which it imitates – was inspired by a long platonic affair with Doña Leonor de Millán, the wife of the Conde de Gelves, though she was never named in his verse or otherwise openly identified. He also wrote three patriotic *canciones*, odes stylistically indebted to the Old Testament. *Canción al señor don Juan de Austria vencedor de los moriscos en las Alpujarras* celebrates Don John of Austria's part in defeating the Moorish uprising in Granada (1568–71); *Canción por la pérdida del Rei Don Sebastián* concerns the death of the king of Portugal in a battle against the Moors in 1578; and *Canción por la victoria del Señor Don Juan* celebrates the naval victory of Lepanto in 1571.

After Doña Leonor's death in 1591, Herrera wrote mainly in prose but most of these works are lost. He edited the works of Garcilaso de la Vega (*Obras*, 1580). In the form of *anotaciones* he included a formulation of his own poetics: he holds clarity of expression as a principle and emphasizes the craftsmanlike and learned skills of writing verse.

Herrera, Francisco, the Elder (1576–1656) Spanish painter and engraver. A native of Seville, Herrera was influenced by the mannerist Juan de las *Roelas in his early works, which also bore the influence of sixteenth-century Flemish prints and of Caravaggio. His early pieces include an engraving of St Ignatius Loyola (1610), a Pentecost painting (1617; Casa y Museo del Greco, Toledo), and scenes from the life of St Bonaventura (c. 1627; Prado and Villandry), upon which Francisco de Zurbarán also worked. In about 1638 he moved to Madrid, shortly afterwards painting his masterpiece, *St Basil Dictating his Doctrine* (1639; Louvre). Other notable works include the *Triumph of St Hermengild* (c. 1624; Museo de Bellas Artes, Seville) and *St Joseph* (1648; Museo Lázano Galdeano, Madrid). Among his pupils were his son Herrera the Younger and, possibly for a brief period (1611–12), Velázquez.

Herrera, Juan de (c. 1530–97) Spanish architect. The most influential architect in Spain during the Renaissance, Herrera was born in Mobellán and educated at Valladolid, after which he travelled with Philip II to Flanders and Italy (1547–51). During this time Herrera indulged his primary interest in the sciences, but also became familiar with the ideals of contemporary Italian artists. In 1563 he was appointed assistant to Juan Bautista de Toledo (died 1567), the court architect in charge of the building of the *Escorial; in 1572 he was given command of the project and was able to develop the austere style, known as *desnudo* or *desornamentado*, for which he is chiefly remembered.

Herrera also designed a palace at Aranjuez (1569) and the exchange at Seville (1582), both of which were executed in his characteristic simplified manner. Later, in his role as royal inspector of monuments, he worked on but did not complete the cathedral at Valladolid (1585). His style was copied by his successors in the post of royal architect and others, and his designs inspired a large number of imitators throughout Spain and its colonies, although several of them revolted against the severity of his architectural style. Of all his buildings, the most influential were the west façade and church of the Escorial. He also amassed a notable library of mathematical and scientific books, invented navigational instruments, and founded the academy of mathematics at Madrid (1582).

Hervetus, Gentian (1499–1584) French scholar and humanist. He came from a poor family near Orleans and had to earn a living as a tutor. In Paris he met Thomas Lupset (?1498–1530) and published with him an edition of Galen. Lupset invited him to England where he became tutor to the younger brother of Cardinal Pole; he accompanied his pupil to Rome where he translated many of the Greek Fathers into Latin. He became professor at Bordeaux but then returned to Rome, to the service of Cardinal Cervini (Pope Marcellus II, 1555) and was a participant in the Council of Trent (1545). He died at Reims where he had been a canon since 1562. Apart from his translations Hervetus produced polemical works against the Calvinists. He also worked on the edition of the Bible projected by the Council of Trent, published a French translation of its decrees (1564), and collated the Codex Bezae (*see under* Beza). His French version of Augustine's *Civitas dei* was published in 1572.

Hilliard, Nicholas (c. 1547–1619) English miniaturist. The son of an Exeter goldsmith, Hilliard was trained as a jeweller and by 1560 was already painting miniatures. He was appointed court miniaturist and goldsmith (c. 1570), and in his official role he designed a Great Seal for Elizabeth I and was sent to France (1576–78) attached to the queen's suitor *Francis, Duke of Alençon. Until the 1600s he remained the leading miniaturist in England, rivalled only by his pupil Isaac *Oliver. His eminent sitters included Sir Philip *Sidney, the earl of Southampton, Sir Walter *Raleigh, Sir Francis *Drake, Sir Christopher Hatton, the earl of Cumberland, and the queen herself. In 1600 he wrote a treatise, *The Arte of Limning*, in which he

HILLIARD Alice Hilliard. *Hilliard was apprenticed to the royal goldsmith, Robert Brandon, and married his daughter Alice in 1576. (1578; Victoria and Albert Museum, London)*

detailed his approach to miniature painting and recorded among other things the queen's agreement with him that such works were better done in a linear style without shadows. He also makes it clear that, while he regarded himself as following in Holbein's footsteps, he treated miniatures as something more than small-scale oils and considered them to have a subtlety of their own, exemplified in such works as the *Young Man Among Roses* (c. 1590), which combines the artist's skills as a jeweller and a portraitist to achieve an exquisite work of art. Other notable paintings, most of which were painted on vellum mounted on card, include *Mrs Mole*. He also occasionally worked on a larger scale, for instance in his portrait of Elizabeth painted around 1575. His son Laurence (1582–post-1640) was also a limner.

historiography The study and writing of history during the Renaissance differed considerably from that of the Middle Ages. Medieval monks had written chronicles of events from the Creation to the Last Judgment in an attempt to justify God's ways. Starting in Italy, humanist historians broke with tradition and initiated the "modern" and "scientific" (because critical) study of history. Renaissance historiography is flawed by its excessive concentration on military and political history and on kings and queens. Sometimes, like *biography, it was mainly a vehicle for royal propaganda with little claim to be regarded as history. Yet these faults were far outweighed by the positive contributions made by Renaissance historians. First, they pioneered the division of history into three parts; ancient history until the last days of the Roman empire, the dark or middle ages from the fall of Rome to the beginning of

their age, and their own modern age, which they considered one of optimism and light after darkness. Second, they secularized history, looking for natural explanations rather than explaining causality in terms of the supernatural or God's will. Third, they were more selective and often focused their work on the history of one state, as, for instance, Peruta did on Venice. Fourth, believing men could learn from history, they undertook comparative studies or selected events which could help men to understand the world they lived in. Finally, they approached previous history with a healthy scepticism and used original sources.

In the fifteenth century Florence was the nursery of a thriving school of historians, among them Leonardo *Bruni and Flavio *Biondo; *Machiavelli and Francesco *Guicciardini were later representatives of this tradition. Depending on subject matter, historians looked to Julius Caesar, Livy, Tacitus, or Sallust as classical models for their style. *Baronius was a pioneer in applying the new historiographical techniques to ecclesiastical history.

Hoby, Sir Thomas (1530–66) English diplomat and translator. Born in Leominster, Hoby went to Cambridge before undertaking extensive travels on the Continent. An expert linguist, he was knighted and sent as ambassador to France in 1566, but died in Paris a few months later. His fame rests on his elegant translation of *Castiglione's *Il cortegiano* (The *Courtier*), which appeared in 1561 and in four later editions before 1603. Hoby's wife Elizabeth (1528–1609) was also a skilled linguist.

Hoefnagel, Georg (1542–1600) Flemish painter. The son of an Antwerp diamond dealer, Hoefnagel travelled extensively, visiting Spain and France (1561–67), England (1569), and Italy (1577), before entering the service of first the *Fugger family and eventually of *Rudolf II (from 1591). His travels, often accompanied by his friend the geographer *Ortelius, resulted in his numerous depictions of towns in Braun and Hogenberg's great topographical work *Civitates orbis terrarum* (1572–1618). In Prague he made exquisite drawings of natural history subjects and also created his masterpiece, the illustrations to a work on calligraphy by a Hungarian, George Bocskay. Hoefnagel's son Jakob (1575–c. 1630) followed him as a miniature painter in the imperial service.

Holbein, Hans, the Elder (c. 1465–1524) German painter. A native of Augsburg, Holbein worked there between 1494 and 1517, mainly producing altarpieces and other religious subjects in the late Gothic style for ecclesiastical patrons. His early work reveals the influence of contemporary

Netherlands painters, but works of his last period, such as the *Well of Life* (1519; Lisbon), show incipient awareness of Italian Renaissance motifs. Like his more famous son of the same name, the elder Holbein was an accomplished portraitist. He died at Isenheim.

Holbein, Hans the Younger (1497/8–1543) German painter. Born in Augsburg, the son of Hans *Holbein the Elder (c. 1465–1524), he began by training in his father's Augsburg studio. By 1515 he was working for a painter in Basle with his brother. He also executed designs for the humanist publisher *Froben, through whom he met Erasmus in about 1516. The drawings he did for the paintings of Burgomaster Meyer and his wife (1516; Basle) were probably more mature than the paintings themselves. After visiting Lucerne and proba-

HOLBEIN Jane Seymour. *The sitter was the short-lived third wife of Henry VIII and mother of Edward VI. Holbein also painted a formal portrait of the queen in state. (c. 1537; Royal Library, Windsor Castle, England)*

bly Italy (1517–19), Holbein returned to Basle, where he was commissioned to paint the council chamber. Disturbances connected with the Reformation, however, interrupted this work, which was not finally completed until 1530; other paintings from this period include *Bonifacius Amerbach* (1519; Basle) *Christ in the Tomb* (1521; Basle), and *Madonna and Child with Saints* (1522; Solothurn). Holbein also designed the *Dance of Death* (1523/24) and the *Alphabet of Death* (1524) series of woodcuts, illustrated the Luther Bible (1522), and painted three portraits of Erasmus (1523), which established his international reputation.

In 1526, possibly because of continuing religious unrest, Holbein moved to London and met Sir Thomas *More, whose family he painted in the first group portrait of full-length figures in their domestic setting in European art (the painting now exists only in sketches and copies). After eighteen months he returned to Basle, there executing designs for stained glass and a portrait of his own family whom he painted with an honesty he curbed with influential sitters. Then religious strife again prompted him to seek his fortunes (c. 1532) in England. As More was now out of favour, Holbein won the patronage of the German merchants of the Steelyard, producing for them many portraits of considerable virtuosity. Possibly through the good offices of Thomas *Cromwell he obtained the commission in 1533 for his great double portrait *The Ambassadors* and then the patronage of *Henry VIII, for whom he undertook his most celebrated work in England, the wall painting in Whitechapel Palace of the king with his mother and Jane Seymour (destroyed in 1698 but preserved as a cartoon and in copies). Subsequent portraits for Henry VIII included *Jane Seymour* (1537; Vienna), *Anne of Cleves* (1539/40; Louvre), *Catherine Howard* (1540/41; Toledo, Ohio), and *Christina, Duchess of Milan* (1538; London). Although it seems likely that Holbein never realized the full depth of his talent at the English court, he did also produce other portraits, miniatures, and designs for goldsmiths' work which has now perished. He died in London of the plague.

Holl, Elias (1573–1646) German architect. Holl was born into a prominent Augsburg family of masons. He visited Venice briefly (1600–01) and some Palladian influence is to be seen in his work. He was the city architect, or master builder, of Augsburg from 1602 to 1635, at a time when Augsburg was the largest city in Germany and one of the most important. It is for his Augsburg building programme (which included schools, guildhalls, warehouses, houses, and city gates) that he is known, although he also executed commissions outside the city. His first building in office was the arsenal (constructed 1602–07), carrying out a design by Joseph Heintz. The style here was mannerist verging on baroque, especially in the sculpture erected over the portal. Holl's own designs are based on a primarily functional approach, symmetry, and fine proportions – in fact a far more restrained classicism, almost severe in its lack of elaborate detailing. This style can be seen particularly in St Anne's grammar school (1613–15) and in Holl's most acclaimed building, the town hall (constructed 1615–20). This combines classical with Germanic and other features (such as onion domes) in a very plain, functional, but pleasantly proportioned building. Holl's career reflects the fate of Renaissance architecture in Germany, being brought to an abrupt close by the Counter-Reformation and the Thirty Years' War. Along with 8000 Augsburg citizens, Holl went into temporary exile when Protestant worship was forbidden in the city in 1629; in 1635 his Protestantism finally lost him his post. Widely celebrated in his own day, Holl is considered the most important German Renaissance architect.

Holland, Philemon (1552–1637) English translator. Holland was born at Chelmsford, Essex, the son of a Protestant clergyman who fled to the Continent during Mary's reign. He took his MA at Cambridge in 1574 and subsequently studied medicine. He then settled in Coventry where he spent the rest of his life teaching, practising medicine, and making his renowned translations from the classics: of Livy (1600), Pliny's *Natural History* (1601), Plutarch's *Moralia* (1603), Suetonius (1606), Ammianus Marcellinus (1609), and Xenophon's *Cyropaedia* (1632). In addition he translated Camden's *Britannia* into English (1610), and some medical translations were issued posthumously. His translations are characterized by immense learning combined with a fine feeling for the emotional tone of the original.

Hollanda, Francisco da *see* Francisco da Hollanda.

holy brotherhood *see hermandad.*

Holy League Any military alliance that includes the papacy. In the Renaissance period the term was applied to several such alliances. Pope *Julius II inspired the Holy League (1511–13) of the papacy, Venice, Spain, England, and Emperor *Maximilian I to fight the French threat to Italy. The French won at Ravenna (1512), but were defeated by the league's Swiss mercenaries at Novara (1513). This league collapsed after quarrels among its members and Julius II's death. In 1571 Spain, the papacy, Venice, and other Italian states formed the Holy League to fight the Turkish threat. Their navy practically annihilated the Ottoman fleet at *Lepanto (1571).

Holy Roman Empire During the Renaissance, a loosely organized collection of between three hundred and four hundred states, varying greatly in size. The term itself dates back to 1254. These mainly Germanic territories covered central Europe from the Alps in the south to the Baltic in the north, and from France in the west to Hungary and Poland in the east. The empire's population, about twenty million in 1450, was the largest in Europe.

The Golden Bull (1356) had established an electoral empire, but heads of the *Habsburg family ruled the empire continuously from 1438 to 1740. In many ways the emperor was a nominal ruler; real power lay with the princes, especially the seven electoral princes.

The Holy Roman Empire faced serious problems. In the fourteenth and fifteenth centuries local and factional warfare brought it close to disintegration. Emperors often only survived because they were too weak to be a threat to their powerful subjects. In the sixteenth century *Ottoman Turks reached the gates of Vienna, the Habsburg-Valois conflict strained the empire's resources, and the empire was torn apart by religious wars. In the seventeenth century it was devastated by the Thirty Years' War. Some emperors tried to centralize the empire and to make it into a modern sovereign state like France and England, but they were defeated by its size, its diversity, and its powerful vested interests. Only *Charles V in the sixteenth century might have managed to weld it into a modern European power.

Homer (?ninth century BC) Greek epic poet. Although the stories of the *Iliad* and *Odyssey* were known in the West in the Middle Ages, the almost universal ignorance of Greek prevented any widespread appreciation of the poems themselves. Various Latin paraphrases, commentaries, and secondary material were available (*see* Troy, legend of) and these accounted for the medieval picture of Homer as a great and venerable poet. Dante, for instance, refers to him in the *Divine Comedy* as "Omero poeta sovrano". The earliest humanist Latin translations of the *Iliad* and *Odyssey* were made in the fourteenth century at the instigation of *Petrarch and *Boccaccio; *Bruni and *Valla in the following century were responsible for Latin prose versions and *Politian for one in Latin hexameters.

The growth of *Greek studies in western Europe from the mid-fifteenth century eventually ensured a readership for the Homeric poems in their original tongue. The *editio princeps* was printed in Florence in 1488. Inevitably Homer was compared with his Roman epic counterpart *Virgil. *Ronsard was one of the earliest critics to contrast "la naïve facilité d'Homère" with "la curieuse diligence de Virgile". *See also* epic.

Hondius, Jodocus (Josse de Hondt; 1563–1612) Flemish cartographer. Raised in Ghent, Hondius moved to London around 1583, where he established himself as an engraver and type founder and met many geographers and scientists, including Hakluyt. Hondius engraved Molyneux's globes (1592), before moving to Amsterdam in 1593. His most celebrated works were his two world maps on the *Mercator projection. One was the illustrated Christian Knight map, the other depicted the voyages of Drake and Cavendish. Hondius made other maps and globes and engraved the maps for John Speed's *Theatre of the Empire of Great Britain* (1611–12), but the latter part of his career was successfully involved with the work of Mercator, whose plates he bought in 1604. He published a Mercator atlas with thirty-seven new plates two years later. Hondius's work is less scientific but more attractive than Mercator's, and is notable for its decorative calligraphy. His sons, Jodocus (1593–1629) and Henricus (1597–1644), and also later descendants, continued his business, capitalizing on the phenomenal success of the Mercator-Hondius atlas.

Hooft, Pieter Cornelisz. (1581–1647) Dutch poet, playwright, and historiographer. Hooft's father was a prosperous merchant of Amsterdam, who obtained a good classical education for his son. Hooft then travelled in France and Italy (1598–1601); his literary encounters in these countries made a deep impression, turning him away from the indigenous tradition nurtured in the *chambers of rhetoric (he was a member of De Egelantier in Amsterdam) and towards the Renaissance poets such as *Petrarch, *Ariosto, *Tasso, and *Ronsard. His brilliance as a lyricist manifested itself not only in the love lyrics he wrote in the decade after his return but also in the lyrical passages of his plays such as the pastoral *Granida* (1605), which is influenced by *Sannazaro. After studying law at Leyden (1606–09), Hooft was appointed sheriff of Muiden, where he restored the castle and lived the rest of his life. There he played host to a distinguished literary and musical circle, known as the Muiderkring. His play *Geeraerdt van Velzen* (1613) was inspired by the story of a late thirteenth-century occupant of the castle at Muiden; it was followed by *Baeto* (1617), another historical drama on a Netherlands theme, and in both plays Hooft displays his interest in statecraft

and the nature of power. The comedy *Ware-nar*, written in 1614, adapts Plautus' *Aulularia* to an Amsterdam setting.

Even more important than his poems and plays was Hooft's output in prose, of which he was an outstanding master. He wrote histories of Henry IV of France (1624), and the Medici (1638), but his greatest achievement was his twenty-seven book *Nederlandsche Historiën* (1624, 1654) on the history of the Dutch struggle against Spain in the years 1555–87. Its style and presentation are deeply indebted to Tacitus. Hooft died while visiting The Hague and was buried in the Nieuwe Kerk in Amsterdam.

Hooker, Richard (?1554–1600) English theologian and scholar. Hooker was born near Exeter into a poor family and was sent to Oxford through the generosity of Bishop John Jewel (1522–71), to whose defence of the Church of England, *Apologia ecclesiae Anglicanae* (1562), Hooker's own great work was to be deeply indebted. Hooker became a fellow of Corpus Christi College (1577) and deputy professor of Hebrew (1579) but had to leave Oxford on his marriage. About the same time (1581) he took holy orders and in 1584 was appointed rector of Drayton Beauchamp in Buckinghamshire. In 1585 he was made master of the Temple before returning to parochial duties, first (1591) in Boscombe, Wiltshire, and finally (1595) in Bishopsbourne, Kent, where he died.

The first four books *Of the Lawes of Ecclesiasticall Politie* appeared in 1594, followed by the fifth book in 1597. The remaining three books did not appear in Hooker's lifetime. The treatise is a masterly defence of the Elizabethan settlement of 1559, defending the Church of England against the implications of the Puritans' literal interpretation of the scriptures. Hooker's interpretation of natural law as the manifestation of God's reason had important repercussions on the political theories of seventeenth-century writers like John Locke. He is also important as a prose stylist, writing a clear and vigorous English that was unusual in theological debate in his time. A biography of Hooker was published by Isaak Walton in 1665.

Hop(f)fer, Daniel (c. 1470–1536) German engraver and designer. Hopfer was born at Kaufbeuren, but was a citizen of Augsburg from 1493. He is claimed as the first to have made prints on paper by etching iron plates (as opposed to *engraving). He produced some of the earliest original etched portraits, a number of religious illustrations (on Reformation lines), scenes of everyday life, such as village festivals, and a large number of reproductions of Italian art, which made him a significant popularizer of the Italian style in

Germany. He was also a designer of decoration, publishing fifty plates of ornamental motifs, which included Gothic foliage and Renaissance grotesques. Like other engravers of the time, he etched decoration on ceremonial parade armour, which formed a major part of his work.

Horace (Quintus Horatius Flaccus; 65–8 BC) Roman poet. Born in the Latin colony of Venusia, Horace was educated in Rome and Athens. He lost his estate in the civil war that followed the murder of Julius Caesar, but in about 33 BC *Maecenas gave him a farm which inspired some of his most beautiful poetry on country life. The *Odes* and *Epodes*, in a range of lyric metres, cover personal, political, and patriotic themes, and were much admired and imitated from the time of Petrarch onwards. *Celtis even had some of the odes set to music to be sung after his lectures. The two books of *Satires* were also admired for their urbanity, as were the *Epistles*. Another epistle, to Piso, is better known as the *Ars poetica*. Before the full text of *Aristotle's *Poetics* was in general circulation, Horace's treatise was the main source for Renaissance knowledge of literary theory in the ancient world.

horology The science of measurement of time. Time in antiquity was measured by several devices, chief among them the water clock or clepsydra and the sundial. The use of both, however, was limited, the former by frost and the latter by cloud or darkness. The mechanical *clock emerged in the late thirteenth century. In its earliest forms it was powered by a descending weight and controlled by the verge and foliot escapement. Although free from the disabilities of clepsydrae and sundials, early clocks operated more as planetaria and alarm bells than as a means of measuring time. So inaccurate were they that it was only in the late fifteenth century that it was deemed worthwhile to fit them with a minute hand. *Brahe, for example, still used a clepsydra in the late sixteenth century to make his more precise measurements, and clocks only became reliable and accurate enough for scientific use with the development of the pendulum clock in the late seventeenth century. *See also* watches.

Hosius, Stanislaus (Stanislaus Hosen; 1504–79) Polish churchman. He studied law in his native Cracow and at Bologna and Padua. Ordained priest in 1543, he was appointed bishop of Kulm (1549) and then of Ermland (1551). In his struggle with the Protestants in his diocese he approved the use of force against them. This course of action was based on his conviction that Catholicism was the only true Christianity; Hosius attempted to prove this in his *Confessio catholicae fidei christiana* (1552–53), a work that was frequently reprinted and translated in the next twenty-five years. In 1558 he was summoned to Rome to advise the pope about Poland and Prussia. Two years later he was papal nuncio to Emperor Ferdinand I and reclaimed his son (later Maximilian II) for the Roman Church. He was made a cardinal in 1561 and attended the Council of Trent as papal legate. He died at Capranica, near Rome.

Hospitallers *see* Knights Hospitaller.

Hothby, John (c. 1410–87) English music theorist and composer. Hothby was a Carmelite monk who travelled through Germany, France, Spain, and northern Italy. He had settled at Lucca by 1467, becoming choirmaster, teacher, and chaplain at the cathedral there. He died on his way back to England. Nine of his compositions survive, but he is remembered as a theorist. His treatises include texts on the rudiments of music, *musica speculativa*, notably his *Calliopea legale*, and polemical works, such as *Dialogus Johannis Ottobi Anglici in arte musica*, in which he attacks the ideas of *Ramos and defends traditional foundations of music.

Houtman, Cornelis (died 1598) Dutch explorer. Houtman was a key figure in the Dutch exploration movement inspired by *Linschoten. In 1595 Houtman headed a four-ship expedition which sailed from Texel in search of trade routes to Asia. Although his voyage was disrupted by illness, he

HOROLOGY *This miniature watch, set in an imperial seal ring, was made by Johann Buz of Augsburg. Such watches were ingenious toys or items of jewellery, rather than accurate timepieces. (c. 1610–20; Kunsthistorisches Museum, Vienna)*

eventually arrived at Java. After exploring the surrounding area and visiting Bantam, Houtman was imprisoned because the native inhabitants and the Portuguese merchants resented the presence of the Dutch, but on his release he negotiated a commercial treaty before sailing home. The voyage cost Houtman one ship and two-thirds of his men. He attempted a second voyage in 1598, during which he was killed by the inhabitants of Sumatra. Houtman's account of his first voyage was published in 1597.

Howard, Henry, Earl of Surrey *see* Surrey, Henry Howard, Earl of.

Huber, Wolfgang (c. 1490–1553) German artist. One of the masters of the *Danube school, he was born in Feldkirch (Vorarlberg) and was probably Altdorfer's assistant around 1510. Like him, Huber frequently depicted poetic landscapes in both drawings and paintings. He also made some experiments in figure composition and perspective, but is chiefly remembered for his studies of wind-blown trees and views of the Danube valley. From 1515 he worked in Passau, incurring the dislike of the local painters. He was also a notable draughtsman and engraver.

Huguenots The name given to French Protestants from the mid-sixteenth century, apparently derived from a King Hugo in a medieval romance. By the early 1520s *Luther's ideas were circulating in France and a reform movement was established. The first French Protestant martyr was burnt in 1523. After the appearance of posters attacking the Mass (1534) many Protestants, including *Calvin, had to leave France, but Protestantism still spread, attracting members of the nobility like Antoine de Bourbon (father of Henry of Navarre who became *Henry IV). At a synod in Paris (1559) the Huguenots drew up a confession of faith (*see* Gallican Confession) which was strongly influenced by Calvin; hence they became a Calvinist rather than Lutheran movement.

The Huguenots were fiercely opposed by the *Guise family and their Catholic supporters (*see* Religion, (French) Wars of). After the Edict of *Nantes (1598) granted them religious and political freedom the Huguenots prospered, but the revocation of the edict (1688) drove most of them into exile.

humanism In general, any system of belief that places human affairs at its centre. In the Renaissance context humanism is associated with the rediscovery of the culture of the Greco-Roman world, particularly Greek literature and philosophy (*see* Greek studies). The medieval world had some knowledge of classical Latin literature; indeed, individual scholars such as Alcuin and John of Salisbury show an impressive range of reference, but this cannot properly be described as humanism. The term *humanismus* itself seems first to have been used by Petrarch and his contemporaries to express the spirit of intellectual freedom by which man asserted his independence from the authority of the Church. Characteristically, Petrarch was influenced by the use of the term *humanitas* by Cicero and Varro to define their educational ideal. By the sixteenth century humanistic concepts had become inextricably involved with theological controversy but even the earliest humanists, by their exaltation of personal freedom, challenged the hierarchical structure of the medieval theocracy. Humanism grew up in the cities and communes of Italy which were fighting for their political autonomy against the control of pope or emperor, both personifications of fundamentally medieval institutions.

According to orthodox theology, man was born sinful and was incapable of virtue without the aid of divine grace. Humanism offered an alternative, which said that man could freely choose his destiny and by the exercise of his own will could act rightly. *Pico della Mirandola expressed this idea most comprehensively in his *Oratio de dignitate hominis* but other humanists took up and developed the idea. For such men Prometheus, the foresighted Titan, is the prototype of the humanist "wise man". This did not necessarily mean a rejection of religion; on the contrary many humanists strove to synthesize the new approaches with Christianity, a Christianity which came more and more to depend not on the interpretations of ecclesiastical authority but on the scientific study of original texts. The methods of classical scholarship which were evolved to deal with secular literature were applied to the scriptures and the Church Fathers (*see* patristic studies) and the same standards of coherence and connection were demanded (*see* criticism, textual). The interaction of humanism with religion produced another consequence – a search for some underlying principle which would unite the warring elements of different doctrines. This search made many humanists more tolerant of religious differences; Pico for example aimed at nothing less than a demonstration of the accord between Plato, Aristotle, classical and Jewish esoteric wisdom, and the spectrum of patristic interpretation and exegesis. He felt that the diversity of belief reflected partial but not contradictory glimpses of the original One to which humanism sought to return (*see also* Neoplatonism, Renaissance).

Renaissance humanism also helped to create the conditions that led to the scientific revolution. The revival of interest in classical doctrines of the nature of the physical universe, the insistence on autopsy of original texts, the shift away from the *ipse dixit* of scholasticism, all helped to stimulate a spirit of critical objective inquiry. By stressing that man is a natural being, the humanists implied that he could understand his physical environment by using the tools that nature gave him, namely his senses.

Another of the major contributions of Renaissance humanism to the stock of western European concepts is the idea of historicity. Medieval thinkers had little sense of the difference between the ancient world and their own time. The humanists, by virtue of their own self-consciousness about their relationship with the ancient world focused sharply on precisely those differences and coined the term "Middle Ages" to express that historical awareness (*see also* historiography).

As humanism diffused beyond the bounds of Italy it became increasingly involved in theological controversy. The potential for such controversy was always there, and frequently it was only the direct intervention of humanist popes like Nicholas V, Pius II, or Eugenius IV that protected humanists from ecclesiastical wrath. In France and Germany humanism was associated first with the movement for reform within the Church, then with the more radical reformers; it was said that Luther hatched the egg that Erasmus laid.

It is difficult to assess briefly the lasting contribution of Renaissance humanism to Western civilization. Many of its features have mainly historical interest today. But the central belief of the early humanists that the human personality is worth cultivating and developing to its fullest extent for its own sake is a continuing inspiration.

Hurtado de Mendoza, Diego de (1503–75) Spanish humanist, poet, and historian. Born to a noble family at Granada and a descendant of *Santillana, he received an excellent humanist education, learning Hebrew and Arabic as well as the classical languages. After serving with the Spanish armies, he entered on a distinguished diplomatic career. As ambassador to Venice, he sponsored the recovery of 300 Greek manuscripts from Greece and Mount Athos and was a patron of the *Aldine press. From 1547 to 1554 he exercised the highest authority in Italy, but was recalled to Spain in 1555 on the accession of Philip II, who eventually dismissed him from court (1568). He returned to Granada and participated in suppressing a Moorish rebellion there, in the Alpujarras (1568–71). This forms the subject of *La guerra de Granada* (published 1610, 1627, 1630, in various versions), the first objective military history written in Spanish. Modelled on Sallust, the work is remarkable for its brilliant style and its impar-

tiality. As a poet, Hurtado de Mendoza practised the Italian metres introduced by *Boscán and his own contemporary, *Garcilaso de la Vega. His poems were published in *Obras* (1610). At one time he was believed to be the author of *Lazarillo de Tormes*. At his death his manuscript collection was added to that of the Escorial.

Huss, Jan (1369–1415) Czech theologian and religious reformer. Together with Jerome of Prague, Huss, who was rector of Prague university from 1403, initiated the reform movement that resulted in the creation of a strong national Church in Bohemia by the mid-fifteenth century. Huss came into prominence as the keenest defender of the fourteenth-century English theologian John Wyclif in Prague during the early years of the fifteenth century. As part of a growing movement that sought greater religious egalitarianism, Huss included in his demands vernacular translations of the Bible, lay communion, and a reduction of clerical power. Opposition to Huss was aroused not only because of the possible heresy in his teachings but also because he became the hero of the Czech nationalist movement. In 1408 Archbishop Zbyneck of Prague suspended him from his teaching office and in 1411 he was excommunicated by Pope John XXIII. Taking refuge in southern Bohemia, he wrote a major treatise *De ecclesia* (1413), which was to be used as the chief pretext for his condemnation by the Council of *Constance. He attended the council under a false promise of safe conduct from Emperor Sigismund and was burned as a heretic upon its decision in July 1415. Whether the charge of heresy could be substantiated is debatable, especially since he rejected many of the more obviously heretical Wycliffite claims. His execution and that of Jerome the following year, proved disastrous for the orthodox party, since it ensured a successful radical Hussite revolution in Bohemia and the spread of Hussite doctrine throughout Europe.

Hutten, Ulrich von (1488–1523) German humanist. After an early life of apparently aimless wandering from his native Steckelberg around the universities of Germany and Italy, Hutten found fame as a controversialist and pamphleteer. His first work, an attack on Duke Ulrich of Württemberg, was inspired by a family quarrel, but about the same time (1515) Hutten also became a major contributor to the famous humanist satire, *Epistolae obscurorum virorum*. In 1517 Hutten entered the service of the archbishop of Mainz and the following year published an edition of *Valla's *Donation of Constantine* with a sarcastic dedication to the pope. In 1520 his enthusiastic support of Martin *Luther (expressed in several Latin and

German tracts) resulted in his dismissal from the archbishop's service, and Hutten resumed his wanderings. He died soon afterwards, under the protection of Ulrich *Zwingli at Zürich.

hydraulics Before the development of the steam engine, and excluding animal power, much of the energy available to Western man derived from hydraulic power. Vitruvian mills, with vertical wheels and horizontal axles, were introduced into Rome in the first century BC. They were mainly used to grind corn. From the tenth century AD new uses began to be found for them. With suitable gearing and connections a water mill could be used to power a trip hammer or a mechanical saw, to beat cloth, to pound ore, to pump water, to ventilate galleries, and to operate numerous other devices. Many of these machines can be seen illustrated in the pages of Georgius *Agricola and *Ramelli. Advances were also made in canal design. Pound locks replaced primitive flash locks in the fifteenth century and soon spread across Europe. At approximately the same time the mitregate, reputedly designed by *Leonardo da Vinci and still in use today, began to replace the more cumbersome portcullis.

At a more theoretical level, Renaissance mathematicians sought to advance beyond the foundations established by Archimedes in antiquity. *Stevin in his *Hydrostatics* (1586) formulated the so-called hydrostatical paradox, the principle that the force exerted by a fluid on the bottom of a vessel is proportional to the bottom's area, the height of the fluid, and its specific gravity, but is not necessarily equal to the weight of the fluid. Further insight came from Leonardo da Vinci, who presented the continuity equation, relating the flow of a volume of water to its cross-sectional area. He was less successful, however, in determining the water's velocity. This required a more sophisticated mathematics than was available to the Renaissance.

Hypnerotomachia Polifili A romance, describing a lover's search for his mistress, written by the Dominican monk Francesco Colonna (1433–1527) and published by Aldus *Manutius in Venice in 1499. The large book is outstanding for the beauty of its typography and woodcut illustrations, as well as for its fine printing. The unknown artist may reflect the influence of both *Mantegna and Giovanni *Bellini, and some of his work records contemporary garden designs. The text, a mixture of Latin and Italian, was translated into French by Jean Martin and Jacques Ghorry in 1546 and published, with extra pictures, in a format almost as beautiful as the original. *The Strife of Love in a Dreame*, an incomplete English version by Robert Dallington, appeared in a scruffy little book in 1592.

I

iatrochemistry The medical theory that disease results from a chemical reaction and that it can be both defined and treated chemically. The idea was originally associated with the remarkable Swiss physician *Paracelsus. For iatrochemists the creation of the universe itself, as well as most natural processes, were essentially chemical operations; it followed inevitably that medicine would be absorbed into the scheme. Iatrochemistry was helped by the total failure of traditional medicine to control the spread of syphilis and *plague. Its practitioners, with their use of such potent chemical medicines as arsenic and antimony, seemed initially to be successful, and the movement prospered. This early success is signalled in the growing tendency for the printed *pharmacopoeia to include chemical preparations. Although opposition was encountered in Paris, where the authorities declared antimony a poison and banned its therapeutic use, elsewhere, and particularly in Britain and Germany, iatrochemistry spread rapidly and widely.

iconoclasm The breaking or destruction of images set up for religious veneration, especially practised by Protestants during the century of the Reformation. Protestants based their hostility to images on the Old Testament prohibition (Exodus 20:4–5) and on their belief that religious statues and pictures encouraged superstition among the ignorant multitude. Not all reformers shared this view: *Luther approved of religious pictures as an aid to piety, and intervened forcibly at Wittenberg to restrain Carlstadt and his supporters, who were bent on their destruction (1522). *Calvin, however, attacked superstitious practices with particular severity, and many of the most violent episodes were perpetrated by his followers, notably the so-called "Iconoclastic Fury" in the Netherlands (1566). Van *Mander records among the losses paintings by Aertsen, Bosch, and Scorel, and other famous works such as the Eyck brothers' *Ghent altarpiece only narrowly escaped destruction. Such outbursts were widely deplored, and even Protestant regimes hostile to images usually tried to secure their orderly removal, in order both to discourage riotous conduct and to prevent plunder. But undoubtedly iconoclasm resulted in the destruction of many priceless works of art and the defacement of numerous church buildings.

iconography The study of icons, that is, images which are often, though not necessarily, sacred and which express in a concentrated visual way some deep moral or spiritual truth. The Church in the Middle Ages had elaborated a complex set of rules for the interpretation of icons and these were based on assumptions about the nature of the relationship between the image and the object it depicts. The Renaissance, in this area as in so many others, took over medieval concepts and modified them. Renaissance icons had to satisfy a number of requirements. First was the principle of decorum; the icon had to be appropriate to the situation or object. For example, a representation of Vulcan's smithy was a suitable decoration for a fireplace. However, an image had also to convey a moral message so an even better subject would be Croesus about to be burnt on his pyre and recalling Solon's saying that no man should be considered happy until he had finished his life happily. Symbols could be drawn in this way from the whole range of classical and biblical sources, and many handbooks were published classifying and explaining their application, thus evolving a shared vocabulary of symbols current throughout educated Europe. Perhaps the most representative of these was the *Iconologia* of Cesare Ripa (1593). Ripa takes as his starting point the theory of metaphor developed by Aristotle in the *Rhetoric* and *Poetics*, and the four-fold definition by types of causes, material, efficient, formal, and final. The deviser of images has the same freedom to work within these four categories as the formulator of verbal definitions. The other strand of iconography in the Renaissance was the Neoplatonic. This owed much also to Christian mysticism, particularly the works of Dionysius the Areopagite. These fused Neoplatonic and Christian ideas to produce a theory of symbolism which made the image the medium by which the deepest truths were expressed in the most concise way. Platonism assumed that unity was superior to multiplicity and the icon seemed to Renaissance Platonists to have a precision which was denied to discursive language. This made the designing of icons one of the most serious tasks for the philosopher, as it was by means of the image that one approached the ineffable Reality which was the Divine Oneness.

From this it will be clear that the study of icons in the Renaissance requires not only an extensive knowledge of the possible sources for such images but also an awareness of the philosophical subtleties which determined the choice of a particular image in a particular situation. Thus, much ingenuity has been exercised by historians of art in expounding the Neoplatonic programme that underlies the images of Botticelli's *Primavera and by literary critics in explaining the inner significance of such verbal icons as those created by Spenser in such passages as the Masque of Cupid or the Bower of Bliss in his *Faerie Queene. See also emblems; *imprese*.

Ignatius Loyola, St (1491–1556) Spanish mystic, founder of the *Jesuits. Ignatius was born at his family's castle in the Basque province of Gúipuzcos, the youngest of thirteen children. After his leg had been shattered in battle at Pampeluna in 1521, he went on pilgrimage and retreat for a year, during which time he drafted his *Ejercicios espirituales* (*Spiritual Exercises*), eventually printed at Rome in 1548. He was brought before the Inquisition because of his preaching, but was released. In 1534 he and six other students founded the Society of Jesus in Paris and took their first vows. In 1539 they presented their plans for the order to Pope Paul III, and the order was approved the following year. Ignatius was appointed the first superior-general. He sent his companions as missionaries to found Jesuit schools, colleges, and seminaries throughout Europe. Ignatius wrote the Jesuit *Constitutions*, which were adopted in 1554. These regulations created a monarchical organization and stressed absolute obedience to the pope. The Jesuits thus became a major factor in the success of the *Counter-Reformation.

Ignatius was a mystic who believed in a rigorously ordered spiritual life. His ideal became the Jesuit motto: *ad maiorem dei gloriam* ("All things for the greater glory of God"). He died in Rome and was canonized in 1622.

imprese Devices embodying a picture and a motto in such a way that they reciprocally interpret each other. It is thus a sub-type of the *emblem; the difference, according to Carpaccio (1592), was that the emblem had only to feed the eyes, the device the mind – the former was only concerned with a moral, the latter aimed at the concept of things. While the design of the emblem allowed much greater freedom of personal choice, the rules of the *impresa* were fixed by the academies, and one of the tasks a court humanist would be expected to perform was the devising of suitable *imprese*. The concept of the *impresa* came into Italy from courtly French society in the reign of Louis XII, specifically during the occupation of Milan from 1499. The correspondence of Isabella d'Este shows how much importance was attached to *imprese*, which were believed to present in a peculiarly concentrated form the various operations of mind and spirit to produce a distillation of the owner's personality; medals bearing a portrait of the owner on one side and a riddling *impresa* on the other were favourite tokens among humanist courtiers. Thus Lorenzo di Pierfrancesco de' Medici had depicted on the obverse of his medal a variation on the ancient Egyptian hieroglyph of a serpent biting its tail, an emblem of perfection or eternity; the hint conveyed to the initiated by this serpent is that the soul although descended to earth still partakes of its heavenly nature. Paolo Giovio (*Dialogo dell' imprese militari et amorose*, 1555) established five requisites for the *impresa*: it should show just proportion; it should not be too obscure or too transparent; it should make a fine show; there should be no human figure; the motto should be in a different language from that of the author of the device.

incunabula (Latin: swaddling clothes) Books printed before the end of the year 1500. The term was first used in reference to printing by Bernard von Mallinckrodt, dean of Münster cathedral, in *De ortu et progressu typographicae* (Cologne, 1639), a bicentenary celebration of *Gutenberg's invention. The author describes the period up to 1500 as *prima typographicae incunabula* ("the time when printing was in swaddling clothes"), a phrase that other writers soon copied. In the eighteenth century the word "incunabula" alone began to be applied to the products of early printing. The singular form "incunabulum", now often anglicized or gallicized to "incunable", is used to refer to a single book from this period. The German equivalent is *Wiegendruck* ("cradle-book"). The choice of the year 1500 as the end of the first period suggests a clear break in the development of printing, an implication that is not confirmed by the work produced early in the sixteenth century.

Index Librorum Prohibitorum A list of books which Roman Catholics were forbidden to read, on pain of excommunication. Its aim was to protect faith and morals, especially to prevent the spread of heresy and to regulate the reading and editing of scripture. From the fourth century onwards, the works of heretics were condemned, and several popes issued decrees listing recommended and forbidden books. From about 1540 lists of proscribed works were produced by universities and bishops. In 1557 Pope *Paul IV ordered the Congregation of the Holy Office to compile the first official printed list or Index, which condemned some authors entirely and certain works of others: there were rules for the guidance of readers. It was issued in 1559 and revised several times by the popes and by the Council of *Trent in 1562. In 1571 a separate Congregation for the Index was established, which was reorganized in 1588; the secretary was always a Dominican. The system has remained substantially unchanged till modern times. *See also* censorship.

Inquisition The Inquisition has a long history, starting in the thirteenth century. Following the crusade called by the pope and led by the northern French nobility against the Cathars of southern France (which also reduced the southern French nobility), an inquisition investigated communities for Albigensian heresy. The most famous case is that in the Bas-Pyrenées between 1294 and 1324, when Jacques Fournier (later Pope Benedict XII) conducted an inquisition into the diocese of Montaillou. Except for the Languedocian region of southern France, inquisitorial activity declined in the fourteenth century.

After the mid-sixteenth century, the Inquisition became an important arm of the *Counter-Reformation. Individual communities (e.g., Rome, Modena, Venice, and Spain) had their own inquisitorial bodies; the most famous are the *Spanish Inquisition and the Roman Inquisition. The former was founded by Tomás de *Torquemada and was infamous for its severity. In Spain, confiscated properties went to the royal coffers, and the Spanish Inquisition was entirely independent of Rome. The Roman Inquisition (reestablished in 1542) was given strict procedural rules by Francisco Peña. No matter whether in Madrid, Rome, or Modena, the Inquisition was a dread instrument for heresy hunting. Once charged with heresy by a delator (informer), the accused was imprisoned and intensely questioned about his heresy. It was said that in the Inquisition's prisons one's diet consisted of "the bread of sorrow and the water of tribulation". If the charge was not too severe, the accused might be imprisoned for several years or, occasionally, released after the trial and sentencing. In more serious cases, if the accused was found to be unrepentant or was a relapsed heretic, the sentence was death. The heretic was then "relaxed" to the secular authorities who burned him at the stake.

In the late sixteenth and early seventeenth centuries, the local and Roman inquisitions were active against both famous intellectuals and village eccentrics whose theological ideas went beyond the rather straitened bounds of Counter-Reformation orthodoxy. Among the victims of the Inquisition's investigations during this period were the philosophers Francesco *Patrizi, Giordano *Bruno, and Tommaso *Campanella, and the scientist *Galileo Galilei. Of these, only Bruno was executed; Galileo ended his days under house arrest and Campanella spent many years in prison.

Inquisition, Spanish *see* Spanish Inquisition.

Institutes The popular English name for *Calvin's *Christianae religionis institutio*, the principal text of the Calvinist or reformed church. The first edition, published at Basle in 1536, was a brief manual of six chapters based on the framework of the catechism and intended as a short textbook of reformed orthodoxy. Its success prompted Calvin to expand it considerably, so that by the time of the definitive edition of 1559 it was five times its original length. Its eighty chapters and four books now comprised a complete handbook of the reformed religion: a systematic theology based on the Bible, a manual of ethics, a guidebook to the Protestant creed, and a comprehensive survey of Reformation theological controversy. The clearest and ablest systematic exposition of the ideals that inspired the Reformation, the *Institutes* was translated into the languages of those countries influenced by Calvinism, including French (1541; by Calvin himself), Dutch (1560), and English (1561).

interlude (Latin *interludium*: "between-play") In the theatre, a short dramatic piece, usually comical or farcical and possibly including music, mime, and acrobatics, performed as a diversion between the acts of a longer play. In Italy the *intermedii* or *intermezzi* of the late fifteenth and early sixteenth centuries was a slight, often comic entertainment, frequently on a classical or mythological theme, inserted as relief between the acts of a more substantial work. The related French *entremets* was a similar comic or satirical interpolation. The Spanish *entremés* evolved in Castile from comic interludes performed in public theatres and became a separate independent genre, popularized especially by Luis Quiñones de Benavente (c. 1583–1631) and practised by most Golden Age playwrights including *Cervantes and Lope de *Vega.

In England, "interlude" was applied to a very wide range of dramatic works written in the transitional period (c. 1500–76) between the medieval religious drama (mystery, morality, and miracle plays) and Elizabethan drama as performed in theatres by professional companies. John Heywood (c. 1497–1580) was the first English playwright to treat it as an independent dramatic genre (as, for example, his farcical interlude *The Pardoner and the Friar*).

But the term continued to be used very loosely in England and could as easily describe a late mystery play or John *Bale's *King John* as a "classical" comedy (for example, Nicholas *Udall's *Ralph Roister Doister*).

intermedii (*or intermezzi*) Either instrumental interludes played out of sight of the audience, or, more popularly, stage spectacles by singers, dancers, and actors in costume, first performed in the Renaissance between the acts of plays. Sometimes the subject matter of the *intermedii* was connected with that of the play, though more often unrelated pastoral scenes with allegorical figures were presented. While *intermedii* were first performed in the fifteenth century at the court in Ferrara, the Medici court in Florence was the scene of many of the most lavish entertainments; the most spectacular was that performed in 1589 at the wedding of Christine of Lorraine and Ferdinando de' Medici, for which the music was provided by leading composers, including *Marenzio and *Caccini. In its combination of music and drama, the *intermedio* can be regarded as a forerunner of opera.

Isaac, Heinrich (c. 1450–1517) Flemish composer. Though Isaac was born in Flanders, the first definite reference to him is in Innsbruck (1484) en route for Florence to enter the service of Lorenzo de' Medici. In Florence Isaac sang in the Cantori di S Giovanni and was regularly employed at the cathedral from 1485. After the death of Lorenzo (1492) Isaac met Maximilian I, and in 1497 became his court composer. While in the emperor's employ he maintained his Florentine connections and eventually resettled there in 1514. Isaac was one of the few Netherlanders active in Germany. He wrote a wide range of music; among his Masses, motets, German lieder, Italian songs, and instrumental pieces, his *Choralis constantinus* (1550–55), a posthumous collection of Mass propers, stands out as a monumental achievement. Isaac contributed considerably to the *Tenorlied*, as his skilful settings of "Innsbruck, ich muss dich lassen" demonstrate.

Isabella (I) of Castile *see* Ferdinand II.

Isabelline style *see under* plateresque.

Italian language In many respects the closest of the romance languages to Latin, Italian is used, at least as a written or second language, by more than sixty million people in Italy, Switzerland, and elsewhere. By the beginning of the Christian era, Latin had largely supplanted a number of early peninsular languages with which it originally co-existed. Ligurian, Etruscan, Oscan, Umbrian, Rhaetian, and Punic had disappeared or been reduced to insignificance, though some (Etruscan and Punic) may have survived for a while in ritual use. Greek is still spoken in areas of southern Italy, but whether it is continuous with that of Roman times is doubtful. Between 476 and 960 three waves of Germanic invaders entered Italy. Romanized Goths under Theodoric (489) had slight effect on vocabulary and were soon submerged by Justinian's reconquest (555). Lombards (Langobards) occupied areas north of the latitude of Spezia-Rimini and further south in Benevento and Spoleto, donating some 280 words to Italian and many more to various dialects. Franks (from 773) reached northern and central regions, but it is difficult to determine which Frankish words (e.g. *barone, feudo, ligio* (liegeman), *galoppare, bargagnare*) date from the era of Charlemagne and which from the later era of chivalry.

Evidence that a vernacular language is about to be born exists from the late eighth or early ninth century in the *Indovinello veronese*. This is a riddle, of uncertain interpretation but generally comparing ploughing to writing (plough: pen, oxen: fingers, white meadows: parchment, black seed: ink). By 960 legal documents record testimonies in the vernacular. Like all romance languages, Italian developed certain features: simplification of gender with loss of the neuter; loss of the deponent; definite and indefinite articles; a passive with *esse* and compound tenses with *habere*; prepositional constructions replacing genitives and datives; comparatives with *plus* replacing Latin synthetic comparatives; *quia* assuming a modern function (as *che*). Other typical changes can be exemplified in such words as *più* (from *plus*), *poi* (*post*), *buono* (*bonum*) and *fatto* (*factum*). The earliest literary document is the *Ritmo laurenziano* (c. 1150) and a number of other poems in various dialects are found by about 1200. The Albigensian crusade caused Provençal poets to migrate to Italy. In the northern courts, the *langue d'oc* (*see* French language) competed with Tuscan as a literary language. At the court of Frederick II, however, the poets of the Sicilian school, while writing in the troubadour tradition, did so in some variety of Italian, perhaps a refined version of the local dialect (a *volgare illustre*); their compositions was then passed to the north in tuscanized form and had an immense influence (*see* dolce stil nuovo). In Umbria, St Francis and Jacopone da Todi inspired the writing of religious verse, such as the *Laudes creaturarum* (or *Cantico di Frate Sole*), by St Francis (c. 1225). By the end of the thirteenth century, there is an awareness of Tuscan primacy in vernacular usage; the prestige of the so-called *Tre Corone*, *Dante, *Petrarch, and *Boccaccio, eventually assured Tuscan, and Florentine, pre-eminence.

A temporary setback occurred in the first half of the fourteenth century, however, when humanist devotion to Latin radically depreciated the vernacular in all fields of learning. But the vernacular foundations were strong and the fifteenth century saw the triumph of the vernacular humanism which *Alberti, *Politian, Lorenzo de' *Medici, and others cultivated. Printing (from 1470), in which the earliest priorities were the works of Petrarch, Boccaccio, and Dante (in that order), in time assisted in standardizing the language. Pietro *Bembo's *Prose della volgar lingua* (1525) and the founding of the Accademia della Crusca (1582) mark the final stages in resolving the *questione della lingua* and establishing the standard embodied in the Cruscan *Vocabolario* (1612).

In speech, though Italian has now gained ground and dialects are becoming increasingly italianized, an extreme diversity persists that is due to the historical fragmentation of Italy and the lack of a centralizing impetus (before unification in 1861) able to counterbalance the civic pride of the urban centres. (It has even been suggested that Venice produced no substantial body of literature out of pique at the preference for Tuscan over her own dialect.) In *De vulgari eloquentia* (c. 1303) Dante listed major dialect groups, noting further differences within them (as between Siena and Arezzo in Tuscany) and even between districts of a city. The present picture is scarcely less complex, with up to four levels of usage occurring in one area (Italian for writing and a regional variety with two local dialects as well for spoken use in certain circumstances). The dialects may vary greatly, Piedmontese and Sardinian, for example, having less in common that Spanish and Portuguese. Recently over 200 concepts or things surveyed in a study of fifty-four Italian regions produced only one item known to all informants by the same word (*espresso*); for other items, between two and thirteen different words or expressions were used. In such conditions, the establishment of a standard language at the end of the Renaissance was an achievement of unique and lasting importance.

Italy, Wars of (1494–1559) A series of conflicts that involved most Italian states, Spain, the Holy Roman Empire, France, and Switzerland. They began with *Charles VIII's triumphal invasion and coronation in Naples (1494–95) and the expulsion of France from Naples by Spain and its Italian allies (1496). In the second French invasion *Louis XII took Milan and tried to regain Naples. Initially he co-operated with *Ferdinand of Aragon, but the Aragonese later expelled the French from southern Italy (1504).

The conflict continued when *Maximilian I joined Pope *Julius II, some other Italian states, France, and Spain in the League of *Cambrai against Venice (1508), but quarrels over the spoils led to the formation of the anti-French *Holy League in 1511. The Swiss entered the wars and forced Louis XII out of Milan, which his successor, *Francis I, regained after his victory at Marignano (1515).

In the relatively quiet period that followed, both Ferdinand (1516) and Maximilian (1519) died. War resumed in the 1520s in the wider context of the European struggle between the Habsburgs under *Charles V and the Valois under Francis I. At the battle of *Pavia (1525) Charles V defeated and captured Francis I, who had to renounce his Italian claims. In the anti-Habsburg reaction that followed, France, the papacy, and other Italian states formed the League of Cognac against Charles. The notorious sack of *Rome (1527) by imperial troops followed. By 1529 several setbacks compelled Francis I again to surrender his Italian claims in the treaties of Barcelona and Cambrai. The last phase of the wars (1529–59) saw limited foreign involvement in Italy and ended with France's final renunciation of its Italian claims in the treaty of *Cateau-Cambrésis (1559).

J

Jacobean style The English architectural and decorative style associated with the reign (1603–25) of James I. It is also known as Early Stuart and is a natural development of the preceding *Elizabethan style. Its general tendency was to fine down and restrain the exuberant inventiveness of earlier craftsmen and builders in their attitude to classical models and motifs. While *furniture was still made predominantly of oak, some new forms of chairs and tables began to make their appearance.

In architecture there was renewed interest in the correctness of classical proportions and a tendency to use stone again for important buildings. Forerunner of the revival of building according to classical canons in late Stuart England was the architect Inigo *Jones, whose important commissions and careful study of the work of *Palladio initiated the fashion for pure Italian Renaissance architecture.

Jacobello del Fiore (c. 1370–1439) Italian artist. The son of Francesco del Fiore, the president of the guild of painters in Venice (1415–36), Jacobello was a pupil of *Gentile da Fabriano and adopted a similar approach in the International Gothic style when he began painting in 1394. His earliest surviving work is the *Madonna della Misericordia* (1407); other works include the *Lion of St Mark* (1415; Palazzo Ducale, Venice) and the *Coronation of the Virgin* (1438), a copy of the well-known painting by Gauriento.

James I (1566–1625), King of England and Ireland (1603–25), King of Scots (as James VI; 1567–1625) The son of *Mary, Queen of Scots, and Henry Stewart, Lord Darnley, James was the first monarch to rule both Scotland and England. His long minority was plagued by Scotland's religious and political turmoil, but after 1583 he succeeded in imposing his authority on the warring factions. In England he had less success, failing to understand the English and their institutions; they in turn mocked his personal habits and his liking for handsome young courtiers. They also resented his policy of seeking peace with Spain. In his attempts to assert himself James had bitter disputes with his parliaments, usually over money. His schooling under George *Buchanan had given him a taste for learning, and he wrote treatises on several subjects (witchcraft, tobacco, the divine right of kings) but his greatest contribution to literature was made in 1604 when he commissioned the Authorized Version of the Bible.

James IV (1473–1513), King of Scotland (1488–1513) The son of James III, he succeeded to the throne when his father was killed at the battle of Sauchieburn (1488) fighting against a rebellion of nobles. In 1503 he married Margaret, daughter of Henry VII of England. An energetic and popular ruler, he promoted efficient administration, improved the working of the judicial system, and attempted to assert royal authority in the Highlands and Western Isles. He encouraged learning, supporting the foundation of King's College, Aberdeen (1495), which became a centre of humanist learning, patronizing the poet William Dunbar, and granting a patent to the first Scottish printers (1507). In general he avoided war, but in 1513 treaty obligations with France compelled him to invade England. He was defeated and killed at the battle of Flodden.

Jamnitzer family The leading family of German goldsmiths and silversmiths in the sixteenth and seventeenth centuries, working in Nuremberg. Wenzel Jamnitzer (1508–85), the greatest of the family, moved with his father Hans (died c. 1549) and brother Albrecht (died 1555), both goldsmiths, to Nuremberg from Vienna sometime before 1534. His pre-eminence as a craftsman and contribution to the city's prosperity were recognized in his appointment as master of the city mint (1552) and in further civic positions. He was court goldsmith to four Habsburg emperors. His work, which was extremely ornate, includes elaborate table centres, goblets, and a richly ornamented jewel casket. A design also exists for a magnificent bearing sword for Charles V. Particularly famous is the table fountain (about 3 metres high) made for Emperor Rudolf II, an allegory both of Habsburg rule and of the various types of knowledge (1578). Jamnitzer worked in the mannerist style, and is known particularly for using naturalistic casts of insects, lizards, grasses, and shells as decoration, setting the fashion

JAMNITZER FAMILY *An exceptionally ornate piece by Christoph Jamnitzer, this jug depicts the triumphs of Fame (on the side shown) and Truth. (Kunsthistorisches Museum, Vienna)*

for this in Germany (it was already established in Italy). An example is his mother-of-pearl and silver-gilt ewer in the shape of a snail (c. 1570). His figures, such as the caryatids for Rudolf's table fountain, show him to have been a gifted sculptor. He also made mathematical and astronomical instruments, and published a book on mathematics, mechanics, and architecture, *Perspectiva corporum regularium* (1568).

Wenzel's son Hans (c. 1538–1603) and Albrecht's son Bartel (c. 1548–c. 1596) carried on the workshop and produced several fine pieces. Christoph (1563–1618), the son of Hans the Younger, was again a highly talented craftsman, approaching his grandfather's brilliance. His more complex work, in a mannerist style verging on the Baroque, includes a goblet in the form of an angel and a table fountain in the form of an elephant. He probably visited Italy, and he too produced work for Emperor Rudolf II. In 1610 he published his *Neuw Groteszken Buch*, a collection of decorative designs which included grotesque fantasies.

Janequin, Clément (c. 1485–1558) French composer. He may have been educated in his native Châtellerault. In 1505 he was a "clerc" in Bordeaux, and in 1523 he entered the service of the bishop there. He collected various ecclesiastical appointments, and in the 1530s was *maître de chapelle* in the cathedrals of Auch and Angers. He probably moved to Paris in the 1540s, but was certainly there from 1549, and he spent the rest of his life there. In 1530 he wrote a chanson to celebrate the entry of Francis I into Bordeaux, but it was not until the 1550s that he joined the court as a singer and then *compositeur ordinaire*. He is best remembered for his chansons, ranking with *Sermisy as the foremost exponent of the genre. His lengthy programmatic chansons such as *Le chant des oiseaux* and *La bataille* are well known, but the bulk of his output comprises short, pithy works with a good deal of imitation and clearly defined rhythmic patterns. There is often a popular or rustic aspect to these works. Janequin also set metrical versions of psalm texts and a small number of motets and two Masses. The Masses are both closely based on two of his own chansons.

Jena A city in south central Germany on the River Saale. Probably of ninth-century origins, the city was chartered in 1230 and ruled by the Margraves of Meissen from the mid-thirteenth century until it passed to the elector of Saxony (1423). The university, founded in 1548 and granted university status in 1577, was a stronghold of Lutheran scholarship. Notable buildings which have survived from the Renaissance period include the Black Bear inn (where *Luther sheltered after his flight from Wartburg), the fourteenth-century town hall, and St Michael's church (1438–1528).

Jenson, Nicolas (1420–80) French type designer and printer. Jenson was born at Sommevoie, near Troyes, and after learning to print in Germany, perhaps at Mainz, he settled in Venice about 1470. There he perfected the roman type-face first used in Strasbourg and Rome by 1467, following a roman manuscript hand. In the following decade he issued about seventy books, mostly Latin or Greek classics; among them Pliny's *Historia naturalis* (1472) is one of his finest productions. Many of his books were illuminated and decorated by hand, as though they were manuscripts, and special copies of some were printed on vellum.

Jesuits A Roman Catholic religious order established to strengthen the papacy and the Catholic Church against Protestantism. The Jesuits came into being when *Ignatius Loyola and ten followers, all committed to missionary work, met in Venice in 1537 to become the Society of Jesus. This put into effect plans made in Paris three years earlier, when Loyola and six companions dedicated themselves to a life of service to God. Their order was recognized by Pope Paul III in 1540.

Representing a new religious technique rather than new doctrine, the Jesuits' spiritual discipline is contained in the *Spiritual Exercises*, first composed by Loyola in 1522 but continually revised until the appearance of a printed version in 1548. The *Exercises*, reinforced by Loyola's *Constitutions* (first drafted 1547–50), are fundamental to the self-discipline and organization that are the hallmark of the society. Divided into four parts, each part to be studied for a week, the *Exercises* provide a meditative experience based upon the themes of sin, Christ's life, the Passion, and the Resurrection. The overall effect of the programme was the fostering of a greater awareness of sin and salvation, continually refreshed through study and confession. United in a devotion to the pope and organized into congregations superintended by a general, the society proved to be a highly effective mission. By the time of Loyola's death (1556) it had over a thousand members and was set to become a major force in the *Counter-Reformation.

Dedicated to personal humility and reliant on alms, the Jesuits soon became renowned for their courage, tenacity, and zeal, as demonstrated in the heroic exploits of one of the original companions of Loyola in Paris, *Francis Xavier, whose mission lay in the Indies and Far East. The Jesuit mission to reconvert England, undertaken in 1578, also produced many acts of bravery and several martyrs. The Jesuits were opposed by the Jansenists and other movements within the Catholic Church and were persecuted in several European countries during the late seventeenth and eighteenth centuries, but their suppression was incomplete. The society once again flourishes and plays a leading part in modern Roman Catholicism, particularly in its educational aspects (*see also* Gregoriana).

Jeux Floraux, les *see under* academies.

jewellery The jeweller's art flourished in the Renaissance, fuelled by the rivalry between courts and noble families that expressed itself in ostentatious display. Many outstanding artists designed jewellery, among them *Botticelli, *Giulio Romano, and *Holbein the Younger; some even initially trained as goldsmiths. Because Renaissance jewellery was so elaborate, the value of the workmanship usually exceeded the intrinsic value of the material, and much therefore survives. Contemporary portraits offer excellent evidence of the opulence and variety of Renaissance jewellery (see Plate XIV). Women's hair ornaments emphasized the movement of loose hair and braids. Necklaces were particularly popular, either in the form of a heavy gold chain with a central pendant or multiple ropes of pearls; those of extreme length were worn looped up to the bodice. Numerous brooches and rings were worn together, pearls dangled from the points of lace ruffs and stiff caps, and frequently the whole female dress would be jewel encrusted.

Pendants were an important form as a frame for a cameo or portrait miniature. Many were polychromatic with inset gemstones and enamelling. Jewelled or enamelled cases for miniatures and watches were also popular. Other pendants developed into complicated openwork creations in which the bizarre shape of a baroque pearl suggested to the artificer the body of a sea monster or centaur. Rings were often made in architectural high relief and some had concealed compartments for poisons or love charms. Pendant crosses became highly decorative, their original religious significance submerged in their ornamental function.

Jewellery often shared with medals an emblematic or symbolic role. Queen Elizabeth I, for example, in a portrait (c. 1575) by Nicholas *Hilliard wears at her breast a pendant of a phoenix rising from the flames as a symbol of her uniqueness and her chastity. Portraits of James I show him wearing in his hat a jewel called the Mirror of Great Britain, made for him in 1604 to symbolize the union of the kingdoms and comprising four main stones – three diamonds and a ruby.

Jodelle, Étienne (1532–73) French dramatist and poet. A member of the *Pléiade, Jodelle applied the principles of the group to dramatic composition and succeeded in producing the first modern French tragedy and comedy, utterly different in every way from the morality and mystery plays then occupying the French stage. He is chiefly remembered for the tragedy *Cléopâtre captive* (acted before the court in 1552), which excited great interest in humanist circles for its careful construction, elegiac atmosphere, long declamatory speeches, and characters in the grand style. Together with *Didon* (c. 1560) and his comedy *Eugène* (1552), this play broke new ground and prepared the way for the great neoclassical dramatists Racine and Corneille. Despite these successes, Jodelle died in Paris in extreme poverty.

Johannes de Muris *see* Muris, Johannes de.

John Fisher, St (1469–1535) Roman Catholic martyr, churchman, and scholar. As chancellor of Cambridge university Fisher encouraged Hebrew studies and brought his friend *Erasmus to England to teach. He was bishop of Rochester from 1504 until 1534. Strongly opposed to Protestantism, Fisher spearheaded the Catholic cause. He enraged *Henry VIII by denouncing the divorce of Catherine of Aragon and by refusing to accept Henry as supreme head of the Church of England. Shortly before Fisher's trial and execution for treason on Tower Hill the pope made him a cardinal. He was canonized in 1935.

John of Austria, Don (1545–78), Spanish prince. He was born at Regensburg, the illegitimate son of Emperor Charles V and a local magnate's daughter, and brought up in Spain in ignorance of his parentage. Recognized in Charles's will, John was received into the royal family (1559) with the title Don Juan de Austria. His military ambitions soon manifested themselves in fighting Algerian corsairs (1568), crushing a revolt of moriscos in Granada (1569–70), and commanding the Christian fleet at *Lepanto (1571). Philip II, alarmed at his half-brother's schemes, refused to back his projects, including his short-lived capture of Tunis (1573), but instead appointed him governor-general of the now openly defiant Netherlands (1576). Reluctantly brought in 1577 to comply with the terms of the Pacification of *Ghent, Don John repudiated the agreement when he realized how strong Prince William of Orange had become. Reinforced by troops under Alessandro *Farnese, Don John defeated the rebels at Gemblours (1578) but was unable to follow up the success and died of fever the same autumn.

John of the Cross, St (Juan de Yepes; 1542–91) Spanish Carmelite reformer and mystic. He was born the youngest son of a Toledan silk weaver at Fontiveros and after studying with the Jesuits in Salamanca he went to university there. He abandoned the idea of following in his father's trade and joined the Carmelites in 1563 and was ordained in 1567. He soon met *Teresa of Ávila and promoted her cause of reforming the Carmelite order (see Carmelites, Reform of the). In 1568 Antonio de Heredia, José de Cristo, and he founded the male Discalced Carmelites. In 1572 Teresa of Ávila summoned John of the Cross (as he now termed himself) to Ávila to serve as the spiritual adviser of her reformed Convent of the Incarnation.

Because of a conflict with a Carmelite superior who disapproved of John's and Teresa's reformist activities, John was imprisoned for a short while in Toledo. During this period his spiritual experiences intensified and he wrote the mystical poems *The Dark Night of the Soul* and *The Spiritual Canticle*. In 1578 he escaped from prison and resumed his former activities. Finally in 1579 the Discalced Carmelites became a recognized order, one of the several new orders of the Counter-Reformation. Between then and his death John founded several new houses for the order. In 1591 his enemies managed to have him relieved of all his offices and even attempted to expel him from the order. Seriously ill, he nevertheless went to Ubeda where he received scant welcome. There he died. He was canonized in 1726 and was named Doctor of the Church in 1926.

Jonas, Justus (Jodocus Koch; 1493–1555) German Lutheran jurist and theologian. Jonas was born at Nordhausen and proved to be an able scholar whose precocious talents attracted the notice of *Erasmus. He became professor of law at Erfurt in 1518, and in 1521 professor of theology at Wittenberg. A firm friend and admirer of *Luther, Jonas took a prominent part in the Protestant cause. He attended both the Colloquy of Marburg (1529) and the Diet of Augsburg (1530), and translated a number of Luther's Latin works into German, along with the *Loci communes* of *Melanchthon. In 1541 Jonas left Wittenberg to take up a post in Halle, where as superintendent of the area's churches he supervised the organization of the local reform. Forced to leave Halle by the Schmalkaldic war (see Schmalkaldic League) he eventually settled in Eisleben, where he remained until his death.

Jones, Inigo (1573–1652) English architect and stage designer. The son of a London clockmaker, Jones probably trained as a painter, although little is known of his early life. He became acquainted with the ideals of the Italian Renaissance during visits to Italy (1598–1603, 1613), where he studied both classical architecture and the theories of Andrea *Palladio. After a short period at the Danish court of Christian IV, Jones was brought to the court of James I, where he executed costume and set designs for numerous masques and plays, notably those by Ben *Jonson. After being consulted on the building of Hatfield House and the New Exchange for Merchants (now destroyed), he was appointed surveyor of works to James I in 1615 and he subsequently held the same office under Charles I.

Jones's earliest surviving structure is the Queen's House at Greenwich, London (1616–35), which was built in the style of an Italian villa and was the first strictly classical English building. His greatest work, however, was the building of the Banqueting Hall in Whitehall (1619–22), which owed much to the ideas of Palladio, and subsequent designs for the rebuilding of the whole of Whitehall Palace. The only other surviving royal

Jonghelinck, Jakob

INIGO JONES The Fallen House of Chivalry. *A design for* Barriers, *a court entertainment scripted by Ben Jonson, in which James I's heir, Prince Henry, was hailed as the reviver of chivalry. Reminiscent of a ruined Roman amphitheatre, the drawing incorporates elements of classical buildings which Jones may have seen on his visit to Italy. (1610; Devonshire Collection, Chatsworth, England)*

building by Jones is the Queen's chapel at St James's Palace (1623–27), the first English church in the classical style. Jones also designed London's first piazza (at Covent Garden in 1630), including the Palladian church of St Paul, and several country houses, and directed the restoration of St Paul's Cathedral (1632–42); this last work was unfortunately lost in the Great Fire of London (1666). Jones's career ended with the civil war in the 1640s, but his influence upon later English architects was profound.

Jonghelinck, Jakob (1530–1606) Netherlands medallist and sculptor. After studying in Milan with Leone *Leoni, Jonghelinck, who was born in Antwerp, returned to the Netherlands in 1555. Between 1558 and 1566 he executed the tomb of Duke *Charles the Bold of Burgundy, who had died nearly a century earlier, for the church of Our Lady in Bruges. As this tomb was situated beside the late fifteenth-century tomb of Charles's daughter, Mary of Burgundy, Jonghelinck imitated the style of the earlier artist, an example of antiquarianism rare in sixteenth-century art, which customarily eschewed the Gothic past in favour of neoclassicism. Although Jonghelinck's life-size bronze of the infamous duke of *Alba in the Antwerp citadel was destroyed during the revolt of 1577, its appearance is reflected in a bust of the same sitter now in New York. Jonghelinck's bronzes are technically very accomplished and his portraits have considerable characterization.

Jonson, Ben(jamin) (1572–1637) English dramatist, poet, and critic. Jonson received a classical education under *Camden at Westminster school in his native London, but then followed his stepfather's trade of bricklaying. In the 1590s he fought in Flanders and later became an actor. His first great success as a dramatist was *Every Man in his Humour* (1598), the forerunner of "the comedy of humours" at which he excelled, but the same year he was imprisoned for killing a fellow-actor and barely escaped hanging. He converted to Catholicism in gaol and remained a Roman Catholic for twelve years. In 1605 he was again in trouble, along with *Chapman and Marston, for anti-Scots satire in *Eastward Ho!* He nonetheless became a favourite producer of entertainments and masques for James I's court, usually in collaboration with Inigo *Jones (*see* masque). In 1616 the king awarded him a pension.

Johnson's great comedies – *Volpone* (1606), *Epicoene* (1609), *The Alchemist* (1610), and *Bartholomew Fair* (1614) – are outstanding for their energy and comic invention. His tragedies – *Sejanus* (1603) and *Catiline* (1611) – were less popular, but are models of classical construction and contain some fine blank verse. In 1612–13 he accompanied Raleigh's turbulent son, young Walter, as his tutor on a continental tour. After publishing his collected *Works* (1616) Jonson abandoned the stage for a decade, but his reputation as a man of letters continued to grow. He was a great mentor to younger writers ("the tribe of Ben"), thirty-three of whom contributed elegies to the commemorative volume *Jonsonus Virbius* (1638) after his death. Among the troubles of his later years were a fire that destroyed his library and unpublished manuscripts (1623), the failure of several plays, a paralytic stroke (1628), financial distress, and a feud with Inigo Jones, whom he satirized in *The Tale of a Tub* (1634).

Jonson's chief work in prose was *Timber, or Discoveries made upon Men and Matter* (1640), but his recorded conversations with William Drummond of Hawthornden, whom he met in Scotland in 1618, give the most vivid impression of his ideas on poetry and people. He also wrote some magnificent lyrics for his masques, such as "Queen and huntress, chaste and fair" from *Cynthia's Revels* (1600), and the famous epitaph on the child actor Salathiel Pavy (published in *Epigrams*, 1616).

Josquin Des Prés *see* Des Prés, Josquin.

Journée des Barricades (12 May 1588) A Catholic revolt in Paris, which was one of the decisive events in the final stages of the French wars of religion. The Parisians, many of whom supported the

Catholic League by which Duke Henry of Guise (*see* Guise family) hoped to secure his succession to the throne, had grown increasingly anxious during the 1580s about the threat from Huguenot force and they were also weary of the vacillations of the ineffectual King *Henry III. They invited Duke Henry to come to their aid, which he did in defiance of the king's ban against his entering Paris, and the Parisians then erected barricades against their sovereign. The king fled to Chartres and, unable to recover his position, determined upon the assassination of Guise and his brother in December that year.

Julius II (1443–1513), Pope (1503–13) Giuliano *della Rovere came from an impoverished noble family in Liguria. When his uncle became Pope *Sixtus IV (1471) he gained a cardinal's hat and many benefices. He served on papal missions and helped defend Rome against Naples, but had to leave Rome when his enemy Rodrigo Borgia became Pope *Alexander VI (1492). When Alexander VI died (1503) Cardinal della Rovere returned to Rome and was elected pope after Pius III's short reign. Once elected, Julius broke his promises to continue the war against the Turks, to call a general council within two years, and to consult the cardinals on all important matters.

Julius took some interest in Church reform; he issued a bull against simony and encouraged the reform of the Benedictines. He also summoned the fifth Lateran Council in 1511. Julius was primarily a military leader and statesman who did much to restore the papacy's temporal power. After defeating Cesare *Borgia (1504) he commanded an expedition which forced Perugia and Bologna to submit to papal authority (1506). He joined the League of Cambrai against Venice (1509) and after Venice's defeat joined the anti-French *Holy League (1511). With *Maximilian I's support he foiled *Louis XII's attempts to depose him and isolated France. He occupied Modena (1510) and took Mirandola (1511).

Julius was a clever financial administrator, but is best remembered for his generosity to such great artists as *Raphael, *Michelangelo, and *Bramante. He expanded the Vatican Library, collected ancient sculpture, and laid the cornerstone of *St Peter's basilica, Rome.

Juni, Juan de (c. 1507–77) French-born sculptor. Although probably a native of Burgundy, Juni became a part of the Spanish artistic tradition, arriving at León in 1533. He settled in Valladolid in 1540. His early works include portrait medallions (1536) for the façade of S Marcos, León, but he is best known for the polychromed wood group *The Entombment of Christ* (1539–44; Valladolid museum), which testifies to Juni's great technical skill and emotionalism. Other pieces include a large reredos (1545–61; Valladolid cathedral) for Sta Maria la Antigua and other altarpieces. He also executed works in Salamanca and Zamora. His later pieces anticipated the Baroque in Spain.

Junta press *see* Giunti (*or* Junta) press.

Justus of Ghent (Joos van Wassenhove; active 1460–c. 1480) Flemish painter. Between 1473 and 1475 "Giusto da Guanto" (the Italian form of Justus of Ghent) is documented as the painter of the *Communion of the Apostles* altarpiece in Urbino. He is identical with Joos van Wassenhove, active at Antwerp in 1460 and recorded at Ghent in 1464–69. A document of 1475 states that he was an associate of Hugo van der *Goes and that he had gone to Rome. A handful of early pictures have been attributed to Justus by comparison with his only documented work, the *Communion* altarpiece. The most important of these is the *Mount Calvary* triptych in St Bavon, Ghent. Justus is usually identified with the anonymous painter of a group of pictures in a Netherlandish style executed for the Urbino court: these include twenty-eight portraits of *Famous Men* and *Federico da Montefeltro and his son Guidobaldo* (c. 1473–76) for the ducal study in Urbino, and four fragments from a series of *The Seven Liberal Arts* and *Federico da Montefeltro Attending a Lecture* (c. 1476–80) for a similar study in Gubbio. The former group is divided between Paris and Urbino; the latter between London, Windsor, and (prior to destruction in 1945) Berlin. Pedro *Berruguete probably assisted Justus with both schemes.

Justus is the only fifteenth-century Flemish painter with surviving works known to have been produced in Italy. These reveal his increasing mastery in the handling of illusionistic perspective and the representation of Italianate subject matter. He is thus an important forerunner of the assimilation of Italian ideas by northern artists during the early sixteenth century.

K

Kempeneer, Pieter de *see* Campana, Pedro de.

Kepler, Johannes (1571–1630) German astronomer. Born near Wittenberg, the son of a mercenary, Kepler was educated at Tübingen university where, as a student of Michael *Maestlin, he was introduced to astronomy and where he became an early convert to the *Copernican system. Here also he began to consider the problem of why there were only six planets (according to the contemporary count) and why they were sited in their particular orbits. In his *Mysterium cosmographicum* (1596) he proposed that God had modelled the universe on the pattern of the five regular solids of 4, 6, 8, 12, and 20 sides respectively. Before he could advance further, he realized, he would need fuller and more accurate data.

Access to such data came in 1599 when he was invited by Tycho *Brahe, the leading observer of his day, to join him at his Prague observatory. The death of Brahe soon afterwards (1601) left Kepler in charge of all his observations. With them Kepler was able to reshape astronomy. After several years' struggling to make sense of the orbit of Mars, Kepler finally saw in 1605 that planetary orbits were elliptical, not circular as had previously been thought. This result, since known as Kepler's first law, was revealed in his *Astronomia nova* (1609). The debt to Brahe was repaid after many years with the publication of his observations in 1627 as the Rudolfine Tables. Ever convinced, however, that the universe was built to some divine design, Kepler continued to search for the key to the cosmic mystery. His final thoughts on the matter were contained in his *Harmonices mundi* (1619), a work in which he also first formulated his third law.

Kepler's personal life was to prove less successful. Although he succeeded Brahe in 1601 as imperial mathematician to *Rudolf II he found the duties irksome and often unpaid. In 1612 he moved to Linz as provincial mathematician. The outbreak of the Thirty Years' War in 1618, religious controversies, domestic troubles, and the need to defend his mother against a charge of witchcraft, together with a perennial shortage of funds, ill health, and intense intellectual labours, made the latter part of Kepler's life both hectic and unpredictable. After abandoning Linz in 1627, he settled in Silesia in 1628 in the service of the statesman and general Wallenstein. He died at Regensburg, while travelling to Linz to collect a debt. *See also* astronomy.

Key, Lieven de (1560–1627) Netherlands stonemason and architect. Key was born in Ghent and after working in England for some years, he moved to Haarlem (1591), where he remained for the rest of his life. His highly ornamental style was largely a development of that of his predecessor in Haarlem, Willem den Abt. His finest works are the Haarlem meat hall (1602–03) and the tower of the Nieuwe Kerk (1613). Both buildings are basically traditional in type, but are distinguished by a taut sense of form and a brilliant handling of decorative details. While Key stands out in comparison with many of his sixteenth-century predecessors for his vigorous and personal sense of decorative design, he nevertheless remained a provincial figure, rooted in an essentially Dutch architectural tradition.

Keyser, Hendrick de (1565–1621) Dutch architect and sculptor. The son of a cabinet maker, Keyser studied in his native Utrecht under Cornelis Bloemaert and was appointed city sculptor and architect of Amsterdam in 1594. In London in 1607 he met the English sculptor Nicholas Stone, who became his assistant and son-in-law. Keyser's major buildings include the Zuiderkerk, the Westerkerk, and the exchange, all in Amsterdam, and Leyden town hall. Like Lieven de Key, Keyser was a leading figure in the last phase of Dutch Mannerism. However, unlike his colleague, he outgrew this increasingly provincial tradition, to become one of the founders of seventeenth-century Dutch classicism.

Keyser was also the most significant Dutch sculptor of the early seventeenth century, working in a style loosely derived from that of the Italian mannerists. He produced numerous small bronzes and pieces of architectural sculpture. His chief sculptural work, the tomb of William the Silent in the Nieuwe Kerk at Delft, was commissioned in 1614 but was not complete by the time of his own death.

Khair ed-Din *see* Barbarossa.

Plate I

ANDREA DEL SARTO   Last Supper

Less dramatic than Leonardo's version, this fresco in the refectory of the Vallombrosan abbey of S Salvi, just outside Florence, is nonetheless notable for its highly individualized portraits and rich colouring. (?1527: S Salvi)

Plate II

ARCIMBOLDO Rudolf II as Vertumnus
Arcimboldo composed a number of similar bizarre "portraits" for his imperial patron, whose taste inclined towards the grotesque. Vertumnus was the ancient Roman god who presided over the changing seasons of the year and their produce. (c. 1590; Baron von Essen Collection, Nationalmuseum, Stockholm)

Plate III

GIOVANNI BELLINI Sacred Allegory

The subject is possibly taken from a medieval French allegory. Le pèlerinage de l'âme. (c. 1500: Uffizi, Florence)

Plate IV

BOOK ILLUSTRATION

The frontispiece of Cristoforo Landino's Italian translation of Giovanni Simonetta's
Sforziada, *a biography of Francesco Sforza, the first Sforza duke of Milan. Printed in Milan in 1490, this deluxe copy, for presentation to Francesco's son, Lodovico "il Moro", was printed on vellum and magnificently decorated by hand – a reminder that the new craft of printing did not immediately put manuscript illuminators out of work. (1490; British Library, London)*

Plate V

BOTTICELLI Birth of Venus

Classical literary and graphic sources, well known to the contemporary Neoplatonists of Florence, inspire the iconography of Botticelli's vision of the new-born goddess of love wafted over the sea in her scallop shell by zephyrs. The personification of spring stands ready to cast a flowery cloak about her. (c. 1485; Uffizi, Florence)

Plate VI

JAN BRUEGHEL Allegory of Sight

One of a series on the senses, this painting shows a room cluttered with examples of the fine and decorative arts and optical instruments. The double portrait behind the seated female figures shows the Archdukes Albert and Isabella, patrons of Brueghel and also of Rubens, on whose studio the room may be based. (1617; Prado, Madrid)

Plate VII

CARAVAGGIO The Supper at Emmaus

Caravaggio's daring use of foreshortening and chiaroscuro captures the drama of the moment when Christ reveals his identity to the disciples at Emmaus, when, as Luke's gospel (24:31) says, "Their eyes were opened and they knew him." (c. 1598; National Gallery, London.

Plate VIII

DOSSO DOSSI Circe and her Lovers in a Landscape

The subject is taken from the section of Homer's Odyssey describing how the enchantress Circe turned her discarded lovers into animals. Painted without any of the moralizing content with which the Middle Ages endowed the fable, this sensuous Circe in her luxuriant surroundings might be an illustration of the enchantress Alcina from the Orlando furioso of Dossi's friend Ariosto.
(Kress Collection, National Gallery of Art, Washington)

Plate IX

GIAMBOLOGNA

The colossal statue of the Apennines, symbol of untamed natural forces, gazes at its own reflection in a pool at the Villa Demidoff at Pratolino, on the outskirts of Florence. (c. 1580)

Plate XII

HUGO VAN DER GOES   The Portinari altarpiece *(central panel)*
Originally set up in the church of Sant'Egidio in the hospital of Sta Maria Nuova, this work was the first
sizable example of Netherlandish art to be seen in Florence, and was attentively studied by late Quattrocento
Florentine artists. The grotesque rusticity of the shepherds on the right contrasts with the idealized beauty
of the adoring angels and with the exquisite naturalism of the flower still life in the foreground.
(c. 1475/77; Uffizi, Florence)

Plate XIII

EL GRECO   The Adoration of the Name of Jesus
*Sombrely clad, Philip II of Spain kneels in the foreground, his back to a devouring hell-mouth, while men
on earth and the heavenly host unite in worship of the holy monogram* IHS (*Iesus Hominum Salvator —
Jesus, Saviour of Men*). (*c. 1580; Escorial, Madrid*)

Plate XIV

JEWELLERY
An unknown artist depicts Elizabeth Vernon, Countess of Southampton, at her dressing-table, on which are displayed the contents of her jewel box. (c. 1600; the collection of the Duke of Buccleuch, K.T., Boughton House, England)

Plate XV

BATTLE OF LEPANTO

This panoramic view by an unknown artist clearly shows the rows of oars that provided the motive power for both Christian and Turkish ships and the use of artillery that determined the outcome in favour of the Christians. The entrance to the Gulf of Corinth is marked by the two small forts on the right.

(c. 1571; National Maritime Museum, Greenwich, London)

Plate XVI

MANTEGNA   The Triumph of Caesar
This canvas panel is one of a series of nine originally intended for the Gonzaga palace in Mantua but which passed into the collection of Charles I of England in 1627. The numerous quotations from ancient Roman sculpture show the depth of Mantegna's interest in the antique. (1487–94; Hampton Court Palace, England)

Plate XVII

SIMONE MARTINI Guidoriccio da Fogliano

The striking colours of the horse and rider show up brilliantly against the bare landscape as Guidoriccio, commander's baton in hand, rides to the siege of Montemassi in 1318. (1328: Palazzo Pubblico, Siena)

Plate XVIII

MASACCIO   St Peter Giving Alms
*Vasari praised Masaccio's "vivid colours, formidable drawing, outstanding figures", now revealed afresh in
the Brancacci Chapel frescoes after cleaning and restoration work undertaken in 1984.
(c. 1426; Brancacci Chapel, Sta Maria del Carmine, Florence)*

Plate XIX

MICHELANGELO Ignudo

Twenty of these naked youths adorn the vault of the Sistine Chapel, interspersing the religious and symbolical scheme with figures that extol human grace, beauty, and delight. (1508–12: Sistine Chapel)

Plate XX

MUSIC

In Hans Mielich's miniature Kapellmeister *Orlando Lassus (at left) directs music making at the Bavarian court. (Bayerische Staatsbibliothek, Munich)*

Plate XXI

ISAAC OLIVER   Edward Herbert, 1st Baron Herbert of Cherbury
*Lord Herbert appears in the dual role of man of action (suggested by the armour and horses in the background)
and the melancholic philosopher. The motto on his shield refers to the theory of sympathetic magic, which was
based upon the Neoplatonic concept of occult influences. (c. 1610–15; the collection of
the Earl of Powis, Powis Castle, Wales)*

Plate XXII

PALMA VECCHIO Flora
*A Venetian courtesan poses as the goddess of flowers, but the slight symbolic content of the portrait is
overwhelmed by the erotic appeal of the rich colours, flowing blonde hair, and exposed breast. A portrait
by Titian of a similar subject, similarly titled, is in the Uffizi. (c. 1520; National Gallery, London)*

Plate XXIII

PARMIGIANINO Madonna and Child with St Zacharias
Painted for Bonifacio Gozzadini of Bologna, where Parmigianino had sought refuge after the sack of Rome, this treatment of the Madonna and Child theme is laden with foreboding, from the visionary head of St Zacharias in the foreground to the brooding sky above. The thoughtful Christ Child seems to shrink from the embrace of the infant St John the Baptist while behind them St Mary Magdalene holds up her jar of ointment, emblem of Christ's Passion and death. (1527–31; Uffizi, Florence)

Plate XXIV

PIERO DELLA FRANCESCA Federico da Montefeltro
*The imposing profile of the great condottiere and patron of the arts dominates the serene
light-filled landscape against which it is painted, creating an icon of intellectual, moral,
and physical power. (1465–70; Uffizi, Florence)*

Plate XXV

PINTURICCHIO   Aenea Silvio Piccolomini crowned Laureate by Emperor Frederick III
This is the third in a series of ten scenes from the life of Pope Pius II.
(1502–07; Piccolomini library, Siena cathedral)

Plate XXVI

RAPHAEL   School of Athens

Painted on the wall facing the Disputa, the School of Athens represents the noblest expression of the human intellect, which the Renaissance believed to have been embodied in the philosophers of ancient Greece. Plato and Aristotle pass through the centre of a vaulted portico (clearly based on the Roman Baths of Caracalla); Plato points heavenwards, indicating the metaphysical nature of his speculations, while Aristotle gestures towards the physical world before him. Around them are their followers or representatives of other philosophical schools; several of these are portraits of Raphael's contemporaries and in the extreme right-hand corner Raphael has included himself and Sodoma. (1509–11; Stanza della Segnatura, Vatican)

Plate XXVII

SEBASTIANO DEL PIOMBO Pope Clement VII
*Within the limits of a conventional pose for papal portraits, Sebastiano has created a
powerful and subtle impression. At about the time the picture was painted Clement abandoned
his former ally, Charles V, in favour of an alliance with France, a decision that led to
the sack of Rome by imperial troops the following year. Something of these political
manoeuvres is suggested in the sitter's half-averted head and watchful gaze.
(1526; Capodimonte, Naples)*

Plate XXVIII

SIGNORELLI The Fall of the Damned

Signorelli's Last Judgment frescoes, of which this is a part, acknowledge a debt to Dante as well as to classical and medieval Christian iconography. (1499–1503; Capella della Madonna di S Brizio, Duomo, Orvieto)

Plate XXIX

TAPESTRY   Battle of Pavia *(detail)*

These Flemish tapestries, woven to the designs of Bernard van Orley, commemorate the victory of the imperial forces over Francis I of France in 1525. It was this battle that finally established the supremacy of firearms over the cavalry lance and pike. (Capodimonte, Naples)

Plate XXX

TITIAN   Danaë

According to the ancient Greek myth, Danaë was imprisoned by her father in a tower after he had been warned by an oracle that she would bear a son who would kill him. Her lover, the god Zeus, frustrated these precautions by coming to her in a shower of gold. The ugly maidservant, with her greedy gesture, introduces a witty contrast to the voluptuous nude Danaë. (1554; Prado, Madrid)

Plate XXXI

UCCELLO   A Hunt in a Forest

The brightly coloured huntsmen with their horses and hounds, streaming away into the green recesses of the forest, are an exercise in the use of perspective in which Uccello so greatly delighted, as they draw the eye towards the vanishing point of their quarry.

(c. 1460: Ashmolean Museum, Oxford)

Plate XXXII

VERONESE   The Family of Darius before Alexander

In a magnificent Renaissance courtyard a famous episode from ancient history is re-enacted; the presentation of the womenfolk of Darius of Persia to the conquering Alexander. In her confusion, Darius' mother kneels to Alexander's comrade Hephastion, who corrects her mistake with a gesture indicating the king. The honourable treatment accorded by Alexander the Great to the family of his enemy was legendary; the picture therefore represents one of the qualities most prized in Renaissance princes – that of magnanimity. (c. 1570; National Gallery, London)

Kid, Thomas *see* Kyd (*or* Kid), Thomas.

Klonowic, Sebastian Fabian (c. 1545–1602) Polish poet. Klonowic was born in Sulmierzyce but worked mainly in Lublin, where he was a teacher and held civic offices and described the social life of a Polish town in his satirical and descriptive verse. He wrote in both Latin and Polish; his major works in the former are *Roxolania* (1584) and the allegory *Victoria deorum* (1587), and in the latter *Flis* (1595) and *Worek Judaszów* (1600).

Knights Hospitaller (Knights of the Order of the Hospital of St John of Jerusalem) A religious order founded in the eleventh century in the Holy Land for the medical care and armed defence of pilgrims. After the fall of Acre (1291) the order moved first to Cyprus and then settled in Rhodes (1309), which they held with superlative military skill against repeated Muslim attacks until 1522, when the victorious Suleiman the Magnificent allowed them to withdraw to Crete. They then established themselves on Malta (1530), where they withstood a famous siege by the Ottoman fleet in 1565. The Knights' military prowess was a key factor in checking Ottoman naval expansionism in the Mediterranean for nearly three centuries.

Knights of Malta *see* Knights Hospitaller.

Knights of Rhodes *see* Knights Hospitaller.

Knights Templar A military religious order founded in 1118 in Jerusalem to protect the holy places against the Muslims. Following the fall of Jerusalem (1187) to Saladin the Templars continued to fight until the Christians were ejected from the Holy Land after the siege of Acre (1291), in which the master of the order was killed. Meanwhile the order prospered to the extent that their headquarters in London and Paris were repositories of immense wealth. This brought upon them the envy of the French monarchs, who, on a series of trumped-up charges, persuaded Pope Clement V to suppress the order at the Council of Vienne in 1312.

Knox, John (c. 1513–72) Scottish religious reformer. Although trained at Glasgow for the Catholic priesthood Knox converted to Protestantism in the 1540s. He was a preacher at St Andrews when the town was attacked by the French and suffered two years' imprisonment. On his release he became a leading figure in Edward VI's religious reforms in England (1549–53) but fled to Geneva on *Mary I's accession. While there he published *The First Blast of the Trumpet against the Monstrous Regiment of Women* (1558), a violent attack on Mary of Guise's regency in Scotland, and the following year he returned to Scotland to join the fight against Catholicism, particularly as represented by Mary of Guise and her daughter *Mary, Queen of Scots. In 1560, in the terms of the Scottish Confession, Knox shaped the moderate Calvinist doctrines of the Church of Scotland. After Mary, Queen of Scots had to abdicate (1567), Knox, with the support of the regent, the Earl of Moray, directed Scotland's religious affairs and the organization of the Church of Scotland on democratic lines.

Koch, Jodocus *see* Jonas, Justus.

Kochanowski, Jan (Johannes Cochanovius; 1530–84) Polish poet. A native of Sycyn, Kochanowski was educated at Cracow and Padua. He then visited Königsberg and Paris, meeting *Ronsard in the latter. He returned to Poland (1559) with a thorough knowledge of classical and Italian literature and a sympathy with the Renaissance literary ideals, which until then he had expressed only in accomplished Latin verse. His *Foricoena*, not published until 1584, dates from this period, as do his Latin lyrics and elegies. Attaching himself to the court, where he attained (1567) the position of royal secretary, Kochanowski began to write in Polish as well as Latin. His *Szachy* (?1566) is based on the mock-heroic *Scacchia Ludus* by *Vida. In 1570 he retired from the court to settle on an estate at Czarnolas, where he farmed and wrote some of the masterpieces of Renaissance Polish verse; his work refined the language, exercising a formative influence upon the vernacular and upon later poets. *Treny* (1580) is a cycle of laments for his infant daughter Urszula (died 1579). *Fraski* (Trifles; 1584) is a collection of sparkling epigrams. *Pieśni* (Songs; 1586) is much influenced by the odes of Horace, as are his lyrical renderings of the psalms. He wrote one verse play, *Odprawa posłów greckich* (The Dismissal of the Greek Envoys: 1578) based on an incident in the third book of the *Iliad* and modelled on the lines of classical Greek tragedy.

Kolman family *see* Helmschmied (*or* Kolman) family.

Kraf(f)t, Adam (c. 1460–1508/09) German sculptor. Kraft's work was all produced in his native Nuremberg, where he was given the most prestigious commissions. He was a close friend of Peter Vischer the Elder (*see* Vischer family). As a stone carver he worked in the late Gothic style, but with a new realism and expressiveness and particular clarity and simplicity. All these qualities are apparent in his seven reliefs of the Stations of the Cross near the entrance to St John's church (1505–08).

His best-known work is the tabernacle in the church of St Lawrence (1493–96), for which he made not only the sculptures but also the whole imaginative architectural edifice – a kind of tiered spire about 62 feet (19 metres) high. Among the numerous figures of humans and animals decorating it are portraits of Kraft and two apprentices, kneeling and supporting the base of the structure.

Krump(p)er, Hans (c. 1570–1634) German sculptor, architect, and painter. Born at Weilheim, he joined the court of Duke Wilhelm V in Munich in 1584, and became a pupil of the sculptor Hubert *Gerhard. He was sent to Italy to complete his training (1590–92). In 1599 he succeeded Friedrich *Sustris as court architect and artistic director (having already married his daughter). Wilhelm's successor, Duke Maximilian I, appointed him also court painter (1609), although Krumper's chief assignment at this time was to oversee the alterations to the Munich palace (the Residenz). He worked in the mannerist style, producing not only sculpture, but also many designs for goldsmiths (lamps, altars, reliquaries, etc.).

Kulmbach, Hans Suess von (1475/80–1522) German painter. About 1500 he left his native Kulmbach for Nuremberg, where he studied in Dürer's workshop and was also influenced by the visiting Venetian artist Jacopo de' Barbari. In 1511 Kulmbach obtained citizenship of his adopted town and became an independent artist. As a young man, he collaborated with Dürer in designing woodcuts, and after 1508 he designed numerous stained-glass windows. When Dürer gave up the execution of altarpieces in 1510, Kulmbach emerged as a major painter of triptychs. Of his dozen or so altarpieces, three were exported to Cracow in Poland. He also painted a number of portraits of considerable charm. Next to *Baldung, Kulmbach was Dürer's most important pupil, with a personal style quite distinct from that of his master.

Kyd (*or* **Kid**), **Thomas** (1558–94) English playwright. Kyd was the son of a London scrivener, who sent him to the Merchant Taylors' school (1565); he seems, for a time at least, to have followed his father's profession, though the details of his life are obscure and what information there is often derives from the gossip of Kyd's contemporaries on the London literary scene. His claim to fame is the Senecan-based *Spanish Tragedy* (1594). It was probably written in the middle of the decade 1582–92 and ushered in the Elizabethan vogue for revenge tragedies. The melodramatic plot, violent actions, overwrought emotions, and murderous finale, along with such devices as the madness of the hero, appealed strongly to the contemporary audience, both in England and on the Continent; the play is also well constructed and its hero, Jeronimo, is a genuinely moving figure. Kyd also wrote a tragedy on the subject of Cornelia (1594), and *Soliman and Perseda* (c. 1592) is ascribed to him. His connection with the so-called Ur-Hamlet (*see Hamlet*) has aroused much speculation.

L

Labé, Louise (c. 1524–c. 1566) French poet. The beautiful wife of a wealthy ropemaker (*cordier*), Louise Labé was nicknamed "La Belle Cordière". She was also an accomplished horsewoman, skilled in swordsmanship: one of the many legends attached to her alleged that in her adventurous youth she had ridden to war disguised as a soldier. She was a member of the group of poets, led by Maurice *Scève, that flourished in her native Lyons in the sixteenth century. Her poetic works, published in 1555, comprise three elegies and twenty-four sonnets, which express with intense passion and realism, inspired by personal experience, the joys and anguish of love. She also wrote the prose *Débat de Folie et d'Amour.*

La Boétie, Étienne de (1530–63) French magistrate and man of letters. La Boétie was born at Sarlat and became a colleague of *Montaigne in the *parlement de Bordeaux:* their acquaintance developed into a close friendship that was to have a profound influence on Montaigne's life and works. La Boétie is remembered for his *Discours sur la servitude volontaire* or *Contr'un* ("Against One"), an antimonarchical treatise written in his youth and published posthumously in 1576; his other works include translations of Xenophon and Plutarch, the *Mémoire sur l'édit de janvier,* demanding nonviolent Catholic reform, and a number of sonnets stylistically influenced by *Ronsard. La Boétie's premature death, the result of a bout of dysentery, was movingly described by Montaigne in a letter to his father, his first published work.

Lafreri, Antonio (Antoine Lafréry; 1512–77) French-born Italian engraver and publisher. Born in Orgelet, Lafreri settled in Rome as an engraver (1544), but by 1553 had moved into publishing. A particularly sumptuous production was his *Speculum Romanae magnificentiae* (1575), but he was also known for his output of prints by Marcantonio *Raimondi. Lafreri had the idea of binding sheet maps by various cartographers into a single volume according to the individual customer's requirements; these compilations, of which no two are exactly the same, are known generically as Lafreri atlases, although other publishers in Rome and Venice were naturally quick to take up this profitable scheme. Lafreri's own imprint occurs on a number of such atlases issued between 1556 and 1572, the later ones under the title of *Tavole moderne di geografia.*

Laib, Konrad (fl. c. 1431–60) German painter. Laib was born in Swabia and is recorded as working in Nördlingen in 1431; he moved to Salzburg around 1440. An early German proponent of the realistic style, he established this style in Salzburg. His realism is apparent in his depiction of the folds of fabric and reflections in polished metal, and particularly in his portraiture and interest in facial expression. His ability to portray individuals is seen, for example, in his portrait of Emperor Sigismund (c. 1437) and in the crowds of figures in his altar panels (e.g. the Viennese *Crucifixion* of 1449).

Lamb, Adoration of the (*or* **The Mystic Lamb**) *see* Ghent altarpiece.

Lambert, Francis (1486–1530) French-born religious reformer. The son of a papal official at Avignon, Lambert joined the Franciscan Order there (1507) and became famous as a preacher. After 1517 he travelled through France, Italy, and Switzerland, and his study of the Bible and the religious reformers he encountered caused him to abandon his order and travel to Wittenberg (1523), where he was assisted by *Luther. Moving to Strasbourg (1524) he met such hostility that he was forced to move on. In 1526 he was summoned to Hesse by the landgrave, Philip, who entrusted Lambert with the setting up of a reformed Church in his domains and appointed him as professor of exegesis at his new university of Marburg (1527). In 1529 Lambert openly adopted the Zwinglian line in the debate over the Eucharist, thus alienating his Lutheran supporters. The following year he died of the plague, leaving a number of works that include a polemic against Erasmus (1525) and commentaries on the Song of Songs (1524) and the Book of Revelation (1528).

Landini, Francesco (Francesco Landino; c. 1325–97) Italian composer. A Florentine by birth, Landini was a leading exponent of the *ars nova.*

Although he was blind (and was therefore referred to by contemporaries as "il Cieco"), he was famous as an organist and also played the lute and other instruments. He spent most of his life in Florence but also visited Venice, where he was highly acclaimed. As a composer he is remarkable for his madrigals and *caccie*, both forms that later underwent considerable development.

Landino, Cristoforo (1424–92) Italian humanist scholar. Born in Florence, Landino was one of the group of able men who gathered round Lorenzo de' *Medici in the *Platonic Academy. He became professor of poetry and rhetoric (1457), and later of Latin literature, a post which he held until his death. He published commentaries on Virgil and Horace and translated Pliny's *Natural History*. His edition of Dante (1481) and lectures on Petrarch reveal the humanist interest in vernacular literature which seemed to measure up to classical standards. His *Camaldolese Disputations* (?1480), a dialogue modelled on the *Tusculan Disputations* of Cicero, gives an intimate glimpse of the kind of discussion engaged in by members of the Florentine academy. The poetry of Virgil is one of the main topics, but the interpretations are still those of the medieval allegorists. The other subjects discussed, for example the comparative advantages of the active and the contemplative life, show the extent to which classical concepts permeated the Medicean circle.

landsknechts *see under* mercenaries.

Languet, Hubert (1518–81) French writer and diplomat. Born at Vitteaux in Burgundy, he was educated by Jean Perrelle, a distinguished Greek scholar, and then studied at Poitiers (1536–39), Bologna, and Padua. In 1549, after meeting *Melanchthon at Wittenberg, he became a Protestant. He travelled widely in Europe before entering the service (1559) of Augustus I, Elector of Saxony, whom he represented at the French court (1561–72). He narrowly escaped the *Massacre of St Bartholomew and later served Augustus at the imperial court (1573–77) before retiring to the Netherlands and dying at Antwerp. Languet's extensive correspondence is a valuable source for sixteenth-century history; among his friends and correspondents was Sir Philip *Sidney. The anonymous *Vindicia contra tyrannos* (1579) expounding the doctrine of resistance to tyranny by constitutional means, is attributed to him, but this attribution is still disputed. He may also have helped *William the Silent draft his *Apologia* against the king of Spain (1581).

La Noue, François de (1531–91) French soldier and writer. La Noue was born in Nantes and converted to Protestantism in 1558. He fought on the *Huguenot side in the wars of religion; his nickname "Bras de Fer" ("Iron Arm") derived from the replacment "arm" he wore after an injury sustained in battle. Following the *Massacre of St Bartholomew he spent four years in the Huguenot defence at La Rochelle. Fighting against the Spanish in the Netherlands La Noue was captured and imprisoned for five years; he used this enforced leisure to reflect on his military career in *Discours politiques et militaires* (1587), a patriotic account of France's problems, advocating reconciliation between Catholics and Protestants, combined with his personal memoirs as a soldier. On his return to France La Noue entered the service of Henry IV and died in action.

Larivey, Pierre (c. 1540–1619) French playwright. Of Italian extraction, Larivey was born in Champagne. He was responsible for the introduction of Italian Renaissance comedy into France through his versions of nine plays by various Italian authors. Six (*Le Laquais*, *La Veuve*, *Les Esprits*, *Le Morfundu*, *Les Jaloux*, *Les Écoliers*) were published in 1579 and a further three in 1611.

Las Casas, Bartolomé de (1474–1566) Spanish priest. Las Casas was born in Seville and studied law before being ordained (c. 1510). In Cuba from 1512 onwards he quickly became incensed at the conquistadores' treatment of the Indians. From 1514 he devoted his life to the preservation of Indian rights, pleading their cause before the king (1515) and publishing books in their defence. Most of Las Casas's humanitarian schemes failed because of Spanish opposition and because he had overestimated the capabilities of the Indians, as highlighted by the failure of his model colony at Cumuná, Venezuela. Established in 1520, Cumuná was destroyed by an Indian revolt one year later. Back in Spain he advised the Council of the Indies (1539–44), obtaining several decrees protecting the Indians. His tenure of the Mexican bishopric of Chiapas (1544–47) was rendered impossible by local Spanish hostility. In 1550 he had a famous debate with the humanist scholar Ginés de Sepúlveda (?1490–?1573) concerning exploitation of aboriginal populations.

Lassus, Orlando (1532–94) Franco-Flemish composer. Lassus was born in Mons, and at the age of twelve he entered the service of Ferrante Gonzaga, a general in the service of Charles V. Lassus accompanied him to Mantua, Sicily, and Milan, and then went to Naples and Rome, becoming *maestro di cappella* at the church of St John Lateran in 1553. A year later he left to visit his parents and in 1555 was in Antwerp. In 1556 he was appointed as a singer at the court of Duke Albrecht V in Munich, and in 1563 took over the post of *Kapellmeister*, which he held until his death. Lassus's duties here included a wide range of liturgical responsibilities, as well as music for such special occasions as state visits, banquets, and hunting parties. In the years following his appointment he travelled much, often at the invitation of kings and dukes, and was received with high honour; in 1574 he received the Knighthood of the Golden Spur from Pope Gregory VIII. His works were published in Venice, Antwerp, Paris, Frankfurt, and Munich, and were widely disseminated. Lassus was a prolific and versatile composer; his compositions embrace all sixteenth-century forms of vocal music from drinking songs to Masses. About 200 Italian madrigals and villanelles, 150 chansons, and ninety German lieder survive of his secular music, which covers a wide range of moods; Lassus was a master in all three styles. He was most prolific in motet composition; over 500 survive, in which both liturgical and nonliturgical texts are set. As in all Lassus's music, the words of the motets generate most of the expressive content of the composition. The largest collection of motets is the posthumous *Magnum opus musicum* (1604). Around sixty Masses, 101 Magnificats, and numerous other liturgical works survive, in which Lassus's skilful counterpoint, rhetorical treatment of the text, and succinct manner are demonstrated to great effect. He was more cosmopolitan than his great contemporary *Palestrina, and their musical styles differ considerably.

Last Supper (*Cenacolo*) A major work by *Leonardo da Vinci, executed in the refectory of Sta Maria delle Grazie, Milan, between 1495 and 1497. One of Leonardo's most important paintings, the *Last Supper* differed from the numerous earlier treatments of the same subject by concentrating on the psychological content at the moment that Christ reveals that one among the present company will betray him. The figures of the apostles themselves were based upon some of Leonardo's contemporaries. Because Leonardo chose to paint with oil directly onto the plaster, the painting deteriorated rapidly, even within Leonardo's own lifetime, and suffered further from inadequate restoration in the eighteenth and nineteenth centuries – as well as from damage in the Napoleonic wars, in World War II, and from the monks themselves, who cut a door through it. Nonetheless, the painting effectively launched the High Renaissance and has been properly restored in recent years.

La Taille, Jean de (c. 1535–c. 1607) French dramatist. La Taille, like his younger brother Jacques (1542–62), also a playwright, was born at Bondaroy. He is notable for having written vernacular religious tragedies in the style of Seneca – *Saül le furieux* (1572) and *La Famine, ou les Gibéonites* (1573) – and an influential treatise on dramatic theory, *De l'art de la tragédie* (1572), in which Aristotelian principles are expounded. Of his prose comedies, *Le Négromant* is a translation from Ariosto.

Latin studies Throughout the Middle Ages Latin remained the language of the Church, used for a variety of purposes. It was also the language of polite literature, certainly until the tenth or eleventh century when the vernacular languages first began to be used in a self-consciously artistic way. Medieval Latin had developed its own characteristics which made it a distinct language, and the rediscovery of the classical Latin writers gradually influenced humanists and scholars in their own use of Latin. The letters of *Petrarch show evidence that he had begun to assimilate the style of the recently discovered Ciceronian correspondence. For the first generation of Italian humanists, work on Latin authors took second place as a rule to the work of editing Greek texts and translating them (into Latin), but as the fifteenth century went on scholars became more anxious about their personal standards of Latinity. Latin gradually ceased to be a living language used with flexibility and variety and became increasingly restricted by an artificial canon of rules formulated from the works of Cicero. *Erasmus did much by ridicule and by example to weaken the influence of this Ciceronianism, but the classical writers remained models for imitation and criteria by which contemporary products were judged.

The study of classical Latin literature itself began with work on the interpretation of texts. The earliest humanists regarded classical Latin authors as in some sense contemporaries; Petrarch responded to the revelations of the weaknesses in Cicero's character which followed the discovery (1345) of the letters to Atticus as if responding to the discovery that a trusted friend had feet of clay. This sense of the contemporaneity of classical authors passed into a desire to produce the most accurate texts, to treat Latin authors as testimony to a remote past. This is an important aspect of that historical sense which so sharply distinguished the later Renaissance from the Middle Ages. The second half of the fifteenth and the sixteenth century saw the skills of textual analysis refined (*see* criticism, textual); Lorenzo *Valla's demonstration (1440) that the Donation of Constantine was a forgery depended on a very accurate knowledge of Latin usage in the fourth century AD. Work of this kind led finally to the encyclopedic editions of Latin authors produced by Casaubon, Scaliger, and others. Latin became the language of scholarship and ceased to evolve except within a very limited sphere. Once the styles of ancient Latin authors were more fully appreciated and understood, the next stage was the investigation of the material remains of the Roman world, and the late sixteenth- and seventeenth-century editions embodied the latest researches in archaeology, numismatics, and legal and religious history.

Latin also continued to be used as a medium for creative writing, and an immense quantity of Latin verse was produced by Renaissance writers on every conceivable subject. The writings of *Bembo, *Fracastoro, *Sannazaro, and *Sadoleto, to name but four, show the extent to which the Latin language could be exploited by humanist poets. Often a scholar's international reputation depended on his skill as a versifier; *Buchanan in Scotland and Milton in England are examples of writers whose Latin poems reached a European audience. The Latin eclogues (1498) of Mantuan (*Spagnoli) were a crucial influence upon the development of *pastoral poetry in the vernacular throughout Europe.

Laurana, Francesco (c. 1430–c. 1502) Dalmatian sculptor. Laurana was born at Zara, but little is known of his early life. He produced works in Italy, France, and Sicily, sometimes in collaboration with his relative Luciano *Laurana. He is first recorded as working on the triumphal arch of Alfonso I at Castelnuovo in Naples (1453), after which he moved to the court of *René of Anjou, for whom he executed some notable medals. Laurana is best known, however, for a series of portrait busts of women connected with the royal house of Naples, including those of Battista Sforza (Bargello, Florence) and Beatrice of Aragon (Kunsthistorisches Museum, Vienna). Besides these, he also produced a number of reliefs and worked on the Mastrantonio chapel at the church of S Francesco in Palermo, Sicily (1468).

Laurana, Luciano (c. 1422–79) Dalmatian architect. A relative of the sculptor Francesco *Laurana, Luciano was born at Lo Vrana, near Zara, and is first recorded as working in Urbino in about 1465. By 1468 he had been appointed principal architect on the construction of the ducal palace of Urbino, which became the site of his best work. Laurana was responsible for the courtyard of the palace and the façade, which resembled the triumphal arch of Alfonso I at Castelnuovo in Naples, upon which he may have worked in the 1450s. The palace at Urbino was later completed by the Sienese architect *Francesco di Giorgio and is known to have inspired Bramante.

Laurenziana, Bibliotheca A library in Florence, formerly the library of the Medici family. The library was built to house the valuable collection of books and manuscripts founded by Cosimo de' Medici and enlarged by other members of the Medici family in the fifteenth and sixteenth centuries. It was opened to the public in 1571. The library building was designed by *Michelangelo for Pope Clement VII (Giulio de' Medici) in 1523 in the cloisters of the church of S Lorenzo and includes such features as a carved ceiling, mosaic floor, and carved benches all made to Michelangelo's designs. The library's staircase was completed by Bartolommeo *Ammanati and Giorgio *Vasari in 1559. Among the library's 10 000 manuscripts are some of the most important surviving classical texts, including a fifth-century copy of Virgil, and the oldest complete Latin Bible known, the eighth-century Codex Amiatinus. In 1808 the Medici library at the convent of S Marco (*see* Marciana, Bibliotheca) was combined with the Laurenziana to form the present Bibliotheca Medicea Laurenziana.

Lazarillo de Tormes An episodic narrative published in 1554 (though evidence suggests there may have been an earlier edition). It is remarkable for its social satire, and its scathing anticlerical passages caused it to be put on the Index in 1559, but its continued popularity was such that Philip II authorized an expurgated edition in 1573 (*Lazarillo castigado*). Authorship has never been determined; among the candidates proposed are Fray Juan de Ortega, Diego de *Hurtado de Mendoza, and the brothers *Valdés. The tale relates the adventures of Lázaro, a boy from the dregs of society. He learns the art of survival as he moves from one corrupt or deluded master to another: as helper to a blind beggar who starves him, as altar-boy to a priest who is even meaner, as servant to an impoverished *hidalgo*, and so on. The hero ends, optimistic and contented, as a towncrier in Toledo married to the mistress of an archpriest – in other words, in a dismally low position and a cuckold. The book introduced the realistic autobiographical narrative and is thus the forerunner of the *picaresque novel. It was translated into English in 1586.

Lebrija, Elio Antonio de *see* Nebrija, Elio Antonio de.

Lefèvre d'Étaples, Jacques (Faber Stapulensis; c. 1453–1536) French humanist and theologian. Born at Étaples, Lefèvre became a priest and a

LUCIANO LAURANA
The courtyard of the Palazzo Ducale, Urbino, on which Laurana began work in the late 1460s.

teacher of philosophy in Paris. He visited Italy in the late fifteenth century and embarked on the study of Greek classics, translating and editing some of the works of Aristotle. Around 1505 he was teaching Greek in Paris. He subsequently turned his attention to the scriptures, publishing his *Commentaires sur les épîtres de Saint Paul* in 1512; by 1530 he had completed the first French translation of the Bible. Lefèvre's approach to religion and to the study of biblical texts made him a leader of the pre-Reformation movement in France and an enemy of the Sorbonne; in 1525 he was forced to abandon his post as vicar-general to the bishop of Meaux and take temporary refuge in Strasbourg. After a brief period of service as tutor to the children of Francis I he retired to Nérac, where he enjoyed the protection of *Marguerite de Navarre for the last five years of his life.

Leicester, Robert Dudley, Earl of (?1532–88) English nobleman, courtier, and soldier. He was the fifth son of the duke of Northumberland and shared his family's disgrace over the abortive attempt (1553) of his sister-in-law, Lady Jane Grey, to ascend the throne. Mary I however pardoned him, and on the accession of Elizabeth I he rapidly rose in royal favour, becoming a strong contender for the queen's hand. In 1560 his wife Amy Robsart died from a fall in suspicious circumstances; rumour had it that Dudley was implicated in her death to facilitate his marriage with the queen. This

marriage was now out of the question, but he nonetheless remained a royal favourite and Elizabeth created him earl of Leicester in 1564.

Leicester was a generous patron of writers, particularly those with a strongly Protestant, even Puritan, bias; his nephew *Sidney, *Spenser, and Edward Dyer were the most distinguished of his literary protégés. He was also a patron of *Hilliard, apparently promoted Federico *Zuccaro's visit to England, and sat for his portrait over a dozen times. His anti-Catholic policies embroiled him in the catastrophic expedition (1585–87) to aid the Dutch against their Spanish Habsburg overlords (*see* Netherlands, Revolt of the). By his marriage (1578) to Lettice, widow of the 1st earl of Essex, he became stepfather to Robert Devereux, Earl of *Essex.

Leipzig A central German city where Germans were settled in the later Middle Ages. After obtaining municipal status (1170), Leipzig prospered on account of its position on important trade routes. Its two annual markets, which became imperial fairs in 1497, and further commercial privileges from the empire ensured continuing prosperity during the period of the Renaissance, especially from the fur trade. By the sixteenth century Leipzig was known for its publishing and for its annual book fairs. Its university (founded 1409) was known for its humanist and Greek studies by 1500. In 1519 Leipzig was the site of the famous disputation between *Luther and *Eck. Many historic landmarks were restored after World War II.

Leipzig, Interim of (1548) Articles of religion imposed on his subjects by Maurice, Elector of Saxony. It was a Lutheran modification of the *Augsburg Interim, intended to preserve the unity of the Church until the disputed doctrines should be resolved by the Council of Trent. This compromise was abandoned at the Peace of Augsburg in 1555.

Leo X (1475–1521) Pope (1513–21) Born Giovanni de' Medici at Florence, the second son of Lorenzo the Magnificent, he received a humanistic education from Ficino, Politian, and Pico della Mirandola and studied canon law at Pisa (1489–91). In 1492 he became a cardinal and went to live in Rome. Lorenzo's death recalled him to Florence the same year, but he was exiled with the rest of his family (1494). After travelling in Europe he returned to Rome (1500) and in 1503 he became the head of the Medici family. The revolution of 1512 allowed the Medici to return to Florence and in 1513, aged only thirty-seven, Giovanni was elected pope. He was thus able to gratify his humanistic tastes, patronizing scholars and artists and spending papal wealth lavishly on the construction of St Peter's and on the accumulation of books and manuscripts.

One of Leo's concerns was the removal of foreign influence from Italy; this was initially achieved by the victory of Novara (1513) over the French, but the death of Louis XII with the accession of Francis I brought fresh hostilities. These were resolved through negotiation; by the Bull Primitiva (1516) relations between the French monarchy and the papacy were regulated and the concordat agreed at Bologna that year remained in force until 1789. The most significant event of Leo's papacy was the attack by Luther on the Roman Catholic Church, inspired by the sale of indulgences to cover the ever-increasing costs of the papacy. Leo excommunicated Luther in 1521. One of Leo's last acts was to confer the title "Defender of the Faith" on Henry VIII of England for his stance against Luther.

León, Fray Luis de see Luis de León, Fray.

Leonardo da Vinci (1452–1519) Italian painter. Vasari justly began the third part of his *Lives* (the High Renaissance section) with Leonardo, commenting that the artist "endowed his figures with motion and breath." Leonardo was born at Anchiano, the illegitimate child of a notary, Piero da Vinci, and a peasant woman, Caterina. By 1469 Leonardo, his father, and stepmother, had moved to Florence, where, because of his aptitude in drawing, Leonardo was apprenticed to the studio of *Verrocchio. He became a member of guild of St Luke in 1472; about the same time he painted portions of Verrocchio's *Baptism of Christ* (Uffizi). The kneeling angel in the left foreground displays the young artist's deft handling of colour and brush. Other early works traditionally attributed to Leonardo include the *Annunciation* (c. 1474; Uffizi) and the portrait of Ginevra de' Benci (c. 1474 or c. 1480; National Gallery of Art, Washington). The Benois *Madonna* (c. 1478; Hermitage, Leningrad) reveals a figurative animation which will characterize his later paintings.

Leonardo's first major independent commission was the *Adoration of the Magi* (Uffizi), begun in 1481, for the monastery of S Donato a Scopeto outside Florence. The unfinished panel contains only the underdrawing with areas of light and shadow indicated; among the preliminary studies is a fine linear perspective study for the architecture of the left background (Uffizi). The composition of the *Adoration of the Magi* features a pyramidal grouping of Mary, the Christ Child, and the three Magi surrounded by a semicircular gathering of worshippers. The predilection for geometrical compositions reveals Leonardo's belief, common in the Renaissance, that mathematics and geometry "embrace everything in the universe". While he was working on the *Adoration* panel, Leonardo began to experiment with a more fully activated *contrapposto* figure, counterpositioning the shoulders and legs to create a vigorous movement. Leonardo's invention, explored in a drawing of *St Sebastian* (Kunsthalle, Hamburg), would be known in the sixteenth century as *figura serpentinata* (serpentine figure), and would have great impact, especially on Michelangelo, who, like Leonardo, saw figurative movement as reflecting psychological life. Another unfinished work from this period is the painting of *St Jerome* (Vatican museum, Rome).

Around 1482 Leonardo left Florence to seek employment at the court of Lodovico Sforza "il Moro" in Milan. A draft of his letter to Duke Lodovico survives; the areas in which Leonardo cites expertise include the construction of bridges and irrigation canals, the designing of military weapons, and architecture, as well as painting and sculpture. He offers to construct the colossal bronze equestrian monument which Lodovico desired to have made in memory of his father Francesco. Leonardo entered the service of Lodovico, directing festivals, displaying his talent as a musician, working on architectural projects, and studying anatomy and painting; one portrait, known as the *Lady with an Ermine*, is of Cecilia Gallerani, Lodovico's young mistress (c. 1483; Czartoryski museum, Cracow). Two paintings from this time pose particular problems regarding their mutual relationship, an early *Madonna of the Rocks* (c. 1484; Louvre) and a later copy of the same painting (c. 1488, perhaps reworked c. 1506; National Gallery, London); the extent of Leonardo's hand in the London painting is uncertain. The Louvre painting skilfully demonstrates Leonardo's use of *sfumato*, a subtle modelling revealed through a thin veil of atmosphere, delicately blending the lines and colours. From 1495 to 1497 Leonardo worked on the *Last Supper in the refectory of Sta Maria della Grazie, Milan, a composition that exemplifies the ideals of High Renaissance art, with its convincing illusionism, heroic scale, and psychological reactions displayed by the apostles to Christ's prophecy of immiment betrayal. It embodies Leonardo's maxim: "Painted figures ought to be done in such a way that those who see them will be able to easily recognize from their attitudes the thoughts of their minds."

Leonardo left Milan in 1499 just after French troops entered the city to put an end to the rule of Lodovico Sforza. He travelled to Mantua and Venice, but by April 1500 was back in Florence, where, in 1503, he had his name reinscribed in the roll of guild painters. The brilliant maturity of Leonardo's art was, according to Vasari, viewed by excited crowds of Florentines who were astonished at his cartoon of the *Virgin and Christ Child with St Anne* (now lost). The cartoon was probably similar to the Burlington House cartoon of the *Virgin and Child with St Anne* (1500–05; National Gallery, London) and the panel of the *Virgin and Child with St Anne* (c. 1508; Louvre); both works displayed a masterful command of modelling, creating in illusory forms the palpability of sculpture. During this Florentine period Leonardo painted *Mona Lisa, whom Vasari identified as the wife of Francesco del Giocondo. Vasari praised the portrait for its naturalism; only in the nineteenth century did critics begin to read personal psychological revelations in the picture. From 1503 to 1505 Leonardo worked on the *Battle of Anghiari* (now lost, although studies for it survive) for the Sala del Gran Consiglio of the Palazzo Vecchio; Michelangelo, in 1504, was contracted to paint an adjoining fresco in the same council hall. Between 1506 and 1513 Leonardo worked in both Florence and Milan; he journeyed to Rome in 1513. A late work, *St John the Baptist* (c. 1515; Louvre) is perhaps his most enigmatic; the intense *chiaroscuro* is prophetic of later baroque painting.

For Leonardo, art as he wrote, "truly is a science." Nowhere is his belief observed more completely than in the over 3500 surviving pages of his notebooks, which contain detailed observations on the widest variety of natural phenomena, including mathematics, perspective, modelling, colour, optics, anatomy, painting media, sculpture, philosophy, architecture and urban planning, astronomy, engineering, and the earth sciences. Visual form was given to his observations and ideas in numerous drawings which, more than any other medium, express the freedom of his mind, the subtlety of his observing eye, and the talent of his hand. In 1516 Leonardo travelled to France at the invitation of Francis I. Among the projects he proposed to the French king was a scheme for regulating the waters of the Loire. He died at Clos-Luce, near Amboise, in the manor given to him by Francis.

Leone Ebreo (Judah Abarbanel; ?1465–?1530) Portuguese Jewish philosopher and physician. The son of Isaac *Abarbanel, he was born in Lisbon and lived in Toledo from 1483 until the expulsion of the Jews from Spain in 1492. He then practised as a physician in several Italian towns and fell under the influence of *Pico della Mirandola. Around 1502 he wrote, probably in Spanish or Hebrew, his *Dialoghi di amore*, first published in an Italian translation in 1535. It was soon translated into Latin and became a highly influential text for Christian Neoplatonists throughout Europe, with its doctrine that "in God the lover, the beloved, and their love are all one and the same," and that love, identified with God, is the principle underlying and animating the universe. Leone Ebreo died in Naples.

Leoni, Leone (c. 1509–90) Italian sculptor, engraver, and goldsmith. Leoni was born at Arezzo and trained as a goldsmith, but none of his work in that medium has survived. He is best known for his bronze portraits and funerary monuments and for his medals of patrons, rulers, and artists such as Michelangelo. He is said to have rivalled *Cellini, not only in his work but also in the notoriety of his personal life. Leoni first worked in Venice and then in Rome, where he was coin engraver at the papal mint (1537–40). He held the same post at the mint in Milan from 1542. As court sculptor and medallist to Emperor Charles V (from 1546; see p. 240) Leoni travelled to Germany and Brussels, besides attending the emperor on his visits to Italy. Later he executed portraits of Philip II of Spain, Empress Isabella, and Maria of Portugal and collaborated with his son Pompeo *Leoni on statuary for the *Escorial. His sculptural style was one of strong elegant naturalism. He spent the last years of his life at his base in Milan, where the tomb of Gian Giacomo de' Medici in the cathedral (1560–62) is an example of his work.

Leoni, Pompeo (?1531–1608) Italian sculptor, goldsmith, and medallist. Like his father, Leone *Leoni, Pompeo is best known for his funerary

LEONE LEONI *Statue of Charles V suppressing Tumult, made in Augsburg after Charles's victory at Mühlberg. Like the Roman emperor Augustus, whose feat was praised by Virgil, Charles conquers "Furor" and binds him with brazen chains. (c. 1548; Prado, Madrid)*

monuments and his expressive sculpture portraits. He spent much of his life in Spain finishing bronze statues that had been cast and sent to him from Milan by his father. He also produced his own work for Spanish princes and cardinals and for his patron Philip II. The church of the *Escorial contains his most famous sculptures, the larger-than-life-size bronze statues flanking the main altar.

Lepanto, Battle of (7 October 1571) A naval battle fought off Lepanto, in the Gulf of Corinth, in which the forces of the *Holy League, commanded by Don John of Austria (half-brother of Philip II of Spain), defeated the *Ottoman Turks

under Ali Pasha, governor of Alexandria. The dominant naval power in the Mediterranean for thirty years, the Turks had invaded Cyprus, Venice's wealthiest colony, in 1570. Spain joined Venice and the pope in the Holy League (1571), contributing respectively a half, a third, and a sixth of the forces, and, fired by crusading zeal against the infidel, the Christian fleet sought out the Turks in their home waters. The fleets, at 300 ships apiece, were roughly equal in strength; the Turks lost about 117, the Christians between fifteen and twenty. The victory was widely celebrated as proof that the Turks were not invincible, but the practical results were minimal: the Turks built another fleet and retained control of Cyprus, which the Venetians formally surrendered in 1573. See Plate XV.

Lescot, Pierre (c. 1510–78) French architect. Born into a wealthy family of lawyers, Lescot probably never visited Italy but became acquainted with classical ideals through books and study of Roman ruins in France. He executed his most famous work at the *Louvre, where he designed a square court known as the Cour Carrée (1546–51). His final design combined classical and traditional French features and was further embellished with low-relief sculptures by Jean *Goujon; it was completed under Claude Perrault in the seventeenth century. Other major works included the Fontaine des Innocents (1547–49) in Paris and the Hôtel de Ligneris (now the Musée Carnavalet; 1545). Other works, which exercised an important influence upon subsequent French design and decoration, have been largely destroyed.

Leto, Pomponio Giulio (Julius Pomponius Laetus; 1428–98) Italian humanist. Born in Calabria, an illegitimate member of the Sanseverini family, he was educated by *Valla. He was a dedicated Latinist, refusing even to learn Greek, and he deliberately cultivated an antique lifestyle, with his behaviour modelled on the life of Cato the Elder. Leto was the moving spirit behind the *Roman Academy which developed in imitation of the more famous one in Florence. The academy was accused of being a conspiracy to overthrow the papal administration (1468) but Leto escaped serious punishment and the academy revived under Sixtus IV. Leto's main influence was as a lecturer and as an example of how far enthusiasm for the ancient world would carry the humanists.

Leyden A city in the Netherlands. Leyden grew up around a twelfth-century castle. During the Renaissance period prosperity came to the city through the textile industry, which was first developed in the fourteenth century by weavers from

Ypres and greatly expanded in the late sixteenth century by refugees from the Spanish-ruled parts of the Netherlands. During the revolt of the *Netherlands Leyden bravely resisted a Spanish siege (May–October 1574) and was saved when the dykes were breached so that Dutch ships could bring supplies to the citizens across the flooded fields. In recognition of the city's heroism *William (I) the Silent founded the university of Leyden (1575) as a centre for science, medicine, and reformed theology. The classical scholar Joseph *Scaliger held a chair at the university in the late sixteenth century and Arminius, leader of the *Remonstrants, became professor of theology there (1603). After 1580 the *Elzevir press made Leyden an important centre of publishing. Van Goyen in 1596 and Rembrandt in 1609 were both born in Leyden. The Pilgrim Fathers spent some years there before sailing for New England. Landmarks from the Renaissance period include the fifteenth-century Hooglandse Kerk, the botanic gardens (1587), and the Gemeenlandshuis van Rijn (1596).

Leyden, Lucas van see Lucas van Leyden.

L'Hôpital, Michel de (1507–73) French lawyer. He became councillor of the *parlement* of Paris (1537), *Henry II's envoy to the Council of *Trent (1547), master of requests, responsible for petitions to the king (1553), president of the *chambre des comptes* (1555), and chancellor of France (1560–68). As chancellor he worked for judicial reform and joined the moderate Catholics (*politiques*) in their search for a compromise to end religious conflict. He was the author of impressive presentations of the case for religious toleration. With the resumption of the Wars of *Religion in 1567 *Catherine de' Medici lost confidence in L'Hôpital and his policy of religious toleration, so he retired to his estates and wrote. His *Epistolarum seu sermonum libri VI* appeared posthumously (1585).

Libavius, Andreas (c. 1560–1616) German chemist. Born at Halle, the son of a weaver, Libavius studied at Jena university, then worked initially as a doctor. From 1588, however, he was a teacher of history and literature, first at Jena, and thereafter at Rothenburg (1591–1607) and Coburg (1607–16). A prolific writer and controversialist, he is best known for his *Alchemia* (1597; expanded edition, entitled *Alchymia*, 1606), a work often described as the first recognizable textbook of modern chemistry. Though of little interest theoretically, it nonetheless, with over two hundred illustrations, is a prime source for the organization of the sixteenth-century chemical laboratory.

liberal arts Those arts which, according to a classification made first in antiquity, were worthy of study by a free (Latin *liber*) man. In contrast with the *artes liberales* were the *artes vulgares* (or *artes sordidae*); this roughly corresponded with the distinction between intellectual occupations and those for which slaves or trained performers were engaged. The system was further refined in the early Middle Ages by Boethius (died 524), who divided the liberal arts into the *trivium* (grammar, *rhetoric, and logic) and *quadrivium* (astronomy, geometry, music, and arithmetic). It should be noted that music featured among the liberal arts purely in its theoretical form, musical performance being in the sphere of the vulgar arts. The *trivium* and *quadrivium*, together with philosophy, underpinned the entire medieval educational system. In practice the subjects often covered a wider range of topics than their names now suggest; for instance, geography was often included under geometry and some study of literature would be part of the grammar course.

The exclusion of the arts of painting and sculpture from the liberal arts category resulted in the artist's being held in low esteem. *Leonardo da Vinci was one of the earliest to protest against this perception of the artist as a "mere" artisan; he and *Michelangelo led the way in winning proper recognition of the great artist's creative powers and raising the status of the arts of *disegno*. One reason for the enthusiasm with which the study of *perspective and proportion was pursued was that it provided the visual arts with a theoretical basis and so made them a respectable intellectual subject, like music in the medieval schools.

The liberal arts themselves were often personified during the Middle Ages, following the lead of the fifth-century AD poet Martianus Capella. They were depicted as seven ladies, each holding an identifying attribute, and often accompanied by an eminent practitioner of the art they represent, for example, Pythagoras accompanying Geometry. The full scheme can be seen in the frescoes of the Spanish chapel of Sta Maria Novella, Florence, executed in about 1355 by Andrea da Firenze and depicting the triumph of St Thomas Aquinas. Later artists also used and sometimes expanded on the scheme. *Agostino di Duccio combined the liberal arts with the Muses in his programme of reliefs for the *Tempio Malatestiano. *Pinturicchio's decorations in the Appartamento Borgia in the Vatican (1492–95) depict the seven liberal arts enthroned and attended by groups of their adherents. They also appear, with the addition of Philosophy, Theology, and "Prospettiva", on the bronze reliefs on the tomb of Sixtus IV (1493; now Museo Storico Artistico, St Peter's, Rome) by *Pollaiuolo.

Liberale, Antonio (Liberale da Verona; c. 1445–c. 1526) Italian miniaturist and painter. Liberale was born in Verona, trained as a book illuminator, and spent about a decade from the late 1460s illustrating liturgical books at Monte Oliveto Maggiore, near Siena, and in Siena itself. Some of his exquisite work in this genre, together with that of Girolamo da Cremona, by whom he was influenced, is housed in the cathedral (Piccolomini) library, Siena, and the techniques of the miniaturist are visible even in his large-scale paintings. Liberale also worked in Florence and Venice, but by 1488 was back in Verona. His *Madonna with Saints* (1489; Berlin) initiated a series of religious paintings that confirmed his standing as a major representative of the Veronese school. His Munich *Pietà* is possibly his most impressive work. Other paintings are still to be found in Verona, including an *Adoration of the Magi* (1490; Duomo). His sensitivity to the decorative qualities of architecture is apparent in his *St Sebastian* (Brera, Milan), set against the backdrop of a Venetian canal, and in his *Dido on the Pyre* (National Gallery, London).

Ligorio, Pirro (c. 1500–83) Italian architect. Born in Naples, Ligorio is best known for his work (1550–69) on the Villa d'Este at Tivoli, which he designed for his patron Cardinal Ippolito d'Este. Incorporating both landscape features and a terraced garden, Ligorio's plan shows the influence of both Bramante and Raphael and has survived largely intact. Ligorio also built (1558–62) the Casino in the Vatican gardens for Pope Pius IV, but was later dismissed as Michelangelo's successor at St Peter's after altering Michelangelo's designs (1565). He was also known as a painter and an antiquarian, although he was suspected of forging certain Roman antiquities. Several of Ligorio's buildings were also adorned with stucco decorations by him, including the Casino in the Vatican.

Ligozzi, Jacopo (c. 1547–1626) Italian painter. Ligozzi was born in Verona but moved to Florence, where he became a court painter to the Medici (1575). In this role he painted scenes from Florentine history for the Palazzo Vecchio, Florence. His paintings in Ognissanti, Florence, show his characteristic use of warm colour. He was also a fine draughtsman, noted for his detailed pen drawings, some of which are in the Ashmolean Museum, Oxford.

Lily, William (?1468–1522) English educationist. Born at Odiham, Hampshire, Lily was the godson of *Grocyn. He entered Magdalen College, Oxford (1486), graduated there, and then travelled to Jerusalem, pausing on his return journey to study Greek and Latin in Italy. He was the friend of *More, with whom he collaborated in the translation of Greek epigrams into Latin elegiacs (*Progymnasmata*, 1518) and of *Colet, who appointed him first high-master of St Paul's School, London (1512). His Latin syntax with rules in English, *Grammatices rudimenta*, was published with Colet's *Aeditio* in 1527, and in revised forms this volume was the standard Latin grammar in England for over two centuries.

Linacre, Thomas (c. 1460–1524) English physician and humanist. Linacre was born at Canterbury and educated at Oxford. He then spent several years in Italy, where he met many humanist schol-

LIGORIO *Decoration of the Casino in the Vatican (detail). Ligorio's enthusiasm for the antique Roman decorative style is manifested in his stucco and painted ornamentation.*

ars and studied Greek in Florence and medicine in Padua. To promote the revival of classical learning he translated works of Aristotle, Galen, and Proclus from Greek into Latin. He also published Latin grammars, one of which was reprinted some fifty times before the end of the sixteenth century. Linacre's own career was advanced through his service at court, first (1500–02) as tutor to Henry VII's eldest son, Arthur, and then as physician (from 1509) to Henry VIII, and finally tutor (1523) to Princess Mary. Many eminent statesmen and scholars were among his patients and friends. His most lasting contribution remains, however, his foundation (1518) of the College of Physicians, forerunner of the Royal College of Physicians.

lingua cortigiana see under Italian language; questione della lingua.

Linschoten, Jan Huyghen van (1563–1611) Dutch traveller and author. A native of Haarlem, Linschoten is famous for his epic journey to India (1583–88) as clerk to the archbishop of Goa, during which he gathered information about the lands bordering the Indian and western Pacific oceans. This was published in his Itinerario (1595–96). He also made a two-year stay (1589–91) in the Azores following a shipwreck, and while at Flores he collected first-hand evidence of the battle there between England and Spain in 1591 involving Sir Richard Grenville of the Revenge. Later he played a major role in promoting Holland's search for a *northeast passage, accompanying *Barents on his second voyage (1595), which he described in his Journalen (1601). He died at Enkhuizen.

Lippi, Filippino (1457/58–1504) Italian painter. The son of Fra Filippo *Lippi, by whom he was trained in Spoleto, Filippino was born at Prato and moved at the age of twelve, after his father's death, to Florence. There he became the pupil of *Botticelli, whose influence is evident in early paintings attributed to him. He was commissioned to paint the Annunciation on two tondi in S Gimignano (now in the Pinacoteca there) in 1483 and then received a major commission in 1484 to complete the frescoes alongside those of *Masaccio in the Brancacci chapel of Sta Maria del Carmine, Florence. The Vision of St Bernard (1486; Badia, Florence) is generally considered his masterpiece. Filippino's frescoes in the Strozzi chapel in Sta Maria Novella illustrate his later style and his interest in classical art. In 1488 he went to Rome where he decorated the Caraffa chapel in Sta Maria sopra Minerva. His popularity was then at its height and he was asked to replace the Adoration of the Magi (completed 1496; Uffizi), which *Leonardo da Vinci had begun in 1481 for the monks of S Donato

a Scopeto near Florence and had left unfinished. During his last years in Rome he painted many panels and was able to study antique remains. As a result of this all his paintings included fragments of antiquity, entirely for their own sake.

Lippi, Filippo (c. 1406–69) Italian painter. Lippi was an orphan and became a Carmelite monk in his native Florence at the age of eight, taking orders in 1421. His earliest works, the damaged fresco of the Relaxation of the Carmelite Rule in the cloister of Sta Maria del Carmine (c. 1432), is heavily influenced by *Masaccio's bold three-dimensional style, suggesting that he was indeed the pupil of Masaccio, who was painting the Brancacci chapel in the same Florentine church during the 1420s.
Filippo Lippi's first important work, the Tarquinia Madonna (1437), shows a lessening of this influence and an interest in *Donatello and Flemish painting. In the Barbadori altarpiece (Louvre), also begun in 1437, with its complicated composition and decorative features there is almost none of Masaccio. In about 1438 he painted the Annunciation in S Lorenzo, Florence, remarkable at the time for its careful composition and use of perspective. In 1442 Filippo Lippi became the rector and abbot of the parish of S Quirico at Legnaia near Florence. Among other paintings during this period was the Bartolini tondo, a Madonna and Child with Scenes from the Life of the Virgin (1452; Palazzo Pitti, Florence), which shows his mastery of spatial organization.
The frescoes in the cathedral at Prato, begun in 1452 and completed twelve years later, are generally considered his finest achievement. They showed a revival of interest in Gothic features, using a Gothic landscape and an increasingly dramatic style which included several events in one area of space. In 1456 while chaplain at the convent of Sta Margherita, where he painted a large altarpiece, he met the nun, Lucrezia Buti, who became the mother of his son, Filippino *Lippi; she is supposed to have been the model for Salome in the Banquet of Herod fresco in Prato cathedral. In his later years he painted several beautiful Nativities, notably the Uffizi Madonna and Child, set in landscapes filled with gold light, full of religious feeling, and more poetical than his early works. His last work at Spoleto cathedral, where he went with his son in 1466 to paint frescoes, was unfinished at his death and completed by pupils and assistants. As well as influencing fifteenth-century artists such as *Botticelli, who was his pupil, the style which Lippi developed served as an inspiration for the Pre-Raphaelites in the nineteenth century.

Lipsius, Justus (1547–1606) Netherlands scholar and teacher. Born at Issche and educated at the Catholic university of Louvain, he then went to Italy as secretary to Cardinal *Granvelle. Returning via Vienna he then taught at the Lutheran university of Jena, where he became a Lutheran. He married a Catholic and returned to lecture at Louvain. In 1579 he accepted an invitation to the Calvinist university of Leyden where he was professor of Roman history for twelve years. He then reverted to Catholicism and spent the last fourteen years of his life teaching at Louvain, where he died. His major editions of Tacitus (1574; second edition, 1600) and Seneca (1605), combine critical insight with wide knowledge of Roman social and political history. His much admired and translated *De Constantia* (1584) advocates a Christianized form of the ancient philosophy of Stoicism on which he was an acknowledged expert.

Little Masters (of Nuremberg) A group of sixteenth-century engravers, influenced by Dürer, whose work was mainly on a small scale. The English phrase translates the German *Kleinmeister*, which would more informatively be rendered "masters in little". Hans Sebald Beham (1500–50) and his brother Bartel (1502–40) were foremost in the group, which also included Georg Pencz (c. 1500–50), Jakob Binck (died c. 1569) and Heinrich *Aldegrever. Their characteristic work was small, finely worked illustrations of biblical, mythological, and historical scenes, with a strong decorative interest.

Livy (Titus Livius; 59 BC–17 AD) Roman historian. Livy was born at Patavium (Padua), but spent much of his adult life in Rome, where he was befriended by Augustus. He wrote the history of Rome, *Ab urbe condita* (from the foundation of the city) in 142 books, of which only books 1–10 and 21–45 survived complete into the Middle Ages and so down to the present. The whole work was divided into "decads" of ten books, and the contents of the incomplete or missing decads are known from summaries.

Livy's patriotism, idealization of the Roman republic, and flair for description of characters and events recommended him first to *Petrarch, who compiled from separate manuscripts a text that brought together almost all the surviving parts of Livy's work. *Valla emended the text (1448) and the first printed edition appeared at Rome in about 1469. Livy's appeal to students of statecraft received its greatest tribute in *Machiavelli's *Discorsi della prima deca di Tito Livio*. Despite charges of Patavinity (stylistic provincialisms), Livy was the acknowledged model for Renaissance historians until supplanted in the later sixteenth century by *Tacitus.

Lodge, Thomas (1558–1625) English author and physician. A Londoner by birth, Lodge attended the Merchant Taylors' School there before going to Oxford and then studying law. *Daniel, *Drayton, and *Greene were among his literary friends. Lodge attempted several genres: literary controversy in his *Defence of Plays* (1580) against Stephen Gosson's *Schoole of Abuse* (1579); social criticism in *An Alarum against Usurers* (1584); verse romance in *Scillaes Metamorphosis* (1589; reissued as *Glaucus and Scilla*, 1610); pastoral romance in *Rosalynde, Euphues Golden Legacie* (1590), which was a successful exercise in *Euphuism and was dramatized by Shakespeare in *As You Like It*; poetry in *Phillis* (1593); the play *The Wounds of Civill War* (1594); and satire in *A Fig for Momus* (1595). He twice made long voyages, to the Canaries in 1585 and to South America in 1591–93; the latter resulted in *A Margarite of America* (1596). Around this time he converted to Roman Catholicism and began to study medicine, which he practised successfully in London from 1600. Apart from *A Treatise of the Plague* (1603), Lodge's later works are translations: of Josephus (1602), Seneca (1614), and *du Bartas (1625).

Lodi, Peace of A peace agreement signed at Lodi, near Milan, between Milan and Venice in 1454. Later the same year this was extended into a mutual non-aggression pact to which Florence and, early in 1455, the papacy and Naples also became parties. Despite periods of tension, such as that arising from papal involvement in the *Pazzi conspiracy, these five principal Italian powers in the main kept the peace among themselves and their adherents until the outbreak of generalized turmoil occasioned by the French invasion of 1494 (*see* Italy, Wars of).

Lomazzo, Giovanni Paolo (1538–1600) Italian painter and art theoretician. Lomazzo was born in Milan and trained as a painter under Gaudenzio *Ferrari, but as the age of thirty-three he went blind. He therefore turned to writing on the theory of art. His first major work was *Trattato dell'arte de la pittura* (1584), which was widely used as a handbook for over two hundred years after his death. The work is in seven parts, dealing with proportion, movement, colour, light, perspective, technique, and history. In 1587 his *Rime* was published, and in 1590 *Idea del tempio della pittura*. His writings can be considered to represent the outlook and ideas of the later mannerists, particularly the renunciation of the belief in nature as the source of all beauty.

Lombard, Lambert (1506–66) Netherlands painter, architect, and art theorist. A pupil of Jean Demeuse at his birthplace, Liège, Lombard subsequently studied under Arnold de Beer at Antwerp and Gossaert at Middelburg. In 1537–38/39 he visited Italy, principally Rome, and he is also reputed to have visited Germany and France. Only a very small number of paintings can be attributed to him with certainty, and many have been lost, but he executed a considerable number of drawings, nearly seventy of which were engraved by Hieronymus Cock. The latter reveal his figural style to have been conditioned largely by a study of classical and contemporary Italian sculpture. Lombard's chief significance was as an educator. In 1565 he sent Vasari details about northern artists and requested in return sketches of Italian Trecento paintings for comparison with northern stained glass. His students included Frans *Floris and Willem Key. Long after his death, Lombard was praised by van *Mander as "a father of our art of drawing and painting".

Lombardo family A family of sculptors and architects, originally from Lombardy, who established a major workshop in Venice during the fifteenth and sixteenth centuries. Pietro (c. 1435–1515), born at Carona the son of the architect Martino, was the most important member of the family. He executed monuments in Padua, for example that of *Gattamelata's son Giannantonio (died 1455) in Il Santo, before moving to Venice in about 1467. His Venetian sculptures included the monuments of Doge Pasquale Malipiero (died 1462), of Doge Pietro Mocenigo (died 1476), and of Doge Niccolò Marcello (died 1474) in the church of SS Giovanni e Paolo, as well as the church of Sta Maria dei Miracoli (1481–89), on which he worked as both architect and sculptor. Other works by Pietro included the effigy and tomb of Dante in Ravenna (1482), the Zanetti tomb in Treviso cathedral (1485), and the Palazzo Vendramin-Calerghi on the Grand Canal in Venice, which he completed (c. 1500–09) to designs by *Codussi.

Pietro's sons Tullio (c. 1460–1532) and Antonio (c. 1458–c. 1516) assisted their father in his workshop and were much influenced by classical models, as seen in such works as their decoration of Sta Maria dei Miracoli. Among Tullio's best works are the tombs of Doge Giovanni Mocenigo (died 1485) and Doge Antonio Vendramin (died 1478) in SS Giovanni e Paolo, Venice, the effigy of Guidarello Guidarelli (1525; Accademia, Ravenna), and reliefs of classical subjects such as the *Bacchus and Ariadne* in the Kunsthistorisches Museum, Vienna. Antonio worked with his brother on reliefs depicting the miracles of St Anthony for Il Santo, Padua, and worked independently (1506–

16) on reliefs of mythological subjects (now mainly in Leningrad) to decorate the Camerini d'Alabastro in Alfonso I d'Este's Castello at Ferrara. Antonio's sons, Aurelio (1501–63), Girolamo (c. 1504–c. 1590), and Lodovico (c. 1507–75) were also active as sculptors.

London The capital city and port on the River Thames in southeast England. By the Renaissance period London included the two cities of London and Westminster, the buildings in the two-mile gap between the cities, the surrounding areas, and the areas south of the river that were linked to the cities by a single stone bridge, London Bridge. A Roman administrative centre from the first century AD, the City of London declined in importance during the Saxon period although it was the site of the first St Paul's cathedral (founded 597). The importance of the City of London was firmly established by the Norman rulers in the eleventh and twelfth centuries. The City of Westminster was important from the reign of Edward the Confessor (1042–66), when Westminster became the royal capital and Westminster Abbey was consecrated (1065).

In the fourteenth and fifteenth centuries Westminster was an administrative centre, the home of parliament, the royal court, and the law courts. In 1476 *Caxton set up England's first movable type printing press at Westminster. The City of London was the commercial and trading capital of England with great fairs and markets (such as the Corn Exchange, Leadenhall, and Billingsgate), busy docks, flourishing silk, pottery, and glass industries, and energetic mercantile communities of Danes, Dutch, Gascons, Germans, and Italians.

During the sixteenth century the capital expanded rapidly. Between 1530 and 1600 the City of London's population grew from 25 000 to 75 000; by the early seventeenth century the population of the two cities and surrounding areas was close on 250 000, probably the largest centre of population in Europe. Notable sixteenth-century developments include the development of London's commerce with the building of Gresham's Royal Exchange (1567) and the formation of such great trading companies as the *Muscovy Company (1552), the Turkey Company (1581), and the *East India Company (1600).

Sixteenth-century London was externally transformed by the use of bricks in housing and by the conversion of York Place to the royal palace of Whitehall from 1529. The later sixteenth and earlier seventeenth centuries were the period of the great literary age of England, and London became a European centre of culture. Most of the City of London's notable Renaissance buildings were destroyed by the Great Fire (1666).

Lope de Vega *see* Vega Carpio, Lope Félix de.

López de Ayala, Pedro ("El Canciller"; 1332–1407) Spanish chronicler and poet. A member of a distinguished noble family, he was born at Vitoria, Castile, and played a prominent role at the court of Peter (I) the Cruel (1350–69), and under the succeeding Trastámara kings, Henry II, John I, and Henry III. His nickname derives from his appointment as chancellor of the realm (1399). During this period of unrest, foreign powers took part in the dynastic struggles of Castile, and Ayala was twice taken prisoner of war: briefly by the Black Prince (the English had invaded to support Peter I) and in 1385 for two years by the Portuguese. His work as official historian, the *Crónicas* (completed 1393; published 1526), cover the years 1350–90. They contain remarkably objective first-hand accounts recorded with a clarity Ayala learned from translating Livy. The verse miscellany, *El rimado de palacio* (1385–1407), begun during his captivity in Portugal, is penitential in tone, with satirical passages on a courtier's life. It contains a confession, an attack on contemporary corruption, a "mirror for princes" section, and concludes with an adaptation of Gregory the Great's *Moralia* on the Book of Job. It is the last example of the medieval stanzaic form known as *cuaderna vía*, though Ayala also used the new metre, the *arte mayor*. Ayala also translated Boethius, Isidore of Seville, and Boccaccio's *De casibus virorum illustrium* (*Cayda de príncipes*).

Lorenzetti, Ambrogio (fl. 1319–47) Italian painter. Brother of Pietro, Ambrogio formed in style a link between the schools of his native Siena and Florence, extending a trend towards realistic narration and emotional intensity. Although probably a pupil of *Duccio in Siena he also worked periodically in Florence between 1318 and 1332 and was a member of the painters' guild in Florence in 1324. In much of his work therefore the predominant influence is that of *Giotto. His earliest dated work, the *Madonna and Child* (1319) at Vico l'Abate, near Florence, illustrates this influence and also that of the contemporary sculptor Giovanni *Pisano. His most important works are the frescoes of *Good and Bad Government* in the Palazzo Pubblico of Siena (1337–39). Those representing good government in the town and in the country are noted respectively for the unusually accurate perspective for that time and for the exceptionally evocative representation of a landscape. Ambrogio's *Presentation in the Temple* (1342; Uffizi) again illustrates a realism and use of perspective considered to be a hundred years ahead of their time. Other important panel paintings are scenes from the legend of St Nicholas of Bari

(1327–32; Uffizi) and *Madonnas* and an *Annunciation* (1344) in the Pinacoteca in Siena. It is thought that Ambrogio may have died in the plague of 1348.

Lorenzetti, Pietro (fl. 1305–45) Italian painter. Like his brother Ambrogio, Pietro was Sienese born and was influenced by the schools of both Siena and Florence. His work was similarly concerned with emotional expression and realism of form. His earliest dated painting, the polyptych in the parish church (Pieve) at Arezzo (1320), shows an already mature style but more influenced by *Duccio than Ambrogio's works are. Of his frescoes those at the lower church of S Francesco, Assisi, are the most important, illustrating the influence of *Giotto in their expressive simplicity. Among his paintings the altarpiece from the Carmine in Siena (1329) and *The Birth of the Virgin* (1342), both in the Museo dell'Opera, Siena, are the best known and demonstrate his narrative power.

Lorenzo Monaco (c. 1370–c. 1425) Italian artist. A native of Siena, Lorenzo settled in Florence where he entered the monastery of Sta Maria degli Angeli (1391). His early works were influenced by Agnolo *Gaddi and include several altarpieces, notably two versions of the *Coronation of the Virgin* (1414), one in the Uffizi and the other in the National Gallery, London. The decorative and naturalistic style of his early works was replaced in his mature paintings by the International Gothic approach of such artists as Lorenzo Ghiberti, as seen in the massive frescoes *Life of the Virgin* (1420–22; Bartolini chapel, Sta Trinità, Florence) and the *Adoration of the Magi* (c. 1422; Uffizi), which was one of his best works. Lorenzo was also known as a painter of miniatures, but no such works can be attributed to him with certainty.

Lorenzo Veneziano (active 1356–79) Italian painter. The leading Venetian painter in the latter part of the fourteenth century, Lorenzo may have been a pupil of Paolo Veneziano (died c. 1360). His own work was Gothic in style and comprises a number of polyptychs such as those in the Duomo at Vicenza (1356), the Accademia, Venice (1357), and S Giacomo Maggiore, Bologna (1368). Other works are preserved in the Museo Civico, Padua, and the Museo Correr, Venice.

Loris, Heinrich *see* Glareanus, Henricus.

Lotto, Lorenzo (c. 1480–1556) Italian painter. He trained in the studio of Giovanni *Bellini, probably alongside *Giorgione and *Titian, and later under Alvise *Vivarini in his native Venice. From 1508

to 1512 Lotto was in Rome, but although he is known to have been employed in the Vatican there is no surviving record of his work there. After leaving Rome he spent most of his life in Bergamo, where his principal frescoes were done, and in Venice and neighbouring towns, where many churches contain altarpieces by him. He also worked in Ancona. His pictures reveal a wide variety of influences during this period but always retain a very personal character. His portraits, for example, though derived from *Titian, are more direct and show a penetrating and highly individual insight into character, as in his portrait of a young man against a white background (c. 1505; Kunsthistorisches Museum, Vienna). Lack of material success is suggested by his account book, which he kept from 1538 onwards. In 1552 he settled in the monastery of the Sta Casa in Loreto and became a lay brother in 1554.

Louis XII (1462–1515), King of France (1498–1515) Louis, who was duke of Orleans from 1465, first married (1476) Louis XI's saintly but handicapped daughter Jeanne. He was imprisoned for rebellion in 1488, but was reconciled to *Charles VIII three years later. On his accession Louis agreed to support Pope *Alexander VI's son, Cesare *Borgia, in Romagna in exchange for the annulment of his marriage to Jeanne. He then married (1499) Anne of Brittany, widow of Charles VIII.

In Italy Louis pursued the claim to Naples inherited from Charles and the claim to Milan via his *Visconti grandmother. He captured Milan and ruled there from 1500 to 1512. Then, in cooperation with *Ferdinand of Aragon, he conquered and partitioned Naples (1501–02), but the Spaniards later drove the French out (1504). France joined the anti-Venetian League of *Cambrai (1508), but quarrelled with its allies who then formed the *Holy League against it (1511). The Swiss then drove the French out of Italy and invaded Burgundy, Spain took southern Navarre, and *Henry VIII invaded northern France. Peace with Henry and Louis's marriage to Henry's sister Mary (1514) partly retrieved the situation.

Although his Italian ventures caused France severe financial problems, Louis was popular. Internal peace, low taxation, judicial reforms, and measures protecting the poor from oppression earned him the title "the father of the people".

Louvre, the The national art gallery and museum of France. Built on the right bank of the Seine in Paris on the site of a former royal fortress and residence, the present building was begun on the orders of Francis I, who commissioned the French architect Pierre *Lescot to design four wings around a square court in 1546. Noted as a great collector of Renaissance art, Francis I gathered about him many celebrated Italian artists, including *Leonardo da Vinci, *Andrea del Sarto, *Primaticcio, and Benvenuto *Cellini, and established the basis of the royal collection to be housed in the Louvre. After Lescot had completed the west wing of the complex, with sculptures by Jean *Goujon, work on the Louvre and the adjoining *Tuileries was continued by *Bullant and *Delorme and in the seventeenth century by Lemercier, Jacques II Ducerceau, and others, while the decoration of the Grande Galerie was entrusted to Poussin and his assistants (1641). The court moved into the Louvre in 1652, after which many alterations were made to the original design by such noted artists as Bernini and Perrault before the building was dedicated as a museum in 1678. The overall complex was completed in the nineteenth century during the reign of Napoleon III.

Loyola, St Ignatius *see* Ignatius Loyola, St.

Lucas van Leyden (?1489–1533) Netherlands painter and print maker. According to Carel van Mander, Lucas was born in 1494, although this seems unlikely in view of the evident maturity of his earliest dated engraving, *Muhammad and the Murdered Monk* (1508). Between 1514 and 1529 the artist is repeatedly documented in his native Leyden and in 1521 he met Dürer in Antwerp. He is probably identical with the "Lucas of Holland" listed as a visiting artist in the registers of the Antwerp guild for 1522. According to van Mander, he visited Zeeland, Flanders, and Brabant at the age of thirty-three, a journey which presumably occurred in 1522, rather than 1527. Although Lucas was apparently trained by his father Huygh Jacobsz. and by Cornelis Engebrechtsz., his earliest surviving painting, *The Chess Players* (before 1508; West Berlin) has a psychological intensity which is entirely novel. He was profoundly influenced by the graphic work of Dürer and Marcantonio Raimondi, as well as by Jan Gossaert and Jan van Scorel. From these sources, without ever visiting Italy, he formulated a post-classical mannerist style which reached its ultimate expression in the Leyden *Last Judgment* tryptych (1526) and the Boston *Moses Striking the Rock* (1527). Despite his evident skills as a painter, Lucas's chief claim to fame rests upon the formal variety and technical virtuosity of his engravings, which rival those of Dürer himself. In his short lifespan he emerged as the most accomplished Dutch artist of the early 1500s. See p. 248.

Lucca A city state by the River Serchio in Tuscany, northern Italy. In turn Etruscan, Roman, Gothic,

LUCAS VAN LEYDEN
Engraving of grotesques (1523). Such patterns show the northern artist's ready assimilation of the latest trends in Italian art.

Byzantine, and Lombard, Lucca was granted an imperial charter of liberties (1118) and was the most powerful Tuscan city until overtaken by Florence in the late Middle Ages. It continued to prosper however until family feuds in the fourteenth century left it unable to resist domination by other Italian cities. From 1369 imperial protection brought a measure of security, although the Milanese briefly occupied Lucca between 1430 and 1433. Despite some years under a *signoria*, Lucca was generally a republican oligarchy during the period of the Renaissance. Its silk industry and position on roads linking Florence, Parma, Pisa, and Rome made the city rich. Surviving landmarks include the cathedral, completed in the fourteenth century, the impressive ramparts (begun in the 1560s), and several fine sixteenth-century palaces.

Lucretius Carus, Titus (?99–?55 BC) Roman poet. Lucretius' long philosophical poem *De rerum natura* (*On the nature of things*) was known in the Middle Ages only through excerpts. Poggio *Bracciolini discovered a complete manuscript in 1417, but even after the text was printed (c. 1473) suspicion of the author's philosophy, which is heavily indebted to the notorious *Epicurus, prevented its attaining great influence. Giordano *Bruno was one of its few Renaissance followers, and Lucretius' atomism attracted some scientists, among them William *Gilbert.

Luini, Bernardino (c. 1481–1532) Italian painter. Little is known for certain about his early life and work before 1512. He appears to have been influenced by Bramantino and other Milanese artists,

of whose school he was a follower. At first he worked in a fresh and light-hearted style, as demonstrated in the fresco fragments from a villa at Monza, but his popularity in the sixteenth century, and later with Victorians such as Ruskin, was chiefly due to his later works, which consisted of sentimentalized imitations of *Leonardo's style. These survive in large numbers, mainly in Milan.

Luis de León, Fray (?1527–91) Spanish poet, writer, and translator. Born the eldest son of a judge at Belmonte, La Mancha, Luis de León entered the university of Salamanca (c. 1541), in which town he spent virtually his entire life, and then joined the Augustinian order, taking vows in 1544. He was elected to the chair of St Thomas Aquinas in 1561. After the decrees of the Council of Trent were promulgated in Spain (1564), there was pressure to impose orthodoxy on university teachers. For various reasons (a translation of the Song of Songs made privately for a cousin who was a nun, public criticism of the Vulgate, and perhaps even the fact that a great-grandmother was a *conversa*), Luis de León fell foul of the Inquisition (he was secretly denounced by rival professors) and was imprisoned for five years (1572–76). Finally acquitted, he returned to Salamanca, holding the chairs of moral philosophy (1578) and biblical studies (1579). He became provincial of the Augustinian order in Castile shortly before his death.

Luis de León's twenty-nine poems (not published until 1631) were influenced by Virgil, Horace, and Neoplatonic philosophy and are, like those of St *John of the Cross, highly personal expressions. They include odes that are among the best examples of the *lira* stanza introduced by *Garcilaso de la Vega. In his lifetime Luis de León was recognized as the greatest prose writer of his age. His masterpiece, *De los nombres de Cristo* (1583), is a Platonic discussion of the scriptural names of Christ (the Way, Shepherd, Bridegroom, etc.) in the form of a Ciceronian dialogue which was composed while he was in prison. He also wrote *La perfecta casada* (1583), a commentary on chapter 31 of the Book of Proverbs expounding the duties of a married woman. He was as fluent a writer in Latin as in Spanish, and also translated works by Pindar, Seneca, Tibullus, Bembo, and della Casa.

Luis of Granada (Luis Sarriá: 1505–88) Spanish preacher and religious writer. Leaving his native Granada, he studied at Valladolid before moving to Cordova (1534–45), where he restored the Dominican convent and studied devotional works. In 1547 he became prior at Badajoz, and about 1555 was invited by Cardinal Infante (later King) Henry to Portugal, where he was provincial of the Portuguese Dominicans (1556–60). Among his works were *Libro de la oración* (1554) on prayer and meditation, *Guía de pecadores* (1555), a guide to the Christian virtues for sinners, and *Memorial de la vida cristiana* (1566) on the ascetic life. He was influenced by Savonarola and Erasmus, emphasized the importance of the inner life, and regarded ceremonies as unimportant. In 1559 the *Libro de la oración* and the *Guía* were put on the Index.

Luna, Álvaro de (?1390–1453) Spanish statesman and poet. An illegitimate member of a family of wealthy *conversos*, de Luna rose by being tutor to the young King John II of Castile. When John came of age (1419) he totally relied upon de Luna, who, despite the hostility of the king's Trastámara cousins and their supporters among the old aristocracy, became virtual ruler of Castile. He was appointed constable of Castile in 1423. Although driven from court in 1427, he was recalled the following year and consolidated his power, but his attempt to raise a crusade against the Moors of Granada (1431) ultimately failed. After the Castilian defeat of the Aragonese at Olmedo (1445) he was elected grand master of the Order of Santiago. The hostility of the king's second wife, Isabella of Portugal, brought about his downfall, and he was executed at Valladolid after a mock trial for witchcraft. His poems appeared in the *Cancionero de Baena* (1445) and he also wrote a treatise in defence of women, *Libro de las virtuosas e claras mugeres* (1446).

Lusiad, The (*Os Lusíadas*; 1572) The national poem of Portugal, written by *Camões, and one of the most important and successful epics of the Renaissance. The title refers to the Portuguese (the Lusitanians), whose heroic achievement in discovering the sea route to India the poem celebrates. Although in historical time the action spans the two years of Vasco da *Gama's voyage of 1497–98, it includes a visionary expanse of Portuguese history both backward and forward to Camões's day. The poem, consisting of ten cantos (1102 stanzas) of *ottava rima*, is thoroughly Virgilian and classical and yet firmly based on historical events and draws on Camões's seventeen years' experience in India and the Orient. After an introduction, the invocation and a dedication to King Sebastian, the action begins at the point when the Portuguese are sailing off the coast of East Africa in the Indian Ocean. The mythological action (with Venus protecting and Bacchus opposing the enterprise) is skilfully combined with the historical narrative, which incorporates outstanding descriptive passages and a variety of historical and fictitious episodes before its triumphant conclusion.

Luther, Martin (1483–1546) German reformer. The son of a prosperous copper miner at Eisleben, Luther received a thorough education, first at school in Magdeburg, then at the local university in Erfurt. He graduated MA in 1505 and began to study law, but soon abandoned his legal studies and entered the Augustinian priory at Erfurt. The year after his ordination (1507) Luther was appointed a lecturer in the new university at Wittenberg, where he became a doctor of theology in 1512 and then professor of scripture. During his years in Wittenberg Luther's intensive theological studies brought him into an increasingly troubled relationship with established Catholic doctrine: his mounting impatience with scholastic theology and his preference for the Bible over the Church as a final arbiter in matters of faith and practice both grew steadily more apparent in his sermons and lectures. About this time (1512–15) Luther seems also to have come to his new understanding of justification, with the realization (based on his reading of St Paul's Epistle to the Romans) that faith alone justifies without works. This doctrine, of justification by faith, was to be the cornerstone of his future creed.

Luther's impatience with traditional Catholic theology and its abuses finally found voice with his Ninety-five Theses against Indulgences published in November 1517. The indulgence, granted by Pope Leo X for the renovation of St Peter's in Rome and preached with little restraint by the Dominican friar Johann Tetzel, was widely resented in Germany, and Luther's Theses found a ready audience. Within a month they had spread throughout Germany, making their author a major public figure. In the fierce controversy that now arose Luther gradually elaborated his theology and broadened his attack on the Church. At the Leipzig Disputation with Johann *Eck (1519) he denied the primacy of the pope and the infallibility of a general council. The following year, 1520, he published the three great tracts that marked the final break with the Roman establishment. The appeal *An den christlichen Adel deutscher Nation* (*To the Christian Nobility of the German Nation*) urged the princes to take ecclesiastical reform into their own hands. *De captivitate Babylonica ecclesiae* (*The Babylonian Captivity of the Christian Church*), published in German as well as Latin, denounced Catholic abuse of the sacraments and condemned the doctrine of transubstantiation. *Von der Freiheit eines Christenmenschen* (*The Freedom of a Christian Man*) developed the doctrine of salvation by faith. Finally, in December, Luther burnt the papal Bull condemning his teaching (*Exsurge domine*, June 1520), leaving the pope no alternative but to pronounce his excommunication (January 1521).

Luther's fate now depended to a large extent on political events within the empire. Summoned to appear before Emperor Charles V at the Diet of *Worms (March 1521) Luther refused to recant, but he was protected in his defiance by *Frederick the Wise, Elector of Saxony, and in 1522 Luther was able to return to Wittenberg. Here he remained for the rest of his life, writing and watching over the gradual growth of the reformed movement. In 1534 he completed his new German translation of the Bible based on the original texts, destined to be the most enduring of his literary productions. The Greater Catechism and Shorter Catechism (1529) also played an important role in spreading his teaching among the people. Luther also wrote an enormous number of small pamphlets and tracts in which his love of controversy and capacity for abuse found full expression. In middle age Luther became increasingly irrascible, stubbornly resisting any attempt to develop or refine his theological insights. The result was a series of damaging disputes, of which the eucharistic controversy with the Swiss reformer Ulrich *Zwingli (*see* Marburg, Colloquy of) was the most serious. By the time of Luther's death a Lutheran church was well established over large areas of Germany, but it was increasingly troubled by internal dissensions.

Luther married in 1525 and enjoyed a happy family life: the *Table Talk* recorded by his students faithfully preserves the flavour of life in his household.

Lutheranism The movement for evangelical reform in Germany, led by Martin *Luther. Although the term "Lutheran" was originally coined by Luther's Catholic opponents, it soon came into general use to describe his supporters. As the movement gathered pace the need for a clearer definition of doctrine than that provided by Luther's own writings became evident; this process of definition led to the establishment of a distinct Lutheran church and to the exclusion of many non-Lutheran reformers. The first authoritative expression of Lutheran doctrine was the Confession of *Augsburg, drawn up by *Melanchthon with Luther's approval. Its twenty-one doctrinal articles included a clear exposition of justification by faith, together with an affirmation of the Real Presence (of Christ's body in the sacrament, the point which had already caused a breach between Luther and the Swiss reformer *Zwingli). Although Melanchthon issued a substantially revised version in 1540 (the *Variata*), more acceptable to reformed theologians, it was the original text which was incorporated into the Book of *Concord in 1580, the definitive statement of Lutheran orthodoxy. Also influential in defining Luther's teaching were his two catechisms (1529) and the *Schmalkaldic Articles (1537).

Lutheranism achieved its greatest success in Germany, where many cities and princes adopted the Reformation between 1524 and 1535. Lutheran state churches were subsequently established in much of the empire, including the important states of Saxony, Brandenburg, Brunswick, and Hesse. Outside Germany Lutheran churches were permanently established only in Scandinavia (in Denmark in 1530 and Sweden in 1531–37) and the Baltic lands. In other parts of Europe where the Reformation had made early headway Lutheranism was generally superseded by the more robust Calvinist tradition. After Luther's death (1546) his movement was increasingly rent by internal divisions, resulting in the virtual exclusion of the Melanchthonite wing in the Formula of *Concord (1577).

Luzzaschi, Luzzasco (c. 1545–1607) Italian composer. Luzzaschi studied with *Rore in Ferrara and in 1561 became a singer at the Este court there. In 1564 he became court organist, but was also active as a composer and teacher. Frescobaldi was among his pupils. Luzzaschi was also organist at Ferrara cathedral and the Accademia della Morte. By 1570 he was directing the duke's chamber music. It was here that the celebrated "singing ladies" of Ferrara, remarkable virtuoso singers, performed for private audiences, and Luzzaschi composed madrigals for them. His *Madrigali per cantare, et sonare a 1–3 soprani* (1601) contains some of these pieces with their fully notated keyboard accompaniments. From 1597 Luzzaschi served Cardinal Pietro Aldobrandini, who took over Ferrara from the Este when the city passed to the papacy. Luzzaschi wrote some sacred works, but his madrigals are his best-known compositions. His five-part madrigals were his most popular works, and, while not very innovatory in style, they are skilfully composed; the later ones show an increased use of homophony.

Lyly, John (?1554–1606) English novelist and playwright. The son of a Kentish gentleman, Lyly took his MA at Oxford (1575) before trying to earn his living as a writer in London. He was appointed vice-master of St Paul's choir school (1585), and the Paul's boys gave the first performances of several of his plays before Queen Eliza-beth; these highly polished prose comedies on mythological themes included *Alexander and Campaspe* (1584), *Sapho and Phao* (1584), *Endimion* (1591), *Gallathea* (1592), and *Midas* (1592). Lyly contributed the pro-bishop *Pappe with an Hatchet* (1589) to the *Marprelate controversy, but his main achievement in prose was *Euphues*, a romance published in two parts – *The Anatomy of Wit* (1578) and *Euphues and his England* (1580). He was MP successively for Hindon, Aylesbury, and Appleby (1589–1601), but never achieved his longed-for court post of master of the revels. If he wrote the exquisite lyrics in his plays, he was also an accomplished poet. *See also* Euphuism.

M

Mabuse *see* Gossaert, Jan.

Machaut, Guillaume de (c. 1300–?1377) French composer and poet. Probably born in Reims, Machaut entered the service of John of Luxembourg, King of Bohemia, in around 1323, and was his secretary until the king's death at Crécy (1346). Machaut was given canonries by Pope John XXII at Verdun, Arras, and Reims in the 1330s, and after the king of Bohemia's death, he was patronized by, among others, the king of Navarre, the duke of Berry, and the future King Charles V. Machaut's autobiographical poem "Voir dit" gives some insight into his compositional methods. He is generally regarded as the most important figure of the French *ars nova* and was highly revered by his contemporaries. He wrote little sacred music, but notable among it is his *Messe de Notre Dame*, one of the earliest polyphonic settings of the Ordinary of the Mass. His secular output consists of around twenty motets and well over a hundred pieces in song forms (lais, virelais, rondeaux, and *ballades*). The lais and virelais are for one voice in the troubadour tradition, but the rondeaux and *ballades* are polyphonic, based on isorhythmic tenor lines. Here Machaut is at his most innovatory, using syncopation and musical rhyme to great effect.

Machiavelli, Niccolò (1469–1527) Italian political theorist and dramatist. From 1498, after the fall of Savonarola, Machiavelli served in the republican administration of his native Florence, in the chancery and as secretary (1498–1512) to the Ten of War, the body concerned with diplomacy and warfare. He acquired a thorough knowledge of political affairs and travelled extensively in legations to various courts, meeting such leaders as *Louis XII of France, Pope *Julius II, Emperor *Maximilian I, and Cesare *Borgia. With the return to power of the Medici in 1512, Machiavelli was forced to retire from public life because of his association with the republican government; he was also suspected of involvement in a plot against the Medici in 1513. Apart from insignificant and temporary appointments, he devoted the rest of his life to his writings, living at S Andrea in Percussina, several miles from Florence.

Two of Machiavelli's works were published in his lifetime: *La mandragola* (*The Mandrake Root*; 1518), an instant success still acknowledged as one of the most brilliant of Italian comedies, and the treatise *Dell'arte della guerra* (*The Art of War*; 1519–20), set in the intellectual gatherings of the *Orti Oricellari. It was there that he read a version of his first major commentary on government, *Discorsi sopra la prima deca di Tito Livio* (*Discourses on the First Decade of Livy*; 1531), written about 1517. His other works include a history of Florence (written 1520–25), the comedy *Clizia* (written c. 1524), and his political masterpiece, *Il principe* (*The *Prince*). *Dell'arte della guerra* and *Istorie fiorentine* were translated into English in 1560 and 1595 respectively, but by that time Machiavelli's name had undeservedly become a byword for godlessness, cynicism, and treachery, exemplified in the prologue to Marlowe's *The Jew of Malta* in which the ghost of "Machevill" is made to say, among other scandalous sentiments: "I count Religion but a childish Toy, And hold there is no sinne but Ignorance."

Machuca, Pedro (died 1550) Spanish architect and painter. Machuca became familiar with Italian Renaissance theories while studying in Italy. He returned to Spain in 1520. He is best known for his design of the palace of Charles V in the Alhambra at Granada, begun in 1531. This was the first building of its kind in Spain, exhibiting many Italian features and decorated in the mannerist style; it was never completed. Other works included the colouring of a carved reredos in Jaén cathedral, several altarpieces at Granada (1521–49), and an early panel, the *Madonna del Suffragio* (1517; Prado, Madrid), executed in Italy.

Madrid The capital city of Spain, situated on the central Castilian plateau. At first a small Moorish town named Majrit, Madrid was reconquered by the Christians in 1083. Although its first *cortes* was summoned in 1329 and various monarchs spent some time in the city, Madrid only became an important centre in 1560 when *Philip II established his court there. Madrid was chosen presumably because it was not associated with the historic divisions of Spain. In 1607 Philip III made Madrid

Spain's official capital. Surviving landmarks include the town hall and the Plaza Mayor from the early seventeenth century.

madrigal In the fourteenth century, a setting of a secular poem of eight to eleven lines for two voices. In the sixteenth century the genre re-emerged in Italy, and became the most popular secular form in the second half of the sixteenth century. The sixteenth-century madrigal was a freer musical form than its predecessor and was generally for four or five voices. The poetry of Petrarch was revived, used, and also imitated in countless pieces. Two of the earliest exponents were *Verdelot and *Festa; madrigals by both were published in 1530. *Arcadelt published one of the most popular madrigal collections in Venice; his first book was reprinted around forty times before the mid-seventeenth century. In it he uses imitative counterpoint and chordal declamation according to the contour of the text.

Venice became an important centre for the publication and composition of madrigals during the 1540s; *Willaert and his pupils composed madrigals in which the form of the music is dictated by the text. In the 1550s declamation of the text remained important, requiring a supple rhythm with a chordal texture; composers started to experiment with harmonies, using chromaticism to some effect. The influence of Willaert and *Rore remained strong; in the second half of the sixteenth century composers all over Italy imitated them, notably Andrea *Gabrieli in Venice and *Wert in Mantua. Gabrieli and other Venetian composers wrote in a new style which was freer, polyphonically complex, and of a light texture. From the 1580s *Marenzio helped to make Rome and Ferrara centres of madrigal composition. As a new style of singing with great ornamentation, fostered in particular by the dukes of Ferrara, became established, composers wrote virtuoso music full of contrasts, both harmonic and textural.

In the 1590s another new style emerged, led by Marenzio, *Luzzaschi, and *Gesualdo, in which the text was increasingly the master of the music; these texts were almost always of great emotional intensity and as such inspired the use of dissonance, bold harmonies and rhythms, and unusual melodic leaps. The compositions of composers active in Italy were imitated throughout Europe. *Ferrabosco composed madrigals in England in the 1560s and 1570s, but it was not until the 1580s and 1590s that English composers interested themselves in the genre. *Morley, *Weelkes, and *Wilbye wrote with great expressiveness, depicting dramatic contrasts in the text.

Madrigal, Alfonso de (c. 1400–55) Spanish philosopher and theologian. Often referred to as "El Tostado", after his father Alfonso Tostado, Madrigal was born at Madrigal de la Sierra, Ávila, and first taught at Salamanca. He later went to Rome, where he came to the notice of Pope Eugenius IV. He entered the Carthusian Order at the Scala Dei monastery in Catalonia, but King John II of Castile persuaded him to leave the contemplative life and secured his appointment as bishop of Ávila. He is one of twenty-four eminent men at the court of Henry IV who are memorialized in the *Libro de los claros varones de Castilla* (Book of the Famous Men of Castile; 1486). Madrigal was a proverbially voluminous writer in Spanish and Latin (*escribir más que el Tostado* – "to write more than el Tostado"). In addition to works on moral philosophy and religious subjects, he translated Seneca's *Medea* and wrote a commentary on Eusebius. The first edition of his *Opera omnia* (Venice, 1507–31) was published in twenty volumes.

Maecenas, Gaius (74/64–8 BC) Roman statesman and patron. He was the trusted adviser of Emperor Augustus and the friend and patron of *Virgil, *Horace, and other major Roman poets, who eulogized him in their poetry. His name became synonymous with discerning *patronage, and he is often invoked in Renaissance writers' dealings with their own patrons.

Maestlin, Michael (1550–1631) German astronomer. Educated at Tübingen university, Maestlin became in 1576 a Lutheran pastor. He also served as mathematics professor at the universities of Heidelberg and Tübingen. Having observed the *new star of 1572 and the comets of 1577 and 1580, Maestlin began to express privately his support for the *Copernican system, but in public and in his *Epitome astronomiae* (1582), he continued to expound the *Ptolemaic system. He must have been more daring in conversation, for it was from Maestlin that *Kepler, as a student at Tübingen, received his first serious introduction to Copernican astronomy. Maestlin also edited Kepler's Copernican treatise, *Mysterium cosmographicum* (1596).

Maestro Giorgio *see* Andreoli, Giorgio.

Magellan, Ferdinand (c. 1480–1521) Portuguese explorer. Born near Villa Real of noble parentage, Magellan served in the court of Queen Leonor from an early age. In 1505 he sailed to the East Indies with Francisco de Almeida, acquiring during the voyage a comprehensive knowledge of navigational techniques. From then until 1510 Magellan was perpetually on the move, helping to establish a fort in Mozambique and fighting at the battle of Diu (1509), which confirmed Portuguese supremacy in the Indian Ocean. He also played a major role in the conquest of Malacca (1511), the gateway to the Far East. Back in Portugal (1512) Magellan took part in an expedition against Morocco (1513), but he then lost favour with King Emanuel.

Magellan responded by offering his services to Spain. In 1518 he and the exiled Portuguese astronomer Ruy Faleiro were commissioned by Charles I of Spain (later Emperor Charles V) to sail west and ascertain that the Spice Islands were within Spanish territory (see Tordesillas, Treaty of). To reach his destination, Magellan navigated the southern tip of America, discovering the straits which now bear his name. He then took the unprecedented decision to return home by continuing to sail westwards. On 6 September 1522 the *Vittoria* arrived back in Seville, but Magellan himself had been killed a year earlier in battle against the natives of Mactan in the Philippines. Consequently, his deputy, Sebastian del *Cano, is acclaimed as the first actual circumnavigator.

Maggior Consiglio (Great Council) The ruling body of Venice on which all adult males belonging to patrician families had a lifelong hereditary right to sit. The closure (*serrata*) of the membership to all except these families took place in 1297, and from 1325 their names were recorded in the *Libro d'Oro* (Golden Book). Throughout the Renaissance period the Maggior Consiglio functioned mainly as a pool from which members could be drawn for other councils and committees of state, such as the senate (with about 200 members) and the *Council of Ten, all under the chairmanship of the *doge.

The Venetian council was copied in Florence on the fall of the Medici in 1494 and became the basis of the republican constitution there until 1512.

magic In the Renaissance, a specific and essentially literate view of how the universe operates. It was far from the body of superstitious beliefs held by illiterate peasants in many other cultures. One of the fullest accounts of Renaissance magic is to be found in *Agrippa's *De occulta philosophia* (1531). For Agrippa, the universe was divided into natural, celestial, and intellectual worlds, with influences flowing from the intellectual to the celestial to the natural world. There were, thus, three types of magic: natural magic applying to the natural world, celestial magic deriving from the stars and planets, and intellectual magic controlled by ceremony and ritual. As natural magic operated by observing the sympathies and antipathies between natural objects, such as the lodestone and iron, it approximated to some extent to Renaissance science.

Celestial and intellectual magic, whatever their pretensions, soon degenerated into astrology and numerology. Much ingenuity was consequently devoted to extracting, by techniques like that of gematria, important and potent numbers, such as that of God (tetragrammaton), Christ (pentagrammaton), and the Shemhamphorash (the pre-eminent name). In gematria words were converted into numbers by assigning the letters arbitrary values. Thus, given that $Y = 10$, $H = 5$, and $V = 6$, then the name of God, YHVH (the tetragrammaton) takes the value $10 + 5 + 6 + 5 = 26$. In this manner a verse of the Bible containing exactly 26 syllables would be taken by the Renaissance magician as being of special significance.

Less mechanical systems of magic emerged from the work of the Neoplatonists *Ficino and *Pico della Mirandola. Extracted in part from the Corpus hermeticum (*see under* hermeticism) and the Jewish *Cabbala, they sought to identify harmonies and resonances in the universe rather than cast spells or design amulets. From the early seventeenth century, however, all such traditions began to be challenged. *Kepler in his *Harmonices mundi* (1619), for example, and Marin Mersenne in his *Quaestiones in genesim* (1623), began the process of critical appraisal which thereafter assigned magic a more peripheral role in intellectual history.

magus As seen by Renaissance scholars, a man in possession of powerful esoteric knowledge gained from certain secret texts or from another noted magus. His initiation might involve various rites of purification and entailed a code of behaviour of which fasting and sexual abstinence would be the most obvious features. The knowledge gained by the magus in this way was thought to give him power over nature. It could be exercised, as by John *Dee, through the conjuring of demons, or, following *Agrippa, through the manipulation of occult sympathies, celestial influences, and numerological relationships. *See also* magic.

majolica A tin-glazed soft earthenware pottery made at several places in Italy during the fifteenth and sixteenth centuries. It derived from the Islamic Middle East via Spain through the Majorcan trade (hence the name). Sometimes called Raffaele ware (after the influence of *Raphael), majolica was particularly suited to brilliantly coloured painted decoration in the Renaissance taste.

The manufactures include domestic utensils, drug jars, and ornamental display pieces. The painted decoration surpassed previous achievements and consisted of grotesques, arabesques, strapwork, armorial and commemorative statements, and narrative and mythological scenes (see Plate XI).

Many of the centres of manufacture were under noble patronage and developed individual styles. The principal products prized by collectors include wares from: Gubbio (patronized by the dukes of Urbino), famed for ruby metallic lustres by Maestro Giorgio *Andreoli; Deruta (patronized by Cesare *Borgia), making yellow lustres edged with blue; Caffagiuolo (patronized by the Medici family), painting in bright orange, yellow, red, and green on cobalt blue; Florence, where Luca *della Robbia produced tin-glazed bas-reliefs and dark blue Gothic decoration; Castel Durante (now Urbania), remarkable for arabesques and grotesques, often on a blue ground; and Faenza (*see* faenza). An important source for knowledge of Italian majolica in the sixteenth century is *Li tre libri dell'arte del vasaio* (c. 1548) by the nobleman Cipriano Piccolpasso (1524–79) of Castel Durante, in which he describes the techniques used by the potters in making and decorating their wares.

Malatesta, Sigismondo (1417–68) Italian nobleman and condottiere. He succeeded his uncle as lord of Rimini in 1432. A successful condottiere, he served Pope Eugenius IV and Francesco Sforza well, but later, his desertion of King *Alfonso (I) of Naples (1447) and his rejection of *Pius II's peace terms incurred the bitter enmity of other Italian rulers. Pius II launched a crusade against him and seized most of his territories (1459–61). Although reviled on biased papal evidence as immoral, cruel, and reckless, Sigismondo was a man of culture and learning. He took a keen interest in military science and in the work of *Valturio. Under his instruction *Alberti replanned S Francesco in Rimini as a monument for the Malatesta family (*see* Tempio Malatestiano). He was for many years infatuated with Isotta degli Atti, whom he married in 1456 after two previous marriages.

Malatesta family The rulers of Rimini and neighbouring towns in the fourteenth and fifteenth centuries. The Malatesta were originally feudal lords and *condottieri in the service of the papacy. Veruchio Malatesta became lord of the city after expelling the imperial faction (1295), and from 1355 his descendants ruled Rimini as papal vicars, loyal servants of the papacy until Sigismondo *Malatesta rashly challenged papal authority. Despite the efforts of Roberto (died 1482) the power of the Malatesta declined and they became increasingly dependent on Venice. Pandolfo V's brutal regime provoked a rebellion in Rimini (1498) and Pandolfo was expelled by Cesare *Borgia (1500). The family later made two unsuccessful attempts to re-establish itself in Rimini (1522–23, 1527–28).

Maldonado, Juan (1533–83) Spanish theologian. He studied at Salamanca and became a Jesuit in 1562. From 1564 he was a professor at the Jesuit college in Paris, where his lectures on theology were popular. In 1574 the Sorbonne accused him of heresy, but he was vindicated by the bishop of Paris in 1576. His important commentaries on the gospels were published posthumously in 1596–97.

Malherbe, François de (1555–1628) French poet and literary critic. Malherbe was born at Caen and after studying at the universities of Basle and Heidelberg, he took the post of secretary to Henry of Angoulême, governor of Provence, in 1577. His first published poetic work was the baroque *Les Larmes de Saint Pierre* (1587); in 1605 he became court poet to King Henry IV in Paris. Malherbe was not a prolific poet: he wrote slowly and deliberately, developing the clear pure style that was to form the basis of French classicism, in reaction against the neologisms and Latinisms of the *Pléiade, which had been a major stylistic influence in his early works. His prose writings include translations, letters, and a number of critical works, notably a hostile commentary on the poems of his predecessor *Desportes.

Malines (Flemish: Mechelen) A city in Antwerp province in the Netherlands (now Belgium). Founded by St Rumoldus, Malines was ruled successively by the prince-bishops of Liège (915–1333), the counts of Flanders (1333–69), and Burgundy (1369–1477) before passing to the *Habsburgs. *Margaret of Austria held a brilliant court at Malines (1507–30), making it not only the capital of the Netherlands but also a centre of learning and the arts. Malines was long famed for its fine lace. The city suffered extensive war damage in the sixteenth and seventeenth centuries. Landmarks which have survived from the period of the Renaissance include the cathedral of St Rumoldus (thirteenth to fifteenth centuries), the fourteenth-century cloth hall, Margaret of Austria's palace, and the town hall (fourteenth to seventeenth centuries).

Mander, Carel van (1548–1606) Flemish painter and writer. Born into a noble family near Kortrijk, van Mander was taught by Lucas de *Heere and visited Rome (1573) and Vienna (1577) before settling in Haarlem (1583). There he opened an academy with Hendrick *Goltzius and Cornelis *Cornelisz. in order to spread the ideas of the Italian Renaissance. He moved to Amsterdam three years before his death. Van Mander is best

Mannerism

remembered as author of *Het Schilderboeck* (1604), an educational handbook for young artists largely based upon Vasari's *Lives of the Painters* (1550). Divided into three parts, *Het Schilderboeck* constitutes, despite inaccuracies, a unique guide to northern European painters from van Eyck to van Mander's contemporaries. The book also includes an instructional poem summarizing the fundamentals of Renaissance art as the author interpreted them, although this had little impact upon Dutch painting of that period. Often called the "the Dutch Vasari", van Mander was a distinguished artist in his own right, producing works in the mannerist style instilled by his Viennese mentor *Spranger. He wrote several allegorical dramas for which he also painted the scenery. His pupils included Frans Hals.

Mannerism A style in the arts originating in Italy during the sixteenth century. Deriving its name from the Italian word *maniera* (manner), the movement developed first in Rome and Florence in the wake of the High Renaissance around 1520. Mannerism extended to all branches of the arts and depended chiefly upon the exaggeration of such Renaissance features as the use of classical motifs and technical virtuosity. Its effect is one of extreme elegance and sophistication. In architecture the chief exponent in the mannerist style was *Giulio Romano, who was a pupil of Raphael and introduced numerous distinctive devices. Mannerist architects in Florence included *Vasari and *Ammanati; those in northern Europe included de *Vries, Cornelis *Bos, and Cornelis *Floris.
In painting *Michelangelo and others developed the ideas of Raphael and executed many notable works distinguished by distortions of scale, strong colours, and elongated human figures. Italian artists in the mannerist style included *Pontormo, *Parmigianino, Vasari, *Tintoretto, and *Brónzino, whose allegory *Venus, Cupid, Folly, and Time* (1546; National Gallery, London) exemplifies the movement's salient characteristics. From Italy the style was exported to France, where it was used at *Fontainebleau by *Cellini and others, and the Netherlands, where artists included Pieter *Coecke van Aelst, Hendrick *Goltzius, and Antonio *Moro. Other masters associated with mannerist art include El *Greco, Pieter *Brueghel the Elder, and *Altdorfer.
In the field of sculpture Mannerism achieved its highest expression in the bronze figures of *Giambologna, who based his work largely on the late figures of Michelangelo. Cellini and Ammanati were the other most significant exponents. Eventually the style fell from fashion and by 1660 it had been absorbed by the Baroque. Although the term "mannerist" was later used as a derogatory phrase

suggestive of artistic decadence, the movement has since been recognized as an important development in its own right.

Manrique, Jorge (1440–79) Spanish poet and soldier. Born at Paredes de Nava, the son of a famous general, Rodrigo Manrique, Count of Paredes and Grand Master of the military Order of Santiago, Manrique was also the grand-nephew of *Santillana. Like his father he was a professional soldier, fighting for the Castilian Infante Don Alfonso (against his half-brother Henry IV) and later for Alfonso's sister Isabella. He was killed in battle at Calatrava. The author of about fifty lyric poems, he is remembered for a longer elegy, *Las coplas de Jorge Manrique por la muerte de su padre* (*Stanzas of Jorge Manrique for the death of his father*; 1476). The forty-three *coplas* (twelve-line stanzas in a pattern of eight and four-syllable lines known as *pie quebrado*) are an expression of grief but move from a conventional medieval and Christian emphasis on the brevity and vanity of human life to a more humanistic celebration of Count Rodrigo's character and worldly achievements.

Mantegna, Andrea (1431–1506) Italian painter and engraver. Born near Vicenza, Mantegna served his apprenticeship in Padua from 1441 as the pupil and adopted son of the archaeologist-artist Francesco *Squarcione. His earliest works were dominated by the influence of *Donatello, who also worked in Padua, and by the archaeological detail that also characterizes many of his later paintings. Chief of these early works was the fresco decoration for the Ovetari chapel (1448–55), in which Mantegna demonstrated his original mastery of perspective; these frescoes were largely destroyed in 1944. He married the daughter of Jacopo Bellini in 1454. Mantegna then executed an influential altarpiece for the church of S Zeno in Verona (1459), in which he depicted sacred figures in a group instead of the usual triptych (*see sacra conversazione*), before being appointed court painter to the Gonzaga family in Mantua in 1460. Another painting, *St Sebastian* (c. 1460; Vienna), again betrays his passion for antiquity and impressed Vasari, but it was not until 1474 that he painted his best work, the Camera degli Sposi in the Palazzo Ducale in Mantua. This painted room includes portraits of the Gonzaga family and their court, classical motifs, and an illusionistic painted ceiling later imitated by artists of the Baroque. Other major works of Mantagna's later period include the nine-canvas series of the *Triumph of Caesar* (1487–94; Hampton Court Palace; see Plate XVI), *Parnassus* (1497; Louvre), and the *Triumph of Virtue* (c. 1500; Louvre), all of which had a deeper allegorical significance. One of the most important artists of the early Italian Renaissance, Mantegna influenced many later artists, including Giovanni *Bellini and *Dürer.

Mantovano, Battista *or* **Mantuan** *see* Spagnoli, Giovan Battista.

Mantua A city in Lombardy, northern Italy. Protected by lakes on three sides, Mantua was first an Etruscan settlement and then Roman. In the late Middle Ages Mantua was governed by the Bonacolsi family (1276–1328) before the *Gonzaga seized power and ruled for three centuries. With imperial support, astute government, sound administration, and the approval of the city's leading families, the Gonzaga gave Mantua security, independence, and political prestige. Local agriculture and textiles brought prosperity to the city, which attained a population of about 25 000 by 1500. Under the Gonzaga Mantua was a splendid centre of the arts and scholarship. *Mantegna was court painter, the architects Giulio *Romano and *Alberti designed a number of Mantua's buildings, and the humanist educator, *Vittorino da Feltre, made Mantua a centre of learning. The writers *Castiglione and *Tasso also enjoyed Gonzaga patronage. Notable buildings which have survived from the period of the Renaissance include the cathedral (rebuilt in the sixteenth century), the churches of S Francesco (1304), S Sebastiano (1460–70), and S Andrea (begun 1472), the ducal palace (begun 1292), the Palazzo della Ragione (thirteenth to fifteenth centuries), and the Palazzo del *Tè (1525–35).

Manuel, Niklaus *see* Deutsch, Niklaus Manuel.

Manueline style (*Arte Manuelina*) A style in Portuguese architecture associated with the reign (1495–1521) of King Emanuel I, under whom numerous monasteries and churches were built. It was contemporaneous with and partly influenced by the early *plateresque in Spain and, like plateresque, incorporates mudéjar elements and represents a transition from Gothic to Renaissance modes. Its characteristic decorative motif is a carved stone rope, thickly knotted and twisted round windows and doorways, coiled around pinnacles, looped from vaulting, and in many other situations; coral, tree branches, artichokes, and other organic forms, often with a marine connection, are also worked into the designs, which are generally carved in much higher relief than their plateresque equivalents. The monasteries at Tomar, Batalha, Belém, and Alcobaça are examples of Manueline style, and it was also exported to Portuguese possessions overseas.

Manutius, Aldus ((Teob)aldo Mannucci *or* Manuzio; 1449–1515) Italian scholar and printer. After studying Latin and Greek, Aldus became tutor to *Pico della Mirandola's nephews at Carpi. There he conceived the idea of establishing a printing house at Venice to publish classical Greek texts, drawing on the resources of the Venetian libraries and the expertise of the city's community of Greek exiles. The *Aldine press (founded 1494/95) produced the first printed editions of nearly all the major Greek authors, the years 1502–04 alone seeing editions of Demosthenes, Euripides, Herodotus, Sophocles, and Thucydides. The Cretan Marcus Musurus (1470–1517) undertook a large share of the scholarly work involved. Sometime before 1502 Aldus founded his *Neakademia (Academy) to promote Greek studies; the names of about forty members of this club are known and its famous visitors included *Erasmus and Thomas *Linacre. *See also* printing; typography.

Manzoli, Pier Angelo *see* Palingenius.

maps *see under* cartography.

Marburg, Colloquy of (1529) A conference summoned by Philip, Landgrave of Hesse, to effect a reconciliation between the evangelical and reformed churches. It was attended by *Luther and *Melanchthon on the German side and by *Zwingli, *Oecolampadius, and *Bucer on the Swiss. There was agreement on most of the articles, but the Zwinglians refused to accept the doctrine of consubstantiation.

Marciana, Bibliotheca (in Florence) The library of the Dominican convent of S Marco. The basis of the collection was the library of some 800 volumes accumulated by Niccolò *Niccoli and purchased on his death by Cosimo de' *Medici, who entrusted them to the Dominicans, who housed them in a building designed by *Michelozzo (1441). Many were dispersed and destroyed by *Savonarola and his followers. In 1508 the library was bought by Pope Leo X and returned to Florence in 1532 by Clement VII. In 1571 Grand Duke Cosimo I made the Marciana a public library. In 1808 the collection was amalgamated with that of the *Laurenziana.

Marciana, Bibliotheca (in Venice) The library housed in the Libreria Sansoviniana on the Piazzetta. The building, begun in 1536, is considered the masterpiece of its designer *Sansovino. It was finished by *Scamozzi in the 1580s and inside it is adorned with stuccoes by *Vittoria and paintings by *Titian, *Tintoretto, *Veronese, and Andrea *Schiavone.

The foundation of the collection was the gift of manuscripts made by Cardinal *Bessarion to the Venetian senate in 1468. Among its treasures are the Grimani Breviary, bought in 1489 by Cardinal *Grimani from a former Milanese ambassador in Flanders, and the *Camaldolese Chart. Associated from its beginnings with Greek studies, it contains many Greek items among its 13 000 manuscripts.

Marenzio, Luca (1553/4–99) Italian composer. Born at Coccaglio, near Brescia, Marenzio probably spent his early years as a singer in the service of the Gonzagas in Mantua. He moved to Rome to join the household first (c. 1574–78) of Cardinal Cristoforo Madruzzo, and then (1578–86) of Cardinal Luigi d'Este, serving both as a singer but also publishing many madrigals, for which he became internationally famous. In 1588 he entered the employ of Ferdinando de' Medici in Florence, and contributed to his wedding celebrations (1589). Later in 1589 he returned to Rome, where his chief patron was Virginio Orsini, Duke of Bracciano. Another patron, Cardinal Cinzio Aldobrandini, recommended Marenzio as *maestro* to the king of Poland. Marenzio arrived in Poland in 1596 and remained for two years. He then returned to Rome, where he died.

Marenzio wrote a small amount of sacred music, but it is for his madrigals that he is celebrated. During his life eighteen madrigal books (1580–99) for four to ten voices were published, as well as five books of villanelles and two books of motets. The early madrigals (written before 1587) are frequently settings of pastoral texts by, among others, *Petrarch; these were greatly imitated throughout Europe, and in England by *Morley. The mood of the madrigals became increasingly serious throughout Marenzio's career, with melancholy texts and greater use of dissonance and chromaticism.

Margaret of Austria (1480–1530), regent and governor of the Netherlands for *Charles V (1507–15; 1519–30) She was the daughter of *Maximilian I and Mary of Burgundy. After her brief marriage to the Spanish heir (1497) ended with his death, she married (1501) Philibert II of Savoy, who died in 1504. In the Netherlands Margaret extended Habsburg domination. She pursued a foreign policy favourable to England and hostile to France, but did negotiate the "Ladies' Peace" between Spain and France at Cambrai (1529). She employed the sculptor Konrad *Meit of Worms and the painter Bernard van *Orley and encouraged writers and scholars. The palace built for her at Malines (1507–26) combined Renaissance

MARGARET OF AUSTRIA *Tomb in the church of Brou, Bourg-en-Bresse. The tombs at Brou were commissioned originally from Michel Colombe, but he died before he had proceeded beyond the stage of making models, and the work was completed by the Flemish artist Jan Roome (or Jan of Brussels) with sculptures by Konrad Meit.*

decoration with a basically Gothic structure.

Margaret of Austria (1522–86) *see* Margaret of Parma.

Margaret of Parma (Margaret of Austria; 1522–86), Duchess of Parma (1547–86) Margaret was the illegitimate daughter of Emperor Charles V by a Flemish woman, Margaret of Ghent, and she was brought up in the Netherlands by her aunts *Margaret of Austria and *Mary of Hungary, who were successively regents there. She was first married (1533) to Duke Alessandro de' Medici of Florence, who was assassinated in 1537, and she later (1542) married Ottavio Farnese of Parma, by whom she became the mother of the general Alessandro *Farnese. Appointed regent of the Netherlands (1559) by her half-brother Philip II, she was confronted by a gathering storm of opposition to Spanish tyranny and religious persecution, made worse by Philip's inflexible stance. After the rejection of the Compromise of Breda (1566) the revolt of the *Netherlands began in earnest. Resigning her post to the duke of *Alba, Margaret retired (1567) to Italy where she lived the rest of her life.

Marguerite de Navarre (Marguerite d'Angoulême; 1492–1549) French patron and writer. Sister of Francis I of France and widow of Charles, Duke of Alençon, Marguerite married Henry d'Albret, King of Navarre, in 1527: their daughter Jeanne was the mother of the future King Henry IV of France. Marguerite was respected as a patron of literature and philosophy; her court became a place of refuge for persecuted writers and supporters of religious reform, such as *Lefèvre d'Étaples, *Des Périers, and *Marot. The best known of Marguerite's own works is the *Heptaméron* (1558–59), a collection of seventy-two tales of love and passion influenced in form by Boccaccio's *Decameron*; she also wrote poetry, notably *Le Miroir de l'âme pécheresse* (1531; translated as *A Godly Meditation of the Soul*, 1548) and *Les Marguerites de la Marguerite des princesses* (1547), and a number of plays.

Mariana, Juan de (?1535–1624) Spanish historian. The illegitimate son of the dean of the collegiate church of Talavera de la Reina, Mariana entered the Jesuit novitiate (1554), studied at Alcalá, and was ordained in 1561. He became a professor of theology at Rome and also lectured in Sicily, Paris, and Flanders before returning to Spain. He lived in Toledo from 1574 until his death.
Historiae de rebus Hispaniae libri XX (1592) was enlarged to thirty books (1605) and a two-volume Spanish version by Mariana was published in the meantime (1601). An uncritical work that drew on every source available and included a wealth of legendary and anecdotal material, Mariana's history of Spain covered events from the earliest times to the death of Ferdinand (1516) and was written in an impeccable style modelled on Livy. He also wrote a number of essays on political theory and other subjects, several of them controversial; *De rege et regis institutione* (1599), on kingship, for instance, contained arguments in favour of tyrannicide. His works reflect an enlightened and liberal point of view and independence of judgment.

Marlowe, Christopher (1564–93) English dramatist. Born and sent to school in Canterbury, Marlowe took his BA at Cambridge in 1584. Thereafter he lived, like other *University Wits, in London, or travelled abroad on secret government service. *Raleigh, *Nashe, and other prominent writers were among his friends or admirers. He had a reputation for atheism, and at the time of his death at the hands of Ingram Frisar in a tavern stabbing at Deptford, a warrant was out for his arrest.
The two parts of *Tamburlaine*, Marlowe's earliest play, published in 1590, were probably written in 1587 and 1588; like his other tragedies, they were immediately successful and often revived. His mastery of blank verse (which Jonson called Marlowe's "mighty line") and ability to create a powerful central character were already apparent. *Dr Faustus* (1604) and *The Jew of Malta* (1633) were probably written in, respectively, 1588/89 and 1589/90, with *Edward II* (1594), his best play in terms of construction, following in about 1593. *Dido, Queen of Carthage* (1594) was completed by Nashe. All Marlowe's poems were published posthumously: his translations of Ovid's *Amores* (c. 1597) and the first book of Lucan's *Pharsalia* (1600), the erotic fragment *Hero and Leander* (1598) in heroic couplets (completed by *Chapman), and his famous song "Come live with me, and be my love" (in *The Passionate Pilgrim*, 1599).

Marnix, Philipp van, Lord of Ste-Aldegonde (1538–98) Netherlands Calvinist theologian and statesman. Born a member of the lesser Netherlands nobility in Brussels, Marnix studied in Geneva as a young man and became a personal disciple of *Calvin and *Beza. He took part in the insurrection against Spain in 1566 and was consequently forced to go into exile in Germany, where he helped organize the important Synod of Emden (1571). Returning to Holland in 1572 he became a close political and religious adviser of William of Orange and played a prominent part in drafting the Pacification of Ghent (1576). An author of some skill, Marnix wrote a number of influential polemical works, including the famous *De biënkorf der heilige roomsche kerche* (*The Beehive of the Holy Roman Church*; 1569), a satirical attack on the old Church in the style of Rabelais, which was translated into English in 1579.

Marot, Clément (?1496–1544) French poet. Clément Marot was born at Cahors, the son of Jean Marot, court poet to Anne of Brittany. He entered the service of the future *Marguerite de Navarre in 1518 or 1519 and, after the death of his father in 1526, became *valet de chambre* to Francis I. His first collection of poetry, *Adolescence Clémentine*, appeared in 1532. Twice arrested for eating meat during the Lenten period, Marot was suspected of Lutheran sympathies and found himself obliged to leave Paris in 1534. He took refuge first with Marguerite de Navarre, then with Renée de France at Ferrara, Italy.

On his return to France in 1536 Marot was reinstated as court poet and continued his metrical translation of the Psalms, a task he had undertaken before his exile. The first part of this work, *Trente Psaumes* (1541), was condemned on publication by the Sorbonne; Marot was forced to flee once again, this time to Geneva, where he published a second edition of his Psalms (1543), and thence to Turin. Marot's contribution to French poetry was influenced by his periods of residence in Italy: he introduced several new forms, such as the epigram and the eclogue, and composed some of the earliest French sonnets. His other works include numerous rondeaux, ballades, and chansons; *L'Enfer* ("The Inferno"; 1542), an allegorical poem inspired by his first term of imprisonment; and editions of *Le Roman de la rose* (1527) and the works of François Villon (1533).

Marprelate controversy An English theological controversy initiated in 1588 by attacks on the episcopal system of Church government by an unidentified writer calling himself "Martin Marprelate". Seven Marprelate pamphlets, printed (1588–89) on a secret press, are known; they are important not so much for their content as for their vivid satirical prose style. *Lyly and *Nashe were among the writers who took the bishops' side. Of the two puritans arrested on suspicion of being "Martin Marprelate", John Penry (1559–93) was executed and John Udall (*or* Uvedale; ?1560–92) died in prison.

Mars In Roman mythology, the god of war, often equated with the Greek god Ares. The fable about him that most appealed to Renaissance artists was his affair with the goddess of love, *Venus.

Martini, Francesco di Giorgio *see* Francesco di Giorgio Martini.

Martini, Simone (c. 1285–1344) Italian painter. Born in Siena, Martini was the pupil of *Duccio di Buoninsegna, from whom he inherited a liking for sumptuous colour. His earliest documented work was the *Maestà* (1315), an enormous fresco painted on the end wall of the Sala del Mappamondo of the Palazzo Pubblico in Siena. Retouched by Martini in 1321, this work imitates a similar piece by Duccio, although with an added Gothic element. In 1317 Martini painted a notable altarpiece *Louis of Toulouse Crowning his Brother, King Robert of Anjou* (1317; Museo di Capodimonte, Naples) and subsequently executed a number of elegant court paintings, such as the influential *Madonna* polyptych (1319; Museo

Nazionale, Pisa), which reflected French Gothic art. Equally important was his *Guidoriccio da Fogliano* (1328; Palazzo Pubblico, Siena; see Plate XVII), a portrait of a Sienese general, in which the central equestrian figure is placed in a panoramic landscape – an innovation in that this was probably the first Sienese painting not serving a religious purpose. His best-known work was the *Annunciation* (1333: Uffizi), painted in collaboration with his brother-in-law, Lippo Memmi (active 1317–47). Martini spent his last years in Avignon, where he met Petrarch. Other notable works include scenes from the life of St Martin of Tours (c. 1330; lower church of S Francesco, Assisi) and *Christ returning to his Parents after disputing with the Doctors* (1342; Liverpool).

Martyr, Peter *see* Peter Martyr (Pietro Martire d'Anghiera).

Martyr, Peter *see* Peter Martyr (Pietro Martire Vermigli).

Mary, Queen of Scots (1542–87), Queen of Scotland (1542–67), Queen consort of France (1559–60) The only child of James V of Scotland to survive him, Mary was sent to be educated at the French court (1548) and in 1558 married the future Francis II of France. From 1558 many people, including herself, regarded her as the legitimate queen of England, on the grounds that *Elizabeth I was a bastard. After Francis's death, she returned to Scotland (1561), a Catholic queen of an officially Protestant (but in fact divided) country. At first she successfully pursued an even-handed course, but after her marriage (1565) to Henry Stuart, Lord Darnley, she more openly favoured Catholics. Darnley, however, earned her hatred by murdering (1566) her secretary and favourite, David Rizzio. Darnley was assassinated in 1567, probably by James Hepburn, Earl of Bothwell, whom Mary afterwards married. Scottish opinion, already discontented with her policies, was outraged, both by the marriage and Mary's widely suspected complicity in Darnley's death. A rebellion by Protestant nobles forced her abdication (24 July 1567), and she fled to England (1568). Elizabeth I kept her confined in various castles, but she was the focus of several conspiracies to place her on the English throne. In 1586 the government acquired proof of her involvement in the Babington plot, and she was tried and executed at Fotheringay castle.

Mary I (1516–58), Queen of England and Ireland (1553–58) The daughter of *Henry VIII and his first wife, Catherine of Aragon, Mary was declared illegitimate (1533) after her parents' divorce. She remained loyal to her mother and to her faith, but was compelled to acknowledge her illegitimacy and to renounce Catholicism. In 1544 the crown was entailed upon her after any lawful child of Henry VIII. Despite attempts to place Lady Jane Grey on the throne, Mary succeeded her half-brother, *Edward VI, in 1553. Her marriage to *Philip II of Spain caused revolts, but Mary was determined to return England to the Catholic Church, and in 1555 papal authority was restored in England. The ensuing martyrdom of around 300 Protestants (1555–58) earned Mary the nickname "Bloody Mary". In 1557 England's alliance with Spain in the war against France cost her Calais, the last English stronghold on the Continent. Mary died without a child to continue the Catholic succession.

Mary of Hungary (1505–58), Queen consort of Hungary (1522–26) The younger sister of Emperor Charles V, she was known as Mary of Austria before her marriage to King Louis II of Hungary and Bohemia in 1522. When the childless Louis was killed at the battle of *Mohács (1526) his realms passed to the Habsburgs. It was Mary who persuaded an assembly of Hungarian nobles at Pressburg to elect her brother Ferdinand (later Emperor *Ferdinand I) as their king, and she later mediated between Ferdinand and Charles in their quarrel over the succession to the empire. Mary was appointed regent of the Netherlands in 1531, a post that she held until 1556, the year of Charles's abdication. She retired with him to Spain, settling at the castle of Cigales, near Valladolid, where she died.

Despite the growth of Protestantism in the Netherlands during her regency, Mary's sway was generally moderate and the enforcement of edicts against heretics was carried out in a manner that did not provoke widespread discontent. She was a keen patron of the arts, employing Jacques *Dubroeucq as architect at her castles of Binche and Mariemont and furnishing them with pictures by the great Flemish masters and by *Titian.

Masaccio, Tommaso (Tommaso di Giovanni di Simone Guidi; 1401–28) Italian painter. Nicknamed Masaccio ("slovenly Tom") because of his slipshod appearance, he was born at Castel S Giovanni di Altura and moved to Florence in 1417, where he joined the Arte dei Medici e Speziali in 1422. Only a handful of paintings are definitely attributed to him, the earliest of which was the polyptych painted for the church of Sta Maria del Carmine in Pisa (1426), which is now largely destroyed. The central panel, *Madonna and Child Enthroned*, survives in the National Gallery, London, and indicates the debt Masaccio owed to *Giotto, to *Brunelleschi's approach to linear perspective, and to *Donatello's ideas about the construction of the human figure. Similar influences are evident in his fresco of the *Trinity* (1425–27), painted for Sta Maria Novella in Florence, and again in his masterpiece, the frescoes for the Brancacci chapel of Sta Maria del Carmine in Florence. Although some of these latter frescoes have been lost, those that remain – painted in association with Filippino *Lippi and *Masolino – illustrate Masaccio's masterly control of *chiaroscuro* and revolutionary concentration upon the humanistic spirit of his subjects. Such scenes as *The Expulsion of Adam and Eve, Tribute Money*, and *St Peter Giving Alms* (see Plate XVIII) in this chapel became models for subsequent artists in the naturalist school, despite the fact that Masaccio's work there was probably unfinished at the time of his death in Rome at the age of twenty-seven. Sometimes referred to as the forerunner of Michelangelo, Masaccio was, with Donatello and Brunelleschi, one of the founders of the Florentine Renaissance. Among other works often attributed to him is the triptych in S Giovenale at Reggello, near Florence.

Masolino da Panicale (Maso di Cristofano Fini Masolino; c. 1383–c. 1447) Italian painter. Born in Panicale, Masolino trained in Florence and may have worked with *Ghiberti on the baptistery doors (1403–07). His earliest dated work is the *Madonna and Child* (1423; Kunsthalle, Bremen), which shows the influence of Lorenzo Monaco and the International Gothic style, and was painted in the same year that he became a member of the painters' guild in Florence. Masolino first collaborated with *Masaccio on his *Virgin and Child with St Anne* (c. 1420; Uffizi) and was soon producing work that was almost indistinguishable from that of the master. From 1425 to 1427 Masolino worked with Masaccio on the frescoes illustrating the life of St Peter in the Brancacci chapel in Sta Maria del Carmine, Florence. In 1427 he went to Hungary. After Masaccio's death Masolino reverted to the more decorative style of his early years, producing fresco cycles in Rome (1428–31) and Castiglione d'Olona (c. 1435).

masque An amateur form of entertainment in sixteenth- and seventeenth-century courts, involving a spectacle created by sets and costumes, with music and dance. In the masque's later, developed form, verse speeches or dialogue were specially written for the performance, often based on allegorical themes and classical mythology. The masque evolved from folk and religious traditions, such as those of Twelfth Night, which featured the arrival of masked visitors, the presentation or exchange of gifts, and a final dance in which the entire assembly joined. The proceedings culminated in an unmasking, in which the royal person or persons and other maskers were revealed in their true identities. The emphasis was on the visual spectacle, music, and dance or mime, but a classical "fable" might be used to provide a theme and appropriate speeches; the "parts" were, of course, always played by royal or noble amateurs.

The masque first acquired a definite shape in Italy and was imbued with great sophistication by Lorenzo the Magnificent; fantastic sets were made possible by complex machinery devised by Brunelleschi and other major artists. In France it influenced similar courtly entertainments like the *ballet de cour and mascarade and the comédie-ballet as developed in the seventeenth century by Molière. In England the lively traditions of morris dancing, "disguising", and mummers' plays merged in the court masque, and here the form reached its most elaborate, and final, state in the collaborations of Ben *Jonson and Inigo *Jones for the Stuart court (1605–31). Jones supervised and designed outstanding sets for these productions, while Jonson, who argued for the central importance of the poetic text, introduced a new dramatic unity in the "fable", as in their Masque of Blacknesse (1608). Although Jonson eventually lost his argument to Jones's emphasis on the visual spectacle, it was not before they had together created a number of perfect examples of the type. Jonson was also responsible for introducing the antimasque, a brief contrastive grotesque and comic section performed before the concluding dance.

Mass In music, the Mass comprises two parts: the Ordinary and the Proper. The Ordinary consists of the Kyrie, Gloria, Credo, Sanctus with Benedictus, and the Agnus Dei which are fixed; the Proper consists of the Introit, Gradual, Alleluia, Tract, Offertory, and Communion, which vary according to season.

The early fifteenth century saw a more progressive style of Mass composition led by *Ciconia, who began to use imitative passages alternating with chordal ones. Around this time English composers took the lead; *Dunstable wrote one of the earliest examples of a cyclic Mass, with sections based on the same tenor melody. Contemporary continental composers, such as *Binchois and *Dufay, wrote Mass movements singly or in pairs, with the top voice carrying the chant. By 1450 the Ordinary of the Mass was the most important compositional form, and in the late fifteenth century the cantus firmus Mass predominated with the tenor part carrying the chant throughout. Masses were sometimes based on secular melodies: *Dufay's Missa Se la face ay pale is probably the earliest example. Composers often competed by setting the

same melody. The late fifteenth-century Mass culminated in the works of Josquin *Des Prés and *Obrecht; both used traditional styles in combination with new techniques of free composition, and the basing of a Mass composition on a freely invented subject. Composers borrowed entire polyphonic pieces as the basis of a composition and this "parody mass" became the most popular form throughout the sixteenth century.

*Palestrina became the first Italian to contribute substantially to the composition of Mass settings after a long period of dominance by northern composers. The Council of Trent instructed that all settings be intelligible, and Palestrina paid great attention to the text. He was the most prolific composer of Masses (104) in the century, and his compositions were widely disseminated. Other figures who dominated Mass composition are *Victoria, *Lassus, and *Byrd.

Massacre of St Bartholomew (23–24 August 1572) The massacre of some 3000 Huguenots by the Paris mob. The queen dowager of France, *Catherine de' Medici decided at the urging of the *Guise faction that it was necessary to assassinate the Huguenot leader, the Comte de *Coligny, Admiral of France. On 22 August a Guise agent shot but failed to kill him. As tension rose in Paris, Catherine panicked and persuaded King Charles IX to authorize the elimination of all the Huguenot leaders, who were gathered in the capital for the wedding of Henry of Navarre. Only a few were to be killed; the duke of Guise himself stabbed Coligny in his bed at 2 a.m. on 24 August. However, the virulently Catholic Paris mob took matters into their own hands, and spontaneously began a general massacre of Huguenots.

Similar massacres occurred in provincial towns during the autumn, causing perhaps 10 000 deaths. The long-term effect was to destroy Catherine's image as conciliator and to throw the Huguenots on the defensive, making them safeguard their own position rather than seek to control France.

Massys, Quintin see Metsys, Quintin.

Master E. S. (mid-fifteenth century) Anonymous German artist also known as the Master of 1466. An engraver and goldsmith, he was an early user of copperplate engraving and was possibly the inventor of the cross-hatch technique, with which he produced subtle tonal effects. He was remarkable too for the extent of his works. Three hundred of the engravings attributed to him have survived, although only eighteen are signed E. S. His skilful use of line engraving can be seen in his religious subjects such as the Annunciation, Nativity, or Man of Sorrows. He covered a wide range of subjects however and progressed from technically accomplished early engravings with careful detail work to a more vigorous mature style.

Master of Flémalle *see* Campin, Robert.

Masters of Nuremberg, Little *see* Little Masters (of Nuremberg).

mathematics The Renaissance was a somewhat transitional period in the history of mathematics. Its first task was to collect, edit, publish, and absorb the main classical mathematical texts. Thereafter mathematicians sought to work out a more convenient formalism and to express within it some of the basic mathematical operations. Thus, in *arithmetic not only did the Hindu numerals win acceptance, but the basic algorithms of addition, multiplication, division, and subtraction were worked out for both integers and fractions. Considerable advances were also made in *algebra. Equations came increasingly to be written in a standard form, and general solutions were found in the sixteenth century to cubic equations. In *trigonometry the main functions were defined in modern terms, while comprehensive tables were provided by *Rheticus. Development was less apparent in the field of *geometry, but understanding nonetheless improved sufficiently to prepare the way for the enormous advances made in the seventeenth century by such mathematicians as Descartes, Fermat, and Newton.

Matteo di Giovanni (c. 1435–95) Italian painter. A leading member of the Sienese school, Matteo di Giovanni was probably a pupil of *Vecchietta although *Pollaiuolo also heavily influenced his decorative linear style, which made generous use of gold, particularly in his numerous *Madonnas*. In 1465 he completed a polyptych for his native Borgo S Sepolcro, of which the central panel, the *Baptism of Christ*, is now in the National Gallery, London. Other works include four versions of the *Massacre of the Innocents,* three (1482–91) painted in a realistic manner and one in inlaid marble in the floor of Siena cathedral, and an *Assumption* (1475; National Gallery, London).

Matthias Corvinus (Matthias I Hunyadi; 1440–90), King of Hungary (1458–90) Matthias was the second son of János Hunyadi (c. 1387–1456), hero of the Hungarian resistance against the Turks, especially the siege of Belgrade (1456). Despite the opposition of some nobles, he was elected king of Hungary, but the malcontents then crowned Emperor *Frederick III in Matthias's stead (1459) and it was not until 1464 that Matthias had sufficiently established his position against his foreign

and domestic enemies for his coronation to take place. In 1469 he was also elected king of Bohemia, but after years of fighting he was forced to relinquish his claim to Ladislaus of Poland.

Frederick III offered to recognize Matthias as king of Hungary on condition that he should succeed him if Matthias died without an heir. Matthias declared war (1481) and drove Frederick from Vienna (1485), which he occupied henceforth as his capital. He also extended his territories by conquest and consolidated his position by alliances, thus making himself the principal power in central Europe. He was still attempting to secure the succession for his illegitimate son János Corvinus (1473–1504), a plan fiercely resisted by his childless third wife, Beatrice of Naples, when he unexpectedly died.

Matthias was a ruler of outstanding qualities, combining statesmanship with military prowess, administrative adroitness with a passion for learning and the arts. It was on his initiative that the university of Budapest was founded in 1475. Some of the greatest Italian scribes copied books for Matthias's royal library; one Florentine aptly wrote in 1489 that Matthias "means to outdo every other ruler in respect of his library – as he does in all other respects." Such a tribute is a measure of Matthias's success in presenting himself upon the European stage as the ideal of a Renaissance prince.

Mattioli, Pierandrea (1501–77) Italian physician and botanist. He was born in Siena, studied in Padua, and travelled widely in Italy to collect plants. His lengthy *Commentarii* on the *herbal of Dioscorides were intended as practical advice for physicians. The book was first published in Venice in 1544 and went into many editions and translations, the first in Latin, following three Italian ones, in 1554. The commentaries go beyond Dioscorides' plants to include Mattioli's own discoveries and reports from his correspondents. The two series of illustrations, one first published in the Venice edition of 1554, the larger ones appearing in a Prague version of 1562, and both copied repeatedly, are unusual in representing massed foliage, fruit, and flowers instead of single twigs or plants.

Maurice of Nassau (1567–1625), Prince of Orange (1618–25) and Count of Nassau (1584–1625) The son of *William (I) the Silent and Anne of Saxony, he succeeded his father as commander-in-chief of the Dutch forces and became stadtholder of most Dutch provinces. In a brilliant military campaign he took Breda (1590) and had driven the Spanish out of the northern and eastern provinces by 1598. After years of inconclusive struggle he reluctantly agreed a twelve-year truce with Spain in 1609, and was then embroiled in a bitter religious and political conflict with his former loyal supporter, the great statesman and advocate of the truce, Johan van *Oldenbarneveldt. Maurice gained an infamous triumph by Oldenbarneveldt's execution (1619). In 1621 he resumed the fight against Spain, but with little success.

Mauro, Fra *see under* Camaldolese Chart.

Maximilian I (1459–1519), Holy Roman Emperor (1493–1519) The son of *Frederick III and Eleonora of Portugal, Maximilian had great abilities; he was a daring huntsman and a brave knight, an expert on infantry, and a man of letters who probably wrote part of an allegory and a treatise on hunting. He was a popular ruler, but also a gullible man who embarked on unrealistically ambitious ventures. In the empire at large his reforms failed, but in Austria they laid the foundations of a unified administration. His dynastic arrangements greatly strengthened Habsburg power and influence.

Maximilian's marriage (1477) to Mary, heiress of Burgundy, brought war with Louis XI of France, but in the name of his son, Philip, he secured Flanders and the Netherlands (1482) and Franche-Comté and Artois (1493). Maximilian expelled the Hungarians who were occupying much of Austria (1490) and drove the Turks out of Carinthia (1492). His second marriage, to Bianca Maria Sforza of Milan (1494), encouraged his Italian ambitions, but after years of futile and expensive effort he had to abandon Milan to France and Verona to Venice (1516). The Swiss effectively established their political independence from the empire in 1499.

In his attempts at reform, Maximilian persuaded the imperial diet to promulgate public peace (1495), which banned private warfare. He set up the *Aulic Council and his own court of justice, but his constant absences from Germany and obstruction from its princes foiled his efforts. He was strong enough to block the efforts of the princes to increase their power in the empire and was largely responsible for the failure of the *Reichsregiment*, an executive committee of princes established in 1500.

Perhaps Maximilian's greatest achievements were dynastic. In addition to securing most of the Burgundian inheritance he obtained Tyrol (1490) peacefully by negotiation with his cousin. He arranged the marriage of his son, Philip, to the Infanta Joanna, thus bringing the Spanish inheritance to his grandson, *Charles V. The marriage of his two grandchildren to Hungarian royalty brought Bohemia and Hungary to the Habsburgs

after the death of Louis II of Hungary at the battle of *Mohács (1526).

Maximilian II (1527–76), Holy Roman Emperor (1564–76) Maximilian was the eldest son of Emperor *Ferdinand I and Anna of Hungary. Born in Vienna but educated mainly in Spain, he was early involved in the business of empire. He married his cousin Maria, daughter of *Charles V, in 1548. During the 1550s he was principally involved in protecting Austria against the Turks. Like his father, he adopted a tolerant policy in religious matters, and was even accused of being a crypto-Lutheran. In 1562 he was chosen king of the Romans and succeeded to the empire on his father's death (1564).

Maximilian inherited his father's taste for the arts and sciences; he tried unsuccessfully to lure *Palestrina and *Giambologna to his court in Vienna and employed the painters *Arcimboldo and *Spranger and the architect and sculptor Hans Mont of Ghent. The business of his reign, like that of his father, was chiefly taken up with defending the empire's eastern border against the Turks and trying to ensure peaceful coexistence between Catholics and Protestants in Habsburg lands. The ambiguity of Maximilian's own theological position is highlighted by his deathbed refusal to receive the Catholic sacrament. He was succeeded by his son *Rudolf (II).

May, Jan *see* Vermeyen, Jan Cornelis.

Mazarine Bible *see under* Gutenberg, Johann.

Mazzoni, Guido (Paganino; c. 1450–1518) Italian sculptor. Born at Modena, Mazzoni worked there and at Ferrara, Venice, and Naples, specializing in dramatic and realistic Nativity and Lamentation scenes. In 1495 he travelled with Charles VIII from Naples to France and helped to popularize the ideals of the Italian Renaissance there. In 1498 he worked on a monument to Charles VIII in the abbey of St Denis (destroyed in 1793) and later executed an equestrian statue of Louis XII at Blois. Subsequently he was approached by Henry VIII of England to design a monument for Henry VII in Westminster Abbey, a project which was later undertaken by Pietro *Torrigiano. Much of the realism in these works was achieved through Mazzoni's frequent use of both life and death masks. In 1516 he returned to Modena, where he died.

Mechlin (*or* **Mechelen**) *see* Malines.

medals *see under* numismatics.

Medici, Cosimo de' (1389–1464) Italian financier and patron of artists and scholars. The son of the very successful banker, Giovanni, Cosimo was exiled from Florence by the *Albizzi (1433) but promptly recalled by a newly elected council (1434). He used his wealth to establish Medici power. While overtly respecting republican forms of government he put his supporters in control of Florentine institutions, notably the *balìa* (committee of magistrates). Cosimo brought prosperity and stability to Florence, spending generously on art and public works. *Brunelleschi, *Michelozzo, *Ghiberti, *della Robbia, *Alberti, Fra *Angelico, and *Uccello all lived in Florence in Cosimo's time. Cosimo also protected Marsilio *Ficino and encouraged the study of Greek.

In Italian affairs Cosimo brought the struggle against Milan to a successful conclusion at the Peace of Cavriana (1441), but his main concern was to preserve stability and freedom from foreign intervention. Cosimo played an important part in the formation of the Italian League (*see* Lodi, Peace of). He allied Florence with Francesco Sforza, Duke of Milan, from 1450. After his death he was honoured with the title "*pater patriae*" (father of his country), which is signified by the letters P.P. carved on his chair in the posthumous portrait of him by *Pontormo (1519; Uffizi).

Medici, Lorenzo de' (Lorenzo the Magnificent; 1449–92) Italian scholar-prince. Although Lorenzo respected republican traditions and never adopted a formal title, he governed Florence with the splendour of a typical Italian Renaissance prince. His lavish entertainments made him popular and his manipulation of Florentine institutions gave him near autocratic power. He arranged noble marriages for his family and procured a cardinal's hat for his son Giovanni, later Pope *Leo X. Lorenzo integrated the administration of Florence with Tuscany and tightened his control through the Council of Seventy and the *balìa* (committee of magistrates). He clashed with Pope *Sixtus IV, whose nephew organized the *Pazzi conspiracy (1478), in which Lorenzo's brother was murdered at Mass. Lorenzo ended the war with the papacy that followed (1478–79) by persuading the pope's ally, Naples, to make peace.

Lorenzo supported artists and scholars like *Politian, *Pico della Mirandola, *Botticelli, and *Verrocchio. Despite *Savonarola's denunciations of Florence's pagan pleasures and loss of republican freedoms from 1489, Lorenzo admired and tolerated the preacher.

Medici family A dynasty powerful in Florence and Tuscany from the thirteenth to the eighteenth century and renowned for its statesmanship and for its patronage of letters and the arts. The family included four popes (*Leo X, *Clement VII, Pius IV, Leo XI) and two queens of France (*Catherine and Marie de' Medici). The first prominent Medici, Chiarissimo, served on Florence's council (1201), and his descendants joined Florence's elite. After the exile of Salvestro, who supported the *ciompi in 1378, another branch of the family headed by the banker Giovanni (died 1429) became dominant. Giovanni's son, Cosimo de' *Medici (1389–1464), established the family's political power; Cosimo's grandson, Lorenzo de' *Medici (1449–92), ruled Florence without any formal designation other than the courtesy title of "il Magnifico". Lorenzo's son, Piero, was expelled from Florence (1494), but the family was restored in 1512. After the second expulsion of the Medici (1527–30) Pope Clement VII installed Alessandro (died 1537), the illegitimate son of his second cousin Lorenzo (died 1519), as duke of Florence. After Alessandro's assassination a junior branch of the family, headed by *Cosimo I (1519–74), established a dynasty of grand dukes of Tuscany (1569–1737). See p. 266.

medicine Renaissance medicine inherited an erroneous but well-worked-out and comprehensive theory of disease. Formulated in antiquity by Hippocrates and developed by Galen (*see* Galenism, Renaissance), it assumed that man was compounded from four elements (fire, earth, water, and air) which, in turn, revealed themselves as the four humours: yellow bile (bilious or choleric), black bile (melancholic), phlegm (phlegmatic), and blood (sanguine). Any imbalance between the four humours, whether caused by diet, meteorological factors, or other conditions, led to sickness. The physicians' task was to restore the initial harmony that once existed between the humours in a person's constitution.

While the theory itself found widespread support among Renaissance physicians, there was still considerable disagreement about how best to treat an illness. Traditionalists aimed to conform to Hippocratic practice by treating disease conservatively with diet, rest, and simple herbal medicines. Such moderate therapies proved of little value against the spread of bubonic *plague in the fourteenth century and the introduction of syphilis into Europe a century later. The failure of traditional remedies against savage epidemics of this kind invited competition from a growing number of alternative therapies. The most prominent of these was linked with the name of *Paracelsus, who saw disease as a specific rather than a general condition. It was, further, analysable in chemical terms. Thus, whereas traditional physicians had argued that contraries cure, the Paracelsians turned

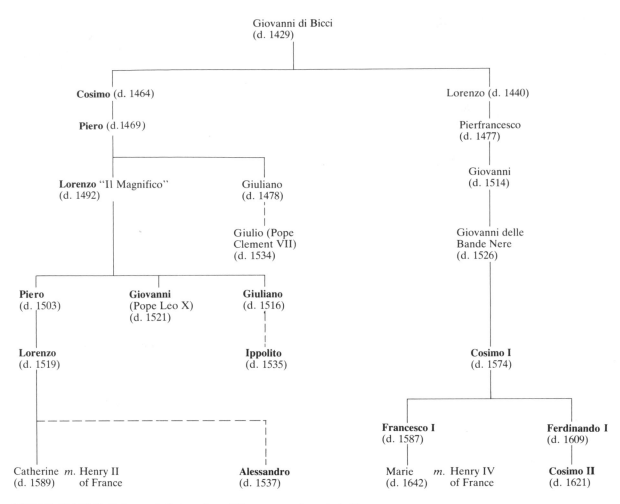

Giovanni di Bicci
(d. 1429)

Cosimo (d. 1464)   Lorenzo (d. 1440)

Piero (d.1469)   Pierfrancesco
(d. 1477)

Lorenzo "Il Magnifico"   Giuliano   Giovanni
(d. 1492)   (d. 1478)   (d. 1514)

Giulio (Pope   Giovanni delle
Clement VII)   Bande Nere
(d. 1534)   (d. 1526)

Piero   **Giovanni**   **Giuliano**
(d. 1503)   (Pope Leo X)   (d. 1516)
(d. 1521)

Lorenzo   **Ippolito**   **Cosimo I**
(d. 1519)   (d. 1535)   (d. 1574)

Francesco I   **Ferdinando I**
(d. 1587)   (d. 1609)

Catherine *m.* Henry II   **Alessandro**   Marie *m.* Henry IV   **Cosimo II**
(d. 1589)   of France   (d. 1537)   (d. 1642)   of France   (d. 1621)

MEDICI FAMILY *Rulers or* de facto *rulers of Florence are shown in bold.*

from bland and harmless vegetables to powerful poisons. Syphilis was treated by the traditionalists with guaiac wood; the Paracelsians tackled it with mercury and antimony. The debate continued for much of the sixteenth century, with the Paracelsians being accused of using lethal poisons and the traditionalists being pilloried as ineffective. A third tradition, linked with the name of *Fracastoro, argued that disease was caused and spread by specific contagious *seminaria*. While explaining much, there were too many obvious objections to theories of contagion to make them at all plausible. If the plague was contagious, why did some members of a household survive, despite frequent contact with their infected kin? Furthermore, talk of invisible *seminaria* accorded badly with a growing scientific reluctance to accept supposedly occult qualities as causes.

Not all patients, however, needed the services of a physician. Frequent wars, fought increasingly with artillery and firearms, had added to the calls made upon surgeons. Although they were incor-

porated by a royal charter in England in 1540 their status remained low; ignorant of Latin, and summoned only in the direst emergency, they could not compete in status with the learned graduates of Oxford and Padua who ran the College of Physicians. Consequently, while Henry VIII's physician received a salary of £126.13s.4d., his surgeon had to be satisfied with £26.13s.4d. a year.

Whether surgeons or physicians, Renaissance doctors had little power to help their patients. With a neo-natal mortality of over 30 per cent and with a life expectancy at birth of under 40, the quality of the average European's life was little affected by the medical profession, especially as physicians were few and expensive enough to place them beyond the reach of the bulk of the population. As a result, most people consulted herbalists, empirics, sorcerers, and anyone with a reputation for healing. Such practitioners worked well outside any tradition developed by Hippocrates and Paracelsus. The greatest failure of Renaissance medicine, however, was to ignore problems of public health. While the small populations of antiquity could escape such indifference, the growing urban concentrations of Renaissance states did so at their peril. *See also* anatomy; iatrochemistry; pharmacopoeia; plague.

Meistergesang A form of sung poetry which developed in Germany during the fourteenth and fifteenth centuries and flourished in the sixteenth. It was performed solo by members of guilds of *Meistersinger* (mastersingers), according to strict rules of versification and music. At first religious but later also secular, it developed out of the medieval courtly song (*Minnesang*) as the practice of poetry and music became a form of relaxation for members of the urban trade guilds. The guilds of *Meistersinger* had five hierarchies of membership, from beginner to *Meister*; the latter had to have written both words and music of at least one new song. Singing contests were held, in which the judge (*Merker*) watched for breaches of the rules. Although the best-known *Meistersinger*, Hans Sachs, the cobbler of Nuremberg (1494–1576), composed over 4000 songs, the rulebound nature of the composition and the exclusiveness of the guilds condemned the form to mediocrity and prevented its development.

Meit, Konrad (c. 1480–1551) German sculptor. Meit was born at Worms and from 1506 to 1510 he worked at the court of Frederick, Elector of Saxony, in Wittenberg. The rest of his life was spent in the Netherlands, where he was court sculptor to the regent, *Margaret of Austria. Working mainly in boxwood, alabaster, and metal, he made many small portrait busts and statuettes in a classical style. His alabaster nude, *Judith* (c. 1510–15), is noted as his most successful sculpture in fusing Italian and northern elements in a sensuous and polished Renaissance style. He also produced monumental sculptures for the tombs of Margaret, her husband, and mother-in-law (1526–32) at Brou, Bourg-en-Bresse. Little work remains from Meit's period in Antwerp after Margaret's death (1530).

melancholia According to Renaissance psychological theory, the humour capable of producing intellectual distinction in those in whom it predominated. This theory was grounded in the ancient physiological scheme of the four humours (*see* Galenism, Renaissance); melancholia was the cold, dry humour, which, in certain manifestations, was the hallmark of the philosopher, poet, and scholar. It was also, under the equally ancient system of astrological correspondences, linked with the planet Saturn, patron of mathematics and sciences. This concept is embodied in Dürer's famous engraving *Melancholia I* (1514), which depicts the

MELANCHOLIA Melancholia I. *Engraving by Dürer (1514).*

essence of melancholic contemplation in the figure surrounded by mathematical instruments. A verbal equivalent of Dürer's engraving is Milton's early poem *Il Penseroso* (written c. 1632), describing the pleasures and preoccupations of the melancholic. The most extensive Renaissance treatment of the subject is Robert Burton's *Anatomy of Melancholy* (1621), which affirms that "melancholy men of all others are most witty."

Melancholia was suffered or affected by numerous eminent Renaissance figures, among them Michelangelo and Raphael. As a cult it was imported from Italy into England in the late 1580s. Melancholics, whose condition was often caused by unrequited love, advertised their plight by both dress and behaviour; a black hat with a large brim (to be pulled down over the face) was *de rigueur*, as were folded arms and heavy sighs. Such affectation naturally lent itself to ridicule, and satirists were not slow to home in on a tempting target; in Jonson's *Every Man in his Humour* (1598), for instance, the two fops, Stephen and Matthew, vie with each other in their claims to melancholic distinction, as witness Matthew's boast, "I am melancholy myself divers times, sir, and then do I no more but take pen and paper presently, and overflow you half a score, or a dozen of sonnets, at a sitting."

Melanchthon, Philipp (Philipp Schwarzerd; 1497–

1560) German humanist and reformer. He was born at Bretten, near Karlsruhe, the son of Georg Schwarzerd, a locksmith and armourer, and a great-nephew of *Reuchlin, whose ideas on the pronunciation of Greek he publicized in his *Institutiones linguae Graecae* (1518). Melanchthon studied at Heidelberg and Tübingen, and in 1518 became the first professor of Greek at Wittenberg. He supported *Luther, and in 1521 published *Loci communes* (Commonplaces), a systematic statement of evangelical theology. His gentle manner contrasted with Luther's vehemence. A significant figure in education, he founded secondary schools (*gymnasia*) at Eisleben, Nuremberg, and elsewhere, reformed ancient universities, and was instrumental in establishing new ones at Marburg, Jena, and Königsberg (Kaliningrad). While rejecting the debased Aristotelianism of the later scholastics, Melanchthon encouraged the study of Aristotle's own works; he was influenced by Stoicism, and his belief in natural theology and reason was partly derived from this source. In 1530 he attended the Diet of Augsburg and formulated the Confession of *Augsburg, the "articles of religion" of the evangelical churches of Germany and Scandinavia. In 1546 he succeeded Luther as leader of the Protestants, but was criticized for his willingness to compromise with both the Romanists and the more radical reformers. His biography was written by *Camerarius (1566).

Melozzo da Forlì (1438–94) Italian painter. Melozzo trained in his native Forlì and in Urbino and came under the influence of *Piero della Francesca. Although Melozzo was acclaimed in his own time as master of illusionism in his wall-paintings and ceiling decorations, none of his frescoes have survived intact. In 1475 he moved to Rome where he painted *Sixtus IV investing Platina as Vatican Librarian* (1477; Vatican museum) and the fresco of the *Ascension* (1477–80) in the church of SS Apostoli, now preserved in the Vatican and the Quirinale Palace, Rome. In these and other works Melozzo devised a style of extreme foreshortening known as *sotto in sù*. Other works include frescoes at Loreto and for the dome of S Biagio at Forlì (1493; destroyed in 1944).

Melville, Andrew (1545–1622) Scottish reformer and humanist. He was born at Baldovie, near Forfar, and learnt Greek at Montrose grammar school from Pierre de Marsiliers. From 1564 to 1566 he read oriental languages, law, and mathematics at Paris, where he was influenced by the new methods of Petrus *Ramus, and later occupied the chair of humanity (Latin) at Geneva (1568–73). From 1574 he held academic posts in Scotland. Several times moderator of the general assembly of the church, he opposed the remnants of episcopacy and was largely responsible for the presbyterian constitution. At the *Hampton Court conference in 1606, he criticized the royal supremacy and was imprisoned in the Tower of London. In 1611 he went to France and spent the rest of his life as professor of biblical theology at Sedan.

Memling, Hans (Hans Memlinc; active 1465–94) Flemish painter. Born in Seligenstadt but based in Bruges, Memling may have been trained by Rogier van der *Weyden, although the influence of Dirk *Bouts is also apparent in his work. He enjoyed a wide circle of patronage and several of his most important pictures were produced for foreign clients. These include the Donne triptych (London), a *Last Judgment* altarpiece (destined for Florence, but now in Gdańsk) and a *Passion* altarpiece (Lübeck). The finest collection of his work is that in the Hans Memlingmuseum (Sint Janshospitaal), Bruges. Many of his paintings are precisely datable, but Memling's style changed little and the exact chronology of his œuvre is elusive. His numerous altarpieces and portraits are very highly accomplished but add little to the repertory established by earlier Netherlands painters.

memory, art of The training and exercise of the memory, partly as an adjunct to *rhetoric, widely practised in both antiquity and the Renaissance. Its effectiveness can be judged by St Augustine's report of a certain Simplicius able to recite the whole of Virgil backwards. The classical tradition survived the medieval period and found its most extravagant Renaissance deployment in the scheme devised by Giulio Camillo (1480–1544) and published in his posthumous *L'idea del theatro* (1550). The basic idea of such a system was to aid memory by systematically linking items to be memorized to a series of striking images. Camillo thus conceived of a theatre divided into a large number of blocks of seats, each one of which could be used as a memory locus. Matteo *Ricci constructed a "memory palace" which he used to good effect in his missionary work at the imperial Chinese court. Alternative systems were presented by, among others, *Bruno and *Fludd. For these, it has been argued, the art was more than a mnemonic device and had deep links with Renaissance occultism. Although the art continues to be cultivated today it has long since returned to its mnemonic role.

Mena, Juan de (1411–56) Spanish poet and writer. Educated in his native Cordova and at Salamanca and Rome, he returned to Spain to become Latin secretary to King John II of Castile and later official court chronicler. The king and Álvaro de

*Luna were his patrons, though he also maintained a friendship with Luna's great opponent, *Santillana. The first Spanish poet to put his vocation above all else, he showed a fine disregard for pleasing the public in his own work. He refined Spanish style, both in poetry and prose, bringing to bear the influences of Virgil, Ovid, Lucan, and Italian poets, especially Dante and Petrarch. In poetry one problem was the rapid, regular, strongly accented beat of traditional Spanish verse. Mena, imitating Dante and Petrarch, introduced a hendecasyllabic line and paved the way for a more varied and subtle metre. He thus popularized the *arte mayor* and was known as *El Ennio español* ("the Spanish Ennius", after the poet who had introduced the Latin hexameter). He ignored colloquial usage, developed an elaborate syntax, introduced neologisms, and employed a range of rhetorical devices to create a new, learned humanistic poetry. His major work, *El laberinto de fortuna* (*The Labyrinth of Fortune*; written 1444, published 1481–88), is an allegorical vision inspired by Dante and much indebted to Ovid. Mena was the first translator of the *Iliad* into Spanish (1519) from a medieval prose version in Latin.

"Mentzer, Der" *see* Fischart, Johann.

Merbecke, John (c. 1508–c. 1585) English composer and writer. In 1531 Merbecke was employed at St George's Chapel, Windsor, as clerk and organist. In 1543 he was condemned to death for his Calvinist views but was reprieved by Henry VIII. His concordance of the English Bible, the first complete edition, was published in 1550. After Edward VI's accession, Merbecke compiled his *Booke of Common Praier Noted* (1550). The first book of its kind, it used adaptations of plainsong as well as similar melodies composed by Merbecke himself, with syllabic underlay of the text. Merbecke's other surviving compositions comprise a large-scale Mass, two motets, and an anthem.

Mercator, Gerardus (Gerhard Kremer; 1512–94) Flemish geographer and cartographer. Mercator was born in Rupelmonde, East Flanders. He studied at Louvain before being employed by his mentor *Gemma Frisius as his assistant. In 1537 Mercator made a map of Palestine, followed by one of the world a year later, and a survey of Flanders (1537–40). He also published a terrestrial globe for use on board ship (1541). In 1551 Mercator presented Charles V with a celestial globe and other accessories, along with written instructions on their use.
The following year, prompted by religious persecution on account of his newly adopted Protestantism, Mercator moved to Duisburg where he established a workshop and lectured. Over the next twenty years his key works appeared. His maps of Europe in 1554 (fifteen sheets) and Britain in 1564 (eight sheets) set new standards in precision, presentation, and detail and broke free from the shackles of Ptolemy's geography that had hampered earlier cartographers. His masterpiece was his 1569 world chart, drawn on the so-called "Mercator projection", which has the parallels of latitude and meridians of longitude at right angles. The sophisticated mathematics of the projection however militated against its immediate acceptance by mariners. Mercator spent his later years consolidating his maps into a series of publications, notably his *Atlas*, the first part of which appeared in 1585 and which was completed by his son Rumold (died 1602) in 1595.

mercenaries Paid professional soldiers who replaced ill-trained feudal levies in many armies of Renaissance Europe. As technological innovations made *warfare more complex and expensive, the new princes created new armies which were heavily dependent on mercenaries. In France Charles VII founded *compagnies d'ordonnance* (1439), French soldiers paid by the king. Monarchs however usually preferred foreign mercenaries as being less likely to become embroiled in the domestic politics of their employer's country. Highly trained and disciplined Swiss mercenaries served French kings well in the fifteenth and sixteenth centuries and the *Swiss Guard has served the papacy from the early sixteenth century. The German landsknechts, modelled on the Swiss, often served abroad. In Italian warfare *condottieri played a dominant part, and Venice relied on her *stradiotti* for numerous policing and garrison duties.
Mercenaries were expensive and, lacking patriotic motivation, could be untrustworthy. On the eve of battle mercenary captains might demand handsome bonuses for their continued loyalty, and in peacetime mercenaries could threaten law and order by using their redundant military skills to prey on civilians.

Mercury *see* Hermes.

Merulo, Claudio (1533–1604) Italian composer and organist. Born at Correggio, Merulo was appointed cathedral organist at Brescia (1556), and a year later as one of the organists at St Mark's, Venice. While in Venice he composed for many official occasions, including the state visit of Henry III of France (1574). In 1586 he became organist to the duke of Parma, then organist also at Parma cathedral (1587), and in 1591 organist to the company of La Steccata, a post he held until his death. A renowned player, Merulo was also a publisher of his own and other composers' music. He wrote madrigals and church music in a style similar to that of Andrea *Gabrieli, but is best remembered for his keyboard music. He developed the ricercar and canzona, but his finest works are his toccatas. Merulo moved away from the practice of basing instrumental music on vocal models; contrapuntal sections are joined by improvisatory, virtuoso passages, without the ensemble textures normally encountered in contemporary keyboard music.

metallurgy The craftsmen of antiquity had developed techniques for the extraction and working of gold, silver, copper, tin, and lead. They had also, since about 1500 BC, begun to work with iron, but as they were able to attain temperatures no higher than 1200°C, well below the 1528°C melting point of iron, production was restricted to wrought iron. A major metallurgical advance, however, took place in the fifteenth century with the emergence of the blast furnace. The molten iron thus attainable could be cast into a variety of forms, using techniques learnt by working in bronze. Chief among these objects were the *cannon and cannonballs increasingly being demanded by warring Renaissance princes. Gunners at the two-month

METALLURGY *Woodcut from Lazarus Ercker's* Beschreibung. *(Prague, 1574)*

siege of Magdeburg (1631), for example, expended as many as 18 000 cannonballs daily.

Demand also increased for precious metals. While world gold production almost doubled between 1500 and 1700, silver production increased ninefold in the sixteenth century alone. Much of this was made possible by improved extraction processes. Methods for separating silver from copper became established in the early fifteenth century, while the Mexican process for extracting silver by amalgamation was well understood by the midsixteenth century. Most of this increased production went into the mints of western Europe.

Copper also played a significant role in Renaissance industry. It was used as an ingredient of bronze in the manufacture of cannon and bells and by itself for the minting of coins. Details of all aspects of Renaissance metallurgy are available in the illustrated volumes of Georgius *Agricola, *Ramelli, *Biringuccio, and Lazarus Ercker.

Metsys, Quintin (Quintin Massys; 1465/66–1530) Netherlands painter. Presumably trained in his native Louvain, Metsys entered the Antwerp painters' guild in 1491. His earliest work indicates points of contact with *Bouts and his followers. His Antwerp *Lamentation* triptych (1507–09) is a grand composition, drawing on the fifteenth-century Netherlandish tradition, and his *Banker and his Wife* (1514; Louvre) is an antiquarian exercise in the style of Petrus *Christus. In the Brussels *Holy Kindred* triptych (1509) figure types derived from Robert *Campin coexist with classicizing architectural details of recent Italian derivation. Metsys's early interest in grotesque facial types was fortified by sketches by Leonardo da Vinci; works such as the Paris *Old Man* of 1513 and the presumably contemporary London *Old Woman* are probably copies after the Florentine painter's work. Metsys also excelled as a painter of more conventional portraits, of which the most famous is the divided diptych of *Erasmus* (Rome) and *Peter Giles* (Longford Castle). His two sons Jan (1509–75) and Cornelis (1511–65) became painters at Antwerp in 1531.

Michelangelo Buonarroti (Michelangiolo di Lodovico Buonarroti-Simoni; 1475–1564) Italian sculptor, painter, architect, and poet. For Vasari, Michelangelo, who was his friend in later years, was the "perfect exemplar" of the arts of *disegno*, representing the culmination of the previous two centuries of progress and accomplishment in Italian art.

Against his father's wishes, the young Michelangelo, who was born in Caprese, decided on a career in art and was apprenticed to the Florentine workshop of Domenico *Ghirlandaio in 1488.

Among his initial drawings are sketches after paintings by earlier masters of Italian art, including Giotto and Masaccio. Michelangelo also made, as an exercise in *fantasia*, a copy of *Schongauer's engraving, *The Temptation of St Anthony*. A year later Michelangelo was training under Bertoldo di Giovanni, a student of Donatello, who was curator of the Medici sculpture collection (whether the Medici garden was actually a school is debated by scholars). Catching the eye of Lorenzo de' Medici, Michelangelo was invited to live in the Medici palace (c. 1490–91). There he came to know the proponents of *Neoplatonism, the philosophy that would guide many of his creative endeavours. An early relief, the *Battle of the Centaurs* (c. 1491; Casa Buonarroti, Florence), demonstrates his precocious talent and understanding of antique art; the *Battle* relief also established his penchant for the human figure, the nobility of which, for Michelangelo, must always be viewed within its symbolic significance as a microcosm, reflecting the perceived order of the universe. Continually assimilating the experience of past masters, Michelangelo carved a *schiacciato* relief, *The Madonna of the Stairs* (c. 1491; Casa Buonarroti) in the manner of Donatello.

As the French army threatened Florence, Michelangelo travelled to Bologna and Venice (1494–95). In Bologna he completed three statuettes for the tomb of St Dominic and had the opportunity to view the expressive furore of Jacopo della *Quercia's sculpted figures. Between 1496 and 1501 Michelangelo was in Rome; two surviving works from this period are the *Bacchus* (c. 1496–98; Bargello, Florence), which treats an antique theme with a new and revealing interpretation, and a *Pietà* (1498–99; St Peter's, Rome), which displays his consummate mastery in communicating both the anatomical and psychological expression of the human form. Michelangelo returned to Florence in 1501 where, until 1504, he was engaged in carving the colossal *David* (Accademia, Florence) from a block of marble quarried in 1464 and left "misshapen" (Vasari) after earlier attempts to carve a figure from it had failed. David's intense scowl reflects the *terribilità* of his psychological state, while the heroically accomplished sculpture reveals the *terribilità* of Michelangelo's creative prowess. The *David*, originally conceived as part of the cathedral prophet series programme, was placed at the entrance of the Palazzo Vecchio, symbolizing the virtue of Florentine republicanism, defiant against the Medici. During this time Michelangelo also worked on a cartoon (now lost) for a fresco intended as a pendant for Leonardo's *Battle of Anghiari* in the Palazzo Vecchio; this *Battle of Cascina* was never painted. With the unfinished *St Matthew* (1504–08; Accademia,

Florence) Michelangelo explored the energetic counterpositioned movement of the *figura serpentinata* (serpentine figure) which would dramatically characterize his later figurative art.

In 1505 Michelangelo was summoned to Rome by Pope Julius II, who then commissioned the sculptor to fashion the pope's tomb; work on the *Moses* (S Pietro in Vincoli, Rome) may have begun in 1506 or later around 1513. (The tomb project, which Condivi, Michelangelo's biographer in 1553, called the "tragedy of the tomb", proved burdensome for Michelangelo. It was completed, four contracts later, in 1542, in a much reduced version of the original scheme.) From 1508 to 1512 Michelangelo, again contracted by Julius II, painted the vaulted ceiling of the *Sistine Chapel with the story of Creation, exalting the human figure throughout the composition (see Plate XIX). Following the completion of the ceiling, work resumed on the tomb project; two figures, the *Dying Slave* and the *Rebellious Slave* (c. 1514; Louvre) were begun. In 1516 Michelangelo, again in Florence, was occupied with numerous commissions. Work on the Julius II tomb continued, the triumphant *Victory* (c. 1527; Palazzo Vecchio) was carved, but the progress was slowed by Medici contracts, including the Medici Chapel (begun 1519) and the Bibliotheca *Laurenziana (1523). The Medici Chapel combines Michelangelo's organically expressive architecture with herculean figures bearing allegorical conceits. In the vestibule of the Laurenziana Michelangelo's unique licence of architectural invention is on display; here, the classical vocabulary of architecture has been refashioned to an imaginative, yet judicious aesthetic.

Late in 1533 Michelangelo settled in Rome. From 1534 to 1541 he painted a *Last Judgment* on the altar wall of the Sistine Chapel; considering the copious variety of figural positions, displayed with dramatic foreshortenings, Condivi rightly observed, "Michelangelo expressed all that the art of painting can do with the human figure, leaving out no attitude or gesture whatever." During this time Michelangelo's friendship with Vittoria *Colonna and Tommaso de' Cavalieri inspired many of his finest poems; his status as an artist rose to that of a cult figure. Two frescoes in the Pauline Chapel, *The Conversion of Paul* and *The Crucifixion of Peter*, were completed by 1550. Throughout this period Michelangelo was continually absorbed in architectural projects in Rome, including work on the Capitoline Hill, the Palazzo Farnese, and St. Peter's, of which he was chief architect from 1546. A second *Pietà* (Museo dell'Opera del Duomo, Florence) intended for his own tomb was begun before 1550; one night about 1556 Michelangelo attempted to destroy the sculpture, betraying the spiritual anxiety which found ardent expression in the late Crucifixion drawings and poems. (In the mid-1550s Michelangelo wrote, "No brush, no chisel will quiet the soul, once it is turned to the divine love of Him who, on the cross, outstretched His arms to take us to Himself.") Work on a third *Pietà* (1555–64; Castello Sforzesco, Milan) continued to a week before his death. Michelangelo died in Rome, but his body was transported to Florence for burial, with a solemn funeral in his parish church of Sta Croce. His tomb in that church is by Vasari.

Michelozzo di Bartolommeo (1396–1472) Italian sculptor and architect. Born in Florence and first documented (c. 1420) as assisting *Ghiberti, Michelozzo subsequently established a workshop with *Donatello with whom he executed a number of important tombs, such as that of the anti-pope John XXII (died 1419) in the baptistery in Florence, as well as the pulpit (began 1428) in the Duomo at Prato. In 1420 he designed S Francesco al Bosco at Caffagiuolo, near Florence, and became increasingly involved in architectural projects. His pragmatic approach to design, involving the marrying of Gothic forms with a free use of antique motifs, endeared him to Cosimo de' *Medici for whom he built a number of *palazzi* and villas. The Palazzo Medici-Riccardi, begun in 1444, with its heavy classical cornice and symmetrically aligned courtyard, was hailed by Flavio *Biondo as being "comparable to the work of the Roman emperors" and established the prototype for Tuscan palace architecture.

Michelozzo's work from 1437 in the cloisters and library of S Marco, Florence, displays a new formal vocabulary in the use of plain Ionic capitals and columns on pedestals. However, his centrally planned choir in SS Annunziata (c. 1444; Florence), based on the design of the temple of Minerva Medica, Rome, sparked controversy in its disregard for the liturgical requirement to separate clergy and laity. Through his work on the Medici bank in Milan (1462) Michelozzo was responsible for the introduction of Florentine Renaissance architecture to Lombardy.

microscopes Early, though obscure, references to magnifying glasses can be found in the twelfth-century writings of Roger Bacon. One of the first Renaissance works to deal specifically with the theory of lenses was the posthumously published *Photismi* (1611) of Francesco Maurolico (1494–1575) (*see also* optics). The first work, however, to describe an optical instrument constructed with "glasses concave and convex of circular and parabolical formes" was the 1571 edition of Leonard Digges's *Pantometria*. The first compound

microscope was constructed by Zacharias Janszoons. (There were other Dutch claimants to the invention, including *Drebbel, and *Galileo seems to have been an early user, if not maker, before 1610.) Its first published scientific use is for the series of drawings of the honeybee included in Francesco Stelluti's *Descrizzione dell'ape* (1625).

Milan A powerful northern Italian city state in the basin of the River Po in Lombardy. First Gallic and then Roman, Milan was devastated by Attila the Hun and the Goths, but survived to become an independent commune (1045). Under *Visconti and *Sforza rule in the fourteenth and fifteenth centuries Milan reached the peak of its political power and cultural splendour, at times threatening to take over most of northern Italy. The Visconti ruled from 1311 until the extinction of the male line in 1447. Following the short interlude of the *Ambrosian Republic (1447–50), the Sforza family ruled (1450–99) with great magnificence until they were displaced by the French during the Wars of *Italy. In the early sixteenth century the Sforza were twice restored to Milan, but in 1535 the city fell to *Charles V, who invested his son Philip (later *Philip II of Spain) with the duchy of Milan in 1540. Thereafter Milan continued under Spanish rule until passing to Austria in 1713.

Visconti and Sforza splendour were supported by sound administrative measures and a thriving economy. By 1500 Milan's population was probably close to 100 000. The city prospered through trade, textiles, and metalwork; it was famous for the quality of its weapons and armour (*see* Missaglia family). Canals for irrigation and communication were built and agriculture was encouraged, particularly the cultivation of rice from 1475. The first Greek book to be printed in Italy, Constantine Lascaris's *Erotemata*, was issued at Milan in 1476. The Visconti and Sforza were generous patrons of the arts and scholarship. They encouraged humanist learning, scientific studies, and great public works. *Petrarch owed much to Visconti patronage. In the late fifteenth century Lodovico ("il Moro") Sforza (1451–1508) and his wife, Beatrice d'Este made their court into a showpiece of culture and learning, supporting *Leonardo da Vinci among others; Lodovico also commissioned for Milan several buildings by *Bramante. Under Spanish rule in the sixteenth century Milan's political prestige and cultural glories were in decline, but it was then the home of one of the leading figures in the *Counter-Reformation, St *Charles Borromeo.

Notable buildings surviving from the period of the Renaissance include the enormous cathedral (begun 1386), the Dominican monastery of Sta Maria, containing Leonardo's *Last Supper*, the

Bibliotheca *Ambrosiana (founded 1609), and the Palazzo di Brera (present façade 1615).

mineralogy In ancient, medieval, and Renaissance times no distinction was made between minerals, rocks, and fossils. All were described as "fossils", a word that meant no more than that they had been dug out of the ground. A number of medieval lapidaries survive and, like the best known of these, the *De mineralibus* (1260) of Albertus Magnus, they derive mainly from Pliny and are predominantly concerned with supposedly magical and medicinal properties of selected stones. Early texts, consequently, were full of such wonders as the bezoar, found in a toad's head and considered an antidote against all poisons. Much of this tradition survived the Renaissance intact.

Minerva The Roman goddess of wisdom and the arts, often identified with the Greek goddess Athene (*or* Pallas Athene). Like her Greek counterpart, Minerva was also associated with the arts of war, and she is generally depicted as armed with a helmet, shield, spear, and coat of mail. She was depicted in Renaissance allegorical scenes as the embodiment of rational, intellectual power; in a picture now in the Louvre, but originally carried out for Isabella d'Este by *Mantegna, the armed Minerva is shown driving a motley and grotesque crowd of personified vices from an arcaded garden pool. Perhaps the most haunting of Renaissance images of Minerva is *Botticelli's painting (Uffizi) of her taming a centaur, symbol of brute physical strength and passion; in this picture she does not carry the accoutrements of the classical goddess but subdues the centaur by the twist of its hair in her right hand, rather than by the huge halberd which she also carries.

Miranda, Francisco de Sá de (1481–1558) Portuguese poet and dramatist. The illegitimate son of a canon at Coimbra, Miranda read law, obtained a degree, and taught in Lisbon. His first works as a poet at the court of Emanuel I were in the traditional forms and metres of medieval Portugal and Spain. Some of these were published in Resende's *Cancioneiro geral* (1516). He inherited property after his father's death (1520) which allowed him to make a long visit to Italy (1521–26). Through his distant relative, Vittoria *Colonna, he met *Sannazaro, *Ariosto, and others. He returned to Portugal through Spain, where he may have met *Garcilaso de la Vega and *Boscán. He married in 1530.
With the patronage of King John III and his inheritance, Miranda was able to devote himself to his poetry and live in rural seclusion. He introduced

to Portugal the eleven-syllable line and the main Italian verse forms: the Petrarchan sonnet, the *canzone*, *terza rima*, and *ottava rima*. His two plays, *Comédia dos estrangeiros* (1559) and *Comédia dos Vilhapandos* (1560), are written in prose, carefully plotted, and thoroughly classical in style. A tragedy, *Cleopatra*, is lost.

Missaglia family Italian makers of weapons and armour. In the fifteenth century their workshop in Milan was a European leader in this field. Tommaso (died c. 1454), who retired in about 1451, handed over to his son Antonio (died c. 1495), who fulfilled commissions for a number of important clients. Some of his work is preserved in the Wallace Collection, London. After Antonio's death the family's place as leading armour manufacturers in Milan was taken by the *Negroli family.

Mohács, Battle of (1526) A Turkish victory over Christian forces in southern Hungary. Led by Suleiman (I) the Magnificent, the *Ottoman Turks destroyed the army of Louis II of Hungary before sweeping north to take Buda and Pesth and to occupy most of Hungary; from here Suleiman could threaten the very heart of Europe. Since King Louis, who drowned while fleeing from Mohács, left no male heir, the elective crowns of Bohemia and Hungary passed to his Habsburg brother-in-law, Ferdinand (later *Ferdinand I, Holy Roman Emperor). In 1687 at a second battle of Mohács the imperial Christian forces defeated the Turks.

Mona Lisa A panel painting executed by Leonardo da Vinci (1503–06; Louvre). Also known as *La Gioconda*, the painting depicts the wife of a Florentine official, Francesco del Giocondo, and ranks among Leonardo's finest works. The psychological content of the painting, epitomized by the sitter's famous enigmatic smile, coupled with the fantastic mountainous landscape in which she is set, profoundly influenced contemporary artists and effectively reformed portraiture of the period. Also notable for Leonardo's *sfumato* technique, the painting later provided the base for Raphael's portrait of Maddalena Doni. See p. 274.

Monet, Jan (c. 1480–c. 1550) Flemish sculptor. Monet was born in Metz but by 1497 he was active in Barcelona. In 1512–13 he was in Aix-en-Provence, whence he had returned to Barcelona by 1516. The following year he worked beside Bartolomé *Ordóñez on the decoration of the choir of the cathedral there, after which he may have visited Naples. In 1521 he met Dürer at Antwerp and the following year Emperor Charles V appointed him a court artist. From about 1524/25 until his death

MONA LISA *The apparent simplicity of Leonardo's famous portrait, with none of the usual trappings of social status or emblematic allusions, has led generations of commentators to concentrate upon the riddle of the sitter's expression.* (1503–06; Louvre, Paris)

he was resident at Malines. Monet's chief works were alabaster altarpieces, such as those at Halle (1533) and Brussels (1538–41). In a sense, these works were the first Renaissance sculptural altarpieces in the Netherlands, in that their architectural and stylistic repertory consists entirely of classical or Italianate motifs. However, their overall compositions lack classical repose and seem to seethe with an uneasy motion, more reminiscent of Spanish late Gothic than contemporary mannerism.

Monluc, Blaise de *see* Montluc, Blaise de Lasseran-Massencôme, Seigneur de.

Montagna, Bartolommeo (Bartolommeo Cingano; c. 1450–1523) Italian painter. Born near Brescia, Montagna probably trained as a painter in Venice and may have been a pupil of Andrea *Mantegna, by whom he was greatly influenced. He was influenced also by Giovanni *Bellini, Antonio *Vivarini, and *Antonello da Messina. Montagna settled in Vicenza around 1474 and was soon recognized as Vicenza's leading artist. His control of geometric composition and taste for grand architectural settings is most clearly seen in his altarpiece for S Michele, Vicenza (1499; Brera, Milan), although subsequent portraits also underline his sensitivity to character. His son Benedetto

(c. 1481–c. 1558) was also a painter and engraver of note.

Montaigne, Michel Eyquem de (1533–92) French essayist. Montaigne was born at the château de Montaigne (near Bordeaux), the son of Pierre Eyquem, a wealthy merchant whose grandfather had bought himself into the nobility; his mother, Antoinette de Louppes, was a Catholic of Spanish-Jewish origin. For the first six years of his life he spoke only Latin, his German tutor having no knowledge of the French language. He subsequently attended the Collège de Guyenne in Bordeaux and went on to study law. In 1557, after three years' service in the *cour des aides*, Montaigne became a magistrate at the *parlement de Bordeaux*, where he made the acquaintance of *La Boétie; the two men remained close friends until the latter's premature death in 1563, an event that caused Montaigne deep and lasting distress.

Never enthusiastic about his legal career, Montaigne resigned his office in 1570, two years after the death of his father, and retired to the family château to write. His translation of Raymond de Sebonde's *Theologia naturalis* had already appeared in 1569; in 1571 he published an edition of La Boétie's works and began to set down in *essay form the reflections inspired by his reading and his meditations on life and death. After the publication of the first two books of *Essais* (1580) Montaigne embarked on an eighteen-month tour of Europe, the subject of his *Journal de voyage*; on his return to France he served for four years as mayor of Bordeaux. During a visit to Paris in 1588, possibly on behalf of Henry of Navarre, Montaigne was arrested and briefly imprisoned in the Bastille; the main purpose of his trip had been to supervise the publication of a new edition of the *Essais*, containing the third volume. In the same year he met Marie de Gournay, his *fille d'alliance* (adopted daughter), who edited his final additions and amendments to the *Essais* and published the augmented work in 1595.

Montano, Benito Arias (y) *see* Arias (y) Montano, Benito.

Montchrestien, Antoine de (c. 1575–1621) French dramatist, poet, and economist. Montchrestien was a native of Falaise. As a youth he was almost killed in a fight and later had to flee abroad after taking part in a duel. He travelled in Holland and England, a keen observer of commercial activities, and established steelworks in France after his return. Although a Catholic he was killed at a tavern while fomenting a Huguenot uprising in Normandy.

Montchrestien's six tragedies (published 1601, except *Hector*, 1604) – based on classical myth and history, biblical subjects, and contemporary history – are notable for their baroque lyrical and descriptive passages. They are: *Sophonisbe*, *L'Écossaise* (on the death of Mary, Queen of Scots), *Les Lacènes* (on the Spartan king Cleomenes), *David* (on David and Bathsheba), *Aman* (on Haman, Esther, and Ahasuerus), and *Hector*. Also published in 1601 were *Susane* (a long poem on Susanna and the Elders) and *Bergerie*, a pastoral play. His *Traité de l'économie politique* (1615), one of the earliest works on the subject, influenced Richelieu and Colbert.

Monte, Philippe de (1521–1603) Flemish composer. Born in Malines, Monte went to Italy while still young. From 1542 to 1551 he served the Pinelli family in Naples as singer, teacher, and composer. In 1554 he travelled to England, and sang in the private chapel of the queen's husband, Philip II of Spain. In 1568 he became *Kapellmeister* to Emperor Maximilian II at Vienna. From this time he composed prolifically and published many of his works. Though he remained in the imperial service for the rest of his life, he also held various nonresidential positions at Cambrai cathedral. He died in Prague. Among Monte's friends were *Lassus and *Byrd. About forty-eight Masses, 300 motets, forty-five chansons, and an amazing 1100 madrigals survive. The Masses are largely based on motets by contemporary composers. His madrigals show close attention to the text (usually by contemporary pastoral poets such as *Guarini); later madrigals become simpler in form and tend towards increased homophony. Monte's secular music was widely sung, as the distribution of his publications and manuscripts testifies.

Montefeltro family A family prominent in the Romagna from the thirteenth to the sixteenth century as *condottieri and rulers of Urbino. The Montefeltro fought for the Ghibelline (imperial) forces until Guido submitted to Pope Boniface VIII in 1295. They first ruled Urbino in 1234, but lost and regained power on several occasions. Antonio, who recovered Urbino in 1377, made peace with the pope and ruled as papal vicar until his death (1403). His son, Guidantonio, papal vicar and lord of Urbino (1403–44), married a *Colonna and enjoyed papal support against the *Malatesta. Federico (1422–82; see Plate XXIV), who succeeded his father in 1444, was an outstanding military leader in the service of Pope *Sixtus IV, who created him duke of Urbino (1474); he also served Lorenzo de' *Medici. Federico consolidated his family's power and spent his earnings as a condottiere on art, his palace, and other public works. Federico's son, Guidobaldo, was the last

Montefeltro to rule Urbino (1482–1508); his court in 1506 was the setting for *Castiglione's *The Courtier*. *See also* della Rovere family.

Montemayor, Jorge de (c. 1519–61) Portuguese writer and poet. Montemayor was born at Montemor o Velho, near Coimbra, into a Portuguese *converso* family and became a soldier and a professional musician. He served the Infanta Juana, the Spanish wife of Prince John of Portugal and mother of King Sebastian. He followed her to Spain after the death of her husband and was subsequently in the service of Philip II, whom he accompanied to England in 1554 and also probably to the Netherlands. He was killed in Italy, apparently in a duel resulting from a love affair. His works, written in Spanish, include a *Cancionero* published at Antwerp (1554), which was reprinted with a *Segundo cancionero espiritual* (1558). The latter, which sought to render the style of the Psalms in Italianate hendecasyllabic verse, was banned by the Inquisition (1559). Montemayor's most important work, which introduced the pastoral romance from Italy to Spain, was *La *Diana*.

Montluc, Blaise de Lasseran-Massencôme, Seigneur de (c. 1500–77) French soldier. Montluc was born at St-Puy and spent his early years at court, as page and archer to the duke of Lorraine. His military career began in 1521 and culminated in his appointment as *maréchal de France* in 1574; during the intervening years he had taken part in five pitched battles and more than 200 skirmishes. As governor of Siena (1554–55) Montluc distinguished himself in the heroic defence of that city against imperial and Florentine forces; as lieutenant-general of Guyenne and a supporter of the Guise in the early years of the Wars of *Religion he was remembered for his severe repression of the *Huguenots. Montluc's *Commentaires*, published posthumously in 1592, are an autobiographical record of his military career, its successes and its failures: his colourful description of sixteenth-century warfare is particularly valuable for its detailed accounts of individual operations.

Montmorency, Anne de (1493–1567) French soldier and nobleman. The boyhood friend of *Francis I, Montmorency was made marshal of France (1522) after his bravery in the Wars of *Italy. Captured at *Pavia (1525), he negotiated Francis I's release from captivity (1526). He exercised great influence at court, becoming constable of France (1538) after his successes against imperial forces in Provence and Savoy, but intrigues brought about his downfall (1541). Restored to royal favour in the reign of *Henry II (1547–59), Montmorency fought bravely against Spain until his capture at *St-Quentin (1557). The *Guise family drove him from Francis II's court (1559–60), but he joined the duke of Guise in the triumvirate against Protestantism (1561), and fought on the Catholic side in the Wars of *Religion until he was killed at the siege of Paris.

Montorsoli, Giovanni Angelo (1507–c. 1561) Italian sculptor in marble. Born at Montorsoli, near Florence, he was taught by Ferrucci and influenced by the work of *Michelangelo, whom he assisted in the 1520s. In 1531 Montorsoli became a brother in the Servite order and during the next five years executed commissions for the Servites in the church of the SS Annunziata in Florence. After three years in Naples, Montorsoli went to Genoa in 1539 and in 1547 to Messina in Sicily. Here, as master of the works at the cathedral, he created his two best-known works: the fountain of Orion and the fountain of Neptune. Between 1558 and 1561 he worked in Bologna before finally returning to his convent in Florence.

Mor, Anthonis *see* Moro, Antonio.

Morales, Luis de (El Divino; c. 1509–86) Spanish painter. Generally considered the greatest Spanish artist in the mannerist style before El Greco, Morales spent most of his life in his birthplace, Badajoz. He may have studied under the Dutch artist Hernando Sturmio and was influenced by the art of both the Flemish school and Leonardo's followers. Morales acquired his nickname on account of the religious intensity of his works (he never undertook profane subjects), which include a series of about twenty paintings for the church of Arroyo del Puerco (1563–68) and five panels in Badajoz cathedral. Notable works include a *Virgin and Child* (National Gallery, London) and a *Pietà* (Academia de S Fernando, Madrid). Morales also worked for a time upon the decoration of the Escorial, at the behest of Philip II, and executed commissions at Elvas and Évora in Portugal. Other influences upon his highly personal style included the German artists *Schongauer and *Dürer.

More, St Thomas (1478–1535) English statesman, scholar, and author. The son of a London barrister, More was brought up in Cardinal Morton's household before being sent to Oxford (c. 1492–94). There he met *Linacre (who taught him Greek) and *Grocyn. Returning to London to study law, he continued his scholarly interests, and became friends with *Lily, *Colet, and *Erasmus. After four years (1499–1503) during which he seriously contemplated entering holy orders, More entered parliament instead (1504) and commenced a highly successful legal career, which led to his becoming under-sheriff of London (1510–19). His house was a centre for humanists, and he also made two journeys to France and Flanders (1508, 1515), during the second of which he sketched out his *Utopia.

More's talents, learning, and personal charm recommended him to *Wolsey, and from 1518 he held official posts that brought him into constant contact with *Henry VIII, with whom he was a personal favourite. Accompanying Henry to the *Field of the Cloth of Gold (1520), he met *Budé, and later *Holbein came to England (1526) under More's patronage. He also used his position at court to promote the new learning in England. In 1529 he was made lord chancellor, but relations with Henry cooled on account of More's continued support for Queen Catherine during the king's divorce proceedings against her. In 1532 More resigned and went into retirement, but Henry insisted on his taking the oaths recognizing the new Act of Succession in favour of Anne Boleyn's children (1534) and denying the authority of the pope. More was willing to agree to the former, but would not compromise his religious convictions by swearing to the second. He was arrested and imprisoned in the Tower of London. There he wrote A Dialogue of Comfort against Tribulation (not published until 1553) and other religious treatises and astounded everyone by his calm and even humorous demeanour. He was found guilty on perjured evidence of high treason and executed. He was hailed as a martyr in Catholic Europe and canonized in 1935.

More's private life is mainly known from the biography by his son-in-law William Roper, first published in 1626. He himself published an English version of the Latin biography of *Pico della Mirandola (1510), but most of his works, apart from Utopia, were not published until long after his death. These include his biography of Richard III, Latin epigrams, Latin translations of dialogues of Lucian, and controversial pamphlets in both Latin and English.

Moreelse, Paulus Jansz. (1571–1638) Dutch painter and architect. A founder-member of the St Lucas guild (1611), Moreelse was born and worked in Utrecht and was known chiefly as a portraitist. His portraits of children are particularly attractive. Influenced by Mierevelt, whose pupil he was, he also produced a number of pastoral portraits of shepherds and shepherdesses. His architectural works include the Catherine gate and the façade of the Utrecht meat market.

Moretto, Alessandro Bonvicino; (c. 1498–1554) Italian painter. He was a pupil of Ferramola, with whom he decorated the choir of the cathedral in his native Brescia (1518). He worked mainly in the Brescia and Bergamo districts before visiting Milan and Verona in the 1540s. His paintings, mainly of religious subjects, are notable for their silvery colours, strength of composition, and the homely flavour which Moretto often imparted to elevated subjects. The influence of *Raphael can be seen in his treatment of form. He was also an outstanding portrait painter, influenced by *Lotto and *Titian, and he is said to have introduced the full-length portrait into Italy (The Nobleman, 1526; National Gallery, London).

Morley, Thomas (1557–1602) English composer. Morley was born in Norwich, and in 1583 was appointed organist and master of the choristers at the cathedral there. He was a pupil of William *Byrd, though it is not known when. In 1588 he gained the Oxford BMus. and a year later became organist at St Paul's Cathedral, London. He was appointed a gentleman of the Chapel Royal in 1592, and in 1598 obtained the monopoly for music printing that had belonged to Byrd. His treatise, A Plaine and Easie Introduction to Practicall Musicke (1597), criticizes some English compositional styles and promotes Italian methods.

Morley's contribution to the madrigal in England, through the publication of Italian music and his arrangements of Italian pieces, is unrivalled. The most famous collection for which Morley was responsible is The Triumphs of Oriana (1601). This contains madrigals by Morley and twenty-two English contemporaries; one of Morley's two contributions shows the influence of *Croce, on whose Il trionfo di Dori the collection was modelled. Morley's sacred and keyboard music is influenced by that of Byrd; his madrigals, canzonets, and balletts are more Italianate in style, but his Consort Lessons (1599), arrangements of English popular music for broken consort, are more typically English.

Moro, Antonio (Anthonis Mor van Dashorst; c. 1519–c. 1576) Dutch painter. Born in Utrecht, Moro was a pupil of Jan van *Scorel, whose influence can be clearly seen in Moro's Two Jerusalem Pilgrims (1544: Berlin). After visiting Italy Moro came under the influence of Titian, as his portrait of his patron Cardinal Granvelle (1549; Vienna) shows, although subsequent portraits by him tend towards a more austere approach. He visited Portugal and in 1554 went to London and painted his masterpiece: the portrait of Mary I commissioned by Philip II of Spain. By 1560 he had become painter to the Spanish court and was painting portraits of the Habsburgs in Spain and the

Netherlands. Other works include the portraits *Maximilian II* (1550; Prado), *Sir Henry Lee* (1568; National Portrait Gallery, London), and the *Man with a Dog* (1569; National Gallery, Washington). Moro's pupils included Alonso Sánchez *Coelho.

Morone, Giovanni (1509–80) Italian churchman. A Milanese by birth, he was appointed bishop of Modena in 1529, and in 1536 was sent by the pope on a diplomatic mission to Germany, to prepare for a general council. He was present at the diets of Hagenau (1540), Regensburg (1541), and Spires (1542). In 1542 he became a cardinal and was later also bishop of Novara (1553–60). He was imprisoned on a charge of heresy (1557–59), but later absolved, and served as the last president of the Council of Trent from 1563. In 1570 he became bishop of Ostia, and acted as protector of the English College in Rome.

Moroni, Andrea (died 1560) Italian architect. Moroni was active in Padua, where his chief monument is the courtyard (1552) of the university, with its Tuscan and Ionic columns. He was also responsible for building the church of Sta Giustina, modifying as he did so the original plans (1502) by *Riccio, and for the classical courtyard of the Municipio, formerly the Palazzo del Podestà.

Moroni, Giovanni Battista (c. 1525–78) Italian painter. Born near Bergamo, Moroni studied under *Moretto da Brescia and also absorbed the influence of *Lotto. More than any other artist of the Renaissance he specialized in portraiture, chiefly of family groups and single figures of the people of Bergamo. His most famous painting is the undated *Tailor* (National Gallery, London), although he also produced some less distinguished religious paintings for the churches of Bergamo.

Moser, Lukas (early fifteenth century) German painter. Although almost nothing is known about his life and only one work by him survives, Moser is generally acknowledged as one of the most important German painters at a time when a national style was beginning to develop. His altarpiece of the Magdalene (1431) at Tiefenbronn, near Pforzheim, was executed in the International Gothic style and is comparable with similar realist works by the German Swiss artist Konrad *Witz and Jan van *Eyck. The painting includes a lament for the state of contemporary art: "Cry out, art, cry out and wail! No one wants you now. So alas, 1431."

Mostaert, Jan (1472/73–1555/56) Dutch painter. In 1507 Mostaert was appointed dean of the painters' guild in his native Haarlem. By 1521 he was a court artist to *Margaret of Austria, and, although she resided at Brussels and Malines, Mostaert retained his principal base in his home town. His earliest work, the Amsterdam *Tree of Jesse*, is influenced by Geertgen tot Sint Jans and even his Brussels *Passion* altarpiece (c. 1520) reveals a debt to Rogier van der *Weyden. Mostaert's *West Indian Landscape* (c. 1542) in Haarlem has overtones of *Patinir but seems to have been partly based upon sketches brought back from the New World. He also painted numerous highly accomplished portraits, although none of his likenesses of the imperial household has survived. The landscape backgrounds of his portraits sometimes include small figure compositions, for example, the legend of St Hubert in his Liverpool *Portrait of a Man*.

motet A musical work sung in Latin and, though not liturgical, often heard during church services. During the Renaissance motets were frequently composed for ceremonial events or in honour of a person. The medieval technique of isorhythm was continued in motet composition into the early fifteenth century; a late example is *Dufay's *Nuper rosarum flores*, written for the dedication of Florence cathedral (1436). In England *Dunstable led the way towards the devotional votive motet, with more use of Marian texts. Continental composers used English pieces as models, experimenting with fauxbourdon and improvised counterpoint, and in France composers adopted the style of secular songs in three-part writing. In the second half of the fifteenth century a compositional tradition of motet writing became established in which parts were evenly balanced in polyphonic texture, and the tenor *cantus firmus* part, though retained, became less distinguishable from the others. *Cantus firmi* continued in motets throughout the sixteenth century, though composers also composed freely with no reference to chant; *Ockeghem's *Ave Maria, gratia plena* is an example of free composition with equal use of counterpoint in each voice. Josquin *Des Prés developed the motet in many ways: the canonic doubling of the tenor *cantus firmus*; the quotation of secular melodies; homophonic declamation; free counterpoint; variation in texture as duos and trios are used in alternation with the full choir; and a change of metre from binary to ternary. These compositional procedures were continued by Josquin's successors; *Palestrina accepted chant as an important element, and in his motets imitative polyphony alternates with homophony. *Lassus's style of motet writing is more rhetorical with more depiction of the text and more homophony; this style was disseminated throughout Europe. Giovanni *Gabrieli sowed the seeds of a new style in which choirs of voices or voices and instruments interchange in short homophonic phrases, paving the way for the baroque motet.

Mudo, El *see* Fernández de Navarrete, Juan.

Mühlberg, Battle of (1547) A victory gained at the German town of Mühlberg, on the bank of the River Elbe, by forces under the personal command of Emperor *Charles V over a Lutheran alliance led by John Frederick, Elector of Saxony. By this triumph Charles hoped he was in a position to achieve religious harmony in his German realms and at Augsburg the following year he attempted to draw up the necessary settlement (*see* Augsburg, Interim of).

Müller, Johann *see* Regiomontanus.

Munich (German: München) A city on the River Isar in Bavaria, southern Germany. Founded by Henry the Lion, Duke of Bavaria, in 1157, the city passed to the Wittelsbach family in the late twelfth century, and from 1255 it was the Wittelsbach home and capital city. In the early fourteenth century Emperor Louis (IV) the Bavarian greatly extended Munich. Under the leadership of the dukes of Bavaria and influenced by the Jesuits, Munich remained loyal to the Catholic faith in the sixteenth century and was an important centre of *Counter-Reformation activity. Notable buildings which have survived from the period of the Renaissance include the cathedral (1468–88), the town hall (1470–80), and the Renaissance style Michaelkirche (1583–97).

Münster, Sebastian (1489–1552) German theologian and geographer. Münster was born at Ingelheim and educated at the universities of Tübingen and Heidelberg. He became a Franciscan monk in 1505, but after converting to Protestantism in 1529 he moved to Switzerland and was appointed to the chair of mathematics at Basle university (1536). A formidable linguist, he produced Hebrew and Chaldean grammars as well as an edition of the Hebrew Bible (1534–35). He is best known for his *Cosmographia universalis* (1544), a comprehensive survey, rich in woodcuts and maps, of the known world. Although weak on the New World and Asia it contained much impressive detail on Germany and western Europe. Münster also published *Horologiographia* (1531) on dialling and an edition of Ptolemy's *Geography* (1540). He died of the plague.

Muret, Marc-Antoine (Muretus; 1526–85) French humanist scholar. Born at Muret, near Limoges, Muret attracted the attention of Julius Caesar *Scaliger and soon made a reputation for himself as a teacher of Latin. He was also friendly with members of the *Pléiade and sympathetic towards their poetic programme. His early success, notably a course of lectures in Paris in the early 1550s attended by a numerous audience that included the French king, brought him many enemies and he was thrown into prison. From 1555 he made his home in Italy, settling in Rome in 1559 under the patronage of Cardinal Ippolito d'Este. Apart from a brief return visit to France (1561–63) he remained in Rome for the rest of his life, lecturing and building up an immense reputation as a Latin stylist. *Montaigne, a student of his, called him "le meilleur orateur du temps". As a classical scholar he wrote commentaries on Cicero, Sallust, Plautus, and the elegiac poets, and his *Variae lectiones* was published in Venice in 1559.

Muris, Johannes de (c. 1300–c. 1350) French music theorist. Born in Normandy, he studied in Paris and spent some time at the Collège de Sorbonne there, otherwise travelling extensively through France. He knew Philippe de *Vitry, and was influential in developing a theory of measured music. His *Ars nove musice* (1321) is his most important work, dealing with the notions of sound and musical proportions.

Murner, Thomas (1475–1537) German satirist. Born in Alsace, Murner grew up in Strasbourg and took orders as a Franciscan friar there (1491). He then studied theology and taught at Fribourg, Cologne, Paris, Rostock, and Cracow, and later studied law at Basle. His popular appeal was evident in both his preaching and his writing, in his use of familiar sayings and imagery combined with a love of the grotesque and scurrilous. More biting than *Brant's gentle satire, Murner's was directed first at folly in general, as in the rhyming verses of *Die Narrenbeschweerung* ("Fools' Exorcism"; 1512), modelled on Brant's *Narrenschyff*. Although highly critical of Church corruption, he found Luther too iconoclastic and took up the cudgels for Catholicism. In *Von dem grossen Lutherischen Narren, wie in doctor Murner beschworen hat* ("Of the Great Lutheran Fool, as Doctor Murner has exorcised him"; 1522), he vitriolically attacked the Reformation. Other works apart from satires include anti-Lutheran pamphlets, theological works in Latin, and a translation of Virgil's *Aeneid* into German verse.

Muscovy Company (*or* Russian Company) A group of English merchants trading with Russia. The company was founded in 1552 by merchants desiring a *northeast passage to China and India.

In 1553 the founders sponsored a three-ship expedition under Sir Hugh Willoughby (died 1554), but only one reached Russia. Its captain, Richard Chancellor (died 1556), was entertained by Tsar Ivan IV, who promised free trade rights. In 1555 the company obtained a monopoly on Anglo-Russian trade. A thriving relationship with Russia developed, although attempts in the late 1550s to establish a similar link with Persia, principally through the efforts of the traveller Anthony Jenkinson (died 1611), proved abortive. In the seventeenth century the company lost its privileges in England and Russia, and was forced to compete with other English and Dutch companies, but survived to re-emerge as a prominent force in eighteenth-century trading.

Muses The nine goddesses who, in classical mythology, were patronesses of various individual art forms. Although they were the daughters of Zeus and Mnemosyne, they are often depicted as companions of *Apollo in their role of inspirers of music and the divine creative power. Their names and the arts over which they presided were: Calliope, epic poetry; Clio, history; Erato, erotic poetry; Euterpe, lyric poetry; Melpomene, tragedy; Polyhymnia, sacred music; Terpsichore, dancing; Thalia, comedy; Urania, astronomy. Each was depicted with her conventional attributes: Urania with a staff and globe, Euterpe with a flute, etc. They feature collectively or individually in Renaissance allegorical and decorative schemes, and the appropriate Muse was conventionally invoked by writers.

music In the Renaissance period musicians, like artists and writers, began to sense the emergence of a new age. Writing in 1477, *Tinctoris stated that music written more than forty years previously was not worth hearing. He goes on to list the composers of his own period who had brought the art to its current state of perfection: those, like *Ockeghem, who learned from the example set by *Dunstable, *Binchois, and *Dufay. After the barren period of the Dark Ages, composers sought models for their works. Unlike those active in other fields, musicians had no direct examples to follow in trying to resurrect the learning and styles of the classical era. This proved frustrating at a time when sculptors and architects, at least in Italy, were discovering the legacy of antiquity all around them. The musician was forced to look to trends in other arts to discover which direction his own should take.

Of the sparse references to music in classical writings the most influential was surely the Platonic dictum that the music should be subservient to the text. This continued to influence musicians throughout the Renaissance, and the principle was even cited as the reason for the advent of another "new age" which we now call the early Baroque. Late Renaissance enthusiasm for such humanist ideals led to some rather extreme applications, such as *Baïf's Académie de la poésie et de la musique; the word setting practised by those associated with this institution rigidly adhered to the poetic metres – no deviation was countenanced in this *musique mesurée*. Though theorists continued to discuss music as a branch of mathematics, in practice musicians became more text-orientated, and the carefully devised numerical structures present in so much earlier music were only occasionally discernible.

Another trend in favour of verbal clarity, affecting musical idioms, manifested itself in ecclesiastical reforms, notably those of the Council of Trent. This assembly was concerned about the lack of intelligibility of the text in composed liturgical settings. A purging of musical idioms was called for in order to right the position. Again there were a number of extreme reactions, but a more rational response to the council is evident in the works of most composers, notably *Palestrina. Polyphonic compositions became organized in such a way that there was greater coincidence of words between the differing vocal lines; earlier this had generally been only a secondary consideration.

Italy has been regarded as the cradle of the Renaissance but, at least until the second half of the sixteenth century, most influential composers hailed from the Netherlands and northern France. It was not until the early sixteenth century that Italians themselves gained any status as composers; in fact, foreigners were crucial in the early development of the *madrigal, a genre that more than any other embodied a sophisticated synthesis of Italian poetry and music. Many northerners found employment in Italy at sophisticated courts and in high ecclesiastical posts. But it is questionable whether these Franco-Flemish musicians, or indeed their music, can be considered as products of the same cultural development that gave birth to contemporaneous works of literature and fine art. Their native Italian patrons were certainly men of the Renaissance, but few were equipped to exert any substantial influence on the manner in which their servants actually wrote. They could, of course, control the creative life of the musician as far as it fell to them to decide which occasions merited musical participation; the current level of prosperity determined what forces would be available for any particular event.

While musicians, like other artists, were bound by the strictures of their patrons, there was a developing sense of the composer as a creator, rather than one who merely sought to reflect the order already present in the created universe. Theoretical writings of the Renaissance demonstrate the marked decline in interest in *musica theorica* in favour of a view of music in which sound and harmony were all important, and the ears were the ultimate judge. Trained ears were necessary to the appreciation of the more recondite areas of musical performance. With the emphasis on this man-centred notion of music came the practice of reflecting nature, particularly in the madrigal.

Despite the dominance of the Netherlanders in this period, music also flourished outside the courts and churches where they were active. England had a strong and individual tradition of florid church music which was brought to an abrupt end by the Reformation. In Germany a parallel, though less severe, hiatus was the result of religious changes there. In the Iberian peninsula liturgical music was produced which could worthily be heard alongside the sacred output of many musicians active in Italy. There is no doubt that the fifteenth and sixteenth centuries were a flourishing period for musical composition. Connections can be made between some of the tendencies which emerge in the music of the period and those in fine art, the field in which the term "Renaissance" was originally applied. It is perhaps wrong to emphasize too strongly the term when dealing with the music of this period. There are certain ways – the lingering interest in numerology, for instance – in which the music is still a product of the medieval era. On the other hand Renaissance music so closely resembles in concept the Baroque in its attitude to the central issue of text that to delineate the characteristics of a single period too minutely is to misunderstand its place in the historical continuum. *See also ars nova.*

See Plate XX.

Muziano, Girolamo (1528–92) Italian painter and engraver. Based in Brescia, near his birthplace of Acquafreddo, Muziano was a pupil of *Romanino, by whom he was greatly influenced. Muziano also shared with Titian a taste for strong colour and dramatic landscape, as seen in his *St Jerome* (Accademia Carrara, Bergamo). Around 1548 he went to Rome and was influenced by the work of Michelangelo and Raphael. He produced some attractive landscape drawings, now in the Uffizi.

Myconius, Oswald (Oswald Geisshäusler; 1488–1552) Swiss reformer. One of the pioneering figures of Swiss humanism, Myconius was born at Lucerne and studied in Rottweil and Basle before coming to Zürich to teach in the cathedral school there. He played an influential role in securing the appointment of his friend Ulrich *Zwingli as minister and was a close collaborator in his reforming

work. In 1531 Myconius was called to Basle, where he succeeded *Oecolampadius as chief minister and remained for the rest of his life. He supervised the publication of the Basle Confession of 1534 and helped draft the first Helvetic Confession of 1536. His writings included a number of biblical commentaries and the first biography of Zwingli (1536).

mythology The classical myths had caused serious problems for the Middle Ages. Their solution was either to characterize the pagan gods as devils, a method sanctioned by St Augustine, or to allegorize them as symbols of Christian ethics and morality, a method exemplified in the countless manuscripts of the work known as *Ovid Moralized*. Renaissance scholars inherited both these approaches and added something of their own. A number of handbooks of mythology had been transmitted to the Renaissance; the *Bibliotheke* (*Library*) of Apollodorus and two works attributed to Julius Hyginus provided a basis for the study of the classical myths. The late antique period produced a number of commentaries – Servius' on Virgil (early fifth century) is the best known – which supplemented the handbooks.

The first Renaissance scholar to draw on these resources was *Boccaccio, who compiled (1350–75) *De genealogiis deorum*, an encyclopedia of mythology, geography, and history. He also made use of Leonzio Pilato's notes to his translation of Homer and of Lactantius Placidus' commentary on the *Thebaid* of Statius. For Boccaccio a knowledge of classical mythology is an essential part of a poet's equipment; the fourteenth book of the *Genealogia* is in fact devoted to this proposition. He adopted the Stoic position that myths are allegories of deeper truths, and this was to have a profound influence on later students of mythology. Boccaccio's popular work circulated widely in manuscript and was printed with a commentary by Micyllus in 1532. It was the primary source of information about classical myth for poets and artists; Chaucer made use of it and its influence can be seen in the Renaissance painter's love of allegory. It was finally superseded by the *Mythologia* of Natalis Comes (1551), which provided a codification, with emblematic illustrations, of contemporary knowledge of classical mythology. Mythology not only provided the raw material for decoration; it was also a way of conveying the truths of Neoplatonic philosophy. Plato himself had used myth as an integral part of his dialectic method. The first Neoplatonists, particularly Plotinus and Porphry, developed this aspect of their master's work to an extravagant degree and Origen made the technique respectable from the Christian point of view. The Florentine Platonists found this approach especially congenial. The choice of *Hercules, the judgment of the arms of Achilles, and the cave of the nymphs are typical of the classical myths which received allegorical or mystical interpretations. In the visual arts *Botticelli led the way for this kind of treatment in his introduction of pagan subject matter in major paintings.

Renaissance scholars frequently misunderstood their authorities and these misunderstandings were sometimes more fruitful than a more pedantic accuracy would have been. Boccaccio for example begins his genealogy of the gods with Demogorgon, who went on to have a long history in the works of many European writers. The reference comes from a misreading by a medieval scribe of a word in Lactantius Placidus' commentary on Statius. *See also* iconography.

N

Nanni di Banco (Giovanni di Antonio di Banco; c. 1384–1421) Italian sculptor. A native of Florence, Nanni trained under his father, the sculptor Antonio di Banco, with whom he worked on pieces for Florence cathedral. His first major work was the statue *Isaiah* (c. 1408), a life-sized marble figure that was a companion piece to Donatello's marble *David* and was executed in a notably Gothic manner. A more classical influence is evident, however, in his masterpiece, the *Quattro Santi Coronati* (c. 1411–13), a group of marble figures for Orsanmichele, Florence. His last major work was the *Assumption of the Virgin Mary* (begun c. 1414) over the Portale della Mandorla of Florence cathedral; it was probably finished by Luca *della Robbia, who may have been Nanni's pupil.

Nantes, Edict of (April 1598) The proclamation by *Henry IV of France that ended the Wars of *Religion. By it the *Huguenots were granted some religious toleration, including complete freedom of conscience and the right to worship freely in parts of France. Their pastors were paid by the state. They enjoyed full civic rights and were assigned certain towns as strongholds. A special Catholic and Huguenot court was to judge disputes arising from the settlement. The Catholic Church resented the edict; Cardinal Richelieu revoked the political clauses (1629) and Louis XIV revoked the entire edict in 1685. The revocation was followed by the emigration of hundreds of thousands of Huguenots, depriving France of many industrious and enterprising citizens.

Naogeorgus, Thomas (Thomas Kirchmaier; 1511–63) German polemical dramatist. Naogeorgus was born near Regensburg and became a Protestant pastor. He used the Latin drama, revived by the humanists, as a vehicle for his Reformation polemic against the pope and higher echelons of the Catholic Church. His *Pammachius* (1538), representing the pope as Antichrist, is one of the best examples of this drama and was acted in Cambridge in 1545. *Mercator* (1540) is an Everyman play. The many plays that followed were less successful. Naogeorgus also translated Sophocles' tragedies into Latin.

Napier, John (1550–1617) Scottish mathematician. The son of a wealthy laird, Napier was born at Merchiston Castle near Edinburgh. After attending St Andrews university and a period of foreign travel, he returned to Scotland to manage the family estates. A fanatical Protestant, Napier sought to demonstrate the identity of the pope and anti-Christ in his *Plaine discovery of the Whole Revelation of St John* (1593), a work that also predicted that the world would end between 1688 and 1700. Today Napier is remembered for his *Mirifici logarithmorum canonis descriptio* (1614; translated by Edward *Wright as *A Description of the Admirable Table of Logarithmes*, 1618), the work that introduced logarithms to the world. Other methods of computing, of which the best known is "Napier's bones" (a set of ten wooden or ivory rods), are described in his *Rabdologiae* (1617). *See also* Bürgi, Jost.

Naples (Italian: Napoli) A city and port in Campania, southern Italy, formerly capital of the kingdom of Naples. Originally colonized by Greeks, Naples was in turn Roman, Byzantine, and Norman before it was ruled by the Angevins (1282–1442), the king of Aragon (1442–58), and the illegitimate Aragonese line (1458–95). In pursuit of the Angevin claim, *Charles VIII of France briefly took over Naples (1495–96); after a period of confusion the city and kingdom of Naples were restored to Aragonese and Spanish rule (1504). Naples was then ruled by Spanish governors until the early eighteenth century.

During the fourteenth and fifteenth centuries Naples was the capital of a kingdom still organized largely on feudal lines; it lacked a substantial middle class and its commercial and economic development lagged behind that of cities in northern Italy. The prosperity of the city depended on the presence of the royal court and on the agriculture of the region. Yet, the growth of the city's population in the Renaissance era was remarkable, rising from about 30 000 in 1300 to about 60 000 in 1400 and close to 300 000 in 1600.

Royal patronage made Naples an important centre of learning and the arts. The city had a fine university (founded 1224), schools of humanist studies in the second half of the fifteenth century, printing presses (from 1471), and one of the oldest conservatories of music (founded 1537). In the 1530s the influential religious thinker and reformer, Juan de *Valdés, studied and wrote in Naples. *Caravaggio painted for the Neapolitan court in the late sixteenth and early seventeenth centuries. Neapolitan monarchs encouraged grand public works in their capital city; the Castel Nuovo (1279–82), the cathedral (1294–1333), and the Castel Sant'Elmo (rebuilt 1537–46) are among the buildings that have survived.

Nardi, Jacopo (1476–1563) Italian politician and historian. Nardi was born in Florence and belonged to the intellectual circle of the *Orti Oricellari. His earliest works were two comedies based on tales in Boccaccio: *L'Amicizia* (written between 1502 and 1512) and *I due felici rivali* (performed in 1513). A committed republican, he held various offices after the exiling of the Medici in 1494 and played an active role in their second expulsion in 1527. On their return in 1530 Nardi himself was exiled. Most of the rest of his life was spent in Venice. His chief work *Istorie della città di Firenze* (1582), covering the period 1498–1537, is mainly valuable for the period 1512–30, when Nardi was in the thick of political events on the anti-Medicean side.

Nashe, Thomas (1567–?1601) English writer. Nashe was born in Lowestoft, went to Cambridge university (1582), and then travelled in France and Italy before settling (c. 1588) in London. There he quickly embroiled himself in literary feuds, publishing his *Anatomie of absurditie* (1589) in which he attacked recent writers, and under the pseudonym of Pasquil he contributed pro-bishop pamphlets to the *Marprelate controversy. The Cambridge pedant Gabriel *Harvey was a special target of Nashe's lively satire until, after the publication of *Have with you to Saffron Walden* (1596), officialdom intervened to terminate the dispute. The picaresque novel *The Unfortunate Traveller, or the Life of Jack Wilton* (1594) shows Nashe's narrative and inventive powers at their best, while *Lenten Stuffe* (1599), a mock panegyric on Yarmouth herrings, is a bravura performance in burlesque. Nashe also wrote for the stage; in 1597 he was imprisoned for his share in the lost comedy *The Isle of Dogs*. Another comedy, *Summers Last Will*, was published in 1600, and he completed Marlowe's *Dido, Queen of Carthage* (1594) after the latter's death.

natural philosophy Throughout the Renaissance, and indeed long after, the term widely used to refer to the systematic investigation of nature. Science, as we know it today, emerged in the seventeenth

century but its roots lay in Renaissance thought. This is most clearly seen in astronomy. The work of *Copernicus had shown that the universe is heliocentric and was followed by *Kepler's discovery of the three laws of planetary motion. What, though, of motion itself? Two problems faced the Renaissance natural philosopher; to develop techniques to describe and analyse all kinds of motion and to explain its various forms. On the first issue scholars began with the work of medieval mathematicians such as *Oresme, who had developed simple graphical techniques to describe the motion of bodies, whether uniform or accelerating. Using their techniques, *Galileo succeeded in deriving the basic equations of motion relating acceleration, time, distance, and velocity. They were, however, expressed as geometrical ratios rather than the algebraic equations familiar today. Galileo's grasp of the nature of motion was equally limited. Although he was able to break with tradition in a number of respects, he failed to recognize the essential role of inertia in physics.

Nor was any greater progress made when scholars turned their attention to the nature of matter. While some rejected the traditional four-element theory of matter (*see* Aristotelianism, Renaissance), few could agree on its replacement. *Paracelsus and his followers argued that bodies were composed of salt, sulphur, and mercury, without ever making it clear what was meant by these terms. Others, however, proposed the existence of two, four, five, or more elements. With no clear concept of the nature of an element, and without an authoritative theory, Renaissance chemistry inevitably lacked cohesion. This condition was made worse by the secretiveness and suspicion brought about by the close contact between Renaissance chemistry and *alchemy.

If old disciplines proved hard to reform, more impressive results were achieved in newer areas of research. Thus William *Gilbert in *De magnete* (1600), with no traditional constraints to worry about, virtually founded the scientific study of magnetism. Galileo, too, in his *Due nuove scienze* (1638), could achieve similar results on the cohesion of bodies and the resistance they offer to fracture. Much of this success depended on the growing reliance on experiment and observation, exemplified especially in the works of Gilbert and Galileo. The theory justifying this approach was presented by Galileo himself and, even more so, by *Bacon.

Less progress was made in the study of organic nature. While knowledge, of sorts, was accumulated, and some fresh attempts were made to systematize that knowledge (*see* zoology), the subject remained too constrained by its own theological assumptions to develop into new areas. At a more fundamental level natural philosophy during the Renaissance found itself under strong attack from supporters of *magic. To an uncommitted sixteenth-century witness it cannot have been entirely clear whether a better understanding of nature could be derived from the magical techniques of someone like *Agrippa, or the work of the young mathematician Galileo. In the event, the vision of Galileo and Kepler prevailed over that of *Ficino and Agrippa and prepared the way, in the process, for the science of Descartes and Newton.

Naumburg Convention (1561) A meeting of German princes and Protestant theologians, designed to achieve doctrinal unity in accordance with the Confession of *Augsburg. It failed because the Lutherans insisted on the original articles of 1530 (*invariata*) and the Calvinists preferred those of 1540 (*variata*). A papal invitation to send delegates to the Council of Trent was declined.

Navagiero, Andrea (1483–1529) Italian scholar, historian, poet, and diplomat. Navagiero was born into an eminent Venetian family. He studied in Padua where he learned Greek and particularly interested himself in the odes of Pindar; the Greek *editio princeps* of Pindar (1513) was dedicated to Navagiero by Aldus *Manutius, for whose press Navagiero edited Latin authors, most notably Cicero. In 1506 Navagiero was appointed to succeed *Sabellico as librarian of S Marco and this position, together with his membership of the *Neakademia, placed him in the centre of Venetian intellectual life. Among his friends was *Fracastoro, who made Navagiero the mouthpiece for his views on poetry in the dialogue *Naugerius* (1555); the garden setting for this dialogue recalls Navagiero's own interest in natural science and his renowned garden at Murano. He was also friendly with *Bembo, with whom he visited Rome, with *Raphael, who painted his portrait, and with *Ramusio.

Besides writing a history of Venice, Navagiero served the republic as ambassador. In 1526 he was in Spain, where he met *Boscán and introduced him to Italian poetic metres, which Boscán was the first to naturalize in Spanish. Navagiero brought back with him from Spain to Italy the then newly discovered potato and other exotics, including possibly a banana. He was next sent on an embassy to Francis I of France, but died while at Blois. His *Orationes duae carminaque nonnulla* were published posthumously at Venice (1530).

Navarrete, Juan Fernández de *see* Fernández de Navarrete, Juan.

navigation Renaissance navigation was fundamentally a combination of the Arab astronomy that guided medieval travellers and latter-day technological developments. The forerunner of the numerous scientific navigational instruments created by Renaissance inventors was the compass in the thirteenth century. In the wake of its popularization, the first known navigational book, *Lo compasso di navigare*, began to circulate in 1296. Around the same time, the Carta Pisana (Pisan chart) displayed the horizon in terms of compass points, although directions, especially in the Mediterranean area, were still mainly determined by major winds. Also, early compasses were based on dead reckoning, with no allowances for magnetic variation. Along with instruments, *cartography flourished during the Renaissance period. In the fifteenth century Portuguese cartographers developed the use of latitude to permit navigators unprecedented certainty in determining their whereabouts; it was assessed by the position of either the Pole Star or the midday sun. Various methods were proposed to establish longitude; *Gemma Frisius suggested the use of a clock in 1530, but a sufficiently accurate timepiece was not available until the chronometer was developed in the eighteenth century, and mariners until then had to rely on very uncertain methods of dead reckoning.

Although navigational techniques improved throughout the Renaissance period, most of the major gaps were filled by instruments invented by German or Flemish scientists such as *Apian and *Regiomontanus in the late fifteenth and early sixteenth centuries. Improvements to *astrolabes made them more useful to mariners, while *quadrants, cross-staffs, and *backstaffs were also invented or refined. The development of practical literature and of printing processes suitable for cartography was invaluable to the spread of navigational knowledge. For example, Regiomontanus's *Ephemerides* (1474) proposed the principle of working out longitude from lunar distances, and the idea was taken up again by Werner (1514), Apian (1524), Gemma Frisius (1530), and *Nunes (1560). See p. 286.

Neakademia (New Academy *or* Aldine Academy) The academy founded by Aldus *Manutius in Venice around 1500 for the propagation of Greek scholarship. Under its constitution, which was drawn up in Greek, only Greek was to be spoken at its sessions; fines for violation of this rule were accumulated to provide occasional banquets in imitation of Plato's symposia. The Neakademia had between thirty-five and forty members, about a third of them Greeks. Members were divided into sections to undertake specific publishing projects

NAVIGATION *A gathering of Dutch mariners with their nautical instruments and charts adorns the frontispiece of Willem Jansz. Blaeu's sea atlas* Het Licht der Zeevaerdt. *Among the instruments shown are an astrolabe, a cross-staff, terrestrial and celestial globes, a compass, and a mariner's astrolabe.*

for the *Aldine press, with proofreaders and correctors attached to each section. *Aleandro and *Bembo were among its distinguished members, and the academy also welcomed visiting scholars like *Erasmus and *Linacre.

Neapolitan Academy A literary society that first emerged as a coherent group in Naples in the 1440s under the patronage of *Alfonso (I) the Magnanimous and the leadership of *Beccadelli. A little later it became known as the Accademia Pontaniana after its new leading member, *Pontano.

Nebrija (*or* Nebrissa *or* Nebrixa), Elio Antonio Martínez de Cala de (1444–1522) Spanish humanist. He was born at Lebrija (Latin name: Nebrissa), Seville, and studied at Salamanca and from 1461 to 1470 at Bologna, concentrating on classical languages but reading widely in law, medicine, and theology. He taught grammar and rhetoric at Salamanca from 1475. In 1502 he was one of the group of scholars gathered by Cardinal *Ximénes de Cisneros at Alcalá to produce the *Complutensian Polyglot Bible. He was also appointed royal chronicler (1508–09). Failing to succeed to the chair of grammar at Salamanca in 1513, he moved to the university of Alcalá.

The greatest Spanish humanist of the Renaissance, Nebrija published the first sound Latin grammar in Spain, *Introductiones latine* (1481), which he later translated into Spanish for Queen Isabella. *Interpretatio dictionum ex sermone latino in hispaniensem* (1492), a Latin-Spanish dictionary, listed 30 000 words. In the same year he published the first scientific grammar of any European vernacular language, *Gramática sobre la lengua castellana* (1492). He also published a Spanish-Latin dictionary (c. 1495, expanded 1516), a volume attempting to regularize spelling (*Reglas de orthographia en la lengua castellana*, 1517), a classics-based educational manual, and commentaries on Persius and Prudentius.

Negretti, Jacomo *see* Palma Vecchio.

Negretti, Jacopo *see* Palma Giovane.

Negroli family Italian makers of weapons and armour. They succeeded the *Missaglia family as the leading Milanese manufacturers in this field in the first half of the sixteenth century. Leading members were Jacopo and Filippo (active 1525–50) who made embossed parade armour as well as more practical suits. Among their clients were

Emperor Charles V and Francis I of France.

neo-Latin literature The quantity and quality of original Latin writing in the Renaissance tend to be underestimated as few people possess the necessary facility in Latin to appreciate it, very little of it has been translated, and interest has generally been focused upon the emergent literature in the *vernacular. In these circumstances it is easy to forget that the Latin writings of *Petrarch were as widely known and imitated as his innovatory Italian poems (*see* sonnet), since Latin as the universal language of the learned easily transcended national boundaries. The major controversy connected with the creation of a body of humanistic Latin literature – the Ciceronian debate (*see* Cicero) – also flourished across Europe. Virtually every humanist demonstrated his proficiency in Latin with a volume of Latin verse, though these were often juvenile or occasional productions; other writers produced Latin poetry that had a major impact upon poetic developments in the vernaculars (*see* Latin studies; pastoral).
In prose *Salutati was one of the first humanists to win renown as a stylist, followed by *Bruni, *Ficino, *Pico della Mirandola, and other Florentine writers. Juan Luis *Vivès was the leading Spanish Latinist, and in northern Europe *Erasmus and *Muret were among those whom contemporaries singled out as stylistic models, the former colloquial and fluent, the latter more polished and correct.

Neoplatonism, Renaissance Neoplatonism developed in the second and third centuries AD, mainly in Alexandria where Greek, Jewish, and oriental ideas had a natural meeting place. Its greatest exponent was Plotinus, who in the *Enneads* developed a complex structure of mysticism and allegory which, while using aspects of Plato's doctrines as a starting point, introduced an element of the irrational which was far removed from Plato's own ideas. Gnostic concepts were also incorporated and in its fully developed form the system constituted a serious challenge to Christianity. This philosophical school never completely died out in Constantinople and when Greek teachers migrated to Italy in the fifteenth century they brought with them Neoplatonism in its Byzantine form.
Gemistus Plethon's work is typical of the writings that conveyed Neoplatonic ideas to the Renaissance. Though ostensibly a Platonist, he was heavily influenced by the Alexandrian school, and by Stoicism and oriental religions such as Zoroastrianism. In his major work *Nomoi* (Laws) he attributed souls to the stars, accepted metempsychosis (transference of souls), and derived his social morality from natural law in a way that scandalized

the orthodox Western Christians. These and similar ideas were congenial to many Renaissance thinkers, and Neoplatonism spread from Florence to other Italian centres. The work of *Ficino, who translated Plotinus into Latin in 1492, and of *Pico della Mirandola helped to popularize Neoplatonic ideas and the transcendentalism of Plethon's philosophy appealed to those who were looking for a unifying principle and already using *magic, hermetic theories, and heterodox Christian mysticism as elements to further that search (*see also* Egyptian studies). Neoplatonism exercised a powerful influence on creative writers in the Renaissance. Its characteristic mode was allegory and the exegetical potential of the allegorical approach was attractive to both poets and prose writers. Spenser's *Faerie Queene*, for instance, has many Neoplatonic elements.
It is in fact almost impossible to draw rigid distinctions between Platonism and Neoplatonism in the Renaissance; striking evidence of this is the fact that the discussions of the *Platonic academy at Florence were concerned far more with essentially Neoplatonic ideas than with authentic Platonism.

Neri, St Philip *see* Philip Neri, St.

Neri di Bicci (1419–c. 1491) Italian painter. Born in Florence, Neri trained under his father Bicci di Lorenzo (1373–1452), although the influence of other eminent contemporary Florentine artists, such as Fra Angelico and Fra Filippo Lippi, can also be seen in his large output. He himself became a sought-after teacher. Examples of his work are to be found in several Florentine churches, and his journal, covering the years 1453–75, is in the Uffizi.

Neroccio (di Bartolommeo) dei Landi (1447–c. 1500) Italian painter and sculptor. Based in his native Siena, Neroccio was the partner of *Francesco di Giorgio for several years (1467–75) and typified the charming poetic quality of the Sienese school. His most important works include *Madonna with Saints*, *Antony and Cleopatra*, and *Portrait of a Girl*, all in the National Gallery, Washington. Two particularly attractive treatments of the *Madonna and Child* theme are in the Pinacoteca in Siena.

Netherlands, Revolt of the (1566–1609) The Dutch rebellion against Spanish rule, caused by Spanish attempts to suppress Dutch Calvinism and political freedoms. Mounting discontent led wealthy Dutch burghers and noblemen to draft the Compromise of *Breda (1566), which they presented to the regent, *Margaret of Parma, as a petition. The scornful rejection of the petitioners as "ces gueux" (these beggars) was followed by

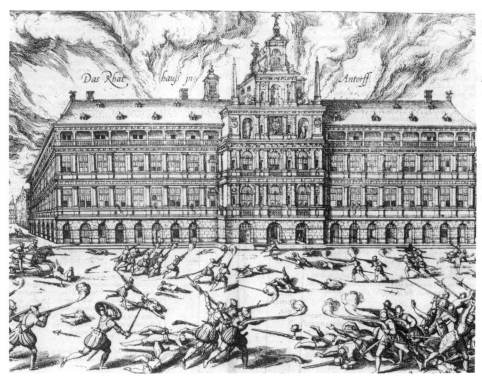

attacks on Catholic clergy and churches.

In 1567 *Philip II of Spain sent the duke of *Alba with 20 000 troops to crush the rebel Dutch, and a reign of terror was instituted by the Council of Troubles, nicknamed the *Tribunal of Blood. Led by *William (I) the Silent from 1568, the Dutch suffered setbacks, but Spanish repression only stiffened their resistance.

After the *sea-beggars seized Brill (1572) and took towns in Holland and Zeeland Alba was recalled to Spain in disgrace (1573). The struggle continued inconclusively under the governor-generalship (1573–76) of Luis de Requisens and then under Don *John of Austria until the conciliatory policies of Alessandro *Farnese, Duke of Parma (governor 1578–92), won the southern Catholic provinces back to Spain. It was too late to win back the north, where the seven provinces had organized themselves into the Union of Utrecht (1579) and in 1581 proclaimed their independence as the Republic of the United Netherlands, with William the Silent as their hereditary stadtholder.

After William's assassination (1584), *Maurice of Nassau led the Dutch and drove the Spanish out of the seven northern provinces by 1594. The struggle continued until Spain came close to recognizing Dutch independence in the truce of 1609. By the Treaty of Westphalia (1648) the European powers formally recognized Dutch independence.

new star (stella nova) The supernova (a star that temporarily becomes up to one hundred million times brighter than the sun) observed in 1572 in the constellation Cassiopeia by Tycho *Brahe. Its observation among the "fixed stars" challenged the Aristotelian view, already under attack from the Copernican (heliocentric) hypothesis, that the celestial region was immutable. *See also* astronomy; cosmology.

Niccoli, Niccolò (1363–1437) Italian bibliophile. A member of the learned Medici circle in Florence, Niccoli avoided public life and concentrated on the collecting of manuscripts and on encouraging scholars to edit, copy, and translate classical texts. In this he was helped by Cosimo de' Medici who gave him unlimited credit at the Medici bank. Niccoli also exploited the Medici commercial network, using their agents to search for manuscripts; among those he discovered was the oldest manuscript of the minor works of Tacitus. Despite his collection of Greek manuscripts Niccoli knew no Greek himself. He was noted for the elegance of his life-style and the generosity with which he opened his library to scholars. On his death he left his library to a group of trustees, including Leonardo *Bruni. Cosimo took over the collection to cancel the overdraft, and it was housed in the monastery of S Marco and catalogued by Tommaso Parentucelli, later Pope *Nicholas V. Niccoli's life was written by Vespasiano da *Bisticci.

Niccolò dell'Arca (c. 1440–94) Italian sculptor.

Sometimes known as Niccolò di Bari or Niccolò da Puglia after his birthplace, Bari in Apulia, he worked in Venice in the 1460s, but his main work was executed in Bologna – hence his other name of Niccolò da Bologna. In 1469 he undertook the contract for the decorated canopy of the tomb (*arca*) of St Dominic in the church of S Domenico, Bologna; he also contributed some of the small free-standing figures on the tomb. Elsewhere in Bologna are several fine terracottas by him, including a *Madonna* (1478) in the Palazzo Communale and a *Pietà* (post-1485) in Sta Maria della Vita.

Nicholas of Cusa *see* Cusanus, Nicholas.

Nicholas V (1397–1455), Pope (1447–55) He was born Tommaso Parentucelli at Sarzana, and after studying law at Bologna, he acted as tutor to two Florentine families who introduced him to humanistic ideas. He was the friend of Cosimo de' *Medici, whom he advised (1439–40) on the collection of texts for his library. In 1444 he was made bishop of Bologna by *Eugenius IV, whom he succeeded as pope three years later. In 1449 he resolved the schism occasioned by the Council of *Basle, and the following year he held a jubilee at Rome. In 1452 he crowned *Frederick III emperor, the last time such a coronation took place in Rome. Nicholas V was the first humanist pope. He employed dozens of scholars to edit and copy classical texts and founded a library which had grown by his death to 9000 volumes; this collection formed the basis for the *Vatican Library. His own library room was decorated (1449) with portraits of pagan and Christian authors by Fra *Angelico. Himself a scholar, Nicholas mixed on equal terms with the humanists who crowded to Rome, among them, *Valla, *Filelfo, and *Bessarion. The most significant event of his pontificate was the fall of Constantinople (1453) to the Ottoman Turks, which Nicholas saw as a blow to scholarship as much as to religion. He called a crusade to eject the Turks, but could arouse no response. His plan for extending and beautifying Rome, over which he consulted *Alberti, among others, met with serious opposition, and in 1453 there was an unsuccessful conspiracy to overthrow him.

Noot, Jan Baptista van der (Jonker Jan van der Noot; c. 1540–c. 1595) Dutch poet and prose writer. Noot was born in Brecht and was sheriff of Antwerp until (1567) he was forced to take refuge in England on account of the political and religious turmoil. He later moved on to France and Germany. Noot was deeply affected by the Renaissance ideals embodied in the work of the *Pléiade, especially *Ronsard, and his *Het Bosken*, published in London in 1570 or 1571, is the first true volume of Renaissance verse in Dutch. *Het Theatre oft toon-neel* (1568), a Calvinistic prose tract, was also published in London and was translated into French the same year, into English (possibly partly by *Spenser) in 1569, and German in 1572. In 1578 Noot returned to Antwerp where he struggled to make a living by writing and eventually died. His *Olympiados* (1579) is an epic interspersed with sonnets; the full text is known only from a German translation, *Das Buch Extasis* (1576).

North, Thomas (1535–?1601) English translator. Born into a good London family, North seems to have suffered financial difficulties throughout his life. In 1574 he accompanied his brother on a embassy to France and about 1591 he was knighted. Otherwise his fame rests entirely on his translations. The first of these to appear was of Antonio de *Guevara's *Reloj de príncipes*, via an intervening French version, under the title *The Diall of Princes* (1557). *The Morall Philosophy of Doni* (1570) was a translation of a collection of oriental fables made by the Italian Anton Francesco *Doni. *The Lives of the Noble Grecians and Romans* (1579), dedicated to Queen Elizabeth, is a translation of Amyot's 1559 version of Plutarch; as such it is neither scholarly nor accurate, but it was nonetheless immensely and deservedly successful, not least because of North's clear and vigorous style. Shakespeare drew heavily upon North's Plutarch for his Roman plays.

northeast passage A passage from Western Europe to China and India through north European and Russian waters. The merchant Robert Thorne (died 1527), writing to Henry VIII in 1527, proposed a northeast, *northwest, or polar route to the Indies as being shorter than the southerly routes taken by the Spaniards and Portuguese. Sir Hugh Willoughby led the first of many unsuccessful attempts at discovery in 1553, perishing in the endeavour (*see* Muscovy Company). Another notable but unsuccessful explorer in this direction was the Dutchman Willem *Barents, and all attempts over the next three centuries were defeated by the harsh climate and dangerous currents. The first successful passage was achieved in 1878 when a Norwegian ship, *Vega*, sailed to Japan through the Arctic Ocean.

northwest passage A route from Europe to China and India along the northern coast of America. An intense search for this passage was sponsored by English, Dutch, and French merchant companies in the sixteenth century, as Europe yearned for rapid access to Asia's riches, but the adverse climatic conditions rendered most expeditions abortive and claimed many lives. Sebastian *Cabot in 1509 sailed northwest from Newfoundland, perhaps as far as the Hudson Strait, until ice and threatened mutiny forced him to retreat. French expeditions followed (1523, 1534), leading to the exploration of Canada (see Cartier, Jacques), and in 1576 Sir Humfrey Gilbert refired enthusiasm for the search with his *Discourse of a Discoverie of a new passage to...Cathay*. This resulted in the voyages (1576–78) of Martin Frobisher, John Davis (1585–87), Henry Hudson (1607–10), and William Baffin (1615–16) – all names commemorated on the map of Canada's Arctic region – but the question of a route northwest from Hudson's Bay remained unresolved for more than two centuries.

Nostradamus (Michel de Nostredame; 1503–66) French astrologer. Born at St-Remy, Provence, the son of a Jewish-Italian doctor, Nostradamus studied medicine at Montpellier (1522–25). He then spent four years tending sufferers from plague, acquiring a reputation as a healer. Moving to Agen, he married (c. 1534), but his family was killed by plague. In 1538 he was accused of heresy and left Agen to wander across Europe; during this time stories of his prophetic powers began to circulate. From 1550 onwards he produced a yearly almanac. In 1555 the first part of his *Centuries*, a book of prophecies, was published and made a great impression, resulting in a summons to the French court (1556). However, the remainder of the work was not published until 1568, probably because of the dangers of investigation for practising magic. For the same reason, the *Centuries* were written in a deliberately obscure style. They still exert an influence in occult circles.

novella The prose tale, ancestor of the short story, originated and flourished in Italy from the thirteenth to the seventeenth century. It was established as a respectable literary genre by Boccaccio's *Decameron*, though Boccaccio invented neither the term *novella* nor the form. *Novelle* drew on many sources for their plots, which were straightforward, often anecdotal. Folk tales, classical and oriental sources, the Bible, *exempla*, romances of chivalry, and *fabliaux* all provided material. The narratives were direct, sometimes conversational in style, reflecting contemporary everyday life, especially of the urban merchant class. They were published in collections, usually with a frame (*cornice*) in imitation of the *Decameron*. The outstanding collection before the mid-fourteenth-century *Decameron* is the anonymous Tuscan *Cento novelle antiche* (or *Novellino*), anecdotal narratives presented as models for inculcating polite speech and manners. Fourteenth-century collections written after the *Decameron* include the

Trecentonovelle (223 stories) of Franco *Sacchetti, who dropped the framing device and wrote in a lively colloquial style; *Percorone* (*Numskull*, a reference to a number of stupid characters in the tales; c. 1378) by Ser Giovanni Fiorentino, fifty stories including one having the plot of Shakespeare's *Merchant of Venice*; and the 155 *Novelle* of Giovanni Sercambi of Lucca (1347–1424), much indebted to the oral tradition of storytelling. Resembling secular *novelle* in some respects are the exemplary tales found in two religious works, *Vite dei santi padri* by Domenico Cavalca (1270–1342) and *Lo specchio di vera penitenza* by Jacopo Passavanti (c. 1302–57). Fifteenth-century humanist Latin examples are *Historia de duobus amantibus* (1444) by Aenea Silvio Piccolomini (later Pope Pius II) and the bawdy *Facetiae* of Poggio *Bracciolini. Giovanni Gherardi da Prato (c. 1366–c. 1446) in *Paradiso degli Alberti* (c. 1426) portrays a learned gathering, which includes Coluccio *Salutati and Luigi Marsigli, telling tales but mainly conversing during a stay at Antonio degli Alberti's villa (Paradiso) in 1389. The *Novelle* (1424) of Gentile Sermini of Siena and the Bolognese Giovanni Sabadino degli Arienti's *Le Porrettane* (The Ladies of Porretta; 1475) refer, in their frames, to life at spas, which permitted a certain licence and relaxed humour. The fifty tales in the *Novellino* of Masuccio Salernitano (c. 1415–c. 1480) are notable for harsh polemical passages against friars and women; one story is a source for the Romeo and Juliet plot. Sixteenth-century contributions include *Firenzuola's uncompleted *Ragionamenti d'amore* (ten *novelle*), *Doni's *La zucca* (1551), the *Novelle de' novizi* (1560) by Pietro Fortini (1500–62), *Le cene* by Anton Francesco *Grazzini, the seventy-five *novelle* of *Le piacevole notte* (1550, 1553) by Gianfrancesco Straparola (c. 1490–1557), the 214 *Novelle* (1554, 1573) by Matteo *Bandello, source of many plots for later playwrights, *della Casa's *Galateo* (1558), and *Cinthio's *Hecatommithi* (1565), which contained the sources for Shakespeare's *Othello* (III, 7) and *Measure for Measure* (VIII, 5).

Noye, Sebastian van (Sebastian van Noyen or van Oye; c. 1493–1557) Netherlands architect. He was born in Utrecht and worked as military architect for Emperor Charles V; the star-shaped fortress at Philippeville (now in Belgium) was one of his constructions. In 1550 he also built the Brussels palace of Cardinal *Granvelle, an important building in true Italian Renaissance style.

numismatics The collecting and studying of coins and medals. The science of numismatics originated with the enthusiasm of Italian noblemen for all aspects of the classical world during the early

NUMISMATICS *The personal medal of Giovanni Pico della Mirandola. The three Graces are depicted on the reverse, with the inscription* PULCHRITUDO-AMOR-VOLUPTAS *(beauty – love – pleasure).*

Renaissance. Such scholars as *Petrarch formed large collections of Greek and Roman coins, especially prizing specimens of particular historical interest or rarity. The popularity of coin collecting in Italy also precipitated the growth of a lucrative trade in counterfeits. Jacopo *Strada in the 1550s was one of the earliest collectors to publish his coin collection. The Medagliere Mediceo, a vast collection of Italian medals, was begun by Lorenzo de' Medici and is now housed in the Bargello, Florence.

The striking of medals, usually as commemorative items, was known in the classical world but was extensively revived during the Renaissance, when it reached its highest level of artistry. The usual formula for the design of medals reflected the practice of imperial Rome: a portrait head in profile on the obverse and on the reverse a symbol or device. Considerable ingenuity was often expended in the Renaissance upon the choice of *imprese* for the reverses of medals. The metals commonly used were lead or bronze. *Pisanello, effectively launched the art of the Renaissance medal with his bronze medal of the Byzantine emperor John VIII Palaeologus in 1438. This was the first of a series of notable portrait medals; among those who commissioned medals from him were several members of the Gonzaga family, Duke Filippo Maria Visconti of Milan (1441), Leonello d'Este (1442), Sigismondo Malatesta (1445), and Alfonso I of Naples (1449).

Pisanello's success inspired a number of contemporary imitators, among them Antonio Marescotto of Ferrara (active 1444–62), Matteo de' *Pasti of Verona, and, slightly later, *Adriano Fiorentino. All early medals were cut entirely by hand but innovations were gradually made by leading medallists, such as the architect Donato *Bramante, who invented a press for leaden seals. Pre-eminent among medallists of the sixteenth century was Benvenuto *Cellini, who also made improvements in methods of engraving dies. Other important Italian medallists included *Sperandio in Ferrara, Bologna, and Venice, Niccolò Fiorentino (Niccolò Spinelli; 1430–1514) and Cellini's pupil Pier Paolo Romano (c. 1520–84) in Florence, Caradosso (Cristoforo Caradosso Foppa; 1452–1527) in Rome, *Antico in Mantua, and Pastorino de' Pastorini (1508–92) in Siena.

Outside Italy, there developed a notable medal-striking tradition in Germany during the first half of the sixteenth century, where Peter *Flötner, Ludwig Krug (c. 1490–1532), and others established a leading school at Nuremberg. Albrecht Dürer also produced several designs, although he probably never actually struck the medals himself. The Milanese Antonio Abondio (1538–91) made bronze medals in Vienna for the emperors Maximilian II and Rudolf II, and his son Alessandro (1575–c. 1645) followed in his footsteps. French medallists dominated the art during the seventeenth century, especially François *Briot, Guillaume Dupré (c. 1576–1643), who was also in charge of France's coinage, and Jean Warin (1604–72). A younger relative of François Briot, Nicolas Briot (1580–1646) settled in England (1625), worked for the Mint, and instructed the English medallists and engravers Thomas Rawlins (?1620–70) and Thomas Simon (1618–65). Thomas Simon's brother Abraham (1617–92) and the Antwerp-born John Roettiers (1631–1703) maintained a belated Renaissance medallic tradition after the Restoration; among the Simon brothers' notable medals were a famous portrait of Cromwell (1656) and a gold one of General Monck (1660).

Nunes, Pedro (1492–1577) Portuguese geographer and mathematician. Born at Alcacer do Sal, Nunes was a brilliant student and quickly rose to become professor of mathematics at Lisbon. In 1529 he was appointed royal cosmographer to promote Portugal's claim to possession of the Spice Islands. He translated part of Ptolemy's works (1537) and wrote a treatise *De arte atque ratione navigandi* (1546). He recognized (1537), but did not pursue, the navigational problem solved by *Mercator in his projection, and in *De crepusculis* (1542) explained the phenomenon of afterglow or second twilight. His *Libro de Algebra en Arithmetica y Geometria* appeared in 1567. Between 1538 and 1544 he worked in Spain but he died at Coimbra as professor of mathematics.

Nuremberg (German: Nürnberg) A city on the River Pegnitz in Bavaria, southern Germany. During the thirteenth century Nuremberg became an imperial free city and joined the Confederation of the Rhine. By the early fourteenth century its craftsmen had brought prosperity to Nuremberg, and in the fifteenth century further prosperity arose from its situation on the trade route linking Italy and the Netherlands. There were rich metal and mineral deposits nearby and Nuremberg produced very fine gold and silver plate. Surplus capital was used to make Nuremberg one of the first major European banking centres outside Italy.

Prosperity and close links with Italy placed the city at the forefront of the northern Renaissance. Willibald *Pirckheimer made it a centre of humanist scholarship, and the astronomer and mathematician *Regiomontanus also worked there. The Nuremberg geographer Martin Behaim made the oldest surviving terrestrial globe in 1492, epitomizing the city's reputation as a producer of scientific instruments. Anton Koberger the publisher produced at least 236 books in Nuremberg between 1573 and 1613. Other distinguished citizens included the painter and engraver Albrecht *Dürer, the woodcarver Veit *Stoss, the bronze-founder Peter *Vischer, the sculptor Adam *Kraft, and the poet and dramatist Hans Sachs. Rather extensively restored buildings which have survived include the Marthakirche and Frauenkirche (both fourteenth century), and the Lorenzkirche (thirteenth to fifteenth centuries).

Nuremberg, Little Masters of *see* Little Masters (of Nuremberg).

O

Obrecht, Jacob (c. 1450–1505) Flemish composer. In 1476 Obrecht became master of the choristers at Utrecht, then (1479–84) held the same post at the church of St Gertrude, Bergen-op-Zoom (probably his native town), and at Cambrai cathedral (1484–85). He was appointed succentor at St Donatien, Bruges, in 1486, and became *maître de chapelle* there in 1490, after a visit to Ferrara at the invitation of Duke Ercole I d'Este in 1487. In 1494 he was employed at the church of Notre Dame in Antwerp but in 1496 was again in Bergen-op-Zoom. After further short spells in Antwerp and Bruges he retired in 1500, made a second trip to Ferrara in 1504, and died there of the plague. As Duke Ercole d'Este's invitation to Obrecht testifies, he was greatly respected as a composer in his day, regarded as second only to Josquin *Des Prés. Obrecht wrote some secular music, notably chansons and arrangements of Dutch popular tunes, but is best known for his writing of sacred music, in particular for the Mass. Some twenty-six Masses survive, in which Obrecht uses the *cantus firmus* in varying ways. Sometimes, as in the *Missa Je ne demande*, the melody on which the work is based is segmented, while in the *Missa Sub tuum praesidium* the plainsong *cantus firmus* melody is joined progressively by three other borrowed melodies, all four combining together in the Agnus Dei.

Ockeghem, Johannes (c. 1410–97) Franco-Flemish composer. The first mention of Ockeghem is as a singer at Notre Dame, Antwerp, in 1443. It is thought that he studied with *Binchois and had connections with the ducal chapel of Burgundy. He entered the employ of Charles, Duke of Bourbon, around 1445, and was active in the court of King Charles VII of France in 1453, being favoured with the office of treasurer of the church of St Martin-de-Tours. On Charles VII's death (1461) Ockeghem continued in the service of Louis XI, and in 1463 became a canon at Notre Dame, Paris. In 1470 he travelled to Spain as part of a diplomatic retinue and sometime probably visited Italy. He died in Paris, still in the service of the French court.
Even in his own day, Ockeghem was renowned as a composer and as a singer. He wrote some secular

works (around twenty-two chansons in a traditional style survive), but it is his sacred works, particularly his Masses, which are important. Although his output is comparatively low – ten complete Masses, some settings of the Ordinary, and a few motets – he is regarded as one of the greatest composers of the second half of the fifteenth century. The Masses are of two kinds; those based on pre-existing material, like the *Missa L'homme armé*, and those which are freely composed. In both kinds smooth counterpoint is used to great effect, with a skilful use of varied textures.

Oecolampadius, John (Johann Hussgen; 1482–1531) German theologian and reformer. Oecolampadius was born at Weinsberg, at that time in the Palatinate. After visiting Bologna, he studied theology at Heidelberg and in 1515 was appointed preacher at Basle cathedral, where his strong reforming tendencies became plain. In 1520 he published a Greek grammar and was invited to preach in Augsburg, but a period of doubt then caused him to withdraw for a time to a monastery. In 1522, his reforming faith restored, he moved to Ebernburg, and then returned to Basle where he spent the rest of his life as a leader among the reformers. In 1528 he married, and the same year he and *Zwingli caused the reformed faith to be adopted at Berne and the Mass to be discontinued at Basle. In 1529 he attended the Colloquy of *Marburg.

Okeghem, Jean de *see* Ockeghem, Johannes.

Oldenbarneveldt, Johan van (1547–1619) Dutch statesman. Oldenbarneveldt was born at Amersfoort. He studied law at Louvain, Bourges, and Heidelberg, where he became a Protestant, and in 1568 he supported the revolt against Spain. In 1579 he joined *William the Silent, Prince of Orange, in negotiating the Union of Utrecht, which united the northern provinces of the Netherlands. He was attorney-general of the union and secretary to the provincial estates of Holland. After the assassination of William the Silent in 1584, he took charge of domestic and foreign affairs, while Prince *Maurice of Nassau commanded the armed forces.

He negotiated an alliance with France and England in 1596 and a controversial twelve-year truce with Spain in 1609. He worked to maintain the dominance of the province of Holland within the union and in religious affairs supported the Arminians against the Calvinists; this brought him into conflict with Maurice. Accused of subverting church and state, he was beheaded at The Hague.

Oliver, Isaac (c. 1560–1617) English painter. Born in Rouen, the son of French Huguenots, Oliver was brought to England in 1568 and studied painting under Nicholas *Hilliard. Although he also painted life-size portraits (see Plate XXI) and religious and classical scenes, Oliver is remembered chiefly as a painter of miniature portraits. He travelled in the Netherlands (1588) and to Venice (1596) and by 1595 he had become Hilliard's chief rival. Oliver's patrons included Anne of Denmark (1604) and later Henry Frederick, Prince of Wales, of whom he painted a striking portrait miniature (c. 1610). The large-scale equestrian portrait of the prince in the Venetian manner, formerly attributed to Oliver, is now assigned to Robert Peake. In his later years Oliver adopted a more naturalistic style and painted historical and biblical scenes in the mannerist tradition. His son Peter (1594–1647) also executed paintings in his father's later style.

Olivetan (Pierre Robert; c. 1506–38) French Protestant reformer and translator. Born at Noyon, Picardy, a cousin of Jean *Calvin, Olivetan was forced to abandon his studies at Orleans and flee to Strasbourg after his conversion to Protestantism. He became actively involved in the Reformation, preaching to the Waldenses in Piedmont, and undertook the translation of the Bible into French; this was published at Serrières, near Neuchâtel, in 1535. Extensively revised by Calvin and others during the sixteenth century, Olivetan's Bible ranked with that of *Lefèvre d'Étaples as a major source for subsequent French translations of the scriptures.

Ollanda, Francisco d' *see* Francisco da Hollanda.

optics Considerable advances were made in antiquity in the study of geometrical optics. Ancient scientists distinguished between *catoptrics*, the study of reflection, and *dioptrics*, the corresponding study of refraction. While they had managed to formulate the basic laws of reflection they were less successful in their work on refraction. Ptolemy had established no more than that the angle of incidence was always greater than the angle of refraction, whatever the media. It was not until the early seventeenth century that Willebrord

*Snell established the true relationship. The ratio of the sines of the angles of incidence and refraction, he demonstrated, were constant for any media.

Renaissance scientists also made significant advances in the development of optical instruments. The period of the late sixteenth and early seventeenth centuries is especially significant as the time when the *microscope and the *telescope were invented. Equally of concern to scientists was the nature of light and its mode of propagation. Two main theories had emerged in antiquity. Some considered that light was emitted from the eye, the object, or both, and operated by travelling between the eye and the visible object. Others, following Aristotle, denied that anything travelled between eye and object, and argued instead that light was a state of the medium acquired instantaneously from the presence in it of a luminous object. Aristotle's view found wide acceptance among Renaissance scholars. If light did travel, it was asked, why, unlike sound, was no interval noted between the occurrence of an event and its perception? Against this view, supported by *Kepler and Descartes, scholars such as Francesco Maurolico (1494–1575), in his posthumously published *Photismi* (1611), argued that light emanated from the observed body and travelled directly and rectilinearly to the eye of the observer. It was not clear, however, where the image of the object was formed. Traditionally it had been supposed that the lens was the recipient of vision and that the lens was placed in the centre of the eye. The lens was first sited correctly by the anatomist Matteo Colombo (c. 1516–59), while the retina was first proposed as the site of image formation by Felix Plater (1536–1614) in 1583. *Leonardo da Vinci had earlier recorded how the image, as it formed on the retina, became inverted, a phenomenon that was duly accounted for by Kepler in his *Ad Vitellionem* (1604).

There remains the question of colour and such related phenomena as the rainbow and the prism. No one before Newton in 1672 suspected that white light was a compound mixture of the primary colours. Aristotle had thought, and in this he had been followed by all medieval and Renaissance scholars, that white light was a simple quality; colour was produced by a weakening or modification of light as it was reflected, refracted, or corrupted by the medium. The rainbow, consequently, had been held to be caused by reflection from the drops of water sited in a conveniently placed cloud. Against this Maurolico argued that the rainbow resulted from internal reflections within the raindrop, while Kepler considered it to be due to both internal reflections and refractions. Further progress in this and other optical problems awaited a clearer understanding of the nature of light.

Oratorians *see under* Philip Neri, St.

Orcagna (Andrea di Cione; c. 1320–c. 1368) Italian painter, sculptor, and architect. The son of a goldsmith, Orcagna (whose name was Florentine argot for "archangel") was admitted to the guild of painters in his native Florence in about 1343 and to the guild of stonemasons nine years later. Inclined to paint in a fashion that predated Giotto, Orcagna painted an altarpiece in the Strozzi chapel of Sta Maria Novella, Florence (1354–57), which is now the only painting definitely attributed to him. Probably also by him was the trilogy of frescoes for the nave of Sta Croce, Florence (c. 1350), and the *St Matthew* altarpiece (1367; Uffizi, Florence), which was finished by his brother Jacopo di Cione (d. 1398) after Orcagna fell ill. His best-known sculptural work was the ambitious tabernacle in Orsanmichele (1359). As an architect he directed the construction of the cathedral in Orvieto (1359–62) and also advised on the building of the cathedral in Florence.

Ordóñez, Bartolomé (c. 1490–1520) Spanish sculptor. Born into a wealthy family in Burgos, Ordóñez studied in Italy, probably under Sansovino in Florence, and later imported many features of the High Renaissance into his native Spain. While still in Italy, he produced a marble relief, the *Epiphany* (c. 1516–18), for the Caracciolo chapel in Naples, on which he worked with Diego de *Siloe, and the marble tomb of Andrea Bonifacio (c. 1518; SS Severino e Sosia, Naples). He then moved to Barcelona, where he executed important wood and marble carvings for the cathedral. In 1519 he was commissioned by Charles V to produce the tomb for Philip the Handsome and Joanna the Mad in the royal chapel in Granada cathedral; when Ordóñez died the following year at Carrara, where he was working on the monument, the commission was almost completed. After his death his style was much imitated, especially in Naples and Flanders.

Oresme, Nicolas (c. 1320–82) French mathematician and physicist. Oresme, who was born at Caen, flourished under the patronage of Charles V of France, and after serving as tutor to the future Charles VI he was appointed bishop of Lisieux in 1377. In his most original work, *De configurationibus qualitatum* (c. 1350), Oresme tried to show in the inadequate mathematics of his day how changing "qualities", such as speed, could be handled geometrically. He also, in his *Livre du ciel et monde* (c. 1377), a commentary on Aristotle's *De caelo*, considered the question of the earth's rotation. Despite appearing to have disposed of the traditional objections to such a possibility, he affirmed, nonetheless, his commitment to the *Ptolemaic system. In a further work, the *Algorismus proportionum*, he introduced into mathematics for the first time the notion of fractional exponents.

Orichovius *see* Orzechowski, Stanisław.

Orlando furioso The epic written by Ludovico *Ariosto continuing the story begun in the *Orlando innamorato* of *Boiardo. The poem is structurally very elaborate, often seeming to be a tangled web of adventures sustained only by the tremendous energy of Ariosto's narrative, but three main strands of story are clearly discernible: the madness of the hero Orlando, chief of Charlemagne's paladins, caused by his love for the beautiful princess Angelica; the wars between Christians and Saracens; and the love story of Ruggiero and Bradamante, destined to marry and found the house of Este, in whose service Ariosto passed his life and in whose celebration the poem is ostensibly written.
Orlando furioso appeared in three editions during Ariosto's lifetime (1516, 1521, 1532), and in its final form comprised forty-six cantos written in *ottava rima*. This third edition, in particular, reveals the influence of *Bembo in matters of language and style. The poem successfully welds together medieval chivalric and folk traditions with humanistic neoclassicism to form a complex whole of which the dominant note is one of brilliant gaiety. (This gaiety is excellently captured in the English translation (1591) by Sir John *Harington.) It was immediately accepted as a classic, and during the late sixteenth-century controversy on *epic it became the representative of one form of the genre against the more unified concept exemplifed in Tasso's *Gerusalemme liberata*.

Orlando innamorato *see under* Boiardo, Matteo Maria.

Orley, Bernard van (c. 1492–1542) Netherlands painter and designer of tapestries and stained glass. Trained by his father Valentin van Orley, Bernard was principally active in Brussels, where he was born. In 1515 he was commissioned to paint portraits of the children of Philip the Handsome for presentation to the king of Denmark. Three years later he was formally appointed a court painter to the regent, *Margaret of Austria. In 1530 he accepted a similar position from her successor, *Mary of Hungary. Van Orley was influenced by the Italianate repertory of Jan Gossaert and by Dürer, whom he met in 1520/21. Although he does not appear to have visited Italy, he appropriated motifs from a range of Italian prints and was personally familiar with the Raphael cartoons for the Sistine Chapel, which were woven into tapestries in Brussels between 1514 and 1519. There is a tension in van Orley's work, between the northern naturalistic tradition in which he was principally trained and the Italianate schooling which he received as a young painter. For example, in his Job altarpiece (1521; Brussels), the careful observation of individual details actually makes the overall composition more difficult to read as a single entity. By contrast, the magnificent landscape vistas in van Orley's tapestry cycle of the *Hunts of Maximilian* (c. 1550; Paris) belong beside the paintings of Pieter Brueghel as major monuments of the Netherlandish landscape tradition. See Plate XXIX.

Orpheus In classical legend, a Thracian poet who was given a lyre by *Apollo and taught by the Muses to play it so exquisitely that wild animals, and even inanimate trees and rocks, were drawn to its sound. When his wife Eurydice died of a snake bite, Orpheus journeyed to Hades, hoping to win her back by his music; this he succeeded in doing, but lost her forever when he broke the conditions imposed upon him and looked back at her before they had reached the upper world. Grief then led him to fall foul of the maenads, who tore him to pieces in their frenzied worship of *Bacchus. There are several elements in this story attractive to graphic artists, but the "Orpheus and the animals" theme gained particular favour. Allegorically interpreted, it demonstrated the power of art to subdue nature. It also afforded scope for depicting an exotic assemblage of creatures, a kind of pagan Garden of Eden in which no creature injures or preys upon another. The human figures predominate in Giovanni *Bellini's treatment of the theme (Widener Collection, National Gallery of Art, Washington), but are totally overwhelmed by the fauna and the landscape in the numerous versions by the mannerist *Savery.

As the supposed author of the Orphic hymns and source of the mystic cult of Orphism in ancient Greece, Orpheus was a subject of intense interest to the Florentine Neoplatonists. *Pico della Mirandola in *De hominis dignitate* states his belief that the Orphic hymns contain profound religious revelations under the guise of poetic fables and that the concealed truth is apparent only to a small band of initiates. Both Pico and Lorenzo de' *Medici (prompted by Plato's exegesis in the *Symposium*) read the Eurydice episode as a fable of the proximity of love and death in the experience of religious initiates.

The Orpheus legend of course also lent itself to musical and dramatic treatment. *Politian's pastoral drama *Orfeo*, performed in Mantua in 1480, contained songs which set the subject on the road towards opera. The earliest surviving works that count as true opera were produced in Florence in 1600 and 1602; these are two settings of Rinuccini's text *L'Euridice*, the first by Jacopo Peri (1561–1633) with additions by *Caccini and the second by Caccini alone. This pastoral treatment of the story has a happy ending (*lieto fine*), as does *L'Orfeo* by Monteverdi (1567–1643), produced in Mantua in 1607.

Orsi (da Novellara), Lelio (1511–87) Italian painter. Born at Novellara, Orsi became a prominent figure of the Parmesan school. He was influenced by *Correggio and *Michelangelo as well as by German woodcuts. *The Walk to Emmaus* (National Gallery, London) reveals a taste for dramatic lighting, while other works such as *The Rest on the Flight into Egypt* (York) are more elegant and subtly coloured, in the style of *Parmigianino. The majority of his frescoes are lost.

Ortelius, Abraham (Abraham Oertel; 1527–98) Dutch cartographer. Born at Antwerp, Ortelius trained as an engraver before establishing himself as a dealer in maps and more general antiquities. He travelled widely to collect and sell maps, many of which he illustrated or coloured before sale. He made many contacts (*see* Hoefnagel, Georg), but it was his friendship with *Mercator that prompted his active involvement in cartography. Throughout the 1560s Ortelius built his reputation as a map maker. His most famous creation was a heart-shaped map of the world (1564), followed by maps of Egypt and Asia.

Ortelius's masterpiece was a collection of maps by eighty-seven different cartographers including himself. Entitled *Theatrum orbis terrarum* (1570), it consisted of special engravings of the best maps in the world and covered all areas of the globe. It ran to seven editions by the end of the century, and translated and abridged versions also appeared. In 1575, despite suspicions that he might have Protestant inclinations, Ortelius was appointed geographer to *Philip II of Spain.

orthography Interest in spelling reform and standardization was an aspect of interest in the *vernacular which manifested itself in most European countries during the Renaissance. The wide dissemination of books made possible by *printing increasingly rendered unacceptable the variations in spelling that reflected various dialectal pronunciations; when printers could adopt a standard and adhere to it, the prospects for reliable versions of texts were brighter than in the situation when individual scribes could "myswrite" or "mysmetre for defaute of tonge" – as Chaucer feared would befall his *Troilus and Criseyde* (V 1795–96). However, two centuries later Gabriel *Harvey was still maintaining, in a letter to *Spenser published in 1580, that the one essential prerequisite for a proper grammar and prosody of English was "universally to agree upon *one and the same Ortographie (sic)*"; for lack of a better, he recommended the system proposed by Sir Thomas *Smith, which had originated in the latter's interest in the controversy over the pronunciation of Greek (*see* Greek studies).

Thoughtful users of the vernaculars recognized that the Roman alphabet was inadequate to render all the sounds current in speech, so proposals for rationalization of spelling abounded. An early entrant in the field was the Spanish humanist *Nebrija. *Trissino evolved a system for Italian, which he promoted vigorously in the 1520s; among other innovations the Greek letters ε and ω were drafted in to render the different sounds expressed in written Italian by the simple vowels e and o. In France Louis Meygret (1545), Jean-Antoine de *Baïf, and *Ramus tried and failed to achieve a rational phonetic spelling in place of a learned, etymologically based standard. The use of grave and acute accents (è and é) to denote different qualities of e became standard French printing practice in this period. The most thoroughgoing phonetician in England was John Hart, whose *Orthographie* (1569) sets out an admirable phonetic alphabet which he says would be equally applicable to Italian, Spanish, German, and French.

Orti Oricellari

Orti Oricellari (Rucellai Gardens) The gardens in Florence that became the meeting place for the revived Florentine Academy, successor to *Ficino's Accademia Platonica. The grounds were laid out by Bernardo Rucellai (1448–1514), who assembled there statuary looted from the Medici after their expulsion in 1494. *Machiavelli attended the discussions in the Orti Oricellari in the period after 1513 and read his *Discorsi* (1513–21) to the members, some of whom he made participants in his dialogues *Dell'arte della guerra* (1521).

Orzechowski, Stanisław (Orichovius; 1513–66) Polish polemicist and theologian. Born at Przemyśl, Orzechowksi was a Roman Catholic priest and a zealous participant in all manner of controversies. Among his Latin works are tracts urging a crusade against the Turks (1543) and opposing celibacy (1551). He also wrote in Polish on the benefits of theocracy (1563, 1564). His history of Poland from the reign of Sigismund I was published posthumously (1611). Orzechow-

ski's vigorous prose style was important in the development of vernacular prose writing.

Osiander, Andreas (1498–1552) German Protestant theologian. After studying in Ingolstadt and being ordained (1520), Osiander returned to Nuremberg, near which he had been born, and became a leading figure in the local reforming movement. He represented the city at both the Colloquy of Marburg (1529) and the Diet of Augsburg (1530), and was one of the original signatories of the Schmalkaldic Articles (1537). Forced to leave Nuremberg by the imposition of the Augsburg Interim (1548), Osiander settled in Königsberg, where he became professor at the newly founded university. His controversial views on justification (*De iustificatione*, 1550) brought him into conflict with *Melanchthon and were eventually repudiated by the Lutherans in the Formula of *Concord (1577). His other writings include a revised edition of the Latin Vulgate and a harmony of the gospels, the first of its kind. His niece Margaret married Thomas *Cranmer.

ottava rima An Italian stanza form usually comprising eight lines of eleven syllables each, rhyming abababcc. Its virtues as a vehicle for narrative were most amply demonstrated by Ariosto's *Orlando furioso*. It was adopted into English in the sixteenth century using the English five-stress (decasyllabic) line, often with a feminine rhyme. One of the earliest practitioners was *Drayton, who, on rewriting his *Mortimeriados* (1596) as *The Barrons Warres* (1603), changed the seven-line stanza of the former to *ottava rima* and observed "this sort of stanza hath in it majesty, perfection, and solidity."

Ottoman Turks A Turkic people who migrated from central Asia to Asia Minor, where they adopted Islam. They took their name from their first sultan, Osman (ruled c. 1288–1326), who founded a state in Anatolia, bordering on Christian territory. At this time they adopted the concept of *jihad* (holy war to extend Islam). As the Renaissance developed in Italy the Ottomans established their first settlement in Europe (1354) and took Adrianople in Thrace (1361). From Thrace they advanced to conquer the Balkans, overrunning Bulgaria (1382), Serbia (1459), most of Greece (1461), and Bosnia (1463). Taking advantage of the Byzantine empire's weakness, they occupied the eastern Mediterranean and conquered Constantinople itself (1453), which became the Ottoman capital. By the early sixteenth century they had conquered Persia, Syria, and Egypt, and Suleiman (I) the Magnificent (sultan 1520–66) took the *jihad* into the heart of Europe. He captured Belgrade

(1521) and, after crushing the Christian army at Mohács (1526), occupied most of Hungary. By 1529 the Ottoman forces had reached the gates of Vienna, but they returned to Constantinople after a short siege. Although the main expansionist drive of the Ottomans to the northwest was now over, Renaissance Europe remained aware of them as a constant threat on its eastern flank, to be contained by crusading ventures such as the battle of *Lepanto. In 1683 Ottoman troops again reached the gates of Vienna, but were repulsed by the Christian forces.

Overbury, Sir Thomas (1581–1613) English courtier and prose writer. He was born at Compton Scorpion, Warwickshire, and educated at Oxford before becoming a member of the Middle Temple (1597). Robert Carr, Earl of Somerset, was his friend and patron, but when Overbury opposed the earl's marriage with the divorced countess of Essex, he was imprisoned in the Tower of London on a trumped-up charge and slowly poisoned by the countess's agents. The murder came to light and at the ensuing trial, for which the prosecution was conducted by Francis *Bacon, the earl and countess were found guilty and condemned to house arrest; four of their accomplices were hanged. Apart from his lead role in "the Overbury Affair", Overbury is remembered as a writer of "characters"; these are a sub-form of the essay evolved by the third-century BC Greek Theophrastus and comprise short and vivid descriptions of various human types and their characteristic behaviour.

Oye, Sebastian van *see* Noye, Sebastian van.

OTTOMAN TURKS *A miniature from the Topkapi Serai Museum, Istanbul, depicts the army of Suleiman the Magnificent besieging Vienna in 1529. The city was only saved by the onset of winter, which made the Turks withdraw.*

P

Pacheco, Francisco (1564–1654) Spanish painter and art theorist. Pacheco was born at Sanlúcar de Barrameda, but when still young he moved to Seville, where he became a canon at the cathedral and opened an art academy which attracted numerous pupils. An enthusiast for Italian art, Pacheco collected Italian Renaissance drawings, but his own work chiefly comprised academically correct, if somewhat lifeless, religious paintings. Many of these are still to be seen in or around Seville. He was also a sought-after portraitist. A visit to Madrid and Toledo (1611) brought him into contact with El Greco, whose interest in *chiaroscuro* he then came to share. Pacheco's *Arte de la pintura* (?1640) is a significant text in the development of Spanish art. Velázquez was his son-in-law and most famous pupil.

Pacher, Michael (active 1462–98) Austrian sculptor and painter. Pacher is first recorded in 1467, at Bruneck in the Tyrol; it seems likely that he was born in this region, though he travelled extensively. His key surviving works are the incomplete altar at Gries, near Bolzano (1471–88), the high altar at St Wolfgang, near Salzburg (1471–88), and the painted *Fathers of the Church* altarpiece in Munich (c. 1479–82). At the time of his death, he was putting the finishing touches to his colossal high altar at Salzburg parish church, which was almost entirely destroyed during the eighteenth century. Early influences upon Pacher were Hans Multscher (active in the Tyrol during the 1450s) and Nikolaus Gerhaert (active 1462–73), whose sculptural style was disseminated by the engravings of the *Master E. S. Pacher's Gries and St Wolfgang altars suggest that he visited the Netherlands between 1469 and 1471, where he encountered the paintings of Hugo van der *Goes and Jan van *Eyck. His fragmentary and undated altarpieces of St Thomas (Graz) and St Lawrence (Vienna and Munich) indicate that he visited Padua, probably before 1465, where he was profoundly influenced by the frescoes of *Mantegna and took note of the altar by *Donatello in the Santo. Pacher ignored the classical formal vocabulary of Italian art, but became a master of one-point perspective and foreshortening. In his large composite altars, with polychromed carved central panels and pinnacles and painted shutters, his mastery of pictorial space helped to bridge the gap between sculptural and pictorial elements. Out of his various sources Pacher forged a lyrical and expressive style that breathed new life into the traditional German carved wooden altar. He had a large circle of followers.

Pacification of Ghent *see under* Ghent.

Pacioli, Luca (c. 1445–1517) Italian mathematician. Little is known about Pacioli's life other than that he was born at Burgo in Tuscany, became a Franciscan friar some time after 1471, taught mathematics in several towns of northern Italy, and was a friend of *Leonardo da Vinci. He wrote numerous mathematical works, the best known of which, *Somma di aritmetica, geometria, proporzioni e proporzionalità* (1494), is one of the earliest printed mathematical texts. Though entirely derivative, it manages to convey in the vernacular, and in an improved notation, the new mathematics first developed by Leonardo of Pisa in his *Liber abaci* (1202). Pacioli was well aware of the needs of commerce and consequently devoted considerable space to the application of the new arithmetic to book-keeping and trade. He was also responsible for a Latin translation of Euclid (1509) and a more original geometrical text, *De divina proportione* (see p. 300), including designs after Leonardo.

Paciotto, Francesco (Francisco Pachote; 1521–91) Italian architect. A native of Urbino, Paciotto was a pupil of *Genga. Around 1540 he was in Rome but in 1553 he was appointed tutor to Alessandro *Farnese, for whose mother, *Margaret of Parma, he designed the never-completed Cittadella at Piacenza (1558). The same year he accompanied Philip II to the Netherlands where he was commissioned to design a palace for the Habsburg governors of the Netherlands in Brussels. This was never built. Paciotto also worked on harbour defences at Nice for the duke of Savoy (1559) and in 1561 went to Spain where he contributed to the plans for the *Escorial. He was much in demand as a military architect, building a fortress at Antwerp (1564) and working for

PACIOLI *Geometric constructions from* De divina proportione *(1509)*.

several Italian princes from his base at Urbino, where he spent his latter years.

Padua (Italian: Padova) A city on the River Bacchiglione in Veneto, northern Italy. Padua was known to the Romans as Patavium and survived to become an important and prosperous commune in the later Middle Ages. During the Renaissance it was ruled by *signori* from the Carrara family (1318–1405) before being annexed by Venice (1405–1797). Venice allowed Padua's municipal government considerable power and dignity, even after Padua's unsuccessful rebellion in 1509.

During the Renaissance Padua was an important centre of learning and the arts, and its university (founded 1222) was famous for its medical, legal, and philosophical faculties. Celebrated figures connected with the university include the teachers and anatomical researchers, *Vesalius and *Falloppio, William Harvey who graduated as a

doctor there (1602), and *Galileo, who held the post of professor of mathematics (1592–1610). The philosophers followed Averroes and the Aristotelian tradition and Elia del Medigo was the leading student of Hebrew philosophy. The botanic garden, founded in 1545, is among the oldest in Europe. Great artists who worked in Padua include *Giotto and *Donatello.

Surviving buildings from the Renaissance period include the *Arena Chapel or Capella degli Scrovegni (1303–05) with its Giotto frescoes, Il Santo or the basilica (1232–1307) of the town's patron saint, St Anthony, which has in front of it Donatello's famous equestrian statue of *Gattamelata (1453), the rebuilt cathedral (1552), the Palazzo della Ragione (rebuilt 1306), and the Palazzo del Capitano (1532).

Paganino *see* Mazzoni, Guido.

painting If the key term "Renaissance" is used in its widest, general sense as no more than a historical label for the two centuries of European history between about 1400 and 1600, then all paintings produced in this area and period may be described as "Renaissance" artefacts. However, in the context of the visual arts, this key term has a very specific meaning which, if analysed, permits the categorization of two hundred years of European painting into a series of sub-groups, more or less closely identified with "Renaissance" values.

At the heart of the matter lies the rebirth of interest in classical antiquity which started in Italy during the early fifteenth century and subsequently spread to most other regions of Western Europe. Originally a purely literary movement, the roots of which may be traced back to the middle of the fourteenth century, its influence on the visual arts was somewhat belated. Given that Roman sculptural remains constituted its principal visual source, it is not surprising that sculptors, such as *Donatello, were motivated by the rebirth earlier than painters, such as *Masaccio. What made *the* Renaissance different from earlier, analogous movements, such as the so-called "Carolingian Renaissance", is that it entailed an appreciation of both classical form *and* content, rather than of the one or the other in isolation. Together with this imitation of antique style and subject matter came a growing interest in naturalistic values. In part the latter was fostered by the former. For example, there can be no doubt that Masaccio's study of ancient marbles assisted his portrayal of human character and emotion. However, other tools utilized by the Renaissance artist in pursuit of naturalistic visual effects, such as one-point *perspective, were original inventions unknown to the ancients. It must be stressed that, while the revival of classical form and content was central to the Renaissance, naturalism was secondary. It is because Giotto's profoundly innovatory and naturalistic style neither derives from nor reflects the values of classical antiquity that it cannot meaningfully be labelled as a manifestation of Renaissance art.

Florence was the principal centre of literary humanism and had been, for more than a century, the home of the most innovatory school of painting in Italy before it became the birthplace of Renaissance painting. These first stirrings were promoted by a wealthy and erudite bourgeois ruling class which commissioned works of art both individually and corporately. Without such patrons as Felice Brancacci, for whom Masaccio executed the revolutionary fresco cycle in Sta Maria del Carmine, there would have been no material basis for the Florentine awakening which set the tone of most subsequent developments in Renaissance painting. Although Masaccio's *Trinity* fresco (c. 1427) in Sta Maria Novella demonstrates a familiarity with classical forms of drapery and architecture and reveals the power of one-point perspective, the manifesto of Renaissance painting, Leon Battista *Alberti's treatise *Della pittura* (1435), was written by a humanist observer from the Florentine ruling class, rather than a professional artist. The Florentine painters Fra *Angelico, *Domenico Veneziano, Paolo *Uccello, and *Andrea del Castagno elaborated further on the three essential tools of the Quattrocento avant-garde: the study of antique remains, use of one-point perspective, and direct observation of the human body and, especially, the nude.

Gradually these originally Florentine preoccupations spread more widely in Italy. At Borgo S Sepolcro in the Marches of central Italy, *Piero della Francesca had an appreciation of weight and volume and an understanding of light effects which far surpassed that of the painters of Florence, where he was trained. His contemporary, the Paduan Andrea *Mantegna, who worked principally as a court artist of the Gonzaga princes of Mantua, developed a hard-edged style informed by a meticulous study of antique remains and was the most virtuoso exponent of one-point perspective of his generation. In Venice, Giovanni *Bellini evolved a more contemplative manner, combining classicizing forms and one-point perspective with delicate light effects, the latter derived partly from Netherlandish models. In Florence, during the second half of the fifteenth century, Antonio *Pollaiuolo refined the depiction of the nude in motion and devised tightly structured symmetrical compositions. The last principal element of Renaissance style to fall into place, the reunification of classical form and classical subject matter, did so

only towards the end of the century, in such pictures as *Botticelli's *Birth of Venus* (c. 1485).

Many hundreds of miles to the north, in the Netherlands, a new school of naturalistic painting was established almost simultaneously with the new developments in Florence. The style of its founder, Jan van *Eyck, may be seen, already fully formed, in his earliest dated work, the *Ghent altarpiece of 1432. Jan's success depended upon a seemingly infinite patience in the rendering of the minutest detail, embodied by a newly developed method of painting, in superimposed translucent glazes of oil paint, which permitted effects of light and texture to be delineated with a fidelity hitherto beyond the reach of artists working with opaque tempera. At about the same time, in Tournai, a similar but rather less accomplished style was formulated by Robert *Campin, sometimes known as the Master of Flémalle. Jan's pupil, Petrus *Christus, had few followers, but Campin's student, Rogier van der *Weyden, became the most influential northern painter of the fifteenth century. Abroad, the style of the early Netherlandish painters was introduced to Germany, Austria, and Switzerland by Lukas *Moser, Konrad *Laib, and Konrad *Witz, to France by the Master of Aix, and to Spain by Luis *Dalmau. In Sicily *Antonello da Messina was trained by a Netherlander. Even the Florentine painters were affected by such works as Hugo van der *Goes's *Portinari altarpiece, imported from Ghent in about 1475. Jan van Eyck was something of an antiquarian in as much as he was intrigued by twelfth-century architecture, but the early Netherlandish painters had little or no interest in classical antiquity. Nevertheless, northern painters of the fifteenth century are best considered under the "Renaissance" head of account, because they were contemporary with the Italian avant-garde, were commonly interested in naturalism, devised the oil technique subsequently adopted throughout Europe, and fathered the Italianate northern schools of the sixteenth century.

The term "High Renaissance" is customarily reserved for the three decades of Italian art from the beginning of the sixteenth century to the sack of Rome in 1527. Central to this epoch are the earlier works of *Michelangelo, the mature period of *Raphael, and most of *Leonardo da Vinci's paintings. To this pantheon may be added the Florentines Fra *Bartolommeo and *Andrea del Sarto and, with less assurance, the Venetians *Giorgione and the young *Titian. No northern painters are included, although it may be argued that Albrecht *Dürer's work of the period between about 1500 and 1509 has much in common with what we traditionally perceive as "High Renaissance" values. The view of this period as one in which painters in assured control of the techniques forged in the previous century attained a pure, classical harmony, free of superfluous detail, may be traced back to that of Giorgio *Vasari, whose *Lives* was first published in 1550. While the validity of this concept, which derives from the evolutionary cycle of rise, maturity, and decay, is highly suspect, it has proved remarkably alluring. Like the brief "classical" epoch of Greek art, the High Renaissance remains one of the essential fixed points in Western art history.

Some great northern painters, principally Michael *Pacher, Jean *Fouquet, and *Justus of Ghent (Joos van Wassenhove), visited Italy during the fifteenth century and devised Italianate styles of considerable distinction. Nevertheless, they constitute the exceptions which prove the general rule that most northerners were indifferent to the achievements of the Italians. Albrecht Dürer's visits to Venice in 1495 and 1505–07 were fundamentally different to those of his predecessors in that they stimulated the artist to seek a thorough understanding of the first principles of perspective and proportion. These Dürer publicized not only in paintings and numerous prints, but also in a series of treatises.

Dürer had little, if any, first-hand experience of ancient art. The first northern painters to retrace the steps of Masaccio and Mantegna to the antiquities of Rome were the Netherlanders Jan *Gossaert, Jan van *Scorel, and Maarten van *Heemskerck. By the fourth decade of the sixteenth century, three principal centres of Italianate northern painting had been established: southern Germany, the Netherlands, and *Fontainebleau, where Francis I entrusted the decoration of his palace to expatriate Italians. Thence a variety of more or less Italianate styles rapidly became the norm throughout northern Europe. Remarkably, the most outstanding northern painter of the mid-sixteenth century, Pieter *Brueghel, eschewed the trappings of contemporary Italianism in favour of a more traditional naturalism, which drew upon fifteenth-century Netherlandish painting and was yet prophetic of Dutch landscape pictures of the following century.

Widespread use of the term "*Mannerism" in different contexts has dissipated its meaning, which was originally quite specific. Vasari regarded *maniera* as a positive quality, evocative of stylishness. Its principal exponents were *Rosso Fiorentino, *Pontormo, and *Giulio Romano. While deeply attached to traditional Italian artistic precepts, especially the primacy of figure drawing, these painters rejected the serenity of High Renaissance art in favour of a powerful but subjective and emotional style, which drew somewhat upon Raphael's last paintings and was profoundly influenced by Michelangelo's late grand manner. The principal northern Italian exponent of this style was *Parmigianino. Venice was too profoundly conditioned by the work of Titian to be much affected by these new developments, although some aspects of *Tintoretto's style have been characterized as mannerist.

It was largely as a result of the initiative of these "first generation" mannerists that a new canon of drawing, which emphasized complexity of pose and gesture and popularized elongated figure types, became widely established. In northern Europe where the mainstream of painting had been abruptly redirected, Mannerism found fertile soil. Its principal Flemish exponent, Frans *Floris, established a trend which endured, through the paintings of such artists as Joachim Wittewael (c. 1566–1638), Hans von *Aachen, and Hendrick *Goltzius. Ultimately "Mannerism" as broadly applied, constituted the final international phase of Renaissance painting. Moreover, it set the scene for the more truly European style which was to follow, the *Baroque.

Palatina, Bibliotheca Originally the library of the university of Heidelberg, which was founded in 1386. The library was named in honour of the electors of the Palatinate, several of whom increased its holdings, especially Philip, Ludwig III, Ludwig V, Friedrich, and Otthenrich, the first Protestant elector, who lived in Heidelberg from 1556 to 1559. In 1584 it received a donation of manuscripts and books from Ulrich *Fugger of the Augsburg bankers. When Heidelberg fell to the Catholic league in 1622, Maximilian I of Bavaria presented its 3542 manuscripts and 5000 books to Pope Gregory XV and these form the Palatini collection in the *Vatican Library, except for 852 manuscripts returned to Heidelberg by the Vatican in 1816.

Palatinate A territory on the middle Rhine, inherited by Conrad, half-brother of Emperor Frederick I, who made Conrad count palatine in 1155. Conrad combined his administrative and judicial duties in the empire with his inherited territories. Both office and territories passed to a branch of the Bavarian Wittelbachs, who were confirmed as counts palatine by the treaty of Pavia (1329). The Golden Bull (1356) confirmed the count palatine as one of the seven imperial electors. Frederick III, Elector Palatine, established Calvinism in the Palatinate in 1563. The defeat of Frederick V (*see* Winter King) by Catholic forces in the Thirty Years' War led to a reduction of the elector palatine's powers, and the treaty of Rijswijk (1697) restored Catholicism in the Palatinate.

Palestrina, Giovanni Pierluigi da (1525–94) Italian composer. Palestrina is arguably the most important composer of the late sixteenth century and he was widely admired and imitated in his day. Palestrina was probably born in the town of that name outside Rome, and by 1537 was a choirboy at the Roman church of Sta Maria Maggiore. In 1544 he became organist at the cathedral in Palestrina, where he remained until 1551. In that year he was appointed *maestro* at St Peter's, and in 1554 his first book of Masses, the earliest by an Italian composer, was published. This was dedicated to Pope Julius III, his most powerful patron. In 1555 he became a member of the Cappella Sistina and *maestro di cappella* at St John Lateran, but left the latter post after a dispute over funds for musicians (1560). He returned to Sta Maria Maggiore, and in the summer of 1564 organized music at the Villa d'Este for Cardinal Ippolito II d'Este, whose service he entered in 1567. His fame was spreading, and he was offered the post of *maestro* at the court of Emperor Maximilian II in Vienna, but declined. He was also patronized by the Gonzaga family in Mantua. In 1571 Palestrina returned to Rome, to the Cappella Giulia, and remained there until his death.

Palestrina was a prolific composer; 104 Masses, around 375 motets, and many other liturgical works survive. He also composed around 140 spiritual and secular madrigals and eight *ricercari*. His sacred music, written in a conservative but uniquely harmonious style much influenced by the precepts of the Counter-Reformation, ensured Palestrina's fame and earned him the sobriquet "The Prince of Music". The Council of Trent advised that sacred texts set to music should be intelligible and that the music should contain no secular elements; it is possible that the famous *Missa Papae Marcelli* was composed for a commission of cardinals assembled to hear Masses and check that the words were intelligible. Many of Palestrina's early Masses are based on *cantus firmi*, whereas the later ones frequently employ the more modern "parody Mass" technique, and are based on pre-existing polyphonic compositions by himself and other composers. Despite the later codification of the Palestrina style by Fux, his later works provide evidence of a developing musical trend which in its harmony and texture was clearly heading in the direction of the Baroque.

Palingenius (Pier Angelo Manzoli; c. 1500–c. 1543) Italian poet. He was born at La Stellata, near Ferrara, and was attached to the court circle of *Renée de France, who married Ercole d'Este in 1528. She provided a refuge for persecuted French Calvinists at Ferrara, and Palingenius's only work, the *Zodiacus vitae* (1535–36), reflects the Calvinist outlook. This extensive moralistic poem in Latin hexameters was banned by the Inquisition, but was well received in Protestant Europe. The Polish moralist *Rej based his *Wizerunek* (1558) on it, and an English translation by Barnaby Googe (?1540–94) of the first six books appeared in 1565.

Palissy, Bernard (c. 1510–90) French naturalist and potter. Trained as a glass painter, Palissy settled in Saintes in about 1540 and tried to develop his own distinctive style of pottery. His pond-like dishes bordered with realistically modelled animals soon won him commissions from the French court. They also gained him, as a Huguenot, some much needed protection. Although he escaped the 1572 St Bartholomew massacre the respite proved only temporary; he was arrested in 1586 and died in the Bastille. In 1580 he published his *Discours admirables* in which "Practice" instructs "Theory" on, among other things, the origin of springs and rivers and in which he argues for the organic origin of marine fossils; the tenth section of this work expounds his own discoveries in the arts of ceramics and enamelling.

Palladio, Andrea (1508–80) Italian architect. A native of Padua, Palladio was born Andrea di Pietro della Gondola and began his career as a stonemason in Vicenza, where much of his work survives. In 1536 he came under the influence of the humanist poet Giangiorgio *Trissino, who became Palladio's patron and was responsible for renaming the young mason after the mythological patron of the arts, Pallas Athene. Trissino encouraged Palladio's interest in the buildings of antiquity and introduced him to leading scholars of the time, probably including the mannerist architect Sebastiano *Serlio. In 1540–42 Palladio executed his first design for a villa, the Villa Godi-Valmarana at Lonedo, north of Vicenza, which incorporated many of the features of classical buildings, such as symmetrical wings and a walled courtyard, that were to become hallmarks of his style. At about this time Palladio also designed his first palace, the Palazzo Civena, which again made use of classical models.

In 1541 Palladio had visited Rome with Trissino for the first time and made an extensive study of the many ancient buildings there; his findings were published as the treatise *Le antichità di Roma* (1554). (Two years after this publication he collaborated with Daniele *Barbaro on a new edition of *De architectura* by Vitruvius, thus identifying himself further with the geometry and harmony of classical architecture.) In 1545 Palladio was given his first important commission, the rebuilding of the Basilica in Vicenza, which provided him with an opportunity to put into practice his understanding of the proportions and motifs of antiquity. Subsequent Vicentine buildings of note that echoed ancient ideals included the Palazzo Chiericati (1550), the Palazzo Iseppo da Porto (1552), the Palazzo Antonini (1556), and the Palazzo Thiene (c. 1545–50). In the 1560s Palladio also designed a villa for Barbaro at Maser, near Asolo, which was decorated by *Veronese and *Vittoria.

Of his later works, which included churches, palaces, and country villas, probably the most influential was the Villa *Rotonda in Vicenza, which imitated the design of the Roman Pantheon both in its symmetrical structure and in its classical ornament. He built two highly successful churches in Venice: the Redentore (begun 1577), which was built in thanksgiving for Venice's deliverance from the plague in the preceding year, and S Giorgio Maggiore (1565–80), conspicuously situated on an islet across the Canale di S Marco. Although some of Palladio's designs owed a small debt to the ideas of contemporary mannerists, they were derived chiefly from the architect's understanding of antique structures, which he explored most fully in the hugely influential *Quattro libri dell'architettura* (1570), which took twenty years to complete and profoundly influenced architects throughout Italy and the rest of Europe, including Inigo Jones in England. Palladio's last commission (c. 1579) was for the Teatro Olimpico in Vicenza, completed by his pupil Vincenzo *Scamozzi in 1585 (*see* theatres).

Pallas (Athene) *see* Minerva.

Palma Giovane (Jacopo Negretti; 1544–1628) Italian painter. He was born in Venice, the great-nephew of *Palma Vecchio and the son of Antonio Negretti. His first training was with his father and probably with *Titian, whose *Pietà* he completed after Titian's death. He then visited Urbino and studied in Rome for about three years. Following his return to Venice (c. 1570) he produced pictures for the doge's palace and Venetian churches in a style that combined the influence of Mannerism with that of *Titian and *Veronese and of *Tintoretto, whose style dominated Venetian painting at that time. Palma increasingly rivalled Tintoretto and became the dominant figure in Venice after Tintoretto's death.

Palma Vecchio (Jacomo Negretti; 1480–1528) Italian painter. He was born at Serimalta, near Bergamo, and was almost certainly trained in the studio of Giovanni *Bellini, possibly with *Titian and *Giorgione, although the first mention of Palma in Venice is not until 1510. It was at about this time that he began to paint the pictures of ample female figures that made him so popular and which he continued to produce throughout his career. These blonde ladies of generous proportions appeared sometimes as mythological and sometimes biblical personages in rich sensuous pictures of simple composition (see Plate XXII). Many of the works are *sacre conversazioni* with several female saints, such as his masterpiece *Sta Barbara and Other Saints* in Sta Maria Formosa, Venice. Among the artists that he influenced are *Moretto and *Romanino.

Palmieri, Matteo (1406–75) Italian writer and poet. Born into a Florentine mercantile family, Palmieri studied under some of the leading humanists of his day and held a number of governmental posts in the republic. He wrote several historical works in Latin, including a history of Florence (*Historia florentina*, published in the eighteenth century), and in the vernacular a lengthy religious poem, *La città di vita*, heavily indebted to Dante. His major work, written about 1430, is the dialogue *Della vita civile* (1529). Drawing on arguments in Cicero and Quintilian, the treatise is a discussion and a defence of the active life of civic responsibility based on humanist principles, as against a life of contemplative scholarship.

Paludanus, Guilielmus (Willem van den Broeck; 1530–80) Netherlands sculptor. Possibly born at Malines, he matriculated in St Luke's guild of artists in Antwerp (1557) and was granted citizenship two years later. He carved architectural details for the Antwerp town hall, built by Cornelis *Floris, as well as two reliefs with Christ's Passion for Augsburg (1560–62). Paludanus is not recorded as having travelled to Italy, but his style shows a knowledge of the Italian High Renaissance, possibly gained from studying engravings and the work of Leone *Leoni, who visited the imperial court in Brussels (1556–59). A male anatomical statuette of *St Bartholomew*, excellently modelled in terracotta (dated 1569; Kunsthistorisches Museum, Vienna) attests his skill and possible contact with *Giambologna. In 1571 he made narrative reliefs for the base of Jacques *Jonghelinck's monument in Antwerp to the duke of Alba (destroyed) and began a choir screen for export to S Leonardo, Alba (Spain), now lost. An altar in Antwerp cathedral was destroyed (1582) during the wars of religion.

Pannemaker family The most famous of the sixteenth-century Flemish tapestry weavers, based in Brussels. Pieter I Pannemaker (active from 1510) was a follower of Pieter van Aelst, who in 1514 was commissioned by Pope Leo X to weave the tapestries from Raphael's cartoons of New Testament subjects. In 1518 Pieter was the first of his family to gain imperial patronage, with a commission from Maximilian I, and he subsequently (1523) also worked for *Margaret of Austria. Pieter II and Willem continued to work for the Habsburgs. Among their prolific output was the series of twelve tapestries depicting Charles V's campaign to capture Tunis (1535), after designs by *Vermeyen. At the end of the 1570s the pre-eminence of the Pannemakers was overtaken by the Geubels family.

Pantagruel see Gargantua and Pantagruel.

Panvinio, Onofrio (1529–68) Italian humanist scholar. Panvinio studied in his native Verona, in Padua, and in Naples. His first published work was an edition of the *Fasti Consulares* (1556). He also published studies of the pedigrees of contemporary Roman families, ancient games, the Roman triumph, sacrifices, and the Sibylline books. Most of this antiquarian work was based on the collection of nearly 3000 inscriptions which he hoped would eventually form the basis for a complete edition of Roman inscriptions. In 1568 he visited Sicily and died at Palermo; he was buried at Rome. Panvinio's work typifies the sort of antiquarian studies characteristic of the later Renaissance. His manuscript collections are now in the Vatican. Titian painted a fine portrait of him.

Paracelsus, Philippus Aurcolus (Theophrastus Bombastus von Hohenheim; 1493–1541) German physician, chemist, and alchemist. The son of a physician, Paracelsus was born near Zürich and began his career working the Fugger silver mines at Hutenberg. He soon abandoned mining for medicine and in 1526 began to practise in Basle. He immediately gained a notable success by curing the famous printer *Froben of a leg infection while his orthodox rivals were advising amputation. Although appointed city physician Paracelsus proved to be too quarrelsome ever to occupy an official post more than briefly: nor was his tenure helped by the sudden death of Froben in 1527. Thereafter Paracelsus led the life of an itinerant teacher and physician, travelling through, but never long welcome in, the provinces of Austria, Bohemia, Switzerland, and Bavaria. As a physician he proclaimed the total inadequacy of the classical tradition, burning the works of Avicenna in 1527, and declaring in his own adopted name that he had advanced well beyond Celsus. His main innovation involved the adoption of such therapeutic drugs as mercury and antimony rather than pursuing the humoural approach of traditional medicine. In chemistry his name is linked with the claim that matter was ultimately reducible to the three elements: salt, sulphur, and mercury. Both proposals were fertile enough to establish a Paracelsian tradition which survived late into the seventeenth century.

Paré, Ambroise (c. 1510–90) French surgeon. The son of an artisan at Laval, Paré qualified as a master barber-surgeon in 1536. He immediately joined the army with which he practised his skill on a number of campaigns. He also served as court surgeon to Henry II, Charles IX, and Henry III. One of the major problems facing the military surgeon of Paré's day was how to deal with the fearsome wounds produced by cannon and other firearms introduced into warfare in the fourteenth century. The orthodox technique of cauterization could prove as crippling as the wound itself. During the siege of Turin in 1536, Paré tried instead the alternative technique of applying dressings; he found it just as satisfactory. Later, in his *Dix livres de la chirurgie* (1563), he described a second and even more revolutionary technique: the use of the ligature in such wounds, an innovation which would eventually permit surgery to extend its domain considerably. Paré's attitude to his art is epitomized in his dictum: "I treated him, God cured him."

Paris The capital city of France on the River Seine in northern France. Paris was founded by the Parisii, a Gallic tribe, and (as Lutetia) was a capital under the Romans, and later under the Merovingians and the Capetian founders of modern France. As the Capets restored order and stability during the later Middle Ages the population and prosperity of Paris grew. The twelfth century saw the establishment of the first guilds. In the thirteenth century the university of Paris gained royal recognition (1200), the Sorbonne was founded (1257), and a royal charter gave Parisians the right to levy duties on incoming goods (1220).

At the beginning of the fourteenth century Paris probably possessed the largest urban population in Europe, about 100 000; this was halved by the Black Death (1348–49) and the Hundred Years' War (1337–1453). Paris was torn apart by the struggle between the Burgundian and Armagnac factions (1407–35) and occupied by the English and the Burgundians in 1418. After Paris was recaptured by Charles VII's forces (1435) the city enjoyed a period of comparative peace and its population rose to 200 000 by the middle of the sixteenth century. The municipality was reorganized (1450) and the *parlement* of Paris became France's most powerful court of justice. The installation of the first printing press (1470) was followed by the development of Paris as most prolific centre of publishing in Europe; during the sixteenth century 25 000 editions were published in Paris. During the second half of the fifteenth century many churches were restored and work started on such magnificent private residences as the Hôtel de Sens and the Hôtel de Cluny. The first half of the sixteenth century saw the start of work on the rebuilding of the *Louvre and the construction of the Hôtel de Ville. During the second half of the sixteenth century the Louvre became the royal residence and work was begun on the *Tuileries palace.

Paris prospered and its population expanded until the sectarian turmoil (see Religion, (French) Wars of) of the second half of the sixteenth century. Although Paris had been a centre of humanist scholarship under the inspiration of *Lefèvre d'Étaples in the late fifteenth century it became a stronghold of Catholic reaction during the *Reformation. In 1535 the appearance of placards denouncing the Mass had led to the first persecution of French Protestants. Although French Protestants held their first synod in Paris (1559), later in the century it was the scene of the *Massacre of St Bartholomew (1572) and the bastion of the Catholic League and the *Guise family. By the time Paris finally accepted *Henry IV as its king (1594) its population had dropped to about 180 000.

Notable landmarks which have survived from the period of the Renaissance include the *Louvre and the Pont-Neuf (1599–1604).

Parker, Matthew (1504–75) English clergyman and scholar. Born at Norwich and educated at Cambridge, Parker was ordained in 1527 and rose in the ecclesiastical hierarchy to become chaplain to Anne Boleyn in 1535. During the reign of Mary (1553–58) he found it necessary to retire into private life, but under *Elizabeth I he was consecrated archbishop of Canterbury (1559). In this role he staunchly defended the moderate character of the Anglican Church against Puritan extremism. Parker was also a scholar of note, being particularly concerned with the collection and preservation of the many medieval documents released by the dissolution of the monasteries. Some of these he edited and published, such as the chronicle of Matthew Paris (1571), while others formed the basis for his *De antiquitate ecclesiae* (1572), in which he contentiously tried to trace the roots of the Elizabethan Church to St Augustine.

Parma A city in the Emilia-Romagna region of northern Italy. Parma was originally Etruscan, then Roman, and emerged in the late Middle Ages as an independent commune. Threatened by Milan and Verona and weakened by rivalry between the Correggio and Rossi families, Parma enjoyed only short spells of independence before long periods of subjection to Milan (1346–1447, 1450–1500). Under both the *Visconti and *Sforza rulers of Milan Parma was allowed a good measure of self-government. During the wars of Italy Parma was subject in turn to France (1500–12), the papacy (1515–15), France (1515–20), and the papacy again (1520–45). In 1545 Pope *Paul III made Parma and Piacenza into a duchy for his illegitimate son, Pierluigi Farnese. The *Farnese, who made the ducal court a centre of arts and learning, ruled Parma until the eighteenth century.

Although its population was modest (about 15 000 in 1500), Parma prospered on account of local agriculture and the woollen industry. It boasted two great sixteenth-century artists, *Correggio and *Parmigianino. Notable churches that have survived from the period of the Renaissance include S Giovanni Evangelista (rebuilt 1498–1510), with frescoes by Correggio and Parmigianino, the baroque SS Annunziata (1566), and the church of Sta Maria della Steccata, reputedly built (1521–39) to *Bramante's original plan for St Peter's, Rome. Secular buildings include the Palazzo Ducale (1564) and the Palazzo della Pilotta (begun 1583).

Parmigianino, Il (Francesco Mazzola; 1503–40) Italian painter and graphic artist. In the early 1520s he was already executing commissions for frescoes in the cathedral in Parma, his birthplace and the city after which he was named, and in the church of S Giovanni Evangelista, where *Correggio was also working. Although Parmigianino's personal mannerist style was already established, his work was influenced by Correggio and later by the painting of *Pordenone, *Raphael, and *Michelangelo. Around 1523 he left for Rome, where he appears to have concentrated on graphic arts, particularly etching. He was one of the first artists to produce original etchings from his own designs, and these, which were widely distributed, together with reproductions of his paintings in engravings and woodcuts, helped to increase the extent of his influence in Italy and the rest of Europe.

At the sack of Rome (1527), Parmigianino was captured, but he soon escaped to Bologna. He began to experiment with the use of landscape as a background (see Plate XXIII) and his work influenced Niccolò dell'*Abbate. After visiting Verona and Venice he spent the 1530s in Parma. To this period belongs the well-known *Madonna dal collo lungo* (Uffizi), one of the most extreme examples of Parmigianino's mannerist elongation of limbs, particularly, in this case, of the neck and hands. His main commission during these years was a series of frescoes in Sta Maria della Steccata but so little of it was completed that he was imprisoned briefly in 1539 for breach of contract. According to *Vasari he had by this time undergone a change of personality from an amiable and elegant person to a long-haired, untidy, and almost savage man. The following year Parmigianino's short career came to an end in Casalmaggiore. As well as the types of work already mentioned he also left behind him a number of portraits, such as the self-portrait in a mirror (1521; Kunsthistorisches Museum, Vienna) and the portrait of a woman (Museo di Capodimonte, Naples), probably his mistress, Antea "La Bella"; many of these convey a sense of deep spiritual insight.

Paruta, Paolo (1540–98) Italian historian. A member of a patrician Venetian family, Paruta was educated at Padua and from 1561 occupied a number of official positions in the republic, among them that of city historian, an office previously held by *Bembo, to which he was appointed in 1579. In this capacity he was able to consult state records and his careful use of these sources lend a special interest to his historical works in Italian which he was officially commissioned to write. These include *Istorie veneziane* (1605), a history of the republic from 1513 to 1552, and *Storia della guerra di Cipre* (c. 1573), a history of the Cyprus war (1570–73). The conservative and reflective viewpoint of a Venetian nobleman informs the works written on his own account. The dialogue *Della perfezione della vita politica* (1579) is a discussion of civic ideals in which Paruta supports the argument for the active life of political involvement against the contemplative religious life. His *Discorsi politici* cover questions in history and politics earlier introduced by *Machiavelli, for example, the causes of the greatness of ancient Rome and the character of the ideal state.

Pasquier, Étienne (1529–1615) French lawyer and man of letters. Pasquier studied law at Toulouse and was called to the bar in his native Paris in 1549: he made his name as a lawyer with his successful defence of the university of Paris in its suit with the Jesuits. Having served as commissioner in the assize courts of Poitiers and Toulouse, in 1585 he was appointed advocate-general for Henry III at the *chambre des comptes* in Paris. In 1560 Pasquier produced the first volume of his *Recherches de la France*, an encyclopedic collection of information on the country's history, culture, and institutions; this major work was to occupy much of his leisure time in the later years of his life and was first published in its entirety in 1621. His other writings include the anti-Jesuit pamphlet *Le Catéchisme des Jésuites* (1602), *Lettres* (1586, 1619), and a number of collections of poetry.

Passarotti, Bartolommeo (1529–92) Italian painter. Born in Bologna, he studied with Giacomo Barozzi da *Vignola and then became the assistant of Taddeo *Zuccaro in Rome, where he lived from about 1551 to about 1565. His *Martyrdom of St Paul* can be seen in the church of S Paolo alle tre fontane. On his return to Bologna he continued to paint altarpieces and also portraits, mainly of popes and cardinals, at which he excelled. He created a type of genre and still-life painting depicting peasants with flowers and fowls and he produced a number of etchings. As his style moved further towards the Baroque his studio became a focal point for many of Bologna's artists, among whom his most distinguished disciple was Agostino Carracci.

Passerat, Jean (1534–1602) French poet and humanist. Passerat was born at Troyes and after studying at the university of Paris and teaching at the Collège du Plessis, he was appointed to the chair of Latin at the Collège de France (1572). His prose writings include commentaries on Catullus, Propertius, and other Latin poets; among his better-known poetic works are the ode "Du premier jour de mai" and the villanelle "J'ai perdu ma tourterelle". A supporter of Henry of Navarre, Passerat was one of the authors of the *Satire Ménippée* (1594).

Pasti, Matteo de' (c. 1420–c. 1467) Italian architect and artist. Pasti was born in Verona and executed a number of works in Venice. He included Sigismondo Malatesta, Leonello d'Este, and Piero de' Medici among his patrons. Notable examples of his work in various genres are the illuminations for Piero de' Medici's copy of Petrarch's *Trionfi* (1441), the Palazzo Rucellai in Florence (c. 1446–c. 1451) as designed by *Alberti, and several portrait medals in the style of *Pisanello, of whom he was a follower. Other works included the unfinished reconstruction of the church interior of S Francesco in Rimini, on which he also collaborated with Alberti (*see* Tempio Malatestiano).

pastoral A type of literature concerned with idealized rustic life, especially the lives and loves of shepherds living in a golden age of simplicity and innocence. The style is often artificial, always unrealistic, and frequently coloured by the nostalgia felt by the urbanized author and his audience. Pastoral (or bucolic) elegy, romance, and drama developed as important genres in the Renaissance. The pastoral poem originated in Sicily. The *Idylls* of Theocritus, who was probably born at Syracuse around 270 BC, include six pastorals (nos. 1, 3, 4, 5, 6, 10) which reflect ancient Sicilian life and are structured dramatically as verse dialogues or contests (known as Amoebean or "responsive" verses) between rural characters. Other of the *Idylls* contain pastoral elements, for example, no. 15: although set in Alexandria, it describes the Adonia-zusae or festival of Adonis and concludes with a hymn in his honour. Idyll 1 contains a "Lament for Daphnis", the legendary Sicilian shepherd who invented the pastoral (in Theocritus' version, he dies of unrequited love visited on him by Aphrodite as a punishment for his having earlier refused love himself). Theocritus' successors were Bion, born at Smyrna (c. 100 BC), and the Syracusan Moschus (born c. 150 BC). Bion wrote six pastorals, imitating Theocritus most successfully in his "Lament for Adonis". The "Lament for Bion", traditionally attributed to Moschus but probably by one of Bion's disciples, completes the Greek models for what in the Renaissance was conventionalized as the pastoral elegy. Milton's "Lycidas" (1638) is the outstanding English example of the type.

Virgil's ten *Eclogues* (c. 42–37 BC) imitate Theocritus and refine pastoral conventions: the unrequited love of Corydon for Alexis (2), song and verse contests between shepherds (3, 7), the death of Daphnis (5). The fourth eclogue, which foretells the return of a golden age under the rule of a newborn child, was read by early Christians as a Messianic prophecy of the coming of Christ, and Virgil's use of allegory in the *Eclogues* exercised a strong influence on later poets. Far removed from the classical tradition, the medieval *pastourelle* (Provençal *pastorela*) was especially popular among Old French poets in the thirteenth century, though it was Provençal in origin. A short narrative poem about the meeting of a knight and a shepherdess, it had no characteristic formal features and was defined merely by its often crude subject matter. *Cavalcanti's "In un boschetto trova' pasturella" is an example. The classical pastoral, with a decided allegorical emphasis, was revived in the Latin poems of *Dante (two eclogues), *Petrarch (twelve eclogues), and in *Boccaccio's *Bucolicum carmen.* His "Ninfale fiesolano" (Nymph of Fiesole; 1344–46), which qualifies as the first vernacular idyll, dealt with Ovidian transformations to explain Tuscan river names and incorporated pastoral elements. *Pontano's Latin eclogues and idylls (three of each; Aldine edition, 1518) stand at the beginning of a Neapolitan revival of the pastoral tradition which culminated in *Sannazaro's *Arcadia.* (Sannazaro's innovative *Piscatoria* (1526) substituted fishermen for shepherds; in this he was imitated by Phineas *Fletcher.) Among *Boiardo's earliest poems are Italian eclogues imitating Virgil. *Spagnoli's (Mantuan's) ten Latin eclogues (1498) developed satirical motifs by using conventional pastoral

characters to attack the follies of church, court, and the female sex.

The pastoral romance is usually traced to Boccaccio's *Ameto* (1342), which mixed a long prose narrative with *terza rima* lyrics in a complicated plot involving pastoral characters. *Ameto* owes most, however, to medieval allegory. Sannazaro's *Arcadia* (1504) was the first true, and definitive, pastoral romance, the model for later authors (*see also* Arcadia). The pastoral drama of the sixteenth century developed in the wake of the immense popularity of *Arcadia* and drew on the dramatic potentials of the pastoral eclogue: the dialogues and verse contests, the loves of shepherds and nymphs, the allegorical elements and allusions to contemporary people and events, and the contrast between the golden age of rustic simplicity and the sophistication of the court life of the audience. The court of Ferrara in particular gave the impetus to these developments and its poets produced the two most influential pastoral plays: *Tasso's *Aminta* (1573), the best example of the type, which became the model for *Guarini's *Il pastor fido* (1589), the first pastoral tragicomedy. Other important Italian pastoral plays (or plays with significant pastoral elements) are Poliziano's *Favola di Orfeo* (1472), Epicuro's *Mirzia* (1535), *Cinthio's *Egle* (1545), and Beccari's *Il sacrificio* (1554).

The fashion for pastoral spread throughout Europe, encouraged by the Italian example or by direct contact with the classical models. The eclogues of Alexander Barclay (?1475–1552), the earliest in English (1515, 1521), are based directly on Spagnoli's, as are the pastoral poems of *Marot in French. Both Mantuan (Spagnoli) and Marot are acknowledged by *Spenser as sources for his *Shepheardes Calender* (1579).

In the field of pastoral romance, La *Diana* (1559) by Montemayor was immensely popular in its original Spanish and in translation. *Sidney's *Arcadia* (1590) is one of its offspring, and several Elizabethan prose writers tried their hand at the genre, most successfully perhaps in the case of *Lodge, whose *Rosalynde* (1590) is the source for *Shakespeare's *As You Like It.* In France the best-known novel in this kind is d'Urfé's *L'Astrée* (1607–27).

Besides plays, pastoral also had its uses in court entertainments and *masques; rustic characters could be introduced for merriment while more refined shepherds and shepherdesses could pay delicate compliments to the powerful and sophisticated audience, and courtiers could themselves take on bucolic roles and enjoy the game of pastoral make-believe.

Pastor fido, Il *see under* Guarini, Battista; pastoral.

Patinir, Joachim (c. 1480–1524) Netherlands painter. Patinir, who was born at Dinant, is first recorded in 1515 on his admission to the painters' guild at Antwerp, where he remained for the rest of his life. In 1521 he met Dürer who described him as "the good landscape painter". An early inventory states that the figures in Patinir's Madrid *Temptation of St Anthony* are by Quentin *Metsys. The landscape background in Joos van Cleve's Liverpool *Virgin and Child with Angels* is identical with one in a painting by Patinir in Lugano and may actually have been painted by him. Accordingly, Patinir emerges as the first landscape specialist, initiating a trend which flourished in Flemish painting of the early sixteenth century. Patinir's dramatic late landscapes, such as the Oxford *Destruction of Sodom and Gomorrah*, with heaped-up rocks of great size and irregular shape, strongly influenced subsequent Flemish mannerist landscapes.

patristic studies Early humanists made no distinction between the texts of classical authors and those of the Church Fathers. Petrarch collected texts of Cicero and St Augustine with equal enthusiasm and studied both for their moral content, preferring, as he himself said, to be made good rather than learned. As philological awareness advanced, however, scholars realized that there was a difference between the Latin prose style of Cicero and that of third- or fourth-century AD writers. *Valla, a leader in this field of study, observed in his *Elegantiae* (1444) that the Church Fathers were indebted to Cicero for their eloquence and exalted Ciceronian Latin as the model to be followed. He castigated St Jerome for deficiencies in his Latin style that he considered deformed the "truth" of the Greek original text of the New Testament which Jerome translated.

As the religious controversies of the sixteenth century got under way, Catholics and Protestants alike appealed to the venerable authority of the Church Fathers for guidance on biblical interpretation and for their teaching on such matters as justification by faith and the operation of divine grace. To do this it was necessary for authoritative texts to be available. An early leader in the field of patristic printed texts was Johannes *Amerbach at Basle, whose successor, *Froben, was the chief publisher of *Erasmus. Erasmus showed phenomenal zeal in his patristic publications: his nine-volume St Jerome appeared in 1516, his ten-volume St Augustine in 1529, and his two-volume Origen, which had taken up the last months of his life, in 1536; these were in addition to texts of Sts Ambrose, Cyprian, Hilary, Irenaeus, and John Chrysostom.

The Council of *Trent explicitly endorsed the authority of the Fathers in biblical exegesis, thus giving a further stimulus to patristic studies in Catholic countries. The first important printed collection of patristic texts, the *Bibliotheca SS patrum*, appeared in Paris in eight volumes in 1575, and in increasingly expanded editions over the next century. Apologists of the Church of England found the Fathers an invaluable source of doctrine, uncontaminated, as they saw it, by Romanist corruptions. Isaac *Casaubon and Georg *Cassander were just two scholars who were greatly influenced in their theological opinions by their patristic studies.

Patrizi, Francesco (Franjo Petrić *or* Patritius; 1529–97) Dalmatian philosopher, mathematician, and scholar. Born at Cherso, Istria, he studied at Padua and Venice where he developed an interest in Platonism through reading the *Theologia Platonica* of *Ficino. After service in France, Spain, and Cyprus he became professor of Platonic philosophy at Ferrara (1578). In 1592 he was called to Rome by Pope Clement VIII and died there as professor of philosophy at the university. Pure scholarship was not his only interest; he also published practical manuals of military strategy. He produced a number of works presenting art, history, and philosophy in a Platonic interpretation challenging the dominant Aristotelianism of his day, most notably *Della historia* (1560), *Della retorica* (1562), and *Nova de universis philosophia* (1591). Patrizi sought to combine Christianity, Platonism, and the hermetic writings in a metaphysical synthesis but failed through lack of a sufficiently rigorous method of argument.

patronage In considering the cultural bond linking creative artists and the grandees who supported them, the Renaissance looked back for its model to a famous relationship in classical antiquity: the patronage bestowed by Maecenas, the friend and minister of the Roman emperor Augustus, upon the epic poet Virgil. As the epigrammatist Martial said, "Sint Maecenates, non deerunt...Marones" (As long as there are Maecenases... Virgils will not be lacking). Maecenas was thus perceived as the epitome of the liberal and discerning patron, and it was a standard compliment from Renaissance literati to refer to an actual or intended patron as a "Maecenas" (*see* Sidney, Philip).

At its most basic, the patron's duty was to provide the artist with financial security, either through long- or short-term employment or by commissioning specific works from him. The degree of enlightened encouragement that a patron could provide naturally varied with the patron's own tastes, discernment, and interests. Poets, musicians, and painters, along with competent falconers or riding masters, might well be considered no more than desirable personnel in the entourage of any nobleman who wished to cut a dash among his fellows, but ideally both sides conceived the patronage relationship as considerably more than a crude transaction whereby monetary advantage was traded for gross flattery. Present enjoyment and display naturally mattered to a patron, but the quality of his artists' output mattered too, because in a world in which military glory and political power were seen to be frail and transitory the discriminating prince could hope to achieve lasting renown through his association with works that would be admired by future generations.

This idealistic view of patronage applied particularly to literature, less so to the visual arts, and hardly at all in the case of music. Even so, writers were seldom primarily employed for literary ends, as was the case with *Ariosto, who was sent on various diplomatic missions by his *Este employers. The relationship between painters, sculptors, and architects and their patrons varied considerably. Some artists had little, if any, more status than other household employees, but great figures such as Michelangelo, Titian, and Cellini were highly mobile and were sought after by popes and emperors. On the other hand, such artists needed the scope provided by huge and expensive projects for such patrons as Pope Julius II, Emperor Charles V, and Francis I of France to realize their artistic vision. Music, while an integral part of Renaissance life, is scarcely included within the exalted concept of patronage; princes, great churches, or municipal corporations generally just hired the best men available to compose and perform music for grand occasions and for everyday requirements.

While some patronage relationships in the visual arts are well documented, especially the stormy ones like that between Michelangelo and Pope Julius II, most evidence for the system in the Renaissance derives from literature. Compliments to patrons could be integral to the work itself (as in Ariosto's glorification of the Este in *Orlando furioso*) or the patron's association with it could be proclaimed via the dedication. With the spread of printing the latter practice was easily debased, with some authors claiming as "patrons" eminent persons whom they scarcely knew, in the hope of a cash hand-out.

Paul II (1417–71), Pope (1464–71) A wealthy Venetian by birth, at the age of twenty-three Pietro Barbo was created a cardinal by his uncle, Pope *Eugenius IV. Paul II failed to gain Emperor Frederick III's cooperation in organizing a crusade against the Turks, but he enjoyed more success in his fight against heresy in Bohemia, where he

excommunicated and deposed King George of Podebrady for his Hussite sympathies. Paul supported the candidature of the more loyal Catholic, King *Matthias Corvinus of Hungary, who was elected king of Bohemia in 1469. Paul II made little progress in restoring papal authority in the Papal States, but his restoration of ancient monuments made Rome a more worthy papal capital; he also amassed a collection of ancient coins and bronzes. Paul II founded the first printing presses in Rome, but clashed with the humanist scholars at the *Roman Academy, led by Pomponio *Leto. He temporarily closed the academy in 1468 and arrested its members; one of them, *Platina, was tortured.

Paul III (1468–1549), Pope (1534–49) After enjoying the benefits of a humanist education in the circle of Lorenzo de' *Medici, Alessandro Farnese became through papal patronage cardinal deacon (1493), bishop of Parma (1509), and papal legate to the Lateran Council (1512). He gave up his mistress before his ordination (1519) and subsequently led an irreproachable private life, although as pope he indulged in nepotism. Paul III wished to unite Catholic Europe against Turks and Protestants, but could not persuade Emperor *Charles V and *Francis I of France to settle their differences.

By supporting agriculture, the construction of fortifications, and major projects in Rome Paul brought prosperity and security to his domains, but his attempts to assert his authority elsewhere provoked the Perugian *Salt War. Paul III supported reform. He appointed virtuous men as cardinals, favoured new religious orders like the *Jesuits, and established the Italian Inquisition (1542). He summoned the Council of *Trent, the first meeting (1545) of which marked the beginning of the *Counter-Reformation and led to major administrative and spiritual reforms. A patron of the arts and learning, Paul III added to the Vatican Library, restored the university of Rome, completed the plans for the new St Peter's, and persuaded *Michelangelo to finish *The Last Judgment* in the *Sistine Chapel.

Paul IV (1476–1559), Pope (1555–59) Giampietro Caraffa was born into an aristocratic Abruzzi family. Having served as papal nuncio in England and acted as adviser to the papacy on means of counteracting heresy, he was co-founder of the *Theatine Order (1524). As cardinal archbishop of Naples from 1536 he was an active ecclesiastical reformer whose reorganization (1542) of the Italian Inquisition made it a feared defender of Catholic orthodoxy. An austere and authoritarian pope, he curbed clerical abuses in Rome, disciplined erring clergy, and forced Jews to live in a Roman ghetto and to wear badges. He joined France in a war against Spain, but Spain's victory compelled him to make peace with *Philip II (1557). Paul's unwillingness to compromise led him to charge Cardinal *Pole with heresy and facilitated the Protestant victory in England. In 1559 Paul issued the first *Index Librorum Prohibitorum.

Paumann, Konrad (c. 1410–73) German composer and organist. Paumann, who was born blind, was organist at the church of St Sebald in his native Nuremberg from at least 1446; the next year he was appointed town organist. In 1450 he became court organist to Duke Albrecht III of Bavaria in Munich, a post he retained for the rest of his life. Famous throughout Germany as an organist, from 1450 Paumann travelled widely through France, Italy, Germany, and Austria, playing and examining instruments at the courts of dukes and princes. Few of Paumann's compositions survive, probably because he was unable to write them down; it is thought by some, however, that he was the inventor of German lute tablature. His treatise, *Fundamentum organisandi* (1452), gives examples of the ornamentation of chant, with keyboard arrangements of chants and secular melodies.

Pavia, Battle of (24 February 1525) A victory by the forces of Emperor Charles V, numbering some 23 000, against Francis I of France. Francis had invaded Italy in 1524 and beseiged Pavia, near Milan, with 28 000 men, as a preliminary to attacking Milan itself. The imperial force's attempt to relieve the town resulted in a battle in which the French army was destroyed and the king captured. The battle established the Habsburgs as the dominant power in Italy, and Charles was able to dictate the terms of Francis's release in the treaty of Madrid (1526); but France's power was not broken, and the threat of Habsburg domination in Europe attracted allies to the French king. Pavia was also significant in conclusively demonstrating the superiority of *firearms over cavalry lances. See Plate XXIX.

Pazzi conspiracy (1478) A plot by Francesco and Girolamo Pazzi, of the Florentine banking family who were longtime rivals to the Medici, to assassinate *Lorenzo de' Medici and his brother Giuliano. Their fellow-conspirators included the archbishop of Pisa, and the plot had the tacit support of Pope Sixtus IV because of Lorenzo's efforts to thwart consolidation of papal rule over the Romagna. The Medici brothers were to be killed in the cathedral in Florence after Mass on Easter Day (26 April); in the event, Giuliano was killed, but Lorenzo escaped with only slight injuries. Simultaneous attempts to raise the populace against the Medici met with no support. Subsequent executions (including that of the archbishop of Pisa) and exiles broke the influence of the Pazzi family and strengthened the Medici hold on Florence.

Pecock, Reginald (c. 1393–1461) English churchman. He was born in Wales, became a fellow of Oriel College, Oxford, and in 1431 was appointed master of Whittington College, London. He was created bishop of St Asaph, in Wales (1444), and of Chichester (1450) and he was also made a privy counsellor. He wrote extensively and preached against the Lollards; many of his works have not survived. The Lancastrian dukes of Gloucester and Suffolk were his patrons, and the hostility of the Yorkists resulted in his expulsion from the privy council and citation before the archbishop of Canterbury for denying the authority of the Apostles' Creed (1457). Despite a public recantation he had to resign his bishopric, and from 1459 he was confined in Thorney Abbey, near Cambridge, where he probably died. His writings are remarkable for their clarity, rationality, and critical power in presenting a theological argument, but read oddly on account of his having frequently to coin words or borrow foreign expressions to make up for the limitations of the unsophisticated vernacular in this period.

Peele, George (?1558–?1597) English poet and dramatist. Little is known for certain of Peele's life except that he was at Oxford in the early 1570s and in 1579 was ejected from his father's house in Christ's Hospital, London, for dissipation. He wrote a number of plays and pageants in the 1580s and 1590s; these are notable principally for their highly accomplished lyrics. *The Arraignment of Paris* (1584), a pastoral comedy, was his first play, performed perhaps as early as 1581. It was followed by the chronicle play *Edward I* (1593), *The Battle of Alcazar* (1594), *The Old Wives Tale* (1595), and *The Love of King David and fair Bethsabe* (1599).

Peffenhauser (*or* Pfeffenhauser), An (c. 1525–1603) German armourer. One of the best-known sixteenth-century German armourers, Peffenhauser came from an Augsburg family of armourers. As plate armour was by then ceremonial parade armour rather than practical, and was magnificently decorated, Peffenhauser's work was both extremely elaborate and beautifully crafted. His clients included German princes and members of the court of Philip II of Spain. The suit of armour made for King Sebastian of Portugal is one of the most ornate ever made. Examples of his work still survive, for instance in the Tower of London.

Pellegrini, Pellegrino de *see* Tibaldi, Pellegrino.

Pérez, Antonio (c. 1540–1611) Spanish courtier and writer. Pérez was born in Madrid, the illegitimate son of an imperial secretary. Educated in Italy and Flanders, he himself rose to become the favourite minister of Philip II; in 1573 he was appointed head of the bureau through which Philip governed his domains. In 1578 Pérez engineered the assassination of one of Philip's enemies, an act that eventually brought about his downfall, when the king, to prevent his complicity in the murder becoming public knowledge, arranged for Pérez's imprisonment and torture by the Inquisition (1589). Pérez escaped, leaving behind in Spain a fine picture collection, which Philip promptly confiscated.

Received first at the Navarrese court at Pau, Pérez subsequently moved to Paris and then England. His *Relaciones* (1598) and epigrammatic letters effectively blackened the character and conduct of Philip while exonerating his own. Despite later efforts to win a pardon from Philip III, Pérez died in exile in Paris.

perspective The graphical representation of three-dimensional objects on a two-dimensional surface, as developed chiefly during the Italian Renaissance. There are generally three recognized types of perspective: visual, linear, and aerial. Visual perspective – the simple overlapping of objects – was known to the ancient Greeks and Romans, but the laws governing the use of linear perspective, in which objects are arranged along parallel lines that apparently converge on a distant point (the "vanishing point") on the horizon line, were only discovered by *Brunelleschi in the fifteenth century. These properties were also explored by such notable artists as *Alberti (who wrote an early treatise on the subject) *Uccello, *Piero della Francesca, and *Masaccio. *Leonardo da Vinci also used linear perspective in some of his greatest paintings, including his *Last Supper, in which the parallel lines converge on the vanishing point of Christ's head. Other leading artists, such as *Mantegna, *Botticelli, and Fra Filippo *Lippi refined the Italian idea of perspective, sometimes using more than one vanishing point in order to intensify the illusion of depth. Considerable use was also made of the third type of perspective, aerial perspective, in which distant colours are made paler and outlines of distant objects are less clearly defined.

Perugia A city in Umbria, central Italy. Perugia was originally an Umbrian foundation, then Etrus-

can, Roman, and Lombard. It was annexed by the papacy in 1303. During the fourteenth and fifteenth centuries Perugia was the scene of bitter internal conflicts from which the *Baglioni family had emerged with the greatest success in the fifteenth century. Rome allowed Perugia considerable autonomy until 1540, when Pope *Paul III abolished Perugia's municipal powers after the city's unsuccessful revolt against papal authority in the *Salt War.

During the fourteenth century the university of Perugia (founded 1308) was an important centre for the study of Roman law under the direction of Bartolus of Sassoferrato. In the fifteenth century it was the focus of the Umbrian school of painting, with which such distinguished artists as *Perugino, *Pinturicchio, and the young *Raphael were associated. Notable Renaissance landmarks include the thirteenth-century walls, the cathedral (1345–1430), the oratory of S Bernardino (1457–61) with its façade by *Agostino di Duccio, and the Collegio del Cambio (1452–57) with frescoes by Perugino.

Perugino, Pietro Vanucci (c. 1445–1523) Italian artist. Born at Città della Pieve, near Perugia, Perugino possibly began his career under the tutelage of *Piero della Francesca, although little is known for certain about his early training. He then moved to Florence, where he probably worked in the workshop run by *Verrocchio – possibly alongside Leonardo da Vinci – and became familiar with oil painting techniques. In 1472 he was listed as one of the painters of the company of S Luke in Florence, and by 1481 he was well known enough to be employed by Pope Sixtus IV on the frescoes for the Sistine Chapel. Working there alongside Rosselli, Ghirlandaio, Botticelli, and others, and with Pinturicchio as his assistant, Perugino executed such influential paintings as *Christ Delivering the Keys to St Peter* (1482), upon which his reputation was established. Other works from this period included an important altarpiece, the *Crucifixion with Saints* (1481; National Gallery of Art, Washington), which is remarkable for its use of an extensive landscape as a setting. Such a sense of space, with the figures close to the front of the composition, is characteristic of much of Perugino's work.

During the 1490s Perugino, who was always prolific, produced further notable works, including the *Vision of S Bernard* (1491–94; Alte Pinakothek, Munich), a *Pietà* (1494–95; Uffizi), and a *Madonna with Saints* (1491–92; Louvre). Between 1498 and 1500 Perugino undertook the decoration of the audience chamber of the Collegio del Cambio at Perugia, working alongside his pupil *Raphael; among the biblical, allegorical, and classical figures there is Perugino's famous self-portrait in a red cap. This shows the naturalism that appears in several of his portraits, for example that of Francesco delle Opere in the Uffizi, in contrast to the idealized and gracefully decorative figures of his religious and allegorical pictures. After Raphael's death, Perugino completed several of his unfinished paintings, although his own works after 1500 showed a marked decline in standard, becoming increasingly sentimental in tone. Among his later works is the fresco of the *Adoration of the Magi* (1504) in the church of Sta Maria dei Bianchi in his native town. By 1506 his style had become outmoded and Perugino retired to Perugia, where he died.

Peruzzi, Baldassare (Tommaso) (1481–1536) Italian painter, architect, and stage designer. Born in Siena, Peruzzi moved to Rome in 1503, where he came under the influence of Bramante and Raphael and contributed designs for St Peter's. Peruzzi's first major architectural achievement was the Villa *Farnesina (1509–21) in Rome, a building in the High Renaissance style in which he also executed notable frescoes and experimented with the use of false perspectives. After Raphael's death Peruzzi continued in his attempts at illusionist architectural painting when he became (1520) one of the architects for St Peter's; on this he worked until the sack of Rome in 1527, once again producing designs that employed the use of multiple perspectives. After a period in Siena he returned to Rome in about 1532 to embark on his last major architectural undertaking, the Palazzo Massimo alle Colonne, which was completed in about 1535.

With its dramatic portico and curved façade, this was one of the first mannerist buildings and is unusual in its decorations and irregular plan. Other works by Peruzzi include frescoes in the Cappella S Giovanni in Siena cathedral and stage designs, most of which are now lost.

Peter Martyr (Pietro Martire d'Anghiera; 1459–1526) Italian humanist. Born in Angera, near Arona on Lake Maggiore, he used his humanist education to secure secretaryships in Rome. From there he accompanied the Castilian ambassador back to Spain (1487), where he spent the rest of his life in the service of the Spanish crown. He fought in the campaigns that resulted in the reconquest of Granada (1492), ran a school to introduce young courtiers to the elements of humanist learning, went on an embassy to Cairo (1501–02), and was increasingly employed in matters relating to administration of Spain's overseas empire, becoming an official historian to the council for the Indies in 1510.

Peter Martyr had taken a keen interest in *Columbus and seems quickly to have grasped the significance of the great navigator's discoveries; in a letter dated 1494 he is apparently the first person to use the phrase "western hemisphere". His *Decades de orbe novo* appeared in three instalments: 1511, 1516, and (first complete edition) 1530. The work was the first full public chronicle of the voyages of discovery and was responsible for spreading knowledge of Spain's explorations throughout Europe; its accuracy and completeness appear even to have embarrassed the Spanish authorities, who would have preferred to keep

PERUZZI The convex front of the Palazzo Massimo alle Colonne, Rome, was Peruzzi's response to the challenge of a narrow and irregular site.

some of the information secret. Peter Martyr was renowned for his pleasant Latin style, which was particularly apparent in his history of the years 1488–1525, written in the form of letters and published as *Opus epistolarum* (1530).

Peter Martyr (Pietro Martire Vermigli; 1500–62) Italian reformed theologian. Born in Florence and becoming a member of the Augustinian order, Peter Martyr held several important offices before his evident sympathy for the evangelical movement led to accusations of heresy by the Inquisition. After sheltering for a time in Rome, in 1542 he left Italy and settled in Strasbourg, where *Bucer secured for him an appointment as professor of theology. In 1547 he was invited to England by *Cranmer and appointed regius professor of divinity at Oxford, where he defended the reformed doctrine of the Eucharist in an important disputation (1549). Forced to leave England in 1553 by the accession of Mary I, he first returned to Strasbourg and then moved to Zürich (1556), where he remained until his death. A prolific writer, Peter Martyr defended a Zwinglian sacramental theology, but was temperamentally inclined to ecumenicism. His most popular work, the *Loci communes* (Commonplaces), was published posthumously in 1563.

Peter of Alcántara, St (Pedro Garavito; 1499–1562) Spanish mystic, founder of the Discalced Franciscans. He studied at Salamanca and became a Franciscan Observant friar (1515). Ordained priest, he preached in Estremadura, where he was elected provincial of his order in 1538. His desire for a yet more rigorous observance of the rule led him to establish a friary at Pedrosa (c. 1556), from which his movement for reform spread. The Discalced Franciscans went barefooted, consumed no meat or wine, and spent much time in solitude and contemplation. As confessor to St *Teresa of Ávila he encouraged her to initiate reform among the Carmelites. He was the author of a popular treatise on prayer and meditation (1556).

Petrarch (Francesco Petrarca; 1304–74) Italian poet and humanist. Petrarch was born in Arezzo after his father, a notary, was exiled from Florence by the Black faction of the Guelph party. In 1311 the family settled in Provence, soon after the establishment of the papacy at *Avignon. Apart from his travels, chiefly to Italy, Petrarch lived in Provence, mainly at his villa in Vaucluse, until 1353. Thereafter he lived in Italy under the protection of powerful rulers: in Milan, of the Visconti; in Venice, of the senate; and in Padua, of Francesco da Carrara, Il Vecchio. He first studied at Carpentras under Convenevole da Prato, a Tuscan; after

reading law at Montpellier and Bologna, he returned to Avignon in 1326 and in 1330 took minor orders, which required a vow of celibacy but little else. Nevertheless he had two illegitimate children: Giovanni (born 1337) and Francesca (born 1343). The Colonna became the first of many patrons and this support, together with the benefices he received, enabled Petrarch to devote himself to writing and to cultivate classical scholarship, which was to assure him an unassailable reputation in the eyes of humanists of the fifteenth century. On 6 April 1327 Petrarch had his first glimpse of Laura (Sonnet 211). (Historically little is known of her; she died in the plague of 1348.) His love for her is the central theme of 366 Italian poems collected in *Canzoniere*, a work apparently completed towards the end of his life which had a momentous effect on European poetry. Petrarch did not invent the *sonnet which bears his name or introduce other innovations in the *Canzoniere*; rather, he brought a refinement and subtlety to the tradition of Provençal and Sicilian verse that led his successors to rank him even above *Dante and inspired a host of "Petrarchan" imitators, especially in the sixteenth century. (*See also* concetto; dolce stil nuovo; questione della lingua; stilnovismo.)

Except for an unfinished allegorical poem, *I trionfi* (written after 1350), Petrarch's other works and all of his prose were written in Latin. The epic *Africa* on Scipio Africanus, which he considered his greatest poetic achievement, and a collection of Roman biographies, *De viris illustribus*, were started before his coronation but never completed. In Rome on 8 April 1341 he was crowned poet laureate, the first modern poet so honoured, after being examined by *Robert of Anjou, King of Naples. *Secretum* (1342–43) reflects a tension discernible in other works between Petrarch's humanistic ideals and an otherworldly Augustinian tendency. *De vita solitaria* (1346) attempts to strike a balance and in several invectives, especially *Contra medicum*, Petrarch vigorously defended humanistic pursuits, but the medieval and Christian view dominates again, for example, in the later dialogues of *De remediis utriusque fortunae*. His history, *Rerum memorandum libri* (begun 1343), was left unfinished.

Petrarch continually worked to unearth and emend classical texts. By his early twenties he was at work on putting together a complete text of Livy, obtaining exemplars from as far away as Chartres cathedral. His researches turned up texts of Propertius, Cicero's *Pro Archia*, and Seneca's tragedies, and the discovery of Cicero's letters to Atticus at Verona (1345) inspired the collection of his own *Epistolae familiares* and *seniles*. Around forty-four surviving manuscripts have been identified as having belonged to Petrarch's personal collection; among them is his copy of Servius' commentary on Virgil, written about 1325 in Avignon, with a frontispiece by Simone *Martini (Bibliotheca Ambrosiana, Milan).

The republican cause of Cola di *Rienzo at first attracted his enthusiastic encouragement, but he took no part in political activity after its defeat (1347), a change of heart also probably related to the deaths of Laura and his patron Cardinal Colonna in 1348. The final six years of his life were spent at Arquá, near Padua, on land presented to him by Francesco da Carrara.

Petri, Olaus (Olof Petersson; 1493–1552) *and* **Laurentius** (Lars Petersson; 1499–1573) Swedish reformers. The brothers were born at Orebro, and Olaus studied at Wittenberg (1516–18), where he was taught by Luther and Melanchthon. He returned to Sweden as a teacher, supported the breach with Rome in 1527, and helped to produce the first Swedish New Testament (1526) and liturgies (1529, 1531). He became a favourite of King Gustavus Vasa and was made chancellor (1531–33) but he fell out with the king and in 1540 was condemned to death for treason. This sentence was commuted to a fine. He later became pastor of the principal church (*storkyrkan*) in Stockholm.

Laurentius became the first Protestant archbishop of Uppsala in 1531. He and Olaus were chiefly responsible for the Swedish Bible (Gustavus Vasa Biblc) of 1541. Laurentius's book on church order (1571) helped to make the Swedish church less subject to the state than other Lutheran churches.

Petrucci, Ottaviano (1466–1539) Italian music printer. Petrucci was probably educated at the court of Guidobaldo I, Duke of Urbino. Around 1490 he went to Venice and in 1498 the doge granted him the exclusive right to print measured music. Until then only chant had been printed in Germany and Italy, but Petrucci's new method meant that polyphony could be printed from type; in his first publication, *Harmonice musices odhecaton A* (1501), a collection mainly of French chansons, the new process is used. This entailed three impressions – one of staves, one of notes, and one of the text. In 1507 Petrucci published lute tablature. In 1511 he returned to his native Fossombrone and continued to print music, obtaining a privilege from Pope Leo X to print mensural music and organ tablature in the Papal States. Back again in Venice from 1536 he printed Latin and Italian classical texts. Petrucci's success meant that the works of composers such as Josquin *Des Prés and *Obrecht were widely disseminated in their day.

Peuerbach, Georg (1423–61) Austrian mathematician and astronomer. Educated in Vienna and Italy, Peuerbach began his career as court astrologer to Ladislaus V of Hungary. He was appointed later to the chair of mathematics and astronomy at Vienna. Much of Peuerbach's short life was devoted to the study of the *Almagest* (*see* Ptolemaic system). Wtih Cardinal *Bessarion he planned to obtain an accurate copy of the Greek text, but died before he could even begin the project. He did succeed in drafting the first six chapters of his *Epitome* of the *Almagest*, a task completed by his pupil *Regiomontanus, and managed to finish his *Theoricae novae planetarum*; this elementary survey of planetary astronomy served as a popular textbook well into the sixteenth century. His *Tabulae eclipsium*, probably completed in 1459, were also used for many years.

Peutinger, Konrad (1465–1547) German humanist scholar. Between 1482 and 1488 Peutinger travelled in Italy, where he met *Politian and *Pico della Mirandola, and became deeply imbued with the spirit of the Italian Renaissance. He remained in correspondence with his Italian teachers, published extracts from their lectures, and copied Leto's *Roman Academy in the foundation of his *Sodalitas literaria Augustana* in his native Augsburg. As town clerk of Augsburg (1497) Peutinger was on terms of friendship with Emperor Maximilian I. He published Roman inscriptions, and among his collection of antiquities was the map known as the *Tabula peutingeriuna*, a thirteenth-century copy of the late Roman original depicting military roads, which he inherited (1508) from Konrad *Celtis.

pharmacopoeia A standard list of drugs with information on their preparation and use. In antiquity scholars, of whom Dioscorides is the best known, produced *materia medica* devoted almost exclusively to the medicinal properties of plants. The tradition persisted throughout the medieval period with Albucasis, a tenth-century Arab physician and other scholars, adding to the classical heritage. Albucasis's work, the *Liber servatoris*, first published in the West in 1471, became well known to Renaissance physicians. Thereafter the modern pharmacopoeias began to appear. Initially they began as local collections representing the medical wisdom of a particular area. The first appeared in Florence (1498) and was followed by similar items from Nuremberg (1546), Augsburg (1564), Cologne (1565), and London (1618). One feature of the pharmacopoeias was their growing willingness to accept the chemical remedies proposed by *Paracelsus and his followers. Thus, though absent from early issues of the Augsburg pharmacopoeia, they were introduced into the 1613 edition.

Philip II (1527–98), King of Spain (1556–98) He was born at Valladolid, the son of Emperor *Charles V and Isabella of Portugal. Philip's first wife, Maria of Portugal, died in 1545. During his second marriage (1554–58), to *Mary I of England, he was joint sovereign of her realms. His third marriage, to Elizabeth of Valois (1559–68), produced two daughters. His heir, the ineffectual Philip III (1578–1621), was the only surviving son of his fourth marriage (1570–80), to Anne of Austria.

Even without the Habsburg possessions in Germany, which went to Charles's brother, *Ferdinand I, Philip inherited vast territories. He ruled Spain, Milan, Naples and Sicily, the Netherlands, and the New World territories of the Caribbean, Mexico, and Peru. In 1580 he annexed Portugal.

As a young man Philip travelled in Italy, Germany, and the Netherlands, but as king he preferred the semi-seclusion of El *Escorial, the palace he had built near Madrid (1563–84). From his study he used viceroys to govern his provinces. His officials were obliged to submit regular and exhaustive reports and to obey his detailed instructions. Philip's ability to deal with up to 400 documents a day led one historian to describe him as the "arch bureaucrat".

Philip saw himself as a devout Catholic and a staunch opponent of both Turk and Protestant. At times he seemed to be trying to establish a Spanish Catholic hegemony over Europe. His forces checked the *Ottoman Turks at *Lepanto (1571), but he enjoyed less success against the Protestants. The destruction of the *Spanish Armada (1588) demonstrated his inability to subdue the English, and he failed to suppress the revolt of the *Netherlands. Yet, he was a leading force in the *Counter-Reformation and did much to secure the Catholic faith in Italy, Spain, and Belgium.

Despite his reputation as the "most Catholic King" Philip was prepared to use the *Spanish Inquisition not just as a weapon against heresy but also as an instrument of his royal power, as in the case of Antonio *Pérez. He also did not hesitate to oppose papal policies that seemed hostile to the Habsburg interests. An austere and dedicated ruler, Philip lived frugally, but he spent lavishly on the books and paintings he loved, continuing his father's patronage of *Titian and Leone *Leoni and employing Federico *Zuccaro and *Tibaldi on major projects. See Plate XIII.

Philip Neri, St (1515–95) Italian religious, founder of the Oratorians. The son of a lawyer in Florence, Neri abandoned an intended commercial career for a life of lay piety. Moving to Rome (1533), he tutored and lived an ascetic life. Neri then founded the Oratory in Rome, composed of like-minded laymen and clergy living together without vows for the purpose of prayer, fasting, and a more intense spiritual life. The Roman Oratory also organized help for Roman children, the sick, and pilgrims visiting the Holy City.

Neri's was but one of several confraternities organized during the Catholic Reformation of the early-to-mid-sixteenth century, and it lies at the heart of that movement. The Oratory used traditional medieval mystical texts, and its themes were joy and love. Neri's prayer meetings were often accompanied by the music of his friend *Palestrina, and this gave birth to the "oratorio". Neri finally took priestly vows in 1551. He led afternoon excursions to Roman churches, music sessions, and picnics, practices censored by Pope Paul IV because the pope had been warned that Neri had formed a heterodox sect. Pius IV rehabilitated Neri's reputation and he was allowed to build a new church on the site of Sta Maria in Vallicella. In 1575 Gregory XIII recognized the Oratorians as a congregation. Neri's most famous follower was Cesare *Baronius, and his advice was sought by *Ignatius Loyola, *Charles Borromeo, and *Francis de Sales. He has been called the "Apostle of Rome". He died in Rome and was canonized in 1622.

Philips, Peter (c. 1560–1628) English composer and organist. Philips sang in the choir of St Paul's Cathedral as a boy. In 1582 he fled to Rome because of his Catholic beliefs, and was received there at the English College, of which he became organist. In 1585 Philips entered the service of Lord Thomas Paget, and in the next five years travelled through Italy, Spain, and France, settling in Brussels in 1589. On the death of Paget (1590) Philips moved to Antwerp. In 1593, returning from a visit to hear Sweelinck play in Amsterdam, he was arrested on suspicion of being party to a plot to assassinate Queen Elizabeth. He was released, and in 1597 entered the Brussels household of Archduke Albert, where he remained until the archduke's death in 1621. Philips was probably the most famous English composer in northern Europe. His collections of madrigals and motets were reprinted many times in Antwerp; these are Roman in style, with Italianate word-painting and polyphony. Philips also wrote much keyboard music, some of which is preserved in the Fitzwilliam Virginal Book. This belongs to the English tradition, the most inventive pieces being those based on madrigals and chansons.

Philip the Bold (1342–1404), Duke of Burgundy

(1363–1404) and Count of Flanders (1384–1404) The title of "the Bold" was given him for his conduct at the battle of Poitiers (1356), after which he accompanied his father, John II of France, into captivity in England. When the duke of Burgundy died without an heir, his domains reverted to the French crown, and John II granted the duchy to Philip in 1363. Philip's domains were further enlarged through his marriage (1369) to Margaret, heiress of Flanders, Artois, and Franche-Comté. During the minority (1380–88) of his nephew, Charles VI of France, Philip was regent. When Charles went mad in 1392 Philip resumed the regency and, despite the rival claim of the duke of Orleans (Charles VI's brother), virtually ruled France until his death. He fought England and the Netherlands, and tried to heal the *Great Schism within the Church.

Philip the Good (1396–1467), Duke of Burgundy (1419–67) Philip succeeded his assassinated father, John the Fearless. During his reign the Burgundian court was the most splendid in Europe and his domains enjoyed their greatest eminence and prosperity, but he failed to create a national state out of his inheritance. The splendour and chivalric aspirations of his court were most clearly expressed in his institution of the Order of the *Golden Fleece (1429) to honour his marriage to Isabella of Portugal. He was an ally of England from 1420 to 1435, recognizing Henry VI of England as king of France, but subsequently he supported the French king. When the dauphin, later Louis XI, fled (1456) from his father, Philip gave him asylum, and later recognized his accession (1461). Philip was much troubled by rebellions in the Netherlands, most notably in Ghent (1432, 1448, 1453).

physic gardens see botanic (or physic) gardens.

Piagnoni (the Snivellers) The most devout supporters of *Savonarola.

Piarists (or Regulares pauperes Matris Dei scholarum piarum) A teaching order founded in Rome in 1602 by the Spanish priest (later St) Joseph Calasanctius (1556–1648). It grew from his work among the neglected and homeless children of the city, for whom he had set up a free elementary school in 1597. In 1621 Pope Gregory XV recognized the Piarists as an order, whose members took a vow to dedicate themselves to the teaching of children. It subsequently flourished in many parts of southern Europe and spread from Spain to Latin America.

picaresque novel In sixteenth- and seventeenth-century Spain, a popular realistic episodic narrative in autobiographical form relating the life of a rogue (pícaro) in a corrupt world, with moral or religious reflections giving the final views of the repentant sinner.*Lazarillo de Tormes (1554) established the model of lowlife first-person narrator, but typical picaresque novels are later in date, for example *Guzmán de Alfarache (1599, 1604) by Mateo *Alemán, the earliest, and El Buscón (The Rogue; written 1603–08, published 1626) by Francisco Gómez de Quevedo y Villegas (1580–1645), perhaps the most brilliant and malicious of the type. Others are La pícara Justina (1605), with a female protagonist, Marcos de Obregón (1618), Alonso, mozo de muchos amos (Alonso, Servant of Many Masters; 1624–26) by Jerónimo Alcalá Yáñez, and Estebanillo González (1646), an apparently real autobiography set in the Thirty Years' War, after which the vogue for the picaresque died out. Two of *Cervantes's Novelas ejemplares, Rinconete y Cortadillo and La ilustre fregona (The Illustrious Kitchenmaid; both 1613) are shorter examples. The picaresque represents a reaction against idealized chivalric literature. There is no reason to discount the moral content of the novels, however, as merely a means to appease the censor. A forerunner of the picaresque novel in England was The Unfortunate Traveller (1594) by *Nashe.

Piccinino, Niccolò (1386–1444) Italian condottiere. Born near Perugia, Piccinino took up the profession of mercenary to escape from following his father's trade as a butcher. In 1424, on the death of his commander, Piccinino assumed leadership of the band, selling their services first to Florence and then (1426) to Duke Filippo Maria Visconti of Milan. His ambitions and his military prowess however soon alarmed his employer, who sought to win Francesco Sforza, at that time commander of Venice's forces and a personal enemy of Piccinino, over to his side. The uneasy relationship between the Milanese duke and the two condottieri on whom, in their different ways, he relied continued throughout the 1430s, but in 1443 Sforza resoundingly defeated Piccinino in battle. Piccinino died of dropsy the following year.

Piccolomini, Aenea Silvio see Pius II.

Piccolpasso, Cipriano see under majolica.

Pico della Mirandola, Giovanni (1463–94) Italian philosopher and humanist. The nephew of Marsilio *Ficino, he was born at Mirandola near Modena. He studied law at Bologna but found these studies unsatisfying and at the age of eighteen travelled extensively in France and Italy, accumulating a large library and acquiring a wide range of knowledge sacred and profane, which his prodigious memory made readily accessible. In 1486 he arrived in Rome and proposed 900 theses or propositions, dealing, as he said, "*de omni re scibili*" (with everything knowable), inviting all comers to debate them with him and offering to pay their travelling expenses if poverty prevented their taking up the challenge. However, Pope Innocent VIII intervened by a Bull in 1487 to prevent the discussion. Thirteen theses were singled out and condemned as heretical. Pico withdrew to Florence and defended himself in an *Apology* (1489) but the attacks continued until Alexander VI absolved him of the taint of heresy and protected him from further persecution. Under the influence of *Savonarola Pico withdrew to a life of austere piety and died of fever aged thirty-one.

Like so many Renaissance philosophers Pico sought to reconcile theology and philosophy. He approached the problem through a variety of avenues, notably the study of the *Cabbala, in which he believed he had found the quintessential truth that would harmonize the scriptures and secular philosophy. A graphic description of the impact of Pico's personality on contemporaries comes from Politian, who described him as "the Phoenix of the wits". Pico's biography was written by his nephew Giovanni and translated into English (?1510) by Sir Thomas More.

Pienza The model Renaissance city created out of the rebuilding of the village of Corsignano, near Siena, birthplace of Pope *Pius II. The pope initiated the project in 1459, with Bernardo *Rossellino as architect in charge. In 1462 the town's name was changed from Corsignano to Pienza by papal Bull. The main piazza was handsomely constructed in Florentine style and a grid of streets was also laid out, the earliest Renaissance example of symmetrical town planning. The deaths of both pope and architect in 1464 brought work at Pienza to an end before more than a few houses could be built. Nonetheless the Palazzo Piccolomini, begun in 1460, is considered to be Rossellino's masterpiece; other notable buildings from this period are the cathedral, the Palazzo Communale, and the Palazzo Vescovile.

Pierino da Vinci (c. 1530–c. 1554) Italian sculptor and silversmith. Born at Vinci, the nephew of *Leonardo da Vinci, from the age of twelve Pierino attended the academy of *Bandinelli in Florence and was a pupil of *Tribolo. He then spent a year in Rome before moving to Pisa. His work illustrated the influence of *Michelangelo on composition in sculpture; with this influence he combined an engaging tender quality typical of Tuscan art. A number of his sculptures can be seen in the palaces of Florence and there are also examples in

European museums. He died of a fever in his mid-twenties.

Pierino del Vaga (Pietro Buonaccorsi; c. 1501–47) Italian painter. Born near Florence, he lost his indigent parents when young and was put under the protection of an artisan named Andrea de' Ceri. After studying under Ridolfo Ghirlandaio, he adopted the name of Pierino del Vaga and went to Rome. In Rome he worked under *Raphael with *Giulio Romano and others executing designs in the Vatican, and after Raphael's death he was among those employed to finish these works. According to *Vasari he was very highly regarded as a designer. He fled to Genoa after the sack of Rome (1527) and worked there on the decoration of the Palazzo Doria. Returning to Rome (1540) he was put in charge of decorative schemes in the Vatican and Castel S Angelo.

Piero della Francesca (1410/20–1492) Italian painter. Piero was born the son of a shoemaker at Borgo S Sepolcro, with which he maintained a lifelong connection and where he eventually died. In 1439 he is recorded as assisting *Domenico Veneziano on the frescoes of S Egidio in Florence (now destroyed). He returned to his birthplace in 1442, was made a councillor there, and in 1445 was commissioned to paint the *Madonna della Misericordia* polyptych (Palazzo Communale, Borgo S Sepolcro), which apparently shows the influence of *Masaccio. His *Baptism of Christ* (National Gallery, London) probably dates from this time or a little later, and he also worked in Ferrara for the Este family before going to Rimini to paint a fresco in the *Tempio Malatestiana, showing Sigismondo *Malatesta kneeling before his patron saint (1451). There he met and was deeply influenced by *Alberti, whose interest in perspective and architectural practice is reflected in many of Piero's later paintings; notable among these is the *Flagellation of Christ* (c. 1457; Palazzo Ducale, Urbino), with its enigmatic foreground figures and complex mathematical construction.

The work generally acclaimed as Piero's masterpiece is the fresco cycle of the *Legend of the True Cross* in the church of S Francesco at Arezzo (c. 1452–c. 1464). These frescoes show Piero's skill in handling a range of scenes and emotions from the pathos of the dying Adam to the drama of the discovery of the True Cross, from the motionless figures of the dream of Constantine to the hectic action of Heraclius' victory over Chosroes. During this period Piero also worked in the Vatican on frescoes that were painted over by Raphael and painted the *Madonna del Parto* for the cemetery chapel of Monterchi (his mother's birthplace). In the late 1460s he painted the portraits in profile of

Federico da Montefeltro of Urbino (see Plate XXIV) and his wife, Battista Sforza, in a diptych on the reverse of which are allegorical "triumphs" (Uffizi). For Borgo S Sepolcro in the same period he painted the powerful and moving *Resurrection* (Palazzo Communale), one of his finest works, and the now dismembered polyptych for the high altar of the church of S Agostino (panels in Lisbon, Milan, London, and New York).

From about 1470 Piero's vigour as an artist began to decline, perhaps on account of failing eyesight. His latest commission from Federico da Montefeltro, an altarpiece depicting the duke adoring the Madonna and Child with saints and angels (Brera, Milan) shows his skill at depicting imposing and solemn figures in an opulent architectural setting, but increasingly Piero's later work relied upon the help of assistants. His interest in the mathematical aspects of aesthetic theory was set down in treatises from his last years. *De prospettiva pingendi*, dedicated to Federico da Montefeltro, was written sometime before 1482 and an autograph manuscript in Italian survives in Parma; a Latin version, with autograph notes by Piero, is in Milan. His other works, one in Italian on geometry and arithmetic and the other in Latin on the five regular solids, survive in Florence and the Vatican in autograph or partially autograph form.

Piero di Cosimo (1462–?1521) Italian artist. A native of Florence, Piero was born Piero di Lorenzo but later assumed the Christian name of Cosimo *Rosselli, of whom he was a pupil. In about 1481 he was assisting Rosselli with the frescoes in the Sistine Chapel. Piero's early conventional religious scenes show the influence of Botticelli and Ghirlandaio, but subsequent works owe more to the style of Signorelli and Leonardo da Vinci. Piero was renowned for his unconventional

character, and his eccentricity expressed itself most clearly in the mythological paintings for which he is best known. Such works as *The Discovery of Honey* (c. 1500; Worcester, Mass.), *The Battle of the Centaurs and the Lapiths* (1486; National Gallery, London), and *A Forest Fire* (c. 1486; Ashmolean Museum, Oxford) bear witness to Piero's taste for the bizarre and idiosyncratic with their depictions of distorted humans and wild animals. His masterpiece, *The Death of Procris* (c. 1490–1500; National Gallery, London), combines a sense of tenderness with elements of both mythology and natural detail. Other works include such portraits as the head-and-shoulders of Simonetta Vespucci (c. 1498; Musée Condé, Chantilly). Piero was a recluse in his later years, often painting purely for his own pleasure. His pupils included Andrea del Sarto.

Pigafetta, Antonio (c. 1491–?1526) Italian historian. Raised in Vicenza by his well-to-do family, Pigafetta is known as the official historian of Magellan's circumnavigation of the world. His journal of the voyage, first published in 1525, is a vivid and detailed account, both flawed and coloured by lengthy accounts of Pigafetta's personal feelings and experiences. The work is of great historical significance and presents particularly valuable accounts of the discovery and passage of the Magellan Straits. Pigafetta also claims to have tried to dissuade Magellan from the battle on Mactan in which Magellan was killed; Pigafetta himself was wounded. Pigafetta's reports of the voyage earned him a reception at the court of Francis I of France in 1523, a meeting that inspired Francis to promote France's belated entry into the realm of exploration.

Pilon, Germain (1537–90) French sculptor. Born

PIERO DI COSIMO Mars and Venus. *(Staatliche Museen, Berlin-Dahlem)*

in Paris, Pilon was the son of a sculptor and specialized in monumental tombs executed in an elongated mannerist style. He was heavily influenced by *Primaticcio, with whom he worked on a monument for Henry II (c. 1560; Louvre), as well as by Domenico del Barbiere and *Bontemps. His later works were executed in the more fluid naturalistic manner of *Pontormo and *Michelangelo, as seen in his finest piece, the tomb (1563–70) for Henry II and his wife Catherine de' Medici. As sculptor royal from 1568, Pilon also served in the post of controller of the mint and produced many notable portrait medals as well as busts of the French royal family. Other works include a bronze figure of René de Birague (1583–85; Louvre), a contribution to the tomb of Francis I at St-Denis, an *Annunciation* in the Chapelle de la Vierge at Valmont, a statue of the Virgin in Notre-Dame-de-la-Couture, Le Mans (1571), and a bronze bust of Charles IX (Wallace Collection, London).

Pinto, Fernão Mendes (1510–83) Portuguese writer and adventurer. Born in Coimbra, Pinto enjoyed a lifetime of varied and pioneering activity. He sailed for Goa in 1537, and thereafter lived as a soldier, pirate, and merchant, working from East Africa to Japan. In twenty-one years he was captured thirteen times, enslaved seventeen times, and shipwrecked on several occasions.
Pinto's voyages to Indo-China opened new trade markets for Europeans, although his greed caused the Chinese to torture him after he robbed a sacred tomb at Calempluy. After escaping from China, he became one of the first Europeans to visit Japan. He later met St *Francis Xavier and subsequently became a Jesuit novice. However, he was unsuited to the life of the Jesuits and returned to Portugal (1558), where he became famous. Pinto's life story, the *Peregrinação*, was not published until 1614. He had done so much that the book was considered a fantasy (the possible reason for the delay in publication), but it is now acknowledged as both thorough and accurate, if somewhat embellished.

Pinturicchio, Bernardo, il (Bernardino di Betto; c. 1454–1513) Italian painter. Pinturicchio was a native of Perugia. Among his earliest work are two panels in a series depicting the miracles of St Bernardino of Siena (c. 1473; Galleria Nazionale dell'Umbria, Perugia). In the early 1480s Pinturicchio accompanied *Perugino to Rome and collaborated with him on two frescoes in the Sistine Chapel, but he also became a member of the painters' guild in Perugia (1481) and executed work there, including a number of decorative *Madonnas* of a type for which he became famous.
He was also much in demand as a painter of frescoes, and examples of his work in this genre occur in several towns in Umbria. His first major independent commission however was in Rome: the cycle on St Bernardino of Siena in the Bufalini chapel in Sta Maria in Aracoeli (c. 1485–90). Cardinal Giuliano della Rovere (later Pope *Julius II) commissioned him soon afterwards to decorate part of the Palazzo Colonna, and della Rovere patronage continued in commissions for decorations for chapels in Sta Maria del Popolo, Rome. Pope Innocent VIII was another patron, but Pinturicchio's work for him on the Belvedere at the Vatican is almost entirely lost. Innocent VIII's successor, *Alexander VI, employed Pinturicchio on the great decorative scheme for the Borgia apartments in the Vatican (1492–95). Outside Rome, Pinturicchio worked in the 1490s on frescoes in the Eroli chapel in the cathedral at Spoleto (1497). One of his best paintings also dates from this period, the *Madonna and Saints* altarpiece for a Perugian church (1495; Galleria Nazionale dell'Umbria).
In the early 1500s Pinturicchio was at work in Siena. One of his most successful decorative schemes is the cycle of frescoes (1502–07) in the Piccolomini library there; ten scenes from the life of Pope *Pius II are placed in attractive architectural settings and peopled with varied and graceful figures (see Plate XXV). At about the same time he also painted frescoes in the chapel of St John the Baptist in the cathedral and in about 1509 he decorated the Palazzo del Magnifico (his paintings from there are now dispersed, with a number in the Metropolitan Museum, New York). In 1507 he paid a final visit to Rome to decorate the choir of Sta Maria del Popolo for his old patron, Julius II. He continued his prolific output right up to his death in Siena.

Pirckheimer, Willibald (1470–1530) German humanist. Pirckheimer was born at Eichstätt into a wealthy Nuremberg commercial family with scholarly interests. He was sent to Padua and Pavia to study law, but showed more interest in Greek, philosophy, the sciences, and other subjects. From his return in 1495 until 1523 he was a Nuremberg city councillor, and he led a contingent from Nuremberg in the Swiss war of 1499. This experience resulted in his vivid historial account of the war, *Bellum Helveticum*, not published until 1610. A renowned scholar, Pirckheimer edited Greek and Latin works and made many translations from Greek into Latin and from Greek and Latin into German. At the request of Emperor Maximilian I, he translated the *Hieroglyphica* of the Egyptian Horapollo from Greek into Latin, with illustrations by his lifelong friend Albrecht *Dürer. This work introduced German scholars to *Egyptian studies. In recognition of this and other imperial commissions, Pirckheimer was appointed imperial councillor. His wealth enabled him to build up one of the largest private libraries in Germany, to collect ancient coins, and to hold open house for other scholars. He corresponded with many other humanists, including *Celtis, *Erasmus, von *Hutten, *Melanchthon, and *Reuchlin.

Pisa A city state on the River Arno in Tuscany, central Italy. Pisa was a Roman colony from 180 BC and by the late Middle Ages it was a major Tuscan city state, with a population of about 40 000 in 1300. Despite the destruction of its fleet by Genoa (1284), Pisa continued as a major port during the period of the Renaissance. Even after silting blocked the passage of laden galleys up the Arno, Pisa maintained its sea trade by using the nearby port of Livorno, which was linked to Pisa by a canal. Tanning, textiles, and the manufacture of soap and hats also brought prosperity to the city.

Political feuds weakened Pisa and brought about its annexation by Florence in 1406. During the wars of Italy Pisa declared its independence (1495), but it was reconquered by Florence (1509) after the Pisan war. Despite public works and the reopening of the university of Pisa (1543) by *Cosimo I de' Medici, Pisa suffered economic and cultural decline during the sixteenth century. After the *Pisano family of sculptors in the thirteenth and early fourteenth centuries Pisa produced no great artists, but it was the birthplace of Galilei *Galileo, who studied and taught at the university of Pisa before going to Padua.

The romanesque Duomo and Gothic baptistery contain important sculptures by Niccolò and Giovanni Pisano, and the campanile ("Leaning Tower") is a famous landmark, completed in the mid-fourteenth century. *Vasari designed the church of S Stefano dei Cavalieri (1565–69) and modernized the Palazzo dei Cavalieri for the Knights of St Stephen, an order founded (1561) by Cosimo I. Several Renaissance *palazzi*, the university courtyard (1550), and the Logge di Banchi (1603–05) also survive, despite the damage suffered by Pisa in World War II, in which the Camposanto (cemetery) was wrecked, with the loss of many antique, medieval, and Renaissance monuments and frescoes.

Pisa, Council of (1409) A Church council convened at Pisa to deal with the situation arising from the *Great Schism – the existence of two popes, at that time Gregory XII at Rome and Benedict XIII at Avignon. The council deposed both and elected Alexander V, who resided at Bologna, but the others refused to submit. It was not until the Council of *Constance that Gregory abdicated, and the others were deposed. It is consistent to regard Gregory as the only lawful pope till his abdication, and his deposition by the prelates at Pisa as unlawful. The Pisan council's further resolution to reform ecclesiastical abuses was not effective.

Pisanello (Antonio Pisano; c. 1395–c. 1455) Italian painter and medallist. After training in Verona, probably under Stefano da Zevio, Pisanello collaborated with *Gentile da Fabriano on frescoes at the doge's palace in Venice (1415–20) and at the Lateran Basilica in Rome (1431–32), all now destroyed. The only surviving fresco cycles by Pisanello are the *Annunciation* (1423–24; S Fermo, Verona) and the *St George and the Princess* (c. 1437–38; Sta Anastasia, Verona), in both of which fantasy and fact are combined in the International Gothic style favoured by Gentile da Fabriano. Richness of detail characterizes other works such as the *Vision of St Eustace* and the *Madonna with SS Anthony and George* (both National Gallery, London), but Pisanello's best works, for which he was most celebrated in his day, were his portrait medals. Drawing upon similar works produced in antiquity, Pisanello made the finest and most delicate medals of his period for several of the contemporary ruling families, notably for *Alfonso I of Naples, for whom he executed a whole series (*see* numismatics). He also painted a number of striking portraits, including those of Margherita

PISANELLO *The reverse of a portrait medal of King Alfonso I of Naples. Above the antique motif of a nude youth killing a boar is the inscription* VENATOR INTREPIDUS *(fearless hunter); Pisanello has signed the design, which fits the circular space brilliantly, beneath the feet of the hound.*

Gonzaga (c. 1438; Louvre) and Leonello d'Este (c. 1440; Accademia Carrara, Bergamo). Pisanello's keen sense of observation also shows itself in the Vallardi Codex (Louvre), an important collection of animal studies and miscellaneous sketches.

Pisano, Andrea (Andrea da Pontedera; c. 1290–c. 1348) Italian sculptor. Born in Pontedera and possibly trained in Pisa, Pisano is first recorded through his commission (1329) for a pair of bronze doors for the south portal of the baptistery of Florence cathedral. Consisting of twenty scenes from the life of St John the Baptist and depictions of eight Virtues, the doors were decorated in the Italian Gothic style practised by Giotto and influenced Ghiberti's baptistery doors of fifty years later. In 1337 Pisano succeeded Giotto as the chief architect of the campanile of Florence cathedral and executed several marble panel reliefs; statues of David and Solomon there have also been attributed to him. In all these works, and the few others sometimes credited to him, Pisano demonstrates his artistic restraint and debt to Giotto. After his death while master of works at Orvieto cathedral, Pisano's son Nino (died ?1368), noted by his contemporaries as a goldsmith, architect, and sculptor, succeeded him there. Nino produced a number of free-standing life-size marble sculptures of sacred subjects.

Pisano, Giovanni (c. 1250–c. 1314) Italian sculptor and architect. The son of Niccolò *Pisano, Giovanni was born in Pisa and was trained by his father, whom he assisted from the mid-1260s, first with the Sienese pulpit and later with the great fountain in Perugia. Before 1284 Giovanni produced a series of monumental figures of saints and prophets for the exterior of the Pisan baptistery, and after this date he worked in Siena on the lower part of the façade of the cathedral. This great Gothic sculptural scheme was designed to glorify the Virgin Mary.
Giovanni also contributed to the cathedral of S Cerbone at Massa Marittima (1287) and carved pulpits for the church of S Andrea at Pistoia (1301) and Pisa cathedral (1302–10). He executed several sculptures on the Madonna and Child theme, among them a small ivory in the sacristy of Pisa cathedral, a majestic standing Madonna in the Arena Chapel, Padua (c. 1305), and the *Madonna della Cintola* (c. 1312) in Prato cathedral. His last known commission (1313) was for the tomb of Margaret of Brabant (died 1311), wife of Emperor Henry VII, in the former church of S Francesco, Genoa; a portrait head from this tomb survives in the Palazzo Bianco, Genoa. Widely acknowledged as the greatest Italian sculptor of his day and occupying a position comparable to that of Giotto

in painting, Giovanni Pisano exercised a profound influence on later Trecento artists in his integration of classical and Gothic elements.

Pisano, Niccolò (c. 1220–c. 1278) Italian sculptor. He began his career in Apulia, at a time when Emperor Frederick II was encouraging artists there to take a renewed interest in classical motifs, and he then moved to Pisa, probably shortly before 1250. His first known work there was the hexagonal pulpit in the baptistery (c. 1260), on which the relief scenes from the life of Christ are composed along the lines of the scenes on the antique sarcophagi in the Camposanto. Between 1265 and 1268 Niccolò produced an even more magnificent octagonal pulpit for Siena cathedral, although in this work the influence of French Gothic predominates over the classicizing impulse in his Pisan sculptures. His last major commission, in which he was assisted, as on the Sienese pulpit, by his son Giovanni *Pisano, was the fountain (c. 1275) for the former Piazza dei Priori (now Piazza IV Novembre), Perugia. Besides Giovanni, Niccolò's followers included Fra Guglielmo da Pisa (1256–c. 1312), who carved the pulpit of S Giovanni Fuorcivitas, Pistoia, and the Arca di S Domenico, Bologna, and Arnolfo di Cambio (died c. 1302), who was an architect as well as a sculptor, working in Florence and Rome.

Pistorius, Johann, the Younger (1546–1608) German physician and theologian. Pistorius was born at Nidda, the son of Johann Pistorius the Elder (1503–83), one of the first Catholic converts to Lutheranism. He studied theology, law, and medicine at Marburg and Wittenberg and in 1575 became court physician to Charles II, Margrave of Baden-Durlach. He became disillusioned with Luther's doctrines and after a brief period as a Calvinist he returned to the Catholic faith. He published polemical religious works in Latin and in German, edited collections of the works of early German and Polish historians, and produced a volume of cabbalistic texts and studies (1587).

Pius II (1405–64), Pope (1458–64) Italian humanist and historian. Aenea Silvio Piccolomini was born at Corsignano, near Siena, the eldest of eighteen children of an impoverished aristocratic family. His extensive knowledge of classical literature came largely from private study, though he was for a time a pupil of *Filelfo in Florence. He attended the Council of Basle (1432) with the cardinal of Fermo, then travelled in Germany and to Scotland. He was crowned poet laureate by Emperor *Frederick III (1442) and worked in the emperor's chancery (1442–55). Eugenius IV made him a papal secretary, overlooking his previous service to the antipope Felix V. His rise through the ecclesiastical hierarchy was steady; he became bishop of Trieste (1447) and of Siena (1450) and was made cardinal in 1456. He was elected pope with the help of Rodrigo Borgia, later Pope *Alexander VI, and took the name Pius in honour of Virgil's hero Aeneas. At the Congress of Mantua (1459) he was active in organizing a crusade against the Turks to avenge the fall of Constantinople (1453). He died at Ancona, whither he had gone to assemble his fleet for this expedition.

Pius wrote a history of the Council of Basle and an autobiography (*Commentarii*), as well as more secular works. The *Commentarii* gives a frank picture of his attitudes and motivations. His letters, a precious source of information, are models of humanistic Latin. His career is the subject of frescoes by *Pinturicchio in the Piccolomini library of Siena cathedral (see Plate XXV). Pius was also important for the stimulus he gave to classical studies in northern Europe; in 1459 he signed the foundation charter for the university of Basle, which thus began its existence as a centre of humanistic learning. He also encouraged humanists to join the college of papal secretaries – *Platina was one employed in this way – but he demanded rather stricter standards of Christian conduct than his predecessor, *Nicholas V. Pius II's works were published in folio at Basle in 1551, and his other lasting monument was his model city of *Pienza.

Pizarro, Francisco (c. 1471–1541) Spanish soldier, conqueror of Peru. Born in Trujillo, Estremadura, Pizarro was illegitimate and illiterate. He went to Darien in 1509, accompanying *Balboa on his discovery of the Pacific, before settling in Panama. In 1522 Pizarro and Diego de Almagro were commissioned to claim Peru for Spain. Their first expedition (1524–25) was abortive, but the following year, sailing down the west coast of South America, they reached the Isla del Gallo. Pizarro then continued to the Peruvian coast with about twelve men. Returning to Spain (1528), Pizarro appealed to the emperor, who appointed him governor of Peru (New Castile) in 1529. In 1531 he marched with 183 men, including his two brothers, to Cajamarca, where he seized the Inca Atahuallpa, extorting a huge ransom. Reinforced by Almagro, Pizarro murdered Atahuallpa in 1533 and entered the Inca capital at Cuzco. He founded Lima in 1535, but soon afterwards territorial disputes broke out between the Pizarro brothers and Almagro. The latter was defeated and executed (1538), but his supporters then conspired and assassinated Pizarro at Lima.

plague An infectious disease transmitted by rat fleas, especially in overcrowded or insanitary conditions. In 1348 three galleys brought bubonic plague to Genoa from the East. The Black Death, as it became known, spread with great rapidity and fearsome mortality throughout Europe. By 1350 the first wave of the disease had worked itself out, killing about a third of Europe's population – some twenty-five million deaths, including one and a half million in England alone. At frequent intervals over the following three centuries the plague returned, bringing with it disruption and death. At Venice, for example, some twenty epidemics of bubonic plague are recorded between 1348 and 1630. The impact on society was considerable. The decline in the market and the labour shortage resulting from the Black Death were largely to blame for the economic depression of the late fourteenth century. The safest strategy, open only to the rich and powerful, was flight and isolation. Of those who stayed and were forced back on their own or other's remedies, many died. In the face of panic and desperation there was little room for any medical orthodoxy to emerge. While a few physicians, such as *Fracastoro, began to suspect that the disease spread by contagion, the majority attributed the epidemic outbreaks to astrological, theological, or meteorological conditions, against which they were helpless. *See also* medicine.

Plantin press The printing house founded in Antwerp by Christophe Plantin (c. 1520–89). Plantin was a Frenchman who had worked in Caen and Paris before settling in Antwerp as a bookbinder in 1548. The first book from his press, Giovanni Bruto's *La institutione di una fanciulla nata nobilmente* (1555) has a parallel text in Italian and French. It was followed by about 1500 others, including liturgical, scientific, and medical books, classics, dictionaries, Waghenaer's *Spieghel der Zeevaerdt* (1584–85) (*see* waggoners), and the Antwerp Polyglot Bible or *Biblio regia* (1568–73) subsidized by *Philip II of Spain and edited by *Arias Montano. By 1576 Plantin had sixteen presses at work. He also published books produced by other printers. His illustrated books, among them many *herbals, used the products of a team of draughtsmen led by Pieter van der Borcht, reproduced at first in woodcuts and later in engravings. The Plantin stock of pictures was used by other printers too; for example, the second edition of *Gerard's *Herball* (1633) drew its illustrations from this source, though even the first (1597) had a dragon tree based on a Plantin orginal. Type was also carefully chosen and arranged, with *Granjon among the designers commissioned.

Plantin was driven from Antwerp by the Spanish attack of 1576. He remained in exile until 1585, leaving the press in the hands of his sons-in-law

Francis Raphelengius (who in 1585 succeeded Plantin as printer to the university of Leyden) and Jan Moretus, whose descendants kept the press going until 1876. In that year the city of Antwerp bought the archives, library, presses, and other material to found the Musée Plantin-Moretus, which encapsulates the history of printing.

plateresque A style of architecture and ornament in Spain during the early Renaissance. Meaning "silversmith-like", the term *plateresco* was apparently first used in an architectural context in reference to the façade of León cathedral by the humanist writer Cristóbal de Villalón in 1539. The salient feature of plateresque decoration is the richness of its detail, a feature that it shared with much contemporary metalwork. Heraldic shields, pilasters, roundels, and trellis patterns were carved, usually in low relief, on surfaces with little reference to an overall structural unity, except that imposed by the presence of strong horizontal lines, as on the portal of the university library at Salamanca. The plateresque is generally regarded as being divided into two phases. The first, often known as Gothic-plateresque, was in the ascendant in the last two decades of the fifteenth century and the first two of the sixteenth; it combined traditional Spanish features with others imported from the Netherlands and Germany. Exponents included Juan *Guas and Enrique de *Egas. The Capilla del Condestable (1482–94) at Burgos, designed by Simón de *Colonia (whose family, as the name suggests, came from Cologne), is a prime example of the early plateresque style. Another name for this style is Isabelline, in acknowledgment of the impetus given to its development by the patronage of Queen Isabella (*see* Ferdinand II).

The second phase, often called Renaissance-plateresque, entailed the rejection of the more ornate features of the first phase as the influence of the Italian High Renaissance reached Spain. The architectural theorist Diego de Sagredo encouraged the change of emphasis with his publication of *Medidas del Romano* (1526), which promoted Vitruvian canons. Examples of this phase include the façades of the universities of Salamanca (completed 1529) and Alcalá de Henares (1541–53), Diego de *Riaño's Ayuntiamento at Seville, and the chancel screen of Toledo cathedral (1548) by Francisco Villalpando. The plateresque style was also utilized in Mexico and other Spanish possessions in the New World, for example, in the façade of S Domingo cathedral and in the ruined cathedral of Antigua, Guatemala (both 1540s).

Platina, Il (Bartolommeo Sacchi; 1421–81) Italian humanist and biographer. Called after his birthplace, Platina, near Cremona, he studied at Mantua after a military career, then moved to Florence to perfect his knowledge of Greek. During the five years he spent at Florence he formed a close friendship with the Medici. In 1467 he became secretary to Cardinal Gonzaga. As a leading member of the *Roman Academy he was closely associated with its founder Pomponius *Leto. When Paul II suppressed the academy in 1468 Platina, along with other leading figures, was imprisoned and tortured. After his release he became Vatican librarian (1475–81) under Sixtus IV. His works include biographical studies of the popes and ethical treatises on true and false goodness and on true nobility. The first anniversary of Platina's death was commemorated with ceremonies described by Jacopo Volterrano.

Plato (c. 427–348 BC) Greek philosopher. From about 407 he was the pupil of Socrates in Athens, and after Socrates' death he travelled abroad before returning to Athens to found his Academy. This was the model for the *Platonic Academy in Quattrocento Florence, where discussion was based upon the understanding of the methods of Plato's school obtained from his dialogues. Greek manuscripts of these began to reach the West from Constantinople around 1400, and *Ficino translated the entire corpus into Latin. Among the dialogues were many that raised matters of key interest to later philosophers: for example, the *Theaetetus* on the nature of knowledge, the *Timaeus* on the nature and origin of the universe, the *Phaedo* on Socrates' views on death and the immortality of the soul, the *Symposium* on the nature of love, the *Phaedrus* on true rhetoric, the *Meno* on the teaching of virtue, and the *Laws* on legislation for a new state. The Platonic theory of Ideas, developed in the *Republic*, deals with the relationships between the unseen eternal world and the phenomenal world; the supreme Idea of the Good was particularly assimilable by Christian philosophers.

The elaboration of Platonic thought in the later antique world by *Plotinus and his followers was often merged with *Platonism in the understanding of medieval and Renaissance scholars (*see* Neoplatonism, Renaissance).

Platonic Academy An informal body of scholars and humanists first assembled in Florence around Cosimo de' *Medici after the Council of Florence (1439). The main influence was Gemistos *Plethon, who had come to Florence to represent the Eastern Church. Subsequent leading members of the academy were Marsilio *Ficino who translated the dialogues of Plato, *Politian, *Landino, and *Pico della Mirandola. *Alberti, *Michelangelo, and *Pulci were all at one time or another members of this or successor associations (*see* Orti Oricellari). The main preoccupation of the fifteenth-century academicians was the reconciliation of Christian and pagan philosophy; the method used was mysticism rather than exact reasoning, and the allegorical approach derived more from medieval exegesis than from the approaches that were being developed for contemporary literary criticism.

Platonism, Renaissance To the Middle Ages the main classical philosopher was Aristotle. His works circulated in Latin translations, many of them translated from Arabic versions. The *Summa Theologia* of Aquinas achieved a fusion of Christian and Aristotelian ideas that became the basis for subsequent theological training. The emphasis was on logic and in an appeal to the subtleties of the intellect. As part of the general reaction against medieval ideas, the Renaissance inevitably turned to Plato as a challenge to the dominance of Aristotle (*see* Aristotelianism, Renaissance).

There were two important problems associated with the study of Plato in the Renaissance. The earliest Platonists were Greeks from Constantinople, whose adherence to the Orthodox Church (in schism since the eleventh century) made their ideas suspect to traditionalists in Western Christendom. Furthermore it was difficult to make direct contact with Platonic texts because the founder of Platonic studies in Italy, Gemistus *Plethon, was himself strongly influenced by Neoplatonic ideas. The mysticism inherent in some, though not the most characteristic, parts of Platonic philosophy appealed to Renaissance thinkers. They saw it as the major difference from the rationalism of Aristotle and it seemed to offer a greater possibility of reconciliation with Christianity. Moreover it made a powerful appeal to the emotions.

The influence of Plethon can be seen in his disciples *Ficino and *Pico della Mirandola. Their approach was uncritical and eclectic; their admiration for Plethon blinded them to the many absurdities and inconsistencies in his system. They failed to see that Platonic theology was only a background to Plato's ethical, political, and educational theories, and they were thus prevented from using these theories as a starting point for their own speculations. The allegorizing which was so characteristic of Byzantine Platonism struck a responsive chord in men who were already familiar with the method as used by Christian exegetes.

The contribution of the Renaissance to the serious study of Plato is now only of historical importance. The willingness of scholars to accept the amalgam of Near Eastern theosophy and Neoplatonic mysticism as authentic Platonism made almost impossible to develop any serious discussion of Plato's ideas. The most lasting contribution the Renais-

sance Platonists made was in the sphere of translation. Even after the Aldine press's publication of Marcus Musurus's *editio princeps* of Plato (1513), the Latin translation (1482) made by Ficino in 1477 continued to circulate, and the availability of a complete Plato in the original and in accurate translation increased the accessibility of authentic texts.

Plautus, Titus Maccius (c. 254–184 BC) Roman comic playwright. Twenty of his plays, which are largely based on earlier Greek comedies, have survived. They have a background of Roman middle-class life and generally feature a number of stock characters: the young lovers (whose romance is complicated by the girl's being a slave until it is discovered that she is really of free birth), a devious slave who promotes their interests, a braggart soldier, a miserly or lecherous old man, and a grasping pimp. Eight of Plautus' plays were known in the fourteenth century, and Nicholas *Cusanus found a manuscript with twelve more in Cologne in 1425. The staging of Plautine comedies began in earnest in Ferrara, in 1486, under the patronage of the Este family. Meanwhile translations and imitations of Plautus began to proliferate, and, with *Terence, he can be accounted the founder of the modern tradition of *comedy.

Pléiade A group of seven French poets of the sixteenth century. They were Pierre *Ronsard, Joachim *du Bellay, Rémy *Belleau, Jean-Antoine de *Baïf, Pontus de *Tyard, Étienne *Jodelle, and either Peletier du Mans or Jean *Daurat (according to some scholars Daurat became a member of the Pléiade after the death of Peletier; others reject his membership altogether). The name was originally applied to seven tragic poets of the third century BC and is ultimately derived from the seven stars of the constellation known as the Pleiades. Originally known as the "Brigade", the group was formed by Ronsard with some of Daurat's other students at the Collège de Coqueret; the name "Pléiade" was adopted in 1556. Its principal aims, set out in du Bellay's manifesto *Défense et illustration de la langue française* (1549), involved the reform of French poetry and the French language through imitation of the linguistic and stylistic techniques of classical antiquity and the Italian Renaissance, notably the odes of Pindar and Horace, the epics of Virgil and Homer, and the sonnets of *Petrarch, and through the revival of archaisms, the adoption of dialect words and technical terms, and the coining of neologisms.

Plethon, George Gemistus (c. 1355–1450) Greek philosopher. Plethon was born in Constantinople. Brought to the Council of Florence (1438) by

Emperor John Palaeologus from his position as leader of the Platonic school at Mistra, he vigorously opposed the prevailing Aristotelianism of the Italians. In Florence he became an inspiration to the circle of humanists around Cosimo de' *Medici. Pletho (the name is a synonym for Gemistus – both mean "full" – and also close to Plato in pronunciation) developed a philosophical system that owed much to the Neoplatonism of Alexandria. He emphasized the mystical side of Plato's teaching and evolved a system in which Greek mythology fused with Greek logic. This blend struck a chord in the Florentines; his followers regarded him as the reincarnation of Plato. Some time before 1441 Plethon returned to Greece where his ideas were attacked by *Gennadius, who accused him of paganism. In 1455 Plethon's body was exhumed and reburied in the *Tempio Malatestiana at Rimini by Sigismondo *Malatesta. Plethon's influence on *Ficino and *Pico della Mirandola was fundamental in determining the mystical character of Florentine Platonism.

Plotinus (c. 205–c. 262) Egyptian-born philosopher. He settled around 244 at Rome, where he included among his disciples the Greek philosopher Porphyry, who later edited his *Enneads*. His profoundly mystical nature strongly influenced his interpretation of Platonic philosophy, and he is hailed as the founder of Neoplatonism. A Latin translation with commentary was published (1492) by *Ficino, but the Greek text was not printed until 1580. *See also* Neoplatonism, Renaissance.

Plutarch (c. 46–c. 120) Greek biographer and moral philosopher. Plutarch exercised a major influence on two Renaissance literary genres: on *biography through his *Parallel Lives* of Greek and Roman notables and on the prose treatise through his *Moralia*. The *Lives* appealed to the Renaissance emphasis on the individual and the *Moralia* to the prevailing interest in ethics. Lost to the Middle Ages, Plutarch's works first became accessible to humanists through epitomes and through the Latin translations of *Bruni, *Guarino da Verona, and others, and these texts, of variable accuracy, became the basis for subsequent vernacular versions. The translations of the *Lives* into French (*see* Amyot, Jacques) and English (*see* North, Thomas) were enormously influential in their respective countries, and *Montaigne and Francis *Bacon were indebted to the *Moralia* in their development of the *essay form. The *editiones principes* of the Greek texts were the work of the Aldine press, the *Moralia* appearing in 1509 and the *Lives* in 1519.

podestà An administrator responsible for law and

order in an Italian city. If conditions were right, an opportunist official could turn this post into the basis for the acquisition of permanent power.

poesy (poesia) In art, a painting of a mythological or arcadian character, created purely for aesthetic pleasure and without ideological or symbolic content. The most famous paintings of this kind are probably the "Poesy" series painted in the 1550s by *Titian for Philip II of Spain, depicting eight scenes from Ovid's *Metamorphoses*.

Poggini, Domenico (1520–90) Italian sculptor, medallist, and goldsmith. Poggini was born in Florence and worked mainly there until he moved to the court of Pope Sixtus V in Rome in 1585. From the 1550s he produced an interesting series of medals. As a sculptor he was more successful in bronze than in marble. His elder brother Gianpaolo (1518–?1582) was also a medallist who worked for Philip II in Brussels and from 1559 in Madrid.

Poggio Bracciolini *see* Bracciolini, Poggio.

Pole, Cardinal Reginald (1500–58) English Catholic churchman. Pole was the grand-nephew of Edward IV. He was educated at Oxford and spent some time in Italy from 1521. After challenging *Henry VIII's assumption of supremacy over the English Church he was forced into exile (1532), and his rebuke to the king, *Pro ecclesiasticae unitatis defensione*, was presented to Henry in 1536, causing deep offence. Pole's home at Viterbo became a centre for Catholic reformers, and his saintly character and hostility to the English Reformation earned him a cardinal's hat in 1536. The infuriated Henry attainted his family (1539) and executed his mother (1541). Pole returned to England as papal legate (1554) and was *Mary I's close adviser during the Catholic reaction. He became the last Roman Catholic archbishop of Canterbury in 1556, but clashed with Pope *Paul IV, who deprived Pole of his authority on suspicion of heresy. Pole died just twelve hours after Mary I.

Polidoro Caldara da Caravaggio (c. 1500–43) Italian painter. A pupil of *Raphael, he spent the early part of his career in Rome, where he became famous for the masterly monochrome imitations of classical reliefs with which he decorated house façades. He also worked as an assistant on decorative works in the Vatican. He was one of the earliest classical landscape painters, and works such as his fresco in the church of S Silvestro al Quirinale anticipate the paintings of Claude and Poussin. Following the sack of Rome (1527), Polidoro worked in Naples and in Messina, where he was murdered.

Politian (Angelo Ambrogini; 1454–94) Italian humanist scholar and poet. Politian (or Poliziano) took his adopted name from his birthplace of Montepulciano. Entering the university of Florence at the age of ten, he was taught Latin by Landino, Greek by Callistus and Argyropoulos, and philosophy by Ficino. Lorenzo de' Medici appointed him tutor (1475) to his sons Piero and Giovanni. In 1480, after a brief sojourn in Mantua, he became professor of Greek and Latin at Florence and won a European reputation. He translated the *Iliad* into Latin hexameters, lectured on Hellenistic Greek writers, and produced material for an edition of the *Pandects* of Justinian which is still of critical value. His prologues to his lectures were elegant poems in Latin hexameters, published under the title *Silvae*, and he even composed Greek epigrams. Unusually for a classicist, he was also a very competent writer in the vernacular: his pastoral drama, *Orfeo*, was produced at Mantua in 1480, and he published a collection of Tuscan ballads and songs entitled *Rime*. His *Stanze per la giostra del Magnifico Giuliano*, begun in 1475 but never finished, commemorates the victory of Giuliano de' Medici (died 1478) in a tournament and Giuliano's love for Simonetta Vespucci (died 1476).

Politian was the first Western scholar who could compete with the Greek immigrants in knowledge of the ancient language. Evidence for Politian's scholarship comes from the books in his own library which were extensively annotated with readings from his collations of manuscripts. He also seems to have invented the method of designating manuscripts by an individual letter (*siglum*) which made for easy reference. His major scholarly publication was his *Miscellanea* (1489) in which he offered critical comments on a wide range of Greek and Latin texts. As a teacher his influence was very great; his pupils included *Reuchlin, *Linacre, and *Grocyn. His private life was marred by scandal and his personal reputation at his death was dubious.

Pollaiuolo, Antonio del (1432–98) Italian painter, sculptor, engraver, and goldsmith. With his brother, Piero (c. 1441–96), he ran one of the most successful, innovative, and influential workshops in their native Florence. It is usually assumed that their better paintings were executed mainly or wholly by Antonio because they reveal a mastery of the human form which can only be matched by the bronze works of Antonio and not in works known to have been done by Piero alone. Influences visible in Antonio's work include *Donatello,

*Mantegna, and *Andrea del Castagno, under whom Antonio's brother may have studied. But the most important factor that shaped Antonio's work was his analysis of the human form. He was one of the first scientific artists who practised dissection in order to understand muscular structure, as *Leonardo da Vinci was to do later. His drawings and engravings such as *Battle of the Nude Men* (c. 1470) exemplify the link between art and research into nature that was to be such a feature of Leonardo's work. In this engraving and in Pollaiuolo's masterpiece, the *Martyrdom of St Sebastian* (1475; National Gallery, London), the figures have clearly defined muscular structures and the pictures are composed to show poses from a variety of angles.

Pollaiuolo's second main innovation was the introduction of landscape interest to Florentine art through paintings like *Hercules and Nessus* (Yale Art Gallery, New Haven) which set the figures in a lyrical landscape. His most important sculptures were carried out with Piero in St Peter's in the 1490s. They are the bronze tombs of Sixtus IV (1493) and of Innocent VIII (c. 1495). The latter included the first sepulchral effigy to depict the living man, and features of both tombs were widely copied. See p. 328.

Pollaiuolo, Simone del *see* Cronaca, Simone, Il.

Polybius (c. 202–120 BC) Greek historian. Polybius had a distinguished career in Greek public life, was the friend of the great Roman general Scipio Aemilianus, and after 146 BC organized the Roman administration in Greece. His wide military and diplomatic experience made him exceptionally well qualified to observe and discuss the causes of Rome's rise and the decadence of the Greek cities. Much of his narrative and viewpoint in the first five books of his *History* (all that survive intact out of the original forty) was exceptionally interesting to Renaissance students of statecraft, warfare, and the role of the individual in history. Fragments of the sixth book survive in excerpts, including a passage on the Roman constitution that appears to have influenced *Machiavelli. A Latin translation, made in 1452–53 for Pope Nicholas V, was printed in 1473, and the *editio princeps* appeared in 1530.

Pomponazzi, Pietro (1462–1525) Italian physician and philosopher. Pomponazzi was born at Mantua. After medical studies at Padua (1487) he was appointed professor of philosophy there and lectured on Aristotle's *Physics* until 1509, when the closure of the Paduan schools sent him to Ferrara. There he began the studies in Aristotelian psychology which were to lead him to develop heretical

POLLAIUOLO The Annunciation. *The setting is a complex Renaissance interior; through the window above the angel's head, a view of the city of Florence, dominated by Brunelleschi's dome, can be seen (detail, right). (?1470; Staatliche Museen, Berlin-Dahlem)*

views concerning the nature of the soul. In 1512 he went to Bologna as professor of natural and moral philosophy, a post which he held until his death. In 1516 he published *De immortalitate animae*, a treatise on the immortality of the soul that generated much opposition, as it conflicted with both the accepted (Thomist and Averroist) views on Aristotle. Pomponazzi tried to separate his speculations from his own personal belief and made a formal submission to the Church on matters of faith, but it required the intervention of Cardinal *Bembo with Pope Leo X to save him from suffering as a heretic.

Pontano, Giovanni (1422–1503) Italian humanist statesman and poet. Educated in his native Umbria, he entered the service of the Aragonese king of Naples, *Alfonso I, becoming a royal secretary. Under his successor *Ferdinand I (Ferrante), Pontano was appointed secretary of state (1486) and played a leading role in the political and military affairs of the kingdom until the conquest by the French under Charles VIII (1495).

Early in his career Pontano had become a dominant influence in the *Neapolitan Academy and acted as its official head from 1471. His devotion to classical learning, which led him to adopt the name Jovianus (or the Italianized form, Gioviano) Pontanus, inspired his many and varied Latin works in prose and verse. His prose works include a number of stories and essays or dialogues, often on conventional moral subjects (generosity,

fortune, etc.) and on philology and astrology; and a history, *De bello napoletano*, on the war between the French and the house of Aragon. His poetry was held by some contemporaries, among them Erasmus, to rival or surpass its classical models, such as Theocritus and Virgil. It includes three pastoral eclogues (*Acon, Quinquennius, Maeon*) and three idylls (*Meliseus, Lepidina, Coryle*), published by the Aldine press in 1518, that greatly influenced the revival of interest in classical pastoral verse in the Renaissance.

Pontelli, Baccio (1450–c. 1492) Italian architect. Pontelli, who was born in Florence, first trained as a woodcarver and worked in the cathedral in Pisa and in Urbino. He probably learned the technique of castle construction from *Francesco di Giorgio Martini and during the 1480s and 1490s he built fortresses in Ostia, Iesi, Osimo, and Senigallia. He also fortified the Santuario della Sta Casa at Loreto (1490–94) and built other churches and religious buildings, many of them for the popes Sixtus IV and Innocent VIII. He died in Urbino.

Pontormo, Jacopo da (Jacopo Carrucci; 1494–1557) Italian painter. Born near Empoli, the son of the painter and draughtsman Bartolommeo Carrucci, Pontormo probably became a pupil of Leonardo da Vinci in about 1511. He was then apprenticed to Albertini and Piero di Cosimo before becoming the assistant of *Andrea del Sarto, by whom he was profoundly influenced.

Early works in the style of Andrea del Sarto include the *Visitation* (1514–16; SS Annunziata, Florence), but a more individual approach is evident in the complex painting *Joseph in Egypt* (1518–19; National Gallery, London), which owes a clear debt to Dürer and includes a portrait of Pontormo's pupil and adopted son Angelo *Bronzino. In about 1520 Pontormo decorated the Medici family villa at Poggia a Caiano with mythological scenes, after which he executed further decorations for the Certosa near Florence in a mannerist style. Pontormo then embarked upon his masterpiece, a cycle of paintings in the Capponi chapel of Sta Felicità, Florence (1525–28), loosely based upon Michelangelo's *Pietà*. These works included an entombment scene with a self-portrait of the artist and the *Deposition*. Later works include the *Visitation* (1528–30; Carmignano, Pieve) and fresco decorations for the choir of S Lorenzo, Florence (1554–57), a major work, influenced by Michelangelo, of which only the original drawings survive. A recluse in his later years, Pontormo wrote a diary (1554–57) that vividly illuminates his obsessive and neurotic character.

Pordenone (Giovanni Antonio de Sacchis; c. 1484–1539) Italian painter. Born in Pordenone in Friuli, Pordenone was a pupil of Pellegrino da S Daniele, although early influences also included Giorgione and Mantegna. In about 1515 he moved to Rome where he was further influenced by the works of Michelangelo, Correggio, and Raphael and developed his taste for highly dramatic illusionistic painting. His masterpiece was the cycle of frescoes on the Passion in Cremona cathedral (c. 1521), painted in a distinctly mannerist style that is also evident in his painted dome in Treviso cathedral (1520–22) and his frescoes at Piacenza (1531; Madonna di Campagna). He eventually settled in Venice where, for a brief time, he rivalled Titian. Both Titian and Rubens adopted elements of his style.

Portinari altarpiece (c. 1475/77) A large-scale triptych commissioned from Hugo van der *Goes by Tommaso Portinari, the Italian agent of the Medici in Bruges, for the church of the hospital of Sta Maria Nuova, Florence (now in the Uffizi; see Plate XII). The Adoration scene on the central panel is flanked by portraits of the donor and his family with their patron saints on the wings. An Annunciation, painted in grisaille, is revealed when the wings are closed.

portolans Sailors' charts based on practical navigational experience and giving details of features of interest to ships' pilots. Inland features are seldom marked. In use from at least the late thirteenth to the late fifteenth century, the portolans' main function was to record bearings, distances, coastal landmarks, and hazards for the guidance of mariners. They were generally hand written on parchment, and were based on the assumption that the Earth is flat. Most portolans were of southern European origin and many famous ones can be found in the thirteenth-century *Compasso di navigare*, a comprehensive survey of the Mediterranean and the Black Sea. *See also* Catalan Atlas.

Portuguese language The romance language of more than eighty-five million speakers in Portugal, Brazil, the Azores, and a few formerly colonial areas of Africa and Asia. Galician or Galego, spoken in northwestern Spain, is a dialect of Portuguese. Brazilian Portuguese differs in generally minor details of pronunciation, vocabulary, and grammar from the language of the mother country. The region of the Iberian peninsula known as Lusitania took its name from the Celts who settled there about 1000 BC and were particularly concentrated in the Serra da Estrela. Some of these tribes for a time successfully resisted Roman attempts at colonization in the second and first centuries BC, while others, such as the Conii in Algarve, accepted Roman rule. Roman conquest of the region was completed by Julius and Augustus Caesar.
Portuguese derives from the Vulgar Latin spoken in the province, but, like Spanish, reflects the influences of later invasions (Germanic and Arabic) and the country's subsequent cultural (French and Italian borrowings) and imperial (African and Amerindian words) history. Germanic tribes invaded the whole of the Iberian peninsula in the fifth century AD. The kingdom of the Suevi (Swabians) in the north was taken over by the dominant Visigoths towards the end of the sixth century. In 711 the Moors occupied all areas except Asturias (east of Galicia, the present province of Oviedo) and the Basque homeland. Portugal's national identity, which assured the separate development of the language, evolved during the slow process of the reconquest. The Moors were driven from Galicia in the eighth century and from Coimbra in 1064 (by Ferdinand I of Castile), and by the twelfth century the foundation of national independence had been established.
The earliest extant documents in which Portuguese has quite distinctive features date from about 1190, but the language had probably developed its characteristics by the tenth century. The earliest literary texts (Portuguese and Galician) are the three thirteenth-century *cancioneiros* (*da Ajuda*, *da Vaticana*, and *Colocci-Brancuti*), which reveal a thorough absorption of Provençal poetry. Portuguese was standardized in the sixteenth century on

the basis of the dialect of Lisbon and Coimbra, though the orthography of some words remains unsettled, despite several official efforts to reform spelling. Grammatically the language retains some complex features lost in modern Spanish, for example a number of subjunctives. Among phonetic characteristics are the nasalization of vowels and diphthongs (which can be indicated by the tilde) and the tendency to pronounce final *s* and *z* as a sound like English *sh*. As in French, acute, grave, and circumflex accents are used to indicate pronunciation, mark contractions, and distinguish homonyms. Important early lexicographical works include the bilingual *Dictionarium lusitanico-latinum* (1611) by Bishop Augustinho Barbosa (1590–1649) and the *Diccionario de lingua portugueza* (1789) by Antonio de Moraes e Silva (1755–1824), which has been continually revised and reissued.

Postel, Guillaume (1510–81) French orientalist, linguist, and visionary. Postel was born at Barenton. A member of Francis I's embassy to Constantinople in 1537, he travelled in the Middle East before returning to Paris; at the Collège de France he taught Greek, Hebrew, and Arabic and became the first professor of oriental languages. He entered the priesthood (1544) and returned to the Orient to preach reconciliation between Christians and Muslims. In Italy, where he spent ten years, he was imprisoned by the Inquisition. In his writings Postel expounded his ideal of the *concordia mundi*: his works include *De orbis terrae concordia* (1544), *Protévangile de Jacques* (1552), and *Les Très Merveilleuses Victoires des femmes* (1553).

Pourbus family A family of Flemish artists who in three generations were active as portrait painters. Pieter Pourbus (c. 1510–84) was a native of Gouda but by 1538 was in Bruges as the pupil of Lancelot *Blondeel. A *Last Judgment* in Bruges museum shows a debt to Michelangelo. He also worked as a surveyor for Charles V and for the city of Bruges and painted a number of portraits, among them one of Jan van der Gheenste (1583; Brussels museum). His son, Frans the Elder (1545–81), was born in Bruges and became a disciple of Frans *Floris. His altarpiece of *Christ and the Doctors* (1571; St Bavon, Ghent) contains portraits of some eminent contemporaries, and he also practised as a portraitist in a more conventional sense. Frans's son, Frans the Younger (1569–1622), was born in Antwerp and became one of the most distinguished court portraitists of his time. He worked from 1592 for the Habsburg archducal court at Brussels before moving in 1600 to Mantua, where he worked at the court of Duke Vincenzo I Gonzaga. Examples of his output in Italy are in

the Pitti gallery, Florence. In 1609 he was summoned to Paris by Queen Marie de' Medici, for whom he worked until his death.

Prague (Czech: Praha) The capital city of Bohemia (now part of Czechoslovakia), situated on the River Vltava. Celts, Slavs, and Avars lived on the site before Prague was founded in the ninth century. Under Přemyslid rule from the ninth century to 1306, Prague was the nucleus of Bohemia, and the city prospered on account of its position on major trade routes during the late Middle Ages. Prague developed as a major European city during the reign (1346–78), of Emperor Charles IV, who founded the Charles university (1348) and encouraged civic expansion. By the late sixteenth century Prague's population had risen to over 50 000.
During the early fifteenth century Prague became a centre of the Hussite reformers (*see* Huss, Jan); there followed the first *Defenestration of Prague and the popular rising (1419) which led to the Hussite wars. After the death of King Louis II of Hungary at *Mohács (1526), Prague and Bohemia passed to the Catholic Habsburgs who were determined to suppress Bohemian Protestantism; in the 1540s a Jesuit school for young nobles was founded in Prague. *Rudolf II made his permanent residence in Prague's Hradschin palace and there assembled his great art collection. In 1618 the second *Defenestration of Prague was followed by the outbreak of the Thirty Years' War (1618) and the crushing of Bohemian Protestantism at the battle of the *White Mountain near Prague (1620). The Charles university was an important centre of mathematical and astronomical studies which in the reign of Rudolf II attracted Tycho *Brahe and Johannes *Kepler. St Vitus's cathedral was begun in 1344 and parts of the new town and the Jewish ghetto survive from the fourteenth century.

Prague, Compacts of *see under* Basle, Council of.

Praise of Folly, The (*Encomium Moriae*) A prose satire written in Latin by Erasmus in 1509 and first published in 1511. It was composed in its earliest form at the Chelsea home of Sir Thomas *More, and its original title is a pun on More's name, as Erasmus's dedication to him makes plain. In it the goddess Folly, in a formal oration, addresses the multitude of her disciples and congratulates herself on how all mankind is enrolled in her train: princes, courtiers, statesmen, scholars, poets, lawyers, philosophers, and, most pointedly, theologians. The satire on the follies of churchmen was the heart of the work and provoked much fury from its victims. The work was an extraordinary best-seller; forty-two Latin editions appeared in Erasmus's lifetime and it was soon translated into French (1520), German (1520), and English (1549).

Prato A town in Tuscany 12 miles (20 km) from Florence. It was a prosperous wool-manufacturing centre as early as the thirteenth century and its cathedral exhibits fine work by *Donatello, *Michelozzo, and Fra Filippo *Lippi. The church of Sta Maria delle Carceri (1485–91) is by Giuliano *Sangallo. The "Merchant of Prato", Francesco di Marco *Datini, is buried in the church of S Francesco.

Primaticcio, Francesco (1504–70) Italian painter and architect. Bolognese by birth, Primaticcio learned his decorative skills as the assistant of Giulio Romano during the decoration of the Palazzo del *Tè, Mantua (1525–32). In 1532 he was summoned to France by Francis I to work on the decoration of the château at *Fontainebleau. Although much of the important work he did there has been destroyed, some rooms, such as the Chambre de la Duchesse d'Étampes (c. 1541–45) and the Galerie Henri II (1552–56), survive in an altered form. After the death of *Rosso, with whom he worked there, Primaticcio became head of the workshop at Fontainebleau, despite the opposition of Cellini, and continued to produce sumptuous paintings in a mannerist style that favoured mythological subjects and elongated nudes after the fashion of Parmigianino. Other works include the Valois chapel at St-Denis and the Aile de la Belle Cheminée at Fontainebleau (1568).

Primavera, La One of a series of paintings on pagan mythological subjects made by *Botticelli probably in the early 1480s. It is likely that it was commissioned by Lorenzo di Pierfrancesco de' Medici for the Villa di Castello just outside Florence. The picture shows the entourage of Venus, as conceived in Horace's *Odes* and Ovid's *Fasti* and expounded in Renaissance Florence by *Politian, but the significance of the figures in terms of Neoplatonic allegory has been much debated. Over the head of Venus in the centre of the picture, blindfolded Cupid aims his dart at the central one of the three dancing *Graces, while the god Mercury (*see* Hermes) stands on the left. In the right of the picture Zephyr, the wind of spring, catches hold of the nymph Chloris, who is instantly transformed into the goddess Flora, spreading the earth with flowers, a metamorphosis described in the *Fasti*.

Prince, The (*Il principe*; 1532) A political treatise in twenty-five chapters by *Machiavelli, with a conclusion urging the redemption of Italy from barbarian forces. It was originally written in 1513 and dedicated to Giuliano de' Medici but was revised in 1516 and dedicated to Giuliano's nephew Lorenzo before he became duke of Urbino. Machiavelli's ideas had developed during his active career (1498–1512) in the Florentine republic, when he had become familiar with all manner of political problems and conflicts and had, as a member of important missions, directly dealt with such powerful figures as Cesare Borgia.
The Prince concerns what is necessary for the successful seizure and exercise of political power and considers the means available to achieve this end, without reference to individual morality or ultimate religious truths. The secular point of view and the ambiguous tone arising from Machiavelli's procedure of presenting his firmly held opinions in a purely descriptive guise were largely responsible for the work's unjustified reputation in the later sixteenth century as an epitome of atheism and wickedness. Although it was not translated into English until 1640, it and its author were frequently alluded to in Elizabethan writings.

printing After *Gutenberg began printing in Mainz, other craftsmen, many of them German, soon followed his example elsewhere. Cologne, Strasbourg, and Basle had their own printers by the mid-1460s, followed closely by Nuremberg and Augsburg. Printers found it sensible to settle in thriving commercial towns, so that the *book trade grew alongside others, making use of the fairs already in existence at Frankfurt and Lyons and supplying buyers all over Europe. University cities were also obvious centres, providing a ready market for the sale of quantities of identical copies of essential texts. Paris had its first press in 1470, under the wing of the Sorbonne, and *Badius and the *Estienne family continued the scholarly tradition. Italian printing started at Subiaco, near Rome, in 1464/65, but Venice, beginning in 1469, attracted more fifteenth-century printers than any other town, with the greatest of them, including *Jenson and Aldus *Manutius, having a profound influence on both the *typography and the content of early printed books. Once the Italian introduction of roman and italic types made smaller and cheaper formats a possibility, books were able to be acquired easily by individuals as well as by institutional libraries. Pocket editions of the classics were a great improvement on chained folios for private study.
Printing in *vernacular languages soon began to oustrip Latin and other learned tongues. A good example is *Caxton's production, nearly three-quarters of which was in English, starting even before he took his press to London in 1476. Private patrons were important in Caxton's success, as they

PRINTING *The personnel and equipment of an early sixteenth-century printing house are depicted on the titlepage of a publication by the Parisian printer Jodocus Badius Ascensius. While the pressman pulls the bar to operate the press, an assistant behind him rubs two inkballs together; the compositor, composing stick in his left hand, sits at the type frame. Paper ready for printing and printed sheets lie on a table handy to the pressman.*

were in that of other contemporary printers. Books in the vernacular, one more way of bringing new ideas to the growing number of those able to read, facilitated other changes too, among them those promoted by Martin *Luther, who was the making of the Wittenberg printer, Hans Lufft. Thirty vernacular Bible translations, mostly German, appeared before 1500, and during the sixteenth century virtually every part of Europe acquired its own version. As printed books became more familiar objects they inevitably began to standardize the languages in which they were written. Caxton was influential once again in the stabilization of written English (*see* English language), while Robert Estienne gave French its acute and grave accents. The demands of the market affected the choice of material from the earliest days, for the first vernac-

ular scientific book was a *herbal printed by Schöffer in 1485.

The first half of the sixteenth century has been labelled a golden age of printing, helped by the development of *engraving and the consequent improvement in *book illustration, with engraved or decorated title-pages as well as vignettes or head- or tail-pieces in the text. Many printers became publishers of other people's books as well, like Christophe *Plantin, or even left printing for publishing, like Anton Koberger of Nuremberg. The influence of Italy was later overtaken by that of Germany and the Netherlands, with Plantin in Antwerp and the *Elzevirs further north, all flourishing once Spanish control of the region was ended.

The basic equipment, the wooden printing press, changed very little until the eighteenth century, except for the enlargement of the printing surface and consequently the output of printed sheets. However, as the power of the press became evident, both Church and state attempted to impose some control over the material being disseminated. Such measures included the foundation of the Stationers' Company in London in 1557 as the self-regulating body of the English book trade and the establishment of the *Index Librorum Prohibitorum in Rome in 1559. *See also* censorship.

Provoost, Jan (c. 1465–1529) Flemish painter. He was born at Bergen and trained at Brussels and Valenciennes, where he married the widow of the miniaturist Simon Marmion (died 1489). From 1494 he worked in Bruges, where he painted a *Last Judgment* (c. 1524; Bruges museum) for the town hall. His other works, none of which is signed, show him moving away from a style predominently influenced by Gerard *David towards one with an Italianate flavour. Provoost entertained Dürer on the latter's 1521 visit to the Netherlands.

Prutenic Tables *see under* astronomy.

Psyche The heroine of a fable in Apuleius' *Golden Ass*, whose name is Greek for "soul". The tale of the many vicissitudes that befell her as the result of her love for *Cupid and her eventual union with him in heaven was allegorized in the Renaissance as the yearning of the human soul for divine love. The story inspired the fresco cycle designed by *Raphael for the Villa Farnesina (c. 1518).

Ptolemaic system The definitive system of ancient astronomy as fully described by Ptolemy (fl.127–161 AD) in his *Almagest*. All observation suggested that the heavens revolved around the earth; it also seemed obvious, given the stability of buildings and the behaviour of falling bodies, that the earth was

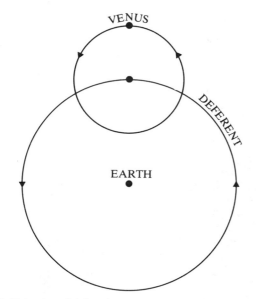

Fig. 1. Epicycle and deferent

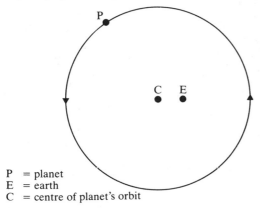

P = planet
E = earth
C = centre of planet's orbit

Fig. 2. Eccentric orbit

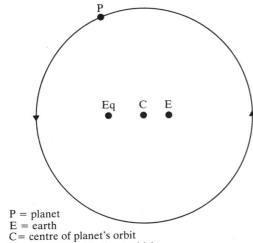

P = planet
E = earth
C = centre of planet's orbit
Eq = equant point about which
      P moves with uniform velocity

Fig. 3. Equant

PTOLOMAIC SYSTEM

stationary. It was further assumed that all celestial motion was "perfect" and as such must be both circular and uniform (*see* cosmology, Fig. 1). Such assumptions were, however, too simplistic and soon required considerable modification. They could not, for example, account for the varying brightness of Venus, or for the unequal length of the seasons. The system was consequently adapted in a number of ways. Planets, like Venus, were assigned a secondary epicyclic motion (Fig. 1). Or, as with the sun, they could be given an eccentric orbit (Fig. 2). A third and more controversial construction, the equant (Fig. 3), identified a point distinct from both the earth and the planet's orbital centre, around which the planet moved uniformly. Despite these, and other complications, the Ptolemaic system survived intact until the sixteenth century when it was replaced by the *Copernican system.

Puglia, Niccolò da (*or* Niccolò di Bari *or* Niccolò da Bologna) *see* Niccolò dell'Arca.

Pulci, Luigi (1432–84) Italian writer and poet. Born into a patrician but impoverished Guelph family in Florence, Pulci was helped by a friend who was close to Pierfrancesco de' Medici, in whose house he studied under the poet and humanist Bartolommeo *Scala. From the age of twenty-nine, Pulci was a member of Lorenzo de' Medici's circle, and his numerous poems reflect Lorenzo's enthusiastic interest in popular Tuscan verse. His masterpiece, the epic *Il Morgante* (1478; expanded version, 1483), draws on such anonymous popular material: a fourteenth-century version of the Roland story and an account of the adventures of Charlemagne's peers (*see* Charlemagne, legend of). Though loosely structured and digressive, Pulci's fantastic chivalric epic is enlivened by some mock-heroic comic inventions, especially the giant Morgante, dedicated to gluttony, and the demigiant Margutte, who manages to confess to seventy-seven mortal sins. (*Rabelais was much indebted to the comic grotesque of *Il Morgante*.) The irreverent and occasionally bitter note in Pulci's writings contributed to his being charged, by Ficino among others, with heresy, and he was not afforded a Christian burial. His other works include *Vocabolista* (*Lexicon*; 1465), a compilation of Latinisms, and *La Beca de Dicomano* (before 1470), which parodies *La Nencia da Barberino*, a pastoral by Lorenzo de' Medici.

Pulci's brothers Luca (1431–70) and Bernardo (1438–88) were also poets. Luca, like Luigi, exploited the *materia cavalleresca* in his *Ciriffo Calvaneo*, and Bernardo's best-known work is the sacred play *Barlaam e Josafat*.

Q

quadrants Observational instruments consisting of a quarter circle, the curved edge of which is graduated from 0° to 90° and which is fitted with a movable sight and plumb line. It was first proposed by Ptolemy who recognized that an arc was easier to graduate than a full circle. Quadrants reappeared in Western astronomy in the sixteenth century when astronomers like *Brahe first began to appreciate the serious inaccuracies in the available planetary tables. Accordingly in 1568 he designed a nineteen-foot oak quadrant divided into 5400 minutes. When he moved to Uraniborg some years later he designed for his own use a seven-foot mural quadrant. As the fixed position of such an instrument could be unduly restrictive Brahe also built a rotatable quadrant mounted on a pillar. Such large instruments, however, tended to warp if made of wood or suffer from thermal expansion if made of metal. Small quadrants, on the other hand, proved difficult to graduate accurately. Suitably modified, the basic quadrant also found use among surveyors, navigators, engineers, and gunners. A specialized form, Gunter's quadrant, was described by Edmund Gunter (1581–1626) in his *De sectore et radio* (1623). Also known as the astrolabe quadrant, it allowed, in the manner of *astrolabes, the time to be determined.

Quattrocento (Italian: four hundred) A term denoting artistic and cultural development in Italy during the fifteenth century. Beginning with the competition to design the baptistery doors in Florence in 1401 and ending with the election of Pope Julius in 1503, this period saw the revival of classical ideals in Italian culture and the first development of the mannerist movement. Leading figures of the time, who prospered in such artistic centres as Florence, Rome, Naples, Ferrara, Venice, and Padua, included *Boiardo in literature, *Brunelleschi, *Alberti, the elder *Sangallo brothers, and *Filarete in architecture, *Donatello, *Ghiberti, and *della Robbia in sculpture, and *Masaccio, *Uccello, Fra *Angelico, *Botticelli, the *Bellini family, *Piero della Francesca, and *Mantegna in painting.

Quercia, Jacopo della (c. 1374–1438) Italian sculptor. Born in Siena, Quercia was an unsuc-

JACOPO DELLA QUERCIA The Expulsion from the Garden of Eden. *A strong dramatic composition contrasts the implacability of the angel with the attempted resistance of Adam and the submissiveness of Eve. (c. 1430; S Petronio, Bologna)*

cessful candidate for the first set of doors for the baptistery in Florence (1401), later executed by *Ghiberti. His earliest surviving work is the marble tomb of Ilaria del Carretto (c. 1406) in the cathedral of Lucca, in which elements of both classical and Gothic styles are combined. Subsequent works include the statue of the Virgin and Child in Ferrara (1408; Museo dell'Opera del Duomo), marble reliefs in the Trenta chapel at S Frediano in Lucca (c. 1413–22) and the Fonte Gaia for the Piazza del Campo in Siena (1414–19; Palazzo Pubblico, Siena). From 1417 to 1434 he worked on reliefs for the baptistery in Siena, on which Donatello and Ghiberti also worked, before embarking upon his greatest decorations, the biblical reliefs on the main portal of S Petronio in Bologna (1425–38). This last work was much admired by Michelangelo. In 1435 della Quercia was appointed architect of Siena cathedral.

questione della lingua The controversy over what should be the preferred form of a national language in Italy reached its climax in the early sixteenth century. The roots of the problem lay in the competing dialects of the urban centres (with their dependent regions) and the political fragmentation of the peninsula. The controversy in effect concerned the establishment of a literary or written standard, and indeed the question was successfully resolved by the early seventeenth century; however, dialectal diversity in speech and in many nonliterary works (private correspondence, diaries, and official documents) continued up to the present century, and only recently has something approaching the uniformity of written Italian begun to emerge in the spoken language.

Although the *vernacular in literary composition had apparently won the day against Latin during the thirteenth century – *Boccaccio could still question *Dante's choice of the vernacular to treat the weighty matters of the *Divine Comedy* – there remained the issue of which of the many regional dialects was the best. In *De vulgari eloquentia* Dante examined a number of them (for the purposes of poetic composition only), finding none perfect but each with useful features. Tuscan had early acquired a certain advantage since the works of the poets of the Sicilian School (written under Frederick II and his son Manfred, between about 1230 and 1266) had been transcribed in a Tuscanized form by copyists and so passed to later poets. Several positions were taken in the controversy. *Trissino and *Castiglione argued for an eclectic *lingua cortigiana*, of mixed usage but essentially Tuscan, such as already prevailed in the great courts of Milan, Rome, and Ferrara, where courtiers of diverse backgrounds communicated in the same language. *Machiavelli argued for current spoken Florentine. The position that eventually triumphed was that taken by Pietro *Bembo in *Prose della volgar lingua* (1525). Just as Virgil and Cicero had become the paradigms of Latin style, so Bembo proposed *Petrarch and Boccaccio as models for Italian. Their fourteenth-century language was not, he pointed out, that of contemporary Florence and Tuscany. His views, strongly supported by Leonardo *Salviati, were adopted by the *Accademia della Crusca and so reflected in the Cruscan *Vocabolario* (1612), which settled most aspects of spelling, grammar, and vocabulary.

Quevedo y Villegas, Francisco Gómez de (1580–1645) Spanish satirist, poet, and novelist. Quevedo's parents held positions at court in Madrid, where he was born, but his father died soon after his birth and his mother left him in the charge of tutors. Although born lame and with poor eyesight, he attended the university of Alcalá; there he developed an active belligerent character and was intellectually brilliant, mastering Greek, Latin, and Hebrew, and later Italian, French, and some Arabic. About 1600 he was at the court in Valladolid and moved with it to Madrid in 1606. He produced a constant flow of satirical verses and pamphlets, made a lifelong enemy of *Góngora, cultivated a friendship with *Cervantes, and corresponded with *Lipsius. He wrote an outstanding *picaresque novel, *El Buscón* (1603–08), and in 1606 the first of five *Sueños* (Visions). Published in 1627, these scathing prose satires, influenced by Dante and Lucian, contain passages of grotesque brilliance.

In 1611 Quevedo was forced to leave court – according to rumour, for having murdered a man – and in 1613 became an agent of the duke of Osuna in Italy. Deeply involved in Osuna's plots against Venice, Quevedo, thanks to excellent Italian, barely escaped with his life when the Venetians struck back at the conspirators. When Olivares came to power with the accession of Philip IV (1621), all former ministers of Osuna were punished. Quevedo, however, eventually regained favour by dedicating to Olivares a "mirror of princes" work (which he thought his best), the *Política de Dios* (1617; published 1626). The period to 1639 was the happiest of his life, despite an unfortunate marriage (1634); both parties welcomed an agreed separation in 1636. In 1639 Philip IV found under his napkin at table some anonymous verses attacking Olivares. Quevedo was held to be guilty – how, exactly, he was involved is not certain – and was confined in a monastery in Léon until after Olivares's death in 1643. Too ill to return to court, he spent his final years on his estate.

Quevedo was unexcelled as a stylist, his works being particularly associated with the "wit" (*agudeza* – a term approximating the "wit" of English Metaphysical poetry) of *conceptismo* (often, inaccurately, taken as the antithesis of the mannered rhetorical style of Góngora and *culteranismo*). He carried on a continual polemic against Góngora and his followers and edited the works of Fray *Luis de León as a corrective against *culteranismo*. Over a thousand of his poems were anthologized posthumously, but an accurate edition of his prolific output is more recent, the first volume of *Obras completas*, ed. J. M. Blecua, appearing in 1963.

Quiñones, Francisco de (1480–1540) Spanish Franciscan reformer. Quiñones, who was born at León, adopted the name Francisco de los Angeles when he joined the Order of Friars Minor sometime before 1507. He served as minister-general of the order (1523–28), was named cardinal (1527), and was bishop of Coira (1531–33). Quiñones was a pre-Tridentine reformer, advocating humanist learning, the training of Franciscan youth, and the use of retreat houses to promote an intense spiritual life. He was also interested in missionary activity and in 1523 sent the mission of the "Twelve Apostles" to New Spain, to which he hoped to go as papal nuncio and Spanish viceroy. Pope Clement VII instead employed him on secret missions to Charles V's court where, following the sack of Rome (1527), he won the pope's freedom and prepared the treaties of Barcelona (1528) and of Cambrai (1529).

At the pope's behest, Quiñones prepared a simplified breviary, often referred to as "the Breviary of the Holy Cross". Between 1535 and 1558, 100 editions were published, totalling about 100 000 copies, and it influenced the Church of England's Book of Common Prayer. The Council of Trent suppressed the Quiñones breviary. Quiñones died in Veroli, Italy.

Quintilian (Marcus Fabius Quintilianus; c. 35–c. 95) Spanish-born Roman rhetorician. After a distinguished teaching career in Rome Quintilian devoted the remainder of his life to writing the *Institutio oratoria*. Despite the title, it deals not only with the training of orators but with the general principles of *education. After suffering an eclipse in the Middle Ages, the work was immensely important to the Renaissance; *Petrarch knew it only through an imperfect copy, Poggio *Bracciolini unearthed a complete text (1416), and it was first printed in 1470. The *Institutio*'s insistence upon linking knowledge and oratorical ability with excellent moral character was the keynote of most Renaissance educational programmes – in the words of Sidney, "the ending end of all earthly learning being verteous action" (*Defence of Poesie*). Quintilian's assessment of ancient authors in his tenth book played a significant role in Renaissance literary judgments.

R

Rabelais, François (?1483–1553) French satirist, humanist, and physician. The son of a wealthy lawyer, Rabelais was born near Chinon. He may have studied law before entering the Church, becoming a Franciscan novice at La Baumette, near Angers, and subsequently moving to the convent of Puy-St-Martin at Fontenay-le-Comte, where he was ordained priest. Suspected of heretical tendencies on account of his study of Greek, he transferred to the Benedictine convent of Maillezais (1524) and became secretary to Geoffroy d'Estissac, Bishop of Maillezais.

By 1530 Rabelais had abandoned religion for medicine, which he studied at Montpellier; in 1532 he was appointed physician to the hospital of the Hôtel-Dieu in Lyons. The same year saw the publication of his edition of Hippocrates' *Aphorismes*, the first novel of his **Gargantua* and *Pantagruel* cycle (which appeared under the anagrammatic pseudonym Alcofribas Nasier), and the *Pantagruéline Prognostication*, a parody of the almanacs that were fashionable at the time. As physician to the brothers Jean and Guillaume du Bellay (*see* du Bellay, Joachim), Rabelais accompanied the former on diplomatic missions to Rome and the latter to Piedmont, relinquishing his post at the Hôtel-Dieu; after the publication of *Gargantua* in 1534 he appears to have written nothing until the *Tiers Livre* (1546), the third novel of the cycle, which was dedicated to **Marguerite de Navarre. The Sorbonne's condemnation of this work forced Rabelais into temporary exile at Metz; his *Quart Livre*, which first appeared in its entirety in 1552, was also banned on publication. Rabelais died in Paris, probably in 1553, having resigned his benefices at Meudon and Jambet. The authenticity of the *Cinquième Livre*, published posthumously in 1564, has been disputed.

One of the most influential French writers of the Renaissance, Rabelais combined insight and imagination with a talent for verbal invention that made a profound impression on his contemporaries and has been a valuable and lasting source of inspiration for subsequent satirists and humorous writers everywhere.

Raffaele ware *see under* majolica.

Ragusa (Serbo-Croatian: Dubrovnik) A Dalmatian city and port on the Adriatic. Founded in the seventh century by Roman refugees, Ragusa enjoyed considerable autonomy under Venetian suzerainty (1205–1358). After a period under Hungarian rule (1358–1420) Ragusa was restored to Venice, but became a free city in all but name. During the period of the Renaissance shipbuilding, commerce, and the Ottoman trade brought prosperity to Ragusa. By the sixteenth century Ragusan ships were sailing to the Indies and the Americas (the word "argosy", meaning a ship with a rich cargo, derives from the Italian phrase for "ship of Ragusa"). A number of refugees fled to Ragusa from the Ottoman advance, making the city an important literary and artistic centre from the fifteenth to the seventeenth centuries and earning it the title of the "Athens of the South Slavs". Fine paved streets and handsome palaces still bear witness to the enlightened civic policies and wealth of Ragusa's rulers at this time.

Raibolini, Francesco *see* Francia, Francesco Raibolini.

Raimondi, Marcantonio (c. 1480–1534) Italian engraver. Born near Bologna, Raimondi was trained by the goldsmith and painter **Francia and is notable chiefly for his engravings of paintings by his contemporaries. After moving to Venice in about 1506, and later Rome (c. 1510), he was greatly influenced by the woodcuts of Dürer and became famous for his engravings of works by Raphael, Michelangelo, and others. Although he became financially very successful, his reputation suffered after his arrest for engraving obscene designs by Giulio Romano and he died in obscurity in Bologna. The technique of engraving brought by Raimondi to a high degree of perfection enabled accurate copies of works of art to be produced and disseminated in large quantities, thus contributing greatly to the spread of iconographic and stylistic information in the Renaissance.

Rainolds, John (1549–1607) English divine and humanist. Rainolds was born at Pinhoe, near Exeter, and became (1568) a fellow of Corpus Christi College, Oxford, where he was tutor to

Richard *Hooker. From 1573 he was college reader in Greek and lectured on Aristotle's rhetoric. Owing to internal disputes in his college, he resigned in 1578, and became a fellow of Queen's. Although two of his brothers, William and Edmond, were Roman Catholics, John was a Calvinist; in 1592 he was rebuked by Queen Elizabeth for his reforming zeal. In the following year, he became dean of Lincoln, but returned to Oxford in 1598 as president of Corpus Christi College. In 1604 he led the Puritan faction at the *Hampton Court Conference and was designated one of the translators of the Authorized Version of the Bible (1611).

Raleigh, Sir Walter (?1552–1618) English mariner and writer. The son of an obscure Devonshire gentleman, Raleigh went to Oxford but did not graduate. He then fought in the French Wars of Religion and in Ireland. From 1581 he was in attendance on Queen Elizabeth, and his wit, sincerity, and handsome appearance established him as a favourite. His long poem "The Ocean to Cynthia " expresses aspects of their relationship. Knighted in 1584, Raleigh gained grants of land and trading privileges from Elizabeth, guaranteeing his financial security. An expedition sponsored by him (1584) claimed Virginia for England, naming the territory in Elizabeth's honour, and Raleigh spent £40,000 over the next three years trying to establish a colony there. Despite its failure, it drew attention to the merits of expansionism and the economic possibilities of America.

From the late 1570s Raleigh had been involved in various seafaring adventures, mainly against Spain, and in 1592 he was recalled from one and thrown into the Tower because of his clandestine marriage to one of Elizabeth's maids of honour. His expedition to Guiana (1595) and key role in the sacking of Cádiz (1596) more or less restored him to favour, although Essex was now Elizabeth's principal favourite. On the accession of James I, with his policy of peace with Spain, Raleigh's numerous enemies ensured his downfall; in 1603, at a sham trial, he was convicted of treason. Given an eleventh-hour reprieve from the scaffold, he then spent twelve years in prison, where he made alchemical experiments and wrote many letters, poems, and his influential, but inappropriately titled *History of the World* (1614). In 1616 James released him to search for gold along the Orinoco. The expedition was a disaster, and, contravening James's explicit instructions, Raleigh's followers attacked a Spanish settlement. On his return to England Raleigh was beheaded on the 1603 charge.

Rambaldoni, Vittorino de' *see* Vittorino da Feltre.

Ramée, Pierre de la *see* Ramus, Petrus.

Ramelli, Agostino (c. 1537–c. 1608) Italian engineer. Ramelli was born at Ponte Tresa, near Como, and is first heard of as a military engineer in the service of Gian Giacomo de' Medici. He later moved to France where he seems to have settled sometime in the 1570s. Ramelli is remembered today as the author of *Le diverse et artificiose machine* (1588), a volume published with French and Italian texts on facing pages. The 195 full- or double-page illustrations serve as a primary source for the state of Renaissance engineering. About one hundred depict pumps and pumping machinery; the remainder show a variety of devices, including windmills, tilt hammers, screw jacks, water wheels, and revolving bookcases. Many of these, though feasible designs, were likely to have been beyond the capacity of the craftsmen of Ramelli's day.

Ramist controversy The long-running dispute over the issues with which *Ramus chose to concern himself, namely, the nature of logic, dialectic, and rhetoric. Ramus rejected the Aristotelian tradition, opting instead to follow Cicero as he had been presented by Rudolf *Agricola. Whereas Aristotle had distinguished between logic, which argued to a necessary conclusion, and dialectic, which permitted only probable conclusions, Ramus insisted there was only one *ars disserendi* (art of discourse), called indifferently by him logic or rhetoric. At a less abstract level he extolled the virtues of the practical over the theoretical, and the particular over the general. Thus, geometry was defined by him as "the art of measuring well", while ethics, he said, should be taught through biography and history. This practical approach to philosophy was echoed in the work of John *Dee, William *Gilbert, and Francis *Bacon. It was also readily accepted throughout much of Protestant Europe and found support in Puritan New England. Such support was still being expressed long after the death of Ramus in the writings of Milton and Leibniz, among others.

Opposition arose, however, in Catholic Europe. Jacques Charpentier in France, and other so-called anti-Ramists, insisted upon the distinction between logic and dialectic and argued that "the standard and norm of logic" lay elsewhere than in the popular speech studied by the Ramists. A third group, the curiously named semi-Ramists, or Philippo-Ramists, was identified by Franco Burgersdyck in 1626; this group sought a compromise between the Ramists and the followers of *Melanchthon. Despite the intensity of the dispute, its historical significance was limited by the emergence of the more central concerns and potent method of Descartes.

Ramos de Pareja, Bartolomé (c. 1440–c. 1491) Spanish music theorist. Ramos taught music at the university of Salamanca and appears to have gone to Bologna in about 1472, where he lectured in music. After 1484 he went to Rome and was still there in 1491. Ramos wrote several theoretical works, but only his *Musica practica* (1482) survives. In it he attacked contemporary musical procedures, such as notation, classification of the modes, and, in particular, the theories of Boethius on tuning. Ramos argued that many of the theories of the past were too complicated and impractical for performers. Although he was widely criticized, his ideas were used by later theorists, including *Glareanus and *Zarlino.

Ramus, Petrus (Pierre de la Ramée; 1515–72) French logician and humanist. Ramus was born near Soissons and educated at the university of Paris. In 1536 he defended for his MA the thesis that everything written by Aristotle is false. The claim was made more publicly in his *Aristotelicæ animadversiones* (1543) and resulted in a ban forbidding him from teaching philosophy. The ban was lifted in 1547 by *Henry II and in 1551 Ramus was appointed professor of philosophy at the Collège Royal in Paris. Much of his later work was concerned with the reform of traditional logic, thought, and education (*see* Ramist controversy). His views were widely disseminated in his best-known work, *Dialectique* (1555), the first work on logic to be published in French. After converting to Calvinism in 1561 Ramus abandoned France for some time to avoid the dangers of the religious wars. He settled once more in Paris in 1570 and died as one of the victims of the *Massacre of St Bartholomew.

Ramusio, Giovanni Battista (1485–1557) Italian writer and geographer. Born at Treviso, Ramusio was raised in an environment of discovery and innovation. He worked in the Venetian public service, rising steadily to become secretary of the Council of Ten by 1533. Around 1520 he became friends with Girolamo *Fracastoro, who inspired him to collect a diversity of geographical material, much of it gathered through personal contact with leading explorers and humanists of his day. This was published as the three-volume *Delle navigationi et viaggi* (1550–59), a masterpiece widely acknowledged as the definitive geography book of the sixteenth century.

Raphael (Raffaello Sanzio; 1483–1520) Italian painter and architect. Raphael was born in Urbino, the son of the painter Giovanni Santi, but little of his early career is documented. He probably joined *Perugino's workshop before 1500, establishing contacts within the Urbino court as well as with important patrons in Perugia and Città di Castello. The St Nicholas altarpiece (fragments in Capodimonte, Naples, and Pinacoteca Tosio-Martinengo, Brescia) shows that by 1500 Raphael had already established a reputation as a competent artist. The Mond *Crucifixion* (c. 1502; National Gallery, London) demonstrates his ready assimilation of Perugino's style.

By 1504 he had learnt all his master had to teach him and, armed with an introduction from the Urbino court, Raphael went to Florence to face the artistic challenges posed by *Leonardo da Vinci and *Michelangelo. Drawings played a vital role in Raphael's absorption of the Florentine concerns with mass, form, light, and movement. A drawing in the British Museum adapting the *contrapposto* of Leonardo's *Leda* onto a representation of Michelangelo's *St Matthew* displays an eclecticism typical of Raphael. The evolution of Raphael's style from the static Umbrian mould towards a more fluid and emotive idiom is documented in the series of drawings connected with the Baglioni *Entombment* (1507; Galleria Borghese, Rome). Raphael began with a Peruginesque *Lamentation*, which subsequently developed into a dramatic, if not wholly successful, composition imbued with the Florentine emphasis on emotive narrative compositions. One of Raphael's earliest Florentine works, the *Madonna del Granduca* (c. 1505; Palazzo Pitti, Florence) displays a new simplicity of form and unity in composition that suggests contact with Fra *Bartolommeo and Leonardo. Motifs from Leonardo's cartoon *Virgin and Child with St Anne* (c. 1501; now lost) are reflected in a number of Raphael's Madonna compositions, particularly that of the Carnigiani *Holy Family* (c. 1505; Prado, Madrid), where the figures, placed in a pyramidal composition, relate to one another in a significant and harmonious fashion. Leonardo's *Mona Lisa* introduced a new portrait type taken up in Raphael's *Maddalena Doni* (c. 1507; Palazzo Pitti, Florence), while Leonardo's *Adoration of the Magi* (1481; Uffizi) which incorporated over forty figures circling in and out of a dark penumbra, was to influence many of Raphael's works, including drawings for the *Disputa* (1509; Vatican).

In 1508, possibly at the behest of fellow-Umbrian *Bramante, Raphael went to Rome. Pope Julius II had commissioned a team of artists to redecorate part of the Vatican palace, but by 1509 Raphael had been made solely responsible for the designs of the Stanze. The theme of the Stanza della Segnatura (painted 1509–11) is human versus divine intellect (see Plate XXVI). In their harmonious repose and classical purity, the frescoes in this room represent the zenith of High Renaissance painting. Clarity and logic dominate the designs, particularly in the *Disputa*, where the elevated Host acts as both the vanishing point and the narrative pivot linking earthly with heavenly realms. The Stanza dell'Eliodoro (1511–14), representing divine intervention on behalf of the Church, was executed in a more theatrical vein, befitting the drama of the potent political message. The Stanza dell'Incendio (1515–17) was mainly the work of assistants, for by now Raphael was beleaguered by commissions. He executed a number of works for the wealthy banker, Agostino *Chigi, decorating his villa in Trastevere (*see* Farnesina, Villa), with a classically inspired fresco cycle of *Cupid and Psyche* (c. 1518) and designing his chapel in Sta Maria del Popolo (c. 1513–16), where antique funerary motifs, expressed in architecture, sculpture, and painting, proclaimed the ascent of Chigi's soul to heaven. Raphael was also much in demand as a portrait painter; his *Julius II* (c. 1511; National Gallery, London) and *Baldassare Castiglione* (c. 1515; Louvre) are just two outstanding examples of his skill in this field.

In 1514 Pope Leo X appointed Raphael architect of St Peter's and in 1515, superintendent of Roman antiquities. Raphael's architectural works displayed his increasing appreciation of classical vocabulary. His design for the Chigi stables (1514–18; now destroyed) incorporated column bases modelled on those of the Forum of Nerva, while the incomplete Villa Madama (c. 1518) owes much to the classical villas of Pliny the Younger. While Raphael's *tapestry cartoons of the *Acts of the Apostles* (c. 1515–19; royal collection, Victoria and Albert Museum, London) still display a classical majesty, his last work, the *Transfiguration* (1518–20; Vatican museum, Rome) suggests a new departure in its dramatic chiaroscuro and violently twisting figures. Unfinished at his death, it was displayed over his coffin in the Pantheon.

Ratdolt, Erhard (c. 1447–1528) German printer and type cutter. He worked in Venice for ten years from 1476 and, on his return to his native Augsburg (1486), issued the first known specimen sheet, showing ten sizes of gothic type, three roman, and one Greek. In Venice his innovations included the first title-page, in *Regiomontanus's *Kalendarius* (1476), which also had diagrams of solar and lunar eclipses printed in colour, and the 400 diagrams in his edition of Euclid's *Elementa* (1482), the first to be printed. Decorated initials and borders were used with woodcuts in the missals and breviaries that Ratdolt also produced.

Ratisbon, Colloquy of *see* Regensburg, Colloquy of.

Raymond of Sebonde (died ?1436) Spanish philosopher, doctor, and theologian. He was born in Barcelona and in the 1430s he was professor at Toulouse, where he died. There he composed his most important work, the *Liber creaturarum seu naturae*, which was printed about 1480 under the title *Theologia naturalis*. Raymond sought to reach an understanding of God through the "two books", that of the creatures and that of sacred scripture. This approach united the claims of reason and faith. Raymond's work attracted the criticism of the Church, and the prologue to the *Theologia* was suppressed and put on the Index (1595). *Montaigne translated the work into French (1569), and one of his best-known essays is *L'Apologie de Raimond Sebon*, defending the Spaniard's emphasis on the "book of nature".

rederijkers *see under* chambers of rhetoric.

Reformation The movement for the reform of western Christianity which led in the sixteenth century to its division into opposed Catholic and Protestant churches. The roots of the Reformation are now usually seen in the reform movement of the medieval period, the failure of which left many still dissatisfied with numerous aspects of Church government and teaching. This dissatisfaction found an important outlet in the writings of humanist scholars such as *Erasmus and *Reuchlin. By their sustained criticism of abuses within the Church, and still more by their encouragement of textual analysis (thereby undermining the claims of the Church to be the final arbiter on matters of faith), such scholars played an important role in creating the climate of opinion in which protest (like that of *Luther) against unpopular papal practices could gain a following (*see* humanism). Luther's protest against indulgences in 1517 thus belonged to a well-established tradition; its novelty lay in the speed with which it spread throughout Germany (its diffusion assisted by printing, a comparatively recent invention) and the determination with which Luther pressed home his charges of papal corruption. In his great tracts of 1520 Luther developed his criticism into a systematic denunciation of the old Church, emerging as a worthy leader of the movement; the Roman hierarchy, in contrast, responded with hesitation and indecision, influenced by political considerations which dictated caution in dealing with the German princes and with Emperor Charles V. With this encouragement the evangelical movement spread very rapidly. By 1535 most of the imperial free cities and many of the princely states had embraced the Reformation. When they banded together in a military association to defend Protestantism (*see* Schmalkaldic League) its future within the empire was largely secure.

The great interest shown in Luther's writings outside Germany strongly assisted the spread of the Reformation. In Switzerland the lead was taken by Ulrich *Zwingli, who between 1522 and 1525 introduced in Zürich a radically reformed church polity. Zwingli's teaching, with its greater emphasis on communal values and a more emphatic rejection of Catholic practice, achieved a substantial following in Switzerland and south Germany, despite a serious disagreement with Luther over sacramental doctrine which a personal meeting failed to resolve (*see* Marburg, Colloquy of). After Zwingli's death the leadership of the Swiss Reformation passed eventually to John *Calvin, the reformer of Geneva. Calvin introduced into Geneva a strongly theocratic church polity, based on a tightly organized reformed theology which preserved much of the best from both the Lutheran and non-Lutheran reforming traditions (*see Institutes*).

The spread of *Calvinism after 1550 helped revive a movement which showed signs of flagging in the face of an increasingly determined Catholic counter-offensive. In France early interest in reform (characterized by groups such as Briçonnet and the Circle of Meaux) had given way to a sustained persecution which forced most of the leading French Protestants to seek safety in exile. But between 1555, when the first church was founded in Paris, and 1562 over 2000 Calvinist communities were planted (*see* Huguenots), a rate of growth that destabilized the weak French monarchy and precipitated the French Wars of *Religion. Although the Reformation never attained full success in France the Edict of Nantes (1598) guaranteed the Huguenot churches the status of a privileged minority. In the Netherlands Calvinism also made rapid progress, building on the foundations established by a robust native evangelical tradition. Although forced to take their first constitutional steps in exile (Synod of Emden, 1571) the Calvinist communities returned in time to play a major role in the war of independence which freed the northern Netherlands from Spain. In 1622 Calvinism was established as the official state religion of the United Provinces. Calvinism also achieved a notable triumph in Scotland, where the Reformation again prevailed as part of a movement of national self-determination (1559–61). Under the leadership of John *Knox the Scottish ministers succeeded in establishing a strongly presbyterian church order. Other important Calvinist churches were planted in central Europe (Bohemia, Poland, Hungary), while Lutheranism achieved permanent success outside

Germany only in the Baltic and Scandinavia.

The Reformation in England conformed fully to neither of these patterns, the breach with Rome having been initiated by the otherwise orthodox King Henry VIII for entirely political reasons. The introduction of a genuine Protestant polity was achieved only in the reign (1547–53) of Henry's son Edward VI under the guidance of Thomas *Cranmer, who was responsible for the Book of Common Prayer (1549). After a brief Catholic restoration (1553–58) under Mary I, the accession of Elizabeth signalled the final triumph of Protestantism. The Anglican Church preserved its individuality in a determinedly erastian form of church government (*see* Erastianism), although in doctrinal terms it was essentially Calvinist.

The Reformation inevitably spawned a great variety of religious thinkers who owed allegiance to none of the major church leaders. Luther was confronted with the problem of radical dissent in Wittenberg as early as 1521 (Münzer and the Zwickau Prophets), and Zwingli faced a similar challenge from the Swiss Brethren. The most coherent force beyond the Protestant mainstream was the anabaptist movement, which made rapid progress in Germany and northern Europe. Drawn together by a shared practice of adult baptism, the *Anabaptists were persecuted by Catholics and Protestants alike, particularly after the collapse of the radical anabaptist kingdom of Münster (1535). Anabaptism, however, proved extremely resilient, particularly in the Netherlands under the leadership of Menno Simons (1496–1561), whose followers were known as Mennonites.

The cultural and political effects of the Reformation were profound if unpredictable. Ultimately it may be said to have assisted the process of nation-building, by breaking the moral and economic power of the old Church, although for a time Calvinism mounted its own challenge to the developing trend towards absolutist monarchies. In cultural terms the negative impact of the reformers' hostility towards traditional religious art was balanced by their encouragement of church music and the incentive they provided for a new artistic tradition, as in the case of Rembrandt. Certainly the Reformation helped create the magnificent diversification of European culture which marked the succeeding centuries.

Regensburg, Colloquy of (1541) A conference of Roman Catholic and Protestant theologians convened by Emperor Charles V in the Bavarian city of Regensburg (formerly Ratisbon). The Roman Catholic representatives were Johann *Eck, Julius Pflug (1499–1564), and Johann Gropper (1503–59) and the Protestants Martin *Bucer, Philipp *Melanchthon, and Johann Pistorius the Elder (1503–83). The quest for reconciliation on doctrinal issues was largely successful, but the colloquy had no practical outcome, mainly due to Luther's implacable opposition to any compromise with Rome.

Regiomontanus (Johann Müller; 1436–76) German mathematician and astronomer. His Latin name derives from his birthplace, Königsberg. Educated at Vienna university, Regiomontanus travelled to Italy with Cardinal *Bessarion in search of important Greek scientific texts. After six years in Italy, and a brief period at the Hungarian court of *Matthias Corvinus, Regiomontanus settled in Nuremberg. He planned to set up the world's first printing press devoted primarily to the publication of scientific texts, and a catalogue of twenty-two titles was issued. Called to Rome in 1476 to advise on calendrical reform he died suddenly, reportedly of poison, his programme scarcely begun. He did, however, complete the first printed *Ephemerides* (1474), and his *De triangulis* (1533) is one of the earliest works of modern trigonometry. He also completed the *Epitome* of his teacher *Peuerbach which finally appeared in 1496, long after the death of both scholars.

Régnier, Mathurin (1573–1613) French satirical poet. A nephew of *Desportes, Régnier was born at Chartres, entered the Church at the age of nine, and accompanied the Cardinal de Joyeuse on a number of diplomatic missions to Rome. His lack of discretion and dissolute behaviour, however, prevented him from fulfilling his parents' aspirations and from inheriting the lucrative benefices enjoyed by his uncle. In 1609 he became a canon of Chartres cathedral. In his *Satires* (1608–09) Régnier imitated the style of the classical satirists Horace and Juvenal and was heavily influenced by a number of other Renaissance writers, notably *Ariosto, *Rabelais, and *Ronsard. He attacked the purist literary reforms proposed by *Malherbe and, in lighter vein, painted lively and realistic portraits of a wide range of characters from all walks of life: poets and courtiers, prostitutes and procurers. His thirteenth satire, *Macette*, against religious hypocrisy, is generally considered his masterpiece.

Reinhold, Erasmus (1511–53) German astronomer. Appointed professor of mathematics at Wittenberg university, Reinhold, together with his colleague *Rheticus, became one of the first astronomers to embrace publicly the newly published *Copernican system. He saw his immediate task as that of compiling a new set of tables, based on Copernican assumptions, to replace the inaccurate thirteenth-century Alfonsine Tables. The resulting

Prutenic Tables (1551) proved to be no more than a marginal improvement. Reinhold died in his native Saalfeld, having fled Wittenberg in the previous year (1552) to escape the plague.

Rej, Mikołaj (1505–69) Polish poet, playwright, and prose writer. Rej was a country gentleman at Nagłowice, born at Żórawno and largely self-educated. His conversion to Calvinism (1546) emphasized the moralistic stance adopted in his numerous works in different genres. His first important work (1543) was a satirical dialogue in verse. His plays *Żywot Józefa* (1545) and *Kupiec* (1549) are based respectively upon the *Coemedia sacra Joseph* by *Crocus and *Mercator* by *Naogeorgus. The long poem *Wizerunek* (1558), based on the *Zodiacus vitae* by *Palingenius, describes the moral education of a young man. He also wrote miscellaneous volumes in verse and prose; one of his most famous prose pieces describes the ideal life of a Polish country gentleman. His grasp of theology is demonstrated in his works of biblical exegesis and he also made an influential prose translation of the psalms, *Psalterz Dawidów* (1546). As the first major writer to make exclusive use of Polish, Rej made an important contribution to acceptance of the vernacular in several literary genres.

Religion, (French) Wars of (1562–98) French civil wars between Catholics and Protestants (*Huguenots). During the 1550s tension grew between Huguenots eager to make converts to Calvinism and Catholics who felt that their faith was threatened. *Catherine de' Medici, then regent for Charles IX, sought a compromise through the Edict of St-Germain (January 1562), granting Huguenots freedom of conscience and the right to worship away from town centres. The discovery of Huguenots worshipping in Vassey led to the first war (1562–63), ended by the Pacification of Amboise. Uneasy peace followed; it was broken in 1567 by the Huguenot attempt to seize both regent and king at Meaux, leading to the second and third wars (1567–68; 1568–70). The Catholics, having failed to follow up their victories, agreed to a compromise peace at St-Germain (1570), but, remembering Meaux, the regent decided to end the Huguenot threat with the *Massacre of St Bartholomew (1572). Shocked by the death of thousands of their fellows, the Huguenots defied the crown and established governments in southern and western France. The war (1572–73) which followed ended with the granting of liberty of conscience and the right to worship freely in Huguenot towns. At the end of the fifth war (1575–76) the Huguenots made further gains, but the sixth and seventh wars (1577; 1580) were inconclusive. Finally, the War of the Three Henrys (1585–89) was provoked by the Catholic *Guise faction, which feared the accession of the Huguenot Henry of Navarre. He survived to become *Henry IV (reigned 1589–1610), but had to convert to Catholicism. *See also* Nantes, Edict of.

Remonstrants The name given to the followers of Arminius, the Dutch theologian whose lectures at Leyden challenged the orthodox Calvinist doctrine of predestination. After Arminius's death (1609) his followers drew up the Remonstrance of 1610, setting out the Arminian position. They held that predestination is not absolute, but conditioned by man's response (thus reintroducing an element of free will); that grace may consequently be received or denied; and that the offer of salvation is directed to all men. Their manifesto provoked the Contra-Remonstrance of 1611, setting out the orthodox position, and a bitter controversy ensued. This quickly achieved a political dimension, since the advocate of the States of Holland, *Oldenbarneveldt, took the side of the Remonstrants, and *Maurice of Nassau the contrary position. The Arminians were finally condemned at the Synod of *Dort (1618–19), and more than 200 ministers were ejected from their pulpits, although a degree of toleration returned after Maurice's death (1625). *See also* Arminianism.

Renée de France (1510–75), Duchess of Ferrara (1534–59) Born at Blois, the daughter of King Louis XII of France and Anne of Brittany, Renée was the subject of several abortive wedding negotiations before she was married (1528) to Ercole d'Este, heir to the dukedom of Ferrara. She encouraged men of letters at her court, particularly those who favoured the reforming side in religion; among these were *Palingenius and *Marot, and in April 1536 *Calvin himself paid a brief visit to Ferrara under an assumed name. Renée subsequently embraced Calvinism, much to the anger of her husband who adopted draconian measures to force her to renounce her new faith, at least as far as outward forms were concerned. Returning to her lands in France after Duke Ercole's death (1559), Renée made her château at Montargis in Loiret a stronghold of the Protestant faith. In 1562 it was even besieged by her son-in-law, the Duke of Guise, and she suffered harassment by Catholic forces on other occasions during the wars of religion.

René (I) of Anjou (1409–80), Duke of Bar (1430–80), Duke of Anjou and Count of Provence (1434–80). As duke consort of Lorraine, titular king of Naples, and claimant to Sicily and Jerusalem, René spent his youth vainly trying to establish his wife's claim to Lorraine and his own claims to Naples, where he had been chosen as successor by Queen Joanna II (*see also* Alfonso I). In his last years, after quarrelling with Louis XI of France, he spent more time in his French domains, where his interest in legal reforms and his patronage of literature and the arts earned him the title of "René the Good". It has even been suggested that the manuscript illuminator known as the Master of King René, who illustrated *Le livre des tournois du roi René* (c. 1446; Bibliothèque National, Paris) and a manuscript of Boccaccio's *Teseida* (1468; Vienna), was King René himself. At his death without a male heir his territories and the Angevin claims passed to the French crown.

Reni, Guido (1577–1642) Italian painter. He spent most of his life in his native Bologna, where he was a pupil of *Calvaert. Much influenced by Ludovico *Carracci and during a period in Rome (1600–14) by the naturalism of *Caravaggio, he soon developed his own style in the Renaissance tradition of *Raphael. His classicism is evident in his two best-known works: *Aurora*, a fresco painted for the Casino Rospigliosi in Rome (1613), and *The Massacre of the Innocents* (1611; Pinacoteca, Bologna). It was his religious compositions which, bringing him great popularity during his own lifetime among the fashionable circles of Rome and Bologna, were eventually criticized by Ruskin for their sentimentality and caused his fall from favour in the nineteenth century. His style, particularly latterly, was noted for its simple sketchlike designs, pale colours, and soft outlines. He also painted portraits and mythological subjects, among the latter the Naples *Atalanta and Hippomenes* and the Munich *Apollo and Marsyas*.

Reuchlin, Johann (Capnion; 1455–1522) German humanist scholar. Reuchlin was born at Pforzheim and educated at Fribourg and Paris, where he began to study Greek. After periods in Basle and Orleans, he joined the entourage of Eberhardt, Count of Württemberg, with whom he travelled to Italy (1482). There he completed his Greek studies with *Argyropoulos. On his second visit to Italy (1490), he met *Pico della Mirandola, who introduced him to Jewish mystical literature. From 1492, with the help of the Jewish physician Jacob Loans, he mastered Hebrew and began to study the *Cabbala, on which he published *De verbo mirifico* in 1494. His pro-Jewish sympathies brought him into conflict with the bigoted Jewish convert Johann Pfefferkorn, who advocated such antisemitic measures as the destruction of Hebrew books. The resulting controversy (*see* Epistolae obscurorum virorum) involved nearly all the northern humanists, becoming a war between Renaissance intellectual inquiry and ecclesiastical authoritarianism. Reuchlin's Latin comedy *Sergius* (1496) is a devastating satire on the monkish obscurantists. After years of virulent controversy, the case against Reuchlin was referred to Pope *Leo X, who quashed it (1516). Reuchlin spent his last years quietly teaching and studying in Ingolstadt and Tübingen. *De arte cabalistica* appeared in 1517 and the following year *Melanchthon published Reuchlin's advocacy of the manner of pronouncing Greek used by contemporary Greeks (against the supposed "ancient" pronunciation advocated by Erasmus). However, perhaps the most important of all his works was his Hebrew grammar and lexicon, *De rudimentis hebraicis* (1506), which laid the foundations of Hebrew scholarship for later humanists.

Rhenanus, Beatus (1485–1547) German humanist scholar. Rhenanus studied in Paris (1503–07) and from 1511 was attached to the circle of scholars around *Froben in Basle, for whose press he edited classical and patristic texts. In 1526 he returned to his native Schlettstadt. His *Rerum Germanici libri tres* (1531) was a significant contribution to German historical research. A disciple and friend of *Erasmus, he published the first collected edition of the latter's works, in nine volumes (1540–41), including Rhenanus's life of the great humanist. Rhenanus's fine library was bequeathed to his native town, where it remains.

Rheticus (Georg Joachim von Lauchen; 1514–76) Austrian astronomer and mathematician. Born at Feldkirch, he called himself after his native region of Rhaetia. The son of a physician beheaded for sorcery in 1528, Rheticus was appointed (1536) to teach mathematics at Wittenberg university. In 1539 he visited *Copernicus in Frauenburg and thereafter, as an ardent disciple, strove to both publicize and publish his work. To this end he published the first account of the Copernican system in his *Narratio prima* (1540). Subsequently he persuaded Copernicus to allow him to publish his long-since-completed *De revolutionibus*. Academic duties, however, forced Rheticus to leave the task to others, and in 1542 he became professor of mathematics at Leipzig university. Forced to resign in 1551 as a result of a sexual scandal, Rheticus spent the rest of his life practising medicine in Poland and Hungary. His *Opus Palatinum de triangulis*, a comprehensive set of trigonometrical tables, appeared posthumously in 1596.

rhetoric One of the seven liberal arts taught in the Middle Ages and defined as the art of using language to persuade or influence others. In the medieval academic scheme rhetoric was in the lower group, called the *trivium*, which also included grammar and logic. During the Renaissance period, its importance increased, and it was recognized, with grammar, history, poetry, and morals, as one of the *studia humana* (humane studies). The traditional teaching of Aristotle, Cicero, and Quintilian was modified by the influence of *Ramus; there was less connection with logic and more importance was attached to elocution, pronunciation, and gesture. Figures of speech were elaborated, but mere verbal decoration was to be avoided; there was always a moral purpose, to unite an elegant style with the promotion of virtue. The application of rhetorical principles to works and speeches in the vernacular languages was studied no less than traditional Latin oratory.

In the fifteenth century Lorenzo *Valla, in his *Dialecticae disputationes* and *Elegantiae linguae Latinae*, attacked the received ideas and tried to reduce the number of traditional categories. A far more conservative treatise was *The Arte of Rhetorique* (1553), by Thomas Wilson (c. 1525–81), English secretary of state, who maintained the classical teaching of Aristotle and denounced the pedantry of French and Italian idiom. Abraham Fraunce's *Arcadian Rhetorike* (1588) follows the Ramist approach in English and draws its examples from the best ancient and contemporary European writers, including Tasso and Boscán. The most important French treatises were those of Tonquelin (1555) and Courcelles (1557).

The political climate created by authoritarian rulers may have limited the scope of public oratory, but there was a greatly increased demand for sermons in the vernacular; among the most effective preachers were *Savonarola, *Luther, and John *Knox. At the same time, there was a great increase in international diplomatic activity and in written communications between heads of state; this called for a class of men skilled in the art of persuasive argument, from which the ambassadors, ministers, and secretaries could be recruited. Eloquence as well as knowledge was required of those who practised as advocates in the law courts. The spoken word was of paramount importance in education, which was still largely oral. Public disputations on subjects of academic controversy were still frequently held at the universities. Sir Henry Wotton (1568–1639) provost of Eton, advised the boys there "not to neglect rhetoric, because Almighty God has left mankind affections to be wrought upon" (Walton's *Lives*). The influence of Renaissance rhetorical teaching lasted well into the nineteenth century, especially in the grammar schools.

Riaño, Diego de (died 1534) Spanish architect. Riaño worked mainly in southern Spain and in

1523 was appointed cathedral architect at Seville. His masterpiece, however, was the Renaissance-plateresque Ayuntiamento (city hall) of Seville (1527–35), in which classical motifs are applied with extraordinary exuberance and inventiveness to give an effect of great richness and variety.

Ribadeneyra, Pedro de (Pedro Rivadeneyra *or* Ribadeneira; (1527–1611) Spanish biographer and religious writer. Born Pedro Ortiz de Cisneros at Toledo, he adopted the name of his maternal grandmother. The turning point of his life occurred in Rome, where he met *Ignatius Loyola, whose friend and devoted disciple he became and to whom he was affectionately known as "Perico". He joined the recently constituted Society of Jesus (its statutes had been approved in 1540). In the year of Ignatius's death and beatification (1556), Ribadeneyra was given charge of the Jesuit mission to Belgium. Although Loyola left his own account of his life (*Autobiografía y Diario espiritual*), Ribadeneyra's *Vita Ignatii Loyolae* (Naples, 1572) became the "classic" biography of the future saint. His Spanish translation of it was published in 1583. Ribadeneyra also wrote a two-volume history of the "schism" in England (*Historia ecclesiástica del scisma del Reyno de Inglaterra*; 1588, 1593), a consolatory work addressed to Spaniards after the disaster of the *Spanish Armada (*Tratado de la tribulación*; 1589), and two volumes of saints' lives (*Flos sanctorum*; 1599, 1601).

Ribalta, Francisco de (c. 1565–1628) Spanish artist. Born in Valencia, Ribalta probably trained at the *Escorial under Juan *Fernández de Navarrete and at Madrid. His earliest known work is *Christ nailed to the Cross* (1582; Hermitage, Leningrad), a minor mannerist painting, but after moving to Valencia in about 1599 and establishing a large studio there he adopted a grander realist style, influenced by Caravaggio. Later works, typical of the Spanish Baroque, include *The Vision of Father Simeon* (1612; National Gallery, London) and two paintings commissioned by the Capuchins in about 1620, *The Vision of St Francis* (Prado, Madrid) and *St Francis embracing Christ* (Valencia museum). His son Juan (c. 1597–1628) was also a painter.

Ribeiro, Bernadim (1482–1552) Portuguese poet and novelist. Ribeiro, who was born at Torrão, was a friend of Sá de *Miranda, was perhaps a converted Jew, and belonged to the group of courtly poets whose works appeared in Resende's *Cancioneiro geral* (1516). Little else is known of his life. His *Éclogas* were the first written in Portuguese and established a fashion for this type. These

and a fragmentary pastoral novel, *Minina e Moça*, which is extremely sentimental in rendering the lovers' unappeasable passion, were published posthumously (1554), together with the *Trovas de Crisfal* attributed to Cristóvão Falcão (c. 1518–c. 1554). This work, if not in fact by Ribeiro, is a very close and successful imitation of his style.

Ricci, Matteo (1552–1610) Italian Jesuit missionary and writer. Born in Macerata, Ricci obtained a wide-ranging education in Rome. He went to Goa in 1578 and Macao in 1582, before following Michael Ruggieri to China. After an unsettled beginning, Ricci developed a comprehensive knowledge of Chinese language and culture, before settling at Chao-king in 1583. In 1589 the new viceroy expelled him and he moved on to Shao-chow, then Nanking (1599), and Peking (1601), where in the same year he was received by the emperor. Wherever he went, Ricci shone as a missionary of outstanding ability. He achieved numerous conversions by placing Christian doctrine within the context of Chinese culture, rather than attempting to inflict alien values on confused or resistant proselytes. Ricci also impressed the Chinese with many European innovations, including clocks and maps. His methods upset the religious hierarchy in Europe, but delighted the Chinese. He wrote a number of works in Chinese, notably *The True Doctrine of God* (1595), and translated Christian texts for missionary work into their language.

Riccio, Andrea di Ambrogio Briosco (c. 1470–1532) Italian sculptor and goldsmith. Born in Trento, Riccio was probably a pupil of Bellano and an assistant of Donatello, and had settled in Padua by about 1497. His most famous work is the sumptuous bronze Easter candelabrum in S Antonio at Padua (1507–16), which is notable for its classical figures and technically brilliant decoration. He also executed many small bronze statuettes in the humanist style then prevalent in Padua, including *Boy Milking a Goat* (Bargello, Florence), *Shouting Warrior on Horseback* (Victoria and Albert Museum, London), and *Arion* (Louvre). He also executed numerous small items in terracotta.

Richier, Ligier (c. 1500–67) French sculptor. Born at St Mihiel, Richier worked mainly for the dukes of Lorraine, but in later life became a Protestant and was compelled to move to Geneva. The tomb (1545) of René de Chalons in the church of St Etienne at Bar-le-Duc is considered to be Richier's masterpiece, featuring a gruesomely realistic cadaver. There is a wooden Christ by Richier in the church of Notre-Dame in the same town, and a *Christ carrying the Cross* in the church of St

Riemenschneider, Tilman

Martin at Pont-à-Mousson is also attributed to him. His recumbent effigy of Philippe de Gueldres, Duchess of Lorraine (died 1547), is in the former church of the Cordeliers, Nancy. He also sculpted an *Entombment* (1553) for the church of St Etienne in his native town.

Riemenschneider, Tilman (c. 1460–1531) German woodcarver and sculptor. Although born in Osterode am Harz, Riemenschneider was based in Würzburg from 1483, eventually becoming mayor of the town (1520–21). He is particularly famous for his beautiful limewood carvings, both individual figures and whole altarpieces, which combine the powerful emotionalism of Veit *Stoss with Adam *Kraft's vigorous realism. Of his works in stone, the most famous is in Bamberg cathedral, the magnificent marble tomb (c. 1513) of the cathedral's founder, Emperor Henry II and his wife Cunigunde. As well as his major commissions for Würzburg and Bamberg, Riemenschneider also produced work for churches in several neighbouring towns: an altarpiece for Münnerstadt (1490–92), a triptych for Windsheim (c. 1508), and a sandstone *Lamentation* group for Maidbronn (1519–23), among others.

Rienzo, Cola di (Nicolà di Rienzo; ?1313–54) Italian populist leader who tried to restore the greatness of Rome. He has been honoured in literature and his life inspired Wagner's *Rienzi*. Rienzo summoned a Roman assembly on the Capitoline Hill in May 1347 and assumed the title of tribune with dictatorial powers, with the aim of replacing the power of the aristocrats and the absentee pope (then resident in Avignon) with a popular government in Rome. He executed reforms and prepared for the election of a Roman emperor of Italy, but was overthrown by the Roman nobles (December 1347). He went into exile, but triumphantly resumed power in August 1354. His dictatorial ways made him unpopular and he hacked to death by a Roman mob soon afterwards.

rilievo schiacciato (*or rilievo stiacciato*) *see schiacciato*.

Rimini An Adriatic port and city state in Emilia-Romagna, northern Italy. At first Umbro-Etruscan, Rimini was subsequently under the sway of Romans, Byzantines, Goths, Lombards, and Franks. By the early fourteenth century Rimini had accepted papal suzerainty, but was actually governed by the *Malatesta family, who were recognized as lords of Rimini from 1334. In return for political and military support successive popes supported the creation of a city state based on Rimini. In the mid-fifteenth century Sigismondo

RIEMENSCHNEIDER Mary Salome and Zebedee. *These glazed limewood figures formed part of a group of the Holy Kindred. (c. 1520; Victoria and Albert Museum, London)*

*Malatesta's quarrel with Pope *Pius II and his defeat (1463) led to Sigismondo's exile and the restriction of the Malatesta state to Rimini itself. The fortunes of Rimini declined, and after some years of conflict Rimini became directly subject to Rome (1527). Notable landmarks have survived from the period of the rule of Sigismondo Malatesta. These include the fortifications, the castle, and the so-called *Tempio Malatestiano.

Rivadeneyra, Pedro de *see* Ribadeneyra, Pedro de.

Rizzo, Antonio di Giovanni (c. 1440–c. 1500) Italian sculptor and architect. A native of Verona, Rizzo worked chiefly in Venice, where he settled in 1466. He worked with *Amadeo on the Certosa di Pavia, but is better known for his tomb of Doge Niccolò Tròn (c. 1480; Sta Maria dei Frari, Venice), which is notable for its scale and detail. Later works included *Adam and Eve* (c. 1485) for the Arco Foscari of the Palazzo Ducale, Venice, upon which he worked with Antonio Bregno (c. 1420–1501), clearly under the influence of Flemish or German artists. The Scala dei Giganti of the palace is likewise his work, as is the façade on the eastern side of the Cortile, rebuilt after the fire of 1483.

Robert Bellarmine, St (Roberto Francesco Romolo Bellarmino; 1542–1621) Italian cardinal and theologian. He was born at Montepulciano, entered the Society of Jesus in 1560, and studied in Rome, Mondovii, and Padua, before being sent to Louvain in 1569. The following year, after ordination, he began lecturing, and achieved celebrity upon his return to Rome (1576) as professor at the Jesuit Collegium Romanum (*see* Gregoriana). He lectured and wrote on a variety of controversial subjects, and was both applauded and castigated for treating Protestant views fairly. His most important writings were the three volumes of lectures published under the title *Disputationes de controversiis Christianae fidei adversus huius temporis haereticos* (1586–93). These contained a scholarly and cogent appraisal of Roman Catholic doctrine, which was divided into four sections: the Church, the sacraments, Christ, and the grave.
Pope Clement VIII made Bellarmine a cardinal in 1599, and he was archbishop of Capua (1602–05) until ill health caused his retirement; he moved first to Montepulciano and then to Rome, where he eventually died. Bellarmine continued to write prolifically, his most important work in later life being *De scriptoribus ecclesiasticis* (1613). He was also an early critic of Galileo, and the two men shared a mutual respect. He was not canonized until 1930 because of his opposition to papal authority in temporal matters.

Roberti, Ercole de' *see* Ercole de' Roberti.

Robert of Anjou (1278–1343), King of Naples (as Robert I, 1309–43) Son of Charles II of Naples, Robert spent much of his youth as a hostage in Aragon. His ambitions led him to support the Guelf faction in their struggle against the papacy – with little success. He was known as a patron of literature and the arts, numbering *Giotto and Simone *Martini among his protégés, and was particularly interested in *humanism. He is also credited with the authorship of moral and theological treatises.

Robusti, Jacopo *see* Tintoretto.

Roelas, Juan de las (c. 1558–1625) Spanish painter. The son of an admiral, Roelas was born in Seville but became acquainted with Italian art while a student in Venice, being especially influenced by Titian and Tintoretto. In 1603 he was appointed prebendary of the chapel at Olivárez, where after some years in Madrid and Seville, he lived from 1624. Roelas was recognized as the most important artist in Seville and did much to free the Seville school from the last influence of Romanism. His best paintings, all still in Seville, included the *Circumcision* (c. 1606; university church), the *Martyrdom of St Andrew* (1609–13; museum), and a *Pentecost* (1615). His pupils included Pablo Legote (c. 1598–1671) and Francisco de Zurbarán (1598–1664).

Rojas, Fernando de (c. 1465–1541) Spanish writer. Born the son of converted Jews (*conversos*) at Puebla de Montalbán, Toledo, Rojas studied at Salamanca. He moved from his birthplace because of discrimination against *conversos* and settled in Talavera, where he became mayor and lived the rest of his life. The work for which he is known was first published anonymously at Burgos with the title *La comedia de Calisto y Melibea* (1499), a novel in dramatic form in sixteen acts (*auctos*). In a later, expanded version of twenty-one acts, it was retitled *La tragicomedia de Calisto y Melibea* (1502), and Rojas's authorship is announced acrostically and in a prefatory claim that he completed the work of an anonymous original author. The most influential work of sixteenth-century Spain, the novel was apparently intended for dramatic reading aloud and not as a play. It is better known by its popular name, that of a central character, *La *Celestina*.

Roman Academy The society founded in Rome in the late 1450s by Pomponio *Leto with the aim of encouraging scholarly interest in all aspects of classical Roman culture. Its members adopted Latin or Greek names and met at Leto's house on the Quirinal. Its fame spread all over Europe, but its enthusiasm for all things Roman, including pagan rituals, caused Pope *Paul II to imprison and even torture its leading members and to order its closure (1468). Later it was revived and numbered two popes (*Julius II and *Leo X) among its members, but it was finally dissolved after the sack of Rome (1527).

Romanino, Girolamo (c. 1484–c. 1562) Italian artist. A native of Brescia, Romanino was a fellow-pupil of Moretto and was profoundly influenced by Giorgione, to whom several of his paintings have been attributed, Titian, Savoldo, and Lotto. He executed numerous sacred pictures and frescoes in provincial churches throughout northern Italy, including an *Enthroned Madonna with Saints and Angels* (Museo Civico, Padua) and *St Matthew and the Angel* (S Giovanni Evangelista, Cremona). His best works are the frescoes with mythological figures at the Castello del Buon Consiglio at Trento; other works include portraits and the *Passion* at Cremona cathedral (1519).

Romano, Gian (*or* **Giovanni**) **Cristoforo** (c. 1470–1512) Italian sculptor. He was born in Rome and studied under Andrea *Bregno, before working in a number of northern Italian cities – Cremona, Ferrara, Milan, Mantua, Pavia, and Urbino – to which he introduced elements of the Roman classical style. His most important work is the tomb of Giangaleazzo Visconti in the Certosa di Pavia (1493–97). He had considerable talent as a portraitist; Federico da Montefeltro and Francesco Sforza were among his sitters (both Bargello, Florence), and of Isabella d'Este he made a portrait medal as well as the marble bust now in the Louvre.

Romano, Giulio *see* Giulio Romano.

Rome The capital city of Italy situated on the River Tiber 15 miles (24 km) from the Mediterranean in central Italy. During the Middle Ages and early Renaissance Rome was a wretched place, described as a city filled with huts, thieves, and vermin. Bitter factional strife and conflict between imperial, papal, and republican forms of government brought such chaos to Rome that the papacy removed itself to Avignon (1309). During the Avignon papacy, disorder and the Black Death (1348–49) devastated Rome and reduced its population to little more than 20 000. In 1347 and 1354 Cola di *Rienzo tried in vain to re-establish the glories of ancient Rome and the powers of its citizens. The return of the papacy to Rome (1378) was followed by the *Great Schism, only ended in 1417 with the election of Pope Martin V, who began to lay the foundations of a system of govern-

ment that made Rome the capital of a major Renaissance power – the Papal States.

*Nicholas V (pope 1446–55) was the first of the Renaissance popes; he and his successors embarked on the rebuilding of Rome and attracted artists and scholars to the city. By the late fifteenth century Rome had become an important centre of humanist and Greek studies, following the initiative of Nicholas V in organizing the translation of Greek classics and the work of the *Roman Academy under the leadership of Pomponio *Leto. By 1500 Rome's financial basis was secured by the local alum deposits and banking.

It was during the early sixteenth century that the efforts of *Julius II (pope 1503–13) and *Leo X (pope 1513–22) and the genius of such artists as *Bramante, *Michelangelo, and *Raphael enabled Rome to displace Florence as the pre-eminent Renaissance city. The beginning of the rebuilding of St Peter's basilica during Julius II's pontificate provided many opportunities which attracted men of talent and genius to Rome.

The sack of Rome (1527) by *Charles V's troops was a setback from which the city recovered later in the century under such *Counter-Reformation popes as Sixtus V (pope 1585–90), the initiator of Domenico *Fontana's huge programme of civic planning. By the late sixteenth century Rome was again prosperous and cosmopolitan, with a population of about 100 000.

Fifteenth-century buildings which have survived include the Palazzo Venezia (1445), Sta Maria del Popolo (1472–77), S Agostino (1479–83), and the Cancelleria (1486–98). During the sixteenth century the new St Peter's (from 1506) and the Quirinal palace (1574) were built, and the Lateran and Vatican palaces were remodelled. Two of the great works of art which have survived are Michelangelo's frescoes in the *Sistine Chapel (1508–12) and Raphael's frescoes in the papal apartments (begun 1509).

Rome, Sack of (1527) The pillage of Rome by imperial troops after their commander was killed in their successful assault on the city. Following the battle of *Pavia, Pope Clement VII joined (1526) the French-led League of Cognac to resist the threatened Habsburg domination of Europe. Emperor Charles V appealed to the German diet for support and raised an army, which entered Italy in 1527 and joined the imperial forces from Milan, commanded by the duke of Bourbon. This army marched on Rome, hoping to detach the pope from the league. The many Lutherans in its ranks boasted that they came with hempen halters to hang the cardinals and a silk one for the pope; in addition, by the time they reached Rome, the troops were mutinous because of lack of pay.

Rome fell on 6 May 1527, Bourbon being killed in the first assault. Discipline collapsed, and the city was savagely pillaged for a week before some control was restored. The pope initially took refuge in the Castel S Angelo before surrendering. The imperial army occupied Rome until February 1528. While achieving its immediate objective by bringing the pope firmly under imperial control, the sack shocked the Christian world. Charles's enemies were quick to take advantage, France and England declaring war on him in 1528.

rondeau A verse form used in French song from the thirteenth century and in French poetry in the fifteenth century. The typical rondeau consists of three stanzas of five, three, and five lines, based on two rhymes, usually in the pattern aabba, aab, aabba; the opening words (or, in the sung rondeau, the opening lines) of the first stanza are repeated as a refrain at the end of the second and third stanzas. The rhyming pattern, number of stanzas, and overall length of the rondeau are subject to considerable variation: the *rondeau redoublé* consists of six four-line stanzas in the pattern abab, baba, etc., in which the four lines of the first stanza are used in turn as the fourth lines of the second, third, fourth, and fifth stanzas. Notable exponents of the rondeau include Guillaume *Dufay, Clément *Marot, and Charles d'Orléans.

Rondelet, Guillaume (1507–56) French zoologist. Although trained in medicine Rondelet was enabled to indulge his interest in natural history while travelling throughout Europe with his patron, Cardinal Tournon. He returned to his native Montpellier in 1545 to teach medicine. In the main work of his life, *Universae aquatilium historiae* (1555) he described 245 species of marine animals. *See also* zoology.

Ronsard, Pierre de (?1524–85) French poet. Born near Couture into a noble family of the Vendôme, Ronsard entered the French court in 1536 as page to the royal family. He visited Scotland in the course of his duties and subsequently accompanied Lazare de Baïf on a diplomatic mission to Alsace. Forced to abandon his court career after an illness that left him partially deaf, Ronsard turned to literature; at the Collège de Coqueret he studied Greek and Latin poetry under the humanist Jean *Daurat and, in association with Joachim *du Bellay and others, formed the school of poets that became known as the *Pléiade. Ronsard's early verse collections, *Odes* (1550, 1552), containing the famous "Mignonne, allons voir si la rose...", and *Amours* (1552), were heavily influenced by Pindar, Horace, and *Petrarch; his *Bocage* (1554) and *Continuation des Amours* (1555) were inspired by

the Greek poet Anacreon and the *Hymnes* (1555–56), a series of longer poems, by Callimachus. By 1560 Ronsard had become established as court poet to Charles IX: during the Wars of *Religion his ardent and patriotic support of the royalist and Catholic cause found expression in the political poems *Discours des misères de ce temps* (1562), *Remonstrance au peuple de France* (1562), and the unfinished epic *La Franciade* (1572). Under Henry III, however, Ronsard found himself supplanted by *Desportes; in semi-retirement at his priory of St-Cosme at Tours he continued to write, publishing the *Sonnets pour Hélène*, one of his best-known collections of love poetry, in 1578. His nostalgic *Derniers Vers* appeared in 1586, the year after his death. Ronsard had numerous imitators and translators among sixteenth-century English poets, but the criticisms of *Malherbe, Boileau, and others led to a decline in his reputation in France in the seventeenth and eighteenth centuries. Sainte-Beuve's *Tableau historique et critique de la poésie française et du théâtre français au XVIe siècle* (1828), however, brought about a new appreciation of Ronsard's work and re-established his position among the principal French poets of the Renaissance.

Rore, Ciprien de (c. 1515–65) Franco-Flemish composer. Born at Malines, Rore appears to have been in Venice in the 1540s, and by 1547 was *maestro di cappella* at the Este court at Ferrara, where he remained until the death of Duke Ercole II (1559). After a brief period of employment with *Margaret of Parma, governor of the Netherlands, in 1561 he entered the service of her husband, Ottavio Farnese, in Parma. In 1563 he succeeded *Willaert as *maestro* at St Mark's, Venice, but returned to Parma a year later, where he died. Rore composed much sacred music; his parody Masses and motets follow the style of composers of the previous generation, but it is for his madrigals that he is chiefly remembered. Of these, 125 survive; Rore set many Petrarchan texts in his earlier madrigals, and in the later ones sensitive treatment of the text became increasingly important. He is recognized as a strong influence on Monteverdi.

Rosicrucianism The movement that combined several strands of esoteric wisdom – *hermeticism, the *Cabbala, and *alchemy – in a mysterious secret society of the learned that apparently originated in Protestant Germany in the early seventeenth century. The two basic Rosicrucian texts were both printed in Kassel: the German *Fama Fraternitatis*, of which the first known printed edition appeared in 1614 (it had earlier circulated in manuscript), and the Latin *Confessio Fraternitatis R.C.* (1615). The *Fama* relates how "Christian

Rosencreutz", who was purportedly born in 1378, journeyed to the East and returned with secret wisdom which he then imparted to members of the order he founded; the "discovery" (dated to 1604) of the emblematic tomb of "Rosencreutz" and his disciples is then described, together with the refounding of the order. The *Confessio* sets out the order's programme for universal Christian reformation and enlightenment. The author or authors of the *Fama* and *Confessio* are unknown, but the Lutheran pastor and mystic Johann Valentin Andreae (born 1586) was indisputably the author of a third Rosicrucian text *Chymische Hochzeit Christiani Rosencreutz* (1616), and the anonymous writers probably belonged to his circle in Württemberg and the Palatinate.

The Rosicrucian manifestos caused a stir throughout Europe. Several English scholars, among them Robert *Fludd, claimed to be or to be in touch with a member of the society. Disillusionment set in when the "brothers of the Rosy Cross" remained obstinately invisible and elusive. However, some of the Rosicrucian enthusiasm for utopian restructuring of society through knowledge resurfaced in the ideals of early members of the Royal Society.

Rosselli, Cosimo (1439–1507) Italian painter. The pupil of Benozzo *Gozzoli, Rosselli established an important workshop in his native Florence, where his own pupils included Fra *Bartolommeo and *Piero di Cosimo. He produced a number of fairly pedestrian works himself, including frescoes in the cloister of the Annunziata and the church of S Ambrosius in Florence. In 1481 he was also commissioned to help with the frescoes for the Sistine Chapel, despite the fact that few would class him with such colleagues on the project as Botticelli and Ghirlandaio.

Rossellino, Bernardo (1409–64) and **Antonio** (1427–79) Italian sculptors. The brothers were born in Settignano and worked in Florence, where Bernardo executed a number of architectural works, including the Palazzo Rucellai (1446–51). His masterpiece, however, is the Palazzo Piccolomini (1460–63) in *Pienza. Bernardo's most notable sculptural achievement is the tomb of Leonardo *Bruni in Sta Croce in Florence (1444–47), which was based upon Donatello's classical tomb of Pope John XXII. He was also employed for a time on work at St Peter's in Rome (1451–53) by Pope Nicholas I.

Bernardo's younger brother Antonio was also influenced by Donatello and for a while was Bernardo's pupil. His greatest work, the tomb of the cardinal-prince of Portugal in S Miniato al Monte in Florence (1461–66), was highly innovative and more sophisticated than his brother's

work. Other works by Antonio include the portrait busts of Giovanni Chellini (1456; Victoria and Albert Museum, London) and of Matteo Palmieri (1468; Bargello, Florence). Both brothers also executed decorative works.

Rosso Fiorentino (Giovanni Battista di Jacopo; 1495–1540) Italian painter. Rosso probably trained with Pontormo under Andrea del Sarto, whose influence is strong upon Rosso's early painting. Rosso's earliest surviving work is the fresco of the Assumption (1517) in the church of SS Annunziata in Florence, in which his taste for drama and violent colour is already evident. Equally emotional in treatment was the famous *Deposition* (1521; Galleria Pittorica, Volterra), which Rosso painted shortly before leaving for Rome, where he came under the influence of Michelangelo. After the sack of Rome (1527) Rosso wandered Italy for several years before being summoned to France by Francis I to work on the design and decoration of the château at *Fontainebleau. Here, with *Primaticcio, he founded the French mannerist school, executing such influential works as the Galerie François I. Other major works include the impressive *Moses and Jethro's Daughters* (c. 1523; Uffizi) and *Dead Christ with Angels* (1525–26; Museum of Fine Arts, Boston).

Rotonda, Villa An Italian villa designed by Andrea *Palladio and built on a hilltop site at Vicenza. The Villa Rotonda, which is also known as the Villa Capra, was begun in about 1549 but not completed until 1606 by *Scamozzi for Giulio Capra. It consists of a domed central hall with four symmetrical rooms leading off it, each with an identical Ionic portico. The proportions, balance, and classical ornamentation of the villa caught the imagination of architects throughout Europe. Chiswick House (1730–36) in west London is just one of the numerous buildings to be built in imitation of the Villa Rotonda.

Rucellai family Wealthy Tuscan merchants who, from the late thirteenth century onwards, lived in Florence studying and cultivating the arts. *Alberti designed the Palazzo Rucellai for Giovanni (1403–81), whose son, Bernardo (1448–1514), designed the Rucellai Gardens; Bernardo was a humanist historian who was an early user of the phrase "the balance of power" in his history of *Charles VIII's invasion of 1494–95. Giovanni's grandson, also Giovanni (1475–1525), was a didactic poet, the author of *Le Api* (1539), based on Virgil's fourth *Georgic*, and *Rosamunda* (1525), a classical tragedy in verse based on an incident in Lombard history. Cosimo, Bernardo's grandson, presided over gatherings of intellectuals in the Rucellai Gardens (*see* Orti Oricellari).

Rudolf II (1552–1612), Holy Roman Emperor, King of Bohemia and Hungary, Archduke of Austria (1576–1612) Rudolf was the son of Emperor Maximilian II and Mary, daughter of Emperor *Charles V. A scholar who suffered from poor health, he spent many years in semi-seclusion in Prague. He dabbled in chemistry, medicine, astronomy, alchemy, and astrology and, with the help of his court antiquary Jacopo *Strada, acquired an impressive collection of rare works of art. He was a patron of *Arcimboldo, *Savery, and *Spranger, and, in the scientific realm, of Tycho *Brahe and *Kepler. Perhaps because he was educated in Spain, Rudolf was an uncompromising Catholic, determined to eradicate Protestantism in his domains. He reversed the tolerant

RUDOLF II *Wenzel Maller's wax relief of the emperor with his hound, although superficially similar, is a strong contrast in terms of personal dignity with the portrait of Charles V by Titian. (1606; Victoria and Albert Museum, London)*

religious policies of his father and supported the Jesuits and the other religious orders in their efforts to further the *Counter-Reformation.

By the beginning of the seventeenth century Rudolf was suffering from fits of morbid depression which made him incapable of governing effectively. His attacks on Protestantism in Austria led to the collapse of government and the division of the country into warring religious leagues, and similar campaigns against political and religious liberties in Hungary occasioned a revolt (1604–05) that only terminated when the Habsburg archdukes insisted that Rudolf entrust the government of Hungary to his brother, Matthias. Under similar circumstances he was forced in 1608 to hand over the government of Austria and Moravia to Matthias. Bohemia, where Protestantism was very well established, rebelled, and in 1611 Rudolf had to abdicate and to accept the election of Matthias by the Bohemian estates as king of Bohemia.

Rudolfine Tables *see under* astronomy; Brahe, Tycho; Kepler, Johannes.

Rueda, Lope de (c. 1510–65) Spanish actor and playwright. The first Spanish professional actor about whom anything is known, Rueda was born in Seville and as a youth joined a troupe of wandering actors performing at inns or other venues permitted by town councils. He became an actor-manager, performing before the future Philip II in 1551 and in plays staged in Philip's honour in 1554. Rueda's works were published posthumously in three series (1567–70). With one exception his several comedies are in prose. Crudely constructed and with no attempt to develop characterizations, they draw on Italian material. The best, *Eufemia*, is based on a tale in Boccaccio's *Decameron*. More important are his *pasos*, one-act farcical interludes with realistic dialogue and stereotype characters borrowed from *commedia dell' arte*: the *fanfarrón* (braggart), *rufián* (pimp), *gracioso* (the wit, or comic servant), and others. Twenty-four of some forty *pasos* survive; about half were written for interpolation in his own comedies. By the end of Rueda's life, acting acquired the status of a full-time profession and permanent public theatres soon opened in Madrid (Teatro de la Cruz, 1579), Seville, and other cities.

Ruiz de Alarcón y Mendoza, Juan (1580–1639) Spanish dramatist. The son of a wealthy superintendent of mines, Alarcón was born in Mexico City. He went to Spain, was educated at Salamanca and settled in Madrid (1611). Between 1615 and 1625 he wrote twenty-five plays, which established him as a leading playwright of the Siglo de Oro. In the meantime he was appointed to the Council of the Indies, an office he held for the rest of his life.

Alarcón was a hunchback and was mercilessly ridiculed by literary rivals such as Lope de Vega, Góngora, and Quevedo. These attacks did nothing, however, to obscure the outstanding quality of his work, written with much greater care than the plays of contemporaries, who were accustomed to turning them out by the hundreds. Most of his plays were collected for print during his life: *Parte primera de las comedias* (1628) contained eight plays and *Parte segunda* (1634), thirteen, including his best known, *La verdad sospechosa*, concerning a hero incapable of telling the truth. Alarcón's subjects cover a wide range but the plays dealing with contemporary manners have a moral and comic subtlety, matched by a classical construction and versification, that associates them more with eighteenth-century comedy than with the baroque style of Counter-Reformation Spain.

Rustici, Giovanni Francesco (1474–1554) Italian sculptor. Nothing is known about Rustici's early years but that he was born at Florence and as a young man became a close friend of *Leonardo da Vinci. His best-known works are the three bronze figures of John the Baptist preaching, flanked by a Levite and a Pharisee, over the north door of the baptistery in Florence, begun in 1506 and installed in 1511. A number of his marble statues, less assured than his work in bronze, are now in the Bargello and the Palazzo Vecchio and he also worked in terracotta (statue of a victorious knight in the Museo Horne, Florence). Two paintings in the Uffizi may be his; his drawings have all been lost. In 1528 Rustici went to France at the invitation of Francis I to work on an equestrian monument which he never finished. He died in Tours.

rutters Mariners' charts. The English word derives from the French "routier". Rutters were mainly manuscript compilations until the publication of Waghenaer's *Spieghel der Zeevaerdt* (1584–85) introduced a more sophisticated kind of guide for pilots (*see* waggoners).

S

Sabellico, Marcantonio (Marcantonio Coccio; ?1436–1506) Italian humanist scholar and historian. He lived and worked in Venice, where he lectured and held the post of librarian of S Marco, in charge of the bequest of books by Cardinal *Bessarion, which formed the nucleus of the Bibliotheca *Marciana. He wrote *Historiae rerum Venetarum* (1487) and followed this with a universal history, *Enneades* (1498–1504), as well as the vernacular treatise *Del sito di Venezia città* (1502). His two-volume *Opera* were published posthumously (1538).

Sacchetti, Franco (c. 1333–1400) Dalmatian-born writer and poet. Although he was born at Ragusa (Dubrovnik), Sacchetti was from an old established Florentine family and played an active role in the public life of Florence, holding many important posts. He claimed to have little learning or knowledge of Latin, but it is obvious he was widely read in vernacular literature. A prolific poet, he wrote some of the outstanding lyric poems of the century and collected his verse in *Libro delle rime* (c. 1362). His major prose work, *Trecentonovelle* (*Three Hundred Tales*; 1392–97), of which 223 complete tales survive, acknowledges Boccaccio as model but is very different from the *Decameron*. There is no frame and no complexity in point of view; the tales are short, anecdotal, with explicit morals, like *exempla*; historical characters (e.g. Pope Boniface, Dante) appear occasionally; the comedy is low, often involving a cruel practical joke (*beffa*), but seldom indecent; the language is conversational. Sacchetti is also the author of a short burlesque epic poem and of vernacular prose commentaries on the gospels, *Sposizioni di Vangeli* (1381).

Sack of Rome *see* Rome, Sack of.

sacra conversazione (sacred conversation) A pictorial formula favoured especially in the Italian Renaissance, in which the Madonna is depicted in apparent conversation with a small intimate group of saints. This style of composition succeeded earlier altarpieces in which the various figures are painted on separate panels. Renaissance artists who employed the device included Mantegna, Fra Angelico, Fra Filippo Lippi, Giovanni Bellini, Titian, Holbein, Reni, and Tintoretto.

sacra rappresentazione A form of sacred drama of popular origin performed in public squares or other open spaces, especially in fifteenth-century Tuscany. The plays, often by anonymous authors and mainly written in *ottava rima*, dealt with biblical events, saints' lives, or similar religious subjects but included elements of realistic characterization and description and allusions to contemporary life. There were no divisions into acts and scenes and no fixed length, but a variety of sets were used with scene changes as required. Presentations were sponsored by lay confraternities.

The plays apparently evolved from sung or spoken dialogues that developed in the singing of the *lauda*, a popular religious song of praise derived from the liturgy. *Laudes* flourished in Umbria among the flagellants (c. 1260), and the form, with its octosyllabic line, was adopted by the Franciscan Jacopone da Todi (1236–1306) and spread to the rest of Italy. Among writers of the *sacra rappresentazione* are Feo Belcari (1410–84), author of *La rappresentazione di Abram ed Isac* (1449), *Savonarola, Jacopo *Nardi, and Lorenzo de' *Medici, whose *Rappresentazione dei SS Giovanni e Paolo* (1491) was performed towards the end of his life. During the sixteenth century texts of the plays were published but public performances gradually declined.

Sadeler family A dynasty of late sixteenth- and seventeenth-century artists, best known for their vast output of engravings, mainly reproduced after the designs of other painters. The head of the family was Johannes I (1550–c. 1600), who was born in Brussels, a member of the Antwerp guild, and was also active in Frankfurt and at the court of Wilhelm V of Bavaria, as well as in Florence, Verona, Rome, and Venice. His brother Raphael I (1560–1628/32), born in Antwerp, accompanied him to Germany. His son Justus (1583–1620) was also an editor, and his nephew Aegidius (c. 1570–1629) was both painter and engraver. After visiting Germany and Italy he moved to the court of Rudolf II at Prague (1597), where he died. Raphael I had three sons, Raphael II (1584–1632), Philip (active 1610s) and Johannes II (died 1665), all of whom were active at Munich. As a number of their prints are signed simply with an initial, it is sometimes difficult to distinguish the work of one member of the family from that of another.

Sadoleto, Cardinal Jacopo (1477–1547) Italian humanist and churchman. Sadoleto was born in Modena and studied Latin at Ferrara and Greek at Rome. He gained a reputation for his Latin style and for his hexameter poem on the newly discovered statue of Laocoön. Pope Leo X made him his secretary (1513) and bishop of Carpentras (1517). He wrote many moral and pastoral works and a commentary on the Epistle to the Romans which was placed on the Index because of suspicions that it contained crypto-Protestant ideas. Sadoleto certainly felt that the Church was in need of serious reform and was sympathetic to those pressing for change, but he did not advocate the rejection of papal authority, and in 1539 he attempted to win Geneva back to the Catholic Church with an eloquent appeal to Christian unity. In a letter to Clement VII after the sack of Rome (1527), he interpreted the catastrophe as a divine punishment. In 1536 he was made a cardinal by Paul III. He was buried in S Pietro in Vincoli, Rome. His correspondence is a valuable primary source because of his contacts with many of the leading noble Italian families. He also wrote the educational treatise *De pueris recte instituendis* (1533).

St Bartholomew's Day, Massacre of *see* Massacre of St Bartholomew.

St Peter's, Rome The central basilica of the Roman Catholic Church. The first church, often referred to as Old St Peter's, was dedicated in about 330 AD by Constantine I but was demolished in the sixteenth century after it had fallen into a state of disrepair. In 1506 Pope Julius II commissioned *Bramante to design a new church over the tomb of St Peter. The new building, often called New St Peter's, was originally modelled on a Greek cross plan, although the designs underwent many changes after Bramante's death (1514), with modifications being made by his successors, who included *Raphael, Fra *Giocondo, *Peruzzi, and Antonio *Sangallo the Younger. In 1546 *Michelangelo was appointed chief architect; he made a number of changes to Bramante's centralized plan, enlarged the size of it, and worked on the massive dome, which was completed after Michelangelo's death by Giacomo *della Porta. The two small cupolas were the work of *Vignola. Further extensions were executed by Carlo Maderno in the seventeenth century, when St Peter's square was also laid out (1656–67) by Giovanni Bernini. The present basilica contains many notable works of art, including the first great *Pietà* (1498–99) by Michelangelo.

St-Quentin, Battle of (10 August 1557) A Spanish victory over the French at St-Quentin in northern France. In March 1557 a French army entered Italy to challenge Habsburg domination there and in reply a Spanish army invaded France from the Netherlands. The Spanish general beseiged the fortress of St-Quentin; a relief force under Anne de *Montmorency, Constable of France, was destroyed. Montmorency and many other nobles were captured and the way to Paris lay open, but a bankrupt Spain was unable to press home its advantage. *See also* Cateau-Cambrésis, Peace of.

Salamanca A city in western Spain on the River Tormes. The town was captured by Hannibal (222 BC) from the original inhabitants and then passed to the Romans, Visigoths, and Moors; the Moors were finally expelled around 1055. Salamanca's fame in the Middle Ages and Renaissance depended on its university, founded about 1230 by Alfonso IX of León and renowned throughout Europe first for its faculties of canon and civil law and later for its theology school. The new cathedral, begun in 1509 and from 1513 constructed to designs by Juan Gil de Ontañon, and several other ecclesiastical and university buildings date from the Renaissance period.

Sales, St Francis de *see* Francis de Sales, St.

Salinas, Francisco de (1513–90) Spanish organist and music theorist. Salinas, who was born at Burgos, went blind about the age of ten. He studied philosophy and classics at Salamanca and then entered the service of Pedro Sarmiento de Salinas, who in 1538 became a cardinal. Salinas accompanied his employer to Rome, where he was ordained a priest. He became organist at the vice-regal chapel at Naples (1533–58), and in 1559 organist at Sigüenza cathedral. He later became organist at León and, in 1567, professor of music at Salamanca. Salinas's theoretical work, *De musica libri septem* (1577) deals with the questions of consonant and dissonant intervals and proportions.

Salt War (1540) A rebellion by the city of Perugia against Pope *Paul III's authority. In 1538 Pope Paul III raised the price of salt by 50 per cent throughout the Papal States. Perugia claimed his action violated an agreement not to increase its tax burdens, but the pope rejected this claim and excommunicated the city (March 1539). The Perugians chose twenty-five citizens as leaders and put Ridolfo Baglioni in command of their army.

Paul III sent his son, Pierluigi Farnese, to Perugia with 13 000 soldiers. After minor skirmishes the Perugians submitted to papal power. Perugia had to accept rule by a papal legate and to pay for the construction of Paul III's fortress, the Rocca Paolina, in their city.

Salutati, Lino Coluccio (1331–1406) Italian humanist and politician. Salutati was born near Lucca and educated in rhetoric at Bologna. He became chancellor of Florence in 1375. Salutati rejected Petrarch's abstract patriotism and for thirty years was an active politician. He united *studia humanitatis* with the life of action and this had a profound influence on the development of Renaissance Florence. His voluminous correspondence has still not been fully edited. In 1392 he arranged for an ancient manuscript of Cicero's *Epistolae ad familiares* to be copied; this work made a lasting impact on Renaissance concepts of the interaction between literary culture and political activity. Salutati accumulated a large library – over 800 volumes, 111 of which are still extant and identified – and he opened it to scholars. In his youth he wrote poetry and he always maintained the superiority of poetry to prose. His major work was an allegorical treatment of the labours of *Hercules, begun 1378–83 and left incomplete at his death. He was not a fruitful scholar and he knew only a few words of Greek but he was instrumental in bringing the Greek teacher *Chrysoloras to Florence.

Salviati, Francesco (Il Cecchino; 1510–63) Italian painter. He was born in Florence and having studied with *Andrea del Sarto, he moved to Rome, where he was patronized in the early 1530s by Cardinal Giovanni Salviati, whose surname he adopted. In 1539 he went to Venice via Parma, where the paintings of *Parmigianino influenced him. Other influences on his work were *Michelangelo, *Pontormo, and the Venetians. He became a notable portrait painter and one of the leading fresco painters of the Florentine-Roman school. He decorated part of the Palazzo Vecchio in Florence in the 1540s, and in 1554 he was invited to the French court, but his restless nature brought him back to Rome the following year. His most important work in Rome was a set of frescoes in the Palazzo Farnese.

Salviati, Leonardo (1540–89) Italian scholar and academician. Born into an eminent Florentine family, Salviati studied under Piero *Vettori and rapidly established himself in literary circles, first publishing a *Dialogo dell'amicizia* (c. 1560), indebted to Cicero's *De amicitia*. His life's work, the promotion of the Tuscan vernacular, was announced in his *Orazione in lode della fiorentina favella* (1564) delivered before the Accademia Fiorentina. In the funeral oration for Benedetto *Varchi (1565), Salviati revised the definition of *humanism to include, in addition to classicists, those teaching and writing the language of Florence. A purist for whom Boccaccio was the ideal model, Salviati criticized Tasso's style on the publication of *Gerusalemme liberata* (1581). He was one of the founders of the *Accademia della Crusca, taking the academic name l'Infarinato ("the one covered with flour"), and his linguistic views were effectively embodied in the Cruscan *Vocabolario* (1612). He produced an expurgated version of the *Decameron* (1582), not from prudishness but in order to end suppression of the text (it had been placed on the Index in 1559) and restore its influence. Of continuing interest are his linguistic comments in *Avvertimenti della lingua sopra'l Decamerone* (*Remarks on the Language of the Decameron*; 1584–86). He also wrote two comedies, *Il granchio* (*The Crab*; 1566) and *La spina* (*The Thorn*; 1592). *See also questione della lingua*; vernacular.

Sánchez Coelho, Alonso *see* Coelho, Alonso Sánchez.

Sangallo family Italian architects. The family originated in the vicinity of Florence. Giuliano (c. 1443–1516), who was also a sculptor in wood and a military engineer, was a follower of Brunelleschi, whose influence is clear on several of Giuliano's buildings. Giuliano's church of Sta Maria delle Carceri, Prato (1485–91) combines features of Brunelleschi's Pazzi chapel in Florence and of Alberti's S Sebastiano in Mantua. As Lorenzo de' Medici's favourite architect, Giuliano also executed work for the Medici family in Florence, notably the villa at Poggia a Caiano (1485), and designed Florence's defensive fortifications (1478). Other works include designs for St Peter's in Rome, as Bramante's successor, and for the façade of Brunelleschi's S Lorenzo in Florence (1516). Giuliano's son Francesco (1494–1576), known as Il Margotta, was also active as a sculptor and medallist.

Antonio I (1455–1535), Giuliano's younger brother and pupil, also executed work as a military engineer but is best known for his one great work, the church of the Madonna di S Biagio at Montepulciano (c. 1518–29). This dramatic classical building draws on Giuliano's church at Prato but is much more powerful in impact, despite the fact that it was never finished. Antonio II (1483–1546), the nephew of Giuliano and Antonio I, was influenced chiefly by Bramante for whom he worked in Rome (c. 1503). He undertook several projects

355

for the Farnese family, including the initial stages of the Palazzo *Farnese. Other works include designs for St Peter's, of which he was an architect from 1520, and the Palazzo del Banco di S Spirito (1523–34) in Rome. Another member of the Sangallo clan was Antonio I's nephew Aristotele (1481–1551), also called Bastiano, who was a painter and theatre decorator at the Medici court.

Sanmicheli, Michele (1484–1559) Italian architect. The son of a Veronese architect, Giovanni Sanmicheli, he trained at a very early age in Rome, where he was influenced by *Bramante, *Raphael, and the *Sangallo family. From 1509 to 1528 he worked in Orvieto as *capo-mastro* (master builder) of the cathedral. Among his works in Orvieto is Capella Petrucci in the church of S Domenico. Returning to Verona, he began a career as a military architect, working in an elaborate mannerist style throughout the Venetian empire and. in Cyprus and Crete. His two fortified gates in Verona, the Porta Nuova and the Porta Palio (1533–41), are among his best works. From the 1530s Sanmicheli also built a number of palaces, mainly in Verona, showing the influence of Bramante, *Giulio Romano, and Roman antiquity. Notable examples are the Bevilacqua, Canossa, and Pompei palaces.

Sannazaro, Jacopo (1457–1530) Italian poet. Of aristocratic birth, Sannazaro spent almost all his life in or near his native Naples. With the backing of *Pontano he became a member of the Neapolitan Academy, taking the academic name Actius Syncerus. King Federico also recognized his erudition, giving him the Villa Mergellina in 1499. He remained devoted to the Aragonese royal house after its downfall and followed the king into exile in France in 1501, returning to Mergellina after Federico's death in 1504. He thereafter lived in retirement and was buried in Sta Maria del Parto in a tomb he had himself designed.

Sannazaro's earliest poetry, about a hundred Petrarchan sonnets and *canzoni*, was published posthumously (*Rime*, 1530). By the end of the 1480s he had completed most of his major work, the pastoral romance *L'Arcadia*, in which poetic eclogues alternate with prose narrative. It appeared in some fifty editions in the sixteenth century, from 1504 onwards. Initially depicting the tranquil idyllic world of shepherds, the poem shifts to a more dramatic and tragic mood with the introduction of themes of mutability, unrequited love, and political protest. The principal figure, Sincero, suffers from *melancholia, the first of many heroes thus afflicted. Although anticipated by Boccaccio's *Ameto* (1342), *L'Arcadia*, which rifled virtually the entire classical heritage of bucolic poetry, estab-

lished the *pastoral in European verse for the next two centuries. Sannazaro's Latin poems, influenced by Pontano, are among the outstanding examples of the Renaissance. These include epigrams and three books of *Elegies* (1535), five *Eclogae piscatoriae* (1526), in which fishermen replace the conventional shepherds, and *De partu virginis* (*On the Parturition of the Virgin*; 1526), a Christian epic in Virgilian hexameters dedicated to Pope Clement VII.

Sano di Pietro (Ansano di Pietro di Mencio; 1406–81) Italian painter. Born in Siena, Sano di Pietro was a pupil of *Sassetta and *Gentile da Fabriano and established a reputation for his decorative and religious paintings and illustrations. His large body of work includes altarpieces, panels, predellas, and numerous scenes from the life of St Bernardino, of whom he was a follower. Most notable of these is the *Sermon of St Bernardino* (Siena cathedral); other works are the *Coronation of the Virgin* (Palazzo Pubblico, Siena) and *St Francis receiving the Stigmata* (Nantes).

Sansovino, Andrea (Andrea Contucci; c. 1460–1529) Italian sculptor and architect. He was born at Monte S Sovino, near Siena, and having trained in Florence under Antonio *Pollaiuolo and *Bertoldo he worked there until 1491, when he was sent by Lorenzo de' Medici to Portugal. The years 1493–96 he spent in Florence working on the baptistery and he then returned to Portugal until 1499, but very little is known of the reason for his two visits there. After his eventual return to Florence he began one of his best-known works: the *Baptism of Christ* over the central door of the baptistery. The style of this work, which was completed by Danti nearly seventy years later, reflects the transition to the High Renaissance. It was, however, during his stay in Rome (1502–12) that he executed his most famous works: the tombs in Sta Maria del Popolo of the cardinals Ascanio Sforza (1505) and Girolamo della Rovere (1507). These were influential works and the sleeping attitudes of the deceased were an innovation that was widely copied. In his later years Sansovino worked mainly in Loreto, supervising decorative and building work. He died in Monte S Sovino.

Sansovino, Jacopo (Jacopo Tatti; 1486–1570) Italian sculptor and architect. A Florentine by birth, he was the pupil and most important follower of Andrea *Sansovino, whose name he adopted. In 1505 he went to Rome to carry out a commission for Pope Julius II to restore ancient statues. With the Florentine architect Giuliano *Sangallo he also studied examples of ancient architecture. Before his move to Venice in 1527,

JACOPO SANSOVINO
The library of S Marco (Bibliotheca Marciana) is housed in the Libreria Sansoviniana on the Piazzetta, Venice. Begun by Sansovino in 1536, it was eventually completed by Scamozzi in the 1580s.

Sansovino worked in Florence and then again in Rome, producing mainly sculptures; some of these showed the influence of *Michelangelo, while others derived more from ancient models and from the style of Andrea Sansovino. However, like many other artists, he fled after the sack of Rome in 1527 and two years after his arrival in Venice he was made chief architect of the city. It was in this post, which he held until his death, that he carried out the designs for which he is most famous. Chief among these was the library of S Marco (1536), one of the major architectural works of the sixteenth century and one which *Palladio described as the richest and most ornate building since antiquity. Sansovino's other designs in Venice include the Palazzo Corner della Ca' Grande (1533) and the Zecca (mint) (1537). His most famous sculptures are the large statues of Mars and Neptune (1554–56) on the Scala dei Giganti of the doge's palace, which show his severe late style. He remained an exponent of the restrained style of the High Renaissance despite the increasing dominance of Mannerism in Italy.

Santi di Tito (1536–1603) Italian painter. He was born at Borgo S Sepolcro, near Florence, and was trained by *Bronzino and then probably by *Bandinelli. He also studied in Rome, where he was influenced by the Roman masters and by antiquity, before returning to settle in Florence. *Vasari says that he painted in the Belvedere of the Vatican and on the catafalque of *Michelangelo but his best-known works are to be seen in the churches of Florence, such as his *Madonna* in S Salvatore and *Burial of Christ* in S Giuseppe. Many of his paintings are notable for their use of architectural perspectives. He was also a portrait painter and there are examples in the Uffizi.

Santillana, Íñigo López de Mendoza, Marqués de (1398–1458) Spanish, poet, critic, and patron. The son of the admiral of Castile and nephew of *López de Ayala, Santillana was born at Carrión de los Condes, near Burgos. The most powerful man in Castile after his defeat of the Infantes Juan of Navarre and Enrique of Aragon at the battle of Olmedo (1445), he also led the successful opposition to the constable Álvaro de *Luna, the favourite of King John II. Though he could not read Latin or Greek, he collected classical manuscripts and formed a great library at his palace, open to all who wished to use it. He commissioned translations of the *Iliad*, *Aeneid*, Seneca's tragedies, and the *Divine Comedy* and had Petrarch's *Canzoniere* copied in the original. The *Prohemio* introducing a selection of his own poems sent to Don Pedro, the constable of Portugal, is the first work of literary criticism in Spanish (*Prohemio é carta… envió al condestable de Portugal*; 1449). In it he calls for a patron of Iberian poets, discusses the importance of studying Italian and French models, while ranking poetry in Latin and Greek highest (cultivated vernacular poetry is only middling and popular ballads are lowest in rank). Despite this judgment, his own most memorable verses are short lyrics belonging to the popular troubadour tradition, especially ten *serranillas*, poems similar to the *pastourelle*, in which a knight encounters a mountain girl (a *serrana*). His forty-two less successful *Sonetos fechos al itálico modo* (1438–58) are the first Petrarchan sonnets in Spanish. He also wrote a number of longer allegorical, dream-vision, and didactic poems, mainly in octosyllabic verse.

Saravia, Hadrian à (1531–1613) Protestant theologian. Born in Hesdin, Artois, of Hispano-Flemish parentage, Saravia came to England as a religious refugee in 1559. He interspersed periods serving as a minister in the Netherlands with ten years as a schoolmaster in Guernsey and Southampton (1563–66, 1571–78). He settled in England permanently in 1587, and wrote a number of important tracts defending episcopacy and the Anglican Church settlement. His *De diversis ministrorum evangelii gradibus* (1590) provoked a response from *Beza, to which Saravia in turn replied (*Defensio*, 1594). A further treatise of 1593 (*De imperandi authoritate*) was an early exposition of the divine right of kings. Saravia also contributed to the new translation of the Bible which became the Authorized Version of 1611.

Sarpi, Fra Paolo (1552–1623) Italian philosopher, historian, and theologian. Sarpi, who was born at Venice, entered the Servite order around 1565, was elected provincial in 1579, and later held the office of procurator-general (1585–88). His friendly relations with Protestants, including the British ambassador to the Venetian republic, Sir Henry Wotton, made him suspect in Rome. He also maintained an extensive international circle of correspondents. In 1606 he became theological counsellor to the republic during its dispute with Pope Paul V concerning secular controls over ecclesiastical buildings and the donation of property to the Church and he helped to render the papal interdict on the Venetians ineffective, though at the cost of his own excommunication (1607). His *History of the Council of Trent* was published in Latin and English in 1619, strongly influencing northern views on papal machinations at the council. His letters indicate sympathy with some forms of Protestantism, but his secret *Pensieri* suggest an altogether more sceptical outlook on Christianity. He had a genuine interest in contemporary science, especially optics.

Sarto, Andrea del *see* Andrea del Sarto.

Sassetta, Stefano di Giovanni (1392–c. 1450) Italian painter. Probably trained in his native Siena, Sassetta was influenced by the International Gothic style of *Masolino and *Gentile da Fabri-

SASSETTA The Betrothal of St Francis to Lady Poverty. *The decorative charm of Sassetta's style was a particular characteristic of the Sienese school, of which Sassetta was a leading figure. (Musée Condé, Chantilly)*

ano, which he combined with Florentine realism. His first work was an altarpiece for the Arte della Lana chapel in Siena (1423–26), which was followed by another altarpiece, the *Madonna of the Snow* (1423–26; Contini Bonacossi Collection, Florence), painted for Siena cathedral. His masterpiece was the double-sided altarpiece (1437–44) executed for S Francesco, Borgo S Sepolcro, which includes panels illustrating the legend of St Francis (National Gallery, London and Musée Condé, Chantilly) and fuses religious sincerity with naturalistic observation. Other works include a polyptych painted for S Domenico at Cortona (c. 1437) and scenes illustrating the legend of St Anthony Abbot (Yale University Art Gallery, New Haven). Noted for his mystical imagination, Sassetta bridged the gap between the traditional Gothic style and the humanist elements of the High Renaissance. He died in Siena.

Satire Ménippée A satirical pamphlet in prose and verse published in 1594 by opponents of the

French Catholic League. A parody of the league's *États géneraux*, convoked (1593) to elect a king other than Henry of Navarre, the *Satire Ménippée* was compiled by Jean Leroy, a canon of Rouen, in collaboration with a number of scholars, lawyers, ecclesiastics, and others, notably Pierre Pithou, Jacques Gillot, Nicolas Rapin, Florent Chrestien, and Jean *Passerat. The most important and influential element of the work, a solemn and eloquent harangue by a representative of the Third Estate, is preceded by a burlesque introduction, satirical attacks on prominent members of the league, and a series of comic speeches; the final part of the composition takes the form of a collection of satires and epigrams. The immense success of the *Satire Ménippée* is attributable not only to its literary merit but also to its strategic publication at the moment of the league's final defeat.

Saturn In Roman mythology, the god of agriculture, who was later identified with the Greek Kronos. His reign, after he had overthrown his father Uranus, was a legendary Golden Age, the *Saturnia regna* celebrated by Virgil in the fourth eclogue. He was believed to be the father of Jupiter (Zeus) and several of the other major deities in the pagan pantheon.

In astrological terms the planet Saturn was predominantly a malign force. The metal associated with it was lead, and the qualities of slowness, coldness, and heaviness were supposed to manifest themselves in the characters of those under the planet's influence. In certain cases the gloomy temperament of the saturnine man was accompanied by intellectual and creative prowess (*see* melancholia).

Savery, Roelant (c. 1576–1639) Flemish painter. He was born in Courtrai but studied in Amsterdam under Jacques Savery (died 1602), who was probably his brother. Around 1604 he entered the employment of Emperor *Rudolf II and spent about eight years in Prague, where he became one of the emperor's favourite artists in the symbolic mannerist mode that Rudolf particularly liked. Savery specialized in precise depiction of animals, observing from life some of the more exotic species in the emperor's menagerie; he painted at least twenty variations on the theme of *Orpheus and the animals, and his famous *Paradise* (National Gallery, Prague) is another example of his fantastic *mélanges* of exotic and domestic birds and beasts. He also produced some fine mountain landscapes, the fruit of travels in the Alps and Tyrol (1606–08) at the emperor's behest. His exquisite flower paintings are among the earliest of their kind, although not so frequent in his prolific output. After working for Rudolf's successor, Matthias, in

Vienna (1612–16), Savery returned to the Netherlands and settled at Utrecht in 1619, where his fame and ability brought him many admirers and followers.

Savile, Sir Henry (1549–1622) English mathematician and humanist. Savile was born at Bradley, near Halifax, and educated at Oxford university where he was appointed warden of Merton College in 1585. He also served Queen *Elizabeth as Greek tutor and Latin secretary, and from 1596 he was provost of Eton. He wrote or edited a number of books, the most substantial being his eight-volume Greek edition of St John Chrysostom (1610–13) to which he contributed £8000 of his own money. He also helped his friend Bodley to found the *Bodleian Library. He is best remembered, however, for his attempt to reintroduce science into Oxford by founding in 1619 the Savilian chairs of geometry and astronomy, the first recognizably scientific chairs to be established at any English university.

Savini, Guido di (Guido Andries; died 1541) Italian potter. He first worked at Castel Durante (now Urbania), near Urbino, but by 1508 had moved to Antwerp, where he introduced the making of *majolica. Three of his sons were later responsible for transferring the technique to England.

Savoldo, Giovanni Girolamo (c. 1480–c. 1548) Italian painter. Born in Brescia, Savoldo trained in Florence but worked chiefly in Venice, apart from a few years spent in Milan (c. 1529–35). He was influenced by Titian, Giorgione, Bellini, and Lotto and became known for his skilful handling of light effects, especially in night scenes. His masterpiece, the *Transfiguration* (Uffizi), anticipates the realism of Caravaggio, while other paintings such as *Magdalene* (National Gallery, London) and *Gaston de Foix* (Louvre), which follows the contemporary fashion of linking painting with sculpture, illustrate Savoldo's mastery of texture and materials. Other works include the *Nativity* (1527; Hampton Court), the altarpiece for Sta Maria, Verona (1523), and *St Jerome* (National Gallery, London).

Savonarola, Girolamo (1452–98) Italian preacher and politician. Savonarola was born in Ferrara and became a Dominican friar at Bologna in 1475. From 1482 he lectured at the convent of S Marco, Florence, of which he became prior in 1491. Despite the patronage of Lorenzo de' Medici, he preached in favour of ecclesiastical reform and against the high-handed and materialistic rule of the Medici; the emotional power of his sermons made him a valuable ally for the forces in Florence that brought about the exile of the Medici in 1494. His moral teaching was narrow-minded and puritanical, and during his ascendancy he presided over bonfires of "vanities", exercised strict control over religious art, and tried to eliminate gambling and licentious dress and behaviour. His influence was extraordinary, especially with the young.

He became the leader of a republic, set up with Florence's ancient democratic institutions that had fallen into disuse under the Medici. His actions, especially his support for Charles VIII's invasion of Italy, incurred the enmity of the duke of Milan, Pope Alexander VI, and the Franciscans. He also ignored papal briefs summoning him to Rome, ordering him to return to Bologna, and forbidding him to preach. In 1496 he was deprived of his post at S Marco by the amalgamation of the congregation with that of another church. He responded by calling for a general council of the Church, maintaining that it could and should depose the pope. One of his disciples unwisely accepted a challenge to resort to ordeal by fire, to settle his disputes with his opponents; this proved a fiasco, and the tide of popular opinion turned against Savonarola. In spite of the fact that he was an orthodox Catholic in all matters but papal authority, he was tried for heresy, tortured, and condemned by the ecclesiastical authorities to be hanged and burnt.

Among his works are Latin poems against worldly and ecclesiastical corruption, *De ruina mundi* (1472) and *De ruina ecclesiae* (1475), a tract *Della semplicita della vita Christiana* (1496), and writings against astrology.

Savoy, house of The Franco-Italian noble family originally based on the western Alps, where France, Italy, and Switzerland now converge. The founder of the family, Humbert I, held the county of Savoy and other territories east of the Rhône River and south of Lake Geneva in the eleventh century. His successors expanded their inheritance by marriage, conquest, and diplomacy until they eventually ruled Italy (1861–1945). Amadeus VII (count 1383–91) acquired Nice (1388). Amadeus VIII (1383–1451), who annexed Piedmont, was created duke of Savoy by Emperor Sigismund (1416), but abdicated (1439) to become the (anti)pope Felix V (1439–49). The fortunes of the house of Savoy then declined and France occupied most of its territory (1536–59). After the restoration of Savoy to its ruling house (1559) Emanuel Philibert (duke 1553–80) reconstructed and enlarged his inheritance. He encouraged commercial and agricultural development and successfully welded the feudal lords and cities of Savoy into a centralized state by the time of the accession of his son *Carlo Emanuele I.

Saxon Confession (1551) A statement of Lutheran doctrine, drawn up by *Melanchthon at the request of the Emperor Charles V, for submission to the Council of *Trent. It was less conciliatory than the Confession of *Augsburg. The argument was developed from two articles of the Creed, concerning the forgiveness of sins and the Church; it was held that the former excluded the doctrine of merit, or justification by works, and that the latter referred to a spiritual community of believers. The principle that the sacraments are valid only in use was maintained.

Saxton, Christopher (c. 1542–1611) English cartographer. Saxton, who was born in Yorkshire, is renowned as the compiler of the first provincial atlas of any country. In 1572 the MP and court official Thomas Seckford commissioned Saxton to map the counties of England and Wales, an undertaking supported by the queen herself who granted a royal licence in 1577. Enhanced by expert engraving, the maps were published as *An Atlas of the Counties of England and Wales* in 1579. The atlas influenced English cartography for many years. Saxton's subsequent works included an engraved map of England and Wales (1583).

Scala, Bartolommeo (1430–97) Italian humanist. Born the son of a miller at Florence, Scala received a sound education and studied law first in Florence and then in Milan under the humanist Francesco *Filelfo. He was appointed to a post in the household of his patron Pierfrancesco de' Medici before becoming secretary to the Parte Guelfa (1459). Supported by the Medici, he held the chancellorship of Florence from 1465 during the lifetime of Lorenzo de' Medici, but later wrote a defence of the republic under Savonarola. He was knighted (1484) by Pope Innocent VIII. In addition to some unremarkable philosophical works, he wrote (c. 1480–97) a history of Florence from the foundation of the city to 1450.

Scaliger, Joseph Justus (1540–1609) French scholar and editor of Italian descent. He was educated briefly at Bordeaux but mostly by his father Julius Caesar *Scaliger. Though his training was mainly in the classics he also developed an interest in science. His father disapproved of Greek and it was not until the latter's death that the younger Scaliger, aged nineteen, went to Paris to learn Greek. He mastered the language with amazing speed and within two years had read all the available Greek literature, translating much of it into Latin. He also studied oriental languages.

He was attached to an aristocratic Poitevin family for thirty years (1563–93) and with one of them travelled in Italy collecting inscriptions. He became a Calvinist (1562 or 1566) and was involved on the fringes of the religious wars. In 1593 he went to Leyden where he held a non-teaching post until his death. Scaliger is a giant among classical scholars; he had an outstanding knowledge of archaic Latin, edited many texts, and made fundamental contributions in several areas of study, notably chronology. His *Thesaurus temporum* (1606) made the ancient sources available with a brilliantly intuitive commentary.

Scaliger, Julius Caesar (1484–1558) Italian humanist. Scaliger was born at Riva, Lake Garda, and, according to his own account, from the age of twelve he served Emperor Maximilian as a soldier for seventeen years before studying at the university of Bologna. He migrated to France (1526) and settled at Agen. In the quarrel with *Erasmus over Ciceronianism he championed the Ciceronians' cause. He published several volumes of Latin verse and his *Poetices* (1561) was a key text in Renaissance literary theory, especially in its formulation of Aristotle's doctrine of the unities in tragedy. His main importance is as a philosopher; his commentaries on Aristotle and Theophrastus show acute power of reasoning and wide knowledge but retain a fundamental acceptance of the authority of Aristotle.

Scamozzi, Vincenzo (1552–1616) Italian architect and theorist. Born in Vicenza, Scamozzi was trained by his father and executed important commissions in Rome and Padua. He was greatly influenced by Andrea *Palladio, three of whose buildings he completed after Palladio's death, including the Villa *Rotonda on which Scamozzi modelled his own Rocca Pisani at Lonigo (1576). Scamozzi's original works incorporate many Palladian features, notably in the Procuratie Nuove in Venice, begun in 1584. He was also the architect of two theatres, the Teatro Olimpico in Vicenza (1584) and the Teatro di Vespasiano Gonzaga in Sabbioneta (1588). Scamozzi travelled widely and was the author of an influential treatise, mainly written in the 1590s, *L'idea dell'architettura universale* (1615); this summarized his views of baroque art and had a considerable impact upon English neoclassical architecture. He also produced designs for Salzburg cathedral and the Italian fortress of Palmanova.

Scève, Maurice (c. 1501–c. 1564) French poet. The son of a magistrate, Scève made his name in the literary world with his alleged discovery of the tomb of *Petrarch's Laura at Avignon and with

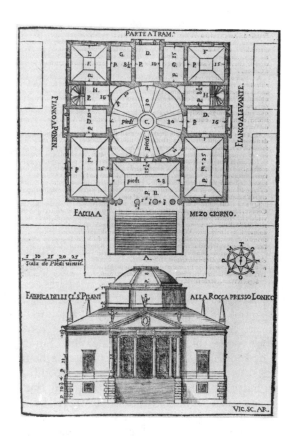

SCAMOZZI *The symmetry of the exterior of the Rocca Pisani at Lonigo, near Vicenza, is repeated in the plan of the interior, as shown in an illustration in Scamozzi's architectural treatise.*

his first anthology, *Blasons* (c. 1536). He became leader of a group of poets in his native Lyons, whose other members included Antoine *Héroet, Pernette du Guillet (c. 1520–45), and Louise *Labé: Pernette du Guillet is believed to have been the inspiration for much of Scève's poetry. *Délie, objet de plus haute vertu* (1544) is a series of 449 decasyllabic ten-line stanzas that deals in symbolic and metaphysical terms with the subject of love, and is heavily influenced by Plato and Petrarch; the title of the poem has been the subject of some speculation, "Délie" being interpreted by certain scholars as an anagram of "l'idée" ("the idea"). Scève's other works include the pastoral poem *La Saulsaye, eglogue de la vie solitaire* (1547) and *Microcosme* (1562), an epic account of the fall and redemption of mankind.

Schardt, Jan Jorisz. van der (c. 1530–81) Netherlands sculptor. Born at Nijmegen and initially trained in the Netherlands, Schardt was active in Italy during the 1560s. After executing works for Emperor Maximilian II and King Frederick II of

Denmark, he had arrived in Nuremberg by 1570. There he executed such works as the life-size terracotta bust of Willibald Imhof (Berlin) and the painted faience medallions of Paul von Praun (now divided between Nuremberg and Stuttgart). Although the latter is known to have owned dozens of terracottas and some bronzes by Schardt, very few of these can be traced. Schardt's severe realism owes more to the Italian tradition than to his experiences in Italy. Although a foreigner, he may be counted as the last major luminary in the sixteenth-century Nuremberg school of sculptors.

Schäufelein, Hans Leonhart (c. 1480–c. 1538) German painter and illustrator. A pupil of *Dürer in his native Nuremberg, Schäufelein clearly shows his master's influence, especially in his early work. He also worked for Hans *Holbein the Elder in Augsburg for a while (c. 1509). In 1515 he became a citizen of Nördlingen, his home until his death. His own style, particularly suited to characterization and portrait painting, was imaginative, sensitive, and tasteful. His paintings include a number of altarpieces and paintings for churches, such as the *Dead Christ* for Nuremberg cathedral, and a fresco of the siege of Bethulia for Nördlingen town hall. A gifted book illustrator, and one of the most prolific of his time, he drew the designs for numerous woodcuts and engravings, although he did not execute them himself. He provided many of the illustrations for Emperor Maximilian I's book *Theuerdank* (1517).

Scheiner, Christoph (1573–1650) German astronomer. A prominent Jesuit, Scheiner was appointed professor of mathematics and Hebrew at Ingolstadt university in 1610. He served later at the court of Maximilian I, Elector of Bavaria, and in Rome from 1624 to 1633. In 1612, under the pseudonym Apelles, he published the first account of sunspots. The work led to a long and bitter controversy with *Galileo. The issue was revived once more by Scheiner in his *Rosa ursina* (1626–30) and ended only with Galileo's summons to Rome in 1632. Scheiner himself, it was widely believed, was not unconnected with the decision to prosecute his rival. Scheiner was also one of the first scholars, in his *Oculus* (1619), to identify the retina as the seat of vision.

schiacciato (or *stiacciato*) A technique of marble carving in a very low relief, evolved by *Donatello and also practised in the Quattrocento by *Desiderio da Settignano and *Agostino di Duccio. Despite the shallowness of the carving, the sculptors' understanding of perspective enabled them to achieve effects of depth comparable to those produced by contemporary painters.

Schiavone, Andrea Meldolla (c. 1515–63) Italian painter. Born in Sebénico, Dalmatia, Schiavone was known as "the Slavonian" on account of his origin. He settled in Venice, where he produced a number of religious and mythological scenes and may have been a pupil of Parmigianino, whose influence is apparent upon his engravings and etchings. He combined this mannerist element with the rich colours of Titian in a style that was much admired by Tintoretto and imitated by him in his early works. Schiavone also painted several secular subjects and portraits, including pictures of philosophers in the great hall of the Bibliotheca *Marciana, Venice.

Schidone, Bartolommeo (c. 1570–1615) Italian painter. He was born at Modena, but little else is known about Schidone's life. He may have received his training under the *Carracci brothers but his work bears little resemblance to theirs and indicates more the influences of *Correggio and *Caravaggio. He spent most of his life in Parma, apart from the period 1602–06, when he worked for the duke of Modena. His most important work in Modena was his series of emblematical figures in the Palazzo Pubblico depicting the history of Coriolanus. Many of his other paintings are in the museums of Parma and Naples. His later works reveal the influence of baroque trends in Rome. He is said to have been a gambler and to have died in Parma after amassing in one night a huge debt that he could not pay off.

Schmalkaldic Articles (1537) A statement drawn up by Luther at the request of John Frederick, Elector of Saxony, for submission to a council of the Church to be held at Mantua. The first part, which was not controversial, dealt with the Creeds; the second, concerning the office of Christ, attacked the doctrine of the Mass and other Roman teachings; the third was about differences between Protestants in eucharistic doctrine. An appendix by *Melanchthon conceded the supremacy of the pope by human right. The articles were approved by a convention of theologians at Schmalkald, in Germany and, though never formally adopted by the evangelical churches, they were widely accepted.

Schmalkaldic League An alliance of Protestants formed in 1531 at Schmalkald, in Germany, against Charles V. It united Lutherans and Zwinglians, north German princes and southern cities, including Strasbourg. It was ruined by the defection of Maurice of Saxony and defeated by Charles at the battle of *Mühlberg in 1547.

Scholarius, George *see* Gennadius.

Schongauer, Martin (c. 1440–91) German engraver and painter. He was the son of Kaspar Schongauer, a goldsmith from Augsburg who had settled in Colmar, where Martin was born and spent most of his life. The only painting definitely attributed to him is the altarpiece for the church of St Martin, Colmar, the so-called *Madonna in the Rose Bower* (1473); this shows the attention with which Schongauer must have studied the work of fifteenth-century Flemish artists, especially Rogier van der *Weyden. Schongauer's main importance resides in his innovative copper engravings of religious subjects; 113 of them are known, signed with his initials. These were widely disseminated, spreading Schongauer's influence far beyond the school for engravers he ran at Colmar; some of the works of the *Little Masters of Nuremberg show a clear debt to him, and had it not been for Schongauer's death *Dürer would have carried out his intention of studying with him when he visited Colmar in 1492.

Schwabach, Articles of *see under* Augsburg, Confession of.

Schwänke Comic anecdotes written in prose or verse, collections of which were popular reading matter in fifteenth- and sixteenth-century Germany. They often centred on the exploits of legendary rogues, such as the hero of *Till Eulenspiegel* (1515), a witty mischief-maker who revelled in tricking good burghers. Another extremely successful collection was *Das Rollwagenbüchlein* (1555) by Jörg *Wickram. During the sixteenth century the *Schwank*, in the form of the humorous everyday scene, also served as the basis for drama in Shrovetide plays (*Fastnachtspiele*). The *Schwank* reflected the shift of emphasis in German literature from courtly chivalric concerns to the homelier ones of town and village. It also represented one of the earliest forms of German prose literature, which scarcely existed before the thirteenth century. Hans Sachs, the cobbler of Nuremberg (1494–1576), was a master of the *Schwank*. *See also facetiae.*

Schwarz, Hans (c. 1492–post-1532) German medallist and sculptor. Schwarz was born in Augsburg but travelled extensively in northern Europe. A talented portraitist, he produced numerous portrait medallions in the Italian style, showing faces in profile or three-quarters view. As a sculptor, he worked particularly in low relief, using fine stone, and followed the style of paintings of the period by including effects of perspective and even elements of landscape. His work includes sculptures for the *Fugger family chapel (executed from sketches by Dürer).

science *see* natural philosophy.

Scorel, Jan van (1495–1562) Netherlands painter. He was born at Schoorl, near Alkmaar, and was probably first trained by Cornelis Buys the Elder in Alkmaar. Scorel was then apprenticed to Jacob Cornelisz. van Oostsanen in Amsterdam in 1512. In about 1517/18 he may have visited Gossaert in Utrecht. In 1519 he undertook an extensive trip to Carinthia via Basle and Nuremberg, where he may have worked briefly in Dürer's shop. In Obervellach, in Carinthia, he executed an altarpiece heavily influenced by Dürer. By 1520 Scorel was in Venice, whence he took ship for Jerusalem. His *Entry of Christ into Jerusalem* (1527; Utrecht) includes a vista of the holy city which reveals a personal study of its topography. In 1521 Scorel was back in Italy, first at Venice and subsequently in Rome. The following year the Dutch Pope Adrian VI appointed him curator of the papal collection of antiquities in the Belvedere. However, Scorel's tenure was terminated by the pope's death (1523)

SCOREL Adam and Eve. (*Metropolitan Museum of Art (gift of Mrs Stanford White), New York*)

and he returned home. From 1524 he resided in Utrecht, save for short visits to the southern Netherlands and France and a period in Haarlem between 1527 and 1529/30.

Scorel was deeply influenced by a range of Italian artists, including Michelangelo, Raphael, Giorgione, and Palma Vecchio. His *Death of Cleopatra* (c. 1522; Amsterdam) repeats a formula of reclining female nude popular in Venice, but with a musculature reminiscent of Michelangelo's sculptures. While the composition of his *Baptism of Christ* (c. 1528; Haarlem) harks back to Dirk *Bouts in some respects, it includes figure types derived from both Raphael and antique art. His *Rest on the Flight* (c. 1530; Washington) incorporates a background heavily indebted to ancient Roman wall paintings, with which the artist would have become familiar as curator of the Belvedere. Scorel was also a fine portrait painter of both individual figures and groups. A key figure in the assimilation of Italian style in northern Europe, Scorel has a significance in the development of the sixteenth-century Dutch school second only to that of *Lucas van Leyden. The style of Scorel's pupil, Maarten van *Heemskerck, is a creative development of his own, but seems mannered and uneasy by comparison.

sculpture Like its sister arts, *painting and *architecture, sculpture was a medium that gave tangible form to Renaissance ideals. Mirroring the growth of cultural and intellectual currents, the origins of Renaissance sculpture are found in those of the period itself. The newly matured humanist movement stimulated a historical self-consciousness which prompted comparisons of contemporary culture with that of the ancient Greeks and Romans. Ancient texts about art became a source of inspiration and a touchstone against which to measure artistic achievements. Verisimilitude, the imitation of nature, gained signal importance in the artists' vocabulary. Contemporaneously, the lay spirituality of the Franciscan movement gave force to the renewed interest in nature and man.

Monumental stone sculpture had been revived as a component of architectural decoration in the Romanesque period. Figural sculpture was reintroduced into the artistic vocabulary of Europe in the Gothic period principally through the evolution of portal jamb colonnettes into jamb figures. This process adumbrated the revival of the ancient Vitruvian association between the human form and the column. In Italy, ingrained classical traditions ensured that figures and reliefs on pulpits, tombs, and church façades had a greater independence from their architectural setting than did those on northern Gothic structures.

Classicism and Gothic naturalism combined in the art of Niccolò *Pisano, a sculptor from Apulia, working in Tuscany. His son, Giovanni *Pisano, a contemporary of Giotto, enlarged the expressive capabilities of figures. Quotations from classical sculpture continued to appear side by side with stylistic elements imported from the Gothic north throughout the Trecento. By the end of the century, the Italian and northern traditions merged momentarily, producing the phenomenon of the International Gothic style, whose chief exponent in the north was Claus *Sluter.

A series of commissions for public sculpture in Florence in the first decades of the Quattrocento was the catalyst for the emergence of new directions in sculpture. The protagonists were a group of young craftsmen, mostly trained as workers of precious metal or stone in the International Gothic style. Challenged to give tangible form to a new ideal of the individual – of man's special place in the world order – they carved and cast a race of heroes, saints, and gods and won acclaim for their own genius. This concept of virtu, represented by the image as well as the maker, became a leitmotif of Renaissance sculpture.

Within this context, two strains in sculpture emerged, a refined, elegant mode and a vigorous, classical one, sparked respectively by the different temperaments of the two leading artists, Lorenzo *Ghiberti and *Donatello. Throughout the century materials, motifs, and formats were reintroduced under the guidance of ancient art. Figures in classical *contrapposto stance, clothed or nude, life-size and over life-size, sometimes free-standing, reappeared. Artists in the service of the cult of the individual created portrait busts, equestrian statues, and a special brand of funerary monument for a clientele who wished to perpetuate their memory or to commemorate their achievements. *Donatello, a leader in these developments and undisputed creative genius of his generation, also evolved a new method of low-relief carving (*schiacciato). He took advantage of that method to offer provocative interpretations of traditional subjects, heightening psychic energy and incorporating the newly developed Brunelleschian one-point perspective into complex vistas. In addition to marble and bronze, terracotta was revived as a primary sculptural material; among the most important workshops, that of the *della Robbia family produced glazed, polychromed reliefs and statues, meant principally to decorate the coolly rational pietra serena and plaster spaces of the new architectural style. The third quarter of the century witnessed the emergence of a group of virtuoso marble carvers (*Desiderio da Settignano, Antonio *Rossellino, *Benedetto da Maiano) working in the so-called "sweet style". Perhaps best known for their reliefs of the smiling Virgin and Child, they focused their production on church furnishings, including pulpits and tabernacles. By the last quarter of the Quattrocento, technical mastery of materials and an emerging scientific knowlede of anatomy combined in a new ability on the part of sculptors to display the body in motion. A primary vehicle for the exploration of the figure in action (and in the round) was the bronze statuette, though experiments of this kind found their way into sculpture on a large scale as well. Leading the field were *Verrocchio and Antonio del *Pollaiuolo, masters who were distinguished by the fact that they were also painters. Greater facility gained through the combined use of drawings and models further enhanced the potential for experimentation.

The Tuscan style was disseminatd to other cultural centres; Donatello spent about a decade in Padua, while artists of lesser rank sought work in the courts of northern and southern Italy or in Rome. In most cases Quattrocento sculpture outside Tuscany was characterized by a more sharply exaggerated local classicism, meant to suggest ties to Roman and early Christian traditions specific to that area.

In general, fifteenth-century sculptors outside Italy continued working in a late Gothic idiom which featured figures of either tall, slender proportions or Sluteresque robustness swathed in drapery. The figures, for the most part, appear embedded in fantastic and elaborate Gothic settings as part of architectural schemes or church furnishings. Sculptors worked primarily in wood and stone; polychromy was a significant feature. Among the greatest northern sculptors are counted Hans Multscher (c. 1400–67), Nicolaus *Gerhaert von Leyden, Tilmann *Riemenschneider, Veit *Stoss, and Adam *Kraft. Of the sculpture that was independent of an architectural framework, votive figures, such as Pietà groups and Madonnas, were especially popular. In France the popularity of groups of near life-size figures in stone (representing, most typically, Entombments, as at Auch and Bourges) may have inspired a similar phenomenon in Italy, although in terracotta. Niccolò dell'*Arca exploited the latter medium, producing highly active figures charged with great expression. The appeal of tableaux vivants (which also included Annunciation and Nativity scenes) in polychromed terracotta, wood, or wax, is explained by their uncanny realistic qualities. This vogue culminated in the episodic set of tableaux of the life of the Virgin and of Christ at the Sacro Monte of Varallo in the Sesia valley northwest of Milan.

A number of conditions continued to affect the course of the development of sculpture in Italy, which was virtually dominated by the Florentines in the fifteenth and sixteenth centuries. The technological advances of the Quattrocento and the increasing significance of archaeological finds inspired a concept of perfection which characterizes the art of the sixteenth century. The study of collections of antiquities, like that of Lorenzo de' *Medici, inspired young sculptors in the 1490s to formulate a new ideal of beauty, grace, and harmony. The challenge not only to match but also to outdo antique sculpture prompted a shift to colossal scale in sculpture for public places and funerary projects. The relationship of sculpture and its architectural setting was tuned to a perfect harmony. The creative power of the artist, filtered through an aesthetic vision of perfection, provided the potential to surpass nature; expression of the artifice of art replaced verisimilitude as the primary objective. The evolution of art theory in the sixteenth century and the corollary notion of the artist-philosopher was critical to the formulation of the concept of the artist as genius and led to the establishment of academies of design by mid-century. *Michelangelo, the premier artist of the age and recognized master of painting, sculpture, and architecture, became the principal exponent of the concept of *disegno*, explaining it as the unifying factor among those arts. His avowed allegiance to sculpture above all secured the principal position in the hierarchy for this medium.

The political and religious climate following the sack of Rome in 1527 and in the wake of the *Counter-Reformation further affected artistic production. The strengthening of a powerful international aristocracy was mirrored by the growing importance of more localized Italian courts. Patrons favoured suave, attenuated figures crafted of precious materials which represented intellectualized encores of the work of Michelangelo, Raphael, and Leonardo, either on a grand scale or translated into decorative motifs on *objets de virtu*. *Cellini, Vincenzo *Danti, and Bartolommeo *Ammanati were among the most important exponents of this style. In contrast, the new Counter-Reform piety in Rome and strong tendencies towards realism in Venice tempered the excessive refinements of the *maniera* (see Mannerism) in those cultural centres.

From the late fifteenth century, but especialy in the sixteenth century, Italian artists in all media were called to work in the courts of England, France, Spain, Portugal, and Poland; artists from the north and from Spain travelled to Italy to gain firsthand experience. Most artistic production throughout Europe carried an Italianate stamp. In Germany, Konrad *Meit, for example, produced small statuettes in alabaster, bronze, and wood, classical in style and subject. Florentine mannerism enjoyed primacy at the French court, evoking a response from the talented native sculptors Jean *Goujon, Germain *Pilon, and Ligier *Richier.

Appropriately, in the last decades of the sixteenth century, northern and southern traditions fused in the work of the Flemish sculptor *Giambologna, who lived principally in Florence. His technical and compositional virtuosity represented a culmination of Renaissance ideals and set a course for the development of the European Baroque.

sea-beggars Dutch Calvinist privateers who played a vital part in the successful Dutch revolt against Spanish rule. They took their name from a scornful reference by a Spanish nobleman to Dutch petitioners for religious toleration in the Compromise of *Breda (1566). In 1572 they achieved an important breakthrough in their struggle against Spain when they took the port of Brill in the name of *William (I) the Silent. The conquest of Flushing soon followed. *See* Netherlands, Revolt of the.

Sebastiano del Piombo (Sebastiano Luciani; c. 1485–1547) Italian painter. Born in Venice, Sebastiano trained and studied under Palma Vecchio, Titian, Giovanni Bellini, and Giorgione. After Giorgione's death (1510) Sebastiano completed several of his paintings, while his own work *Salome* (1510; National Gallery, London) is clearly influenced by Giorgione's style. In 1511 Sebastiano settled in Rome, where he remained, apart from a brief period in Venice (1528–29). He became one of Raphael's circle, working upon the Villa *Farnesina, before falling out with Raphael and becoming an adherent of Michelangelo. Sebastiano's *Raising of Lazarus* (c. 1517–19; National Gallery, London) was painted for Cardinal Giulio de' Medici in direct competition with Raphael, while Michelangelo himself contributed the cartoon for Sebastiano's *Pietà* (c. 1520–25; Musico Civico, Viterbo). Sebastiano also painted a number of notable portraits, including those of Pope Clement VII (1526; Capodimonte, Naples; see Plate XXVII) and Cardinal Pole (c. 1537; Leningrad). In 1531 he received a papal sinecure as keeper of the curial seal (which was made of lead – hence his nickname "Piombo"); after this he executed few further works. Other major works include *St John Chrysostom with other Saints* (1510–11; S Giovanni Crisostomo, Venice), *Portrait of a Young Man* (1514; Uffizi), and *Holy Family with a Donor* (1517–18; National Gallery, London).

Secundus, Janus (Jean Second *or* Jan Nicolaesz. Everaerts; 1511–36) Netherlands poet. Secundus was born at The Hague into a distinguished Netherlands family and studied law at Bourges before becoming secretary (1533) to the archbishop of Toledo. It was while he was in Spain that he wrote his *Basia*, a series of amatory poems with Catullan undertones; written, like all Secundus's work, in elegant humanist Latin, the *Basia* has been translated into many languages. In 1534 Secundus accompanied Emperor Charles V to Tunis before returning briefly to the Netherlands to become secretary to the bishop of Utrecht. His increasing fame as a writer of Latin verse led Charles to offer him the post of private Latin secretary, but he died of fever near Tournai en route to join the emperor in Italy. Besides *Basia*, Secundus also wrote odes, epigrams, elegies, and an account of his travels. He was interested in painting and sculpture and several portrait medals have been attributed to him.

Sellaio, Jacopo del (1442–93) Italian painter. A Florentine by birth, Sellaio was known by the name that reflects his father's trade of saddlemaker. He was a pupil of Filippo Lippi and also influenced by Botticelli and Ghirlandaio. He is represented by Madonnas in the Palazzo Pitti, Florence, and in the Ca' d'Oro, Venice, and by panels depicting the triumphs of love, chastity, and time in the Museo Bandini, Fiesole.

Sendivogius, Michael (Michael Sendivow; 1556–post-1630) Polish alchemist. Sendivogius was widely known in his day as the possessor of a powder obtained from the Scot Alexander Seton (died 1604) and supposedly capable of transmuting lead into gold. Successful demonstrations were reportedly given to *Rudolf II in Prague and to King Sigismund of Poland in Warsaw. Shortly afterwards, in 1607, Sendivogius lost the remainder of Seton's dwindling stock of powder. Thereafter little is known of him until 1625 when he reappeared in Warsaw peddling a variety of nostrums. There was, however, a more serious side to Sendivogius. In such works as *Novum Lumen Chemicum* (1604; translated as *A New Light of Alchemy*, 1650) he developed a theory of metals which was to prove highly influential among a later generation of alchemists and chemists.

Seneca, Lucius Annaeus, the Younger (c. 4 BC–65 AD) Roman philosopher and dramatist. He was the son of the rhetorician Lucius Annaeus Seneca, the Elder (c. 55 BC–c. 37 AD), and became a leading Stoic philosopher in Rome, as well as participating in public life there. His literary reputation brought his appointment as tutor to Nero, over whom at first he exercised some beneficial influence, but he was eventually ordered by the emperor to commit suicide. His calmness and courage at his death contributed substantially to his standing as a moralist.

In the Middle Ages Seneca was known as the author of a book on natural phenomena but primarily for his philosophical dialogues, treatises, and epistles. The temper of these was so congenial to the medieval mind that many people believed that Seneca had been a Christian, and the appeal of both his sentiments and style continued unabated among the Florentine philosophers of the fifteenth century. His tragedies too were known and their moral character highly praised. The medieval definition of *tragedy as a great man's fall from prosperity to adversity owes much to the argument of Seneca's plays.

It is no exaggeration to say that the revival of tragedy on the Renaissance stage was entirely founded on Seneca's nine dramas on Greek mythological subjects. Although probably based on ancient Greek originals, they deviate considerably in mood and treatment from surviving Greek tragedies. The latter were barely accessible to the fifteenth century, as no printed texts existed and very few people could have read them if there had been any, so Seneca's plays were the sole ancient models available. It is likely that they were written for recitation rather than acting, and their style is highly rhetorical, declamatory in tone, and recondite in allusion, combining excessive moralizing with bizarre horrors. These features were avidly incorporated in neo-Latin and vernacular imitations.

Senfl, Ludwig (c. 1486–c. 1542) Swiss composer. From 1496 to 1513 Senfl sang in the *Hofkapelle* of Emperor Maximilian I in Vienna, Augsburg, and Constance. He worked with his teacher, the *Kapellmeister* *Isaac, in copying a large amount of music which was later published as part of Isaac's *Choralis constantinus* (1550–55), a task Senfl completed in around 1520 after Isaac's death. He took over Isaac's position at the *Hofkapelle* in 1517. After Maximilian's death (1519) Senfl travelled extensively. In 1523 he became court composer in the *Hofkapelle* of Duke Wilhelm of Bavaria in Munich, where he remained until he died. Senfl did compose some sacred music, but his numerous German lieder are his main achievement; traditional German melodies are treated in imaginative ways, ranging from chordal harmonization to canons.

Serlio, Sebastiano (1475–1554) Italian architect, painter, and architectural theorist. Born in Bologna, Serlio trained as a painter under his father before moving to Rome where he studied architecture and antiquarianism under Baldassare *Peruzzi. After the sack of Rome (1527) Serlio travelled to Venice; there he remained until 1540, when he was invited to France by Francis I to help in the building of the palace at Fointainebleau. By this time Serlio was already famous for the first

instalment of his great treatise, *Tutte l'opere d'architettura e prospettiva* (1537–75), in which he set out the principles of classical architecture with accompanying illustrations by Bramante, Peruzzi, and his own hand. This influential work helped to spread Renaissance ideas in northern Europe, appearing in Dutch in 1606 and English in 1611, and was the first such work to manifest a practical rather than a theoretical approach to architecture. Serlio also produced a short book on portals, the *Libro extraordinario* (1551), and introduced innovations in stage design based upon the classical theories of Vitruvius. The only two surviving architectural works by Serlio are a doorway at Fontainebleau and the château at Ancy-le-Franc (begun in 1546).

Sermisy, Claudin de (c. 1490–1562) French composer. Known as Claudin in his day, Sermisy sang at the Ste-Chapelle and in the king's private chapel. He may have accompanied Francis I to Bologna in 1515 and to the *Field of the Cloth of Gold (1520). In 1532 he was *sous-maître* at the royal chapel and in 1533 was nominated canon at the Ste-Chappelle. Sermisy must have lived in Paris for much of this period and eventually died there. He wrote about 110 sacred works, including motets, Masses, and a Passion, but is chiefly remembered for his 175 or so chansons. These are in a simpler, more homophonic and syllabic style than those of his contemporaries, with attractive melodies. Many were so popular that other composers arranged them for all kinds of vocal and instrumental forces.

Servetus, Michael (1511–53) Spanish theologian and physician. The son of a notary, Servetus travelled and studied in Spain, France, Italy, and Germany before settling (1532) in Lyons, where he worked, under the pseudonym Michel de Villeneuve, as a publisher. This cover was adopted to protect him from the notoriety gained by his earlier antitrinitarian work, *De trinitatis erroribus* (1531). Servetus's interests then turned to medicine and, after graduating from the university of Paris, he worked in France as a physician to the archbishop of Vienne (1541–53). He then produced a further antitrinitarian work, *Christianismi restitutio* (1553), in which he described the circulation of the blood from the heart's left side via the lungs to the right side. Charged with heresy, he fled, but, most unwisely, went to Geneva where, under the direction of *Calvin, he was burnt at the stake as a heretic.

Seusenhofer family One of the most important German families of armourers in the fifteenth and sixteenth centuries. Konrad Seusenhofer (1460–

1517) moved from Augsburg to Innsbruck in 1504 to set up a court armoury for Emperor Maximilian I, and was later succeeded as court armourer by his brother Hans (1470–1555) and Hans's son Jörg (c. 1505–80). During the sixteenth century, when plate armour had become ceremonial rather than practical, the family made richly elaborate armour, often decorated by inlaying, gilding, etching, or carving, for the European monarchies. Konrad was instrumental in evolving the type of fluted armour, known as "Maximilian", popular in the first three decades of the sixteenth century (a fusion of the German and Italian styles of armour). A fashion in armour during the 1520s was to simulate the puffing and slashing of the dress of the period; an early example is the armour made by Konrad for Archduke Charles in 1514. Other clients of Konrad's included Henry VIII of England and James IV of Scotland.

Another fashion of the mid-sixteenth century was for garnitures – complete "wardrobes" of matching pieces of armour for different occasions. A famous example of this is the "Eagle" garniture made by Jörg Seusenhofer for Ferdinand, Archduke of Tyrol, in 1547, which comprised over sixty separate pieces.

Seville A city and river port on the Guadalquivir in Andalusia, southern Spain, 54 miles (86 km) from the Atlantic. Seville was in turn Roman, Visigoth, and Moorish before the Christian reconquest (1248). By the early Renaissance period Seville's silk and woollen textile industries had brought it prosperity, but it was the establishment in 1503 of the city's Casa de Contratación (house of trade), with a monopoly of trade with the Americas, that made Seville very rich. Foreign merchants flocked in, and Seville's population increased from 25 000 in 1517 to 90 000 in 1594, making it Spain's largest city. During the seventeenth century competition from Cádiz led to Seville's decline.

Seville's religious history was troubled. It was a prime centre of the activities of the *Spanish Inquisition; Jews were expelled as early as 1483 and altogether some 2000 suspected heretics were burned in *autos da fé* there during the 1480s. In the early years of *Philip II's reign further *autos da fé* (1559, 1560) brutally suppressed the city's incipient Protestant movement. Notable buildings from the Renaissance period include one of the largest cathedrals in the world (1403–1506). *Pacheco established his painting academy in Seville, and Francisco *Herrera the Elder and *Roelas both worked in the city.

Sforza family Originally, prosperous farmers from Romagna, whose fortunes were made by two noted *condottieri. The family's founder was Muzio Attendolo (1369–1424), who assumed the name Sforza (force). His son Francesco, also a condottiere, was hired to protect the short-lived *Ambrosian Republic (1447), but Francesco, who had married (1441) Bianca Maria, illegitimate daughter of the last *Visconti duke, instead made himself duke of Milan (1450). He gave Milan great public works and lavish entertainments to make his despotism acceptable. Francesco's son Galeazzo ruled capably and encouraged agriculture, commerce, communications, learning, and the arts. After his assassination (1476) he was succeeded by his young son Giangaleazzo (1469–94), whose power was usurped by his ruthless and unpopular uncle, Lodovico "il Moro", husband of Beatrice d'Este (*see* Este family). Lodovico was expelled by *Louis XII of France (1499). Lodovico's son Massimiliano was briefly restored (1513–16) by the Swiss and then expelled by the French and Venetians. Finally, *Charles V supported the rule (1522–35) of Massimiliano's brother Francesco Maria, but when Francesco died without heirs Milan passed to Charles V. See Plate IV.

sfumato The technique of effecting a gradual transition from one colour to another, practised by many painters of the High Renaissance. To critics like Vasari it was an indicator of the maturity of art as manifested in the paintings of *Leonardo da Vinci and *Giorgione, in contrast to the hard outlines and abrupt colour transitions of Quattrocento painters. Taking its name from the Italian word *sfumare*, meaning "to evaporate like smoke", *sfumato* was used in both paintings and drawings for various purposes, including the emphasis of relief effects. Leonardo and other major artists also advocated its use on more philosophical grounds, stressing its value as a means of merging human figures with the natural landscapes in which they are set.

Shakespeare, William (1564–1616) English dramatist. Shakespeare was born and educated at Stratford-upon-Avon, Warwickshire, the eldest son of a prosperous glover who had married into the local gentry. Little is known (though much is conjectured) about Shakespeare's early life. In 1582 he married Anne Hathaway and possibly supported her and their children, Susanna (born 1583), and the twins Hamnet and Judith (born 1585), by working as a schoolmaster. At some unknown date, maybe in the late 1580s, Shakespeare moved to London.

The erotic poems *Venus and Adonis* (1593) and *The Rape of Lucrece* (1594), with dedications to Lord Southampton, were Shakespeare's first published works, but he had already had several plays

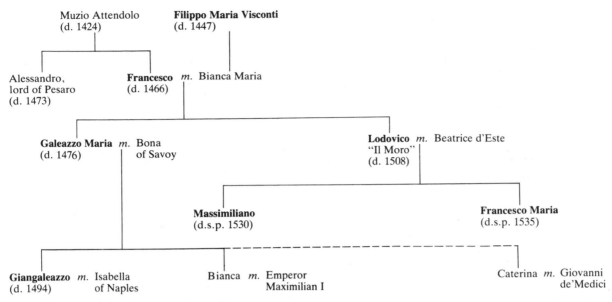

Muzio Attendolo
(d. 1424)

Filippo Maria Visconti
(d. 1447)

Alessandro,
lord of Pesaro
(d. 1473)

Francesco *m.* Bianca Maria
(d. 1466)

Galeazzo Maria *m.* Bona
(d. 1476)   of Savoy

Lodovico *m.* Beatrice d'Este
"Il Moro"
(d. 1508)

Massimiliano
(d.s.p. 1530)

Francesco Maria
(d.s.p. 1535)

Giangaleazzo *m.* Isabella
(d. 1494)   of Naples

Bianca *m.* Emperor
Maximilian I

Caterina *m.* Giovanni
de'Medici

SFORZA FAMILY *The Sforza dukes of Milan. Through her third marriage (1496), to Giovanni di Pierfrancesco de'Medici, Galeazzo Maria's illegitimate daughter Caterina became the grandmother of Duke Cosimo (I) of Florence.*

produced (the three parts of *Henry VI, Richard III,* and the Plautine *Comedy of Errors*). He was also probably writing sonnets, about which speculation has continued to rage since their collection and publication in 1609. From 1594 Shakespeare's theatrical company was the Lord Chamberlain's Men, for whom in the next five years he wrote the plays of his early maturity, among them *Romeo and Juliet, A Midsummer Night's Dream, Much Ado about Nothing, As You Like It, The Merchant of Venice,* and the history plays *Richard II, 1* and *2 Henry IV,* and *Henry V.* In 1596 his father acquired a grant of arms and the following year Shakespeare purchased New Place at Stratford, both evidence of the family's standing and prosperity.

The Globe Theatre at Bankside, south of the Thames in London, was opened in 1599, and for it Shakespeare wrote his seven great tragedies (*Julius Caesar, *Hamlet, Othello, King Lear, Macbeth, Antony and Cleopatra,* and *Coriolanus*). Apart from *Twelfth Night,* his comedies of the period 1599–1608 (*Measure for Measure, All's Well that Ends Well,* and *Troilus and Cressida*) are more sombre and ambiguous than those of the 1590s. In 1608 Shakespeare's company, known since 1603 as the King's Men, took over the indoor Black-friars Theatre, for which Shakespeare wrote the romantic comedies *Pericles, Cymbeline, The Winter's Tale,* and *The Tempest*; the last, probably written in 1611, is generally read as the playwright's farewell to the stage. Shakespeare retired to Stratford, where he died. In 1623 his old friends and colleagues in the theatre, John Heminge and Henry Condell, published the first collected edition of

Shakespeare's works, known as the First Folio; it contained thirty-six plays, of which only nineteen had been printed during the playwright's lifetime.

Sibyls Classical prophetesses, originally associated with oracles of Apollo, but famous in post-classical times as the reputed authors of the Sibylline Oracles. This collection of prophecies had supposedly been obtained from the Sibyl of Cumae and was kept in the Capitol in ancient Rome and only consulted in national crises. The Capitoline collection was destroyed in 405 AD, but meanwhile purported texts of the prophecies had been put into circulation and overlaid with Jewish and Christian accretions, making them of great interest to the Middle Ages. The Sibyls therefore passed into medieval and Renaissance lore as true prophets, fit to associate in iconographical schemes with the biblical seers.

Most commonly, the number of Sibyls was computed at nine: Cumaean (alternatively known as the Erythraean), Tiburtine (or Albunean), Hellespontine, Samian, Eritrean, Delphic, Libyan, Persian, and Cimmerian. The list, however, can vary. The Tiburtine Sibyl was particularly famous, as among her supposed utterances was one foretelling the coming of Christ, and she is sometimes shown without her sisters, as in a fresco (1528) by Peruzzi over the altar of the Fontegiusta church, Siena, in which she announces the birth of Christ to the Roman emperor, Augustus. The Sibyls were portrayed as either young or very old women holding scrolls or books. They are depicted in inlaid marble slabs in the pavement of the aisles of Siena cathedral (mainly fifteenth century), and in association with prophets in the *Tempio Maletestiano, in Michelangelo's ceiling in the *Sistine Chapel, and in scores of humbler decorative schemes, even in domestic surroundings, as at Chastleton House, Oxfordshire, England (early seventeenth century).

Sidney, Philip (1554–86) English writer, courtier, and soldier. Born on his father's estate at Penshurst, Kent, Sidney was brought up in court circles, went to Shrewsbury school (1564) and Christ Church, Oxford (1568–71), and then spent three years travelling on the Continent, where he made a profound impression on many eminent scholars and statesmen. On his return he was much favoured by Queen Elizabeth. He wrote the entertainment *The Lady of May* (1578) for her, but in 1579 quarrelled with the earl of Oxford and, rejecting the queen's wish that he should apologize, he retired from court. He then incurred further displeasure by sending her, at the instigation of his uncle, the earl of *Leicester, an outspoken memorandum (1580) against her proposed marriage with Duke *Francis of (Anjou-)Alençon. While in retirement at Wilton, home of his sister Mary Herbert, Countess of Pembroke (1561–1621), Sidney probably completed the first version of *Arcadia* and with Mary composed metrical versions of the Psalms. In 1581 his prolonged courtship of Penelope Devereux (?1562–1607) was terminated by her marriage to Lord Rich; Sidney, who had been addressing sonnets to her under the name "Stella", expressed his continuing passion in some of the finest sonnets in the sequence *Astrophel and Stella* (1591). In the early 1580s he also wrote his famous *Defence of Poesie* (1595; also entitled *Apologie for Poetrie*), justifying the social utility of verse as "delightfull teaching". In 1583 he was knighted and married Frances Walsingham, daughter of the queen's adviser, both events taking place with the queen's reluctant consent, but two years later he made peace with the queen and was appointed governor of Flushing on Leicester's expedition to the Netherlands. The following autumn he was mortally wounded while fighting the Spaniards at Zutphen and died at Arnhem.
Sidney's lifelong friend Fulke *Greville wrote (c. 1610–14) a biography of Sidney (1652) which idealizes him as the embodiment of Elizabethan greatness and Christian chivalry. His integrity, charm, courage, and learning made him universally mourned. He was a considerable patron of writers (Greville calls him "a generall Maecenas of learning "), among them *Spenser, who wrote the pastoral elegy "Astrophel" upon his death. The Countess of Pembroke published the revised *Arcadia* (1590), more moralistic in tone than the original "toyfull booke", and continued to encourage her brother's literary protégés.

Siena A city and city state in Tuscany, central Italy. Siena was subject to, in turn, Etruscans, Romans, and Lombards before attaining its independence in the twelfth century. By the early fourteenth century Siena was a great banking and commercial centre, but its economy and population then declined on account of foreign warfare, raids by mercenaries, the Black Death (1348–49), Florentine expansionism, divisive constitutional arrangements, and Florence's commercial supremacy in Tuscany. Siena was briefly ruled by the *Visconti of Milan (1399–1404), but then resumed its communal constitution until the *signoria* of the Petrucci family (1487–1524). From 1530 the city had to accept a Spanish garrison, but rebelled against *Charles V's plan to build a fort there (1552). Spanish and Florentine forces subdued Siena (1555) and Spain sold Siena to Florence two years later.
Siena had a university (founded 1240) and a sixteenth-century literary society called the Intronati, but it is best known for its fourteenth-century school of artists (*Duccio, Simone *Martini, Ambrogio *Lorenzetti). *Pinturicchio lived in Siena in the early sixteenth century. The architects *Francesco di Giorgio Martini and Baldassare *Peruzzi were Sienese-born, as was the sculptor Jacopo della *Quercia. Renaissance Siena boasted two saints: Catherine (1347–80) and Bernardino (1380–1444). Surviving landmarks include the Palazzo Pubblico (1297–1310), the Torre del Mangia (1338–48), and numerous handsome palaces such as the Palazzo Piccolomini "delle Papesse", begun in 1460 to designs by Bernardo *Rossellino.

Siglo de Oro The golden age of Spanish literature, roughly the sixteenth and seventeenth centuries. The term, first applied by a minor nineteenth-century romantic writer, is imprecise, there being no agreement on the exact boundaries of the period. The accession of *Ferdinand and Isabella (1474) or 1500 have been advanced as *termini a quo*, and as *termini ad quem*, the death of the last major writer, Calderón (1681), or 1700. In either case, most Spanish "classics" fall within the period. Literary developments do not parallel but lag behind those of Renaissance Italy; nevertheless, a new European orientation emerged during this era as writers responded to humanist ideals. Particularly notable, from this point of view, are (in poetry) the publication of the works of *Boscán and *Garcilaso de la Vega (1543), and (in prose) Boscán's translation (1534) of The *Courtier and the Erasmian influence spread by the works of the brothers *Valdés.

signatures, theory of A theory that seems to have originated with *Paracelsus, who stated: "By the outward shapes and qualities of things we may know their inward Vertues, which God hath put in them for the good of man." Thus, St John's wort was held by Paracelsus to be good for wounds because the leaves had a similar "porositie" to that of the skin, and its flowers "when putrified are like blood". Paracelsus went on to derive the secondary principle that "what Climate soever is subject to any Particular disease, in the same place there grows a Cure." Consequently, it was pointless to search for foreign drugs. But what of the objection that not all plants clearly advertised their virtues? God, it was answered, has signed some plants to put man on the right track. Thereafter man must search more strenuously. The Paracelsian doctrine was picked up and publicized by *della Porta in his *Phytognomonica* (Plant Indicators; 1588), after which it remained current for many years although rejected by such botanists as John Ray (1627–1705).

Signorelli, Luca (c. 1441–1523) Italian painter. Signorelli was born in Cortona, the cathedral of which houses some of his major late works, including *The Institution of the Eucharist* (1512). His earliest known works, fragments in Città di Castello (1474), show some influence of *Piero della Francesca, whose pupil he is thought to have been; this is evident in the sculptural style of his figures. He was greatly influenced however by the contemporary Florentine school of *Pollaiuolo and *Verrocchio, as is shown by his interest in the representation of movement and exaggerated muscular development. Between 1479 and 1481 he painted frescoes in the cupola of the sacristy of the Santuario della Sta Casa at Loreto, and in the 1480s he worked on the Sistine Chapel frescoes with *Perugino, *Botticelli, *Rosselli, and others. His masterpiece is the fresco cycle at Orvieto cathedral (1499–1503). Begun by Fra *Angelico in 1477, it is a series of compositions entitled *The End of the World* and *The Last Judgment*. Signorelli uses the grotesque to convey his vision of the theme with brutal intensity, as in the packed, writhing figures in *The Fall of the Damned* (see Plate XXVIII). The frescoes are also noted for their brilliant draughtsmanship and the representation of nude figures in action, which influenced *Michelangelo. The interest in the nude was also manifest in the overtly pagan *Pan and other Gods* (c. 1490), which was destroyed in Berlin during World War II.

signoria (lordship) The characteristic form of government in Italian city states from the thirteenth to the sixteenth century. It replaced the older republican governments which were often torn apart by rival factions. The lord or despot of the *signoria* was ideally a strong ruler who ensured efficient government and peace for his people; he fostered civic pride through magnificent public works and lavish patronage of arts and letters. The *signoria* helped pave the way for the modern nation state. In Florence the ruling magistrates formed the *signoria*.

Sigüenza, Fray José de (?1544–1606) Spanish historian. Named after his birthplace, Sigüenza was librarian of the *Escorial and later became prior of the Jeronymite monastery there. He is known for one work of dull but authoritative scholarship, *Historia de la Orden de San Jerónimo* (*History of the Order of St Jerome*; three volumes, 1595, 1600, 1605), of which order he had been a friar since 1567. The third volume contains a full description of the Escorial that has never been superseded and the work offers fascinating glimpses of Philip II's role in the building of the great complex and his relationships with artists who decorated it.

Siloe, Diego de (c. 1495–1563) Spanish architect and sculptor. Born in the city of Burgos, Diego was the son of the sculptor Gil de *Siloe and was trained largely in Italy. His earliest documented piece is the marble Caraccioli reredos (1514–15; S Giovanni a Carbonara, Naples), on which he collaborated with his fellow-Spaniard Bartolomé *Ordóñez. In 1519 he returned to Burgos, where he executed a number of designs, including one for the tower of Sta Maria del Campo. His major work in that city, however, was the Escalera Dorada (1519–26), a magnificent gilded staircase in the cathedral. Diego is best known for his design of Granada cathedral (1528–43), where he succeeded Enrique Egas as architect. On Egas's Gothic foundations Diego erected a great domed church that combined elements of Italian, Gothic, and Spanish Muslim styles in a manner known as *plateresque, also employing features of the design of the Church of the Holy Sepulchre in Jerusalem. Later works included the church of El Salvador at Ubeda (1536), the cathedrals of Málaga and Guadix (1549), and S Gabriel at Loja.

Siloe, Gil de (active 1486–99) Spanish sculptor. Possibly born in Orleans or Antwerp, Gil was one of the last great sculptors in the Gothic style in Spain. The few works by Gil that have survived include a number of elaborate tombs, including those of John II of Castile and his second wife Isabella of Portugal, Infante Alfonso, and Juan de

Padilla (1489–93; all in La Catuja, Miraflores). Also for the monastery of Miraflores near Burgos, Gil executed a notable altarpiece (1496–99); other works include four reredoses for churches in Valladolid and Burgos. All his works show the influence of Spanish Muslim and Flemish styles but themselves had little artistic impact upon subsequent sculptors working in the Italian style, such as his son Diego de *Siloe.

Simone Martini *see* Martini, Simone.

Sistine Chapel The papal chapel in the Vatican palace, Rome. Commissioned by Pope Sixtus IV, the chapel was built (1473–81) under the supervision of Giovanni de Dolci and is famous as the meeting place of the Sacred College of Cardinals. The chapel is also celebrated for its series of fourteen frescoes, commissioned between 1481 and 1483 and painted by leading artists of the day. The south wall is decorated with frescoes by *Pinturicchio, *Botticelli, *Rosselli, *Piero di Cosimo, Luca *Signorelli, and Bartolommeo della Gatta (1448–c. 1502). The north wall has frescoes by *Perugino, Pinturicchio, Botticelli, *Ghirlandaio, Rosselli, and Piero di Cosimo. Most remarkable of all the paintings in the chapel, however, are those by Michelangelo. The west wall is covered by Michelangelo's *The Last Judgment* (1533–41), while the barrel-vaulted ceiling was also decorated by him with scenes from Genesis (see Plate XIX). On ceremonial occasions parts of the side walls are covered by tapestries depicting biblical scenes, designed by *Raphael and woven in Brussels (1515–19). The chapel also contains a marble screen and cantoria probably made in the Roman workshop of Andrea *Bregno.

Sixtus IV (1414–84), Pope (1471–84) Born Francesco della Rovere of a poor family near Savona, he became a Franciscan friar and teacher. He was made minister-general of the Franciscans (1464) and cardinal (1467). As pope Sixtus initially campaigned unsuccessfully for a crusade against the Turks, but later concentrated more on Italian politics and the aggrandizement of the *della Rovere family. Like other Italian princes he ruled his domains firmly and became involved in Italian quarrels, notably wars against Florence (1478–79) and Venice (1482–84).
In foreign affairs, relations with France were strained over the Pragmatic Sanction of *Bourges, but he allowed *Ferdinand and Isabella of Spain to establish the *Spanish Inquisition (1478) and to make ecclesiastical appointments in Spain and the New World. Sixtus IV was a great nepotist who made five nephews and one grand-nephew cardinals; one of them was later Pope *Julius II.

Sixtus IV administered the church and its domains well. He was personally devoted to the Blessed Virgin Mary and instituted (1476) the Feast of the Immaculate Conception. As a patron of letters and the arts, Sixtus IV repaired Roman churches, had the *Sistine Chapel built, established the Sistine choir, commissioned *Botticelli and *Pollaiuolo, and opened the Vatican Library to scholars.

Sixtus V (1521–90), Pope (1585–90) Born in Ancona of a poor family, Felice Peretti joined the Franciscans at the age of twelve. He became known as a harsh reformer, especially when inquisitor-general in Venice (1557–60). He was vicar-general of the Franciscans (1566–72) and was created cardinal in 1570.
As pope he was concerned with the lawlessness and the financial problems of the Papal States, dealing ruthlessly with the bandits and making the papacy rich by introducing heavy new taxes. He embarked on an expensive building programme, including the completion of St Peter's dome and work on the Lateran Palace and the Vatican Library. Sixtus V reorganized the Curia, limiting the number of cardinals to seventy and establishing fifteen congregations (or departments) to perform the work of the papacy. He also inaugurated (1589) a revision of the Vulgate, the *editio Sistina.*

Skarga, Piotr (1536–1612) Polish theologian and writer. Skarga was born into a bourgeois family at Grójec and joined the Jesuits in 1569. His appointment in 1579 as head of the academy at Vilna gave him scope for the Counter-Reformation teachings for which he became famous. His book on the lives of the saints, published the same year, became a classic. In 1588 he became a preacher at the court of King Sigismund III, where his influence exacerbated the religious intolerance then beginning to afflict Poland. Nonetheless he gained a unique eminence as a Polish patriot on account of his *Kasania Sejmowe* (Parliamentary Sermons; 1597); these combine moral and political exhortation, prophecies of the downfall of the Polish state, and patriotic sentiment, expressed in powerful and compelling prose that won many admirers.

Sleidanus, Johannes (1505–56) German religious historian. He was born at Schleiden, near Aachen, and having studied both law and the classics, in 1537 he entered the service of France as secretary to Cardinal du Bellay. Between 1537 and 1544 he represented Francis I in several important negotiations with the German Protestant powers. In 1544 he was appointed on the recommendation of Martin *Bucer as official historian of the Reformation and was granted access to archive material in Saxony, Hesse, and the Palatinate. His work *De* *statu religionis et republicanae Carolo V Caesare commentarii*, which was published in Strasbourg in 1555, was an immediate success and was translated into many languages (first English edition, 1560). It remains the most valuable contemporary record of Reformation times, largely on account of its large collection of documents.

Sluter, Claus (c. 1350–1406) Netherlands sculptor. Possibly born at Haarlem, Sluter worked for *Philip the Bold of Burgundy on the Charterhouse of Champmol on the outskirts of Dijon, where he was master of the works from 1389. He worked first on the portal of the church, but his masterpiece is the calvary (1395–1404) there, of which the base, known as the Puits de Moïse, survives. Fragments of the rest are preserved in the Musée Archéologique, Dijon, including a magnificent head of Christ. The imposing figures of the prophets on the Puits de Moïse confirm Sluter's position as one of the great innovators in the history of sculpture; in their powerful realism and characterization they represent a complete break with the decorative formulae of earlier northern European art. Sluter also executed the tomb of Philip the Bold at Champmol (now in the Musée Archéologique), notable particularly for the treatment of the drapery of the mourning figures. In 1404 Sluter retired to the Augustinian monastery at Dijon. His influence continued long after his lifetime and far beyond the boundaries of Burgundy.

Smith, Sir Thomas (1513–77) English statesman, lawyer, and scholar. The son of a wealthy landowner at Saffron Waldon, Smith was educated at Cambridge. After a period of foreign travel he returned to Cambridge in 1544 as regius professor of civil law. He also served from 1547 to 1554 as provost of Eton and was first elected to parliament in 1559. Later much of his time was spent at court, advising Queen Elizabeth on a number of issues. From 1562 to 1566 he served as ambassador to France, negotiating at the Peace of Troyes (1564) Elizabeth's abandonment of her claim to Calais. Smith's most famous work, *De republica anglorum* was published posthumously (1583); in it he describes the basis of the Tudor constitution.

Snell, Willebrord (1581–1626) Netherlands physicist and mathematician. The son of Rudolf Snell (1546–1613), a mathematician at Leyden, Snell succeeded his father as professor of mathematics at Leyden university in 1613. He published a number of mathematical books, notably *Eratosthenes Batavus* (1617), and worked on the practical problem of measuring, by triangulation, the length of a degree. He is best known, however, for his discovery in 1621 of the law of refraction (for any two media, the ratio of the sine of the angle of incidence to the sine of the angle of refraction is constant), since known as Snell's law. The law itself, possibly derived from Snell's unpublished manuscripts, was first published in *Dioptrique* (1637) by Descartes.

Society of Jesus *see* Jesuits.

Soderini, Piero (1452–1522) Italian nobleman. A member of a prominent Florentine family, Piero Soderini came to power during the period of the Medici exile from the city after the ejection of Piero de' Medici in 1494. As the egalitarian system of government set up by *Savonarola faltered, Soderini was proclaimed *gonfaloniere* for life (1502). It was under his leadership that Florence recaptured Pisa, but this success could not stem the rising tide of opposition to Soderini's increasingly oligarchic rule. In 1512 the opposition of Medici supporters within the city, the withdrawal of his French allies from Italy, and the threatened attack on Florence by the Spanish papal army forced Soderini to resign, and he went into permanent exile in Ragusa.

Sodoma (Giovanni Antonio Bazzi; 1477–1549) Italian painter. According to Vasari, Sodoma earned his nickname for his homosexuality and

SODOMA Christ Bound to the Column. (*Pinacoteca, Siena*).

outrageous behaviour for which he became notorious. He trained in his native Vercelli under the Piedmontese artist Giovanni Martino Spanzotti (c. 1456–c. 1526), although the influence of Leonardo da Vinci is strong upon his early work. His earliest known works are the frescoes in Sta Anna in Camprena, Pienza (1503–04), and the thirty-one frescoes of the life of St Benedict at Monte Oliveto Maggiore, near Siena (1505–08). In 1508 Sodoma visited Rome and came under the influence of Raphael and Baldassare Peruzzi. His most notable works are the frescoes painted at the Villa Farnesina, Rome, including *The Marriage of Alexander and Roxane* (c. 1514); his other major fresco cycle is *The Life of St Catherine* (1526; S Domenico, Siena). His reputation as Siena's greatest artist of the sixteenth century was later eclipsed by *Beccafumi.

Solis, Virgil (1514–62) German engraver, designer, and illustrator. Solis's birthplace is not known, but his workshop in Nuremberg was producing engravings and woodcuts from around 1540. Among editions he illustrated were the Bible and Walter Rivius's famous *Vitruvius Teutsch* (1548). His workshop also produced a large number of engraved designs for the construction and decoration of gold- and silverware and for jewellery and other items. These were primarily fashionable rather than original, but were widely popular until after the turn of the century, not only among metalworkers but also among cabinet makers and stuccoists. The styles used ranged from early Renaissance (basically late Gothic with classical motifs) to the mannerist grotesque (for example, a ewer with lizards crawling over its surface and a snake as its handle), employing motifs popularized by the *Jamnitzer family.

sonnet (Italian *sonetto*, little song) A fourteen-line poem in iambic pentameter (in France typically iambic hexameter), the main types of which are customarily distinguished by their different rhyme schemes. The earliest, the Italian or Petrarchan sonnet, both in rhyme and logical construction consists of an octave (abbaabba) and a sestet (cdecde or cdcdcd). The English or Shakespearean sonnet, more suited to the difficulty of rhyming in English, consists of three quatrains and a couplet (abab cdcd efef gg). Other types are the Spenserian (abab bcbc cdcd ee) and the Miltonic, which is Petrarchan in rhyme but often with an extended logical development which blurs the *volta*, or turn in thought, between the octave and sestet. The sonnet seems to have derived from the lengthening of a very early Italian single-stanza form, the Sicilian *strambotto*, which rhymed variously; in Sicily it was usually eight hendecasyllabic lines, in

Tuscany the preferred length was six lines. The poems of Jacopo da Lentino (c. 1215–33) are considered the earliest forms of sonnet (abababab cdecde), and the division into octave and sestet was fixed by his contemporaries. Guittone d'Arezzo (1230–94) introduced the octave rhyming abbaabba, which was adopted by *Dante and *Petrarch and so firmly established.

As the vogue for the sonnet spread throughout most of Europe during the fifteenth and sixteenth centuries, the form tended to become trivialized as the vehicle for standard Petrarchan love sentiments. It was given new life, however, by *Tasso, *Michelangelo, *Bembo, and *Castiglione. The earliest theoretical comment on the form is found in Antonio da Tempo's *Summa artis rithimici* (1332). Besides the famous Italian sonneteers, the form was practised in England by *Wyatt, *Surrey, *Sidney, *Shakespeare, and *Spenser, among others; in France by members of the *Pléiade; in Spain by *Boscán and *Garcilaso de la Vega; and in Portugal by *Camões.

Spagnoli, Giovan Battista (1448–1516) Italian poet and author of biographical and religious works. Commonly known as Mantovano or Mantuan after his birthplace, Spagnoli was educated at Padua, became a Carmelite, and was elected Carmelite vicar-general in Mantua in 1483. From 1513 until his death he served as head of the order as a whole. He was canonized by Pope Leo XIII in 1883. His literary reputation mainly rests on ten Latin pastoral eclogues, eight of which were composed while he was a student and two after he entered the Carmelites. Imitations of Virgil and of Petrarch and Boccaccio, the eclogues were published in 1498; they were widely influential in Europe and were imitated in turn, as in Spenser's *Shepheardes Calender* (1579). *Parthenices* (*Hymns to the Virgin*; 1481), a series of seven poems, contains a depiction of hell and an assembly of fallen angels that became a source for comparable passages in Milton's *Paradise Lost*.

Spalatin, Georg (Georg Burckhardt; 1484–1545) German theologian and humanist reformer. Spalatin took his name from Spalt, near Nuremberg, where he was born. He was educated at Nuremberg and Erfurt. He became a close friend of Luther and in 1514 was appointed chaplain and secretary to *Frederick (III) the Wise, Elector of Saxony. From then on his activities involved him with most of the events of the German Reformation. His close connection with Frederick took him to the Diet of Augsburg (1518) and he shared in the negotiations with *Cajetan. He also attended the Diet of *Worms. After Frederick's death (1525) Spalatin served his successor John and in his later years he concerneed himself mainly with reforming churches and schools in Saxony. His works included Latin translations of the writings of Luther and Melanchthon and a German translation of Erasmus. He also wrote a history of the Lutheran reform movement (*Chronicon et annales reformationis*). He died in Altenberg, where he had lived since 1525.

Spanish Armada The fleet sent by *Philip II of Spain to invade England (1588). The 130 ships and 27 000 men under the inexperienced command of the duke of Medina-Sidonia reached the Channel in July. Hampered by unfavourable winds and harassed by English ships, the Armada made its way to Calais and waited in vain to rendezvous with the duke of Parma's army from the Netherlands. Taking advantage of the English fleet's greater mobility and its able captains, its commander, Lord Howard of Effingham, ordered the attack on 8 August 1588. The Armada suffered heavy losses off Gravelines and fled north, suffering further losses in storms off Scotland and Ireland. Seventy-six ships limped back to Spain. The defeat of the Armada foreshadowed Spain's decline and England's emergence as a great power.

Spanish Inquisition At the request of *Ferdinand and Isabella, Pope Sixtus IV in 1478 united the inquisitions of the Spanish kingdoms under the control of Tomás de *Torquemada. The Spanish monarchs wanted to deal with the "problem" of *conversos* or *morranos* (Jewish converts to Christianity who secretly practised their ancestral faith and rites). Torquemada has the reputation of a cruel monster; a more accurate characterization might be to say that he was an energetic administrator who shared the intolerance of his age and who tried to regulate the affairs of the Spanish Inquisition and prevent it from pursuing policies intended only to aggrandize or enrich the inquisitors. Devoid of personal ambition, Torquemada imprinted his own austerity on the entire institution of the Inquisition in Spain. The Spanish Inquisition was also aimed against *moriscos* (converted Muslims who were thought still to be secret practitioners of the Islamic faith). They were brutally treated by Diego Lucero, the inquisitor of Cordova, after the expulsion of the Moors from Spain in 1492, but his brutality was so blatant that he was eventually removed from office and imprisoned (1507). The Spanish Inquisition was also active in the sixteenth century against *alumbrados*, spiritualists whose mystic tendencies went beyond orthodox bounds. This illuminism was practised especially in Franciscan circles, although it may have had its origins in Jewish and Muslim mystical traditions in Spain which had influenced radical

Franciscans. As Spain closed its borders to outside ideas in the course of the sixteenth century – against Erasmian currents and Lutheran heterodoxy especially – the Spanish Inquisition acted as the safeguard of Spanish Catholic orthodoxy.

The hallmarks of the Spanish Inquisition were its Spanish Catholic orthodoxy and its *autos-da-fé*. The latter were ceremonies in which the inquisitors publicly charged their prisoners with and convicted them of various heresies. After these ceremonies, those convicted of unrepentant heresy or of having relapsed into heresy were burned at the stake. Others, convicted of lesser charges, were imprisoned, had their property confiscated (which then went into royal coffers), were turned over to the Spanish galleys, or suffered other humiliations.

The Inquisition also reached New Spain. There were many *autos-da-fé* in Mexico, but there charges were not directed against *conversos*, *moriscos*, or *alumbrados*, but against sorcerers. Thus, the Spanish Inquisition rarely acted against theological heresy in the New World, but more often against what was called demonic magic. The Spanish Inquisition survived until the nineteenth century when it was suppressed by Napoleon (1808) and, after his fall, by royal decree in 1834.

Spanish language The romance language deriving from the dialect of Castile, which is spoken in the Iberian peninsula (together with Catalan, Basque, and Galician-Portuguese), in part of Morocco, and in the countries of the former Spanish empire (chiefly those of Central and South America, with the major exception of Brazil). Like other romance languages, Spanish descends from spoken or Vulgar Latin, the day-to-day speech of Roman colonists, and has evolved by acquiring distinctive features different from Latin: a heavy stress accent (with certain effects on the stressed vowel and the unstressed syllable, as *tierra* from *terra* (land), *mesa* from *mensa* (table), and *ojo* from *oculus* ("eye"), for example); a simplification of genders and inflectional endings (replaced by analytic structures, like prepositional phrases); definite and indefinite articles; differences in the method of forming verbal tenses; and many semantic developments.

Spanish also reflects, in varying degrees, a number of other influences, both pre- and post-Roman. Among pre-Roman influences are the Phoenicians (and Carthaginians), Greeks, Iberians, Basques, and Celts. Later, Germanic, Arabic, and Amerindian languages also affected the character of Spanish. Pre-Roman traces are seen mainly in place names, for example Málaga (Phoenician *malka*, "trading factory"), Ibiza (from Carthaginian), Ampurias (Greek *emporion*, "market"), and Ebro (Iberian *Iberus*, whence the patronymic of these people, who may have been a number of unrelated migrant tribes). A few common nouns, like *manteca* ("butter") and *bruja* ("witch"), are also pre-Roman. Castilian has some similarities to the agglutinative non-Indo-European language of the Basques. An important phonological detail is the lack of the Latin *f*-sound in Basque, comparable to the Castilian loss of Latin *f* in some contexts, for example *hablar*, "to speak" (Latin *fabulare*) and *hacer*, "to do, make" (Latin *facere*). Celtic migrations around 900 and 600 BC left their mark both in place names and in some common nouns: Segovia (Celtic *sego*, "victory") and *cerveza* ("beer"). With the decline of Rome, Germanic tribes (Suevi, Asding and Siling Vandals, and Alans) invaded the peninsula (409), followed (415) by a contingent of romanized Visigoths from Toulouse who were sent as protection against them. As a result about 2500 Spanish place names are traceable to these Germanic settlers (for example, Andalusia, via Arabic *al-Andalus*, from *-andal-*, "Vandal") as are typical personal names – *Fernando, Gusmán* ("good man"), *Ramón, Bermudo, Manrique, Rodrigo*, etc. The Moorish invasion of 711 had a telling effect on vocabulary, contributing about 4000 lexical items, with the Arabic in a number of instances replacing the Latin term. Many of these words, especially in science, became part of a common European vocabulary (*alcohol, algebra, alquimia, nadir, elixir*, etc.). At various more recent stages Spanish vocabulary has been influenced by French, Italian, and classical Latin (through learned borrowings in the Renaissance and later). The American empire provided a number of Indian words for common products – *tomate, chocolate, coca, maíz, patata, hamaca*, etc.

With the completion of the reconquest of Andalusia by Ferdinand in 1492, Castilian was assured the position of dominant dialect, though previously it had been one of four major forms of Spanish, the other three being Aragonese (in Aragon and Navarre), Leonese (in León), and Mozarabic (the Spanish of those who chose to remain under Moorish rule after 711). *Nebrija's *Gramática* (1492) was the earliest scientific grammar of any European vernacular language, and the *Tesoro de la lengua castellana o española* (1611) of Sebastián de Covarrubias y Orozco (fl. 1545–72) was the first major Spanish dictionary. The Real Academia Española was founded in Madrid in 1713, one of its primary purposes being the compilation of an authoritative dictionary of the language. Six volumes were subsequently published (1726–37).

Speed, John (?1552–1629) English cartographer and historian. Born in Farringdon, Cheshire, Speed began his career as a tailor. Through Fulke *Greville's patronage he was allowed to present maps to Queen Elizabeth in 1598. He earned the admiration of the Society of *Antiquaries, whose members helped him compile and publish his two most famous works. *The Theatre of the Empire of Great Britain* (1611–12) was an atlas based on existing maps. This work was a prologue to the rather less valuable *Historie of Great Britaine* (1611). These works were often republished and were influential for many years, as was Speed's world atlas, *A Prospect of the Most Famous Parts of the World* (1627).

Spenser, Edmund (?1552–99) English poet. Spenser was born in London and attended the Merchant Taylors' School there before going to Cambridge. At Cambridge he became friends with the scholar Gabriel Harvey, with whom he corresponded about poetics, but soon made more influential acquaintances in the earl of Leicester's circle (*see* Areopagus). To one of these, Sir Philip *Sidney, he dedicated his first major publication, the set of twelve eclogues entitled *The Shepheardes Calender*. In 1580 he went as secretary to the lord deputy, Lord Grey, to Ireland, where he spent much of the rest of his life. From 1589 to 1598 he lived on his estate at Kilcolman; despite the friendship of *Raleigh and later the earl of *Essex, he obtained little recognition at court, apart from a £50 pension. When Kilcolman was sacked during Tyrone's revolt (1598), Spenser withdrew to London, where he died.

Spenser probably began work on The *Faerie Queene* before his departure for Ireland; only six books and a fragment of a seventh were completed before his death. His other poetic works include *Complaints* (1591), an assortment of original poems and translations; *Colin Clouts Come Home Again* (1595), recording his fruitless journey to court in 1590/91 in search of patronage; "Astrophel" (1595), an elegy on Sidney's death; *Amoretti* (1595) and "Epithalamion", a sonnet sequence and bridal ode commemorating his marriage to Elizabeth Boyle; and *Fowre Hymnes* (1596) on Platonic themes of love and beauty. His *View of the Present State of Ireland*, written between 1594 and 1597, was not published until 1633.

Sperandio, Savelli (c. 1425–c. 1504) Italian medallist, goldsmith, and sculptor. Possibly born in Mantua, Sperandio was the pupil of his father Bartolommeo. He also worked in Ferrara, Milan, and Faenza, and in 1482 completed the terracotta monument to Pope Alexander V in S Francesco, Bologna. In 1496 he moved to Venice. He executed a number of portrait medals, but the strong designs are sometimes marred by careless workmanship.

Speroni, Sperone (1500–88) Italian humanist and

literary critic. Speroni was born at Padua and educated at Bologna under *Pomponazzi, graduating in philosophy and medicine in 1518. His main importance was as a critic and student of literary language. He used the dialogue as a medium for his ideas; his most important work was the dialogue *Delle lingue* (1542) in which he maintained that the Italian language was capable of achieving any of the effects of Latin. He also wrote a tragedy *Canace* (1542) in an irregular metre which Tasso and Guarini borrowed and produced critical works on Dante, Virgil, and Ariosto, which treated vernacular literature as worthy of serious discussion.

Speyer, Diets of see Spires, Diets of.

spheres, armillary see armillary spheres.

spheres, celestial see celestial spheres (or globes).

Spiegel, Hendrick Laurensz. (1549–1612) Dutch writer. He was a native of Amsterdam and a member of the Egelantier chamber of rhetoric, who made himself the centre of a distinguished literary circle based at his country estate on the Amstel. He was the main author of the *Twespraack van de Nederduitsche letterkunst* (1584), to which his friend *Coornheert contributed the preface; it was influential in promoting notions of correctness in the use of the Dutch language. Although brought up as a poet in the *rederijker* tradition, Spiegel became after 1578 an exponent of Renaissance poetic metres, principally the alexandrine. His major work, *Hertspiegel* (published posthumously in 1614), is a long allegorical poem written in this metre and blending Christian and Platonic philosophy. Spiegel also wrote the play *Numa*, drawn from Plutarch, and a hymn of praise for the defeat of the *Spanish Armada.

Spires, Diets of (1526, 1529) Assemblies (*Reichstage*) of the Holy Roman Empire at Spires (Speyer) in southern Germany. At the 1526 meeting, on the grounds that the emperor was now at war with the pope, the princes repudiated instructions previously received from Charles V to cease innovations and enforce the Edict of Worms. It was agreed that each prince should determine the established religion of his own territory, and that others should be tolerated. Luther agreed to union with Rome, provided that only biblical institutions and ceremonies were regarded as essential, and others were reserved for decision by a general council of the Church.

At the 1529 assembly there was a large majority of Roman Catholics, and toleration of dissenters in Catholic territories was revoked. Six princes and fourteen cities made a formal protest against this decision; this was the origin of the term "protestant".

Spiritual Exercises see under Ignatius Loyola, St; Jesuits.

Spranger, Bartholomäus (1546–1611) Flemish painter. Born in Antwerp, Spranger studied landscape painting there under Jan Mandijn and Cornelius van Dalem. He then spent some years in Paris, Rome, and other Italian cities (1565–75), where he learnt figure painting from *Parmigianino and Federico *Zuccaro. In Rome he met the Flemish painter van *Mander, who later spread Spranger's style through Flanders. In 1575 he was at the court of Emperor Maximilian II in Vienna, and after the emperor's death (1576) Spranger worked for Maximilian's son, Emperor Rudolf II, in Prague. As Rudolf's taste was for the erotic, expressed through mythological and allegorical themes, Spranger's work consists largely of nudes in formalized scenes from Greek and Roman

SPRANGER The Triumph of Wisdom over Ignorance. *The blend of eroticism and learned allusion seems to have had a particular attraction for Spranger's patron, Rudolf II. Minerva tramples the figure of Ignorance, who is shown with an ass's ears; the female figures represent the arts and sciences. (Kunsthistorisches Museum, Vienna)*

mythology, such as *Minerva Conquering Ignorance* (c. 1591) and *Hercules and Omphale* (both Vienna). Spranger probably came closest of all German and Dutch artists to the spirit of Italian Mannerism, although his work still retained a northern restlessness. It was extremely popular and influential, and much copied.

sprezzatura A term in *Il cortegiano* (*The *Courtier*) by *Castiglione, sometimes translated as "nonchalance". The ideal courtier must be formidably accomplished, but it is essential that he avoid offensive or undignified display. *Sprezzatura* refers to the easy grace and superiority required to "make whatever is done or said to appear to be without effort".

Squarcialupi, Antonio (1416–80) Italian organist. The son of a Florentine butcher, Squarcialupi became organist at Orsanmichele in Florence in 1431, and in the next year was appointed organist at the cathedral there, a post he held until his death. Squarcialupi was probably the most famous organist of his day, and is known to have corresponded with *Dufay. The Squarcialupi Codex, a famous manuscript containing secular works of the Trecento, belonged to him.

Squarcione, Francesco (1397–1468) Italian painter. He was born the son of a notary in Padua, and, as a teacher of as many as 157 pupils, he is traditionally described as the founder of the Paduan school, a term associated with painters such as *Mantegna, *Zoppo, Giorgio Schiavone, and *Tura, who were either taught or influenced by Squarcione. In his youth he travelled in Greece and Italy collecting antique sculpture and paintings, which resulted in the interest in classical architecture and antique works often associated with the Paduan style. His only surviving paintings are a *Madonna* (Staatliche Museen, Berlin) and a damaged polyptych (1449–52; Museo Civico, Padua). These show the influence of the Florentine sculptor, *Donatello, who worked in Padua between 1443 and 1453. Little remains of the frescoes of scenes from the life of St Francis which Squarcione painted on the exterior of S Francesco at Padua (c. 1452–66) but they would indicate that, among other artists, he spread the early Renaissance style of Florence in his native city.

Stampa, Gaspara (c. 1523–54) Italian poet. She was born in Padua but lived in Venice after 1531, cultivating her literary interests, entertaining leading figures in her salon, and becoming known for her poetry, musical ability, and beauty. As "Anassilla" she was a member of the Accademia dei Pellegrini. Some critics have speculated that she became a courtesan. *Rime* (1554), published posthumously by her sister Cassandra and dedicated to Giovanni *della Casa, consists of some three hundred Petrarchan lyrics, mostly sonnets, inspired by her love for Collaltino di Collalto, Count of Treviso, whom she met in 1549 and who eventually deserted her for another. Not widely known until rediscovered by nineteenth-century romantics, the work is notable for its spontaneity and narrative continuity.

Stefano da Verona (Stefano da Zevio; c. 1375–c. 1450) Italian painter. The town of Zevio, just east of Verona, was reputedly the painter's birthplace, but his career is associated with Verona itself, where he was a leading exponent of the International Gothic style. The influence of *Altichiero can be seen in his work; frescoes by them both appear in several Veronese churches. The *Madonna del Roseto* (Castelvecchio, Verona) is a good example of his style, but his only dated work is the late *Adoration of the Magi* (1435; Brera, Milan).

Stephanus *see* Estienne press.

Stevin, Simon (1548–1620) Belgian mathematician and engineer. Little is known of Stevin's life other than that he was born at Bruges, started life as a merchant's clerk in Antwerp, and then served as quartermaster-general of the Dutch army. He is best known as the author of *De thiende* (The Tenth; 1585) in which he introduced decimal fractions into Western mathematics. Translated into English in 1608, it contained the first English use of the word "decimal". In works on statics and hydrostatics Stevin made a number of mechanical advances, the most important of which was his formulation of the triangle of forces. Stevin was also an engineer, publishing in 1594 a work on fortification which tackled the problem of designing forts capable of withstanding *artillery assaults.

stiacciato (*or rilievo stiacciato*) *see schiacciato*.

stilnovismo Collectively, the practitioners of the poetic style described by *Dante as the *dolce stil nuovo* (*Purgatorio* XXIV 57). The names originally mentioned by Dante are Guinizelli, *Cavalcanti, Lapo Gianni, Cino da Pistoia, and himself. They were apparently those poets who shared certain literary ideals, rather than a formally constituted movement. Later scholarship has extended this list by the addition of Gianni Alfani, Dino Frescobaldi, Guido Orlandi, and Guido Novello da Polenta. *Petrarch transmitted the style to the whole of Europe. A number of other Italian poets are categorized as *stilnovisti*, for example Franceschino degli Albizzi, Sennuccio del Bene, *Boccaccio, Matteo Frescobaldi, Giovanni Gherardi da Prato, and Cino Rinuccini, and later heirs include Lorenzo de' *Medici, *Michelangelo, and Torquato *Tasso.

Stimmer, Tobias (1539–84) Swiss artist. Stimmer was born into a family of artists at Schaffhausen, where he decorated the Haus zum Ritter with frescoes of figures from ancient stories. After 1570 he was active mainly in Strasbourg and painted the case of the astronomical clock in the cathedral there. The portraits of Jakob Schwyzer and his wife (Basle museum) demonstrate his proficiency as a portraitist. Besides these undertakings, the versatile Stimmer was significant as a draughtsman, designer of woodcuts and glass paintings, book illustrator, and poet.

Stoss, Veit (c. 1450–1533) German woodcarver and sculptor. Leaving his native Nuremberg in 1476, Stoss went to Cracow where he created the huge and complex altarpiece of the Virgin Mary for the Marienkirche (1477–89). The intensely dramatic and moving central panel depicts the Dormition of the Virgin with the Assumption above; the heads of the mourning apostles are vividly individualized and the intricately folded drapery adds to the richness of effect. Stoss also made the red marble tomb of King Casimir IV Jagellon (died 1492) in Cracow cathedral. In 1496 Stoss returned to Nuremberg where he carried out some major commissions in the city's churches. Among his other carvings, a *St Roch* in unpainted limewood (1516; SS Annunziata, Florence) elicited high praise from Vasari; generally, however, Stoss's statues were polychromed in accordance with the prevailing Gothic style.

Strada, Jacopo (?1515–88) Italian-born artist, antiquarian, and collector. Although he was born in Mantua, Strada belonged to a Netherlandish family. At an early age he began collecting antique coins, on the basis of which he published his *De consularibus numismatibus* in the 1550s. In the late 1540s he moved to Augsburg, where he lived in the house of Johann Jakob Fugger before moving on to Paris and Lyons. In France he acquired from *Serlio the manuscript and plates of the seventh book of his great work on architecture; Strada published this in 1575. In 1553 Strada issued a major work on the Roman emperors illustrated from coins, *Epitome thesauri antiquitatum*, and the following year he returned to Rome to enter the papal service. He then moved to Nuremberg, where he worked for the Fuggers as artist and goldsmith. In Nuremberg Strada attracted the attention of Archduke Ferdinand of Austria (later Emperor *Ferdinand I) and from 1557 he was in his employ-

ment. Under Ferdinand's successors, Maximilian II and Rudolf II, Strada attained the position of court antiquary and was instrumental in obtaining for the emperors all manner of antiquities, books, and *objets d'art*. Titian's portrait of Strada (1567/68) shows him holding an antique statuette, with a torso and ancient coins on the table before him. He was also the possessor of a remarkable library, said to have comprised over 3000 volumes in thirteen languages. At his death he left numerous manuscripts dealing with antiquities and problems in mechanics; his work on various sorts of mill was published in part by his grandson in 1617. Strada's daughter Katharina was for many years the mistress of Rudolf II and bore him several children.

Stradano, Giovanni *see* Straet, Jan van der.

stradiotti Cavalrymen from various parts of the Balkans, employed by Venice to guard her sea empire. They were usually posted away from their homes because they also performed policing duties. Armed with lances, scimitars, and shields, the *stradiotti* fought bravely and loyally for Venice in various Italian wars during the sixteenth century and became the republic's main protection. They were much admired by European rulers and were also employed in Germany and France in the sixteenth century. From the mid-sixteenth century *stradiotti* helped to maintain law and order on the Venetian mainland.

Straet, Jan van der (Giovanni Stradano; 1523–1605) Netherlands painter and designer of tapestries. Born in Bruges and a pupil of Pieter *Aertsen, van der Straet became a master in 1545. Shortly afterwards he travelled via Lyons and Venice to Florence, where he joined *Vasari's circle. There he assisted Vasari in the decoration of the Palazzo Vecchio and designed tapestries, the most important of which was a series of hunting scenes for the Medici villa of Poggio a Caiano (1567). Although he was based in Florence, he also visited Rome and Naples and even returned to the Netherlands between 1576 and 1578. His early works reveal the impress of his northern training but his later style was heavily conditioned by that of Vasari.

Strigel, Bernhard (1460–1528) German painter. Trained by his father and uncle in his home town of Memmingen, Strigel first worked on their altars for Disentis and Obersaxen. His work of the 1490s reveals the influence of *Bouts and Bartholomäus Zeitblom of Ulm. By 1499 he had come into contact with Emperor Maximilian I, whom he painted many times. In Memmingen Strigel held a number of municipal and guild offices and even served as an ambassador. He also continued to paint religious pictures, such as the wings of the Schussenried altarpiece (c. 1515; Berlin). Strigel never entirely outgrew his original late Gothic style, which served him well in profile portraits. His court portraits have an almost heraldic monumentality of form but little psychological intimacy.

Strigel, Victorinus (1524–69) German evangelical theologian. Strigel was born at Kaufbeuren, near Kempten, and educated at Fribourg and Wittenberg, where he was influenced by *Melanchthon. He taught at Erfurt, and in 1548 was appointed first professor and rector of the secondary school (gymnasium) at Jena. He worked with Justus *Jonas, opposed the stricter forms of Lutheranism, and lectured on Melanchthon's *Loci communes*. In 1563 he was appointed professor at Leipzig and in 1567 at Heidelberg. He was the author of a commentary on the Bible and of philological and historical works.

Striggio, Alessandro (c. 1540–92) Italian composer and lira da gamba player. Of noble birth, Striggio was a leading composer in the Medici court in Florence in the 1560s, where he collaborated with other composers to provide *intermedii* for great festivities. His fame must have spread, as in 1568 his forty-part motet, *Ecce beatam lucem*, was sung at the marriage of Duke Albrecht IV of Bavaria. The patronage of music at the Medici court declined in the 1570s, and little is known of Striggio's activities at this time. In 1584 he visited the court at Ferrara, and later that year returned to his native Mantua, where he remained until his death, patronized by both the Gonzaga and Medici. Striggio was a virtuoso lira da gamba player, but it is for his madrigals that he is chiefly renowned. Often highly descriptive, they were much admired abroad. His son, Alessandro the younger (1573–1630), also served the Gonzaga and was a friend of Monteverdi.

Strozzi family Italian bankers. A member of a noble Florentine banking family, Filippo I (1428–91) returned to Florence from exile in 1466; he prospered and became Lorenzo de' *Medici's trusted adviser in foreign affairs. Filippo began (1489) the construction of the magnificent Palazzo Strozzi. His grandson Filippo II (1488–1538), despite his marriage to a Medici, opposed Medici power and was a leader of the rising (1527) that expelled the Medici from Florence. He went into exile when the Medici were restored (1530) but then led a band of republican exiles in an unsuccessful attack on Florence (1537); he was caught and tortured before his death in captivity. The Strozzi

clan then moved to France, where several members became valued servants of the French kings.

Stuart style *see under* Jacobean style.

Sturm, Johannes (1507–89) German educationist. A native of Schleiden, Sturm underwent the usual humanistic training at Liège and at Louvain, where he started a printing press. He then went to Paris, where under the influence of Martin *Bucer he became a Protestant. In 1537 he became professor of rhetoric and dialectic at the Collegium Praedicatorum in Strasbourg, and there in 1538 he founded the first gymnasium in northern Europe. He remained its principal for forty-three years. Sturm was a zealous supporter of the Swiss reformers and engaged in lively controversies with the Lutherans. He wrote numerous educational works, in which, as in his school, he promoted his ideal of wise and eloquent piety, produced an edition of Cicero (1557) and a Latin translation of Aristotle's *Rhetoric*, and wrote the biography of Beatus *Rhenanus.

Suarez, Francisco (1548–1617) Spanish Jesuit theologian and philosopher. Born in Granada, he became a Jesuit in 1564, was ordained in 1572, and studied canon law, theology, and philosophy at the universities of Ávila, Segovia, Valladolid, Alcalá, Salamanca, and Rome. In 1597 Philip II appointed Suarez professor of philosophy at the university at Coimbra, where he remained until 1615. At Pope Paul V's request, he wrote *De defensione catholicae fidei* (1613) against James I of England and *De immunitate ecclesiastica* against the antipapalism of Venice (1615). He was a prolific writer and his *Opera omnia* (Venice, 1747) totalled twenty-three volumes. Although a Thomist, he was not the ape of St Thomas Aquinas nor of Aristotle, and he founded a school of thought called Suarism. He represents a late Renaissance resurgence of scholasticism, the more universal success of which was thwarted by the new science, and he is still considered one of the founders of modern international law, mainly by virtue of his summary of the principles of the law in *De legibus* (1612). He died in Lisbon.

Sully, Maximilien de Béthune, Duke of (1560–1641) French Huguenot statesman. As *Henry IV's most important minister, Sully did much to aid France's recovery from the religious wars, in which he had served with distinction. He encouraged agriculture, improved the posts and roads, and started major canals. An honest man in an age of corruption, Sully, as superintendent of finances (1598–1610), rescued French finances from bankruptcy. He removed the worst abuses of the fiscal system, cut extravagance at the court, and introduced a system of book-keeping to check on tax-farmers and officials. In 1602 he was made governor of the Bastille. In 1606 he was created a duke. He retired in 1610, the year after Henry IV's assassination, and devoted his last thirty years to writing his memoirs.

Surrey, Henry Howard, Earl of (1517–47) English poet and courtier. The elder son of Thomas Howard, who became 3rd duke of Norfolk in 1524, Surrey was brought up with an illegitimate son of Henry VIII and travelled to France (1532) with the royal entourage. He led a tempestuous life at court, alternately distinguishing himself and being in disgrace for various offences. In 1545–46 he held military commands in France, but was recalled after losing a fight at St-Étienne and was beheaded on several charges of treason.

Surrey's poetic output, although small, shows his awareness of continental Renaissance trends in verse. He wrote successful versions of Petrarchan sonnets and some other fine lyrics, as well as biblical paraphrases in poulter's measure (couplets of lines of twelve and fourteen syllables). His most interesting achievement is his translation of books two and four of Virgil's *Aeneid*, the earliest blank verse poem in English. Many of his poems were first published in the anthology Tottel's *Miscellany* in 1557. He wrote a fine elegy for *Wyatt ("Wyatt resteth here, that quick could never rest"), with whom his name is often linked as being the first Renaissance poets in England.

surveying The skill traditionally involving the ability to determine and represent the height, distance, and direction (azimuth) of an object from a particular reference point. The first book to deal with the subject, Hero of Alexandria's *Dioptra*, dates from about 100 AD. Techniques described were simple. A trough of water to find a level, a plumb line, and a hodometer to measure distance, together with a few instruments to measure angles, constituted the surveyor's stock-in-trade. To these the medieval period added the cross-staff (*see under* backstaffs).

Political and social conditions in the Renaissance – increased wealth, a growing population, the demands of ballistics, and the spread of the enclosure movement – made extra demands on the surveyor, and new techniques and instruments were developed to meet his needs. The most fundamental was the technique of triangulation, first proposed by *Gemma Frisius in the early sixteenth century. With triangulation all distance measurements, apart from the original base line, could be ignored. A high premium was consequently placed on the accuracy of the original measurement and

its correct plotting. To this end two sixteenth-century innovations were crucial: the theodolite and the plane table. The theodolite, initially described by Leonard *Digges in *Pantometria* (1571), consisted of a horizontal circle divided into 360°, on which an adjustable semi-circle had been placed at right angles. The plane table was first described in 1551 by Abel Foullon, a Frenchman at Henry II's court. Once fully developed into workable instruments they permitted a genuinely geometrical form of surveying to emerge before 1600.

Sustris, Frederik Lambertsz. (c. 1540–99) Italian-born painter of Netherlands descent. The son of Lambert *Sustris, Frederik was born in Venice and was presumably trained by his father during the latter's decade in Padua, which began about 1554. In 1560 Frederik visited Rome and between 1563 and 1567 he lived in Florence, where he assisted Vasari in the decoration of the Palazzo Vecchio and, in 1565, became a member of the Florentine academy of drawing. Anton *Fugger summoned him to Munich in 1568, where he worked beside Antonio Ponzano and Alessandro Paduano on the decoration of the Fugger palace. In 1573 he entered the service of Wilhelm von Landshut, later duke of Bavaria. The latter employed him on numerous important court commissions, such as the decoration of the Jesuit Michaelkirche (begun 1583) and the layout of the garden and grotto of the ducal Residenz between 1582 and 1586. Sustris also worked beside Pieter de *Witte on the decoration of the Munich Antiquarium. The chief artist and designer at the Munich court, Sustris's role was analogous to that of Vasari as court artist of the Medici dukes.

Sustris, Lambert (Alberto da Olanda; c. 1515/20– c. 1584) Netherlands painter. Sustris was born in Amsterdam but nothing is known of his training prior to his arrival at Titian's Venetian studio in the mid-1540s. There he seems to have specialized in the painting of landscape backgrounds. In 1548 and 1550–51 he accompanied Titian to Augsburg. The portraits which he painted in Germany are a successful synthesis of the northern tradition and the style of Titian. On his return to Italy, Sustris was influenced by the mannerist styles of Tintoretto and Schiavone, as well as by the prints of Parmigianino. Although thoroughly Italianized, the mature Sustris remained expert in the Netherlandish genre of landscapes peopled with numerous little figures. After moving to Padua in 1554, he returned to Venice during the late 1560s. There he superseded Tintoretto as a painter of official portraits, of which the latest known is dated 1584. See p. 382.

LAMBERT SUSTRIS
Venus and Cupid.
(Louvre, Paris)

Swiss Guard The special military guardians of the pope and the Vatican Palace since the early sixteenth century. *Julius II (pope 1503–13) agreed to pay Swiss cantons for the services of Swiss soldiers, who were excellent fighters and unlikely to become involved in Roman politics. The Swiss Guard now consists of about 100 men recruited from the Swiss cantons. They wear a distinctive parade uniform, designed by Michelangelo, of tunic, breeches, and boldly striped stockings.

Sylvester, Joshua (1563–1618) English poet and translator. Born in Kent, Sylvester was sent to school in Southampton, where he acquired an excellent knowledge of French. He earned a living in trade, but infinitely preferred poetry, at which he was prolific if undistinguished. His fame rests with his translations of *du Bartas; parts of his translation of *La Semaine* appeared from 1592 onwards and the first complete version, *Du Bartas his Devine Weekes and Works*, was issued in 1605–06. In 1606 Prince Henry gave him a small pension, but on the prince's death (1612) he obtained a post in the Company of Merchant Venturers (1613) and was sent to Middelburg in Holland, where he died. Sylvester's version of du Bartas's long poem remained influential in England until the Restoration.

T

Tacitus, Cornelius (c. 55–c. 117) Roman historian and provincial governor. His *Histories* cover the reigns of the Roman emperors from Galba to Domitian, partly overlapping his own lifetime, and his *Annals* cover the earlier period from the accession of Tiberius; both are only partially preserved and were virtually unknown in the Middle Ages. *Boccaccio apparently possessed a manuscript of the *Annals* and *Histories* containing sections of the works unknown before the fourteenth century, possibly from the monastery of Monte Cassino. Niccolò *Niccoli obtained a codex with minor works of Tacitus from the German library of Fulda. Tacitus' *Germania* was edited by *Celtis (1500) and *Rhenanus (1519) as being of particular interest to northern European antiquarians. The history of imperial Rome did not appeal to the fifteenth-century Italians with their republican ideals, and Tacitus' importance was only fully recognized through the work of *Lipsius in the late sixteenth century.

Taddeo di Bartolo (c. 1363–c. 1422) Italian painter. The last major representative of the Trecento tradition in his native Siena, Taddeo frescoed the chapel of the Palazzo Pubblico there (1407–14) and also executed commissions in the Palazzo Piccolomini and several churches. He also worked in Pisa and is represented by several pictures in the Galleria Nazionale dell'Umbria in Perugia. *Sassetta was one of his closest followers.

Taille, Jean de la *see* La Taille, Jean de.

Tallis, Thomas (c. 1505–85) English composer. Tallis is first mentioned as organist at Dover priory in 1532. He served at the church of St Mary-at-Hill, London, in 1537, probably as organist, and in about 1538 moved to Waltham abbey, where he was organist until its dissolution (1540). In 1541–42 he was a lay clerk at Canterbury cathedral, and he probably served as a full-time gentleman of the Chapel Royal from the following year until his death at Greenwich. In 1575 he was granted an exclusive patent to print and publish music with William *Byrd. Of his forty-two motets, seventeen appear in their joint publication of that year, *Cantiones sacrae.*

Tallis was one of the most important English composers whose work spanned the period of the English Reformation. His early, Latin compositions are florid in style, but there is a tendency away from this in the last years of Henry VIII's reign, under the influence of Cranmer. The trend was reversed in the reign of Mary, when Tallis wrote one of his richest compositions, *Gaude gloriosa Dei mater* for six voices. On the abolition of the Sarum rite in 1559, Tallis's Latin settings were probably no longer used liturgically. He was one of the first musicians to compose for the Anglican liturgy of 1547–53; his settings from this period are succinct, with little polyphony and more use of chords. Tallis's music thus embraces several styles largely dictated by the religious upheavals of the time; his forty-part motet, *Spem in alium*, is a curiosity of the mid-Tudor contrapuntal style, while his Anglican anthems tend towards homophony and simplicity. A few keyboard works survive, among which are the earliest datable English plainsong settings.

Tansillo, Luigi (1510–68) Italian courtier and poet. From 1535 Tansillo, who was born at Venosa, served in administrative and military posts under the Spanish viceroys of Naples, taking an active part in many campaigns. A prolific author, he was influenced by *Pontano and *Sannazaro. His work, associated with Mannerism, is various, formally ranging from Petrarchan sonnet and eclogue to religious verse suggestive of the Baroque and didactic poetry. *Il vendemmiatore* (*The Grape Harvester*; 1532) gained notoriety for supposedly licentious passages and was put on the Index. To make amends, Tansillo devoted years to his epic *Le lagrime de S Pietro* (*The Tears of St Peter*; 1585), notable mainly as the model for *Malherbe. Numerous lyrics, anthologized in Venice by Gabriele Giolito (1552), achieved wide circulation. The didactic *La balia* (*The Nurse*; 1566) was written to encourage mothers to nurse their own babies.

tapestry During the fifteenth century most European requirements for tapestries were met by workshops in France and Flanders. In Italy small workshops under noble patronage flourished sporadically, only that at Ferrara, founded (c.

1445) by Leonello d'Este, being of much importance. Using Flemish weavers, it executed cartoons by the local painter *Tura. Throughout the Italian Renaissance tapestry weaving was subordinated to painting, so that for instance the famous *Acts of the Apostles*, commissioned in Brussels by Pope Leo X after cartoons by Raphael, made no concession to the possibilities of tapestry as a medium. When war brought about the decline of the fifteenth-century centres of Arras and Tournai, Brussels became the main source for European tapestry (*see also* Pannemaker family). Its characteristic Renaissance style was established by the Flemish painter Bernard van *Orley (see Plate XXIX). His early work reflects medieval influence but later on that of the Raphael cartoons prevails. In designs based on biblical and historical narrative van Orley attempted to harmonize the Flemish taste for genre and narrative and the Italian preference for monumentality with the artistic potential of tapestry. A famous example of his work is the series the *Hunts of Maximilian I* (c. 1530; Louvre). Other minor centres in sixteenth-century Flanders, such as Oudenaarde, produced verdures.

In France tapestries were made at *Fontainebleau under the patronage of Francis I from 1538, using Flemish weavers to execute cartoons by the king's Italian painters. These were the first tapestries to imitate paintings in the *trompe l'oeil* manner. In Italy, where the warmer climate made wall-hangings less essential to comfort in draughty palaces, the most important workshop was established (1545) by Duke Cosimo I de' Medici at Florence. Run by Flemish craftsmen, such as Jan Rost (*or* Rossi; died 1564), who came from Brussels via a sojourn (1536–45) in Ferrara, it worked from cartoons by the leading Florentine mannerists, Pontormo and Bronzino. It also executed some fine tapestries designed by Bachiacca (1490–1557) of grotesques on a yellow ground (Uffizi).

Tartaglia, Niccolò (1499–1557) Italian mathematician. Born Niccolò Fontana at Brescia, Lombardy, Tartaglia derived his name "stammerer" from the impediment to his speech caused by the wounds he received at the hands of the French in 1512. Largely self-educated, Tartaglia began his mathematical career giving private tuition in Verona. He soon, however, established his reputation by claiming to be able to solve any cubic equation of the form $x^3 + qx = r$. The claim was justified publicly in a competition with del Fiore in Venice in 1535. Shortly afterwards he was appointed to the chair of mathematics at Venice. Although he refrained from publishing his general solution of cubic equations, he was persuaded to reveal the solution to *Cardano who, despite swearing an oath of secrecy, disclosed the result in his *Ars magna* (1545). Tartaglia also worked on the application of mathematics to artillery, publishing his conclusions in *Nova scientia* (1537), and on the geometrical concepts behind military architecture; his book on fortification, *Quesiti, et inventioni diverse* (1546) was dedicated to Henry VIII. He also published and extensively annotated the first Italian translation of Euclid (1543) and composed a major treatise on arithmetic and number theory, the two-volume *Trattato di numeri et misure* (1556–60).

Tasso, Bernardo (1493–1569) Italian poet. Tasso was born into a patrician family from Bergamo and entered the service of Ferrante Sanseverino, Prince of Salerno. By his Neapolitan wife Porzia de' Rossi he was the father of Torquato *Tasso. In 1552 his patron fell into disfavour with the Spanish rulers of Naples and was exiled; the elder Tasso followed him into exile. In 1557 he moved to the court of Guidobaldo II, Duke of Urbino. He died at Ostiglia to which he had been sent as governor by the duke of Mantua. He wrote poems (*Rime*, 1560) and some interesting letters, but his chief claim to fame is the epic poem *Amadigi di Gaula* (1560) based on the Spanish prose romance *Amadís de Gaula*. It attempts to marry the Aristotelian theory of heroic poetry to the metre and material of Ariosto – with long-winded and tedious results.

Tasso, Torquato (1544–95) Italian poet. Tasso was born at Sorrento and as a boy accompanied his father Bernardo *Tasso into political exile, spending a short time at the court of Urbino and studying at the universities of Padua and Bologna. *Rinaldo* (1562), a chivalric romance, demonstrated a youthful poetic competence. In 1565 he joined the retinue of Cardinal Luigi d'Este and in 1572 won the patronage of Duke Alfonso II d'Este and was appointed (like *Ariosto before him) as court poet of Ferrara. He produced his *Aminta*, one of the outstanding *pastoral plays of the Renaissance, before the court in the summer of 1573. By 1575 he had completed the first of many versions of his masterpiece, the epic *Gerusalemme liberata*.

Soon afterwards Tasso betrayed signs of the mental instability that had a tragic effect on the rest of his life. In 1577, after a violent outburst in the presence of Lucrezia d'Este, Tasso was briefly confined but soon fled to the south. After two years of restless wandering throughout Italy, he returned to Ferrara, but after another episode in which he violently abused the duke in public, he was confined in the hospital of Sant'Anna (1579–86). After his release (authorized by Alfonso), he continued wandering, but now with the protection of prominent men and welcomed by various academies and religious orders. He settled finally at the monastery of Sant'Onofrio in Rome, dying before his coronation as poet laureate, which Pope Clement VIII had intended for him, could take place. His other works include almost 2000 formally composed letters; twenty-eight *Dialoghi* on various subjects; *Discorsi del poema eroico* (1594), a critical study that throws light on his own poetry; the tragedy *Torrismondo* (1587), based on Sophocles' *Oedipus Rex*; *Rime* (1593), comprising more than 1000 of his shorter poems; and the long hexameral poem in blank verse, *Il mondo creato* (1594).

Tatti, Jacopo *see* Sansovino, Jacopo.

Tausen, Hans (1494–1561) Danish religious reformer. The son of a peasant at Birkende, Tausen was converted to Lutheran teachings at Wittenberg (1523). On returning to Denmark he was imprisoned for spreading heretical ideas, but, undeterred, he soon afterwards established the first Danish Lutheran congregation at Viborg. He was appointed royal chaplain (1526) and his preaching at Copenhagen won support from the Danish national assembly (1529); he then drew up a radical confession of faith for the Danish Church, but this was later rejected in favour of the more conciliatory Confession of *Augsburg. A firm believer in the use of the vernacular for ecclesiastical purposes, Tausen wrote sermons and hymns and translated sections of the Old Testament. In 1542 he was appointed bishop of Ribe.

Taverner, John (c. 1490–1545) English composer. Taverner served as a lay clerk at the collegiate church of Tattershall in Lincolnshire in the early 1520s, and in 1525 was invited by the bishop of Lincoln to become the first choirmaster at Cardinal College (now Christ Church), Oxford. He took up the post in 1526, but left four years later when the college began to be run down on Wolsey's fall from favour. He returned to Lincolnshire and became master of the choristers at the parish church of St Botolph, Boston. By 1537 he had left the post but remained in Boston, where he died as a highly respected, wealthy local dignitary. Generally regarded as the greatest English composer of the early sixteenth century, he wrote eight Masses, twenty-eight motets, and three secular pieces. The motets include antiphons, Magnificat settings, and responds; in the last, plainsong *cantus firmi* with equal note values are treated polyphonically. There are three six-voice festal Masses written in an archaic style based on a plainsong material with long melismas and constructional devices; these are the last examples from almost a century of the English festal Mass. Taverner's famous *Western*

Wynde Mass is on a smaller scale. It is for four voices and consists of a series of variations on a popular melody.

Tè, Palazzo del The palace on the outskirts of Mantua constructed (c. 1525–35) by *Giulio Romano for Federico II Gonzaga. Challenging classical principles and combining the elegance and sophistication of Raphael and Michelangelo, Giulio created the structure in brick and terracotta (local stone being unavailable) as one of the earliest masterpieces of mannerist architecture. The most dramatic of the palace's decorative features is the Sala dei Giganti, painted from floor to ceiling with frescoes of the fall of the Titans with over-lifesize bodies of tumbling giants and hurtling rocks (see Plate X).

Teatro Farnese *see under* theatres.

Teatro Olimpico *see under* theatres.

technology The Renaissance saw a number of major technological innovations, four of which (*printing, *gunpowder, mechanical *clocks, and the mastery of ocean *navigation) brought about fundamental changes in the nature of society and transformed the course of world history. The first of these, printing, dates from the invention of movable type in the period 1440–50. This in turn was only made possible by the introduction of paper, via China and Islam, into early fourteenth-century Italy. Before 1500 some twenty million *incunabula were published, an operation scarcely conceivable without the benefit of printing and paper. Gunpowder, an earlier invention attributed to Roger Bacon in the thirteenth century, was first seen in its full significance in Europe in the early fourteenth century. At the same time mechanical clocks began to spread across Europe. A century later improvements in ship design, the development of more efficient sails, and the introduction of *cannon on the main deck gave the merchants of Europe the basic equipment with which to dominate world trade.

Within Renaissance Europe itself, the main sources of power remained wind and water. The windmill first arrived in Europe in the late twelfth century in the form of the post-mill, in which a change in wind direction required the whole of the mill's superstructure to be realigned. The less cumbersome tower-mill first appeared in the late fourteenth century. Although initially used for grinding corn they later came to be used mainly for raising water. More versatile and more ancient were the water wheels which spread so extensively throughout Europe that by the beginning of the Industrial Revolution some 600 000 had been constructed. With their aid a range of new industries became possible. Used to drive tilt hammers, mechanical saws, bellows, pumps, and beaters they were partly responsible for the growth of, among others, the paper, iron, tanning, and fulling industries. Before power could be conveniently deployed, however, it was first necessary to convert the rotary motion of the mill into the reciprocating motion of the hammer or saw. It was also necessary to provide efficient and adaptable systems of gears. To this end the Renaissance engineer displayed his ingenuity with the deployment of cranks, compound cranks, flywheels, and cam shafts.

The Renaissance also saw the development of a number of smaller if more specialized industries. In ceramics, for example, a growing confidence in the use of glazes allowed fourteenth-century Italian potters to produce *majolica ware. At about the same time coloured *glass began to be produced in Venice. Both these, and such other industries as distilling, dyeing, and tanning, depended at least partly on the skills of the chemist who began to figure more prominently in the technology of his age. Less successful were the attempts of Renaissance engineers to improve means of inland transport (*see* communications). The same means and speeds suffered by the fourteenth-century traveller were precisely those endured by a comparable eighteenth-century figure. Goods could, thus, take longer to travel a few miles by road than to be shipped scores of miles by water. Significant improvements came only with the development of the steam engine and better road-building methods long after the Renaissance had ended.

telescopes Optical instruments for making distant objects appear larger. The first undisputed description of a telescope, in the official Hague records for 1608, attributes the invention to Hans Lippershey, a spectacle maker of Middelburg, Holland. Details are scarce and the precise nature of the instrument is unknown. The claim was challenged immediately by James Metius of Alkmaar and Zacharias Janzoon of Middelburg. It is now known that all three had in fact been anticipated by Thomas *Harriot. All such instruments were refractive telescopes and operated with a bi-convex object lens and bi-concave eye lens. Word of the new invention spread quickly, for in 1609 in Padua a similar refractor capable of magnifying thirty-three times had been made by *Galileo. Such instruments, known as Dutch telescopes, produced an erect image (which fitted them well for military and naval applications) but presented an unacceptably small field of view. The latter defect was overcome by *Kepler in 1611, by using two bi-convex lenses, though at the price of producing an inverted image. This was not a serious drawback

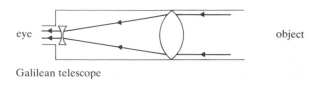

Galilean telescope

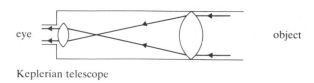

Keplerian telescope

TELESCOPES *The operation of the two kinds of refractive telescope produced by the early pioneers in the field, Galileo and Kepler.*

for astronomers, and Kepler's arrangement became known as the "celestial" telescope – as opposed to the "terrestrial" or Galilean instrument.

More serious faults remained. The images produced were distorted and often surrounded by coloured rings. The defects, known respectively as spherical and chromatic aberration, were in fact inherent properties of refracted light. At best they could be minimized by constructing telescopes, the so-called aerials, with very long focal lengths. Instruments 150 feet long were in fact constructed, but proved too impractical. The solution – to construct reflective rather than refractive telescopes – came much later (1672) with Isaac Newton. *See also* optics.

Telesio, Bernardino (1509–88) Italian natural philosopher. Telesio was born at Cosenza and was educated by his uncle who taught him Greek, thus enabling him to make direct contact with Greek scientific works. He studied at Padua where he became disillusioned with contemporary Aristotelianism, influenced as it was by Arabic interpretations. After he left Padua he spent some years developing his own views, which amount to a return to the authentic opinions of Aristotle. In 1565 he published his first book, *De rerum natura iuxta propria principia*, a work which he continued to expand and which reached its final form in 1586. In 1566 he founded the Academia Telesiana, a scientific society. He died at Cosenza.

Telesio believed that sense is the only basis for speculation about nature. His importance lies in his use of Aristotelian concepts to present an essentially physical explanation of natural phenomena. His system depends on two active natures, heat and cold, and an inert mass on which the two natures react. Telesio also introduced approaches to space and time which in some ways foreshadowed Newtonian physics, and he numbered *Campanella and Giordano *Bruno among his followers.

Téllez, Gabriel *see* Tirso de Molina.

Tempesta, Antonio (1555–1630) Italian engraver, painter, and etcher. Tempesta trained in his native Florence under Jan van der *Straet and also assisted Vasari on the decorative schemes for the Palazzo Vecchio. For much of his life, however, he was based in Rome, where he contributed to the decoration of several palaces, including the Vatican, and of the Villa Farnese at Caprarola. His prints, mainly of hunting and battle scenes, were widely disseminated and copied by other artists.

Tempio Malatestiano The "temple" of Sigismondo Malatesta at Rimini. Conceived by Sigismondo as a temple dedicated to the arts and philosophy and as a monument to himself and his third wife, Isotta degli Atti, the Tempio is a remodelling of the thirteenth-century Gothic church of S Francesco. The interior was begun in 1450 by Matteo de' *Pasti, whose work obliterated earlier frescoes by *Giotto. Chapels were built for Sigismondo and Isotta, with reliefs, notably, of the

TEMPIO MALATESTIANO *A bronze medal by Matteo de' Pasti preserves Alberti's original design for the temple, which was to have been surmounted by a huge hemispherical dome. (1450; Kress Collection, National Gallery of Art, Washington)*

Arts and Sciences by *Agostino di Duccio and a fresco (1451) by *Piero della Francesca that depicts Sigismondo kneeling before St Sigismund. The exterior is the work of *Alberti, who designed a classical shell to encase the earlier building. The structure is based on the motif of the Roman triumphal arch, inspired by the arch of Augustus nearby, and was to be surmounted by a dome. Because of his conflict with Pope Pius II, Sigismondo abandoned work on the Tempio in 1460.

Templars *see* Knights Templar.

Ten, Council of *see* Council of Ten.

Ten of War (*dieci di libertà et pace*) The Florentine council concerned with the conduct of diplomacy and warfare. It was accountable to the *signoria* but had considerable freedom in the way it arranged embassies and ran the military establishment. *Machiavelli was its secretary for fourteen years (1498–1512), and his correspondence from this period gives a detailed picture of the Ten's operations.

Terence (Publius Terentius Afer; 195/185–159 BC) Roman comic playwright. An African-born slave, Terence was received into the cultivated Roman circle of Scipio Aemilianus, to whose taste his plays catered. The plays number six, with four of them being adaptations from the Greek comedy of Menander. Terence was much admired by later Roman writers for the purity of his style, and he similarly appealed to Renaissance pedagogues who recommended his plays for school reading and acting. Although he used much the same material as *Plautus, Terence's sentiments are generally more refined, affording, as Renaissance educationists saw it, moral edification as well as stylistic benefit to students.

Teresa of Ávila, St (Teresa Sánchez de Cepeda y Ahumada; 1515–82) Spanish Carmelite reformer and mystic. She was born near Ávila and, already infused with a heightened religious enthusiasm at the age of seven, Teresa and her brother Rodrigo set off for Moorish territory to be beheaded for Christ. Her uncle stopped them. After her mother died she was placed in the Augustinian convent of Sta Maria de Gracia in 1531. Her spiritual ardour finally compelled her to take up the religious habit and pursue an ascetic life. She entered a Carmelite nunnery in Ávila in 1538 and later fell ill and was paralysed as a result of her self-deprivations. In 1554 she recorded her first visions and ecstatic union with God. She became an ardent reformer and in 1562 founded the Convent of the Incarnation of Discalced Carmelite nuns. In subsequent years she wrote *The Way of Perfection* as a guide for the nuns of her Ávila convent and *Meditations on the Canticle*. In 1567 she and St *John of the Cross began founding other Discalced Carmelite monasteries. Their opponents, the Calced Carmelites, tried to deport her to New Spain but succeeded only in limiting her activities to Toledo. During this difficult time she wrote her most famous work, *The Interior Castle*. She died in Alba shortly after founding yet another Discalced Carmelite house at Burgos. In 1617 the Spanish *cortes* declared her "Patroness of Spain", and she was canonized in 1622, along with *Ignatius Loyola, *Francis Xavier, and *Philip Neri.

St Teresa of Ávila represents, along with St John of the Cross, the most intense mysticism of the Counter-Reformation. As a woman in sixteenth-century Spain, she was not educated in a formal sense, and her writings display a rustic style. Although historians commonly say that in her writings her rapturous religious fantasies are mixed with intense sensual and erotic sentiments, this assertion is exaggerated; in this respect her writings are more moderate than those of St John of the Cross. The mystical enthusiasm of Teresa has been well captured by Bernini's renowned sculpture *St Teresa in Ecstasy* (1645–52; Sta Maria della Vittoria, Rome).

terza rima A type of rhymed verse introduced by Dante in the *Divine Comedy*. It consists of triplets of usually eleven-syllable lines, the triplets being joined by a *rima incatenata* or linked rhyme having the pattern aba bcb cdc ded ... etc. The *chiusa* or conclusion is a single line, e.g. ... xyx yzy z. Perhaps derived from Provençal forms (*sirventes*) or from types of sonnet, *terza rima* acquires a powerful and obvious symbolic value in the *Divine Comedy*. It was later adapted to many different uses, including satire. *Petrarch, *Boccaccio, and in English *Chaucer, *Wyatt, *Daniel, Byron, and Shelley have written poems in *terza rima*.

Teutonic Knights A military religious order founded in the twelfth century and originally attached to the German hospital of St Mary in Jerusalem. In the thirteenth century they were granted territory in eastern Germany from which to subdue Prussia, and with papal support, rapidly increased in wealth and numbers. From 1308 the order's headquarters was Marienburg on the River Vistula. They protected the merchants of the *Hanseatic League, who brought great prosperity to many towns in the Knights' Baltic territories of Prussia and Livonia. Conflict with Poland brought the crushing defeat of the Knights at Tannenberg (1410) from which the order never wholly recovered, and under the peace of Torun (1466)

Poland obtained west Prussia, confining the Knights to the east, which they held as a Polish fief. On their eastern frontiers they continued active into the sixteenth century against Russian encroachments but the growing nationalism of Poland-Lithuania effectively ended their territorial independence.

Theatine Order (the Congregation of Clerks Regular of the Divine Providence) A religious order founded in 1524 by Gaetano da Thiene (St Cajetan) and Giampietro Caraffa, Bishop of Chieti (Theate), who later became Pope *Paul IV. Members were bound by vows and lived in common; they held no property, but were not mendicants, and they were distinguished from the secular clergy by their white socks. They engaged in pastoral work to combat heresy, were zealous promoters of the Counter-Reformation, and sought to remove abuses and encourage piety in the life of the Church. The order spread from Italy to Spain and central Europe and from 1583 it included some nuns.

theatres The important Renaissance innovations in theatre building occurred in fifteenth- and sixteenth-century Italy. Interest in the plays of Palutus and Terence led to the rise of the *commedia erudita*; accompanying this was an interest in authentic classical staging. In 1414 the discovery at the monastery of St Gall of Vitruvius' *De architectura*, book five of which dealt with theatre design, provided the classicizing stimulus to Italian innovators. The manuscript was printed without its illustrations in about 1486, with them in 1511, and in Italian translation in 1521. Vitruvius' principles and his emphasis on symmetry, proportion, and acoustics were eagerly adapted, with varying results. A famous woodcut in an edition of Terence (1493) illustrates the imposition of classical style on earlier traditions of staging. (The *theatrum* (auditorium), placed above a ground storey of arches (*fornices*), had three tiers for spectactors who faced a *proscenium* (stage wall), which was divided by columns with curtains between them.) *Periaktoi* (or, later, *telari*), triangular devices at either side of the stage, the faces of which were painted with rudimentary scenes and revolved to indicate scene changes, were also adapted from the classical model and were increased in number and improved by Bastiano *Sangallo. Knowledge of perspective had also vastly improved painted sets, a feature that much impressed *Castiglione at the 1513 staging of *Bibbiena's *La calandria* in Urbino. By the early sixteenth century several temporary theatres had been constructed from the Vitruvian model. Although Ferrara had led the way in classical performances (Plautus' *Menaechmi* was staged by Duke Ercole d'Este in the palace courtyard in 1486), Vicenza became the centre of theatre construction. In the 1530s Sebastiano *Serlio built a classically inspired temporary theatre for the Vicenzan Accademia Olimpica. He also recorded detailed plans for building a stage and auditorium in a banqueting hall (*Regole generali di architettura*, Book 2); the stage sets behind the shallow playing area, were designed with pronounced perspective effects, and comedy, tragedy, and satire each had its own characteristic set – a street of palaces for tragedy, houses for comedy, and woodland for satire. *Palladio, himself a member of the Accademia Olimpica, was commissioned to build the permanent theatre. Based on Daniele *Barbaro's commentary on Vitruvius (1556), Palladio's Teatro Olimpico, completed by *Scamozzi and opened in 1585 with a performance of Sophocles' *Oedipus Rex*, was the culmination of neoclassical design, though, with its fixed scenery of a piazza and perspective streets, it proved to be dead-end and impractical for performances, even of Roman comedy. A far more flexible arrangement was that of the Teatro Farnese in Parma (1618; destroyed in World War II), built to designs by Giovanni Battista Aleotti (c. 1546–1636); there the proscenium arch and curtained stage made their appearance, with a U-shaped (instead of the previous semicircular) auditorium. Further developments, such as the horseshoe auditorium adopted for opera and ballet, belong to a somewhat later period.

As in other fields, Italian Renaissance experimentation was far in advance of the rest of Europe in responding to classical ideas. However, new theatres having their own national characteristics multiplied in the sixteenth century. The first and only permanent theatre in Paris, a long narrow structure, the Théâtre de l'Hôtel de Bourgogne, rue Mauconseil, was built in 1548 by the Confrérie de la Passion, a lay society dedicated to performing *mystères*; after 1578 it was occasionally let to professional companies. Spanish and Elizabethan English stages remained open air. In Spain the typical stage was raised on scaffolding in a courtyard and surrounded by spectators on balconies or at windows. The unroofed London theatres, such as the Globe and Swan, reflected a similar evolution from the performances of wandering players given at inn yards, although the acting companies also used indoor theatres, such as Blackfriars.

Theotokopoulos, Domenikos *see* Greco, El.

Tibaldi, Pellegrino (1527–96) Italian painter, sculptor, and architect. He was born at Puria di Valsolda, near Milan, and following his early train-

ing in Emilia, he lived in Rome (1549–53), where he was greatly influenced by *Daniele da Volterra and even more by *Michelangelo. This is evident in works such as his *Adoration of the Christ Child* (1549; Galleria Borghese, Rome). He later worked in Bologna, where he built the Palazzo Poggi (now the university), decorating the Sala di Ulisse there (c. 1554) with illusionistic frescoes, and designed and decorated a chapel in the church of S Giacomo Maggiore (c. 1555). In Milan in the 1560s and 1570s he was mainly involved in architecture, building the Jesuit church of S Fedele (begun 1569) and the round church of S Sebastiano (1576). In 1567 Cardinal (later St) Charles Borromeo put him in charge of architectural and sculptural additions to Milan cathedral; Tibaldi designed several parts of the Duomo including the screen between the choir and ambulatory. In 1588 he went to Madrid to execute sculpture and paintings for Philip II in the *Escorial, only returning to Milan shortly before his death. The same mannerist style which is found in his paintings is evident in the huge frescoes in the Escorial, in which he breaks down forms into geometric shapes. He was in part responsible for diffusing *Mannerism outside Rome.

Tinctoris, Johannes (c. 1435–?1511) Franco-Flemish music theorist and composer. Born at Nivelles, he may have known *Dufay while a singer at Cambrai in 1460. In 1463 Tinctoris was instructor of the choirboys at Orleans cathedral. Around 1472 he was appointed tutor to the daughter of the king of Naples and maintained connections with the court there for at least the next fifteen years. Tinctoris composed some music, but is remembered as one of the most important music theorists of his day; he wrote twelve treatises, two of which were printed. The most important of these is his *Terminorum musicae diffinitorium*, the oldest printed music dictionary, in which 299 musical terms are defined. His other writings treat the aesthetics of music, its educational and therapeutic roles, its use in religion, composition, and improvisation. His writings furnish great insight into the music of the Renaissance.

Tintoretto (Jacopo Robusti; 1518–94) Italian painter. Born in Venice, where he spent most of his life, Tintoretto acquired his nickname (meaning "little dyer") by reference to his father's trade as a dyer (*tintore*). Although few details of his life are known, Tintoretto was briefly (according to his 1642 biographer, Ridolfi) a pupil of Titian, from whom he certainly learnt much about the handling of colour. He was also familiar – possibly through prints and engravings – with the works of Michelangelo from whom he inherited a deep interest in draughtsmanship. Ridolfi is the source for the story that Tintoretto wrote up in his studio as his prescription for painting: "Il disegno di Michelangelo ed il colorito di Tiziano." Tintoretto also apparently used wax and clay models which he set in a box with a light in order to experiment with different lighting effects. His early paintings are notable for their daring use of colour and unconventional groups of figures: among them are his masterly *Last Supper* (1547; S Marcuola) and *St Mark Reviving a Slave* or *The Miracle of the Slave* (1548; Accademia, Venice), the latter being one of four commissioned by the Scuola di S Marco, the enthusiastic reception of which established Tintoretto's fortunes.

Tintoretto was later influenced by Paolo *Veronese with whom he collaborated on the important commission for the decoration of the interior of the doge's palace in Venice after the fire of 1577; there he executed the massive paintings of *The Siege of Zara* (1584–87) and *Paradise* (1588) and a portrait sequence of seventy-two doges, among numerous other paintings glorifying Venice. A deeply religious man, Tintoretto often worked for religious institutions, most notably the Scuola di S Rocco, for whom he painted an extensive cycle of wall and ceiling paintings (1565–87), including scenes from the Old and New Testaments, in which he demonstrated his skill in depicting different light effects and experimented with certain illusionistic devices.

Always a prolific artist, he completed the huge *Crucifixion* in the Sala dell'Albergo there in 1565, and the decorative scheme for the Scuola and adjacent church comprise over fifty major paintings. The dramatic swooping flight of the angels and the startled Virgin in the *Annunciation* are just one example of Tintoretto's ability to imbue familiar scenes with drama, and his manipulation of figures and *chiaroscuro* in these paintings mark him out as a leading artist in the mannerist mode. Tintoretto had learnt to paint rapidly as a young man while collaborating with *Schiavone on frescoes in the Palazzo Zen. In later years his sons Domenico and Marco and his daughter Marietta worked as his assistants. Other notable works include many portraits and the famous *Susanna Bathing* (c. 1550; Kunsthistorisches Museum, Vienna). The voluptuous Venetian nude exemplified in the figure of Susanna also found a place in several of Tintoretto's paintings on mythological subjects, such as the Dresden *Liberation of Arsinoe* and the London *Origin of the Milky Way*. Tintoretto died of a fever and was buried in the church of the Madonna dell'Orto, for which he had painted three of his greatest pictures, the virtuoso pyramidal composition of *The Presentation of the Virgin*, *The Worship of the Golden Calf*, and *The Last Judgment*.

Tirso de Molina (pseudonym of Gabriel Téllez; 1583–1648), Spanish playwright. Very little is known for certain of Tirso's early life. It has been argued that he was the illegitimate son of the duke of Osuna but there are serious objections to the theory. He studied at Alcalá, became a Mercedarian friar (1601) and probably lived in Toledo (1605–15), where he may have written the first of some 400 plays, about eighty-six of which (some of doubtful ascription) are extant. He travelled extensively and after 1625, when he was reprimanded by the council of Castile for too frankly portraying vice on stage, abandoned the theatre. He became official chronicler of his order in 1637, producing a recently discovered *Historia general de la orden de Nuestra Señora de las Mercedes*, and died as a prior of a Mercedarian monastery.

Five collections of his plays were published during his lifetime, as well as two miscellanies (1621, 1635) of tales, plays, and poems set in *Decameron*-like frameworks. The most distinguished disciple of Lope de *Vega, Tirso wrote comedies of intrigue and plays on historical and religious themes. A number of these are notable for the prominent roles given to women. His most popular intrigue comedy was *El vergonzoso en palacio* (The Shy Man in the Palace; 1611); but he is now best known for two plays on theological issues of faith, the acceptance or refusal of grace, and salvation: *El condenado por desconfiado* and *El burlador de Sevilla* (both 1620s). The last introduced one of the most memorable of Spanish fictions, the story of Don Juan Tenorio.

Tisi, Benvenuto see Garofalo, Il.

Titian (Tiziano Vecellio; c. 1490–1576) Italian painter. The old tradition that Titain attained the age of ninety-nine is very doubtful, and his birth date is plausibly given by Vasari as around 1490. Titian was born in Pieve di Cadore and moved south to Venice at the age of nine to train as a painter. There he was taught by Gentile and Giovanni Bellini and he then assisted *Giorgione, by whom his early work was strongly influenced, with frescoes commissioned for the German merchants' warehouse. He visited Padua in 1511 to paint frescoes in the Scuola del Santo and then returned to Venice where he executed a number of works that show him gradually moving beyond the Giorgionesque idiom. These include some celebrated half-lengths of beautiful women (the so-called *Vanity* in Munich and the Uffizi *Flora* among them), some accomplished portraits, the allegories of *The Three Ages of Man* (Edinburgh, Sutherland loan) and *Sacred and Profane Love* (Galleria Borghese, Rome), and the first of his great mythological pieces, *The Worship of Venus* (Prado, Madrid) and *Bacchus and Ariadne* (National Gallery, London). Also in this period he received his first major public commission: an *Assumption of the Virgin* for the high altar of Sta Maria dei Frari, Venice (1516–18), a masterpiece of dramatic animation and vivid colouring. He also painted the *Madonna di Ca' Pésaro* (1523) for the same church. Another early altarpiece (1522) is the *Resurrection* triptych, with its notable figure of St Sebastian, in SS Nazaro e Celso, Brescia.

In 1516 Titian had obtained the post of official painter to the Venetian Republic but that did not stop him from accepting commissions from Duke Alfonso d'Este of Ferrara (1516), the Gonzagas in Mantua (1523), and the della Rovere in Urbino (1532). He painted fine portraits for all of these, and his portrait (1535–38; Kress Collection, National Gallery, Washington) of Doge Andrea Gritti exemplifies Titian's extraordinary ability to capture both the dignity and pathos of the old age of the powerful. In 1530 Titian was introduced to Emperor Charles V at Bologna, and his full-length portrait of the emperor with his hound (1532; Prado) ensured his appointment as court painter, with the title of count palatine (1533). Titian also painted several other portraits of Charles that are now lost, but two that have survived are those painted in Augsburg in 1548: an equestrian portrait commemorating Charles's victory at *Mühlberg (Prado) and a full-length seated figure in black (Alte Pinakothek, Munich). On a second visit to Augsburg (1550–51), Titian was probably entrusted with the commission for the great devotional picture known as the *Gloria* or *Trinity* (1551–54; Prado), in which the emperor, wrapped in his winding sheet, kneels in adoration. The emperor's sister, *Mary of Hungary, regent of the Netherlands, was also an enthusiastic collector of Titian's work.

Philip II of Spain continued his father's patronage of Titian. At the end of 1548 the artist travelled to Milan to meet the prince; one fruit of this first encounter may have been the *Venus with Cupid and an Organist* (Berlin), in which the organist appears to be a portrait of Philip. The famous series of erotic poesies (*see* poesy) for Philip was begun in the early 1550s with *Danaë* (Prado; see Plate XXX). Titian was also invited to paint a *Martyrdom of St Laurence* (1564–67) for the central altar of the church of the *Escorial. *The Allegory of the Battle of Lepanto* (1571–75; Prado) was the last of Titian's works to be sent to Spain and shows how heavily the aged artist was by then relying upon his assistants.

Besides the pictures painted for his Habsburg patrons and the ducal families of Italy, Titian continued to execute commissions for the Venetian Republic, including the lost *Battle of Cadoro*, completed in 1538, for the Sala del Gran Consiglio. Another of Titian's patrons was Pope Paul III, the first portrait of whom was painted in Bologna in 1543. In 1545 Titian travelled to Rome, where he met Michelangelo and painted another portrait of the pope, this time with his grandsons (1546; Capodimonte, Naples); the group poignantly captures the tension between the frail elderly pope, the scheming Ottavio, and the indifferent Alessandro. The charming portrait of two-year-old Clarice Strozzi (1542) shows a very different aspect of Titian's abilities. In the 1550s he also painted several portraits of his daughter Lavinia and a self-portrait now in Berlin.

Although Titian's output of portraits, and religious, mythological, and historical paintings was aided, particularly in his declining years, by numerous assistants in his Venetian studio – Vasari, who visited Titian in 1566, describes their practice – the quantity and quality of the work he produced throughout his long life is astonishing. His last painting was a *Pietà* (1576; Accademia, Venice) intended for his own tomb in the Frari. He left it unfinished and it was completed by *Palma Giovane.

Toledo A city in south central Spain, by the River Tagus. Toledo was a Roman colony (founded 193 BC), a Visigoth capital, and an important Moorish city (712–1085). After the Christian reconquest (1085) Toledo was a great Castilian city where Arabs, Jews, and Christians met; it was known for its Hebrew studies until the expulsion of the Jews in the late fifteenth century. Despite its part in the revolt of the *Comuneros (1520–21) Toledo was a favourite residence of King Charles I of Spain (Emperor *Charles V). When *Philip II made Madrid his capital (1560) Toledo's importance declined, but it continued to prosper from its cloth and silk industries and the manufacture of fine steel goods, notably swords.

During the Renaissance the great Catholic reformer, Cardinal *Ximénes, was archbishop of Toledo and an important patron of scholarship. El *Greco lived in Toledo from 1577 until his death in 1614. Notable buildings include the Moorish quarter, the cathedral (1226–1493), the monastery of San Juan de los Reyes and the Casa de la Santa Hermandad (both built in the late fifteenth and sixteenth centuries), and the Alcázar (begun 1531), with its façade by Juan de *Herrera.

Topsell, Edward (1572–1625) English naturalist. Little is known of Topsell's life other than that he was a clergyman and held a number of livings in southeast England. His interest in zoology appears to have been stimulated by the need to identify the various animals referred to in the Bible. The result of his researches was his *Historie of Four-footed Beastes* (1607) and *Historie of Serpents* (1608). Both works are entirely uncritical and derivative; they are, nonetheless, the first illustrated natural history works to be published in English. *See also* zoology.

Tordesillas, Treaty of (7 June 1494) The agreement between Portugal and Spain intended to settle conflicting claims in the New World and to exclude other rivals. In 1493 Pope *Alexander VI established a line of demarcation from pole to pole 100 leagues west of the Cape Verde islands. Portugal was to have the monopoly of exploration to the east of the line and Spain to the west, but neither should occupy territories already under Christian rule. Portugal was understandably dissatisfied; after prolonged negotiations the Portuguese and Spanish ambassadors agreed on the Treaty of Tordesillas, which confirmed the papal idea of demarcation but moved the line 270 leagues further west. This enabled Portugal to claim Brazil when *Cabral landed there (1500). Pope *Julius II approved the treaty in 1506.

Torquemada, Tomás de (1420–98) Spanish Dominican inquisitor. As confessor to the Spanish monarchs *Ferdinand and Isabella, Torquemada, himself born of Jewish descent in Valladolid, encouraged them to attack openly practising Jews and *conversos*. In 1478 the queen persuaded Pope Sixtus IV to unify the inquisitions of Castile and Aragon under Torquemada's control, giving him power to appoint, dismiss, and hear appeals from other inquisitors. He organized the Spanish Inquisition under five territorial tribunals, with one supreme appellate council directed by himself. The Ordinances he issued (1484) regulated inquisitorial procedures in Spain for the next 300 years. From 1483 onwards Torquemada used these vast policing and judicial powers to try and punish spiritual offenders on a grand scale: 2000 were executed during his tenure of office, and vast numbers were punished with imprisonment and confiscation of property. Torquemada used an alleged ritual murder of a Christian baby by Jews in La Guardia as a pretext to expel non-*converso* Jews and Muslims from Spain in 1492.

Torres Naharro, Bartolomé de (?1485–?1524) Spanish playwright. He was born at La Torre de Miguel Sesmero, near Badajoz, and was probably educated at Salamanca. For a time he served as a soldier, was captured by pirates, sold into slavery in Algiers, and later ransomed. He was then ordained a priest and spent his life in Italy, at Rome and Naples, where a number of prelates were his patrons. A collection of comedies together with some poems and a theoretical "Prohemio" on comedy was published in 1517 as *Propalladia*. (Literally, "the first things of Pallas", the title suggests that a further volume of works was to follow, but none was published.) The collection was widely read and reprinted a number of times with additional comedies (ultimately six, after the addition of *Calamita*, 1520, and *Aquilina*, 1524).

In the "Prohemio" Torres Naharro defines comedy as an ingenious arrangement of incidents with a happy ending. He follows the five-act structure and divides comedies into two types: *comedias a noticia*, realistic plays about the lower social orders; and *comedias a fantasía*, imaginative plays. To the latter category of romantic comedy belong *Serafina*, *Himenea*, *Calamita*, and *Aquilina*. *Comedia Himenea*, his best play, owes something to *La *Celestina* and was the earliest *capa y espada* (cape and sword) play on the theme of honour; it introduced such conventional characters as the lover (*galán*), the lady (*dama*), and the comic servant (*gracioso*). His realistic *comedias a noticia* are *Comedia Soldadesca* and *Comedia Trinellaria*. His works were placed on the 1559 Index, but an expurgated edition was allowed in 1573.

Torrigiano, Pietro d'Antonio (1472–1528) Italian sculptor. A native of Florence, Torrigiano is notorious for breaking the nose of Michelangelo when they were fellow students, for which he was vilified by Cellini, Vasari, and other contemporaries. After wandering about Italy for some time as a soldier, Torrigiano visited Antwerp and in about 1511 reached England, where he executed his finest works. The first representative of the Italian Renaissance in English art, he was commissioned to produce the tombs of Henry VII and his wife Elizabeth (1511–18) in Westminster Abbey, and also that of Henry's mother Margaret, Countess of Richmond. Other works in England included an altar (1517, destroyed in 1641), a medallion of Sir Thomas Lovell, and the tomb of Dr John Yonge (1516; Public Record Office). Moving to Seville during the 1520s, Torrigiano was imprisoned by the Spanish Inquisition and starved himself to death. Works executed in Seville include two polychromed terracottas, *St Jerome Kneeling in Penitence* and a *Virgin and Child*.

Toscanelli, Paolo dal Pozzo (1397–1482) Italian mathematician and geographer. He was educated at Padua and became an official astrologer at Florence, where he moved in a circle of distinguished humanists. His theories that most influenced his contemporaries concerned perspective and the possibility of a sea route westwards across the Atlantic to China; his calculations on the latter issue, which overturned those of the geographers of antiquity, may have inspired *Columbus.

Tostado, El *see* Madrigal, Alfonso de.

Totentanz *see* dance of Death.

Tournèbe, Adrien (Turnebus; 1512–65) French humanist scholar. He was born at Les Andelys, Normandy, and studied at Paris before becoming professor of belles-lettres at Toulouse. Returning to Paris in 1547 he became *lecteur royal* at the Collège de France and in 1552 succeeded Robert *Estienne as director of the royal press. In this role he oversaw the production of major new texts of Aeschylus and Sophocles (1552–53) and the *Iliad* (1557). He was also renowned for his knowledge of ancient Greek philosophy, and his extensive interests were demonstrated in his *Adversaria* (1564–65) and in his complete works, published by his son Étienne in 1600.

tragedy In the Middle Ages tragedy, like *comedy, was understood in literary rather than dramatic terms. It concerned the fall of a prince or other great personage from prosperity to adversity and illustrated the mutability of Fortune. The remedy, most eloquently stated in Boethius' *De consolatione philosophiae*, was faith in divine providence. Attachment to wordly things binds man to the wheel of Fortune; awareness of his true end frees him from its inevitable fluctuations. In this thoroughly Christian context, tragedy in the classical mode was not possible. No action was complete in this life but extended beyond; the ultimate outcome was a matter for comedy, in Dante's sense. Thus even Adam's sin and the fall of man involved the paradox of the *felix culpa* in that it led to the Incarnation and the redemption of mankind by Christ. Such conceptions continued in the Renaissance and are found, for example, in works by *Petrarch, *Boccaccio, and *Chaucer.

Towards the beginning of the sixteenth century, however, there was a renewed, classically inspired interest in tragedy as drama. Seneca whose closet dramas on Greek models had coloured the medieval literary view of tragedy, was translated into Italian in 1497. His influence was a dominant strand in Renaissance tragedy and in Elizabethan England was responsible for the vogue of the revenge play. In Italy an improved Latin translation of Aristotle's *Poetics* was published in 1498 and the Greek text in 1508. At the turn of the century appeared the Aldine edition of the Greek tragedians, and Erasmus's Latin translations of Euripides' *Hecuba* and *Iphigenia* were published in Paris in 1506. *Trissino's *Sophonisba* (1515; performed 1562) is the earliest Renaissance tragedy in purely classical style, a direct imitation of Greek models. *Cinthio's *Orbecche* (1541) established the Senecan model (a five-act structure with horrendous carnage and appropriate moralizing). Other notable Italian plays were Giovanni Rucellai's *Rosamunda* (1525), *Alamanni's *Antigone* (1533), *Speroni's *Canace e Macereo* (1542), Pietro *Aretino's *Orazia* (1546), *Groto's *Dalida* (1572), *Tasso's *Torrismondo* (1587), and Federico della Valla's *Reina di Scozia* (1595). The pressure of classical imitation restricted the development of Italian tragedy; it failed to achieve successes equal to the less purist (and more popular) English examples and was soon displaced by the taste for tragicomedy and opera.

Although there are no significant French tragedies before the era of Corneille and Racine, some sixteenth-century works of note are: Lazare de Baïf's translation of Sophocles' *Electra* (1537), the Bordeaux-based Scot George Buchanan's Latin versions of Euripides (*Medea* and *Alcestis*, written c. 1539) and his own *Baptistes sive calumnia* and *Jephthes sive votum* (written c. 1540 and 1542, respectively), Marc-Antoine *Muret's *Julius Caesar tragoedia* (1544), Jean Bochetel's translation of Euripides' *Hecuba* (1544), and the first original French tragedy, Étienne *Jodelle's *Cléopâtre captive* (acted 1552).

In Spain Jerónimo Bermúdez (c. 1530–99), Cristóbal de Virués (c. 1550–1614), and Lupercio Leonardo de Argensola (1559–1613) wrote Senecan plays. Juan de la *Cueva produced four tragedies, but *Cervantes' *El cerco de Numancia* is the most distinguished example before Lope de *Vega and the heyday of the Spanish theatre. In England publication of the historical chronicles of Edward Hall (1548) and Raphael Holinshead (1577), Jasper Heywood's translations of Seneca (from 1559), and Thomas North's version of Plutarch's *Lives* (1579) all stimulated the making of tragedies. The earliest was *Gorboduc* (1561), a Senecan drama by Thomas Sackville and Thomas Norton, which introduced blank verse to the English stage. Thomas Preston's clumsy and incoherent *Cambises* (1569) was followed by the great tragedies of *Marlowe, *Kyd's *Spanish Tragedy*, and *Shakespeare's masterpieces.

translation The translation of texts was one of the characteristic activities of the Renaissance, enabling a wider range of people than ever before to profit from contact with the literature of ancient Greece and Rome (*see* translations (of classical authors)) and with the major works written in other European tongues (*see* translations (of contemporary authors)). Similarly, the numerous vernacular versions of the Bible (*see* Bible, translations of) were both motive and product of the religious ferment of the times.

The principles governing translation had been discussed in antiquity – by Cicero, Horace, and St Jerome, among others – and the debate was continued by the early humanists. *Bruni, one of the busiest of the early translators, expounded his theory of translation in introductions to his Latin versions of Greek masters, and in his *De interpretatione recta* he castigated the medieval translators while attempting a formal justification of his own method. Translators' "apologies" became a standard feature of translations and often throw interesting light on the contemporary status of the author translated as well as on a whole range of linguistic and literary values. Gavin *Douglas, for instance, wrote a 500-line prologue to his Scots *Eneados*, in which he expresses some very characteristic preoccupations: extreme reverence for his author ("Virgillis volume maist excellent"), outrage at earlier botched attempts at translation (in this case Caxton's 1490 *Eneydos*, taken from a French version), and diffidence about his own ability and that of his native "Scottis" tongue ("my rurall vulgar gros") to do justice to the conception and dignity of Virgil's poem.

The point about the insufficiency of the vernacular as a vehicle for the thoughts of the great writers of antiquity was one that vexed most early translators. In the long run their efforts, even if they sometimes stretched the language beyond its limits, had a beneficial effect of raising the level of stylistic awareness and of testing the flexibility of a vernacular in a variety of genres. Douglas regrets that he had to resort on occasions to "Sum bastard Latyn, French or Inglys oys [usage]/Quhar scant was Scottis – I had nane other choys." Such necessity became in many instances a virtue, enlarging and enriching the vocabulary of the vernaculars (*see also* vernacular).

Another question frequently raised by translators was that of fidelity to the words of the original versus fidelity to the spirit. Even those translators who professed the greatest reverence for the original frequently indulged in practices that would be frowned upon by modern scholars; for example, Douglas silently incorporates in his text, at points where he thinks his readers may require it, explanatory material taken from *Badius' prose paraphrase of the poem. Likewise a modern translator would not adopt the cavalier attitude to cuts and omissions displayed by *Harington in his preface to his English *Orlando Furioso* (1591), where he admits tht he has left out "matters impertinent to us" and "tediouse flatteries of persons that we never heard of".

The status of translation in this period accords with the humanistic and patriotic high-mindedness of most translators. The desire to be useful to one's fellow-citizens and to improve their cultural environment runs strongly through their accounts of their motives; underpinning this was the theory that it was beneficial to copy a good model (*see* criticism, literary). As Harington observed, it was preferable "to be called rather one of the not worst translators then one of the meaner makers". Certainly in the hands of *Amyot in France or *Holland in England the translator's profession attained a literary dignity that it has seldom, if ever, attained since.

translations (of classical authors) The earlier Renaissance was preoccupied with the need to make Greek literature accessible to a Latined audience, and the first translations reflected this need. They also reflected the intellectual priorities of the first humanists; prose precedes verse, and philosophy and history precede other types of prose. Leonardo *Bruni translated Aristotle's *Economics* (1419/20), *Ethics* (before 1416), and *Politics* (1437), and by 1480 most of the major Aristotelian works had been made available in Latin translations from the Greek. Translations of Plato began in 1414, Bruni again leading the way with the *Apology*, and reached a climax with *Ficino's comprehensive rendering, completed in 1477. The Greek historians attracted attention as well as the more historical public speeches of Demosthenes. The chief works here were Valla's incomplete version of Herodotus (1457) and his complete translation of Thucydides (1452). By 1460 all the important Greek historians were available and the indefatigable Bruni had translated *On the Crown*, the *Olynthiacs*, and *On the False Embassy*, among other public speeches in the Demosthenic corpus. Poetry and purely literary texts were less commonly translated. The *Iliad* was translated into Latin prose as far as book sixteen by Valla (1442–44). Some of Lucian's *Dialogues* were translated by Bruni and many more by *Erasmus, who also translated *Hecuba* and *Iphigenia* by Euripides (1506).

As the ideas of the Renaissance began to spread they were diffused to an audience which has no access to the classical languages. The prestige of the classics made more people eager to make contact with ancient literature and the increased affluence of the mercantile classes created a market for vernacular translations to satisfy a public who had neither time nor inclination to submit themselves to the long apprenticeship of learning Latin and Greek. A common feature of vernacular translations is the expressed desire of the translators to benefit their audience either in practical ways or by increasing the general level of cultivation in society. The number of vernacular translations in the period before 1620 was huge, and the quality inevitably varied.

Classical works for translation into the vernacular were selected on different criteria than those used by scholars turning Greek into Latin for the benefit of the learned community. Although improvement of the reader was a prime (expressed) aim, entertainment and relaxation were also important. Fidelity to the original was not high on the list of priorities; rather, the aim was to make the ancient author "live" again in the translator's native tongue. Some highly successful translations were not even taken from the original text but from an intervening translation, as was the case with Plutarch's *Lives* (1579) translated by Thomas *North from the French version (1559) of *Amyot.

translations (of contemporary authors) The perceived inferiority of the *vernacular among many Renaissance savants dampened the impulse to translate original works in these tongues into other vernaculars. Proficiency in European tongues other than one's own only gradually gained ground as an educational accomplishment, and then it was ambassadors, merchants, and other travellers, rather than scholars, who were responsible for vernacular to vernacular translations. The automatic respect accorded to ancient Latin and Greek authors (*see* translations (of classical authors)) recommended them to the translators' attention, while a contemporary writer, however esteemed in his own country, might be suspect on religious, political, or moral grounds.

The international organization of the *book trade enabled books, especially in Latin, to circulate easily throughout Europe, and popular and controversial contemporary texts like Erasmus's *Encomium Moriae* (*see Praise of Folly*), More's *Utopia, and Calvin's *Institutes* were quickly translated. Sometimes a vernacular work was translated into Latin to increase its readership, as in the case of Sebastian *Brant's *Das Narrenschyff* (1494); Jakob Locher made a free Latin translation (*Stultifera Navis*, 1497), which was again freely interpreted by Alexander Barclay in his *Ship of Fools* (1509). By such processes Renaissance translations sometimes came to bear little resemblance to their purported originals.

Vernacular to vernacular translations were a product both of the international book trade and of fashions in travel. The young Englishmen who visited Italy in the second half of the sixteenth century, for instance, promoted an interest in the Italian language and literature, which manifested itself in translations of works ranging from bawdy tales to moral tracts. Books on morals and manners seem to have achieved a particularly wide circulation in translation. *Castiglione's *Il cortegiano* (1528) progressed quickly into Spanish (1534) and French (1538), then English (1561) and Polish (1566), and a Latin version in 1571. A trilingual (Latin, French, Spanish) version of *Il Galateo* (1558) by *della Casa appeared in 1598. Guevara's *Reloj de príncipes* (1539) spawned French, Italian, and English versions within two decades of publication. The admiration accorded to Ariosto's *Orlando furioso* as the pre-eminent epic of the early Renaissance is reflected in numerous partial or complete translations: into Spanish (1549), a French prose version (1555), Latin extracts (1588), English (1591; *see* Harington, John), Dutch (1615), and German (1636), among others. Two Spanish prose narratives that attracted the translators and became influential throughout Europe in their respective genres were the pastoral romance La *Diana* (1559) by *Montemayor and *Cervantes's novel *Don Quixote. See also* translation.

Traversari, Ambrogio (Fra Ambrogio *or* Ambrose of Camaldoli; c. 1386–1439) Italian humanist. He entered the Camaldolese Order in 1400, at the monastery of Sta Maria degli Angioli at Florence. From 1431 he was general of the order. At the Council of *Florence he strove to promote the union between the Eastern and Western Churches. A scholar of refined taste and the owner of a renowned collection of Greek patristic manuscripts, he translated many of the Greek Fathers into Latin. He supported the movement within the Roman Catholic Church for the reform of abuses. Although never canonized, he is commemorated on 20 November. His letters and speeches were published in 1759.

Trecento (Italian: three hundred) A term denoting artistic and cultural development in Italy during the fourteenth century. This period was a prelude to the Renaissance of the following two centuries and witnessed the gradual transition from Gothic ideals, despite the disruption caused by the Black Death in 1348. Focused upon such cultural centres as Florence, Siena, and Venice, the Trecento saw the emergence of *Dante, the chief literary figure of the time, the dominance of the *Pisano family in the field of sculpture, and the influence of *Duccio, Simone *Martini, the *Lorenzetti brothers, and *Giotto and his followers over painted art, most profoundly in their emancipation from Byzantine tradition.

Tremellius, John (1510–80) Hebrew scholar and reformer. Born a Jew in Ferrara, he converted to Catholicism (1538) under the influence of Cardinal *Pole. He then came under the influence of *Peter Martyr and became a Protestant, fleeing to Basle

(1542) and then to Strasbourg and England, where he became King's Reader of Hebrew at Cambridge (1549) and made the acquaintance of Matthew *Parker. The death of Edward VI (1553) caused Tremellius to return to Europe where, after extensive travelling and a brief period of imprisonment, he settled at Metz. He spent his last years teaching Hebrew at Sedan, where he died. Tremellius's great work was the translation of the Bible from Hebrew and Syriac into Latin (1569–79). Despite its errors, this became the standard Latin translation used by the reformers to replace the Vulgate.

Trent, Council of The ecumenical council of the Roman Catholic Church, convened at Trent (Trento) in northern Italy, which met in three sessions (1545–47, 1551–52, 1562–63) and ushered in the *Counter-Reformation. There had long been calls for an ecumenical council to reform abuses in the Church, but early sixteenth-century popes had been reluctant to call such a council. There were many reasons for this reluctance. Reforming councils in the late fourteenth and early fifteenth centuries had ventured to limit the power of the popes. (They had achieved this by voting in "nations", according to which the "Italian nation" was always outvoted, even though the Italian bishops present outnumbered those from the "French" and "German" "nations".) More immediately, the Protestant revolt made the situation still more difficult. Emperor Charles V wanted desperately to settle the religious question in the empire, as the Lutheran heresy there sapped his power. (The Lutheran princes were always interested in limiting the power of the emperor.) Charles was willing to compromise and in fact, in the 1548 Interim of *Augsburg, he offered such concessions as clerical marriage and Communion in both kinds (bread and wine) to the Protestant negotiators. In a sense, it was in the interest of Rome to call the reforming council, lest the emperor call a German council and settle the religious question in his domains without taking into account the interests of the papacy. Nor did the French king have much interest in backing the papal call for a council, for he feared the collusion of pope and emperor. The Gallican Church always strove to be independent of the papacy, so much so that there was a point in mid-century when the French king almost followed the example of Henry VIII in breaking with Rome. Rome itself was not overly anxious to compromise with the Protestants, a reluctance that frustrated the emperor.

Finally, however, the council was called, to be held in the small city of Trent. The first session began on 13 December 1545. Few delegates attended this first meeting; there were only thirty-one bishops and fifty theologians and canonists in attendance.

At one time or another during the three sessions of the council, 270 bishops attended. There were 187 Italians, thirty-one Spaniards, twenty-six French, and only two German bishops, figures which might lead one to think that the pope could easily have had his way, since voting was by individual bishop rather than by "nation". However, the Milanese and Neapolitan bishops were constrained to some degree by the wishes of their temporal overlord, Charles V, while the Venetian bishops shared the strong antipapal feeling of Venice. In the third session (1562–63), the very orthodox and unbending Spanish bishops strove to work as a disciplined group, even though they were outnumbered. They resisted any doctrinal novelty and they tried to make the episcopate and the council independent of the pope. Their goal was to allow the pope a primacy of honour but not of power, and they intended to shelter the Spanish national Church from direct papal interference. In addition, the twenty or so French bishops, invested with a Gallican spirit, were intent upon safeguarding the independence of their national Church. However, since all these groups conflicted with each other, the pope eventually prevailed.

Notwithstanding these contradictory forces, the Council of Trent was able to accomplish a great deal. While in the second and third decades of the sixteenth century it had not always been clear what was Protestant doctrine and what Roman Catholic and what clergyman or layman belonged to which confession, the doctrinal decrees of the first two sessions left no doubts on these questions. Henceforth Roman Catholicism could be readily distinguished from Protestantism, as the Tridentine definitions on scripture, justification, and sacraments indicate. Whereas the Protestant churches claimed there was only one authority, holy scripture, Trent declared that there were two: scripture and the teaching tradition of the Church whose *magisterium* was embodied in the papacy. While Trent did not forbid vernacular editions of the Bible, it did declare the Latin Vulgate to be the only authentic text and stressed the right of the *magisterium* "to judge of the true sense and interpretation of holy scripture". On the question of justification, while Protestants claimed that man is justified by faith alone without the works of the Mosaic law, the Council of Trent asserted that man is saved by faith in combination with good works. Regarding sacraments, the Protestant churches held that there were only two (baptism and the Eucharist) and that they were not vehicles of grace; Trent reaffirmed the seven sacraments (baptism, penance, the Eucharist, confirmation, holy orders, marriage, and extreme unction) as vehicles of saving grace. Finally, the last session of the council redefined and reaffirmed almost every belief that humanist scholars like Erasmus had considered superstitious (and therefore not obligatory for the believer): the making of vows, belief in Purgatory, the invocation of saints, the veneration of relics, and the giving of indulgences. On 13 November 1564 (the year that John Calvin died), the pope summed up the Roman Catholic faith as taught at Trent in the Creed of Pope Pius IV. This was a fitting capstone to the Council, as it was truly a victory for the papacy and a closing off of all possibility of negotiated compromise with Protestantism for the next four hundred years.

Tribolo, Niccolò (Niccolo de' Pericoli; 1500–50) Italian sculptor. He was born in Florence, where much of his work is to be seen. Tribolo was influenced by Michelangelo, of whose works he made copies (Bargello). His own most successful genre was fountain statuary, such as the fountain of Hercules and Cacus at the suburban Villa di Castello (Florence), where Tribolo also laid out the gardens (c. 1540).

Tribunal of Blood (*or* Council of Blood) The popular name for the Council of Troubles, established in 1567 by the Spanish governor of the Netherlands, the duke of *Alba, to try the cases of those suspected of treason during the Dutch revolt (*see* Netherlands, Revolt of the). In the next six years it heard some 12 203 cases, producing 9000 convictions and just over 1000 executions. The slaughter has been exaggerated by propaganda, but fear of the tribunal did drive many rebels and Calvinists out of the Netherlands, 60 000 (2 per cent of the population) fleeing during Alba's rule. The tribunal was abolished by his successor, Don Luis de Requesens, in 1573 in an attempt to conciliate the Dutch.

Tridentine Of, or relating to, the Council of *Trent.

trigonometry The main achievements of Renaissance mathematicians in the field of trigonometry were two-fold. Their first task involved the identification and definition of the main trigonometric ratios. Although trigonometry was developed by ancient Greek mathematicians, it was in fact based on quite different presuppositions. The Greeks were interested in establishing tables of chords. Abandoning this approach, Renaissance mathematicians based their work on the assumption that the trigonometric ratios could be expressed as functions of angles. The first modern attempt to develop trigonometry in this way, though restricted to sines and cosines, was made by *Regiomontanus in *De triangulis* (1464; published in 1533). The

system was extended to the other trigonometric ratios by *Rheticus in his *Canon doctrinae triangulorum* (1551). The success of this programme imposed on mathematicians the second task of constructing the appropriate tables. After more than a decade of intense labour Rheticus succeeded in completing detailed tables of all six trigonometric functions. They were published posthumously in his *Opus Palatinum de triangulis* (1596).

Trissino, Giangiorgio (1478–1550) Italian classicist, critic, dramatist, and poet. Born to a patrician family in Vicenza, Trissino studied Greek in Milan (1506) and went to the court of Ferrara in 1512. He attended meetings of the Orti Oricellari in Florence in 1513 and the following year moved to the court of Pope Leo X in Rome. He was highly regarded by successive popes, who entrusted him with several important diplomatic missions.

Sophonisba (1515; first performed 1562), inspired by an episode in Livy, led the way in introducing a vernacular tragedy based directly on Greek models and Aristotelian principles, instead of on Seneca. Written in blank verse, it was also structurally close to Greek tragedy in alternating episode and chorus and in maintaining the unities of action and time. His comedy *I simillimi* (*The Look-Alikes*; 1548) drew on Plautus' *Menaechmi* but again imitated the Old Comedy of Aristophanes in structure. His blank-verse epic in twenty-seven books, *La Italia liberata da' Gotthi* (1547–48), recounting Belisarius' sixth-century conquest of Italy under Justinian, aimed at a purely Homeric style. Trissino also wrote Pindaric odes, the first imitation of a Horatian ode in Italian, and a number of Petrarchan poems.

Though influential examples of the careful imitation of classical models, Trissino's drama and poetry are perhaps of less interest today than his critical and linguistic works. These include an *Epistola* to Clement VII (1524) on spelling reform; the treatises *Grammatichetta*, *Dubbii grammaticali*, and *Il castellano* (all 1529); and the important critical work, *La poetica* (1529). Trissino also translated Dante's *De vulgari eloquentia* (1529), finding in it support for his own views in the *questione della lingua* controversy, in which he took a leading role. With *Castiglione, he favoured an eclectic solution to the problem of a national language.

Trithemius, Johann (Johann Heidenberg; 1462–1516) German reformer and scholar. He took his Latin name from his native town of Trittenheim. An associate of John Camerarius at Heidelberg, he had heard Erasmus lecture at Cologne and was influenced by the ideas of Christian humanism. In 1485 he became abbot of the Benedictine monastery at Sponheim and in 1506 abbot of St James,

Wurzburg, where he died. Trithemius was a leader of the Catholic reformation advocated by Nicholas *Cusanus. He wrote an ecclesiastical history and planned a history of Germany for which he collected many documents. Unfortunately his historical works are unreliable, though the information in *Catologus illustrium virorum Germaniae* (1491) is more trustworthy. His *Polygraphia* (1518) is a pioneering work on *cryptography.

Troubles, Council of *see* Tribunal of Blood.

Troy, legend of The stories connected with the Trojan war, as originally related by Homer and Virgil and expanded by the pseudo-historical medieval authors known as Dares Phrygius and Dictys Cretensis. The latter two purported to have been participants in the events leading to the fall of Troy, and were consequently highly regarded as sources in the Middle Ages. Hints in them were taken up by poets such as Benoît de Ste-Maure, author of the twelfth-century French *Roman de Troie* and the first to treat at any length the love story of Troilus and Cressida. This story was later detached from the cycle and treated as an autonomous narrative by, among others, *Boccaccio, Chaucer, Henryson, and *Shakespeare. In the thirteenth century the Italian Guido delle Colonne made a Latin prose version of Benoît's *Roman*, in which form the expanded Troy legend circulated widely in the Renaissance.

The myth that refugees from Troy or their descendants founded kingdoms and dynasties all over Europe was a potent and attractive one for Renaissance writers eager to compliment their patrons by attributing to them a venerable genealogy (*see also* Arthur, legend of; Charlemagne, legend of). In France, the imaginary Francus the Trojan had long been claimed as the progenitor of the French race. *Ariosto traces the lineage of Bradamante, the fictional ancestress of his *Este patrons, to "The noble blood that came of ancient Troy" (*Orlando furioso* III 18, Harington's translation), and Lydgate in his *Troy-book* (written 1412–20) was just one of numerous English poets to describe a Trojan settlement of Britain under Brutus, the grandson of Virgil's hero Aeneas, founder of Rome. In these stories London is often referred to as "Troynovant" or "New Troy".

Tudor, house of The family of Welsh origin that ruled England from 1485 to 1603 and England and Ireland from 1540 to 1603. Owen Tudor (c. 1400–61), who married (c. 1429) Henry V's widow, Catherine of Valois, established the family's fortunes. Their son, Edmund Tudor (?1430–56), was created earl of Richmond by his half-brother *Henry VI and married (1455) Margaret

*Beaufort, a Lancastrian descendant of Edward III. Their son, later Henry VII, claimed the English throne through his mother, and seized it after invading England and defeating the Yorkist king, Richard III, at Bosworth (1485). Henry VII (reigned 1485–1509) married Elizabeth of York to unite the Yorkist and Lancastrian branches of the royal family. Their son, *Henry VIII, broke with Rome and initiated the English Reformation. During the reign (1547–53) of his young son *Edward VI, Protestant doctrine was established in England, and despite the attempts of Henry VIII's elder daughter, *Mary I (reigned 1553–58), to restore Catholicism to England, the Protestant settlement was concluded by the last Tudor monarch, *Elizabeth I (reigned 1558–1603). The Elizabethan age saw the high point of the English Renaissance which had begun during Henry VIII's reign, the triumphant victory over Catholic Spain, and the continuation of the overseas maritime exploration which led to the development of the British empire.

Tudor style The prevalent architectural and decorative style in England in the period 1485–1558. The reign (1485–1509) of the first Tudor monarch, Henry VII, brought the stability that enabled his son and grandchildren to preside over a resurgence of interest in the arts (*see also* Elizabethan style), and Renaissance influences, although often in misunderstood or debased forms, began to percolate across the Channel to England during the early sixteenth century. Foreign workmen produced some notable artefacts in the new style; one example is the Westminster Abbey tomb of Henry VII himself, commissioned from the Florentine *Torrigiano in 1512.

Ecclesiastical architecture, which after the 1520s was affected by the turmoil of the Reformation, continued to favour the Perpendicular style, the final phase of English Gothic. Domestic architecture, on the other hand, saw major developments, notably the increasingly widespread use of brick, often in conjunction with timber framing and with the bricks laid in herringbone or other decorative patterns. Great houses no longer needed to be heavily fortified, so attention could be paid to aesthetic considerations in their construction. Battlements reduced to ornaments and large, elaborately decorated chimneys, often formed in a barleysugar twist, were new exterior features, while decorative fireplace surrounds and wooden panelling, carved in the shallow pattern known as linenfold, were innovations inside. The shallow, four-centred arch was the characteristic shape for doorways, and oriel windows grew in size and prominence. Compton Wynyates in Warwickshire and the parts of *Hampton Court Palace built under Henry VIII are important examples of Tudor buildings.

Tuileries A former palace on the right bank of the Seine in Paris. Named after the tile factories (*tuileries*) that existed in the area in the thirteenth century, the Tuileries palace was commissioned in 1564 by *Catherine de' Medici and originally designed by the famous architect Philibert *Delorme. Jean *Bullant and Jacques *Ducerceau also worked on the palace which gradually became recognized as the source of a national style of decoration. As a royal residence the Tuileries became the target of rioters during the French Revolution. In 1871 the palace was burnt down during the Commune of Paris. The site is now occupied by the Tuileries gardens.

Tunis, Battle of (July 1535) A Christian victory over the Ottoman Turks in North Africa. In 1534 the admiral of the Turkish fleet, the corsair *Barbarossa, captured Tunis from its Moorish king. This posed a threat to Spanish provinces in Italy, and the king of Spain, Emperor Charles V, resolved to meet the danger decisively. Crossing in person to North Africa with a large army, and with Andrea *Doria as admiral of his fleet, he took Tunis by storm and restored its former ruler as his vassal. This was regarded as a great Christian triumph over the infidel, but it failed to check continued growth of Turkish naval power. Tunis was reconquered by the Turks in 1547.

Tura, Cosimo (Il Cosmè; 1430–95) Italian painter. He was the founder and the first great artist of the school of his native Ferrara. As court painter to the Este dukes he is well known for the series of wall paintings depicting the magnificence of court life with which he decorated the Palazzo Schifanoia in Ferrara (1469–70). It is thought he was trained by Francesco *Squarcione in Padua and the sculptured style of his figures show this influence, as well as that of *Mantegna and *Piero della Francesca. His paintings such as *Primavera* (c. 1460), an allegorical figure from his early period, a *St Jerome* from his later years (both National Gallery, London), and the *St George* organ shutters (1469; Museo del Duomo, Ferrara) illustrate the personal style he developed within the tradition of Squarcione. He used careful detail and rich metallic colours to produce what is often described as a mannered and nervous quality.

Turks *see* Ottoman Turks.

Turner, William (1508–68) English divine, physician, and naturalist. His *New Herball*, published in London (1551) and Cologne (1562–68), was written in English for the benefit of ignorant physicians. Its woodcuts, taken from a 1545 edition of *Fuchs's herbal, reflect Turner's intention of making known the work of the continental botanists he met during his exile in Mary's reign, necessitated by his belligerent Protestantism.

Tyard, Pontus de (1521–1605) French poet. From the family château in Bissy, his birthplace, Tyard combined the careers of poet, scholar, ecclesiastic, courtier, and epicure. An associate of *Scève's group of Lyonnaise poets and a member of the *Pléiade, he produced the first volume of his *Erreurs amoureuses*, containing some of the earliest examples of the French sonnet, in 1549; the influence of *Ronsard is discernible in *Le Livre des vers lyriques* (1555). Tyard's prose works, which include a series of treatises on poetry (*Solitaires*), "Discours de la vérité de divination par astrologie", and writings on astronomy and philosophy, were published in the encyclopedic *Discours philosophiques* (1587). In 1578 Tyard was appointed bishop of Chalon-sur-Saône; his defence of the king during the latter years of the wars of religion caused him to suffer at the hands of the ultra-Catholic party and he resigned his office in 1594.

Tychonic system The cosmological system devised by Tycho *Brahe. In 1543 *Copernicus had argued that, contrary to the *Ptolemaic system, the earth and all other celestial bodies orbited around the sun. Brahe rejected the crystalline spheres of antiquity on the ground that comets seemed to pass unobstructed through them, but was equally dismissive of the heliocentric system of Copernicus.

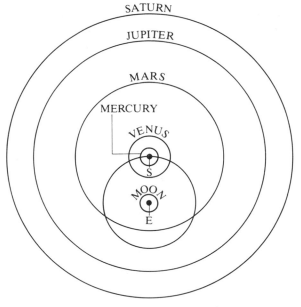

TYCHONIC SYSTEM

The earth's supposed solar orbit, Brahe argued, should lead to a detectable displacement (parallax) in the position of a number of stars. Failing to detect any such effect he sought for an alternative system. The resulting geoheliocentric compromise (see illustration) proposed that the planets and the fixed stars did in fact orbit the sun, but that the sun in turn moved around the earth. Brahe's system was first revealed in his *De mundi aetherei recentioribus phaenominis* (1588). The system found little support, receiving its final formulation in the *Almagestum novum* (1651) of G.B. Riccioli (1598–1671).

Tyndale, William (?1494–1536) English translator of the Bible and religious reformer. Tyndale studied in both Oxford and Cambridge before returning to preach in his native Gloucestershire. Having conceived his project of an English translation of the Bible, and receiving no encouragement from the English ecclesiastical authorities, Tyndale retired abroad, first to Hamburg (1524), and later to Wittenberg, where he met *Luther. The publication of his New Testament (completed at Worms in 1526) increased the hostility of the English bishops, who made repeated efforts to have him arrested. Tyndale spent most of his remaining years in Antwerp, revising his translation and publishing several other important works, including *The Obedience of a Christian Man* (1528), which is his major constitutional and theological treatise, an attack on *Wolsey and the royal divorce (*The Practice of Prelates*, 1530), and a defence against Sir Thomas *More. He was arrested at Vilvorde near Brussels in 1535 and executed the following year.

typography The design of metal types for printing at first closely followed prevailing manuscript trends (*see* calligraphy). Thus, the first types to be cut for German printers such as *Gutenberg were based on the gothic script that had evolved in northern Europe from the script known as Carolingian minuscule. These types formed the gothic or black-letter family of types. In Italy Renaissance scribes practised a more rounded variant of Carolingian minuscule, which became the source for the roman family of types. The first successful roman fount was introduced by *Jenson in Venice in 1470; it was revived in the USA in 1915 under the name of Centaur. Also in Venice, Aldus *Manutius commissioned a highly succesful roman face which he used in 1495 to publish a tract by *Bembo; the twentieth-century adaptation of the face, still called Bembo, is much used in modern bookwork. The third family of typefaces, the italic, was also an Aldine introduction (1501); with its numerous ligatures, it was an attempt to imitate yet another form of humanist script. A rather different italic fount, with numerous modern descendants, was designed in 1523 by the papal calligrapher Arrighi, who derived it from the chancery hand of the papal scribes.

Aldine roman and italic types were greatly admired and imitated with differing degrees of competence all over Italy and France. Typeface usage varied from country to country; in sixteenth-century Italy, for instance, whole books were often printed in italic, but elsewhere, as in modern practice, italic faces were mainly used as differentiation types. In northern Europe black-letter founts remained the norm for the early years of the sixteenth century (and in Germany long after), but the greater legibility of roman ensured its ultimate predominance. This came about at different speeds in different countries: in England, for example, works in Latin were often printed in roman, but those in the vernacular were generally in black-letter until the 1580s, after which roman gradually superseded it except in ballads and inexpensive prose items, which continued to be printed in black-letter until the mid-seventeenth century.

U

Uccello, Paolo (Paolo di Dono; 1397–1475) Italian painter. A Florentine by birth, Uccello was praised by Cristoforo *Landino in 1481 for his skill in foreshortening and for his understanding of the technique of perspective. Uccello's few surviving works demonstrate an interest in the innovations of early Quattrocento artists, especially foreshortening and Brunelleschi's scientific perspective, but united with a strong personal taste for decorative patterns and repeated colours.

Uccello is documented as a youthful assistant to Ghiberti in the workshop creating the north doors for the Florentine baptistery, was admitted as a painter to the Compagnia di S Luca in 1414 and the Arte dei Medici e Speziali in 1415, and worked as a mosaicist at S Marco in Venice in the late 1420s. His stylistic development is exemplified in the *terra verde* Old Testament frescoes of the cloister of Sta Maria Novella, Florence, which were executed in two campaigns; the earlier paintings (?1420s) are still in the International Gothic style, while the later *Flood* (?1440s) demonstrates a fascination with Renaissance perspective, foreshortening, and complex drawing problems that threaten to submerge the theme.

In 1436 the supervisors of Florence cathedral commissioned Uccello to execute a frescoed equestrian monument to Sir John Hawkwood (died 1394), the English condottiere who had been employed by the Florentines; Uccello had to repaint his first version, perhaps because it emphasized the foreshortened illusion of the tomb, horse, and rider, as seen from below, at the expense of the portrait. The completed work is ambivalent in viewpoint, but Uccello's subtle surface modelling and his application of geometric shapes to horse and rider alike create a dignified and sculpturesque monument, while the Renaissance interest in the antique is evident in the influence of the horses at S Marco, Venice. For Florence cathedral during the 1440s Uccello undertook two projects: a frescoed clock face with four illusionistic *Heads of Prophets*, and designs for a *Nativity* and *Resurrection* for stained glass rondels in the drum of Brunelleschi's dome in a programme that included designs by Andrea del Castagno, Donatello, and Ghiberti.

Uccello's *St George and the Dragon* (c. 1455; National Gallery, London) demonstrates how his interest in certain aspects of Renaissance science and his lively imagination could together produce a charming fantasy; it can be related to Landino's praise of Uccello as "a great master of animals and landscape", as can *A Hunt in a Forest* (c. 1460; Ashmolean Museum, Oxford; see Plate XXXI). Uccello's three large panels of the *Battle of S Romano* (before 1456; Uffizi; National Gallery, London; Louvre) were painted for the Medici palace, perhaps as decoration for the bedroom of the young Lorenzo de' Medici, who was born in 1449. They honour a victory of 1432 won by a Medici general, Niccolò da Tolentino, but the content is less militaristic than decorative; they offer a delight in patterns of form and colour especially appropriate for a secular decoration. Uccello's demonstration of how to represent horses, men, and military equipment in foreshortening is impressive, but the poor state of preservation of the paintings had simplified the once subtle modelling. Vasari reported that Uccello was so enamoured of foreshortening that, when his wife called him to bed, she would find him muttering, "Oh what a delightful thing is perspective."

Udall, John *see under* Marprelate controversy.

Udall, Nicholas (1505–56) English schoolmaster and playwright. Born in Southampton, Udall was educated at Winchester and Oxford, but was forced to leave the latter (1529), probably on account of his Lutheran tendencies. He was headmaster of Eton (1534–41) until dismissed on charges of dishonesty, but this did not prevent his obtaining the patronage of Queen Catherine Parr and Princess Mary (later Mary I), and he helped the latter translate part of Erasmus's *Paraphrases* (1548). He also translated Erasmus's *Apophthegmata* (1542) and Peter Martyr's *Tractatio de sacramento eucharistiae* (c. 1550). Edward VI favoured Udall, and he became a canon of Windsor in 1551. In 1555 he was appointed headmaster of Westminster school. His most famous literary production was *Ralph Roister Doister*, published in 1567, but probably written in the early 1550s for a London school. The earliest surviving English comedy, it grafts native comic elements onto a dramatic structure similar to the Latin plays of Plautus and Terence.

Uffizi A palace in Florence, now housing the world's finest collection of Italian Renaissance works of art. The palace was commissioned in 1560 by *Cosimo I de' Medici and designed by *Vasari in the mannerist style. Artistic treasures in the Uffizi include works by such Italian masters as *Cimabue, *Giotto, *Gentile da Fabriano, *Uccello, Fra *Angelico, Fra Filippo *Lippi, *Botticelli, *Leonardo da Vinci, *Michelangelo, *Raphael, *Parmigianino, *Titian, and *Veronese. Artists from other countries represented in the Uffizi include *Dürer and *Altdorfer from Germany, Rogier van der *Weyden and Hugo van der *Goes from the Netherlands, and various French artists. Many of these works were passed to the Uffizi from collections assembled by the Medici family. The palace also houses fine collections of antique sculpture and tapestries, as well as prints and drawings.

Ugo da Carpi (c. 1450–c. 1525) Italian artist. Born at Carpi, near Modena, Ugo was in Venice in 1516, when he requested from the Venetian senate a patent for his technique for making *chiaroscuro* *woodcuts. As the first Italian practitioner of the technique (his earliest known print dates from 1518), Ugo da Carpi was successful in achieving quite complex effects by the use of three blocks. Among his best products are a *Descent from the Cross* (after Raphael) and *Diogenes* (after Parmigianino).

Umbrian school The school of painting associated with the towns of the hilly district of Umbria in central Italy, particularly with Perugia, Todi, and Orvieto. Umbrian art was characterized by qualities described as "softness" and "sweetness". *Perugino and *Pinturicchio were its most famous figures and the young *Raphael was trained in the Umbrian style.

universities The usual medieval term for a university, *studium generale*, implied a teaching centre open to all. The word *universitas*, which gradually superseded *studium generale*, applied to any corporate body and is a reminder that the earliest universities were originally groups of scholars and teachers, who formed themselves, like any trade guild, into a body for reasons of self-protection and self-interest. From the thirteenth century many of these bodies put themselves on a more formal footing by obtaining from pope, king, or emperor a licence enabling them to confer degrees; degrees themselves were licences to teach. Later medieval universities were generally founded by papal bull.

By 1400 there were sixty-five of them spread throughout Europe from Oxford to Prague.

In their earliest form universities were specialist institutions intended to enlarge the scope of *education available through Church schools; thus Salerno was dedicated to medicine, Bologna to law, and Seville to linguistic studies. Paris began as a school for logic but in 1231 gained the right to establish several faculties, of which the theology faculty (the Sorbonne) gained a pre-eminence which it retained until the Reformation. By the fourteenth century many universities possessed four faculties: the arts faculty, which offered a preliminary course, and the three higher faculties of theology, medicine, and law. In many places this pattern of studies prevailed throughout the Renaissance period and beyond as universities became centres of conservatism, dedicated to repressing the effects of humanist studies and religious dissent. On the other hand, with Latin as the universal medium of instruction, students and teachers could and did migrate freely across Europe. The cosmopolitan nature of the academic community was reflected in the frequent subdivision of universities into "nations", for example French, Norman, Picard, and English at Paris.

Over thirty new universities were founded during the fifteenth century, but the rise of *humanism in Italy was fuelled not so much by them as by individual patrons and by the *academies. The university of Florence made the temporary appointment of Manuel *Chrysoloras as professor of Greek in 1395; a century later *Greek studies had found their way into many academic institutions. *Hebrew studies too secured an academic footing in the fifteenth century, principally because, like Greek, they were adjuncts to theological scholarship. With the advent of printing the universities' traditional role of supervising the production of accurate manuscript texts for the use of their students became obsolete; instead university presses began to be founded, the Sorbonne leading the way in 1470, when three Germans set up their press there for a couple of years.

The Reformation posed a massive challenge to the universities in so far as their authority derived from the Roman Catholic Church. The influence of great teachers, like *Erasmus at Fribourg and *Reuchlin at Tübingen, promoted humanist studies, but in many places the teaching of Greek fell under suspicion of encouraging heresy. Institutions like the Dominican-dominated university of Cologne led the anti-humanist, anti-reformist backlash (*see Epistolae obscurorum virorum*). New colleges and new universities however were founded, more receptive to new ideas. The university of Wittenberg, nursery of the Reformation, was founded in 1502 by imperial decree, although with papal approval. Corpus Christi College, Oxford, founded in 1517, made special provision for Greek instruction in its statutes; feelings in Oxford ran so high over the question of Greek that there were street brawls between the pro-Greek faction and its opponents (dubbed, inevitably, "Trojans").

The first Protestant university was founded at Marburg (1527) by Luther's supporter, Philip of Hesse; it soon attracted students from all over Europe. Other famous Lutheran universities were Königsberg (1544), Jena (1558), and Helmstedt (1575). Calvin's *Genevan Academy, although a theological college rather than a university, similarly welcomed students from other countries. In Scotland the universities of St Andrews (founded 1411) and Glasgow (1459) readily embraced Protestantism, the latter being John *Knox's university, while in England Cambridge became a stronghold of Puritanism. Leyden, the first Dutch university to be founded (1575), quickly established an association with *Arminianism; in the seventeenth century it also became famous for its science, a rare phenomenon among universities at a time when advances in science were generally made by individuals in the teeth of opposition from the Church and the traditional academic establishment or were left to private enterprise, like the college endowed in London by Sir Thomas *Gresham.

The universities' potential for assisting the *Counter-Reformation was speedily recognized by the Church, spearheaded by the Jesuits, who had their own university, the *Gregoriana, in Rome. As early as 1556 they established themselves at Ingolstadt, which had long been a bulwark against the reformers. Secular rulers sympathetic to the Counter-Reformation cause might even found a university and hand it over to the Jesuits to run, as Duke Charles III of Lorraine did at Pont-à-Mousson in 1572. Indeed, by 1600 the Jesuits had established a virtual monopoly over higher education in France, with the exception of Paris. The universities of Spain, heartland of Catholic orthodoxy, were renowned in the sixteenth century for their study of scholastic philosophy, revitalized at Salamanca by *Vitoria.

University Wits The name given by the critic G.E.B. Saintsbury (1845–1933) to a distinct group of educated young men in England who, lacking patrons, made their living by writing for the theatres and bookstalls of the 1580s. Chief among them were *Lodge and *Peele from Oxford, and *Greene, *Marlowe, and *Nashe from Cambridge.

Urbino A city and former ducal capital in the Marches of central Italy. Umbrians, Etruscans, Celts, Gauls, Romans, and the Church ruled Urbino until it passed to the *Montefeltro (1234–1508) and *della Rovere families (1508–16, 1521–1631). As the ducal capital (1474–1536) Urbino was an important centre of culture and learning, despite the political weakness of the duchy. When the capital was moved to Pesaro (1536) Urbino itself became a minor mercantile centre, known mainly for its *majolica ware.

During the reigns (1474–1508) of the two Montefeltro dukes, Federico and Guidobaldo, the city was admired throughout Italy for its humanist learning and cultivated ways. The court was the setting for *Castiglione's *The Courtier*, the splendid ducal palace and library were built to house the Montefeltro treasures and manuscripts, the mausoleum of S Bernardino was constructed, and the university was founded in 1506. The fifteenth-century cathedral was destroyed by earthquake in the eighteenth century. *Bramante and *Raphael were born in Urbino, and Luciano *Laurana, *Piero della Francesca, Girolomo *Genga, and (probably) *Francesco di Giorgio Martini were involved in the construction of the Palazzo Ducale. Later Federico *Barocci was the city's principal artist.

Urfé, Honoré d' (1567–1625) French author. D'Urfé was born in Marseilles but as an active supporter of the Catholic party, he was forced to leave France after its defeat by Henry IV; he took refuge in the duchy of Savoy, fighting for the duke, with whose family his mother was connected, in the war between Savoy and Genoa. D'Urfé's best-known work is *L'Astrée* (1607–27; translated as *Astrea*, 1657–78), a pastoral romance in five parts set in the fifth century: the plot centres on the love of the shepherd Céladon for the shepherdess Astrée, their individual adventures, and the lovers' eventual reunion. *L'Astrée* had a considerable influence on seventeenth-century literature and outshone d'Urfé's earlier writings, which include *Epîtres morales* (1598), inspired by the Platonic theory of love, and the pastoral poem *Sireine* (1604).

Ursulines A religious order for women founded at Brescia in 1535 by St *Angela Merici. Its primary purpose was the education of women, and to this end it was intended by the founder that members should live unenclosed. The order was approved by Pope Paul III in 1544 but underwent a radical change in 1572 when communal life was introduced. In 1612 the Ursulines of Paris adopted strict enclosure and solemn vows, following a version of the Augustinian rule.

Utopia A social and political satire written in Latin by Sir Thomas *More, whose friend *Erasmus arranged its publication in Louvain in 1516. Part of *Utopia* was drafted while More was on an embassy in Flanders in 1515, and the book's framework is the narrative of Raphael Hythloday, a fictitious traveller whom More purports to have met in Antwerp. In the first book Hythloday outlines the shortcomings of English society and in the second describes the perfect society of the imaginary island of Utopia (literally, "Nowhere"), which he visited in the New World. The Utopians are ruled by a monarch elected for life, hold all property in common, extend religious toleration to all, operate a system of universal education for men and women, never make war except in self-defence, limit working hours to six a day, and promote cultural activities in the citizens' leisure time. Wrong-doers are enslaved until they amend, an aspect of the system that has been much criticized.

Public sanitation, hygiene, and housing are all much in advance of those in sixteenth-century England.

Utopia spawned several later Renaisance imitations, such as *Campanella's *Città del sole*, and has given its name to the political philosophy that insists upon the creation of a perfect society. Immediately popular, it was frequently issued in Latin during the sixteenth century and translated into German (1524), Italian (1548), French (1550), English (1551), and Dutch (1553).

Utrecht, Union of *see under* Netherlands, Revolt of the.

Uvedale, John *see under* Marprelate controversy.

Uvedale, Nicholas *see* Udall, Nicholas.

V

Vaenius *see* Veen, Otto van.

Valdés, Alfonso de (c. 1490–1532) Spanish humanist and writer. Born like his brother Juan at Cuenca, Valdés, a *converso*, became a Latin secretary (1526) to Charles V and left Spain with the imperial court in 1529. Like Juan, he was a disciple of Erasmus, with whom he carried on a correspondence. His two dialogues, biting satirical attacks on the corruption of the Church, written in an austere, ironic Erasmian style, were published together in 1530 and reprinted several times in the sixteenth century. Although he was reported to the Inquisition, he died as a Catholic, a victim of the plague in Vienna.
Diálogo de las cosas acaecidas en Roma is a defence of the sack of Rome by the imperial armies in 1527, which is seen as a divine punishment of the papal Curia and the clergy in general for their failure to heed criticisms of writers like Erasmus. *Diálogo de Mercurio y Carón* continues the justification of Charles V's imperial policy and broadens the anticlerical satire by contrasting *exempla* of corrupt clergy, dedicated to the letter, and good clergy, dedicated to the spirit, of religion.

Valdés, Juan de (c. 1491–1541) Spanish humanist and religious writer. A *converso*, born at Cuenca, he studied classical languages at Alcalá and, like his brother Alfonso, became a committed follower of Erasmus, with whom he corresponded. *Diálogo de doctrina cristiana* (1529) caused him to be denounced for heresy and he moved to Rome in 1531 to escape the Inquisition. He lived the final years of his life in Naples where he gathered a circle of followers who shared his Protestant, though not strictly Calvinistic or Lutheran, religious views on justification by faith, biblical exegesis, and dogma. His theological thought is summed up in *Ciento y diez consideraciones divinas* (One Hundred and Ten Religious Considerations; 1539), written with his brother. His most important work, however, is *Diálogo de la lengua* (written c. 1535, published 1737), a dialogue in which two Italians and two Spaniards (one called "Valdés") discuss the Spanish language in all aspects of vocabulary, spelling, style, etc. The work was influenced by Bembo's *Prose della volgar lingua* (1525).

Valdés recommends an unadorned plain style and mocks the excesses of the chivalric narratives. The Italians are encouraged to improve their Spanish by considering faultlessly chosen literary examples and some 200 proverbs that are models of terseness.

Valencia A city in eastern Spain, on the River Turia, close to the Mediterranean. It was a Roman settlement in the second century BC, was taken by the Visigoths (413), and subsequently changed hands between Moors and Christians several times before becoming part of Aragonese territory (1238). It was the site of Spain's first printing press (1474), and its university was founded around 1500. From the late fourteenth century Valencia had a thriving school of artists, the early ones mainly anonymous, but the later ones including Luis *Dalmau and *Ribalta. It was also famous for its exported majolica wares, especially in the fifteenth century.

Valerianus, Pierius (Giovanni Pietro delle Fosse; 1477–1558) Italian humanist scholar and poet. He was born in Belluno and became the protégé of Giulio de' Medici (Pope *Clement VII), who employed him as tutor to his wards Ippolito and Alessandro de' Medici in Rome and made him his apostolic protonotary. Among his contemporaries Valerianus had a phenomenal reputation for learning and is primarily remembered for his contribution to *Egyptian studies in his *Hieroglyphica* (1556), the first book to ascertain the historical truth about the writing system of ancient Egypt on the basis of the *Bembine Table, inscriptions on Roman obelisks, the *Hieroglyphica* of Horapollo, and hints in other ancient writers. Around 1516 he also wrote an interesting contribution to the *questione della lingua*, advocating the use of the *lingua cortigiana* as a basis for literary Italian rather than the local dialect of Florence; this *Dialogo della volgar lingua* was not published until 1620. Besides scholarly works in Latin he also published love poetry, the *Amorum libri* (1549).

Valla, Lorenzo (1407–57) Italian humanist scholar. Valla was born at Rome and studied and taught at Pavia before becoming secretary to

*Alfonso I at Naples in 1437. Returning to Rome in 1447, he became papal secretary and taught at the university until his death. He wrote a renowned eulogy on classical Latin composition *Elegantiarum linguae Latinae* (1444), of which fifty-nine editions were printed before 1536. He also wrote philosophical treatises on pleasure and free will, *De voluptate* (1431) and *De libero arbitrio* (c. 1440), and his *Dialecticae disputationes* (1439) was a cogent attack on medieval Aristotelianism. His forcefully stated views on both philology and philosophy provoked confrontations with other humanist scholars, including Poggio *Bracciolini. His most famous work was his exposure (1440) of the Donation of Constantine as a medieval forgery. This document purported to be a grant from Constantine the Great to the pope of authority over the empire. Using philological analysis Valla demonstrated that the language of the Donation was incompatible with the age of Constantine, a discovery that undermined papal claims to supremacy over secular rulers and was useful to his then employer, Alfonso. Valla's reasoning foreshadowed later developments in the attack on Catholic claims by Protestant reformers. Valla also produced influential Latin translations of Thucydides (1452) and Herodotus (1457), whose works became far better known in the Renaissance through Valla's translations than in the original.

Valladolid A city on the River Pisuerga in northwest Spain. Valladolid was granted to the Ansurez family in 1074 and passed to the Castilian crown in 1208. During the late Middle Ages and the Renaissance the city became important as a favoured residence of the Castilian and Spanish courts. *Ferdinand II of Aragon and Isabella of Castile were married there in 1469. The city was a centre of the revolt of the *Comuneros (1520–21) and of a shortlived movement for religious reform which was crushed by the *Spanish Inquisition in the late 1550s. Valladolid's university (founded 1346) is one of the oldest in Spain. Notable buildings from the period of the Renaissance include the cathedral, begun by Juan de *Herrera in 1585, the fifteenth-century Colegio de S Gregorio, and the Colegio de Sta Cruz (1479–92), built in the *plateresque style. Alonso *Berruguete, Juan de *Juni, and Gregório *Fernández all worked in Valladolid.

Valois, house of The family that ruled France from 1328 to 1589. Its founder was Charles of Valois, younger son of the Capetian king, Philip III, who awarded Charles the county of Valois in 1285. When the direct Capetian line died out Philip of Valois became Philip VI of France. There was a direct line of succession until the death of Charles

VIII (1498) without issue. *Louis XII, head of a junior branch of the family, the Valois-Orleans, then succeeded to the throne. When Louis XII also died childless (1515) the throne passed to *Francis I, head of another junior branch, the Valois-Angoulême.

Despite the English claim to the French throne and many setbacks in the Hundred Years' War against England, the Valois established their power in France, defeating overmighty feudal lords and unifying the country under their authority. During the late fifteenth and early sixteenth centuries Valois claims in Italy led to bitter conflict with the house of *Habsburg. The Renaissance flourished in France during the reigns of Francis I (1515–47) and *Henry II (1547–59), but the Wars of *Religion considerably weakened the power of the last Valois monarchs. When *Henry III died without an heir (1589) the throne passed to Henry of Navarre and the house of Bourbon.

Valturio, Roberto (1405–75) Italian military adviser and expert. After some years of legal work for the papacy Valturio returned to his birthplace of Rimini and the service of the lord of Rimini, Sigismondo *Malatesta. In 1472 he published his

VALTURIO *Woodcut of a warship from the 1472 edition of Valturio's* De re militari.

twelve-book treatise on the art of war (*De re militari*). This included beautifully executed woodcuts of military machines (possibly by Matteo de' *Pasti) and many practical comments on contemporary warfare. Some of the ideas for military devices were impractical, like the plan for a cart driven by windmills geared to its wheels, but the book was widely influential, appearing in both Italian (1483) and French (1532) versions.

van Eyck, Hubert *and* **Jan** *see* Eyck, Hubert van *and* Jan van.

Varchi, Benedetto (1503–65) Italian scholar and critic. Varchi was born and lived most of his life in Florence, but was influenced in his critical theories by a spell as a student at Padua, where he was imbued with the prevailing Aristotelianism. Believing in the classical ideal of republicanism, he supported the exiling of the Medici rulers of Florence in 1527, and was himself exiled on the restoration of the Medici in 1530. Despite taking part in Piero Strozzi's abortive expedition against the Medici (1537), he was recalled in 1543 to the service of Duke *Cosimo I de' Medici and provided with a pension to write his *Storia fiorentina*, a history of Florence from 1527 to 1538; notable for its careful documentation, the sixteen-book history was eventually published in 1721. Varchi also wrote poems (*Sonnetti*, 1555–57), plays, and translations from classical authors. Among his critical works, *L'Ercolano* (1560) supports the use of the vernacular in literature.

Vasari, Giorgio (1511–74) Italian painter, architect, and art historian. The son of a potter at Arezzo, Vasari came as a boy to the notice of Cardinal Silvio Passerini, who sent him to Florence to be educated with the young Ippolito and Alessandro de' Medici. Patronage by the Medici continued throughout his career. They and other prominent benefactors encouraged his prolific output, but his posthumous artistic reputation has not remained as high as it was among his contemporaries. Examples of his work as a painter (and decorator) are the posthumous portrait of Lorenzo the Magnificent and decorations in various parts of the Palazzo Vecchio in Florence and the work in the Sala Regia in the Vatican. He was the architect of the *Uffizi in Florence and the modernized Palazzo dei Cavalieri (1562) in Pisa.

It was as the first art historian, the author of *Vite ...* (*Lives of the Most Excellent Painters, Sculptors, and Architects*; 1550, revised 1568), that Vasari has exercised the most profound influence. The biographies were carefully researched and included coverage of technical matters and critical judgments. The book also introduced the idea of a rebirth, or renaissance, of painting and analysed its development in three anthropomorphic stages corresponding to childhood (c. 1250), youth (c. 1400– c. 1500), and maturity (to the death of Michelangelo, 1564), citing representative artists (*Giotto; *Masaccio; *Leonardo, *Raphael, and *Michelangelo) for each stage. This conception of the Renaissance of art and its progressive development has influenced critical judgments and taste up to the present.

Vasconcelos, Jorge Ferreira de (c. 1515–c. 1563) Portuguese playwright and novelist. His birthplace is unknown and little else is known of his early life, though his familiarity with Coimbra and his obvious learning suggest that he may have studied there. He was an attendant of Prince Edward at the court of King John III until 1540 and thereafter became secretary of the treasury and secretary of the India House. His three prose comedies are perhaps better classified as dramatic dialogues intended for reading, in the tradition of *La *Celestina*, rather than as plays for stage performance. *Eufrosina* (between 1537 and 1543), in which youthful love happily ends in marriage, is set in the academic city of Coimbra and is obviously indebted to *Celestina*. *Ulisipo* (a learned form of "Lisbon"; c. 1554) attacks the materialism of the Lisbon middle class. *Aulegrafia* (c. 1555) is concerned with courtiers. Vasconcelos's novel, *Memorial da Segunda Távola Redonda* (c. 1554), defends the old values of chivalry; lyrical passages are interspersed in a narrative that involves both the Arthurian knights of the Round Table and deities from classical mythology.

Vatican Library (Bibliotheca Apostolica Vaticana) The library housing the papal collections in the Vatican City, Rome. The Vatican Library developed from a library established in Rome in the fifteenth century by Pope Nicholas V, who gathered together valuable manuscripts from Germany, England, Greece, and other countries and presented them to the public view, although an inventory (1295) of 443 works survives of an earlier papal collection in the time of Boniface VIII (pope 1294–1303). The present building was erected by Domenico *Fontana at the end of the sixteenth century and the collection was moved from the Floreria beneath the Borgia apartments by Sixtus V (pope 1585–90). In later years the library has been enriched by a number of major bequests and now houses about 60 000 manuscripts, 7000 incunabula, and 950 000 other printed books. The present library comprises twelve basic collections, including the Palatini (*see* Palatina, Bibliotheca), the Reginenses (formerly belonging to Queen Christina of Sweden), the Borghesiani, and the Barberiniani.

Vecchi, Orazio (1550–1605) Italian composer. Born in Modena, Vecchi took holy orders. He is known to have been active in Venice, and became *maestro* at Salò cathedral in 1581. Three years later he was appointed to the same post at Modena. In 1586 he worked for a short period in Reggio Emilia and then became *maestro* at Correggio. He returned to his original post at Modena in 1593, and in 1598 also became *maestro* at the court chapel of Duke Cesare d'Este. In this capacity he was celebrated as a composer of entertainments; though a priest and a composer of sacred works, it is for his madrigals and canzonettes that Vecchi is remembered. His most famous work is his *L'Amfiparnaso* (1597), a madrigal comedy comprising fourteen madrigals for five voices setting a *commedia dell'arte* text.

Vecchietta, Lorenzo di Pietro, Il (c. 1412–80) Italian painter, sculptor, and architect. A native of Siena, Vecchietta was a pupil of *Sassetta and was greatly influenced by Florentine art. The influence of Donatello is particularly strong upon Vecchietta's masterpiece, the painting *The Assumption of the Virgin* (1461–62; Pienza cathedral), which is distinguished by its linear but naturalistic style. The influence of Donatello is also evident upon his marble and bronze sculptures, notably the relief *The Resurrection* (1472; Frick Collection, New York). Other works include an illuminated codex of the *Divine Comedy* (British Museum), a ciborium in Siena cathedral (1467–72), the painting *St Bernardino Preaching* (Liverpool), and frescoes (1441–49) in the Ospedale di Sta Maria della Scala, Siena. His pupils included *Matteo di Giovanni.

Veen, Otto van (Vaenius; 1556–1629) Flemish painter. Van Veen, who although illegitimate was of patrician birth, studied under Isaac Swanenburgh in his native Leyden before moving briefly to Liège (1573). He then spent time in Italy (1575–80), during which he acquired under Federico *Zuccaro in Rome an Italian mannerist overlay to his original Flemish style. On his return to the Catholic Netherlands, he became court painter (1585–92) to the duke of Parma and later held the equivalent post with the archduke Albert. Between 1596 and 1600 Rubens did his final training in van Veen's Antwerp studio. Religious, historical, and allegorical subjects feature among van Veen's output, and his self-portrait with his extensive family is in the Louvre.

Veer, Gerrit de (late sixteenth century) Dutch explorer and surgeon. Veer accompanied Willem *Barents on his three voyages in search of the *northeast passage, and his *Waerachtighe beschryvinghe van de drie seylaegien by Noorden* (1598) gives a lively account of these journeys, in particular the winter of 1596/97 passed by Barents' men in their makeshift shelter on the ice of Novaya Zemlya. The book quickly became famous, and was translated into English (1609) and other European languages.

Vega Carpio, Lope Félix de (1562–1635) Spanish dramatist, poet, and novelist. He attended a Jesuit school in his native Madrid, perhaps studied at Alcalá, and spent a period at Salamanca. He had numerous love affairs throughout most of his life. That with Elena Osorio in the 1580s inspired in part his dialogue novel *La Dorotea* (1632). Shortly after marrying the aristocrat Isabel de Urbina, he sailed with the *Spanish Armada (1588), which he survived. In 1590 he became secretary to the duke of Alba; his pastoral novel, *La Arcadia*, dates from this period. His wife died in 1594, and in 1598 he married Juana de Guardo, while continuing an affair with Micaela de Luján. In 1610 he settled in Madrid. After his second wife died in 1613, he had several love affairs but nevertheless prepared to be ordained as a priest. His final tragic affair was with Marta de Nevares Santoyo, whom he met in 1616. She gradually became blind and then insane, dying in 1632. Though long famous, he himself died poor. Lope established the form of Spanish comedy in the seventeenth century. Of more than 1500 theatrical works credited to him by contemporaries, about one third survive, including *entremeses* (farcical interludes) and *autos* (religious plays) as well as *comedias* (published 1604–47 in twenty-five volumes, with occasional additional volumes since). His three-act verse plays draw on the widest possible range of subject matter (Spanish history, legend, and balladry, mythology, chivalric romance, Italian *novelle*, pastoral, and biblical and religious literature). The plays often have a comic sub-plot related to the main action, an unforeseen dénouement, and characters not portrayed with deep realism but with speech suited to their class; they are intended as moral instruction as well as entertainment. Lope brought to full development a number of stock characters like the *gracioso* (comic servant). His formula for writing plays was set forth in an ironic poem, *Arte nuevo de hacer comedias* (New Art of Making Comedies; c. 1607). The theme of honour, he noted there, was particularly popular. The *capa y espada* (cape and sword) type, with upper-class characters and appropriate sword-play, form the largest group of his comedies. To mention but a few, his plays include *El caballero de Olmedo*, *Fuenteovejuna*, *La discreta enamorada*, *El castigo sin venganza*, and *Peribáñez*.

Almost equally prolific as a poet and adept in a number of genres, Lope wrote Petrarchan and religious sonnets, ballads, poems in the elaborate style of *Góngora (whom he attacked but imitated), and philosophical works. His lyrics, collected by friends, were published in *La Vega del Parnaso* (1637). He also wrote several epics (*La hermosura de Angélica*, *La Jerusalén conquistada*, *Andromeda*, and *La Dragontea*, the last-named an attack on Drake and the English) and a burlesque battle of cats, *La gatomaquia*.

Vegio, Maffeo (1407–58) Italian poet and humanist. Born at Lodi, he studied at Milan and Pavia before publishing (1427) his own thirteenth book of the *Aeneid* as testimony to his admiration for Virgil. This supplement, covering Aeneas' death and deification and the subsequent greatness of Rome, remained an accepted part of the text of the *Aeneid* for about 150 years. This made his reputation and he was appointed secretary of briefs and canon of St Peter's (1444). He taught poetry at the university of Pavia and produced much Latin verse on a variety of subjects, including mythology (*The Golden Fleece* in four books), as well as epigrams and a poem on the Vatican which gives a picture of the building before it was demolished and reconstructed by Nicholas V. Vegio also wrote the educational treatise *De educatione liberorum* (1445–48).

Veleslavín, Daniel Adam of (1546–99) Czech humanist, printer, and historian. Veleslavín lived and worked in Prague where he was a professor at the Charles university until disqualified from his post by marriage. His father-in-law ran the city's major publishing house, and under Veleslavín's management (from 1580) this press put out some important historical compilations and dictionaries. Several of these were Veleslavín's own work, including *Silva quadrilinguis* (1598), a multi-lingual dictionary reflecting the international culture of contemporary Prague. Veleslavín's own prose style was much admired and imitated.

Venetian Academy *see* Neakademia.

Venetian School During the Renaissance, those painters working in or near Venice whose art evolved in a manner distinct from that of other northern Italian towns in the fifteenth century. The movement away from the prevailing Byzantine and Gothic modes began with the Bellini family, in particular with Giovanni *Bellini, who had numerous disciples. The prolific *Vivarini workshop at Murano was also significant in establishing the separate identity of Venetian painting, while another Venetian characteristic, the description of

landscape and townscape, surfaces in the work of *Carpaccio.

With *Giorgione and *Titian Venetian painting reached its apogee, and artists even from northern Europe came to Venice to study there. The quality that above all distinguished Venetian art of the Cinquecento was its warmth and richness of colour, which these two painters exemplified to an extraordinary degree. Other Venetian masters included *Palma Vecchio, Paolo *Veronese, and *Tintoretto, while *Sebastiano del Piombo, Dosso *Dossi, and Lorenzo *Lotto, although not settled in Venice, retained a Venetian flavour to their works as a result of early influences. In the later sixteenth century Mannerism, as exemplified by *Palma Giovane, prevailed over the characteristically Venetian style and the school lost its identity, which only re-emerged in the great eighteenth-century masters, Canaletto and Guardi.

Venice A northern Italian city and port, built on the islands of an Adriatic lagoon, formerly a city state and ruler of a maritime empire. Venice has long been famous for its waterways; in the fifteenth century the Grand Canal was described as "the finest street in the world". Venice originated with the arrival of refugees from the Lombard invasions (568); by the ninth century Venice was a city ruled by a popularly elected *doge and associated with the Byzantine empire. By the late Middle Ages the doge had lost much of his executive power to elected councils and Venice was a great trading state competing with Constantinople.

During the fourteenth and fifteenth centuries Venice was one of the great political, mercantile, and maritime powers of Europe. It ruled over an eastern Mediterranean empire and obtained great wealth from its trade with the Levant, Mediterranean countries, and northern Europe, while through its Egyptian depots it monopolized the import of spices from the Far East. Its dependence upon the sea for its power and wealth was symbolized in the annual ceremony of the *spozalizio del mar* (*see under bucintoro*). Venetian shipbuilding was based on the Arsenale which employed up to 16 000 workers and at one stage produced a galley every day for one hundred days for the war against the Turks. Although great patrician merchant families dominated Venice, its constitution was regarded as a model of co-operation between the monarchical, oligarchic, and democratic elements of society. Greek refugees in the late fifteenth century made Venice a magnet for European scholars; their activities focused on the *Neakademia of Aldus *Manutius, whose *Aldine Press placed the city in the forefront of *printing in Europe. Venice's great power and wealth led it into conflict both with its Italian neighbours and with major

European powers. Maritime rivalry resulted in war with Genoa in the fourteenth century, and Venetian territorial expansion led to war with Milan in the fifteenth. Venice was so greatly feared that its Italian neighbours, the papacy, Aragon, and France combined against it in the League of *Cambrai (1508). From the second half of the fifteenth century Venice also spent many years in wars against the Turks and suffered a number of setbacks. By the sixteenth century numerous wars, the Portuguese discovery of an alternative route to the rich spice trade of the Far East, and Venice's inability to compete effectively with the new nation states of western Europe led to the beginning of Venice's centuries-long decline.

During the period of the Renaissance Venice was renowned for its banks in the Rialto, the site of Europe's first bank in the twelfth century. The wealth of Venice supported the work of the numerous artists of the *Venetian school. Venice has many great palaces and churches. Notable Renaissance constructions include the doge's palace (fourteenth century), the Arsenale (founded in the twelfth century), the Rialto bridge (c. 1590), and the Bridge of Sighs (1600). The medieval St Mark's square and the basilica are still the heart of the city.

Venus The Roman goddess of love, beauty, and fertility, frequently identified in classical antiquity, and later, with the Greek goddess Aphrodite. One of the earliest Renaissance paintings to celebrate a pagan subject was *Botticelli's *The Birth of Venus* (see Plate V), which recreates the Greek myth telling of Aphrodite's birth from the foam of the sea. The choice of subject was intended to recall one of the most famous works of art of antiquity – Apelles' lost painting known as *Aphrodite Anadyomene* (or *Aphrodite rising from the Sea*).

In the Greek pantheon Aphrodite was married to the lame smith god Hephaestos (Roman Vulcan), but was unfaithful to him and became the mistress of the god of war, Ares (Roman Mars). Depictions of the lovers were a favourite theme in Renaissance art, often presented as an allegory of War subdued and disarmed by Love, but also as erotic art for its own sake; Botticelli, *Piero di Cosimo, and *Veronese in their different renderings of the subject show little Cupids carrying off and playing with Mars's warlike accoutrements (*see also* Cupid). Another scene that appealed to painters as offering the scope for depicting female nudes in a pastoral landscape was the judgment of Paris, who, according to the story, was appointed as arbiter by the goddesses Aphrodite, Hera, and Athene in their contest to decide which of them was the most beautiful. Besides Cupid or Cupids, Venus is often depicted with roses and myrtles, the

VENUS *Adriano Fiorentino's bronze figurine follows antique models in the pose known as the* Venus pudica *(modest Venus). (Philadelphia Museum of Art)*

plants traditionally associated with her, and with doves, sparrows, or swans, who either carried messages for her or drew her chariot. The frequent inclusion of sea shells in these scenes is a reminder of her marine origin, and occurs, with the birds, in a low-relief panel of the goddess in the Tempio Malatestiano, possibly by Matteo de' *Pasti.

Several antique statues of Venus, mainly Roman copies of Hellenistic originals, were known to the Renaissance, among them the Medici Venus (Uffizi), discovered in Rome in the sixteenth century. These inspired some imitations, and the Mars and Venus theme was also taken up by mannerist and baroque sculptors.

Verdelot, Philippe (c. 1475–pre-1552) French composer. Born in northern France, Verdelot presumably went to Italy early in his career. He became *maestro* at the baptistery in Florence (1523–25) and at the cathedral there (1523–27). He is also known to have been in Rome around 1523. Verdelot wrote two Masses, a Magnificat, about fifty-seven motets, and nine volumes of madrigals. Though his church music was popular throughout Europe (his motets were parodied by, among others, *Lassus and *Palestrina), it is for his madrigals that he is chiefly remembered, as he was one of the earliest exponents of the genre. In some he adopts a syllabic approach to the text and in others he uses more imitation. The madrigals were popular in Verdelot's day and influenced other madrigalists.

Vergil, Polydore (c. 1470–1555) Italian historian. Born at Urbino and educated in Italy, Vergil was sent to England as deputy to the collector of Peter's Pence (1502). He remained in England for the following fifty years, naturalized in 1510, and held a number of positions in the English Church. Before leaving Italy he published a pioneering history of inventions, *De inventoribus rebus* (1499). In England, however, his attention turned to British history. His most important work in this field was his *Anglica historia* (1534). It began by censuring such traditional parts of British history as the Arthurian legends and went on to present an equally traditional view of British history as leading inevitably to the Tudor monarchy. He also published the first scholarly edition of the earliest history of Britain, Gildas's sixth-century *De excidio et conquesta Britanniae* (On the Ruin and Conquest of Britain; 1526).

Vermeyen, Jan Cornelis (Jan May; c. 1500–59) Netherlands painter and engraver. Born at Beverwijk, near Haarlem, Vermeyen may have studied under Gossaert. He held the post of court painter (1525–29) to *Margaret of Austria and subsequently was attached to the entourage of Emperor Charles V, with whom he was a great favourite. He accompanied the emperor on his Tunis campaign (1535) and designed the series of tapestries commemorating it. His style as a painter was influenced by that of his friend Jan van *Scorel. Numerous engravings by him have survived. Vermeyen's nickname "Jan met de Baard" or "Barbalonga" refers to his fine beard, which he wore so long that he sometimes trod on it.

Vermigli, Pietro Martire *see* Peter Martyr (Pietro Martire Vermigli).

vernacular The rise of the vernacular languages of Europe to accepted status as literary media was a phenomenon closely associated with the Renaissance, even if it was not completed during this period. The original lowly status of these languages is indicated by their name, "vernacular" being derived from the Latin word *verna*, a household slave. In medieval Europe culture and education were Latin-based and Church-mediated, which meant in practice that they were accessible only to males destined for an ecclesiastical career or one of its professional offshoots such as the law. Poetry and chivalric romances in the vernacular, some of which are now recognized as being of the very highest quality, were produced for the recreation of certain aristocratic societies, notably by the Provençal troubadours and German Minnesingers; no contemporary claims however were made for their significance as "great" literature entitled to the attention either of posterity or of anyone beyond the immediate cultural circle for which they were produced. The idea of immortalizing a beloved in a sonnet ("So long as men can breathe or eyes can see,/So long lives this, and this gives life to thee," as Shakespeare boasted) arises from self-conscious and self-confident assumptions about the status of vernacular literature alien to the spirit of medieval verse. In practical terms, limited literacy, the vagaries of scribes, the vulnerability of manuscripts, and the condition of the principal languages themselves (fragmented into numerous dialects, lacking any accepted *orthography) meant that medieval bards were realistic in not setting too much store by posterity or a wider audience.

The *Italian language was the first to begin to undergo the evolutionary process that transformed the despised vernacular into a respectable literary medium. In this process the works of the great Florentine writers of the fourteenth century – *Dante, *Petrarch, and *Boccaccio – played a key role; later the *questione della lingua* debate raised issues of linguistic analysis and the concept of "correctness" that encouraged both interest and pride in the use of the vernacular. A similar route was followed by other languages, and the spread of *printing throughout Europe reinforced the tendency towards standardization. Confidence in a vernacular's qualities as a literary medium to replace or at least equal Latin developed at different speeds in different countries, either helped by *humanism, as in Italy, where it was promoted by scholars like Leonardo *Salviati and Sperone *Speroni, or hindered by it, as in Germany (*see* German language). The process was consolidated once there was a sufficient body of literature in the vernacular of a quality that demanded serious attention from the literary critics (*see* criticism, literary). On the other hand, the use of Latin for serious works on such subjects as law or religion, remained unchallenged until the seventeenth century and even later in cases where the writer wished to reach an international audience.

*Translation was a major factor in the advance of the vernaculars during the Renaissance (*see also* Bible, translations of; translations (of classical authors); translations (of contemporary authors)). Although motives for translating the Bible differed from those for translating the classical Greek and

Latin authors, the acknowledged standing of the original texts in both cases compelled their translators to exert themselves to the utmost to find an appropriate style in the vernacular, with generally beneficial results. Translation between vernaculars became an important means of creating a new European secular culture, accessible to women and laymen.

Verona A city on the River Adige in the Veneto region of northern Italy. Verona became a Roman colony in 89 BC; it was later ruled by Ostrogoths and taken by Charlemagne (774). By the twelfth century Verona was an independent commune frequently torn apart by factional conflicts; the story of Romeo and Juliet is based on family feuds in Verona at the start of the fourteenth century. From 1260 the *della Scala family began to establish its authority over Verona first as *capitani* and from 1300 as hereditary *signori*. In 1387 Verona passed to the *Visconti of Milan and in 1405 to Venice. Venice ruled Verona until 1797, except for when the town was occupied by Emperor *Maximilian I.

During the period of the Renaissance Verona was not only a prosperous centre of trade but also an important centre of humanist studies and artistic output. The artists *Pisanello and *Veronese worked in Verona. Notable buildings include the Castelvecchio (1354), the cathedral (rebuilt in the fifteenth century), the church of Sant'Anastasia, and the fortifications and triumphal gates designed by Verona's great architect, Michele *Sanmicheli.

Veronese, Paolo (Paolo Caliari; c. 1528–88) Italian artist. Born in Verona, from which he acquired the name by which he is better known, Veronese was apprenticed to the local painter Antonio Badile (1486–1541) at the age of fourteen. Badile's influence is strong upon Veronese's earliest known work, the Bevilacqua-Lazise altarpiece (1548). Other early influences include those of Giulio Romano and Titian, whose use of colour and control of illusionistic devices is reflected in Veronese's frescoes for the Villa Soranza, executed in collaboration with G.B. Zelotti (1532–78) but now largely destroyed. Veronese was also moved by the influence of Michelangelo in such paintings as the *Temptation of St Anthony* (1552), executed for Mantua cathedral.

In about 1553 Veronese arrived in Venice, where he established himself as a leading painter in the mannerist style. As a prolific artist who specialized in huge paintings on allegorical, biblical, or historical themes, Veronese was in high demand: typical of his early work was his decoration of the church of S Sebastiano, begun in 1555, in which he sought the effective integration of painting with architec-ture and continued his experiments with foreshortening and light effects. Particularly brilliant in these respects was his decoration of the interior of the Villa Barbaro at Maser (c. 1561), in which Veronese abandoned his mannerist style in order to react freely to Palladio's design. Subsequent works included several notable paintings, including the *Marriage at Cana* (1562–63; Louvre), *The Family of Darius before Alexander* (c. 1570; National Gallery, London; see Plate XXXII), and *The Adoration of the Magi* (1573; National Gallery, London). His famous *Feast in the House of Levi* (1573; Accademia, Venice), caused a considerable stir by its unconventional inclusion of such details as a dog and soldiers in what purported originally to be a version of the Last Supper. Veronese was called before the Inquisition and, despite his spirited defence of the intellectual liberty of the artist, was obliged to change the painting's title to its present form.

Towards the end of his life Veronese received so many commissions that he had to rely heavily on workshop assistance. From 1577 he was involved, with *Tintoretto, in the redecoration of the doge's palace after a serious fire there. His brother, Benedetto Caliari (1538–98), assisted him with this work, which included the magnificent *Apotheosis of Venice* (c. 1585) in the ceiling of the Sala del Maggior Consiglio.

Verrazzano, Giovanni da (died 1528) Italian explorer. Born in Florence of a noble family, Verrazzano was sponsored by a group of bankers to find a western route to China. He sailed from Brittany with a crew of fifty in a French ship, *La Dauphine*, in 1524. On reaching America, he mistook Pamlico Sound, North Carolina, for a strait leading to the Pacific and sent home reports which misled explorers and cartographers for a hundred years and caused an imaginary Sea of Verrazzano (Mare de Verrazana) to appear on North American maps. The search for a passage to China was Verrazzano's sole objective, and although he did stop in New York Bay, the first European to do so, he left when he realized it did not lead to a strait. He continued north to Newfoundland before admitting defeat and returning home. Evidence for his later voyages is less certain but it is said that a southerly voyage in 1528 cost Verrazzano his life, when he landed on an island, possibly Guadeloupe, and was killed by cannibals.

Verrocchio, Andrea del (1436–88) Italian goldsmith, sculptor, and painter. A native of Florence, Verrocchio was probably a pupil of *Donatello, after whose death he worked at the court of Lorenzo de' Medici. Many artists were

VERROCCHIO *Terracotta portrait bust of Lorenzo de' Medici. (National Gallery of Art, Washington)*

trained in Verrocchio's workshop, in its heyday the biggest in Florence; among them were *Leonardo da Vinci and *Perugino. Few paintings attributed to Verrocchio survive; one is a *Baptism of Christ* (c. 1474–75; Uffizi) in which it is possible that the head of one angel was painted by the young Leonardo. Verrocchio's sculptural style illustrates the developing interest of Florentine art in naturalism and movement. In the bronze statue of David (c. 1476; Bargello, Florence) Verrocchio conveyed the arrogance of a young man through expression as well as through the aggressive pose (and incidentally criticizes Donatello's suaver treatment of the same subject). In the bronze *Putto with a Dolphin* (c. 1480; Palazzo Vecchio), designed for a fountain at the Medici villa at Careggi, he successfully presented movement in three dimensions so that the pattern in the work appears to change from each angle. The famous lifesize bronze equestrian statue of Bartolommeo *Colleoni (c. 1479–88; Campo S Zanipolo, Venice), completed after his death, shows Verrocchio's interest in another type of figure than that of youth – the strong, dynamic, and ruthless warrior. His most important work in Florence is perhaps the bronze *Christ and St Thomas* (1467–83), on the outside of Orsanmichele. Examples of his fine portrait busts are those of a noblewoman holding flowers (Bargello, Florence) and of Lorenzo de' Medici (National Gallery, Washington). He is regarded as one of the most influential Florentine artists of his time.

Vesalius (Andrea Vesalio; 1514–64) Belgian-born

anatomist. The son and grandson of physicians who had practised at the imperial court, Vesalius, after studying medicine in Paris and Padua, followed the family tradition and served successively Emperor *Charles V and his son, *Philip II of Spain. He began his anatomical work with the publication of six detailed plates in his *Tabulae sex* (1538), and completed his programme with the most comprehensive and lavishly illustrated of all Renaissance anatomical texts, *De humani corporis fabrica* (On the Structure of the Human Body; 1543). Although Vesalius attempted to base his *anatomy on human *dissection, cadavers were too scarce to allow his programme to be realized. Consequently, at several points, he was compelled to fall back reluctantly on the authority of Galen (*see* Galenism, Renaissance). In 1562, for unknown reasons, Vesalius left the service of Philip II. He died in mysterious circumstances while returning from a pilgrimage to the Holy Land and was buried on the Ionian island of Zakynthos (Zante).

Vespasiano da Bisticci *see* Bisticci, Vespasiano da.

Vespucci, Amerigo (1454–1512) Italian explorer. Born in Florence, Vespucci was introduced to astronomy and geography by an uncle. He studied law at Pisa before entering the service of the Medici family around 1480. From 1494 he worked for them as a shipping agent in Seville. When Columbus's administration of Hispaniola was called in question (1497), Vespucci sailed there with the commission of investigation, thus beginning a career in active exploration. He made several voyages to the New World, although exactly how many and their destinations are unclear. In 1498–99 he sailed with Alonso de Ojeda, exploring the Gulf of Mexico and possibly northern Brazil.
In 1500 Vespucci and Gonzalo Coelho led a three-ship Portuguese expedition down the coast of Brazil. This voyage was extensively documented and charted, and one of Vespucci's letters describing it, *The New World* (*Mundus Novus*), was the first document to define America as a continent and separate from Asia. The cartographer Martin Waldseemüller was the first to christen the new land mass America in Vespucci's honour on his world map of 1507, and *The New World* soon appeared in Italian, French, and German editions. Back in Spain Vespucci held the post of pilot major from 1505 until his death.

Vettori, Piero (Petrus Victorius; 1499–1585) Italian humanist scholar. Vettori was born in Florence and attended Pisa university. He then spent some time in Rome before returning to Florence, where he held the university chairs in

Greek, Latin, and moral philosophy. A dominant figure in European classical studies of his time, Vettori conducted an extensive correspondence; Pope Julius III, Henry III of France, and Grand Duke Cosimo of Florence were among his admirers. His letters were collected and published in 1577 and 1597.

Vettori's editions and commentaries show the astonishing scope of his Greek scholarship: editions of Euripides, Aeschylus, and Sophocles; commentaries on Aristotle's *Rhetoric*, *Poetics*, *Politics*, and *Nicomachean Ethics*; editions of Porphyry, Dionysius of Halicarnassus, and Clement of Alexandria. Among the Latin authors who attracted his attention were Cicero (his annotations on Cicero's letters (1587) are particularly important), Cato, Varro, and Columella. His other observations on classical writers were collected in twenty-five books of *Variae lectiones* (1553; subsequently enlarged to thirty-eight books, 1569, 1582).

Vicente, Gil (?1465–?1537) Portuguese playwright and poet. Biographical details are few concerning the dramatist sometimes called the father of the Portuguese theatre and perhaps the country's greatest poet after *Camões. He may have been born at Guimarães and educated at Coimbra. It has also been suggested that he started life as a goldsmith and in this role created the fantastically elaborate gold and enamel Belém monstrance (1506; Lisbon museum) in the Manueline style. He married in 1500 and his two children edited his works (1562). Attached to the courts of Emanuel I and John III, he supervised dramatic productions at court. His works, particularly his religious *autos*, were influenced by Juan del *Encina; they were also indebted to Erasmus, who compared him to Plautus.

Virtually all of Vicente's lyric poetry, which draws on the traditional and folk verse of medieval Portugal and Spain, is contained in his plays and reflects the fact that he was a musician as well as a poet. His forty-four plays consist of *autos*, tragicomedies for courtly audiences, and comedies and farces for popular audiences. Sixteen of these are in Portuguese, eleven (including many of his best non-religious plays) in Spanish, and seventeen in a mixture of the two languages. The tragicomedy *Dom Duardos* (1525) is sometimes considered his masterpiece; other examples of his work are *Comédia del Viudo* (1514), *Comédia de Rubena* (1521), *Auto da Feira* (1528), and *Amadis de Gaula* (1533). The opposition of the Inquisition, introduced in Portugal in 1536, the fashion for Italianate verse, and the popularity of Lope de *Vega checked the growth of a Portuguese national theatre, which Vicente's work seemed to herald.

Vicentino, Nicola (1511–76) Italian composer and theorist. Born in Vicenza, Vicentino studied in Venice under *Willaert and took holy orders. He later moved to Ferrara, where he was employed by Cardinal Ippolito d'Este and taught music to the ducal family. Vicentino travelled throughout Italy with his patron, but by 1563 he had become *maestro* at Vicenza cathedral. The following year he left and went to Milan, where he died of the plague. Vicentino wrote motets and madrigals but is principally noted for his theoretical works. In *L'antica musica ridotta alla moderna prattica* (1555) he advances modal theories which encouraged composers towards equal temperament and describes the arcicembalo, an instrument with a thirty-one note octave.

Vicenza A city in the Veneto region of northern Italy, and the centre of a rich agricultural region. During the period of the Renaissance Vicenza prospered from its woollen cloth industry. The city was ruled by Romans, Lombards, by the *della Scala of Verona (1311–87), by the *Visconti of Milan (1387–1405), and by Venice from 1405. Vicenza's most famous citizen was the architect *Palladio, whose work in the city was continued by Vincenzo *Scamozzi. Palladian structures which survive include the Basilica (1549–1614), the Villa *Rotonda (1553–89), the Loggia del Capitano (1571), and the Teatro Olimpico (1580–84). Among other well-known Vicentines are the poet *Trissino and the navigator *Pigafetta, and the painter Bartolommeo *Montagna spent much of his working life in the city.

Victoria, Tomás Luis de (1548–1611) Spanish composer. Victoria sang as a boy at the cathedral of his native Ávila, but by 1565 he was enrolled as a singer at the German College, Rome. From 1569 he was employed at the Roman church of Sta Maria di Monserrato and in 1571 taught music at the German College, being appointed *maestro* in 1573. After taking holy orders (1575) he became chaplain at the church of S Girolamo della Carità in 1578. From 1587 Victoria served Empress Maria, widow of Maximilian II, as chaplain at the monastery of Las Descalzas de Sta Clara in Madrid, a post he held until his death, although he continued to visit Rome frequently. Victoria is generally regarded as the greatest Spanish composer of the Renaissance. All his compositions are sacred and comprise twenty Masses, fifty-two motets, and many other liturgical pieces. His works are in a style as sophisticated as *Palestrina's, whose pupil he may have been, but of an emotional intensity rarely equalled elsewhere. Perhaps best known are his motet *O quam gloriosam* and the Mass which he based upon it.

Victorius, Petrus *see* Vettori, Piero.

Vida, Marco Girolamo (?1485–1566) Italian prelate and poet. Born at Cremona and educated in Mantua Vida went in 1510 to Rome and the papal court of Leo X, where he became acquainted with *Castiglione, *Bembo, and other eminent literary figures. He was consecrated bishop of Alba in 1535 and took part in the Council of Trent. His works are important contributions to neo-Latin literature in the Renaissance. His *Christus* or *Christiad* (1535), written in Virgilian hexameters, adapted the epic to Christian matter in presenting Christ as the heroic redeemer. The episode of a council in Hell, borrowed from Boccaccio's *Filocolo*, influenced similar scenes in *Tasso's epic and, through Tasso, Milton's *Paradise Lost*. *De arte poetica* (1527), in the tradition of critical essays that extends from Horace to Pope, is concerned with epic style and imitation of classical models. Among other works are the didactic poems *Scacchia ludus* (*The Game of Chess*; 1527), which expounds chess in the guise of a mock-heroic account of a match between Apollo and Mercury, and *De bombyce* (*On the Silkworm*; 1527), on the production of silk.

Vienna (German: Wien) The capital city of Austria on the River Danube. Celts and Romans lived on the site, but Vienna's history is continuous only from the early twelfth century. The city was granted its charter in 1147 and as the capital of the dukes of Babenberg from 1156 became a centre of courtly patronage. When the Habsburgs took over in 1278 they made Vienna their capital and from 1558 it became the capital of the Holy Roman Empire, although under Emperor *Rudolf II its primacy was usurped by Prague. It was not only its capital status but also its position on important trade routes that brought prosperity to the city. Vienna was temporarily occupied by the Hungarian monarch in the late fifteenth century and it heroically resisted the siege by the *Ottoman Turks in 1529. Both in 1529 and in 1683 it was the bastion against the Turkish advance into the heart of Europe. Under Habsburg rule Vienna was a centre of the Counter-Reformation in southern and eastern Europe. Vienna possesses a number of fine fourteenth-century Gothic churches and the cathedral of St Stephen (1137–1578).

Viète, François (1540–1603) French mathematician. Although the greatest French mathematician of the century, Viète, who was born at Fontenay-le-Comte, trained initially in law at the university of Poitiers. Much of his early life was spent in politics. He served as a member of the Brittany *parlement*, practised law in Paris, and in 1580 was appointed an officer of the Paris *parlement*. As Henry IV's cryptographer, he broke an elaborate cipher used by Spanish agents. It is, however, as an algebraist that he is mainly remembered. In his *In artem analyticam isagoge* (1591) Viète introduced such basic algebraic conventions as using letters to represent both known and unknown quantities, while improving the notation for the expression of square and cubic numbers. Further advances in the solutions of cubic and quartic equations were described by Viète in the posthumously published *De aequationum recognitione* (1615).

Vigarni, Felipe (Felipe Biguerny; died 1543) Burgundian-born sculptor. Vigarni was active chiefly in Spain after 1498. Combining features of northern European art with Italian ideas, Vigarni executed work for Burgos cathedral and the chapel royal at Granada (1520–21) before embarking upon his best-known work at Toledo cathedral. In collaboration with Diego Copin and Cristiano from Holland, Rodrigo the German, Sebastián de Almonacid, and the painter Juan de Borgoña, Vigarni executed the high wooden altar (1498–1504), designed by Peti Juan. His other works included a number of medals, such as that of Cardinal *Ximénes de Cisneros (before 1517; Madrid university).

Vigenère, Blaise de (1523–96) French diplomat and cryptographer. Vigenère, who was born at St-Pourcain, began his career as a secretary to *Francis I in 1540. Shortly afterwards he entered the service of the duke of Nevers with whom, apart from several diplomatic missions, he remained for the rest of his life. He first came into contact with cryptology while in Rome in 1549 on diplomatic business. In 1570 Vigenère retired from the court to write. Of the more than twenty books he published two are still remembered. The first, *Traicté des cometes* (1578), was one of the earliest works to suggest that comets were natural phenomena, bringing no special dangers for monarchs and princes. Many great kings, he pointed out, had died unheralded by any comet. In the second and more important work, *Traicté des chiffres* (1586), Vigenère laid the foundations of modern *cryptography.

Vignola, Giacomo Barozzi da (1507–73) Italian architect. Named after his birthplace of Vignola, near Modena, Vignola worked in the mannerist style and is best known for his highly influential treatise upon Vitruvius, the *Regola delle cinque ordini d'architettura* (1562). The ideals expressed in this work, which was translated into most European languages, were reflected in many of

Vignola's own designs and were themselves derived from his study of antique models during his training in Bologna and Rome. In 1541 he widened his horizons with work at Fontainebleau, returning to Italy two years later in order to produce his own designs.

After executing plans for the Palazzo Bocchi at Bologna (1545), Vignola moved to Rome where he was appointed papal architect by Pope Julius III in 1550. In 1551 he began work on the Villa Giulia in collaboration with Vasari and Ammanati, basing the design closely on classical examples. At about the same time, however, he also began work on the designs for the churches of S Andrea (1550–54) in the Via Flaminia and Anna dei Palafrenieri (begun 1565), which constituted a radical break with the classical tradition and anticipated Baroque architecture. After Michelangelo's death (1564) Vignola led the architectural team working to complete *St Peter's.

Vignola's most important building, the church of Il Gesù in Rome, was nonetheless designed in the classical style. Begun in 1568, the church was built for the Jesuits and had a profound influence on later architects, even though it was completed after Vignola's death in a form somewhat different from the original plans. Another highly original building by Vignola was the Villa Farnese at Caprarola, a polygonal structure begun by Antonio da *Sangallo the Younger and *Peruzzi for which Vignola designed (1559) a circular courtyard and magnificent spiral staircase. He also wrote a treatise on perspective, *Le due regole della prospettiva pratica* (1583).

Villamediana, Don Juan de Tassis y Peralta, Count of (1580–1622) Spanish poet, satirist, and courtier. Born at Lisbon, the son of a diplomat, Villamediana was a gambler and libertine, who, on being banished from court in 1608, travelled and fought in Italy. Returning in 1617, he soon made himself so unpopular with his savage lampoons that he was forced to withdraw from Madrid again, but in 1621 he was appointed gentleman-in-waiting to the young Queen Isabel, wife of Philip IV. His attentions to her soon attracted the notice of his many enemies. During the performance of his masque *La Gloria de Niquea* in May 1622 a fire broke out and Villamediana's rescue of the queen caused further scandal. Three months later he was assassinated at the instigation of the king and his minister Olivares.

Villamediana was the friend and patron of *Góngora, by whose style his own was deeply influenced. His satires combine concentrated venom with polished versification, and he also wrote some fine love poems and poetical fables.

villanelle A verse form developed in sixteenth-century France by the poets *du Bellay, *Desportes, *Passerat, and others and revived in the nineteenth century. The term "villanelle" is derived from *villanella*, a type of Italian rustic song or dance: the content of the villanelle is usually of a pastoral or popular nature. The villanelle consists of a variable number of three-line stanzas (usually five) with the rhyming pattern aba, followed by a four-line stanza with the rhyming pattern abaa. The first and third lines of the first stanza are used alternately as the third lines of the second, third, fourth, and fifth stanzas; both lines reappear as the third and fourth lines of the final stanza.

Vinck(e)boons, David (1576–1632) Netherlands painter and print designer. In 1579 Vinckboons's family moved from his birthplace of Malines to Antwerp, where he received his initial training from his father Philip, a watercolourist. After the return of the Spanish army, the family moved on (1591) to Amsterdam, where Vinckboons studied under another Flemish émigré, Gillis (III) van Coninxloo. The latter's influence was decisive upon Vinckboons's many landscapes populated by numerous tiny figures. However, in such works as the *Kermis* (c. 1610; Dresden), the influence of the peasant scenes of Pieter *Brueghel the Elder is paramount. Vinckboons was one of the most popular and prolific painters and print designers of his day. His work constitutes a bridge between the Netherlandish genre traditions of the sixteenth and seventeenth centuries.

Virgil (Publius Vergilius Maro; 70–19 BC) Roman poet. Born near Mantua, where he later farmed, Virgil studied philosophy and rhetoric at Rome. There he was accepted into the literary circle surrounding *Maecenas and the future Emperor Augustus. Virgil's three great works – the *Eclogues* (37 BC), the *Georgics* (30 BC), and the *Aeneid* (virtually complete at the poet's death) – have had an incomparable influence over subsequent European literature. Known, copied, and studied throughout the Middle Ages, these poems were accorded a veneration that partially offset the dubious reputation acquired by their author as a powerful wizard. On the credit side, however, it was believed that Virgil's Fourth Eclogue was a prophecy of the birth of Christ, and it was the more positive assessment of Virgil in medieval tradition that led Dante to appoint him as his guide in the first two parts of the *Divine Comedy.

The *Eclogues* comprise ten short poems in hexameters, written in imitation of the *Idylls* of the third-century BC Greek poet Theocritus. From him Virgil adapted such motifs as the incantations used by a country girl to draw back a faithless lover from the town, a singing match between shepherds, and laments for unrequited love; these recur in countless Renaissance imitations in Latin and in the vernaculars. Theocritus, who was virtually rediscovered in the early fifteenth century, and Virgil together laid the foundations of the *pastoral.

The *Georgics* are four didactic poems, also in hexameters, on the subject of farming. They deal respectively with the cultivation of crops, the growing of trees, cattle rearing, and bee-keeping. The *Georgics* had fewer Renaissance admirers, but among them was *Fracastoro, who imitated them in his *Syphilis*. One reason for the comparative lack of enthusiasm for the *Georgics* was Aristotle's strictures on didactic poetry, aired particularly by *Castelvetro.

The *Aeneid* was the virtually unchallenged model for a national *epic in the Renaissance, greatly preferred to *Homer by, among others, *Vida and Julius Caesar *Scaliger. The text known to the Renaissance was generally supplemented by a thirteenth book, added in 1428 by Maffeo *Vegio. Finding an adequate metre to reproduce the dignity and power of Virgil's Latin hexameters was one of the major tasks of his translators and imitators.

Vischer family A family of sculptors and bronze founders in Nuremberg, Germany. The foundry was started in 1453 by Hermann the Elder (died 1488), whose most important work was the bronze font (1457) in the Stadtkirche, Wittenberg. His son Peter the Elder (c. 1460–1529), the most renowned member of the family, gave the foundry its wide reputation. A gifted sculptor, he made many of the models for his work himself. He worked in the late Gothic naturalistic style with a touch of classicism, which was apparent, for example, in the monument of Archbishop Ernst of Saxony in Magdeburg cathedral (1494–95). To him is attributed the "Bough-Breaker" (1490; Munich), a key work of German bronze sculpture because of its early three-dimensionality and interest in movement. Another important work was the pair of bronze statues of Theodoric and King Arthur for the tomb of Emperor Maximilian I at Innsbruck (1513). Peter's most famous work is the large and impressive reliquary shrine of St Sebald for the church of St Sebald in Nuremberg, erected in 1519. Peter was assisted in this by his talented sons who carried on the foundry, Hermann the Younger (c. 1486–1517), Peter the Younger (1487–1528), and Hans (c. 1489–1550). The first two visited Italy (c. 1512–15), and Italian influence is apparent in their work, including the St Sebald shrine. The design of the whole structure and the main figures of the apostles are still essentially Gothic, but much of the decoration is mannerist, including a profusion of biblical, mythological, and allegorical figures. Hermann cast many funeral monuments, including the tomb of Elisabeth and Hermann VIII of Henneberg at Römhild (probably after 1507). Peter produced medals and plaques in a full-blown Renaissance style, as well as monuments. Hans's work includes reliefs for the Fugger chapel in Augsburg (1537–40). Hans's son Georg (1520–92) made small decorative items in bronze.

Visconti family A family predominant in Milan from the late thirteenth century. The careers of Ottone Visconti (1207–95; archbishop of Milan, 1262–95), who ousted the rival della Torre family, and his great-nephew Matteo (captain of the people, 1287–1302; imperial vicar, 1311–22) were the basis of the Visconti family fortunes. In 1349 the council of the commune bestowed upon Matteo's heirs the perpetual title of *Signore*. Despite papal opposition, they extended their lands and influence throughout Lombardy and Piedmont. The height of Visconti power came under Giangaleazzo (1351–1402), who succeeded his father Galeazzo II (c. 1321–78) in the western part of the family's lands in 1378 and ousted his uncle, Bernabò (1323–85), from the remainder in 1385. He was made duke of Milan in 1395, and by his death only Florence stood out against Visconti overlordship of northern Italy. Giangaleazzo was succeeded by his weak son Giovanni Maria (1388–1412; duke, 1402–12); after a troubled reign, during which he relied heavily on the support of Facino *Cane and his *condottieri*, he was succeeded by his brother, Filippo Maria (1392–1447; duke, 1412–47), who restored Visconti power, but was thwarted in his dreams of wider expansion by Florence and Venice in a war that lasted from 1423 to 1428. Increasing reliance upon *condottieri* in his later years did not prevent his suffering heavy territorial losses, including that of Genoa, which he had seized in 1412. He produced no male heirs and at his death the line was extinguished. Power passed briefly to the *Ambrosian Republic, and then (1450) to Filippo Maria's son-in-law, Francesco Sforza. See p. 418.

Vitoria, Fray Francisco de (?1483–1546) Spanish theologian. He may have been born at Burgos, where, having entered the Dominican Order (c. 1502), he studied at the convent of S Pablo, before going to Paris in 1506. There he was ordained priest (1509), taught arts and philosophy (1512–17), and became a doctor of theology (1523). After lecturing on theology at Valladolid (1523–26), he was appointed to the first chair of theology at Salamanca, where he reformed theological studies by his changes to the curriculum and his insistence upon a humanistic approach to the subject.

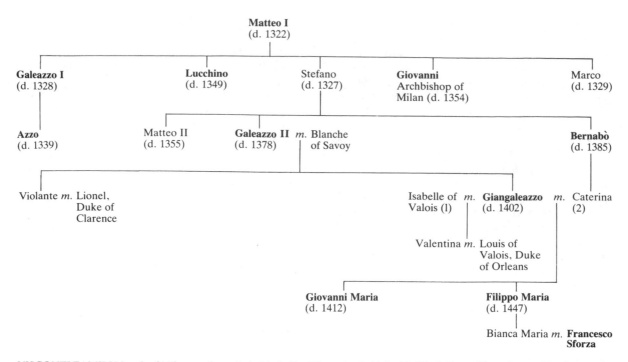

VISCONTI FAMILY *Lords of Milan are shown in bold; the first Visconti to hold the title "Duke" was Giangaleazzo. The direct male line of Visconti rulers of Milan died out with Duke Filippo Maria, but the dynastic marriages of the previous eighty years had raised Milan to the status of a European power. It was through Valentina's marriage to Louis of Orleans that the French royal house made their claim to Milan.*

Melchior *Cano was among his pupils. His *Relectiones* (1557, 1565, 1604) covered many of the moral questions of the time, including the conquest of the American Indians (he was critical of Spanish methods) and the concept of a just war (war is only held to be justifiable if undertaken to redress a wrong already inflicted).

Vitruvius Pollio (active c. 50–26 BC) Roman military engineer. He is important as the author of *De architectura*, the only treatise on the subject surviving from the ancient world (*see* architecture). Copies of the work were known in Italy in the Middle Ages, but interest in it escalated with Poggio *Bracciolini's discovery of a superior manuscript of this notoriously problematical text. It was avidly studied by *Alberti and *Palladio, among others, and it provided the basis for a theory of architecture in conscious opposition to Gothic practice, as well as providing models for buildings such as *theatres for which there was no medieval equivalent.

Vitry, Philippe de (1291–1361) French music theorist, poet, and composer. Vitry studied at the Sorbonne, was a canon at the cathedrals of Cambrai, Clermont, and Verdun among others, and became bishop of Meaux in 1351. For much of his life he was active in the French court as secretary to Charles IV, Philip VI, and John II. Vitry was recognized in his day as a leading intellectual; his famous treatise, *Ars nova musicae* (c. 1320), is a fundamental source of information on rhythmic notation in which Vitry developed the mensural system of notation (*see ars nova*). Of Vitry's compositions only motets survive; these are often lyrical in quality and demonstrate the use of isorhythm and the hocket.

Vittoria, Alessandro (1525–1608) Italian sculptor. A native of Trent in northern Italy, Vittoria was active after 1543 chiefly in Venice where he became the leading sculptor in the city. A friend of *Titian, *Tintoretto, *Palladio, and other notable mannerists, Vittoria was a pupil of Jacopo *Sansovino and undertook work in several different media – marble, bronze, and terracotta. Among his best-known work is the elaborate stucco decoration of the Scala d'Oro (1555–59) in the doge's palace in Venice, where he also created three statues in the Sala delle Quattro Porte (1587) and other pieces, both before and after the fire of 1577. He also produced a number of important religious works for the church of Sta Maria de' Frari and other

Venetian churches. Other works included stucco decorations at Daniele *Barbaro's Palladian Villa Barbaro (now Villa Volpi) at Maser, near Asolo, and several important tombs, numerous portrait busts, and bronze figurines. His own particular brand of Mannerism survived after his death in the styles of several of the pupils of the school he founded.

Vittorino da Feltre (Vittorino de' Rambaldoni; 1378–1446) Italian humanist educator. Vittorino is generally called after his birthplace, Feltre, north of Treviso. He studied and then taught at Padua university, met *Guarino da Verona, and began to evolve the educational theories that laid the foundation of humanistic pedagogy. In 1423 he was invited to Mantua by Gianfrancesco Gonzaga to establish a school for the children of the Gonzaga court. For twenty-two years Vittorino administered every aspect of the intellectual, moral, and physical development of about seventy boys, including some paupers, who were boarded in the Gonzaga villa, the Casa Giocosa.

The basis of the curriculum was the teaching of Latin and Greek grammar, and the classical ideal of the eloquent and virtuous citizen was held up for the pupils to emulate. Mathematics, music, and philosophy (both Platonic and Aristotelian) were also taught, but there was also an emphasis on sound Christian doctrine, and physical education was not neglected.

Vivarini family A family of artists in fifteenth-century Venice. The founder of the Vivarini workshop at Murano was Antonio Vivarini (c. 1415–84), also known as Antonio da Murano. His early commissions included a number of Madonnas, such as that painted for the Oratorio dei Filippini in Padua (c. 1440). A prolific artist, Antonio favoured a more naturalistic approach in his later works, many of which were executed with the collaboration of his brother-in-law Giovanni d'Alemagna (d. 1450). The two men together produced several gilded and elaborate altarpieces for churches in Venice and also collaborated upon Antonio's masterpiece, the polyptych *Virgin and Child Enthroned with Saints* (1448; Pinacoteca Nazionale, Bologna), which also exhibits the influence of Antonio's younger brother Bartolommeo (1432–91). From 1447 to 1450 Antonio and Giovanni d'Alemagna lived in Padua, where they worked alongside Andrea *Mantegna and Niccolò Pizzolo upon a fresco cycle in the Ovetari chapel of the church of the Eremitari (destroyed in World War II) that reflected the influence of *Gentile da Fabriano and *Masolino. Antonio's son Alvise (1445–1505) was influenced by *Antonello da Messina and Giovanni *Bellini and produced a number of original works, including *Christ Blessing* (1498; Brera, Milan) and *St Anthony of Padua* (undated; Museo Correr, Venice).

Vivès, Juan Luis (1492–1540) Spanish humanist scholar and educator. Vivès was born and educated in Valencia and subsequently studied at Paris (1509–c. 1512), Bruges, and Louvain. While in Paris (1519) he met *Erasmus, who already knew of him through Thomas *More. In 1520 Vivès was appointed lecturer at Louvain, and soon afterwards began work at Erasmus's request on a commentary on St Augustine's *City of God* (1522). When Henry VIII and Catherine of Aragon visited Bruges (1521), Vivès was presented to them, and they and Wolsey welcomed him when he moved to England in 1523. He made his home at Oxford, becoming a fellow of the newly founded Corpus Christi College. His support for Catherine over the royal divorce proceedings cost him Henry's favour and even led to his being placed under house arrest for six weeks. He then withdrew to the Continent, where, between 1528 and 1531 he wrote his famous treatise on education *De tradendis disciplinis* (1531). This ranks as his major educational work but he also wrote a book on the education of women, translated into English as *The Instruction of a Christian Woman* (1540), and *Linguae Latinae exercitatio* (1539) to provide practice in Latin for schoolchildren. His educational theories marked an important development in Christian humanism. In philosophy, his *De causis corruptarum artium* (1531) embodied his opposition to scholasticism and *De anima et vita* (1538) offered a fresh approach to psychology. He died in Bruges of fever.

Volterra, Daniele (Ricciarelli) da *see* Daniele (Ricciarelli) da Volterra.

Vos, Maarten Pietersz. de (1532–1603) Netherlands painter and print designer. De Vos was born in Antwerp and trained by his artist father Pieter de Vos and by Frans *Floris. He seems to have visited Italy, possible in the company of Pieter Brueghel. He is reputed to have worked at Venice in the studio of Tintoretto as an assistant in the painting of landscapes. In 1558 he returned to Antwerp, where he joined the artists' guild and in 1572 became its dean. Having Lutheran sympathies, de Vos became involved with the liberal, reformist circle of the famous geographer Abraham *Ortelius. These connections did not prove incompatible with his work as a painter of altarpieces, to replace those which had been destroyed by

ADRIAEN DE VRIES
Rudolf II Leads the
Arts and Sciences into
Bohemia. *The river god
and lion (left foreground)
symbolize, respectively, the
River Vltava and Bohemia.
(Windsor Castle, England)*

iconoclastic riots. De Vos also designed illustrations for Christopher *Plantin and, in 1594, collaborated with Ambrosius Francken on the decorations for the triumphal entry of Archduke Ernest of Austria. As a painter of historical, religious, and mythological scenes, de Vos continued the style of Frans Floris, somewhat modified by a colouristic sense derived from his Venetian experiences.

Vredeman de Vries, Hans (1527–?1604) Netherlands architect and designer. Born at Leeuwarden, Friesland, Vredeman de Vries was a student of Cornelis *Floris, whose style he plagiarized, primarily in a long series of variations upon the design of Antwerp town hall. Several of these variants are reproduced, together with numerous other architectural fantasies, in his *Varia architecturae formae* (1601). Vredeman de Vries does not appear to have been an architect in the generally accepted sense of the term, in that no known buildings can be securely attributed to him. However, his journeys through the Netherlands and Germany and his books of prints popularized his designs, reflections of which may be seen in the guildhalls of Antwerp and the butchers' hall of Namur. A seminal, rather than an original figure, Vredeman de Vries's influence may be traced well into the seventeenth century.

Vriendt, Cornelis de *see* Floris, Cornelis.

Vriendt, Frans de *see* Floris, Frans.

Vries, Adriaen de (1546–1626) Dutch sculptor. Adriaen de Vries was born in The Hague and became a pupil of *Giambologna in Florence. His first major commissions were the Mercury fountain and the Hercules fountain, completed respectively in 1599 and 1602, for Augsburg. Although de Vries designed both works, he did so in Rome; the actual casting and finishing was done, from his models, by other sculptors in Augsburg. As early as 1593 de Vries was already executing commissions for Emperor Rudolf II, including the famous *Abduction of Psyche by Mercury* in Paris. In 1601 he moved to Prague, where he worked mainly for the emperor on portrait busts, allegorical reliefs, and the like. After the emperor's death in 1612 and the removal of the imperial court to Vienna, de Vries widened his circle of patrons. For Count Ernst of Schaumburg he executed the font in Bückeburg parish church and the count's tomb in Stadthagen, as well as a pair of bronze groups, since lost, for the bridge leading to Bückeburg castle. All of this work was designed and cast in Prague, being subsequently transported to north Germany by road. De Vries collaborated with Hans von *Aachen and was influenced by artists as diverse as Raphael and Dürer, but his principal model remained Giambologna. Adriaen de Vries was the last great northern mannerist sculptor and a leading light in the international "hothouse" culture which briefly and spectacularly flourished in imperial Prague at the turn of the sixteenth and seventeenth centuries.

waggoners Navigational guides containing charts and sailing instructions. The word is an English corruption of the Dutch name "Waghenaer". Lucas Jansz. Waghenaer's *Spieghel der Zeevaerdt* (1584–85; translated as *The Mariners Mirrour*, 1588) popularized printed sailing charts, standardized navigational techniques, and brought the best contemporary mathematical and astronomical data within reach of the ordinary mariner.

warfare Wars in all their varieties constantly swept Renaissance Europe. The *Holy Roman Empire never fully reintegrated itself after local and religious wars; the Hundred Years' War (1337–1453) and the Wars of *Religion (1562–98) brought France close to collapse; the Habsburg-Valois conflict raged over Europe for over sixty years; the Turkish army twice threatened Vienna. At the same time as warfare advanced technically and the horrors of *firearms became more apparent there was a growing awareness of the brutality of war and correspondingly less emphasis on its romantic glories.

The English longbow was the most effective fourteenth-century weapon, but the introduction, probably by the English at Crécy (1346), of *gunpowder was the most significant development. Warfare became more technical and more expensive; this favoured the evolution of royal and national armies and weakened the private feudal armies. Monarchs relied more on skilled *mercenaries and less on untrained feudal levies. By the fifteenth century the new *cannon could demolish medieval castle walls, a further blow to the power of feudal lords. The arquebus, a firearm which a man could carry, was developed. The study of tactics, artillery, and techniques were all part of the more professional approach to warfare, with military experts like *Valturio and theoreticians like *Machiavelli commanding an attentive audience.

In the sixteenth century pistols and muskets were invented. At the battle of *Pavia (1525) General Fernando de Avalos proved the worth of the musket in the rout of the French cavalry by Spanish musketeers. The sixteenth century also saw great advances in naval warfare. Admirals like Sir Francis *Drake, Andrea *Doria, and Don *John

of Austria made effective use of lighter and more manoeuvrable ships.

Wars of Italy *see* Italy, Wars of.

Wars of Religion (French) *see* Religion, (French) Wars of.

Wassenhove, Joos van *see* Justus of Ghent.

watches The first watches appeared shortly before 1500, supposedly the invention of Peter Henlein (c. 1479–1542), a Nuremberg locksmith. More plausibly, they emerged in several centres as a natural development from small table *clocks. These, in turn, were made possible by the invention in the late fifteenth century of the spring-driven escapement. Thereafter no further fundamental advance in watch design and accuracy took place before the invention of the balance spring in 1675. Before this, without minute or second hands, the Renaissance watch was valued more as an item of jewellery or a toy than as an instrument for measuring time. Watches were accordingly expensive, highly decorated luxuries produced mainly to satisfy the whims of the wealthy. Typical of such pieces are, for example, the two very expensive watches bought by Francis I in 1518 to fit into the hilt of his dagger or the miniature timepiece Elizabeth I had made to fit into her ring.

Wechel family A dynasty of printers based from the 1520s in Paris and from 1572 in Frankfurt and other German towns. The first in the line was Christian (fl. 1520–54), who worked in Paris, where he established the firm's special line in medical books and parallel Greek and Latin texts of the classics. He also produced *Agrippa's *De occulta philosophia* (1531), several editions of the Latin, French, and German texts of Alciati's *emblem book, the earliest in 1534, and the third book of *Pantagruel* (1546). Wechel's son Andreas (died 1581) took over in 1554 and moved for religious reasons to Frankfurt in 1572, where he produced a number of historical and geographical works, both classical and modern. Other members of the family continued printing at Frankfurt, and also at Hanau and Basle, until the outbreak of the

Thirty Years' War effectively strangled humanistic publishing enterprise. The international and eclectic scope of the Wechel presses after 1572 is indicated by the variety of their modern authors: *Sadoleto, *Buchanan, *du Plessis-Mornay, *Falloppio, *Fernel, Giacomo *Zabarella, *Serlio, *Paracelsus and his disciples Thomas Moffett and Gerard Dorn, *Bruno, Giambattista *della Porta, *Dee, and *Ramus and authors on both sides of the *Ramist controversy.

Weelkes, Thomas (c. 1576–1623) English composer. Nothing is known of Weelkes's early life. In 1598 he was appointed organist at Winchester College, where he probably remained until at least 1601, when he became organist and choirmaster at Chichester cathedral. In 1602 he was awarded the Oxford BMus. degree. Weelkes's employment at Chichester was tempestuous: he was periodically reproved for unruliness, drunkenness, and neglect of duty, and in 1617 he was even dismissed from the post, though he later resumed it. He died in London. Weelkes is important as a composer of both church music and madrigals. He wrote ten Anglican services and around forty anthems, of which *When David heard* is perhaps one of the finest. The madrigals are in a less restrained style, often for four, five, and six voices. In his four published collections, Weelkes demonstrated to great effect his intricate style, using fine counterpoint and brilliant imagery. A contemporary of Thomas *Morley, he contributed to the collection, *The Triumphs of Oriana* (1601).

Weerbeke, Gaspar van (c. 1445–post-1517) Franco-Flemish composer. By 1472 Weerbeke was in the employ of the Sforza family in Milan, and around 1481 he joined the papal choir in Rome. He returned to the Sforza court in 1489. From 1495 he was associated with Philip the Handsome, Archduke of Austria and Duke of Burgundy. He probably returned to Milan in 1498 and then to Rome in 1500, where he again sang in the papal choir. He is last documented as a canon at St Maria ad Gradus in Mainz. Weerbeke worked with Josquin *Des Prés at the Sforza court. Some eight Masses, twenty-eight motets and several other liturgical works survive, including substitution Masses. Five of his Masses were published by *Petrucci.

Weiditz, Hans (I) (Hans Wydyz; active 1497–1510) German sculptor. Weiditz was a wood carver working in a sculptural, three-dimensional style. He settled in Fribourg im Breisgau, and his altarpieces include the Schnewlin altar for a choir chapel in the minster there (c. 1512–14), depicting the *Rest on the Flight into Egypt* (after an etching by

*Dürer). He also produced small-scale figures and groups, such as his *Adam and Eve* (c. 1510).

Weiditz, Hans (II) (pre-1500–1536) German illustrator. Presumed to be the son of Hans (I) Weiditz, he was probably born in Fribourg and worked in Augsburg and later Strasbourg. He is known as the gifted illustrator of numerous humanist, classical, sacred, and scientific books, for which he designed woodcuts. These included Cicero's *De officiis* (1531), which was extremely popular at the time, and *Brunfels's *Herbarum vivae eicones* (1530–36). His illustrations often satirize particular sections of society, such as the clergy and nobility.

Weigel, Valentin (1533–88) German mystic. He was a Lutheran pastor near Chemnitz in the latter part of his life, but his writings show him to have held highly unorthodox ideas on the nature of the universe, some of which can be traced to the influence of *Paracelsus. He himself influenced Jakob *Boehme. Although his writings, and those ascribed to him, were not published until twenty years after his death, they circulated widely in manuscript during Weigel's lifetime.

Buchenschell. Backerkraut.

HANS (II) WEIDITZ *Weiditz's careful observation of living plants is exemplified in this woodcut of a pasque flower (*Pulsatilla vulgaris) *for Brunfels's* Herbarum vivae eicones.

Wert, Giaches de (1535–96) Flemish composer. Wert went to Italy as a child to sing at the court of the marchese della Padulla at Avellino near Naples. By 1558 he was in the employ of Count Alfonso Gonzaga at Novellara. He sang in choirs in Parma and Milan, and from 1565 until his death was *maestro* at the Gonzaga chapel of Sta Barbara in Mantua. He also travelled to Augsburg and Venice, and is known to have had associations with the Este court in Ferrara in the 1570s and 1580s. Wert was a prolific composer; numerous Masses, motets, and Magnificats survive, but his most celebrated compositions are his madrigals. A strong influence on Monteverdi, he published thirteen madrigal collections, often with texts of a high quality, declamatory in style and with the three upper voices frequently emphasized; these were written for virtuoso court singers, and in particular the Ferrarese *concerto delle donne*.

Weyden, Rogier van der (1399/1400–1464) Netherlands painter. Rogier is first heard of in 1427 as the student of Robert *Campin. In 1432 he entered the guild of his native Tournai but by 1435 had already moved to Brussels where he settled permanently. Rogier attracted commissions from numerous patrons, both within the Netherlands and abroad, and was civic painter of Brussels. None of his paintings is exactly dated and his œuvre presents numerous attributional problems, as he had many followers. Rogier's earliest surviving work, such as the Louvre *Annunciation*, was strongly influenced by Campin. Later, the Boston *St Luke Drawing the Virgin* incorporates motifs borrowed from Jan van *Eyck. The Madrid *Descent from the Cross* (second half of the 1430s) is probably the artist's greatest work. In this composition, Rogier compressed ten nearly life-size figures within a gilded niche, simulating the appearance of a sculptured altarpiece of polychromed wood.
In 1439–41 Rogier worked on the four panels of his only secular narrative cycle, *The Justice of the Emperor Trajan and Count Herkinbald*, which decorated Brussels town hall until their destruction in 1695. The artist's fame had already spread to Castile by 1445, when King John II donated his altarpiece of the *Virgin* (now in Berlin) to the Charterhouse at Miraflores near Burgos. Rogier painted the enormous *Last Judgment* altarpiece in the hospital founded by Nicholas Rolin at Beaune, near Dijon, during the late 1440s. With its gold background, sculptural associations, and emotional intensity, it is closely comparable with the earlier *Descent from the Cross*. In 1449–51 Rogier was executing commissions for the Este of Ferrara and, in 1450, he visited Rome. Shortly after his return home, he executed two altarpieces for the Medici, the Frankfurt *Madonna and Child with Four Saints* and the Uffizi *Entombment*. Rogier's Braque triptych in Paris reinterprets a Tuscan format of the Trecento, but is innovative in its juxtaposition of half-length figures against a landscape background – an idea subsequently adopted in the portraits of *Memling and others. His last work is probably the *St Columba* altarpiece in Munich, which is remarkable for its formal and colouristic harmony. In addition to religious works, Rogier painted numerous portraits in which he developed a new mode of aristocratic likeness by subjectively manipulating the appearance of his sitters. Rogier's numerous exported works and his large *atelier*, which even attracted students from Italy, broadcast his style throughout Europe, making him the most influential northern painter of the fifteenth century.

White Mountain, Battle of the (1620) An important Catholic victory early in the Thirty Years' War. Following the election of the Calvinist *Winter King, Frederick V, Elector Palatine, to the Bohemian throne, Emperor Ferdinand II promised Bohemia to Maximilian of Bavaria if he drove out the Calvinists. The Calvinists, led by Christian of Anhalt, met the imperial forces under Maximilian at the White Mountain near Prague. The decisive imperial victory led to Frederick's expulsion from Bohemia (1620) and the Palatinate (1623). It was followed by harsh Catholic retribution in Bohemia. The scale of the victory brought a number of Protestant powers into the war against the Habsburgs.

Wickram, Jörg (1505–c. 1560) German novelist and dramatist. The illegitimate son of a municipal official, Wickram himself became an official in his native Colmar and later town clerk of Burgheim. Wickram, who was a *Meistersinger*, founded a school of *Meistergesang* in Colmar in 1549. He was influential in the development of the German novel out of the medieval chivalric romance; the chivalric roots are still clear in, for example, his *Ritter Galmy uss Schottland* ("Sir Galmy from Scotland"; 1539). Gradually, however, the world and values of the knight are replaced by those of peasant and burgher in his work, which becomes increasingly didactic and moralizing, as in *Der Jungen Knaben Spiegel* (1554). Wickram's most popular work was his *Rollwagenbüchlin* ("Stagecoach Booklet"; 1555), a collection of anecdotes and *Schwänke (a popular literary form then), intended as entertainment for travellers and lacking all didacticism. Wickram's plays are largely *Fastnachtspiele* (comic Shrovetide plays) and biblical tragedies, such as *Tobias* (1550).

Wiericx, Anthonie (c. 1552–1624), **Hieronymus** (c. 1553–1619) *and* **Johan** (c. 1549–1615) Netherlands engravers. Born in Antwerp and trained by their painter father, also named Anthonie, the brothers were child prodigies, as is indicated by their ages (prefixed *aet*), which appear on their line engravings. Johan's copies of Raimondi's *Venus and Cupid* and Dürer's *Fall of Man* date from when he was, respectively, fourteen and sixteen years old. Hieronymus executed copies of Dürer's *St George* and *St Jerome* when he was, respectively, only twelve and thirteen. It should be stressed that these copies are, probably, the best in existence, following the originals virtually line for line. Given the remarkable sophistication of Dürer's engraved technique, the quality of the Wiericx brothers' copies reveals astonishing technical virtuosity. The brothers produced more than 2000 prints, many of which were small devotional works of a type popularized by the Jesuits in their campaign against the Protestant reformers. Although the Wiericx workshop also produced the brothers' own designs, the early copies after Dürer may be counted as its finest achievement.

Wilbye, John (1574–1638) English composer. Born at Diss, Norfolk, Wilbye worked from 1598 for the Kytson family at Hengrave Hall near Bury St Edmunds, where he remained for twenty-eight years. In 1628, on the death of Lady Elizabeth Kytson, he moved to Colchester. Influenced by *Morley and *Ferrabosco, Wilbye is one of the finest English madrigalists. He published only two books of madrigals (1597, 1609), but the second is generally regarded as one of the greatest English madrigal collections. It contains arguably the finest of Wilbye's madrigals, "Draw on sweet Night", in which major and minor tonalities are used to depict intense melancholy.

Willaert, Adrian (c. 1490–1562) Flemish composer. Probably born in Bruges, Willaert studied music with Jean Mouton (c. 1459–1522) in Paris. From 1515 he was employed as a singer in the household of Cardinal Ippolito d'Este in Ferrara, travelling widely with him and spending two years in Hungary. On the cardinal's death (1520) Willaert transferred to the service of Duke Alfonso I d'Este. In 1527 he was appointed *maestro* at St Mark's, Venice, where he remained until his death. Here he presided over a flourishing musical scene. His pupils included important composers, such as *Rore, *Vicentino, and Andrea *Gabrieli, and he was regarded as a major figure in the development of Italian music.

Willaert was a most prolific and versatile composer; he published a great deal of church music, many madrigals, chansons, villanelles, and a few instrumental pieces. His *Salmi spezzati* (1550) contains music for double choirs and set a tradition for polychoral music in St Mark's. As a madrigalist Willaert paid great attention to the text. His collection of motets and madrigals, *Musica nova* (1559, though probably written much earlier), is arguably his most important work.

William (I) the Silent (1533–84), Prince of Orange (1544–84) and Count of Nassau (1559–84). The son of William of Nassau and Juliana of Stolberg, William inherited Orange and substantial territories in Brabant and Franche-Comté from a cousin in 1544. At *Charles V's insistence William was educated in Orange as a Catholic. He enjoyed the favour of Charles, who made him commander of the army in the Netherlands and governor of Holland, Zeeland, and Utrecht in 1555. William also served *Philip II of Spain against France and negotiated the preliminaries of the peace of *Cateau-Cambrésis (1559) between Spain and France.

Despite his concern at the persecution of Dutch Protestants in the early 1560s, William remained loyal to Philip II until the duke of *Alba began his reign of terror in the Netherlands. William then resigned his offices, refused to take the oath of loyalty to Alba, and in 1568 openly declared his Protestant faith. He then embarked on his long struggle to drive the Spanish from the Netherlands. His efforts enjoyed little success until the *sea-beggars seized Brill (1572) and flew the flag of Orange over its walls. Other towns followed, and in 1579 the seven northern states formed the Union of Utrecht. In 1581 they declared their independence and settled the hereditary stadtholdership on William, who was henceforth acclaimed as founder of the Republic of the United Netherlands. His assassination by a Catholic three years later gave the Dutch a martyr and inspired them to continue their struggle for full independence for the Netherlands.

William (IV) the Wise (1532–92) Landgrave of Hesse-Kassel (1567–92). In 1552 William fought for the Protestant cause against Emperor *Charles V, and helped secure the release of his father, Philip the Magnanimous, from five years' captivity. William succeeded his father as landgrave, but had to share the inheritance with his three brothers. He was an outstanding administrator and organizer with a considerable talent for economics. The survey, Ökonomische Staat, compiled for him in 1585 is a model of administrative statistics. William had a particular interest in astronomy; he constructed astronomical instruments and calculated stellar positions and was a friend of Tycho *Brahe and patron of Jost *Bürgi.

Wimpfeling, Jakob (1450–1528) German humanist and educator. The son of a saddler at Schlettstadt, Alsace, Wimpfeling was educated at the universities of Fribourg, Erfurt, and Heidelberg. He also taught at Heidelberg (1471–84, 1498–1500), becoming rector there from 1481 until 1484. In Strasbourg (1501–15) he founded a literary society with Sebastian *Brant and Johannes Geiler. Although a critic of ecclesiastical abuses, as his satirical *Stylpho* (performed in 1480—the first Latin comedy by a German humanist) makes clear, he could never endorse the Reformation. His ideas on education were expressed in two books: *Isidoneus germanicus* ("Guide to the German Youth"), in which he argued for moral teaching in education and also recommended the reading of selected pagan Latin authors (many educators totally rejected their use), and the highly successful *Adolescentia* ("Youth"), a collection of ideas and advice from other authors. The patriotic element of Wimpfeling's humanism (in reaction to Italian cultural domination) is seen in his polemical treatise *Germania* (1501), in which he claimed that Alsace was incontestably German, and in his *Epitome rerum germanicarum* (1505; translated as *A Short History of Germany*), the first attempt at a systematic history of Germany. He died in Schlettstadt, where he had become involved in controversy with younger humanists over their blanket endorsement of the pagan poets.

Winter King The sobriquet of Frederick V (1596–1632), Elector Palatine (1610–23), on account of the brevity of his reign as king of Bohemia (1619–20). He married (1613) Elizabeth, daughter of *James I of England; she became known as the Winter Queen. As head of the Protestant Union, Frederick accepted the Bohemian throne from nobles in rebellion against the Catholic Habsburgs, but at the *White Mountain (1620) the imperial forces defeated the Protestants and went on to drive Frederick out of both Bohemia (1620) and the Palatinate (1623).

Witte, Pieter de (Pietro Candido; c. 1548–1628) Netherlands painter. Born in Bruges, from about 1570 Witte was active in Florence, Rome, and Volterra (hence the Italian form of his name "Pietro Candido"). In 1586 he arrived in Munich where he worked beside Frederik Sustris on the decoration of the Antiquarium, the first museum of antiquities to be built in modern times, which was itself destroyed during World War II. From 1587 he worked on the decorations of the grotto court, also at the ducal palace. In 1588 he executed a *Martyrdom of St Ursula* for the Michaelkirche and in 1620 painted the high altarpiece at the Frauenkirche. He also designed series of tapestries of the *Months* and the life of Otto of Wittelsbach. Highly praised by Joachim von Sandrart for his versatility, he incorporated both Venetian and Tuscan elements in his mannerist style and remained dominant in Munich until the arrival of Rubens's style in Bavaria in 1619.

Wittenberg A capital city in Saxony, on the River Elbe. First mentioned in the twelfth century, Wittenberg was granted its municipal charter in 1293 and became the capital of the Ascanian dukes and electors of Saxony until 1423, when it passed to the house of Wettin. Wittenberg continued to be the capital of Saxony until 1547, when the

WINTER KING *The castle and gardens at Heidelberg during the time of Frederick V. The inventor Salomon de Caus laid out the famous gardens, shown here in an engraving by Merian for de Caus's* Hortus Palatinus *(1620).*

electorate passed to the Albertine line of the house of Wettin. The university of Wittenberg (founded 1502) was made famous by two of its teachers who were leading religious reformers – *Luther and *Melanchthon. The *Reformation is taken as beginning in Wittenberg in 1517 when Luther posted his Ninety-five Theses on the doors of the church of All Saints. Lucas *Cranach was court painter at Wittenberg from 1505. Notable buildings from this time include the castle (1490–99) and the town hall (1524–40). The Augusteum, erected (1564–83) on the site of the Augustinian monastery associated with Luther, became a Lutheran seminary in the eighteenth century.

Witz, Konrad (c. 1400–c. 1445) German painter. Witz was probably born near Württemberg or near Baden; little is known of his life, although his father was an artist working for the duke of Burgundy, and Witz probably travelled with him to France and Flanders. His work shows the influence of contemporary Flemish painting. He moved to Basle around 1430, and all his known work was executed in Basle and Geneva. Witz stands at the end of the Gothic artistic tradition, rejecting its patterns and elegant curves for an accurately observed realism, and using light in his paintings in a dramatic and innovatory way. His surviving works are panels from altarpieces, of which the latest, *Christ Walking on the Water and the Miraculous Draught of Fishes* from the St Peter altarpiece (1444; Geneva), is a remarkable achievement. The figures, the water, the reflections, and the various effects of light are all finely observed, and the landscape around the lake is clearly that of Lake Geneva. This represents one of the earliest depictions in European art of a real, recognizable landscape.

Wolf, Hieronymus (1516–80) German humanist scholar. Wolf was born in Oettingen and was the pupil of both *Melanchthon and *Camerarius. Despite a peripatetic life, he managed to produce editions of the Greek orators Isocrates (1548) and Demosthenes (1549) that formed the basis of a definitive critical edition (1572) unsuperseded for more than 200 years. From 1551 to 1557 he was employed as secretary and librarian to the *Fugger family in Augsburg. In the latter year he began publication of the works of Byzantine historians, with the object of assembling the complete corpus of Byzantine historiography. Also from that year he was head of the Protestant school in Augsburg, a post which he combined with that of city librarian until his death.

Wolgemut, Michael (1434–1519) German artist. A native of Nuremberg, Wolgemut was appren-ticed to his father Valentin. The altarpieces attributed to him at Zwickau in Saxony (1479), Feuchtwangen (1484), and Schwabach (1508) show him painting in a predominantly Netherlandish style. His major importance resides however in his development of the *woodcut as a medium for *book illustration. The blocks for the famous and handsome Nuremberg Chronicle (1493) were a product of Wolgemut's prolific workshop, but most important of all, he was *Dürer's master in the technique of woodcut, and the refinements that Wolgemut had introduced were brought to fruition in the work of the younger artist.

Wolsey, Thomas (c. 1473–1530) English statesman. The son of an Ipswich butcher, Wolsey attended Magdalen College, Oxford, of which he was bursar, before becoming chaplain to Henry VII (1507). He was appointed almoner under Henry VIII (1509) and had become a leading councillor by 1513, when his efficient organization of a military expedition to France recommended him to the king. His willingness to manage the routine of government and most affairs of state appealed to the pleasure-loving Henry, and Wolsey virtually governed England from 1515, when he became chancellor, until his fall from favour in 1529, over his failure to secure the annulment of Henry's marriage to Catherine of Aragon. He died the next year at Leicester, on his way to London to answer charges of treason.

Wolsey's main interest was foreign affairs, in which he strove to maintain England's security in a Europe dominated by the Habsburg-Valois rivalry, while also preserving his own position as papal legate (from 1518) and indulging Henry VIII's unrealistic desire to revive the glories of the Hundred Years' War. He was not unsuccessful until 1529, when a temporary Habsburg-Valois *rapprochement* left England isolated. In domestic affairs he was no great innovator but an energetic administrator who kept the government functioning efficiently. His most enduring achievement was the firm establishment of the court of chancery as the court of equity in civil cases. As archbishop of York from 1514 and a cardinal from 1515, he ruled the English Church by virtue of his legatine commission, reducing the archbishop of Canterbury to a cipher. Perhaps his weakest area was finance, where he consistently failed either to obtain sufficient taxes or to cut expenditure.

Wolsey used his position to amass a large personal fortune. Its basis was his collection of ecclesiastical posts: in addition to the archbishopric of York he held other bishoprics in England – Lincoln (from 1514), Bath and Wells (1518–24), Durham (1524–29), and Winchester (1529–30) – and was bishop of Tournai (1513–18) and abbot of St Albans (from

1521). His annual income was as high as £35,000 (six times that of the richest peer), enabling him to found colleges at Ipswich and Oxford (Cardinal College, 1525; refounded as Christ Church, 1546), build *Hampton Court Palace, and enjoy an ostentatious way of life.

woodcuts Woodcut is a relief printing process, whereby an image is printed from a block of wood onto a sheet of paper, in much the same way as text is printed from movable type. The image is first drawn, in reverse, on the block. Those areas of the block's surface corresponding to those parts of the print which the artist wishes to appear white are then gouged out with special knives. After cutting, the untouched wood which stands out corresponds to the black lines of the resultant print. This remaining surface of the block is then inked and pressed firmly against a sheet of paper, transferring the image from the former to the latter. As the woodblock is less malleable than the plate used in *engraving it is more suitable for printing large editions, such as those required by publishers of illustrated books. However, the technique is less subtle than engraving and less amenable to the printing of fine detail.

The earliest European woodcuts, such as the "Bois Protat", date from about 1400 and may originally have been used for textile printing. The technique was also used from an early date for the printing of playing cards which, for obvious reasons, had to appear as much like one another as possible. Some illustrated books were published from large woodcuts, with text and illustrations cut on the same block. After *Gutenberg's invention of *printing with movable metal type in the 1450s, such experiments were abandoned, and the woodcut illustration, together with the metal type, became the two essential components in the printing of illustrated books. At the beginning of the sixteenth century, the so-called "*chiaroscuro woodcut*" was developed, initially by Hans *Burgkmair and Lucas *Cranach in Germany and by *Ugo da Carpi in Italy. This technique utilizes a series of blocks, printed one after the other to create colour effects. As it was both expensive and complicated, this technique was used for individual prints rather than for books during the Renaissance.

From the earliest times, artists supplied the designs for woodcuts, while the task of cutting the block was entrusted to specialist block cutters, who were actually a kind of highly trained carpenter. During the fifteenth century, woodcut, like printing itself, was essentially a German art form, which reached its highest expression in deluxe illustrated books, such as the *Nuremberg Chronicle* (*Liber chronicarum*) of Hartmann Schedel, published by Koberger

with numerous woodcuts by Michael *Wolgemut at Nuremberg in 1493. Initially the Italians lagged somewhat behind, but by 1499 a distinctively Italian aesthetic of woodcut illustration had been created, in such works as the *Hypnerotomachia Polifili* of Francesco Colonna, published by Aldus Manutius in Venice with numerous unsigned woodcuts of superb quality. Albrecht *Dürer revolutionized the woodcut as an artistic medium by refining its technique to a level of subtlety that had previously only been found in engravings. To achieve this, he must necessarily have trained a team of block cutters to his own, uniquely exacting standards.

However, despite this technological leap, there is a gradual falling off in the artistic quality of later woodcuts. Holbein's *Dance of Death* (1523/24) cycle is, arguably, the last great Renaissance masterpiece in this technique. Although later woodcuts were often of outstanding technical virtuosity and of considerable formal and iconographic variety, this technique steadily became less the province of avant-garde artists than of publishers and printers (*see* book illustration).

Worms, Diet of (1521) An assembly (*Reichstag*) of the estates of the Holy Roman Empire, the most important business of which was the condemnation of Martin *Luther. The case against Luther, who had already been excommunicated, was stated by the papal legate, Girolamo *Aleandro, in the presence of Emperor *Charles V. In a famous act of defiance Luther refused to retract his antipapal writings and was outlawed. At the same diet, the estates agreed to the establishment of a government council (*Reichsregiment*) to function in the absence of the emperor, and Charles made over the government of Austria to his brother *Ferdinand (I).

Wotton, Edward (1492–1555) English physician and naturalist. Wotton was educated at his native Oxford and at Padua. On his return to England he practised medicine in London and held office, including the presidency (1541–43), in the College of Physicians. He was also the author of *De differentiis animalium* (1551) which, though published in Paris, was the first serious work on natural history written by an Englishman. The work itself is derivative and contains little that cannot be found in *Gesner.

Wright, Edward (1558–1615) English mathematician. Wright was born in Garveston, Norfolk, and educated at Cambridge. He became aware of the inadequacies of current navigational practice during a voyage in 1589 to the Azores. The conventional plane chart with its parallel lines of latitude and longitude prevented mariners from setting an accurate course directly on the chart; nor were the mathematically sophisticated innovations of *Mercator much help to the average seaman. Wright worked on the problem, publishing tables in his *Certaine Errors in Navigation* (1599) which allowed mariners to make the necessary adjustments on their charts; for the first time nautical triangles could be plotted, showing the correct relation between direction and distance. After 1614 he lectured on mathematics for the East India Company. Wright's translation into English of *Napier's work on logarithms was published in 1616.

Württemberg Confession (1552) The Protestant confession of faith drawn up by the Württemberg reformer Johann Brenz (1499–1570) with the specific aim of presenting the Protestant viewpoint at the Council of *Trent. Comprising thirty-five articles, it is based on the Confession of *Augsburg, and so is generally Lutheran in its stance, though with some Calvinist elements. Consulted by Archbishop *Parker, the confession played a role in the evolution of the Thirty-nine Articles of the Church of England.

Wyatt, Sir Thomas (c. 1503–42) English poet and diplomat. Educated at Cambridge, he found favour at Henry VIII's court, where he excelled at tournaments, music, and languages. He was thought to have been a lover of Anne Boleyn before she was courted by the king. Wyatt served as high marshal of Calais (1529–30), but in 1536 he was detained in the Tower, probably to give evidence against Anne. In 1537 he was knighted and sent abroad on diplomatic missions. Wyatt's enemies accused him of involvement in Thomas *Cromwell's treachery; in the Tower again, he confessed to some faults and was pardoned by Henry VIII in 1541. He died suddenly of a fever.

Waytt's fame rests mainly on his poetry. He was the first to introduce the Petrarchan sonnet form to England. His poems and songs, which convey a strong personal quality, were printed in *Certayne Psalmes...drawn into Englyshe meter* (1549) and *Tottel's Miscellany* (1557). His son, Sir Thomas Wyatt the younger (?1521–54), was executed for instigating Wyatt's Rebellion (1554), an abortive protest against *Mary I's proposal to marry *Philip II of Spain.

Wyttenbach, Thomas (1472–1526) Swiss reformer. He was born at Biel and attended university in Tübingen. As a lecturer at Basle he taught *Zwingli, whom he encouraged to study the Bible without reliance upon the scholastic commentaries, and interested himself in the implications of the new humanist approach to literary studies. From 1515 he was pastor in his native town, but eight years later publicly aligned himself with the Reformation and in 1524 lost his post upon his marriage.

XZ

Xavier, St Francis *see* Francis Xavier, St.

Ximénes de Cisneros, Cardinal Francisco (1436–1517) Spanish churchman, politician, and scholar. A Castilian by birth, he studied at Alcalá and Salamanca, becoming doctor in both canon and civil law. In 1492 Isabella of Castile chose him as her confessor and in 1495 he became archbishop of Toledo. He was an energetic reformer, seeking a return to more austere standards of Christian life, and he encouraged the conversion of the Moors of Granada. In 1507 Ximénes became cardinal and inquisitor-general. From January 1516 until his death (November 1517) at Valladolid, he was governor of Castile and consolidated the unification of Spain achieved by Ferdinand and Isabella. Cardinal Ximénes spent his income lavishly on educational projects and public works; he founded the university of Alcalá (1500) and was its great benefactor. His main monument is the great polyglot Bible known as the *Complutensian Polyglot (Complutum was the Roman name for Alcalá), which provided for the first time a printed text of the scriptures in their original languages.

Zabarella, Cardinal Francesco (1360–1417) Italian canonist. After studying at Bologna, Zabarella taught canon law at Florence (1385–90) and Padua (1390–1410). He attended the Council of *Constance as legate of Pope John XXIII, who created him cardinal in 1411. In 1408 he wrote *De iurisdictione imperiali* in which he insisted that the pope was only the highest servant of the Church to whom executive power was entrusted. An ecumenical council had the power to discipline a pope and he could be deposed if it seemed necessary to such a council. The Council of Constance accepted this doctrine and its corollary of regular ecumenical councils. Had this become established practice, Zabarella would have effected a fundamental change in the government of the Church.

Zabarella, Giacomo (1533–89) Italian philosopher and humanist. Zabarella was the leading representative of Aristotelianism in his native Padua during the sixteenth century. He engaged in controversy with Francesco Piccolomini over his interpretation of Aristotle's logic, which gained him great notoriety among his contemporaries, but modern students have shown more interest in Zabarella's work on the immortality of the soul. There are close similarities between his solution to this problem and that proposed by *Pomponazzi: he excluded the notion of a prime mover and insisted on the soul's independent and autonomous nature. Zabarella also published *De rebus naturalibus libri XXX* (1589) in which he discussed the traditional problems of Aristotelian physics.

Zarlino, Gioseffo (?1517–90) Italian composer and music theorist. Born in Chioggia, Zarlino was educated by the Franciscans, whom he joined in 1521. In 1536 he was a singer at Chioggia cathedral. From 1539 he was organist there before moving to Venice in 1541, where he became a pupil of *Willaert. In 1565 he was appointed *maestro* at St Mark's and remained in this post until his death. Zarlino wrote motets and madrigals, but is most significant as a theorist. His major work, *Le istitutioni harmoniche* (1558), caused Willaert's methods of contrapuntal writing to become models of the style. In it he also discusses theories of modes and intervals, as well as looking back to classical models.

Zenale, Bernard(in)o (c. 1450–1526) Italian painter. Zenale was born at Treviglio, for the cathedral of which, in collaboration with his fellow-townsman Butinone (c. 1450–c. 1507), he painted the splendid polyptych that is his best-known work. They also worked on frescoes depicting the life of St Ambrose (1490) in the church of S Pietro in Gessate, Milan. Zenale also wrote a treatise on perspective.

zoological collections Animals for both hunting and display had long been kept by important nobles. One such collection of wild animals was established in 1252 by Henry III at the Tower of London. The custom was extended by Renaissance noblemen to include in their newly created *musei* natural history specimens, along with their antiquities and their art collections. One of the earliest such *musei* was founded by Lorenzo de' Medici (the Magnificent) in Florence in the fifteenth century. He was soon followed by the Este in

Ferrara and the Montefeltro in Urbino. Some 250 such collections were established in sixteenth-century Italy, one of them by *Aldrovandi in Bologna. Scholars also began, on a much smaller scale, to assemble their own more specialized collections. Known as *cabinets, they provided the Renaissance scholar with his basic research material. *Gesner, for example, based his *De omni rerum fossilium genere* (1565) on his own cabinet of fossils.

zoology Considerable zoological knowledge was collected by Aristotle and presented in his *Historia animalium* and other works, but the Aristotelian tradition, technical, detailed, and pedestrian, held little appeal for medieval scholars. In its place two more imaginative approaches flourished. One, typified by Solinus (fl. 200 AD) and his *Collecteana rerum memorabilium*, concentrated almost exclusively on such wonders as men with dog's heads or ants as large as lions which guarded the gold of India. An alternative tradition, clearly seen in the medieval bestiaries, looked on nature as a source of moral inspiration; thus the phoenix inevitably is a reminder of Christ, and the fox, because of its skill in entrapping its victims, recalls the devil. Both traditions persisted throughout much of the Renaissance.

Although the leading Renaissance zoologists, *Aldrovandi and *Gesner, devoted much less space to moralistic or mythological themes, neither they nor their disciples were entirely free from such preoccupations. Much less gullible than Solinus, they still found space for dragons, unicorns, basilisks, and the phoenix. Nor were their works restricted to specifically zoological data; their encyclopedic scope embraced all facts, whether linguistic, mythological, historical, or gastronomic. Aldrovandi, for example, after devoting a page or two to the various breeds of chicken, went on to present a further 300 pages on folklore about the bird. A clear example of the literary nature of Renaissance zoology is provided by Ermolao Barbaro's *Castigationes Pliniae* (1492) in which he sought to do no more than identify the numerous errors of Pliny. When genuinely zoological issues were tackled they tended to be dealt with in an unambitiously Aristotelian manner. Classification at higher levels depended, accordingly, on whether the animals were oviparous or viviparous, and became trivially alphabetical at the level of species. One area in which zoology did advance was in the field of experimental embryology. Volcher Coiter (1534–c. 1576) made a detailed study of the development of embryonic chickens. Further advances were made by *Fabricius, whose *De formato foetu* (1600), the first modern work on comparative embryology, described the development of man, various domestic animals, the dogfish, and the viper.

The Renaissance also saw the emergence of the zoological monograph. Some, like the work of Jacob Bondt (1592–1631) on the East Indies, were regional studies, others like the *De omni rerum fossilium genere* (1565) of Gesner were restricted to a single topic. Works of this kind tended to be more singleminded in their pursuit of zoological issues than the better known encyclopedic collections. Missing completely, however, from Renaissance zoology are any of the great theoretical issues that would puzzle scientists of a later period. For the Renaissance zoologist animals had been created

ZOOLOGY *The illustration of a whale sinking a ship, taken from Gesner's* Historiae animalium, *owes more to the medieval bestiary tradition than to personal observation.*

by God as described in Genesis and were linked with man as constituents of the great *chain of being. How then, it was asked, did the alpaca and guanaco get to Peru? Were they created there? And, if so, what of Noah? The orthodox answer came from *Acosta. All animals came out of the ark and dispersed over long-since-flooded land bridges to the environments best suited to them. Few voices were heard in dissent before the eighteenth century.

Zoppo, Marco (Marco d'Antonio di Ruggero; 1433–78) Italian painter and draughtsman. Born near Bologna, Zoppo was probably a pupil of *Tura and later, at the age of twenty-one, he became the adopted son of and assistant to *Squarcione in Padua. Zoppo was also active in Venice (1455, 1468–73) and executed further works in Bologna, including a triptych for the Collegio di Spagna. Influenced by *Mantegna and by Jacopo and Giovanni *Bellini, Zoppo produced paintings in a distinctively harsh and precise style and an album of drawings formerly attributed to Mantegna (British Museum, London).

Zuccaro, Federico (c. 1540–1609) Italian painter. Born at Vado, south of Bologna, Zuccaro began his artistic career as assistant and pupil to his older brother Taddeo. In 1565 he was in Florence, working under Vasari, after which he visited France and the Netherlands (1574) and then England (1575), where he drew (and perhaps painted) full-length portraits of Elizabeth I and the earl of *Leicester (British Museum, London). Subsequently he helped in the painting of the dome of Florence cathedral (1575–79) and executed the painting *Barbarossa Making Obeisance to the Pope* (1582), influenced by Tintoretto and Raphael, for the doge's palace in Venice. Summoned to Spain by Philip II, Zuccaro produced several works, chiefly altarpieces, for the Escorial (1585–88), which failed to win the royal approval. He returned to Italy, and in 1593 he established the Accademia di S Luca in his own house in Rome, later becoming the academy's first president. Other works included the *Adoration of the Magi* (1594; Lucca cathedral), paintings in the Sala Regia of the Vatican, a book on aesthetic theory, *L'Idea de' pittori, scultori, et architetti* (1607), and a series of ninety drawings illustrating Dante's *Divine Comedy* (Uffizi). Through the medium of prints his accomplished mannerist style became widely known in Italy and beyond.

Zuccaro, Taddeo (1529–66) Italian painter. Born, like his brother and pupil Federico, at Vado, Taddeo Zuccaro became a leading painter in the mannerist style in Rome, where he settled in 1551. He was largely self-trained and was influenced chiefly by the works of Correggio, which he had encountered at Parma. The body of Taddeo Zuccaro's works consisted of decorative frescoes and religious paintings, many of which were later completed by Federico. His most influential work was the series of frescoes and stucco decorations executed (1561–66) for the Villa Farnese at Caprarola, in which elements of northern Italian art and the manner of Michelangelo and Raphael were fused. Other works included a fresco cycle in the Sala Regia of the Vatican and another in the Cappella Frangipane, S Marcello al Corso, Rome, incorporating the altarpiece *The Conversion of St Paul* (c. 1563).

Zürich Agreement (1549) The formulation of a common sacramental doctrine agreed at Zürich between *Bullinger, who represented the Zwinglian churches of German Switzerland, and *Calvin and *Farel representing Geneva and the Protestant churches of French Switzerland. *Zwingli had supported a purely symbolic interpretation of the Eucharist, resulting in a split with *Luther that led to a rift between the German and Swiss churches (*see* Marburg, Colloquy of). Calvin's position, midway between the Swiss and the Lutheran, was more acceptable to the Zwinglians, and the Zürich Agreement proved an important milestone on the road to a distinctive form of Swiss Protestantism.

Zurita, Jerónimo de (1512–80) Spanish historian. The son of a doctor at the court of Ferdinand II of Aragon, Zurita was born at Zaragoza, educated at Alcalá, and became official chronicler of Aragon (1548). *Anales de la corona de Aragón* (six volumes, 1562–80) covered the history of the kingdom from the Moorish invasion to the death of Ferdinand (1516). An index was published in 1604. (The third edition, in seven volumes (1610–21), is considered the best.) Though it lacks literary distinction, Zurita's history is the first in Spanish to be compiled critically and methodically. He took pains to read primary materials, excluded supernatural matter, and took account of conflicting evidence.

Zwingli, Ulrich (1484–1531) Swiss reformer. The son of a well-to-do farmer at Wildhaus, Zwingli studied in Basle and Berne before embarking on a conventional church career. He was ordained in 1506 and from 1506 to 1516 served as parish priest at Glarus. While there he continued his humanistic studies and published his first original work, a verse satire criticizing the involvement of Swiss mercenaries in the dynastic quarrels of the European powers (*De bello Judaico*, 1510). In December 1518 Zwingli was elected a stipendary priest in the minster at Zürich, where his preaching and lectures on the New Testament evoked an enthusiastic response. Zwingli's sermons, in which he moved to an increasingly forthright denunciation of purgatory, monasticism, and other Catholic dogma and practices, paved the way for the Zürich reformation, carried through between 1522 and 1525 under Zwingli's leadership.

By this time too Zwingli had begun to develop his characteristic eucharistic doctrine, which diverged significantly from that of *Luther. In rejecting transubstantiation Zwingli also rejected any sort of Real Presence, expounding a purely symbolic interpretation of the sacrament. The ensuing conflict between the two men, which a personal meeting (*see* Marburg, Colloquy of) could not resolve, led to a permanent division between the Swiss and German strands of Protestantism. Zwingli remained until his death the key figure in the Swiss Reformation, and played a leading role in the promotion of Protestantism in the other Swiss cantons.

BIBLIOGRAPHY

The following suggestions for further reading, divided into primary and secondary sources, barely touch the surface of a huge literature which, in the case of the secondary sources, is constantly expanding. However, many of the works listed in the secondary sources section contain valuable bibliographies, which will enable students to pursue particular lines of inquiry. The primary sources listing is intended to direct the student's attention to just a few of the authors and works that were exceptionally influential in their own day or which give extraordinary insight into the literary, intellectual, or social climate of the times.

Primary Sources

ALBERTI The original Latin text of *De re aedificatoria* was printed in Florence in 1485 with a prefatory letter by Politian addressed to Lorenzo de' Medici. This Latin version was reprinted in Paris in 1512 and Strasbourg in 1541. The first Italian translation (Venice, 1546) was soon superseded (1550) by Cosimo Bartoli's version, which was also the first edition of the work to be illustrated. Giacomo Leoni (1686–1746), a Venetian architect living in England, published his English translation in 1726, with engravings based on his own drawings after the woodcuts of the 1550 Bartoli edition. Leoni's translation was twice reprinted in the eighteenth century (1739, 1755); the 1755 edition was the basis of a photographic reprint edited by Joseph Rykwert (London, 1955; New York, 1966).

ALCIATI One of the best sellers of the sixteenth century, the *Emblemata* was first published at Augsburg in 1531 in an edition containing 103 emblems; an edition revised by the author and enlarged to 211 emblems appeared at Lyons in 1550. The work was rapidly disseminated throughout Europe, both in complete and abridged versions of the Latin original and in French (1536), German (1542), and Spanish (1549) rhyming translations. Many of the emblems are reproduced in the great compilation *Emblemata* by A. Henkel and A. Schöne (Stuttgart, 1967), which also provides valuable comparative material from other emblem books. P. M. Daly (ed.) in *Andreas Alciatus* (Toronto, 2 vols., 1985) prints the emblems in Latin and also provides English translations, along with useful indexes.

ALEMAN J. Mabbe's lively translation of *Guzman de Alfarache*, under the title of *The Rogue* (1622), is still the best; it was reprinted in the Tudor Translations series (4 vols., 1924; repr. 1967). T.

Roscoe also translated the work for his Spanish Novelists collection (1832).

ARIOSTO *Orlando furioso*, which came out first in Italian between 1516 and 1532, soon achieved a following outside Italy with a Spanish version in 1549 and a French prose version in 1555. Harington's English verse translation (1591) is available in an edition by G. Hough (London, 1963). There are modern prose translations by A. H. Gilbert (New York, 3 vols., 1954) and by G. Waldman; the latter, which first appeared in 1974, has been reissued in the World's Classics series (Oxford, 1983). A verse translation by B. Reynolds was published by Penguin (Harmondsworth, 1975).

BOCCACCIO Despite the popularity of stories from the *Decameron*, many of which were familiar in various forms to English readers from the fourteenth century, the first full-scale translation of the work into English was not published until 1620. This anonymous version has sometimes been ascribed to John Florio. J. Payne's 1886 translation is available in an edition revised and annotated by C. S. Singleton (Berkeley, Calif., 3 vols., 1982). In this century the translation by R. Aldington (New York, 1930) has often been reprinted. The Penguin Classics version (Harmondsworth, 1972) is by G. H. McWilliam.

CALVIN A modern edition of the *Institutes of the Christian Religion*, edited by J. T. McNeill with translation from the Latin by F. L. Battles, comprises vols. 21 and 22 in the Philadelphia Library of Christian Classics (1960; repr. 1980). The French text appeared in a critical edition with notes by J.-D. Benoit (Paris, 1957–63).

CAMÕES *Os Lusiadas* has been edited with an introduction and notes by F. Pierce (Oxford, 1973; repr. 1981). R. Fanshaw's version (1655), the first and most successful of the English verse translations, has been republished in editions by J. D. M. Ford (Cambridge, Mass., 1940) and G. Bullough (London, 1963). Sir Richard Burton's abstruse rendering (London, 2 vols., 1880) is a curiosity rather than a valid attempt at interpretation. W. C. Atkinson made the prose translation for Penguin Classics (Harmondsworth, 1952; repr. 1973).

CASTIGLIONE Following its first publication in 1528 Castiglione's *Il cortegiano* reached an audience all over Europe in the course of the sixteenth century, with versions in Spanish (1534), French (1538), English (1561), Polish (1566), and Latin (1571). The 1561 translation by Hoby, *The Book of the Courtier*, remains a perennial favourite and has frequently been reprinted this century. G. Bull, retaining Hoby's title, made a modern translation for the Penguin Classics series (rev. edn., Harmondsworth, 1976).

CELLINI Cellini's *Vita* was first published in Naples in 1728. The original manuscript then vanished for many years before being rediscovered in the early nineteenth century; it is now housed in the Laurenziana library in Florence. English versions have been variously titled *Life*, *Memoirs*, or *Autobiography*. The first English translation, made by Thomas Nugent (1771), has often been reprinted, as has the later version by J. A. Symonds (2 vols., 1888). A more recent version of the *Autobiography* is that by G. Bull in the Penguin Classics series (Harmondsworth, 1956).

CERVANTES *Don Quixote* was first translated into English between 1612 and 1620 by Thomas Shelton, whose version was republished in the Tudor Translations series (1896; repr. 1967); an edition of this version published in 1901 has illustrations by Frank Brangwyn. J. M. Cohen's translation, *The Adventures of Don Quixote*, has appeared as a Penguin Classic (Harmondsworth, 1950; frequently repr.).

COPERNICUS *De revolutionibus orbium coelestium*, first printed at Nuremberg in 1543, was republished during the Renaissance at Basle (1566) and Amsterdam (1611). There are facsimiles of the 1543 edition (Amsterdam, 1943) and of the 1566 Basle edition (Prague, 1971); the latter is edited by Z. Horský and contains Tycho Brahe's commentary on Copernicus's work, as well as an introduction and notes in Czech, English, French, German, and Russian. There is an annotated English translation by A. M. Duncan, *On the Revolutions of the Heavenly Spheres* (Newton Abbot, 1976).

DANTE The first printed edition of the *Divine Comedy* (Foligno, 1472) was followed in the same year by others printed at Mantua and Iesi. In all, just under fifty editions appeared before 1600 and there was also a substantial secondary literature in Latin and the vernacular. English-speaking admirers of Dante, of which there were always some from Chaucer onwards, read the *Divine Comedy* in Italian until the first complete translation in blank verse by H. Boyd (1802). It was soon superseded by H. F. Cary's version (1814), also in blank verse. The annotated translation by D. L. Sayers and B. Reynolds (Harmondsworth, 3 vols., 1955–62) is in blank verse and *terza rima*. For an Italian text with facing English translation and commentary see the three-volume edition by

J. D. Sinclair originally published in 1939 (New York, 1961, 1981).

DELLA CASA *Il Galateo* was one of the most frequently translated texts in Europe during the second half of the sixteenth century. Robert Peterson translated it into English in 1576 under the title *A Treatise of the Maners and Behaviours*; a facsimile of this edition was produced at Amsterdam in 1969. For a modern translation see *Galateo, or the Book of Manners* by R. S. Pine-Coffin (Harmondsworth, 1958).

ERASMUS The *Opera omnia*, ed. J. Le Clerc, have been made available in ten volumes (London, 1962), with an eleventh volume containing a facsimile of the 1703–06 Leyden edition. The University of Toronto Press is issuing a new English translation of all Erasmus's writings under the title *The Collected Works of Erasmus* (1974–); the earliest volumes to appear contain his highly readable letters. The publishing history of *The Praise of Folly* has been partially covered in the text article. Sir Thomas Chaloner's 1549 English translation has been reissued as vol. no. 257 in the Early English Text Society collection (Oxford, 1965). *The Praise of Folly* is also available in modern English in the Penguin Classics series, translated by B. Radice, with introduction and notes by A. H. T. Levi (Harmondsworth, 1971). A convenient introduction to the *Adagia* is M. M. Phillips's *Erasmus on his Times* (Cambridge, 1968).

GALILEO The *Dialogo sopra i due massimi sistemi del mondo Tolemaico, e Copernicano* (Florence, 1632), Galileo's famous defence of the Copernican system, was translated into Latin in 1635. After its author's notorious trial by the ecclesiastical authorities the work was placed on the Index Librorum Prohibitorum, where it remained until 1823, thus curtailing its circulation in Catholic Europe. It was translated into English in 1661 by T. Salusbury for a compilation of mathematical texts; this version, *Dialogue on the Great World Systems*, has been reprinted separately (London & Chicago, 1953). The translation by S. Drake, *Dialogue Concerning the Two Chief World Systems, Ptolemaic and Copernican* (Berkeley, Calif., 1953) has a foreword by Einstein.

GUARINI Admirers of the pastoral genre throughout Europe ensured the continuing popularity and influence of *Il pastor fido* for at least 150 years after its publication in 1589. Its first English translator was Sir Edward Dymoke, who had visited Guarini while travelling in Italy (c. 1590–91) and whose *Faithfull Shepheard* was published in 1602 (repr. 1633). The most enduring

English translation however was that by Sir Robert Fanshawe (1647). It has been republished in a critical edition by W. F. Staton Jr. and W. E. Simeone (London & New York, 1964) and also in an edition by J. H. Whitfield (Edinburgh, 1976).

LOYOLA The *Spiritual Exercises* were translated from the Latin text into English by C. Seager in 1847. J. Norris and others worked from the Spanish text for their 1880 translation, which has been several times reprinted. A recent version is by T. Corbishley. English recusants of the sixteenth and seventeenth centuries were supplied with English texts based on the *Exercises* printed by Catholic presses overseas; Tomas de Villacastin's *Manuall of devout meditations and exercises* was published at St Omer in 1618, with further editions in 1623 and 1624, and *Annotations to the exercise* appeared about 1630 at Rouen.

MACHIAVELLI *Il principe* was the subject of an anonymous Tudor translation of about 1560, which was edited by Hardin Craig and first published at Chapel Hill in 1944. The first printed English translation (1640) was by E. Dacres, who had earlier (1636) published the first English translation of Machiavelli's *Discorsi*; Dacres's version, entitled *Nicholas Machiavel's Prince*, was reprinted in the Tudor Translations series (1905). Despite the opprobrium loaded on the author, H. Nevile's edition of Machiavelli's *Works* (1675) was twice reprinted before the end of the seventeenth century (1680, 1694). *The Prince* forms part of the second volume of C. E. Detmold's edition of Machiavelli's *Historical, Political, and Diplomatic Writings* (Boston, 1882) and is also included in A. H. Gilbert's *The Chief Works of Machiavelli* (Durham, N.C., 1965). G. Bull's translation of *The Prince* was first issued in the Penguin Classics series in 1961, and there is an Oxford World's Classics edition by P. Bondanella, with the translation by P. Bondanella and M. Musa (Oxford, 1984). Parallel Italian and English texts feature in Musa's earlier edition of the work (New York, 1964).

MONTAIGNE The evolution of the text of the *Essais* is outlined in the text article. Of English translations, that by John Florio (1603) was the earliest and also the most frequently reprinted, for instance in the Tudor Translations series (1892–93). An accessible modern version is that by J. M. Cohen (Harmondsworth, 1958). The *Essays* have also been translated by D. M. Frame in an edition of the *Complete Works* of Montaigne (Stanford, Calif., 1957); this translation was subsequently reissued separately (Stanford, 1958; New York, 1960).

MORE The original Latin edition of More's *Utopia* (1516) appeared at Louvain and its popularity was such that it was quickly followed by editions printed at Paris (1517), Basle (1518), and Vienna (1519). The Basle editions of 1518 and 1520 have illustrations by Holbein. It was translated into German (1524), Italian (1548), and French (1550) before the issue of the first English version by Raphe Robinson (1551). A facsimile of the 1516 Latin edition was issued by the Scolar Press (Leeds, 1966) and a facsimile of the Robinson version of 1551 was issued in Amsterdam in 1969. In 1963 Yale University Press began publication of the *Complete Works of St. Thomas More*, in which *Utopia*, ed. E. Surtz and J. H. Hexter, comprises Vol. IV (1965). A handy modern translation is the Penguin Classics version by Paul Turner (Harmondsworth, 1965).

RABELAIS The text article gives the titles and outline details of the publication of the *Gargantua* and *Pantagruel* novels. The first part of Urquhart's vigorous but free English translation, apparently the first to be published in Britain, appeared in 1653. This version was completed by Motteux (1708) after Urquhart's death, and although Motteux fails to capture the spirit of either Rabelais or Urquhart this Urquhart-Motteux version was several times reprinted in the eighteenth and nineteenth centuries, and C. Whibley edited it for the Tudor Translations series (3 vols., 1900). A ponderous Victorian version by W. F. Smith (1893) has valuable notes. J. M. Cohen's version for the Penguin Classics series (Harmondsworth, 1955) has often been reprinted.

TASSO *Aminta*, like Guarini's *Il pastor fido*, helped shape, and shared to a marked degree in, the fashion for pastoral in the seventeenth century. An almost complete English version in hexameters was published by A. Fraunce in 1591 under the title *The Affectionate Life and Unfortunate Death of Phillis and Amyntas*. There followed *Aminta Englisht* (1628) by H. Reynolds and later in the seventeenth century there were versions by J. Dancer (1660) and J. Oldmixon (1698). Leigh Hunt produced a verse translation in 1820, as did F. Whitmore in 1900. E. Grillo published an edition with parallel Italian and English texts (London & New York, 1924) and L. E. Lord published a prose version in 1931. *Gerusalemme liberata* was first partially translated into English by R. Carew in 1594, who published five cantos in octaves, with parallel Italian and English texts. The major English translation is E. Fairfax's version in Spenserian stanzas, under the title *Godfrey of Bulloigne* (1600). This was reprinted in 1624 and 1687 and has appeared most recently in a critical

Bibliography

edition by K. M. Lea and T. M. Gang (Oxford, 1981).

VASARI   The massive compilation of Vasari's *Vite* was first completely translated into English by Mrs J. Foster between 1850 and 1885. An abridged version of her text by B. Burroughs appeared in 1960, and it has also been published in a two-volume format (New York, 1967). A. B. Hinds's translation has recently appeared in a revised edition by W. Gaunt (London, 4 vols., 1980). An illustrated selection of lives entitled *Artists of the Renaissance* (London, 1978) was made by G. Bull, who also translated the extracts in the Penguin Classics volume (Harmondsworth, 1965).

VESALIUS   *De humani corporis fabrica libri septem*, first issued in Basle in 1543, appeared in a number of editions in several countries within a few years of its initial publication. The remarkable illustrations were plagiarized in England as early as 1545 by the engraver Thomas Geminus for an abridged version of Vesalius' work entitled *Compendiosa totius anatomie delineatio*; this abridgement was translated into English by Nicholas Udall (1553; repr. 1559). A modern English version is *The Epitome of Andreas Vesalius* by C. R. Lind (Cambridge, Mass., 1969).

Secondary Sources

BACKGROUND

Allen, J. W., *A History of Political Thought in the Sixteenth Century* (3rd edn., London, 1977)

Bietenholz, P. & Deutscher, T. B. (eds.), *Contemporaries of Erasmus: A Biographical Register of the Renaissance and Reformation*, Vol. I (A–E) (Toronto, 1985)

Braudel, F., *The Mediterranean and the Mediterranean World in the Age of Philip II* (1949; London & New York, 1972)

Elliott, J. H., *Europe Divided: 1559–1598* (London, 1968)

Elton, G. R., *Renaissance and Reformation, 1300–1648* (3rd edn., New York, 1976)

Hale, J. R., *Renaissance Europe, 1480–1520* (London, 1971; Berkeley, Calif., 1978)

Huizinga, J. H., *The Waning of the Middle Ages* (1924; London, 1968)

Major, J. R., *Age of the Renaissance and Reformation* (New York, 1970)

Mandrou, R. L. R. (transl. B. Pearce), *From Humanism to Science, 1480 to 1700* (Harmondsworth, 1978)

Mates, J. & Cantelupe, E. (eds.), *Renaissance Culture* (New York, 1968)

New Cambridge Modern History: Vol. I *The Renaissance, 1493–1520*, ed. G. R. Potter (Cambridge, 1957); Vol. II *The Reformation, 1520–59*, ed. G. R. Elton (Cambridge, 1958); Vol. III *The Counter-Reformation and Price Revolution, 1559–1610*, ed. R. B. Wernham (Cambridge, 1968)

Schwoebel, R., *Renaissance Men and Ideas* (New York, 1971)

Snyder, J., *The Northern Renaissance* (New Jersey, 1985)

Trevor-Roper, H., *Religion, the Reformation and Social Change* (London, 1967)

University of Chicago Readings in Western Civilization: Vol. V *The Renaissance*, ed. J. W. Boyer & J. Kirshner (Chicago, 1986)

Italy

Bouwsma, W. J., *Venice and the Defense of Republican Liberty: Renaissance Values in the Age of Counter Reformation* (Berkeley, Calif., 1968)

Burke, P., *Civilization and Society in Renaissance Italy, 1420–1540* (London, 1972)

Chamberlin, E. R., *The World of the Italian Renaissance* (London, 1983)

Gilbert, F., *Machiavelli and Guicciardini: Politics and History in Sixteenth-Century Florence* (1965; New York, 1984)

Hay, D., *The Italian Renaissance in its Historical Background* (2nd edn., Cambridge, 1977)

Hersey, G. L., *Alfonso II and the Artistic Renewal of Naples, 1485–1495* (New Haven, Conn., 1969)

Laven, P., *Renaissance Italy, 1464–1534* (London, 1966)

Martines, L., *Power and Imagination: City-states in Renaissance Italy* (London, 1980)

Mitchell, B., *Rome in the High Renaissance: The Age of Leo X* (Oklahoma, 1973)

Origo, I., *The Merchant of Prato* (1957; London, 1963)

France

Febvre, L. (transl. M. Rothstein), *Life in Renaissance France* (Cambridge, Mass., 1979)

Fowler, K., *The Age of Plantagenet and Valois: the struggle for supremacy, 1328–1498* (London, 1967)

Knecht, R. J., *Francis I* (Cambridge, 1982)

Lewis, P. S., *Late Medieval France: the polity* (London, 1968)

Britain

Briggs, J., *This Stage-Play World* (Oxford, 1983)

Caspari, F., *Humanism and the Social Order in Tudor England* (1954; Chicago, 1968)

Ferguson, A. B., *Clio Unbound: Perception of the Social and Cultural Past in Renaissance England* (Durham, N.C., 1979)

Levine, M., *Tudor England, 1485–1603* (Cambridge, 1968)

McConica, J., *English Humanists and Reformation Politics* (Oxford, 1965)

Yates, F., *Astraea: the Imperial Theme in the Sixteenth Century* (London, 1975)

Netherlands

Geyl, P., *The Revolt of the Netherlands, 1555–1609* (London, 1958)

Grierson, E., *The Fatal Inheritance: Philip II and the Netherlands* (London, 1969)

Tex, J. den, *Oldenbarnevelt* (Cambridge, 1973)

Vaughan, R., *Philip the Good: the apogee of Burgundy* (London, 1970)

Vaughan, R., *Charles the Bold: the last Valois duke of Burgundy* (London, 1973)

Northern Europe

Christiansen, E., *The Northern Crusades: the Baltic and the Catholic frontier* (London, 1980)

Dickens, A. G., *The German Nation and Martin Luther* (London, 1974)

Dollinger, P., *The Hansa* (London, 1970)

Evans, R. J. W., *Rudolf II and his World* (Oxford, 1973)

Hoffmeister, G., *The Renaissance and Reformation in Germany: An Introduction* (New York, 1977)

Spain

Hillgarth, J. N., *The Spanish Kingdoms, 1250–1516* (Oxford, 2 vols., 1976, 1978)

Pierson, P., *Philip II of Spain* (London, 1975)

Thompson, I. A. A., *War and Government in Habsburg Spain, 1560–1620* (London, 1976)

PHILOSOPHY

Bamborough, J. B., *The Little World of Man* (London, 1952)

Baron, H., *From Petrarch to Leonardo Bruni* (Chicago, 1968)

Cassirer, E., *The Individual and the Cosmos in Renaissance Philosophy* (New York, 1964)

Garin, E. (transl. P. Munz), *Italian Humanism* (Oxford, 1965; New York, 1976)

Gilmore, M. P., *The World of Humanism* (New York, 1962)

Kristeller, P. O., *Renaissance Thought* (New York, 1961)

Kristeller, P. O., *Eight Philosophers of the Italian Renaissance* (Stanford, Calif., 1964)

Robb, N. A., *Neoplatonism of the Italian Renaissance* (London, 1969)

Schellhase, K. C., *Tacitus in Renaissance Political Thought* (Chicago, 1977)

Schmitt, C. B., *Aristotle and the Renaissance* (Cambridge, Mass., 1983)

Trinkaus, C., *The Scope of Renaissance Humanism* (Ann Arbor, Mich., 1983)

Vickers, B. (ed.), *Occult and Scientific Mentalities in the Renaissance* (Cambridge, 1986)

Walker, D. P., *Spiritual and Demonic Magic from Ficino to Campanella* (London, 1958; Notre Dame, Ind., 1975)

Walker, D. P., *The Ancient Theology* (London, 1972)

Weiss, R., *Humanism in England during the Fifteenth Century* (2nd edn., Oxford, 1957)

Weiss, R., *The Spread of Italian Humanism* (London, 1964)

Wind, E., *Pagan Mysteries in the Renaissance* (1958; Oxford, 1980)

Yates, F., *Giordano Bruno and the Hermetic Tradition* (London, 1964)

Yates, F., *The Art of Memory* (London, 1966)

SCIENCE & TECHNOLOGY

Caspar, M., *Kepler* (London, 1959)

Castiglioni, A., *The Renaissance of Medicine in Italy* (New York, 1979)

Cipolla, C. M., *Guns and Sails in the Early Phases of European Expansion, 1400–1700* (London, 1966)

Cipolla, C. M., *Public Health and the Medical Profession in the Renaissance* (Cambridge, 1976)

Debus, A. G., *Man and Nature in the Renaissance* (Cambridge, 1979)

Garin, E., *Science and Civic Life in the Italian Renaissance* (Garden City, N.Y., 1969)

Guilmartin, J. F., Jr., *Gunpowder and Galleys* (Cambridge, 1975)

Hannaway, O., *The Chemists and the Word: the Didactic Origins of Chemistry* (Baltimore, Md., & London, 1975)

Heninger, S. K., Jr., *The Cosmographical Glass: Renaissance Diagrams of the Universe* (San Marino, Calif., 1977)

Koyre, A., *Astronomical Revolution* (new edn., London, 1980)

Koyre, A., *Galileo Studies* (Brighton, 1977)

Kuhn, T. S., *The Copernican Revolution* (2nd edn., New York, 1959)

Landes, D. S., *Revolution in Time: Clocks and the Making of the Modern World* (Cambridge, Mass., & London, 1983)

Lovejoy, A. O., *The Great Chain of Being* (Cambridge, Mass., 1936)

Pagel, W., *Paracelsus: An Introduction to Philosophical Medicine in the Era of the Renaissance* (Basle & New York, 1958)

Parsons, W. B., *Engineers and Engineering of the Renaissance* (Boston, Mass., 1968)

Webster, C., *From Paracelsus to Newton: Magic and the Making of Modern Science* (Cambridge, 1982)

Bibliography

Wightman, W. P., *Science and the Renaissance* (Aberdeen, 1962)

RELIGION

Bentley, J., *Humanists and Holy Writ* (Princeton, 1983)

Collinson, P., *The Religion of Protestants: the Church in English Society 1559–1625* (Oxford, 1982)

D'Amico, J., *Renaissance Humanism in Papal Rome: Humanists and Churchmen on the Eve of the Reformation* (Baltimore, Md., 1983)

Dickens, A. G., *Reformation and Society in Sixteenth-Century Europe* (London, 1966)

Dickens, A. G., *The Counter-Reformation* (London, 1968)

Kaminsky, H., *A History of the Hussite Revolution* (Berkeley, Calif., 1967)

Stinger, C. L., *Humanism and the Church Fathers: Ambrogio Traversari (1386–1439) and the Revival of Patristic Theology in the Early Italian Renaissance* (New York, 1977)

CALVIN Höpfl, H., *The Christian Polity of John Calvin* (Cambridge, 1982)

Kendall, R. T., *Calvin and English Calvinism to 1649* (Oxford, 1980)

LUTHER Brook, P. N. (ed.), *Seven-Headed Luther* (Oxford, 1983)

Haile, H. G., *Luther, a Biography* (London, 1980)

SAVONAROLA Ridolfi, R., *The Life of Girolamo Savonarola* (London, 1959)

ZWINGLI Potter, G. R., *Zwingli* (Cambridge, 1976)

SCHOLARSHIP & EDUCATION

Black, R., *Benedetto Accolti and the Florentine Renaissance* (Cambridge, 1985)

Borchardt, F., *German Antiquity in Renaissance Myth* (Baltimore, Md., 1971)

Cochrane, E., *Historians and Historiography in the Italian Renaissance* (Chicago, 1985)

Goldschmidt, E. P., *The Printed Book in the Renaissance* (Cambridge, 1950)

Jayne, S., *John Colet and Marsilio Ficino* (Oxford, 1963)

Kearney, H., *Scholars and Gentlemen* (London, 1970)

Kelley, D., *Foundations of Modern Historical Scholarship* (Columbia, 1970)

Simon, J., *Education and Society in Tudor England* (1966; Cambridge, 1979)

Ullman, B. L., *The Humanism of Coluccio Salutati* (Padua, 1963)

Wardrop, J., *The Script of Humanism, Some Aspects of Humanistic Script, 1460–1540* (Oxford, 1963)

Woodward, W. H., *Studies in Education during the Age of the Renaissance, 1400–1600* (Aberdeen, 1962)

Yates, F., *The French Academies of the Sixteenth Century* (London, 1959)

ERASMUS Huizinga, J., *Erasmus and the Age of Reformation* (New York, 1957)

Sowards, J. K., *Desiderius Erasmus* (Boston, Mass., 1975)

MORE Marius, R. C., *Thomas More* (London, 1985)

Sylvester, R. S. & Marc'hadour, G. P., *Essential Articles for the Study of Thomas More* (London, 1977)

PETRARCH Mann, N., *Petrarch* (Oxford, 1984)

Trinkaus, C., *The Poet as Philosopher: Petrarch and the Formation of Renaissance Consciousness* (New Haven, Conn., 1979)

Wilkins, E. H., *Life of Petrarch* (Chicago, 1961)

RAMUS Ong, W. J., *Ramus: Method and the Decay of Dialogue* (Cambridge, Mass., 1958)

SCALIGER Grafton, A., *Joseph Scaliger* (Oxford, 1983)

MUSIC

Arnold, D., *Giovanni Gabrieli and the Music of the Venetian High Renaissance* (1979; Oxford, 1985)

Brown, H. M., *Music in the Renaissance* (London & Englewood Cliffs, 1976)

Cazeaux, I., *French Music in the 15th and 16th Centuries* (Oxford, 1975)

Le Huray, P., *Music and the Reformation in England, 1549–1660* (2nd edn., Cambridge, 1978)

New Oxford History of Music: Vol. III *Ars Nova and the Renaissance, 1300–1540*, eds. G. Abraham & A. Hughes (Oxford, 1960); Vol. IV *The Age of Humanism, 1540–1630*, ed. G. Abraham (Oxford, 1968)

Palisca, C. V., *Humanism in Italian Renaissance Musical Thought* (New Haven, Conn., 1986)

Watkins, G. E., *Gesualdo* (Oxford, 1973)

EXPLORATION

Elliott, J. H., *The Old World and the New, 1492–1650* (Cambridge, 1969)

Hale, J. R., *Renaissance Exploration* (New York, 1972)

Iglesia, R., *Columbus, Cortes and Other Essays* (Berkeley, Calif., 1969)

Madariaga, S. de, *Christopher Columbus: Being the Life of the Very Magnificent Lord Don Christobal Colon* (London, 1979)

Parry, J. H., *The Age of Reconnaissance* (New York, 1964)

Taylor, E. G. R., *The Haven-Finding Art: a history of navigation from Odysseus to Captain Cook* (London, 1956)

LITERATURE

Forster, L., *The Icy Fire: Five Studies in European Petrarchism* (Cambridge, 1969)

Highet, G., *The Classical Tradition* (1949; Oxford, 1975)

Levin, H., *The Myth of the Golden Age in the Renaissance* (Oxford, 1969)

Nelson, J. C., *The Renaissance Theory of Love* (New York, 1958)

Pelican Guide to European Literature: *The Continental Renaissance, 1500–1600,* ed. A. J. Krailsheimer (Harmondsworth, 1971)

Smeed, J. W., *The Theophrastan "Character"* (Oxford, 1985)

Tayler, E., *Nature and Art in Renaissance Literature* (New York, 1964)

Italy

Boyde, P., *Dante Philomythes and Philosopher* (Cambridge, 1981)

Brand, C. P., *Torquato Tasso* (Cambridge, 1965)

Grayson, C., *The World of Dante* (Oxford, 1980)

Hanning, R. W. & Rosand, D., *Castiglione: The Ideal and the Real in Renaissance Culture* (New Haven, Conn., 1983)

Hathaway, B., *The Age of Criticism: The Late Renaissance in Italy* (Ithaca, N.Y., 1962)

France

Armstrong, E., *Ronsard and the Age of Gold* (Cambridge, 1968)

Castor, G. & Cave, T., *Neo-Latin and the Vernacular in Renaissance France* (Oxford, 1984)

Coleman, D. G., *Rabelais* (Cambridge, 1971)

Jondorf, G., *Robert Garnier and the Themes of Political Tragedy in the Sixteenth Century* (Cambridge, 1969)

McFarlane, I. D. & Maclean, I. W. F. (eds.) *Montaigne: Essays in Memory of Richard Sayce* (Oxford, 1982)

Screech, M., *Rabelais* (London, 1979)

Britain

Buxton, J., *Sir Philip Sidney and the English Renaissance* (London, 1964)

Craig, H., *The Enchanted Glass* (1952; New York, 1975)

Greenblatt, S., *Renaissance Self-Fashioning: From More to Shakespeare* (Chicago, 1980)

Javitch, D., *Poetry and Courtliness in Renaissance England* (Princeton, N.J., 1978)

Norbrook, D., *Poetry and Politics in the English Renaissance* (London, 1984)

Rosenberg, E., *Leicester, Patron of Letters* (Columbia, 1955)

Schoenbaum, S., *Shakespeare: The Globe and the World* (New York, 1980)

Southall, R., *The Courtly Makers* (Oxford, 1964)

Stevens, J., *Music and Poetry at the Early Tudor Court* (London, 1961)

Northern Europe

Butler, E. M., *The Fortunes of Faust* (Cambridge, 1979)

Pascal, R., *German Literature in the Sixteenth and Seventeenth Centuries* (London, 1968; repr. 1979)

Taylor, A., *Problems in German Literary History of the Fifteenth and Sixteenth Centuries* (New York, 1939; repr. 1966)

Spain

Brenan, G., *St. John of the Cross* (Cambridge, 1973)

Wilson, E. M. (ed. D. Cruickshank), *Spanish and English Literature of the Sixteenth and Seventeenth Centuries* (Cambridge, 1981)

VISUAL ARTS

Painting

Antal, F., *Florentine Painting and its Social Background* (London, 1947)

Baxandall, M., *Painting and Experience in Fifteenth Century Italy* (Oxford, 1972)

Benesch, Otto, *The Art of the Renaissance in Northern Europe* (2nd edn., London, 1965)

Berenson, B., *The Italian Painters of the Renaissance* (1952; 3rd edn., Oxford, 1980)

Biatostocki, J., *Art of the Renaissance in Eastern Europe* (London, 1976)

Blunt, A., *Artistic Theory in Italy, 1450–1600* (Oxford, 1962)

Blunt, W., *The Art of Botanical Illustration* (London, 1950)

Borsook, E., *The Mural Painters of Tuscany* (1960; Oxford, 1980)

Burckhardt, J., *The Civilization of the Renaissance in Italy* (new edn., Oxford, 1981)

Cole, B., *Masaccio and the Art of Early Renaissance Florence* (Bloomington, Ind., 1980)

Freedberg, S. J., *Painting of the High Renaissance* (Cambridge, Mass., 2 vols., 1961)

Friedländer, M. J. (ed. F. Grossmann), *From Van Eyck to Bruegel* (new edn., Oxford, 1981)

Hale, J. R., *Italian Renaissance Painting from Masaccio to Titian* (Oxford, 1977)

Klibansky, R., Panofsky, E., & Saxl, F., *Saturn and Melancholy* (London, 1964)

Letts, R. M., *The Renaissance* (Cambridge, 1983)

Lytle, G. F. & Orgel, S. (eds.), *Patronage in the Renaissance* (Princeton, N.J., 1981)

Murray, L., *The High Renaissance* (London, 1967)

Murray, L., *The Late Renaissance and Mannerism* (London, 1967)

Bibliography

Panofsky, E., *Renaissance and Renascences in Western Art* (London, 1970)

Shearman, J., *Mannerism* (Harmondsworth, 1967)

Stechow, W., *Northern Renaissance Art, 1400–1600* (New Jersey, 1966)

Trevor-Roper, H., *Princes and Artists* (London, 1976)

Turner, A. R., *The Vision of Landscape in Renaissance Italy* (Princeton, 1966)

Ullman, B. L., *Studies in the Italian Renaissance* (Rome, 1955)

Waterhouse, E. K., *Italian Baroque Painting* (2nd edn., London, 1968)

INDIVIDUAL ARTISTS

Baldass, L. von, *Hieronymus Bosch* (London, 1960)

Berti, L., *Masaccio* (Pennsylvania, 1967)

Clark, K., *Leonardo da Vinci: an Account of his Development as an Artist* (Harmondsworth, 1975)

Clark, K., *Piero della Francesca* (2nd edn., Oxford, 1982)

Ettlinger, L. D. & H. S., *Botticelli* (London, 1976)

Ettlinger, L. D. & H. S., *Raphael* (Oxford, 1983)

Hirst, M., *Sebastiano del Piombo* (Oxford, 1981)

Horster, M., *Andrea del Castagno* (Oxford, 1980)

Hulten, P. (ed.), *The Arcimboldo Effect* (Milan, 1987)

Kemp, M., *Leonardo da Vinci, the Marvellous Works of Man and Nature* (Cambridge, Mass., 1981)

Knappe, K. A. (ed.), *Dürer: the Complete Engravings, Etchings and Woodcuts* (London, 1965)

Levey, M., *Dürer* (London, 1964)

Panofsky, E., *The Life and Art of Albrecht Dürer* (Princeton, 1955)

Pedretti, C., *Leonardo, a Study in Chronology and Style* (New York & London, 1982)

Pignatti, T. (ed.), *Titian* (London, 1981)

Richter, J. P. (ed.), *The Literary Works of Leonardo da Vinci* (3rd edn., New York, 1970)

Wasserman, J., *Leonardo da Vinci* (New York, 1984)

Sculpture

Avery, C., *Florentine Renaissance Sculpture* (London, 1970)

Baxandall, M., *The Limewood Sculptors of Renaissance Germany* (Yale, 1980)

Bober, P. P., & Rubinstein, R. O., *Renaissance Artists and Antique Sculpture: A Handbook of Sources* (Oxford, 1987).

Pope-Hennessy, J., *Italian Renaissance Sculpture* (1958; 3rd edn., Oxford, 1986)

Pope-Hennessy, J., *Italian High Renaissance and Baroque Sculpture* (1963; Oxford, 1986)

Seymour, C., *Sculpture in Italy, 1400–1500* (Harmondsworth, 1966)

INDIVIDUAL SCULPTORS

Condivi, A., *The Life of Michelangelo* (Baton Rouge, La., 1976)

Ettlinger, L. D., *Antonio and Piero Pollaiuolo* (Oxford, 1978)

Goldschneider, L., *Michelangelo: Paintings, Sculptures, Architecture* (London, 1975)

Greenhalgh, M., *Donatello and his Sources* (London, 1982)

Hibbard, H., *Michelangelo* (New York, 1974)

Janson, H. W., *The Sculpture of Donatello* (Princeton, 1957)

Krautheimer, R., *Lorenzo Ghiberti* (Princeton, 2 vols., 1970)

Passavant, G., *Verrocchio* (London, 1969)

Pope-Hennessy, J., *Luca della Robbia* (Oxford, 1980)

Seymour, C., *Jacopo della Quercia, Sculptor* (Yale, 1973)

Seymour, C., *The Sculpture of Verrocchio* (London, 1971)

Summers, D., *Michelangelo and the Language of Art* (Princeton, 1981)

Tolnay, C. de, *Michelangelo* (Princeton, 5 vols., 1943–60)

Wilde, J., *Michelangelo: Six Lectures* (Oxford, 1978)

Architecture

Girouard, M., *Robert Smythson and the Architecture of the Elizabethan Era* (London, 1966)

Hale, J. R., *Renaissance Fortification: Art or Engineering?* (London, 1978)

Hall, M. B., *Renovation and Counter-Reformation* (Oxford, 1979)

Hitchcock, H. R., *German Renaissance Architecture* (Princeton, 1981)

Kubler, G., *Building the Escorial* (Princeton, 1982)

Lotz, W., *Studies in Italian Renaissance Architecture* (Cambridge, Mass., 1977)

McAndrew, J., *Venetian Architecture of the Early Renaissance* (Cambridge, Mass., 1980)

Wittkower, R., *Architectural Principles in the Age of Humanism* (3rd edn., London, 1962)

INDIVIDUAL ARCHITECTS

Ackerman, J. S., *Palladio* (Harmondsworth, 1966)

Battisti, E., *Brunelleschi* (London, 1981)

Borsi, E., *Leon Battista Alberti* (Oxford, 1977)

Bruschi, A., *Bramante* (London, 1977)

Howard, D. J., *Jacopo Sansovino: Architecture and Patronage in Renaissance Venice* (New Haven, Conn., 1975)

CHRONOLOGICAL TABLE

Note: this table does not attempt comprehensive coverage of European history in the period 1300–1620, but is intended to provide a chronological framework for the events and personalities described in the text.

POLITICS & SECULAR EVENTS	RELIGION	EMPERORS	KINGS & PRINCES
1300			
1300 Edward I of England invades Scotland	1302 Papal Bull *Unam Sanctam* declares papal authority supreme		1301 Edward I of England creates his son prince of Wales
1301 Dante exile from Florence	1305 Clement V pope		1307 Edward II king of England (→1327)
1302 Flemings defeat French at Courtrai	1309 Papacy at Avignon (→1377)	1308 Henry VII of Luxembourg (→ 1313)	1309 Robert of Anjou king of Naples (→1343)
1309 Emperor recognizes Swiss League; Knights Hospitallers settle in Rhodes			
1310			
1314 Scots defeat English at Bannockburn	1312 Council of Vienne	1314 Louis IV of Bavaria (→ 1347)	
1315 Florentines defeated by Pisans at Montecatini	1316 John XXII pope		
1319 Sweden and Norway united under Magnus VII			
1320			
1320 Peace of Paris (between France and Flanders)		1324 Louis IV excommunicated	1327 Edward III king of England (→1377)
1326 Ottoman Turks capture Bursa		1328 Louis IV crowned emperor in Rome	1328 Philip VI first Valois king of France (→ 1350)
1329 Compact of Pavia			

441

POLITICS & SECULAR EVENTS	RELIGION	EMPERORS	KINGS & PRINCES
1330			
1330 Treaty of Hagenau			1333 Casimir III king of Poland (→ 1370)
1336 Van Artevelde revolt in Flanders	1334 Benedict XII pope		
1337 Outbreak of Hundred Years' War			
1340			
1340 English defeat French at Sluys	1342 Clement VI pope		1342 Louis I king of Hungary (→1382)
1346 English defeat French at Crécy			1343 Joanna I queen of Naples (→1381)
1347 Plague reaches Italy	1348 Pope purchases town of Avignon	1347 Charles IV of Luxembourg (→1378)	
1348 Black Death in England			
1350			
1351 Zürich joins Swiss League	1352 Innocent VI pope		1350 John II king of France (→1364)
1356 English defeat French at Poitiers; Golden Bull issued		1355 Charles IV crowned emperor in Rome	
1357 Turks capture Adrianople (Edirne)			
1358 Jacquerie (peasants' revolt) in France			

POLITICS & SECULAR EVENTS	RELIGION	EMPERORS	KINGS & PRINCES
1360			**KINGS & PRINCES**
1360 Treaty of Brétigny			
1361 Denmark at war with Hanseatic League	1362 Urban V pope		
1363 Austria obtains Tyrol			1364 Charles V king of France (→1380)
1367 English defeat Castilians at Nájera		1365 Charles IV crowned king of Burgundy at Arles	1369 Henry II first Trastamara king of Castile (→1379)
1370			
1370 English sack Limoges	1370 Gregory XI pope		1371 Robert II first Stuart king of Scotland (→1390)
1375 War of the Eight Saints			1377 Richard II king of England (→1399)
	1378 Great Schism begins	1378 Wenceslas of Luxembourg (→1400)	
1380			
1380 Norway and Denmark united under Olaf IV			1380 Charles VI king of France (→1422)
1381 Peasants' Revolt in England			
1382 Turks capture Sofia			
	1384 Death of Wyclif		1385 John I first Avis king of Portugal (→1433)
1386 Treaty of Windsor between England and Portugal; Portuguese defeat Castilians at Aljubarrota			1386 Ladislas II first Jagellon king of Poland (→1434)
1389 Turks defeat Serbs at Kossovo			

POLITICS & SECULAR EVENTS	RELIGION	EMPERORS	KINGS & PRINCES
1390			1393 Niccolò III d'Este created first marquis of Ferrara
			1395 Giangaleazzo Visconti created first duke of Milan
1396 Turks complete conquest of Bulgaria			1399 Henry IV king of England (→1413)
1397 Union of Kalmar unites Norway, Sweden, and Denmark			
1400	1401 First Lollard martyr	1400 Robert of Bavaria (→1410)	
	1409 Council of Pisa		
1410		1410 Sigismund of Luxembourg (→1437)	1413 Henry V king of England (→1422)
1410 Ladislas II of Poland defeats Teutonic Knights at Tannenberg			1414 Joanna II queen of Naples (→1435)
1415 Portuguese capture Ceuta	1415 Council of Constance; martyrdom of Huss		
	1417 Election of Martin V as pope ends Great Schism		
1419 Defenestration of Prague	1419 Outbreak of Hussite Wars		

POLITICS & SECULAR EVENTS	RELIGION	EMPERORS	KINGS & PRINCES
1420			
1420 Treaty of Troyes makes Henry V heir to French throne			1422 Henry VI king of England (→1461)
1423 Council of Pavia			
1429 Siege of Orleans lifted			1429 Charles VII of France crowned
1430			
1431 Joan of Arc burned	1431 Council of Basle; Eugenius IV pope		1433 Gianfrancesco I Gonzaga first marquis of Mantua
1432 Portuguese discover Azores	1433 Compacts of Prague	1433 Sigismund crowned emperor	1434 Cosimo de' Medici returns to Florence
	1434 Revolt in Rome forces pope to flee to Florence		1435 Rene of Anjou king of Naples (→1442)
1435 Congress of Arras allies Burgundy with France	1438 Pragmatic Sanction of Bourges; Council of Ferrara	1438 Albert II of Habsburg (→1439)	
	1439 Council of Florence		
1440			
		1440 Frederick III of Habsburg (→1493)	1442 Alfonso I (Alfonso V of Aragon) king of Naples (→1458)
	1442 Council of Rome		
	1443 Papacy returns to Rome		
1444 Turks defeat Poles at Varna			1446 John Hunyadi elected regent of Hungary
1447 Ambrosian Republic in Milan	1447 Nicholas V pope		1447 Casimir IV king of Poland (→1492)
1449 French take Rouen			

POLITICS & SECULAR EVENTS	RELIGION	EMPERORS	KINGS & PRINCES
1450			
			1450 Francesco Sforza first Sforza duke of Milan (→1466)
1453 French victory at Castillon ends Hundred Years' War; Turks capture Constantinople			
1454 Peace of Lodi			
1455 Outbreak of Wars of the Roses in England	1455 Calixtus III pope		
1456 John Hunyadi raises Turkish siege of Belgrade; Cape Verde Islands discovered			
1457 Poles capture Marienburg			
	1458 Pius II pope		1458 Matthias Corvinus king of Hungary (→1490); Ferdinand I king of Naples (→1494)
1459 Turks overrun Serbia			
1460			1460 Death of Henry the Navigator
			1461 Louis XI king of France (→1483); Edward IV king of England (→1483)
1462 Castilians capture Gibraltar from Arabs			
1463 Turks overrun Bosnia			
	1464 Paul II pope		
1466 Peace of Torun			
			1467 Charles the Bold duke of Burgundy (→1477)
			1469 Marriage of Isabella of Castile and Ferdinand II of Aragon; Lorenzo the Magnificent head of the Florentine republic (→1492)

POLITICS & SECULAR EVENTS	RELIGION	EMPERORS	KINGS & PRINCES
1470			
	1471 Sixtus IV pope		1471 Ercole I d'Este created first duke of Ferrara
1471 Portuguese capture Tangier			
1472 Portuguese reach Fernando Po			1474 Isabella queen of Castile (→1504); Federico II da Montefeltro created first duke of Urbino
1476 Swiss defeat Burgundians at Morat		1477 Frederick's heir, Maximilian, marries Mary of Burgundy	
1478 Pazzi conspiracy			1479 Ferdinand II king of Aragon (→1516)
1479 Union of Aragon and Castile			
1480			
	1484 Innocent VIII pope		1483 Richard III king of England (→1485); Charles VIII king of France (→1498)
1485 Matthias Corvinus takes Vienna from Frederick III			1485 Henry VII, first Tudor king of England (→1509)
1487 Diaz rounds Cape of Good Hope			1488 James IV king of Scotland (→1513)
1489 Cyprus ceded to Venice			

POLITICS & SECULAR EVENTS	RELIGION	EMPERORS	KINGS & PRINCES
1490			
1491 Treaty of Pressburg recognizes Habsburg rights to Bohemia and Hungary	1492 Alexander VI pope	1493 Maximilian I (→1519)	1495 Charles VIII of France crowned king of Naples
1492 Conquest of Granada completes *Reconquista*; Jews expelled from Spain; Columbus lands in New World			1498 Louis XII king of France (→1515)
1494 Charles VIII of France invades Italy; Medici expelled from Florence; treaty of Tordesillas			
1495 Holy League against the French		1496 Marriage of Maximilian's heir, Philip the Handsome, to Joanna, heiress of Spain	
1497 Cabots reach Nova Scotia	1498 Savonarola burned		
1498 Vasco da Gama reaches India			
1499 Peace of Basle effectively ensures Swiss independence; Louis XII occupies Milan			

448

POLITICS & SECULAR EVENTS	RELIGION	EMPERORS	KINGS & PRINCES
1500			
1500 Treaty of Granada agrees French/Spanish partition of Italy; Cabral discovers Brazil			1501 Cesare Borgia created duke of Romagna
1501 Basle joins Swiss League			
1504 France cedes Naples to Spain under treaty of Lyons	1503 Pius III pope; Julius III pope		1507 Margaret of Austria regent of Netherlands (→1530)
1505 Portuguese reach Sri Lanka			1508 Francesco Maria I first della Rovere duke of Urbino
1508 League of Cambrai against Venice	1507 Indulgence for building of St Peter's		1509 Henry VIII king of England (→1547)
1509 Venice defeated at Agnadello; Spaniards conquer Oran			
1510			
1510 Portuguese capture Goa	1512 Fifth Lateran Council		1513 James V king of Scotland (→1542)
1512 Medici restored in Florence	1513 Leo X pope		
1513 English defeat French at battle of the Spurs and Scots at Flodden; Balboa discovers Pacific Ocean	1514 Tetzel sells Indulgences		1515 Francis I king of France (→1547)
1515 French defeat Milanese at Marignano	1516 Concord of Bologna		
	1517 Luther's Ninety-five Theses	1519 Charles V (→1556)	
1519 Magellan sets out on voyage of circumnavigation			

449

POLITICS & SECULAR EVENTS	RELIGION	EMPERORS	KINGS & PRINCES
1520			
1520 Field of the Cloth of Gold	1520 Luther excommunicated		
1521 Cortes discovers Mexico City	1521 Diet of Worms	1521 Ferdinand (I) regent of Austria	
1522 Turks expel Knights Hospitallers from Rhodes; del Cano completes circumnavigation	1522 Adrian VI pope		
	1523 Clement VII pope		1523 Gustavus I Vasa king of Sweden (→1560)
1525 Battle of Pavia; Milan becomes Habsburg territory			
1526 Treaty of Madrid; League of Cognac; battle of Mohács			
1527 Sack of Rome; Medici expelled from Florence			
1528 Andrea Doria in power in Genoa			
1529 Peace of Cambria; Turks besiege Vienna	1529 Colloquy of Marburg; Articles of Schwabach		
1530			
1530 Charles V gives Malta to Knights Hospitallers; Medici restored in Florence	1530 Confession of Augsburg	1530 Charles V crowned emperor	1530 Federico II Gonzaga created first duke of Mantua
	1531 Schmalkaldic League		1531 Mary of Hungary regent of Netherlands (→1556)
	1533 Henry VIII of England excommunicated		
	1534 Ignatius Loyola founds Jesuits; Henry VIII supreme head of Church in England; Paul III pope		
1535 Battle of Tunis	1536 Dissolution of English monasteries begins; first Helvetic Confession		
1536 French occupy Savoy-Piedmont; Cartier claims Canada for France			

450

POLITICS & SECULAR EVENTS	RELIGION	EMPERORS	KINGS & PRINCES
1540			
1540 Spaniards discover California; Perugian Salt War	1541 Colloquy of Regensburg		1542 Accession of infant Mary, Queen of Scots
1542 English defeat Scots at Solway Moss	1542 Roman Inquisition re-established		
1544 English capture Boulogne	1545 First session of the Council of Trent		1545 Pierluigi Farnese created first duke of Parma
1547 Battle of Mühlberg	1548 Interim of Augsburg		1547 Edward VI king of England (→1553); Henry II king of France (→1559)
	1549 Zürich Agreement		
1550			
1550 Peace of Boulogne between England, France, and Scotland	1550 Julius III pope		1553 Mary I queen of England (→1558)
	1551 Council of Trent reconvoked		
	1553 England reconciled with papacy	1554 Charles' heir Philip marries Mary I of England	1556 Philip II king of Spain (→1598)
1555 Spaniards capture Siena; Muscovy Company founded	1555 Peace of Augsburg; Protestants persecuted in England; Marcellus II pope; Paul IV pope	1556 Charles V abdicates; Ferdinand I emperor (→1564)	1558 Elizabeth I queen of England (→1603)
1557 Battle of St Quentin			1559 Francis II king of France (→1560); Margaret of Parma regent of Netherlands (→1567)
1558 French recover Calais from English	1559 Protestantism re-established in England; Pius IV pope; Gallican Confession; first issue of Index		
1559 Peace of Cateau-Cambrésis			

451

POLITICS & SECULAR EVENTS	RELIGION	EMPERORS	KINGS & PRINCES
1560			
	1560 Church in Scotland set up on presbyterian principles		1560 Charles IX king of France (→1574) with Catherine de' Medici as regent
	1561 Colloquy of Poissy attempts reconciliation of French Catholics and Huguenots; Belgic Confession		
1562 Outbreak of religious wars in France	1562 Edict of St Germain; Council of Trent reconvoked for final sessions; Heidelberg Catechism		
		1564 Maximilian II (→1576)	
1565 Turks besiege Malta			
1566 Compromise of Breda	1566 Pius V pope; second Helvetic Confession		
1567 Duke of Alba sent to Netherlands	1567 Conspiracy of Meaux		1567 Mary, Queen of Scots, compelled to abdicate; James VI king of Scotland (→1625)
1568 Tribunal of Blood			1569 Cosimo I of Florence created grand duke of Tuscany
1569 Union of Lublin unites Poland and Lithuania			
1570			
	1570 Elizabeth I of England excommunicated; Peace of St Germain		
1571 Battle of Lepanto			1572 Sigismund II, last Jagellon king of Poland, dies
1572 Sea-beggars seize Brill and Flushing, marking start of Dutch war of independence	1572 Massacre of St Bartholomew; Gregory XIII pope		
1574 Relief of Leyden by sea-beggars			1574 Henry III king of France (→1589)
1576 "Spanish Fury" at Antwerp		1576 Rudolf II (→1612)	
	1577 Formula of Concord		1578 Alessandro Farnese appointed governor of Netherlands
1579 Union of Utrecht; peace of Arras			

POLITICS & SECULAR EVENTS	RELIGION	EMPERORS	KINGS & PRINCES
1580			
1580 Drake completes circum-navigation; Philip II of Spain occupies Portugal 1583 Gilbert claims New-foundland for England 1585 Drake raids Spanish possessions in New World; first attempt to found colony in Virginia 1586 Battle of Zutphen 1587 Drake's raid on Cádiz 1588 Spanish Armada; assassin-ation of duke of Guise	1585 Sixtus V pope	1583 Rudolf II moves his capital to Prague	1580 Carlo Emmanuele I duke of Savoy (→1630) 1584 Assassination of William I of Orange 1587 Execution of Mary, Queen of Scots 1589 Death of Catherine de' Medici; Henry of Navarre (Henry IV) first Bourbon king of France (→1610)
1590			
1590 Henry IV defeats Catholic forces at Ivry; Paris besieged 1594 Philip II of Spain closes port of Lisbon to Dutch ships 1595 O'Neill's revolt in Ireland Raleigh explores Guiana 1596 Sack of Cádiz 1598 Ferrara passes to papacy; southern Netherlands handed over to Archdukes Albert and Isabella	1590 Urban VII pope; Gregory XIV pope 1591 Innocent IX pope 1592 Clement VIII pope 1593 Henry IV of France converts to Catholicism; Swedes accept Lutheran catechism 1598 Edict of Nantes		1598 Philip III king of Spain (→1621)

POLITICS & SECULAR EVENTS	RELIGION	EMPERORS	KINGS & PRINCES
1600			
1600 English East India Company granted charter			
1602 Dutch East India Company granted charter			*1603* James I (VI of Scotland) first Stuart king of England (→*1625*)
	1604 Hampton Court Conference		
1605 Gunpowder Plot	*1605* Leo XI pope; Paul V pope		
		1608 Rudolf forced to cede Hungary to Matthias	
1609 Twelve-year truce agreed between Netherlands and Spain	*1609* Rudolf II grants concessions to Bohemia Protestants under Letter of Majesty		
1610	*1610* Arminian Remonstrance		*1610* Louis XIII king of France (→*1643*) with Marie de' Medici as regent
1611 War of Kalmar between Denmark and Sweden			*1611* Gustavus II Adolphus king of Sweden (→*1632*)
		1612 Matthias (→*1619*)	*1613* Michael first Romanov tsar of Russia (→*1645*)
1617 War between Sweden and Poland		*1617* Ferdinand of Styria elected king of Bohemia	
1618 Defenestration of Prague	*1618* Synod of Dort		
1619 Execution of Oldenbarneveldt		*1619* Ferdinand of Styria (Ferdinand II) (→*1637*)	
1620			
Battle of the White Mountain, first major engagement of Thirty Years' War			